Putnam's Contemporary Dictionaries

Italian–English
Inglese–Italiano

Putnam's Contemporary German Dictionary
Putnam's Contemporary Italian Dictionary
Putnam's Contemporary French Dictionary
Putnam's Contemporary Spanish Dictionary

PUTNAM'S CONTEMPORARY ITALIAN DICTIONARY

ITALIAN ENGLISH
ENGLISH ITALIAN

ISOPEL MAY, B.A., Ph.D.

Revised by:
ANTONIA SANSICA STOTT, DOTT. LETT.
Lecturer in Italian,
University of Glasgow

CATHERINE WILSON
Special Editor to the American Edition

BERKLEY BOOKS, NEW YORK

Published by arrangement with G. P. Putnam's Sons.

G. P. Putnam's Sons
200 Madison Ave.
New York, N.Y. 10016

Library of Congress Catalog Card Number: 72-97576

SBN 0-425-04363-0

BERKLEY MEDALLION BOOKS are published by
Berkley Publishing Corporation
200 Madison Avenue
New York, N.Y. 10016

BERKLEY MEDALLION BOOKS ® TM 757,357

Printed in the United States of America

Berkley Medallion Edition, JANUARY, 1977

General Editor: J. B. Foreman, M.A.
Executive Editor: Isaebail C. Macleod, M.A.

Tenth Printing

Contents

Contenuto

Introduction

It is opportune to remind the user of the Dictionary that, although a standard pronunciation exists both in English and in Italian—and this we have used here—pronunciation both in Italy and in the English-speaking world varies from one region to another.

Italian Consonants

The consonants *s* and *z* may be voiced or unvoiced. When they are voiced this sound is indicated in the Dictionary by a dot under the letters *s* and *z*.

Accents used in the Italian-English section of the Dictionary

In this Dictionary, to help the student, the accent has been inserted in all words, marking the open sounds with the 'grave' accent, and the close ones with the 'acute.'

Genders

Rules concerning masculine and feminine forms are indicated in the Supplement. However, to help the student, the feminine form in *-trice* and exceptions to the rules have been indicated in the Dictionary.

Irregularities and Peculiarities in Italian Plurals

All exceptions in plurals of nouns and adjectives ending in the singular in *-cia* and *-gia* and in *-io*, and the plural of all the words, regular or exceptions, nouns or adjectives, of *two* or *more* syllables ending in the singular in *-co* and *-go* have been indicated in the Dictionary.

Some nouns in Italian change their gender in the plural. Some nouns have two plurals with different meanings. Some compounds, as well as certain single nouns, have the same form both for the singular and for the plural; some compounds form their plural either changing both parts of the word, or only one. All these plurals are duly indicated in their place in the Dictionary.

English Pronunciation

In the English-Italian section of the Dictionary the letters and symbols of the International Phonetic Association have been used.

English Irregular Plurals

All irregular plurals have been indicated.

Proper Names and Geographical Names

The most important proper names and geographical names have been incorporated in the main part of the Dictionary.

Abbreviations used in the Dictionary—Abbreviazioni usate nel Dizionario

aggettivo	**a**	adjective
abbreviazione	**abbr**	abbreviation
accusativo	**acc**	accusative
avverbio	**ad**	adverb
agricoltura	**agr**	agriculture
anatomia	**anat**	anatomy
aggettivo e nome femminile	**a nf**	adjective and noun feminine
aggettivo e nome maschile	**a nm**	adjective and noun masculine
aggettivo e nome maschile o femminile	**a nmf**	adjective and noun masculine or feminine
arcaico	**arc**	archaic
architettura	**arch**	architecture
astronomia	**astr**	astronomy
automobile	**aut**	automobile
ausiliare	**aux**	auxiliary
aviazione	**av**	aviation
biblico	**Bibl**	Biblical
botanico	**bot**	botanical
chimica	**chem**	chemistry
cinema	**cin**	cinema
congiunzione	**cj**	conjunction
collettivo	**coll**	collective
commerciale	**com**	commercial
cucina	**cook**	cooking
cosmetici	**cosm**	cosmetics
articolo definito	**def art**	definite article
dimostrativo	**dem**	demonstrative
ecclesiastico	**eccl**	ecclesiastical
economia	**econ**	economics
elettricità	**el**	electricity
femminile	**f**	feminine
familiare	**fam**	familiar
figurato	**fig**	figuratively
finanziario	**fin**	financial
femminile plurale	**fpl**	feminine plural
geografico	**geogr**	geographical
geologia	**geol**	geology
geometria	**geom**	geometry
grammatica	**gram**	grammar
storico	**hist**	historical
impersonale	**impers**	impersonal
industria	**ind**	industry
articolo indefinito	**indef art**	indefinite article
interiezione	**interj**	interjection
interrogativo	**interrog**	interrogative
legale	**leg**	legal
letterario	**liter**	literary
maschile	**m**	masculine
matematica	**math**	mathematics
meccanica	**mech**	mechanics
medicina	**med**	medicine
metallurgia	**metal**	metallurgy
militare	**mil**	military
minerale	**min**	mineral
maschile plurale	**mpl**	masculine plural
musica	**mus**	music
nome	**n**	noun

nautico	**naut**	nautical
nome femminile	**nf**	noun feminine
nome maschile	**nm**	noun masculine
nome maschile o femminile	**nmf**	noun masculine or feminine
nominativo	**nom**	nominative
nome proprio	**n pr**	proper noun
nome femminile plurale	**nf pl**	noun feminine plural
nome maschile plurale	**nm pl**	noun masculine plural
nome femminile proprio	**nf pr**	proper noun feminine
nome maschile proprio	**nm pr**	proper noun masculine
ornitologia	**ornit**	ornithology
filosofia	**phil**	philosophy
fotografia	**phot**	photography
fisica	**phys**	physics
plurale	**pl**	plural
poesia	**poet**	poetry
politico	**pol**	political
possessivo	**poss**	possessive
participio passato	**pp**	past participle
proprio	**pr**	proper
predicativo	**pred**	predicative
preposizione	**prep**	preposition
pronome	**pron**	pronoun
qualcosa	**qc**	something
qualcuno	**qlcu**	someone
radio	**rad**	radio
reciproco	**recip**	reciprocal
riflessivo	**refl**	reflexive
relativo	**rel**	relative
religione	**relig**	religion
ferrovia	**rly**	railway
singolare	**sing**	singular
gergo	**sl**	slang
qualcuno	**s.o.**	someone
qualcosa	**sth**	something
tecnico	**tec**	technical
telefono	**tel**	telephone
teatro	**theat**	theatre
televisione	**tv**	television
tipografica	**typ**	typography
Stati Uniti, americano	**US**	United States, American
generalmente	**usu**	usually
vedere	**v**	see
veterinario	**vet**	veterinary
verbo intransitivo	**vi**	verb intransitive
verbo passivo	**vp**	verb passive
verbo riflessivo	**vr**	verb reflexive
verbo transitivo	**vt**	verb transitive
verbo transitivo e intransitivo	**vti**	verb transitive and intransitive
volgare	**vulg**	vulgar
zoologia	**zool**	zoology

Italian Pronunciation—Pronuncia Italiana

The Italian alphabet

The Italian alphabet consists of twenty-one letters, of which five are vowels (**vocali**) **a, e, i, o, u**; the others are consonants (**consonanti**).

A a	**G** gi	**O** o	**U** u
B bi	**H** acca	**P** pi	**V** vi
C ci	**I** i	**Q** qu	**Z** zeta
D di	**L** elle	**R** erre	
E e	**M** emme	**S** esse	
F effe	**N** enne	**T** ti	

The letters **k, w, x, y** (kappa, vi doppio, ics, ipsilon) are used only in words of foreign origin. The letter **j** (i lungo) is no longer in use.

The Vowels (Le Vocali)

Every vowel in Italian, stressed or unstressed, has a single, distinct sound.

a	[ɑ]	as *a* in father	
e	open [ɛ]	as *e* in seven	unaccented **e** is always close
	close [e]	as *a* in hate	(without the short 'i' sound)
i	[i]	as *i* in ravine	
o	open [ɔ]	as *o* in cot	unaccented **o** is always close
	close [o]	as *o* in note	(without the short 'u' sound)
u	[u]	as *oo* in moon	

Stress in Pronunciation

Most words have the stress on the vowel in the last but one syllable; some on the final vowel, others on the vowels in the third last or fourth last syllable. No written (or printed) accent, however, is used except where the final vowel is stressed, and to avoid ambiguity. (See *Written Accents*)

Diphthongs

Diphthongs are made (1) of the combination of **a, e,** or **o** with unaccented **i** or **u**; (2) when **i** and **u** are combined with each other. In (1) the stress falls on **a, e,** or **o**; in (2) sometimes on **i**, sometimes on **u**; e.g. **fiàba, manièra, fióre; lúi, guida.**

Hiatus

Hiatus occurs when two vowels are pronounced separately: **pa-úra, le-àle.**

The Consonants (Le Consonanti)

The consonants **b, d, f, l, m, n, p, t, v** are pronounced as in English. In double consonants each consonant is distinctly sounded in order to give a double effect within the same sound, as in: **bèllo, bírra, còccola, fàccia.**

c is soft, or palatal [tʃ] before **e** and **i** (as in cheese): **cénere, bàcio, cibo, fàccia.**

c is hard or guttural [k] before **a, o, u** and consonants (like **k**): **calamàio, còsa, cuòre, chièsa, clorúro.**

ch (only found before **e, i**) is hard, or guttural (as in chemist): **chílo, che.**

g is soft or palatal [dʒ] before **e** and **i** (as in general): **generàle, gelóso, ginnàsio.**

g is hard or guttural [g] before **a, o, u,** : (as in god, gruesome): **gàra, godiménto, gústo, grído.**

gh (only found before **e, i**) is hard, or guttural (as in **ghetto,** guinea): **ghétto, ghinèa.**

gl is hard or guttural [gl] before **a, o, u, e** (as in **gland**): **glàndola, glèba, glòbo, glucòsio.**

gli a single, palatal sound [ʎ] (as in brilliant): **gli, fíglio, móglie, màglia.**
Exceptions: **Anglia, glicerína, negligènte, geroglífico, gànglio,** where the sound is guttural.

gn a single, palatal sound [ɲ] (similar to opinion, companion): **campàgna, agnèllo, bàgno, magnífico, sógno.**

h is never pronounced.

qu [kw] (as in question): **quàdro, questióne, quínto, quòta.** If preceded by **c** this sound is kept separate from **qu** giving the effect of a slightly double sound; **àcqua, acquirènte, acquísto, nàcque.**

r [r] must be distinctly pronounced: **ràro, rósso, àrte, tortúra.**

s unvoiced (**s aspra, s sorda**) [s] (as in silk): **sèrvo, séta.**
voiced (**s dolce, s sonora**) [z] (as in rose): **ròsa, úso, spòsa.**
This sound is shown in the Dictionary by a dot under the letter **s.**

sc before **e, i** has a single, palatal sound [ʃ] (as in **shell**): **scèna, scéndere.** Before **a, o, u** it has a guttural sound [sk] (as in scholar): **scàtola, scolàro, scuòla.**

z unvoiced (**z aspra, z sorda**) [ts]: **zàmpa, zòccolo.**
voiced (**z dolce, z sonora**) [dz]: **zàino, zèro, zínco, zòtico.**
This sound is shown in the Dictionary by a dot under the letter **z.**

Written Accents

Three written accents are in use in Italy, the acute (ʹ), the grave (ˋ) and the circumflex (^). The circumflex accent is employed only to indicate that the word has been abbreviated by the omission of part of it. As for the other two accents, there is considerable variation concerning their use. They are invariably indicated as follows: (a) on words in which the accent falls on the last syllable: **città, virtù, caffè** (See *Stress in Pronunciation*); (b) on monosyllables ending with a diphthong: **già, giú, piú**; (c) on monosyllables which, if accented, change meaning; **dà** (part of the verb **dare**), **da** (from, by to); **sé** (himself), **se** (if) *etc*; (d) on words which change meaning depending on the position of the accent; **àncora** (anchor), **ancora** (still, yet), **príncipi** (princes), **princìpi** (principles). The acute and grave accents are stress marks, the acute over **i** and **u**, the grave over **a**. With **e** and **o** they are pronunciation as well as stress marks, the acute being used for the close sounds, the grave for the open. In many texts, however, only the grave accent is indicated, irrespective of whether the sound may be open or close. In the Italian-English part of this we have inserted the accent in *all* words, marking the open sounds with the 'grave' accent, and the close ones with the 'acute'.

Apostrophe

This indicates the omission of the last vowel of a word and it occurs when the next word begins with a vowel: *eg* **la amíca, l'amíca,** the girl friend; **un bèllo àlbero, un bell'àlbero,** a beautiful tree. The apostrophe is not to be used between plural feminine articles and nouns: *eg* **le èrbe.**

Syllable Division

Italian words are divided into syllables, each syllable normally starting with a consonant.

Double consonants are always separated: ex. **màm-ma; pàl-la; sàs-so.**

When **s** is followed by one or more consonants it belongs to the subsequent syllable: *eg* **vi-schio; pò-sta; à-sma.**

Vowels in diphthongs are not separated: *eg* **fià-ba; fió-re** except when hiatus occurs: *eg* **pa-ú-ra; le-à-le.**

When a word is carried from one line to another, if the word is apostrophized the apostrophe cannot be left at the end of the line. The apostrophe must either be accompanied by the first part of the following word, or it must not be used at all and the full, unapostrophized form should be used instead: *eg* **un'a-/mica** or **una/amíca;** *not* **un'/amíca.**

Pronuncia Inglese—English Pronunciation

Vocali e Dittonghi inglesi

Simbolo	*Esempio inglese*	*Esempio italiano o Spiegazione*
[ɑː]	f*a*ther ['fɑːðə]	p*a*dre
[ʌ]	b*u*t [bʌt] c*o*me [kʌm] bl*oo*d [blʌd]	quasi *a*
[æ]	m*a*n [mæn] c*a*t [kæt]	*e* molto aperta
[ɛə]	th*e*re [ðɛə] b*ea*r [bɛə]	*e* aperta seguita da un suono di *a* e da una brevissima *r*
[ai]	fl*y* [flai] h*igh* [hai] n*i*ne [nain]	m*ai*
[au]	h*ow* [hau] h*ou*se [haus]	f*au*na
[ei]	d*ay* [dei] n*a*me [neim] ob*ey* [ɔ'bei]	é[i] *e* chiusa seguita da un leggero suono di *i*
[e]	g*e*t [get] b*e*d [bed]	p*e*tto *e* breve e stretta
[əː]	b*i*rd [bəːd] h*ea*rd [həːd] w*o*rd [wəːd]	*eu* francese
[ə]	*a*go [ə'gou] conc*e*rn [kən'səːn]	*a* brevissima, quàsi priva di suono
[iː]	t*ea* [tiː] s*ee* [siː] c*ei*ling ['siːliŋ]	p*i*no, v*i*no
[i]	*i*t, [it] b*i*g [big]	*i* breve e stretta, quasi come in f*i*tto, r*i*tto
[iə]	h*e*re [hiə] h*ea*r [hiə]	*i* + *a* come in z*ia*, m*ia* + un brevissimo suono di *r*
[ou]	g*o* [gou] n*o*te [nout] sl*ow* [slou]	ó[u] *o* chiusa seguita da un lieve suono di *u*
[ɔː]	s*aw* [sɔː] *a*ll [ɔːl] bef*o*re [bi'fɔː]	*o* aperta e prolungata come in m*o*le
[ɔ]	h*o*t [hɔt] w*a*sh [wɔʃ] l*o*ng [lɔŋ]	*o* aperta e breve come in n*o*tte
[ɔi]	b*oy* [bɔi] *oi*l [ɔil]	p*oi*
[uː]	t*oo* [tuː] y*ou* [juː] sh*oe* [ʃuː] t*rue* [truː]	*u* prolungata, come in f*u*ne, l*u*na

[u]	p*u*t [put] b*oo*k [buk]	*u* breve, come in t*u*tto, p*u*lpito
[uə]	p*oor* [puə] s*ure* [ʃuə]	*u* prolungata + un breve suono di *a* + un brevissimo suono di *r*

Consonanti inglesi

Simbolo	*Esempio inglese*	*Esempio italiano o Spiegazione*
[b]	*b*een [bi:n] gra*b* [græb]	*b* italiana
[d]	*d*ay [dei] ha*d* [hæd]	*d* italiana
[f]	*f*ather ['fɑ:ðə]	*f* italiana
[g]	*g*o [gou] bi*g* [big]	*g* dura, come in *g*occia, *g*hiaccio
[ŋ]	lo*ng* [lɔŋ] si*ng* [siŋ]	la *n* è prolungata. La *g* non si pronuncia
[h]	*h*ouse [haus]	*h* aspirata
[j]	*y*oung [jʌŋ] *y*es [jes] mill*i*on ['miljən]	*i* italiana
[k]	*c*ome [kʌm] mo*ck* [mɔk] s*ch*ool [sku:l] *k*ey [ki:]	*c* dura, come in *c*osa, s*c*uola, *c*hiosco
[l]	*l*ook [luk]	*l* italiana
[m]	*m*uch [mʌtʃ] la*mb* [læm] colu*mn* ['kɔləm]	*m* italiana
[n]	*n*oo*n* [nu:n]	*n* italiana
[ŋk]	i*nk* [iŋk] fra*nk* [fræŋk]	*n* + *c* dura
[p]	*p*ush [puʃ] ho*p*e [houp]	*p* italiana
[r]	*r*ed [red] b*r*ead [bred]	*r* non fortemente marcato
[s]	*s*tand [stænd] *s*and [sænd] ye*s* [jes] de*c*ide [di'said]	*s* aspra, come in *s*orte
[z]	(s between vowels or at the end of a word) ro*s*e [rouz] hi*s* [hiz] base*s* ['beisiz] *z*eal [zi:l]	*s* dolce e *z* dolce, come in ro*s*a e *z*aino
[ʃ]	*sh*all [ʃæl] ma*ch*ine [mə'ʃi:n] mo*t*ion ['mouʃən] spe*c*ial ['speʃəl] mi*ss*ion ['miʃən]	*sc* come in *sc*ene, *sc*ia, *sc*ialle, *sc*iogliere

[tʃ]	*ch*in [tʃin] ri*ch* [ritʃ] pi*c*tur*e* ['piktʃə]	*c* palatale, come in *c*ento
[t]	*t*ennis ['tenis] swee*t* [swi:t]	*t* italiana
[v]	*v*ery ['veri] li*v*e [liv]	*v* italiana
[w]	*w*ater ['wɔ:tə] *wh*ich [witʃ]	*u* italiana
[ʒ]	vi*s*ion ['viʒən] plea*s*ure ['pleʒə] gara*g*e ['gærɑ:ʒ]	*j* francese, come in *j*ournal
[dʒ]	*g*erm [dʒə:m] *j*ust [dʒʌst] bri*dg*e [bridʒ]	*g* dolce italiana, come in *g*enio, *g*iusto
[ð]	*th*e [ðə] fa*th*er ['fɑ:ðə]	Questo suono non esiste in italiano. È un suono dolce che si ottiene mettendo la lingua tra i denti. Potrebbe, approssimativamente, rappresentarsi con *dh*
[θ]	*th*ink [θiŋk] me*th*od ['meθəd]	Questo suono non esiste in italiano. È un suono forte, come l'emissione di un soffio tra i denti. Si avvicina alla *c* spagnola, come nella parola *cec*eo
[x]	(Scottish) lo*ch* [lɔx]	suono aspirato duro, come nella parola tedesca na*ch*

: indica che la vocale precedente è lunga.
L'accento principale è indicato dal simbolo ['] che è posto prima della sillaba accentata. L'accento secondario è indicato dal simbolo [ˌ]
Il simbolo fonetico è indicato entro parentesi quadra.

Italian-English

A

a *prep* at, in, to, by, for, on.
abàte *nm* abbot, abbé.
abbacinàre *vt* to blind, dazzle; deceive.
àbbaco *pl* **-chi** *nm* elementary arithmetic book; (*arc*) abacus.
abbadéssa *nf* abbess.
abbagliaménto *nm* dazzling, dimness of sight.
abbagliànte *a* dazzling; *nm* (*aut*) driving beam, high beam.
abbagliàre *vt* to dazzle, fascinate, deceive, astonish.
abbaiàre *vi* to bark.
abbaíno *nm* skylight, garret window, garret.
abbandonàre *vt* to leave, quit, abandon; **-rsi** *vr* to give oneself up to, despair.
abbandonataménte *ad* freely, passionately.
abbandonàto *a* abandoned, forsaken, deserted, desolate.
abbandóno *nm* abandonment, desertion.
abbarbicàre *vi* to take root; **-rsi** *vr* to cling (as ivy).
abbaruffàre *vt* to ruffle; **-rsi** *vr* to come to blows.
abbassaménto *nm* lowering, humiliation.
abbassàre *vti* to lower, lessen, abase, humble; **-rsi** *vr* to humble oneself, fall.
abbàsso *ad* below; *interj* down! down with!
abbastànza *ad* enough, fairly, rather.
abbàttere *vt* to throw down, depress, slaughter; to shoot down (a plane); **-rsi** *vr* to lose heart, fall.
abbattiménto *nm* knocking down, felling, overthrow, depression.
abbattúto *a* depressed, cast-down.
abbazía *nf* abbey.
abbecedàrio *nm* first spelling book.
abbelliménto *nm* embellishment, ornament.
abbellíre *vt* to adorn, embellish.
abbeveràre *vt* to water (animals).
abbeveratóio *nm* watering place, drinking trough.
abbiccí *nm* alphabet, rudiments.
abbiènte *a* well-to-do.
abbigliaménto *nm* clothes, clothing, finery.
abbigliàre *vt* to deck, dress.
abbinàre *vt* to pair, link together.
abbindolàre *vt* to wind (skeins); cheat, trick.
abbisognàre *vi and impers* to need, want.
abboccaménto *nm* interview, conversation, talk.
abboccàre *vti* to seize with the mouth; (*fig*) to be deceived; **-rsi** *vr* to have an interview, confer.
abboccàto *a* brimful; (*in speech*) nice; (*of wine*) sweet.
abbonacciàre *vt* to calm, pacify; **-rsi** *vr* (*sea*) to grow calm.
abbonaménto *nm* subscription, discount, season ticket.
abbonàre *vt* to accept as subscriber; (*com*) to deduct, pass (a doubtful account); **-rsi** *vr* to subscribe.
abbonàto *nm* subscriber, season-ticket holder, commuter; (*gas, el*) consumer.
abbondànte *a* abundant, plentiful.
abbondànza *nf* abundance, plenty.
abbondàre *vi* to abound.
abbordàbile *a* accessible, approachable.
abbordàggio *nm* (*naut*) boarding.
abbordàre *vt* to board (a ship), accost; **-rsi** *vr* (*naut*) to collide.
abbórdo *nm* access, approach; (*naut*) boarding.
abbottonàre *vt* to button (up); **-rsi** *vr* to button up, become secretive.
abbozzàre *vt* to outline, sketch, rough-hew.
abbòzzo *nm* rough draft, sketch; **a. d'uomo** manikin.
abbracciaménto, abbràccio *nm* embrace.
abbracciàre *vt* to embrace, contain, include.
abbrancàre *vt* to grasp, seize; **-rsi** *vr* to cling to, grasp.
abbreviàre *vt* to abridge, shorten.
abbreviazióne *nf* abbreviation, abridg(e)ment.
abbronzàre *vt* to tan, bronze, make brown.
abbronzatúra *nf* sunburn, tan, bronzing.
abbruciacchiàre *vt* to scorch, burn slightly.
abbrunàre *vt* to brown, darken; **-rsi** *vr* to go into mourning.
abbruníre *vti* to darken, grow dark, become tanned.
abbrustolíre *vt* to toast, crisp; **-rsi** *vr* to turn brown.
abbrutíre *vt* to brutalize.
abbuiàre *vt* to obscure; **-rsi** *vr* to grow dark, cloud over.

abbuòno *nm* discount, deduction.
abburattàre *vt* to sift.
abdicàre *vi* to abdicate.
abdicazióne *nf* abdication.
aberrazióne *nf* abberration, deviation.
abetàia *nf* fir-wood.
abéte *nm* fir-tree.
abiètto *a* abject, base.
abiezióne *nf* abjectness, baseness.
àbile *a* able, capable, clever, skillful.
abilità *nf* ability, dexterity, skill.
abilitàre *vt* to enable, qualify.
abilitazióne *nf* qualification.
Abissínia *nf* Abyssinia.
abissíno *a nm* Abyssinian.
abísso *nm* abyss, chasm; (*fig*) ruin.
abitàbile *a* habitable.
abitànte *nmf* inhabitant.
abitàre *vti* to inhabit, live in, live.
abitàto *a* inhabited; *nm* inhabited place.
abitazióne *nf* dwelling, house.
àbito *nm* dress, clothes, suit, habit, custom; **a. borghése** civilian clothes.
abituàle *a* habitual, customary.
abituàre *vt* to accustom; **-rsi** *vr* to get accustomed.
abitúdine *nf* habit, custom.
abitúro *nm* hovel.
abiúra *nf* abjuration, recantation.
abiuràre *vt* to abjure, recant.
ablatívo *nm* ablative case.
abluzióne *nf* ablution, purification.
abnegazióne *nf* self-denial, abnegation.
abolíre *vt* to abolish, repeal.
abolizióne *nf* abolition, repeal.
abominàre *vt* to abominate, detest.
abominazióne *nf* abomination, detestation.
abominévole *a* abominable.
abomínio *nm* abomination, shame.
aborígeno *a* aboriginal.
aborríre *vt* to abhor.
abortíre *vi* to miscarry, abort, fail.
abòrto *nm* miscarriage, abortion, still-born child; failure.
Abràmo *nm pr* Abraham.
abraşióne *nf* abrasion, graze.
abraşivo *a nm* abrasive.
abrogàre *vt* to abrogate, repeal.
abrogazióne *nf* abrogation, repeal.
abruzzése *a* of the Abruzzi; *nm* native of the A.
Abrúzzi e Molişe *nm pl* (*geogr*) Abruzzi e Molise.
àbside *nf* apse.
abuşàre *vt* to abuse, misuse, trespass on.
abuşívo *a* abusive, improper.
abúşo *nm* abuse, misuse, infringement (of the law).
A.C. Avànti Cristo *ad* B.C.
acàcia *pl* **-cie** *nf* acacia-tree.
accadèmia *nf* academy.
accadèmico *pl* **-ici** *a* academic; *nm* academician.
accadére *vi* to happen, occur.
accadúto *nm* event.
accagliàre *vi* **-rsi** *vr* to curdle.
accalappiàre *vt* to catch, ensnare, deceive.
accalcàre *vi* to crowd up; **-rsi** *vr* to crowd.
accaldàrsi *vr* to get heated, excited.
accaldàto *a* heated (with running *etc*).
accaloràre *vt* to heat; **-rsi** *vr* to get heated.
accampaménto *nm* encampment, camp.
accampàre *vi* to camp; *vt* (*reasons etc*) to adduce; **-rsi** *vr* to pitch camp.
accaniménto *nm* fury, ardor.
accanírsi *vr* to rage, to concentrate doggedly.
accaníto *a* pitiless, fierce, obstinate.
accànto *ad* beside, near.
accantonàre *vt* to billet.
accaparraménto *nm* earnest money, deposit; buying up, cornering.
accaparràre *vt* to conclude (a bargain) by paying earnest money; to buy up, corner.
accapigliàrsi *vr* to scuffle, to quarrel.
accappatóio *nm* bathrobe, wrap.
accapponàre *vi* **fàre a. la pèlle** to make the flesh creep; **la pèlle mi si accappona** I've got gooseflesh.
accarezzaménto *nm* caress.
accarezzàre *vt* to caress.
accartocciàre *vt* to wrap up, to crumple up.
accasàre *vt* to marry; **-rsi** *vr* to marry, set up house.
accasciaménto *nm* dejection.
accasciàre *vt* to depress; **-rsi** *vr* to fall to the ground, lose heart.
accatastàre *vt* to heap up, stack.
accattabríghe *nm* quarrelsome fellow.
accattàre *vi* to beg.
accattonàggio *nm* begging.
accattóne *nm* beggar.
accavalcióne, a cavalcióni *ad* astride.
accecaménto *nm* blinding, confusion, obstruction.
accecànte *a* blinding, dazzling.
accecàre *vt* to blind: **-rsi** *vr* to become blind.
accèdere *vi* to approach, enter.
acceleràre *vt* to accelerate, quicken, speed up.
acceleràto *a* accelerated; (*of a train*) slow.
acceleratóre *nm* accelerator.
accelerazióne *nf* acceleration.
accèndere *vt* to light, kindle; **-rsi** *vr* to catch fire, grow angry.
accendíno *nm* (cigarette) lighter.
accendisígaro *nm* cigarette-lighter.
accennàre *vti* to indicate, hint, nod.
accénno *nm* sign, hint.
accensióne *nf* lighting; (*aut*) ignition.
accènto *nm* accent.
accentuàre *vt* to accentuate.
accerchiàre *vt* to encircle, surround.
accertaménto *nm* ascertainment,

assurance, check; (*of account*) settlement.
accertàre *vt* to ascertain, (*com*) to settle, to assess; **-rsi** *vr* to make sure.
accéso *a* alight, flushed, bright.
accessíbile *a* accessible, approachable.
accèsso *nm* access, fit, paroxysm.
accessòrio *a nm* accessory.
accétta *nf* hatchet, axe.
accettàbile *a* acceptable.
accettàre *vt* to accept, agree to; **accettànte** *nm* (*com*) accepter.
accettazióne *nf* acceptance.
accètto *a* received with pleasure, welcome, (*com*) honored.
acchiappàre *vt* to catch, trap.
acciaccàre *vt* to bruise, enfeeble.
acciàcco *pl* **-àcchi** *nm* infirmity, ailment.
acciaiería *nf* steelworks.
acciàio *nm* steel.
accidentàle *a* accidental, casual.
accidentalménte *ad* accidentally.
accidentàto *a* (*of ground*) broken.
accidènte *nm* accident, misfortune.
accidènti! *interj* (*annoyance*) damn it!; (*surprise*) Good Heavens!
accídia *nf* idleness, sloth.
accidióso *a* idle, slothful.
accigliaménto *nm* frown, sullen air.
accigliàrsi *vr* to frown, look sullen.
accigliàto *a* frowning, sullen.
accíngersi *vr* to set about, prepare oneself.
acciocché *cj* in order that, so that.
acciuffàre *vt* to seize by the hair, grasp.
acciúga *nf* anchovy.
acclamàre *vt* to acclaim; *vi* to clap hands, cheer.
acclimàre, acclimatàre *vt* to acclimatize.
acclimatàrsi *vr* to grow acclimatized.
acclúdere *vt* to enclose.
acclúso *a* enclosed.
accoccolàrsi *vr* to crouch, squat.
accogliènte *a* welcoming, cozy.
accogliènza *nf* reception, welcome.
accògliere *vt* to receive, welcome.
accollàre *vt* to put round the neck, yoke; (*fig*) burden, saddle with; **-rsi** *vr* to undertake.
accollàto *a* high-necked.
accoltellàre *vt* to stab, knife.
accomandànte *nm* (*com*) sleeping partner.
accomandatàrio *nm* (*com*) acting partner.
accomàndita *nf* (*com*) limited partnership.
accomiatàre *vt* to dismiss; **-rsi** *vr* to take leave of.
accomodaménto *nm* adjustment, agreement, compromise.
accomodàre *vt* to repair, mend, arrange, adjust, (*com*) settle; **-rsi** *vr* to sit down, make oneself comfortable, come to terms; **s'accòmodi** take a seat, please.
accompagnaménto *nm* accompaniment, retinue.
accompagnàre *vt* to accompany, escort; **-rsi** *vr* to keep company, join, match; (*mus*) accompany oneself.
acconciàre *vt* to dress (the hair), adorn, arrange; **-rsi** *vr* to deck oneself.
acconciatúra *nf* hair style.
accóncio *a* fit, suitable.
accondiscéndere *vi* to consent, condescend.
acconsentíre *vi* to consent.
accontentàre *vt* to content; **-rsi** *vr* to be satisfied, be content with.
accónto *nm* (*com*) part payment.
accoppiàre *vt* to couple, pair, yoke; **-rsi** *vr* to join together, couple.
accoraménto *nm* grief, affliction.
accoràre *vt* to grieve deeply; **-rsi** *vr* to be grieved to the heart.
accorciàre *vt* to shorten; **-rsi** *vr* to grow shorter.
accordàre *vt* to grant; (*mus*) tune, harmonize, (*gram*) make agree; conciliate; **-rsi** *vr* to agree, be in harmony with.
accòrdo *nm* agreement, arrangement, (*mus*) chord, (*fig*) harmony, accord; **èssere d'a.** to agree.
accòrgersi *vr* to perceive, notice, realize, be aware of.
accorgiménto *nm* circumspection, prudence, device.
accórrere *vi* to run up, to go to help.
accortézza *nf* prudence, sagacity, cunning.
accòrto *a* wary, shrewd, prudent.
accostàre *vt* to approach, bring near(er); leave ajar; **-rsi** *vr* to approach, draw near.
accòsto *ad* beside, hard by.
accostumàre *vt* to train, accustom; **-rsi** *vr* to get accustomed.
accovacciàrsi *vr* to cower, crouch.
accozzàglia *nf* medley, disorderly mass; **un'a. di gènte** motley crowd.
accreditàre *vt* to give credit to, to accredit; **-rsi** to gain credit.
accréscere *vt* to increase.
accresciménto *nm* increase, growth.
accudíre *vi* (*of household duties*) to attend to.
accumulàre *vt* to accumulate, heap up; **-rsi** *vr* to accumulate.
accumulatóre *nm* (*el*) storage cell.
accumulazióne *nf* accumulation.
accuratézza *nf* accuracy, care.
accuràto *a* accurate, neat.
accúṣa *nf* accusation, charge.
accuṣàre *vt* to accuse, charge, blame, show, complain of, (*com*) acknowledge; **-rsi** *vr* to accuse oneself, confess.
accusatívo *a nm* accusative.
accuṣàto *nm* accused, defendant.
accuṣatóre *nm* accuser, prosecutor; **púbblico a.** public prosecutor.
acerbità *nf* acerbity, asperity.

acèrbo *a* unripe, sour, (*fig*) sharp.
àcero *nm* maple-tree.
acetilène *nm* acetylene.
acéto *nm* vinegar.
acetóne *nm* acetone.
acetóso *a* vinegary, sourish.
acidità *nf* acidity, sourness.
àcido *a nm* acid.
àcino *nm* grape, grape-stone.
àcne *nm* acne.
àcqua *nf* water; **a. corrènte** running water; **a. dólce** fresh water; **a. mineràle** mineral water; **a. potàbile** drinking water; **a. di sèltz** soda-water.
acquafòrte *nf* etching.
acquàio *nm* sink.
acquaplàno *nm* aquaplane.
acquaràgia *nf* turpentine.
acquartieràre *vt* (*troops*) to quarter; **-rsi** *vr* to take up quarters.
acquasantièra *nf* holy water stoup.
acquàta *nf* heavy shower.
acquàtico *pl* **-ici** *a* aquatic.
acquattàrsi *vr* to crouch, squat.
acquavíte *nf* gin, brandy.
acquazzóne *nm* sudden and heavy shower, downpour.
acquedótto *nm* aqueduct.
acquerellísta *nmf* painter in water-colors.
acquerèllo *nm* water color, water-color painting.
acquerúgiola *nf* drizzle.
acquiescènza *nf* acquiescence.
acquietàre *vt* to appease, pacify.
acquirènte *nmf* purchaser, buyer.
acquiṣíre *vt* to acquire, obtain.
acquistàre *vt* to acquire, buy; (*fig*) gain, improve.
acquísto *nm* acquisition, purchase, gain.
acquitríno *nm* marsh, swamp.
acquitrinóso *a* marshy, boggy.
acquolína *nf* **far veníre l'a. in bócca** to make somebody's mouth water.
acquóso *a* watery.
àcre *a* sharp, sour, harsh.
acrèdine *nf* bitterness, sourness; (*fig*) acrimony.
acrimònia *nf* acrimony.
acrimonióso *a* acrimonious.
acròbata *nmf* acrobat.
acrobazía *nf* acrobatics *pl*.
acuíre *vt* to sharpen, whet.
acúme *nm* quickness of wit, acumen.
acuminàre *vt* to point, sharpen.
acústica *nf* acoustics *pl*.
acutézza *nf* acuteness, wit, penetration.
acúto *a* acute, pointed, sharp.
adacquàre *vt* to water, irrigate.
adagiàre *vt* to lay down, make comfortable; **-rsi** *vr* to arrange oneself comfortably; *nm* proverb, saying.
adàgio *ad* slowly, softly, at leisure.
Adàmo *nm pr* Adam.
adattàbile *a* adaptable, applicable.
adattabilità *nf* adaptability.
adattàre *vt* to fit, adapt, adjust; **-rsi** *vr* to adapt oneself.
adàtto *a* fit, proper, right, suitable.
addebitàre *vt* to debit.
addensàre *vt* to make thick; **-rsi** *vr* to grow dense, thicken.
addentàre *vt* to bite.
addentràrsi *vr* to penetrate, probe.
addéntro *ad* within, inside.
addestràre *vt* to train, drill, instruct; (*horse*) break in; **-rsi** *vr* to train oneself, practice.
addétto *a* belonging to, attached; **a. ad un'ambasciàta** attaché at an embassy.
addí *ad* on the (day) of.
addiètro *ad* behind, back(wards), ago.
addío *ad nm* good-bye.
addirittúra *ad* downright, immediately, outright.
addírsi *vr and impers* to suit, become.
additàre *vt* to point out, show, indicate.
addizionàre *vt* to add (up).
addizióne *nf* addition, supplement.
addobbàre *vt* to furnish, decorate.
addòbbo *nm* decorative furnishing, hangings.
addolcíre *vt* to sweeten, soften, alleviate.
addoloràre *vt* to afflict, grieve; **-rsi** *vr* to be grieved, grieve.
Addoloràta (l') *nf* Our Lady of Sorrows.
addòme *nm* abdomen.
addomesticàre *vt* to tame; **-rsi** to become tame, become more sociable, grow familiar.
addormentàre *vt* to put to sleep; (*fig*) calm; **-rsi** to fall asleep.
addossàre *vt* to lay upon, place on the back of, place against, charge, load, burden; **-rsi** *vr* to undertake, charge oneself with.
addòsso *ad* on, upon, close by, above; **avére a.** to have on, wear; **tiràrsi a.** to bring upon oneself.
addúrre *vt* to adduce, cite.
adeguàre *vt* to equalize, balance, conform.
adeguàto *a* sufficient.
Adèle *nf pr* Adela.
adémpiere, adempíre *vt* to fulfill, perform; **-rsi** *vr* to come true.
adempiménto *nm* fulfillment, accomplishment, execution.
aderènte *a* adherent, close-fitting; *nmf* supporter.
aderènza *nf* adherence, adhesion; (*fig pl*) high connections.
aderíre *vt* to adhere, agree.
adescàre *vt* to lure, entice.
adeṣióne *nf* adhesion, adherence, consent.
adeṣívo *a* adhesive.
adèsso *ad* now, at present.
adiacènte *a* adjacent, adjoining, next.

adiacènza *nf* adjacency, vicinity.
adibíre *vt* to destine for use.
àdipe *nm* fat, grease.
adiposità *nf* fatness, plumpness.
adipóso *a* fat, plump.
adiràre *vt* to make angry, provoke; **-rsi** *vr* to get angry.
àdito *nm* entry, access; **dàre a. a** give rise to.
adocchiàre *vt* to eye, ogle.
adolescènte *a nmf* adolescent.
adolescènza *nf* adolescence, youth.
Adòlfo *nm pr* Adolph.
adombràre *vt* to shade, conceal; suggest, symbolize; **-rsi** *vr* to take umbrage.
adoperàre *vi* to use, employ; **-rsi** *vr* to exert oneself, endeavor.
adoràbile *a* adorable, charming.
adoràre *vt* to adore, worship.
adorazióne *nf* adoration, worship.
adornàre *vt* to adorn, deck; **-rsi** *vr* to adorn oneself.
adórno *a* adorned, trimmed.
adottàre *vt* to adopt.
adottívo *a* adoptive, adopted.
adozióne *nf* adoption.
Adriàno *nm pr* Adrian, Hadrian.
Adriàtico *a nm* Adriatic.
adulàre *vt* to flatter.
adulatóre *nm* **-tríce** *nf* flatterer.
adulatòrio *a* adulatory, flattering.
adulazióne *nf* adulation, flattery.
adulteràre *vt* to adulterate, taint, falsify.
adultèrio *nm* adultery.
adúltero *nm* adulterer.
adúlto *a nm* adult, grown-up.
adunànza *nf* assembly, meeting.
adunàre *vt* to assemble, bring together, convoke; **-rsi** *vr* to come together, assemble, (*mil*) fall-in.
adunàta *nf* (*mil*) fall-in; assembly; **a. popolàre** mass meeting.
adúnco *pl* **-chi** *a* hooked, curved.
aeràre *vt* to air, aerate.
aèro *a* of the air, aerial, airy, unsubstantial; *nm v* **aeroplàno.**
aerocèntro *nm* air center.
aerodinàmica *nf* aerodynamics *pl*; **aerodinàmico** *pl* **-ici** *a* aerodynamic, streamlined.
aeròdromo *nm* aerodrome, airfield, airport.
aeronàutica *nf* aeronautics *pl*, aviation, air force.
aeroplàno *nm* flying machine, airplane; **a. da càccia** fighter plane; **a. da bombardaménto** bomber; **a. a reazióne** jet plane; **a. di línea** airliner.
aeropòrto *nm* airport.
aerosòl *nm* (*chem*) aerosol.
àfa *nf* sultry heat.
affàbile *a* affable, friendly.
affabilità *nf* affability.
affaccendàrsi *vr* to occupy oneself, be very busy.
affaccendàto *a* busy.
affacciàre *vt* to bring forward, show; **-rsi** *vr* to show oneself, occur; **-rsi su** to face (a place).
affamàre *vt* to starve.
affamàto *a* hungry, famished, starving.
affannàre *vt* to trouble, vex; **-rsi** *vr* to toil, strive, fret, be anxious.
affannàto *a* breathless, panting, distressed.
affànno *nm* shortness of breath, asthma; trouble, anxiety.
affannóso *a* suffocating, troublesome, wearisome, troubled.
affàre *nm* affair, matter, business; **uòmo d'affàri** businessman.
affarísta *nm* unscrupulous businessman.
affaróne *nm* good bargain.
affascinànte *a* fascinating.
affascinàre *vt* to fascinate, enchant.
affastellàre *vt* to tie up in bundles, jumble up.
affaticàre *vt* to tire, harass; **-rsi** *vr* to get tired, toil, strive.
affàtto *ad* entirely; **niènte a.** not at all.
affermàre *vt* to affirm; **-rsi** *vr* to assert oneself, make a name for oneself.
affermatíva *nf* affirmative.
affermatívo *a* affirmative.
affermazióne *nf* statement, assertion, achievement.
afferràre *vt* to seize, grasp, comprehend.
affettàre *vt* to cut in slices; affect, pretend.
affettàto *a* sliced; affected, prim; *nm* sliced ham, salami.
affettazióne *nf* affectation.
affètto *a* affected, afflicted; *nm* affection, love.
affettuosaménte *ad* lovingly, affectionately.
affettuóso *a* affectionate.
affezionàre *vt* to make fond; **-rsi** *vr* to become fond of, attached to.
affezióne *nf* affection, attachment.
affiancàre *vt* to flank, place side by side.
affiatàre *vt* to bring together; **-rsi** *vr* to get on well together.
affibbiàre *vt* to buckle, clasp; (*fig*) give.
affibbiatúra *nf* buckle, clasp.
affidàre *vt* to entrust, confide; **-rsi** *vr* to trust, rely on.
affievolíre *vt* to weaken; *vi and* **-rsi** *vr* to grow weak.
affíggere *vt* to affix, stick (up), attach.
affilàre *vt* to whet, grind; **-rsi** *vr* to become thin.
affiliàre *vt* to affiliate; **-rsi** *vr* to become a member, join.
affiliazióne *nf* affiliation.
affinàre *vt* to refine, improve, sharpen, make thin; **-rsi** *vr* to become refined, improve, become sharper, become thinner.

affinatóio *nm* refining furnace.
affinché *cj* so that, in order that.
affíne *a* akin, kindred; *nm* kinsman, relative; **a. di** *cj* in order to, so as to.
affinità *nf* affinity, attraction.
affiocàre, affiochíre *vt* weaken, dim, render hoarse, *vi* become hoarse.
affiochiménto *nm* hoarseness.
affioràre *vi* to come to the surface.
affissàre *vt* to affix, gaze at.
affissióne *nf* bill-posting; **vietàta l'a.** post no bills.
affísso *a* fixed, posted up; *nm* bill, placard, poster.
affittacàmere *nm* landlord; *nf* landlady.
affittàre *vt* to let, rent, hire, lease.
affítto *nm* rent, hire; **dàre in a.** to let; **prèndere in a.** to rent.
afflíggere *vt* to afflict, torment; **-rsi** *vr* to be grieved.
afflítto *a* afflicted, sad.
afflizióne *nf* affliction.
affluènza *nf* crowd, large audience; abundance.
affluíre *vi* to flow, flock.
affogàre *vt* to drown, (*fig*) smother; *vi* to be drowned; **-rsi** *vr* to drown oneself; **uòvo affogàto** poached egg.
affollàre *vt* to crowd, throng; **-rsi** *vr* to crowd together.
affondàre *vti* to sink, founder, ruin; **-rsi** *vr* to sink, founder, go to the bottom.
affossaménto *nm* trench, entrenchment, sinking.
affrancàre *vt* to free, exempt; (*letter*) stamp; **-rsi** *vr* to be freed; grow strong.
affrancatúra *nf* postage.
affrànto *a* broken, crushed, overcome.
affratellàre *vt* to make as brothers; **-rsi** *vr* to fraternize.
affrésco *pl* **-chi** *nm* fresco.
affrettàre *vt* to hasten, speed; **-rsi** *vr* to hurry, make haste.
affrontàre *vt* to confront, face, attack; **-rsi** to meet face to face fight.
affrónto *nm* affront, insult.
affumicàre *vt* to fumigate, smoke-dry, blacken; **-rsi** *vr* to be smoked, grow black.
affústo *nm* (*mil*) gun-carriage.
afóso *a* sultry, heavy.
Àfrica *nf* Africa.
africàno *a nm* African.
Àgata *nf pr* Agatha.
agènda *nf* notebook, agenda.
agènte *nm* agent, factor, manager; **a. di polizia** policeman.
agenzía *nf* agency; **a. di turísmo** travel agency.
agevolàre *vt* to facilitate, make easy, help.
agévole *a* easy, manageable.
agganciàre *vt* to hook (up).
aggéggio *nm* gadget, device; trifle.
agghiacciàre *vt* to freeze, turn to ice; **-rsi** *vr* to freeze, grow cold.
aggiogàre *vt* to yoke.
aggiornàre *vt* to postpone; bring up to date; *vi* to dawn.
aggiornàto *a* up-to-date.
aggiotàggio *nm* stock-jobbing.
aggiràre *vt* to go round; deceive; **-rsi** *vr* to wander; deal with.
aggiúngere *vt* to add; **-rsi** *vr* to join, be added.
aggiúnta *nf* addition.
aggiúnto *a* added, additional; *nm* adjunct, assistant.
aggiustàre *vt* to adjust, regulate, set to rights, tidy, settle; **-rsi** *vr* to adjust oneself, tidy oneself, come to an agreement.
agglomeràre *vt* **-rsi** *vr* to agglomerate.
agglomeràto *a* agglomerate; *nm* agglomerate, agglomeration.
aggomitolàre *vt* to wind into a ball; **-rsi** *vr* to curl up.
aggranchíre *vt* to benumb.
aggrappàre *vt* to grapple, grasp; **-rsi** *vr* to cling to, lay hold (of).
aggravànte *a* aggravating; *nm* (*leg*) aggravating circumstance.
aggravàre *vt* to aggravate, weigh upon, oppress; **-rsi** *vr* (*illness*) to grow worse.
aggràvio *nm* heavy burden, expense, charge; **a. fiscàle** tax.
aggredíre *vt* to attack, assault.
aggregàre *vt* to aggregate.
aggregàto *a* joint, united; *nm* aggregate; block of houses; temporary clerk.
aggregazióne *nf* aggregation.
aggressióne *nf* aggression, attack.
aggressività *nf* aggressiveness.
aggressívo *a* aggressive; *nm* chemical agent used in warfare.
aggressóre *nm* aggressor, assailant.
aggrinzàre *vt* to wrinkle; **-rsi** *vr* to wrinkle, shrivel (up).
aggrottàre *vt* to frown; **a. le ciglia** to frown, knit one's brows.
aggrumàre *vt* to curdle, clot.
aggruppàre *vt* to group, collect, gather; **-rsi** *vr* to form a group.
agguàglio *nm* comparison.
agguantàre *vt* to seize.
agguàto *nm* ambush.
agguerríre *vt* to inure to war, train to arms.
agiatézza *nf* ease, comfort, easy circumstances *pl*.
agiàto *a* in easy circumstances, well-off, comfortable.
àgile *a* agile, nimble.
agilità *nf* agility, nimbleness.
àgio *nm* ease, comfort, leisure.
agíre *vi* to act, operate, behave; (*leg*) proceed.
agitàre *vt* to agitate, upset, excite; **-rsi** *vr* to get agitated.

agitazióne *nf* agitation, excitement.
àglio *nm* garlic.
agnèllo *nm* lamb.
Agnèse *nf pr* Agnes.
àgo *pl* **àghi** *nm* needle.
agognàre *vt* to yearn for, covet.
agonía *nf* agony, anguish.
agonizzàre *vi* to be in agony, be at the point of death.
agoràio *nm* needle-case.
Agostíno *nm pr* Augustine.
agósto *nm* August.
agràrio *a* agrarian.
agrèste *a* rustic, rural.
agrézza *nf* sourness, tartness.
agrícolo *a* agricultural.
agricoltóre *nm* farmer.
agricoltúra *nf* agriculture.
agrifòglio *nm* holly.
agrimensóre *nm* land surveyor.
àgro *a* sour, sharp; *nm* sourness; field; country surrounding a town.
agrodólce *a* bittersweet; *nm* sweet-and-sour sauce.
agrúmi *nm pl* citrus fruits *pl.*
aguzzàre *vt* to whet, sharpen, point; (*fig*) stimulate, sharpen.
agúzzo *a* sharp-pointed.
ahi *interj* oh!, ouch!
ahimè *interj* alas!
àia *nf* threshing floor.
aitànte *a* strong, sturdy; brave.
aiuòla *nf* flowerbed.
aiutànte *nmf* helper, assistant; (*mil*) **a. di càmpo** aide-de-camp.
aiutàre *vt* to help, assist, lend a hand; **-rsi** *vr* to make use of.
aiúto *nm* help, assistance; helper, assistant.
aizzàre *vt* to instigate, enrage, incite, set on (dogs).
àla *nf* wing; **a. a dèlta** (*av*) delta-wing.
alabàstro *nm* alabaster.
àlacre *a* willing, quick.
alacrità *nf* alacrity, quickness.
alàno *nm* mastiff.
alàre *nm* andiron, firedog.
Alàsca *nf* (*geogr*) Alaska.
alàto *a* winged.
àlba *nf* dawn.
albagía *nf* haughtiness, conceit.
albanése *a nmf* Albanian.
Albanía *nf* (*geogr*) Albania.
àlbatro *nm* albatross; (*tree*) arbutus.
albeggiàre *vi* to dawn.
albergàre *vt* to lodge, to harbor.
albergatóre *nm* hotel-owner.
albèrgo *pl* **-ghi** *nm* hotel.
àlbero *nm* tree; ship's mast.
Albèrto *nm pr* Albert.
albicòcca *nf* apricot.
àlbo *nm* roll, list; **èssere iscrítto all'a. degli avvocàti** to be called (admitted) to the bar.
albóre *nm* dawn.
àlbum *nm* album.
albúme *nm* albumen, white of egg.
alcalíno *a* alkaline.
alcalizzàre *vt* to alkalize.
àlce *nm* elk.
alchímia *nf* alchemy.
alcióne *nm* kingfisher.
àlcool *nm* alcohol; **alcoòlico** *pl* **-ici**, **alcoolizzato** *a nm* alcoholic.
alcoolísmo *nm* alcoholism.
alcúno *pron* somebody, anybody, (*preceded by* **non**) nobody; *a* any (*preceded by* **non**) no; **alcuni** *a and pron pl* some, a few *pl.*
Àldo *nm pr* Aldous.
àlea *nf* chance, risk; **córrere l'a.** to run the risk.
aleggiàre *vi* to flutter, try to fly.
Alessàndria *nf* (*geogr*) Alexandria (in Egypt).
Alessàndro *nm pr* Alexander.
alétta *nf* fin; (*av*) tab.
alettóne *nm* (*av*) aileron.
alfabètico *pl* **-ici** *a* alphabetical.
alfabèto *nm* alphabet.
alfière *nm* (*mil*) ensign, standard bearer; (*chess*) bishop.
alfíne *ad* at last.
Alfrèdo *nm pr* Alfred.
àlga *nf* seaweed.
àlgebra *nf* algebra.
Algería *nf* Algeria.
Algèri *nf* Algiers.
algeríno *a nm* Algerian.
aliànte *nm* glider.
àlibi *nm* (*leg*) alibi.
alíce *nf* anchovy.
Alíce *nf pr* Alice.
alienàre *vt* to alienate, estrange; **-rsi** *vr* to be estranged.
alienàto *a* estranged, crazy; *nm* lunatic, mentally deranged person.
alienazióne *nf* alienation, estrangement, mental derangement.
alièno *a* alien, adverse.
alimentàre *a* alimentary; *vt* to feed, nourish.
alimentàrio *a* alimentary.
alimentatóre *nm* nourisher; (*mech*) feeder.
alimentazióne *nf* nourishment, food, diet; (*mech*) feeding.
aliménto *nm* food, nourishment.
alisèi, vènti *nm pl* trade winds *pl.*
aliscàfo *nm* hydrofoil.
àlito *nm* breath, breathing; breeze.
allacciàre *vt* to lace, connect, entangle.
allagaménto *nm* inundation.
allagàre *vt* to inundate, overflow, submerge.
allampanàto *a* emaciated.
allargàre *vt* to enlarge, extend, widen.
allarmàre *vt* to alarm, disturb; **-rsi** *vr* to be alarmed.
allàrme *nm* alarm, alert.
allàto *ad* beside.
allattàre *vt* to suckle, breast-feed.
alleànza *nf* alliance, league.
alleàrsi *vr* to make an alliance.
alleàto *a* allied; *nm* ally.
allegàre *vt* to allege, enclose; (*teeth*) to set on edge.

allegazióne *nf* allegation.
alleggeríre *vt* to lighten, relieve; **-rsi** *vr* to put on lighter clothing, relieve oneself of.
allegoría *nf* allegory.
allegraménte *ad* cheerfully, merrily.
allegrézza *nf* gaiety, cheerfulness.
allegría *nf* mirth, gladness.
allégro *a* gay, cheerful, merry; (*mus*) allegro.
allenaménto *nm* training.
allenàre *vt* to train, strengthen, invigorate.
allenatóre *nm* trainer, coach.
allentàre *vt* to slacken, relax, diminish; **-rsi** *vr* to get slack; unlace or undo one's clothing.
allergía *nf* allergy.
allèrgico *pl* **-ici** *a* allergic.
allestíre *vt* to prepare, make ready.
allettaménto *nm* allurement.
allettànte *a* alluring.
allettàre *vt* to allure, entice; **-rsi** *vr* (*in illness*) to take to one's bed.
allevaménto *nm* bringing-up, breeding.
allevàre *vt* to bring up, breed.
allevatóre *nm* **-trice** *nf* breeder.
alleviàre *vt* to relieve.
allibíre *vi* to be amazed.
allietàre *vt* to gladden.
allièvo *nm* pupil, student, cadet.
allignàre *vi* to take root, grow.
allineàre *vt* to align, set in rows.
allocuzióne *nf* address, allocution.
allòdola *nf* skylark.
alloggiàre *vti* to lodge, stay, billet.
allòggio *nm* lodgings *pl*, billet, inn.
allontanaménto *nm* removal, distance, estrangement.
allontanàre *vt* to remove, send away; **-rsi** *vr* to go away, withdraw.
allóra *ad* then, at that time.
allorché *cj* when.
allòro *nm* laurel.
allucinàre *vt* to hallucinate; **-rsi** *vr* to suffer from hallucination, deceive oneself.
allucinazióne *nf* hallucination.
allúdere *vi* to allude, refer, hint.
allumínio *nm* aluminum.
allungàre *vt* to lengthen, prolong; (*wine etc*) water; hand; **-rsi** *vr* to grow longer, stretch oneself.
allușióne *nf* allusion.
almanaccàre *vi* to fancy, build castles in the air, puzzle one's brain.
almanàcco *pl* **-àcchi** *nm* almanac, calendar.
alméno *ad* at least.
àlno *nm* alder-tree.
alóne *nm* halo.
alpèstre *a* mountainous, wild.
Àlpi (le) *nf pl* the Alps *pl*.
alpigiàno *nm* inhabitant of a hilly district, mountaineer.
alpinișmo *nm* mountaineering.
alpíno *a* alpine; **A.** *nm* soldier of a special Italian alpine division.
alquànto *a* some, a good deal; *ad* somewhat, rather.
Alsàzia *nf* (*geogr*) Alsace.
alsaziàno *a nm* Alsatian.
alt *interj* halt, stop.
altaléna *nf* swing, seesaw.
altaménte *ad* highly, greatly.
altàre *nm* altar; **a. maggióre** high altar.
alteràre *vt* to alter, change; **-rsi** *vr* to get angry, go bad.
alterazióne *nf* change, deterioration, falsification.
altercare *vi* to quarrel.
alterézza, alterigia *nf* haughtiness, pride, insolence.
alternàre *vt* to alternate.
alternatíva *nf* alternative, alternation.
alternativaménte *ad* alternately, alternatively.
alternatívo *a* alternate, alternative.
altèro *a* dignified, proud, haughty.
altézza *nf* height; (*of cloth*) width; depth; highness; **A. Reàle** Royal Highness.
altezzóso *a* haughty, arrogant.
altíccio *a* tipsy.
altipiàno *nm* plateau, tableland.
altitúdine *nf* altitude, height.
àlto *a* high, tall, loud, deep; (*of cloth*) wide; (*geogr*) upper, northern; **ad àlta vóce** aloud.
Àlto Àdige *nm* (*geogr*) South Tyrol.
àlto-atesíno *a nm* South-Tyrolese.
altofórno *nm* blast furnace.
altolocàto *a* high-ranking, important.
altoparlànte *nm* loudspeaker.
altresí *cj* likewise, too.
altrettànto *ad* equally, as much (again); *interj* the same to you!
àltri *pron sing and pl* someone, another, some *pl*.
altrièri, l' *ad* the day before yesterday.
altriménti *ad* otherwise.
àltro *pron and a* (an)other, different, next; (something) else; *interj* not at all!; **per a.** anyhow.
altrónde, d' *ad* besides, on the other hand.
altróve *ad* elsewhere, somewhere else.
altrúi *pron* others, other people *pl*; *a* of other people; **l'a.** *nm* other people's property.
altúra *nf* height, elevation.
alúnno *nm* pupil, schoolboy.
alveàre *nm* beehive.
àlveo *nm* channel, bed of a river.
alzàre *vt* to raise, lift, build; **a. le càrte** to cut the cards; **a. le spàlle** to shrug one's shoulders; **-rsi** *vr* to get up, rise.
alzàta *nf* rise, elevation, shrug.
amàbile *a* amiable, kind, agreeable.
amabilità *nf* amiability, kindness.
amalgamàre *vt* to amalgamate.

amànte *a* loving, fond; *nmf* lover, sweetheart.
amàre *vt* to love, like, be fond of.
amareggiáre *vt* to embitter; **-rsi** *vr* to grow bitter.
amarèna *nf* sour black cherry.
amarézza *nf* bitterness, grief.
amàro *a* bitter, grievous, cruel.
amarràre *vt* to moor.
amatóre *nm* **-tríce** *nf* lover; amateur.
amàzzone *nf* Amazon, horsewoman.
ambascería *nf* embassy, deputation, diplomatic mission.
ambàscia *nf* shortness of breath, anxiety.
ambasciàta *nf* embassy, message.
ambasciatóre *nm* **-tríce** *nf* ambassador.
ambedúe *pron and a pl* both (of).
ambiènte *nm* atmosphere, circle, environment, room.
ambiguità *nf* ambiguity, doubt.
ambíguo *a* ambiguous, doubtful.
àmbio *nm* amble.
ambíre *vt* to long for, covet.
ambizióne *nf* ambition, love of finery, vanity.
ambizióso *a* ambitious, vain, fond of finery.
àmbra *nf* amber.
Ambrógio *nm pr* Ambrose; **ambrosiàno** *a* Ambrosian.
ambulànte *a* walking, itinerant.
ambulànza *nf* ambulance.
ambulatòrio *nm* out-patients' department, first-aid post.
Ambúrgo *nf* (*geogr*) Hamburg.
àmen *nm* amen.
amenità *nf* amenity, agreeableness.
amèno *a* pleasant, agreeable.
Amèrica *nf* America.
americàna *nf* cycle relay race.
americàno *a nm* American.
ametísta *nf* amethyst.
amíca *nf* (woman) friend.
amichévole *a* friendly, amiable.
amicízia *nf* friendship.
amíco *pl* **-íci** *a* friendly; *nm* friend, boy-friend.
àmido *nm* starch.
Amlèto *nm pr* Hamlet.
ammaccàre *vt* to bruise, crush; **-rsi** *vr* to get bruised.
ammaestraménto *nm* teaching, instruction, training of animals.
ammaestràre *vt* to teach, instruct; (*animals*) train, tame.
ammainàre *vt* (*sails*) to strike; (*flag*) haul down, lower.
ammalàre *vi* **-rsi** *vr* to fall sick, sicken.
ammalàto *a* sick, ill; *nm* patient.
ammaliàre *vt* to bewitch.
ammànco *pl* **-chi** *nm* shortage, deficit.
ammanettàre *vt* to handcuff.
ammansàre, ammansíre *vt* to make tame, gentle; **-rsi** *vr* to grow tame, gentle.
ammantàre *vt* to mantle, cover, hide, disguise.
ammaràre *vi* (*av*) to alight (on water).
ammassàre *vt* to amass, heap up; **-rsi** *vr* to come together, crowd.
ammàsso *nm* heap, accumulation, (*com*) pool.
ammattíre *vi* to go mad.
ammazzàre *vt* to kill, murder; **-rsi** *vr* to kill oneself; (*fig*) toil hard.
ammazzasètte *nm* braggart, bully.
ammazzatóio *nm* slaughter-house.
ammènda *nf* amends *pl*, fine.
ammendàre *vt* to amend, reform; **-rsi** *vr* to improve, get better.
ammennícolo *nm* gadget, trinket, trifle, pretext, cavil.
amméttere *vt* to admit, allow, receive.
ammezzàre *vt* to halve.
ammezzàto *nm* mezzanine.
ammiccàre *vt* to wink, beckon, (*with the eyes*) make a signal.
amministràre *vt* to administer, rule.
amministratívo *a* administrative.
amministrazióne *nf* administration, government, trusteeship.
ammiràbile *a* admirable, wonderful.
ammiragliàto *nm* admiralty.
ammiràglio *nm* admiral.
ammiràre *vt* to admire.
ammirazióne *nf* admiration, wonder.
ammissíbile *a* admissible.
ammissióne *nf* admission; **tàssa d'a.** entrance fee.
ammobiliàre *vt* to furnish.
ammòdo *a* nice-mannered, respectable; *ad* nicely, carefully.
ammogliàre *vt* to give a wife to; **-rsi** *vr* to take a wife.
ammollàre *vt* to steep, soften; **-rsi** *vr* to be soaked, get wet.
ammollíre *vt* to soften, move (to compassion); **-rsi** *vr* to get soft.
ammoníaca *nf* ammonia.
ammoniménto *nm* admonition, warning.
ammoníre *vt* to admonish, warn, advise.
ammonizióne *nf* admonition, reproof, warning.
ammontàre *nm* (*com*) amount; *vt* to heap; *vi* to amount; **-rsi** *vr* to accumulate.
ammorbidíre *vt* to soften; **-rsi** *vr* to grow soft.
ammortíre *vt* to weaken, deaden.
ammortizzare *vt* to deaden; (*debt*) redeem.
ammorzàre *vt* to extinguish, put out.
ammostàre *vt* (*grapes*) to press.
ammostatóio *nm* wine-press.
ammucchiàre *vt* to heap up.
ammuffíre *vi* to grow stale.
ammutinaménto *nm* mutiny, revolt.
ammutinàrsi *vr* to mutiny, revolt.
amnesía *nf* amnesia.

amnistía *nf* amnesty.
àmo *nm* fish-hook; **abboccàre all'a** to take the bait; (*fig*) to swallow the bait.
amóre *nm* love, affection; **a. pròprio** self-esteem; **per a. di** for the sake of; **fàre all'a.** to make love.
amoreggiàre *vt* to flirt.
amorétto *nm* flirtation, love affair.
amorévole *a* loving, kind.
amoríno *nm* Cupid, little darling; (*bot*) mignonette.
amorosaménte *ad* lovingly.
amoróso *a* loving; *nm* lover, gallant.
ampiézza *nf* ampleness.
àmpio *a* ample, wide, spacious.
amplèsso *nm* embrace.
ampliàre *vt* to enlarge, extend; **-rsi** *vr* to become larger, extend.
amplificàre *vt* to amplify, exaggerate.
amplificatóre *nm* amplifier.
amplitúdine *nf* amplitude.
ampólla *nf* phial, ampoule.
ampollosità *nf* bombast.
ampollóso *a* bombastic.
amputàre *vt* to amputate.
amputazióne *nf* amputation.
amuléto *nm* amulet, talisman.
anabbagliànte *a* anti-glare.
anacorèta *nm* anchorite, hermit.
anacronísmo *nm* anachronism.
anàgrafe *nf* registry office.
analfabèta *a nmf* illiterate.
analfabetísmo *nm* illiteracy.
anàlisi *nf* analysis.
analizzàre *vt* to analyze.
analogía *nf* analogy.
ananàsso *nm* pineapple.
anarchía *nf* anarchy.
anàrchico *pl* **-ici** *a nm* anarchic, anarchist.
anatomía *nf* anatomy.
anatòmico *pl* **-ici** *a* anatomic(al); *nm* anatomist.
anatomizzàre *vt* to anatomize, dissect.
ànatra *nf* duck.
ànca *nf* hip, haunch.
ànche *ad* also, too, even.
àncora *nf* anchor.
ancóra *ad* yet, still, again, even, more, longer.
ancoràggio *nm* anchorage.
ancoràre *vi* to anchor.
andaménto *nm* gait, carriage, trend.
andànte *a* current, common, cheap, plain; (*style*) flowing; **artícolo a.** cheap article.
andàre *vi* to go, call on, proceed; please, suit, happen; **a. a pièdi** to go on foot; *nm* going, gait; **a lúngo a.** in the long run; **andàrsene** to go away.
andàta *nf* going; **a. e ritórno** (going) there and back; **bigliétto di a.** single ticket.
andatúra *nf* gait.
andàzzo *nm* trend, passing fashion.
Ànde (le) *nf pl* (*geogr*) the Andes *pl*.
andirivièni *nm pl* coming and going of people, digressions, windings *pl*.
àndito *nm* passage, entrance.
Andrèa *nm pr* Andrew.
andróne *nm* portal, entrance (hall).
anèddoto *nm* anecdote.
anelàre *vi* to long for, pant, be breathless.
anèllo *nm* ring, ringlet, thimble; (*of a chain*) link.
anemía *nf* anemia.
anèmico *pl* **-ici** *a* anemic.
anestètico *pl* **-ici** *a nm* anesthetic.
anfíbio *a* amphibious; *nm* amphibian.
anfiteàtro *nm* amphitheatre.
anfràtto *nm* ravine, gorge.
angariàre *vt* to vex, harass, ill-treat.
Àngela *nf pr* Angela.
angèlico *pl* **-ici** *a* angelic.
àngelo *nm* angel.
anghería *nf* vexation, oppression, ill-treatment.
angína *nf* angina, quinsy.
angipòrto *nm* blind alley.
anglicàno *a nm* Anglican.
anglosàssone *a nmf* Anglo-Saxon; British and American.
angolàre *a* angular.
àngolo *nm* angle, corner.
angòscia *nf* anguish, affliction.
angoscióso *a* afflicted, grievous.
anguílla *nf* eel; elusive, nimble person.
angúria *nf* water-melon.
angústia *nf* narrowness; want, distress.
angustiàre *vt* to grieve, vex, harass; **-rsi** *vr* to be distressed, be afflicted.
angústo *a* narrow.
ànice *nm* aniseed.
ànima *nf* soul, spirit, person.
animàle *a nm* animal.
animàre *vt* to animate, enliven; **-rsi** *vr* to grow animated, take courage, get excited.
animàto *a* living, lively, animated; **cartóne a.** animated cartoon.
animèlla *nf* sweetbread.
ànimo *nm* mind, heart, courage; **fàrsi a.** to pluck up courage; **pèrdersi d'a.** to lose heart.
animosità *nf* animosity.
animóso *a* courageous, valiant.
anisétta *nm* anisette.
ànitra *nf* duck.
anitròccolo *nm* duckling.
Ànna *nf pr* Anna, Anne, Ann.
annacquàre *vt* to water, dilute; (*fig*) moderate.
annaffiàre *vt* to water, sprinkle.
annaffiatóio *nm* watering-can.
annàli *nm pl* annals *pl*.
annàta *nf* year; year's profits *pl*, produce *etc*.
annebbiàre *vt* to cloud, dim, darken; **-rsi** *vr* to grow dim, be overcast.
annegàre *vt* to drown; *vi* to be drowned; **-rsi** *vr* to drown oneself.

anneríre *vt* to blacken, tarnish.
annessióne *nf* annexation.
annèsso *a* attached, annexed; *nm* annex.
annèttere *vt* to annex.
annichilíre *vt* to annihilate; (*fig*) dismay.
annidàrsi *vr* to nestle, nest, hide.
annientaménto *nm* annihilation, destruction.
annientàre *vt* to annihilate, destroy; **-rsi** *vr* to come to nothing; (*fig*) abase oneself.
anniversàrio *a nm* anniversary.
ànno *nm* year; **capo d'a.** New Year ('s Day).
annodàre *vt* to knot; **a. amicízie** to make friends.
annoiàre *vt* to bore, vex, tire; **-rsi** *vr* to get tired, be bored.
annòna *nf* victuals *pl*, provisions *pl*.
annonàrio *a* connected with provisions.
annóso *a* old, ancient.
annotàre *vt* to note, annotate.
annotazióne *nf* annotation, note.
annottàre *vi* **-rsi** *vr* to grow dark.
annoveràre *vt* to number, count.
annuàle *a* annual, yearly.
annualità *nf* annuity.
annuàrio *nm* annual, trade directory; (*of members*) list.
annuíre *vi* to nod.
annuità *nf* yearly installment.
annullaménto *nm* annulment, repeal.
annullàre *vt* to repeal, annul.
annunciàre, annunziàre *vt* to announce, predict.
annunciazióne *nf* annunciation; **fèsta dell'A.** Lady Day.
annúncio, annúnzio *nm* announcement, advertisement.
Annunziàta *nf* Our Lady of the Annunciation.
ànnuo *a* annual, yearly.
annusàre *vi* to sniff, smell.
anodíno *a nm* anodyne.
ànodo *nm* (*el*) anode.
anomalía *nf* anomaly.
anòmalo *a* anomalous.
anònimo *a* anonymous.
anormàle *a* abnormal.
anormalità *nf* abnormality.
ànsa *nf* handle.
ansàre *vi* to pant.
ànsia *nf* anxiety.
ansietà *nf* anxiety, anxiousness.
ansimàre *vi* to pant.
ansióso *a* anxious, eager.
antagonismo *nm* antagonism.
antagonista *nmf* antagonist, opponent.
antàrtico *pl* **-ici** *a* antarctic.
antecedènte *a nm* antecedent.
antecedènza *nf* precedence, priority.
antecessóre *nm* predecessor.
antefàtto *nm* preceding event.
anteguèrra *a* pre-war; *nm* pre-war times *pl*.
antemuràle *nm* rampart, bulwark.
antenàto *nm* ancestor.
anténna *nf* feeler, aerial, antenna; **a. d'emissióne** transmitting aerial; **a. di ricezióne** receiving aerial.
antepórre *vt* to put before, prefer.
anteprima *nf* preview.
anterióre *a* prior, former, fore(most).
antiabbagliànte *a* anti-glare.
antiaèreo *a* (*mil*) anti-aircraft.
antibiòtico *pl* **-ici** *a nm* antibiotic.
anticàglia *nf* old rubbish, old curiosity.
anticàmera *nf* anteroom, hall.
anticàrro *a* (*mil*) anti-tank.
antichità *nf* antiquity.
anticipàre *vt* to anticipate, pay in advance, forestall; *vi* arrive earlier.
anticipazióne *nf* anticipation, advance payment.
antícipo *nm* advance, earnest; (*aut*) spark advance.
anticlericàle *a nmf* anti-clerical.
antíco *pl* **-íchi** *a* ancient, antique, obsolete.
anticomunísta *a nmf* anti-communist.
antidiluviàno *a* antediluvian.
antídoto *nm* antidote.
antifascísta *a nmf* antifascist.
antifúrto *a nm* antitheft.
antílope *nm* antelope.
antimeridiàno *a* antemeridian.
antimilitarismo *nm* antimilitarism.
antipàsto *nm* hors d'œuvres *pl*.
antipatía *nf* antipathy, dislike.
antipàtico *pl* **-ici** *a* unpleasant, disagreeable.
antípodi *nm pl* Antipodes.
antipòrta *nf* outer door.
antiquàrio *nm* antiquarian.
antiquàto *a* antiquated, old-fashioned, out-of-date.
antirúggine *a* antirust.
antisemíta *nmf* anti-Semite.
antisemítico *pl* **-ici** *a* anti-Semitic.
antisemitismo *nm* anti-Semitism.
antisèttico *pl* **-ici** *a nm* antiseptic.
antistànte *a* before, in front of.
antivigília *nf* the day before the eve.
antologia *nf* anthology.
Antònia *nf pr* Antonia.
Antònio *nm pr* Ant(h)ony.
antracíte *nf* anthracite.
àntro *nm* cave, den.
antropòfago *pl* **-gi, -ghi** *a nm* maneater, cannibal.
antropologia *nf* anthropology.
anulàre *nm* ring finger.
Anvérsa *nf* (*geogr*) Antwerp.
ànzi *prep* before; *cj* rather, on the contrary.
anzianità *nf* seniority.
anziàno *a* elderly, old, senior; *nm* elder.
anziché *cj* instead of, rather than.
apatía *nf* apathy.
apàtico *pl* **-ici** *a* apathetic.
àpe *nf* bee.
aperitívo *nm* aperitif.

apèrto *a* open, frank; **all'a.** in the open air; *ad* frankly.
apertúra *nf* aperture, opening, hole, span.
apiàrio *nm* beehive.
àpice *nm* apex, top, summit.
apocalísse *nf* Apocalypse.
apòcrifo *a* apocryphal.
apogèo *nm* apogee, acme.
apòlide *a nmf* stateless (person).
apolítico *pl* **-ici** *a* non-political.
apología *nf* apology.
apòlogo *pl* **-ghi** *nm* apologue.
apoplessía *nf* apoplexy.
apoplèttico *pl* **-ici** *a* apoplectic.
apòstata *nmf* apostate.
apostolàto *nm* apostleship.
apostòlico *pl* **-ici** *a* apostolic.
apòstolo *nm* apostle.
appagàre *vt* to satisfy, content; **-rsi** *vr* to be satisfied.
appaiàre *vt* to pair, match, couple; **-rsi** *vr* to pair, unite.
appallottolàre *vt* to roll into a ball; **-rsi** *vr* to coil up.
appaltàre *vt* to let out or lease out, farm.
appàlto *nm* undertaking, contract.
appannàggio *nm* appanage, inheritance.
appannàre *vt* to tarnish, dim; **-rsi** *vr* to grow dim, tarnish.
apparàto *nm* apparatus, adornment, pomp; (*theat*) scenery.
apparecchiàre *vt* to prepare, furnish, lay the cloth; **-rsi** *vr* to get ready.
apparécchio *nm* receiver (telephone) apparatus, set; airplane; **a. cinematogràfico** (film) projector; **a. fotogràfico** camera; **a. trasmitténte** transmitting set; **a. televisívo** television set.
apparènte *a* obvious, visible.
apparènza *nf* appearance; **in a.** apparently.
apparíre *vi* to appear, show oneself.
appariscènte *a* gorgeous.
appariscènza *nf* appearance, showiness.
apparizióne *nf* apparition, vision.
appartaménto *nm* flat, apartment; **a. ammobiliàto** furnished flat.
appartàre *vt* to set apart, separate; **-rsi** *vr* to withdraw, retire.
appartàto *a* secluded, remote, solitary.
appartenére *vi* to belong, concern.
appassionàre *vt* to move, excite; **-rsi** *vr* to be excited, eager (about).
appassionàto *a* eager, enthusiastic.
appassíre *vi* to fade, wither.
appellàre *vt* to call, name; **-rsi** to appeal.
appèllo *nm* appeal, roll-call; **fare l'a.** to call the roll.
appéna *ad* hardly, scarcely.
appèndere *vt* to hang up.
appendíce *nf* appendix, addition.
appendicíte *nf* appendicitis.
Appennìni *nm pl* (*geogr*) the Apennines.
appesantíre *vt* to make heavy, weigh down; **-rsi** *vr* to become heavier, stouter.
appetíre *vt* to long for, desire.
appetíto *nm* appetite, strong desire; **avére a.** to be hungry.
appetitóso *a* appetizing, tempting.
appianaménto *nm* leveling.
appianàre *vt* to level, smooth.
appiattàre *vt* to flatten, conceal; **-rsi** *vr* to squat down, hide oneself.
appiccàre *vt* to join, hang (up), start; infect; **-rsi** *vr* to cling.
appiccicàre *vt* to stick; **-rsi** *vr* to stick together, hang on.
appiccicatíccio *a* sticky.
appiccicóso *a* sticky.
appiè *ad* at the foot, at the bottom.
appièno *ad* fully, completely.
appigionàre *vt* to let, rent, (*house*) lease.
appigliàrsi *vt* to cling to, hold on to; (*advice etc*) follow.
appíglio *nm* pretext.
appiómbo *ad* perpendicularly; *nm* perpendicularity; self assurance.
appisolàrsi *vr* to doze off.
applaudíre *vt* to applaud.
applàuso *nm* applause.
applicàre *vt* to apply, enforce, appoint; **-rsi** *vr* to apply oneself, study.
appoggiàre *vt* to lean, prop, support; **-rsi** *vr* to lean against, depend upon, trust.
appoggiàto *a* leaning, supported.
appòggio *nm* prop, support, favor.
appollaiàrsi *vr* to roost, perch.
appórre *vt* to affix, insert; (*fig*) impute.
apportàre *vt* to bring, cause.
appòsito *a* special, suitable.
appòsta *ad* on purpose.
appostaménto *nm* ambush, (*mil*) emplacement.
appostàre *vt* to waylay; **-rsi** *vr* to lurk.
apprèndere *vt* to learn, get to know.
apprendísta *nmf* apprentice.
apprendistàto *nm* apprenticeship.
apprensióne *nf* apprehension.
apprensívo *a* apprehensive, fearful, quick to perceive.
apprèsso *prep* near, by, after, behind; *ad* close by, shortly after.
apprestàre *vt* to prepare; **-rsi** *vr* to get ready.
apprezzaménto *nm* appreciation, estimate, appraisement.
apprezzàre *vt* to value, rate, appreciate.
appròccio *nm* approach.
approdàre *vi* to come to shore, land.
appròdo *nm* landing place.
approfittàre *vi* to profit; **-rsi** *vr* to avail oneself, take advantage.
approfondàre, -díre *vt* to dig, deepen, search out, go into thoroughly.
appropriàre *vt* to use properly,

adapt; **-rsi** *vr* to appropriate to oneself.
approssimàre *vt* to place near; **-rsi** *vr* to approach, draw near.
approssimatívo *a* approximate, rough.
approvàre *vt* to approve, pass.
approvazióne *nf* approval.
approvvigionàre *vt* to victual, provision.
appuntaménto *nm* appointment.
appuntàre *vt* to point, sharpen, pin, tack, blame.
appuntíno *ad* just in time, exactly, neatly.
appúnto *nm* note; *ad* precisely, exactly.
appuràre *vt* to verify, ascertain; (*com*) clear.
apribottíglie *nm* bottle-opener.
apríle *nm* April.
apríre *vt* to open, unlock, split, disclose, begin; **-rsi** *vr* to open, expand; (*weather*) clear.
apriscàtole *nm* tin-opener, can-opener.
aquàrio *nm* aquarium.
àquila *nf* eagle; (*fig*) genius.
aquilóne *nm* north wind; (*toy*) kite.
Aquisgràna *nf* (*geogr*) Aachen.
Aràbia *nf* Arabia.
aràbico *pl* **-ici** *a* Arabic, Arabian.
àrabo *a* Arab, Arabian; *nm* Arabic, Arab.
aragósta *nf* lobster.
aràldica *nf* heraldry.
aràldo *nm* herald, harbinger.
arància *nf* orange.
aranciàta *nf* orangeade.
arâncio *a nm* orange, orange (tree).
aranciόne *a nm* (*color*) orange.
aràre *vt* to plow, cultivate.
aratóre *nm* plowman.
aràtro *nm* plow.
aràzzo *nm* tapestry.
arbitràggio *nm* speculation on the exchange; umpiring.
arbitràre *vi* to arbitrate, umpire, referee; **-rsi** *vr* to take the liberty (to do).
arbitràrio *a* arbitrary.
arbitràto *nm* arbitration.
arbítrio *nm* will, absolute power.
àrbitro *nm* arbiter, umpire, referee.
arbòreo *a* arboreal.
arboréto *nm* grove.
arboscèllo *nm* small tree, shrub.
arbústo *nm* shrub.
àrca *nf* chest, coffer, tomb; **a. di Noè** Noah's Ark.
arcàico *pl* **-ici** *a* archaic.
arcaismo *nm* archaism.
arcàngelo *nm* archangel.
arcàno *a* secret, mysterious; *nm* mystery.
arcàta *nf* archway, arcade.
archeología *nf* archaeology.
archeològico *pl* **-ici** *a* archaeological.
archeòlogo *pl* **-gi, -ghi** *nm* archaeologist.
archétto *nm* small arch; (violin) bow.
architettàre *vt* to draw the plan of; (*fig*) plot, contrive.
architétto *nm* architect.
architettúra *nf* architecture.
archívio *nm* archives *pl*, record office.
archivísta *nmf* archivist.
Arcibàldo *nm pr* Archibald.
arcidúca *nm* archduke.
arciduchéssa *nf* archduchess.
arcière *nm* archer.
arcígno *a* gruff, surly.
arcipèlago *pl* **-ghi** *nm* archipelago.
arciprète *nm* (*eccl*) dean.
arcivescovàdo *nm* archbishopric.
arcivèscovo *nm* archbishop.
àrco *pl* **-chi** *nm* bow, arch.
arcobaléno *nm* rainbow.
arcuàto *a* arched, bent.
ardènte *a* burning, ardent, eager, spirited.
àrdere *vi* to burn, glow, be on fire, shine.
ardèsia *nf* slate.
ardiménto *nm* boldness, daring.
ardíre *vi* to dare, be bold; *nm* daring, valor.
arditézza *nf* daring, hardihood.
ardíto *a* daring, hardy, bold.
ardóre *nm* ardour, enthusiasm, passion.
àrduo *a* arduous, difficult, dangerous.
àrea *nf* area, surface.
aréna *nf* sand, amphitheatre.
arenàre *vi* to run aground; **-rsi** *vr* to stick fast, be in difficulties.
argentàre *vt* to silver, silver plate.
argentàto *a* silvery, silver, silver-plated.
argentatúra *nf* silver-plating; **a. galvànica** electroplating.
argentería *nf* silverware.
argentiére *nm* silversmith.
Argentína *nf* Argentina.
argentíno *a nm* Argentine.
argentíno *a* silvery.
argènto *nm* silver; **a. vívo** mercury, quicksilver.
argentóne *nm* German silver, nickel silver.
argílla *nf* argil, potter's clay.
argillóso *a* clayey.
arginàre *vt* to dam, dike, embank; (*fig*) stem.
àrgine *nm* bank, embankment, dam (*also fig*).
argomentàre *vt* to argue, reason.
argoménto *nm* argument, subject, topic, occasion, synopsis.
arguíre *vi* to infer.
argutézza *nf* finesse, quibble, witticism.
argúto *a* subtle, witty, ingenious.
argúzia *nf* subtlety, piquancy, joke.
ària *nf* air, wind, appearance, song; **all'a. apèrta** out-of-doors.
aridità *nf* aridity, barrenness.
àrido *a* arid, barren, dry.

arieggiàre *vt* to air; *vi* to resemble.
arínga *nf* herring; **a. affumicàta** kipper, smoked herring.
arióso *a* airy.
aristocràtico *pl* **-ici** *a* aristocratic; *nm* aristocrat.
aristocrazía *nf* aristocracy.
aritmètica *nf* arithmetic.
aritmètico *pl* **-ici** *a* arithmetical; *nm* arithmetician.
arlecchíno *nm* harlequin, buffoon.
àrma *nf* weapon; (*mil*) branch, service; coat of arms.
armacòllo, ad *ad* in a sling.
armàdio *nm* cupboard, wardrobe.
armaiuòlo *nm* gunsmith, armorer.
armaménto *nm* armament, arming, weapons *pl*.
armàre *vt* to arm, equip, provide; **-rsi** *vr* to arm oneself, take up arms.
armàta *nf* army, navy; **corpo d'a.** army corps.
armàto *a* armed, equipped; (*el*) armored; (*building*) reinforced; **a màno armàta** by force of arms.
armatúra *nf* armor, armoring, framework; (*el*) armature.
Armènia *nf* (*geogr*) Armenia.
armèno *a nm* Armenian.
arménto *nm* herd of cattle.
armistízio *nm* armistice.
armonía *nf* harmony, concord.
armonizzàre *vt* to harmonize.
Arnàldo *nm pr* Arnold.
arnése *nm* tool, utensil.
àrnia *nf* beehive.
arròma *nf* aroma, fragrance.
àrpa *nf* harp.
arpeggiàre *vi* to play the harp, play in arpeggios.
arpía *nf* harpy.
arpióne *nm* hook, hinge.
àrra *nf* earnest money, pledge.
arrabbiàre *vt* to make angry; **-rsi** to get angry.
arrabbiàto *a* furious; rabid.
arrampicàrsi *vr* to climb.
arrecàre *vt* to bring, cause.
arredaménto *nm* furnishings.
arredàre *vt* to fit out, furnish.
arrèdo *nm* furniture, furnishings.
arrèndersi *vr* to surrender, yield, submit.
arrestàre *vt* to stop, seize, arrest; **-rsi** *vr* to stop.
arrèsto *nm* arrest, stop, pause; **in a.** under arrest.
arretràre *vt* to pull back, withdraw; **-rsi** *vr* to draw back, recoil.
arretràto *a* backward; (*com*) outstanding, in arrears; *nm* (*also pl*) arrears *pl*.
arricchíre *vt* to enrich, embellish; *vi* **-rsi** *vr* to grow rich, thrive.
arricchíto *nm* profiteer, nouveau riche.
arricciàre *vt* to curl; **a. il nàso** to frown, show disgust.
arrídere *vi* to smile upon.
Arrígo *nm pr* Henry.
arrínga *nf* harangue, speech.
arringàre *vi* to harangue.
arrischiàre *vt* to risk, hazard; **-rsi** *vr* to venture, dare.
arrischiàto *a* risky, venturesome, rash.
arrivàre *vi* to arrive; (*fig*) to achieve, succeed, happen, understand, fit, be reduced to.
arrivàto *a* successful; *nm* a successful man.
arrivedérci(-la) *interj* goodbye.
arrivísmo *nm* social climbing.
arrivísta *nmf* social climber, go-getter.
arrívo *nm* arrival.
arrochíre *vt* to make hoarse; **-rsi** *vr* become hoarse.
arrogànte *a* arrogant, overbearing.
arrogànza *nf* arrogance.
arrolàre *vt* to enroll, register; **-rsi** *vr* to enroll oneself, enlist.
arrossíre *vi* to blush, be ashamed.
arrostíre *vt* to roast, toast.
arròsto *nm* roast meat.
arrotàre *vt* to whet, grind, wear smooth.
arrotíno *nm* knife-grinder.
arrotolàre *vt* to roll up.
arrotondàre *vt* to round; **-rsi** *vr* to become round, plump.
arrovellàrsi *vr* to get angry, worry.
arroventàre *vt* to make red-hot.
arrovesciàre *vt* to turn inside out, overthrow; **-rsi** *vr* to capsize, turn over.
arrovèscio, a rovèscio *ad* against the grain, on the wrong side, the reverse way.
arruffàre *vt* to ruffle, tousle, confuse; **-rsi** *vr* to get ruffled, confused.
arruginíre *vi* **-rsi** *vr* to rust, grow rusty.
arsèlla *nf* mussel.
arsenàle *nm* arsenal.
arsènico *nm* arsenic.
àrso *a* burnt, dried up.
arsúra *nf* burning heat, drought, thirst.
àrte *nf* art, skill, profession, artifice.
artéfice *nm* artificer, artisan, creator.
artèria *nf* artery; thoroughfare.
àrtico *pl* **-ici** *a* arctic, northern.
articolàre *vt* to articulate, pronounce; *a* articular.
articolàto *a* articulate; jointed, hinged.
artícolo *nm* article; **a. di fóndo** (*in newspapers*) leading article, leader, editorial; **articoli sportívi** *pl* sports goods, sporting goods.
artificiàle *a* artificial.
artifício *nm* artifice, contrivance, cunning.
artificióso *a* artful, crafty, sly.
artigianàto *nm* artisans *pl*, handicraft, small industry.
artigiàno *a* (of an) artisan; *nm* artisan, craftsman.
artiglière *nm* gunner, artilleryman.

artiglieria *nf* (*mil*) artillery.
artiglio *nm* claw, talon, clutch.
artista *nmf* artist, artiste, actor, actress, singer.
artistico *pl* **-ici** *a* artistic.
àrto *nm* (*anat*) limb.
Artúro *nm pr* Arthur.
arzigogolàre *vt* to cavil, follow a fantastic argument.
arzigògolo *nm* cavil, whim.
arzillo *a* sprightly, nimble.
ascèlla *nf* armpit.
ascendènte *a* ascending, ascendant, -ent; *nm* ascendency, ascendant, ancestor.
ascendènza *nf* ancestors *pl*; ascendancy.
ascéndere *vi* to ascend, rise; amount to.
ascensióne *nf* ascent, ascension, Ascension Day.
ascensóre *nm* lift, elevator.
ascésa *nf* ascent, accession.
ascèsso *nm* abscess.
ascèta *nm* ascetic, recluse.
ascètico *pl* **-ici** *a* ascetic.
ascetismo *nm* asceticism.
àscia *nf* axe, hatchet.
asciugacapélli *nm* hair-drier.
asciugamàno *nm* towel.
asciugàre *vt* to dry, wipe.
asciugatríce (automàtica) *nf* spin-drier.
asciútto *a* dry, thin, penniless; **all'a.** in a dry place; **restàre all'a.** to be without money, news *etc.*
ascoltàre *vt* to listen, hear, attend; (*med*) sound.
ascoltatóre *nm* **-tríce** *nf* listener, hearer.
ascoltazióne *nf*, **ascólto** *nm* listening, hearing; (*med*) auscultation; **stàre in ascólto** to listen; **dàre ascólto** to lend an ear.
asfàlto *nm* asphalt.
asfissía *nf* asphyxia.
asfissiàre *vt* to asphyxiate.
Àsia *nf* Asia.
asiàtico *pl* **-ici** *a nm* Asiatic, Asian.
asilo *nm* refuge.
asinàta *nf* foolish action, foolish remark.
asinería *nf* stupidity, foolish action, foolish remark.
àsino *nm* ass.
àsma *nf* asthma.
asmàtico *pl* **-ici** *a* asthmatic.
àsola *nf* buttonhole.
aspàrago *pl* **-gi** *nm* asparagus.
aspèrgere *vt* to sprinkle.
asperità *nf* asperity, harshness.
aspettàre *vt* to wait for, await; **-rsi** *vr* to expect, look for.
aspettatíva *nf* expectation, hope; temporary discharge; **in a.** *ad* on the reserve list.
aspettazióne *nf* expectation.
aspètto *nm* aspect, appearance, look; **sàla d'a.** *nf* waiting room.
aspirànte *a* aspiring to, sucking up; *nmf* candidate, competitor.
aspirapólvere *nm* vacuum cleaner.
aspiràre *vt* to inhale, suck up; *vi* aspire to, be a candidate for.
aspirína *nf* aspirin.
asportàbile *a* removable.
asportàre *vi* to remove, extirpate.
asportazióne *nf* removal.
asprézza *nf* bitterness, harshness, roughness, sharpness.
asprígno *a* sourish.
àspro *a* bitter, rough, sharp, severe, hard.
assaggiàre *vt* to sample, taste, try.
assàggio *nm* trial, testing, sampling.
assài *nm* plenty; *ad* much, very, enough.
assalíre *vt* to assail, attack.
assaltàre *vt* to assault, attack.
assàlto *nm* assault, attack, onset.
assaporàre *vt* to savor, taste; (*fig*) to relish.
assassinàre *vt* to assassinate, murder.
assassínio *nm* assassination, murder.
assassíno *nm* assassin, murderer.
àsse *nm* axis; *nf* board, plank.
assecondàre *vt* to favor, support.
assediàre *vt* to besiege, crowd round.
assèdio *nm* siege; (*fig*) pestering.
assegnaménto *nm* assignment, allotment; reliance.
assegnàre *vt* to allow, assign, award, fix.
assegnazióne *nf* assignment, allotment.
asségno *nm* allowance, check; **a. bancàrio** (*com*) draft; **a. postàle** money order.
assemblèa *nf* assembly, meeting.
assembraménto *nm* throng, concourse, assembling.
assembràre *vt* to assemble; **-rsi** *vr* to assemble.
assennatézza *nf* commonsense, wisdom, prudence.
assennàto *a* sensible, wise, prudent.
assènso *nm* assent, consent.
assènte *a* absent; *nmf* absentee.
assentíre *vi* to assent, consent, approve.
assènza *nf* absence.
assènzio *nm* absinthe.
asseríre *vt* to assert, affirm.
asserragliàre *vt* to barricade; **-rsi** *vr* to barricade oneself.
asserzióne *nf* assertion, declaration.
assessóre *nm* assessor, magistrate.
assestaménto, assèsto *nm* arrangement, settlement.
assestàre *vt* to arrange, settle, set in order, adjust; deliver (a blow).
assetàto *a* thirsty, dry, eager.
assettàre *vt* to arrange, trim, put in order; **-rsi** *vr* to adorn oneself, tidy oneself up.
assètto *nm* good order, trim; **méttere in a.** to put in order, trim.
asseveràre *vi* to assert, affirm, declare.

assicuràre *vt* to secure, assure, declare, insure; (*post*) register; **-rsi** *vr* to fasten oneself, secure for oneself, make sure, insure oneself.
assicurazióne *nf* assurance, insurance, pledge.
assideraménto *nm* **assiderazióne** *nf* frostbite.
assideràre *vt* to chill, benumb; *vi* be benumbed, freeze.
assiduità *nf* assiduity, diligence.
assíduo *a* assiduous, diligent.
assième *ad* together.
assillàre *vt* to urge; harass.
assimilàre *vt* to assimilate, absorb.
assimilazióne *nf* assimilation.
assíse *nf* assizes *pl.*
assistènte *nmf* attendant, assistant; **a.** di vólo air hostess.
assistènza *nf* assistance, aid, help.
assístere *vti* to assist, help; be present.
àsso *nm* ace; **piantàre in a.** to leave in the lurch.
associàre *vt* to associate, join, take into partnership; **-rsi** *vr* to join, become a partner, subscribe.
associazióne *nf* association.
assodàre *vt* to consolidate, harden; make sure.
assoggettàre *vt* to subject, subdue; **-rsi** *vr* to subject oneself, submit.
assolàto *a* exposed to the sun, sunny.
assoldàre *vt* to recruit; **-rsi** *vr* to enlist.
assòlto *a* acquitted, absolved, released.
assolutaménte *ad* absolutely.
assolúto *a* absolute, positive.
assoluzióne *nf* absolution, acquittal.
assòlvere *vt* to acquit, absolve, release.
assomigliàre *vt* to compare; *vi* to resemble; **-rsi** *vr* to be alike, resemble each other.
assonnàto *a* sleepy, drowsy.
assopíre *vt* to make sleepy, appease; **-rsi** *vr* to doze off.
assorbènte *a* absorbent; **càrta a.** blotting paper; **a. igiènico** *nm* sanitary towel, sanitary napkin.
assorbíre *vt* to absorb.
assordaménto, *nm* deafening.
assordànte *a* deafening.
assordàre *vt* to stun, deafen.
assordiménto *nm* deafening.
assordíre *vt* to deafen; *vi* to become deaf.
assortiménto *nm* assortment, stock.
assortíre *vt* to stock; (*fig*) to match.
assortíto *a* assorted, stocked, matched.
assòrto *a* absorbed.
assottigliàre *vt* to thin, sharpen, diminish; **-rsi** *vr* to grow thin, diminish.
assuefàre *vt* to accustom, inure; **-rsi** *vr* to grow accustomed, inured.
assúmere *vt* to assume, take on, engage, raise (to a dignity), undertake, take up.
assúnto *nm* undertaking, charge, assumption.
assunzióne *nf* assumption, accession, Assumption.
assurdità *nf* absurdity.
assúrdo *a* absurd; *nm* absurdity.
àsta *nf* pole, staff, rod, lance; (*of writing*) stroke; auction.
astànte *a* present, standing by; *nmf* bystander, spectator; **mèdico a.** doctor on duty.
astantería *nf* first-aid post.
astèmio *a* abstemious; *nm* abstainer.
astenérsi *vr* to abstain.
astensióne *nf* abstention.
astinènte *a* abstinent.
astinènza *nf* abstinence.
àstio *nm* hatred, envy, grudge, spite.
astióso *a* rancorous, spiteful.
astràrre *vt* to abstract; **-rsi** *vr* to turn one's mind from.
astràtto *a* abstract, abstracted; *nm* abstract.
astrazióne *nf* abstraction, absentmindedness.
astringènte *a* astringent.
àstro *nm* star.
astrología *nf* astrology.
astrològico *pl* **-ici** *a* astrological.
astròlogo *pl* **-gi, -ghi** *nm* astrologer.
astronàuta *nm* astronaut.
astronàutica *nf* astronautics.
astronomía *nf* astronomy.
astronòmico *pl* **-ici** *a* astronomical.
astrònomo *nm* astronomer.
astrúso *a* abstruse, obscure.
astúccio *nm* box, case, sheath.
astutézza *nf* astuteness, cunning.
astúto *a* crafty, cunning, deceitful.
astúzia *nf* astuteness, artfulness, trick.
ateísmo *nm* atheism.
Atène *nf* Athens; **atenièse** *a nmf* Athenian.
atenèo *nm* athenaeum, university.
àteo *a* atheistic; *nm* atheist.
atlànte *nm* atlas.
atlàntico *pl* **-ici** *a* gigantic, Atlantic; *nm* (*geogr*) the Atlantic.
atlèta *nmf* athlete.
atlètica *nf* athletics.
atlètico *a* athletic.
atmosfèra *nf* atmosphere.
atòmico *pl* **-ici** *a* atomic.
àtomo *nm* atom.
atonía *nf* atony.
àtono *a* unstressed.
àtrio *nm* porch, vestibule.
atróce *a* atrocious, terrible, cruel.
atrocità *nf* atrocity.
atrofía *nf* atrophy.
atrofizzàre *vt* to atrophy; **-rsi** *vr* to atrophy, waste away.
attaccabottóne *nm* bore, talker.
attaccabríghe *nm* wrangler.
attaccaménto *nm* attachment.
attaccapànni *nm* hatstand, coathanger.

attaccàre *vt* to tie, fasten, stick, sew on, attack; (*horses*) harness; hang up; *vi* take root; be contagious; **a. un bottóne** (*fig*) to buttonhole someone; **-rsi** *vr* to stick, to become attached to; quarrel.
attaccatíccio *a* sticky; (*med*) contagious; *nm* burnt taste.
attàcco *pl* **-àcchi** *nm* attack, assault; (*el*) connection, plug.
attecchíre *vi* to take root, thrive.
atteggiaménto *nm* attitude.
atteggiàre *vt* to express in gesture; **-rsi** *vr* to assume an attitude, expression, pose as.
attempàto *a* elderly.
attendàrsi *vr* to camp, pitch tents.
attendènte *nm* (*mil*) orderly, batman.
attèndere *vt* to await, expect; *vi* to wait for, attend to.
attendíbile *a* reliable.
attenérsi *vr* to conform (to).
attentàre *vi* to attempt; **-rsi** *vr* to dare.
attentàto *nm* attempt, outrage.
attènti! *interj* (*mil*) attention!
attènto *a* attentive, careful.
attenuànte *a* extenuating; *nf* extenuating circumstance.
attenuàre *vt* to attenuate, lessen, extenuate.
attenzióne *nf* care, application.
atterràggio *nm* (*av*) landing.
atterràre *vti* to knock down; (*av*) to land; (*fig*) humiliate.
atterríre *vt* to frighten, terrify; **-rsi** *vr* to become terrified.
attésa *nf* waiting, expectation, suspense.
attéso *a* awaited, expected, longed for.
attestàre *vt* to attest, testify.
attestàto *nm* attestation, certificate, proof, token.
attestazióne *nf* attestation, testimony, token.
attiguità *nf* contiguity.
attíguo *a* contiguous, adjacent, next.
attillàrsi *vr* to dress smartly, dress so as to show off one's figure.
attillàto *a* close-fitting, smartly dressed.
àttimo *nm* moment, instant.
attinènte *a* pertaining, belonging to, relating.
attinènza *nf* affinity, relation.
attíngere *vt* (*water etc*) to draw; (*information etc*) to get.
attiràre *vt* to attract, draw, entice; **-rsi** *vr* to draw upon oneself.
attitúdine *nf* aptitude, skill; attitude.
attivaménte *ad* actively, busily.
attivàre *vt* to activate, set in motion.
attivísmo *nm* activism.
attivísta *nmf* activist.
attività *nf* activity, assets *pl*.
attívo *a* active; (*com*) receivable; *nm* (*com*) assets *pl*, credit account.
attizzàre *vt* to stir up, incite.
attizzatóio *nm* poker.
àtto *a* fit, apt; *nm* act, action, deed, gesture, certificate, (*com*) bill; *pl* proceedings, minutes.
attònito *a* astonished, amazed.
attòrcere, attorcigliàre *vt* to twist, wring.
attorcigliaménto *nm* twisting.
attóre *nm* actor.
attorniàre *vt* to enclose, surround.
attórno *prep* about, around; *ad* roundabout.
attossicaménto *nm* poisoning.
attossicàre *vt* to poison.
attraènte *a* attractive.
attràrre *vt* to attract, allure.
attrattíva *nf* attraction, charm.
attraversàre *vt* to cross, pass through; thwart.
attravèrso *prep* across, through.
attrazióne *nf* attraction.
attrezzàre *vt* to equip, fit out, supply with, rig.
attrezzatúra *nf* equipment, plant, organization, rigging.
attrézzo *nm* tool, implement.
attribuíre *vt* to ascribe, attribute, assign; **-rsi** *vr* to claim.
attribúto *nm* attribute.
attríce *nf* actress.
attristàre *vt* to sadden.
attríto *nm* friction, (*fig*) dissension.
attruppàrsi *vr* to gather in crowds, flock together.
attuàbile *a* practicable, feasible.
attuàle *a* present, real, actual.
attualità *nf* actuality, present, reality.
attuàre *vt* to effect, execute, perform, realize.
attuazióne *nf* carrying out, realization.
attuffàre *vt* to immerse, plunge, dip; **-rsi** *vr* to dive, plunge into the water.
attutíre *vt* to calm, ease, deaden.
audàce *a* audacious, bold.
àudio *nm* (*tv*) sound; **a. visívo** *a* audio-visual.
auditóre *nm* hearer, junior judge.
auditòrio *nm* auditorium.
audizióne *nf* audition.
àuge *nm* apogee; **èssere in a.** *vi* to be at the zenith of one's fortune.
auguràre *vt* to wish, augur, foretell; **-rsi** *vr* to hope.
augúrio *nm* good wish, augury, omen.
augústo *a* august, royal.
àula *nf* hall, classroom.
aumentàre *vti* to augment, increase, enlarge, grow.
auménto *nm* growth, increase; (*in pay*) raise.
àureo *a* golden, gold.
aurèola *nf* halo, glory.
auròra *nf* dawn.
ausiliàre *a nmf* **-àrio** *a* auxiliary.
auspício *nm* auspice; protection, patronage.
austerità *nf* austerity.
austèro *a* austere, severe.

Austràlia *nf* Australia.
australiàna *nf* pursuit cycle race on a track.
australiàno *a nm* Australian.
Àustria *nf* Austria.
austríaco *pl* **-aci** *a nm* Austrian.
aut-aut *nm* dilemma.
autarchía *nf* autarchy, economic self-sufficiency.
autèntica *nf* authentication, authoritative approval.
autenticàre *vt* to authenticate, prove; **còpia autenticàta** certified copy.
autenticità *nf* authenticity.
autèntico *pl* **-ici** *a* authentic.
autísta *nm* driver, chauffeur.
àuto *nf* motor car.
autobiografía *nf* autobiography.
autoblínda *inv*, **autoblindàta** *nf*, **autoblíndo** *inv* armored car.
àutobus *nm* bus, omnibus.
autocarovàna *nf* motor convoy.
autocàrro *nm* lorry, truck.
autocorrièra *nf* long-distance bus.
autocrazía *nf* autocracy.
autodidàtta *nmf* self-taught person.
autodifésa *nf* self-defense.
autòdromo *nm* autodrome, circuit.
autògrafo *a* autographic; *nm* autograph.
autòma *nm* automaton.
automàtico *pl* **-ici** *a* automatic.
automazióne *nf* automation.
automèẓẓo *nm* motor vehicle.
automòbile *nf* motor car, automobile; **a. di piàzza** taxi.
automobiliṣmo *nm* motoring.
automobilísta *nmf* motorist.
automobilístico *pl* **-ici** *a* motor; **còrsa a.** motor race.
autonomía *nf* autonomy, self-government; (*av, aut*) range.
autònomo *a* autonomous, self-governing.
autoparchéggio, autopàrco *pl* **-chi** *nm* car park, parking, parking lot.
autopómpa *nf* fire-engine.
autopsía *nf* autopsy.
autóre *nm* author.
autorespiratóre *nm* aqualung.
autorévole *a* authoritative, competent.
autoriméssa *nf* garage.
autorità *nf* authority.
autoriẓẓàre *vt* to authorize.
autoriẓẓazióne *nf* authorization, permit.
autoscàtto *nm* (*phot*) automatic release.
autoscuòla *nf* driving school.
autostòp *nm* hitch-hiking; **autostoppísta** *nmf* hitch-hiker; **fàre l'a.** to thumb a lift, hitch-hike.
autostràda *nf* motorway.
autotrèno *nm* motor lorry with trailer, truck.
autríce *nf* authoress.
autunnàle *a* autumnal.
autúnno *nm* autumn, fall.
avallàre *vt* to guarantee (*also fig*).
avàllo *nm* (*com*) guarantee (*also fig*).
avambràccio *nm* forearm.
avàna *nm* Havana (cigar); *a* light brown.
avanguàrdia *nf* vanguard.
avànti *ad and prep* before, forward, in front of, rather (than); *interj* forward!
avantièri *ad* the day before yesterday.
avanzaménto *nm* advancement, progress, promotion.
avanzàre *vt* to put forward, advance, promote, surpass, improve, save, put by, be creditor for; *vi* to advance, be left; **-rsi** *vr* get on, advance.
avanzàta *nf* advance.
avànzo *nm* remainder, remnant, residue, ancient ruin; **d'a.** *ad* over and above.
avaría *nf* damage.
avariàre *vt* to damage.
avarízia *nf* avarice, niggardliness.
avàro *a* avaricious, miserly; *nm* miser.
Àve *interj* Hail!
avéna *nf* oats.
avére *vt and aux* to have, obtain, have on, have to, possess; *nm* property, wealth, credit.
aviatóre *nm* airman, **-trice** *nf* airwoman.
aviazióne *nf* aviation.
avidaménte *ad* avidly, greedily, eagerly.
avidità *nf* avidity, greed, eagerness.
àvido *a* avid, greedy.
aviolínea *nf* airline.
avioriméssa *nf* hangar.
avório *nm* ivory.
avvallaménto *nm* cavity, subsidence.
avvallàre *vt* to lower; guarantee; **-rsi** *vr* to fall in, subside.
avvaloràre *vt* to strengthen; give value to; **-rsi** to become stronger.
avvampàre *vi* to burn, be on fire, be inflamed.
avvantaggiàre *vt* to advantage; **-rsi** *vr* to better oneself, derive advantage.
avvedérsi *vr* to perceive, notice.
avvedutézza *nf* foresight, sagacity.
avvedúto *a* cautious, provident, sagacious.
avvelenaménto *nm* poisoning.
avvelenàre *vt* to poison.
avvenènte *a* charming, agreeable.
avvenènza *nf* attractiveness, grace.
avveniménto *nm* event, incident; (*to the throne*) accession.
avveníre *vi and impers* to happen, *nm* future.
avventàre *vt* to hurl; *vi* to be gaudy; **-rsi** *vr* to throw oneself.
avventàto *a* imprudent, rash.

avventízio *a* temporary, adventitious.
avvènto *nm* advent, arrival; accession.
avventóre *nm* customer, purchaser.
avventúra *nf* adventure, chance.
avventuràre *vt* **-rsi** *vr* to venture.
avventurière *nm* adventurer.
avventuróso *a* adventurous, fortunate.
avveràre *vt* to fulfill, prove; **-rsi** *vr* to come true.
avvèrbio *nm* adverb.
avversàre *vt* to oppose, resist, thwart.
avversàrio *a* contrary, opposing, hostile; *nm* opponent, enemy.
avversióne *nf* aversion, dislike.
avversità *nf* adversity.
avvèrso *a* adverse, contrary.
avvertènza *nf* notice, introduction, care, attention.
avvertiménto *nm* notice, warning.
avvertíre *vt* to inform, advise, warn, perceive; *vi* to take care.
avvezzàre *vt* to accustom.
avvézzo *a* accustomed, used.
avviaménto *nm* setting out, beginning, start.
avviàre *vt* to set going, prepare, begin, start; **-rsi** *vr* to get going, succeed.
avviàto *a* prosperous.
avvicendàre *vi* to alternate; **-rsi** *vr* to take turns.
avvicinàre *vt* to put near; **-rsi** *vr* to approach, draw near.
avviliménto *nm* humiliation, dejection.
avvilíre *vt* to dishearten, abase, humiliate; **-rsi** *vr* to lose heart, humiliate oneself.
avviluppàre *vt* to entangle, wrap up; **-rsi** *vr* to wrap oneself up, get entangled.
avvisàglia *nf* skirmish; foreshadowing.
avviṣàre *vt* to advise, inform, warn; *vi* to judge, think; **-rsi** *vr* to think, consider.
avviṣàto *a* cautious, prudent.
avvíṣo *nm* advice, news, bill, advertisement, announcement, warning; **a mío a.** in my opinion.
avvistàre *vt* to sight.
avvitàre *vt* to screw.
avviticchiàre *vt* to twine, twist; **-rsi** *vr* to be entwined.
avvivàre *vt* to enliven, brighten; **-rsi** *vr* to become lively, (*of fire and fig*) rekindle.
avvizzíre *vi* to wither, fade.
avvocatéssa *nf* lady lawyer.
avvocàto *nm* lawyer, advocate, solicitor, defender.
avvocatúra *nf* legal profession.
avvòlgere *vt* to wrap round, entwine; **-rsi** *vr* to wrap oneself, wind round something.
avvoltóio *nm* vulture.
avvoltolàre *vt* to roll up; **-rsi** *vr* to roll oneself up, wallow.
aẓiènda *nf* business, firm, management.
azionàre *vt* to set in action, set going.
azióne *nf* action, deed, battle, movement; (*com*) share; **a. ordinària** ordinary share, common stock; **a. preferenziàle** preference share, preferred stock.
azionista *nmf* shareholder, stockholder.
azzannàre *vt* to seize with the teeth.
aẓẓardàre *vt* to hazard, risk; **-rsi** *vr* to venture.
aẓẓàrdo *nm* hazard, risk; **giuòco d'a.** game of chance.
aẓẓardóso *a* hazardous, risky.
azzeccàre *vt* to hit the mark, guess, chance on.
àẓẓima *nf* unleavened bread.
aẓẓimàre *vt* to dress smartly; **-rsi** *vr* to dress oneself up.
aẓẓimàto *a* dressed up.
àẓẓimo *a* unleavened.
aẓẓittíre *vt* to silence.
azzuffàrsi *vr* to come to blows, scuffle.
aẓẓúrro *a* blue, azure.

B

babbèo *a* silly, foolish; *nm* blockhead.
bàbbo *nm* (*fam*) daddy.
babbúccia *nf* slipper.
babbuíno *nm* baboon; (*fig*) fool.
babórdo *nm* (*naut*) larboard.
bacàre *vi* **-rsi** *vr* to be worm-eaten, rot.
bàcca *nf* berry.
baccalà *nm* stockfish, cod dried and salted; (*fig*) tall thin person; fool.
baccàno *nm* great noise, tumult.
baccellieràto *nm* bachelor's degree.
baccellière *nm* (*academic*) bachelor.
baccèllo *nm* pod; (*fig*) fool.
bacchétta *nf* rod, staff, stick, wand, maulstick.
bacchettàta *nf* stroke of the cane.
bacchiàre *vt* (*fruit*) to beat down.
Bàcco *nm pr* Bacchus; **per B.** by Jove!
bachèca *nf* show-case.
bacheròzzo *nm* grub, worm.
baciàre *vt* to kiss; **-rsi** *vr* to (exchange a) kiss.
bacíle *nm* basin.
bacíllo *nm* bacillus.
bacinèlla *nf* small basin.
bacíno *nm* basin, wash-hand basin; (*anat*) pelvis; (*naut*) dock; **b. carbonífero** coalfield.
bàcio *nm* kiss.
bàco *pl* **bàchi** *nm* worm, silkworm.
bàda, tenere a *vt* to hold at bay.
badàre *vi* to mind, pay attention to, take care of.
badéssa *nf* abbess.

badía *nf* abbey.
badíle *nm* shovel.
bàffo *nm* moustache, whisker.
baffúto *a* moustached.
bagagliàio *nm* luggage car, baggage car; caboose.
bagàglio *nm* luggage.
bagattèlla *nf* trifle, small matter.
baggianàta *nf* foolery.
baggiàno *nm* fool.
baglióre *nm* flash of light, gleam.
bagnànte *nmf* bather.
bagnàre *vt* to moisten, wet, bath; **-rsi** *vr* to get wet; bathe.
bagnatúra *nf* bathing, bathing season.
bagníno *nm* bathing attendant.
bàgno *nm* bath; **fàre un b.** *vi* to have a bath, to bathe; **stànza da b.** bathroom.
bagórdo *nm* orgy, reveling.
Bahàma (le) *nf pl* the Bahamas *pl.*
bàia *nf* bay; joke, banter.
bàio *a nm* (*color and horse*) bay.
baionétta *nf* bayonet.
bàita *nf* (alpine) hut.
balaústra, balaustràta *nf* balustrade.
balbettàre *vi* to stammer, stutter.
balbettío *nm* **balbúzia** *nf* stammer, stammering.
balbuziènte *a* stammering; *nmf* stammerer.
Balcàni *nm pl* the Balkans *pl.*
balcànico *pl* **-ici** *a* Balkan.
balconàta *nf* balcony, (*theat*) balcony.
balcóne *nm* balcony.
baldacchíno *nm* canopy.
baldànza *nf* boldness, assurance.
baldanzóso *a* bold, confident.
bàldo *a* bold, fearless.
baldòria *nf* bonfire; revel; **fàre b.** *vi* to feast, make merry.
Baldovíno *nm pr* Baldwin.
baléna *nf* whale.
balenàre *vi* to lighten, flash.
balenièra *nf* whaler (ship).
balenío *nm* (continual) lightning.
baléno *nm* lightning; **in un b.** *ad* immediately, in a flash.
baléstra *nf* crossbow.
bàlia *nf* (wet) nurse.
balía *nf* power, mercy.
balística *nf* ballistics.
bàlla *nf* bale, pack; (*sl*) fib.
ballàbile *a* suitable for dancing; *nm* (*mus*) dance.
ballàre *vi* to dance.
ballàta *nf* ballad, ballade.
ballatóio *nm* gallery, platform.
ballerína *nf* dancer, dancing girl, ballet-dancer.
ballerino *nm* dancer, dancing partner.
ballétto *nm* ballet, interlude.
bàllo *nm* ball, dance.
ballonzolàre *vi* to hop about.
ballòtta *nf* boiled chestnut; ballot.
ballottàggio *nm* (second) ballot, ballotage.
balneàre, balneàrio *a* bathing.
baloccàre *vt* to amuse; **-rsi** *vr* to amuse oneself, dally, toy with.
balòcco *pl* **-òcchi** *nm* plaything, toy.
balordàggine *nf* stupidity.
balórdo *a* stupid; *nm* fool, numskull.
balsàmico *pl* **-ici** *a* balmy.
bàlsamo *nm* balm, balsam.
Bàltico *a nm* (*geogr*) Baltic.
baluàrdo *nm* bastion, bulwark.
bàlza *nf* cliff, rock; flounce.
balzàre *vi* to bounce, jump, spring.
bàlzo *nm* jump, spring.
bambàgia *nf* cotton wool.
bambína *nf* little girl.
bambinàia *nf* nursery governess.
bambinésco *pl* **-chi** *a* childish.
bambíno *nm* baby, child, little boy.
bàmbola *nf* doll.
bambù *nm* bamboo.
banàle *a* common, trivial.
banalità *nf* banality, triviality.
banàna *nf* banana; **banàno** banana (-tree).
banca *nf* bank.
bancarèlla *nf* street stall.
bancàrio *a* bank, banking.
bancarótta *nf* bankruptcy; **fàre b.** to go bankrupt.
bancarottière *nm* bankrupt.
banchétto *nm* banquet.
banchière *nm* banker.
banchína *nf* small bench; quay, wharf, waterfront; platform.
banchísa *nf* ice-pack.
bànco *pl* **-chi** *nm* bench, counter, desk, bank, stall, (*of jury*) box; **b. di sàbbia** sand bank; **b. di ghiàccio** ice floe; **b. di ròcce** reef; **b. del lòtto** lottery office.
bancogíro *nm* (*com*) clearing.
banconòta *nf* banknote, note, bill.
bànda *nf* band, side, stripe, gang; **da b.** *ad* aside.
banderuòla *nf* pennon; vane, weathercock.
bandièra *nf* banner, flag.
bandíre *vt* to proclaim, announce; banish.
bandíta *nf* preserve; **b. di càccia** game preserve.
banditísmo *nm* banditry.
bandíto *a* outlawed, exiled; *nm* bandit, outlaw.
banditóre *nm* public crier, auctioneer.
bàndo *nm* ban, banishment; announcement.
bandolièra *nf* shoulder belt.
bàndolo *nm* head of a skein.
bar *nm* bar.
bàra *nf* bier, coffin.
baràcca *nf* booth, stall; barrack, hut.
baraónda *nf* confusion, disorder, tumult.
baràre *vi* (*at play*) to cheat.
bàratro *nm* abyss, gulf.
barattàre *vt* to barter, chaffer, exchange.

baratteria *nf* embezzlement, swindling.
barattière *nm* barterer; embezzler, swindler.
baràttolo *nm* small can or jar.
bàrba *nf* beard; rootlets *pl*; **fàre la b.** *vi* to shave; **fàrsi la b.** to shave (oneself).
barbabiétola *nf* beet.
barbagiànni *nm* owl; simpleton.
barbàglio *nm* dazzle, glare (*of light*).
Bàrbara *nf pr* Barbara.
barbàrico *pl* **-ici, bàrbaro** *a* barbarous, cruel.
barbàrie, barbarità *nf* barbarity.
barbicàre *vi* to take root.
barbière *nm* barber.
barbóne *nm* long beard, long-bearded man, tramp; poodle.
barbóso *a* boring.
barbugliaménto *nm* stammering, stuttering.
barbugliàre *vi* to stammer, stutter.
barbúto *a* bearded.
bàrca *nf* boat; (*fig*) business.
barcàccia *nf* old boat; (*theat*) stage box.
barcaiuòlo *nm* boatman.
barcamenàrsi *vr* to manage cleverly, steer a middle course.
barcaròla *nf* (*mus*) barcarolle.
Barcellóna *nf* Barcelona.
barchétta *nf* **-o** *nm* small boat.
barcollàre *vi* to rock, sway, totter, waver.
barcollío *nm* rocking.
barcóne *nm* barge, large boat.
bardàre *vt* to harness.
bàrdo *nm* bard.
barèlla *nf* stretcher, handcart.
bargíglio *nm* wattle.
baríle *nm* barrel, cask.
barísta *nmf* barman, barmaid.
barítono *nm* baritone.
barlúme *nm* gleam, glimmer.
bàro *nm* cheat, cardsharper.
barocciàio *nm* carter.
baroccíno *nm* small cart, handcart.
baròccio *nm* cart.
baròcco *pl* **-chi** *a* baroque, bizarre; *nm* baroque.
baròmetro *nm* barometer.
baróne *nm* baron.
baronéssa *nf* baroness.
baronétto *nm* baronet.
bàrra *nf* bar, rod, (*naut*) tiller.
barricàre *vt* to barricade.
barricàta *nf* barricade.
barrièra *nf* barrier, palisade.
Bartolomèo *nm pr* Bartholomew.
barúffa *nf* quarrel, brawl.
barzellétta *nf* joke, funny story.
baṣàre *vt* to base, ground; **-rsi** *vr* to base oneself.
bàṣe *nf* base, basis, ground; **b. aèrea** air base.
baseball *nm* baseball.
baṣétta *nf* side whisker.
Baṣiléa *nf* (*geogr*) Basle.
baṣílica *nf* basilica.
baṣílico *pl* **-ichi** *nm* basil.
bassézza *nf* baseness, meanness.
bàsso *a* low, short, mean, (*price*) cheap, (*of material*) narrow, (*mus*) bass.
bassofóndo *nm* (*naut*) shallow; the underworld.
bassorilièvo *nm* bas-relief.
bassòtto *a* stout and short; *nm* tubby man; basset, dachshund.
bassúra *nf* low ground.
bàsta! *interj* enough, stop, that will do.
bastàrdo *a nm* bastard, illegitimate.
bastàre *v impers* to be enough, suffice.
bastiménto *nm* ship, vessel.
bastióne *nm* bastion, rampart.
bàsto *nm* pack saddle.
bastonàre *vt* to beat, cudgel.
bastonàta, bastonatúra *nf* beating, thrashing.
bastóne *nm* stick, cane; cudgel, truncheon; (*cards*) clubs.
batòsta *nf* blow, misfortune.
battàglia *nf* battle.
battagliàre *vi* to fight, struggle.
battaglièro *a* fighting, warlike.
battàglio *nm* bell-clapper.
battaglióne *nm* battalion.
battàna *nf* punt.
battellière *nm* boatman.
battèllo *nm* boat; **b. a vapóre** steamer.
battènte *nm* (*of a door*) leaf; shutter; doorknocker.
bàttere *vt* to beat, knock, thrash, throb; (*of waves*) wash; (*of clocks*) strike; **b. bandièra** to sail under colors; **b. càssa** to ask for money; **b. i dènti** to chatter (with cold); **b. le màni** to clap; **b. monéta** to mint money; *vi* to knock against, insist; **-rsi** *vr* to fight, duel; **bàttersela** *vr* to run away.
battería *nf* battery; set of kitchen utensils.
batteṣimàle *a* baptismal.
battéṣimo *nm* baptism, christening.
battezzàre *vt* to baptize, christen.
battibaléno *nm* **in un b.** in the twinkling of an eye.
battibécco *pl* **-cchi** *nm* quarrel.
batticuòre *nm* palpitation, fear.
battipànni *nm* carpet-beater.
battistèro *nm* baptistery.
battistràda *nm* outrider, guide; (*of tires*) tread.
bàttito *nm* heartbeat, palpitation, throbbing, ticking.
battitóre *nm* beater, thresher; (*sport*) server, batsman, striker.
battúta *nf* beating, remark, cue, (*mus*) bar.
battúto *a* beaten, trodden; (*of iron*) wrought; *nm* (*of meat*) hash, stuffing.
batúffolo *nm* small wad.
baúle *nm* trunk, traveling chest.
bàva *nf* slaver, foam; floss silk.
bavaglíno *nm* child's bib.

bavàglio *nm* gag.
bavarése *a nmf* Bavarian.
Bavièra *nf* Bavaria.
bàvero *nm* coat collar.
bavóso *a* slavering.
bazàr *nm* bazaar.
bàzza *nf* jutting chin; good luck.
bazzècola *nf* nonsense, trifle.
bazzicàre *vt* to frequent, haunt.
beàre *vt* (*poet*) to make happy; **-rsi** *vr* to delight in.
beatificàre *vt* to beatify.
beatificazióne *nf* beatification.
beatitúdine *nf* beatitude, bliss.
beàto *a* happy, blissful, blessed.
Beatríce *nf pr* Beatrice, Beatrix.
beccàccia *nf* woodcock.
beccaccíno *nm* snipe.
beccàio *nm* butcher.
beccamòrti *nm* grave-digger.
beccàre *vt* to peck; **-rsi** *vr* to win, get; (*fig*) to quarrel.
beccheggiàre *vi* (*naut*) to pitch.
becchéggio *nm* (*naut*) pitching.
becchíme *nm* birds' food.
becchíno *nm* sexton.
bécco *pl* **bécchi** *nm* beak; (*of gas*) burner; he-goat; cuckold.
beccúccio *nm* spout.
bécero *nm* (*fam*) low fellow, rascal.
becerúme *nm* cads *pl*.
beduíno *a nm* Bedouin.
Befàna *nf* Epiphany; old woman taking the place of Father Christmas in Italian tales; ugly deformed woman.
bèffa *nf* jest, mockery, trick.
beffàrdo *a* mocking; *nm* mocker.
beffàre *vt* to mock, ridicule; **-rsi** *vr* to deride, make game of.
beffeggiàre *vt* to deride, mock.
bèga *nf* dispute; troublesome business.
beghína *nf* bigot, pietist.
belàre *vi* to bleat.
belàto *nm* bleating.
bèlga *pl m* **bèlgi** *f* **bèlghe** *a nmf* Belgian.
Bèlgio (il) *nm* Belgium.
Belgràdo *nf* Belgrade.
bèlla *nf* belle, sweetheart, girlfriend; (*sport*) final.
belletto *nm* paint, rouge.
bellézza *nf* beauty; **la b. di** as much as.
bèllico *pl* **-ici, bellicóso** *a* warlike, bellicose.
bellimbústo *nm* dandy, fop.
bellíno *a* nice, pretty.
bèllo *a* beautiful, fine, handsome, nice; *nm* beautiful; lover, boyfriend, beau; beauty; *ad* finely, nicely; **il b. è** the best of it is that.
beltà *nf* beauty.
bélva *nf* wild beast.
belvedére *nm* belvedere; **vettúra b.** observation car.
bemòlle *nm* (*mus*) flat.
benché *cj* although.
bènda *nf* band, bandage.
bendàre *vt* to bandage, bind, blindfold.
bène *nm* good, love, happiness, affection; property, wealth; **bèni mòbili** *nm pl* movable property; **bèni stàbili** real estate; *ad* well, quite, right; **per b.** *a* decent, respectable; **star b.** to be well; **volér b. a** *vt* to like, be fond of.
benedettíno *a nm* Benedictine.
benedétto *a* blessed, holy.
benedíre *vt* to bless, consecrate.
benedizióne *nf* benediction, consecration.
beneducàto *a* well-bred.
benefattóre *nm* benefactor.
benefattríce *nf* benefactress.
beneficàre *vt* to benefit, do good to.
beneficénza *nf* beneficence, charity.
beneficiàre *vi* to benefit.
benefício, benefízio *nm* benefit profit; benefice.
benèfico *pl* **-ici** *a* beneficent, beneficial.
benemerènza *nf* merit.
benemèrito *a* deserving, meritorious.
beneplàcito *nm* approval, consent, convenience, option.
benèssere *nm* well-being.
benestànte *a* wealthy, well-to-do.
benestàre *nm* approval, endorsement.
benevolènza *nf* benevolence, favor.
benèvolo *a* benevolent, kind.
Bengàla (il) *nm* Bengal.
bengalése *a nmf* Bengali.
Beniamíno *nm pr* Benjamin.
benignità *nf* benignity, kindness.
benígno *a* benignant, benign.
beníno *ad* pretty well, fairly well.
benintéso *ad* agreed, understood, of course.
beníssimo *ad* very well, all right.
benóne *ad* splendidly, very well.
benpensànte *a* sensible; *nmf* orthodox, right-minded person.
benportànte *a* in good health.
benservíto *nm* testimonial, dismissal.
bensí *cj* but, rather.
bentornàto *a nm* welcome back.
benvenúto *a nm* welcome.
benvolére *vt* to like; **fàrsi b.** *vr* to make oneself liked, win popularity; *nm* benevolence, affection.
benzína *nf* petrol, gasoline, benzine.
bére *vt* to drink, absorb; **-rse una còsa** *vr* to believe implicitly in something; *nm* drinking, drink.
bergamòtto *nm* bergamot.
berlína *nf* pillory; (*aut*) sedan.
Berlíno *nf* Berlin.
Bèrna *nf* Berne.
Bernàrdo *nm pr* Bernard.
bernòccolo *nm* bump, swelling.
bernoccolúto *a* bumpy, knotty.
berrétta *nf* cap, biretta.
berrétto *nm* cap, beret; **b. bàsco** beret.

bersagliàre *vt* to shoot at, harass.
bersaglière *nm* sharpshooter, bersagliere.
bersàglio *nm* aim, butt, mark, target.
bèrta *nf* raillery, mockery; ram; magpie; **dar la b.** to mock.
Bèrta *nf pr* Bertha.
bertúccia *nf* monkey; ugly woman.
bestémmia *nf* blasphemy, oath.
bestemmiàre *vi* to curse, swear; *vt* to blaspheme.
béstia *nf* animal, beast, brute; idiot.
bestiàle *a* bestial, brutal.
bestialità *nf* bestiality, stupidity.
bestiàme *nm* cattle.
béttola *nf* tavern.
betúlla *nf* birch-tree.
bevànda *nf* drink, beverage.
beveràggio *nm* beverage, potion.
bevíbile *a* drinkable, nice to drink.
bevitóre *nm*, **-tríce** *nf* drinker.
bevúta *nf* draft, drinking.
biàcca *nf* white lead.
biàda *nf* corn, oats.
biancàstro *a* whitish.
biancheggiàre *vi* to grow white, show white.
biancheria *nf* linen; **b. personàle** underwear.
bianchétto *nm* white lead, whitewash, bleaching powder.
bianchézza *nm* whiteness.
biànco *pl* **-chi** *a* white, hoary, fair, pale; *nm* white, whitewash; blank; **lasciàre in b.** to leave blank; **di púnto in b.** *ad* point-blank.
biancospíno *pl* **-íni** *nm* hawthorn.
biancúme *nm* mass of white.
biascicàre *vt* to mumble.
biaşimàbile, biaşimèvole *a* blameworthy, reprehensible.
biaşimàre *vt* to blame, reprove.
biàşimo *nm* blame, reproof.
Bíbbia *nf* Bible.
biberon (*French*) *nm inv* feeding-bottle.
bíbita *nf* drink, refreshments *pl.*
bíblico *a* biblical.
bibliografía *nf* bibliography.
bibliogràfico *pl* **-ici** *a* bibliographical.
biblìografo *nm* bibliographer.
bibliotèca *nf* library.
bibliotecàrio *nm* librarian.
bicarbonàto *nm* bicarbonate.
bicchière *nm* drinking glass, tumbler.
bicchieríno *nm* small glass.
biciclétta *nf* bicycle.
bicòcca *nf* small hill fort; hovel.
bidè *nm* bidet.
bidèllo *nm* beadle, janitor, porter, usher.
bidóne *nm* (large metal) receptacle.
bièco *pl* **-chi** *a* grim, squinting; *ad* askance.
biennàle *a* biennial.
biènnio *nm* space of two years.
biètola *nf* beet.
bietolóne *nm* simpleton, fool.
bifólco *pl* **-chi** *nm* plowman, farm laborer, boor.
biforcàrsi *vr* to divide, fork.
bigamía *nf* bigamy.
bígamo *nm* bigamist.
bighellonàre *vi* to idle, loaf, lounge.
bighellóne *nm* idler, loafer.
bígio *a* gray.
bigiottería *nf* trinkets shop.
bigliettàio *v* **bigliettàrio.**
biglietteria *nf* booking office, ticket office; box office.
bigliettàrio *nm* (*of buses etc*) conductor; ticket collector, booking clerk, (*railroad*) ticket agent; box-office attendant.
bigliétto *nm* card, letter, note; ticket; **b. di andàta e ritórno** return ticket, round-trip ticket; **b. d'abbonaménto** season ticket; **b. circolàre** tourist ticket.
bigodíno *nm* (hair-)curler.
bigottería *nf* **bigottíşmo** *nm* bigotry.
bigòtto *a* bigoted; *nm* bigot.
bikíni *nm* bikini.
bilància *nf* balance, pair of scales.
bilanciàre *vt* to balance, ponder.
bilancière *nm* pendulum, balance wheel, fly press, coining press.
bilàncio *nm* (*com*) balance sheet, budget.
bilateràle *a* bilateral.
bíle *nf* bile, anger.
biliàrdo *nm* billiards, billiard room, billiard table.
bílico *pl* **-chi** *nm* equipoise, balance, pivot.
bilíngue *a* bilingual; deceitful.
bilióso *a* bilious, irascible.
bímba *nf* **bímbo** *nm* child, baby.
bimensíle *a* fortnightly.
bimestràle *a* bimonthly.
bimèstre *nm* period of two months.
bimetallíşmo *nm* bimetallism.
bimotóre *nm* two-engined plane.
binàrio *nm* rails, railway track; **único b.** single track; **dóppio b.** double track; *a* binary.
bíndolo *nm* reel, winder, waterwheel; cheat
binòc(c)olo *nm* field-glass, opera-glass, binocular(s).
biòccolo *nm* (*of wool*) flock; (*of cotton*) lump; candle drip; snowflake.
biochímica *nf* biochemistry.
biografía *nf* biography.
biògrafo *nm* biographer.
biología *nf* biology.
biòlogo *pl* **-ogi** *nm* biologist.
biondeggiàre *vi* (*of corn*) to grow yellow, turn golden.
biondèzza *nf* fairness, flaxen color.
bióndo *a* blond, fair, flaxen.
biòssido *nm* (*chem*) dioxide.
bipartíre *vt* to halve; **-rsi** *vr* to diverge, branch off.
bipartizióne *nf* division into two parts.
bípede *a nm* biped.
biplàno *nm* biplane.

bírba *nm* hare-brained youngster, rogue.
birbànte *nm* rogue, dishonest fellow.
birbonàta *nf* roguish act.
birbóne *nm* bad fellow, rascal; **fréddo b.** bitter cold.
birbonería *nf* knavery, roguery.
birichinàta *nf* mischievous trick.
birichíno *a* mischievous, cheeky; *nm* little scamp, urchin.
biríllo *nm* skittle, ninepin.
Birmània *nf* Burma.
birmàno *a nm* Burmese, Burman.
bíro *nf* biro, ball(point) pen.
biroccíno *nm* small cart.
biròccio *nm* cart.
bírra *nf* beer.
birràio *nm* brewer, publican.
birrería *nf* alehouse, pub, brewery.
bís *interj* encore.
biṣàccia *nf* knapsack.
bisàvo, bisàvolo *nm* great-grandfather.
biṣbètico *pl* **-ici** *a* crabbed, shrewish.
biṣbigliàre *vi* to whisper.
biṣbíglio *nm* whisper.
bísca *nf* gambling-house, gaming-den.
Biscàglia *nf* Biscay.
biscaiuòlo *nm* gambler.
biscazzière *nm* gambling-house keeper; (*at billiards*) marker; gambler.
bíscia *nf* adder, snake.
biscottíno, biscòtto *nm* biscuit, cookie.
biṣestíle *a* bissextile; **ànno b.** *nm* leap year.
bisettimanàle *a* bi-weekly.
biṣlàcco *pl* **-àcchi** *a* queer, odd.
biṣlúngo *pl* **-ghi** *a* oblong.
biṣmúto *nm* bismuth.
biṣnònno *nm* great-grandfather.
biṣógna *nf* business, need.
biṣognàre *vi* to need, want, be obliged.
biṣognévole *a* needy, necessary; *nm* requisite.
biṣógno *nm* need, necessity, poverty.
biṣognóso *a* indigent, needy.
bistècca *nf* beefsteak.
bisticciàre *vi* **-rsi** *vr* to dispute, quarrel.
bistíccio *nm* quarrel; pun.
bistrattàre *vt* to ill-treat, offend, wrong.
biṣúnto *a* very greasy.
bitòrzolo *nm* knob, pimple, wart.
bitorzolúto *a* pimply.
bítter *nm inv* bitters.
bitúme *nm* bitumen.
bivaccàre *vi* to bivouac.
bivàcco *nm* bivouac.
bivàlve *a nm* bivalve.
bívio *nm* crossroads *pl*.
biẓantíno *a* Byzantine.
bíẓẓa *nf* freak, whim.
biẓẓàrro *a* bizarre, odd, queer.
bizzèffe *a ad* galore, in quantity.
biẓẓóso *a* irascible, wayward.
blandíẓie *nf* blandishments *pl* wheedling.
blàndo *a* affable, bland, wheedling.
blaṣóne *nm* blazonry.
blèṣo *a* lisping.
blindaménto *nm* **blindatúra** *n* armor-plating.
blindàre *vt* to armor-plate.
bloccàre *vt* to block, blockade.
blòcco *pl* **blòcchi** *nm* block, blockade; (*com*) bulk.
bloc-nòtes *nm* scribbling pad, scratch pad.
blù *a* blue.
bluàstro *a* bluish.
bluffàre *vti* to bluff.
blúṣa *nf* blouse.
bòa *nf* (*serpent, wrap*) boa; (*naut*) buoy.
boàro *nm* cowherd.
boàto *nm* bellowing, thundering.
bobína *nf* reel of cotton, spool, (*el*) bobbin.
bócca *nf* mouth; aperture, opening; **a b. apèrta** *ad* open-mouthed.
boccàle *nm* decanter, jug, mug.
boccapòrto *nm* (*naut*) hatch(way).
boccàta *nf* mouthful.
boccheggiàre *vi* to gasp for air.
bocchíno *nm* pretty mouth; cigarette-holder, mouthpiece.
bòccia *nf* water bottle; bud; (*game*) bowl; **bócce** *nf pl* (*game*) bowls *pl*.
bocciàre *vt* to fail (in an exam).
bocciatúra *nf* failure (in an exam).
bòccio *nm* bud.
bocciòlo *nm* bud.
bocconcíno *nm* titbit.
boccóne *nm* mouthful, bite.
boccóni *ad* prone, face downwards.
Boèmia *nf* Bohemia.
boèmo *a nm* Bohemian.
bofonchiàre *vi* to grumble, mutter.
bòia *nm* executioner, hangman.
boicottàggio *nm* boycotting.
boicottàre *vt* to boycott.
bòlgia *nf* dark hole, pit.
bòlide *nm* meteor, thunderbolt, car driven at great speed.
Bolívia *nf* Bolivia.
boliviàno *a nm* Bolivian.
bólla *nf* blister, bubble; papal bull, seal.
bollàre *vt* to confirm, mark, seal, stamp.
bollatúra *nf* sealing, stamping.
bollènte *a* boiling, fiery.
bollétta *nf* bill, certificate, note, receipt.
bollettíno *nm* bulletin, schedule; **b. meteorològico** weather forecast, weather report.
bollicína *nf* small bubble, pimple.
bollíre *vti* to boil, bubble up.
bollitúra *nf* boiling, bubbling.
bóllo *nm* seal, stamp.
bollóre *nm* boiling, excessive heat.
bolscevíco *pl* **-íchi** *a nm* Bolshevik.
bólso *a* asthmatic.
bómba *nf* bomb, shell; **b. a màno**

hand-grenade; **b. a scòppio ritardàto** delayed action bomb; **b. chímica** gas bomb; **b. esplosíva** high-explosive bomb; **b. fumògena** smoke bomb; **b. incendiària** incendiary bomb.
bombardaménto *nm* bombardment, bombing.
bombardàre *vt* to bombard, bomb.
bómbola *nf* cylinder, bottle; **b. d'ossígeno** oxygen bottle.
bombolóne *nm* doughnut.
bombonièra *nf* bonbonniere, candy box.
bonàccia *nf* (*at sea*) calm, tranquillity.
bonaccióne *nm* good-humored fellow.
bonarietà *nf* good humor, good nature.
bonàrio *a* good-humored.
bongustàio *nm* gourmet.
bonífica *nf* land reclamation.
bonificàre *vt* to reclaim land, put under cultivation; (*com*) to grant an allowance.
bonomía *nf* good nature.
bontà *nf* goodness, kindness.
bontempóne *nm* jolly person.
borbogliàre *vi* to rumble, mutter.
borboglío *nm* rumbling, grumbling.
borbottaménto, borbottío *nm* grumbling, muttering.
borbottàre *vi* to grumble, mutter.
bòrchia *nf* boss, stud.
bordèllo *nm* uproar; brothel.
bórdo *nm* edge, verge, (*of road*) shoulder; border; rim; (*naut*) board; **a b.** *ad* on board.
bòrea *nm* north wind.
borgàta *nf* village, hamlet.
borghése *a* bourgeois; *nmf* middle-class person.
borghesía *nf* middle class.
bórgo *nm* village.
Borgógna *nf* (*geogr*) Burgundy.
bòria *nf* haughtiness, arrogance.
borióso *a* arrogant, vainglorious.
borotàlco *pl* **-chi** *nm* talcum powder.
borràccia *nf* leather bottle, canteen, water bottle.
borraccína *nf* kind of moss.
bórro *nm* ravine.
bórsa *nf* bag, purse, brief-case, Exchange; **b. di stúdio** bursary, scholarship.
borsaiuòlo *nm* pickpocket.
borsanéra *nf* black market.
borseggiàre *vt* to rob, pick someone's pocket.
borséggio *nm* bag-snatching, robbery.
borsellíno *nm* small purse.
borsétta *nf* handbag.
borsísta *nm* stockbroker, scholarship holder.
boscàglia *nf* underwood, wood.
boscaiuòlo *nm* woodcutter.
boscheréccio *a* woody, sylvan.
boschétto *nm* grove, small wood.
boschívo *a* woody.
bòsco *pl* **-chi** *nm* wood, forest.
boscóso *a* wooded.
bòsso, bòssolo *nm* box-plant, box-wood.
botànica *nf* botany.
botànico *pl* **-ici** *a* botanic(al); *nm* botanist.
bòtola *nf* trapdoor.
bòtta *nf* blow; toad.
bottàio *nm* cooper.
bótte *nf* barrel, cask.
bottéga *nf* shop.
bottegàio *nm* shopkeeper.
botteghíno *nm* small shop, box-office, lottery, betting shop.
bottíglia *nf* bottle.
bottiglieria *nf* bar, wine shop.
bottíno *nm* booty.
bòtto *nm* loud bang; blow; (*of bell*) toll; **di b.** *ad* suddenly, directly.
bottóne *nm* button, cufflink; bud; **b. del collétto** collar stud, collar button.
bòve *v* **búe.**
bovíle *nm* ox-stall, byre.
bovíno *a* bovine.
bòzza *nf* bump, swelling; rough draft, proof sheet, sketch.
bozzétto *nm* outline, sketch.
bòzzolo *nm* cocoon.
bràca *nf* sling, tackle; trouser leg; *pl* **bràche** breeches, trousers *pl.*
braccétto, a *ad* arm in arm.
braccìàle *nm* armlet, bracelet, arm-band.
braccialétto *nm* bracelet.
bracciànte *nm* laborer.
bracciàta *nf* armful.
bràccio *pl* **bràccia** (*f*), (*fig*) **bràcci** (*m*) *nm* arm; branch, inlet, fathom.
bracciuòlo *nm* elbow-rest, hand-rail; **sèdia a bracciuòli** armchair.
bràcco *pl* **bràcchi** *nm* hound.
bràce *nf* embers *pl*, charcoal.
bracière *nm* brazier.
braciòla *nf* chop, cutlet, steak.
bràma *nf* desire, longing.
bramàre *vt* to desire, long for.
bramosía *nf* longing.
bramóso *a* eager, longing.
brànchie *nf pl* gills of fishes *pl.*
brànco *pl* **-chi** *nm* flock, herd, band.
brancolàre *vi* to grope.
brancolóni *ad* gropingly.
brànda *nf* folding bed, camp bed, hammock.
brandèllo *nm* rag, tatter, shred.
brandíre *vt* to brandish.
bràno *nm* piece, extract, passage.
Brasíle *nm* Brazil.
brasiliàno *a nm* Brazilian.
bravàre *vt* to defy; *vi* to boast.
bravàta *nf* bravado, boasting.
bràvo *a* clever, good (at something), honest, brave; *nm* cut-throat; *interj* bravo!
bravúra *nf* skill, bravery.
bréccia *nf* breach.

brefotròfio *nm* orphanage.
Bretàgna *nf* Brittany, Britain; Gran B. Great Britain.
bretèlle *nf pl* braces *pl*, suspenders *pl*.
brètone *a nm* Breton.
brève *a* brief, concise, short; *nm* brief; **in b.** *ad* in short.
brevettàre *vt* to patent.
brevétto *nm* patent; (*mil*) commission.
breviàrio *nm* breviary.
brevità *nf* brevity, conciseness.
brézza *nf* breeze.
brícco *pl* **brícchi** *nm* kettle, pot, jug.
bricconàta, bricconería *nf* roguery, trick.
briccóne *nm* rascal, rogue.
bríciola *nf* crumb.
bríciolo *nm* bit, morsel.
bríga *nf* quarrel, trouble; **attaccàre b.** to quarrel; **dàrsi b.** to take pains.
brigadière *nm* (*mil*) brigadier; brigadier general; (*carabinieri*) sergeant.
brigantàggio *nm* brigandage.
brigànte *nm* brigand.
brigantésco *pl* **-éschi** *a* of a brigand.
brigàre *vt* to solicit; *vt* to intrigue, strive.
brigàta *nf* brigade, company, party.
Brígida *nf pr* Bridget, Brigid.
bríglia *nf* bridle, reins *pl*.
brillaménto *nm* glitter; (*of mine*) explosion.
brillànte *a* bright, brilliant; *nm* brilliant.
brillantína *nf* brilliantine.
brillàre *vi* to glitter, shine, sparkle.
bríllo *a* merry, tipsy.
brína, brinàta *nf* hoar frost.
brinàre *vi impers* to be white with frost.
brindàre *vi* to drink a health, toast.
brindèllo *nm* rag, tatter.
bríndisi *nm* toast.
brío *nm* spirit, vivacity.
brióso *a* lively, spirited, vivacious.
Britànnia *nf* Britain.
britànnico *pl* **-ici** *a* British.
britànno *nm* Briton.
brívido *nm* shiver, shudder.
brizzolàto *a* speckled, growing gray.
bròcca *nf* jug, jar, pitcher.
broccàto *nm* brocade.
bròccolo *nm* broccoli.
brodàglia *nf* weak broth, tasteless soup.
bròdo *nm* broth, soup.
brogliàre *vt* to intrigue.
bròglio *nm* intrigue.
bròmo, bromúro *nm* bromide.
bronchiàle *a* bronchial.
bronchíte *nf* bronchitis.
bróncio *nm* pout, sulkiness; **tenére il b.** *vi* to sulk.
brónco *nm* stem, trunk; **brónchi** *pl* bronchi *pl*.
brontolàre *vi* to grumble.
brónzo *nm* bronze.
brucàre *vt* to browse, nibble at, (*leaves*) strip off.
bruciacchiàre *vt* to scorch, singe.
bruciapélo, a *ad* point-blank, suddenly.
bruciàre *vt* to burn.
bruciàta *nf* roast chestnut.
bruciàto *a* burnt; *nm* burning; **gioventù bruciàta** (*sl*) beat generation; **uòmo b.** broken man.
brucióre *nm* smart, burning.
brúco *pl* **-chi** *nm* caterpillar, grub.
brughièra *nf* heath, moor.
brulicàme *nm* swarm.
brulicàre *vi* to swarm, be crawling with.
brulichío *nm* swarming.
brúllo *a* bare, sterile.
brúma *nf* winter mist; ship-worm.
brúno *a* brown, dark; *nm* mourning.
Brúno *nm pr* Bruno.
bruschézza *nf* brusqueness, rudeness.
brúsco *pl* **-chi** *a* brusque, rude, tart.
brúscolo *nm* mote, speck.
brusío *nm* hubbub, buzz, whispering.
brutàle *a* brutal.
brutalità *nf* brutality.
brúto *a* brutal, unreasoning; *nm* brute, wild animal, violent person.
bruttàre *vt* to dirty, soil, stain.
bruttézza *nf* ugliness.
brútto *a* ugly, nasty.
búbbola *nf* hoopoe; idle tale.
búbbolo *nm* harness bell.
bubbóne *nm* (*med*) bubo.
bubbònico *pl* **-ici** *a* bubonic.
búca *nf* hole, cave, cavity; **b. délle lèttere** letter-box.
bucanéve *nf* snowdrop.
bucàre *vt* to bore, pierce, puncture.
bucàto *a* pierced, riddled; *nm* wash(ing), clean linen.
búccia *nf* peel, rind, skin, bark.
búccola *nf* earring, pendant.
bucherellàre *vt* to riddle with holes.
búco *pl* **búchi** *nm* hole, round opening.
budellàme *nm* bowels *pl*, entrails *pl*.
budello *pl* **-a** (*f*), (*fig*) **-i** (*m*) *nm* bowel, gut, intestine.
budíno *nm* pudding.
búe *pl* **buòi** *nm* ox; (*fig*) dunce.
búfalo *nm* buffalo.
bufèra *nf* storm, hurricane, whirlwind; **b. di néve** blizzard.
buffet *nm* sideboard, buffet.
buffétto *nm* fillip, chuck.
búffo *a* comical, comic, droll, funny, queer; *nm* gust, puff.
buffonàta *nf* buffoonery.
buffóne *nm* buffoon, untrustworthy person.
bugía *nf* lie; flat candlestick.
bugiàrdo *a* lying; *nm* liar.
bugigàttolo *nm* very small room, cubby-hole.

búio *a* dark; *nm* dark, darkness; **èssere al b.** *vi* (*fig*) to be in the dark.
búlbo *nm* bulb.
Bulgaría (la) *nf* Bulgaria.
búlgaro *a nm* Bulgarian, Bulgar.
bulíno *nm* (*tec*) graver.
bullóne *nm* bolt.
b(u)ongústo *nm* good taste.
buòno *a* good, sound, kind, right, safe; *nm* good; bond, coupon, permit; **a b. mercàto** *ad* cheap; **di buon'óra** *ad* early; **b. del tesòro** Treasury bill.
burattíno *nm* puppet; flighty person.
burbànza *nf* arrogance, insolent bearing.
búrbero *a* crabbed, morose.
burchièllo, búrchio *nm* small canal boat.
búrla *nf* trick, joke; **per b.** *ad* in fun.
burlàre *vt* to play a trick on, make a fool of; *vi* to joke; **-rsi** *vr* to laugh at, make fun of.
burlésco *pl* **-chi** *a* burlesque, ludicrous.
burlétta *nf* jest, joke.
burlévole *a* laughable, comical, humorous.
burlóne *nm* jester, joker.
buròcrate *nm* bureaucrat.
burocràtico *pl* **-ici** *a* bureaucratic.
burocrazía *nf* bureaucracy.
burràsca *nf* storm, tempest.
burrascóso *a* stormy, tempestuous.
búrro *nm* butter.
burróne *nm* ravine.
búsca *nf* quest, search.
buscàre *vt* to earn, gain; **-rsi** *vr* to bring upon oneself.
buşíllis *nm* difficulty; **qui sta il b.** here lies the difficulty.
bussàre *vi* to knock.
bússe *nf pl* beating, blows *pl*.
bússola *nf* mariner's compass; sedan chair; inner door, screen; **pèrdere la b.** to be at one's wits' end.
bussolòtto *nm* dice-box.
bústa *nf* envelope, case.
bustàia *nf* corset-maker.
bústo *nm* bust; corset, stays *pl*.
buttàre *vt* to throw; **b. all'ària** to throw up, upset; **-rsi** *vr* to throw oneself.
butteràto *a* pock-marked.
bútteró *nm* pock-mark; mounted herdsman.

C

cabína *nf* cabin; **c. telefònica** telephone booth.
cablogràmma *nm* cablegram.
cabotàggio *nm* coasting trade.
cabotièro *a* coasting; *nm* coaster.
cacào *nm* cacao(-tree), cocoa.
càccia *nf* chase, hunt, pursuit, shooting; **andàre a c.** *vi* to go shooting, go hunting.
cacciagióne *nf* game.
cacciàre *vt* to chase, hunt, go hunting, pursue; thrust; **c. un grído** to utter a cry; **-rsi** *vr* to intrude, thrust one's way into.
cacciatóre *nm* **-tríce** *nf* hunter, trapper.
cacciatorpedinière *nf* (torpedo-boat) destroyer.
cacciavíte *nm* screwdriver.
càchi *a* khaki; *nm* persimmon (tree).
càcio *nm* cheese.
cadaúno *pron* (*com*) each.
cadàvere *nm* corpse.
cadavèrico *pl* **-ici** *a* cadaverous, corpselike.
cadènte *a* falling, (*of the sun*) setting.
cadènza *nf* cadence, rhythm, time, step, (*mus*) cadenza.
cadenzàto *a* measured, rhythmical.
cadére *vi* to fall.
cadétto *a* younger, cadet; *nm* cadet.
Càdice *nf* (*geogr*) Cadiz.
caducità *nf* frailty, transiency.
cadúco *pl* **-úchi** *a* frail, transient.
cadúta *nf* fall, ruin.
caffè *nm* coffee, café, **c. concèrto** café-chantant.
caffelàtte *nm* white coffee.
caffettièra *nf* coffee-pot.
caffettière *nm* café proprietor.
cafóne *nm* (*south Italy*) peasant; (*fig*) boor.
cagionàre *vt* to cause, occasion.
cagióne *nf* cause, reason, motive; **a c. di** on account of.
cagionévole *a* sickly, weak.
càglio *nm* rennet.
càgna *nf* bitch.
cagnàra *nf* barking, uproar.
cagnésco *pl* **-chi** *a* currish, surly.
cagnolíno *nm* pretty little dog, puppy.
Calàbria *nf* (*geogr*) Calabria.
calabrése *a nmf* Calabrian.
calabróne *nm* hornet.
calamàio *nm* inkstand; cuttlefish.
calamità *nf* calamity, misfortune.
calamíta *nf* magnet, loadstone.
calamitàre *vt* to magnetize.
calamitóso *a* calamitous, disastrous.
càlamo *nm* reed, quill.
calànte *a* sinking, declining, setting, decreasing; **lúna c.** waning moon.
calaprànzi *nm* dumbwaiter.
calàre *vt* to let down, lower; (*sail etc*) strike; *vi* to decrease, descend, sink, set.
càlca *nf* crowd, throng.
calcàgno *nm* heel.
calcàre *vt* to tread on, lay stress on, (*drawing*) trace.
calcàre *nm* limestone.
càlce *nf* lime; *nm* bottom, foot; **in c.** *ad* at the foot of the page.
calcestrúzzo *nm* concrete.
calciàre *vt* to kick; **c. in pòrta** (*sport*) to kick at goal.
calciatóre *nm* footballer.
calcína *nf* lime, mortar.
calcinàccio *nm* flake of dry plaster.

calcinàio *nm* lime-pit.
calcinàre *vt* to calcine.
càlcio *nm* kick; (*sport*) football; butt-end, rifle stock; (*chem*) calcium; **c. d'àngolo** (*sport*) corner; **c. d'inízio** (*sport*) kick-off; **c. di rigóre** (*sport*) penalty; **c. di punizióne** (*sport*) free kick.
calcístico *pl* **-ici** *a* football.
càlco *pl* **càlchi** *nm* cast, imprint, tracing.
calcògrafo *nm* copperplate engraver.
calcolàbile *a* calculable, computable.
calcolàre *vt* to calculate, compute, reckon.
calcolatóre *m* **-tríce** *f a* calculating; *nm* reckoner, computer; (*fig*) shrewd fellow.
calcolatríce *nf* reckoner, computer, calculating machine; (*fig*) shrewd woman.
càlcolo *nm* calculation, reckoning; (*med*) stone, calculus; (*math*) calculus.
caldàia *nf* boiler.
caldallèssa *nf* boiled chestnut.
caldarròsta *nf* roast chestnut.
caldeggiàre *vt* to favor, foster, protect.
calderàio *nm* coppersmith.
calderóne *nm* cauldron; (*fig*) mixture of things.
càldo *a* warm, hot; *nm* heat.
caleidoscòpio *nm* kaleidoscope.
calendàrio *nm* calendar, almanac.
calèsse *nm* gig, carriage.
calettàre *vt* (*mech*) to couple, key on; *vi* to tally, fit.
calía *nf* gold filing; (*fig*) old stuff.
càlibro *nm* caliber.
càlice *nm* goblet, chalice; (*bot*) calyx.
calígine *nf* thick fog, smog, dimness.
caliginóso *a* foggy, dark.
càlle *nf* (*poet*) path; narrow street in Venice.
callífugo *pl* **-ghi** *nm* corn-plaster.
calligrafía *nf* handwriting.
callísta *nm* chiropodist.
càllo *nm* corn.
callosità *nf* callosity.
callóso *a* callous, hard.
càlma *nf* calm, quiet, tranquillity, quietness.
calmànte *a* soothing; *nm* sedative.
calmàre *vt* to calm, appease, soften; **-rsi** *vr* to calm down, become smooth.
càlmo *a* calm, tranquil, still, cool, (*sea*) smooth.
càlo *nm* loss of weight, fall in price, shrinkage.
calóre *nm* heat, warmth, feverishness.
caloría *nf* calorie.
calorífero *nm* radiator; **impiànto centràle di caloriferi** central heating.
caloróso *a* warm, hearty.
calòscia *nf* galosh.
calòtta *nf* skull-cap, calotte; (*mech*) cap.
calpestàre *vt* to trample on, oppress.
calpestío *nm* trampling.
calúnnia *nf* calumny.
calunniàre *vt* to calumniate, slander.
calunniatóre *nm* **-tríce** *nf* calumniator, slanderer.
calunnióso *a* calumnious, slanderous.
Calvàrio *nm* Calvary, wayside shrine; **calvàrio** *nm* long suffering.
calvízie *nf* baldness.
càlvo *a* bald; *nm* bald-headed person.
càlza *nf* stocking; **fàre la c.** *vi* to knit.
calzamàglia *nf* tights *pl.*
calzànte *a* suitable, appropriate.
calzàre *vt* (*shoes*) to put on, wear; *vi* to fit.
calzatóio *nm* shoehorn.
calzatúra *nf* footwear.
calzíno *nm* sock.
calzolàio *nm* bootmaker, shoemaker.
calzolería *nf* shoemaker's shop.
calzóni *nm* trousers *pl*, slacks *pl*; **c. córti, calzoncíni** shorts *pl.*
camaleónte *nm* chameleon.
cambiàle *nf* (*com*) bill of exchange, draft; **eméttere una c.** to draw a bill.
cambiaménto *nm* change.
cambiamonéte, cambiavalúte *nm* money changer.
cambiàre *vti* to change, alter, turn, exchange; **-rsi** *vr* to change.
càmbio *nm* change, exchange; (*tec*) change gear, (*aut*) gear, gearbox.
càmera *nf* chamber, room; **c. da lètto** bedroom; **C. dei Deputàti** House of Commons, House of Representatives; **C. dei Pàri** House of Lords.
cameràta *nm* comrade; *nf* dormitory.
camerièra *nf* maid, servant, waitress; **-re** *nm* waiter, manservant.
cameríno *nm* (*theat*) dressing room.
càmice *nm* surplice, overall.
camicétta *nf* blouse.
camícia *pl* **-ície** *nf* shirt, wrapper; (*tec*) jacket; **c. da nòtte** nightgown, nightdress; **c. di fòrza** strait-jacket.
caminétto *nm* fireplace.
camíno *nm* fireplace, chimney.
càmion *nm* lorry, truck.
camionétta *nf* (*mil*) jeep.
camioncíno *nm* small van, tradesman's delivery van.
camionísta *nm* lorry driver; truck driver.
cammèllo *nm* camel.
cammèo *nm* cameo.
camminaménto *nm* (*mil*) communication trench.
camminàre *vi* to walk, march; (*of mechanism*) go, work; proceed.
cammíno *nm* way, road, journey; **cammín facèndo** *ad* on the way.
camomílla *nf* camomile.

camòrra *nf* camorra, secret (criminal) society.
camóscio *nm* chamois, shammy.
campàgna *nf* country, estate; campaign.
campagn(u)òlo *a* rustic, country; *nm* peasant, countryman.
campàle *a* (of the) field; **battàglia c.** *nf* pitched battle.
campàna *nf* bell, bell glass.
campanèlla *nf* small bell; (*bot*) harebell.
campanèllo *nm* (*in the house*) bell.
Campània *nf* (*geogr*) Campania.
campaníle *nm* bell-tower, belfry.
campanilismo *nm* local patriotism.
campàno *a nm* (inhabitant) of Campania.
campàre *vt* to save, rescue; (*art*) put into relief; *vi* to live.
campeggiàre *vi* to stand out; camp, encamp.
campéggio *nm* camping, camping place.
campèstre *a* rural, rustic.
Campidòglio (il) *nm* the Capitol (in Rome).
campionàrio *a* sample, trade; *nm* pattern book, sample case.
campionàto *nm* championship.
campióne *nm* champion; (*com*) sample.
càmpo *nm* field, camp; **c. d'aviazióne** airfield; **c. di fortúna** emergency landing-ground; **méttere in c.** *vt* to bring forward, propose.
camposànto *nm* burial ground, cemetery.
camuffàre *vt* to disguise, mask.
Canadà *nm* (*geogr*) Canada.
canadése *a nm* Canadian.
canàglia *nf* mob, rabble, riffraff, rogue.
canàle *nm* canal, channel, pipe; **c. navigàbile** waterway.
canalizzàre *vt* to canalize.
cànapa *nf* hemp.
canapè *nm* couch, sofa.
Canàrie (le) *nf pl* (*geogr*) the Canary Islands, the Canaries *pl*.
canaríno *a* canary-colored; *nm* canary.
canàsta *nf* canasta.
cancellàre *vt* to cancel, erase, obliterate.
cancellàta *nf* railing.
cancellatúra *nf* erasure.
cancellería *nf* chancellor's office, chancery; **artícoli di c.** articles of stationery.
cancellière *nm* chancellor, registrar.
cancèllo *nm* gate, railing.
cancrèna *nf* gangrene.
càncro *nm* cancer.
candeggiàre *vt* to bleach.
candeggína *nf* bleach; **candéggio** *nm* bleaching.
candéla *nf* candle, (*aut*) sparking plug, spark plug.
candelàbro *nm* candelabrum.
candelière *nm* candlestick, (*naut*) stanchion.
candelòra *nf* Candlemas.
candidàto *nm* candidate.
candidatúra *nf* candidature.
càndido *a* white; candid, sincere.
candíre *vt* to candy.
candíto *a* candied; *nm* sugar candy.
candóre *nm* whiteness; candor.
càne *nm* dog, (*of a gun*) cock, (*mech*) catch; **c. da càccia** hound, sporting dog; **c. da guàrdia** watchdog; **c. barbóne** poodle; **c. bastàrdo** mongrel.
canèstro *nm* basket, hamper; basketful.
cànfora *nf* camphor.
cangiàbile *a* changeable, fickle.
cangiànte *a* changing, (*of color*) iridescent; **séta c.** shot silk.
cangùro *nm* kangaroo.
canícola *nf* dog-star; dog-days *pl*.
caníle *nm* kennel.
caníno *a* canine; **tósse canína** whooping-cough.
canízie *nf* white hair, old age.
cànna *nf* cane, reed, tube, (*gun*) barrel, (fishing-)rod, stick, (*measure*) rod.
cannèlla *nf* spout, spigot, tap; cinnamon.
cannéto *nm* reed thicket, cane field.
canníbale *nm* cannibal.
cannocchiàle *nm* binoculars *pl*, opera glass, telescope.
cannonàta *nf* cannon-shot.
cannóne *nm* gun, cannon; **c. anticàrro** anti-tank gun; **c. antiaèreo** anti-aircraft gun.
cannoneggiaménto *nm* cannonade, cannonading.
cannoneggiàre *vti* to cannonade.
cannonièra *nf* gunboat.
cannonière *nm* gunner.
cannúccia *nf* thin cane, (*for drinks*) straw, pen-holder, small tube.
canòa *nf* canoe.
cànone *nm* canon, rule; fee, rent.
canònica *nf* vicarage, rectory.
canònico *pl* **-ici** *a* canonical, regular; **dritto c.** canon law; *nm* canon.
canonizzàre *vt* to canonize.
canonizzazióne *nf* canonization.
canottàggio *nm* rowing, canoeing.
canottièra *nf* vest, singlet, undershirt; straw hat.
canòtto *nm* canoe.
cànova *nf* retail shop for wine *etc*.
canovàccio *nm* dishcloth, canvas; plot.
cantànte *a* singing; *nmf* singer.
cantàre *vti* to sing.
cantatóre *a* singing; *nm* singer.
cantatríce *nf* singer.
canterellàre, canticchiàre *vti* to hum, sing softly.
canteríno *a* singing, warbling, chirping.
càntica *nf* poem, song; **càntico** *nm* canticle, hymn.

cantière *nm* dockyard, ship-building yard.
cantilèna *nf* monotonous song, singsong.
cantína *nf* cellar, wine shop.
cànto *nm* singing, song, poem, canto; corner, side, angle.
cantonàta *nf* corner; blunder.
cantóne *nm* corner; canton.
cantonière *nm* maintenance man on roads, railways *etc*; **càsa cantonièra** roadman's house.
cantóre *nm* singer, chorister.
cantoría *nf* choir, chancel.
cantúccio *nm* corner, bit.
canúto *a* gray-headed, hoary.
canzonàre *vt* to make fun of, tease; *vi* to joke.
canzonatòrio *a* mocking, teasing.
canzonatúra *nf* mockery, teasing.
canzóne *nf* song, ode, ballad.
canzonière *nm* collection of lyrical poems, song book.
càos *nm* chaos, confusion.
caòtico *pl* **-ici** *a* chaotic.
capàce *a* able, capable, capacious.
capacità *nf* ability, capacity.
capacitàrsi *vr* to make out, understand.
capànna *nf* **-no** *nm* hut, cabin.
capannèllo *nm* group of persons, small crowd.
caparbietà *nf* obstinacy, stubbornness.
capàrbio *a* obstinate, stubborn.
capàrra *nf* advance payment, earnest money.
capéllo *nm* hair; **capellóne** *nm* (*sl*) beatnik.
capellúto *a* hairy.
capelvènere *nm* (*bot*) maidenhair.
capèstro *nm* halter, rope.
capezzàle *nm* bolster.
capézzolo *nm* nipple.
capigliatúra *nf* hair, head of hair.
capinéra *nf* (*bird*) blackcap.
capire *vt* to understand, realize; *vi* to be contained.
capitàle *a* capital, principal, main; deadly; *nm* capital, wealth, assets *pl*; *nf* capital (city).
capitalísmo *nm* capitalism.
capitalísta *nm* capitalist.
capitanàre *vt* to captain, head.
capitanería *nf* **c. di pòrto** harbormaster's office.
capitàno *nm* captain, commander.
capitàre *vi* to happen, occur, turn up.
capitèllo *nm* (*arch*) capital.
capitolàre *vi* to capitulate; *a* capitular; *nm* capitulary.
capitolíno *a* Capitoline.
capítolo *nm* chapter, (*of pact or convention*) article.
capitombolàre *vi* to tumble.
capitómbolo *nm* somersault, tumble.
càpo *nm* head; chief, beginning, end, article, item, cape, promontory; **da c.** again; **in c. a** at the end of; **veníre a c. di** to make out, reason out.
capobànda *pl* **capibànda** *nm* bandmaster, gang leader.
capòcchia *nf* head of a nail, pin *etc*.
capocòmico *pl* **-ici, capicòmici** *nm* (*theat*) head of a dramatic company, showman.
capocuòco *pl* **capicuòchi** *nm* head cook, chef.
capofàbbrica *pl* **capifàbbrica** *nm* foreman.
capofítto *ad* head downwards, head foremost.
capogíro *pl* **-íri** *nm* dizziness, giddiness.
capolavóro *pl* **-óri** *nm* masterpiece.
capolínea *pl* **capilínea** *nm* terminus.
capolíno *nm* small head; **fàre c.** to peep in.
capoluògo *pl* **-ghi, capiluòghi** *nm* chief town in a district.
capomàstro *pl* **-tri, capimàstri** *nm* master builder.
caponàggine *nf* obstinacy.
caporàle *nm* corporal.
caporepàrto *pl* **capirepàrto** *nm* head of a department, shopwalker, floorwalker, foreman.
caporióne *pl* **capirióne** *nm* ringleader.
caposàldo *pl* **capisàldi** *nm* essential point of a speech *etc*; (*mil*) stronghold.
caposquàdra *pl* **capisquàdra** *nm* foreman; (*mil*) squad leader.
capostazióne *pl* **capistazióne** *nm* station-master.
capotàvola *pl* **capitàvola** *nm* head of a table.
capotréno *pl* **capitréno** *nm* guard, conductor.
capovérso *pl* **-rsi** *nm* beginning of a line or paragraph.
capovòlgere *vt* to overturn, upset; **-rsi** *vr* to capsize, be upset.
càppa *nf* cape, cloak, cope; the letter K.
cappèlla *nf* chapel.
cappellàno *nm* chaplain.
cappellièra *nf* hat-box.
cappèllo *nm* hat.
càpperi! *interj* goodness!
càppero *nm* caper, caper-bush.
càppio *nm* slip-knot, noose.
cappóne *nm* capon.
cappòtto *nm* cloak, overcoat.
cappuccíno *nm* capuchin friar; coffee with a little cream.
cappúccio *nm* cowl, hood.
càpra *nf* she-goat.
caprétto *nm* kid, young goat.
capríccio *nm* caprice, whim.
capricciόso *a* capricious, whimsical.
caprifòglio *nm* honeysuckle.
capriòla *nf* doe, roe; caper, capriole.
capriòlo *nm* roebuck.
càpro *nm* he-goat; **c. espiatório** scapegoat.
càpsula *nf* capsule, percussion cap.

capuffício *nm* head clerk.
carabína *nf* carbine.
carabinière *nm* carabineer, gendarme.
caràffa *nf* decanter, carafe.
caramèlla *nf* sweet, candy, toffee, taffy, caramel; monocle.
caràto *nm* carat; (*com*) share.
caràttere *nm* character, quality, style, (*typ*) type.
caratterística *nf* characteristic.
caratterístico *a* characteristic.
caratterizzàre *vt* to characterize.
carbonàia *nf* charcoal pit, coal-cellar, bunker.
carbonàio *nm* coalman.
carbònchio *nm* carbuncle.
carbóne *nm* coal; **c. fòssile** pit coal.
carbonèlla *nf* charcoal, coal cinders.
carbònio *nm* carbon.
carbonizzàre *vt* to carbonize.
carburànte *nm* fuel, petrol, gas, gasoline.
carburatóre *nm* carburetor.
carcàme *nm* **-àssa** *nf* carcass.
carceràre *vt* to imprison.
carceràto *nm* prisoner.
carcerazióne *nf* imprisonment.
càrcere *nm* jail, prison.
carcerière *nm* jailer.
carciòfo *nm* artichoke.
cardàre *vt* to card.
cardellíno *nm* goldfinch.
cardíaco *pl* **-íaci** *a* cardiac.
cardinàle *a* cardinal, principal; *nm* cardinal.
càrdine *nm* hinge; (*fig*) foundation.
càrdo *nm* thistle, teasel.
carèna *nf* (*of a ship*) keel.
carenàre *vt* (*naut*) to careen.
carènza *nf* lack, scarcity.
carestía *nf* dearth, famine.
carézza *nf* caress; high price.
carezzàre *vt* to caress, fondle, cherish.
carezzévole *a* caressing, coaxing.
carìàre *vt* to decay, rot.
càrica *nf* position, post; (*mil*) charge; (*el*) charging; winding.
caricaménto *nm* loading, charging, winding up.
caricàre *vt* to charge, load, overburden, exaggerate; **c. un orològio** to wind up a clock.
caricatóre *nm* loader, shipper; (*of firearms*) magazine.
caricatúra *nf* caricature.
càrico *pl* **-chi** *a* charged, loaded, wound up; *nm* load, cargo, burden, charge.
càrie *nf* caries, (*of teeth*) decay.
caríno *a* pretty, nice, dear, sweet.
carità *nf* charity, alms; **per c.** *interj* for heaven's sake.
caritatévole *a* charitable.
carlínga *nf* (*av*) cockpit.
Càrlo *nm pr* Charles.
Carlomàgno *nm pr* Charlemagne.
carlóna, alla *ad* in a slovenly manner.
carmelitàno *nm* Carmelite friar.
carnagióne *nf* complexion.
carnàle *a* bodily, physical, carnal, sensual.
carnalità *nf* carnality, sensuality.
càrne *nf* flesh, meat.
carnéfice *nm* executioner, (*fig*) brutal person.
carneficína *nf* carnage, slaughter.
carnevàle *nm* carnival.
Càrniche (Àlpi) *nf pl* (*geogr*) Carnic Alps.
carnívoro *a* carnivorous.
carnóso *a* fleshy.
càro *a* dear, expensive; *ad* dearly, dear; *nm* high cost; **il carovíta** the high cost of living; **tenér c.** to esteem, value.
carógna *nf* carrion (*also fig*).
Carolína *nf pr* Caroline.
caròta *nf* carrot.
carovàna *nf* caravan, convoy.
càrpa *nf* carp.
carpentière *nm* carpenter.
carpíre *vt* to seize, snatch; cheat.
carpóne, carpóni *ad* on all fours.
carradóre *nm* cartwright.
carràia *nf* cart road.
carreggiàbile *a* practicable for carts.
carreggiàta *nf* track, cart road; gauge; **uscíre di c.** (*fig*) to go astray.
carrèllo *nm* (*tec*) undercarriage, trolley.
carrétta *nf* cart.
carrettàta *nf* cartload.
carrettière *nm* carrier, carter.
carrétto *nm* hand-cart.
carrièra *nf* career, course, speed.
carriòla *nf* wheelbarrow.
càrro *nm* cart, wagon, truck; (*astr*) Great Bear; **c. armàto** (*mil*) tank; **c. leggèro** (*mil*) light tank; **c. fúnebre** hearse.
carròzza *nf* carriage, coach, railway car; **c. belvedére** observation car; **c. ristorànte** restaurant car, dining car; **c. lètto** sleeping car, sleeper.
carrozzàbile *a* practicable for carriages.
carrozzería *nf* body of a car, car-making firm.
carrozzína *nf* perambulator, (*fam*) pram, baby carriage.
carrozzíno *nm* light carriage; (*motorcycle*) sidecar.
carrúcola *nf* pulley, sheave.
càrsico *pl* **-ici** *a* Karst.
Càrso *nm* (*geogr*) Karst.
càrta *nf* paper, document, writing, charter, playing card, map; **c. d'identità** identity card; **c. igiènica** toilet paper; **c. da lèttere** writing paper, notepaper.
cartacarbóne *pl* **cartecarbóne** *nf* carbon paper.
cartàccia, cartastràccia *pl* **cartestràcce** *nf* waste paper.

cartàio *nm* papermaker; (*at cards*) dealer.
cartapècora *pl* **-ore** *nf* parchment.
cartapésta *pl* **cartapéste, cartepéste** *nf* papier-mâché.
cartavetràta *pl* **cartevetràte** *nf* glass paper, sandpaper.
cartéggio *nm* correspondence, collection of letters.
cartèlla *nf* folder, portfolio, writing pad; schoolbag; (*of a manuscript*) sheet; share, bond, score-card, (lottery) ticket.
cartellièra *nf* filing cabinet.
cartèllo *nm* bill, label, signboard, poster.
cartellóne *nm* placard, playbill.
cartièra *nf* paper mill.
cartilàgine *nf* cartilage, gristle.
cartòccio *nm* cornet, paper bag.
cartolàio *nm* stationer.
cartolería *nf* stationer's shop.
cartolína *nf* card; **c. illustràta** picture postcard; **c. postàle** postcard.
cartóne *nm* cardboard; cartoon.
cartúccia *nf* cartridge.
cartuccièra *nf* cartridge belt.
càsa *nf* house, home, family, household; religious community; business firm; **c. di salúte** nursing home.
casàccio, a *ad* at random, haphazard.
casàle *nm* hamlet.
casalíngo *pl* **-ghi** *a* domestic, homely, homemade.
casaménto *nm* tenement house.
casàta *nf* lineage, family.
casàto *nm* surname.
cascàggine *nf* drowsiness, weariness.
cascàre *vi* to fall.
cascàta *nf* fall, waterfall, cascade.
cascemír *nm* cashmere.
cascína *nf* dairy farm, dairy.
caseggiàto *nm* block of houses.
caşeifício *nm* dairy.
casèlla *nf* pigeonhole, small compartment; (*beehive*) cell.
casellànte *nm* level-crossing keeper, signalman.
casellàrio *nm* set of pigeonholes.
caşèrma *nf* barracks *pl*.
casétta, casettína *nf* cottage, small house.
casíno *nm* little cottage; club, gaming-house.
càşo *nm* case; chance, possibility; **a c.** *ad* at random.
casolàre *nm* poor country house.
Càspio, (Mar) *nm* (*geogr*) Caspian (Sea).
càssa *nf* case, chest, coffer, coffin, drum; (*of a gun*) stock; cash, fund; **c. di rispàrmio** savings bank.
cassafòrte *nf* safe.
cassapànca *nf* wooden chest in the form of a bench.
cassàre *vt* to cancel, annul, quash.
cassazióne *nf* annulling, cassation; **corte di c.** (*leg*) court of cassation.
casseruòla *nf* saucepan.
cassétta *nf* box, coach-box, collection box, letter-box, mailbox.
cassétto *nm* drawer.
cassettóne *nm* chest of drawers.
cassière *nm* cashier, teller.
càsta *nf* caste, rank.
castágna *nf* chestnut; **castàgno** *nm* chestnut tree; **c. d'India** horsechestnut(tree).
castagnéto *nm* chestnut grove.
castàno *a* chestnut-colored, brown; **c. scúro** dark brown; **c. chiàro** light brown.
castellàno *nm* lord of a manor.
castèllo *nm* castle, fortress, (*naut*) castle.
castigàre *vt* to punish, chastise, chasten; spoil.
castigàto *a* chaste, pure; (*edition*) expurgated.
castígo *pl* **-íghi** *nm* punishment.
castità *nf* chastity, purity.
càsto *a* chaste, pure.
castòro *nm* beaver.
castràre *vt* to castrate, (*fig*) bowdlerize.
castràto *a* castrated; *nm* mutton.
caşuàle *a* casual; accidental.
caşualità *nf* chance.
casúpola *nf* hovel.
cataclíşma *nm* cataclysm.
catacómba *nf* catacomb.
catalessi *nf* catalepsy.
catalizzatóre *nm* (*chem*) catalyst.
catalogàre *vt* to catalogue.
catàlogo *pl* **-ghi** *nm* catalogue, list.
catapécchia *nf* hovel.
catapláşma *nm* poultice.
catapulta *nf* catapult.
catarifrangènte *nm* reflector, reflex reflector.
catàrro *nm* catarrh.
catàsta *nf* pile, heap, stack.
catàsto *nm* register of lands, land office, land tax.
catàstrofe *nf* catastrophe.
catechíşmo *nm* catechism.
categoría *nf* category, class.
categòrico *pl* **-ici** *a* categorical.
caténa *nf* chain, fetter; (*of hills*) range; **c. cingolàta** (*mil*) caterpillar track.
catenàccio *nm* (*door*) bolt.
catenèlla *nf* small chain.
cateràtta *nf* cataract, sluice.
Caterína *nf pr* Catherine, Katherine.
catinèlla *nf* wash-hand basin; **piòvere a catinèlle** *vi* to rain cats and dogs.
catíno *nm* basin.
catràme *nm* tar.
càttedra *nf* desk, teaching post, chair, professorship, pulpit.
cattedràle *nf* cathedral.
cattivàre *vt* to captivate; **-rsi** *vr* to win (*love, favor etc*).
cattivèria *nf* naughtiness, wickedness.
cattività *nf* captivity.
cattívo *a* bad, naughty, wicked.

Cattolicéṣimo, Cattolicíṣmo *nm* (Roman) Catholicism.
cattolicità *nf* Catholicism, Catholic countries *pl*.
cattòlico *pl* **-ici** *a nm* Catholic.
cattúra *nf* capture, arrest; **mandàto di c.** warrant of arrest.
catturàre *vt* to arrest, capture.
Càucaso (il) *nm* (*geogr*) Caucasus.
caucciù *nm* indiarubber.
càuṣa *nf* cause, origin, reason; (*leg*) law-suit.
cauṣàle *a* causal.
cauṣalità *nf* causality.
cauṣàre *vt* to cause, occasion.
causticità *nf* causticity.
càustico *pl* **-ici** *a nm* caustic.
cautaménte *ad* cautiously.
cautèla *nf* caution, wariness.
càuto *a* cautious, wary.
cauzióne *nf* security, bail, caution money.
càva *nf* quarry, mine.
cavalcàre *vt* to mount (*a horse etc*); *vi* to ride.
cavalcàta *nf* ride, cavalcade.
cavalcatúra *nf* mount.
cavalcavía *nm* fly-over.
cavalcióni *ad* astride; **a c. di** astride.
cavalière *nm* horseman, knight; escort, dancing partner.
cavàlla *nf* mare.
cavallànte *nm* stable-man, horse-rider.
cavalleresco *pl* **-chi** *a* chivalrous, knightly, noble.
cavallería *nf* cavalry, horse *pl*, chivalry.
cavallerízza *nf* riding school, horse-woman; **cavallerízzo** *nm* rider, riding master, ringmaster.
cavallétta *nf* grasshopper.
cavallétto *nm* small horse; easel, trestle; (*torture*) rack.
cavallína *nf* filly; **córrere la c.** to sow one's wild oats.
cavàllo *nm* horse; (*chess*) knight; **c. vapóre** horse-power.
cavàre *vt* to extract, take out, remove, obtain; **-rsi** *vr* to get out of.
cavatàppi *nm* corkscrew.
cavèrna *nf* cave, cavern.
cavézza *nf* halter.
càvia *nf* guinea-pig.
caviàle *nm* caviar.
cavíglia *nf* ankle (bone).
cavillàre *vi* to carp, cavil, split hairs.
cavíllo *nm* cavil, quibble.
cavillóso *a* caviling, quibbling.
cavità *nf* cavity, hole.
càvo *a* hollow, empty; *nm* cable, rope; **c. di orméggio** mooring cable.
cavolfióre *nm* cauliflower.
càvolo *nm* cabbage; **cavolíni di Bruxelles** brussels sprouts.
cazzòtto *nm* punch, blow.
céce *nm* chick-pea.
Cecília *nf pr* Cecily; **Cecílio** *nm pr* Cecil.
cecità *nf* blindness, ignorance.
cèco *pl* **-chi** *a nm* Czech.
Cecoṣlovàcchia *nf* Czechoslovakia.
cecoṣlovàcco *pl* **-chi** *a nm* Czechoslovak.
cèdere *vi* to give in, yield; cave in; *vt* to give up, cede, surrender, transfer.
cedévole *a* yielding; (*of ground*) sinking.
cedíbile *a* transferable.
cèdola *nf* (*com*) coupon.
cédro *nm* cedar, citron.
céfalo *nm* mullet.
cèffo *nm* muzzle, snout.
celàre *vt* to disguise, hide; **-rsi** *vr* to hide (oneself).
celebrànte *nm* officiating priest.
celebràre *vt* to celebrate, praise.
celebrazióne *nf* celebration.
cèlebre *a* celebrated, famous.
celebrità *nf* celebrity.
cèlere *a* nimble, rapid, swift.
celerità *nf* celerity, swiftness.
celèste *a* celestial, divine, heavenly; sky-blue.
cèlia *nf* jest, joke.
celibàto *nm* celibacy.
cèlibe *a* unmarried; *nm* bachelor.
cèlla *nf* (*of prison, monastery*) cell.
cellofàne *nm* cellophane.
cèllula *nf* (*anat, el*) cell.
cellulàre *a* cellular, honey-combed; *nm* jail, prison.
cémbalo *nm* tambourine; harpsichord, spinet.
cementàre *vt* to cement.
ceménto *nm* cement.
céna *nf* supper.
cenàcolo *nm* supper-room, picture of the Last Supper; artistic circle.
cenàre *vi* to sup.
cenciàia *nf* **-io** *nm* rag-picker.
céncio *nm* dishcloth, rag.
cencióso *a* ragged, in tatters.
cénere *nf* ashes *pl*, cinders *pl*; **giórno delle céneri** *nm* Ash Wednesday.
Cenerèntola *nf* Cinderella.
Cenísio, (Monte) *nm* (*geogr*) Cenis.
cénno *nm* nod, sign, signal, gesture, hint; notice, outline; **far c.** to beckon, nod.
censiménto *nm* census.
censíre *vt* to take the census.
cènso *nm* income, wealth, life annuity; census.
censóre *nm* censor.
censòrio *a* censorious.
censúra *nf* censure, censorship.
censuràre *vt* to censor, censure.
centellinàre *vt* to sip.
centenàrio *a nm* centenarian; *nm* centenary.
centennàle *a* centennial.
centèṣimo *a nm* hundredth; *nm* centesimo, centime, cent.
centígrado *a* centigrade.
centigràmmo *nm* centigram.
centímetro *nm* centimeter.
centinàio *nm* hundred; **a centinàia** in hundreds.

cènto *a* hundred.
centràle *a* central, midland; *nf* **c. elèttrica** power station; **c. telefònica** telephone exchange; **c. atòmica** atomic power station.
centralíno *nm* telephone exchange.
centralizzàre *vt* to centralize.
centràre *vt* to center.
cèntro *nm* center, heart, middle.
centuplicàre *vt* centuplicate, multiply.
cèntuplo *a* centuple, hundredfold.
ceppàia *nf* rooty stump.
céppo *nm* (tree) stump, log, (chopping) block; **céppi** *pl* shackles *pl* (*also fig*).
cèra *nf* wax, polish; aspect, face; **c. da scarpe** shoe polish.
ceralàcca *nf* sealing wax.
ceràmica *nf* ceramics *pl*.
cérca *nf* quest, search.
cercàre *vt* to look for, seek, strive, try.
cérchia *nf* circle; encircling walls *pl*.
cerchiàre *vt* to hoop.
cerchiàto *a* (*of eyes*) black-ringed.
cérchio *nm* circle, ring, hoop, tire.
cereàle *a nm* cereal.
cerebràle *a* cerebral.
cèreo *a* waxen, wan.
cerimònia *nf* ceremony.
cerimoniàle *a nm* ceremonial.
cerimonióso *a* ceremonious.
ceríno *nm* wax match, taper.
cernièra *nf* hinge (*of a bag, purse etc*), mount; **c. làmpo** zip-fastener, zipper.
cèrnita *nf* choice, selection, grading.
céro *nm* church candle.
ceròtto *nm* sticking plaster; tedious person.
cèrro *nm* Turkey oak.
certaménte *ad* certainly.
certézza *nf* assurance, certainty.
certificàre *vt* to certify, confirm.
certificàto *nm* certificate, testimonial.
cèrto *a* certain, positive, sure; *ad* certainly, of course.
certósa *nf* Carthusian monastery.
certosíno *nm* Carthusian monk.
certúni *pron pl* a few, some *pl*.
cèrva *nf* hind, doe.
cervellíno *nm* hare-brained person.
cervèllo *nm* brain; brains *pl*, judgment, sense.
cervellòtico *pl* **-ici** *a* fantastic, queer.
Cervíno, (il) *nm* (*geogr*) the Matterhorn.
cèrvo *nm* deer, stag; **càrne di c.** venison; **c. volànte** stag-beetle.
Césare *nm pr* Caesar.
cesellàre *vt* to chisel (*also fig*).
cesèllo *nm* chisel.
cesóie *nf pl* shears *pl*.
cespúglio *nm* bush, thicket.
cessàre *vti* to cease, end, stop.
cessazióne *nf* cessation, end, (*com*) discontinuance.
cessióne *nf* transfer, assignment.
cèsso *nm* water-closet, toilet.
césta *nf* basket, hamper.
cestinàre *vt* to throw into the waste-paper basket.
cestíno *nm* small basket, waste-paper basket.
césto *nm* (*bot*) head; (*basketball*) basket.
cèto *nm* class, rank.
cetriòlo *nm* cucumber.
che *cj and ad* than, that, whether, but, as soon as, lest; *pron and a* that, what, which, who; **che c'è?** what is the matter?
che *interj* what! no! never!
checchessía *pron* whatever.
chèrmisi *nm* crimson.
chetàre *vt* to quiet, silence; **-rsi** *vr* to grow quiet, silent.
chetichèlla, àlla *ad* quietly, secretly.
chéto *a* quiet, silent.
chi *pron interrog* who, whom, which; *pron rel* he who, whom *etc*; whoever; some . . . others.
chiàcchiera *nf* gossip, prattle, tittle-tattle.
chiacchieràre *vi* to chat, gossip.
chiacchieràta *nf* chat.
chiacchierío *nm* chattering.
chiacchieróna *nf* **-óne** *nm* babbler, chatterbox, prattler.
chiàma *nf* rollcall.
chiamàre *vt* to call, name; **-rsi** *vr* to be called; **cóme si chiàma?** what is your name?
chiamàta *nf* call, summons.
chiappàre *vt* to catch, seize.
Chiàra *nf pr* Clara, Clare, Claire.
chiaraménte *ad* clearly, frankly.
chiarézza *nf* clearness, fame.
chiarificàre *vt* to clarify.
chiaríre *vt* to clarify, explain; **-rsi** *vr* to become clear, (*of the weather*) clear up.
chiàro *a* clear, bright, illustrious, *nm* brightness, light, light color; **con quésti chiàri di lúna** (*fig*) in these difficult times; *ad* clearly.
chiaróre *nm* brightness, light.
chiaroveggènte *a* clear-sighted, clairvoyant.
chiaroveggènza *nf* clairvoyance.
chiàsso *nm* noise, uproar.
chiassóso *a* noisy.
chiàtta *nf* lighter, barge.
chiavàrda *nf* bolt.
chiàve *nf* key, spanner, (*mus*) clef.
chiavistèllo *nm* bolt.
chiàzza *nf* spot, stain.
chícchera *nf* cup.
chícco *pl* **-chi** *nm* coffee-bean, grain; hailstone; **c. d'úva** grape.
chièdere *vt* to ask, beg, inquire.
chièrico *pl* **-ici** *nm* priest in minor orders; **chierichétto** *nm* altar-boy, choirboy.
chièsa *nf* church.
chíglia *nf* (*naut*) keel.

chílo *nm* chyle; **fàre il c.** to rest after a meal.
chilo(gràmmo) *nm* kilo(gram).
chilòmetro *nm* kilometer.
chimèra *nf* chimera, illusion.
chímica *nf* chemistry.
chímico *pl* **-ici** *a* chemical; *nm* chemist.
chína *nf* declivity, slope; Peruvian bark.
chinàre *vt* to bend, bow; **-rsi** *vr* to bend down, stoop, submit.
chincàglie *nf pl* **chincaglieria** *nf* fancy goods *pl*, knick-knacks *pl*.
chincaglière *nm* fancy-goods merchant.
chiníno *nm* quinine.
chíno *a* bent.
chiòccia *nf* broody hen.
chiòcciola *nf* snail, sea-shell; screw-nut; **scàla a c.** spiral stair.
chiòdo *nm* nail; **ròba da chiòdi** dishonest thing or person, badly done (or made) thing; **piantàre chiòdi** to run up debts.
chiòma *nf* hair, foliage; (*of a comet*) tail.
chiòṣa *nf* explanatory note, gloss.
chioṣàre *vt* to comment, gloss.
chiòsco *pl* **-òschi** *nm* kiosk, newsstand.
chiòstra *nf* enclosure; (*of teeth*) set; (*of mountains*) range.
chiòstro *nm* cloister; (*fig*) monastic life.
chiòtto *a* silent.
chirurgía *nf* surgery.
chirúrgico *pl* **-ici** *a* surgical.
chirúrgo *pl* **-úrgi, -úrghi** *nm* surgeon.
chissà *interj* who knows!
chitàrra *nf* guitar.
chitarrísta *nmf* guitarist.
chiúdere *vt* to close, enclose, fence; conclude; turn off; **-rsi** *vr* close, close over, close in, shut oneself up, withdraw.
chiúnque *pron rel indef* anyone who, whoever, anyone.
chiúsa *nf* fence, dam, lock, weir; conclusion, close.
chiúso *a* closed, enclosed; (*sky*) overcast; (*com*) settled; *nm* enclosure, pen.
chiusúra *nf* closing, close, fastening, fastener, lock.
ci *pron* us, to us, each other, one another, this, that, it; *ad* here, there.
ciabàtta *nf* slipper.
ciabattíno *nm* cobbler.
ciàlda *nf* **cialdóne** *nm* biscuit, wafer.
cialtróna *nf* slut.
cialtróne *nm* blackguard, rascal.
cialtronería *nf* slatternliness, rascality.
ciambèlla *nf* ring-shaped cake; name given to many objects similarly shaped, as an air cushion, lifebelt *etc*.
ciambellàno *nm* chamberlain.
ciància *nf* idle talk, gossip; **ciànce!** nonsense!
cianciàre *vi* to prate, tattle, gossip.
cianfruṣàglia *nf* trash, odds and ends.
cíano *nm* cornflower.
cianúro *nm* cyanide; **c. di potàssio** potassium cyanide.
ciào *interj* hello!, hi!, (*leaving*) bye-bye.
ciàrla *nf* talkativeness, gossip.
ciarlàre *vi* to talk a lot.
ciarlatanería *nf* quackery.
ciarlatàno *nm* quack, charlatan.
ciascúno *a and pron* each, every, each one, every one.
cibàre *vt* to feed; **-rsi** *vr* to eat, feed upon.
cibària *nf* food, victuals *pl*.
cíbo *nm* food.
cicàla *nf* cicada, chatterbox.
cicatríce *nf* scar.
cicatriẓẓàre *vti* **-rsi** *vr* to cicatrize, heal, skin over.
cícca *nf* cigar-butt, cigarette-end, quid; (*fig*) worthless thing.
ciceróne *nm* cicerone, guide.
ciciṣbèo *nm* gallant, lady's man.
ciclamíno *nm* cyclamen.
ciclíṣmo *nm* cycling.
ciclísta *nmf* cyclist.
ciclóne *nm* cyclone, hurricane.
ciclostilàre *vt* to cyclostyle.
ciclostíle *nm* cyclostyle.
cicógna *nf* stork.
cicòria *nf* chicory.
cicúta *nf* hemlock.
cièco *pl* **-chi** *a* blind; *nm* blind man.
cièlo *nm* sky, heaven; atmosphere, climate; ceiling.
cífra *nf* figure, number, cipher.
cifràre *vt* to write in cipher; (*linen*) mark.
cíglio *pl* **ciglia** (*f*), (*fig*) **cigli** (*m*) *nm* eyelash, eyebrow, edge; **c. della stràda** roadside.
ciglióne *nm* bank, edge.
cígno *nm* swan.
cigolàre *vi* to creak, squeak.
cigolío *nm* creaking, squeaking.
Cíle *nm* (*geogr*) Chile.
cilécca *nf* disappointment, failure.
cilèno *a nm* Chilean.
cilício *nm* hair-shirt, sackcloth.
ciliègia *nf* cherry; **ciliègio** *nm* cherry-tree.
cilíndrico *pl* **-ici** *a* cylindrical.
cilíndro *nm* cylinder, roller.
círna *nf* top, summit, eminence.
cimèlio *nm* relic, antique.
cimentàre *vt* to put to the test, try, risk; **-rsi** *vr* to enter into contest with, strive.
ciménto *nm* test, risk.
címice *nf* bug, bed-bug; drawing pin, thumbtack.
ciminièra *nf* smokestack, chimney, funnel.
cimitèro *nm* cemetery, burial ground.

cimúrro *nm* glanders *pl*; distemper.
Cína *nf* (*geogr*) China.
cinciallégra *nf* tit.
cinedràmma *nm* screenplay.
cinegiornàle *nm* newsreel.
cínema *nm inv v* **cinematògrafo.**
cinematografàre *vt* to film.
cinematografía *nf* cinematography, cinema.
cinematògrafo *nm* cinema(tograph), picture house, pictures, movies.
cinése *a nmf* Chinese.
cingallègra *nf* great tit(mouse).
cíngere *vt* to gird, encircle, surround.
cínghia *nf* belt, strap.
cinghiàle *nm* wild boar.
cíngolo *nm* girdle, (*tec*) caterpillar.
cinguettàre *vi* to chirp, twitter.
cínico *pl* **cínici** *a* cynical; *nm* cynic.
cinísmo *nm* cynicism.
cinquànta *a* fifty.
cinquantèsimo *a* fiftieth.
cinquantína *nf* some fifty, about fifty.
cínque *a* five.
cinquecentísta *nmf* artist or writer of the 16th century.
cinquecènto *a* five hundred; *nm* 16th century.
cinquènnio *nm* period of 5 years.
cínta *nf* city walls *pl*, fence, barrier.
cínto *a* surrounded, girded; *nm* belt; **c. erniàrio** truss.
cintúra *nf* belt, waistband; **c. di salvatàggio** lifebelt.
cinturíno *nm* strap.
ciò *pron* that, this.
ciòcca *nf* (*of hair*) lock, tuft; cluster.
ciòcco *pl* **ciòcchi** *nm* billet of wood, block, log.
cioccolàta *nf* chocolate (*esp. drink*).
cioccolatíno *nm* chocolate (sweet); *pl* chocolates.
cioccolàto *nm* chocolate.
cioè *ad* i.e., namely, that is.
ciondolàre *vi* to dangle; (*fig*) idle about; *vt* to swing, roll (*head etc*).
ciòndolo *nm* pendant, trinket.
ciondolóni *ad* dangling.
ciòtola *nf* bowl.
ciòttolo *nm* pebble.
cipíglio *nm* frown, scowl.
cipólla *nm* onion, bulb.
cipollína *nf* spring onion; **cipollíne sótto acéto** pickled onions.
cíppo *nm* half column, boundary stone.
ciprèsso *nm* cypress.
cípria *nf* face powder.
ciprìòta *a nmf* Cyprian.
Cípro *nf* (*geogr*) Cyprus.
círca *ad* about, nearly; *prep* as to, concerning, with regard to.
círco *pl* **-chi** *nm* circus.
circolàre *vi* to circulate, go round; *a nf* circular.
circolazióne *nf* circulation, traffic.
círcolo *nm* circle, club.
circoncisióne *nf* circumcision.
circondàre *vt* to surround, enclose.
circondàrio *nm* district, neighborhood.
circonferènza *nf* circumference.
circonlocuzióne *nf* circumlocution.
circonvallazióne *nf* belt highway.
circonveníre *vt* to circumvent, entrap.
circoscrívere *vt* to circumscribe, limit.
circoscrizióne *nf* circumscription; area.
circospètto *a* circumspect.
circospezióne *nf* circumspection.
circostànte *a* surrounding.
circostànza *nf* circumstance.
circuíre *vi* to surround, circumvent.
circúito *nm* circuit, compass; **córto c.** (*el*) short circuit.
Cirenàica *nf* (*geogr*) Cirenaica, Cyrenaica.
cisalpíno *a* (*geogr*) cisalpine.
cispadàno *a* (*geogr*) cispadane.
cispositá *nf* bleariness.
cispóso *a* blear-eyed.
císte *nf* cyst.
cistèrna *nf* cistern, tank; tanker.
cistifèllea *nf* gall-bladder.
citàre *vt* to cite, quote, mention; summon.
citazióne *nf* citation, quotation; summons, subpoena.
citòfono *nm* intercom.
citràto *nm* citrate.
città *nf* city.
cittadèlla *nf* citadel.
cittadína *nf* small town.
cittadinànza *nf* citizenship; citizens *pl*.
cittadíno *a* of a town; *nm* citizen, townsman.
ciúco *pl* **ciúchi** *nm* donkey.
ciúffo *nm* forelock, topknot, tuft.
ciúrma *nf* (*naut*) ship's crew.
ciurmàglia *nf* mob, rabble.
ciurmatóre *nm* scoundrel, swindler.
civétta *nf* owl; flirt, coquette.
civettàre *vi* to coquet, flirt.
civettería *nf* coquetry.
cívico *pl* **-ici** *a* civic.
civíle *a* civil, civilian.
civilizzàre *vt* to civilize.
civiltà *nf* civilization, civility.
civísmo *nm* civic virtues *pl*.
clàcson *nm* (*aut*) horn.
clamóre *nm* clamor, outcry.
clamoróso *a* clamorous, noisy.
clandestíno *a* clandestine.
Clàra *nf pr* Clara, Clare, Claire.
clarinétto, claríno *nm* clarinet.
clàsse *nf* class, form, rank, grade; schoolroom; **c. operàia** working class.
clàssico *pl* **-ici** *a* classic(al); *nm* classic.
classífica *nf* classification; (*sport*) position, result.
classificàre *vt* to classify.
classificazióne *nf* classification.
Clàudio *nm pr* Claud.
clàusola *nf* clause.

claustràle *a* cloistral, claustral.
clausúra *nf* seclusion.
clàva *nf* club, bludgeon.
clavicémbalo *nm* (*mus*) harpsichord.
clavícola *nf* collarbone.
clemènte *a* clement, merciful.
clemènza *nf* clemency, mercy.
clericàle *a* clerical.
clericàto *nm* holy orders *pl*, priesthood.
clèro *nm* clergy.
cliènte *nmf* client, customer.
clientèla *nf* clients *pl*, customers *pl*, patronage, practice.
clíma *nm* climate.
climatèrico *pl* **-ici** *a* climacteric.
climàtico *pl* **-ici** *a* climatic; **stazióne climàtica** *nf* health resort.
clínica *nf* clinical medicine; clinic, nursing home.
clínico *pl* **clínici** *a* clinical; *nm* clinical doctor.
clistère *nm* (*med*) enema.
cloàca *nf* sewer, drain.
coabitàre *vi* to live together.
coabitazióne *nf* living together.
coadiuvàre *vt* to assist, help.
coagulàre *vt* to coagulate; **-rsi** *vr* to coagulate, curdle.
coalizióne *nf* coalition.
coàtto *a* forced, compulsory.
coazióne *nf* compulsion.
cobàlto *nm* cobalt.
còc *nm* coke.
cocaína *nf* cocaine.
cócca *nf* (*arrow*) notch; (*of an apron etc*) corner; pet daughter.
coccàrda *nf* cockade.
cocchière *nm* coachman, driver.
còcchio *nm* carriage, coach.
coccinèlla *nf* ladybird.
cocciníglia *nf* cochineal.
còccio *nm* earthenware pot; potsherd.
cocciutàggine *nf* obstinacy.
cocciúto *a* obstinate.
còcco *pl* **còcchi** *nm* coconut, coconut palm; pet, darling.
coccodríllo *nm* crocodile.
còccola *nf* berry.
coccolàre *vt* to fondle; **-rsi** *vr* to make oneself snug, nestle.
cocènte *a* hot, burning.
cocómero *nm* watermelon; blockhead.
cocúzzolo *nm* crown of the head; summit, top.
códa *nf* tail, queue; **fàre la c.** to queue, to line up.
codardía *nf* cowardice.
codàrdo *a* cowardly; *nm* coward.
codésto *a and pron* that, that one.
còdice *nm* code, codex.
codicíllo *nm* codicil.
codificàre *vt* to codify.
codíno *nm* small tail, pigtail; reactionary.
coefficiènte *nm* coefficient.
coeguàle *a* co-equal.
coerède *nmf* co-heir(ess).
coerènte *a* coherent, consistent.
coerènza *nf* coherence, consistency.
coeşióne *nf* cohesion.
coeşístere *vi* to coexist.
coetàneo *a* contemporary.
coèvo *a* coeval.
còfano *nm* coffer, casket; (*aut*) hood.
cogitàre *vi* to cogitate, *v* **ponderàre.**
cògliere *vt* to pick, gather, catch, hit, seize, grasp.
cognàta *nf* sister-in-law; **cognàto** *nm* brother-in-law.
cògnito *a* known.
cognizióne *nf* knowledge.
cognóme *nm* surname.
coincidènza *nf* coincidence; (*of trains*) connection.
coincídere *vi* to coincide.
coinvòlgere *vt* to involve.
colà *ad* there.
colaggiú *ad* below, down there, *v* **laggiù.**
colàre *vt* to strain, sieve, colander; (*metals*) cast; drip; *vi* to drip, trickle, drop, leak.
colassú *ad* up there, *v* **lassù.**
colàta *nf* casting, flow.
colatóio *nm* colander, strainer; crucible.
colazióne *nf* lunch; **príma c.** breakfast.
colèi *pron* she, that woman.
colèra *nf* cholera.
coleróşo *nm* cholera patient.
colibrí *nm* humming bird.
còlica *nf* colic.
colíno *nm* strainer.
còlla *nf* glue.
collaboràre *vi* to collaborate.
collaborazióne *nf* collaboration.
collàna *nf* necklace; (*of literary works*) series.
collàre *nm* collar.
collàsso *nm* collapse; **c. cardíaco** heart failure.
collaudàre *vt* to test, try out; approve.
collàudo *nm* test; approval.
collazionàre *vt* to collate, compare.
còlle *nm* hill.
collèga *nmf* colleague.
collegaménto *nm* connection.
collegàre *vt* to connect, join; **-rsi** *vr* to league, unite.
collègio *nm* boarding school, college; constituency.
còllera *nf* anger, wrath.
collèrico *pl* **-ici** *a* choleric, irascible.
collètta *nf* (*money*) collection, collect.
collettività *nf* collectivity.
collettívo *a nm* collective.
collétto *nm* collar.
collezionàre *vt* to collect.
collezióne *nf* collection.
collezionista *nmf* collector.
collimàre *vi* to agree, tally.
collína *nf* hill.
collinóso *a* hilly.
collírio *nm* collyrium, eyewash.
collişióne *nf* clash, collision.

còllo *nm* neck, collar; piece of luggage; **c. del piède** instep.
collocaménto *nm* placing, employment, situation; **agenzía di c.** employment bureau.
collocàre *vt* to place; give in marriage; invest, employ; **-rsi** *vr* to get a position; get married.
collocazióne *nf* placing, arrangement; (*of library books*) press-mark, call number.
collòquio *nm* conversation, interview.
colluttàre *vi* to scuffle, grapple.
colluttazióne *nf* scuffle, grapple.
colmàre *vt* to fill to overflowing, load, overwhelm.
cólmo *a* full, brimful; *nm* summit, limit.
cólo *nm* sieve, strainer.
colómba *nf* dove; **colómbo** *nm* pigeon; **colómbo viaggiatóre** carrier pigeon.
colombàia *nf* dovecot.
Colómbia *nf* (*geogr*) Columbia.
colombiàno *a nm* Columbian.
colònia *nf* colony, settlement.
Colònia *nf* (*geogr*) Cologne; **àcqua di C.** eau-de-Cologne.
colonizzàre *vt* to colonize.
colónna *nf* column, pillar.
colonnello *nm* colonel.
colòno *nm* farmer, colonist, settler.
colorànte *a* coloring; *nm* dye.
coloràre, coloríre *vt* to color, dye.
coloràto *pp a* colored.
colòre *nm* color, dye; complection, appearance; pretext; (*cards*) suit.
coloríto *a* colored, rosy; *nm* coloring, complexion.
colóro *pron* they, those people.
colossàle *a* colossal.
colossèo *nm* Coliseum, Colosseum.
colòsso *nm* colossus.
cólpa *nf* crime, fault, offense, guilt, blame.
colpabilità *nf* culpability.
colpévole *a* culpable, guilty.
colpíre *vt* to hit, strike.
cólpo *nm* blow, stroke, wound, knock, shot; **ad un c., di c.** *ad* suddenly, unexpectedly.
colpóso *a* (*leg*) culpable, unpremeditated; **omicídio c.** manslaughter.
coltellàta *nf* stab, knife wound.
coltellinàio *nm* cutler.
coltellíno *nm* small knife.
coltèllo *nm* knife.
coltivàre *vt* to cultivate, till.
coltivatóre *nm* **-tríce** *nf* cultivator, farmer.
coltivazióne *nf* cultivation.
còlto *a* cultivated, cultured, educated.
cóltre *nf* coverlet, blanket.
coltróne *nm* quilt.
coltúra *nf* cultivation; breeding, culture.
colúi *pron* he, that man.
comandaménto *nm* command, commandment.
comandànte *nm* commander; **c. in secónda** second-in-command.
comandàre *vt* to order, command.
comàndo *nm* order, command, leadership; (*mil*) H.Q.; (*av*) control.
combaciàre *vi* to fit together, tally.
combattènte *nm* combatant, soldier; **ex c.** ex-serviceman, veteran.
combàttere *vti* to fight, oppose.
combattiménto *nm* fight, fighting, battle, action.
combinàre *vt* to combine; conclude, settle; plan; *vi* to agree; **-rsi** *vr* agree, match; happen.
combinazióne *nf* combination, arrangement; chance, coincidence; (*underwear*) combinations *pl*, union suit.
combríccola *nf* band, gang.
combustíbile *a* combustible; *nm* fuel.
combustióne *nf* combustion.
cóme *ad* like, as, how, that, when, why; *interj* what!; **c. sta?** how do you do?
comèta *nf* comet.
comicità *nf* comicality.
còmico *pl* **-ici** *a* comic, comical, funny; *nm* comicality; comedian.
cominciàre *vti* to begin.
comitàto *nm* committee.
comitíva *nf* company, party.
comízio *nm* assembly, meeting.
commèdia *nf* comedy, play.
commediànte *nmf* player, comedian; (*fig*) hypocrite.
commediògrafo *nm* playwright.
commemoràre *vt* to commemorate.
commemorazióne *nf* commemoration.
commènda *nf* allowance, living; civic honor given in Italy.
commendàbile, -dévole *a* commendable, praiseworthy.
commendàre *vt* to commend, praise.
commendatízia *nf* (*com*) letter of recommendation.
commendatóre *nm* special title given in Italy for civic merit.
commensàle *nm* table companion, guest, fellow-boarder.
commentàre *vt* to comment.
comménto *nm* comment.
commerciàle *a* commercial.
commerciànte *nm* dealer, merchant, trader.
commerciàre *vi* to deal, trade; *vt* to deal in.
commèrcio *nm* commerce, trade, business.
commésso *a* committed, entrusted; *nm* shop assistant, store-clerk; **c. viaggiatóre** commercial traveler, representative.
commestíbile *a* eatable, edible; **-ili** *nm pl* eatables *pl*.
comméttere *vt* to commit, entrust, order.
commiàto *nm* dismissal, leave.

commiseràre *vt* to pity, commiserate.
commiserazióne *nf* pity, commiseration.
commissariàto *nm* (*mil*) commissariat, commissary's office, police station.
commissàrio *nm* commissary, commissioner, superintendent.
commissionàrio *nm* commission agent.
commissióne *nf* errand, commission, order, committee; **fare delle commissióni** *vi* to do errands, go shopping.
commòsso *a* moved, touched, affected.
commovènte *a* moving, touching, affecting.
commozióne *nf* emotion; (*med*) concussion.
commuòvere *vt* to move, touch, affect; **-rsi** *vr* to be moved, touched.
commutàre *vt* to commute.
commutatóre *a* commutating; *nm* commutator, switch; **c. lúci anabbagliànti** (*aut*) dimmer switch.
commutatríce *nf* commutator.
comò *nm* chest of drawers.
comodíno *nm* bedside table.
comodità *nf* comfort, convenience, opportunity.
còmodo *a* comfortable, convenient, useful; well-to-do; *nm* comfort, convenience, ease, leisure; **a súo c.** at your convenience.
compaesàno *nm* belonging to the same district or village.
compaginàre *vt* to join firmly together.
compàgine *nf* connection, joining of parts, structure.
compàgna *nf* female companion, wife.
compagnía *nf* company, society.
compàgno *a* like, similar; *nm* companion, comrade, mate, partner; **c. di giuòchi** playmate.
companàtico *pl* **-ici** *nm* food eaten with bread.
comparàre *vt* to compare.
comparatívo *a* comparative.
comparàto *a* comparative; **anatomía c.** comparative anatomy.
comparazióne *nf* comparison, simile.
comparíre *vi* to appear.
compàrsa *nf* appearance; (*theat*) extra.
compartecipàre *vi* to share (in).
compartiménto *nm* compartment, division.
compartíre *vt* to divide, share.
compassàto *a* stiff, formal.
compassionàre *vt* to pity.
compassióne *nf* compassion, pity.
compassionévole *a* exciting or feeling pity, pitiful.
compàsso *nm* compasses *pl.*
compatíbile *a* compatible, excusable.
compatiménto *nm* compassion, forbearance.
compatíre *vt* to pity, excuse.
compatriòta *nmf* compatriot.
compàtto *a* compact, solid.
compendiàre *vt* to abridge.
compèndio *nm* abridgment, compendium.
compensàre *vt* to compensate, indemnify.
compensàto *nm* plywood.
compènso *nm* compensation, reward, indemnity; **in c.** in return.
comperàre *v* **compràre.**
competènte *a* competent, qualified.
competènza *nf* competence, authority; **competenze** *pl* fees *pl.*
compètere *vi* to compete; be due to.
competizióne *nf* competition, contest.
compiacènte *a* obliging, complaisant.
compiacènza *nf* kindness, complaisance; satisfaction.
compiacére *vt* to please, comply with; **-rsi** *vr* to be pleased to, condescend.
compiaciménto *nm* satisfaction, pleasure; congratulation.
compiàngere *vt* to be sorry for, lament, pity.
compiànto *a* lamented, regretted; *nm* regret, pity, lament.
cómpiere *vt* to accomplish, complete, fulfill, finish.
compilàre *vt* to compile.
compilazióne *nf* compilation.
compiménto *nm* accomplishment, completion, fulfillment.
compíre *v* **compiere.**
compitàre *vt* to spell.
compitézza *nf* courtesy, politeness.
cómpito *nm* homework, task.
compíto *a* courteous, polite.
compiúto *a* accomplished, ended, complete.
compleànno *nm* birthday.
complementàre *a* complementary, supplementary.
compleménto *nm* complement; (*mil*) reserve.
complessióne *nf* constitution.
complessità *nf* complexity.
complessívo *a* comprehensive, total.
complèsso *a* complex, compound; *nm* whole, set; (*mus*) band; **in c.** in general, on the whole.
completaménte *ad* completely, entirely.
completàre *vt* to complete.
complèto *a* complete, whole, full; *nm* (*of clothes*) suit.
complicàre *vt* to complicate, make intricate; **-rsi** *vr* to become complicated, difficult.
complicazióne *nf* complication.
còmplice *nm* accomplice.
complimentàre *vt* to compliment.
compliménto *nm* compliment; **compliménti** *pl* congratulations *pl*;

sènza compliménti frankly, without ceremony.
complimentóso *a* obsequious, ceremonious.
complottàre *vti* to plot, conspire.
complòtto *nm* conspiracy, plot.
componènte *a nmf* component, ingredient, member.
componiménto *nm* arrangement, composition.
compórre *vt* to arrange, compose; conciliate; (*type*) set up; **-rsi** *vr* to consist of.
comportàbile *a* bearable, tolerable; convenient.
comportaménto *nm* behavior.
comportàre *vt* to bear, tolerate; allow, involve; **-rsi** *vr* to act, behave.
compòrto *nm* delay, respite.
compositóre *nm* composer; (*typ*) compositor.
composizióne *nf* composition, agreement, arrangement.
compostézza *nf* composure, self-possession.
compósto *a* compound, composed, sedate, self-possessed; *nm* compound, mixture.
cómpra *nf* purchase.
compràre *vt* to buy, purchase.
compratóre *nm* **-tríce** *nf* buyer.
compravéndita *nf* buying and selling.
comprèndere *vt* to understand, comprehend; comprise, include.
comprendònio *nm* (*fam*) understanding.
comprensíbile *a* comprehensible, intelligible.
comprensibilità *nf* comprehensibility, intelligibility.
comprensióne *nf* comprehension, understanding, sympathy.
comprensívo *a* comprehensive, sympathetic.
compréso *a* included, inclusive.
comprèssa *nf* compress, lozenge.
comprèsso *a* compressed, oppressed.
comprímere *vt* to compress, restrain.
comproméssso *nm* compromise; **mettere in c.** to risk.
comprometttènte *a* compromising.
comprométtere *vt* to compromise, involve.
comprovàre *vt* to prove, give evidence of.
compúnto *a* contrite, sorry.
compunzióne *nf* compunction, contrition.
computàre *vt* to compute, reckon.
computísta *nmf* accountant, bookkeeper.
computisteria *nf* accountant's office; book-keeping.
còmputo *nm* account, reckoning.
comunàle *a* communal, municipal.
comúne *a* common, ordinary; *nm* commune, municipality; town hall.
comunicàre *vt* to communicate, announce; administer the Sacrament; **-rsi** *vr* to take the Sacrament.
comunicatíva *nf* facility in explaining and instructing.
comunicàto *nm* bulletin, comminiqué.
comunicazióne *nf* communication, connection, message.
comunióne *nf* communion, Communion.
comunísmo *nm* Communism.
comunísta *a nmf* Communist.
comunità *nf* community.
comúnque *ad* anyhow, however.
con *prep* with, by, at, from, on, against.
conàto *nm* effort, attempt.
cónca *nf* basin, tub; valley; conch.
concatenàre *vt* to link together.
còncavo *a nm* concave, hollow.
concèdere *vt* to grant, concede, allow.
concedíbile *a* allowable, grantable.
concentraménto *nm* **concentrazione** *nf* concentration; **càmpo di concentraménto** concentration camp.
concentràre *vt* to concentrate.
concentràto *a* concentrated; *nm* extract, concentrated food.
concepíbile *a* conceivable.
concepiménto *vt* conception.
concepíre *vt* to conceive, imagine.
concèrnere *vt* to concern, relate.
concertàre *vt* to conduct, arrange, concert, plan; **-rsi** *vr* to agree, be agreed.
concertatóre *nm* **-tríce** *nf* **maéstro c. e direttóre d'orchèstra** conductor.
concertísta *nmf* concert artist.
concèrto *nm* concert, concerto; agreement; **di c.** unanimously.
concessionàrio *nm* (*com*) concessionaire. agent.
concessióne *nf* concession, permission.
concètto *nm* concept, conception, idea, (*lit*) conceit.
concettóso *a* pithy, sententious.
concezióne *nf* conception, idea.
conchíglia *nf* sea-shell, conch.
cóncia *nf* tanning, curing.
conciàre *vt* to dress (*skins*), tan; (*fig*) ill-treat.
conciatóre *nm* **-tríce** *nf* tanner.
conciatúra *nf* tanning, dressing.
conciliàbile *a* compatible, reconcilable.
conciliàbolo *nm* conventicle, secret meeting.
conciliàre *vt* to conciliate, reconcile; **-rsi** *vr* to agree; win (*affection etc*).
conciliazióne *nf* conciliation, reconciliation.
concílio *nm* council.
concimàre *vt* to manure.
concíme *nm* compost, dung, manure.
cóncio *a* tanned; knocked about; *nm* dung.
concisióne *nf* concision, conciseness.

concíṣo *a* concise, brief.
concitaménto *nm* excitement tumult.
concitazióne *nf* excitement, agitation, emotion.
concittadíno *nm* fellow citizen.
concludènte *a* conclusive, decisive, energetic.
conclúdere *vt* to conclude, infer; do; *vi* be conclusive.
concluṣióne *nf* conclusion, issue; **in c.** finally.
concluṣívo *a* conclusive.
concordàre *vt* to arrange, reconcile; *vi* to agree.
concordàto *a* agreed upon, fixed; *nm* agreement, concordat.
concòrde *a* in agreement, consistent.
concòrdia *nf* harmony, unanimity.
concorrènte *a* concurrent; *nmf* competitor, rival.
concorrènza *nf* concurrence; competition, rivalry.
concórrere *vi* to concur; rival, compete.
concórso *nm* concourse; competition.
concretàre *vt* to make concrete; put into action.
concrèto *a nm* concrete, positive.
concubína *nf* concubine.
concubinàto *nm* concubinage.
concupiscènte *a* covetous.
concupiscènza *nf* concupiscence, lust.
concussióne *nf* concussion; extortion.
condànna *nf* condemnation, conviction.
condannàre *vt* to sentence, condemn.
condensàre *vt* to condense, thicken; **-rsi** *vr* to condense, grow thick.
condensàto *a* condensed.
condensatóre *nm* **-tríce** *nf* condenser.
condensazióne *nf* condensation.
condiménto *nm* seasoning, condiment, dressing, sauce.
condíre *vt* to season, dress.
condiscendènte *a* condescending, compliant.
condiscendènza *nf* compliance, condescension.
condiscéndere *vi* to condescend, yield.
condiscépolo *nm* fellow-disciple, schoolfellow.
condíto *a* seasoned; (*of salad*) dressed.
condivídere *vt* to share.
condizionàle *a* conditional; *nm* (*gram*) conditional; *nf* (*leg*) conditional sentence.
condizionàre *vt* to condition; qualify.
condizionatóre *nm* air conditioner.
condizióne *nf* condition, rank, situation, qualification; **a c.** upon condition.
condogliànza *nf* condolence.
condolérsi *vr* to condole, grieve.
condomínio *nm* joint ownership.
condonàre *vt* to remit, condone.
condótta *nf* conduct, behavior; management; piping system.
condótto *a* **mèdico c.** panel doctor; *nm* duct, conduit, pipe.
conducènte *nmf* driver; leaseholder.
condúrre *vti* to conduct, lead; **-rsi** *vr* to act, behave.
conduttóre *nm* **-tríce** *nf* conductor, driver, guide, leader; (*el*) wire.
conduttúra *nf* conduit, main; **c. d'àcqua** water-pipe.
confabulàre *vi* to confabulate, chat.
confacènte *a* convenient, suitable.
confàrsi *vr* to agree, become, fit, suit.
confederàrsi *vr* to confederate.
confederazióne *nf* confederation.
conferènza *nf* lecture, conference.
conferenzière *nm* lecturer.
conferiménto *nm* bestowal, conferment.
conferíre *vt* to bestow, confer, contribute; *vi* confer (with), agree.
confèrma *nf* confirmation.
confermàre *vt* to confirm, strengthen.
confessàre *vt* to confess, acknowledge; **-rsi** *vr* to go to confession.
confessióne *nf* confession, faith.
confessóre *nm* confessor.
confètto *nm* bonbon, sweet.
confettúra *nf* jam.
confezionàre *vt* to manufacture, prepare, make up; **confezionàto su misúra** made to measure; **artícolo confezionàto** ready-made article.
confezióne *nf* manufacture, preparation; clothes; packing.
conficcàre *vt* to drive in, thrust.
confidàre *vt* to confide, trust; **-rsi** *vr* to confide in.
confidènte *a* confiding, trusting; *nmf* confidant, bosom friend.
confidènza *nf* confidence, secret, intimacy.
confidenziàle *a* confidential, private.
confidenzialménte *ad* confidentially, privately.
confíggere *vt* to nail, thrust.
configuràre *vt* to shape; (*fig*) symbolize.
confinànte *a* bordering, contiguous.
confinàre *vt* to banish, confine; *vi* to border on; **-rsi** *vr* to confine oneself; retire.
confíne *nm* border, frontier, limit.
confíno *nm* political confinement.
confísca *nf* confiscation, forfeiture.
confiscàre *vt* to confiscate, forfeit.
conflagrazióne *nf* conflagration.
conflítto *nm* conflict.
confluíre *vi* to flow together.
confóndere *vt* to confuse, confound; **-rsi** *vr* to get confused; worry.
conformàre *vt* to conform; **-rsi** *vr* to comply (with).
conformazióne *nf* conformation.
confórme *a* conforming, in agreement.
conformiṣmo *nm* conformism.
conformísta *nmf* conformist.

conformità *nf* conformity, accordance.
confortàre *vt* to comfort, console, encourage, fortify; **-rsi** *vr* to console oneself, take courage.
confortévole *a* comforting, comfortable.
confòrto *nm* comfort, consolation, support.
confratèllo *nm* (*relig*) fellow-member.
confratèrnita *nf* brotherhood, confraternity.
confrontàre *vt* to compare, confront; *vi* to agree.
confrónto *nm* comparison.
confuşióne *nf* confusion, shame.
confúşo *a* confused, embarrassed, ashamed; indistinct.
confutàre *vt* to confute, disprove.
confutazióne *nf* confutation.
congedàre *vt* to dismiss; **-rsi** *vr* to resign, take leave.
congèdo *nm* discharge, leave; **in c.** *ad* on leave.
congegnàre *vt* to put together, contrive.
congégno *nm* appliance, gear.
congelaménto *nm* congealment, freezing.
congelàre *vi* to congeal, freeze.
congènere *a* similar.
congènito *a* congenital.
congèrie *nf* heap, mass.
congestionàre *vt* to congest, crowd.
congettúra *nf* conjecture, guess.
congetturàre *vt* to conjecture.
congiúngere *vt* to connect, join; **-rsi** *vr* to join, meet.
congiuntívo *a* conjunctive, (*gram*) subjunctive; *nm* (*gram*) subjunctive.
congiúnto *a* joined, connected, combined; *nm* kinsman, relative.
congiuntúra *nf* conjuncture, circumstance; predicament.
congiúra *nf* conspiracy, plot.
congiuràre *vi* to conspire.
conglomeràre *vt* to conglomerate.
conglomeràto *nm* grouping, conglomerate.
conglutinàre *vt* to conglutinate.
Còngo *nm* (*geogr*) Congo.
congolése *a nmf* Congolese.
congratulàrsi *vr* to congratulate.
congratulazióne *nf* congratulation.
congrèga *nf* gang, set; congregation.
congregàre *vt* to assemble, call together; **-rsi** *vr* to congregate.
congressísta *nmf* member of a congress.
congrèsso *nm* congress, conference.
còngruo *a* congruous, suitable.
conguagliàre *vt* to balance, equalize.
conguàglio *nm* adjustment, balancing, leveling.
coniàre *vt* to coin, (*a medal*) strike.
coniglièra *nf* rabbit-hutch.
coníglio *nm* rabbit.
cònio *nm* coinage; die, brand.
coniugàre *vt* to conjugate; **-rsi** *vr* to marry.
coniugazióne *nf* conjugation.
còniuge *nm* husband; *nf* wife; **còniugi** *pl* married couple.
connazionàle *nmf* compatriot.
connèttere *vt* to connect, join, (*fig*) associate; **non c.** to have confused ideas.
connivènte *a* conniving.
connivènza *nf* connivance.
connotàto *nm* distinctive mark; **connotàti** *pl* description (of a person).
connúbio *nm* marriage, union.
còno *nm* cone.
conòcchia *nf* distaff.
conoscènte *nmf* acquaintance.
conoscènza *nf* knowledge, acquaintance; consciousness, cognition.
conóscere *vt* to know, experience, take cognizance of; **farsi c.** to make oneself known; **-rsi** *vr* to know oneself, know each other.
conoscíbile *a* knowable, recognizable; *nm* knowledge.
conosciménto *nm* knowing, knowledge.
conoscitóre *nm* **-tríce** *nf* connoisseur, good judge.
conosciúto *a* well-known, famous.
conquísta *nf* conquest.
conquistàre *vt* to conquer.
consacràre *vt* to consecrate, dedicate, devote, ordain.
consacrazióne *nf* consecration, ordination.
consanguíneo *a* consanguineous, closely related; *nm* kinsman.
consapévole *a* aware, conscious, acquainted.
consapevolézza *nf* consciousness, knowledge.
cònscio *v* **consapévole.**
conségna *nf* consignment, delivery; **lasciàre in c.** *vt* to deposit.
consegnàre *vt* to consign, deliver.
conseguènte *a* consequent, consistent.
conseguènza *nf* consequence; **in c.** accordingly.
conseguiménto *nm* attainment.
conseguíre *vt* to attain, obtain, reach; *vi* to follow, result.
consènso *nm* consent, assent.
consensuàle *a* (*leg*) by mutual consent.
consentíre *vi* to consent, agree, yield; *vt* to permit.
consenziènte *a* approving, consenting.
consèrva *nf* jam, preserve, preservation, reservoir.
conservàre *vt* to keep, preserve; **-rsi** *vr* to last, keep in good health.
conservatóre, *f* **-tríce** *a* preserving, preservative, conservative; *nm* preserver, keeper; (*pol*) Conservative.
conservatòrio *nm* academy of music.
conservazióne *nf* preservation, care, maintenance.
consèsso *nm* assembly, meeting.

consideràbile *a* considerable.
consideràre *vt* to consider, regard.
consideràto *a* considerate, thoughtful, careful; esteemed.
considerazióne *nf* consideration, esteem.
considerévole *a* considerable, pretty large.
consigliàre *vt* to advise, counsel; **-rsi** *vr* to ask advice, consult.
consiglière *nm* counselor, councilor.
consíglio *nm* advice, counsel, council.
consímile *a* like, similar.
consistènte *a* consistent; firm, substantial.
consistènza *nf* consistence, consistency.
consístere *vi* to consist.
consòcio *nm* associate, partner.
consolàre *vt* to comfort, console; **-rsi** *vr* to take comfort.
consolàre *a* consular.
consolàto *nm* consulate.
consolazióne *nf* consolation, comfort, delight.
cònsole *nm* consul.
consolidàre *vt* to consolidate, strengthen; **-rsi** *vr* to grow firm.
consolidazióne *nf* **consolidaménto** *nm* consolidation, strengthening.
consonànte *a* consonant, agreeing; *nf* consonant.
consonànza *nf* consonance, agreement.
cònsono *a* consonant, agreeing.
consòrte *nmf* consort, husband, wife.
consortería *nf* clique, set.
consòrzio *nm* society, syndicate.
constàre *vi* to consist, be known, be proved.
constatàre *vt* to ascertain, verify, certify.
constatazióne *nf* ascertainment.
consuèto *a* habitual, usual.
consuetúdine *nf* custom, habit, practice.
consulènte *a* consulting, consultant; *nm* consultant, adviser.
consulènza *nf* advice; **c. legàle** legal advice.
consúlta *nf* council.
consultàre *vt* to consult, examine; **-rsi** *vr* to seek advice, consult.
consultazióne *nf* consultation; **gabinétto di c.** (*med*) consulting room; **libro di c.** reference book.
consúlto *nm* consultation, (medical or legal) opinion.
consumàre *vt* to consume, waste, consummate; **-rsi** *vr* to wear out, consume, pine away, waste away.
consumatóre *nm* consumer.
consumazióne *nf* consumption, consummation; drink or food (in a café *etc*).
consúmo *nm* consumption, waste; **úso e c.** wear and tear.
consúnto *a* consumed, worn out; consumptive.
consunzióne *nf* (*med*) consumption.
contàbile *a* book-keeping, calculating; *nm* book-keeper, accountant.
contabilità *nf* book-keeping.
contadína *nf* **-no** *nm* peasant.
contadinésco *pl* **-éschi** *a* rustic.
contàdo *nm* country (round a town).
contagiàre *vt* to infect, contaminate.
contàgio *nm* contagion.
contagióso *a* contagious, infectious.
contagócce *nm* dropper.
contaminàre *vt* to contaminate.
contaminazióne *nf* contamination, pollution.
contànte *a* counting, ready; **denàro c.** cash, ready money; *nm* cash.
contàre *vt* to count; relate; consider; *vi* to count, have authority, rely on; **ciò che cónta** what matters.
contatóre *nm* meter, reckoner; **c. a monéta** slot meter; **c. del gas** gas-meter; **c. per parchéggio** parking meter.
contàtto *nm* contact, touch, connection; **spina di c.** contact plug.
cónte *nm* count, earl.
contèa *nf* earldom, county, shire.
conteggiàre *vt* to count, charge.
contéggio *nm* computation, calculation; **c. all'indiètro** countdown.
contégno *nm* behavior, dignity, gravity.
contegnóso *a* dignified, grave, staid.
contemperàre *vt* to proportion, temper.
contemplàre *vt* to contemplate.
contemplatívo *a* contemplative.
contemplazióne *nf* contemplation.
contemporaneità *nf* contemporaneousness.
contemporàneo *a nm* contemporary.
contendènte *a* contending, opposing; *nm* rival, opponent, competitor.
contèndere *vt* to contest; *vi* to contend, quarrel; **-rsi** *vr* to contend, be rivals for.
contenére *vt* to contain, hold, restrain; **-rsi** *vr* to behave, control oneself.
contentàre *vt* to content, gratify; **-rsi** *vr* to be pleased, satisfied.
contentatúra *nf* contentment; **di fàcile c.** *ad* easy to please.
contentézza *nf* contentment, satisfaction.
contènto *a* content, glad, satisfied; *nm* contentment, happiness.
contenúto *a* contained; *nm* contents *pl*, subject.
contenzióso *a* contentious.
conterràneo *a* of the same country; *nm* countryman.
contésa *nf* contest, dispute, contention.
contéssa *nf* countess.
contestàre *vt* to contest, deny.
contestazióne *nf* contest, dispute; notification.
contèsto *a* interwoven; *nm* context.
contézza *nf* knowledge.

contiguità *nf* contiguity.
contíguo *a* contiguous, adjoining.
continentàle *a* continental.
continènte *a* temperate, continent; *nm* continent.
continènza *nf* continence, self-restraint.
contingènte *a* contingent; *nm* contingency, contingent; (*com*) quota.
contingènza *nf* contingency, emergency, circumstance.
continuaménte *ad* continuously, continually, constantly.
continuàre *vti* to continue, pursue, go on, last.
continuazióne, continuità *nf* continuation, continuity, duration.
contínuo *a* continuous, non-stop, lasting; **di c.** *ad* non-stop, continuously.
cónto *nm* account, bill; computation, reckoning; worth.
contòrcere *vt* to contort; **-rsi** *vr* to twist, wring, writhe.
contornàre *vt* to surround, trim.
contórno *nm* contour, outline; vegetables served with a dish of meat.
contorsióne *nf* contortion.
contrabbandière *nm* smuggler.
contrabbàndo *nm* contraband goods *pl*, smuggling.
contrabbàsso *nm* (*mus*) double bass.
contraccambiàre *vt* to return, reciprocate.
contraccàmbio *nm* exchange, return; **rèndere il c.** to give like for like.
contraccólpo *nm* counter-stroke, rebound.
contràda *nf* countryside, district, wide street.
contraddíre *vt* to contradict.
contraddistínguere *vt* to distinguish, mark.
contraddittòrio *a* contradictory; *nm* debate, cross-examination.
contrad(d)izióne *nf* contradiction.
contraèrea *nf* anti-aircraft artillery; **contraèreo** *a* anti-aircraft.
contraffàre *vt* to counterfeit, forge, imitate; **-rsi** *vr* to disguise oneself.
contraffàtto *a* counterfeit, disguised; deformed.
contraffazióne *nf* counterfeit, forgery.
contrammiràglio *nm* rear-admiral.
contrappélo *nm* the wrong way; **a, di c.** (*fig*) against the grain.
contrappéso *nm* counter-balance, counterpoise.
contrappórre *vt* to contrast, oppose; **-rsi** *vr* to cross, oppose.
contrappúnto *nm* (*mus*) counterpoint.
contrariàre *vt* to thwart, oppose, annoy.
contràrio *a* contrary, opposite, unfavorable, adverse; *nm* contrary, opposite; **al c.** on the contrary.
contràrre *vt* to contract; **-rsi** *vr* to shrink.
contrasségno *nm* countersign, badge, mark.
contrastànte *a* contrasting.
contrastàre *vt* to contest, oppose, resist; *vi* to contrast, clash; **-rsi** *vr* to fight.
contràsto *nm* contrast, opposition, strife, clash.
contrattàcco *nm* counter-attack.
contrattàre *vti* to negotiate, bargain.
contrattèmpo *nm* mishap, hitch; (*mus*) syncopation.
contràtto *a* contracted; *nm* contract, agreement.
contravveléno *nm* antidote.
contravveníre *vi* to contravene, infringe.
contravvenzióne *nf* contravention, infringement; fine; **fàre una c.** impose a fine.
contrazióne *nf* contraction.
contribuènte *nmf* taxpayer.
contribuíre *vi* to contribute, help, share.
contribúto *nm* contribution, share.
contristàre *vt* to afflict, sadden; **-rsi** *vr* to be afflicted, grieve.
contríto *a* contrite, penitent.
contrizióne *nf* contrition, penitence.
cóntro *prep* against, opposite.
controfirmàre *vt* to countersign.
controllàre *vt* to check, control, verify, inspect.
contròllo *nm* check, control.
controllóre *nm* controller, ticket-collector, ticket-inspector.
controlúce *ad* against the light.
contropòrta *nf* double door.
controproducènte *a* having the opposite effect.
contropròva *nf* counter-check, counter-vote, evidence.
contrórdine *nm* counter-order.
Controrifórma *nf* Counter-reformation.
controsènso *nm* misinterpretation, nonsense.
controstòmaco *ad* unwillingly.
controvèrsia *nf* controversy, dispute.
controvèrso *a* controversial, doubtful.
controvèrtere *vt* to controvert, dispute.
contumàce *a* contumacious, guilty of default.
contumàcia *pl* **-àcie** *nf* default, contumacy; quarantine.
contumèlia *nf* contumely, abuse.
contundènte *a* bruising; **àrma c.** blunt weapon.
conturbàre *vt* to disturb, trouble; **-rsi** *vr* to be agitated, fret.
contusióne *nf* bruise, contusion.
contuttochè *cj* although.
contuttociò *ad* however, nevertheless.
convalescènte *a nmf* convalescent.
convalescènza *nf* convalescence.

convalidàre *vt* to confirm, corroborate.
convégno *nm* meeting (place).
convenévole *a* convenient, proper, suitable; **convenévoli** *nm pl* compliments, regards, ceremony.
conveniènte *a* convenient, profitable.
convenienza *nf* convenience, advantage, propriety, proportion.
convenire *vi* to suit; meet, assemble; agree; *vt* to summon.
convènto *nm* convent, monastery.
convenúto *a* agreed (on), fixed; *nm* agreement; defendant.
convenzionàle *a* conventional.
convenzióne *nf* convention, covenant.
convergènza *nf* convergence.
convèrgere *vi* to converge.
convèrsa *nf* lay sister.
conversàre *vi* to converse, talk.
conversazióne *nf* conversation, talk.
conversióne *nf* conversion.
convèrso *a* converse, opposite; *nm* lay brother.
convertíre *vt* to convert; **-rsi** *vr* to be converted.
convertíto *nm* convert.
convessità *nf* convexity.
convèsso *a* convex.
convettóre *nm* convector.
convincènte *a* convincing.
convíncere *vt* to convince, persuade.
convinciménto *nm* **convinzióne** *nf* conviction, persuasion.
convitàto *nm* guest.
convíto *nm* banquet, feast.
convítto *nm* boarding-school.
convivènte *a* living together.
convivènza *nf* cohabitation, living together.
convívere *vi* to cohabit, live together.
convocàre *vt* to convoke, summon.
convogliàre *vt* to convoy, direct.
convòglio *nm* convoy, train.
convulsióne *nf* convulsion, spasm.
convulsívo *a* convulsive, spasmodic.
convúlso *a* convulsive, jerky; *nm* convulsion.
cooperàre *vi* to co-operate.
cooperatíva *nf* (*com*) co-operative society.
cooperazióne *nf* co-operation.
coordinàre *vt* to co-ordinate.
coordinàta *nf* co-ordinate.
copèrchio *nm* cover, lid.
copèrta *nf* blanket, coverlet, rug, cover; (*naut*) deck.
copertína *nf* cover, book-cover, dust-jacket.
copèrto *a* covered, (*of the sky*) overcast; clothed, hidden; *nm* (*at table*) cover, place.
copertóne nm (*tire*) cover; tarpaulin.
copertúra *nf* covering.
còpia *nf* copy, print; plenty, quantity; **c. fotostàtica (fotocòpia)** photostat (photocopy); **c. carbóne** carbon copy; **bèlla c.** fair copy; **brútta c.** rough copy.
copialèttere *nm* letter-book, letter-press.
copiàre *vt* to copy, imitate, transcribe.
copiatívo *a* copying.
copiatúra *nf* copying, transcription.
copióne *nm* (*theat*) script.
copióso *a* abundant, copious.
copísta *nmf* copyist.
copistería *nf* copying office, typing office.
cóppa *nf* cup, goblet; (*aut*) sump, oil pan.
coppellàre *vt* (*metals*) to assay, test.
còppia *nf* couple, pair.
copricàpo *nm* headgear, hat.
coprifuòco *pl* **-fuòchi** *nm* curfew.
coprire *vt* to cover, hide, protect, shelter, hold (a post); **-rsi** *vr* to put on one's hat, wrap oneself up.
copriteièra *nm* tea-cozy, cap.
coprivivànde *nm* dishcover.
còpto *a* Coptic; *nm* Copt, (*language*) Coptic.
coràggio *nm* courage, valor.
coraggiosaménte *ad* bravely.
coraggióso *a* courageous, valiant.
coràle *a* choral; *nm* chorale.
coràllo *nm* coral.
Coràno *nm* Koran.
coràzza *nf* cuirass, armor-plating.
corazzàre *vt* to armor.
corazzière *nm* cuirassier.
còrba *nf* basket.
corbellàre *vt* to make a fool of, make fun of.
corbellería *nf* foolish act.
corbèllo *nm* (small) basket.
corbézzola *nf* arbutus-berry; **corbézzolo** *nm* arbutus-tree.
còrda *nf* cord, rope, (*of a musical instrument*) string; (*mus*) chord.
cordàme *nm* (*naut*) cordage, ropes *pl*.
cordiàle *a* cordial, hearty, warm; *nm* cordial.
cordicèlla *nf* **cordoncino** *nm* fine cord, string.
cordòglio *nm* grief, mourning, sorrow.
cordóne *nm* cord; cordon.
Corèa *nf* (*geogr*) Korea.
coreàno *a nm* Korean.
coriàndolo *nm* paper streamer; **coriàndoli** *pl* confetti.
coricàre *vt* to lay down; **-rsi** *vr* to go to bed, lie down.
coríst̀a *nm* chorister, chorus singer.
cornàcchia *nf* crow; (*fig*) croaker.
cornamúsa *nf* (*mus*) bagpipes *pl*.
cornétta *nf* (*mus*) cornet, horn.
cornétto *nm* ear-trumpet, small horn; *pl* French beans *pl*.
corníce *nf* frame, framework.
cornicióne *nm* cornice.
corniòla *nf* (*min*) cornelian.
còrno *pl* **còrna** (*f*), (*instruments*) **còrni** (*m*) *nm* horn.

Cornovàglia *nf* (*geogr*) Cornwall.
cornúto *a* horned; *nm* cuckold.
còro *nm* chorus, choir.
coróna *nf* crown, wreath, garland; (*mus*) corona.
coronàre *vt* to crown.
coronàrio *a* coronary.
coronazióne *nf* coronation.
corpacciúto *a* burly, corpulent.
corpétto *nm* bodice, waistcoat.
còrpo *nm* body, corpse; mass.
corporàle *a* bodily, corporal, corporeal.
corporatúra *nf* size.
corporazióne *nf* corporation.
corpòreo *a* corporeal.
corpulènto *a* corpulent.
corpulènza *nf* corpulence.
Corràdo *nm pr* Conrad, Konrad.
corredàre *vt* to equip, fit up, outfit.
corredíno *nm* baby's layette.
corrèdo *nm* equipment, furniture, kit, outfit, trousseau.
corrèggere *vt* to correct, revise, upbraid; **-rsi** *vr* to improve, mend one's ways.
correlazióne *nf* correlation.
corrènte *a* running, flowing, current, common; *nf* stream, current; **tenére al c.** to keep informed.
córrere *vi* to run, flow, (*of time*) elapse, circulate, (*of distance*) intervene.
correttaménte *ad* correctly, properly.
correttézza *nf* correctness, propriety, honesty.
corrètto *a* correct, exact, upright, well-bred.
correttóre *nm* **-tríce** *nf* corrector, (*typ*) proof-reader.
correzióne *nf* correction, reform.
corrída *nf* bullfight.
corridóio *nm* corridor, passage.
corridóre *nm* racer, runner.
corrièra *nf* coach, bus, mail-bus, mail-coach.
corrière *nm* courier, messenger, carrier, mail, express company; **a vòlta di c.** *ad* by return of post.
corrispettívo *a* corresponding; *nm* equivalent, compensation.
corrispondènte *a* corresponding, correspondent; *nmf* correspondent.
corrispondènza *nf* correspondence, harmony, connection.
corrispóndere *vi* to correspond, return; *vt* to pay.
corrívo *a* easy-going, lenient, rash.
corroboràre *vt* to corroborate; strengthen.
corroborazióne *nf* corroboration, support.
corródere *vt* to corrode, eat away, wear away; **-rsi** *vr* to corrode, waste away.
corrómpere *vt* to corrupt, pollute, bribe; **-rsi** *vr* to rot, become corrupt.
corroşívo *a nm* corrosive.
corrótto *a* corrupt(ed).
corrucciàre *vi* **-rsi** *vr* to get angry; grieve.
corrúccio *nm* anger, wrath.
corrugàre *vt* to corrugate, frown, knit (one's brows); **-rsi** *vr* wrinkle.
corruscàre *vi* to scintillate, flash.
corruttèla *nf* corruption.
corruttibilità *nf* corruptibility.
corruzióne *nf* corruption, decay.
córsa *nf* race, run, running, trip.
corsàro *nm* corsair, pirate.
corsía *nf* passage; (*of hospital*) ward; dormitory; track.
Còrsica *nf* (*geogr*) Corsica.
corsívo *a nm* cursi[illegible] italic, italics *pl*.
córso *a* passed, plundered; *nm* course, main street, flow.
còrso *a nm* Corsican.
córte *nf* court, hall, tribunal, yard.
cortéccia *nf* bark, crust.
corteggiaménto *nm* courtship, wooing.
corteggiàre *vt* to court, woo.
corteggiatóre *nm* suitor, wooer, lover.
cortéggio *nm* attendants *pl*, retinue.
cortèo *nm* procession, train.
cortéşe *a* courteous, kind, polite.
corteşía *nf* courtesy, politeness.
cortézza *nf* shortness, dullness.
cortigiàna *nf* courtesan.
cortigiàno *nm* courtier.
cortíle *nm* court, courtyard, playground.
cortína *nf* curtain.
córto *a* short, brief, deficient; **èssere a c. di** to be short of, lack.
corvétta *nf* curvet; (*naut*) corvette.
còrvo *nm* raven, crow, rook.
còsa *nf* thing, matter, work; **che còsa?** what?; **tànte còse** regards.
cosàcco *a nm* Cossack.
còscia *nf* thigh, haunch.
cosciènte *a* aware, conscious.
cosciènza *nf* conscience, consciousness, conscientiousness.
coscienzióşo *a* conscientious.
cosciòtto *nm* (*of meat*) leg.
coscrítto *a nm* conscript.
coscrizióne *nf* conscription.
cosí *ad* as, so, thus, therefore; **c. c.** so-so; **per c. díre** so to speak.
cosicché *cj* so that.
cosiddétto *a* so-called.
coşmètico *pl* **-ici** *a nm* cosmetic.
còşmico *pl* **-ici** *a* cosmic.
còşmo *nm* cosmos, universe.
coşmòdromo *nm* cosmodrome, rocket-station.
coşmonàuta *nm* cosmonaut.
coşmopolíta *a nm* cosmopolitan, cosmopolite.
còso *nm* thing, thingummy (*word used instead of the real name of something*).
cospàrgere *vt* to sprinkle, strew.
cospètto *nm* presence.
cospicuo *a* conspicuous; considerable.
cospiràre *vi* to conspire, plot.
cospirazióne *nf* conspiracy.

còsta *nf* coast, declivity; rib; (*of knife, book*) back.
costà *ad* there, in your town.
costaggiù *ad* down there.
costànte *a nf* constant, steady, firm, uniform.
Costantinòpoli *nf* (*geogr*) Constantinople.
costànza *nf* constancy, firmness, perseverance.
Costànza *nf pr* Constance.
Costànza *nf* (*geogr*) **lago di C.** Lake Constance.
costàre *vt* to cost.
costatàre *v* **constatàre.**
costatazióne *v* **constatazióne.**
costàto *nm* flank, ribs *pl*, side.
costeggiàre *vti* to coast, lie along, run along by.
costèi *pron* she, this woman, that woman.
costernàre *vt* to appall, dismay; **-rsi** *vr* to be dismayed.
costì *ad* there, in your town.
costièra *nf* coast, shore.
costipàre *vt* to constipate, give a cold to; **-rsi** *vr* to become costive, catch a cold.
costipàto *a* having a cold; constipated.
costipazióne *nf* (*med*) cold; constipation.
costituíre *vt* to constitute, elect; **-rsi** *vr* to constitute oneself; give oneself up, surrender.
costituzióne *nf* establishment, constitution.
còsto *nm* cost.
còstola *nf* rib; (*of knife, book*) back.
costolétta *nf* chop, cutlet.
costóro *pron pl* they, these (those) people.
costóso *a* costly, expensive.
costríngere *vt* to compel, constrain, compress.
costrizióne *nf* constraint, compulsion, constriction.
costruíre *vt* to build, construct.
costruttívo *a* constructive.
costrútto *nm* construction, profit, meaning.
costruzióne *nf* construction, building.
costúi *pron* he, this man, that man.
costumàre *vi and impers* to be usual, be the fashion, be in the habit of.
costumatézza *nf* decency, good manners *pl*, politeness.
costumàto *a* civil, polite.
costúme *nm* custom, morals *pl*; costume.
costúra *nf* seam.
coténna *nf* pigskin, scalp; turf.
cotésto *a and pron* that, *pl* those.
cotidiàno *a nm* daily.
cotógna *nf* quince; **cotógno** *nm* quince-tree.
cotognàta *nf* quince jam, jelly.
cotolétta *v* **costolétta.**
cotonàto *nm* cotton; silk and cotton fabric.
cotóne *nm* cotton; **c. idròfilo** absorbent cotton.
cotonièro *a* cotton.
cotonifício *nm* cotton-mill.
còtta *nf* baking; surplice; **prèndere una c. per** (*sl*) to have a crush on; get tipsy.
còttimo *nm* job-work, piecework; **lavoràre a c.** to do piecework.
còtto *a* cooked; (*sl*) madly in love; tipsy.
cottúra *nf* cooking.
covàre *vt* to brood, brood over cherish secretly, smolder, hatch.
covàta *nf* brood, hatch.
covíle *nm* den, hole.
cóvo *nm* den.
covóne *nm* (*of grain*) sheaf.
Còzie, (Àlpi) *nf pl* (*geogr*) Cottian Alps.
còzza *nf* mussel.
cozzàre *vti* to butt, collide.
còzzo *nm* butting, collision, shock.
cràc *nm* crash, (financial) failure.
Cracòvia *nf* (*geogr*) Cracow.
cràmpo *nm* cramp.
crànio *nm* skull.
cràpula *nf* excess guzzling, debauch.
cràsso *a* crass, gross.
cratère *nm* crater.
cravàtta *nf* (neck)tie.
creànza *nf* breeding, manners *pl.*
creàre *vt* to create, cause, appoint.
creatívo *a* creative.
creàto *a* created; *nm* creation universe.
creatóre *nm* **-tríce** *nf* creator.
creatúra *nf* creature, child.
creazióne *nf* creation, appointment.
credènte *a* believing; *nmf* believer.
credènza *nf* belief, credit; sideboard, pantry.
crédere *vti* to believe, think, trust; **-rsi** *vr* to believe oneself.
credíbile *a* believable, credible.
credibilità *nf* credibility.
crédito *nm* credit, esteem.
creditóre *nm* **-tríce** *nf* creditor.
crèdo *nm* creed, credo.
credulità *nf* credulity.
crèdulo *a* credulous.
crèma *nf* cream, custard; (*of society*) élite; **c. emolliènte** cold cream; **c. evanescènte** vanishing cream; **c. antivàmpa** suntan cream.
cremàre *vt* to cremate.
crematóio, fórno crematório *nm* crematorium.
cremazióne *nf* cremation.
crèmişi *a nm* crimson.
crèpa *nf* chink, (*in a wall etc*) crack
crepàccio *nm* crevasse, large crack.
crepacuòre *nm* grief, heartbreak.
crepàre *vi* to burst, crack, split; (*fig*) die.
crepitàre *vi* to crackle.
crepitío *nm* crackling.

crepuscolàre *a* crepuscular, of twilight.
crepúscolo *nm* dusk, gloaming, twilight.
crescènza *nf* growth, increase.
créscere *vi* to grow, increase, (*of prices or water-level*) rise; *vt* to raise, bring up.
crescióne *nm* watercress.
créscita *nf* growth, rise.
crèșima *nf* chrism, confirmation.
creșimàre *vt* to confirm; **-rsi** *vr* to be confirmed.
créspa *nf* wrinkle, ripple, crease.
créspo *a* crisp, frizzy, wrinkled, pleated; *nm* crêpe.
crèsta *nf* crest.
crestomazía *nf* anthology.
crèta *nf* chalk, clay.
Crèta *nf* (*geogr*) Crete.
cretinería *nf* foolish act, nonsense.
cretiníșmo *nm* cretinism, idiocy.
cretíno *nm* cretin, idiot.
cricca *nf* gang.
crícco *pl* **crícchi** *nm* (*tec*) jack.
Crimèa, (la) *nf* (*geogr*) Crimea.
criminàle *a nmf* criminal, offender.
crímine *nm* crime, offense.
criminologia *nf* criminology.
crinàle *nm* (*of mountains*) ridge.
críne, críno *nm* horse-hair.
crinièra *nf* mane.
crípta *nf* crypt.
crișantèmo *nm* chrysanthemum.
críși *nf* crisis.
críșma *nm* chrism, consecrated oil.
cristallàme *nm* crystalware, glassware.
cristallería *nf* crystalware, crystal manufactory.
cristallièra *nf* glass case, china cabinet.
cristallíno *a* crystal; crystal-clear; *nm* (*anat*) crystalline lens.
cristallizzàre *vt* **-rsi** *vr* to crystallize.
cristàllo *nm* crystal, glass.
cristianéșimo *nm* Christianity.
cristianità *nf* Christendom.
cristiàno *a nm* Christian.
Cristína *nf pr* Christine, Christina.
Crísto *nm pr* Christ.
Cristòforo *nm pr* Christopher.
critèrio *nm* criterion, judgment.
crítica *nf* criticism, critique, censure.
criticàre *vt* to criticize, censure.
crítico *pl* **-ici** *a* critical, censorious; *nm* critic.
crivellàre *vt* to riddle, sift.
crivèllo *nm* sieve.
cròcchio *nm* gathering, group.
cróce *nf* cross.
crocerossína *nf* Red Cross nurse.
crocevía *nf* crossroads.
crociàta *nf* crusade.
crociàto *nm* crusader.
crocícchio *nm* crossroads.
crocièra *nf* cruise.
crocifíggere *vt* to crucify.
crocifissióne *nf* crucifixion.
crosifísso *a* crucified; *nm* crucifix.
cròco *pl* **cròchi** *nm* crocus.
crogiuòlo *nm* crucible.
crollàre *vi* to collapse, fall down, slump; *vt* to shake.
cròllo *nm* collapse, fall ruin, shake
cròma *nf* (*mus*) quaver, eighth note.
cromàre *vt* to chromium plate.
cromàtico *pl* **-ici** *a* chromatic.
cromàto *a* chromium-plated.
cronaca *nf* chronicle, news.
crònico *pl* **-ici** *a* (*med*) chronic.
croníșta *nm* chronicler, reporter.
cronología *nf* chronology.
cronològico *pl* **-ici** *a* chronological.
cronometràre *vt* to time.
cronòmetro *nm* chronometer, stop watch.
cròsta *nf* crust, scab.
crostàceo *nm* crustacean, shellfish.
crostíno *nm* piece of toast, crouton.
crostóso *a* crusty.
cròtalo *nm* rattlesnake.
crucciàre *vt* to irritate, worry; **-rsi** *vr* to be troubled, worry.
crúccio *nm* grief, trouble, worry.
cruciàle *a* crucial.
crucivèrba *nm* crossword puzzle.
crudèle *a* cruel.
crudelménte *ad* cruelly.
crudeltà *nf* cruelty.
crudézza *nf* crudeness, rawness.
crúdo *a* raw, crude, harsh.
cruènto *a* bloody, dreadful.
crumíro *nm* blackleg, scab, fink, strikebreaker.
crúsca *nf* bran; freckles *pl*.
cruscòtto *nm* (*aut*) dashboard, (*av*) instrument panel.
Cúba *nf* (*geogr*) Cuba.
cubàno *a nm* Cuban.
cúbito *nm* cubit, elbow, forearm.
cúbo *nm* cube.
cuccàgna *nf* abundance, plenty; **paése di C.** land of Cockaigne.
cuccétta *nf* berth, bunk.
cucchiaiàta *nf* spoonful.
cucchiaíno *nm* teaspoon.
cucchiàio *nm* spoon.
cúccia *nf* dog's bed.
cúcciolo *nm* puppy.
cúcco *pl* **cúcchi** *nm* darling, pet; **vècchio c.** childish old man.
cúccuma *nf* coffee pot.
cucína *nf* cooking, kitchen, stove.
cucinàre *vt* to cook.
cuciníno *nm* kitchenette, small kitchen.
cucíre *vt* to sew, stitch.
cucitríce *nf* seamstress; sewing machine.
cucitúra *nf* seam, sewing.
cucú *nm* cuckoo; **orològio a c.** cuckoo clock.
cúculo *nm* cuckoo.
cúffia *nf* bonnet, cap; (*rad*) earphone.
cugína *nf* **-o** *nm* cousin.
cúi *pron* which, whom, whose.
culinària *nf* cookery.
cúlla *nf* cradle.
cullàre *vt* to rock (a cradle), lull.

culminànte *a* culminating, highest.
culminàre *vi* to culminate.
cúlmine *nm* apex, top.
cúlo *nm* buttocks *pl*, rump.
cúlto *nm* cult, worship.
cultúra *nf* culture, cultivation.
cumulàre *vt* to accumulate.
cúmulo *nm* accumulation, heap, pile.
cúneo *nm* wedge.
cuòca *nf* **-o** *nm* cook.
cuòcere *vt* to cook; *vi* to vex, hurt.
cuoiàio *nm* tanner, dealer in leather
cuòio *nm* leather, skin
cuòre *nm* heart, center; courage.
cupidígia, cupidità *nf* cupidity, covetousness, greed.
cúpido *a* eager, covetous, greedy.
Cupído *nm pr* Cupid.
cúpo *a* dark; deep, hollow.
cúpola *nf* cupola, dome.
cúra *nf* care, cure; parish; (*med*) treatment.
curànte, mèdico *nm* doctor in charge of a case.
curàre *vt* to care, take care of, (*med*) treat; **-rsi** *vr* to take care of oneself, mind.
curàto *nm* curate, parish priest.
curatóre *nm* trustee.
cúria *nf* senate house, court of justice, the bar.
curiàle *a* curial; *nm* lawyer.
curiosàre *vi* to be curious about, pry into.
curiosità *nf* curiosity, inquisitiveness.
curióso *a* curious, inquisitive.
cúrva *nf* bend, curve.
curvàre *vt* **-rsi** *vr* to bend, curve.
curvatúra *nf* bending, (*tec*) camber, curvature.
cúrvo *a* bent, crooked, curved.
cuscinétto *nm* small cushion; (*tec*) bearing.
cuscíno *nm* cushion, pillow; (*tec*) buffer.
custòde *nm* attendant, custodian, janitor, door-keeper.
custòdia *nf* custody, keeping, care; case.
custodíre *vt* to guard, keep; **-rsi** *vr* to take care of oneself.
cúte *nf* (human) skin.
cutícola *nf* cuticle.
cutréttola *nf* wagtail.
czar *nm* tzar, tsar, czar.
czèco *pl* **-èchi** *a nm* Czech.

D

da *prep* from, to, at, through, for since, by, in, like, as, when.
dabbàsso, da bàsso *ad* below, down there, downstairs.
dabbenàggine *nf* ingenuousness, simplicity, stupidity.
dabbène *a* good, honest, upright.
daccànto, da cànto *ad and prep* by, close, near.
daccàpo, da càpo *ad* again, once more, over again.
dacché, da che *cj* since, as.
dàdo *nm* die; (*mech*) nut; (*of soup*) cube.
daffàre, da fàre *nm* occupation, work; **un gràn d.** a great to-do.
dàino *nm* fallow deer; buck.
dàma *nf* lady; (*dance*) partner; (*chess, cards*) queen; (*game of*) draughts, checkers.
dameríno *nm* dandy, beau.
damigèlla *nf* maid of honor; young lady.
damigiàna *nf* demijohn.
danàro *v* **denàro.**
danaróso *a* wealthy.
danése *a* Danish; *nmf* Dane.
Danimàrca *nf* (*geogr*) Denmark.
dannàre *vt* to damn; **-rsi** *vr* to be damned, strive hard.
dannazióne *nf* damnation.
danneggiàre *vt* to damage, harm, impair, injure, spoil.
danneggiàto *a* damaged, injured; *nm* (*leg*) the injured party.
dànno *nm* damage, injury, loss.
dannóso *a* harmful, hurtful, detrimental.
dantésco *pl* **-chi** *a* relating to Dante.
dantísta *nmf* Dante scholar.
Danúbio *nm* the Danube.
dànza *nf* dance, dancing.
danzànte *a* dancing; **tratteniménto d.** dance, ball.
danzàre *vi* to dance.
danzatóre *nm* **-trice** *nf* dancer.
dappertútto *ad* everywhere.
dappocàggine *nf* worthlessness, ineptitude.
dappòco *a* inept, worthless.
dappòi *ad* afterwards, then.
dapprèsso *ad* by, close by, near.
dappríma, da príma *ad* at first.
dàre *vt* to give, produce, yield; *vi* to hit, stumble, look on to, burst out; **-rsi** *vr* to devote oneself, give oneself.
dàre *nm* (*com*) debit, liability.
dàrsena *nf* basin, wet-dock.
dàta *nf* date; **di vècchia d.** long-standing.
datàre *vi* to date.
dàto *a* given; *nm* datum; **d. che** *cj* since, as.
datóre *nm* **-tríce** *nf* giver; **d. di lavóro** employer.
dàttero *nm* date, date-palm.
dattilografàre *vt* to type.
dattilògrafo *nm* **-fa** *nf* typist.
dattórno, da tórno *ad* around.
davànti *ad and prep* before, in front of; *a nm* front; **il d. della càsa** the front of the house.
davanzàle *nm* window-sill.
davànzo, d'avànzo *ad* more than enough, over.
Dàvide *nm pr* David.
davvéro *ad* indeed, really, truly; **per d.** in earnest.

dazière *nm* exciseman, customs officer.
dàzio *nm* customs duty, excise, toll; **d. doganàle** customs duty.
dèa *nf* goddess.
debilitàre *vt* to debilitate, weaken.
debitaménte *ad* duly, regularly.
débito *a* due; *nm* debt, duty.
debitóre *nm* **-trice** *nf* debtor.
débole *a* feeble, weak; *nm* weakness.
debolézza *nf* weakness, debility.
debuttànte *nmf* novice, debutante.
debuttàre *vi* to make one's debut.
debútto *nm* debut.
dècade *nf* ten days; decade.
decadènte *a nm* decadent.
decadentismo *nm* school of decadent poets.
decadènza *nf* decline, decay.
decadére *vi* to decay, decline.
decàno *nm* dean.
decantàre *vt* to extol, praise; decant.
decapitàre *vt* to behead, decapitate.
decapitazióne *nf* beheading.
decarburàre *vt* to decarbonize.
decedúto *a* dead, deceased.
decènne *a* ten years old.
decènnio *nm* decade, period of ten years.
decènte *a* decent, seemly.
decentràre *vt* to decentralize.
decènza *nf* decency, seemliness.
decèsso *nm* death, decease; **àtto di d.** death certificate.
decídere *vt* to decide, settle; **-rsi** *vr* to decide, make up one's mind.
decifràre *vt* to decipher, decode.
dècima *nf* tenth part, tithe.
decimàle *a nm* decimal.
decimàre *vt* to decimate.
dècimo *a* tenth.
decína *nf* about ten.
decişaménte *ad* decidedly, definitely.
decişióne *nf* decision, resolution.
decisívo *a* decisive; critical; **voto d.** casting vote.
decíşo *a* decided, determined, resolute.
declamàre *vti* to declaim.
declamatóre *nm* declaimer.
declamazióne *nf* declamation.
declinàre *vt* to decline; *vi* to set, wane, deviate; **d. le pròprie generalità** to give one's particulars.
declíno *nm* decline.
declívio *nm* declivity, slope.
decollàre *vt* to behead; *vi* (*av*) to take off.
decollazióne *nf* decapitation.
decòllo *nm* (*av*) take-off.
decompórre *vt* to decompose; **-rsi** *vr* to decompose, putrefy.
decomposizióne *nf* decomposition.
decoràre *vt* to decorate, adorn.
decorativo *a* decorative.
decoratóre *nm* **-trice** *nf* decorator.
decorazióne *nf* decoration, ornament.
decòro *nm* decorum, dignity.
decoróso *a* decorous, seemly.
decorrènza *n* (*com*) expiration; **con d. dal** beginning from.
decórrere *vi* to have effect, count from.
decórso *a* expired, passed; *nm* passing, period, course.
decrepitézza *nf* decrepitude.
decrèpito *a* decrepit.
decrescènza *nf* decrease, diminution, wane.
decréscere *vi* to decrease, wane.
decretàre *vt* to decree, award.
decréto *nm* decree.
dècuplo *a nm* ten times, tenfold.
dèdica *nf* dedication.
dedicàre *vt* to dedicate, consecrate, devote; **-rsi** *vr* to devote oneself.
dèdito *a* devoted, addicted.
dedizióne *nf* dedication, devotion.
dedúrre *vt* to deduce, infer.
deduzióne *nf* deduction, inference.
defalcàre *vt* to deduct, subtract.
defenestràre *vt* to throw out of the window; (*fig*) drive out of office.
deferènte *a* deferent, respectful.
deferènza *nf* deference, respect.
deferíre *vi* to defer; *vt* to submit.
defezióne *nf* defection, desertion.
deficiènte *a* insufficient, deficient; *nmf* weak-minded.
deficiènza *nf* deficiency weak-mindedness.
definíre *vt* to define, settle.
definitíva, in *ad* after all.
definíto *a* definite.
definizióne *nf* definition, settlement.
deflagrazióne *nf* deflagration.
deflèttere *vi* to deflect; yield.
deformàre *vt* to deform, deface; **-rsi** *vr* to get deformed, lose one's shape.
defórme *a* deformed, ugly.
deformità *nf* deformity.
defraudàre *vt* to defraud, deprive.
defúnto *a* deceased, late.
degeneràre *vi* to degenerate, get worse.
degenerazióne *nf* degeneration, deterioration.
degènere *a* degenerate.
degènte *a* bedridden; *nmf* in-patient.
degènza *nf* period in bed, stay in hospital.
degnàre *vt* to hold worthy; **-rsi** *vr* to deign.
degnazióne *nf* condescension.
dégno *a* deserving, worthy.
degradàre *vt* to degrade, debase; **-rsi** *vr* to degrade oneself.
degustàre *vt* to taste.
degustazióne *nf* tasting, sipping.
deificàre *vt* to deify.
deità *nf* deity, god, goddess, God.
delatóre *nm* **-trice** *nf* informer.
delazióne *nf* secret accusation.
dèlega *nf* (*of authority etc*) delegation, proxy.
delegàre *vt* to delegate, depute.
delegàto *a* delegate(d); *nm* delegate, deputy.

delegazióne *nf* delegation, committee.
deletèrio *a* deleterious, harmful.
delfíno *nm* dolphin; Dauphin.
deliberàre *vt* to deliberate, pass (a resolution).
deliberazióne *nf* deliberation, resolution.
delicataménte *ad* delicately, gently.
delicatézza *nf* delicacy, sensibility, tact; luxury.
delicàto *a* delicate, fastidious, discreet.
delimitàre *v.* to fix the boundaries.
delineàre *vt* to delineate, outline, sketch.
delinquènte *a nmf* delinquent, criminal.
delinquènza *nf* delinquency.
delínquere *vi* to commit a crime.
delíquio *nm* swoon, fainting fit.
deliràre *vi* to be delirious, rave.
delírio *nm* delirium, raving.
delítto *nm* crime.
delittuóso *a* criminal.
delízia *nf* delight.
deliziàre *vt* to charm, delight; **-rsi** *vr* to delight in, take pleasure in.
delizióso *a* charming, delightful.
dèlta *nm* delta; **àla a d.** (*av*) delta wing.
delucidàre *vt* to explain.
delucidazióne *nf* elucidation, explanation; (*textiles*) decatizing.
delúdere *vt* to disappoint, frustrate; escape.
delușióne *nf* disappointment; deception.
demànio *nm* State property.
demarcazióne *nf* demarcation.
demènte *a nmf* insane, lunatic.
demènza *nf* insanity, lunacy.
demeritàre *vti* to forfeit (one's good opinion), be unworthy of.
democràtico *a* democratic.
democrazía *nf* democracy.
demolíre *vt* to demolish, pull down.
demolizióne *nf* demolition.
dèmone, demònio *nm* demon.
demoníaco *a* demoniac(al).
demoralizẓàre *vt* to demoralize.
denàro *nm* money; penny.
denaróso *v* **danaróso.**
denaturàto *a* methylated; **àlcool d.** methylated spirit.
denigràre *vt* to defame, disparage.
denigrazióne *nf* disparagement.
denominàre *vt* to denominate, name.
denominazióne *nf* denomination, name.
denotàre *vt* to denote, signify.
densità *nf* density, thickness.
dènso *a* dense, thick.
dentàta *nf* bite, mark of bite.
dentàto *a* toothed, cogged, dentate, serrated.
dentatúra *nf* (set of) teeth.
dènte *nm* tooth, fang; prong.
dentellàre *vt* to indent, notch.
dentièra *nf* denture, dental plate, false teeth *pl.*
dentifrício *nm* toothpaste.
dentísta *nm* dentist.
dentizióne *nf* dentition, teething.
déntro *ad and prep* inside, within; *nm* inside.
denudàre *vt* to denude, strip.
denúncia *nf* report, notification; **d.** di **matrimònio** marriage banns.
denunciàre *vt* to declare, announce report.
denutríto *a* underfed.
deodorànte *a* deodorizing; *nm* deodorant.
depauperàre *vt* impoverish.
deperiménto *nm* wasting, pining away, decline, deterioration.
deperíre *vi* to waste, pine away, wither, decay.
depilàre *vt* to depilate, remove hairs.
depilatóre *nm* hair remover, depilatory.
depilatòrio *a* depilatory.
depilazióne *nf* hair-removing, depilation.
deploràre *vt* to deplore, lament, blame.
deplorévole *a* deplorable, lamentable, blamable.
depórre *vt* to depose, lay aside, lay down; *vi* to bear witness.
deportàre *vt* to deport, transport.
deportàto *a* deported; *nm* convict.
deportazióne *nf* deportation.
depoșitàre *vti* to deposit, lodge.
depoșitàrio *nm* depository.
depòșito *nm* (*mil*) depot; warehouse; deposit; **d. bagàgli** luggage office, checkroom.
depoșizióne *nf* deposition.
depravàre *vt* to corrupt, deprave.
deprecàre *vt* to deprecate; entreat.
depredaménto *nm* **depredazióne** *nf* depredation, pillage.
depredàre *vt* to pillage, plunder.
depressióne *nf* depression.
deprèsso *a* depressed, low-spirited.
deprezzaménto *nm* depreciation.
deprezzàre *vt* to depreciate, disparage, undervalue.
deprimènte *a* depressing; (*med*) sedative.
deprímere *vt* to depress.
depuràre *vt* to purify, purge.
deputàre *vt* to depute, appoint, fix.
deputàto *a* delegated, deputed; *nm* delegate, deputy.
deputazióne *nf* committee, deputation.
deragliaménto *nm* derailment.
deragliàre *vi* to derail, leave the rails.
derelítto *a* abandoned, derelict.
derídere *vt* to deride, laugh at, ridicule.
derișióne *nf* derision, ridicule.
derișòrio *a* derisive, mocking.
derívа *nf* (*naut*) drift, leeway; **alla d.** *ad* adrift, astray.

derivàre *vi* to derive, spring, result, follow; *vt* to divert, derive.
derivàto *a* derived; *nm* derivative, by-product.
derivazióne *nf* derivation.
dèroga *nf* derogation.
derogàre *vi* to derogate, deviate from, contravene.
derogazióne *nf* derogation.
derràta *nf* foodstuffs, commodity.
derubàre *vt* to rob.
désco *pl* **déschi** *nm* dinner table, butcher's block, bench, stool.
descrittívo *a* descriptive.
descrívere *vt* to describe, relate.
descrizióne *nf* description.
deşèrto *a* deserted, desolate, lonely; *nm* desert.
desideràre *vt* to desire, long for, wish, want.
desidèrio *nm* wish, desire.
desideróso *a* eager, longing for.
designàre *vt* to appoint, designate, name.
designazióne *nf* designation.
deşinàre *vi* to dine; *nm* dinner, meal.
deşinènza *nf* ending, termination.
deşístere *vi* to desist, give up.
deşolàre *vt* to devastate, distress.
deşolàto *a* desolate, devastated, sorry.
deşolazióne *nf* desolation, devastation, grief.
dèspota *pl* **-ti** *nm* despot.
destàre *vt* to (a)wake, excite, rouse, stir up; **-rsi** *vr* to (a)wake, be roused.
destinàre *vt* to destine, assign, appoint, address, decide.
destinatàrio *nm* addressee, receiver.
destinazióne *nf* destination.
destíno *nm* destiny, fate.
destituíre *vt* to dismiss, remove (from office).
destituíto *a* deprived of, removed from, destitute.
destituzióne *nf* dismissal, removal.
désto *a* awake, alert.
dèstra *nf* right hand, right side, (*in politics*) Right.
destreggiàre *vi* to act skillfully, be skillful; **-rsi** *vr* to manage, maneuver, steer one's course.
destrézza *nf* dexterity, skill.
dèstro *a* right; clever, dexterous; *nm* opportunity, right moment; **cògliere il d.** to seize the chance.
desúmere *vt* to deduce, infer.
detenére *vt* to hold, keep, detain.
detenúto *a* kept back, imprisoned; *nm* prisoner.
detenzióne *nf* detention, unlawful possession.
detergènte *a nm* detergent.
deterioràre *vt* to deteriorate, damage; **-rsi** *vr* to deteriorate, get worse.
determinàre *vt* to determine, define, cause.
detersívo *a* cleansing; *nm* detergent, detersive, cleansing agent.
detestàre *vt* to detest, hate, loathe.
detonàre *vi* to detonate.
detonazióne *nf* detonation, explosion.
detràrre *vt* to deduct.
detrattóre *nm* **-tríce** *nf* detractor, slanderer.
detrazióne *nf* deduction, detraction, slander.
detriménto *nm* detriment, damage.
detríto *nm* rubbish, sweepings *pl*.
detronizzàre *vt* to dethrone.
détta *nf* **a d. di** according to.
dettàfono *nm* dictaphone.
dettagliàre *vt* to detail.
dettàglio *nm* detail, particular; **commèrcio al d.** (*com*) retail trade.
dettàre *vt* to dictate.
dettàto *nm* **dettatúra** *nf* dictation.
détto *a* called, named; *nm* saying, word, joke.
deturpàre *vt* to deface, disfigure.
devastaménto *nm* devastation, ravage.
devastàre *vt* to devastate, ravage.
devastazióne *nf* devastation.
deviaménto *nm* deviation, derailment; (*of traffic etc*) diversion.
deviàre *vt* to deviate, be diverted, swerve, divert.
deviatóio *nm* (*tec*) points *pl*, switch.
deviazióne *nf* deviation, (*road*) diversion, detour; (*mech*) deflection.
devoluzióne *nf* devolution, transfer.
devòlvere *vt* to devolve, assign, transfer.
devóto *a* devout; *nm* devotee.
devozióne *nf* devotion, piety.
di *prep* of, from, for, with, at, in, some, any, than.
dì *nm* day.
diabète *nm* diabetes.
diabètico *pl* **-ici** *a nm* diabetic.
diabòlico *pl* **-ici** *a* diabolic(al).
diàcono *nm* deacon.
diadèma *nm* diadem, tiara.
diàfano *a* diaphanous.
diaframma *nm* diaphragm; screen.
diàgnosi *nf* diagnosis.
diagnòstica *nf* diagnostics *pl*.
diagnòstico *a* diagnostic; *nm* diagnostician.
diagonàle *a* diagonal; *nf* (*geom*) diagonal; *nm* (*fabric*) twill.
diagràmma *pl* **-àmmi** *nm* diagram, chart; (*mus*) scale.
dialettàle *a* dialectal.
dialètto *nm* dialect.
diàlogo *pl* **-ghi** *nm* dialogue.
diamànte *nm* diamond.
diàmetro *nm* diameter.
diàmine! *interj* the deuce! of course!
diàna *nf* morning star, reveille.
Diàna *nf pr* Diana.
diànzi *ad* just now, not long ago.
diàpason *nm* tuning fork, diapason, pitch.

diapoșitíva *nf* (*phot*) transparency, slide; (*typ*) direct reversal.
diàrio *a* daily; *nm* diary.
diarrèa *nf* diarrhea.
diatríba *nf* diatribe, quarrel.
diàvolo *nm* devil.
dibàttere *vt* to debate, discuss; **-rsi** *vr* to struggle.
dibàttito *nm* debate, discussion, controversy.
dicastèro *nm* (higher) government office, ministry, department.
dicèmbre *nm* December.
dicería *nf* hearsay, rumor.
dichiaràre *vt* to declare, state; **-rsi** *vr* to declare oneself.
dichiarazióne *nf* declaration.
diciannòve *a* nineteen; **diciannovèsimo** *a* nineteenth.
diciassètte *a* seventeen; **diciassettèsimo** *a* seventeenth.
diciòtto *a* eighteen; **diciottèsimo** *a* eighteenth.
dicitóre *nm* **-tríce** *nf* announcer, speaker, teller.
dicitúra *nf* wording, words.
didascalía *nf* captions, directions, subtitles.
didàttico *pl* **-ici** *a* didactic.
didéntro *ad nm* inside.
dièci *a* ten.
diecína *nf* about ten.
dièta *nf* assembly, diet.
diètro *nm* back; *ad and prep* after, behind.
difàtti, difàtto *ad* as a matter of fact, in fact.
difèndere *vt* to defend, guard, protect; **-rsi** *vr* to defend oneself.
difensíva *nf* defensive.
difensívo *a* defensive.
difensóre *nm* defender.
difésa *nf* defense.
difettàre *vi* to be deficient in, lack.
difettívo, difettóso *a* defective, lacking.
difètto *nm* defect, flaw, fault.
diffàlco *pl* **-chi** *nm* deduction.
diffamàre *vt* to defame, libel.
diffamazióne *nf* defamation.
differènte *a* different; unlike (*s.o., sth.*).
differènza *nf* difference.
differenziàre *vt* to differentiate, distinguish (between); **-rsi** *vr* to differ (from), be different.
differiménto *nm* adjournment, deferment.
differíre *vt* to adjourn, defer, postpone; *vi* to be different, differ, disagree.
diffícile *a* difficult, hard; hard to please.
difficoltà *nf* difficulty, objection.
difficoltóso *a* full of difficulties, fastidious.
diffída *nf* intimation, notice.
diffidàre *vt* to serve a notice; *vi* to distrust, suspect.
diffidènte *a* diffident, distrustful.
diffidènza *nf* diffidence, distrust, suspicion.
diffóndere *vi* to diffuse, pour, spread; **-rsi** *vr* to be diffused, spread.
diffușaménte *ad* diffusely, abundantly.
diffușióne *nf* diffusion.
diffúso *a* diffuse, diffused; long-winded.
difilàto *ad* at once, forthwith.
difteríte *nf* diphtheria.
díga *nf* breakwater, dike.
digerènte *a* digestive.
digeríbile *a* digestible.
digeríre *vt* to digest, assimilate.
digestióne *nf* digestion.
digestívo *a nm* digestive.
digèsto *nm* digest.
digitàle *a* digital; *nf* foxglove; digitalis; **imprònte digitàli** fingerprints.
digiunàre *vi* to fast.
digiúno *a* fasting, devoid of; *nm* fast.
dignità *nf* dignity.
dignitóso *a* dignified.
digradàre *vi* to slope down, decline; diminish, (*of colors*) shade off.
digrassàre *vi* to remove the fat, skim.
digressióne *nf* digression.
digrignàre *vt* to gnash, grind (one's teeth).
digrossàre *vt* to whittle down, rough-hew; teach the first elements.
diguazzàre *vi* to splash about, paddle; *vi* to shake, stir.
dilaceràre, dilaniàre *vt* to tear (to pieces).
dilagàre *vi* to overflow, spread.
dilapidàre *vt* to dilapidate, squander.
dilatàbile *a* dilatable, extensible.
dilatàre *vt* **-rsi** *vr* to dilate, expand.
dilatàto *a* dilated, enlarged.
dilatazióne *nf* dilation, expansion.
dilatòrio *a* delaying, dilatory.
dilazionàre *vt* to adjourn, postpone.
dilazióne *nf* delay, respite.
dileggiàre *vt* to mock, ridicule.
diléggio *nm* derision, mockery.
dileguaménto *nm* disappearance.
dileguàre *vt* to disperse, dissipate; **-rsi** *vr* to dissolve, fade away, vanish.
dilèmma *nm* dilemma.
dilettànte *nmf* amateur, dilettante.
dilettàre *vt* to charm, delight; **-rsi** *vr* to delight, take pleasure in.
dilettévole *a* charming, delightful.
dilètto *a* beloved, darling; *nm* delight, pleasure.
diligènte *a* diligent.
diligènza *nf* diligence; stagecoach.
dilucidàre *vt* to elucidate.
diluíre *vt* to dilute, water.
dilungàre *vt* to lengthen, prolong; **-rsi** *vr* to dwell (on).
dilúngo *ad* straight on.
diluviàre *vi* to pour, deluge, rain in torrents.

dilúvio *nm* deluge, flood.
dimagraménto *nm* growing thin, slimming; (*of ground*) impoverishing.
dimagràre, dimagríre *vt* to make thin; *vi* to grow thin, lose weight.
dimenàre *vt* to shake, (*tail*) wag; **-rsi** *vr* to fidget, toss.
dimensióne *nf* dimension, size.
dimenticànza *nf* forgetfulness, oblivion.
dimenticàre *vt* **-rsi** *vr* to forget.
diméntico *pl* **-chi** *a* forgetful.
dimésso *a* humble, modest.
dimestichézza *nf* familiarity.
dimèttere *vt* to dismiss, remove; forgive; **-rsi** *vr* to resign.
dimezzàre *vt* to halve.
diminuíre *vt* to abate, diminish, lessen, reduce; *vi* to decrease.
diminutívo *a nm* diminutive.
diminuzióne *nf* diminution, reduction.
dimissióne *nf* resignation; **dàre le dimissióni** *vi* to resign.
dimòra *nf* abode, dwelling, stay; **sènza físsa d.** *a* homeless, vagabond.
dimoràre *vi* to live, reside; stay; delay.
dimostràre *vt* to demonstrate, prove, show; **-rsi** *vr* to appear, show oneself.
dimostrazióne *nf* demonstration.
dinàmica *nf* dynamics.
dinàmico *pl* **-ici** *a* dynamic, energetic.
dinamíte *nf* dynamite.
dínamo *nf* (*el*) dynamo, generator.
dinànzi *ad and prep* before, opposite, in front.
dinastía *nf* dynasty.
diniègo *pl* **-ghi** *nm* denial, refusal.
dinoccolàto *a* disjointed, loose-limbed, shambling.
dintórno *ad and prep* about, (a)round; **dintórni** *nm pl* neighborhood.
Dío *nm* God.
diòcesi *nf* diocese.
Dionígi *nm pr* Denis, Dennis.
dipanàre *vt* to wind into a ball; unravel, disentangle.
dipartiménto *nm* department.
dipartírsi *vr* to depart, go away.
dipartíta *nf* (*poet*) departure, death.
dipendènte *a* depending, dependent; *nmf* subordinate, dependant.
dipendènza *nf* dependence, dependency.
dipèndere *vi* to depend (on), derive.
dipíngere *vt* to paint, depict; **-rsi** *vr* to paint oneself.
dipínto *a* painted; *nm* painting.
diplóma *nm* diploma, certificate.
diplomàre *vt* to confer a diploma; **-rsi** *vr* to get a diploma, to graduate.
diplomàtico *pl* **-ici** *a* diplomatic; *nm* diplomat.
diplomazía *nf* diplomacy.
dipòrto *nm* amusement, recreation.
diradaménto *nm* thinning (out), rarefaction.
diradàre *vt* to thin out; **-rsi** *vr* (*of hair etc*) to get thin.
diramàre *vt* to lop, prune; send out; **-rsi** *vr* to branch out, ramify, spread.
diramazióne *nf* branching out, branching off, branch, diffusion.
díre *vt* to say, tell, speak; *nm* speech, words, statement, saying.
direttaménte *ad* directly, direct.
direttíssimo *nm* express train.
direttíva *nf* direction, instruction.
dirètto *a* direct, straight; *nm* fast train; **carròzza dirètta** *nf* through coach (on a train).
direttóre *nm* **-tríce** *nf* director, directress, headmaster, headmistress, manager(ess), (newspaper) editor.
direzióne *nf* direction, course; management, leadership, office; (*tec*) steering-gear.
dirigènte *a* directing, managing; *nm* manager, (*pol*) leader.
dirígere *vt* to direct, address, manage, regulate; **-rsi** *vr* to go towards.
dirigíbile *nm* airship.
dirimpètto *ad* opposite; **d. a** *prep* opposite, in comparison with.
diritta *nf* right, right hand, right side.
dirítto *a* straight, upright, erect, plumb, right; *nm* right, claim, due, law; *ad* directly, straight (on); **dirítti d'autóre** royalties.
dirittúra *nf* straightness, uprightness.
dirizzàre *vi* to straighten, prick up (one's ears); **-rsi** *vr* to draw oneself up.
diroccàre *vt* to demolish, dismantle; **-rsi** *vr* to fall in ruins.
dirótto *a* heavy; **piànto d.** *nm* flood of tears; **piòggia dirótta** heavy rain.
dirozzàre *vt* to rough-hew, civilize, polish; **-rsi** *vr* to become civilized, refined.
dirúpo *nm* rocky precipice.
disabitàto *a* uninhabited.
disabituàre *vt* to disaccustom; **-rsi** *vr* to lose the habit.
disaccòrdo *nm* disagreement, discord.
disadàtto *a* unfit, unsuitable, unbecoming.
disadórno *a* bare, simple, unadorned.
disaffezióne *nf* estrangement, disaffection.
disagévole *a* difficult, uncomfortable.
disagevolézza *nf* difficulty, discomfort.
disaggradévole *a* disagreeable.
disagiàto *a* uncomfortable; poor, needy.
disàgio *nm* discomfort, uneasiness; **sentírsi a d.** to feel uncomfortable.

diṣàmina *nf* examination, investigation.
disaminàre *vt* examine.
diṣappetènza *nf* lack of appetite.
diṣapprèndere *vt* to unlearn, forget.
diṣapprovàre *vt* to disapprove of, blame.
diṣappúnto *nm* disappointment.
diṣarmàre *vt* to disarm; dismantle, (*naut*) lay up (a ship).
diṣàrmo *nm* disarmament.
diṣàstro *nm* disaster, accident.
diṣastróso *a* disastrous, ruinous.
diṣattènto *a* inattentive.
diṣattenzióne *nf* inattention, inattentiveness.
diṣattrezzàre *vt* (*naut*) to dismantle.
diṣavànzo *nm* deficiency, deficit.
diṣavvedutézza, diṣavvertènza *nf* inadvertency.
diṣavventúra *nf* misfortune, mishap.
diṣavvezzàre *vt* to disaccustom.
diṣbórso *nm* disbursement, outlay.
diṣbrigàre *vt* to clear off, dispatch; **-rsi** *vr* to extricate oneself, get out (*of sth*), make haste.
diṣbrígo *pl* **-ghi** *nm* dispatch, settlement.
discàpito *nm* disadvantage, detriment.
discendènte *a* descending; *nmf* descendant.
discendènza *nf* descent; offspring.
discéndere *vi* to descend, go down; spring from; (*of prices, temperature*) fall.
discentràto *a* decentralized; off center.
discépolo *nm* disciple, pupil.
discèrnere *vt* to discern, distinguish.
discernimènto *nm* discernment, judgment.
discésa *nf* descent, fall; (*rad*) lead-in.
dischiúdere *vt* to disclose, reveal.
disciògliere *vt* to dissolve, melt; release, untie; **-rsi** *vr* to dissolve, melt, get loose.
disciplína *nf* discipline.
disciplinàre *vt* to discipline; *a* disciplinary.
dísco *pl* **díschi** *nm* disk, disc; (*mus*) record; (*sport*) discus.
díscolo *a* undisciplined, unruly, wild; *nm* rogue, scamp.
discolpàre *vt* to clear from blame, excuse, defend; **-rsi** *vr* to clear oneself, justify oneself.
disconoscènza *nf* ingratitude.
disconóscere *vt* to disavow, slight, be ungrateful for.
discordànte *a* discordant, clashing, dissonant; disagreeing.
discordànza *nf* discordance, dissonance; disagreement.
discordàre *vi* to disagree; (*mus*) be out of tune.
discòrde *a* discordant, dissonant.
discòrdia *nf* discord, dissension.
discórrere *vi* to discourse, talk.
discórso *nm* discourse, speech, talk.
discòsto *a* distant, far; *ad* at some distance.
discotéca *nf* discotheque.
discreditàre *vt* to discredit; **-rsi** *vr* to damage one's reputation.
discrepànza *nf* discrepancy.
discretaménte *ad* discreetly, fairly.
discretézza *nf* discretion, moderation.
discretíva *nf* power of discernment.
discréto *a* discreet; moderate, passable, reasonable.
discrezióne *nf* discretion; **a d.** according to one's judgment.
discriminàre *vt* to discriminate.
discriminazióne *nf* discrimination.
discussióne *nf* debate, discussion, dispute.
discútere *vt* to discuss, argue.
discutíbile *a* debatable, questionable.
diṣdegnàre *v* **ṣdegnàre.**
diṣdégno *nm* contempt, scorn, haughtiness.
diṣdegnóso *a* contemptuous, scornful.
disdétta *nf* notice to leave; bad luck.
diṣdíre *vt* to annul, cancel, revoke, unsay; *vi* to be unbecoming; **-rsi** *vr* to be unbecoming; go back on one's word.
diṣdòro *nm* dishonor, shame.
disegnàre *vt* to draw, plan.
diségno *nm* design, drawing, plan, purpose.
diṣeredàre *vt* to disinherit.
diṣertàre *vt* to desert; lay waste, ruin.
diṣertóre *a* deserter.
diṣerzióne *nf* desertion.
disfacimènto *nm* destruction, ruin, decay.
disfàre *vt* to undo, break up, take to pieces, untie; **-rsi** *vr* to dispose of, get rid of.
disfàtta *nf* defeat.
disfattísta *a nmf* defeatist.
disfàtto *a* undone, defeated, worn-out.
disfída *nf* challenge, duel.
disfunzióne *nf* (*med*) disorder, irregularity.
diṣgelàre *vi* to thaw; *vt* to defrost.
diṣgràzia *nf* misfortune, ill luck, accident.
diṣgraziàto *a* unfortunate, unlucky; *nm* wretch.
diṣgregàre *vt* **-rsi** *vr* to disintegrate, break up.
diṣguído *nm* (*of post & fig*) going astray.
diṣgustàre *vt* to disgust, sicken, vex; **-rsi** *vr* to take a disgust, dislike for.
diṣgústo *nm* disgust, dislike, loathing.
diṣgustóso *a* disgusting.
diṣillúdere *vt* to disillusion, disenchant.
diṣillusióne *nf* disillusion, disenchantment.

dişimparàre *vt* to unlearn, forget.
dişimpegnàre *vt* to redeem, release, fulfill; (*naut*) clear; **-rsi** *vr* to free oneself, manage one's own affairs.
dişimpégno *nm* disengagement, release.
dişincagliàre *vt* (*naut*) to float (a stranded ship).
dişinfettànte *a nm* disinfectant.
dişinfettàre *vt* to disinfect.
dişinfezióne *nf* disinfection.
dişingannàre *vt* to disillusion, undeceive.
dişingànno *nm* disillusionment. undeceiving.
dişintegràre *vt* **-rsi** *vr* to disintegrate.
dişintegrazióne *nf* disintegration.
dişinteressàre *vt* (*com*) buy out; to make one lose interest; **-rsi** *vr* to disinterest oneself.
dişinteressàto *a* disinterested; unselfish; impartial.
dişinterèsse *nm* disinterestedness, unselfishness.
dişinvòlto *a* easy, free, sure of oneself, unconstrained, impudent.
dişinvoltúra *nf* ease, nonchalance, self-possession, impudence.
dişistimàre *vt* not to esteem, to despise.
dişlivèllo *nm* difference of level.
dişlocàre *vt* to displace.
dişmisúra *nf* excess; **a d.** immoderately.
dişobbligàre *vt* to free from obligation.
dişoccupàto *a* out of work, unemployed; *nm* unemployed person.
dişoccupazióne *nf* unemployment.
dişonestà *nf* dishonesty.
dişonèsto *a* dishonest, indecent.
dişonoràre *vt* to disgrace, dishonor.
dişonóre *nm* disgrace, dishonor, shame.
disópra *nm* top, upper side; *ad and pron* above, on, over, upstairs; **al d. di** *prep* beyond.
dişordinàre *vt* to disorder, disarrange; (*in eating, drinking*) to exceed.
dişordinàto *a* disorderly, untidy.
dişórdine *nm* disorder, confusion, disorderliness, disturbance.
dişorganizzàre *vt* to disorganize.
dişorganizzazióne *nf* disorganization.
dişorientaménto *nm* disorientation, confusion.
dişorientàre *vt* to confuse, disconcert, lead astray, mislead; **-rsi** *vr* to be at a loss, not to know where one is.
disótto *a nm* lower, bottom, lower side; *ad and prep* below, under (neath); **al d. di** inferior to; below.
dispàccio *nm* dispatch; **d. telegràfico** telegram.
disparàto *a* different, disparate, incongruous, unequal.
díspari *a* (*number*) odd; different, unequal.
dispàrte, in *ad* apart, aside, aloof.
dispèndio *nm* expense, outlay.
dispendióso *a* expensive.
dispènsa *nf* distribution; (*of a publication*) number; sideboard, pantry; dispensation, exemption; **dispènse universitàrie** duplicated lecture notes.
dispensàre *vt* to dispense, distribute; exempt.
dispensàrio *nm* dispensary.
dispepsía *nf* dyspepsia.
disperàre *vi* to despair; **-rsi** *vr* to give oneself up to despair.
disperàto *a* despairing, desperate, hopeless, wretched; *nm* destitute creature, desperate creature.
disperazióne *nf* despair, desperation.
dispèrdere *vt* to dispel, disperse, scatter, waste; **-rsi** *vr* to be scattered, disperse.
dispersióne *nf* dispersion, loss; (*el*) leak.
dispèrso *a* missing, dispersed, lost, scattered; *nm* (*mil*) missing soldier.
dispètto *nm* spite, grudge, pique, vexation.
dispettóso *a* spiteful.
dispiacénte *a* sorry; disagreeable.
dispiacére *vi* to dislike, regret; be disagreeable, displease; **mi dispiàce** I am sorry; *nm* displeasure, dissatisfaction, grief, regret.
disponíbile *a* available, free; *nm* (*com*) liquid assets *pl*.
dispórre *vti* to arrange, direct, dispose, order, regulate; **-rsi** *vr* to get ready.
dispoşitívo *nm* (*mech*) contrivance, appliance; (*phot*) adapter; **d. di sicurezza** safety catch.
dispoşizióne *nf* arrangement, disposition, disposal, inclination, order; **avére d. per** to have a talent for; **a súa d.** at your disposal.
dispósto *a* willing, inclined, disposed; arranged; **ben d.** in good order, vigorous.
dispregiàre *etc v* **disprezzàre**.
disprezzàbile *a* contemptible, despicable, negligible.
disprezzàre *vt* to despise, scorn.
disprèzzo *nm* contempt, sorrow.
dísputa *nf* debate, dispute, quarrel.
disputàre *vti* to argue, contend, debate, dispute, quarrel; **-rsi** *vr* to contend (for).
dissanguàre *vt* to bleed; (*fig*) impoverish.
dissanguàto *a* drained of blood; (*fig*) impoverished.
dissapóre *nm* disagreement, misunderstanding.
disseminàre *vt* to disseminate, propagate, scatter, sow.
dissennatézza *nf* craziness, foolishness, rashness.

dissènso *nm* difference of opinion, dissent.
dissentería *nf* dysentery.
dissentíre *vi* to disagree (with).
disseppelliménto *nm* disinterment, exhumation.
disseppellíre *vt* to disinter.
dissertàre *vi* to discourse, expatiate.
dissertazióne *nf* dissertation, thesis.
dissestàre *vt* to ruin, disarrange, derange; **-rsi** *vr* (*financially*) to ruin oneself.
dissestàto *a* in financial straits, badly off.
dissèsto *nm* disorder; financial trouble.
dissetànte *a* refreshing.
dissetàre *vt* to quench (thirst).
dissezióne *nf* dissection.
dissidènte *a nmf* dissentient, dissenter.
dissídio *nm* dissension, discord.
dissigillàre *vt* to unseal.
dissímile *a* unlike.
dissimulàre *vt* to dissimulate, conceal.
dissipàre *vt* to clear up, dissipate, remove; **-rsi** *vr* to disappear, vanish.
dissipazióne *nf* dissipation.
dissociàre *vt* to dissociate.
dissodàre *vt* (*land*) to clear, till.
dissolúbile *a* dissoluble.
dissolubilità *nf* dissolubility.
dissolutézza *nf* dissoluteness, licentiousness.
dissolúto *a* dissolute, licentious.
dissoluzióne *nf* disintegration, dissolution; dissoluteness.
dissolvènza *nf* (*cin*) fade-out.
dissòlvere *vt* **-rsi** *vr* to dissolve, melt.
dissomigliànza *nf* unlikeness, difference.
dissonànte *a* dissonant, discordant.
dissonànza *nf* dissonance, difference.
dissotterràre *vt* to disinter.
dissuadére *vt* to dissuade, deter.
dissuetúdine *nf* disuse.
distaccaménto *nm* (*mil*) detachment.
distaccàre *vt* to cut off, detach, separate, sever; **-rsi** *vr* to become detached, break off.
distàcco *pl* **-chi** *nm* separation, parting, detachment; (*fig*) indifference.
distànte *a* distant, far, remote; *ad* far away.
distànza *nf* distance; difference.
distanziàre *vt* to space (out), leave behind.
distàre *vi* to be distant.
distèndere *vt* to extend, lay (out), spread, relax; **-rsi** *vr* to stretch out.
distendiménto *nm* **distensióne** *nf* spreading, stretching, relaxing.
distésa *nf* expanse, extent.
distillàre *vti* to distill; trickle.
distillatóio *nm* still.
distillería *nf* distillery.
distínguere *vt* to distinguish; **-rsi** *vr* to become famous, distinguish oneself.
distinguíbile *a* distinguishable.
distínta *nf* list, note, schedule; **d. dei prèzzi** price list.
distintaménte *ad* distinctly; (*in letters*) faithfully.
distintívo *a* distinctive; *nm* badge, distinguishing mark.
distínto *a* distinct; clear; distinguished; **distinti salúti** (*in a letter*) yours faithfully.
distinzióne *nf* distinction, regard.
distògliere *vt* to deter, dissuade, distract.
distorsióne *nf* distorsion, sprain.
distràrre *vi* to amuse, distract, divert; **-rsi** *vr* to amuse oneself, let one's attention wander.
distràtto *a* absent-minded, inattentive.
distrazióne *nf* absent-mindedness, inattention; recreation.
distrétto *nm* district.
distribuíre *vt* to distribute, arrange, assign, deliver.
distributívo *a* distributive.
distributóre *a* distributing; *nm* distributor; **d. di benzína** (*aut*) petrol pump, gasoline pump.
distribuzióne *nf* distribution, layout.
districàre, distrigàre *vt* to disentangle, unravel; **-rsi** *vr* to extricate oneself, free oneself.
distrúggere *vt* to destroy, ruin; **-rsi** *vr* to destroy oneself (each other).
distruzióne *nf* destruction.
disturbàre *vt* to disturb, interrupt, trouble; **-rsi** *vr* to put oneself out, take trouble.
distúrbo *nm* disturbance, trouble, inconvenience, disorder.
diṣubbidiènte *a* disobedient.
diṣubbidiènza *nf* disobedience.
diṣubbidíre *vi* to disobey.
diṣuguagliànza *nf* disparity, inequality.
diṣuguàle *a* unequal, dissimilar.
diṣumàno *a* inhuman.
diṣunióne *nf* discord, disunion.
diṣuníre *vt* to disjoin, disunite.
diṣuṣàre *vt* to cease using.
diṣuṣàto *a* disused; out-of-date; unaccustomed.
diṣúṣo *nm* disuse; **cadére in d.** to become obsolete.
ditàle *nm* thimble, finger-stall.
díto *pl* **díti, díta** (*f*) *nm* finger, toe; inch.
dítta *nf* firm, (commercial) house.
dittàfono *nm* dictaphone.
dittattóre *nm* dictator.
dittatúra *nf* dictatorship.
diúrno *a* day, diurnal; **albèrgo d.** *nm* public baths and lavatories *pl.*
díva *nf* goddess; great actress or singer.
divagàre *vt* to amuse, divert; *vi* to

digress, wander; **-rsi** *vr* to amuse oneself, relax.
divagazióne *nf* wandering; digression; recreation.
divampàre *vi* to blaze, flare up.
divàno *nm* couch, divan.
divàrio *nm* difference, diversity.
diveníre, diventàre *vi* to become, get, grow, turn.
divèrbio *nm* altercation, dispute.
divergènte *a* divergent, diverging.
divergènza *nf* divergence, divergency.
divèrgere *vi* to diverge, wander from.
diversaménte *ad* differently, otherwise.
diversificàre *vt* to diversify; *vi*, **-rsi** *vr* to differ.
diversióne *nf* deviation, digression, diversion.
diversità *nf* diversity.
diversívo *a* deviating, diverting; *nm* distraction, amusement.
divèrso *a* different, sundry; **divèrsi** *pl* several; **generi diversi** *nm pl* (*com*) sundries *pl*.
divertènte *a* amusing, entertaining.
divertiménto *nm* amusement, entertainment, recreation.
divertíre *vt* to divert, amuse, entertain; **-rsi** *vr* to amuse oneself, have a good time.
divezzàre *vt* to disaccustom, wean; **-rsi** *vr* to disaccustom oneself.
dividèndo *nm* dividend.
divídere *vt* to divide, share; **-rsi** *vr* to divide, separate.
divièto *nm* prohibition; **d. d'affissióne** 'post no bills'; **d. di sòsta** 'no parking'.
divinaménte *ad* divinely, beautifully.
divinàre *vt* to divine, foretell.
divincolaménto *nm* wriggle, wriggling, writhing, struggling.
divincolàre *vt* to wriggle; **divincolàrsi** *vr* to writhe, wriggle, struggle free.
divinità *nf* divinity.
divíno *a* divine.
divísa *nf* uniform, livery; (*com*) currency; hair parting; motto, device; **d. èstera** foreign currency.
divişàre *vti* to devise, p an, resolve.
divişióne *nf* division, department, discord.
divişòrio *a* dividing, separating; **múro d.** *nm* partition wa l.
dívo *nm* (film)star.
divoràre *vt* to devour eat up.
divorziàre *vti* **-rsi** *vr* divorce, get a divorce.
divòrzio *nm* divorce.
divulgàre *vt* to divulge, spread; **-rsi** *vr* to spread.
dizionàrio *nm* dictionary.
dizióne *nf* diction.
do *nm* (*mus*) C, do.
dóccia *nf* shower(bath), douche; water-pipe; **fàre la d.** *vi* to take a shower.
docènte *nmf* teacher, university lecturer.
docènza *nf* teaching.
dòcile *a* docile; (*of material*) easily worked.
docilità *nf* docility, meekness.
documentàre *vt* to bring documentary evidence, document.
documentàrio *a* documentary; *nm* documentary film, newsreel.
documénto *nm* document, evidence.
dodicènne *a* twelve years old; *nmf* twelve-year-old.
dodicèşimo *a* twelfth.
dódici *a* twelve.
dogàna *nf* customs, customs office, custom-house.
doganàle *a* customs.
doganière *nm* customs officer.
dòglia *nf* ache, pain; **dòglie** *pl* labor pains.
dògma *nm* dogma, principle.
dogmàtico *pl* **-ici** *a* dogmatic.
dólce *a* sweet, mild, soft; *nm* sweetness; pudding, cake.
dolcézza *nf* sweetness, softness.
dolciúmi *nm pl* sweets *pl*, sweetmeats *pl*.
dolènte *a* grieved, sorry; aching.
dolére *vi* to ache; regret; **-rsi** *vr* to be sorry, complain, grieve, lament, regret.
dòllaro *nm* dollar.
dòlo *nm* fraud.
Dolomíti (le) *nf pl* (*geogr*) the Dolomites *pl*.
dolorànte *a* aching, painful.
dolóre *nm* ache, grief, pain, regret.
doloróso *a* painful, grievous, sorrowful.
dolóso *a* fraudulent.
domànda *nf* question, request, demand, application; **fàre d.** apply; **fàre una d.** to ask a question, make a request.
domandàre *vt* to ask, demand, request; **-rsi** *vr* to ask oneself, wonder.
domàni *nm and ad* tomorrow; **d. l'àltro** *ad* the day after tomorrow.
domàre *vt* to break in, tame, conquer, extinguish, subdue, overcome.
domatóre *nm* **-trice** *nf* tamer.
domatúra *nf* (*of horses*) breaking, taming.
doménica *nf* Sunday.
domenicàle *a* (of) Sunday.
domenicàno *a nm* Dominican.
domèstica *nf* maid, servant.
domestichézza *nf* domesticity, fam liarity, intimacy.
domèstico *pl* **-ici** *a* domestic, familiar; *nm* servant.
domiciliàre *vt* to domiciliate, house; **-rsi** *vr* to live, settle, take up one's abode.
domicílio *nm* abode, domicile.

dominànte *a* dominant; prevailing.
dominàre *vt* to command, dominate, govern, overlook, rule; **-rsi** *vr* to control oneself, master oneself.
dominazióne *nf* domination, rule.
domínio *nm* dominion, authority, power, territory, domain.
donàre *vt* to bestow, confer, grant; *vi* to be becoming, suit; **-rsi** *vr* to devote oneself.
donatóre *nm* **donatrice** *nf* donor, giver; **d. di sàngue** blood donor.
donazióne *nf* donation.
dónde *ad* from where, whence, wherefore.
dondolaménto, dóndolo *nm* rocking, swaying, swinging.
dondolàre *vt* **-rsi** *vr* to rock, sway, swing.
dondolóni *ad* dangling.
dònna *nf* woman.
donnaiuòlo *nm* philanderer, ladies' man.
donnésco *pl* **-chi** *a* womanly, feminine, womanish.
dònnola *nf* weasel.
dóno *nm* gift, present; talent.
dópo *ad and prep* after, afterwards, next, later; **e d.?** what next?
dopochè *cj* after, when, since.
dopodomàni *nm* the day after tomorrow.
dopoguèrra *nm* the post-war period.
dopoprànzo *nm* afternoon.
doppiàggio *nm* dubbing.
doppiàre *vt* to double; (*cin*) dub.
doppière *nm* two-branched candlestick.
doppiétta *nf* double-barrelled gun.
doppiézza *nf* double-dealing, duplicity.
dóppio *a* double, deceitful, dual; *nm* double, twice as much.
doppióne *nm* duplicate, (*typ*) double.
doràre *vt* to gild; (*cook*) glaze, brown, sugar-coat.
doratúra *nf* gilding.
dormicchiàre *vi* to doze.
dormiglióne *nm* sleepy fellow, lie-a-bed.
dormíre *vti* to sleep; *nm* sleep.
dormitòrio *nm* dormitory; **d. púbblico** doss house, flophouse.
dormivéglia *nf* (state) between sleeping and waking.
Dorotèa *nf pr* Dorothy, Dorothea.
dórso *nm* back; (*of mountain*) crest.
doṣàre *vt* to dose.
dòṣe *nf* dose.
dòsso *nm* back.
dotàre *vt* to endow, give a dowry.
dotàto *a* gifted, endowed, furnished.
dòte *nf* dowry, gift, talent.
dòtto *a* learned; *nm* scholar.
dottoràto *nm* doctor's degree.
dottóre *nm* doctor, physician.
dottoréssa *nf* (female) graduate, lady doctor.
dottrína *nf* doctrine, learning, catechism.
dóve *ad* where, in the case that, whereas; *nm* where.
dovére *vi* to be obliged, have to, must, ought, should, be indebted, owe; *nm* duty, respects.
doveróso *a* right, dutiful.
dovízia *nf* abundance, plenty, wealth.
dovúnque *ad* anywhere, everywhere, wherever.
dozzína *nf* dozen; board and lodgings.
dozzinàle *a* common, ordinary.
dozzinànte *nmf* boarder.
dràga *nf* (*naut*) dredge.
dragamíne *nf* (*naut*) minesweeper.
dragàre *vt* (*naut*) to dredge.
dràgo *pl* **-ghi** *nm* dragon.
dràmma *nf* drachm(a); *nm* drama.
drammàtica *nf* dramatic art.
drammàtico *pl* **-ici** *a* dramatic.
drammatúrgo *pl* **-ghi** *nm* playwright.
drappèllo *nm* squad.
drappería *nf* drapery, dry-goods store.
dràppo *nm* silk material.
dràstico *pl* **-ici** *a* drastic.
drenàggio *nm* drainage.
drenàre *vt* to drain.
drítta *nf* right; (*naut*) starboard.
drítto *v* **dirítto.**
drizzàre *vt* to straighten, prick up, erect, turn, (*fig*) right; **-rsi** *vr* stand up, straighten up.
dròga *nf* drug, spice.
drogàre *vt* to drug, spice.
drogheria *nf* grocer's shop, grocery.
droghière *nm* grocer.
dromedàrio *nm* dromedary.
dubbiézza *nf* doubt, uncertainty.
dúbbio *a* doubtful, dubious; *nm* doubt, suspense; **èssere in d.** to be doubtful; **méttere in d.** *vt* to question.
dubbióso *a* doubtful, vague.
dubitàre *vi* to doubt, question, mistrust.
Dublíno *nf* (*geogr*) Dublin.
dublinése *a* of Dublin; *nmf* Dubliner.
dúca *nm* duke.
ducàle *a* ducal.
ducàto *nm* ducat; duchy, dukedom.
dúce *nm* chief, leader.
ducentísta *nm* writer of the thirteenth century.
duchéssa *nf* duchess.
dúe *a* two.
duecènto *a* two hundred; *nm* the thirteenth century.
duellàre *vi* to fight a duel.
duèllo *nm* duel.
duemíla *a nm* two thousand.
duétto *nm* (*mus*) duet.
dúna *nf* dune, sand-hill.
dúnque *cj* so, then, well! what! what about it?
duodècimo *a* twelfth.
duodenàle *a* duodenal; **úlcera d.** duodenal ulcer.

duòmo *nm* cathedral.
dúplex *a* **telèfono d.** two-party line telephone.
duplicàre *vt* to double, duplicate.
duplicatóre *nm* duplicator, multigraph, (*rad*) doubler.
dúplice *a* double, twofold.
duplicità *nf* duplicity, double-dealing.
duràbile *a* durable, lasting.
durànte *prep* during.
duràre *vi* to last, continue, remain; *vt* to stand, endure.
duràta *nf* duration, period, wear, endurance.
duratúro, durévole *a* durable, lasting.
durézza *nf* hardness, harshness.
dúro *a* hard, harsh, severe, insensible, stupid; *nm* hard, hardship.
dúttile *a* ductile.

E

e, ed *cj* and; **e . . . e** *cj* both . . . and.
ebanísta *nm* cabinet-maker.
ebanistería *nf* cabinet-maker's shop, cabinet-making.
èbano *nm* ebony.
ebbène *cj* well, well then, what about it?
ebrézza *nf* drunkenness, intoxication, rapture.
èbbro *a* drunk, intoxicated, excited, mad.
èbete *a* dull, stupid; *nm* feeble-minded person.
ebetișmo *nm* feeble-mindedness.
ebollizióne *nf* boiling, ebullition.
ebrèa -o *a* Hebrew, Jewish; *nm* Hebrew, Jew; *nf* Hebrew, Jewess.
ebúrneo *a* of ivory; ivory-white.
eccedènte *a* exceeding, excessive.
eccedènza *nf* excess, surplus.
eccèdere *vti* to exceed, go too far.
eccellènte *a* excellent.
eccellènza *nf* excellence; (*title*) Excellency.
eccèllere *vi* to excel.
eccèlso *a* lofty, sublime.
eccentricità *nf* eccentricity, strangeness.
eccèntrico *pl* **-ici** *a* eccentric; *nm* eccentric person; (*mech*) cam.
eccepíre *vt* to object, except.
eccessívo *a* excessive, immoderate.
eccèsso *nm* excess, overspill.
eccètera *nf* etcetera.
eccètto *prep* except(ing), save, unless.
eccettuàre *vt* to except.
eccezionàle *a* exceptional.
eccezionalménte *ad* exceptionally, extraordinarily.
eccezióne *nf* exception.
eccídio *nm* massacre, slaughter.
eccitàbile *a* excitable.
eccitaménto *nm* **eccitazióne** *nf* excitement.
eccitànte *a* exciting, stimulating; *nm* stimulant.
eccitàre *vt* to excite, rouse, stimulate; **-rsi** *vr* to get excited.
ecclesiàstico *pl* **-ici** *a* ecclesiastic(al), *nm* clergyman, ecclesiastic.
e(c)clissàre *vt* to eclipse, obscure, outdo; **-rsi** *vr* to be eclipsed, disappear, slip away.
ècco *ad* here is, here are, there is (*etc*); *interj* see! look!
echeggiàre *vi* to echo, resound.
eclíssi *nf* eclipse.
èco *pl* **èchi** (*m*) *nf* echo.
economàto *nm* stewardship, steward's office, treasureship, treasurer's office.
economía *nf* economy, saving, thrift; **fàre delle economíe** *vi* to save money.
econòmico *pl* **-ici**; *a* economic(al).
economizzàre *vt* to economize, save.
ecònomo *a* economical, thrifty; *nm* bursar, steward, treasurer.
édera *nf* ivy.
Edgàrdo *nm pr* Edgar.
edícola *nf* news-stand; small chapel; niche.
edificànte *a* edifying.
edificàre *vt* to build; edify.
edifício *nm* building, edifice.
edíle *a* building; **ingegnère e.** building engineer.
edilízia *nf* building, building industry; **edilízio** *a* building.
Edimbúrgo *nf* (*geogr*) Edinburgh.
èdito *a* published.
editóre *nm* publisher, editor.
editríce *af* **càsa e.** publishing house.
edítto *nm* edict.
edizióne *nf* edition.
Edmóndo *nm pr* Edmund, Edmond.
Edoàrdo *nm pr* Edward.
edòtto *a* acquainted (with), aware (of), informed (of).
educandàto *nm* girls' boarding school, convent boarding school.
educàre *vt* to bring up, train, educate.
educatívo *a* educational, instructive.
educàto *a* well-bred, polite, educated.
educazióne *nf* education, training, upbringing, good breeding.
èffe the letter f.
effeminatézza *nf* effeminacy.
effeminàto *a* effeminate, unmanly.
efferatézza *nf* brutality, ferocity.
efferàto *a* brutal, savage.
effervescènte *a* effervescent.
effettívo *a* actual, effective; **effetívi** *nm pl* (*mil*) effectives *pl*.
effètto *nm* effect, result, impression.
effettuàbile *a* practicable, feasible.
effettuàre *vt* to carry out, effect, execute, make, produce; **-rsi** *vr* to take place, happen.
effettuazióne *nf* execution, fulfillment.

efficàce *a* effective, effectual, efficacious.
efficàcia *nf* efficacy, efficaciousness, effectiveness.
efficiènte *a* efficient.
efficiènza *nf* effectiveness, efficiency.
effigiàre *vt* to image, make an effigy of, portray, represent.
effígie *nf* effigy.
effímero *a* ephemeral, fleeting.
efflorescènte *a* efflorescent.
efflússo *a* efflux, outflow.
efflúvio *nm* effluvium.
effóndere *vt* to pour forth, exhale; **-rsi** *vr* to break out into, burst, flow, spread.
effuşióne *nf* effusion, outpouring.
ègida *nf* protection, shelter, shield.
Egídio *nm pr* Giles.
Egítto *nm (geogr)* Egypt.
egiziàno *a nm* Egyptian.
égli *pron* he.
egoíşmo *nm* selfishness, egoism.
egoísta *a* egoistic(al); *nm* egoist.
egrègio *a* egregious, exceptional, remarkable, distinguished.
eguagliànza *nf* equality.
eguagliàre *vt* to (make) equal, level.
eguàle *a* equal, even, like, uniform.
egualménte *ad* equally, alike.
elaboràre *vt* to elaborate, plan, work out.
elargíre *vt* to give liberally, grant, lavish.
elargizióne *nf* donation, generous contribution, gift, grant.
elasticità *nf* elasticity, spring(iness), resilience.
elàstico *pl* **-ici** *a* elastic; *nm* rubber band.
élce *nm* evergreen oak, holm oak.
elefànte *nm* elephant.
elegànte *a* elegant, graceful, (*of speech*) polished.
elegànza *nf* elegance, polish.
elèggere *vt* to choose, elect.
eleggíbile *a* eligible.
elegía *nf* elegy.
elementàre *a* elementary.
eleménto *nm* element, component; -ívi *pl* rudiments *pl*.
elemòşina *nf* alms *pl*, charity.
elemoşinàre *vt* to beg.
elemoşinièra *nf* **-re** *nm* almoner, alms-giver.
Èlena *nf pr* Helen, Helena.
elencàre *vt* to list, catalogue.
elènco *pl* **-chi** *nm* list, catalogue, inventory; **e. telefònico** telephone directory.
Eleonòra *nf pr* Eleanor, Elinor.
elètto *a* chosen, elect, elected.
elettoràle *a* electoral.
elettoràto *nm* electorate, constituency, franchise.
elettóre *nm* **elettríce** *nf* elector.
elettràuto *nm (aut)* electrical repair shop.
elettricísta *nm* electrician.
elettricità *nf* electricity.
elèttrico *pl* **-ici** *a* electric(al).
elettrificàre *vt* to electrify.
elettrizzàre *vt* to electrify, *(fig)* thrill.
elèttrodo *nm* electrode.
elettrodomèstici *nm pl* electrical household appliances *pl*.
elettróne *nm* electron.
elettrotècnica *nf* electrical technology.
elettrotréno *nm* electric train.
elevàre *vt* to elevate, erect, lift, raise; **-rsi** *vr* to make one's way, raise oneself.
elevatézza *nf* elevation, loftiness, nobility.
elevatóre *nm (tec)* elevator.
elevazióne *nf* elevation, raising, rise.
elezióne *nf* election, appointment.
èlica *nf* propeller, screw.
elicòttero *nm* helicopter.
elídere *vt* to elide, suppress.
eliminàre *vt* to eliminate.
eliminatòria *nf (sport)* preliminary heat.
eliminazióne *nf* elimination, removal.
elioterapía *nf* heliotherapy, sun treatment.
eliotròpio *nm* heliotrope.
Elíşa *nf pr* Eliza.
Elişabètta *nf* pr Elizabeth, Elisabeth.
elíso *nm* Elysium; *a* Elysian; elided, suppressed.
elisír *nm* elixir.
élla *pron* she.
èlle the letter l.
ellèboro *nm* Christmas rose, hellebore.
ellísse *nf* ellipse.
ellíssi *nf* ellipsis.
ellíttico *pl* **-ici** *a* elliptic(al).
élmo *nm* helmet.
elocuzióne *nf* elocution.
elogiàre *vt* to praise, commend, eulogize.
elògio *nm* commendation, eulogy.
eloquènte *a* eloquent, fluent.
eloquènza *nf* eloquence.
elòquio *nm* speech.
èlsa *nf (of a sword)* hilt.
elucubràre *vt* to meditate on.
elúdere *vt* to avoid, elude, escape.
eluşívo *a* elusive, evasive.
elvètico *pl* **-ici** *a nm* Helvetic, Helvetian, Swiss.
elzevíro *a nm (typ)* Elzevir; leading literary article in a newspaper.
emaciàrsi *vr* to become emaciated.
emaciàto *a* emaciated.
emanàre *vt* to issue, exhale; *vi* emanate, proceed.
emanazióne *nf* emanation, efflux, issuing.
emancipàre *vt* to emancipate, free; **-rsi** *vr* to get emancipated, free oneself.
emancipazióne *nf* emancipation.

Emanuèle *nm pr* Emmanuel, Immanuel.
embàrgo *nm* (*naut*) embargo.
emblèma *nm* emblem, symbol.
embolía *nf* (*med*) embolism.
embolişmo *nm* (*astr*) embolism.
embrióne *nm* embryo.
emendaménto *nm* **emendazióne** *nf* amendment, amendation, correction.
emendàre *vt* to amend, emend; **-rsi** *vr* to amend.
emergènza *nf* emergency, exigency.
emèrgere *vi* to emerge, stand out.
emèrito *a* emeritus.
emètico *pl* **-ici** *a nm* emetic.
eméttere *vt* to emit, express, give out, issue.
emicrània *nf* headache.
emigrànte *a nmf* emigrant.
emigràre *vi* to emigrate.
emigràto *nm* emigrant, exile, refugee.
emigrazióne *nf* emigration; migration.
Emília *nf pr* Emily, Emilia; **Emílio** *nm pr* Emil.
eminènte *a* eminent, high.
eminènza *nf* eminence.
emisfèro *nm* hemisphere.
emissàrio *nm* emissary.
emissióne *nf* emission, issue.
emittènte *a* issuing; *nm* issuer; **bànca e.** bank of issue; **stazióne e.** (*rad etc*) sending station.
èmme the letter m.
emofilía *nf* hemophilia.
emorragía *nf* hemorrhage.
emorròidi *nm pl* (*med*) hemorrhoids *pl*, piles *pl*.
emotívo *a* emotional, sensitive.
emozionànte *a* exciting, thrilling.
emozionàre *vt* to move, excite.
emozióne *nf* emotion.
émpiere *v* **empíre.**
empietà *nf* impiety, cruelty.
émpio *a* impious, cruel.
empíre *vt* to cram, fill (up).
empírico *pl* **-ici** *a* empiric(al); *nm* empiric, empiricist; quack.
empiríşmo *nm* empiricism.
empòrio *nm* emporium, department store, vast collection.
emulàre *vt* to emulate, vie (with).
emulazióne *nf* emulation, rivalry.
èmulo *a nm* rival, competitor.
emulsióne *nf* emulsion.
encíclica *nf* encyclic(al).
enciclopedía *nf* encyclopedia.
encomiàbile *a* commendable, praiseworthy.
encòmio *nm* encomium, praise; (*mil*) mention in dispatches, citation.
endèmico *pl* **-ici** *a* endemic.
endovenóso *a* intravenous.
Enèa *nm pr* Aeneas.
energía *nf* energy.
enèrgico *pl* **-ici** *a* energetic, powerful.
energúmeno *nm* madman, one possessed.
ènfaşi *nf* emphasis, stress.
enfiagióne *nf* swelling.
enfiàre *vi* **-rsi** *vr* to swell.
enígma *nm* enigma, riddle.
enigmística *nf* **libro di e.** book of riddles and puzzles.
ennèşimo *a* (*math*) nth.
enòrme *a* enormous, huge, incredible.
enormità *nf* hugeness, enormity, nonsense.
Enrichétta *nf pr* Henrietta.
Enríco *nm pr* Henry, Harry.
ènte *nm* being, organization.
entèrico *pl* **-ici** *a* enteric.
enteríte *nf* (*med*) enteritis.
entità *nf* entity, existence, importance.
entomología *nf* entomology.
entràmbi *pron and a pl* both *pl*.
entrànte *a* next, coming.
entràre *vi* to come in, enter, go in, have to do with.
entràta *nf* entrance, entry, admission; income, (*com*) receipts *pl*, revenue.
entratúra *nf* entrance; familiar terms.
èntro *prep* within.
entuşiaşmàre *vt* to enrapture; **-rsi** *vr* to become enthusiastic.
entuşiàşmo *nm* enthusiasm, rapture.
entusiàsta *nmf* enthusiast.
entuşiàstico *pl* **-ici** *a* enthusiastic.
enumeràre *vt* to enumerate.
enunciàre *vt* to enunciate, state, utter.
epàtico *pl* **-ici** *a* (*med*) hepatic, of the liver.
èpico *pl* **èpici** *a* epic, heroic.
epicureíşmo *nm* epicureanism.
epicurèo *a* epicurean; *nm* epicure.
epidemía *nf* epidemic.
epidèrmide *nf* (*med*) epidermis, (outer) skin.
Epifanía *nf* Epiphany.
epígono *nm* imitator, follower; descendant.
epígrafe *nf* epigraph, inscription.
epigràmma *nm* epigram.
epilatòrio *a* depilatory.
epilessía *nf* (*med*) epilepsy.
epilèttico *pl* **-ici** *a nm* epileptic.
epilogàre *v* **riepilogàre.**
epílogo *pl* **-ghi** *nm* epilogue.
episcopàle *a* episcopal.
episcopàto *nm* episcopacy; episcopate.
epişòdio *nm* episode.
epístola *nf* epistle.
epíteto *nm* epithet.
època *nf* epoch, time.
eppúre *cj* and yet, however, nevertheless.
epuràre *vt* to purify, refine, remove, purge.
epurazióne *nf* purge, removal (from office), purification.
equànime *a* calm, tranquil, well-balanced.

equanimità *nf* equanimity, composure.
equatóre *nm* equator.
equazióne *nf* equation.
equèstre *a* equestrian.
equilibràre *vt* to balance, poise.
equilíbrio *nm* balance, equilibrium.
equilibrísta *nmf* tightrope-walker.
equinòzio *nm* equinox.
equipaggiaménto *nm* equipment, rigging.
equipaggiàre *vt* to equip, fit out; (*naut*) man.
equipàggio *nm* (*naut*) crew, equipage.
equiparàre *vt* to make equal, compare.
equipollènte *a* equivalent.
equità *nf* equity, fairness, impartiality, justice.
equitazióne *nf* riding, horsemanship.
equivalènte *a nm* equivalent.
equivalènza *nf* equivalence.
equivalére *vi* to be equivalent.
equivocàre *vi* to equivocate, make a mistake, misunderstand.
equívoco *pl* **-oci** *a* equivocal, ambiguous; *nm* misunderstanding.
èquo *a* equitable, fair, impartial, just.
èra *nf* era, epoch, age.
eràrio *nm* exchequer, public treasury.
èrba *nf* grass, herb; **in e.** *a* green, immature.
erbàccia *nf* weed.
erbàggio *nm pl* pot herbs *pl*, vegetables *pl*.
erbaiòlo *nm* costermonger, street vendor of vegetables and fruit.
erbàrio *nm* herbarium.
erbivèndolo *nm* vegetable dealer.
erborísta *nm* herborist.
erbóso *a* grassy.
erède *nm* heir.
eredità *nf* heritage, inheritance, heredity.
ereditàre *vt* to inherit.
ereditàrio *a* hereditary; **príncipe e.** crown prince.
ereditièra *nf* heiress.
eremíta *nm* hermit.
eremitàggio, èremo *nm* hermitage.
eresía *nf* heresy.
erètico *pl* **-ici** *a* heretical; *nm* heretic.
erètto *a* erect; built; founded.
erezióne *nf* erection.
ergàstolo *nm* galleys *pl*, life sentence.
èrica *nf* heath, heather.
erígere *vt* to erect, raise, institute; **-rsi** *vr* to raise oneself, set up for.
Eritrèa *nf* (*geogr*) Eritrea.
eritrèo *a nm* Eritrean.
ermellíno *nm* ermine.
ermètico *pl* **-ici** *a* hermetic, airtight; (*fig*) secret.
ermetismo *nm* obscurity; (*liter*) a modern Italian school of poetry.
èrmo *a* (*poet*) lonely, solitary; *v* **solitàrio.**
Ernèsto *nm pr* Ernest.
èrnia *nf* (*med*) hernia, rupture; **e. del dísco** slipped disc.
Eròde *nm pr* Herod.
eròe *nm* hero.
erogàre *vt* to bestow, lay out.
eròico *pl* **-ici** *a* heroic.
eroína *nf* heroine; (*drug*) heroin.
eroismo *nm* heroism.
erómpere *vi* to break out, burst out, flow, rush out.
erosióne *nf* erosion.
eròtico *pl* **-ici** *a* erotic.
erotismo *nm* eroticism.
érpice *nm* harrow.
errànte *a* errant, wandering.
erràre *vi* to wander, rove, roam, err.
erràto *a* wrong.
èrre the letter r.
erròneo *a* erroneous, faulty, incorrect.
erròre *nm* blunder, error, mistake.
èrta *nf* slope, steep ascent.
èrto *a* steep.
erudíre *vt* to instruct, teach; **-rsi** *vr* to acquire knowledge, become learned.
erudíto *a* learned, scholarly; *nm* scholar.
erudizióne *nf* erudition.
eruttàre *vti* (*of volcano*) erupt, eject, belch.
eruzióne *nf* eruption.
esacerbàre *vt* to embitter, exacerbate.
esageràre *vti* to exaggerate.
esagerazióne *nf* exaggeration.
esalàre *vti* to exhale, give out.
esalazióne *nf* exhalation.
esaltàre *vt* to exalt, praise; **-rsi** *vr* to get excited, become elated.
esaltàto *a* excited, elated, hotheaded; *nm* hot-head, fanatic.
esàme *nm* examination, investigation; **commissióne di e.** board of examiners.
esaminàre *vt* to examine, inspect, investigate, survey, test.
esaminatóre, *f* **-tríce** *a* examining; *nm* examiner.
esàngue *a* bloodless.
esànime *a* lifeless, dead.
esasperàre *vt* to exasperate; **-rsi** *vr* to get exasperated.
esasperazióne *nf* exasperation.
esattézza *nf* accuracy, exactness, exactitude, punctuality.
esàtto *a* accurate, exact, precise, punctual.
esattóre *nm* **-tríce** *nf* (*of taxes etc*) collector.
esattoría *nf* Revenue Office.
esaudiménto *nm* satisfaction, fulfillment.
esaudíre *vt* to consent, grant, fulfill, satisfy.
esauriènte *a* exhaustive.
esauriménto *nm* exhaustion, depletion; **e. nervóso** nervous breakdown.
esauríre *vt* to exhaust, use up, wear

out; **-rsi** *vr* to exhaust oneself, run out, run dry.
eșauríto *a* exhausted, worn out, sold out, out of print.
eșàusto *a* exhausted.
eșautoràre *vt* to deprive of authority.
eșazióne *nf* collection, exaction.
èsca *nf* bait, decoy, enticement; tinder (for a lighter).
escandescènte *a* choleric, hot-tempered.
escandescènza *nf* outburst, sudden burst of rage.
escavazióne *nf* excavation.
eschimése *a nmf* Eskimo.
esclamàre *vi* to cry out, exclaim.
esclamazióne *nf* exclamation.
esclúdere *vt* to except, exclude, leave out, bar.
esclușióne *nf* exclusion, omission.
esclușíva *nf* patent, exclusive right.
esclușività *nf* exclusiveness.
esclușívo *a* exclusive, sole.
esclúșo *a* excluded, excepted.
escogitàre *vt* to contrive, devise, excogitate.
escoriàre *vt* to graze, excoriate.
escoriazióne *nf* abrasion, graze
escursióne *nf* excursion, trip.
escursionísta *nmf* excursionist.
eșecràre *vt* to execrate.
eșecrazióne *nf* execration.
eșecutívo *a* executive, executory; *nm* executive.
eșecutóre *a* executory; *nm* **-tríce** *nf* executor, performer, executioner.
eșecuzióne *nf* **eșeguiménto** *nm* execution, performance.
eșeguíre *vt* to accomplish, carry out, execute, fulfill, perform.
eșémpio *nm* example, instance, pattern, precedent.
eșemplàre *a* exemplary, model; *nm* specimen, (*of a book*) copy; model.
eșemplificàre *vt* to exemplify.
eșentàre *vt* to excuse, exempt, exonerate, free; **-rsi** *vr* to free oneself.
eșènte *a* exempt, free.
eșenzióne *nf* exemption (*eccl*) dispensation.
eșèquie *nf pl* burial, funeral, obsequies *pl*.
eșercènte *nm* dealer, shopkeeper, trader.
eșercíre *vt* to carry on, keep, practice; **non e. piú** *vi* to have given up (business or practice).
eșercitàre *vt* to exercise, practice, train; **-rsi** *vr* to practice.
eșèrcito *nm* army.
eșercízio *nm* exercise, practice, management, drill; (financial) year.
eșibíre *vt* to display, exhibit, show; **-rsi** *vr* to offer oneself, show oneself.
eșibizióne *nf* exhibition, show.
eșibizionísta *nmf* exhibitionist.
eșigènte *a* exacting, exigent, hard to please.
eșigènza *nf* exigence, exigency, demand, requirement.
eșígere *vt* to exact, require, demand.
eșiguità *nf* exiguity, scantiness.
eșíguo *a* exiguous, slender, scanty.
eșilarànte *a* exhilarating; cheering.
eșilaràre *vt* to cheer up, exhilarate.
èșile *a* slender, slim.
eșiliàre *vt* to banish, exile; **-rsi** *vr* to exile oneself, withdraw from.
eșiliàto *a* exiled; *nm* exile.
eșílio *nm* exile (state).
eșilità *nf* slenderness, weakness.
eșímere *vt* to exempt, excuse; **-rsi** *vr* to excuse oneself, evade.
eșímio *a* excellent, eminent, distinguished.
eșistènte *a* existing, existent, extant.
eșistènza *nf* existence, life; (*com*) stock.
eșístere *vi* to exist, be, be extant.
eșitàre *vi* to hesitate, waver; *vt* (*com*) to sell, dispose of.
èșito *nm* result, outcome, issue, denouement; sale.
eșizièle *a* baneful, fatal.
èșodo *nm* exodus, flight.
eșòfago *nm* esophagus, gullet.
eșoneràre *vt* to exempt, exonerate, free, release, relieve.
eșònero *nm* dispensation, exemption, exoneration.
eșorbitànte *a* exorbitant, excessive.
eșorcizzàre *vt* to exorcize.
esordiènte *a* beginning; *nmf* beginner, novice.
eșòrdio *nm* beginning, exordium.
eșordíre *vi* to begin, start.
eșortàre *vt* to admonish, exhort.
eșortazióne *nf* exhortation.
eșòșo *a* greedy, hateful.
eșòtico *pl* **-ici** *a* exotic, foreign.
espàndere *vt* to spread; **-rsi** *vr* to expand, open one's heart.
espansióne *nf* expansion, demonstration of affection.
espansività *nf* effusiveness.
espansívo *a* expansive, unreserved.
espatriàre *vt* to banish, exile; *vi* to emigrate.
espàtrio *nm* expatriation.
espediènte *a nm* expedient.
espèllere *vt* to expel.
esperiènza *nf* experience; experiment.
esperimentàre *vt* to experience; experiment, test.
esperiménto *nm* experiment, test.
esperíre *vt* to carry out; (*leg*) try.
espèrto *a* experienced; *nm* expert.
espettoràre *vt* to cough up, expectorate.
espiàre *vt* to atone, expiate, make amends for.
espiazióne *nf* amends *pl*, atonement, expiation.
espletàre *vt* to fulfill, accomplish, dispatch.
esplicàre *vt* to develop; explain; **e. un'attività** to carry on an activity.

esplícito *a* clear, explicit, express.
esplòdere *vi* to blow up, burst out, explode.
esploràre *vt* to examine, explore, search, (*mil*) reconnoiter.
esploratóre *nm* explorer, (*mil*) scout; **gióvane e.** (Boy) Scout; **esploratríce** *nf* explorer; **gióvane e.** Girl Guide, Girl Scout.
esplorazióne *nf* exploration, (*mil*) reconnaissance.
esploṣióne *nf* blowing up, discharge, explosion.
esploṣívo *a nm* explosive.
esponènte *nm* exponent.
espórre *vt* to show, exhibit, explain, expose, risk; **-rsi** *vr* to expose oneself, run the risk.
esportàre *vt* to export.
esportatóre *a* exporting; *nm* **esportatríce** *nf* exporter.
esportazióne *nf* export, exportation.
espoṣímetro *nm* (*phot*) exposure meter.
espoṣizióne *nf* exposure, exhibition, exposition, statement.
espósto *nm* statement, petition; foundling.
espressióne *nf* expression.
espressívo *a* expressive, meaningful.
esprèsso *a* express, expressed, precise; *nm* (*letter, parcel, train*) express, special delivery.
esprímere *vt* to declare, express, signify, utter.
espropriàre *vt* to expropriate, dispossess.
espropriazióne *nf* expropriation.
espugnàre *vt* to (take by) storm.
espulsióne *nf* banishment, expulsion.
espúngere *vt* to expunge, delete.
espurgàre *vt* to expurgate.
espurgazióne *nf* expurgation.
éssa *pron* she.
èsse *nm* the letter s.
essènza *nf* essence.
essenziàle *a* essential, main, principal.
èssere *vi* to be, exist, happen, occur; **e. di** to belong to; **e. per** to be on the point of; *nm* being, state, condition.
essiccàre *vt* to dry; **-rsi** *vr* to dry up.
ésso *pron* he.
èst *nm* east.
èstaṣi *nf* ecstasy, rapture.
estaṣiàre *vt* to enrapture, delight; **-rsi** *vr* to be enraptured.
estàte *nf* summer.
estàtico *pl* **-ici** *a* ecstatic.
estemporàneo *a* extemporaneous, extempore, unscripted; **estemporaneamènte** *ad* impromptu, ad lib.
estèndere *vt* to extend, expand; **-rsi** *vr* to extend, stretch.
estensióne *nf* extension, expanse, extent, range.
estenuàre *vt* exhaust; **-rsi** *vr* to become exhausted, weak.
estenuazióne *nf* exhaustion.
Èster *nf pr* Esther.
esterióre *a* exterior, external, outward; *nm* exterior.
esterminàre *vt* to exterminate.
esternàre *vt* to disclose, express, open.
estèrno *a* external, outer; *nm* outside.
èstero *a* foreign; *nm* foreign countries *pl*; **all'e.** abroad.
esterrefàtto *a* terrified, amazed.
estesaménte *ad* extensively.
estéso *a* large, wide, extensive.
estètica *nf* aesthetics *pl*.
estètico *pl* **-ici** *a* aesthetic(al).
èstimo *nm* estimate, valuation, land tax.
estínguere *vt* to extinguish, put out; pay off; **-rsi** *vr* to go out, come to an end, die.
estínto *a* extinguished, deceased; *nm* deceased (person).
estintóre *nm* extinguisher.
estinzióne *nf* extinction, putting out; paying off.
estirpàre *vt* to extirpate, pull out, uproot.
estirpazióne *nf* extirpation, uprooting.
èstone *a nmf* Esthonian.
Estònia *nf* (*geogr*) Esthonia.
estòrcere *vt* to extort.
estorsióne *nf* extortion.
estradizióne *nf* extradition.
estràneo *a* extraneous, not related, alien, foreign; *nm* stranger, foreigner.
estràrre *vt* to dig out, draw out, extract.
estràtto *nm* extract, excerpt, certificate; **e. cónto** (*com*) statement of account.
estrazióne *nf* extraction, digging out; **e. a sòrte** drawing lots.
estremaménte *ad* extremely.
estremità *nf* extremity, end.
estrèmo *a* extreme, farthest; intense, severe; *nm* extremity, extreme.
estrinsecàre *vt* to express, manifest.
estrínseco *pl* **-sechi, -seci** *a* extrinsic.
èstro *nm* inspiration, fancy, freak.
estróso *a* capricious, freakish, whimsical.
estrovèrso *a* extroverted; *nm* extrovert.
estuàrio *nm* estuary, firth.
eṣuberànte *a* exuberant, overflowing.
eṣulàre *vi* to go into exile.
eṣulceràre *vt* to produce sores.
èṣule *nmf* exile (person).
eṣultànte *a* exultant, rejoicing.
eṣultàre *vi* to exult, rejoice.
eṣumazióne *nf* exhumation.
età *nf* age.
ètere *nm* ether.
etèreo *a* airy, ethereal, impalpable.
eternàre *vt* to eternalize, make

endless; **-rsi** *vr* to become eternal, last for ever.
eternità *nf* eternity.
etèrno *a* eternal, everlasting.
ètica *nf* ethics *pl*.
etichétta *nf* etiquette; label.
ètico *pl* **ètici** *a* ethical; (*med*) consumptive.
etimología *nf* etymology.
etimològico *pl* **-ici** *a* etymological.
Etiòpia *nf* (*geogr*) Ethiopia.
etiòpico *pl* **-ici** *a nm* Ethiopian.
etişía *nf* (*med*) consumption.
ètnico *pl* **-ici** *a* ethnic(al).
etrúsco *pl* **-chi** *a nm* Etruscan.
èttaro *nm* hectare (2.47 acres).
Èttore *nm pr* Hector.
Eucaristía *nf* Eucharist.
eufemía *nf* euphemism.
eufemíşmo *nm* euphemism.
eufonía *nf* euphony.
euforía *nf* euphoria, light-heartedness.
eufòrico *pl* **-ici** *a* euphoric, elated.
eugàneo *a* (*geogr*) Euganean.
Eugènio *nm pr* Eugene.
eunúco *pl* **-chi** *nm* eunuch.
Euròpa *nf* (*geogr*) Europe.
europèo *a nm* European.
Èva *nf pr* Eve, Eva.
evacuàre *vt* to clear out, evacuate.
evàdere *vt* to dispatch; evade; *vi* to escape.
evanescènte *a* fading, evanescent.
evanescènza *nf* evanescence; (*rad, tv*) fading.
evangeliẓẓàre *vt* to evangelize.
evangèlo *nm* gospel.
evaporàre *vi* to evaporate.
evaporazióne *nf* evaporation.
evaşióne *nf* escape, evasion.
evaşívo *a* evasive.
eveniènza *nf* contingency, eventuality.
evènto *nm* event, result, outcome; **in ógni e.** at all events.
eventuàle *a* eventual, possible.
evidènte *a* clear, evident, obvious, plain.
evidènza *nf* clearness, evidence, obviousness.
evitàbile *a* avoidable, preventable.
evitàre *vt* to avoid, escape, spare.
evizióne *nf* eviction; recovery of possession.
èvo *nm* age, period, time.
evocàre *vt* to evoke, recall, conjure up.
evoluzióne *nf* evolution.
evvíva *interj* hurrah! long live!
extraconiugàle *a* extramarital.
extraterritorialità *nf* extraterritoriality.

F

fa *ad* ago; *nm* (*mus*) fa, F.
fabbişógno *nm* needs *pl*, requirement; (*com*) estimate of expenditure.
fàbbrica *nf* factory, manufactory, works *pl*, plant; manufacture; building.
fabbricànte *nm* manufacturer; builder.
fabbricàre *vt* to build, manufacture, fabricate.
fabbricàto *nm* building.
fabbricazióne *nf* manufacture; building; invention, forgery.
fàbbro *nm* blacksmith, smith.
fabbroferràio *nm* blacksmith.
faccènda *nf* affair, business, matter.
facchinàggio *nm* porterage.
facchíno *nm* porter.
fàccia *nf* face; **f. tòsta** impudence.
facciàta *nf* façade, front, (*of a page*) side.
facèto *a* facetious.
facèzia *nf* jest, joke, witticism.
fàcile *a* easy.
facilità *nf* facility, ease, easiness.
facilitàre *vt* to facilitate, make easy.
facilménte *ad* easily.
facoltà *nf* faculty, authority, power.
facoltatívo *a* optional.
facoltóso *a* wealthy, well-to-do.
facóndia *nf* eloquence, fluency.
facóndo *a* eloquent, fluent, talkative.
fàggio *nm* beech-tree.
fagiàno *nm* pheasant.
fagiolíno *nm* French bean, string bean.
fagiòlo *nm* kidney-bean; (*fig*) blockhead.
fàglia *nf* (*silk material*) faille.
fagòtto *nm* bundle; (*mus*) bassoon; **fàre f.** *vi* to pack up.
faína *nf* beech marten.
fàlce *nf* scythe, sickle.
falciàre *vt* to cut down, mow.
falciatóre *nm* mower; **-tríce** *nf* mower, mowing machine; **f. da pràto** lawn-mower.
fàlco *pl* **-chi, falcóne** *nm* falcon, hawk.
falconàra *nf* falcon-house; loophole.
fàlda *nf* (snow)flake, layer, slice, slope, (*of hat*) brim, (*of coat*) tail, (*of mountain*) base, foot.
falegnàme *nm* carpenter, joiner.
falèna *nf* moth; flake of ashes.
fàlla *nf* (*naut*) leak.
fallàce *a* deceptive, fallacious.
falliménto *nm* bankruptcy, failure, insolvency.
fallíre *vi* to fail, go bankrupt; *vt* to miss.
fallíto *a* insolvent, unsuccessful; *nm* bankrupt, failure.
fàllo *nm* fault, defect.
falò *nm* bonfire.

falsàre *vt* to alter, distort, falsify.
falsaríga *pl* **-ríghe** *nf* a guide to writing straight; (*fig*) model, example.
falsàrio *nm* forger.
falsificàre *vt* to falsify, forge, misrepresent.
falsificazióne *nf* falsification, forgery.
falsità *nf* falsity, falsehood.
fàlso *a* false, wrong, forged, fictitious, deceitful; (*of door etc*) blind; *nm* falsehood, forgery, error.
fàma *nf* fame, renown, reputation.
fàme *nf* hunger; **avére f.** to be hungry.
famèlico *pl* **-ici** *a* famishing, starving.
famigeràto *a* notorious.
famíglia *nf* family, household.
familiàre *a* domestic, familiar, informal; *nm* relative, intimate, friend, manservant.
familiarità *nf* familiarity, intimacy.
familiarizzàre *vt* to familiarize; **-rsi** *vr* to become familiar.
famóso *a* famous, renowned, well-known.
fanàle *nm* lamp, lantern; (*aut*) light, lamp; **fanàli di posizióne** parking lights.
fanalíno *nm* **f. di códa** (*av*) tail-light; (*aut*) rear light.
fanàtico *pl* **-ici** *a nm* fanatic.
fanatísmo *nm* fanaticism.
fanciúlla *nf* young girl; **fanciúllo** *nm* young boy.
fanciullàggine *nf* childishness.
fanciullésco *pl* **-chi** *a* childish.
fanciullézza *nf* childhood.
fandònia *nf* lie, idle story, tall tale.
fanfàra *nf* brass band, fanfare.
fanghíglia *nf* slush, sludge.
fàngo *nm* mud, mire.
fangóso *a* muddy, miry.
fannullóne *nm* idler, lazybones.
fantasciènza *nf* science fiction.
fantasía *nf* imagination, fancy, fantasy; **gioièlli f.** costume jewelry.
fantàsma *nm* ghost, phantom, phantasm.
fantasticàre *vi* to build castles in the air, daydream.
fantástico *pl* **-ici** *a* fantastic; fanciful; wonderful.
fànte *nm* foot-soldier; (*at cards*) jack.
fantería *nf* infantry.
fantíno *nm* jockey.
fantòccio *nm* puppet (*also fig*).
farabútto *nm* rascal, scoundrel.
faraóne *nm* Pharaoh; (game of) faro.
farcíre *vi* to stuff.
fardèllo *nm* bundle, burden.
fàre *vti* to do, make; have, take, take on, appoint, deem, perform, play, bear, cause; **f. attenzióne** to pay attention; **f. bel tèmpo** to be fine; **f. il bàgno** to take a bath; **f. il mèdico** to be a doctor; **f. fàre una còsa** to have a thing done; **f. lavoràre una persóna** to make a person work; **-rsi** *vr* to become, grow, make oneself, turn; **f. fràte** to turn monk; **f. capíre** to make oneself understood; **f. vedére** to show oneself; *nm* behavior, manner.
farfàlla *nf* butterfly.
farína *nf* flour, meal.
farinàceo *a* farinaceous.
faríngе *nf* pharynx.
farinóso *a* floury, mealy.
farisèo *nm* Pharisee.
farmacèutica *nf* pharmaceutics *pl*.
farmacía *nf* chemist's shop, drugstore, pharmacy.
farmacísta *nm* druggist, pharmacist.
farneticàre *vi* to be delirious, rave; (*fig*) talk nonsense.
fàro *nm* lighthouse.
farràgine *nf* farrago, medley.
fàrsa *nf* farce.
farsésco *a* farcical.
fàscia *nf* band, bandage, cover, swaddling band.
fasciàme *nm* (*tec*) plating, planking.
fasciàre *vt* to bandage, swaddle, wrap.
fasciatúra *nf* bandaging, swaddling; (*wound*) dressing.
fascícolo *nm* (*of a publication*) number; dossier.
fascína *nf* fagot, (*mil*) fascine.
fàscino *nm* charm, fascination.
fàscio *nm* bundle, pile; (*of light*) beam; fasces *pl*.
fascísmo *nm* Fascism.
fascísta *a nmf* Fascist.
fàse *nf* phase, stage, (*aut*) stroke.
fastèllo *nm* bundle of wood, faggot.
fastídio *nm* annoyance, trouble, vexation.
fastidióso *a* annoying, troublesome, intolerant.
fàsto *nm* pomp, splendor, display.
fastóso *a* gorgeous, splendid, ostentatious.
fasúllo *a* false.
fàta *nf* fairy; **paése delle fàte** fairy-land.
fatàle *a* fatal; fated, inevitable.
fatalità *nf* fatality; destiny, fate.
fatíca *nf* fatigue, weariness, hard work, difficulty; **a f.** with difficulty.
faticàre *vi* to toil, work hard.
faticóso *a* exhausting, fatiguing.
fàto *nm* destiny, doom, fate, lot.
fàtta *nf* kind, sort; deed.
fattèzze *nf pl* features *pl*.
fattíbile *a* feasible, practicable.
fattívo *a* effective, active, efficient.
fàtto *a* done, made; ripe, fullgrown, fit; *nm* fact, deed, action, event, matter.
fattóre *nm*, **-tóra, -torèssa** *nf* factor, bailiff, land agent; (*in this sense* **-trice** *f*) maker.
fattoría *nf* farm, land agency, ranch.
fattoríno *nm* message-boy, messenger, page, bellboy (bellhop).

fattúra *nf* make, work, making, workmanship; bill, invoice.
fàtuo *a* conceited, fatuous; **fuòco f.** will-o'-the-wisp.
fàuna *nf* fauna.
fàuno *nm* faun.
fàusto *a* propitious, happy, lucky.
Fàusto *nm pr* Faust, Faustus.
fautóre *nm* **-tríce** *nf* supporter, favorer, protector.
fàva *nf* bean, broad bean.
favèlla *nf* language, speech, tongue.
favellàre *vi* to speak, talk.
favílla *nf* spark.
fàvo *nm* honeycomb.
fàvola *nf* fable, tale, story; laughing stock.
favolóso *a* fabulous.
favóre *nm* favor, kindness, approval; **cambiàle di f.** accommodation bill.
favoreggiàre *vt* to back, favor, support.
favorévole *a* favorable, propitious, well-disposed.
favorevolménte *ad* favorably.
favoríre *vt* to favor, foster, oblige, promote.
favoríto *a* favorite; *nm* favorite; **favoríti** *pl* side whiskers *pl*.
fazióne *nf* faction, party; (*mil*) guard.
fazióso *a* factious, seditious.
fazzolétto *nm* handkerchief.
febbràio *nm* February.
fébbre *nf* fever, temperature; **avére la f.** to have (run) a temperature.
febbríle *a* feverish (*also fig*).
fèccia *nf* dregs *pl*, scum, sediment.
fèci *nf pl* (*med*) stool.
fecondàre *vt* to fecundate, fertilize.
fecondazióne *nf* fecundation; **f. artificiàle** artificial insemination.
fecóndo *a* fecund, fertile, fruitful.
féde *nf* faith, creed, trust, belief, honesty; wedding ring, certificate; **f. di nàscita** birth certificate.
fedéle *a* faithful, loyal, true; *nmf* believer, follower.
fedeltà *nf* faithfulness, fidelity, loyalty.
fèdera *nf* pillow-case.
federàto *a* federate.
federazióne *nf* confederacy, federation.
Federíco *nm pr* Frederic(k).
fedína *nf* police record; whisker.
fégato *nm* liver; (*fig*) courage.
félce *nf* fern.
feld-maresciàllo *nm* (*mil*) field-marshal.
felíce *a* happy, lucky.
feliceménte *ad* happily.
felicità *nf* happiness, felicity.
felicitàrsi *vr* to congratulate.
felicitazióne *nf* congratulation.
felíno *a* feline.
féltro *nm* felt.
fémmina *nf* female, (*contemptuous*) woman.
femmíneo *a* womanly, womanish, effeminate.
femminíle *a* feminine, womanly.
fèndere *vt* to cleave, cut open, split; **-rsi** *vr* to burst, crack, split.
fendinébbia *nm* (*aut*) fog light.
fenditúra *nf* cleft, crack, split.
feníce *nf* (*myth*) phoenix (*also fig*).
fènico *pl* **-ici** *a* carbolic, phenic.
fenicòttero *nm* flamingo.
fenòmeno *nm* phenomenon.
feràce *a* fertile, fruitful, rich (*also fig*).
feràle *a* of death, tragic.
Ferdinàndo *nm pr* Ferdinand.
fèretro *nm* bier, coffin.
fèria *nf* holiday, vacation.
feriàle *a* working; **giórno f.** working day, weekday.
feriménto *nm* wounding.
feríre *vt* to hurt, wound.
feríta *nf* wound, injury, hurt.
feritóia *nf* loophole, embrasure; (*mech*) vent.
férma *nf* (*mil*) service, term of service; (*hunting*) pointing.
fermàglio *nm* brooch, clip, fastener.
fermaménte *ad* firmly, decidedly, positively.
fermàre *vti* to stop, fasten, fix, hold; **-rsi** *vr* to stay, stop, dwell on.
fermàta *nf* halt, stop, pause.
fermentàre *vi* to ferment, leaven.
fermentazióne *nf* fermentation.
ferménto *nm* ferment, leaven.
fermézza *nf* firmness, steadiness.
férmo *a* firm, steady, still; *nm* firmness; (*mech*) catch, stop; (*leg*) provisional arrest; **f. pòsta** poste restante, general delivery.
feròce *a* ferocious, fierce.
feròcia *pl* **-cie** *nf* ferocity, fierceness, savagery.
ferragósto *nm* August holiday (Aug 15th).
ferraménta *nf* hardware, ironmongery, iron fittings.
ferraménto *nm* iron tool.
ferràre *vt* to add iron fittings, shoe (a horse).
ferràto *a* iron-plated, shod; **stràda ferràta** railway.
fèrreo *a* (of) iron; hard, inflexible.
ferrièra *nf* ironworks *pl*, iron foundry, iron mine.
fèrro *nm* iron; *pl* irons, chains; **f. di cavàllo** horseshoe; **f. da càlza** knitting needle; **f. da stíro** (flat) iron; **età del f.** iron age; **lavóro in f.** ironwork.
ferrovía *nf* railway, railroad; **f. sotterrànea** underground, subway.
ferroviàrio *a* (of the) railway; **oràrio f.** *nm* timetable.
ferrovière *nm* railwayman, railroader.
fèrtile *a* fertile, fruitful, prolific.
fertilità *nf* fertility, fruitfulness (*also fig*).

fertilizzànte *a* fertilizing; *nm* fertilizer.
fertilizzàre *vt* to fertilize.
fervènte *a* burning, ardent, fervent.
fèrvere *vi* to be hot.
fèrvido *a* fervent, ardent, fervid.
fervóre *nm* ardor, fervor, zeal.
fesserìa *nf* stupidity (in actions or words).
fésso *a* cleft, cracked; *nm* fool.
fessúra *nf* crack, crevice, fissure, split.
fèsta *nf* feast, festivity, holiday, merry-making, saint's day, birthday.
festeggiàre *vt* to celebrate, feast, give a feast for, solemnize, welcome.
festévole *a* festive, joyous.
festíno *nm* entertainment, party.
festivàl *nm* festival.
festività *nf* festivity, gaiety.
festívo *a* festive.
festóso *a* gay, merry.
feticcio *nm* fetish.
fèto *nm* fetus.
fétta *nf* slice.
fettúccia *nf* tape, ribbon.
fettuccíne *nf pl* noodles.
feudàle *a* feudal.
fèudo *nm* feud, fief.
fiàba *nf* fairy tale, story.
fiàcca *nf* weariness; laziness.
fiaccàre *vt* to exhaust, fatigue, wear out; **-rsi** *vr* to become tired, weak.
fiaccheràio *nm* cabman.
fiacchézza *nf* fatigue, lassitude, weakness, weariness.
fiàcco *pl* **-cchi** *a* exhausted, feeble, tired, weary.
fiàccola *nf* torch.
fiaccolàta *nf* torchlight procession.
fiàla *nf* phial, vial.
fiàmma *nf* flame, blaze; (*naut*) pennant.
fiammànte *a* flaming, glowing, bright; **nuòvo f.** brand new.
fiammàta *nf* blaze, fire.
fiammeggiàre *vi* to blaze, flame, shine.
fiammífero *nm* match.
fiammíngo *pl* **-ghi** *a* Flemish; *nm* Fleming; (the) Flemish (language).
fiancheggiàre *vt* to flank, help, support, border.
fiànco *pl* **-chi** *nm* hip, side, flank.
Fiàndre *nf pl* Flanders.
fiàsca *nf* flask.
fiaschetterìa *nf* wine shop, tavern.
fiàsco *pl* **-chi** *nm* flask; (*fig*) failure, fiasco; **fàre f.** to fail.
fiatàre *vi* to breathe, speak.
fiàto *nm* breath.
fíbbia *nf* buckle.
fíbra *nf* fiber, constitution.
ficcàre *vt* to drive in, thrust in; **-rsi** *vr* to force one's way in, intrude, meddle.
fíco *pl* **-chi** *nm* fig, fig-tree; **f. d'India, ficodíndia** prickly pear.
fidanzaménto *nm* betrothal, engagement.
fidanzàre *vt* to betroth; **-rsi** *vr* to become engaged.
fidanzàto *a* engaged; *nm* fiancé.
fidàre *vt* to entrust; **-rsi** *vr* to trust, confide, rely on; dare.
fidatézza *nf* reliability.
fidàto, fído *a* faithful, trusty.
fído *a* faithful, loyal; *nm* devoted follower; (*com*) credit.
fidúcia *nf* trust, confidence, reliance.
fiducióso *a* trusting, confident.
fièle *nm* gall, bile; (*fig*) rancor, bitterness.
fieníle *nm* hayloft; (*fig*) shabby place.
fièno *nm* hay.
fièra *nf* fair, exhibition; wild beast.
fieraménte *ad* fiercely, proudly, boldly.
fierézza *nf* fierceness, pride, boldness.
fièro *a* fierce, proud, bold, stern.
fiévole *a* feeble, weak, dim.
fífa *nf* plover, lapwing; (*fam*) funk.
fíggere *vt* to fix, fasten; **f. gli òcchi su qualcúno** to stare hard at somebody.
fíglia *nf* daughter; (*com*) counterfoil.
figliàstra *nf* stepdaughter; **figliàstro** *nm* stepson.
fíglio *nm* son, child.
figliòccia *nf* goddaughter; **figliòccio** *nm* godson.
figúra *nf* figure, illustration; (*of a novel etc*) character; symbol; **fàre una bèlla f.** to cut a good figure.
figuràccia *nf* poor figure, sorry figure.
figuràre *vti* to figure, represent, symbolize; look smart, appear, pretend; **-rsi** *vr* to fancy, imagine, picture to oneself.
figuràto *a* figurative; illustrated.
figurinísta *nmf* dress designer.
figuríno *nm* fashion plate, pattern
fíla *nf* line, queue, row.
filànda *nf* spinning mill.
filantropía *nf* philanthropy.
filàntropo *nm* philanthrope, philanthropist.
filàre *vt* to spin; *vi* to run away, take oneself off; *nm* (*of trees etc*) row.
filarmònico *pl* **-ici** *a nm* philharmonic, music-lover.
filastròcca *nf* nonsense rhyme, rigmarole.
filatelía *nf* philately, stamp collecting.
filatèlico *pl* **-ici** *a* philatelic; *nm* philatelist.
filàto *a* spun; consequent; *nm* yarn.
filatóio *nm* jenny, spinning-wheel.
filatóre *nm* **-tríce** *nf* spinner.
filétto *nm* thin thread, border, (*mil*) stripe; (*typ*) rule; fillet.
filiàle *a* filial; *nf* branch, branch-house or office.
filiazióne *nf* filiation.

filibustière *nm* freebooter; (*fig*) adventurer, cad.
filigràna *nf* filigree; (*paper*) watermark.
Filippíne (le) *nf pl* the Philippines.
Filíppo *nm pr* Philip.
film *nm* film, movie.
filmàre *vt* to film.
fílo *nm* thread, flex, wire; trickle; **f. spinàto** barbed wire; **f. flessíbile** flex, extension wire; **f. di tèrra** (*rad*) earth wire, ground wire; *pl* **fíla** *nf* (*fig*) strings.
fílobus *nm* trolley-bus.
filología *nf* philology; study of literary texts.
filóne *nm* (*of mineral*) vein; stream; (*of bread*) long loaf.
filoṣofía *nf* philosophy.
filoṣòfico *pl* **-ici** *a* philosophic(al).
filòṣofo *nm* philosopher.
filovía *nf* trolley-bus line.
filtràre *vti* to filter, percolate.
fíltro *nm* filter, philtre, strainer.
filugèllo *nm* silkworm.
fílza *nf* string, series; **púnto a f.** running stitch.
finàle *a* final, last; *nm* conclusion, finale; *nf* (*sport*) final.
finalménte *ad* finally, at last, lastly.
finalità *nf* finality, aim.
finànche *ad* also, even.
finànza *nf* finance, means.
finanziàrio *a* financial.
finanzière *nm* financier, customs officer.
finchè *cj* as long as; **f. non** till, until.
fíne *a* thin, fine, delicate, refined; *nm* aim; *nf* conclusion, end.
finèstra *nf* window.
finestríno *nm* (*of train, car*) window.
finézza *nf* fineness, finesse, politeness, shrewdness.
fíngere *vi* **-rsi** *vr* to pretend, dissemble, feign.
finiménto *nm* finishing; ornament, harness.
finimóndo *nm* end of the world, great uproar, utter ruin.
finíre *vt* to bring to an end, conclude, finish; *vi* to be over, end, finish, give up.
finítimo *a* bordering, neighboring.
finlandése *a nmf* Finnish, Finn.
Finlàndia *nf* Finland.
fíno *a* fine, thin, sharp; *prep* as far as, to, till, until, from, since; *ad* even.
finòcchio *nm* fennel.
finóra *ad* hitherto, so far, up to now.
fínta *nf* pretense, feint; **fàre f.** *vi* to pretend.
fínto *a* false, sham, artificial; *nm* hypocrite.
finzióne *nf* sham, pretense, fiction.
fío *nm* penalty.
fiocàggine *nf* hoarseness.
fioccàre *vi* to snow in large flakes; (*fig*) shower, abound.
fiòcco *pl* **-chi** *nm* (*of snow*) flake; (*of wool*) knot, tassel; **coi fiòcchi** excellent, first rate.
fiòcina *nf* harpoon.
fiòco *pl* **-chi** *a* hoarse; weak, (*of light*) dim, (*of sound*) faint.
fiónda *nf* catapult, slingshot.
fioràia *nf* **-o** *nm* flower-seller.
fiordalíṣo *nm* cornflower, fleur-de-lis.
fiòrdo *nm* fiord.
fióre *nm* flower, bloom, blossom; (*at cards*) club; **f. di làtte** cream; **f. di quattríni** a lot of money; **a f. d'àcqua** on the surface of the water.
fiorènte *a* blooming, flourishing.
fiorentíno *a nm* Florentine.
fioríre *vi* to flower, thrive.
fiorísta *nmf* florist, flower painter, maker of artificial flowers.
fioríto *a* flowery, full of flowers.
fioritúra *nf* bloom, blossoming; (*fig*) flourishing.
fiòtto *nm* surge, wave.
Firènze *nf* (*geogr*) Florence.
fírma *nf* signature.
firmaménto *nm* firmament.
firmàre *vt* to sign.
fiṣarmònica *nf* accordion.
fischiàre *vt* to hiss, whistle.
físchio *nm* whistle, hiss; (*in the ears*) buzzing.
físco *nm* Exchequer, Inland Revenue, internal revenue; fisc.
fíṣica *nf* physics *pl*.
fíṣico *pl* **-ici** *a* physical; *nm* physique; physicist.
fiṣiología *nf* physiology.
fiṣiològico *pl* **-ici** *a* physiological.
fiṣionomía *nf* countenance, physiognomy.
fiṣioterapía *nf* physiotherapy.
fiṣo *a* fixed; *ad* fixedly.
fissàre *vt* to fix, fasten; gaze at, appoint, arrange, engage, book; **-rsi** *vr* to be fixed, settle, set one's heart on.
fissazióne *nf* fixed idea, obsession, fixation.
físso *a* fixed, settled; *nm* fixed salary; *ad* fixedly.
fítta *nf* sharp pain, pang.
fittízio *a* fictitious.
fítto *a* driven in, dense, thick; *nm* lease; rent; **a càpo f.** headlong.
fiumàna *nf* flood, swollen river, torrent; (*of people*) stream.
fiúme *nm* river.
fiutàre *vt* to smell, sniff, scent; (*fig*) suspect, guess.
fiúto *nm* scent, (sense of) smell.
flagellàre *vt* to flagellate, scourge.
flagèllo *nm* scourge, whip; calamity.
flagrànte *a* flagrant.
flagrànza *nf* flagrancy.
flanèlla *nf* flannel.
flèbile *a* plaintive, feeble.
flèmma *nf* phlegm; calm.
flessíbile *a* flexible, pliable, pliant.
flessióne *nf* flexion, bending.
flessuóso *a* flexuous, supple.
flèttere *vt* to bend, flex.

flirtàre *vi* to flirt.
floreàle *a* floral.
floridézza *nf* floridness, prosperity.
flòrido *a* florid, flourishing, prosperous.
flòscio *a* flabby, flaccid.
flòtta *nf* fleet, navy.
flottíglia *nf* flotilla.
fluidità *nf* fluidity, fluency.
flúido *a nm* fluid.
fluíre *vi* to flow.
fluorescènte *a* fluorescent.
flússo *nm* flood tide, flux, dysentery.
flútto *nm* breaker, surge, wave.
fluttuànte *a* fluctuating, floating.
fluttuàre *vi* to fluctuate, waver.
fluviàle *a* fluvial, river.
fobía *nf* phobia.
fòca *nf* seal.
focàccia *nf* kind of cake.
fóce *nf* river mouth.
focolàio *nm* center of infection.
focolàre *nm* fireplace, hearth.
focóso *a* fiery.
fòdera *nf* lining, sheathing.
foderàre *vt* to line, sheathe.
fòdero *nm* scabbard, sheath.
fòga *nf* impetuosity.
fòggia *nf* fashion, form, manner, way.
foggiàre *vt* to fashion, form, shape.
fòglia *nf* leaf, foil.
fogliàme *nm* foliage, leafage.
fòglio *nm* sheet of paper, bank-note, newspaper, (*of metals*) sheet.
fógna *nf* drain, sewer.
fognatúra *nf* sewage, sewerage.
folclòre *nm* folklore.
folclorísta *nmf* folklorist.
folclorístico *pl* **-ici** *a* pertaining to folklore, folkloristic; (*fam*) folk.
folgoràre *vi* to flash, strike with lightning.
fólgore *nm* thunderbolt.
fòlio *nm* folio.
fòlla *nf* crowd, multitude, throng.
fòlle *a nmf* insane, mad, lunatic; **in f.** (*aut*) in neutral (gear).
follétto *nm* elf, goblin.
follía *nf* folly, insanity, madness.
fólto *a* thick, dense, bushy; *nm* thickness.
fomentàre *vt* to foment, incite, stir up.
fòmite *nm* tinder; (*fig*) cause, source.
fónda *nf* anchorage.
fóndaco *pl* **-achi** *nm* store, warehouse.
fondàle *nm* (*theat*) background.
fondamentàle *a* fundamental, basic, essential.
fondaménto *nm* base, foundation, ground.
fondàre *vt* to build, found, ground, rest; **-rsi** *vr* to be built, founded; rely on.
fondazióne *nf* foundation, institution.
fondènte *a* melting, fusing; *nm* fondant.
fóndere *vt* to melt, fuse, cast, smelt, blend.
fondería *nf* foundry.
fondiària *nf* ground tax.
fonditóre *nm* caster, founder, smelter.
fonditúra *nf* melting, casting.
fóndo *a* deep; *nm* bottom, background, end; fund; **artícolo di f.** leading article.
fonètica *nf* phonetics *pl.*
fonètico *pl* **-ici** *a* phonetic.
fonògrafo *nm* gramophone, phonograph; **f. automàtico a gettóne** jukebox.
fonología *nf* phonology.
fontàna *nf* fountain, source, spring.
fónte *nf* spring, source; *nm* font.
foràggio *nm* fodder, forage.
foràre *vt* to bore, pierce; *vi* to puncture; (*ticket*) to punch.
foratúra *nf* piercing; (*aut*) puncture; hole.
fòrbici *nf pl* scissors, pincers, claws.
forbíre *vt* to furbish, polish.
forbitézza *nf* (*of style*) elegance, polish.
fórca *nf* pitchfork, gallows *pl.*
forcèlla *nf* forked stick; hairpin; (*of chicken*) wishbone; (*of telephone*) cradle; alpine pass.
forchétta *nf* (table) fork.
forcína *nf* hairpin.
forcúto *a* forked.
forènse *a* forensic.
forèsta *nf* forest.
forestàle *a* forestal; **guàrdia f.** forester.
forestière, forestièro *a* foreign, strange; *nm* foreigner, stranger.
fórfora *nf* dandruff, scurf.
fòrgia *nf* forge.
forgiàre *vt* to forge, shape, form.
forièro *a* portending.
fórma *nf* form, shape, figure; formality.
formàggio *nm* cheese; **f. parmigiano** Parmesan cheese.
formàle *a* formal, solemn.
formalità *nf* formality.
formalménte *ad* formally.
formàre *vt* to make, create, fashion, form; **-rsi** *vr* to form, develop.
formàto *a* formed, shaped; *nm* form, size.
formazióne *nf* formation, forming; training.
formíca *nf* ant.
fòrmica *nf* Formica (Registered Trade Name).
formicolàre *vi* to swarm with tingle.
formidàbile *a* formidable, dreadful.
formóso *a* buxom, shapely.
fórmula *nf* formula.
formulàre *vt* to formulate, express.
fornàce *nf* furnace, kiln.
fornàio *nm* baker.
fornèllo *nm* (kitchen) stove.
forniménto *nm* supply, equipment.

forníre *vt* to furnish, provide, supply; **-rsi** *vr* to provide oneself.
fornitóre *nm* **-tríce** *nf* contractor, purveyor, supplier.
fornitúra *nf* stock, supplies *pl*.
fórno *nm* oven, bakery, kiln, furnace.
fóro *nm* hole.
fòro *nm* forum.
fórra *nf* gorge, ravine.
fórse *ad* perhaps.
forsennàto *a* crazy, mad; *nm* madman.
fòrte *a* strong, large, heavy, loud; (*of color*) fast; *nm* fort, forte, sourness; *ad* strongly, loudly, powerfully.
forteménte *ad* strongly, greatly, loudly, bravely.
fortézza *nf* fortress, fortitude.
fortificàre *vt* to fortify, strengthen; **-rsi** *vr* to acquire strength, grow stronger.
fortúito *a* casual, fortuitous.
fortúna *nf* fortune, luck, chance; **atterràggio di f.** forced landing.
fortunàle *nm* storm at sea.
fortunàto *a* fortunate, lucky.
fortunóso *a* eventful, stormy.
forúncolo *nm* (*med*) boil.
forviàre *vt* to lead astray, mislead, misguide.
fòrza *nf* force, power, strength.
forzàre *vt* to compel, force.
forzàto *a* forced; *nm* convict.
forzière *nm* safe, strong-box.
foschía *nf* haze, mist.
fósco *pl* **-chi** *a* dark, dull, gloomy, somber.
fosfàto *nm* (*chem*) phosphate.
fosforescènte *a* phosphorescent.
fosforescènza *nf* phosphorescence.
fòsforo *nm* phosphorus.
fòssa *nf* hole, pit, grave, den, ditch.
fossàto *nm* ditch, moat.
fossétta *nf* dimple.
fòssile *a nm* fossil.
fossilizzàre *vt* **-rsi** *vr* to fossilize.
fòsso *nm* ditch.
fotocèllula *nf* photoelectric cell.
fotocòpia *nf* photocopy.
fotocrònaca *nf* photo reportage.
fotocronísta *nmf* press photographer.
fotografàre *vt* to photograph.
fotografía *nf* photograph, photography; **f. istantànea** snapshot.
fotogràfico *pl* **-ici** *a* photographic; **màcchina fotogràfica** camera.
fotògrafo *nm* photographer.
fotorepòrter *mnf* news photographer.
fotoromànzo *nm* photo strip.
fotostàtico *pl* **-ici** *a* photostatic; **còpia fotostàtica** photostat.
foulard (*French*) *nm* silk scarf.
fra *prep* among, amid, between (two); (*time*) in; *nm* Brother.
frac *nm* evening dress; (*fam*) tails.
fracassàre *vt* **-rsi** *vr* to break in fpieces, smash.
racàsso *nm* crash, fracas, uproar.
fràdicio *a* rotten; wet, wet through.
fradiciúme *nm* mass of wet (or rotten) things.
fràgile *a* brittle, fragile, frail.
fragilità *nf* fragility, brittleness, frailty.
fràgola *nf* strawberry(-plant).
fragóre *nm* crash, loud noise.
fragoróso *a* roaring, very noisy.
fragrànte *a* fragrant, sweet-smelling.
fragrànza *nf* fragrance, aroma.
fraintèndere *vt* to misunderstand.
framassóne *nm* Freemason.
framassonería *nf* Freemasonry.
framménto *nm* fragment.
framméttere *vt* to insert, interpose; **-rsi** *vr* to interfere, interpose, intrude, meddle.
fràna *nf* **franaménto** *nm* fall of earth or rock, landslide, subsidence.
franàre *vi* to fall, sink, (*earth etc*) slide down.
Francésca *nf pr* Frances; **Francésco** *nm pr* Francis.
francescàno *a nm* Franciscan.
francése *a* French; *nm* Frenchman; *nf* Frenchwoman.
franchézza *nf* candidness, frankness, openness.
franchígia *nf* exemption; franchise; (*mil*) time off duty.
Frància *nf* France.
frànco *pl* **-chi** *a* candid, frank; *nm* franc.
francobóllo *nm* (postage) stamp.
Francofòrte *nf* (*geogr*) Frankfort, Frankfurt.
frangènte *nm* breaker, shoal, reef; (*fig*) difficulty.
fràngere *vt* to break to pieces, crush; **-rsi** *vr* to break.
frangétta, fràngia *nf* fringe.
frangiflútti *nm* breakwater.
frangitúra *nf* extraction of oil from olives.
frantóio *nm* (*for olives*) oil-press, stone-crusher.
frantumàre *vt* to break, smash.
frantúmi *nm pl* fragments *pl*, pieces *pl*.
frappé *nm* shake; **agitatóre per f.** milk shaker.
frappórre *vt* to interpose, insert; **-rsi** *vr* to interfere.
frasàrio *nm* jargon; phrasing; collection of phrases.
fràsca *nf* spray, twig; inn sign.
fràse *nf* phrase, sentence.
fraseología *nf* phraseology.
fràssino *nm* ash, ash-tree.
frastagliàto *a* indented, irregular, uneven.
frastornàre *vt* to disturb, trouble, distract.
frastuòno *nm* din, hubbub.
fràte *nm* friar, monk, brother.
fratellànza *nf* brotherhood.
fratellàstro *nm* half-brother.
fratèllo *nm* brother.
fratèrno *a* brotherly, fraternal.

fratricída *a* fratricidal; *nmf* fratricide.
fratricídio *nm* fratricide.
fràtta *nf* briar patch, th cket.
frattànto *ad* in the meantime, meanwhile.
frattèmpo *nm* meantime, interval; **nel f.** meanwhile.
frattúra *nf* fracture, break.
fratturàre *vt* to break, fracture.
fraudolènto *a* fraudulent.
frazióne *nf* fraction; group of houses.
fréccia *nf* arrow; **frecciatína** *nf* pungent remark.
freddaménte *ad* coldly, coolly, calmly.
freddàre *vt* to cool; kill; **-rsi** *vr* to grow cold, cool.
freddézza *nf* coldness, coolness, indifference.
fréddo *a* cold, chilly, cool, indifferent; *nm* coldness, cold; **avére f.** *vi* to be cold.
freddolóso *a* chilly, sensitive to cold.
freddúra *nf* cold; nonsense, silly story, pun.
fregàre *vt* to rub, scrub, cross out; (*vulg*) cheat, swindle; **-rsi** *vr* to rub oneself; (*vulg*) **fregàrsene** not to care.
fregàta *nf* rubbing, scrubbing; (*naut*) frigate.
fregiàre *vt* to decorate, adorn; **-rsi** *vr* to adorn oneself.
frégio *nm* frieze, ornament.
frégola *nf* (*of animals*) heat, (*fig*) mania, immoderate desire.
frèmere *vi* to quiver, thrill, tremble, throb, fume, shudder, rustle.
frèmito *nm* quiver, thrill, throb, roaring.
frenàre *vt* to brake, curb; hinder, repress, restrain; **-rsi** *vr* to keep one's temper; refrain from, restrain oneself.
freneşía *nf* frenzy.
frenètico *pl* **-ici** *a* frantic, raving.
fréno *nm* brake, bridle, curb, restraint; **potènza del f.** brake horsepower.
frenología *nf* phrenology.
frequentàre *vt* to attend, frequent, haunt, consort with.
frequentàto *a* frequented, attended, patronized.
frequènte *a* frequent, quick.
frequenteménte *ad* frequently.
frequènza *nf* frequency, attendance.
frèşa *nf* (milling) cutter.
freşatríce *nf* milling machine.
freschézza *nf* freshness, coolness.
frésco *pl* **-chi** *a* fresh, cool; *nm* coolness, cool; fresco.
frescúra *nf* coolness.
frétta *nf* haste, hurry; **avére f.** *vi* to be in a hurry; **di f., in f.** hastily.
frettolóso *a* hasty, hurried.
fríggere *vt* to fry.
frigidézza frigidità *nf* frigidness, frigidity.
frígido *a* frigid.
frigorífero *nm* refrigerator.
fringuèllo *nm* finch.
frittàta *nf* omelet.
frittèlla *nf* fritter, pancake.
frítto *a* fried; (*fig*) lost, ruined; *nm* fry, fried food.
frittúra *nf* fry, fried food.
frivolézza *nf* frivolity, frivolousness.
frívolo *a* frivolous, trifling.
frizióne *nf* rubbing, massage, friction.
frizzànte *a* sparkling; (*of air*) biting, pungent.
frizzàre *vi* to tingle, sparkle, sting.
frízzo *nm* witticism, gibe.
frodàre *vt* to defraud, swindle.
fròde *nf* fraud, swindle.
fròdo *nm* poaching, smuggling.
fròllo *a* (*of meat*) tender, (*of game*) high; exhausted; **pàsta fròlla** pastry.
frónda *nf* leafy bough, (the) Fronde.
frondóso *a* leafy.
frontàle *a* frontal; *nm* frontal, mantelpiece.
frónte *nf* forehead; *nm* front; **far f. a** to cope with, face, meet.
fronteggiàre *vt* to face, confront.
frontespízio *nm* frontispiece, title page.
frontièra *nf* border, frontier.
frontóne *nm* (*arch*) fronton, gable.
frónzolo *nm* tassel, frill, trinket.
fronzúto *a* leafy.
fròtta *nf* crowd, throng.
fròttola *nf* fib, lie, nonsense; popular song.
frugàle *a* frugal.
frugàre *vt* to rummage; **-rsi** *vr* to search one's pockets.
frúgolo *nm* little, lively child.
fruíre *vi* to make use of, enjoy.
frullàre *vt* to whip, whisk; *vi* to whir, whirl.
frullíno *nm* (*cook*) whisk.
fruménto *nm* wheat.
fruscío *nm* rustle, rustling.
frústa *nf* lash, scourge, whip.
frustàre *vt* to whip, lash, scourge.
frútta *nf* (*coll*) fruit.
fruttàre *vti* to produce, fructify, pay.
fruttéto *nm* orchard.
frutticultóre *nm* fruit-grower.
fruttífero *a* fruit-bearing; fruitful, profitable.
fruttificàre *vi* to fructify.
fruttivéndolo *nm* fruiterer.
frútto *pl* **-i** (*m*), (*table*) **-a** (*f*) *nm* fruit; profit, result, revenue.
fruttuóso *a* fruitful, profitable.
fu *a* late, deceased.
fucilàre *vt* to shoot.
fucilazióne *nf* shooting, execution.
fucíle *nm* gun, rifle.
fucína *nf* forge, smithy.
fucinàre *vt* to forge.
fúga *nf* flight, escape, avoidance; (*mus*) fugue.
fugàce *a* fleeting, transient.
fugàre *vt* to put to flight, rout.

fuggévole *a* fleeting, flying.
fuggiàsco *pl* **-schi** *a nm* fugitive, runaway.
fúggi-fúggi *nm* headlong flight, panic stampede.
fuggíre *vi* to flee, run away, take to flight; *vt* to avoid, shun.
fulgènte *a* shining, refulgent.
fúlgido *a* shining, bright, refulgent.
fulgóre *nm* brightness, splendor, refulgence.
fulíggine *nf* soot.
fulminànte *a* fulminating; *nm* lucifer match, percussion cap.
fulminàre *vt* to strike with lightning, strike dumb; *vi* to flash, lighten.
fúlmine *nm* lightning, thunderbolt.
fulmíneo *a* quick as lightning, sudden.
fúlvo *a* reddish, tawny.
fumai(u)òlo *nm* chimney-pot.
fumànte *a* smoking, steaming.
fumàre *vt* to smoke; **vietàto f.** 'no smoking'.
fumàta *nf* smoke, smoking, puff of smoke, smoke signal.
fumatóre *nm* **-tríce** *nf* smoker.
fumétto *nm usu pl* comic strip, cartoon; **romànzo a fumétti** strip cartoon.
fúmo *nm* smoke, fume, steam.
fumògeno *a* smoke-producing.
fumosità *nf* smokiness.
fumóso *a* smoky.
funàmbolo *nm* tight-rope walker.
fúne *nf* cable, rope.
fúnebre *a* funeral, funereal.
funeràle *nm* funeral.
funèreo *a* funereal, gloomy.
funestàre *vt* to desolate, distress, sadden, ruin.
funèsto *a* baneful, disastrous, sorrowful, fatal.
fúngere *vi* to act as, officiate as.
fúngo *pl* **-ghi** *nm* fungus, mushroom, toadstool.
funicolàre *nf* funicular.
funivía *nf* air cable way.
funzionàre *vi* to act, function, run, work.
funzionàrio *nm* functionary, official.
funzióne *nf* function, office, service (in church).
fuochista *nm* fireman, stoker.
fuòco *pl* **-chi** *nm* fire; (*phot*) focus; **méttere a f.** (*phot*) to focus; **fuochi d'artifízio** firework; **f. di sbarraménto** (*mil*) barrage fire.
fuorché *cj prep* except, but, apart from.
fuòri *ad prep* out, outside, except; **al di f.** *ad* outwards.
fuoribórdo *nm* (*naut*) outboard motor.
fuorilégge *nm* outlaw.
fuorisèrie *nf inv* (*aut*) custom-built.
fuoruscíto *nm* exile, outlaw.
fuorviàre *vt* to mislead; *vi* go astray, stray.
furbería *nf* cunning, slyness.
furbésco *pl* **-schi. furbo** *a* artful, cunning, sly, wily.
furènte *v* **furibóndo.**
furétto *nm* ferret.
furfànte *nm* rascal, scamp.
furfantería *nf* roguery, piece of roguery.
furgoncíno *nm* small van.
furgóne *nm* van, (*railroad*) caboose.
fúria *nf* fury, rage, hurry; **avére f.** to be in a hurry.
furibóndo, furióso *a* furious, raging.
furóre *nm* frenzy, fury, rage; **fàre f.** to be much admired.
furoreggiàre *vi* to be (all) the rage, make a hit.
furtívo *a* furtive, sly, stealthy.
fúrtò *nm* theft, robbery.
fúsa *nf pl* **fare le f.** to purr.
fuscèllo *nm* twig, straw; (*fig*) thin person.
fusièra *nf* pindle-holder.
fuşióne *nf* fusion, melting, smelting, casting, merging.
fúso *a* fused, melted.
fúşo *nm* spindle.
fuşolièra *nf* fuselage.
fustàgno *nm* fustian; corduroy.
fustigàre *vt* to flog.
fústo *nm* stock, stem, trunk; barrel, cask; frame; (*fam*) he-man.
fútile *a* futile, trifling.
futilità *nf* futility, *pl* trifles.
futúro *a nm* future.

G

gabardína *nf* gabardine, overcoat.
gabbàre *vt* to deceive, mock, swindle.
gabbatóre *nm* **-tríce** *nf* deceiver, impostor, swindler.
gàbbia *nf* cage, coop, jail; topsail.
gabbiàno *nm* seagull.
gàbbo *nm* jeering, mockery; **prèndere a g.** to mock.
gabèlla *nf* duty, tax (on goods entering a town).
gabellàre *vt* to tax; (*fig*) **g. per** to pass off as.
gabellière *nm* customs officer.
gabinétto *nm* cabinet; toilet, closet; (*of dentist or doctor*) consulting room, surgery, office; **g. púbblico** public convenience, public comfort station.
Gabrièle *nm pr* Gabriel.
gaèlico *pl* **-ici** *a nm* Gaelic.
gaffe (*French*) *nf* gaffe, blunder.
gaggía *nf* acacia.
gagliardétto *nm* pennon.
gagliàrdo *a* strong, vigorous.
gagliòffo *a* loutish, rascally; *nm* lout, rascal.
gaiaménte *ad* gaily, brightly.
gaiézza *nf* gaiety, brightness.
gàio *a* gay, (*color*) bright.
gàla *nf* finery, gala; **tenúta di g.** (*mil*) full-dress uniform.

galànte *a* courteous, gallant (towards women); *nm* gallant, ladies' man.
galanteggiàre *vi* to play the gallant.
galantería *nf* courtesy, gallantry; delicacy, dainty.
galantína *nf* galantine.
galantuòmo *nm* honest man, man of honor.
galatèo *nm* code of manners *pl*, manners.
galèa *nf* galley.
galeòtto *nm* convict, galley slave.
galèra *nf* galley, jail, hard labor.
Galilèa *nf* (*geogr*) Galilee.
galilèo *a nm* Galilean.
gàlla *nf* gall, blister; **a g.** afloat
galleggiànte *a* floating; *nm* float, buoy, raft.
galleggiàre *vi* to float.
gallería *nf* gallery, tunnel; arcade; (*theat*) gallery, balcony.
Gàlles *nm* (*geogr*) Wales.
gallése *a* Welsh; *nm* the Welsh language, Welshman; *nf* Welshwoman.
gallétta *nf* ship's biscuit, cracker.
gallína *nf* hen.
gallinàccio *nm* turkey-cock: chanterelle.
gàllo *nm* cock, weathercock, Gaul; **g. domèstico** rooster.
gallonàre *vt* to braid.
gallóne *nm* braid, (*mil*) stripe; (*measure*) gallon.
galoppàre *vi* to gallop.
galoppàta *nf* gallop, galloping.
galoppíno *nm* errand boy, messenger; **g. elettoràle** canvasser.
galòppo *nm* gallop.
galòscia *nf* galosh, golosh.
galvànico *pl* **-ici** *a* galvanic.
galvanizzàre *vt* to galvanize.
gàmba *nf* leg; **èssere in g.** *vi* to be fit active, clever.
gambacórta *nm* lame man.
gambàle *nm* legging.
gambàta *nf* kick.
gàmbero *nm* crayfish.
gàmbo *nm* stalk, stem.
gàmma *nf* gamut, range, scale.
ganàscia *nf* jaw.
gàncio *nm* hook, clasp.
gànghero *nm* hinge; **fuòri dei gàngheri** furious.
gànglio *nm* ganglion (*also fig*).
gàra *nf* competition, contest, match.
garage (*Fr*) *nm* garage.
garagísta *nm* motor mechanic, garage owner.
garànte *nm* guarantor, surety.
garantíre *vt* to guarantee, stand surety for, warrant.
garanzía *nf* guarantee, surety, warrant.
garbàre *vi* to be agreeable, to be to one's liking, please, suit.
garbatézza *nf* politeness, kindness.
garbàto *a* civil, polite.
gàrbo *nm* courtesy, grace, manner, politeness; **a g.** gracefully, politely.
garbúglio *nm* entanglement, confusion, disorder.
gareggiàre *vi* to compete, vie.
garganèlla, bere a *vt* to gulp down, toss off.
gargarísmo *nm* gargle.
gargarizzàre *vt* to gargle.
garibaldíno *a nm* (one who) fought under Garibaldi.
garítta *nf* sentry box, look-out turret.
garòfano *nm* carnation, clove.
garrése *nm* (*of horse*) withers *pl*.
garrétto *nm* back of the heel, (*horse*) hock.
garríre *vi* to chirp, warble, screech; (*flag*) flap.
garrulità *nf* garrulity.
gàrrulo *a* garrulous.
gàrza *nf* heron; gauze.
garzóne *nm* apprentice, farm servant, shop-boy.
gas *nm inv* gas; **fornèllo a g.** gas cooker.
gasàto, gassàto *a* aerated.
gassísta *nm* gas-fitter, gasman.
gassómetro *nm* gasometer.
gassósa *nf* aerated drink.
gassóso *a* effervescent, aerated.
gàstrico *pl* **-ici** *a* gastric; **súcco g.** *nm* gastric juice.
gastríte *nf* (*med*) gastritis.
gastronomía *nf* gastronomy.
gastronòmico *pl* **-ici** *a* gastronomic.
gàtta *nf* she-cat; **dàre una g. a pelàre** to give a lot of trouble.
gattabúia *nf* jail, prison.
gattèsco *pl* **-chi** *a* catlike.
gattíno *nm* kitten.
gàtto *nm* cat; **èssere quàttro gàtti** to be very few people.
gattóni *ad* on all fours.
gattopàrdo *nm* leopard.
gaudènte *a* jolly, merry; *nmf* reveler.
gàudio *nm* joy, bliss, happiness; *a* joyful, joyous.
gavazzàre *vi* to revel.
gavétta *nf* mess tin.
gazósa *nf* aerated lemonade.
gàzza *nf* magpie; (*fig*) babbler, chatterer.
gazzàrra *nf* uproar.
gazzèlla *nf* gazelle.
gazzétta *nf* gazette, newspaper.
gelàre *vti* to freeze.
gelatería *nf* ice-cream shop.
gelatière *nm* ice-cream man.
gelatína *nf* gelatine, jelly.
gelàto *a* frozen; *nm* ice(-cream).
gelidaménte *ad* icily, coldly.
gèlido *a* icy, chilly.
gèlo *nm* freezing weather, frost, ice.
gelóne *nm* chilblain.
gelosaménte *ad* jealously.
gelosía *nf* jealousy, great care; shutter.
gelóso *a* jealous.
gèlso *nm* mulberry(-tree).
gelsomíno *nm* jasmine, jessamine.
Geltrúde *nf pr* Gertrude.

gemebóndo *a* moaning, plaintive.
gemèllo *a nm* twin; *pl* **gemèlli** twins *pl*; cufflinks *pl*.
gèmere *vi* to groan, moan, trickle, coo.
geminatúra, geminazióne *nf* gemination.
gèmito *nm* groan, moan.
gèmma *nf* gem, jewel; bud.
gemmàre *vt* to bud.
gemmàto *a* full of buds, studded with gems.
gendàrme *nm* gendarme, policeman.
gendarmería *nf* gendarmerie, police.
genealogía *nf* genealogy.
genealògico *pl* **-ici** *a* genealogical.
generàle *a nm* general.
generalità *nf* generality; (*pl*) particulars *pl*.
generalizzàre *vt* to generalize.
generalizzazióne *nf* generalization.
generalménte *ad* generally, in general.
generàre *vt* to generate, beget, breed, cause, engender, produce.
generatóre *nm* generator; (*aut*) dynamo, generator.
generazióne *nf* generation.
gènere *nm* kind, sort, type; gender; **in g.** *ad* in general; **gèneri** *pl* articles, goods *pl*; **g. di príma necessità** necessaries.
genèrico *pl* **-ici** *a* generic, general.
gènero *nm* son-in-law.
generosaménte *ad* generously.
generosità *nf* generosity.
generóso *a* generous.
gènesi *nf* genesis; **la G.** Book of Genesis.
gengíva *nf* (*in mouth*) gum.
genía *nf* low breed, low set.
geniàle *a* ingenious, clever; genial.
genialità *nf* ingeniousness, talent, genius; geniality.
gènio *nm* genius, talent; **àrma del g.** *nf* (*mil*) engineers *pl*; **andàre a g.** to be to one's liking.
genitàle *a* genital.
gènito *a* born, generated.
genitóre *nm* parent, father; **-tríce** *nf* mother; **-tóri** *pl* parents *pl*.
gennàio *nm* January.
Gènova *nf* (*geogr*) Genoa; **genovése** *a nmf* Genoese.
Genovèffa *nf pr* Genevieve.
gentàccia, gentàglia *nf* mob, rabble.
gènte *nf* people, folk.
gentildònna *nf* gentlewoman, lady of quality.
gentíle *a* courteous, kind, polite; *a nm* Gentile; pagan, heathen.
gentilézza *nf* kindness, politeness, civility.
gentilízio *a* aristocratic, noble; **stèmma gentilízia** *nm* coat of arms.
gentilménte *ad* kindly, politely.
gentiluòmo *nm* gentleman, nobleman.
genuflessióne *nf* genuflection.
genuflèttersi *vr* to genuflect.
genuinità *nf* genuineness.
genuíno *a* genuine, authentic.
genziàna *nf* gentian.
geografía *nf* geography.
geogràfico *pl* **-ici** *a* geographic(al).
geología *nf* geology.
geòmetra *nm* geometer, surveyor.
geometría *nf* geometry.
geomètrico *pl* **-ici** *a* geometric(al).
geràno *nm* geranium.
geràrca *nm* hierarch; leader.
gerarchía *nf* hierarchy.
gerènte *nm* manager, director.
gerènza *nf* management.
gèrgo *pl* **gèrghi** *nm* jargon, slang.
gèrla *nf* pannier.
Germània *nf* (*geogr*) Germany.
germànico *pl* **-ici** *a* Germanic; *nm* (*language*) Germanic.
germàno *a nm* German; *a* germane; **cugíno g.** first cousin; *nm* blood brother; wild duck.
gèrme *nm* germ, shoot, sprout.
germinàre *vi* to germinate.
germogliàre *vi* to bud, sprout.
germóglio *nm* bud, shoot.
geroglífico *pl* **-ici** *a* hieroglyphic; *nm* hieroglyph(ic).
Geròlamo, Gerònimo *nm pr* Jerome.
Gertrúde *nf pr* Gertrude.
Gerusalèmme *nf* (*geogr*) Jerusalem.
gèsso *nm* chalk, plaster of Paris, gypsum.
gèsta *nf pl* deeds, exploits, feats *pl*.
gestànte *a nf* expectant mother.
gestazióne *nf* gestation, pregnancy.
gesticolàre *vi* to gesticulate.
gesticolazióne *nf* gesticulation.
gestióne *nf* management.
gestíre *vt* to gesticulate; manage.
gèsto *nm* gesture, act, action.
gestóre *nm* manager, (*rly*) traffic manager.
Gesú *nm* Jesus.
gesuíta *nm* Jesuit.
gettàre *vt* to throw, cast, fling; **-rsi** *vr* to jump, throw oneself.
gèttito *nm* (*tax*) yield; (*naut*) jettison.
gètto *nm* throw, throwing, jet, sprout, casting; **a g. contínuo** without a break.
gettóne *nm* counter, token.
ghermíre *vt* to claw, collar, seize.
ghétta *nf* gaiter.
ghétto *nm* ghetto.
ghiacciàia *nf* icebox, refrigerator.
ghiacciàio *nm* glacier.
ghiacciàre *vti* **-rsi** *vr* to freeze.
ghiacciàta *nf* iced drink.
ghiàccio *nm* ice.
ghiacci(u)òlo *nm* icicle.
ghiàia *nf* gravel.
ghiànda *nf* acorn.
ghiandàia *nf* jackdaw, jay.
ghiàndola *nf* gland.
ghibellíno *a nm* Ghibelline.
ghigliottína *nf* guillotine.
ghígna *nf* ugly face, grimace.
ghignàre *vi* to sneer.

ghígno *nm* sneer, grin.
ghinèa *nf* guinea.
ghíngeri, in *ad* finely dressed.
ghiótto *a* gluttonous, greedy.
ghiottóne *nm* glutton.
ghiottonería *nf* gluttony; titbit, dainty, rarity.
ghiribízzo *nm* freak, whim.
ghiribizzóso *a* freakish, whimsical.
ghirlànda *nf* garland, wreath.
ghíro *nm* dormouse.
ghísa *nf* cast-iron, pig-iron.
già *ad* already, formerly, once; *interj* of course, yes.
Giacàrta *nf* (*geogr*) Djakarta, Jakarta.
giàcca *nf* jacket; **g. a vènto** windbreaker, anorak.
giacchè *cj* as, seeing that, since.
giacènte *a* lying, lying down, placed; (*of capital*) unproductive.
giacènza *nf* stay, demurrage; stock, (*of books*) unsold copies.
giacére *vi* to lie, be situated.
giacíglio *nm* bed, place for lying.
giaciménto *nm* (*geol*) layer; (*min*) deposit.
giacínto *nm* hyacinth.
Giacòbbe *nm pr* Jacob.
Giàcomo *nm pr* James.
giaggi(u)òlo *nm* Florentine lily, iris.
giaguàro *nm* jaguar.
giallàstro *a* yellowish.
giallézza *nf* yellowness.
giallíno *a* light yellow.
giàllo *a nm* yellow; *nm* thriller; **g. d'uòvo** (egg) yolk.
Giamàica *nf* Jamaica.
giàmbo *nm* iambus.
giammài *ad* never.
Giappóne *nm* Japan.
giapponése *a nmf* Japanese.
giàra, giàrra *nf* jar.
giardinàggio *nm* gardening.
giardinétta *nf* (*aut*) station wagon.
giardinièra *nf* woman gardener; station wagon; flower stand; pickled vegetables.
giardinière *nm* gardener.
giardíno *nm* garden.
giarrettièra *nf* garter; (*men's*) sock suspender, garter.
giavellòtto *nm* javelin.
gibbóso *a* humped, hump-backed.
gibèrna *nf* cartridge box, pouch.
Gibiltèrra *nf* Gibraltar.
gigànte *nm* giant; *a* gigantic.
giganteggiàre *vi* to tower, rise like a giant.
gigantésco *pl* **-schi** *a* gigantic.
gigantéssa *nf* giantess.
gíglio *nm* lily.
gilè *nm* waistcoat.
gincàna *nf* (*sport*) gymkhana.
ginecología *nf* gynecology.
ginecòlogo *pl* **-ogi** *nm* gynecologist.
ginepràio *nm* thicket of junipers; difficult situation.
ginépro *nm* juniper.
ginèstra *nf* broom.
Ginévra *nf* (*geogr*) Geneva.
gingillàre *vi* **-rsi** *vr* to dawdle, play, trifle.
gingillíno *nm* dawdler, loiterer.
gingíllo *nm* knick-knack, trifle.
gingillóne *nm* dawdler.
ginnasiàle *a* of a grammar school, secondary school, high school.
ginnàsio *nm* grammar school, secondary school, high school.
ginnàsta *nmf* gymnast, athlete.
ginnàstica *nf* gymnastics *pl*.
ginocchièra *nf* knee-pad.
ginòcchio *nm pl* **ginòcchi, ginòcchia** *f* knee.
ginocchióni *ad* on one's knees.
Gioacchíno *nm pr* Joachim.
giocàre, giuocàre *vti* to play, stake, work, make a fool of; **-rsi** *vr* to make fun of.
giocàta *nf* game stake.
giocatóre *nm* **-tríce** *nf* player.
giocàttolo *nm* toy, plaything.
giocherellàre *vi* to play, toy, trifle.
giòco *pl* **giòchi** *nm* play, game, sport, gambling, pastime, speculation; (*mech*) clearance.
giocofòrza, èssere *v impers* to be necessary.
giocolière *nm* juggler.
giocondità *nf* gaiety, cheerfulness.
giocóndo *a* gay, joyous.
giocosità *nf* mirth, facetiousness.
giocóso *a* jocose, facetious.
giogàia *nf* chain of mountains, (*of oxen*) dewlap.
giógo *pl* **gioghi** *nm* yoke (*also fig*); mountain ridge, peak.
giòia *nf* joy, delight; jewel.
gioiellería *nf* jewelery, jeweler's shop.
gioiellière *nm* jeweler.
gioièllo *nm* jewel.
gioiosaménte *ad* joyfully, joyously.
gioióso *a* joyful, merry.
gioíre *vi* to be glad, rejoice.
Giordània *nf* (*geogr*) Jordania.
Giordàno *nm* (*geogr*) Jordan.
Giórgio *nm pr* George.
giornalàio *nm* newsagent, newsboy.
giornàle *nm* (news)paper, journal, diary; **cíne g.** newsreel; **g. ràdio** news bulletin.
giornalièro *a* daily; *nm* day laborer.
giornalísmo *nm* journalism.
giornalísta *nmf* journalist, reporter.
giornalístico *pl* **-ici** *a* journalistic.
giornalménte *ad* daily, every day.
giornànte *nf* cleaning woman.
giornàta *nf* day, day's work; **vívere alla g.** to live from hand to mouth.
giórno *nm* day; **èssere a g. di** to be informed of; **di g.** in the daytime.
giòstra *nf* joust, tournament, merry-go-round, roundabout.
giostràre *vi* to joust, tilt.
Giosuè *nm pr* Joshua.
giovaménto *nm* advantage, benefit.
gióvane, gióvine *a* young; *nm*

young man, youth; *nf* young woman.
giovaníle *a* juvenile, youthful.
Giovànna *nf pr* Jane, Jean, Joan.
Giovànni *nm pr* John.
giovanòtto *nm* young man, bachelor.
giovàre *vi* to be of use, be beneficial; **-rsi** *vr* to avail oneself of, benefit by.
giovedì *nm* Thursday.
giovènca *nf* heifer; **giovènco** *pl* **-chi** *nm* bullock, steer.
gioventù *nf* youth, young people.
giovévole *a* beneficial, profitable.
gioviàle *a* jolly, jovial.
giovialità *nf* joviality.
giovinàstro *nm* hooligan, hoodlum.
giovinétta *nf* young girl; **giovinétto** *nm* lad, young fellow.
giovinézza *v* **gioventù**.
giradíschi *nm* record player.
giràffa *nf* giraffe.
giraménto *nm* turning; **g. di tèsta** dizziness.
giramóndo *nm* wanderer, globe-trotter.
giràndola *nf* Catherine wheel; (*fig*) fickle person.
girànte *a* revolving; *nm* endorser.
giràre *vt* to turn, avoid; (*cin*) shoot, act, tour, endorse; *vi* turn, wind, wander; **-rsi** *vr* to turn around.
girarròsto *nm* roasting jack, spit, turnspit.
girasóle *nm* sunflower.
giràta *nf* turn, walk; endorsement.
giratàrio *nm* (*com*) endorsee.
giravòlta *nf* change of front, turning, twirl.
girèlla *nf* pulley, small wheel; (*checkers etc*) piece; (*fig*) political weathercock.
girellàre *vi* to saunter, stroll.
girèllo *nm* small circle; (*children*) go-cart; (*cut of meat*) rump.
girétto *nm* stroll; **fàre un g.** to go for a stroll.
girévole *a* revolving, turning.
giríno *nm* tadpole.
gíro *nm* turn, round, circle, tour, circulation; endorsement; period of time, stroll; **prèndere in g.** to tease.
giróne *nm* (*in Dante's Inferno*) circle; (*football*) series (of games).
gironzolàre *vi* to stroll.
giropilòta *nm* automatic pilot, gyropilot.
girotóndo *nm* dance in a ring; 'ring-a-ring-a-roses'.
girovagàre *vi* to roam, wander.
giròvago *pl* **-ghi** *a* roving, wandering; *nm* wanderer, tramp.
gíta *nf* trip, excursion.
gitànte *nmf* tripper, excursionist.
giú *ad* down; **su per g.** approximately, roughly.
giúbba *nf* jacket, coat.
giubilàre *vi* to exult, jubilate.
giubilèo *nm* jubilee.
giúbilo *nm* jubilation, rejoicing.
Giúda *nm pr* Judas.
giudàico *pl* **-ici** *a* Judaic; Jewish.
giudaísmo *nm* Judaism.
Giudèa *nf* (*geogr*) Judea, Judaea.
giudèo *a nm* Jewish, Jew, Judean.
giudicàre *vti* to judge, think, consider.
giudicàto *a* judged, sentenced; *nm* sentence; **passàre in g.** to be beyond recall.
giúdice *nm* judge, (*title*) Justice.
Giudítta *nf pr* Judith.
giudiziàle, giudizàrio *a* judicial.
giudízio *nm* judgment, opinion, verdict, sentence, prudence; **avére g.** to be sensible; **dènte del g.** wisdom tooth.
giudizióso *a* judicious, sensible.
giudò *nm* judo.
giúgno *nm* June.
Giuliàno *nm pr* Julian.
Giúlie, (Àlpi) *nf pl* (*geogr*) Julian Alps.
Giuliétta *nf pr* Juliet.
Giúlio *nm pr* Julius.
giulívo *a* gay, joyful.
giullàre *nm* jester, minstrel.
giuménta *nf* mare.
giuménto *nm* ass, mule, beast of burden.
giuncàia *nf* **giunchéto** *nm* reed bed.
giuncàta *nf* junket.
giunchíglia *nf* jonquil.
giúnco *pl* **giunchi** *nm* reed, rush.
giúngere *vti* to arrive, reach, go as far as, succeed, join, get at.
giúngla *nf* jungle.
giúnta *nf* addition, increase, makeweight; committee, council; **per g.** in addition, moreover.
giuntàre *vt* to join, sew together.
giuntúra *nf* joint, articulation.
giunzióne *nf* junction, connection.
giuocàre *v* **giocàre**.
giuòco *v* **giòco**.
giuraménto *nm* oath.
giuràre *vti* to swear, take an oath.
giuràto *a* sworn; *nm* juryman.
giureconsúlto *nm* jurisconsult.
giurí *nm* **giuría** *nf* jury.
giurídico *pl* **-ici** *a* juridical.
giurisdizióne *nf* jurisdiction.
giurisprudènza *nf* jurisprudence.
giurísta *nm* jurist.
Giuşèppe *nm pr* Joseph.
Giuşeppína *nf pr* Josephine.
giústa *prep* according to.
giustaménte *ad* justly, rightly.
giustézza *nf* exactness, propriety.
giustificàre *vt* to justify; **-rsi** *vr* to excuse oneself, justify oneself.
giustificazióne *nf* justification, excuse; (*at school*) absence note.
Giustiniàno *nm pr* Justinian.
Giustíno *nm pr* Justin.
giustízia *nf* justice.
giustiziàre *vt* to execute, put to death.
giustiziàto *a* executed; *nm* executed man.
giustizière *nm* executioner, avenger.

giústo *a* fair, just, lawful, proper, right; *nm* just man; **i giústi** *pl* the just, the right; *ad* just, precisely.
glàbro *a* hairless, smooth.
glaciàle *a* glacial, icy.
gladiatóre *nm* gladiator.
gladíolo *nm* gladiolus.
glàndola *nf* gland.
glandulàre *a* glandular.
glassàre *vt* to ice, glaze.
glàuco *pl* **-chi** *a* glaucous, grayish blue or green.
glèba *nf* glebe, soil, earth; **sèrvo della g.** *nm* serf.
gli *art m pl* the; *pron m* (*dat*) to him, (*idiom*) to them.
glicerína *nf* glycerin(e).
glícine *nf* wistaria.
globàle *a* global, total, inclusive.
glòbo *nm* globe; **g. dell'òcchio** eyeball.
glòbulo *nm* globule.
glòria *nf* glory.
gloriàrsi *vr* to boast of, be proud of, pride oneself on.
glorificaménto *nm* **glorificazióne** *nf* glorification.
glorificàre *vt* to glorify.
glorióso *a* glorious, proud.
glòssa *nf* gloss, explanation, annotation.
glossàre *vt* to gloss.
glossàrio *nm* glossary.
glucòsio *nm* glucose.
glúteo *a* gluteal; *nm* (*anat*) gluteus.
glutinàto *a* gluten.
glutinosità *nf* viscosity.
gnaulàre *vi* to mew.
gnòmo *nm* gnome, goblin.
gnòstico *pl* **-ici** *a* gnostic.
gòbba *nf* hump.
gòbbo *a* hump-backed.
góccia, gócciola *nf* drop.
góccio *nm* drop.
gocciolaménto *nm* **gocciolatúra** *nf* dripping, trickling.
gocciolàre *vti* to drip, drop, trickle.
gocciolío *nm* dripping, trickling.
gócciolo *nm* drop.
godè *nm* flare; **gónna a g.** flared skirt.
godére *vti* to enjoy, be glad; **-rsi** *vr* **-rsela** *vr* to enjoy oneself.
goderéccio *a* enjoyable.
godiménto *nm* enjoyment, pleasure; possession, use.
goffàggine *nf* awkwardness, clumsiness.
goffaménte *ad* awkwardly, clumsily.
gòffo *a* awkward, clumsy.
Goffrèdo *nm pr* Geoffrey, Godfrey.
gógna *nf* pillory; **méttere alla g.** to pillory.
góla *nf* throat; gorge; gluttony; **far g.** to be a temptation.
golétta *nf* schooner; narrow gorge; collar.
golf *nm* cardigan, jumper, sweater; golf.
gólfo *nm* gulf.
goliàrdo *nm* university student.
golosaménte *ad* greedily.
golosità *nf* greed, gluttony.
golóso *a* greedy, gluttonous.
gólpe *nf* blight, mildew.
gómena *nf* (*naut*) cable, hawser.
gomitàta *nf* shove with the elbow.
gómito *nm* elbow.
gomítolo *nm* (*of thread etc*) ball.
gómma *nf* rubber, gum, resin; tire.
gommapiúma *nf* foam rubber.
gommàto *a* gummed.
gommóso *a* gummy.
góndola *nf* gondola.
gondolière *nm* gondolier.
gonfalóne *nm* flag, standard.
gonfalonière *nm* standard-bearer.
gonfiàre *vt* to inflate, swell; **-rsi** *vr* to swell (up).
gonfiatóio *nm* inflator, tire pump.
gonfiatúra *nf* swelling, inflation, exaggeration, stunt, adulation.
gonfiézza *nf* swelling.
gónfio *a* swollen, inflated.
gonfióre *nm* swelling.
gongolàre *vi* to rejoice, exult.
goniòmetro *nm* protractor.
gónna *nf* skirt; **gonnellíno** *nm* short skirt; **g. scozzése** kilt.
gónzo *nm* blockhead, foo .
gòra *nf* millrace, millpond, pond.
gorgheggiàre *vi* to trill, warble.
gorghéggio *nm* trilling, warbling.
gorgièra *nf* ruff.
górgo *pl* **-ghi** *nm* whirlpool, abyss.
gorgogliàre *vi* to gurgle, bubble.
gorgoglío *nm* gurgling.
gorílla *nm* gorilla.
gòta *nf* cheek.
gòtico *pl* **-ici** *a* Gothic.
gòto *nm* Goth.
gótta *nf* gout.
gottóso *a* gouty.
governànte *nm* ruler, statesman; *nf* governess, housekeeper.
governàre *vt* to govern, rule, (*naut*) steer, (*av*) control; groom, tend.
governatívo *a* government(al).
governatóre *nm* governor, ruler.
govèrno *nm* government, rule; **g. della càsa** housekeeping.
gózzo *nm* goiter; bird's crop.
gozzovíglia *nf* debauch, revelry.
gozzovigliàre *vi* to revel.
gozzúto *a* goitrous, goitered.
gracchiàre *vi* to caw.
gracidaménto *nm* croaking.
gracidàre *vi* to croak.
gràcile *a* weak, delicate, frail.
gracilità *nf* weakness, thinness.
gradàsso *nm* blusterer, braggart.
gradazióne *nf* gradation, shade.
gradévole *a* agreeable, pleasant.
gradiènte *nm* gradient.
gradiménto *nm* liking, pleasure, satisfaction, approval.
gradinàta *nf* flight of steps.
gradíno *nm* step.
gradíre *vt* to like, wish; accept.
gradíto *a* agreeable, pleasant, welcome.

gràdo *nm* degree, pleasure, rank, will; **èssere in g. di** to be able to.
graduàle *a* gradual.
gradualménte *ad* gradually.
graduàre *vt* to confer (a degree or rank), graduate, grade.
graduàto *a* graded, progressive, graduated; *nm* (*mil*) non-commissioned officer (N.C.O.).
graduatòria *nf* classification, pass list.
graduazióne *nf* graduation; scale.
graffiàre *vt* to scratch.
graffiatúra *nf* scratch.
gràffio *nm* scratch; (*naut*) grapnel.
grafía *nf* writing, spelling.
gràfico *pl* **-ici** *a* graphic; *nm* graph.
grafología *nf* graphology.
gragnuòla *nf* (*fig*) hail, shower.
Gràie, (Àlpi) *nf pl* (*geogr*) Graian Alps.
gramàglie *nf pl* deep mourning.
gramígna *nf* couch-grass, weed.
grammàtica *nf* grammar.
grammaticàle *a* grammatical.
gràmmo *nm* gram.
gràmo *a* miserable, poor, wretched.
gràna *nf* (*tec*) grain; (*fam*) trouble; Parmesan cheese.
granàglie *nf pl* wheat, grain.
granàio *nm* barn, granary.
granàta *nf* broom, brush; grenade.
granatière *nm* grenadier.
granàto *a* garnet red; *nm* garnet.
grancàssa *nf* bass drum.
grànchio *nm* crab; **prèndere un g.** to make a mistake.
grànde *a* great, big, high, tall, grown up, wide; *nm* great man, grandee; **i gràndi** *pl* grown-ups *pl*.
grandeggiàre *vi* to rise to a great height, tower above.
grandézza *nf* greatness, height, size, grandeur; highness.
grandígia *nf* pomp, arrogance.
grandinàre *vti* to hail, shower.
grandinàta *nf* hailstorm (*also fig*).
gràndine *nf* hail.
grandiosità *nf* grandiosity, grandeur.
grandióso *a* grand, grandiose.
grandúca *nm* grand duke; **granduchéssa** *nf* grand duchess.
granducàto *nm* grand duchy.
granèllo *nm* grain, seed.
grànfia *nf* claw, clutch.
granífero *a* grain-producing.
graníre *vt* to grain; (*teeth*) cut; *vi* to seed.
graníta *nf* grated-ice drink, often fruit-flavored.
graníto *nm* granite.
gràno *nm* wheat, corn, grain; (*necklace*) bead; **g. saracèno** buckwheat.
grantúrco *pl* **-chi** *nm* maize, corn.
granulazióne *nf* granulation.
granulóso *a* granulous.
gràppa *nf* clamp, cramp iron, stalk, (*typ*) bracket; brandy.
gràppolo *nm* bunch, cluster.
grassatóre *nm* highwayman.
grassazióne *nf* robbery.
grassétto *a nm* (*typ*) heavy-faced, heavy type.
grassézza *nf* fatness, stoutness; greasiness, abundance.
gràsso *a* fat, abundant, fertile; **martedí g.** Shrove Tuesday.
grassòccio *a* plump.
grassúme *nm* fat substance.
gràta *nf* grating.
graticciàta *nf* trellis-work, fence.
graticcio *nm* hurdle, trellis-work.
gratícola *nf* grill, grate, grating.
gratífica *nf* bonus.
gratificàre *vt* to gratify.
gratificazióne *nf* bonus, gratuity.
gràtis *ad* free, gratis.
gratitúdine *nf* gratitude.
gràto *a* grateful, obliged; welcome.
grattacàpo *nm* problem, trouble.
grattacièlo *nm* skyscraper.
grattàre *vt* to scrape, scratch.
grattúgia *nf* grater.
grattugiàre *vt* to grate.
gratuitaménte *ad* free of charge, gratuitously.
gratúito *a* free, gratuitous.
gravàme *nm* burden, duty, tax.
gravàre *vti* to burden, load, weigh on.
gràve *a* heavy, great, serious, stern, grave; *nm* (*phys*) body; seriousness; **èssere g.** to be seriously ill.
graveménte *ad* gravely, heavily, deeply.
gravézza *nf* heaviness, gravity, weight; tax.
gravidànza *nf* pregnancy.
gràvido *a* pregnant, (*fig*) full, loaded.
gravità *nf* gravity, seriousness, weight.
gravitàre *vi* to gravitate.
gravitazióne *nf* gravitation.
gravosità *nf* heaviness, oppressiveness.
gravóso *a* heavy, oppressive.
gràzia *nf* grace, favor, mercy.
Gràzia *nf pr* Grace.
graziàre *vt* to pardon, grant.
gràzie *interj* thanks, thank you.
graziosità *nf* prettiness, graciousness.
grazióso *a* dainty, pretty, gracious.
Grècia *nf* (*geogr*) Greece.
grecísta *nmf* Hellenist.
grèco *pl* **grèci** *a nm* Greek.
gregàrio *a* gregarious; *nm* (*mil*) private, follower.
grégge *nm* flock, herd.
gréggio *a* (*of materials*) coarse; (*fig*) crude.
Gregòrio *nm pr* Gregory.
grembiúle *nm* apron.
grèmbo *nm* lap, (*fig*) bosom.
gremíre *vt* to crowd, fill; **-rsi** *vr* to fill up, get crowded.

gremíto *a* crowded, packed.
gréppia *nf* crib, manger, rack.
gréppo *nm* cliff, rock; (*of a ditch*) edge.
gréto *nm* pebbly bank.
grettézza *nf* meanness, stinginess.
grétto *a* mean, niggardly, stingy.
grève *a* heavy.
grézzo *v* **gréggio.**
gridàre *vti* to shout, cry, scream, call, proclaim.
grído *nm* cry, shout, scream; **di g.** famous.
grifàgno *a* predatory, fierce.
grífo *nm* snout; griffin, griffon.
grifóne *nm* griffin, griffon.
grigiàstro *a* grayish.
grígio *a nm* gray.
grigiovérde *a* gray-green; *nm* (*mil*) gray-green (Italian) uniform.
gríglia *nf* grate, grating, grill, grid; **alla g.** grilled, broiled.
grillétto *nm* trigger.
grillo *nm* cricket; (*fig*) whim.
grínfia *nf* claw, clutch.
grínta *nf* forbidding face.
grínza *nf* crease, wrinkle.
grinzóso *a* creased, wrinkled.
grippàre *vi* (*mech*) to seize.
grissíno *nm* breadstick.
grisú *nm* firedamp.
groenlandése *a* (of) Greenland; *nmf* Greenlander.
Groenlàndia *nf* (*geogr*) Greenland.
grónda *nf* eaves *pl.*
grondàia *nf* gutter.
grondàre *vi* to stream, drip; *vt* to pour.
gròppa *nf* back, rump.
gròssa *nf* gross (12 dozen).
grossézza *nf* bigness, size, thickness, dullness, coarseness.
grossísta *nm* wholesale dealer, stockist, distributor.
gròsso *a* big, thick; *nm* main body, chief part; **pèzzo g.** bigwig.
grossolanità *nf* coarseness, grossness.
grossolàno *a* coarse, gross, rude.
gròtta *nf* cave, grotto.
grottésco *pl* **-schi** *a* grotesque; *nm* grotesqueness.
grovíglio *nm* tangle, confusion.
gru *nf* crane.
grúccia *nf* crutch, coathanger; (*for birds*) perch, (*door*) handle.
grugníre *vi* to grunt.
grúgno *nm* muzzle, snout.
grúllo *a nm* foolish, silly, foul.
grúmo *nm* clot.
grumóso *a* clotted.
grúppo *nm* group, knot.
grúzzolo *nm* hoard, savings *pl.*
guadàbile *a* fordable.
guadagnàre *vt* **-rsi** *vr* to earn, gain, acquire, win, reach.
guadàgno *nm* gain, profit.
guadàre *vi* to ford, wade.
guàdo *nm* ford.
guài *interj* woe!
guaína *nf* sheath, case.
guàio *nm* trouble, difficulty, accident, misfortune.
guaíre *vi* to whine, yelp.
guaíto *nm* yelp, whine.
gualcíre *vt* to rumple, crease.
Gualtièro *nm pr* Walter.
guància *nf* cheek.
guancièle *nm* pillow.
guantàio *nm* glover.
guantièra *nf* glove box, tray.
guànto *nm* glove.
guardabòschi *nm* forester.
guardacàccia, guardiacàccia *nm* gamekeeper.
guardacòste *nm* coastguard.
guardàre *vt* to look at, gaze at, watch, consider, protect, guard; **-rsi** *vr* to look at oneself, abstain from, beware of, forbear, look at each other.
guardaròba *nf* cloakroom, wardrobe.
guardarobièra *nf* cloakroom attendant, linen maid.
guardasigílli *nm* Lord Privy Seal.
guardàta *nf* look, glance.
guardatúra *nf* way of looking.
guàrdia *nf* guard, watch, look out; **g. del còrpo** bodyguard.
guardiàno *nm* keeper, watchman.
guardína *nf* guardroom.
guardíngo *pl* **-ínghi** *a* cautious.
guarentígia *nf* guarantee.
guarìbile *a* curable.
guarigióne *nf* recovery.
guaríre *vt* to cure, heal; *vi* to recover.
guarnigióne *nf* garrison.
guarníre *vt* to garnish, trim, furnish.
guarnizióne *nf* garnishing, trimming.
Guascógna *nf* (*geogr*) Gascony.
guascóne *a nm* Gascon, (*fig*) gascon, braggart.
guastafèste *nm* spoilsport, wet blanket.
guastamestièri *nm* bungler.
guastàre *vt* to spoil, ruin; **-rsi** *vr* to spoil, be spoiled, quarrel.
guàsto *a* spoiled, damaged, decayed, corrupt; *nm* damage.
guatàre *vt* to gaze, stare.
guàzza *nf* heavy dew.
guazzàre *vi* to paddle, wallow.
guazzétto *nm* stew.
guèlfo *a nm* Guelf, Guelph.
guèrcio *a* squint-eyed.
guèrra *nf* war.
guerrafondàio *nm* warmonger.
guerreggiàre *vi* to (wage) war, fight.
guerrésco *pl* **-chi** *a* (of) war, warlike.
guerrièro *a* warlike; *nm* warrior.
guerríglia *nf* guerrilla war.
gúfo *nm* owl; misanthrope.
gúglia *nf* spire.
Guglièlmo *nm pr* William.
guída *nf* guide, guidance, leadership; (*aut*) drive, steering, driving; **g. telefònica** telephone directory;

patènte di g. driving license; scuòla g. driving school.
guidàre *vt* to guide, lead, manage; drive (*a car etc*); **-rsi** *vr* to conduct oneself, behave.
guiderdóne *nm* recompense.
Guído *nm pr* Guy.
guidoslítta *nf* bobsleigh.
guinzàglio *nm* lead, (*for dogs*) leash.
guísa *nf* manner, way; **a g. di** like.
guizzàre *vi* to dart, flash, flicker, wriggle out.
guízzo *nm* flash, wriggle.
gúscio *nm* shell, pod, cover.
gustàre *vti* to enjoy, taste, like.
gústo *nm* taste, fancy, liking, relish.
gustosità *nf* savoriness, delightfulness.
gustóso *a* tasty, savory, delightful, amusing.
gutturàle *a* guttural.

I

i *art m pl* the.
iàrda *nf* yard.
iàto *nm* hiatus.
iattànza *nf* boasting, bragging.
iattúra *nf* misfortune.
ibèri *nm pl* Iberians.
Ibèria *nf* (*geogr*) Iberia.
ibèrico *pl* **-ici** *a* Iberian.
ibridísmo *nm* hybridism.
íbrido *a* hybrid.
icàstico *pl* **-ici** *a* figurative, graphic.
icòna, icòne *nf* icon.
iconoclàsta, iconoclàste *nm* iconoclast.
Iddío *nm* God.
idèa *nf* idea, notion, opinion, ideal, intention.
ideàle *a nm* ideal.
idealísmo *nm* idealism.
idealista *nmf* idealist.
idealizzàre *vt* to idealize.
ideàre *vt* to imagine, plan.
idèntico *pl* **-ici** *a* identical.
identificàre *vt* to identify.
identificazióne *nf* identification.
identità *nf* identity.
ideología *nf* ideology.
idillíaco, idíllico *a* idyllic.
idíllio *nm* idyll.
idiòma *nm* language.
idiomàtico *pl* **-ici** *a* idiomatic.
idiosincrasía *nf* idiosyncrasy.
idiòta *a* idiotic; *nmf* idiot.
idiotísmo *nm* idiom, idiomatic expression.
idiozía *nf* idiocy.
idolatràre *vt* to worship, idolize.
idolatría *nf* idolatry.
idoleggiàre *vt* to idolize.
ídolo *nm* idol.
idoneità *nf* fitness, ability.
idòneo *a* fit, suitable.
ídra *nf* hydra.
idrànte *nm* hydrant, fire-plug, water-plug.
idràulico *pl* **-ici** *a* hydraulic; *nm* plumber.
ídro *nm* water snake; (*short for*) idrovolànte seaplane.
idroelèttrico *pl* **-ici** *a* hydroelectric; **centràle idroelèttrica** hydroelectric power station.
idròfilo *a* absorbent; **cotóne i.** absorbent cotton.
idròfobo *a* hydrophobic, rabid.
idrògeno *nm* hydrogen.
ídrope *nm* **idropisía** *nf* (*med*) dropsy.
idròpico *pl* **-ici** *a nm* dropsical, dropsical person.
idroplàno *nm* seaplane.
idropòrto, idroscàlo *nm* flying-boat station.
ièna *nf* hyena.
Ièova *nm pr* Jehovah.
ièri *ad* yesterday; **i. l'àltro** the day before yesterday.
iettatóre *nm* **-tríce** *nf* bringer of ill-luck.
iettatúra *nf* evil eye, misfortune.
igiène *nf* hygiene.
igiènico *pl* **-ici** *a* hygienic.
ignàro *a* ignorant, unaware.
ignàvia *nf* sloth.
ignàvo *a* slothful.
ígneo *a* igneous.
ignizióne *nf* ignition.
ignòbile *a* ignoble.
ignomínia *nf* ignominy.
ignominióso *a* ignominious.
ignorànte *a* ignorant.
ignorànza *nf* ignorance.
ignoràre *vt* to be ignorant of, ignore.
ignòto *a* unknown; *nm* unknown person.
ignúdo *a* naked, unclothed.
igròmetro *nm* (*phys*) hygrometer.
il *art m* the.
ílare *a* gay, cheerful.
ilarità *nf* gaiety, hilarity.
Ílda *nf pr* Hilda.
ilíaco *pl* **-aci** *a* (*anat*) iliac; Trojan.
illanguidíre *vt* to weaken; *vi* to grow feeble, languish.
illécito *a* illicit, unlawful.
illegàle *a* illegal, unlawful.
illegalità *nf* illegality.
illeggíbile *a* illegible.
illegittimità *nf* illegitimacy, unlawfulness.
illegíttimo *a* illegitimate, unlawful.
illéso *a* unhurt, uninjured.
illetteràto *a* illiterate, unlettered.
illibatézza *nf* chastity, purity.
illibàto *a* chaste, pure.
illiberàle *a* illiberal.
illimitàto *a* boundless, unlimited.
illividíre *vt* to make livid; *vi* to grow livid.
illògico *pl* **-ici** *a* illogical.
illúdere *vt* to deceive, delude.
illuminànte *a* illuminating, (*fig*) enlightening.
illuminàre *vt* to enlighten, illuminate, light; **-rsi** *vr* to light up.

illuminazióne *nf* illumination, lighting.
illuminísmo *nm* illuminism.
illusióne *nf* illusion, dream.
illusòrio *a* deceptive, illusory.
illustràre *vt* to illustrate, explain, make illustrious.
illustratívo *a* illustrative.
illustrazióne *nf* illustration.
illústre *a* famous, illustrious.
imaginífico *pl* **-ici** *a* with a rich imagination.
Imalàia *nf* (*geogr*) Himalaya.
imbacuccàre *vt* to muffle up, wrap.
imbaldanzíre *vt* to embolden; **-rsi** *vr* to grow bold.
imballàggio *nm* packing, wrapping.
imballàre *vt* to pack, wrap.
imbàllo *nm* (*aut*) racing; packing, wrapping.
imbalsamàre *vt* to embalm, (*animals*) stuff.
imbambolàto *a* bewildered, stunned, dull, drowsy, confused.
imbandieràre *vt* to beflag.
imbandigióne *nf* preparation of a banquet, dish, table.
imbandíre *vt* to prepare a gala meal, lay (the table).
imbarazzànte *a* embarrassing, awkward.
imbarazzàre *vt* to embarrass, perplex, hamper.
imbaràzzo *nm* embarrassment, difficulty; **i. di stòmaco** indigestion.
imbarcadèro *nm* landing-place, pier.
imbarcàre *vt* to put (take) on board, ship; **-rsi** *vr* to embark, take ship.
imbarcatóio *nm* pier.
imbarcazióne *nf* boat.
imbàrco *pl* **-chi** *nm* embarkation, loading.
imbastíre *vt* (*in sewing*) to tack; (*fig*) to improvise, sketch.
imbàttersi *vr* to fall in with.
imbattíbile *a* unbeatable.
imbavagliàre *vt* to gag.
imbeccàre *vt* to feed; (*fig*) prompt.
imbecílle *a nmf* imbecile.
imbèlle *a* cowardly, weak.
imbellettàrsi *vr* to paint one's face.
imbèrbe *a* beardless.
imbestialíre *vi* to grow furious.
imbévere *vt* to imbue, steep; **-rsi** *vr* to become imbued with.
imbiancaménto *nm* whitewashing, bleaching, whitening; (*of hair*) graying.
imbiancàre, imbianchíre *vti* to bleach, whiten, whitewash, turn white, grow gray.
imbianchino *nm* house-painter.
imbizzarríre *vi* **-rsi** *vr* (*of horses*) to rear, grow furious, spirited.
imboccàre *vti* to feed, prompt, enter, fit, flow into.
imboccatúra *nf* **imbócco** *pl* **-chi** *nm* mouth, opening, entrance, mouthpiece.
imboscaménto *nm* hiding, shirking military service.
imboscàre *vt* **-rsi** *vr* to hide, lie in wait, help evade military service, evade military service.
imboscàta *nf* ambush.
imbottigliàre *vt* to bottle.
imbottíre *vt* to pad, stuff.
imbottitúra *nf* stuffing, wadding, quilting.
imbrattàre *vt* to daub, dirty.
imbrigliàre *vt* to bridle, curb.
imbroccàre *vt* to guess right, hit the mark.
imbrogliàre *vt* to cheat, swindle, muddle, entangle; **-rsi** *vr* to get confused.
imbróglio *nm* tangle, confused situation, trick, fraud.
imbroglióne *nm* cheat, swindler.
imbronciàre *vi* **-rsi** *vr* to take offense, sulk.
imbrunàre, imbruníre *vi* to darken, grow dark.
imbruttíre *vt* to disfigure, make ugly; *vi* to grow ugly.
imbucàre *vt* to post, put into a hole; **-rsi** *vr* to creep into a hole.
imburràre *vt* to butter.
imbúto *nm* funnel.
imitàre *vt* to imitate, copy, mimic.
imitatívo *a* imitative.
imitazióne *nf* imitation.
immacolàto *a* immaculate, spotless.
immagazzinàre *vi* to store.
immaginàre *vt* to imagine, fancy; **-rsi** *vr* to fancy, imagine, picture.
immaginazióne *nf* imagination, fancy.
immàgine *nf* image, picture.
immancabilménte *ad* unfailingly, certainly.
immàne *a* enormous, huge, frightful.
immangiàbile *a* uneatable.
immantinénte *ad* at once, immediately.
immateriàle *a* immaterial.
immatricolàre *vt* **-rsi** *vr* to matriculate.
immaturità *nf* immaturity, unripeness.
immatúro *a* unripe, immature.
immedesimàrsi *vr* to identify oneself with.
immediataménte *ad* immediately, directly, forthwith.
immediàto *a* immediate.
immemoràbile *a* immemorial.
immèmore *a* forgetful, unmindful.
immensità *nf* immensity.
immènso *a* immense, vast.
immensuràbile *a* immeasurable.
immèrgere *vt* to immerse, dip, plunge; **-rsi** *vr* to immerse oneself.
immeritàto *a* undeserved, unmerited.
immeritévole *a* undeserving, unworthy.
immersióne *nf* immersion.
immèrso *a* immersed (*also fig*).

immigrànte *a nmf* immigrant.
immigràre *vi* to immigrate.
immigrazióne *nf* immigration.
imminènte *a* imminent, impending.
imminènza *nf* imminence.
immischiàre *vt* to bring into, involve; **-rsi** *vr* to interfere, meddle.
immiṣerìre *vt* to impoverish; *vi* to grow poor.
immissàrio *nm* affluent, tributary.
immòbile *a* immovable, motionless; *nm pl* **gli immòbili** immovables, immovable property, real estate.
immobilità *nf* immobility.
immobiliẓẓàre *vt* to immobilize.
immobiliẓẓazióne *nf* immobilization.
immodèstia *nf* immodesty.
immodèsto *a* immodest.
immolàre *vt* to immolate, sacrifice.
immolazióne *nf* immolation.
immollàre *vt* to wet; **-rsi** *vr* to get wet.
immondézza *nf* uncleanness, filth, garbage.
immondezzàio *nm* garbage heap.
immondízia *nf* garbage, filth.
immóndo *a* unclean, dirty.
immoràle *a* immoral.
immoralità *nf* immorality.
immortalàre *vt* to immortalize.
immortàle *a* immortal.
immortalità *nf* immortality.
immòto *a* motionless.
immúne *a* immune, free, exempt.
immunità *nf* immunity, freedom.
immuniẓẓàre *vt* to immunize; **-rsi** *vr* to become immune.
impaccàre *vt* to pack.
impacchettàre *vt* to make up packets, pack.
impacciàre *vt* to hinder, embarrass, encumber; **-rsi** *vr* to meddle.
impacciàto *a* awkward, embarrassed, self-conscious.
impàccio *nm* encumbrance, obstacle, bother, embarrassment.
impadronírsi *vr* to take possession of, seize, master.
impagàbile *a* priceless, invaluable.
impaginàre *vt* (*typ*) to make up (a book), page.
impagliàre *vt* to cover with straw.
impalàto *a* rigid, stiff.
impalcàre *vt* to board, plank.
impalcatúra *nf* scaffolding.
impallidíre *vi* to turn pale.
impalpàbile *a* impalpable.
impaludàre *vi* **-rsi** *vr* to grow marshy.
impanàto *a* covered with bread crumbs.
impancàrsi *vr* to presume, act like.
impantanàrsi *vr* to sink in the mud, be bogged.
impappinàrsi *vr* to become confused.
imparàre *vt* to learn.
imparatíccio *nm* thing badly learned, beginner's work.
impareggiàbile *a* incomparable.
imparentàrsi *vr* to become related, marry into.
ímpari *a* odd, uneven, unequal.
impartíre *vt* to impart, bestow, give.
imparziàle *a* impartial, unbiased.
impassíbile *a* impassible, impassive.
impastàre *vt* to knead, mix.
impàsto *nm* mixture.
impastoiàre *vt* to shackle, hinder, impede.
impauríre *vt* to frighten; **-rsi** *vr* to get frightened.
impaziènte *a* impatient.
impazientíre *vi* **-rsi** *vr* to lose one's patience.
impazientíto *a* irritated, annoyed.
impaziènza *nf* impatience.
impazzàre, impazzíre *vi* to be crazy about, go mad.
impeccàbile *a* impeccable.
impeciàre *vt* to pitch, tar.
impediménto *nm* impediment, hindrance, obstacle.
impedíre *vt* to prevent, obstruct, hinder.
impegnàre *vt* to bind, engage, pledge, pawn; **-rsi** *vr* to bind, engage oneself, get involved.
impegnatívo *a* binding, exacting.
impègno *nm* engagement, obligation, care.
impenetràbile *a* impenetrable, inscrutable.
impenitènte *a* impenitent.
impenitènza *nf* impenitence.
impensàbile *a* inconceivable, unthinkable.
impensataménte *ad* unexpectedly.
impensàto *a* unthought of, unforeseen, unexpected.
impensierìre *vt* to make uneasy; **-rsi** *vr* to worry.
imperànte *a* ruling, reigning, prevailing.
imperàre *vt* to rule (over).
imperatívo *a nm* imperative.
imperatóre *nm* emperor; **-tríce** *nf* empress.
impercettíbile *a* imperceptible.
imperdonàbile *a* unpardonable.
imperfètto *a nm* imperfect.
imperfezióne *nf* fault, flaw, imperfection.
imperiàle *a* imperial.
imperialiṣmo *nm* imperialism.
imperiosità *nf* imperiousness.
imperióso *a* domineering, imperious.
imperízia *nf* lack of experience, lack of skill.
impermalírsi *vr* to get cross.
impermeàbile *a nm* waterproof.
impermeabilità *nf* impermeability.
imperniàre *vt* **-rsi** *vr* to pivot, hinge.
impèro *nm* empire, command.
impersonàle *a* impersonal.
impersonàre *vt* to impersonate.
impertèrrito *a* undaunted, fearless.
impertinènte *a* impertinent, saucy.

impertinènza *nf* impertinence.
imperturbàbile *a* imperturbable.
imperversàre *vi* (*of diseases, weather etc*) to rage.
impèrvio *a* hard to reach, inaccessible.
ímpeto *nm* impetus, vehemence, impulse, outburst, transport.
impetràre *vt* to ask for, obtain.
impetuosità *nf* impetuosity, impulsiveness.
impetuóso *a* impetuous, vehement.
impiantàre *vt* to establish, set up.
impiantíto *nm* floor.
impiànto *nm* installation, plant, establishment.
impiastràre *vt* to daub, plaster, smear.
impiàstro *nm* plaster; (*fig*) bore.
impiccagióne *nf* hanging (on the gallows).
impiccàre *vt* to hang; **-rsi** *vr* to hang oneself.
impicciàre *etc v* **impacciare** *etc.*
impiccolíre *vt* to make smaller, diminish, lessen.
impiegàre *vt* to employ, spend, invest; **-rsi** *vr* to get a post.
impiegàto *nm* clerk, employee.
impiègo *pl* **-ghi** *nm* employment, job, position, use.
impietosíre *vt* to move to pity; **-rsi** *vr* to be touched.
impietràre, impietríre *vt* to petrify.
impigliàre *vt* to entangle.
impigríre *vt* to make lazy; **-rsi** *vr* to grow lazy.
impinguàre *vt* to fatten, enrich; **-rsi** *vr* to grow fat, get rich.
impiombàre *vt* to seal with lead, splice (a cable), stop (a tooth), lead.
impiombatúra *nf* sealing with lead, stopping (a tooth), splicing (a cable), leading.
implacàbile *a* implacable, relentless.
implicàre *vt* to implicate, involve, imply.
implicazióne *nf* implication.
implícito *a* implicit.
implorànte *a* imploring.
imploràre *vt* to entreat, implore.
implorazióne *nf* entreaty.
impolítico *pl* **-ici** *a* impolitic.
impoltroníre *vt* to make lazy; **-rsi** *vr* to become lazy.
impolveràre *vt* to cover with dust.
imponderàbile *a nm* imponderable.
imponènte *a* imposing, impressive.
imponènza *nf* grandeur.
imponíbile *a* chargeable, taxable.
impopolàre *a* unpopular.
impopolarità *nf* unpopularity.
impórre *vt* to impose; **-rsi** *vr* to impose oneself, make oneself respected, have success.
importànte *a* important, weighty; *nm* important thing.
importànza *nf* importance.
importàbile *a* importable.
importàre *vt* to import, imply, involve, cost; *v impers* to matter, be of importance.
importazióne *nf* importation, import.
impòrto *nm* amount.
importunaménte *ad* importunately, troublesomely.
importunàre *vt* to importune, bother.
importunità *nf* importunity.
importúno *a* troublesome, importunate, untimely; *nm* intruder.
imposizióne *nf* imposition.
impossessàrsi *vr* to take possession of.
impossíbile *a* impossible.
impossibilità *nf* impossibility.
impossibilitàto *a* unable.
impósta *nf* tax, duty; shutter.
impostàre *vt* to post, mail; set up, lay down.
impostazióne *nf* posting, formulation, general lines.
impostóre *nm* impostor, swindler.
impostúra *nf* imposture, fraud.
impotènte *a* impotent, powerless.
impotènza *nf* impotence, powerlessness.
impoveriménto *nm* impoverishment.
impoveríre *vt* to impoverish; **-rsi** *vr* to grow poor.
impraticàbile *a* impracticable, (*road*) impassable.
impratichíre *vt* to train, exercise; **-rsi** *vr* to practice, exercise oneself.
imprecàre *vt* to curse, swear.
imprecazióne *nf* curse, imprecation.
imprecisióne *nf* inaccuracy, lack of precision.
imprecíso *a* inaccurate, vague.
impregnàre *vt* to impregnate.
impremeditàto *a* unpremeditated.
imprèndere *vt* to begin, undertake.
imprenditóre *nm* contractor; **i. di pómpe fúnebri** funeral undertaker.
impreparàto *a* unprepared.
imprésa *nf* undertaking, enterprise, deed, contract, firm; **i. autotraspòrti** road haulage firm, truck line.
impresàrio *nm* contractor, impresario, undertaker.
imprescindíbile *a* that cannot be ignored, indispensable, absolute.
impressionàbile *a* impressionable.
impressionànte *a* striking, impressive.
impressionàre *vt* to impress, frighten; **-rsi** *vr* to be frightened.
impressióne *nf* impression, sensation, imprint.
impressionísmo *nm* impressionism.
imprestàre *etc v* **prestare** *etc.*
imprevedíbile *a* unforeseeable.
imprevidènte *a* improvident.
imprevidènza *nf* improvidence.
imprevísto *a* unexpected, unforeseen; *nm* unexpected event.

imprigionàre *vt* to imprison.
imprimé *nm* printed cloth, print dress.
imprímere *vt* to impress. imprint, print, engrave.
improbàbile *a* improbable, unlikely.
improbabilità *nf* unlikelihood, improbability.
improbità *nf* dishonesty, wickedness.
ímprobo *a* dishonest, wicked, hard.
improduttività *nf* unproductiveness.
improduttívo *a* unproductive.
impróntá *nf* impression, mark, print, stamp.
improntàto *a* stamped, marked with.
impropèrio *nm* abuse, abusive word.
impropriaménte *ad* incorrectly, improperly.
improprietà *nf* impropriety, inaccuracy.
impròprio *a* improper, unsuitable.
improrogàbile *a* that cannot be postponed.
impròv(v)ido *a* improvident, rash.
improvvișaménte *ad* suddenly, unexpectedly.
improvvișàre *vti* to extemporize, improvise.
improvvișàta *nf* surprise.
improvvișàto *a* improvised, extempore, unscripted.
improvvișatóre *nm* **-tríce** *nf* extemporizer, improviser.
improvvișazióne *nf* improvisation.
improvvíșo *a* sudden, unexpected, unforeseen; **all'i.** suddenly.
imprudènte *a* imprudent, rash.
imprudènza *nf* imprudence, rashness.
impudènte *a* impudent, shameless.
impudènza *nf* impudence, shamelessness.
impudicízia *nf* immodesty.
impudíco *pl* **-chi** *a* immodest, shameless.
impugnàre *vt* to impugn; grip, take up (arms).
impugnatúra *nf* grip, hilt.
impulsività *nf* impulsiveness, rashness.
impulsívo *a* impulsive.
impúlso *nm* impulse, impetus.
impunità *nf* impunity.
impuníto *a* unpunished.
impuntàrsi *vr* to be stubborn.
impurità *nf* impurity.
impúro *a* impure, unclean.
imputàbile *a* imputable.
imputàre *vt* to impute, charge, accuse.
imputàto *nm* accused, defendant.
imputazióne *nf* imputation, charge.
imputridíre *vi* to putrefy, rot.
in *prep* in, into, on, to, by, at.
inàbile *a* incapable, unable, unfit.
inabilità *nf* inability, unfitness.
inabilitazióne *nf* disability, disqualification.
inabissàrsi *vr* to sink.
inabitàbile *a* uninhabitable.
inabitàto *a* uninhabited.
inaccessíbile *a* inaccessible.
inaccettàbile *a* unacceptable.
inaccordàbile *a* ungrantable; (*mus*) untunable.
inacerbíre *vt* to embitter, exacerbate.
inacidíre *vt* to sour; *vi* to turn sour.
inadattàbile *a* unadaptable.
inadàtto *a* unfit, unsuitable, improper.
inadeguatézza *nf* inadequacy.
inadeguàto *a* inadequate, insufficient.
inadempiménto *nm* non-fulfillment.
inafferràbile *a* unseizable, elusive.
inalberàre *vt* to hoist, raise; **-rsi** *vr* to get angry.
inalienàbile *a* inalienable.
inalteràbile *a* unalterable.
inamidàre *vt* to starch.
inammissíbile *a* inadmissible.
inamovíbile *a* irremovable.
inàne *a* inane, vain.
inanimàto *a* inanimate.
inanità *nf* inanity, vanity.
inappagàto *a* unsatisfied.
inappellàbile *a* inappellable.
inappetènza *nf* lack of appetite.
inaridíre *vt* to parch, dry up; **-rsi** *vr* to dry up.
inarrivàbile *a* unattainable, incomparable.
inarticolàto *a* inarticulate.
inaspettàto *a* sudden, unexpected.
inaspriménto *nm* embitterment, exacerbation.
inasprire *vt* to embitter, exacerbate; **-rsi** *vr* to become embittered.
inastàre *vt* to hoist.
inattaccàbile *a* unassailable.
inattendíbile *a* unreliable, unfounded.
inattéso *a* unexpected.
inattitúdine *nf* inaptitude.
inattività *nf* inactivity.
inattívo *a* inactive.
inàtto *a* unapt, unfit; *v* **disadàtto.**
inattuàbile *a* impracticable, unfeasible.
inaudíto *a* unheard-of.
inauguràle *a* inaugural.
inauguràre *vt* to inaugurate, open.
inaugurazióne *nf* inauguration, opening.
inavvertènza *nf* inadvertence.
inavvertíto *a* unobserved, careless.
inazióne *nf* inaction.
incagliàrsi *vr* (*naut*) to run aground.
incalcolàbile *a* incalculable.
incallíre *vi* to grow callous, harden.
incaloríre *vt* to heat.
incalvíre *vi* to grow bald.
incalzàre *vt* to chase, press, pursue.
incamminàre *vt* to set going, start; **-rsi** *vr* to set out.
incanalàre *vt* to canalize, direct.

incancellàbile *a* indelible.
incandescènte *a* incandescent, white-hot.
incandescènza *nf* incandescence.
incannàggio *nm* (*of thread etc*) reeling, winding.
incannàta *nf* spindleful.
incantaménto *nm* enchantment, spell.
incantàre *vt* to charm, enchant; **-rsi** *vr* to be enraptured, stop.
incantéşimo *nm* charm, enchantment, spell.
incantévole *a* enchanting, charming.
incantevolménte *ad* enchantingly.
incànto *nm* charm, enchantment; (*com*) public sale; **all'i.** by auction.
incanutíre *vi* to grow gray.
incapàce *a* incapable, unable.
incapacità *nf* incapacity.
incappàre *vi* to get into, fall in (with).
incapricciàrsi *vr* to take a fancy, become infatuated.
incarceràre *vt* to imprison.
incaricàre *vt* to charge, entrust; **-rsi** *vr* to take upon oneself.
incaricàto *a* charged with, entrusted with; *nm* deputy, chargé d'affaires.
incàrico *pl* **-chi** *nm* task, appointment, commission.
incarnàre *vt* to incarnate, embody.
incarnàto *a* incarnate; (*of nail*) ingrowing; *nm* rosiness.
incarnazióne *nf* incarnation, embodiment.
incartaménto *nm* dossier, documents *pl*.
incartàre *vt* to wrap in paper.
incàrto *v* **incartaménto**.
incassàre *vt* to box, cash, set, encase.
incàsso *nm* takings *pl*.
incastonàre *vt* to set (jewels).
incastràre *vt* to embed, drive in; **-rsi** *vr* to fit, get stuck.
incatenàre *vt* to chain, fetter, enthrall.
incàuto *a* incautious, rash.
incavàre *vt* to hollow out, excavate.
incàvo *nm* cavity, hollow, groove, notch, socket.
incendiàre *vt* to set on fire; **-rsi** *vr* to catch fire.
incendiàrio *a nm* incendiary.
incèndio *nm* fire.
inceneriménto *nm* incineration, cremation.
incenerire *vt* to reduce (burn) to ashes.
incensaménto *nm* incensation.
incensàre *vt* to cense; praise.
incènso *nm* incense.
incensuràbile *a* irreproachable.
incentívo *nm* incentive.
inceppàre *vt* to clog, obstruct.
inceràre *vt* to (coat with) wax.
inceràta *nf* oil cloth, tarpaulin.
incertézza *nf* uncertainty, irresolution.
incèrto *a* uncertain, doubtful, irresolute; *nm* uncertainty; **incèrti** *pl* incidental profits *pl*, uncertainties.
incespicàre *vi* to stumble, trip.
incessànte *a* incessant, unceasing.
incèsto *nm* incest.
incestuóso *a* incestuous.
incètta *nf* buying up, cornering.
incettàre *vt* (*com*) to buy up, corner.
incettatóre *nm* **-trice** *nf* monopolizer.
inchiésta *nf* inquest, inquiry.
inchinàre *vt* to incline, bow down; **-rsi** *vr* to bow, stoop.
inchíno *nm* bow, curtsey.
inchiodàre *vt* to nail, rivet, (*also fig*).
inchiòstro *nm* ink.
inciampàre *vi* to stumble, stumble across.
inciàmpo *nm* stumbling block, difficulty.
incidentàle *a* accidental, casual; incidental; parenthetical.
incidènte *nm* accident, incident, dispute.
incidènza *nf* incidence.
incídere *vt* to engrave, etch, record, incise; *vi* to weigh heavily.
incínta *a f* pregnant.
incipiènte *a* incipient.
inciprіàre *vt* to powder.
incişióne *nf* incision, engraving, recording.
incişívo *a* incisive.
incíşo *a* incised, engraved; *nm* digression, parenthesis.
incişóre *nm* engraver, etcher.
incitaménto *nm* incitement, instigation, urge.
incitàre *vt* to incite, spur, urge.
incivíle *a* uncivilized, uncivil.
inciviliménto *nm* civilization, refining.
incivilíre *vt* to civilize, refine; **-rsi** *vr* to become civilized, polite.
inciviltà *nf* incivility, barbarousness.
inclemènte *a* inclement.
inclemènza *nf* inclemency.
inclinàre *vt* to incline, bend; **-rsi** *vr* to incline, lean, slope.
inclinazióne *nf* inclination, slope, propensity.
inclíne *a* inclined, disposed, prone.
ínclito *a* famous, illustrious.
inclúdere *vt* to include, enclose, imply.
inclușióne *nf* inclusion.
inclușívo *a* inclusive.
inclúşo *a* included, enclosed.
incoerènte *a* incoherent.
incoerènza *nf* incoherence.
incògnita *nf* (*math*) unknown quantity, unknown factor.
incògnito *a nm* unknown, incognito.
incollàre *vt* to stick, paste, glue.
incollerire *vi* **-rsi** *vr* to get angry.
incolleríto *a* angry, enraged.
incolóre *a* colorless.
incolpàre *vt* to accuse, inculpate.
incolpévole *a* blameless, innocent.
incólto *a* uncultivated, unkempt.

incòlume *a* unharmed, uninjured, safe.
incolumità *nf* safety.
incombènte *a* impending.
incombènza *nf* errand, charge, task, commission.
incómbere *vi* to impend, hang, fall on.
incominciàre *vt* to begin, commence.
incomodàre *vt* to inconvenience, disturb.
incomodàto *a* indisposed.
incomodità *nf* discomfort, inconvenience.
incòmodo *a* inconvenient, uncomfortable; *nm* inconvenience, trouble.
incomparàbile *a* incomparable, matchless.
incompatíbile *a* incompatible.
incompetènte *a* incompetent, unqualified.
incompetènza *nf* incompetence.
incompiúto *a* unfinished, undone.
incomplèto *a* incomplete.
incompósto *a* disorderly, uncomely, indecent.
incomprensíbile *a* incomprehensible.
incomprensióne *nf* incomprehension.
incompréso *a* not understood.
incomunicabilità *nf* incommunicability.
inconcepíbile *a* inconceivable.
inconciliàbile *a* irreconcilable, incompatible.
inconcludènte *a* inconclusive.
inconclúso *a* unfinished.
incondizionatamènte *ad* unconditionally.
incondizionàto *a* unconditional.
incongruènte *a* incongruous.
incongruènza *nf* incongruency.
incòngruo *a* incongruous.
inconsapévole *a* unconscious, unaware, ignorant.
inconsapevolézza *nf* unconsciousness, ignorance, unawareness.
incònscio *a* unconscious; *nm* the unconscious.
inconseguènte *a* inconsequent.
inconseguènza *nf* inconsequence.
inconsideratézza *nf* inconsiderateness.
inconsideràto *a* inconsiderate, rash.
inconsistènte *a* inconsistent; unsubstantial; unfounded.
inconsolàbile *a* inconsolable.
inconsuèto *a* unusual.
inconsúlto *a* unadvised, rash.
incontentàbile *a* insatiable, exacting.
incontentabilità *nf* insatiability, unappeasability.
incontestàbile *a* indisputable, unquestionable.
incontinènte *a* incontinent.
incontinènza *nf* incontinence.
incontràre *vt* to meet, meet with; *vi* to be a success; **-rsi** *vr* to meet, agree, coincide.
incontrastàto *a* uncontested.
incóntro *nm* meeting; match; *ad* towards, opposite; **i. a** *prep* towards, opposite, against.
incontrollàbile *a* uncontrollable.
inconveniènte *a* inconvenient, unseemly; *nm* inconvenience, disadvantage.
inconveniènza *nf* inconvenience.
inconvertíbile *a* inconvertible.
incoraggiaménto *nm* encouragement.
incoraggiàre *vt* to encourage.
incorniciàre *vt* to frame.
incoronàre *vt* to crown.
incoronazióne *nf* coronation.
incorporàre *vt* to incorporate.
incorpòreo *a* incorporeal, immaterial.
incoraggiànte *a* encouraging.
incorreggíbile *a* incorrigible.
incórrere *vt* to incur, fall (into); **i. in** débiti to incur debts.
incorrótto *a* incorrupt.
incorruttíbile *a* incorruptible.
incorruttibilità *nf* incorruptibility.
incosciènte *a* unconscious; lacking conscience, reckless.
incosciènza *nf* unconsciousness; rashness; lack of conscience.
incostànte *a* inconstant, fickle, changeable.
incostànza *nf* inconstancy.
incostituzionàle *a* unconstitutional.
incredíbile *a* incredible, unbelievable.
incredibilménte *ad* incredibly, extraordinarily.
incredulità *nf* incredulity, unbelief.
incrèdulo *a* incredulous, unbelieving.
incrementàre *vt* to increase, promote, encourage.
increménto *nm* increase, increment.
increscióso *a* unpleasant.
increspaménto *nm* **increspatúra** *nf* rippling, ruffling, curling, wrinkling.
increspàre *vt* **-rsi** *vr* to ruffle, ripple, wrinkle, (*of hair*) curl.
incriminàre *vt* to incriminate.
incrinàre *vt* **-rsi** *vr* to crack.
incrociàre *vti* to cross, cruise; **-rsi** *vr* to cross, meet.
incrociatóre *nm* (*naut*) cruiser.
incrócio *nm* crossing, intersection; (*of breeds*) cross.
incrollàbile *a* unshakable.
incrostàre *vt* to encrust; **-rsi** *vr* to crust.
incrudelíre *vi* to be pitiless, commit cruelties.
incrudíre *vi* to grow harsh, rough.
incruènto *a* bloodless.
incubatríce *af* incubating; *nf* incubator.
incubazióne *nf* incubation.
íncubo *nm* nightmare, incubus.
incúdine *nf* anvil.

inculcàre *vt* to inculcate.
incuràbile *a nmf* incurable.
incurànte *a* careless, indifferent, neglectful.
incúria *nf* carelessness, neglect.
incuriosíre *vt* to make curious, rouse one's curiosity.
incursióne *nf* incursion, inroad; **i. aèrea** air raid.
incurvàre *vt* to bend, curve.
incustodíto *a* unguarded.
incútere *vt* to inspire, rouse.
índaco *pl* **-chi** *nm* indigo.
indaffaràto *a* busy.
indagàre *vt* to inquire, investigate.
indàgine *nf* inquiry, investigation, research.
indebitàrsi *vr* to get into debt.
indébito *a* undue, improper, undeserved, illegal.
indebolíre *vt* to weaken; **-rsi** *vr* to flag, grow weak(er).
indecènte *a* indecent.
indecènza *nf* indecency.
indecifràbile *a* indecipherable.
indecișióne *nf* indecision, hesitation.
indecíșo *a* undecided, hesitant.
indecoróso *a* indecorous, unseemly.
indefèsso *a* indefatigable.
indefettíbile *a* unfailing.
indefiníbile *a* indefinable.
indefiníto *a* indefinite.
indegnità *nf* shame, worthlessness.
indégno *a* undeserving, unworthy, worthless, contemptible.
indelèbile *a* indelible.
indelicatézza *nf* indelicacy.
indelicàto *a* indelicate, tactless.
indemoniàto *a* possessed; *nm* demoniac.
indènne *a* undamaged, unharmed.
indennità *nf* **indenníẓẓo** *nm* indemnity.
indenniẓẓàre *vt* to indemnify.
indéntro *ad* inwards.
inderogàbile *a* that cannot be transgressed.
indescrivíbile *a* indiscribable.
indeterminàto *a* indeterminate, vague, indefinite.
indi *ad* afterwards, thence, then.
Índia *nf* (*geogr*) India.
indiàno *a nm* Indian; **fàre l'i.** to feign ignorance.
indiavolàto *a* demoniac, devilish; (*fig*) furious, violent.
indicàre *vt* to indicate, point out, show.
indicatívo *a nm* indicative.
indicàto *a* suitable.
indicatóre *nm* gauge, indicator, guide; **i. stradàle** traffic sign; **i. di velocità** (*aut*) speedometer.
indicazióne *nf* indication.
índice *nm* forefinger, index, pointer, sign.
indicíbile *a* unspeakable, indescribable.
indietreggiaménto *nm* withdrawal.
indietreggiàre *vi* to fall back, recoil.
indiètro *ad* behind, back, backwards.
indiféso *a* defenseless.
indifferènte *a* indifferent, unimportant.
indifferènza *nf* indifference, unconcern.
indígeno *a* indigenous; *nm* native.
indigènte *a* indigent, needy.
indigènza *nf* indigence, need.
indigeríbile *a* indigestible.
indigestióne *nf* **fàre un' i. di** to eat too much of.
indigèsto *a* indigestible, tiresome.
indignàre *vt* to make indignant; **-rsi** *vr* to grow indignant.
indignazióne *nf* indignation.
indimenticàbile *a* unforgettable.
indimostràbile *a* indemonstrable.
indipendènte *a* independent, self-reliant; (*of flat etc*) self-contained.
indipendenteménte *ad* independently.
indipendènza *nf* independence.
indíre *vt* to announce, call, fix.
indirètto *a* indirect.
indirizzàre *vt* to address, direct; **-rsi** *vr* to address oneself, have recourse to.
indirízzo *nm* address.
indiscerníbile *a* indiscernible.
indisciplína *nf* indiscipline, unruliness.
indisciplinàto *a* undisciplined, unruly.
indiscréto *a* indiscreet, intrusive, prying.
indiscrezióne *nf* indiscretion, impertinence.
indiscutíbile *a* unquestionable.
indispensàbile *a* indispensable, essential.
indispensabilità *nf* indispensability.
indispensabilménte *ad* indispensably, most necessarily.
indispettíre *vt* to vex; **-rsi** *vr* to be angry, vexed.
indispórre *vt* to indispose, irritate, upset.
indisposizióne *nf* indisposition.
indispósto *a* indisposed, unwell.
indisputàbile *a* indisputable.
indissolúbile *a* indissoluble.
indistínto *a* faint, indistinct, vague.
indistruttíbile *a* indestructible.
indisturbàto *a* undisturbed.
individuàle *a* individual.
individualíșmo *nm* individualism.
individualísta *nmf* individualist.
individualità *nf* individuality.
individuàre *vt* to identify, pick out, specify, characterize.
individúo *nm* individual, fellow.
indivișíbile *a* indivisible.
indivíșo *a* undivided, whole.
indízio *nm* indication, sign.
indòcile *a* unruly, intractable.

índole *nf* nature, disposition, temperament, character.
indolènte *a* indolent, lazy.
indolènza *nf* indolence, laziness.
indolenzíre *vt* to benumb, cramp; **-rsi** *vr* to get numb, get stiff.
indolóre *a* painless.
indomàni, l' *nm* (the) next day.
indòmito *a* indomitable, unconquered, untamed.
Indonèṣia *nf* (*geogr*) Indonesia.
indoneṣiàno *a nm* Indonesian.
indoràre *vt* to gild.
indossàre *vt* to put on, wear.
indossatríce *nf* model, mannequin.
indòsso *ad* on.
indovinàre *vt* to divine, guess, foretell.
indovinàto *a* successful, well-done.
indovinèllo *nm* conundrum, riddle.
indovíno *a* prophetic, foreseeing; *nm* fortune-teller.
indú *a nmf* Hindu, Hindoo.
indubbiaménte *ad* undoubtedly.
indúbbio, indubitàbile *a* undoubted.
indugiàre *vti* to postpone, delay, linger.
indúgio *nm* delay.
indulgènte *a* indulgent.
indulgènza *nf* indulgence, leniency.
indúlgere *vt* to indulge.
induménto *nm* garment.
induríre *vt* to harden; *vi* **-rsi** *vr* to harden, get hard.
indúrre *vt* to inspire, induce; **-rsi** *vr* to decide, resolve.
indústria *nf* industry, skill.
industriàle *a* industrial; *nm* industrialist.
industriàrsi *vr* to do one's best.
industrióso *a* industrious.
induzióne *nf* induction, conjecture.
inebriànte *a* inebriating, intoxicating.
inebriàre *vt* to intoxicate, make drunk; **-rsi** *vr* to get drunk, be enraptured.
ineccepíbile *a* unobjectionable.
inèdia *nf* inanition, starvation, boredom.
inèdito *a* unpublished.
ineducàto *a* ill-bred, impolite.
ineffàbile *a* ineffable.
ineffettuàbile *a* unrealizable.
inefficàce *a* ineffective, ineffectual.
inefficàcia *nf* inefficacy.
inefficiènte *a* inefficient.
ineguagliànza, inegualità *nf* inequality.
ineguàle *a* unlike, unequal, irregular.
inelegànte *a* inelegant.
ineleggíbile *a* ineligible.
ineluttàbile *a* inevitable, inescapable.
inenarràbile *a* unspeakable.
inequivocàbile *a* unequivocal, unmistakable.
inerènte *a* inherent, concerning.
inèrme *a* unarmed, defenseless.
inèrte *a* inert, motionless, limp, lifeless, sluggish.
inèrzia *nf* inertness, idleness, inertia.
ineṣattézza *nf* inexactness, inaccuracy, mistake.
ineṣàtto *a* inaccurate, inexact, (*com*) uncollected.
ineṣaudíto *a* ungranted.
ineṣauríbile *a* inexhaustible.
ineṣàusto *a* unexhausted.
inescuṣàbile *a* inexcusable, unjustifiable.
ineṣeguíto *a* unperformed, unfulfilled.
ineṣistènte *a* non-existent.
ineṣoràbile *a* inexorable, relentless.
ineṣorabilità *nf* inexorability.
inesperiènza *nf* inexperience.
inespèrto *a* inexperienced, unskilled.
inesplicàbile *a* inexplicable.
inesploràto *a* unexplored.
inesplóṣo *a* unexploded.
inesprimíbile *a* inexpressible.
inestimàbile *a* inestimable, invaluable.
inettitúdine *nf* ineptitude.
inètto *a* inept, unfit.
inevàṣo *a* (*com*) outstanding.
inevitàbile *a* inevitable, unavoidable.
inevitabilménte *ad* unavoidably.
inèzia *nf* trifle.
infagottàre *vt* to wrap up, muffle.
infallíbile *a* infallible, unfailing.
infallibilità *nf* infallibility.
infamànte *a* disgraceful, shameful.
infamàre *vt* to disgrace, bring shame upon; **-rsi** *vr* to disgrace oneself.
infàme *a* abominable, infamous.
infàmia *nf* infamy, disgrace, shame.
infangàre *vt* to cover with mud.
infànte *nm* infant, child.
infantíle *a* childlike, childish, infantile.
infànzia *nf* infancy.
infarcíre *vt* to stuff, cram.
infarinatúra *nf* covering with flour, (*fig*) smattering.
infàrto *nm* **i. (cardíaco)** heart attack.
infastidíre *vt* to annoy, vex.
infaticàbile *a* indefatigable, untiring.
infàtti *ad* in fact, really.
infatuàre *vt* to infatuate; **-rsi** *vr* to become infatuated.
infatuazióne *nf* infatuation.
infàusto *a* unlucky.
infecóndo *a* barren, unfruitful.
infedèle *a* unfaithful, faithless, false; *nmf* infidel.
infedeltà *nf* unfaithfulness, infidelity.
infelíce *a* unhappy, unlucky, unsuccessful, inappropriate.
infelicità *nf* unhappiness.
inferióre *a* inferior, lower, below, subordinate; *nmf* inferior, subordinate.
inferiorità *nf* inferiority.
inferíre *vt* to infer, deduce, inflict, (*naut*) hoist, bend (a sail).

infermàrsi *vr* to become an invalid.
infermería *nf* infirmary, sick-room.
infermièra *nf* nurse; **infermière** *nm* hospital attendant, male nurse.
infermità *nf* illness, infirmity.
inférmo *a nm* ill, sick, invalid.
infernàle *a* infernal, hellish.
infèrno *nm* hell.
inferocíre *vti* **-rsi** *vr* to make ferocious, become ferocious.
inferriàta *nf* grating, railing.
infervoràre *vt* to fill with fervor; **-rsi** *vr* to get excited.
infestàre *vt* to infest.
infèsto *a* detrimental, harmful.
infettàre *vt* to infect, pollute.
infettívo *a* infectious, contagious.
infètto *a* infected.
infezióne *nf* infection.
infiacchiménto *nm* enervation, weakening.
infiacchíre *vt* to enervate, weaken; **-rsi** *vr* to grow weak.
infiammàbile *a* inflammable.
infiammabilità *nf* inflammability.
infiammàre *vt* to set on fire, inflame; **-rsi** *vr* to catch fire, become inflamed.
infiammazióne *nf* inflammation.
infído *a* untrustworthy, unfaithful.
infieríre *vi* to be pitiless, rage.
infievolíre *vt* to weaken; **-rsi** *vr* to grow weak.
infilàre *vt* to thread, string, run through, insert, enter; **-rsi** *vr* to thread one's way, slip, put on.
infiltràrsi *vr* to infiltrate, penetrate, seep.
infiltrazióne *nf* infiltration.
infilzàre *vt* to pierce, run through, string, stick.
ínfimo *a* lowest, very low.
infíne *ad* at last, after all, finally.
infingardàggine *nf* laziness, slothfulness.
infingàrdo *a* lazy, slothful.
infíngersi *vr* to feign, simulate.
infinità *nf* infinity, large crowd, lot.
infinitèṣimo *a* infinitesimal.
infiníto *a nm* infinite, boundless, endless, infinity.
infioràre *vt* to adorn (strew) with flowers.
infirmàre *vt* to invalidate.
infischiàrsi *vr* not to care for, make light of.
infittíre *vti* to make thick, thicken.
inflazióne *nf* inflation.
inflessíbile *a* inflexible, unmoved.
inflessióne *nf* inflection.
inflíggere *vt* to inflict.
influènte *a* influential.
influènza *nf* influence, influenza.
influenzàre *vt* to influence, affect, bias.
influenzàto *a* influenced; suffering from influenza.
influíre *vi* to influence.
influsso *nm* influx, influence.
infocàre *vt* to make hot, inflamed.
infondatézza *nf* groundlessness.
infondàto *a* groundless.
infóndere *vt* to infuse, instill.
inforcàre *vt* to pitchfork, bestride; **i. gli occhiàli** to put on one's spectacles.
informàre *vt* to acquaint, let (someone) know, inform; **-rsi** *vr* to find out, inquire.
informatívo *a* informative.
informatóre *a* informing; *nm* **-tríce** *nf* informer.
informazióne *nf* (piece of) information; **úfficio i.** inquiry office.
infórme *a* shapeless.
informicolíre *vt* to cause a tickling sensation, cause pins and needles.
informità *nf* shapelessness.
infornàta *nf* batch, ovenful.
infortunàto *a* injured.
infortúnio *nm* accident, misfortune.
infossatúra *nf* hollow, cavity.
infradiciàre *vt* to drench, soak; **-rsi** *vr* to get drenched.
inframmettènza *nf* interference, intrusiveness.
infra(m)méttersi *vr* to meddle.
infràngere *vt* to break, shatter; **-rsi** *vr* to break, smash.
infrangíbile *a* unbreakable.
infrànto *a* shattered, crushed (*also fig*).
infraròsso *a* infra-red.
infrazióne *nf* infraction, infringement.
infreddàrsi *vr* to catch a cold.
infreddatúra *nf* cold.
infreddolíto *a* cold.
infrequènte *a* infrequent.
infrequènza *nf* infrequency.
infrigidíre *vt* to chill, become cold.
infruttífero *a* unfruitful, unprofitable.
infruttuóso *a* fruitless, unsuccessful.
infuòri *ad* out; **all'i. di** *prep* except, but, apart from.
infuriàre *vt* to enrage; *vi* rage; **-rsi** *vr* to fly into a passion, lose one's temper.
infuṣióne *nf* infusion.
infúṣo *a* infused; *nm* infusion.
ingaggiàre *vt* to engage, enlist.
ingàggio *nm* enlistment, engagement.
ingagliardíre *vt* to invigorate, strengthen; **-rsi** *vr* to grow strong, strengthen.
ingannàre *vt* to deceive, beguile, cheat; **-rsi** *vr* to be mistaken.
ingannatóre *a* deceiving; *nm* **-tríce** *nf* deceiver.
ingannévole *a* deceitful, deceptive.
ingànno *nm* deceit, fraud.
ingarbugliàre *vt* to entangle, muddle.
ingegnàrsi *vr* to do one's best, manage.
ingegnère *nm* engineer.
ingegnería *nf* engineering.
ingégno *nm* talent, genius, intelligence; device.

ingegnosità *nf* ingeniousness, ingenuity.
ingegnóso *a* ingenious, clever.
ingelosíre *vt* to make jealous; **-rsi** *vr* to become jealous.
ingeneràre *vt* to engender, cause.
ingènte *a* enormous, huge.
ingentilíre *vt* to refine; **-rsi** *vr* to become refined.
ingenuità *nf* ingenuousness, naïveté, simple-mindedness.
ingènuo *a* ingenuous, naïve.
ingerènza *nf* interference.
ingeríre *vt* to swallow; **-rsi** *vr* to interfere, meddle.
ingessàre *vt* to (set in) plaster.
ingessatúra *nf* plaster, plastering.
Inghiltèrra *nf* (*geogr*) England.
inghiottíre *vt* to swallow (up).
inghirlandàre *vt* to wreathe, garland.
ingiallíre *vi* to make yellow; *vi* to become yellow.
ingigantíre *vt* to magnify, exaggerate.
inginocchiàrsi *vr* to go on one's knees, kneel down.
inginocchiatóio *nm* kneeling-stool.
ingioiellàrsi *vr* to adorn oneself with jewels.
ingiúngere *vt* to order, command.
ingiunzióne *nf* injunction, order.
ingiúria *nf* insult, affront, damage.
ingiuriàre *vt* to abuse, insult.
ingiurióso *a* insulting, offensive.
ingiustaménte *ad* unjustly, wrong.
ingiustificàbile *a* unjustifiable.
ingiustízia *nf* injustice, unfairness.
ingiústo *a* unjust, unfair.
inglése *a nmf* English, the English language, Englishman, Englishwoman.
ingoiàre *vt* to swallow (up).
ingolfàrsi *vr* to form a gulf, plunge into.
ingombrànte *a* cumbersome.
ingombràre *vt* to encumber, obstruct.
ingómbro *a nm* encumbered, obstructed, encumbrance, obstruction.
ingommàre *vt* to gum, stick.
ingordígia *nf* greed(iness).
ingórdo *a nm* greedy, covetous, glutton.
ingórgo *nm* obstruction; **i. stradàle** traffic jam.
ingranàggio *nm* (*tec*) gear, working.
ingranàre *vti* (*tec*) to put into gear, be in gear; get along.
ingranchíre *vt* to benumb.
ingrandiménto *nm* enlargement.
ingrandíre *vt* to amplify, enlarge, exaggerate, increase; **-rsi** *vr* to grow larger, increase.
ingrassàre *vt* to make fat, lubricate, manure, enrich; *vi* **-rsi** *vr* to grow fat.
ingratitúdine *nf* ingratitude.
ingràto *a* ungrateful, thankless, unpleasant, unprofitable.
ingravidàre *vt* to make pregnant; **-rsi** *vr* to become pregnant.
ingraziàrsi *vr* to ingratiate oneself.
ingrediènte *nm* ingredient.
ingrèsso *nm* entry, entrance, admittance; **ingrèssi** (*theat*) standing room.
ingrossaménto *nm* enlargement, increase, swelling.
ingrossàre *vt* to make big(ger), increase, swell; **-rsi** *vr* to grow big(ger), rise, swell.
ingròsso, all' *ad* wholesale.
ingualcíbile *a* crease-resistant.
inguantàto *a* wearing gloves.
inguaríbile *a* incurable.
ínguine *nm* groin.
inibíre *vt* to inhibit, forbid, restrain.
inibizióne *nf* inhibition, prohibition.
inidòneo *a* unfit, unsuited.
iniettàre *vt* to inject.
iniezióne *nf* injection.
inimicàre *vt* to estrange, alienate; **-rsi** *vr* to become estranged from.
inimicízia *nf* enmity, hostility.
inimitàbile *a* inimitable.
inintelligíbile *a* unintelligible.
ininterrótto *a* uninterrupted, unbroken, non-stop.
iniquaménte *ad* wickedly, unjustly.
iniquità *nf* iniquity, wickedness.
iníquo *a* iniquitous, wicked.
iniziàle *a nf* initial.
iniziàre *vt* to begin, initiate.
iniziatíva *nf* initiative, enterprise.
iniziàto *a nm* initiated, initiate.
iniziazióne *nf* initiation.
inízio *nm* beginning, commencement.
innacquàre *vt* to water, dilute.
innaffiaménto *nm* watering.
innaffiàre *vt* to water.
innaffiatóio *nm* watering-can.
innalzàre *vt* to raise, heighten; **-rsi** *vr* to rise.
innamoràre *vt* to charm; **-rsi** *vr* to fall in love.
innamoràto *a* in love, loving; *nm* lover, sweetheart.
innànzi *ad and prep* before, on, towards, further.
innàto *a* innate.
innegàbile *a* undeniable.
inneggiàre *vt* to celebrate, exalt.
innervosíre *vt* to get on people's nerves.
innestàre *vt* to graft, inoculate, insert, join.
innèsto *nm* graft, insertion, inoculation.
ínno *nm* anthem, hymn.
innocènte *a nm* innocent.
innocènza *nf* innocence.
inoculazióne *nf* inoculation.
innòcuo *a* harmless, inoffensive.
innominàbile *a* unnamable, unmentionable.
innominàto *a* unnamed, nameless.
innovàre *vt* to innovate, change.
innovazióne *nf* innovation, change.

innumerévole *a* innumerable, numberless.
inoculàre *vt* to inoculate.
inodóro *a* odorless.
inoffensívo *a* inoffensive, harmless.
inoltràre *vt* to forward, send on; **-rsi** *vr* to advance, penetrate.
inóltre *ad* besides, moreover, furthermore.
inondàre *vt* to flood, inundate.
inondazióne *nf* flood, inundation.
inoperosità *nf* inactivity, idleness.
inoperóso *a* inactive, idle.
inòpia *nf* indigence, poverty, want.
inopinàto *a* unexpected, unforeseen, sudden.
inopportúno *a* inopportune, untimely.
inoppugnàbile *a* unquestionable.
inorgànico *pl* **-ici** *a* inorganic.
inorgoglíre *vt* to make proud; **-rsi** *vr* to become proud.
inorridíre *vt* to horrify; *vi* be horrified.
inosservànte *a* unobservant.
inospitàle, inòspite *a* inhospitable.
inosservànza *nf* non-observance.
inosservàto *a* unobserved.
inossidàbile *a* rustless; **acciàio i.** stainless steel.
inquadràre *vt* to frame; arrange; set.
inquietànte *a* disquieting.
inquietàre *vt* to worry, alarm; **-rsi** *vr* to get angry.
inquietézza *nf* uneasiness.
inquièto *a* restless, uneasy, anxious.
inquietúdine *nf* restlessness, uneasiness, apprehension.
inquilíno *nm* tenant, lodger.
inquinaménto *nm* pollution.
inquinàre *vt* to pollute.
inquirènte *a* inquiring, investigating.
inquişíre *vt* to inquire, investigate.
inquişitóre *nm* **-tríce** *nf* inquisitor; *a* inquiring.
inquişizióne *nf* inquisition.
insaccàre *vt* to put in sacks, stuff.
insaccàto *nm* sausages, salame *etc.*
insalàta *nf* salad.
insalatièra *nf* salad-bowl.
insalúbre *a* unhealthy.
insalubrità *nf* unhealthiness.
insanàbile *a* incurable.
insanguinàre *vt* to cover with blood.
insanguinàto *a* blood-stained.
insània *nf* insanity.
insàno *a* insane, crazy.
insaponàre *vt* to lather, soap.
insapúta, all' (di) *ad* unknown (to).
insaziàbile *a* insatiable.
inscatolàre *vt* to can.
inscenàre *vt* to stage (*also fig*).
inscindíbile *a* inseparable.
inscrutàbile *a* inscrutable.
insediàre *vt* to install; **-rsi** *vr* to take up office, take possession.
inségna *nf* insignia *pl*, badge; colors *pl*, flag; signboard.
insegnaménto *nm* teaching, tuition.
insegnànte *a* teaching; *nmf* teacher; **còrpo i.** teaching staff.
insegnàre *vt* to teach.
inseguiménto *nm* chase, pursuit.
inseguíre *vt* to pursue, run after.
inselvatichíre *vt* to make wild; *vi* to grow wild.
insenatúra *nf* inlet.
insensatézza *nf* senselessness, foolishness.
insensàto *a* senseless, foolish.
insensíbile *a* insensible, unfeeling.
insensibilménte *ad* imperceptibly, unfeelingly.
insensibilità *nf* hard-heartedness, insensibility.
inseparàbile *a* inseparable.
inseriménto *nm* insertion.
inseríre *vt* to insert.
inservíbile *a* useless.
inserzióne *nf* inserting, insertion, advertisement.
inserzionísta *nmf* advertiser.
insetticída *a* insecticidal; *nm* insecticide.
insètto *nm* insect, bug.
insídia *nf* ambush, snare.
insidiàre *vti* to lay snares for, make an attempt on.
insidióso *a* insidious.
insième *nm* whole; *ad* together, at the same time.
insígne *a* famous, notorious.
insignificànte *a* insignificant.
insigníre *vt* to decorate, confer (on).
insincerità *nf* insincerity.
insincèro *a* insincere.
insindacàbile *a* that cannot be criticized.
insinuàre *vt* to insinuate, suggest; **-rsi** *vr* to creep into, penetrate.
insinuazióne *nf* insinuation, suggestion.
insípido *a* insipid, tasteless.
insipiènza *nf* foolishness, ignorance.
insistènte *a* insistent, pressing, urgent.
insistènza *nf* insistence.
insístere *vi* to insist.
ínsito *a* inherent.
insoddisfàtto *a* dissatisfied.
insoddisfazióne *nf* dissatisfaction.
insofferènte *a* intolerant, impatient.
insofferènza *nf* intolerance, impatience.
insolazióne *nf* sunstroke.
insolènte *a* insolent, pert.
insolentíre *vti* to abuse, speak insolently.
insolènza *nf* insolence, pertness.
insòlito *a* unusual.
insolúbile *a* insoluble.
insolúto *a* unsolved, outstanding.
insolvènte *a* insolvent.
insolvènza *nf* insolvency.
insolvíbile *a* unpayable; insolvent.
insómma *ad* in conclusion, in short; *interj* well!
insondàbile *a* unfathomable.
insònne *a* sleepless.

insònnia *nf* insomnia, sleeplessness.
insonnolíto *a* sleepy, drowsy.
insopportàbile *a* insupportable, unbearable.
insórgere *vi* to rebel, rise, arise.
insorgiménto *nm* uprising.
insormontàbile *a* insurmountable.
insórto *nm* rebel, rioter.
insospettàbile *a* beyond suspicion.
insospettàto *a* unsuspected, unexpected.
insospettíre *vt* to make suspicious; **-rsi** *vr* to grow suspicious.
insostenibile *a* untenable.
insozzàre *vt* to soil, sully.
insperàbile *a* beyond hope.
insperataménte *ad* unexpectedly.
insperàto *a* unhoped-for.
inspiegàbile *a* inexplicable.
inspiràre *vt* to inhale; inspire.
instàbile *a* unstable, variable.
instabilità *nf* instability, variability.
installàre *vt* to install; **-rsi** *vr* to install oneself, settle.
installazióne *nf* installation.
instancàbile *a* untiring, indefatigable, tireless.
instauràre *vt* to set up, establish.
instaurazióne *nf* establishment, foundation.
instillàre *vt* to instill.
instradàre *vt* to set on the right road.
insú *ad* up(wards).
insubordinàto *a* insubordinate.
insubordinazióne *nf* insubordination.
insuccèsso *nm* failure.
insudiciàre *vt* to soil, dirty.
insufficiènte *a* insufficient, inadequate.
insufficiènza *nf* insufficiency.
insulàre *a* insular.
insulína *nf* insulin.
insulsàggine *nf* dullness, foolishness.
insúlso *a* dull, foolish.
insultàre *vt* to abuse, insult.
insúlto *nm* insult, affront; (*med*) attack, stroke.
insuperàbile *a* insuperable.
insuperbíre *vt* to make proud; **-rsi** *vr* to grow proud.
insurrezionàle *a* insurrectionary.
insurrezióne *nf* insurrection, rising.
insussistènte *a* non-existent.
insussistènza *nf* non-existence.
intaccàre *vt* to notch; corrode; injure; begin spending.
intagliàre *vt* to engrave, carve.
intagliatóre *nm* engraver, carver.
intàglio *nm* intaglio, carving.
intangíbile *a* intangible.
intànto *ad* meanwhile; **i. che** *cj* while.
intarsiàre *vt* to inlay.
intàrsio *nm* inlay.
intasàre *vt* to choke, obstruct, stop up; **-rsi** *vr* to get stopped up.
intascàre *vt* to pocket.
intàtto *a* intact, uninjured, unsullied.
intavolàre *vt* to board up; put on a board; begin.
integèrrimo *a* honest, upright.
integràle *a* integral; **pàne i.** wholemeal bread.
integràre *vt* to complete, integrate.
integrazióne *nf* integration.
integrità *nf* integrity, uprightness.
íntegro *a* honest, upright, integral.
intelaiatúra *nf* framework, framing.
intellètto *nm* intellect, mind.
intellettuàle *a* intellectual.
intelligènte *a* intelligent, clever.
intelligènza *nf* intelligence, cleverness, knowledge, understanding.
intelligíbile *a* intelligible, comprehensible.
intemeràta *nf* reproof, tirade.
intemeràto *a* irreproachable.
intemperànte *a* intemperate.
intemperànza *nf* intemperance.
intempèrie *nf pl* inclement weather.
intempestívo *a* unseasonable, untimely.
intèndere *vt* to hear; intend, mean; understand; **-rsi** *vr* to be a good judge of; come to an agreement with; understand (each other).
intendiménto *nm* understanding; intention, purpose.
intenditóre *nm* connoisseur, judge.
inteneríre *vt* to soften, move; **-rsi** *vr* to be moved, feel compassion.
intensaménte *ad* intensely.
intensificàre *vt* to intensify, make more frequent.
intensità *nf* intensity.
intensívo *a* intensive.
intènso *a* intense, violent.
intentàre *vt* (*leg*) to bring (an action).
intènto *a* intent; *nm* aim, intent(ion), purpose.
intenzionàle *a* intentional.
intenzióne *nf* intention, wish.
interaménte *ad* entirely, completely.
intercalàre *vt* to insert; *nm* refrain; pet phrase.
intercèdere *vi* to intercede; (*of distance etc*) exist, intervene.
intercessióne *nf* intercession.
intercettàre *vt* to intercept.
intercettazióne *nf* interception.
intercomunàle *nf* (*tel*) trunk call, long-distance call.
intercomunicànte *a* intercommunicating, communicating.
intercórrere *vi* to elapse, pass, happen.
interdétto *a* interdicted, prohibited, disqualified; disconcerted; *nm* interdict.
interdíre *vt* to forbid, interdict, disqualify.
interdizióne *nf* interdiction, disqualification.
interessaménto *nm* interest, concern.
interessànte *a* interesting.
interessàre *vti* to interest, matter; **-rsi** *vr* to take an interest, care.

interessàto *a* interested; *nm* interested party.
interèsse *nm* interest.
interessènza *nf* (*com*) co-interest.
interézza *nf* entirety, integrity.
interferènza *nf* interference.
interferíre *vi* to interfere.
interinàle *a* interim, temporary.
interíno *a* provisional.
interióra *nf pl* entrails *pl*, intestines *pl*.
interióre *a* inner; *nm* interior, inside.
interlineàre *vt* to interline; *a* interlinear.
interlocutóre *nm* **-tríce** *nf* interlocutor.
interloquíre *vi* to put in a word, speak.
interlúdio *nm* interlude.
intermediàrio *a* intermediary; *nm* mediator, (*com*) middleman, go-between.
intermèẓẓo *nm* interval, intermezzo.
interminàbile *a* interminable, endless.
intermissióne *nf* intermission.
intermittènte *a* intermittent.
intermittènza *nf* intermittence.
internaménte *ad* internally, inwardly.
internàre *vt* to intern; **-rsi** *vr* to enter into, penetrate.
internàto *a* interned; *nm* internee; boarding-school.
internazionàle *a* international.
intèrno *a* internal, interior, inner, inside; *nm* interior, inside; **Ministéro degli Intérni** Home Office.
intéro *a* entire, whole; honest; *nm* whole.
interpellànza *nf* interpellation.
interpellàre *vt* to interpellate, ask.
interpolàre *vt* to interpolate, insert.
interpórre *vt* **-rsi** *vr* to interpose, intervene.
interpoṣizióne *nf* interposition, intervention.
interpretàre *vt* to interpret, construe.
interpretazióne *nf* interpretation.
intèrprete *nmf* interpreter.
interpunzióne *nf* punctuation.
interraménto *nm* interment, burial.
interràre *vt* to bury, inter; fill with earth.
interrogàre *vt* to interrogate, question, consult, examine; **i. con contraddittório** cross-examine.
interrogatívo *a* interrogative, questioning; *nm* question.
interrogatório *nm* interrogation, (cross-)examination.
interrogazióne *nf* interrogation, question.
interrómpere *vt* to interrupt, break (off); **-rsi** *vr* to stop.
interrótto *a* interrupted, cut off; (*of road*) blocked.
interruttóre *nm* interrupter, (*el*) switch.
interruzióne *nf* interruption.
intersecàre *vt* to intersect.
interurbàno *a* **telefonàta interurbàna** long-distance call.
intervàllo *nm* interval, space.
intervenire *vi* to intervene, interfere; be present; happen.
intervènto *nm* intervention, interference; presence; (*surgical*) operation.
intervenúto *a* present; *nm* person present.
intervísta *nf* interview.
intervistàre *vt* to interview.
intésa *nf* agreement, understanding.
intéso *a* understood, agreed upon; aiming at.
intèssere *vt* to weave.
intestàre *vt* to enter; head; register; **-rsi** *vr* to be obstinate.
intestàto *a* headed; (*com*) registered; stubborn; intestate.
intestazióne *nf* heading, title, headline.
intestinàle *a* intestinal.
intestíno *a* domestic, internal, civil; *nm* intestine.
intiepidíre *vt* to make lukewarm, warm (up); cool, abate; **-rsi** *vr* to cool down; warm up.
intiéro *v* **intéro.**
intimaménte *ad* intimately, deeply.
intimàre *vt* to intimate, order, notify, enjoin.
intimazióne *nf* order, summons, notification.
intimidazióne *nf* intimidation.
intimidíre *vt* to intimidate; **-rsi** *vr* to become shy, get frightened.
intimità *nf* intimacy, familiarity.
íntimo *a* intimate; inner, deep; private; *nm* intimate friend; heart, depth.
intimoríre *vt* to frighten.
intíngere *vt* to dip.
intíngolo *nm* tasty dish, sauce, gravy.
intirizzíre *vt* to (be)numb, stiffen; **-rsi** *vr* to get benumbed.
intiṣichíre *vi* to grow consumptive.
intitolàre *vt* to entitle; dedicate.
intitolazióne *nf* entitling, title; dedication.
intolleràbile *a* intolerable.
intollerànte *a* intolerant.
intolleranza *nf* intolerance.
intonacàre *vt* to plaster, whitewash, distemper.
intònaco *pl* **-chi** *nm* plaster, whitewash, distemper.
intonàre *vt* to intone; strike up; **-rsi** *vr* to be in tune (harmony) with, tone with.
intonàto *a* in tune, matching.
intonazióne *nf* intonation, tone.
intònso *a* uncut, unshaven, unshorn.
intontiménto *nm* stupor, daze.
intontíre *vt* to stun, daze; **-rsi** *vr* to be stunned, become dazed.
intòppo *nm* hindrance, obstacle,

hitch; i. **stradàle** (*traffic*) hold up, tie-up, traffic jam.
intorbidàre *vt* to make turbid, confuse, trouble; **-rsi** *vr* to become turbid, troubled, grow dim.
intórno *ad* **i. a** *prep* around, round, about.
intorpidíre *vt* to benumb; *vi* **-rsi** *vr* to grow numb.
intossicàre *vt* to poison.
intossicazióne *nf* poisoning.
intraducíbile *a* untranslatable.
intralciàre *vt* to hinder, interfere with, obstruct.
intràlcio *nm* hindrance, obstruction.
intrallàzzo *nm* plotting, swindle; black market.
intraméttere *v* **introméttere.**
intramezzàre *vt* to interpose, alternate.
intramuscolàre *a* intermuscular.
intransigènte *a* intransigent, uncompromising, unmoved.
intransigènza *nf* intransigence.
intransitívo *a nm* intransitive.
intraprendènte *a* enterprising.
intraprendènza *nf* enterprise.
intraprèndere *vt* to undertake, venture on.
intrattàbile *a* intractable.
intrattenére *vt* to entertain; **-rsi** *vr* to linger, stop, dwell upon.
intratteniménto *nm* entertainment.
intrav(v)edére *vt* to catch a glimpse; have a hazy notion; foresee.
intrecciàre *vt* to entwine, interlace, braid.
intréccio *nm* interlacing; (*of a play*) plot.
intrepidézza, intrepidità *nf* intrepidity, bravery.
intrèpido *a* fearless, intrepid.
intricàto *a* intricate, tangled, complicated.
intrigànte *a* intriguing; *nmf* intriguer.
intrigàre *vi* to intrigue; *vt* to entangle; **-rsi** *vr* to meddle.
intrígo *nm* intrigue.
intrínseco *pl* **-ci** *a* intrinsic.
intríso *a* soaked; *nm* mash, mixture.
intristíre *vt* to decay, pine away, wilt; grow wicked.
introdúrre *vt* to introduce, show in; import; **-rsi** *vr* to get in, introduce oneself.
introduzióne *nf* introduction.
introitàre *vt* (*com*) to cash, get in.
intròito *nm* (*eccl*) introit, (*com*) returns *pl*, revenue.
introrésso *a* interposed, introduced, inserted.
introméttere *vt* to interpose, introduce, insert; **-rsi** *vr* to intervene, intrude, meddle.
intromissióne *nf* intervention, intrusion.
intronàre *vt* to deafen, stun.
introspettívo *a* introspective.
introspezióne *a* introspection.
introvàbile *a* not to be found.
introvèrso *a* introverted; *nm* introvert.
intrúglio *nm* hodgepodge, bad concoction, mess.
intrusióne *nf* intrusion.
intrúso *nm* intruder.
intuíre *vt* to perceive by intuition.
intúito *nm* **intuizióne** *nf* intuition.
inuguàle *etc v* **ineguàle** *etc.*
inumanità *nf* inhumanity.
inumàno *a* inhuman, cruel.
inumàre *vt* to inhume, inter.
inumidíre *vt* to moisten, damp.
inurbanità *nf* incivility.
inurbàno *a* uncivil, rude.
inusàto *a* unusual, obsolete.
inusitàto *a* unusual, obsolete.
inútile *a* useless, unnecessary.
inutilità *nf* uselessness.
inutilmènte *ad* uselessly, in vain.
invadènte *a* intrusive; *nmf* intruder.
invadènza *nf* meddlesomeness.
invàdere *vt* to invade, break into.
invaghírsi *vr* to fall in love with, take a liking to.
invalidàre *vt* to invalidate.
invalidità *nf* invalidity.
invàlido *a* invalid, disabled; *nm* invalid.
invàno *ad* in vain, vainly.
invariàbile *a* invariable, unchangeable.
invariàto *a* unvaried, unchanged.
invasaménto *nm* obsession, excitement, infatuation.
invasàre *vt* to obsess, haunt; put in vases.
invasióne *nf* invasion.
invasóre, *f* **invaditríce** *a* invading; *nm* invader.
invecchiàre *vti* to make old, grow old; **-rsi** *vr* to make oneself look old, claim to be older than one is.
invéce *ad* instead, on the contrary; **i. di** *prep* instead of.
inveíre *vi* to inveigh, rail.
inventàre *vt* to invent.
inventàrio *nm* inventory.
inventíva *nf* inventiveness.
inventóre *nm* **-tríce** *nf* inventor.
invenzióne *nf* invention.
inverdíre *vi* to grow green.
inverecóndia *nf* immodesty.
inverecóndo *a* immodest.
invernàle *a* winter, wintry.
inverniciàre *vt* to varnish.
inverniciatúra *nf* varnishing.
invèrno *nm* winter.
invéro *ad* really, truly.
inverosimigliànza *nf* unlikelihood.
inverosímile *a* unlikely, improbable.
inversióne *nf* inversion.
invèrso *a* inverse, opposite, contrary.
invertebràto *a* invertebrate.
invertíre *vt* to invert, reverse.
invertíto *a* inverted; *nm* invert.
investigàre *vt* to inquire into, investigate.
investigazióne *nf* inquiry, investigation.

investiménto *nm* investment; collision.
investíre *vt* to collide with; attack; invest, appoint; **-rsi** *vr* to take a deep interest in; collide.
invetriàta *nf* pane of glass.
invettíva *nf* invective.
inviàre *vt* to send.
inviàto *nm* messenger, representative, envoy, correspondent.
invídia *nf* envy.
invidiàre *vt* to envy.
invidióso *a* envious.
invigilàre *vt* to watch (over).
invigoríre *vt* to invigorate, strengthen; **-rsi** *vr* to grow stronger.
inviluppàre *vt* to envelop, hide; **-rsi** *vr* to wrap oneself up.
invincíbile *a* invincible.
invío *nm* sending, dispatch.
inviolàbile *a* inviolable.
invişíbile *a* invisible.
invíşo *a* disliked, hated.
invitànte *a* inviting, attractive, tempting.
invitàre *vt* to invite, ask; (*at cards*) call.
invitàto *nm* guest.
invíto *nm* call, invitation.
invítto *a* undefeated, unconquered, invincible.
invocàre *vt* to invoke, appeal to.
invocazióne *nf* invocation.
invogliàre *vt* to allure, induce, tempt.
involàre *vt* to steal; **-rsi** *vr* to elope, run away.
invòlgere *vt* to wrap up, envelop, involve.
involontàrio *a* involuntary.
involtàre *vt* to wrap up, pack up.
invòlto *pp of* **invòlgere**; *nm* bundle, parcel.
invòlucro *nm* covering, envelope.
invulneràbile *a* invulnerable.
inzuccheràre *vt* to sugar.
inzuppàre *vt* to dip, drench, soak.
ío *pron* I.
iòdio *nm* iodine.
iònico *pl* **-ici** *a* Ionic.
iònio *a* Ionian; **l'Iònio** *nm* (*geogr*) the Ionian Sea.
iòşa, a *ad* galore.
ipèrbole *nf* hyperbole.
ipersensíbile *a* hypersensitive.
ipertensióne *nf* (*med*) hypertension.
ipnòtico *pl* **-ici** *a* hypnotic.
ipnotíşmo *nm* hypnotism.
ipnotiẓẓàre *vt* to hypnotize.
ipocondría *nf* hypochondria, spleen.
ipocrişía *nf* hypocrisy, cant.
ipòcrita *nmf* hypocrite.
ipotèca *nf* mortgage.
ipotecàre *vt* to mortgage.
ipòteşi *nf* hypothesis.
ìppica *nf* horse-racing.
íppico *pl* **-ici** *a* horse; **còrse ippiche** horse races.
ippocastàno *nm* horse-chestnut.
ippòdromo *nm* racecourse.
ippopòtamo *nm* hippopotamus.
íra, iracóndia *nf* anger, rage, wrath.
iracóndo *a* irascible, choleric.
Iràk *nm* (*geogr*) Irak, Iraq.
Iràn *nm* (*geogr*) Iran, Persia.
iraniàno *a nm* Iranian, Persian.
irascíbile *a* irascible, irritable, hot-tempered.
irascibilità *nf* irascibility.
iràto *a* angry, in a rage.
Irène *nf pr* Irene, Eirene.
íride *nf* iris; rainbow.
iridescènte *a* iridescent.
Irlànda *nf* (*geogr*) Ireland.
irlandése *a* Irish; *nm* Irishman, (*language*) Irish; *nf* Irishwoman.
Írma *nf pr* Irma.
ironía *nf* irony.
irònico *pl* **-ici** *a* ironic(al).
iróso *a* angry.
irradiàre *vti* to (ir)radiate.
irradiazióne *nf* irradiation, fall-out.
irragionévole *a* irrational, unreasonable, absurd.
irragionevolézza *nf* unreasonableness, unfairness.
irrazionàle *a* irrational.
irrazionalità *nf* irrationality.
irreàle *a* unreal.
irrealtà *nf* unreality.
irreconciliàbile *a* irreconcilable.
irrecuperàbile *a* irrecoverable.
irredènto *a* unredeemed.
irredimíbile *a* irredeemable.
irrefutàbile *a* irrefutable.
irregolàre *a* abnormal, irregular.
irregolarità *nf* irregularity.
irreligióso *a* irreligious.
irremissíbile *a* impossible to remit.
irremovíbile *a* irremovable, inflexible.
irreparàbile *a* irreparable.
irreperíbile *a* that cannot be found.
irreprensíbile *a* faultless, irreproachable.
irrequietézza *nf* restlessness.
irrequièto *a* restless.
irresistíbile *a* irresistible.
irresolutézza *nf* irresolution, indecision.
irresolúto *a* hesitant, irresolute.
irresponsàbile *a* irresponsible.
irreversíbile *a* irreversible; **direzióne i.** (*aut*) irreversible steering.
irrevocàbile *a* irrevocable.
irriconoscíbile *a* unrecognizable.
irrídere *vt* to deride, laugh at.
irriducíbile *a* irreducible.
irriflessívo *a* thoughtless.
irrigàbile *a* irrigable.
irrigàre *vt* to irrigate.
irrigazióne *nf* irrigation.
irrigidiménto *nm* stiffening.
irrigidíre *vt* to make stiff; **-rsi** *vr* to grow (stand) stiff.
irríguo *a* well-watered.
irrilevànte *a* insignificant.
irrimediàbile *a* irremediable.
irrişióne *nf* derision, mockery.

irrisòrio *a* derisory; paltry.
irrispettóso *a* disrespectful.
irritàbile *a* irritable; (*of skin*) sensitive.
irritabilità *nf* irritability; (*of skin*) sensitiveness.
irritànte *a* irritating.
irritàre *vt* to irritate, inflame; **-rsi** *vr* to become angry, inflamed.
irritazióne *nf* irritation, inflammation.
irriverènte *a* irreverent.
irriverènza *nf* irreverence.
irrobustíre *vt* to strengthen; **-rsi** *vr* to grow strong(er).
irrómpere *vi* to break into; swarm; overflow.
irruènte *a* impetuous.
irruènza *nf* impetuosity.
irrugginíre *vti* to make (grow) rusty.
irruzióne *nf* irruption.
irsúto *a* hairy, shaggy.
írto *a* bristling, bushy, shaggy.
Isabèlla *nf pr* Isabella, Isabel.
Isàcco *nm pr* Isaac.
iscrítto *a* enrolled, entered, registered, inscribed.
iscrívere *vt* to enroll, register, inscribe; **-rsi** *vr* to enter (for).
iscrizióne *nf* inscription, enrollment, matriculation, entry, membership.
Islàm *nm* Islam.
islàmico *pl* **-ici** *a* Islamic.
islamísmo *nm* Islamism.
Islànda *nf* (*geogr*) Iceland.
islandése *a* Icelandic; *nm* Icelander, Icelandic (language).
ísola *nf* island, isle.
isolaménto *nm* isolation; (*el*) insulation.
isolàno *a* insular; *nm* islander.
isolànte *a* (*el*) insulating; *nm* insulator.
isolàre *vt* to isolate; insulate; **-rsi** *vr* to shun society.
isolatóre *nm* (*el*) insulator.
Isòtta *nf pr* Isolde.
ispanísmo *nm* Hispanicism.
ispettoràto *nm* inspector's office, inspectorship, inspectorate.
ispettóre *nm* **-tríce** *nf* inspector.
ispezionàre *vt* to inspect.
ispezióne *nf* inspection.
íspido *a* bristling, rough, shaggy.
ispiràre *vt* to inspire, instill, infuse into; **-rsi** *vr* to draw inspiration.
ispirazióne *nf* inspiration.
Israèle *nm* (*geogr*) Israel.
israeliàno *a nm* Israeli.
israelíta *a nmf* Israelite, Jew, Jewess.
israelítico *pl* **-ici** *a* Israelite, Jewish.
issàre *vt* to hoist.
istantànea *nf* snapshot.
istantàneo *a* instantaneous, instant.
istànte *a* instant, pressing; *nm* moment; petitioner.
istànza *nf* request, application, petition.
istèrico *pl* **-ici** *a* hysteric(al).
isterísmo *nm* hysteria, hysterics *pl*.
istésso *v* **stesso**.
istigàre *vt* to instigate.
istigazióne *nf* instigation.
istintívo *a* instinctive.
istínto *nm* instinct.
istituíre *vt* to institute, found, appoint.
istitúto *nm* institute, school, bank.
istitutóre *nm* **-tríce** *nf* founder; tutor, governess.
istituzióne *nf* institution, establishment.
ístmo *nm* isthmus.
istoriàre *vt* to adorn with figures, illustrate.
Ístria *nf* (*geogr*) Istria; **istriàno** *a nm* Istrian.
ístrice *nf* porcupine.
istrióne *nm* bad actor, charlatan.
istriònico *pl* **-ici** *a* histrionic.
istruíre *vt* to instruct, teach, inform; **-rsi** *vr* to acquire knowledge, learn.
istruíto *a* educated, well-read.
istrumentàle *a* instrumental.
istruménto *nm* instrument.
istruttívo *a* instructive.
istruttóre *nm* **-tríce** *nf* instructor, teacher; **giúdice i.** examining magistrate.
istruttòria *nf* examination, investigation.
istruttòrio *a* preliminary.
istruzióne *nf* education, instruction, learning, order, teaching; **ministèro della Púbblica I.** *nm* Ministry of Education.
istupidíre *vt* to make stupid; *vi* to become stupid.
Itàlia *nf* (*geogr*) Italy.
italianaménte *ad* after the Italian fashion, in the Italian way.
italianità *nf* Italian feelings, Italian nationality.
Italiàno *a nm* Italian.
itàlico *pl* **-ici** *a nm* Italic, Italian, (*typ*) italics.
iteràre *vt* to iterate, repeat.
iterazióne *nf* iteration, repetition.
itineràrio *nm* itinerary, route.
itterízia *nf* (*med*) jaundice.
Iugoslàvia *nf* (*geogr*) Jugoslavia.
iugoslàvo *a nm* Jugoslav.
iunior, iunióre *a* junior.
iúngla *nf* jungle.
iúta *nf* jute.
Iútland *nm* (*geogr*) Jutland.
ívi *ad* there, therein.

L

la *def art f* the; *pron f* (*acc*) her, it, (*mus*) la.
là *ad* there; **al di là (di)** *ad and prep* beyond.
làbbro *nm, pl m* **làbbri,** *f* **làbbra**

lip; **i làbbri di una feríta** the lips of a wound; **mòrdersi le làbbra** to bite one's lips.
làbile *a* fleeting, ephemeral, weak.
labirínto *nm* labyrinth, maze.
laboratòrio *nm* laboratory, work-room.
laboriosità *nf* laboriousness, industry.
laborióso *a* laborious, industrious, hard-working; difficult.
laburísmo *nm* Laborism.
laburísta *a* Labor; *nmf* Labour Party member (*Eng.*).
làcca *nf* lacquer.
laccàre *vt* to lacquer, enamel.
lacchè *nm* lackey.
làccio *nm* shoelace, string, snare, noose.
lacerànte *a* tearing, rending.
laceràre *v* to lacerate, rend, tear (up); **-rsi** *vr* to tear, get torn.
lacerazióne *nf* laceration, rent.
làcero *a* in rags, rent, torn.
lacònico *pl* **-ici** *a* laconic.
laconísmo *nm* laconism.
làcrima, làgrima *nf* tear; **scoppiàre in làcrime** *vi* to burst into tears.
lacrimàre *vi* to cry, weep, shed tears; water.
lacrimàto *a* lamented, regretted.
lacrimévole *a* tearful.
lacrimògeno *a* lachrymatory.
lacrimóso *a* lachrymose, tearful, weeping.
lacúna *nf* lacuna, blank, gap.
làdro *a* bewitching, thieving; *nm* thief.
ladróne *nm* robber, highwayman.
ladronería *nf* robbery.
laggiú *ad* down there, there below, over there.
lagnànza *nf* complaint.
lagnàrsi *vr* to complain.
làgo *pl* **-ghi** *nm* lake, pool.
làgrima *v* **làcrima.**
lagúna *nf* lagoon.
laicàto *nm* laity.
làico *pl* **-ici** *a* lay; *nm* layman.
laidézza *nf* foulness, obscenity.
làido *a* dirty, foul, obscene.
làma *nf* blade; *nm* (*priest*) Lama; (*zool*) llama.
lambiccàre *vt* to distill; **-rsi il cervèllo** *vr* to cudgel one's brains.
lambícco *pl* **-chi** *nm* still, alembic.
lambíre *vt* to lap, touch lightly.
lamentàre *vt* to lament, mourn, regret; **-rsi** *vr* to complain, mourn.
lamentazióne *nf* lamentation.
laménto *nm* lament, mourning, complaint.
lamentóso *a* mournful, plaintive.
lamièra *nf* plate, sheet iron.
làmina *nf* blade, thin plate (of metal).
laminàto *a* (*metal*) rolled.
laminatóio *nm* rolling-mill.
làmpada *nf* lamp; **l. ad àrco** arc-lamp.
lampadàrio *nm* chandelier, electric-light pendant.
lampadína *nf* (electric) bulb, small lamp; **l. elèttrica (tascàbile)** torch; flashlight.
lampànte *a* clear, obvious.
lampeggiaménto *nm* lightning; flashing.
lampeggiànte *a* flashing.
lampeggiàre *vi* to lighten; flash.
lampionàio *nm* lamp-lighter.
lampioncíno *nm* Chinese lantern, fairylight.
lampióne *nm* street-lamp.
làmpo *nm* lightning, flash; **chiusúra l.** zip fastener, zipper.
lampóne *nm* raspberry.
lamprèda *nf* lamprey.
làna *nf* wool; **l. di vétro** (*ind*) fiberglass; **di l.** wool(len).
lanaiuòlo *nm* wool-comber, wool-worker.
lancétta *nf* (*of watch or clock*) hand; lancet.
lància *nf* lance; (*naut*) launch.
lanciabómbe *nm* trench-mortar.
lanciafiàmme *nm* flamethrower.
lanciàre *vt* to throw, launch; **-rsi** *vr* to fling (launch) oneself.
lanciasilúri *nm* torpedo-tube.
lancière *nm* lancer.
làncio *nm* throwing, launching.
lànda *nf* heath, moor.
lanería *nf* woollens *pl*, woollen goods *pl*.
languènte *a* languishing, pining, drooping.
languidaménte *ad* languidly, languorously.
languidézza *nf* languidness.
lànguido *a* languid, weak; (*of light*) faint.
languíre *vi* to languish, pine; (*of light*) fade.
languóre *nm* languor, weakness, faintness.
lanièro *a* woollen, wool; **commèrcio l.** wool trade.
lanifício *nm* wool factory.
lanóso *a* woolly.
lantèrna *nf* lantern, skylight; **l. di sicurézza** safety-lamp.
lanúgine *nf* down (on the skin).
lapidàre *vt* to stone.
lapidàrio *a nm* lapidary.
lapidazióne *nf* stoning.
làpide *nf* memorial tablet, tombstone.
làpin *French nm* cony, cony (skin).
làpis *nm* pencil.
lapislàzzuli *nm* lapis-lazuli.
lappóne *a* Lapp; *nm* (*language*) Lapp(ish); *nmf* Lapp, Laplander.
Lappònia *nf* (*geogr*) Lapland.
làrdo *nm* bacon.
largaménte *ad* largely, abundantly, at length, extensively.
largheggiàre *vi* to be generous, lavish.
larghézza *nf* breadth, width; **l. di**

mèzzi wealth; **l. di vedúte** broad-mindedness.
largíre *vt* to give liberally.
largizióne *nf* donation, gift.
làrgo *pl* **làrghi** *a* broad, wide, large, generous; *nm* breadth, width; **fàrsi l.** to make a way for oneself.
làrice *nm* larch.
laringe *nf* larynx.
laringíte *nf* (*med*) laryngitis.
làrva *nf* larva, phantom, sham.
larvataménte *ad* by innuendo.
larvàto *a* hidden, latent.
làsca *pl* **-che** *nf* roach.
lasciapassàre *nm* pass, permit.
lasciàre *vt* to abandon, desert, leave (out), let, permit, quit; **l. cadére** to drop; **l. stàre** to let alone; **-rsi** *vr* to allow (let) oneself.
làscito *nm* bequest, legacy.
lascivaménte *ad* lasciviously, lustfully.
lascívia *nf* lasciviousness, wantonness.
lascívo *a* lascivious, wanton.
lassatívo *a nm* laxative.
làsso *a* (*poet*) unhappy, weary; *nm* (*of time*) lapse, period.
lassú *ad* up there.
làstra *nf* (*of glass*) pane, plate, slab.
lastricàre *vt* to pave.
làstrico *pl* **-chi** *nm* pavement; **lasciàre sul l.** to leave penniless.
latèbra *nf* (*poet*) recess, secret place.
latènte *a* concealed.
lateràle *a* side, lateral.
lateranénse *a* Lateran.
Lateràno *a nm pr* Lateran.
laterízi *nm pl* bricks *pl*.
latifondísta *nm* owner of large landed estate.
latifóndo *nm* large landed estate.
latinísta *nmf* Latinist, Latin scholar.
latíno *a nm* Latin.
latitànte *a* absconding; **rèndersi l.** to abscond.
latitúdine *nf* latitude.
làto *nm* side; **a l. di** beside; **dal l. mío** for my part.
latóre *nm* **-tríce** *nf* bearer.
latraménto *nm* barking.
latràre *vi* to bark.
latràto *nm* bark, barking.
latrína *nf* latrine, lavatory, **w.c.**
làtta *nf* tin, can; tin plate.
lattàio *nm* milkman.
lattànte *a* breast-fed; *nm* child at the breast, suckling.
làtte *nm* milk.
lattemièle *nm* whipped cream.
làtteo *a* milky.
lattería *nf* (*farm or shop*) dairy.
latticínio *nm* dairy product.
lattièra *nf* milk-jug, milk-pot, cream-jug, creamer.
lattivéndola *nf* milk-woman; **lattivéndolo** *nm* milkman.
lattonière *nm* tinsmith.
lattòsio *nm* (*chem*) lactose.
lattúga *nf* lettuce.

làuda, làude *nf* laud, hymn of praise, early religious lyric.
làudano *nm* laudanum.
Làura *nf pr* Laura.
làurea *nf* (university) degree.
laureàndo *a nm* final-year undergraduate.
laureàre *vt* to confer a degree on; **-rsi** *vr* to take one's degree.
laureàto *a nm* graduate.
làuro *nm* laurel.
lautaménte *ad* sumptuously, magnificently.
lautézza *nf* magnificence, sumptuousness.
làuto *a* magnificent, sumptuous, abundant.
làva *nf* lava.
lavabiancheria *nf* washing machine.
lavàbile *a* washable.
lavàbo *nm* wash-basin, (*eccl*) lavabo.
lavàcro *nm* (*liter*) bath, font.
lavàggio *nm* washing; **l. a sècco** dry cleaning.
lavàgna *nf* slate, blackboard.
lavamàno *nm* wash-hand basin.
lavànda *nf* lavender; washing.
lavandàia *nf* laundress, washerwoman; **lavandàio** *nm* laundryman.
lavandería *nf* laundry; **l. automàtica** launderette.
lavandíno *nm* sink.
lavapiàtti *a* dish-washing; *nmf* dishwasher, scullery-boy, scullery-maid.
lavàre *vt* **-rsi** *vr* to wash; **l. a sècco** to dry-clean.
lavàta *nf* wash; (*fig*) dressing-down, reprimand.
lavatívo *nm* enema; (*vulg*) tiresome person, bore.
lavatóio *nm* wash-house, wash-board.
lavatríce *nf* washerwoman; washing machine.
lavatúra *nf* washing; **l. a sècco** dry cleaning.
lavorànte *nm* workman; *nf* workwoman.
lavoràre *vti* to work, labor, till.
lavoratívo *a* working; **giórno l.** working day, weekday.
lavoràto *a* worked, processed, manufactured, tilled.
lavoratóre *nm* **-tríce** *nf* worker; *a* working.
lavorazióne *nf* manufacture, working, workmanship, tilling.
lavorío *nm* intense activity, intrigue.
lavóro *nm* work, labor, toil, job; (*theat*) play.
Làzio *nm* (*geogr*) Latium.
Làzzaro *nm pr* Lazarus.
lazzaróne *nm* (Neapolitan) beggar; rogue, idler.
le *def art f pl* the: *pron acc f pl* them; *pron dat f* to her.
leàle *a* loyal, faithful, true, fair.
lealménte *ad* loyally, faithfully, fairly.

lealtà *nf* loyalty, faithfulness, fairness.
lèbbra *nf* leprosy.
lebbróso *a* leprous; *nm* leper.
leccàrda *nf* dripping-pan.
leccàre *vt* to lick.
leccàto *a* affected; **stíle l.** affected style.
léccio *nm* holm-oak.
leccornía *nf* dainty, titbit.
lécito *a* lawful, allowed, right.
lèdere *vt* to offend, harm, injure.
léga *nf* league, union, alloy.
legàccio *nm* string, (*of shoes, boots*) lace.
legàle *a* legal, lawful; *nm* lawyer.
legalità *nf* legality, lawfulness.
legalizzàre *vi* to legalize, authenticate.
legalizzazióne *nf* legalization, authentication.
legalménte *ad* legally, lawfully.
legàme *nm* bond, connection, link, tie.
legaménto *nm* (*anat*) ligament; binding, linking, connecting.
legàre *vt* to bind, fasten, alloy, bequeath.
legatàrio *nm* legatee.
legàto *nm* ambassador, legate; legacy.
legatóre *nm* **-tríce** *nf* (book)binder; (*leg*) testator.
legatoría *nf* (book)binder's.
legatúra *nf* binding, fastening, ligature.
legazióne *nf* legation.
légge *nf* law, (*of parliament*) act.
leggènda *nf* legend.
leggendàrio *a* legendary.
lèggere *vt* to read.
leggerézza *nf* lightness, nimbleness; levity, thoughtlessness.
leggerménte *ad* lightly; thoughtlessly.
leggéro, leggiéro *a* light, slight, nimble, thoughtless, frivolous; **péso l.** (*boxing*) lightweight; **alla leggéra** *ad* lightly, thoughtlessly; **prèndere alla leggéra** *vt* to make light of.
leggiadría *nf* prettiness, grace, gracefulness.
leggiàdro *a* graceful, charming.
leggíbile *a* legible, readable.
leggío *nm* reading-desk, music-stand, lectern.
legióne *nf* legion.
legislatúra *nf* legislature.
legislazióne *nf* legislation.
legittimaménte *ad* legitimately, lawfully.
legittimità *nf* lawfulness, legitimacy.
legíttimo *a* lawful, legitimate.
légna *pl* **légna** *nf* wood, firewood; **portàre l. alla sélva** *vi* to carry coals to Newcastle.
legnai(u)òlo *nm* woodcutter, joiner, carpenter.
legnàme *nm* timber, lumber.
legnàta *nf* blow with a cudgel.
légno *nm* wood, stick; **di l.** wooden; **l. ricostituíto** chipboard; **lavóro in l.** woodwork.
legnóso *a* woody.
legúme *nm* vegetable.
lèi *pron nom and acc f* she, her; you (*polite form m and f*).
Lèida *nf* (*geogr*) Leyden.
lémbo *nm* edge, hem, strip.
léna *nf* breath, energy; **di buòna l.** willingly.
Leningràdo *nf* (*geogr*) Leningrad.
lenire *vt* to soften, soothe.
lenitívo *a* lenitive, palliative.
lenocínio *nm* pandering; (*fig*) artifice.
lenóne *nm* pander, procurer.
lentaménte *ad* slowly.
lènte *nf* lentil; lens.
lentézza *nf* slowness, sluggishness.
lentícchia *nf* lentil.
lentíggine *nf* freckle.
lentigginóso *a* freckled.
lènto *a* slow, sluggish; loose.
lènza *nf* fishing-line, line.
lenzuòlo *nm pl* **-òla** *f* (bed)sheet.
Leonàrdo *nm pr* Leonard.
Leóne *nm pr* Leo, Leon.
leóne *nm* lion; **leonéssa** *nf* lioness.
leopàrdo *nm* leopard.
Leopòldo *nm pr* Leopold.
lepidézza *nf* witticism.
lèpido *a* witty.
Lepontíne, Àlpi *nf pl* (*geogr*) Lepontine Alps.
lèpre *nf* hare.
lércio *a* dirty, filthy, foul.
lésina *nf* awl.
lesinàre *vi* to be stingy; **l. sul prézzo** to haggle over the price.
lesióne *nf* lesion, wound, injury.
léso *a* hurt, injured, offended.
lessàre *vt* to boil.
lèssico *pl* **-ici** *nm* lexicon.
lessicògrafo *nm* lexicographer.
lésso *a* boiled; *nm* boiled meat.
lestaménte *ad* quickly, hastily.
lestézza *nf* agility, quickness, swiftness.
lèsto *a* agile, quick, swift; *ad* quickly.
lestofànte *nm* swindler.
letàle *a* deadly, lethal.
letamàio *nm* dung-heap, hovel.
letàme *nm* dung.
letargía *nf* **letàrgo** *nm pl* **-ghi** lethargy.
letàrgico *pl* **-ici** *a* lethargic.
letízia *nf* gladness, joy.
léttera *nf* letter; **alla l.** literally; **bèlle léttere** *pl* Arts *pl*.
letteràle *a* literal.
letteralménte *ad* literally.
letteràrio *a* literary.
letteràto *a* well-read; *nm* man of letters.
letteratúra *nf* literature.
lettièra *nf* bedstead.
lettíga *nf* stretcher.
lètto *nm* bed.
lettóne *a nmf* Latvian; *nm* Lettish.
Lettònia *nf* (*geogr*) Latvia.
lettoràto *nm* lectureship.

lettóre *nm* **-tríce** *nf* reader, lecturer.
lettúra *nf* reading; **sàla di l.** reading-room.
leucemía *nf* leukemia.
lèva *nf* (*mech*) lever; (*mil*) conscription, draft; **èssere di l.** to be liable to call-up; **la l. del 1960** those called up in 1960.
levànte *nm* East; **vénto di l.** east wind; **il l.** the Levant.
levantíno *a nm* Levantine.
levàre *vt* to lift, raise, remove; **-rsi** *vr* to get out of the way, rise, take off.
levàta *nf* rising; (*postal*) collection.
levatóio *a* **pónte l.** drawbridge.
levatríce *nf* midwife.
levigàre *vt* to smooth.
levrière, levrièro *nm* greyhound.
lèzio *nm* **leziosàggine** *nf* affectation, mannerism.
lezióne *nf* lesson.
lezióso *a* affected, mincing.
lézzo *nm* stink, filth.
li *pron m acc pl* them.
lì *ad* there; **giù di l.** thereabouts; **l. per l.** immediately; **èssere l. l. per** to be within an ace of.
libanése *a nmf* Lebanese.
Líbano *nm* (*geogr*) Lebanon.
líbbra *nf* pound (weight).
libéccio *nm* southwest wind.
libèllo *nm* libel.
libèllula *nf* dragonfly.
liberàle *a* liberal; *nm* Liberal.
liberalísmo *nm* liberalism.
liberalità *nf* liberality.
liberaménte *ad* freely, frankly.
liberàre *vt* to free, clear, exempt, release; **-rsi** *vr* to free oneself, get rid of.
liberazióne *nf* liberation.
Libèria *nf* (*geogr*) Liberia.
liberiàno *a nm* Liberian.
líbero *a* free.
libertà *nf* freedom, liberty.
libertinàggio *nm* libertinage.
libertíno *a nm* libertine.
Líbia *nf* (*geogr*) Libya.
líbico *pl* **-ici** *a nm* Libyan.
libídine *nf* lust.
libidinóso *a* lustful.
líbra *nf* scales.
libràio *nm* bookseller.
libràre *vt* to weigh, balance.
librería *nf* bookshop, book store; library; bookcase.
librétto *nm* (*mus*) libretto; small book; **l. di bànca** bank-book; **l. di circolazióne** (*aut*) log-book.
líbro *nm* book; **l. di càssa** cash-book; **l. giàllo** thriller; **l. maèstro** ledger; **l. di preghiére** prayer-book.
liceàle *a* of a 'liceo'.
licènza *nf* lease, certificate, license; dismissal.
licenziaménto *nm* discharge, dismissal.
licenziàre *vt* to discharge, dismiss; **-rsi** *vr* to resign; get one's diploma.
licenzióso *a* licentious.
licèo *nm* 'Liceo', secondary school.
lído *nm* shore, beach.
Liègi *nf* (*geogr*) Liège.
lietaménte *ad* happily, merrily.
liéto *a* glad, happy, cheerful.
liéve *a* light, slight, easy.
lieveménte *ad* lightly, gently.
lievitàre *vt* to leaven; *vi* (*of bread etc*) rise.
lièvito *nm* yeast, leaven; **l. di bírra** yeast.
lígio *a* faithful, observant.
lignàggio *nm* lineage.
lígure *a nm* Ligurian.
Ligúria *nf* (*geogr*) Liguria.
lílla *nf* lilac; *nm* (*color*) lilac.
Lílla *nf* (*geogr*) Lille.
lillipuziàno *a nm* Lilliputian.
líma *nf* (*mech*) file.
limaccióso *a* miry, muddy.
limàre *vt* to file, polish.
límbo *nm* Limbo.
limitàre *vt* to limit; *nm* threshold.
limitazióne *nf* limitation; **l. dèlle nàscite** birth-control.
límite *nm* boundary, limit.
limítrofo *a* adjacent, neighboring.
límo *nm* mire, mud.
limonàta *nf* lemonade.
limóne *nm* lemon (tree).
limpidézza *nf* clearness, limpidness.
límpido *a* limpid, clear.
línce *nf* lynx.
linciàggio *nm* lynching.
linciàre *vt* to lynch.
líndo *a* clean.
línea *nf* line.
lineaménti *nm pl* features *pl*, lineaments pl.
lineétta *nf* dash, hyphen.
línfa *nf* lymph, sap.
linfàtico *pl* **-ici** *a* lymphatic.
lingòtto *nm* ingot.
língua *nf* tongue, language.
linguàggio *nm* language.
linguísta *nmf* linguist.
linguística *nf* linguistics.
linguístico *pl* **-ici** *a* linguistic.
líno *nm* flax, linen; **séme di l.** linseed.
linòleum *nm* linoleum.
Lióne *nf* (*geogr*) Lyon; **lionése** *anmf* (person from) Lyons.
Lípsia *nf* (*geogr*) Leipzig.
liquefàre *vt* **-rsi** *vr* to liquefy.
liquidàre *vt* to liquidate.
liquidàto *a* liquidated, paid off, ruined.
liquidazióne *nf* liquidation, winding-up.
líquido *a* liquid; (*money*) ready; *nm* liquid.
liquirízia *nf* liquorice.
liquóre *nm* liqueur, liquor.
líra *nf* (*Italian coin*) lira; (*mus*) lyre.
lírica *nf* lyric, lyrical poem or poetry.
lírico *pl* **-ici** *a* lyric, lyrical; *nm* lyric poet.

lirísmo *nm* lyricism.
Lisbóna *nf* (*geogr*) Lisbon.
lísca *nf* fishbone.
lisciaménto *nm* **lisciatúra** *nf* smoothing, polishing.
lisciàre *vt* to smooth, polish; (*fig*) flatter.
líscio *a* smooth, plain, (*of drink*) neat, straight; **mèssa líscia** low mass; *ad* smoothly.
liscíva *nf* lye.
lísta *nf* strip; list, menu.
listàre *vt* to line, border.
listíno *nm* list, price-list.
litanía *nf* litany.
líte *nf* lawsuit, quarrel.
litigànte *nmf* disputant, litigant.
litigàre *vi* to dispute, quarrel.
litígio *nm* dispute, quarrel.
litigióso *a* quarrelsome.
litografàre *vt* to lithograph.
litografía *nf* lithography, lithograph.
litoràle *a* coastal, coast; *nm* littoral, coastline.
lítro *nm* liter.
littorànea *nf* coast road.
littorína *nf* diesel rail-car.
Lituània *nf* (*geogr*) Lithuania.
lituàno *a nm* Lithuanian.
liturgía *nf* liturgy.
litúrgico *pl* **-ici** *a* liturgic(al).
liúto *nm* (*mus*) lute.
livellàre *vt* to level.
livèllo *nm* level; **passàggio a l.** level-crossing, grade crossing; **l. del màre** sea-level.
lívido *a* livid; *nm* bruise.
Lívio *nm pr* Livy.
livóre *nm* envy, hatred.
Livórno *nf* (*geogr*) Leghorn.
livrèa *nf* livery.
lízza *nf* lists *pl.*
lo *def art m* the; *pron acc m* him, it.
lòbo *nm* lobe.
locàle *a* local; *nm* room, premises *pl.*
località *nf* locality.
localizzàre *vt* to locate, localize.
localménte *ad* locally.
locànda *nf* inn.
locandièra *nf* **-re** *nm* innkeeper.
locatàrio *nm* lessee, tenant.
locatóre *nm* **-tríce** *nf* lessor.
locazióne *nf* lease.
locomotíva *nf* locomotive.
locomozióne *nf* locomotion.
locústa *nf* locust.
locuzióne *nf* expression, phrase, idiom.
lodàre *vt* to praise.
lòde *nf* praise.
lodévole *a* praiseworthy, laudable, commendable.
lòdola *nf* lark, skylark.
Lodovíco *nm pr* Ludovic(k).
logarítmo *nm* logarithm.
lòggia *nf* loggia; (*masonic*) lodge.
loggióne *nm* (*theat*) gallery.
lògica *nf* logic.
lògico *pl* **-ici** *a* logical; *nm* logician.
lòglio *nm* darnel.
logoraménto *nm* wearing out, wearing down, wasting away.
logoràre *vt* to wear down, wear out; **-rsi** *vr* to be worn out.
logorío *nm* wear and tear.
lógoro *a* worn down, worn out.
lombàggine *nf* lumbago.
Lombardía *nf* (*geogr*) Lombardy.
lombàrdo *a nm* Lombard.
lombàta *nf* (*of meat*) loin, sirloin.
lómbo *nm* (*human*) loin.
lombríco *nm* earthworm.
Lóndra *nf* (*geogr*) London.
londinése *a* (of) London; *nmf* Londoner.
longànime *a* forbearing, patient.
longanimità *nf* forbearance, patience.
longevità *nf* longevity.
longèvo *a* long-lived.
longitudinàle *a* longitudinal.
longitúdine *nf* longitude.
lontanaménte *ad* vaguely, slightly.
lontanànza *nf* distance; **in l.** at a distance.
lontàno *a* distant, far; *ad* far, far away, far off; **da l.** from a distance; **àlla lontàna** at a distance, slightly.
lóntra *nf* otter.
lónza *nf* panther; (*of meat*) loin.
loquàce *a* loquacious, talkative.
loquacità *nf* loquacity.
loquèla *nf* language, way of speaking.
lordàre *vt* to dirty, soil.
lórdo *a* dirty; **péso l.** *nm* (*com*) gross weight.
lordúra *nf* dirt, filth.
Lorèna *nf* (*geogr*) Lorraine.
lorenése *a* of Lorraine; *nm* Lorrainer.
Lorènzo *nm pr* Laurence, Lawrence.
lóro *pron nom pl* they, you; *acc pl* you, them; *dat pl* to you, to them; *poss a pl* your, their.
Losànna *nf* (*geogr*) Lausanne.
lósco *pl* **-schi** *a* dubious; one-eyed, squint-eyed; **figúra lósca** scoundrel.
lòtta *nf* fight, struggle.
lottàre *vi* to fight, struggle, wrestle.
lottería *nf* lottery.
lòtto *nm* lot, lottery.
lozióne *nf* lotion.
lubricità *nf* lubricity.
lúbrico *pl* **-ici** *a* slippery; indecent.
lubrificànte *a* lubricating; *nm* lubricant.
lubrificàre *vt* to lubricate, oil, grease.
lubrificazióne *nf* lubrication.
Lúca *nm pr* Luke.
lucchétto *nm* padlock.
luccicàre *vi* to glitter, shine.
luccichío *nm* glitter, sparkle.
lúccio *nm* (*fish*) pike.
lúcciola *nf* firefly, glowworm.
lúce *nf* light; **l. abbagliànte** (*aut*) headlight; **l. anabbagliànte** (*aut*) anti-glare light; **lúci della ribàlta** *pl* (*theat*) footlights; **dare alla l.** to give birth to.
lucènte *a* shiny, shining, bright.

lucentézza *nf* brightness, shine, sheen.
Lucèrna *nf* (*geogr*) Lucerne.
lucèrna *nf* oil-lamp.
lucernàrio *nm* skylight.
lucèrtola *nf* lizard.
Lucía *nf* pr Lucy.
Luciàno *nm pr* Lucian.
lucidaménto, lucidatúra *nf* polishing.
lucidàre *vt* to polish.
lucidatóre *nm* polisher.
lucidatríce *nf* polisher, polishing machine.
lucidézza *nf* brightness, sheen.
luciditá *nf* lucidity, clearness.
lúcido *a* bright, shiny, lucid.
lucígnolo *nm* wick.
lúcro *nm* profit, gain.
lucróso *a* lucrative, profitable.
ludíbrio *nm* mockery, scorn.
lúe *nf* (*med*) contagion, syphilis.
lúglio *nm* July.
lúgubre *a* lugubrious, dismal.
lúi *pron m* (*nom*) he; (*acc*) him.
Luígi *nm pr* Louis, Lewis.
Luíșa *nf pr* Louise, Louisa.
Luișiàna *nf* (*geogr*) Louisana.
lumàca *nf* snail; slow person.
lúme *nm* light, lamp; **a quésti lúmi di lúna** in these hard times.
luminàre *nm* great man, luminary.
luminària *nf* public illumination.
lumíno *nm* night-light.
luminosaménte *ad* brightly, luminously.
luminosità *nf* brightness, luminosity.
luminóso *a* luminous, shining, bright.
lúna *nf* moon; **l. di mièle** honeymoon; **chiàro di l.** moonlight.
lunàre *a* lunar.
lunàrio *nm* almanac; **sbarcàre il l.** to make both ends meet.
lunàtico *pl* **-ici** *a* moody.
lunedí *nm* Monday.
lungaménte *ad* for a long time.
lunghézza *nf* length.
lungimirànte *a* far-seeing.
lúngo *pl* **-ghi** *a* long, tall; slow; weak; *prep* along; **a l.** for a long time; **di gran lúnga** by far; **a l. andàre** in the long run.
lungomàre *nm* sea-front.
lungometràggio *nm* feature film.
luògo *pl* **-ghi** *nm* place; **sul l.** on the spot; **l. comúne** commonplace.
luogotenènte *nm* lieutenant.
lúpa *nf* she-wolf; **lúpo** *nm* wolf.
lupacchiòtto *nm* wolf-cub.
lupanàre *nm* brothel.
lupíno *nm* lupin.
lúppolo *nm* hop (plant).
lúrido *a* dirty, filthy.
luridúme *nm* filth, dirt.
lușínga *nf* allurement, illusion, flattery.
lușingàre *vt* to allure, flatter.
lușinghièro *a* alluring, flattering.
lussàre *vt* (*med*) to dislocate.
lussazióne *nf* dislocation.
Lussembúrgo *nm* (*geogr*) Luxembourg.
lússo *nm* luxury.
lussuóso *a* luxurious.
lussureggiànte *a* luxuriant.
lussureggiàre *vt* to be luxuriant, flourish.
lussúria *nf* lust.
lussurióso *a* lustful.
lustràre *vt* to polish.
lustrascàrpe *nm* shoeblack, shoeshine.
lustríno *nm* sequin.
lústro *a* polished, shining; *nm* luster.
luteràno *a nm* Lutheran.
Lutèro *nm pr* Luther.
lútto *nm* mourning; **a l.** in mourning.
luttuóso *a* mournful, sad.

M

ma *cj* but; **macchè** *interj* not at all.
màcabro *a* macabre.
maccheróni *nm pl* macaroni.
màcchia *nf* spot, stain, blot; bush, woodland; **alla m.** clandestinely.
macchiàre *vt* to soil, spot, stain; **-rsi** *vr* to get dirty, disgrace oneself.
macchiétta *nf* speck; caricature; eccentric person, (*theat*) character study.
màcchina *nf* machine, engine; car; **m. a vapóre** steam engine; **m. da scrívere** typewriter; **m. fuòri série** custom-built car; **m. decapotàbile** convertible; **m. lavapiàtti** dish-washing machine (dishwasher).
macchinalménte *ad* mechanically, automatically.
macchinàre *vt* to plot.
macchinàrio *nm* machinery.
macchinazióne *nf* machination, plot.
macchinista *nm* engine driver, engineer.
macedònia *nf* fruit salad, macedoine.
macellàio *nm* butcher.
macellàre *vt* to slaughter, butcher.
macellazióne *nf* slaughter(ing).
macellería *nf* butcher's (shop).
macèllo *nm* slaughter-house, slaughtering, slaughter.
maceràre *vt* to soak, macerate; **-rsi** *vr* to wear oneself out.
maceratóio, màcero *nm* macerating vat.
macerazióne *nf* maceration; (*fig*) mortification (of the flesh).
macèrie *nf pl* debris, remains.
macígno *nm* hard stone; boulder.
macilènto *a* emaciated.
màcina *nf* millstone, grindstone.
macinacaffè (*inv*) *nm* coffee-mill.
macinàre *vt* to grind, mill, crush.
macinatóio *nm* mill, press.
macinazióne *nf* grinding, milling.
macinino *nm* coffee-mill.
maciullàre *vt* to crush, chew.
Maddaléna *nf pr* Magdalene.

Madèra *nf* (*geogr*) Madeira.
màdia *nf* kneading trough, kitchen cupboard.
màdido *a* wet, soaked.
madònna *nf* (*arc*) lady, madonna; **Madònna** the Virgin Mary, (the) Madonna.
madornàle *a* enormous, gross, huge.
màdre *nf* mother; **m. lìngua** mother tongue; **càsa m.** (*com*) head office.
madrepàtria *nf* mother-country, fatherland.
madrepèrla *nf* mother-of-pearl.
madresélva *nf* honeysuckle.
Madríd *nf* (*geogr*) Madrid; **madrilèno** *a nm* of Madrid.
madrigàle *nm* madrigal.
madrína *nf* godmother.
maestà *nf* majesty.
maestóso *a* majestic, stately, magnificent.
maèstra *nf* (school)mistress, teacher.
maestràle *nm* mistral.
maestrànza *nf* skilled workmen *pl*, skilled hands *pl*.
maestría *nf* mastery, skill.
maèstro *a* main, principal, masterly; *nm* schoolmaster, teacher, maestro; **àlbero m.** mainmast; **stràda maèstra** highroad.
màfia *nf* Mafia.
mafióso *a nm* (member) of the Mafia.
magàgna *nf* defect, fault, ailment.
magàri *interj* if only . . . ! *ad* maybe, perhaps, even.
magazzinàggio *nm* storage.
magazzinière *nm* warehouse-man.
magazzíno *nm* store, warehouse, store-house.
maggése *nm* fallow land.
màggio *nm* (*month*) May.
maggioràna *nf* marjoram.
maggiorànza *nf* majority.
maggioràre *vt* (*com*) to increase, put up.
maggiorazióne *nf* (*com*) increase, additional charge.
maggiordòmo *nm* butler.
maggióre *a* bigger, elder, greater, high(er), larger, older, biggest, eldest; *nm* superior, elder; (*mil*) major; *pl* ancestors.
maggiorènne *a* of age; *nm* adult.
maggiorménte *ad* more, much more, all the more.
magía *nf* magic.
màgico *pl* **-ici** *a* magic(al).
magistèro *nm* mastery, teaching.
magistràle *a* magistral, masterly.
magistràto *nm* magistrate.
magistratúra *nf* magistracy.
màglia *nf* stitch; mesh; vest, jersey, (*mech*) link; mail; **lavoràre a m.** to knit.
maglieria *nf* hosiery, knitted goods *pl*.
maglifícío *nm* knitwear factory.
màglio *nm* mallet; (*mech*) hammer.
maglióne *nm* jersey, pullover.
magnanimità *nf* magnanimity.
magnànimo *a* magnanimous.
magnàno *nm* locksmith.
magnàte *nm* magnate, tycoon.
magnèsia *nf* magnesia.
magnèsio *nm* magnesium.
magnète *nm* magnet, magneto.
magnètico *pl* **-ici** *a* magnetic.
magnetismo *nm* magnetism.
magnetizzàre *vt* to magnetize.
magnetòfono *nm* tape-recorder.
magnificàre *vt* to extol, magnify.
magnificènza *nf* grandeur, splendor.
magnífico *pl* **-ici** *a* magnificent, splendid.
magniloquènza *nf* grandiloquence.
màgno *a* great.
magnòlia *nf* magnolia(-tree).
màgo *pl* **-ghi** *nm* sorcerer, wizard; **i Ré Màgi** the Three Kings.
màgra *nf* shallow water, shortage; **tèmpi di m.** hard times.
magrézza *nf* thinness, (*of soil*) poorness.
màgro *a* thin, poor; **giòrno di m.** day of abstinence.
mài *ad* ever, never; **cóme m.?** how is that?; **se m.** in case; if anything.
maiàle *nm* pig, pork.
maiòlica *nf* majolica.
maionése *nf* mayonnaise.
Maiòrca *nf* (*geogr*) Majorca.
màis *nm* maize, corn.
maiúscolo *a* capital; *nm* capitals *pl*.
malaccòrto *a* imprudent, rash.
malacreànza *nf* ill-breeding.
malaféde *nf* bad faith.
malaffàre *nm* **dònna di m.** whore; **gènte di m.** crooks *pl*, scum.
malagévole *a* difficult, hard, unmanageable.
malagiàto *a* uncomfortable, short of money.
malagràzia *nf* bad grace, rudeness.
malaménte *ad* badly.
malandàto *a* in bad repair, in poor health.
malandríno *a* roguish; *nm* robber, rogue.
malànimo *nm* ill will.
malànno *nm* infirmity, misfortune.
malapéna, a *ad* hardly, scarcely.
malària *nf* malaria.
malàrico *pl* **-ici** *a* malarial.
malatíccio *a* sickly.
malàto *a* ill, sick, diseased; *nm* sick person, patient.
malattía *nf* disease, illness.
malauguràto *a* unfortunate, ill-omened.
malaugúrio *nm* bad omen.
malavíta *nf* (criminal) underworld.
malavòglia *nf* unwillingness, ill-will.
malavventuràto *a* ill-fated, unlucky.
malazzàto *a* sickly.
malcapitàto *a* unfortunate, unlucky.
malcóncio *a* in a poor way, in tatters.
malcontènto *a* discontented, dis-

satisfied; *nm* dissatisfaction, discontent.
malcostúme *nm* immorality, corruption, bad habit.
maldèstro *a* awkward, clumsy.
maldicènza *nf* backbiting, slander.
màle *nm* evil, illness, harm; *ad* badly; **mal di dénti** toothache; **mal di góla** sore throat; **mal di tésta** headache; **méno m.** thank Heavens!; **non c'è m.** pretty good; **restàre m.** to be disappointed; **stàre m.** to be ill.
maledètto *a* cursed, damned.
maledíre *vt* to curse.
maledizióne *nf* curse.
maleducàto *a* rude; *nm* ill-bred person.
maleducazióne *nf* bad manners *pl*, rudeness.
malefàtta *nf* mischief.
malefício *nm* witchcraft, spell, misdeed.
malèfico *pl* **-ici** *a* evil, mischievous.
malèrba *nf* weed.
malése *a nmf* Malay.
Malèsia *nf* (*geogr*) Malaya, Malaysia.
malèssere *nm* indisposition, malaise.
malevolènza *nf* ill will, malevolence.
malèvolo *a* malevolent.
malfamàto *a* ill-famed.
malfattóre *nm* **-tríce** *nf* evil-doer, criminal.
malférmo *a* unsteady, shaky; (*of health*) poor.
malfído *a* unreliable, uncertain.
malgàrbo *nm* bad grace, rudeness.
malgovèrno *nm* misgovernment, mismanagement.
malgradíto *a* unwelcome.
malgràdo *prep* in spite of, notwithstanding; **mío m.** against my will; **m. (che)** *cj* although.
malía *nf* witchcraft, charm.
malignità *nf* malignity, wickedness.
malígno *a* evil, malicious, malignant.
malinconía *nf* melancholy, sadness.
malincònico *pl* **-ici** *a* melancholy, sad.
malincuòre, a *ad* unwillingly.
malintenzionàto *a* ill-disposed, malicious.
malintéso *a* mistaken; *nm* misunderstanding.
malízia *nf* malice, cunning, trick.
malizióso *a* mischievous, artful.
mallevadóre *nm* bail, surety.
malleveria, mallevadoría *nf* bail, suretyship.
malmenàre *vt* to ill-treat, ill-use.
malmésso *a* badly dressed, poorly dressed.
malnutríto *a* underfed.
màlo *a* bad, ill, wicked.
malòcchio *nm* evil eye; **vedére di m.** to dislike.
malóra *nf* ruin.
malóre *nm* sudden illness, indisposition.
malsàno *a* unhealthy, unwholesome.
malsicúro *a* unsafe, uncertain, unreliable.
Màlta *nf* (*geogr*) Malta; **maltése** *a nmf* Maltese.
maltalènto *nm* ill-will.
maltèmpo *nm* bad weather.
maltenúto *a* untidy, badly kept.
màlto *nm* malt.
maltòlto *a* ill-gotten; *nm* ill-gotten goods *pl*.
maltrattaménto *nm* ill-treatment.
maltrattàre *vt* to ill-treat, ill-use.
malumóre *nm* ill-humor, spleen.
malvagiaménte *ad* wickedly.
malvàgio *a* wicked.
malvagità *nf* wickedness.
malvísto *a* unpopular.
malvivènte *nm* gangster, criminal.
malvivènza *nf* delinquency, criminality.
malvolentièri *ad* unwillingly.
malvolére *nm* ill-will, dislike, wickedness.
màmma *nf* mama, mum(my), mother.
mammèlla *nf* breast.
mammífero *nm* mammal.
màmmola *nf* violet.
manàta *nf* handful, slap.
mànca *nf* left-hand, left-hand side.
mancànte *a* lacking, missing, deficient; failing, defective.
mancànza *nf* deficiency, lack, shortness, want; **sentíre la m. di** to miss.
mancàre *vi* to lack, be missing, err; **màncano cinque minúti alle dúe** it is five to two; *vt* to miss; **m. il bersàglio** to miss the mark.
mancàto *a* manqué, unsuccessful.
mància *nf* tip, reward.
manciàta *nf* handful.
mancíno *a* left-handed; treacherous.
Manciúria *nf* (*geogr*) Manchuria.
mànco *pl* **-chi** *a* left; *ad* not even.
mandaménto *nm* borough, district.
mandànte *nm* instigator.
mandàre *vt* to send, emit; **m. vía** to send away; **m. all'ària** to ruin.
mandaríno *nm* mandarin; tangerine.
mandàta *nf* batch; (of key) turn.
mandàto *nm* commission, mandate, order, warrant.
mandíbola *nf* jaw.
mandolíno *nm* mandolin.
màndorla *nf* almond; **màndorlo** *nm* almond-tree.
màndra, màndria *nf* flock, herd.
maneggévole *a* easy to handle, manageable.
maneggiàre *vt* to handle, manage, use; **-rsi** *vr* to conduct oneself, manage.
manéggio *nm* handling, use, management; horsemanship, riding-school; intrigue.
manésco *pl* **-chi** *a* ready with one's fists.
manétte *nf pl* handcuffs *pl*.
manganèllo *nm* cudgel.
manganése *nm* manganese.

mangeréccio *a* edible, eatable.
mangiàre *vti* to eat; *nm* eating.
mangiàta *nf* meal, hearty meal.
mangiatóia *nf* crib, manger.
mangiucchiàre *vti* to nibble, pick at one's food.
manía *nf* mania, fixation.
maníaco *pl* **-aci** *a nm* maniac.
mànica *nf* sleeve; **èssere di m. làrga** to be broad minded; **un àltro pàio di màniche** another kettle of fish; **la M.** the (English) Channel.
mànico *pl* **-chi** *nm* handle.
manicòmio *nm* (lunatic-)asylum.
manicòtto *nm* muff; (*mech*) coupling.
manicure (Fr) *nmf* manicurist, manicure.
manièra *nf* manner, way; **in qualúnque m.** anyhow.
manieràto *a* affected, mannered.
manifattúra *nf* manufacture, workmanship.
manifestàre *vt* to manifest, show; **-rsi** *vr* to reveal oneself.
manifestazióne *nf* display; demonstration.
manifèsto *a* clear, obvious; *nm* manifesto, bill, placard, leaflet.
maníglia *nf* handle.
manigóldo *nm* rascal, villain.
manipolàre *vt* to handle, manipulate, adulterate.
manipolazióne *nf* handling, preparation, manipulation, adulteration.
maniscàlco *pl* **-chi** *nm* farrier.
mànna *nf* manna, godsend.
mannàia *nf* axe.
màno *nf* hand; (*of paint*) coat; **a portàta di m.** within reach; **fuòri di m.** out of reach, out of the way; **strétta di m.** handshake; **di secónda m.** second-hand.
manodòpera *nf* labor, workmanship.
manòmetro *nm* manometer, pressure-gauge.
manométtere *vt* to tamper with, violate.
manomissióne *nf* tampering, violation.
manomòrta *nf* (*leg*) mortmain.
manòpola *nf* handle bar grip, knob, fencing glove, cuff.
manoscrítto *a* handwritten; *nm* manuscript.
manovàle *nm* laborer.
manovèlla *nf* crank, handle, winder.
manòvra *nf* maneuver, (*rly*) shunting.
manovràre *vt* to maneuver, shunt, work.
manrovèscio *pl* **manrovèsci** *nm* backhanded blow.
mansàlva *a ad* with impunity.
mansióne *nf* function, duty, office.
mansuefàre *vt* to subdue, tame.
mansuèto *a* meek, mild, docile.
mantèllo *nm* cloak, mantle.
mantenére *vt* to keep (up), maintain; **-rsi** *vr* to keep (oneself).
mantenimento *nm* maintenance' preservation.
màntice *nm* bellows *pl*, (*of a car*) hood.
mànto *nm* cloak, mantle.
Màntova *nf* (*geogr*) Mantua.
mantovàno *a nm* Mantuan.
manuàle *a* manual; *nm* handbook, manual.
manúbrio *nm* handle(-bar), dumbbell.
manufàtto *a* hand-made, manufactured; *nm* hand-made article.
manutenzióne *nf* upkeep, maintenance.
mànzo *nm* steer, beef.
maomettàno *a nm* Mahommedan.
Maométto *nm pr* Mohammed, Mahomet.
màppa *nf* map.
mappamóndo *nm* globe of the world.
marachèlla *nf* trick, prank.
maratóna *nf* marathon (race).
màrca *nf* (*com*) brand, mark, make; **m. da bòllo** revenue stamp; **m. di fàbbrica** trade-mark.
marcàre *vt* to mark.
marchésa *nf* marchioness; **marchése** *nm* marquis.
màrchio *nm* brand, mark; **m. di fàbbrica** trade-mark.
màrcia *nf* (*aut*) gear; march; pus.
marciapiède *nm* pavement, sidewalk; platform.
marciàre *vi* to march.
màrcio *a* bad, rotten, tainted; *nm* rottenness, pus.
marcíre *vi* to decay, go bad, rot, waste.
marciúme *nm* rottenness, rotten things *pl*.
màrco *pl* **-chi** *nm* (*coin*) mark.
Màrco *nm pr* Mark.
marconísta *nm* radio operator.
màre *nm* sea; **in àlto m.** on the high seas; **màl di m.** seasickness.
marèa *nf* tide.
mareggiàta *nf* rough sea.
maresciàllo *nm* marshal; warrant-officer.
marétta *nf* choppy sea.
margarína *nf* margarine.
margheríta *nf* daisy.
Margheríta *nf pr* Margaret.
marginàle *a* marginal.
màrgine *nm* margin, border, edge.
María *nf pr* Mary.
Mariànna *nf pr* Marian(ne).
marína *nf* navy; coast, seaside; **régia m.** Royal Navy; **m. mercantile** merchant navy.
marinàio *nm* sailor, seaman.
marinàra *nf* duffle coat.
marinàre *vt* to pickle, marinate; **m. la scuòla** to play truant.
marinàto *a* pickled, soused.
maríno *a* marine, (of the) sea.
Màrio *nm pr* Marius.
marionétta *nf* marionette, puppet.

maritàre *vt* to marry; **-rsi** *vr* to get married, marry.
marito *nm* husband.
maríttimo *a* maritime, marine.
marmàglia *nf* rabble.
marmellàta *nf* jam; **m. d'arànce** marmalade.
marmítta *nf* saucepan.
màrmo *nm* marble.
marmòcchio *nm* brat.
marmòreo *a* marble, marmoreal.
marmòtta *nf* marmot; (*fig*) lazy-bones.
Màrna *nf* (*geogr*) Marne.
marocchíno *a* Moroccan; *nm* Moroccan, Morocco (leather).
Maròcco *nm* (*geogr*) Morocco.
maróso *nm* billow, wave.
marróne *a* brown; *nm* chestnut; blunder.
Marsíglia *nf* (*geogr*) Marseilles; **marsigliése** *a nmf* of Marseilles, Marseillaise.
Màrta *nf pr* Martha.
martedí *nm* Tuesday; **m. gràsso** Shrove Tuesday.
martellàre *vti* to hammer, throb.
martèllo *nm* hammer.
martinèllo, martinétto *nm* (*mech*) jack.
Martíno *nm pr* Martin.
martín pescatóre *nm* kingfisher.
màrtire *nm* martyr.
martírio *nm* martyrdom.
martirizzàre *vt* to martyrize, torture.
màrtora *nf* marten; (*fur*) sable.
martoriàre *vt* to torment, torture.
marxísmo *nm* Marxism.
marxísta *a nm* Marxist, Marxian.
marzapàne *nm* marzipan.
marziàle *a* martial.
marziàno *a* Martian.
màrzo *nm* March.
mascalzóne *nm* rascal, scoundrel.
mascèlla *nf* jaw.
màschera *nf* mask; (*theat*) usher.
mascheràre *vt* to mask; **-rsi** *vr* to disguise oneself.
mascheràta *nf* masquerade.
mascheróne *nm* mask, grotesque face.
maschiètta, alla *ad* **capélli a. m.** shingled hair.
maschíle *a* male, manly, masculine.
màschio *a* male, manly; *nm* male child; inner keep, tower.
masnàda *nf* gang, set.
masnadière *nm* brigand, robber.
màssa *nf* mass, heap.
massacràre *vt* to massacre, slaughter.
massàcro *nm* massacre, slaughter.
massaggiàre *vt* to massage.
massàggio *nm* massage.
massàia *nf* housewife.
massería *nf* farm.
masserízie *nf pl* household goods *pl*, household utensils *pl*.
massíccio *a* massy, massive, solid; *nm* massif.
màssima *nf* maxim, rule, saying.
massimaménte *ad* chiefly, especially.
màssimo *a* greatest, highest, utmost, best; *nm* maximum.
màsso *nm* big stone, block, boulder.
massóne *nm* Freemason, mason.
massonería *nf* Freemasonry.
massònico *pl* **-ici** *a* masonic.
masticàre *vt* to chew, masticate; stammer; **m. una língua** to have a smattering of a language.
masticazióne *nf* chewing, mastication.
màstice *nm* mastic, putty.
mastíno *nm* mastiff.
màstio *nm* donjon, keep.
mastodòntico *pl* **-ici** *a* huge, colossal.
màstro *nm* ledger, master.
matàssa *nf* skein.
matemàtica *nf* mathematics.
matemàtico *pl* **-ici** *a* mathematical.
materàsso *nm* mattress.
matèria *nf* matter, material, subject; **m. príma** raw material.
materiàle *a* material, rough; *nm* material.
materialísmo *nm* materialism.
materialísta *a* materialistic; *nmf* materialist.
materialménte *ad* materially, physically.
maternità *nf* maternity, motherhood.
matèrno *a* motherly, mother's, materna
Matílde *nf pr* Mat(h)ilda.
matíta *nf* pencil.
matríce *nf* matrix, womb, mold; **regístro a m.** (*com*) counterfoil register.
matrícola *nf* register, roll; freshman.
matricolàre *vt* **-rsi** *vr* to matriculate.
matricolíno *nm* (*student*) freshman, beginner.
matrígna *nf* stepmother.
matrimoniàle *a* matrimonial, wedding; **anèllo m.** wedding ring; **caméra m.** double room; **letto m.** double bed.
matrimònio *nm* marriage, wedding.
mattacchióne *nm* joker, wag.
mattànza *nf* (*naut*) slaughter of tunny fish.
Mattèo *nm pr* Matthew.
matterèllo *nm* (*cook*) rolling-pin.
mattína *nf* **mattíno** *nm* morning.
mattinàta *nf* forenoon, morning, (*theat*) matinée.
mattinièro *a* early rising.
màtto *a* mad; *nm* madman; **scàcco m.** (*at chess*) checkmate.
mattonàto *nm* brick floor.
mattóne *nm* brick; (*fig*) bore, nuisance.
mattonèlla *nf* tile, briquette.
mattutíno *a* morning; *nm* matins.
maturàre *vti* to ripen, mature.
maturazióne *nf* maturity, ripening, maturation.

maturità *nf* ripeness, maturity; **certificàto di m.** leaving certificate.
matúro *a* ripe, mature, (*com*) fallen due.
Maurízio *nm pr* Maurice; **ísola M.** *nf* (*geogr*) Mauritius.
mauṣolèo *nm* mausoleum.
màzza *nf* mallet, sledge-hammer.
mazzàta *nf* heavy blow (*also fig*).
màzzo *nm* bunch; (*of cards*) pack.
mazzolíno *nm* posy, small bunch, bouquet.
me *pron* (*oblique case*) me, myself.
meccànica *nf* mechanics.
meccànico *pl* **-ici** *a* mechanical; *nm* mechanic, mechanician.
meccaniṣmo *nm* gear, mechanism, works; **m. di stèrzo** (*aut*) steering-gear.
mecenàte *nm* Maecenas, patron.
medàglia *nf* medal.
medaglióne *nm* medallion, locket.
medéṣimo *a and pron* same, -self.
mèdia *nf* average; **in m.** on the average.
mediàno *a* median, mean middle; *nm* (*sport*) halfback.
mediànte *prep* by means of.
mediatóre *nm* mediator, (*com*) broker.
mediazióne *nf* mediation, (*com*) brokerage.
medicàbile *a* curable, medicable.
medicaménto *nm* medicament, medicine.
medicàre *vt* to dress, medicate, treat.
medicàstro *nm* quack.
medicazióne *nm* (*wounds*) dressing, treatment; **pòsto di m.** first-aid post.
medicína *nf* medicine, remedy, drug.
medicinàle *a* medicinal; *nm* medicine, drug.
mèdico *pl* **mèdici** *a* medical; *nm* doctor, physician.
mèdio *a* middle, average, medium; *nm* mean, middle finger; **scuòla mèdia** secondary school, junior high school.
mediòcre *a* mediocre, second-rate.
mediocrità *nf* mediocrity.
medioevàle *a* medieval.
medioèvo *nm* Middle Ages *pl*.
meditabóndo *a* pensive, meditative, thoughtful.
meditàre *vti* to meditate, meditate on.
meditàto *a* deliberate.
meditazióne *nf* meditation.
mediterràneo *a* Mediterranean; *nm* (*geogr*) the Mediterranean.
medúsa *nf* jellyfish, Medusa.
megàfono *nm* megaphone.
mèglio *ad and a* better; *nm* best.
méla *nf* apple; **mélo** *nm* apple-tree.
melacotógna *nf* quince.
melagràna *nf* pomegranate.
melanzàna *nf* eggplant, aubergine.
melarància *nf* orange.
melàssa *nf* molasses, treacle.
melènso *a* sheepish, silly.
mellífluo *a* honeyed, mellifluous.
mélma *nf* mire, mud.
melmóso *a* miry, muddy.
melodía *nf* melody.
melòdico *pl* **-ici** *a* melodic.
melodióso *a* melodious.
melodràmma *nm* opera.
melodrammàtico *a* operatic; (*fig*) melodramatic.
melogràno *nm* pomegranate (tree).
melóne *nm* melon.
membràna *nf* membrane.
membranóso *a* membranous.
mèmbro *nm*, *pl* **-bra** *nf* limb; *pl* **-bri** *m* member.
memoràbile *a* memorable.
memoràndum *nm* memorandum; notebook.
mèmore *a* mindful, grateful.
memòria *nf* memory, remembrance, souvenir, record; **a m.** by heart; **imparàre a m.** to memorize; **memòrie** *pl* memoirs *pl*.
menàre *vt* to lead, take, bring; **m. càlci** to kick; **m. un cólpo** to deal a blow; **m. le màni** to fight; **m. il càne per l'àia** to beat about the bush; **m. gràmo** to bring bad luck; **m. buòno** to bring good luck.
mènda *nf* blemish, slight defect.
mendicànte, *a* begging, mendicant; *nmf* beggar.
mendicàre *vti* to beg.
mendicità *nf* begging; beggars *pl*.
mendíco *a* begging; *nm* beggar.
meningíte *nf* meningitis.
méno *a ad prep* less, minus; least; **fàre a m. di** to do without; **le dúe m. cínque** 5 minutes to 2; **a m. che non** unless.
menomaménte *ad* at all, in the least.
menomàre *vt* to lessen, detract from; disable, impair.
menomazióne *nf* reduction, impairment, disablement.
menopàusa *nf* menopause.
mènsa *nf* table; (*mil*) mess; refectory; (*eccl*) altar.
mensíle *a* monthly; *nm* month's pay.
mensilità *nf* monthly installment, monthly payment, monthly occurrence.
mensilménte *ad* monthly.
mènsola *nf* bracket, console.
ménta *nf* mint.
mentàle *a* mental.
mentalità *nf* mentality.
ménte *nf* mind, intellect, intention, memory; **a m.** *ad* by heart.
mentíre *vi* to lie; *vt* to falsify, misrepresent.
ménto *nm* chin.
méntre *ad and cj* while; **in quél m.** at that moment.
menù *nm* menu, bill of fare.
menzionàre *vt* to mention.

menzióne *nf* mention.
menzógna *nf* falsehood, lie.
menzognèro *a* lying, untrue.
meravíglia *nf* wonder, surprise; **a m.** *ad* wonderfully well.
meravigliàre *vt* to amaze, surprise; **-rsi** *vr* to be amazed, wonder.
meravigliosaménte *ad* wonderfully, beautifully.
meraviglióso *a* wonderful; *nm* wonder, the supernatural.
mercànte *nm* merchant, trader; **fàre orécchio da m.** to turn a deaf ear.
mercanteggiàre *vi* to trade, haggle.
mercantíle *a* mercantile, merchant; plain; *nm* cargo boat.
mercanzía *nf* merchandise, goods *pl*, wares *pl*.
mercàto *nm* market; bargain, price; **a buòn m.** cheap, cheaply; **per sópra m.** besides, moreover; **M. Comúne** Common Market.
mercatúra *nf* trade, commerce.
mèrce *nf* goods *pl*, merchandise; **tréno mèrci** freight train
mercè *nf* mercy; **súa m.** thanks to him.
mercéde *nf* pay, reward.
mercenàrio *a nm* mercenary.
mercería *nf* haberdasher's shop; **merceríe** *pl* haberdashery.
merciàio *nm* **merciàia** *nf* dry-goods dealer, haberdasher.
mercoledì *nm* Wednesday; **m. delle cèneri** Ash Wednesday.
mercúrio *nm* mercury, quicksilver.
mèrda *nf* (*vulg*) shit.
merènda *nf* afternoon tea, snack.
meridiàna *nf* sun-dial.
meridiàno *a nm* meridian.
meridionàle *a* south, southern; *nmf* southerner.
meridióne *nm* south.
meríggio *nm* midday, noon.
merínga *nf* meringue.
meritaménte, meritataménte *ad* deservedly, justly.
meritàre *vt* to deserve, earn, be worthwhile, require; **-rsi** *vr* to deserve.
meritévole *a* deserving, worthy.
mèrito *nm* merit; **in m. a** as regards, as to.
meritòrio *a* deserving, meritorious.
merlatúra *nf* battlement; lace trimming.
merlétto *nm* lace.
mèrlo *nm* blackbird; (*arch*) merlon; simpleton.
merlúzzo *nm* cod(fish).
mèro *a* mere, pure, simple.
mesàta *nf* month's salary.
méscere *vt* to pour, mix.
meschinería, meschinità *nf* meanness, stinginess.
meschíno *a* poor, mean, wretched.
méscita *nf* wine shop.
mescolànza *nf* mixing, mixture.
mescolàre *vt* to mix, stir, (*cards*) shuffle; **-rsi** *vr* to mix; interfere.
mése *nm* month, month's pay.
méssa *nf* (*eccl*) Mass; **m. in scéna** (*theat*) staging; **m. in màrcia** (*aut*) starter.
messaggería *nf* haulage trade, mail-coach.
messaggèro *nm* **-ra** *nf* messenger, (*fig*) forerunner.
messàggio *nm* message.
messàle *nm* missal.
mèsse *nf* crop, harvest.
Messía *nm pr* Messiah.
messicàno *a nm* Mexican.
Mèssico *nm* (*geogr*) Mexico.
mésso *a* arranged, disposed, dressed; *nm* messenger, legate.
mestière *nm* trade, occupation, profession, job, craft
mestízia *nf* sadness.
mèsto *a* sad, sorrowful.
méstola *nf* **-lo** *nm* ladle, trowel.
mestruazióne *nf* menstruation.
mèta *nf* destination, aim; (*of straw etc*) pile.
metà *nf* half, middle; **a m. prèzzo** half-price; **a m. stràda** half-way.
metabolismo *nm* metabolism.
metafísica *nf* metaphysics *pl*.
metàfora *nf* metaphor.
metafòrico *pl* **-ici** *a* metaphoric(al).
metàllico *pl* **-ici** *a* metallic, metal.
metàllo *nm* metal; **fatíca del m.** metal fatigue.
metallurgía *nf* metallurgy.
metamòrfosi *nf* metamorphosis.
metàno *nm* methane.
metapsíchico *pl* **-ici** *a* extrasensory.
metèora *nf* meteor.
meteorología *nf* meteorology.
meteorològico *pl* **-ici** *a* meteorologic(al); **bollettíno m.** weather report; **previsióni meteorologiche** weather forecast; **uffício m.** meteorological office, weather bureau.
metíccio *a nm* half-breed.
meticolóso *a* meticulous.
metíle *nm* methyl.
metòdico *pl* **-ici** *a* methodical, business-like.
mètodo *nm* method.
metràggio *nm* length (in meters); (*cin*) **córto m.** short film; **lúngo m.** feature film.
mètrica *nf* prosody.
mètro *nm* (*measure*) meter.
metronòtte *nm* night watchman.
metròpoli *nf* metropolis.
metropolitàna *nf* underground (railway), subway.
metropolitàno *a* metropolitan; *nm* policeman.
méttere *vt* to put, place, set, cause, put forth; *vi* to lead; **-rsi** *vr* to put oneself, get into, begin, put on, turn.
mezzadría *nf* metayage, share-cropping.
mezzàdro *nm* métayer, share-cropper.
mezzalàna *nf* mixed wool and cotton cloth; shady person.

mezzalúna *nf* half-moon, crescent; mincing knife.
mezzaníno *nm* entresol, mezzanine.
mezzàno *a nm* middle, medium; mediator, pimp.
mezzanòtte *pl* **mezzenotti** *nf* midnight, north.
mèzzo *a* half; *ad* half; *nm* middle; **in m. a** *prep* in the middle of; **mèzza età** middle-age.
mezzodí, mezzogiórno *nm* midday, noonday, south.
mezzómbra *nf* half-tone.
mezzotèrmine *nm* compromise.
mezzúccio *nm* mean expedient.
mi *pron acc and dat* (to) me; *refl* myself; *nm* (*mus*) E, mi.
miagolàre *vi* to mew.
míca *nf* crumb, grain; *ad* (*fam*) not at all.
míccia *nf* (*for explosives etc*) fuse.
Michèle *nm pr* Michael.
micidiàle *a* deadly, killing.
mício *nm* tom-cat, (*fam*) pussy.
mícrobo *nm* microbe.
micròfono *nm* microphone.
micromotóre *nm* small motor; motor-scooter.
microscòpico *pl* **-ici** *a* microscopic (al).
microscòpio *nm* microscope.
microsólco *pl* **-chi** *nm* long-playing record, microgroove.
midólla *nf* (bread)crumb, (*fruit*) pulp.
midóllo *nm* marrow, pith.
mièle *nm* honey.
mietere *vt* to reap, mow down.
mietitóre *nm* **-tríce** *nf* reaper, mower.
mietitúra *nf* reaping.
migliàio *nm* about a thousand; **a migliàia** by thousands.
míglio *nm* millet; *nm pl* **míglia** mile; **distànza in míglia** mileage; *pl* **mígli** milestone.
miglioraménto *nm* improvement.
miglioràre *vt* to improve.
miglióre *a* better, best.
miglioría *nf* improvement, amelioration.
mignàtta *nf* leech (*also fig*).
mígnolo *nm* little finger or toe; olive blossom.
migràre *vi* to migrate.
migratòrio *a* migratory.
migrazióne *nf* migration.
Milàno *nf* (*geogr*) Milan; **milanése** *a nmf* Milanese.
miliardàrio *nm* multimillionaire, billionaire.
miliàrdo *nm* billion.
miliàre *a* milestone; (*med*) miliary.
milionàrio *nm* millionaire.
milióne *nm* million; **milionèsimo** *a* millionth.
militànte *a* militant.
militàre *vi* to serve in the army, militate; *a* military; *nm* soldier.
militarménte *ad* militarily.
mílite *nm* militiaman, soldier, warrior; **M. Ignòto** Unknown Soldier.
milízia *nf* army, militia.
millantàre *vt* **-rsi** *vr* to boast (of).
millantatóre *nm* boaster, braggart.
millantería *nf* boast(ing).
mílle *pl* **míla** *a* thousand; **millèsimo** *a* thousandth.
millènnio *nm* millennium.
millepièdi *nm* millepede.
mílza *nf* spleen, milt.
mimetísmo *nm* (*mil*) camouflage.
mimetizzàre *vt* **-rsi** *vr* to camouflage.
mímica *nf* gestures *pl*; mimicry.
mímo *nm* mime; mimer.
mína *nf* mine; (*of pencil*) lead.
minàccia *nf* threat, menace.
minacciàre *vt* to threaten, menace.
minaccióso *a* threatening, menacing.
minàre *vt* to mine, undermine.
minatóre *nm* miner, collier.
minatòrio *a* threatening.
mineràle *a* mineral; *nm* mineral, ore.
mineralogía *nf* mineralogy.
minieràrio *a* mining.
minèstra *nf* soup.
mingherlíno *a* thin, delicate, slender.
miniàre *vt* to paint in miniature, illuminate (*MSS etc*).
miniatúra *nf* miniature.
minièra *nf* mine; **m. di carbóne** coal-mine.
minimaménte *ad* at all.
mínimo *a* least, lowest, smallest; *nm* minimum.
ministèro *nm* office, function, ministry; board, department; cabinet; **púbblico m.** public prosecutor, district attorney.
minístro *nm* minister, secretary of state.
minorànza *nf* minority.
minoràto *a* disabled, maimed; *nm* disabled person, mental deficient.
minorazióne *nf* diminution, disablement, mental deficiency.
minóre *a* less(er), smaller, younger, least, minor *etc*.
minorènne *a* under age; *nm* minor; **tribunàle déi minorènni** juvenile court.
minoríle *a* juvenile; **delinquènza m.** juvenile delinquency; **età m.** minority.
minúscolo *a* small, minute; **léttera minúscola** small letter; *nm* (*typ*) lower-case letter.
minúta *nf* rough copy, minute.
minúto *a* minute, small, detailed, petty; *nm* minute; **al m.** (by) retail.
minúzia *nf* trifle.
minuzióso *a* in detail, minute.
minúzzolo *nm* shred, small bit.
mío *a* my; *pron* mine; **i miéi** *pl* my family, my people.
míope *a* short-sighted; *nm* short-sighted person.
miopía *nf* short-sightedness (*also fig*).

míra *nf* aim, target, purpose.
miràbile *a* admirable, wonderful.
miracolàto *a* miraculously healed; *nm* miraculously healed person.
miràcolo *nm* miracle; wonder.
miracolóso *a* miraculous, wonderful.
miràggio *nm* mirage (*also fig*).
miràre *vt* to look at, admire, aim.
miríade *nf* myriad.
miríno *nm* (*of gun etc*) (fore)sight, (*of camera*) view-finder.
mírra *nf* myrrh.
mirtíllo *nm* bilberry.
mírto *nm* myrtle.
mişantropía *nf* misanthropy.
mişàntropo *nm* misanthrope.
miscèla *nf* mixture, blend; **m. anticongelànte** (*aut*) antifreeze.
miscellànea *nf* miscellany.
míschia *nf* fight, fray.
mischiàre *vt* to mix, shuffle; **-rsi** *vr* to mix (with).
miscredènte *a* unbelieving; *nmf* unbeliever.
miscredènza *nf* unbelief, disbelief.
miscúglio *nm* mixture, medley.
mişeràbile *a* miserable, poor, despicable; *nm* poor wretch.
mişeràndo, mişerévole *a* pitiable.
mişèria *nf* misery, destitution, distress; shortage; trifle; trouble.
mişericòrdia *nf* mercy, pity.
mişericordióso *a* merciful.
míşero *a* poor, wretched, mean.
misfàtto *nm* misdeed, crime.
mişògino *nm* misogynist.
missàggio *nm* (*cin*) mixing; **tècnico del m.** mixer.
míssile *a nm* missile; **m. radiocomandàto** radio-controlled missile.
missilística *nf* rocketry.
missionàrio *nm* missionary.
missióne *nf* mission.
misterióso *a* mysterious.
mistèro *nm* mystery.
misticíşmo *nm* mysticism.
místico *pl* **-ici** *a nm* mystic.
mistificàre *vt* to mystify, deceive.
místo *a* mixed; *nm* mixture; **tréno m.** train for passengers and freight.
mistúra *nf* mixture.
mişúra *nf* measure(ment), size; moderation.
mişuràbile *a* measurable.
mişuràre *vt* to measure, estimate; limit; try on; pace; **-rsi** *vr* to compete; try on.
mişuràto *a* measured; moderate, cautious.
míte *a* gentle, mild, moderate.
mitézza *nf* gentleness, meekness, mildness, moderation.
mítico *a* mythical.
mitigàre *vt* to allay, appease, relieve.
mitigazióne *nf* mitigation, alleviation.
míto *nm* myth.
mitología *nf* mythology.
mítra *nf* miter, submachine gun.
mitràglia *nf* (*mil*) grapeshot.
mitragliàre *vt* to machine gun.
mitragliatríce *nf* machine gun.
mitraglière *nm* machine gunner.
mittènte *nmf* sender.
mòbile *a* mobile, moving, movable, changeable, fickle; *nm* piece of furniture.
mobília *nf* furniture.
mobilière *nm* cabinet-maker.
mobilità *nf* mobility.
mobilitazióne *nf* mobilization.
moccióso *nm* snotty-nosed child; brat.
mòccolo *nm* candle end, small candle; (*fam*) swear word.
mòda *nf* fashion; **di m.** *ad* fashionable.
modalità *nf* modality, formality.
modèlla *nf* model; **modèllo** *nm* model, pattern.
modellàre *vt* to model, mold, fashion.
modenése *a nmf* (native) of Modena.
moderàre *vt* to moderate, curb, reduce; **-rsi** *vr* to restrain oneself.
moderàto *a* moderate.
moderazióne *nf* moderation.
modernità *nf* modernity.
moderniẓẓàre *vt* to modernize.
modèrno *a* modern.
modestaménte *ad* modestly.
modèstia *nf* modesty.
modèsto *a* modest, moderate.
modicità *nf* moderateness, cheapness.
mòdico *pl* **-ici** *a* moderate, cheap.
modífica *nf* alteration, change.
modificàre *vt* to modify, mitigate.
modísta *nf* milliner.
modistería *nf* milliner's shop.
mòdo *nm* manner, way; **ad ógni m.** anyhow, anyway; **a m.** carefully, properly; **persóna a m.** well-bred person; **per m. di dire** so to speak.
modulàre *vt* to modulate, formulate.
modulazióne *nf* modulation.
mòdulo *nm* (printed) form, blank.
mògano *nm* mahogany.
mòggio *nm* bushel.
mògio *a* abashed, quiet, crestfallen.
móglie *pl* **mógli** *nf* wife.
moína *nf* blandishment, wheedling.
mòla *nf* grindstone, millstone.
molàre *a nm* molar; *vt* to grind, whet.
mòle *nf* mass, bulk, size.
molècola *nf* molecule.
molestàre *vt* to molest, bother, vex, tease.
molèstia *nf* trouble, bother.
molèsto *a* troublesome.
mòlla *nf* (*tec*) spring; *pl* tongs *pl*.
mollàre *vti* to loose(n), leave off, yield.
mòlle *a* soft, wet, pliable, flabby, weak, loose; *nm* soft part; **méttere in m.** *vt* to soak, steep.
molléggio *nm* suspension, springing.
molleménte *ad* softly, weakly, languidly.

mollétta *nf* hair-grip, clothespeg, clothespin; *pl* tongs *pl*.
mollézza *nf* softness, feebleness, effeminacy, looseness; *pl* luxury.
mollíca *nf* crumb.
mollúsco *pl* **-chi** *nm* mollusc.
mòlo *nm* pier, quay.
molòsso *nm* mastiff.
moltéplice *a* manifold, multiple.
moltiplicàre *vt* **-rsi** *vr* to multiply.
moltiplicazióne *nf* multiplication.
moltiplicità *nf* multiplicity.
moltitúdine *nf* multitude.
mólto *a* much, (*time*) long; *ad* very, much, greatly; *nm* much, a lot.
momentàneo *a* temporary, passing.
moménto *nm* moment, time, chance; **un m.** *ad* a while.
mònaca *nf* nun.
mònaco *pl* **-aci** *nm* monk.
Mònaco *nf* (*geogr*) Munich; *nm* (*geogr*) Monaco.
monàrca *nm* monarch.
monarchía *nf* monarchy.
monàrchico *pl* **-ici** *a* monarchic(al).
monastèro *nm* monastery.
monàstico *pl* **-ici** *a* monastic.
moncheríno *nm* stump.
mónco *pl* **-chi** *a* maimed, mutilated; *nm* maimed person.
moncóne *nm* stump.
mondanità *nf* worldliness, society life.
mondàno *a* mundane, worldly, society; **víta mondàna** society life; **mondàna** *nf* prostitute.
mondàre *vt* to clean, peel, winnow, (*fig*) cleanse.
mondaríso *nf* rice-picker.
mondiàle *a* worldwide, world, universal.
móndo *a* clean, pure; *nm* world, life, everybody; **un m. di** a world of.
monèlla *nf* tomboy.
monellería *nf* prank.
monèllo *nm* little rogue, street boy, urchin.
monéta *nf* money, coin, small change.
mòngolo *a* Mongolian; *nm* Mongol.
mongolòide *a nm* mongoloid.
moníle *nm* jewel; necklace.
mònito *nm* admonition, warning.
monitóre *nm* monitor, warner.
monòcolo *nm* monocle; one-eyed person.
monogamía *nf* monogamy.
monografía *nf* monograph.
monogràmma *nm* monogram.
monòlogo *pl* **-ghi** *nm* monologue, soliloquy.
monopàttino *nm* scooter.
monoplàno *nm* monoplane.
monopòlio *nm* monopoly.
monopolizzàre *vt* to monopolize.
monopósto *a nm* (*aut av*) single-seater.
monosíllabo *nm* monosyllable.
monotonía *nf* monotony.
monòtono *a* monotonous.
monsignóre *nm* monsignor.
montacàrichi *nm* freight elevator, elevator hoist.
montàggio *nm* (*mech*) assembling, glazing; (*cin*) montage, cutting.
montàgna *nf* mountain.
montagnóso *a* mountainous.
montanàro *a* mountain, of the mountain; *nm* mountaineer, highlander.
montàno *a* mountain; **paése m.** mountain village.
montàre *vti* to mount, set, furnish; climb, rise; (*impers*) to matter; **-rsi** *vr* to get excited; get swollen-headed.
montatóio *nm* footboard, running board, stirrup.
montatúra *nf* fitting, (*of spectacles*) frame.
montavivànde *nm* service lift, dumbwaiter.
mónte *nm* mount, heap; **m. di pietà** pawnbroker's; **andàre a m.** to come to nothing.
montóne *nm* ram, mutton.
montuosità *nf* hilliness, hill.
montuóso *a* hilly.
monumentàle *a* monumental.
monuménto *nm* monument.
mòra *nf* blackberry, mulberry; delay, respite; game of mor(r)a.
moràle *a* moral; *nf* morals *pl*, ethics, moral; *nm* morale.
moralísta *nmf* moralist.
moralità *nf* morality, morals *pl*.
moralizzàre *vti* to moralize.
morbidaménte *ad* softly, tenderly.
morbidézza *nf* softness, leniency.
mòrbido *a* soft, tender.
morbíllo *nm* (*med*) measles.
mòrbo *nm* disease, plague.
morbosità *nf* morbidness.
morbóso *a* morbid.
mordàce *a* biting, pungent, sarcastic.
mordènte *a* biting, caustic; *nm* (*chem*) mordant; (*mus*) mordent.
mòrdere *vt* to bite, sting.
morèllo *a* jet-black; *nm* black horse.
morènte *a* dying, fading; *nmf* dying man, woman.
morésco *pl* **-chi** *a* Moorish.
morétta *nf* brunette, Negro girl; **morétto** Negro boy.
morfína *nf* morphia, morphine.
moría *nf* plague, high mortality.
moribóndo *a* dying, moribund.
morigeràto *a* temperate, moderate, of good morals.
moríre *vi* to die; *nm* death.
mormoràre *vti* to murmur, whisper, grumble.
mormorío *nm* murmur, rustling, whisper, complaining, gossip.
mòro *a* black, dark-skinned; *nm* mulberry tree, Moor, Negro.
moróso *a* defaulting, insolvent; *nm* (*fam*) sweetheart, boy-friend.
mòrsa *nf* (*mech*) vise.
morsicàre *vt* to bite.

morsicatúra *nf* bite.
mòrso *nm* bite; pang; morsel, bit.
mortàio *nm* mortar.
mortàle *a nm* mortal.
mortalità *nf* mortality.
mortarétto *nm* firecracker.
mòrte *nf* death.
mortèlla *nf* myrtle.
mortificàre *vt* to humiliate, mortify, deaden; **-rsi** *vr* to mortify oneself, be mortified.
mortificazióne *nf* humiliation, mortification.
mòrto *a* dead, deceased.
mortòrio *nm* funeral, burial.
mortuàrio *a* mortuary.
mosàico *pl* **-ici** *nm* mosaic.
mósca *nf* fly.
Mósca *nf* (*geogr*) Moscow; **moscovíta** *a nm* Muscovite.
moscatèllo *nm* muscatel grape.
moscàto *nm* muscat(el); **nóce moscàta** nutmeg.
moscerino *nm* gnat, midge.
moschèa *nf* mosque.
moschettière *nm* musketeer.
moschétto *nm* musket.
móscio *a* flabby, soft; (*fig*) dispirited.
moscóne *nm* big fly, bluebottle.
Mosè *nm pr* Moses.
Mosèlla *nf pr* (*geogr*) Moselle.
mòssa *nf* move(ment).
mostàrda *nf* Italian sweet fruit pickles; mustard.
mósto *nm* must.
mostóso *a* full of must.
móstra *nf* exhibition, show, display; pretense.
mostràre *vt* to show, display, point out, prove; pretend; **-rsi** *vr* to show oneself, appear.
mostrína *nf* (*mil*) collar badge.
móstro *nm* monster, prodigy.
mostruosità *nf* monstrosity.
mostruóso *a* monstrous, enormous.
mòta *nf* mire, mud.
motivàre *vt* to give reason for, justify, motivate.
motivazióne *nf* motivation.
motívo *nm* motive, motif; **a m. di** on account of, owing to.
mòto *nm* motion, exercise; revolt; impulse; *nf* motor-cycle.
motocarrozzétta *nf* side-car.
motociclétta *nf* **-ciclo** *nm* motorcycle.
motofurgóne *nm* motorcycle delivery van.
motonàve *nf* motorship.
motopescheréccio *nm* motor trawler.
motóre *nm* motor, engine.
motoríno *nm* **m. d'avviaménto** (*aut*) starter-motor.
motorizzàre *vt* to motorize.
motoscàfo *nm* motor-boat.
motteggiàre *vti* to banter, joke, make fun of.
mòtto *nm* word, saying, motto.
movènte *nm* motive, reason.
movimentàto *a* lively, busy, eventful; **stràda movimentàta** busy street.
moviménto *nm* movement, traffic.
mozióne *nf* motion.
mozzàre *vt* to cut off.
mozzicóne *nm* butt, stub; **m. di sigarétta** cigarette-end.
mózzo *nm* cabin-boy, stable-boy; (*tec*) *a* cut off, docked.
mòzzo *nm* wheel hub.
múcca *nf* cow.
múcchio *nm* heap, pile.
múco *pl* **-chi** *nm* mucus.
múda *nf* molt, molting season.
múffa *nf* mold.
muffíre *vi* to become moldy.
muffíto *a* moldy.
mugghiàre, muggíre *vi* to bellow, howl, roar.
múgghio, muggíto *nm* bellow, roar, howling.
mughétto *nm* lily-of-the-valley.
mugnàio *nm* miller.
mugolàre *vi* to whine, yelp.
mulattièra *nf* mule-track.
mulattière *nm* muleteer.
mulàtto *nm* mulatto.
mulièbre *a* feminine, womanly.
mulinèllo *nm* whirlpool, whirlwind, (*tec*) windlass.
mulíno *nm* mill.
múlo *nm* mule.
múlta *nf* fine.
multàre *vt* to fine.
multicolóre *a* many-colored.
multifórme *a* multiform.
múltiplo *a* multiple.
múmmia *nf* (Egyptian) mummy.
mummificàre *vt* to mummify.
múngere *vt* to milk, (*fig*) exploit.
municipàle *a* municipal, of the town.
município *nm* municipality, town hall.
munificènza *nf* generosity, munificence.
munífico *pl* **-ici** *a* generous, munificent.
muníre *vt* to fortify, furnish; **-rsi** *vr* to equip oneself, fortify oneself.
munizióne *nf* (*mil*) ammunition, munitions *pl*.
muòvere *vt* **-rsi** *vr* to move, stir.
muràglia *nf* wall.
muràle *a* mural, wall.
muràre *vti* to build, wall up; **-rsi** *vr* to shut oneself up.
muratóre *nm* bricklayer, mason.
muratúra *nf* masonry, brickwork.
murèna *nf* moray eel.
múro *nm* wall; *m pl* **múri** walls; *f pl* **múra** (*town*) walls.
Músa *nf* Muse.
muschiàto *a* musky; **ròsa muschiàta** musk-rose.
múschio *nm* musk, moss.
muscolàre *a* muscular.
múscolo *nm* muscle.
muscolóso *a* muscular.
muscóso *a* mossy.

muṣèo *nm* museum.
muṣeruòla *nf* muzzle.
múṣica *nf* music, band.
muṣicàle *a* musical, music.
muṣicànte *nm* musician, bandsman.
muṣicísta *nmf* musician, composer.
múṣo *nm* muzzle, snout; (*fam*) face; **fàre il m.** to pull a long face; **avere il m.** to sulk.
mussàre *vi* to foam, froth.
mussolína *nf* muslin.
mussulmàno *a nm* Mussulman.
mustàcchi *nm pl* moustache.
múta *nf* change, molt, set; (*of hounds*) pack.
mutàbile *a* changeable.
mutabilità *nf* changeability.
mutaménto *nm* change, alteration, variation.
mutànde *nf pl* drawers *pl*, pants *pl*, underpants; **mutandíne** *nf pl* panties; **m. da bàgno** swimming trunks; **m. da ginnàstica** gym shorts.
mutàre *vt* **-rsi** *vr* to change.
mutévole *a* changeable.
mutilàre *vt* to maim, mutilate.
mutilàto *a* maimed, mutilated; *nm* cripple; **m. di guèrra** war cripple.
mutilazióne *nf* mutilation.
mutíṣmo *nm* dumbness, muteness, taciturnity.
múto *a* dumb, mute.
mútua *nf* (**càssa**) **m.** medical insurance.
mutualménte *a* mutually.
mutuànte *a* lending, loan; *nmf* lender.
mutuàre *vt* to borrow, lend.
mútuo *a* mutual, reciprocal; nm loan, mortgage.

N

nàcchere *nf pl* castanets *pl*.
nàfta *nf* naphtha, diesel oil; **a n.** oil-fired.
naftalína *nf* naphthalene; moth-balls *pl*.
nàiade *nf* naiad, water nymph.
nàilon *nm* nylon.
nàno *nm* dwarf; *a* dwarf(ish).
Nàpoli *nf* (*geogr*) Naples; **napoletàno** *a nm* Neapolitan.
nàppa *nf* tassel, tuft.
narcíṣo *nm* daffodil, narcissus.
narcòtico *pl* **-ici** *a nm* narcotic.
narice *nf* nostril.
narràre *vt* to narrate, relate, tell.
narratíva *nf* narrative, fiction.
narratóre *nm* **-tríce** *nf* narrator, story-teller.
narrazióne *nf* narration, tale.
nasàle *a* nasal.
nascènte *a* dawning, rising.
nàscere *vi* to be born, originate, rise.
nàscita *nf* birth; extraction, descent.
nascitúro *a nm* unborn (child).
nascóndere *vt* to conceal, hide; **-rsi** *vr* to hide oneself.
nascondíglio *nm* hiding place.
nascostaménte *ad* secretly; stealthily.
nascósto *a* hidden, secret, underhand; **di n.** secretly, stealthily.
nasèllo *nm* (*fish*) hake, whiting.
nàso *nm* nose; **a lúme di n.** by guesswork.
nàspo *nm* (*tec*) reel, winder.
nàstro *nm* band, ribbon, tape.
nastúrzio *nm* (*bot*) nasturtium, water-cress.
natàle *a* native; **Natàle** *nm* Christmas; **natàli** *nm pl* birth.
natalità *nf* birth-rate.
natalízio *a* (of) Christmas; birthday; *nm* birthday.
natànte *a* floating; *nm* craft.
nàtica *nf* buttock.
natío *a* native.
natività *nf* nativity.
natívo *a* native, natural; *nm* native.
nàto *a* born, risen, sprung up; **nàta** née.
nàtta *nf* wen.
natúra *nf* nature, kind; **pagàre in n.** to pay in kind.
naturàle *a* genuine, natural.
naturalézza *nf* naturalness.
naturaliẓẓàre *vt* to naturalize.
naturaliẓẓazióne *nf* naturalization.
naturalménte *ad* naturally, of course.
naufragàre *vi* to be (ship)wrecked.
naufràgio *nm* (ship)wreck, failure.
nàufrago *pl* **-ghi** *a nm* shipwrecked (man).
nàuṣea *nf* nausea, sickness, loathing.
nauṣeabóndo, nauṣeànte *a* loathsome, nauseous.
nauṣeàre *vt* to disgust, nauseate.
nàutica *nf* nautical science.
nàutico *pl* **-ici** *a* nautical.
navàle *a* naval.
nàve *nf* ship, vessel.
navétta *nf* shuttle.
navicèlla *nf* bark, small ship.
navigàbile *a* navigable; **canàle n.** waterway.
navigànte *nm* sailor.
navigàre *vti* to navigate, sail; **n. in cattíve àcque** to be badly off.
navigàto *a* experienced.
navigatóre *nm* navigator.
navigazióne *nf* navigation.
navíglio *nm* canal; fleet.
nazionàle *a* national; home-grown.
nazionalíṣmo *nm* nationalism.
nazionalità *nf* nationality.
nazionaliẓẓazióne *nf* nationalization.
nazióne *nf* nation.
nazísta *a nmf* Nazi.
naẓẓarèno *a nm* Nazarene.
ne *pron and ad* of him, his, of her, hers; of it, its; of them, theirs; from there; any, some.
né *cj* neither, nor; **né . . . né** neither . . . nor.
neànche *ad* not even; *cj* neither.

nébbia *nf* fog, mist.
nebbióso *a* foggy, hazy.
nebulizzàre *vt* to atomize, vaporize.
nebulizzatóre *nm* atomizer, vaporizer.
nebulósa *nf* nebula.
nebulóso *a* nebulous, hazy.
nécessaire (Fr) *nm* beauty case; **n. per únghie** manicure set.
necessariaménte *ad* necessarily.
necessàrio *a* necessary, needful; *nm* what is necessary.
necessità *nf* necessity, need, poverty.
necessitàre *vt* to necessitate; *vi* to be necessary.
necróforo *nm* gravedigger.
necrològio *nm* obituary, register of deaths.
nefandézza *nf* infamy.
nefàndo *a* abominable, execrable.
nefàsto *a* ill-omened, unlucky.
nefríte *nf* nephritis.
negàbile *a* deniable.
negàre *vt* to deny.
negatíva *nf* denial, negative.
negatívo *a* negative, unfavorable.
negàto *a* denied, unfit; **èssere n. a qc** to be unsuited for sth.
negazióne *nf* denial, negative, negation.
neghittóso *a* slothful.
neglètto *a* neglected, untidy.
negligènte *a* careless, negligent.
negligènza *nf* carelessness, negligence.
negoziàbile *a* negotiable.
negoziànte *nmf* dealer, shopkeeper, tradesman.
negoziàre *vti* to negotiate, deal, trade.
negoziàti *nm pl* negotiation(s).
negózio *nm* shop, store; trade, transaction.
negrièro *nm* slave-trader; (*fig*) slave-driver.
négro *a nm* Negro.
negromànte *nmf* necromancer.
negromanzía *nf* necromancy.
némbo *nm* (storm)cloud.
nemíco *pl* **-ici** *a* hostile, harmful; *nm* enemy.
nemméno *ad* not even.
nènia *nf* dirge, plaintive song.
nèo *nm* blemish, (*on the skin*) mole.
neologismo *nm* neologism.
neomicína *nf* neomycin.
nèon *nm* neon; **inségna al n.** neon sign.
neonàto *a nm* newborn (child).
neppúre *ad* not even.
neràstro *a* blackish.
nerbàta *nf* blow with a whip.
nèrbo *nm* nerve; whip; strength.
néro *a* black, dark; *nm* black.
nervatúra *nf* nervous system, nervation; ribbing.
nèrvo *nm* nerve, vigor; **avére i nèrvi** to be in a bad temper.
nervosità *nf* **nervosismo** *nm* nerves, nervousness.
nervóso *a* nervous, excitable; *nm* irritability.
nèsci: **fare il n.** to pretend ignorance.
nèspola *nf* medlar; **nèspolo** *nm* medlar-tree.
nèsso *nm* connection, link.
nessúno *pron* nobody, no one; *a* no.
nettaménte *ad* cleanly, clearly.
nettapípe *inv nm* pipe-cleaner.
nettàre *vt* to clean, cleanse.
nèttare *nm* nectar.
nettézza *nf* cleanliness; **n. urbàna** garbage collectors *pl*.
nétto *a* clean; distinct; exact; net.
neuròlogo *pl* **-ogi** *nm* neurologist.
neutràle *a nm* neutral.
neutralità *nf* neutrality.
neutralizzàre *vt* to neutralize.
nèutro *a* neutral; *nm* neuter.
nevàio *nm* snowfield, glacier.
néve *nf* snow; **fiòcco di n.** snowflake.
nevicàre *vi* to snow.
nevicàta *nf* snowfall, snowstorm.
nevíschio *nm* sleet.
nevóso *a* snowy.
nevralgía *nf* neuralgia.
nevrastenía *nf* neurasthenia.
nevrastènico *pl* **-ici** *a nm* neurasthenic.
nevrósi *nf* (*med*) neurosis.
nevròtico *pl* **-ici** *a nm* neurotic.
nevvéro? *interj* isn't it (so)?
níbbio *nm* (*bird*) kite.
nícchia *nf* niche.
nicchiàre *vi* to hesitate.
Niccolò, Nicòla *nm pr* Nicholas.
níchel *nm* nickel.
nicotína *nf* nicotine.
nidiàta *nf* brood, nestful.
nidificàre *vi* to build a nest.
nído *nm* nest, haunt.
niènte *pron and nm* nothing.
nientediméno *ad* no less.
Nigèria *nf* (*geogr*) Nigeria.
Nílo *nm* (*geogr*) Nile.
nínfa *nf* nymph.
ninfèa *nf* water-lily.
ninnanànna *nf* lullaby.
ninnàre *vt* to lull, sing to sleep.
nínnolo *nm* trifle, trinket.
nipóte *nmf* grandson, granddaughter; nephew, niece.
nippònico *pl* **-ici** *a* Japanese.
nitidézza *nf* clearness.
nítido *a* clear, distinct.
nitóre *nm* neatness, brightness.
nitràto *nm* nitrate.
nitríre *vi* to neigh.
nitríto *nm* neigh.
nítro *nm* niter, saltpeter.
nitrògeno *nm* nitrogen.
níveo *a* snowy, snow-white.
Nízza *nf* (*geogr*) Nice; **nizzàrdo** *a nm* (native) of Nice.
no *ad* no.
nòbile *a nm* noble.
nobiliàre *a* aristocratic.
nobilitàre *vt* to ennoble.
nobilménte *ad* nobly.
nobiltà *nf* nobility, nobleness.

nòcca *nf* knuckle.
nocchièro *nm* pilot, steersman.
nòcciolo *nm* kernel, stone; (*fig*) point, gist.
nocci(u)òla *nf* hazel-nut; **nocci(u)òla** *nm* hazel tree; **nocciolina americàna** peanut.
nòce *nf* walnut; *nm* walnut tree.
nocívo *a* harmful, hurtful.
nòdo *nm* knot.
nodóso *a* gnarled, knotty.
Noè *nm pr* Noah.
nói *pron* we, us.
nòia *nf* boredom, vexation.
noiosità *nf* boredom, bother.
noióso *a* tiresome, boring.
noleggiaménto *nm* hiring, chartering.
noleggiàre *vt* to hire, charter.
noléggio, nòlo *nm* hire, rental; **a n.** for (on) hire.
nolènte *a* unwilling; **volènte o n.** willy-nilly.
nòmade *a* nomadic; *nmf* nomad.
nóme *nm* name, noun; **n. pròprio** first name, Christian name.
nomèa *nf* reputation, notoriety.
nomenclatúra *nf* nomenclature.
nomígnolo *nm* nickname.
nòmina *nf* appointment.
nominàle *a* nominal.
nominàre *vt* to name, appoint.
nominatívo *a* nominative; *nm* nominative, name.
non *ad* not; **non . . . che** *ad* but, only.
nonagenàrio *a nm* nonagenarian.
nonagèşimo *a nm* ninetieth.
noncurànte *a* careless, heedless.
noncurànza *nf* carelessness, heedlessness.
nondiméno *ad* nevertheless, still, yet.
nònna *nf* grandmother; **nònno** *nm* grandfather.
nonnúlla *nm* nothing, trifle.
nòno *a* ninth.
nonostànte *prep* in spite of, notwithstanding; *ad* nevertheless.
nonpertànto *ad* nevertheless, still.
nonsènso *nm* nonsense.
nontiscordardimé *nm* forget-me-not.
nòrd *nm* north; **a n.** to the north; **n. est** north-east; **n. òvest** north-west.
nòrdico *pl* **-ici** *a* northern; *nm* northerner.
Norimbèrga *nf* (*geogr*) Nuremberg.
nòrma *nf* rule, standard, directions; **a n. di légge** according to law.
normàle *a nm* normal.
normalità *nf* normality.
normalizzàre *vt* to normalize.
normalménte *ad* normally.
Normandía *nf* (*geogr*) Normandy.
norvegése *a nmf* Norwegian.
Norvègia *nf* (*geogr*) Norway.
nostalgía *nf* homesickness.
nostàlgico *pl* **-ici** *a* nostalgic.
nostràle, nostràno *a* domestic, home, of one's own country; **prodòtti nostràli** home produce.
nòstro *poss a and pron* our, ours.
nostròmo *nm* boatswain.
nòta *nf* note, mark, list; **n. a piè di pàgina** footnote; **blòcco per nòte** scribbling block, scratch pad.
notàbile *a nm* notable.
notàio *nm* notary.
notàre *vt* to note, notice; **fàrsi n.** *vr* to attract attention.
notaríle *a* notarial.
nòtes *nm* notebook, agenda.
notévole *a* noticeable, remarkable.
notevolménte *ad* considerably, greatly.
notificàre *vt* to notify.
notífica, notificazióne *nf* communication, notification.
notízia *nf* (piece of) news.
notiziàrio *nm* news bulletin; (*cin*) newsreel.
nòto *a* famous, notorious, (well-) known.
notorietà *nf* notoriety.
notòrio *a* notorious.
nottàmbulo *a* night-walking; *nm* night-walker; somnambulist.
nottàta *nf* (duration of a) night.
nòtte *nf* night; **di n.** by night.
nòttola *nf* bat.
nottúrno *a* night(ly), nocturnal; *nm* (*mus*) nocturne.
novànta *a* ninety; **novantènne** 90-year-old; **novantèsimo** ninetieth.
nòve *a* nine.
novecènto *a nm* nine hundred; twentieth century.
novèlla *nf* short story, tale.
novellière *nm* short-story writer.
novellíno *a* inexperienced; *nm* beginner, inexperienced person.
novellística *nf* short-story writing, fiction.
novèllo *a* new.
novèmbre *nm* November.
nòvero *nm* number, class, category.
novilúnio *nm* new moon.
novità *nf* newness, novelty, news.
noviziàto *nm* apprenticeship, novitiate.
novízio *nm* novice, beginner, apprentice.
nozióne *nf* idea, notion.
nòzze *nf pl* wedding, marriage.
núbe *nf* cloud.
nubifràgio *nm* cloudburst, downpour.
núbile *a* (*of women*) unmarried, marriageable; *nf* spinster.
núca *nf* nape (of the neck).
nucleàre *a* nuclear.
núcleo *nm* nucleus.
nudaménte *ad* nakedly, barely, simply, plainly.
nudità *nf* nakedness, nudity.
núdo *a* naked, bare; *nm* nude.
núlla *nm and pron* nothing.
nullaòsta *nm* (*eccl*) nihil obstat; permit; permission.

nullatenènte *nm f* person who owns nothing.
nullità *nf* nonentity, nullity, worthlessness.
núllo *a* null and void.
núme *nm* deity.
numeràle *a nm* numeral.
numeràre *vt* to number.
numerazióne *nf* numbering.
numèrico *pl* **-ici** *a* numerical.
número *nm* number.
numeróso *a* numerous.
numismàtica *nf* numismatics *pl.*
núnzio *nm* nuncio.
nuòcere *vt* to harm, hurt, damage.
nuòra *nf* daughter-in-law.
nuotàre *vi* to swim.
nuotàta *nf* swim.
nuotatóre *nm* swimmer; **n. subàcqueo** skin-diver.
nuòto *nm* swimming; **passare a n.** to swim across; **n. subàcqueo** skindiving.
nuòva *nf* (piece of) news.
Nuòva York *nf* (*geogr*) New York.
Nuòva Zelànda *nf* (*geogr*) New Zealand.
nuòvo *a* new; **di n.** again.
nutríce *nf* wet nurse.
nutriènte *a* nourishing, nutritious.
nutriménto *nm* nourishment.
nutríre *vt* to feed, nourish, foster; **-rsi (di)** *vr* to feed (on).
nutritívo *a* nourishing, nutritious.
nutrizióne *nf* feeding, nourishment, nutrition.
nùvola *nf* **-lo** *nm* cloud.
nùvolo, nuvolóso *a* overcast, cloudy.
nuziàle *a* wedding.

O

o *cj* or, or else; **o . . . o** either . . . or, whether . . . or; **o l'úno o l'àltro** *pron* either; *interj* oh!
òasi *nf* oasis.
obbediènte *etc v* **ubbidiènte** *etc.*
obbligàre (a) *vt* to compel, force, oblige; **-rsi** *vr* to bind oneself, undertake.
obbligazióne *nf* obligation; (*com*) bond, debenture.
òbbligo *pl* **-ghi** *nm* duty, obligation.
obbròbrio *nm* disgrace.
obesità *nf* obesity.
obèso *a* corpulent, obese.
òbice *nm* (*mil*) howitzer.
obiettàre *vt* to object.
obiettività *nf* objectivity, impartiality.
obiettívo *a* objective, impartial; *nm* objective; lens.
obiezióne *nf* objection.
obitòrio *nm* mortuary, morgue.
oblazióne *nf* donation, oblation.
oblío *nm* forgetfulness, oblivion.
obliquità *nf* obliquity.
oblíquo *a* oblique, underhand.
obliteràre *vt* to obliterate.
oblò *nm* porthole.
òboe *nm* (*mus*) oboe.
òbolo *nm* donation.
òca *nf* goose; **pèlle d'o.** gooseflesh.
occasionàle *a* casual, chance.
occasióne *nf* occasion, opportunity; **d'o.** second-hand.
occhiàia *nf* eye-socket, dark circle under eye.
occhialàio *nm* optician.
occhiàli *nm pl* spectacles *pl*, glasses *pl.*
occhialíno *nm* lorgnette.
occhialúto *a* bespectacled.
occhiàta *nf* glance.
occhieggiàre *vt* to eye, ogle; *vi* to peep, peer.
occhièllo *nm* buttonhole, eyelet.
occhiétto *nm* **fàre l'o. a qlcu** to wink at s.o.
òcchio *nm* eye; **a còlpo d'o.** at first sight; **in un bàtter d'o.** in a twinkling of an eye; **a quàttro òcchi** *ad* privately.
occidentàle *a* west(ern).
occidènte *nm* west.
occorrènte *a nm* necessary, requisite.
occorrènza *nf* circumstance, necessity, need; **all'o.** in case of need.
occórrere *vi impers* to be necessary, need, happen; **occórre mólto tèmpo** much time is required; **mi occórrono sòldi** I need money.
occúlto *a* hidden, occult.
occupànte *a* occupying; *nmf* occupant, occupier.
occupàre *vt* to occupy; **-rsi (di)** *vr* to attend (to), be busy (with), mind.
occupàto *a* engaged, busy.
occupazióne *nf* occupation.
oceànico *pl* **-ici** *a* oceanic.
ocèano *nm* ocean.
ocularè *a* eye, ocular; *nm* eye-piece; **testimóne o.** eye-witness.
oculatézza *nf* cautiousness, circumspection, wariness.
oculàto *a* wary, prudent.
oculísta *nm* eye specialist, oculist.
òde *nf* ode.
odiàre *vt* to hate, detest.
odièrno *a* of today, today's, modern.
òdio *pl* **òdii** *nm* hatred, hate.
odióso *a* hateful, odious.
odissèa *nf* odyssey.
odontoiàtra *nm* odontologist, dentist.
odontoiatría *nf* odontology, dentistry.
odoràre *vti* to smell, scent.
odoràto *nm* (sense of) smell.
odóre *nm* smell, odor, scent.
odoróso *a* fragrant, odorous.
Ofèlia *nf pr* Ophelia.
offèndere *vt* to offend, injure; **-rsi** *vr* to be offended, take offense.
offensíva *nf* (*mil*) offensive.
offensívo *a* offensive, insulting.
offerènte *nmf* bidder, offerer.
offèrta *nf* offer(ing); (*com*) tender, bid.

offertòrio *nm* offertory.
offésa *nf* offense, wrong.
offéso *a* offended, injured.
officína *nf* works, workshop.
offício *v* **ufficio.**
officióso *a* obliging; unofficial.
offríre *vt* to bid, offer.
offuscaménto *nm* dimming, darkening, obscuring.
oggettivaménte *ad* objectively.
oggettívo *a* objective, impartial.
oggètto *nm* article, object, subject.
òggi *ad* today; **o. a òtto** today week.
oggidì, oggigiórno *ad* nowadays.
ógni *a* each, every; **in o. luògo** *ad* everywhere; **in o. mòdo** *ad* anyhow; **o. tànto** *ad* every now and then.
Ognissànti *nm* All Saints' Day.
ognóra *ad* always.
ognúno *pron* each, everybody, everyone.
ohibò *interj* come now!
ohimè *interj* alas!
olà *interj* hello!
Olànda *nf* (*geogr*) Holland.
olandése *a* Dutch; *nm* Dutchman, (the) Dutch (language); *nf* Dutchwoman.
oleàndro *nm* oleander.
oleàto *a* oiled; **càrta oleàta** greaseproof paper, waxed paper.
oleifício *nm* oil mill.
oleodótto *nm* (oil) pipeline.
oleóso *a* greasy, oily.
olfàtto *nm* (sense of) smell.
oliatóre *nm* (*mech*) oil-can, oiler.
olièra *nf* (oil) cruet.
oligarchía *nf* oligarchy.
Olímpia *nf pr* Olympia.
olimpíade *nf* (*usually pl*) (*sport*) Olympic games *pl*, Olympiad.
olímpico *pl* **-ici** *a* Olympic, Olympian; **càlma olímpica** imperturbability.
olimpiónico *pl* **-ici** *a* (*sport*) Olympic; *nm* (*sport*) Olympian.
òlio *nm* oil.
olíva *nf* olive; **olívo** *nm* olive tree.
olivàstro *a* olive(-colored).
olivéto *nm* olive grove.
Olívia *nf pr* Olive, Olivia.
ólmo *nm* elm.
olocàusto *nm* holocaust, sacrifice.
ològrafo *nm* holograph.
oltraggiàre *vt* to outrage, insult.
oltràggio *nm* outrage, insult.
oltraggióso *a* outrageous.
oltrànza, ad *ad* to the bitter end.
óltre *ad and prep* further, beyond, over; **o. a, che** besides.
oltremàre *ad* beyond the sea(s), oversea(s).
oltremòdo *ad* exceedingly.
oltrepassàre *vt* to go beyond, surpass, outrun, exceed.
oltretómba *nm* beyond, hereafter.
omàggio *nm* homage; **còpia in o.** presentation copy; **omàggi** *pl* respects *pl*; **in o.** free.
ombelicàle *a* umbilical.
ombelíco *pl* **-íchi** *nm* navel.
ómbra *nf* shade, shadow; **all'o.** in the shade.
ombreggiàre *vt* to shade.
ombrellàio *nm* umbrella maker.
ombrèllo *nm* umbrella; **ombrellíno** parasol; **ombrellóne** (beach) umbrella.
ombrétto *nm* (*cosm*) eye shadow.
ombróso *a* (*places*) shady; (*people*) touchy.
òmero *nm* shoulder.
Oméro *nm pr* Homer.
omertà *nf* (conspiracy of) silence.
ométtere *vt* to leave out, omit.
omicída *a* homicidal; *nmf* homicide, murderer.
omicídio *nm* homicide, murder.
omissióne *nf* omission.
òmnibus *nm* omnibus, bus.
omogèneo *a* homogeneous.
omòlogo *pl* **-ghi** *a* homologous.
omònimo *a* homonymous; *nm* homonym, namesake.
omosessuàle *a* homosexual.
óncia *nf* ounce.
ónda *nf* wave; **ondàta** *nf* big wave (*also fig*).
ónde *ad* whence; *pron* whereby; *cj* so that, in order that; wherefore.
ondeggiaménto *nm* rocking, swaying; fluttering, wavering.
ondeggiàre *vi* to rock, wave; hesitate.
ondóso *a* undulatory, waving.
ondulàre *vt* to wave; *vi* to undulate; **-rsi i capèlli** to wave one's hair.
ondulàto *a* wavy, undulating, corrugated.
ondulazióne *nf* undulation; (*hair*) wave.
ònere *nm* burden.
oneróso *a* burdensome, onerous.
onestà *nf* honesty, uprightness, fairness.
onestaménte *ad* honestly, modestly, decently.
onèsto *a* fair, honest, upright.
ònice *nf* onyx.
onnipossènte, onnipotènte *a* almighty, omnipotent.
onnisciènza *nf* omniscience.
onnívoro *a* omnivorous.
onomàstico *pl* **-ici** *a nm* name-day.
onomatopèa *nf* onomatopoeia.
onorànza *nf* honor, solemnity.
onoràre *vt* to honor, do credit to; **-rsi (di)** *vr* to be proud (of).
onoràrio *a* honorary; *nm* fee, honorarium; **cittadíno o.** freeman.
onorataménte *ad* honorably.
onoràto *a* honored; honorable.
onóre *nm* honor.
onorévole *a* honorable, (also title of parliamentary deputies).
onorevolménte *ad* honorably.
onorificènza *nf* honor, title, decoration.
onorífico *pl* **-ici** *a* honorific.
ónta *nf* disgrace, shame; **ad o. di** in spite of.

ontàno *nm* alder.
opacità *nf* opacity, opaqueness.
opàco *pl* **-chi** *a* opaque, dull, matt.
opàle *nm* opal.
òpera *nf* work, action; opera; institution.
operàbile *a* operable, workable.
operàio *a* working; *nm* workman.
operàre *vti* to work, act, operate; **o. qlcu** operate on s.o.
operàto *a* (*cloth*) fancy; *nm* conduct, action; one who has been operated upon.
operatóre *nm* operator; (*cin*) cameraman.
operatòrio *a* operative; surgical; **sàla operatòria** operating theatre.
operazióne *nf* operation.
operosità *nf* activity, industry.
operóso *a* active, industrious.
opifício *nm* factory, works.
opinàre *vi* to be of the opinion.
opinióne *nf* opinion, contention.
òppio *nm* opium.
opponènte *a* opposing, opponent; *nmf* opponent.
oppórre *vt* **-rsi** *vr* to oppose, object.
opportunaménte *ad* opportunely, appropriately.
opportunísta *nmf* opportunist.
opportunità *nf* opportuneness; opportunity.
opportúno *a* opportune.
opposizióne *nf* opposition.
oppósto *a nm* opposite.
oppressióne *nf* oppression.
oppressívo *a* oppressive.
opprèsso *a* oppressed.
oppressóre *nm* oppressor.
opprimènte *a* oppressive.
opprímere *vt* to oppress, overwhelm.
oppugnàre *vt* to attack; (*fig*) impugn.
oppúre *cj* or (else).
optàre *vi* to opt.
opulènto *a* opulent, rich.
opulènza *nf* opulence, wealth.
opúscolo *nm* pamphlet.
óra *nf* hour, time; **che óre sóno?** what time is it?; *ad* now; presently; or óra just now; **óra che** *cj* now that.
oràcolo *nm* oracle.
òrafo *nm* goldsmith.
oràle *a nm* oral.
oralménte *ad* orally, verbally.
oramài *ad* by this time, now; from now on.
oràrio *a* per hour; *nm* timetable; **o. d'ufficio** office hours; **segnàle o.** time signal.
oratóre *nm* **-tríce** *nf* orator, speaker.
oratòria *nf* eloquence, oratory.
oratòrio *a* oratorial; *nm* oratory, Sunday school; (*mus*) oratorio.
Oràzio *nm pr* Horace.
orazióne *nf* oration, prayer.
òrbita *nf* eye-socket, orbit.
òrbo *a* blind.
Òrcadi (**le**) *nf pl* (*geogr*) the Orkney Islands.
orchèstra *nf* orchestra.
orchidèa *nf* orchid.
órcio *nm* pitcher.
órco *pl* **órchi** *nm* ogre.
òrda *nf* horde.
ordígno *nm* tool, device.
ordinàle *a* ordinal.
ordinaménto *nm* arrangement, disposition.
ordinànza *nf* order; (*mil*) orderly; **o. municipàle** by-law.
ordinàre *vt* to order, arrange, ordain; **gli ordinài di andàre** I ordered him to go.
ordinariamènte *ad* ordinarily, usually.
ordinàrio *a* ordinary, normal; coarse; *nm* professor.
ordinàto *a* orderly, tidy.
ordinazióne *nf* order; (*eccl*) ordination; **fàtto su o.** *a* made to order.
órdine *nm* order; **o. del giòrno** agenda.
ordíre *vt* to weave; plot.
ordíto *nm* warp, web; plot.
orecchíno *nm* earring.
orécchio *nm* ear; **a o.** by ear; **dúro d'o.** hard of hearing.
orecchióni *nm pl* (*med*) mumps.
orèfice *nm* goldsmith.
oreficería *nf* goldsmith's shop; things made of gold.
òrfano *a nm* orphan.
orfanotròfio *nm* orphanage.
Orfèo *nm pr* Orpheus.
òrfico *pl* **òrfici** *a* Orphic.
organétto, organíno *nm* barrel-organ.
orgànico *pl* **-ici** *a* organic.
organísmo *nm* organism.
organísta *nmf* organist.
organizzàre *vt* to organize.
organizzatóre *a* organizing; *nm* **-tríce** *nf* organizer.
organizzazióne *nf* organization.
òrgano *nm* organ.
orgàsmo *nm* orgasm, excitement.
òrgia *nf* orgy.
orgóglio *nm* pride.
orgogliosaménte *ad* proudly.
orgoglióso *a* proud.
orientàle *a* east(ern), oriental.
orientaménto *nm* orientation, bearings; **o. mediànte ràdio** radio bearing.
orientàre *vt* to set, turn; **-rsi** *vr* to find one's bearings or way.
orïènte *nm* east, orient.
orígano *nm* origan.
originàle *a nm* original, eccentric (person).
originalità *nf* originality, strangeness.
originalménte *ad* originally, ingeniously.
originàre *vti* to give rise to; originate.
originariaménte *ad* originally.
originàrio *a* original, primary.
orígine *nm* origin, beginning, cause.

origliàre *vi* to eavesdrop.
orína *nf* urine.
orinatóio *nm* urinal.
oriúndo *a* native; **èssere o. di Róma** to be of Roman origin.
orizzontàle *a* horizontal.
orizzónte *nm* horizon.
Orlàndo *nm pr* Roland.
orlàre *vt* to edge, hem.
orlatúra *nf* edging, hemming.
órlo *nm* edge, hem.
órma *nf* footprint, mark.
ormài *ad* by now.
ormeggiàre *vt* **-rsi** *vr* to moor.
orméggio *nm* mooring.
ormóne *nm* hormone.
ornamentàle *a* ornamental.
ornaménto *nm* ornament.
ornàre *vt* to adorn, decorate.
ornàto *a* ornate; *nm* decoration.
ornitología *nf* ornithology.
ornitòlogo *pl* **-oghi** *nm* ornithologist.
òro *nm* gold.
orologería *nf* watchmaking, watchmaker's shop, mechanism of a watch (clock).
orologiàio *nm* watchmaker.
orològio *nm* clock, watch.
oròscopo *nm* horoscope.
orrèndo, orríbile *a* horrible, dreadful.
òrrido *a* horrid; *nm* ravine.
orripilànte *a* terrifying; hideous.
orróre *nm* horror, loathing.
orsacchiòtto *nm* bear cub; (*toy*) teddybear.
órso *nm* bear; (*fig*) unsociable person; **Órsa Maggióre** (*astr*) Great Bear; **Órsa Minóre** Little Bear, **o. grígio** grizzly (bear).
Òrsola *nf pr* Ursula.
orsù *interj* come on!
ortàggio *nm* vegetable.
ortènsia *nf* hydrangea.
ortíca *nf* nettle.
orticària *nf* nettlerash.
orticultóre *nm* market gardener, truck farmer.
òrto *nm* kitchen garden.
ortodòsso *a* orthodox.
ortografía *nf* orthography, spelling.
ortolàno *nm* vegetable dealer, truck farmer.
ortopedía *nf* orthopedics.
orzaiòlo *nm* stye (on the eyelid).
orzàta *nf* barley water.
òrzo *nm* barley.
osàre *vti* to dare, risk.
Òscar *nm pr* Oscar; **prémio O.** Oscar (prize), (*US*) Academy Award.
oscenità *nf* indecency, obscenity.
oscèno *a* obscene, horrible.
oscillàre *vi* to swing, hesitate, oscillate.
oscillatóre *nm* oscillator.
oscillatòrio *a* oscillatory, oscillating.
oscillazióne *nf* oscillation, swing (ing), fluctuation.
oscuraménto *nm* darkening.
oscuràre *vt* to darken, obscure; **-rsi** *vr* to grow dark, dim.
oscurità *nf* darkness, obscurity.
oscúro *a* dark, obscure, difficult **èssere all'o. di** to be ignorant of.
ospedàle *nm* hospital.
ospitàle *a* hospitable.
ospitalità *nf* hospitality.
ospitàre *vt* to give hospitality to.
òspite *nmf* host(ess); guest.
ospízio *nm* asylum, home.
ossatúra *nf* (bone) structure, framework.
òsseo *a* bony, osseous.
ossequiàre *vt* to pay one's respects to.
ossèquio *nm* homage, obedience; **ossèqui** *pl* regards, respects *pl*.
ossequióso *a* respectful, obsequious.
osservànza *nf* obedience, observance.
osservàre *vt* to observe, watch, examine.
osservatóre *nm* **-tríce** *nf* observer.
osservatòrio *nm* observatory; (*mil*) observation post, look-out.
osservazióne *nf* observation, remark.
ossessionàre *vt* to obsess, haunt.
ossessióne *nf* obsession.
ossèsso *nm* person possessed.
ossía *cj* or, or rather.
òssido *nm* oxide.
ossídrico *pl* **-ici** *a* oxyhydrogen.
ossigenàto *a* oxygenized; (*of hair*) peroxided.
ossígeno *nm* oxygen.
òsso *nm*; *m pl* **òssi** (*meat*) bone ; (*fruit*) stone; *f pl* **òssa** (human) bone; **di càrne ed òssa** of flesh and blood.
ossúto *a* big-boned, bony.
ostacolàre *vt* to hinder, interfere with.
ostàcolo *nm* hindrance, obstacle; **córsa ad ostàcoli** hurdle-race, steeplechase.
ostàggio *nm* hostage.
òste *nm* innkeeper, publican, saloon keeper, landlord.
osteggiàre *vt* to be hostile to, oppose.
ostèllo *nm* mansion; inn; hostel.
Ostènda *nf pr* (*geogr*) Ostend.
ostentàre *vt* to show off; feign.
ostentazióne *nf* ostentation; pretense.
ostería *nf* inn, tavern.
ostéssa *nf* innkeeper's wife.
ostètrica *nf* midwife.
òstia *nf* (*eccl*) Host, wafer.
òstico *pl* **-ici** *a* difficult, unpleasant.
ostíle *a* hostile.
ostilità *nf* hostility, enmity.
ostilménte *ad* in a hostile manner, with hostility.
ostinàrsi *vr* to insist, persist.
ostinàto *a* obstinate, stubborn.
ostinazióne *nf* obstinacy, persistence.
ostracísmo *nm* ostracism.
òstrica *nf* oyster.
ostruíre *vt* to obstruct, stop (up).

ostruzióne *nf* obstruction.
Otèllo *nm pr* Othello.
otorinolaringoiàtra *nm* ear, nose and throat specialist.
ótre *nm* (goat)-skin bottle.
ottàgono *nm* octagon.
ottàno *nm* (*chem*) octane.
ottànta *a nm* eighty; **ottanténne** *a* eighty-year-old; **ottantésimo** *a* eightieth; **ottantína** *nf* about eighty.
ottàva *nf* octave; **ottàvo** *a nm* eighth; octavo.
ottemperàre (**a**) *vi* to comply (with), obey.
ottenebràre *vt* to darken, cloud.
ottenére *vt* to obtain, gain, get.
ottenìbile *a* obtainable.
òttica *nf* optics.
òttico *pl* **-ici** *a* optic(al); *nm* optician.
ottimìsmo *nm* optimism.
ottimísta *nmf* optimist.
ottimístico *pl* **-ici** *a* optimistic.
òttimo *a* very good, excellent.
òtto *a nm* eight.
ottòbre *nm* October.
ottocènto *a nm* eight hundred; nineteenth century.
ottomàno *a nm* Ottoman.
ottóne *nm* brass, brass instrument.
ottuagenàrio *a nm* octogenarian.
otturàre *vt* to stop (up).
otturazióne *nf* plugging; (*of tooth*) filling, stopping.
ottusità *nf* obtuseness, bluntness.
ottúso *a* obtuse, blunt, dull.
ovàia *nf* ovary.
ovàle *a nm* oval.
ovàtta *nf* wadding, cotton wool, absorbent cotton.
ovazióne *nf* ovation.
óve *ad* where; *cj* if, in case.
òvest *nm* west; **a o.** in, to the west.
Ovídio *nm pr* Ovid.
ovíle *nm* fold, sheep-fold.
ovíno *a* ovine; *nm* sheep.
òvolo *nm* a kind of mushroom.
ovúnque *ad* anywhere, everywhere, wherever.
ovvéro *cj* or.
ovviaménte *ad* obviously, evidently.
ovviàre *vt* to obviate, avoid.
òvvio *a* obvious, evident.
oziàre *vi* to idle, loaf.
òzio *nm* idleness, leisure.
oziosità *nf* idleness, laziness.
ozióso *a* idle.
ozòno *nm* ozone.

P

pacataménte *ad* calmly, quietly.
pacatézza *nf* calmness, quietness.
pacàto *a* calm, quiet.
pacchétto *nm* packet, small parcel.
pàcco *pl* **pàcchi** *nm* parcel, package.
pàce *nf* peace.
pachistàno *a nm* Pakistani.
pacière *nm* **pacièra** *nf* peacemaker.
pacificaménte *ad* peacefully, peaceably.
pacificàre *vt* to pacify, reconcile.
pacificazióne *nf* pacification, reconciliation.
pacífico *pl* **-ici** *a* peaceful; **Pacífico** *a nm* (*geogr*) Pacific (Ocean).
padàno *a* (*geogr*) Po; **la Val Padàna** the Po Valley.
padèlla *nf* frying-pan; bed-pan; **dàlla p. nèlla bràge** out of the frying-pan into the fire.
padiglióne *nm* pavilion, tent.
Pàdova *nf* (*geogr*) Padua; **padovàno** *a nm* Paduan.
pàdre *nm* father.
padríno *nm* godfather; (*in a duel*) second.
padróna *nf* landlady, mistress.
padróne *nm* landlord, master, owner, proprietor.
padronànza *nf* command, mastery; **p. di sè** self control.
padronàto *nm* ownership, possession.
padroneggiàre *vt* to command, master; *vi* to play the master.
paesàggio *nm* landscape.
paesàno *a* country, rustic; *nm* peasant; fellow-townsman.
paése *nm* country; district; village; town.
paesísta *nmf* landscape painter.
paffúto *a* chubby, plump.
pàga *nf* pay, wages *pl*.
pagàbile *a* payable.
pagaménto *nm* payment.
paganèsimo *nm* paganism.
pagàno *a nm* pagan, heathen.
pagàre *vt* to pay, pay for.
pagèlla *nf* (school-)report.
pàggio *nm* pageboy.
pagherò *nm* (*com*) promissory note, I.O.U.
pàgina *nf* leaf, page (of a book).
pàglia *nf* straw; **p. di fèrro** steel wool; **pagliétta** straw-hat.
pagliàccio *nm* buffoon, clown.
pagliàio *nm* straw-rick.
pagliericcio *nm* paillasse.
pagnòtta *nf* loaf.
pàgo *pl* **pàghi** *a* content, satisfied.
pàio *pl f* **pàia** *nm* pair.
Pàkistan *nm* (*geogr*) Pakistan.
pàla *nf* shovel; **ruòta a pàle** paddle-wheel.
palàta *nf* shovelful; blow with a shovel; stroke with an oar.
palatíno *a* Palatine.
palàto *nm* palate.
palàzzo *nm* palace, mansion, building.
pàlco *pl* **pàlchi** *nm* platform, stand; (*theat*) box.
palcoscènico *pl* **-ici** *nm* (*theat*) stage.
palesàre *vt* to disclose, reveal.
palése *a* evident, clear, obvious.
Palestína *nf* (*geogr*) Palestine.
palestinése *a nmf* Palestinian.

palèstra *nf* gymnasium.
palétta *nm* small shovel.
palétto *nm* (*of the floor*) bolt; small pole.
pàlio *nm* horse-race at Siena; silk banner given to winner.
palizzàta *nf* fence, paling, palisade.
pàlla *nf* ball; **p. a bàsi** baseball; **p. a vólo** volleyball; **pallacanèstro** *nf* basketball; **pallacòrda** *nf* lawn tennis; **pallamàglio** *nf* croquet; **pallanuòto** *nf* water polo; **p. da cannóne** shell; **p. da fucíle** bullet.
palleggiaménto, palléggio *nm* (*football*) dribbling; (*tennis*) volleying.
palliatívo *a nm* palliative.
pallidézza *nf* paleness, pallor.
pàllido *a* pale, pallid.
pallína *nf* little ball, small shot; **pallíno** *nm* little ball, small shot, pellet; (*bowls*) jack; **avére il p. di** to have a craze for.
palloncíno *nm* balloon, Chinese lantern.
pallóne *nm* ball, balloon, football.
pallóre *nm* paleness, pallor.
pallòttola *nf* bullet, pellet.
pàlma *nf* palm(tree); (*of the hand*) palm.
palméto *nm* palm-grove.
pàlmo *nm* (*of the hand, or measure*) palm.
pàlo *nm* pole, post, pile, pylon.
palombàro *nm* diver.
palómbo *nm* dogfish; wood-pigeon.
palpàbile *a* palpable, obvious.
palpàre *vt* to feel, handle, touch; (*med*) palpate.
pàlpebra *nf* eyelid.
palpitànte *a* palpitating, throbbing.
palpitàre *vi* to palpitate, tremble, throb.
pàlpito *nm* beat, throb.
paltò *nm* overcoat.
palúde *nf* marsh.
paludóso, palústre *a* marshy.
Pamèla *nf pr* Pamela.
pàmpino *nm* vine leaf.
Pànama *nf* (*geogr*) Panama.
panàre *vt* to cover with breadcrumbs.
pànca *nf* bench, form.
pancétta *nf* bacon.
panchétto *nf* footstool, small bench.
pància *nf* stomach, belly.
panciòlle, in *ad* **stàre in p.** to lounge about.
panciòtto *nm* waistcoat, vest.
Pancràzio *nm pr* Pancras.
pàne *nm* bread, loaf; **buòno cóme il p.** as good as gold.
panegírico *pl* **-ici** *nm* panegyric.
panèllo *nm* oilcake.
panettería *nf* baker's shop.
panettière *nm* baker.
panfrútto *nm* fruitcake.
pània *nf* bird-lime; (*fig*) snare.
pànico *pl* **-ici** *nm* panic.
paníco *pl* **-chi** *nm* millet.
panière *nm* basket.
panifício *nm* bakehouse, bakery.
pànna *nf* cream; (*aut*) breakdown; **p. montàta** whipped cream.
pannéggio *nm* drapery.
pannèllo *nm* (*arch*) panel; **p. di finèstra** window-pane.
pànno *nm* cloth; **pànni** *pl* clothes; **sè io fóssi néi tuòi pànni** if I were in your place (shoes).
pannolíno *nm* (baby's) diaper; sanitary napkin.
panoràmico *pl* **-ici** *a* panoramic.
panpepàto *nm* gingerbread.
pantalóni *nm pl* trousers.
pantàno *nm* bog, swamp.
panteísmo *nm* pantheism.
pantèra *nf* panther.
pantòfola *nf* slipper.
pantomíma *nf* (*theat*) mime, dumbshow.
Pàola *nf pr* Paula, Pauline.
Pàolo *nm pr* Paul.
papà *nm* daddy, papa.
Pàpa *nm pr* Pope.
papàle *a* papal.
papàto *nm* papacy.
papàvero *nm* poppy.
pàpero *nm* gosling; **Paperíno** *nm* Donald Duck.
papíro *nm* papyrus.
pàppa *nf* pap.
pappagàllo *nm* parrot; **pappagallíno** budgerigar, parakeet.
paràbola *nf* parable; parabola.
parabrézza *nm* (*aut*) windscreen, windshield.
paracadúte *nm* parachute.
paracadutísta *nm* parachutist, paratrooper.
paracénere *nm* fireguard.
paradisíaco *pl* **-íaci** *a* heavenly, paradisiacal.
paradíso *nm* heaven, paradise.
paradòsso *nm* paradox.
parafàngo *nm* (*aut*) mudguard, fender.
paraffína *nf* oil, paraffin, kerosene (coal-oil).
paràfrasi *nf* paraphrase.
parafúlmine *nm* lightning conductor.
parafuòco *pl* **-chi** *nm* fireguard.
paràggi *nm pl* neighborhood.
paragonàre *vt* to compare.
paragóne *nm* comparison; **a p. di** in comparison with.
paràgrafo *nm* paragraph.
paràlisi *nf* paralysis.
paralítico *pl* **-ici** *a nm* paralytic.
paralizzàre *vt* to paralyze.
parallelaménte *ad* parallel.
parallèlo *a nm* parallel (*also fig*).
paralúme *nm* lampshade.
paraòcchi *nm pl* blinkers *pl*.
parapètto *nm* parapet.
parapíglia *nm* turmoil.
parapiòggia *nm* umbrella.
paràre *vt* to parry, avert; decorate, lead up to.

parasóle *nm* parasol, (*aut*) sunshield.
parassíta *nm* parasite.
parastatàle *a* state-controlled.
paràta *nf* parade; parry, save; **màla p.** unlucky moment.
paratía *nf* (*naut*) bulkhead.
paratífo *nm* paratyphoid.
paraúrti *nm* (*aut*) bumper.
paravènto *nm* windshield.
parcheggiàre *vt* to park; **parchèggio** *nm* parking (place), parking station, carpark, parking lot.
pàrco *pl* **pàrchi** *a* frugal, moderate; *nm* park.
parécchio *a* a good deal of; *ad* a lot, much; **parècchi** *a and pron m pl* **parècchie** *a and pron f pl* several.
pareggiàre *vt* to balance, level; *vi* (*sport*) to tie; **una scuòla pareggiàta** an officially recognized school.
paréggio *nm* balance; (*sport*) tie.
parentàdo *nm* **parentèla** *nf* kin *pl*, kindred, relations *pl*, relationship.
parènte *nmf* relation, relative; **p. più strétto** next-of-kin.
parèntesi *nf* brackets *pl*, parenthesis.
parére *vi* to seem, look like; *nm* opinion.
paréte *nf* (internal) wall; (*mountain*) face.
pàri *a* equal, (*number*) even; *nm* (*sing and pl*) equal, peer; **càmera déi p.** House of Lords; *nf* par; **àlla p.** au pair; (*com*) at par.
parificàre *v* **pareggiàre**.
Parígi *nf* (*geogr*) Paris; **parigino** *a nm* Parisian.
paríglia *nf* (*horses*) pair; tit for tat.
pariménti *ad* likewise.
parità *nf* equality, parity.
parlamentàre *vi* to parley; *a* parliamentary; *nm* Member of Parliament.
parlaménto *nm* parley; parliament.
parlàre *vi* to speak, talk; **p. chiàro** to be plain, speak one's mind.
parmigiàno *a nm* Parmesan (cheese).
parodía *nf* parody.
paròla *nf* word; **p. d'òrdine** (*mil*) password.
parossísmo *nm* paroxysm.
parricída *a* parricidal; *nm* parricide (*criminal*); **parricídio** *nm* parricide (*crime*).
parròcchia *nf* parish, parish church; **parrocchiàle** *a* parish; **parrocchiàno** parishioner.
pàrroco *pl* **-oci** *nm* parish priest; (Protestant) parson, minister.
parrúcca *nf* wig.
parrucchière *nm* **parrucchièra** *nf* hairdresser.
parsimònia *nf* parsimony, sparingness.
pàrte *nf* part, place, share, side; **la màggior p.** the majority; **da p.** aside; **in p.** partly.
partecipàre *vt* to announce; *vi* to share, participate; **p. àgli útili** to share in the profits.
partecipazióne *nf* participation; announcement.
partécipe *a* informed; participating, sharing.
parteggiàre *vi* to side with, take sides.
Partenóne *nm pr* Parthenon.
partenopèo *a* Neapolitan.
partènza *nf* departure, start(ing).
particélla *nf* particle.
participio *nm* participle.
particolàre *a* particular, special; *nm* particular, detail.
particolareggiàto *a* detailed.
particolarménte *ad* particularly, especially, in particular.
partigiàno *a* partisan; *nm* partisan, supporter.
partíre *vi* to depart, leave, set out, start; **a p. da domàni** starting from tomorrow.
partíta *nf* match; game; party, (*com*) lot, entry.
partíto *nm* (*pol*) party; (*marriage*) match; resolution; **a p. préso** with mind made up.
partitúra *nf* (*mus*) score.
partizióne *nf* division, partition.
pàrto *nm* (child)birth, delivery.
partoríre *vti* to bear, give birth to; *nm* childbearing.
parziàle *a* partial.
parzialità *nf* partiality.
pàscere *vti* **-rsi** *vr* to graze, pasture, feed.
pascolàre *vti* to graze, pasture.
pàscolo *nm* pasture; (*fig*) food.
Pàsqua *nf* Easter; **pasquàle** *a* Easter.
passàbile *a* passable.
passàggio *nm* passage, crossing; (*sport*) pass; **diritto di p.** right of way; **p. a livèllo** level crossing, grade; **p. pedonàle** crossing; pedestrian crossing; **èssere di p.** to be passing through.
passamanería *nf* **passamàno** *nm* trimming.
passamontàgna *nm* Balaclava helmet.
passànte *nmf* passer-by.
passapòrto *nm* passport.
passàre *vti* to pass, spend; **p. da** to call on; **-rsela** *vr* to get on.
passatèmpo *nm* pastime.
passàto *a nm* past.
passeggèro *a* passing, transient; *nm* passenger, traveler.
passeggiàre *vi* to (go for a) walk.
passeggiàta *nf* walk, ride, drive.
passéggio *nm* promenade, walk.
passerèlla *nf* foot-bridge; (*naut*) gangway.
pàssero *nm* sparrow.
passionàle *a* passionate, of passion.
passióne *nf* passion.
passività *nf* passiveness; (*com*) liabilities *pl*.

passívo *a* passive; *nm* passive; (*com*) liabilities *pl*.
pàsso *nm* step, pace; passage; (*geogr*) pass; **a p. d'uòmo** at a walking pace; **di pàri p.** at the same rate.
pàsta *nf* dough, pastry; cake; paste, pulp; **p. dentifrícia** toothpaste; **pastína da tè** teacake, biscuit.
pastèllo *nm* pastel.
pastétta *nf* batter.
pastícca *nf* lozenge, tablet.
pasticcería *nf* confectioner's, confectionary; **pasticcière** *nm* confectioner.
pasticcíno *nm* small cake, tartlet, cookie.
pastíccio *nm* pie; (*fig*) mess; **nèi pastícci** in a fix.
pastíglia *nf* lozenge, pastille.
pàsto *nm* meal.
pastóia *nf* hobble, pastern; (*fig*) fetters.
pastoràle *a* pastoral; *nm* crozier; *nf* pastoral (letter).
pastóre *nm* shepherd, pastor; **pastorèlla** *nf* shepherdess.
pastorizẓàre *vt* to pasteurize.
pastóso *a* doughy, soft, mellow.
pastràno *nm* (man's) overcoat.
pastúra *nf* pasture.
patàta *nf* potato; **patàte frítte** chips, French fries; **patatíne frítte** crisps, potato chips.
patènte *a* open, obvious; *nf* license; **patentàto** *a* trained.
paternàle *nf* scolding.
paternaménte *ad* in a fatherly way, paternally.
paternità *nf* paternity; father's name.
patèrno *a* paternal.
patètico *pl* **-ici** *a* moving, pathetic.
patíbolo *nm* gallows, gibbet.
patiménto *nm* pain, suffering.
patíre *vti* to endure, suffer.
patología *nf* pathology; **patològico** *pl* **-ici** *a* pathologic(al).
pàtria *nf* (one's own) country, fatherland.
patriàrca *nm* patriarch; **patriarcàle** *a* patriarchal.
patrígno *nm* stepfather.
patrimònio *nm* heritage, estate.
pàtrio *a* of one's own country or home.
patriòt(t)a *nmf* patriot.
patriòttico *pl* **-ici** *a* patriotic.
Patrízia *nf pr* Patricia; **Patrízio** *nm pr* Patrick.
patrízio *a nm* patrician.
patrocinàre *vt* to defend, support.
patrocinatóre *nm* defender, sponsor, patron.
patrocínio *nm* defense; **p. gratúito** legal aid.
patróno *nm* patron, defending counsel; **patronàto** *nm* patronage.
patteggiàre *vti* come to terms, negotiate.
pattinàggio *nm* skating.
pattinàre *vi* to skate.
pàttino *nm* (ice)skate; **p. a rotèlle** roller skate.
pàtto *nm* pact, condition.
pattúglia *nf* (*mil*) patrol.
pattuíre *vt* to agree (upon), fix.
pattumièra *nf* dustbin, garbage can.
paùra *nf* fear, fright; **avére p.** to be afraid; **far p. (a)** to frighten; **per p. che** lest.
paurosaménte *ad* fearfully, frighteningly.
pauróso *a* fearful, frightful.
pàusa *nf* pause.
paveșàre *vt* to adorn, beflag.
pavéșe *a nm* (inhabitant) of Pavia; *nm* shield.
paviménto *nm* floor.
pavóne *nm* peacock; **pavoneggiàrsi** *vr* to strut.
pazientàre *vi* to be patient, have patience.
pazïènte *a nmf* patient.
pazïènza *nf* patience; **pèrdere la p.** to lose one's temper; *interj* never mind!
pazzésco *a* mad; foolish.
pazzía *nf* madness, foolish action.
pàzzo *a nm* mad(man), lunatic.
pècca *nf* blemish, defect, flaw.
peccaminóso *a* sinful, culpable.
peccàre *vi* to sin, err.
peccàto *nm* sin; **che p.!** *interj* what a pity!
peccatóre *nm* **-tríce** *nf* sinner.
pécchia *nf* bee; **pecchióne** *nm* drone.
péce *nf* pitch.
pechinése *a nmf* Pekin(g)ese.
pècora *nf* sheep, ewe.
pecoríno *nm* sheep's-milk cheese.
peculàto *nm* peculation.
peculiàre *a* peculiar, special.
peculiarità *nf* peculiarity, characteristic.
pedàggio *nm* toll.
pedagògo *nm* pedagogue.
pedàle *nm* pedal, treadle.
pedàna *nf* dais.
pedànte *a nm* pedant(ic).
pedantería *nf* pedantry.
pedàta *nf* kick; footprint.
pedèstre *a* pedestrian; dull.
pediàtra *nmf* pediatrician.
pedicure (*Fr*) *nm* chiropodist.
pedilúvio *nm* foot-bath.
pedína *nf* piece; (*chess*) pawn.
pedinàre *vt* to follow, shadow.
pedóne *nm* **pedonàle** *a* pedestrian.
pèggio *a nm ad* worse, worst; **àlla p.** if the worst comes to the worst.
peggioraménto *nm* worsening, deterioration.
peggioràre *vt* to make worse; *vi* to worsen.
peggióre *a* worse, worst.
pégno *nm* pawn, pledge, token; **dàre in p.** *vt* to pawn; **giuòco dèi pégni** forfeits *pl*.

pelàre *vt* to skin, peel; (*fig*) fleece; **-rsi** *vr* to go bald.
pellàme *nm* hides *pl*, skins *pl*.
pèlle *nf* skin.
pellegrinàggio *nm* pilgrimage.
pellegrinàre *vi* to wander.
pellegríno *a* rare, strange; *nm* pilgrim.
pelletterìa *nf* leather goods *pl*, leather goods shop.
pellicàno *nm* pelican.
pellicceria *nf* furs *pl*; fur trade; furrier's (shop).
pellíccia *nf* fur (coat).
pelliccìàio *nm* furrier.
pellícola *nf* film.
pelliróssa *nmf* redskin.
pélo *nm* hair, fur; (*cloth*) pile; **per un p.** by a hair's breadth.
pelóso *a* hairy, shaggy.
péltro *nm* pewter.
pelúria *nf* down, fluff.
pèlvi *nf* pelvis.
péna *nf* punishment; pain; trouble; **in p.** anxious; **far p.** to move to pity; **valére la p.** *vi* to be worthwhile; **a màla p.** scarcely.
penàle *a* criminal, penal.
penalísta *nm* criminal lawyer.
penàre (a) *vi* to suffer, find difficulty (in).
pendàglio *nm* pendant.
pendènte *a* hanging, leaning; *nm* earring, pendant.
pendènza *nf* slope, gradient, declivity, grade.
pèndere *vi* to hang; lean, slope.
pendíce *nf* **pendío** *nm* slope, hillside.
pèndolo *nm* pendulum; **pèndola** *nf* clock.
pène *nm* penis.
penetrànte *a* penetrating, piercing, acute.
penetràre *vti* to penetrate.
penetrazióne *nf* penetration.
penicillína *nf* penicillin.
peninsulàre *a* peninsular.
penísola *nf* peninsula.
penitènte *a nmf* penitent.
penitènza *nf* penance, penitence.
penitenziàrio *a* penitentiary; *nm* prison, penitentiary.
pénna *nf* feather; pen.
pennàcchio *nm* plume.
pennellatúra *nf* brushwork; (*med*) painting.
pennèllo *nm* brush, paint-brush; **a p.** perfectly.
Pennìne, (Àlpi) *nf pl* (*geogr*) Pennine Alps.
penníno *nm* nib, penpoint.
pennóne *nm* pennon; (*naut*) yard.
penóso *a* painful.
pentàgono *nm* pentagon.
pensàre *vti* to think.
pensatóre *nm* thinker.
pensièro *nm* thought, idea.
pensieróso *a* thoughtful.
pènsile *a* hanging.
pensilína *nf* (*bus etc*) shelter; awning.
pensionànte *nmf* boarder, lodger.
pensionàre *vt* to pension (off).
pensionàto *a* retired; *nm* pensioner; hostel.
pensióne *nf* pension; board and lodging; boarding house.
pensóso *a* pensive, thoughtful.
pentàgono *nm* pentagon.
Pentecòste *nf* Whitsun(tide), Pentecost.
pentiménto *nm* repentance.
pentírsi (di) *vr* to repent.
péntola *nf* pot, saucepan.
penúltimo *a* penultimate.
penúria *nf* lack, shortage.
penzolàre *vi* to dangle, hang down.
penzolóni, penzolóne *ad* dangling, hanging.
peònia *nf* peony.
pepai(u)òla *nf* pepper-pot.
pépe *nm* pepper.
peperóne *nm* chili, pepper.
per *prep* for, through, by; **p. lo più** generally; **p. l'appúnto** just so; **p. vía aèrea** by airmail.
péra *nf* pear; (*el*) pear-switch.
perbène *a* respectable, nice.
percàlle *nm* cotton cambric.
percentuàle *nf* percentage.
percepíre *vt* to perceive; receive.
percettíbile *a* perceptible.
percezióne *nf* perception.
perché *cj* why?; because; (*with subjunctive*) in order that; *nm* reason.
perciò *ad* therefore, thereby.
percórrere *vt* to pass through, travel over.
percórso *nm* distance, route.
percòssa *nf* blow, stroke.
percuòtere *vt* to strike.
percussióne *nf* percussion.
perdènte *a* losing; *nmf* loser.
pèrdere *vti* to lose, miss; **p. di vísta** to lose sight of; **-rsi** *vr* to get lost, vanish.
pèrdita *nf* loss, waste; **a p. d'òcchio** as far as the eye can see.
perdizióne *nf* perdition.
perdonàbile *a* pardonable.
perdonàre *vt* to forgive, pardon.
perdóno *nm* forgiveness, pardon.
perduràre *vi* to last, persist.
perdutaménte desperately.
perdúto *a* lost.
peregrinàre *v* **pellegrinàre**.
peregríno *a* uncommon.
perènne *a* everlasting, perennial.
perentòrio *a* peremptory.
perfètto *a* perfect.
perfezionaménto *nm* perfecting; specialization.
perfezionàre *vt* perfect, improve; **-rsi** *vr* to perfect oneself; specialize.
perfezióne *nf* perfection.
perfídia *nf* perfidy, wickedness.
pèrfido *a* perfidious.
perfíno *ad* even.

perforàre *vt* to perforate, pierce.
perforatríce *nf* drill, drilling machine.
perforazióne *nf* perforation, drilling.
pergamèna *nf* parchment.
pèrgola *nf* **pergolàto** *nm* pergola, arbor.
pericolànte *a* unsafe.
perícolo *nm* danger, peril.
pericolóso *a* dangerous.
perifería *nf* periphery, outskirts *pl.*
perífrasi *nf* periphrasis.
perímetro *nm* perimeter.
periòdico *pl* **-ici** *a nm* periodical.
período *nm* period; (*gram*) sentence.
peripezía *nf* vicissitude, adventure.
perire *vi* to die, perish.
periscòpio *nm* periscope.
períto *a nm* expert.
peritoníte *nf* (*med*) peritonitis.
perízia *nf* skill; survey.
pèrla *nf* pearl.
perlustràre *vt* to patrol, reconnoiter.
perlustrazióne *nf* patrol, reconnaissance.
permalóso *a* touchy.
permanènte *a* permanent; *nf* permanent wave, perm.
permanènza *nf* stay; **in p.** permanently.
permeàre *vt* to permeate.
permésso *a* permitted; *nm* permission, permit; **p.!** excuse me, allow me.
perméttere (a qlcu di) *vt* to allow (s.o. to); **-rsi** *vr* to take the liberty.
pèrmuta *nf* exchange.
perníce *nf* partridge.
perniciόso *a* pernicious.
pèrno, pèrnio *nm* pivot.
pernottaménto *nm* overnight stay.
pernottàre *vi* to spend the night.
però *cj* but, however.
péro *nm* pear tree.
peronòspora *nf* mildew.
peroràre *vti* to plead.
perorazióne *nf* peroration; pleading, defense.
peròssido *nm* peroxide.
perpendicolàre *a nf* perpendicular.
perpetràre *vt* to commit, perpetrate.
perpetuàre *vt* to perpetuate; **-rsi** *vr* to continue.
perpètuo *a* eternal, perpetual.
perplessità *nf* perplexity.
perplèsso *a* perplexed, puzzled.
perquiṣíre *vt* to search.
perquiṣizióne *nf* search.
persecutóre *nm* persecutor.
persecuzióne *nf* persecution.
perseguíre *vt* to follow, pursue.
perseguitàre *vt* to persecute.
perseverànte *a* persevering.
perseverànza *nf* perseverance.
perseveràre *vi* to persevere.
Pèrsia *nf* (*geogr*) Persia, Iran.
persiàna *nf* shutter, shade.
persiàno *a nm* Persian.
persíno *ad* even.
persistènte *a* persistent, persisting.
persístere *vi* to persist.
pèrso *a* lost; **a tèmpo p.** in one's spare time.
persóna *nf* person, body; **di p.** in person.
personàggio *nm* (*theat*) character, personage.
personàle *a* personal; *nm* staff, personnel, body; **questióne p.** private or personal business.
personalità *nf* personality.
personalménte *ad* personally.
personificàre *vt* to personify.
personificàto *a* personified; **è la bontà personificàta** he is goodness itself.
perspicàce *a* shrewd.
perspicàcia *nf* shrewdness.
perspícuo *a* clear.
persuadére *vt* to persuade, convince.
persuaṣióne *nf* persuasion, conviction.
persuaṣívo *a* persuasive.
pertànto *cj* therefore.
pèrtica *nf* rod, pole, perch.
pertinàce *a* persistent.
pertinàcia *nf* pertinacity.
pertinènte *a* relevant.
pertinènza *nf* pertinence, relevance; **non è di mía p.** it is not my business.
perturbàre *vt* to disturb, perturb.
Perú *nm* (*geogr*) Peru; **peruviàno** *a nm* Peruvian.
perugíno *a nm* (inhabitant) of Perugia.
pervàdere *vt* to pervade.
pervenire *vi* to arrive, reach.
perversióne *nf* perversion.
perversità *nf* wickedness.
pervèrso *a* immoral, wicked.
pervertiménto *nm* perversion.
pervertíre *vt* to lead astray, pervert; **-rsi** *vr* to go astray; **pervèrto** *a nm* pervert(ed).
pervicàce *a* obstinate.
pesànte *a* heavy; wearisome; weighty.
pesantézza *nf* heaviness.
pesàre *vti* to weigh.
pesàto *a* pondered, well-considered.
pèsca *nf* peach.
pésca *nf* fishery, fishing.
pescàre *vt* to fish, catch, (*fig*) fish out.
pescatóre *nm* fisherman.
pésce *nm* fish; **p. rósso** goldfish; **non sapére che pésci pigliàre** to be at one's wits' end; **p. d'apríle** April fool.
pescecàne *nm* shark; (*fig*) profiteer.
pescheréccio *a* fishing; *nm* fishing-boat.
pescheria *nf* fish-market, -shop.
pescivéndolo *nm* fishmonger.
pèsco *nm* peach tree.
péso *nm* weight, burden.
pessimiṣmo *nm* pessimism.
pessimísta *nmf* pessimist.
pessimístico *pl* **-ici** *a* pessimistic.

pèssimo *a* very bad.
pésta *nf* footprint, track; **trovàrsi nèlle péste** to be in difficulties.
pestàre *vt* to crush, pound, tread on.
pèste *nf* plague.
pestèllo *nm* pestle.
pestífero *a* pestilential.
pestilènza *nf* pestilence.
pestilenziàle *a* pestilential.
pésto *a* pounded; **búio p.** pitch dark; **càrta pésta** papier-mâché; *nm* Genoese sauce.
pètalo *nm* petal.
petàrdo *nm* petard; (*firework*) cracker.
petizióne *nf* petition.
petrificàre *vt* to petrify.
petrolièra *nf* (oil-)tanker.
petrolífero *a* oil, petroliferous; **pòzzo p.** oil-well.
petròlio *nm* oil, paraffin, kerosene.
petróso *a* stony.
pettegolàre *vi* to gossip; **pettegolézzo** *nm* gossiping.
pettégolo *a* gossiping; *nm* (*person*) gossip.
pettinàre *vt* to comb; **-rsi** *vr* to do one's hair; **pettinatrice** *nf* hairdresser.
pettinatúra *nf* hairstyle.
pèttine *nm* comb.
pettirósso *nm* robin(redbreast).
pètto *nm* breast, chest; **giàcca a ún (dòppio) pètto** single(double)-breasted jacket.
pettorúto *a* proud, haughty; full-breasted.
petulànte *a* cheeky.
petulànza *nf* arrogance, impertinence.
pèzza *nf* patch, cloth, (*material*) bolt.
pezzènte *nm* beggar.
pèzzo *nm* piece; time; **p. gròsso** bigwig.
piacènte *a* pleasant, attractive.
piacére *vi* to please; **quésto mi piàce** I like this; *nm* pleasure, favor; **avére il p. (di)** to be glad (to); **per p.** please.
piacévole *a* pleasant, enjoyable.
piacevolménte *ad* pleasantly, agreeably.
piàga *nf* sore, evil.
piagnistèo *nm* whine, moaning.
piagnucolàre *vi* to whimper.
piàlla *nf* (*tec*) plane; **piallàre** *vt* to plane.
piallatríce *nf* planing machine.
piàna *nf* plain.
pianaménte *ad* quietly, slowly.
pianèlla *nf* slipper.
pianeròttolo *nm* landing.
pianéta *nm* planet.
piàngere *vti* to cry, weep, lament.
pianificàre *vt* to plan.
pianísta *nmf* pianist.
piàno *a* flat, smooth, plain; *ad* quietly, slowly; *nm* plain, plane; floor; plan.
piano(fòrte) *nm* piano(forte); **p. a códa** grand piano.
piànta *nf* plant; plan, map; sole.
piantagióne *nf* plantation.
piantàre *vt* to plant; fix; quit; **p. in àsso** leave in the lurch; **piàntala!** cut it out!; **-rsi** *vr* to place oneself.
piantatóre *nm* **-tríce** *nf* planter.
pianterréno *nm* ground floor, first floor.
piànto *nm* weeping, tears *pl*.
piantonàre *vt* to keep a watch on, keep under guard.
pianúra *nf* plain.
piàstra *nf* slab, (*of metal*) plate; **piastrélla** *nf* tile.
piastrína *nf* plaque, (*mil*) badge; **p. di riconosciménto** identity disk, identification tag.
piattafórma *nf* platform.
piattíno *nm* saucer.
piàtto *a* flat; *nm* dish, plate; **p. grànde** platter.
piàttola *nf* cockroach; crab-louse; (*fig*) a bore.
piàzza *nf* square; **p. del mercàto** market-place; **p. d'àrmi** parade-ground; **automòbile da p.** taxi; **fàre p. pulíta** to make a clean sweep.
piazzafòrte *nf* stronghold, fort.
piazzàle *nm* large square.
piazzàre *vt* to place, set; **-rsi** *vr* (*racing*) to be placed.
piazzísta *nm* commercial traveler.
piazzuòla *nf* (*aut*) lay-by.
pícca *nf* pique; (*mil*) pike; *pl* (*cards*) spades *pl*.
piccànte *a* spicy, piquant.
piccàrsi (di) *vr* to claim (to); pride oneself (on); persist (in).
picchétto *nm* tent peg, stake; (*mil*) picket; (*cards*) piquet.
picchiàre *vti* to beat, hit, knock, strike; (*av*) dive; **-rsi** *vr* come to blows; **picchiàta** *nf* thrashing; (*av*) dive.
picchiettío *nm* drumming, tapping.
pícchio *nm* blow, knock; woodpecker.
piccíno *a* little; *nm* child.
piccionàia *nf* loft, pigeon-loft; (*theat*) gallery.
piccióne *nm* pigeon; **p. viaggiatóre** carrier pigeon.
pícco *pl* **pícchi** *nm* peak, top; **a p.** perpendicularly; **andàre a p.** (*naut*) to go to the bottom.
piccolézza *nf* smallness, trifle.
píccolo *a* small, young, petty; *nm* child; **i píccoli** the little ones.
piccóne *nm* pickaxe.
piccòzza *nf* axe; **p. da alpinísta** ice-axe.
pidocchiería *nf* stinginess, meanness.
pidòcchio *nm* louse.
pidocchióso *a* filthy; stingy.
piède *nm* foot; **a pièdi** on foot; **a pièdi núdi** barefoot; **stàre in pièdi** to stand.

piedistàllo *nm* pedestal.
pièga *nf* crease, fold, pleat; **prèndere úna brútta p.** to take a bad turn; **mèssa in p.** *nf* (*hair*) set.
piegàre *vti* to fold (up), bend; subdue; submit; turn; **-rsi** *vr* to bend, submit.
pieghettàre *vt* to pleat.
pieghévole *a* folding, pliable; submissive.
Piemónte *nm* (*geogr*) Piedmont; **piemontése** *a nmf* Piedmontese.
pièna *nf* flood; crowd.
pienaménte *ad* fully, completely, entirely.
pienézza *nf* fullness.
pièno *a* full; **in p.** completely.
Pièro *nm pr* Peter.
pietà *nf* pity, mercy; piety; (*art*) pietà.
pietànza *nf* (main) course.
pietóso *a* merciful; pitiful, wretched.
piètra *nf* stone.
pietrificàre *vt* to petrify.
pietrína *nf* (*for lighters*) flint.
Piètro *nm pr* Peter.
piève *nf* country parish (church).
píffero *nm* (*mus*) fife.
pigiàma *nm* pajamas *pl*.
pigiàre *vti* to crush, press; **-rsi** *vr* to crowd.
pigióne *nf* rent; **pigionàle** *nm* tenant.
pigliàre *vt* to seize, take.
pigmèo *nm* pygmy.
pignoraménto *nm* distraint.
pignoràre *vt* to distrain.
pigolàre *vi* to chirp.
pigolío *nm* chirping, chirruping.
pigraménte *ad* lazily, sluggishly.
pigrízia *nf* laziness.
pígro *a* lazy, sluggish.
píla *nf* heap, pile; (*el*) battery; (holy-water) stoup.
pilàstro *nm* pillar.
Pilàto *nm pr* Pilate.
píllola *nf* pill.
pilóne *nm* pillar; (*el*) pylon.
pilòta *nm* pilot.
pilotàre *vt* to pilot.
pinacotèca *nf* picture-gallery.
pinéta *nf* pine-wood.
píngue *a* fat.
pinguèdine *nf* corpulence, fatness.
pinguíno *nm* penguin.
pínna *nf* fin; (*swimming*) flipper.
pinnàcolo *nm* pinnacle.
píno *nm* pine(-tree).
pínza *nf* pliers *pl*, forceps *pl*; **pinzétta** *nf* tweezers *pl*.
Pío *nm pr* Pius.
pío *a* pious, charitable.
pioggerèlla *nf* drizzle, gentle rain.
piòggia *nf* rain; **p. radioattiva** fallout.
piòlo *nm* peg; (*of ladder*) rung.
piombàre *vt* to seal, cover (with lead); (*tooth*) stop; *vi* fall, plunge.
piómbo *nm* (*metal*) lead.
pionière *nm* pioneer.
piòppo *nm* poplar.
piovàno *a* **àcqua piovàna** rain-water.
piòvere *vti* to rain; **p. a dirótto, p. a catinélle** to pour.
pioviggìnàre *vi* to drizzle.
pioviggìnóso, piovóso *a* drizzling, rainy.
piovosità *nf* rainfall.
pípa *nf* (smoker's) pipe.
pipistrèllo *nm* bat.
píra *nf* pyre.
piràmide *nf* pyramid.
piràta *nm* pirate.
pirateria *nf* piracy.
pírica, pólvere *nf* gunpowder.
piròfila *nf* fire-resisting glassware.
piròscafo *nm* steamer, steamship.
pirotècnica *nf* fireworks *pl*, pyrotechnics *pl*.
piscína *nf* fish-pond; swimming-pool.
pişèllo *nm* pea.
pişolíno *nm* nap, snooze.
písta *nf* race course, track; (*av*) runway.
pistàcchio *nm* pistachio.
pistíllo *nm* pistil.
pistòla *nf* pistol.
pistóne *nm* piston.
pitòcco *pl* **-òcchi** *a* stingy; *nm* beggar; miser.
pittóre *nm* **-tríce** *nf* painter.
pittorésco *a* picturesque.
pittúra *nf* painting.
pitturàre *vti* to paint.
più *ad* longer, more, most; **non . . . p.** no longer; **mài p.** never again; **sèmpre p.** more and more; **per di p.** moreover; **per lo p.** generally.
piúma *nf* feather, plume.
piumíno *nm* eiderdown; powder-puff.
piuttòsto (che, di) *ad* rather (than).
píva *nf* bagpipe.
pivière *nm* plover.
pizzería *nf* pizza shop, pizza restaurant.
pizzicàgnolo *nm* delicatessen seller.
pizzicàre *vti* to nip; itch.
pizzichería *nf* delicatessen shop.
pízzico *pl* **-chi** *nm* pinch; **pizzicóre** *nm* itch.
pízzo *nm* lace; pointed beard; (*mountain*) peak.
placàre *vt* to appease, soothe; **-rsi** *vr* subside.
plàcca *nf* plate, plaque; (*in throat*) spot.
plàcido *a* placid, peaceful.
plafóne *nm* ceiling.
plagiàrio *nm* plagiarist.
plàgio *nm* plagiarism.
planàre *vi* (*av*) to glide down.
planetàrio *a* planetary; *nm* planetarium.
plaşmàre *vt* to mold.
plàstica *nf* plastic; modelling; plastic surgery.
plàtano *nm* plane (tree).

platèa *nf* (*theat*) orchestra seats *pl*.
plàtino *nm* platinum.
plauşíbile *a* acceptable, reasonable.
plàuşo *nm* applause, praise.
plebàglia *nf* mob, rabble.
plèbe *nf* common people.
plebèo *a* plebeian, vulgar; *nm* commoner.
plebiscíto *nm* plebiscite.
plenàrio *a* plenary.
plenilúnio *nm* full moon.
plenipotenziàrio *a nm* plenipotentiary.
pleuríte *nf* (*med*) pleurisy.
plíco *pl* **plíchi** *nm* envelope, packet.
plotóne *nm* (*mil*) platoon, squad.
plúmbeo *a* leaden.
pluràle *a nm* plural.
pneumàtico *pl* **-ici** *a* pneumatic; *nm* tire.
po' *v* **pòco**.
pòco *pl* **pòchi** *a pron* little (*pl* few); *ad* (very) little, a little while; **fra p.** soon; **p. fa** not long ago; **un po' per** what with . . .
podàgra *nf* (*med*) gout.
podére *nm* farm.
poderóso *a* mighty, powerful.
podestà *nm* mayor.
podişmo *nm* (*sport*) walking.
poèma *nm* long poem.
poeşía *nf* poem, poetry.
poèta *nm* poet.
poetéssa *nf* poetess.
poètico *pl* **-ici** *a* poetical.
poggiàre *vi* to rest; (*mil*) move.
pòggio *nm* hillock, knoll.
poggiòlo *nm* balcony.
pòi *ad* afterwards, then; **da óra in p.** from now on; **da allóra in p.** from that time on; **o príma o p.** sooner or later.
poichè *cj* since, as, for, after, when.
polàcco *pl* **-àcchi** *a* Polish; *nm* Pole.
polàre *a* polar.
polèmica *nf* controversy, polemic(s).
polènta *nf* corn meal.
poligamía *nf* polygamy.
polígamo *a* polygamous; *nm* polygamist.
poliglòtta *a nm* polyglot.
polígono *nm* polygon.
polímero *nm* (*chem*) polymer.
poliomielíte *nf* poliomyelitis.
pòlipo *nm* polyp; (*med*) polypus.
politeàma *nm* theater.
politècnico *pl* **-ici** *a nm* polytechnic.
politène *nm* polythene.
política *nf* politics, policy.
político *pl* **-ici** *a* politic(al); *nm* politician.
poliviníle *nm* (*chem*) polyvinyl.
polizía *nf* police.
poliziésco *pl* **-chi** *a* police; **film p.** detective film.
poliziòtto *nm* policeman, constable, patrolman.
pòlizza *nf* (*com*) policy, bill.
pollàio *nm* hen-house, poultry-yard.
pollàme *nm* poultry.
pollàstra *nf* pullet; **pollàstro** *nm* cockerel.
pollería *nf* poultry shop.
pòllice *nm* thumb, big toe; inch.
pòlline *nm* pollen.
póllo *nm* chicken, fowl.
polluzióne *nf* pollution.
polmonàre *a* pulmonary.
polmóne *nm* lung.
polmoníte *nf* pneumonia.
pòlo *nm* (*el and geogr*) pole.
Polònia *nf* (*geogr*) Poland.
pólpa *nf* (*fruit*) pulp; boned meat.
polpétta *nf* rissole.
pólpo *nm* octopus.
polsíno *nm* cuff.
pólso *nm* pulse; wrist; **di p.** energetic.
poltíglia *nf* mush, mud, slush.
poltríre *vi* to lie lazily in bed, idle.
poltróna *nf* armchair, easy chair; orchestra seat; **p. a dondolo** rocking chair; **poltroncina** *nf* back orchestra seat.
poltróne *nm* idler.
poltronería *nf* laziness.
pólvere *nf* dust, powder; **p. néra da spàro** gunpowder; **caffè in p.** ground coffee.
polverizzàre *vt* to pulverize.
polveróne *nm* cloud of dust.
polveróso *a* dusty.
pomàta *nf* ointment.
pomèllo *nm* knob, grip; cheek-bone.
pomeridiàno *a* (in the) afternoon.
pomeríggio *nm* afternoon.
pómice *nf* pumice(-stone).
pómo *nm* apple(-tree); head; knob.
pomodòro, pomidòro *pl* **pomodòri, pomidòri** *nm* tomato.
pomogranàto *nm* pomegranate.
pómpa *nf* pump; pomp, display; **far p.** di to display, show off.
pompàre *vt* to pump (up).
pompèlmo *nm* grapefruit.
pompière *nm* fireman; **pompièri (córpo dèi)** fire brigade, fire department.
pompóso *a* pompous.
pònce *nm* (*drink*) punch.
ponderàre *vti* to ponder, consider.
ponderazióne *nf* cautious deliberation, reflection.
ponènte *nm* west.
pónte *nm* bridge; (*naut*) deck.
pontéfice *nm* pontiff, pope.
pontifício *a* papal.
pontíle *nm* landing-stage.
pontóne *nm* pontoon.
popolàno *a* of the (common) people; *nm* man of the people.
popolàre *vt* to populate, people; **-rsi** *vr* to become populated; *a* popular, working-class; **cànto p.** folksong.
popolarésco *pl* **-chi** *a* popular.
popolarizzàre *vt* to popularize.
popolazióne *nf* people, population.
pòpolo *nm* nation, people.
popolóso *a* populous.
popóne *nm* melon.

póppa *nf* (woman's) breast; (*naut*) stern.
poppàre *vti* to suck.
porcellàna *nf* china, porcelain.
porcherìa *nf* dirt, dirty trick.
porcíle *nm* (pig)sty.
pòrco *pl* **-ci** *nm* pig, swine; *a* dirty, horrible.
porcospíno *nm* hedgehog; porcupine.
pòrfido *nm* porphyry.
pòrgere *vt* to give, hand, offer, present, tender.
pòro *nm* pore.
porosità *nf* porousness.
poróso *a* porous.
pórpora *nf* purple.
pórre *vt* to place, put, set.
pòrro *nm* leek; wart.
pòrta *nf* door, gate, gateway, (*football*) goal.
portabagàgli *nm* porter; luggage rack, baggage rack.
portacénere *nm* ashtray.
portacípria *nm* powder-compact.
portaèrei *nf* aircraft carrier.
portafògli *nm* wallet, pocketbook; **portafòglio** *nm* wallet, pocketbook, portfolio.
portafortúna *nm* mascot.
portalèttere *nm* postman.
portaménto *nm* bearing, carriage.
portamonéte *nm* purse.
portaombrèlli *nm* umbrella stand.
portàre *vt* to bear, bring, carry, take; wear.
portaritràtti *nm* photograph frame.
portasapóne *nm* soap-dish.
portasigarétte *nm* cigarette case.
portàta *nf* capacity; course, dish, importance; range; **a p. di màno** (with)in reach; **di gràn p.** far reaching.
portàtile *a* portable.
portatóre *nm* bearer, holder.
portauòvo *nm* eggcup.
portavivànde *nm* dumbwaiter.
portavóce *nm* mouthpiece; megaphone; spokesman.
portènto *nm* marvel, prodigy.
portentóso *a* prodigious, wonderful.
pòrtico *pl* **-ici** *nm* porch, portico; *pl* arcade.
portièra *nf* door curtain; doorkeeper('s wife); (*aut*) door.
portière *nm* caretaker, (hotel-) porte doorman, janitor; (*sport*) goal-keeper.
portinàio *v* **portière**.
portinerìa *nf* porter's lodge.
pòrto *nm* port, harbor; (*com*) carriage; **p. frànco** carriage free.
Portogàllo *nm* (*geogr*) Portugal.
portoghése *a nmf* Portuguese; (*sl*) gatecrasher.
portóne *nm* main door, front door.
porzióne *nf* portion, share.
pòsa *nf* pause; pose; laying; (*phot*) exposure.
posamíne *nm* (*naut*) mine-layer.
posàre *vt* to lay, put (down); *vi* to pose; rest; **-rsi** *vr* to alight, stay.
posàta *nf* article of cutlery.
posàto *a* sedate, calm.
poscrítto *nm* postscript, footnote.
posdomàni *ad* the day after tomorrow.
positíva *nf* (*phot*) positive.
positívo *a* certain, matter-of-fact, positive.
posizióne *nf* position.
pospórre *vt* to place after, postpone.
posposizióne *nf* postponement.
possedére *vt* to possess.
possediménto *nm* possession, property.
possènte *a* powerful.
possèsso *nm* possession, property.
possessóre *nm* owner, possessor.
possíbile *a* possible; **fàre túto il p.** to do one's best.
possibilità *nf* possibility, power.
possidènte *nmf* landowner, property owner.
pòsta *nf* mail, post (office); stake, bet; **p. per l'intérno** inland mails, domestic mails; **a bèlla p.** on purpose.
postàle *a* post, postal; **vagóne p.** mail van, mail car (railway post office).
postàre *vt* to place, station.
postéggio *nm* park, parking; **p. di tassì** cabrank, cabstand.
pòsteri *nm pl* descendants *pl*, posterity.
posterióre *a* back, hind, posterior.
posterità *nf* posterity.
postíccio *a* artificial, false.
posticipazióne *nf* delay, postponement.
postílla *nf* (foot)note.
postíno *nm* postman.
pósto *a* placed, situated; *nm* place, room, seat; job; **c'è p.?** is there any room?
postulànte *nmf* applicant, petitioner.
pòstumo *a* posthumous.
potàbile *a* drinkable, drinking; **àcqua non p.** water unfit for drinking.
potàre *vt* to lop, prune.
potàssio *nm* potassium.
potènte *a* mighty, powerful.
potènza *nf* might, power, strength.
potenziàle *a nm* potential.
potére *vi* to be able (can), be allowed (may); *nm* authority, power; **può dàrsi** it may be.
pòvero *a* poor; *nm* poor man, beggar.
povertà *nf* poverty.
pozióne *nf* draft, potion.
pózza *nf* puddle, pool.
pozzànghera *nf* puddle.
pózzo *nm* well; mine-shaft.
pranzàre *vi* to dine; lunch.
prànzo *nm* lunch, dinner; **sàla da p.** *nf* dining room; **dópo p.** in the afternoon.

Pràga *nf* (*geogr*) Prague.
pratería *nf* grassland, prairie.
pràtica *nf* practice, training; affair; **pràtiche religióse** *nf pl* religious observances.
praticàbile *a* practicable; **stràda p.** passable road.
praticànte *a nmf* practicing, regular church-goer.
praticàre *vt* to practice; frequent.
pràtico *pl* **-ici** *a* practical, experienced; **èssere p. di** *vi* to be familiar with.
pràto *nm* meadow, lawn.
pratolína *nf* daisy.
Preàlpi (le) *nf pl* (*geogr*) the Pre-Alps.
preàmbolo *nm* preamble.
preavvíso *nm* forewarning, notice.
precàrio *a* precarious.
precauzióne *nf* care, precaution.
precedènte *a* preceding, previous; *nm* precedent; **buòni precedènti** good record.
precedenteménte *ad* previously, formerly.
precedènza *nf* precedence, priority; in p. in advance; previously.
precèdere *vt* to go before, precede; *vi* to come first, precede.
precètto *nm* precept, rule, order.
precettóre *nm* **-tríce** *nf* teacher, tutor.
precipitàre *vt* to fling down; *vi* to crash, fall; **-rsi** *vr* to rush, throw oneself.
precipitazióne *nf* fall; haste.
precipitóso *a* hasty, steep.
precipízio *nm* precipice.
precípuo *a* principal, main.
precișaménte *ad* precisely, exactly.
precișàre *vt* to specify.
precișióne *nf* accuracy, exactness.
precíșo *a* accurate, precise, punctual.
preclúdere *vt* to preclude, bar.
precòce *a* precocious, premature.
precocità *nf* precociousness, prematureness.
preconcètto *a* preconceived; *nm* preconception, prejudice.
precursóre *nm* forerunner, precursor.
prèda *nf* prey, plunder.
predatòrio *a* predatory.
predàre *vt* to pillage, plunder, sack.
predecessóre *nm* predecessor.
predestinàre *vt* to predestine.
predétto *a* above-mentioned; foretold.
prèdica *nf* preaching, sermon.
predicàre *vti* to preach.
predicàto *a* preached; exalted; *nm* predicate.
predicatóre *nm* preacher.
predilètto *a nm* favorite.
predilezióne *nf* partiality, fondness.
prediligere *vt* to like better, prefer.
predíre *vt* to foretell, predict.
predispórre *vt* to predispose, arrange.
predizióne *nf* prediction; **p. dell'avvenire** fortune-telling.
predominàre *vti* to (pre)dominate.
predomínio *nm* predominance, supremacy.
predóne *nm* marauder, plunderer.
preeșistènza *nf* pre-existence.
prefabbricàre *vt* to prefabricate.
prefazióne *nf* preface, introduction.
preferènza *nf* preference; **a p. di** rather than; **di p.** preferably.
preferenziàle *a* preferential; **azióni preferenziàli** preference shares, preferred stock.
preferíbile *a* preferable.
preferíre *vt* to prefer, like better.
preferíto *a nm* favorite.
prefètto *nm* prefect.
prefettúra *nf* prefecture.
prefíggersi (di) *vr* to intend (to).
prefiggiménto *nm* determination, resolve.
prefísso *a* intended; *nm* prefix.
pregàre *vti* to pray, ask; **prègo!** *interj* not at all, don't mention it.
pregévole *a* valuable.
preghièra *nf* prayer, request.
pregiàre *vt* to appreciate, esteem, value; **-rsi** *vr* to be honored, have the honor.
pregiàto *a* esteemed; (*com*) favor; valuable; **Pregiatissimo Signóre** (*in letters*) Dear Sir.
prègio *nm* good merit, value.
pregiudicàre *vt* to injure; prejudice.
pregiudicàto *a* bound to fail; *nm* previous offender.
pregiudiziévole *a* prejudicial, detrimental.
pregiudízio *nm* prejudice; detriment.
pregnànte *a* (*lit and fig*) pregnant.
prégno *a* full, impregnated; pregnant.
pregustàre *vt* to anticipate, look forward to.
preistòrico *pl* **-ici** *a* prehistoric.
prelàto *nm* prelate.
prelevaménto *nm* drawing; (*com*) withdrawal.
prelevàre *vt* to draw; withdraw.
prelibàto *a* delicious, excellent.
preliminàre *a nm* preliminary.
prelúdio *nm* prelude.
prematúro *a* premature, untimely.
premeditàre *vt* to plan, premeditate.
premeditazióne *nf* premeditation.
prèmere *vt* to press; *vi* to press; matter.
preméssa *nf* premise, previous statement.
preméttere *vt* to premise, say first, state in advance.
premiàre *vt* to award a prize, reward.
premiazióne *nf* prizegiving.
preminènte *a* pre-eminent.
prèmio *nm* prize, reward; (*com*) premium.
premuníre *vt* to fortify; **-rsi** *vr* to take precautions.

premúra *nf* attention, care; haste.
premurosaménte *ad* solicitously, kindly.
premuróso *a* attentive, solicitous, kind.
prèndere *vt* to take, catch, seize.
prendisóle *nm* sun-suit.
prenotàre *vt* to book, engage.
prenotazióne *nf* booking.
preoccupàre *vt* to make anxious, trouble; **-rsi** *vr* to worry.
preoccupàto *a* anxious, worried.
preoccupazióne *nf* anxiety, care, preoccupation.
preordinàre *vt* to predetermine, prearrange.
preparàre *vt* **-rsi** *vr* to get ready, prepare.
preparatívo *nm* preparation.
preparàto *a* prepared; *nm* (*chemical etc*) preparation.
preparazióne *nf* preparation.
preponderànte *a* predominant, prevailing.
prepórre *vt* to place before, prefer.
preposizióne *nf* preposition.
prepósto *nm* (*eccl*) rector, vicar.
prepotènte *a* overbearing; *nm* bully.
prepotènza *nf* arrogance, bullying.
prerogatíva *nf* prerogative.
présa *nf* grip, hold; seizure; (*el*) (wall-)plug; **màcchina da p.** (*cin*) camera.
preṣàgio *nm* omen, presage.
preṣagíre *vt* to foretell, presage.
preṣàgo *pl* **-ghi** *a* foreboding, having a presentiment of.
prèṣbite *a* long-sighted.
prescégliere *vt* to choose, select.
prescíndere *vi* to leave out of account.
prescrívere *vt* to prescribe, order.
prescrizióne *nf* prescription; regulation.
preṣentàre *vt* to present, introduce; **-rsi** *vr* to present oneself, appear; occur.
preṣentatóre *nm* (*rad and tv*) announcer, (*theat*) master of ceremonies.
preṣentazióne *nf* presentation, introduction.
preṣènte *a nm* present; **tenèr p.** to bear in mind; **i presènti** those present.
presentiménto *nm* presentiment.
presentíre *vt* to have a presentiment, foresee.
preṣènza *nf* presence; **p. di spírito** presence of mind.
preṣèpio *nm* crib.
preservàre *vt* to preserve.
prèside *nm* headmaster, principal.
presidènte *nm* president, chairman.
presidenziàle *a* presidential.
presidiàre *vt* to garrison.
presídio *nm* garrison, defense.
presièdere (a) *vi* to preside (at), be in charge (of).
prèssa *nf* (*mech*) press.
pressànte *a* pressing, urgent.
prèssi *nm pl* neighborhood.
pressióne *nf* pressure.
prèsso *ad* close by, near; *prep* near, beside, with; (*address*) care of; **p. a pòco** *ad* approximately.
pressochè *ad* almost, nearly.
prestabilíre *vt* to pre-arrange.
prestànte *a* good-looking.
prestàre *vt* to lend; pay (*attention etc*); **fàrsi p.** *vt* to borrow; **-rsi** *vr* to be fit for, lend oneself.
prestazióne *nf* performance; **prestazióni** *pl* services.
prestigiatóre *nm* conjurer, juggler.
prestígio *nm* prestige, conjuring.
prèstito *nm* loan; **avére in p.** to borrow; **dàre in p.** to lend.
prèsto *ad* soon, early, quickly; *interj* (be) quick! **far p.** to make haste; **al piú p.** as soon as possible.
preṣúmere *vi* to presume, suppose.
preṣumíbile *a* presumable.
preṣuntuóso *a* conceited, presumptuous.
preṣunzióne *nf* presumption.
presuppórre *vti* to (pre)suppose.
presuppósto *a* presupposed; *nm* presupposition.
prète *nm* priest.
pretendènte *nmf* claimant, suitor.
pretèndere *vt* to claim, want; *vi* to claim, pretend.
pretensióne *nf* pretention, claim.
pretésa *nf* claim; pretense; pretension; **sènza pretése** unpretentious.
pretèsto *nm* pretext, occasion.
pretóre *nm* magistrate.
prètto *a* pure, real.
pretúra *nf* magistrate's court.
prevalènte *a* prevalent, prevailing.
prevalènza *nf* prevalence, supremacy.
prevalére *vi* to prevail.
prevedére *vt* to foresee.
prevedíbile *a* to be expected.
preveggènza *nf* foresight.
prevenire *vt* to precede, forestall, prevent, warn.
preventivàre *vt* (*com*) to estimate.
preventívo *a* preventive; *nm* (*com*) estimate.
prevenzióne *nf* bias, prejudice, prevention.
previdènte *a* provident.
previdènza *nf* foresight; **p. sociàle** social security.
prèvio *a* previous, subject to.
previṣióne *nf* forecast, expectation.
preziosísmo *nm* (*liter*) preciosity.
preziosità *nf* preciousness, preciosity.
prezióso *a* precious, valuable.
prezzémolo *nm* parsley.
prèzzo *nm* price.
prigióne *nf* jail, prison, penitentiary.
prigionía *nf* imprisonment.
prigionièro *nm* prisoner.
príma *ad* before, sooner, first,

formerly; **quànto p.** very soon; **p. di** *prep*, **p. che** *cj* before.
primàrio *a* primary, chief; *nm* chief physician.
primatíccio *a* early.
primàto *nm* pre-eminence; (*sport*) record.
primavèra *nf* spring, springtime.
primaveríle *a* (of the) spring.
primeggiàre *vi* to excel.
primièro *a* first, former, previous.
primitívo *a* primitive, original.
primízia *nf* early fruit or vegetable; novelty.
prímo *a nm* first, former; **di príma màno** first hand; **di prím'òrdine** first rate.
primogènito *a nm* first-born.
primòrdio *nm* beginning.
prímula *nf* primrose.
principàle *a* principal, main; *nm* principal, employer, manager.
principalménte *ad* mainly, chiefly.
principàto *nm* principality.
príncipe *nm* prince; **principéssa** *nf* princess.
principiànte *nmf* beginner.
principiàre *vt* to begin, start.
princípio *nm* beginning; principle.
prióre *nm* prior.
privàre *vt* to deprive, strip.
privataménte *ad* privately.
privatísta *nmf* external student.
privatíva *nf* monopoly; tobacconist's.
privàto *a* private; *nm* private citizen.
privazióne *nf* (de)privation.
privilegiàto *a* privileged; (*com*) preference.
privilègio *nm* privilege.
prívo (di) *a* devoid (of), lacking (in).
prò *nm* advantage, benefit, profit; **a che p.?** what is the use?; **buòn p. gli fàccia!** much good may it do him!
probàbile *a* probable, likely.
probabilità *nf* probability, chance.
probità *nf* honesty, probity.
problèma *nm* problem.
problemàtico *pl* **-ici** *a* difficult, uncertain.
pròbo *a* honest, upright.
probòscide *nf* trunk; proboscis.
procacciàre *vt* **-rsi** *vr* to get, procure, earn.
procàce *a* provocative.
procacità *nf* procacity, sauciness, impudence.
procèdere *vi* to proceed; behave; *nm* process; behavior.
procediménto *nm* conduct; course; process.
processàre *vt* (*leg*) to try; **far p.** to bring to trial.
processióne *nf* procession.
procèsso *nm* process; (*leg*) trial.
procínto *nm* **èssere in p. di** to be on the point of.
proclàma *nm* proclamation.
proclamàre *vt* to proclaim.
proclíve *a* inclined; **proclività** *nf* tendency.
procrastinàre *vti* to postpone, put off.
procreàre *vt* to procreate, generate.
procreazióne *nf* procreation.
procúra *nf* power of attorney, proxy.
procuràre *vt* to get; cause; provide; try; **-rsi** *vr* to get, procure.
procuratóre *nm* attorney, solicitor; (*eccl*) procurator; **P. Generàle** Attorney General.
pròde *a* brave, valiant; *nm* hero.
prodézza *nf* gallant deed, gallantry.
prodigalità *nf* lavishness, prodigality.
prodigàre *vt* to lavish, pour out; **-rsi** *vr* to do one's best.
prodígio *nm* marvel, prodigy.
pròdigo *pl* **-ghi** *a* lavish, prodigal; *nm* prodigal.
proditoriaménte *ad* treacherously.
prodòtto *a* produced; *nm* product, produce.
prodúrre *vt* to produce, yield; cause; **-rsi** *vr* to appear in public; happen.
produttività *nf* productiveness, productivity.
produttívo *a* productive, fruitful.
produttóre *a* producing; *nm* **-tríce** *nf* producer, maker.
produzióne *nf* production, manufacture; exhibition.
proèmio *nm* introduction, preface.
profanàre *vt* to profane, debase.
profanazióne *nf* profanation.
profàno *a* profane, secular; *nm* profane, layman.
proferíre *vt* to utter.
professàre *vt* to profess.
professióne *nf* profession, trade, occupation; **di p.** by profession.
professionísta *nm* professional man; (*sport*) professional.
professóre *nm* (school) master, teacher, (*university*) professor; **professoréssa** *nf* professor, mistress.
profèta *nm* prophet; **profetéssa** *nf* prophetess.
profetàre, profetizzàre *vt* to prophesy.
profezía *nf* prophecy.
profferíre *vt* to offer; utter.
proffèrta *nf* offer.
profícuo *a* profitable, useful.
profilàssi *nf* (*med*) prophylaxis.
profílo *nm* profile, outline.
profittàre *vi* to profit, make progress.
profítto *nm* profit, benefit.
proflúvio *nm* overflow, abundance.
profondaménte *ad* deeply, profoundly.
profóndere *vt* to lavish, squander; **-rsi** *vr* to be lavish.
profondità *nf* depth, profundity.
profóndo *a* deep, profound; *nm* depth.

pròfugo *pl* **-ghi** *nm* refugee.
profumàre *vt* to perfume, scent; **-rsi** *vr* to put on scent.
profumería *nf* perfumer's shop; perfumery.
profumière *nm* perfumer; **negòzio di p.** perfumer's shop.
profúmo *nm* perfume, scent.
profuṣióne *nf* abundance, profusion.
progènie *nf* progeny, descendants *pl*, issue.
progenitóre *nm* ancestor, forefather **-tríce** *nf* ancestor.
progettàre *vt* to plan.
progètto *nm* plan, project, scheme; **p. di lègge** bill.
prògnoṣi *nf* (*med*) prognosis.
prográmma *nm* program, prospectus, syllabus.
progredíre *vi* to advance, (make) progress.
progredíto *a* advanced, civilized.
progrèsso *nm* progress, headway.
proibíre *vi* to forbid, prohibit, prevent.
proibitívo *a* prohibitive.
proibizióne *nf* prohibition.
proiettàre *vti* to project, cast; (*cin*) to screen.
proièttile *nm* projectile, shell.
proiettóre *nm* searchlight, floodlight; projector; (*aut*) headlight.
proiezióne *nf* projection; (*film*) showing, slide.
pròle *nf pl* children, issue.
proletariàto *nm* proletariat.
proletàrio *a nm* proletarian.
prolífico *pl* **-ici** *a* prolific.
prolísso *a* long-winded, prolix.
pròlogo *pl* **-ghi** *nm* prologue.
prolungaménto *nm* prolongation, extension, continuation.
prolungàre *vt* to extend, prolong; **-rsi** *vr* to continue, extend.
proluṣióne *nf* inaugural lecture.
proméssa *nf* promise.
promettènte *a* promising.
prométtere *vti* to promise.
prominènte *a* prominent, jutting.
prominènza *nf* prominence.
promíscuo *a* promiscuous, mixed.
promontòrio *nm* headland, promontory.
promòsso *a* promoted, (*of candidate in exam*) successful.
promozióne *nf* promotion; **avére la p.** to pass (exam).
promulgàre *vt* to promulgate.
promuòvere *vt* to promote, pass; cause.
pròno *a* prone.
pronóme *nm* pronoun.
pronòstico *pl* **-ici** *nm* forecast.
prontaménte *ad* readily, immediately, promptly.
prontézza *nf* quickness, readiness, promptitude.
prónto *a* ready, prompt; (*on telephone*) hello!; **prónta càssa** ready cash.
pronúncia *nf* pronunciation.
pronunciàre *vt* to pronounce, utter; **-rsi** *vr* to express one's opinion.
propagànda *nf* propaganda, advertising.
propagàre *vt* **-rsi** *vr* to propagate, spread.
propàggine *nf* ramification, lineage; (*agr*) layer.
propalàre *vt* to divulge, spread.
propèndere *vi* to incline.
propensióne *nf* propensity.
propènso *a* inclined, ready.
propiziàre *vt* **-rsi** *vr* to propitiate.
propízio *a* favorable, propitious.
proponiménto *nm* resolution, resolve.
propórre *vt* to propose, suggest; **-rsi** *vr* to intend, resolve.
proporzionàle *a* proportional.
proporzionàto *a* proportioned, proportionate; suitable.
proporzióne *nf* proportion.
propòṣito *nm* purpose; **a p.** by the by, by the way; **di p.** on purpose.
propósta *nf* proposal, proposition.
propriaménte *ad* properly, really, exactly.
proprietàrio *nm* owner, proprietor; (*newspaper*) publisher.
pròprio *a* (one's) own, characteristic; *nm* one's own; *ad* exactly, just, really.
propugnàre *vt* to plead for, support.
propulsióne *nf* propulsion.
pròra *nf* (*naut*) bow, prow.
pròroga *nf* adjournment, postponement, extension, respite.
prorogàre *vt* to postpone, put off, extend.
prorómpere *vi* to burst (out), gush.
pròṣa *nf* prose; (*theat*) drama.
proṣàico *pl* **-ici** *a* prosaic.
prosciògliere *vt* to release; (*leg*) acquit.
prosciugaménto *nm* draining, reclamation; drying up.
prosciugàre *vt* to drain, dry, reclaim; *vi and* **-rsi** *vr* to dry (up).
prosciútto *nm* ham.
proscrítto *a* outlawed, exile; *nm* outlaw, exile.
proscrizióne *nf* proscription, banishment.
proseguiménto *nm* continuation.
proseguíre *vt* to continue, go on, pursue.
prosèlito *nm* proselyte.
proṣodía *nf* prosody.
prosperàre *vi* to prosper, thrive.
prosperità *nf* prosperity, wealth.
pròspero *a* prosperous, fortunate.
prosperóso *a* prosperous; healthy, plump.
prospettiva *nf* perspective; prospect, view, outlook.
prospètto *nm* prospect, view; prospectus.
prospiciènte *a* facing, opposite.
prossimaménte *ad* before long, in

the near future; (*in film programs*) coming shortly; *nm* trailer.
prossimità *nf* nearness, proximity, vicinity.
pròssimo *a* near, next; *nm* neighbor; **in un p. avvenire** in the near future.
prostituíre *vt* to prostitute; **-rsi** *vr* to prostitute oneself, sell oneself.
prostitúta *nf* prostitute.
prostituzióne *nf* prostitution.
prostràre *vt* to prostrate, overwhelm; exhaust; **-rsi** *vr* to bow down; get exhausted.
prostrazióne *nf* prostration, exhaustion.
protagonísta *nmf* chief character, protagonist.
protèggere *vt* to protect, defend, support.
proteína *nf* protein.
protèndere *vt* to hold out, stretch; **-rsi in avànti** *vr* to lean forward.
protèsta *nf* protest(ation).
protestànte *a nmf* Protestant.
protestàre *vti* to protest.
protestàto *a* protested (*also com*); **protèsto** *nm* (*com*) protest.
protètto *a* protected, sheltered; *nm* favorite, protégé.
protettóre *nm* **-tríce** *nf* patron, protector.
protezióne *nf* protection, patronage.
protocòllo *nm* protocol; record; **formàto p.** foolscap (size).
protòtipo *nm* prototype.
protràrre *vt* to protract, put off.
protrazióne *nf* protraction, deferment.
protruberànza *nf* protruberance.
protuberànte *a* protuberant, bulging.
pròva *nf* proof; evidence; test; rehearsal.
provàre *vt* to prove; show; try (on); feel; rehearse; **-rsi** *vr* to endeavor, try.
proveniènza *nf* origin, source.
proveníre *vi* to come (from); be caused (by).
provènto *nm* income, proceeds *pl*.
Provènza *nf* (*geogr*) Provence.
provenzàle *a nmf* Provençal.
proverbiàle *a* proverbial.
provèrbio *nm* proverb, saying.
provétta *nf* test-tube.
provètto *a* experienced, skilled.
província *nf* province, district.
provinciàle *a* provincial; **stràda p.** *nf* highway, main road.
províno *nm* test-tube; (*cin*) film-test.
provocànte *a* provocative.
provocàre *vt* to provoke, cause, stir up.
provocazióne *nf* provocation.
provolóne *nm* a kind of cheese.
provvedére (di) *vt* to provide (with); **p. a** *vi* to provide (for); **-rsi** *vr* to provide oneself.
provvediménto *nm* measure, provision.
provvidènza *nf* providence; (*fig*) boon.
provvidenziàle *a* providential.
pròvvido *a* provident, thrifty.
provvigióne *nf* (*com*) commission; provision.
provvisòrio *a* provisional, temporary.
provvísta *nf* supply.
prúa *v* **próra.**
prudènte *a* prudent, careful.
prudènza *nf* prudence, caution.
prúdere *vi* to itch.
prúgna *nf* plum; **prúgno** *nm* plum-tree.
prúno *nm* thorn-bush; thorn.
pruríto *nm* itch(ing).
pseudònimo *a* pseudonymous; *nm* pseudonym, pen-name.
psicanàlisi *nm* psychoanalysis.
psicanalísta *nmf* psychoanalyst.
psichiàtra *nmf* psychiatrist; **psichiatría** *nf* psychiatry.
psicología *nf* psychology; **psicològico** *pl* **-ici** *a* psychological; **psicòlogo** *pl* **-ogi** *nm* psychologist.
pubblicàre *vt* to publish, issue.
pubblicazióne *nf* publication, issue.
pubblicità *nf* publicity, advertising.
pubblicitàrio *a* advertising.
púbblico *pl* **-ici** *a* public; *nm* audience, public.
pubertà *nf* puberty.
pudicízia *nf* modesty.
pudíco *pl* **-chi** *a* modest, bashful.
pudóre *nm* decency, modesty.
pueríle *a* childish, puerile.
puerízia *nf* childhood.
pugilàto *nm* boxing.
púgile *nm* boxer, pugilist.
Púglia *nf* (*geogr*) Apulia.
pugliése *a nm* (inhabitant) of Apulia.
pugnalàre *vt* to stab.
pugnalàta *nf* stab.
pugnàle *nm* dagger.
púgno *nm* fist; blow; handful; **in p.** in one's hands; **fàre a púgni** fight, clash.
púlce *nf* flea.
pulcíno *nm* chick(en).
pulédro *nm* colt, foal.
puléggia *nf* pulley.
pulíre *vt* to clean, polish, wash.
pulíto *a* clean, clear, neat.
pulizía *nf* cleaning; cleanliness, cleanness.
pullman *nm* motor-coach; (*rly*) Pullman car.
pullóver *nm* pullover.
pullulàre di *vi* to be full of, swarm with, pullulate with.
pulvíscolo *nm* fine dust, motes *pl*.
púlpito *nm* pulpit.
pulsànte *a* pulsating, throbbing; *nm* push-button; **p. da campanèllo** bell push.
pulsàre *vi* to beat, pulsate, throb.

pulsazióne *nf* beat, pulsation, throb.
pungènte *a* prickly, stinging, pungent.
púngere *vt* to prick, sting.
pungiglióne *nm* sting.
púngolo *nm* goad, spur.
puníre *vt* to punish.
punizióne *nf* punishment.
púnta *nf* point, tip, end; top; headland; a little; **in p. di pièdi** on tiptoe.
puntàre *vt* to point, aim; push; bet; **p. i pièdi** to dig one's heels in; *vi* to head for.
puntàta *nf* installment; stake; thrust.
punteggiatúra *nf* punctuation.
puntéggio *nm* (*sport*) score.
puntellàre *vt* to prop, support.
puntèllo *nm* prop, support.
puntíglio *nm* punctilio, obstinacy; spite.
puntiglióso *a* punctilious, obstinate.
puntína *nf* (*of record player*) stylus; **p. da disègno** drawing pin, thumbtack.
púnto *nm* point, dot, mark, full stop; stitch; spot; *a* any; **non . . . p.** no, none; *ad* at all; **in p.** exactly; **di p. in biànco** point-blank; **p. e vírgola** semicolon; **dúe púnti** colon.
puntuàle *a* punctual.
puntualità *nf* punctuality.
puntúra *nf* prick, sting; injection.
punzecchiàre *vt* to prick, sting; tease.
pupàzzo *nm* puppet.
pupílla *nf* (*eye*) pupil.
pupíllo *nm* **pupílla** *nf* ward.
púpo *nm* puppet; (*fam*) baby.
purchè *cj* on condition that, provided (that).
púre *ad* also, too; however, yet.
purézza *nf* purity.
púrga *nf* purgative.
purgànte *a nm* purgative, laxative.
purgàre *vt* to purge, purify, expurgate.
purgatívo *a* laxative, purgative.
purgatòrio *nm* Purgatory.
purificàre *vt* to purify, cleanse.
purificazióne *nf* purification.
purità *nf* purity.
puritàno *a nm* Puritan (*also fig*).
púro *a* pure; **p. sàngue** thoroughbred.
purpúreo *a* deep red, purple.
purtròppo *ad* unfortunately.
puşillànime *a* cowardly, fainthearted; *nm* coward.
putifèrio *nm* uproar, hullabaloo.
putrèdine *nf* putridity, rottenness.
putrefàre *vi* **-rsi** *vr* to go bad, putrefy, rot.
putrefazióne *nf* decomposition.
pútrido *a* putrid, rotten.
puttàna *nf* whore.
pútto *nm* (*art*) cherub, child's figure.
puzzàre *vi* to smell bad, stink.
púzzo *nm* bad smell, stench, stink.
púzzola *nf* polecat.
puzzolènte *a* fetid, stinking.

Q

qua *ad* here; **da quàndo in q.?** since when?
quadèrno *nm* exercise book.
quadràngolo *nm* quadrangle.
quadrànte *nm* quadrant, dial, clockface, sun-dial.
quadràre *vt* to square; *vi* to suit.
quadràto *a* square, strong; *nm* square.
quàdro *nm* picture; painting, description; (*mil*) cadre; **quàdri** *pl* (*cards*) diamonds; **a quàdri** (*cloth etc*) checked.
quaggiù *ad* down here.
quàglia *nf* quail.
quàlche *a* some, any; **q. còsa** *pron* something, anything; **in q. luògo** somewhere, anywhere.
qualcòsa *pron* something, anything.
qualcúno *pron* someone, somebody, anyone, anybody; *pl* some, any.
quàle *a pron* which?, what?; as; that, who, whom, whose.
qualífica *nf* qualification; title.
qualificàre *vt* to qualify; call; describe.
qualità *nf* quality, capacity.
qualóra *cj* if.
qualsíasi, qualúnque *a* any, whatever, whichever; **un uòmo q.** an ordinary man.
qualvòlta, ògni *cj* whenever.
quàndo *ad cj* when, if, since; **di q. in q.** from time to time; **quand'ànche** even if.
quantità *nf* quantity, amount.
quànto *a ad pron* how, how much; as, as much as, what; **q. príma** as soon as possible; **per q.** though; **quànti** *pl* as (many), how many.
quantúnque *cj* (al)though.
quarànta *a* forty; **quarantèna** *nf* quarantine; **quarantènne** *a* forty-year-old; **quarantèsimo** *a* fortieth; **quarantína** *nf* some forty.
quaréşima *nf* Lent.
quareşimàle *a* Lenten.
quartière *nm* (*city*) quarter, district; flat, apartment; (*mil*) quarters *pl*; **q. generàle** (*mil*) H.Q.
quartíno *nm* quarter of a liter, about half a pint.
quàrto *a* fourth; *nm* quarter; quarto.
quàşi *ad* almost, nearly; hardly; *cj* as if; **quàsi che** as if.
quassù *ad* up here.
quàtto *a* cowering, crouching; **q. q.** very quietly.
quattórdici *a* fourteen; **quattordicènne** *a nmf* fourteen-year-old; **quattordicèsimo** *a* fourteenth.
quattríno *nm* farthing; **quattríni** *pl* money.
quàttro *a* four.
quattrocènto *a* four hundred; *nm* the 15th century.

quél(lo) *dem a pron* that, that one; whoever; he; the former; **q. che** what.
quèrcia *nf* oak(tree).
querèla *nf* complaint.
querelàre *vt* (*leg*) to proceed against, prosecute; **-rsi** *vr* (*leg*) to bring a complaint.
quésti *dem pron* this man, the latter.
questionàre *vi* to dispute, quarrel.
questionàrio *nm* questionnaire.
questióne *nf* question; dispute, lawsuit.
quésto *dem a pron* this, this one, he, the latter.
questóre *nm* superintendent of police.
quèstua *nf* begging, (*for charity*) collection.
questúra *nf* police station.
questuríno *nm* policeman.
qui *ad* here; **q. vicíno** close by; **fin q.** so far, till now.
quietànza *nf* receipt.
quietàre *vt* to quiet; **-rsi** *vr* to quiet down.
quiète *nf* quiet, calm, peace, silence, rest.
quièto *a* quiet, calm, still, tranquil.
quíndi *ad* hence, therefore, then, thereby.
quíndici *a* fifteen; **quindicènne** *a nmf* fifteen-year-old; **quindicèsimo** *a* fifteenth.
quindicína *nf* some fifteen; **una q. di giórni** a fortnight or so.
quindicinàle *a nm* fortnightly (magazine).
quinquennàle *a* quinquennial.
quínta *nf* (*theat*) wing; **diétro le quínte** *ad* behind the scenes.
quintàle *nm* quintal (100 kilos).
quínto *a* fifth.
Quirinàle *nm* Quirinal.
quòta *nf* share, installment; (*av*) altitude, (*naut*) depth.
quotàre *vt* (*com*) to quote; **-rsi** *vr* to subscribe (a sum).
quotàto *a* (*com*) quoted; esteemed, well-liked.
quotazióne *nf* (*com*) quotation; **quotazióni di Bórsa** Stock-Exchange quotations.
quotidiàno *a* daily; *nm* daily paper.
quoto, quoziènte *nm* quotient.

R

rabàrbaro *nm* rhubarb.
rabberciàre *vt* to botch; patch (up).
ràbbia *nf* anger, fury; hydrophobia, rabies.
rabbíno *nm* Rabbi.
rabbióso *a* furious, angry; rabid.
rabboníre *vt* to calm, pacify; **-rsi** *vr* to calm down.
rabbrividíre *vi* to shiver, shudder.
rabbúffo *nm* rebuke, reprimand.
rabbuiàre *vi* **-rsi** *vr* to grow dark.
rabdomànte *nm* dowser, water diviner.
raccapezzàre *vt* to collect, put together; **-rsi** *vr* to find one's way, make out.
raccapricciànte *a* horrifying, terrifying.
raccapricciàre *vt* to horrify; *vi* **-rsi** *vr* to be horrified, shudder.
raccapríccio *nm* horror.
raccattàre *vt* to pick up, collect.
racchétta *nf* racquet; **r. del tergicristàllo** (*aut*) windscreen wiper, windshield wiper; **r. per la nève** snowshoes.
racchiúdere *vt* to contain, hold.
raccògliere *vt* to pick up; assemble, gather, collect; receive; fold; **-rsi** *vr* to gather, collect one's thoughts.
raccogliménto *nm* concentration, meditation.
raccòlta *nf* collection, gathering; harvest, harvesting.
raccòlto *a* picked, collected; (*fig*) engrossed; cozy, curled up; *nm* crop, harvest.
raccomandàbile *a* reliable, recommendable.
raccomandàre *vt* to recommend; (*mail*) register; **-rsi** *vr* to entreat; commend oneself; **mi raccomàndo** please.
raccomandàta *nf* registered letter; person recommended.
raccomandàto *a* recommended; registered; *nm* protégé.
raccomandazióne *nf* recommendation; registration.
raccomodàre *vt* to mend, repair; arrange; revive.
raccontàre *vt* to narrate, relate, tell.
raccónto *nm* story, tale, report.
raccorciàre *vt* to shorten; **-rsi** *vr* to grow short(er), shrink.
Rachèle *nf pr* Rachel.
rachítico *pl* **-ici** *a* rickety, stunted.
rachítide *nf* **rachitismo** *nm* rickets.
racimolàre *vt* to scrape together, glean.
ràda *nf* (*naut*) roads *pl*, roadstead.
ràdar *nm* radar.
raddolcíre *vt* to soften, soothe, sweeten; **-rsi** *vr* to soften; (*of weather*) become milder.
raddoppiàre *vt* to (re)double.
raddrizzàre *vt* to straighten; correct; **-rsi** *vr* to draw oneself up; improve.
radènte *a* shaving, grazing; **vòlo r.** (*av*) hedgehopping.
ràdere *vt* **-rsi** *vr* to shave (oneself).
radiàre *vt* to expel, strike off.
radiatóre *nm* radiator.
radiazióne *nf* radiation; expulsion.
ràdica *nf* briarwood, root.
radicàle *a nm* radical.
radicàre *vi* **-rsi** *vr* to (take) root.
radíce *nf* root; horse-radish.
radiestesía *nf* sensitivity to radiation.
ràdio *nf* radio, wireless; *nm* radium.

radioascoltatóre *nm* **-tríce** *nf*, **radioauditóre** *nm* **-tríce** *nf* radio listener.
radioattívo *a* radioactive; **piòggia radioattiva** fall-out; **rèndere r.** to activate.
radiocomandàto *a* remote controlled.
radiocronísta *nmf* radio commentator.
radiodiffusióne *nf* broadcasting, broadcast.
radiofònico *pl* **-ici** *a* wireless; **apparècchio r.** wireless set.
radiografía *nf* radiography.
radiología *nf* X-ray treatment.
radioscòpico *pl* **-ici** *a* radioscopic **eşàme r.** X-ray examination.
radióso *a* beaming, radiant, bright.
radiotelegrafísta *nm* wireless operator.
radiotrasmissióne *nf* broadcasting, broadcast.
radiotraşmittènte *a* broadcasting; *nf* broadcasting station.
ràdo *a* rare, thin, infrequent; **di r.** seldom.
radunàre *vt* **-rsi** *vr* to assemble, gather.
radúno *nm* meeting, gathering, rally.
radúra *nf* glade, clearing.
ràfano *nm* horse-radish.
Raffaèle *nm pr* Raphael.
raffermàre *vt* to confirm, renew.
raffèrmo *a* stale.
ràffica *nf* gust of wind, squall.
raffiguràre *vt* to represent.
raffilàre *vt* to sharpen, whet; pare.
raffinaménto *nm* refining.
raffinàre *vt* to refine, thin.
raffinatézza *nf* refinement.
raffinería *nf* refinery.
rafforzàre *vt* to reinforce, strengthen; **-rsi** *vr* to get stronger.
raffreddaménto *nm* cooling, coolness.
raffreddàre *vt* to chill, cool; **-rsi** *vr* to cool, get cold; catch a cold.
raffreddóre *nm* (*med*) cold.
raffrenàre *vt* to check, curb, restrain; **-rsi** *vr* to check oneself.
raffrontàre *vt* to compare.
raffrónto *nm* comparison.
raganèlla *nf* tree-frog; rattle.
ragàzza *nf* girl.
ragàzzo *nm* boy; lad.
raggiànte *a* radiant.
ràggio *nm* ray, beam; radius; spoke.
raggiràre *vt* to cheat, swindle, trick.
raggíro *nm* trick.
raggiúngere *vt* to reach; join; achieve; hit.
raggiustàre *vt* to mend; set in order.
raggranellàre *vt* to scrape together.
raggrinzíre *vt* to wrinkle (up).
raggruppaménto *nm* cluster, group (ing).
raggruppàre *vt* to collect, set in groups; **-rsi** *vr* to cluster, form groups.
raggruzzolàre *vt* to put together, save.
ragguagliàre *vt* to balance, compare; inform.
ragguàglio *nm* balance; comparison; information.
ragguardévole *a* considerable, notable.
ràgia *nf* rosin, resin; **àcqua r.** turpentine.
ragionaménto *nm* reasoning, argument.
ragionàre *vi* to reason, argue, discuss.
ragióne *nf* reason, right; **avèr r.** to be right.
ragionería *nf* accountancy, book-keeping.
ragionévole *a* reasonable.
ragionevolézza *nf* reasonableness.
ragionière *nm* (certified) accountant, book-keeper.
ragliàre *vi* to bray.
ràglio *nm* braying.
ragnatéla *nf* **ragnatélo** *nm* spider's web.
ràgno *nm* spider.
ragú *nm* ragout.
Raimóndo *nm pr* Raymond.
rallegraménto *nm* rejoicing; congratulation.
rallegràre *vt* to cheer, make glad; **-rsi** *vr* to rejoice; congratulate.
rallentàre *vt* to slacken, lessen; **r. il pàsso** to slacken down one's pace; *vi* to slow down.
ramaiòlo *nm* ladle.
ramanzína *nf* telling-off, scolding.
ramàrro *nm* green lizard.
ràme *nm* copper.
ramificàre *vi* **-rsi** *vr* to branch (out), ramify.
ramificazióne *nf* ramification.
ramíngo *pl* **-ghi** *a* roaming, wandering.
ramíno *nm* copper kettle; (*card game*) rummy.
rammaricàrsi *vr* to be sorry, grieve, regret.
rammàrico *pl* **-chi** *nm* grief, regret, bitterness.
rammendàre *vt* to darn, mend.
ramméndo *nm* darn, mending.
rammentàre *vt* to recall, remind; **-rsi** *vr* to recollect, remember.
rammolliménto *nm* softening.
rammollíre *vt* to soften (*also fig*); move to pity.
ràmo *nm* branch; (*com*) line; arm; antler.
ramoscèllo *nm* spray, twig.
ramóso *a* branchy.
ràmpa *nf* flight of steps; steep slope; ramp.
rampicànte *a* climbing, creeping; *nm* (*zool*) climber; (*plant*) creeper.
rampógna *nf* rebuke, reproof.
rampóllo *nm* offspring, shoot.

rampóne *nm* harpoon; crampon.
ràna *nf* frog.
rancidézza *nf* rancidness.
ràncido *a* rancid, rank.
ràncio *nm* (*mil*) rations, mess.
rancóre *nm* grudge, rancor.
randàgio *a* stray, wandering.
randèllo *nm* cudgel.
ranèlla *nf* (*mech*) washer.
Randòlfo *nm pr* Randolph.
ràngo *pl* **rànghi** *nm* rank.
rannicchiàrsi *vr* to crouch, curl up.
rannuvolàre *vi* **-rsi** *vr* to cloud over, grow dark.
ranòcchia *nf* **ranòcchio** *nm* frog.
rantolàre *vi* to breathe heavily, have the death-rattle in one's throat.
ràntolo *nm* heavy breathing, (death-) rattle.
ranúncolo *nm* buttercup.
ràpa *nf* turnip.
rapàce *a* greedy, predatory.
rapacità *nf* greed, rapaciousness.
rapàre *vt* to crop the hair of.
rapidaménte *ad* rapidly.
rapidità *nf* rapidity, swiftness.
ràpido *a* quick, speedy, fast; *nm* express train.
rapiménto *nm* kidnapping; (*fig*) rapture.
rapína *nf* robbery, plunder.
rapinàre *vt* to rob, plunder.
rapinatóre *nm* robber.
rapíre *vt* to abduct, steal, carry off; (*fig*) ravish.
rappacificàre *vt* to pacify, reconcile.
rappezzàre *vt* to patch (up).
rappèzzo *nm* patch.
rappòrto *nm* report, relation, connection; **èssere in buòni rappòrti** to be on good terms.
rappresàglia *nf* reprisal, retaliation.
rappreşentànte *nm* representative, agent.
rappreşentànza *nf* agency; deputation; representation.
rappreşentàre *vt* to represent; (*theat*) perform; **-rsi** *vr* to picture to oneself.
rappreşentatívo *a* representative.
rappreşentazióne *nf* description; performance.
raraménte *ad* seldom.
rarefàre *vt* **-rsi** *vr* to rarefy.
rarità *nf* rarity; scarcity.
ràro *a* rare.
rasàre *vt* to shave; smooth; **-rsi** *vr* to shave.
raschiàre *vt* to scrape, scratch.
ràschio *nm* irritation in the throat.
raşentàre *vt* to graze; border upon.
raşènte (a) *prep* close to.
ràso *a* smooth, shaven; **r. a** *prep* close to; *nm* satin.
rasóio *nm* razor.
raspàre *vt* to rasp, scratch; search through.
rasségna *nf* review, parade.
rassegnàre *vt* to resign; pass in review; **-rsi** *vr* to resign oneself, submit.
rassegnazióne *nf* resignation.
rasserenàre *vt* to brighten, calm; **-rsi** *vr* to clear up, brighten up.
rassettàre *vt* to tidy, mend.
rassicurànte *a* reassuring.
rassicuràre *vt* to (re)assure; **-rsi** *vr* to make sure, be reassured.
rassicurazióne *nf* assurance, reassurance.
rassodaménto *nm* hardening, (*fig*) consolidation.
rassodàre *vti* to harden, strengthen.
rassomigliànza *nf* likeness, resemblance.
rassomigliàre *vi* **-rsi** *vr* to be alike, resemble.
rastrellàre *vt* to rake; ransack; (*mil*) mop up, comb.
rastrellièra *nf* rack; crib.
rastrèllo *nm* (*tool*) rake.
ràta *nf* installment; **véndita a ràte** hire-purchase system, installment plan.
rateàle *a* by installments, partial.
ratífica *nf* ratification.
ratificàre *vt* to ratify.
ràtto *nm* abduction, kidnapping, theft; rat; *a* quick, swift.
rattoppàre *vt* to mend, patch (up).
rattòppo *nm* patch.
rattrappíre *vti* to benumb; contract.
rattristàre *vt* to sadden; **-rsi** *vr* to grieve.
raucèdine *nf* hoarseness.
ràuco *pl* **ràuchi** *a* hoarse.
ravanèllo *nm* radish.
ravvedérsi *vr* to reform, repent.
ravvediménto *nm* reformation, repentance.
ravviàre *vt* to (re)arrange, tidy.
ravvicinàre *vt* to bring closer; reconcile; compare.
ravvişàbile *a* recognizable.
ravvişàre *vt* to recognize.
ravvivàre *vt* to revive (*also fig*).
ravvòlgere *etc v* **avvòlgere** *etc*.
raziocínio *nm* reason(ing), common sense.
razionàle *a* rational.
razióne *nf* ration, portion.
ràzza *nf* race, kind.
ràẓẓa *nf* (*fish*) ray.
razzía *nf* raid; insect-powder.
razziàle *a* racial.
razziàre *vti* to raid, plunder.
ràẓẓo *nm* rocket, missile; spoke.
razzolàre *vi* to scratch about, rummage.
ré *nm* king.
rè *nm* (*mus*) D, re.
reagíre *vi* to react.
reàle *a* real; royal; *nm* the real, reality.
realişmo *nm* realism.
realísta *nmf* realist; royalist.
realístico *pl* **-ici** *a* realistic.
realiẓẓàre *vt* to realize; **-rsi** *vr* to come true.

realizzazióne *nf* fulfillment; realization; (*theat*) production.
realménte *ad* really, in reality.
realtà *nf* reality.
reàme *nm* kingdom.
reàto *nm* crime.
reattívo *a* reactive; *nm* (*chem*) reagent.
reattóre *nm* reactor; (*av*) jet plane; **r. sperimentàle** breeder reactor.
reazionàrio *a nm* reactionary.
reazióne *nf* reaction; **aèreo a r.** (*av*) jet; **motóre a r.** jet engine.
recapitàre *vt* to deliver.
recàpito *nm* address, delivery.
recàre *vt* to bring, carry; cause; **-rsi** *vr* to go.
recensióne *nf* review.
recensíre *vt* to review.
recènte *a* recent, new.
recenteménte *ad* recently.
recèsso *nm* recess.
recídere *vt* to cut off.
recidíva *nf* relapse.
recíngere *vt* to enclose, fence in.
recínto *a* enclosed; *nm* enclosure.
recipiènte *nm* container, vessel.
recíproco *pl* **-oci** *a* mutual, reciprocal.
recíso *a* cut off; resolute; curt.
rècita *nf* performance, recital.
recitàre *vt* to recite, act, play.
recitazióne *nf* recitation; acting.
reclamàre *vt* to claim; *vi* complain.
réclame *nf* (*Fr*) advertising, advertisement.
reclàmo *nm* complaint.
reclusióne *nf* seclusion; imprisonment.
reclusòrio *nm* penitentiary, prison.
rècluta *nf* (*mil*) recruit.
reclutaménto *nm* recruiting.
reclutàre *vt* to recruit.
recòndito *a* hidden, innermost.
recriminàre *vi* to recriminate.
recriminazióne *nf* recrimination.
recrudescénza *nf* recrudescence.
redarguíre *vt* to reproach.
redattóre *nm* **-tríce** *nf* compiler; journalist, writer; (*newspaper*) subeditor, copyreader.
redazióne *nf* compiling; editing; editorial staff; editor's office.
redditízio *a* paying, profitable.
rèddito *nm* income, revenue.
redènto *a* redeemed.
redentóre *nm* **-tríce** *nf* redeemer; *a* redeeming; **il R.** the Redeemer.
redenzióne *nf* redemption.
redígere *vt* to compile, draw up.
redímere *vt* to redeem.
rèdini *nf pl* reins *pl*.
redivívo *a* risen from the dead; new.
rèduce *a* returning; *nm* survivor; ex-serviceman.
réfe *nm* thread.
referènza *nf* reference, testimonial.
refettòrio *nm* refectory.
refezióne *nf* light meal; **r. scolàstica** school meal.
refrattàrio *a* refractory; fireproof.
refrigerànte *a* refrigerating, refrigerant; *nm* refrigerator, icebox.
refrigèrio *nm* cool; relief.
refurtíva *nf* stolen goods *pl*.
regàglie *v* **rigàglie**.
regalàre *vt* to make a present of, present.
regàle *a* regal, royal.
regàlo *nm* gift, present.
regàta *nf* regatta.
reggènte *nm* regent.
reggènza *nf* regency.
règgere *vti* to bear, carry; govern; hold; **-rsi** *vr* to stand; be ruled.
règgia *nf* royal palace.
reggicàlze *nm* suspender belt, garter belt, girdle.
reggiménto *nm* regiment; government.
reggipètto, reggiséno *nm* brassière.
regía *nf* state monopoly; (*theat*) production; (*cin*) direction.
regíme *nm* regime; regimen, diet; **stàre a r.** to be on a diet.
regína *nf* queen.
règio *a* royal.
regióne *nf* region, district.
regísta *nmf* (*theat*) producer, (*cin*) director.
registràre *vt* (*com*) to enter; record, register.
registratóre *nm* **-tríce** *nf* registrar, recorder; **r. su nàstro** tape-recorder.
registrazióne *nf* (*com*) entry; recording, registration.
regístro *nm* register; registry.
regnàre *vi* to reign.
régno *nm* reign; kingdom.
règola *nf* rule; moderation; **di r.** as a rule; **in r.** in order.
regolamentàre *a* regulation.
regolaménto *nm* regulation; (*of accounts*) settlement.
regolàre *a* regular; *vt* to regulate; settle; **-rsi** *vr* to act, behave.
regolarità *nf* regularity.
regolarizzàre *vt* to regularize.
regolatézza *nf* orderliness, moderation.
regolàto *a* orderly, regular, moderate.
regolazióne *nf* regulation; adjustment.
règolo *nm* (*for lines*) ruler; **r. calcolatóre** sliding rule.
reiètto *a* rejected; *nm* castaway, outcast.
reintegràre *vt* to reinstate, restore; compensate.
relativaménte *ad* relatively, comparatively; **r. a** with regard to.
relatívo *a* relative; comparative; **r. a** concerning.
relatóre *nm* reporter.
relazióne *nf* report; relation; acquaintance; affair; **avèr mólte relazióni** to know many people.
relegàre *vt* to confine, relegate.

religióne *nf* religion.
religióso *a* religious; *nm* member of a religious order.
relíquia *nf* relic.
relítto *nm* wreckage.
remàre *vi* to row, paddle.
rematóre *nm* rower, oarsman.
reminiscènza *nf* reminiscence.
remissióne *nf* remission.
remissívo *a* meek, submissive.
rèmo *nm* oar.
remòto *a* distant, remote, secluded.
réna *nf* sand(s).
rèndere *vt* to give back, repay; yield, render; make; **-rsi** *vr* to become, make oneself; **-rsi cónto di** to realize.
rendicónto *nm* report, statement.
rendiménto *nm* rendering, returning (thanks); yield; efficiency.
rèndita *nf* income, revenue.
rène *nm* kidney.
renitènte *a* unwilling, recalcitrant; **r. alla lèva** (*mil*) failing to appear at the call up.
rènna *nf* reindeer.
Rèno *nm* (*geogr*) Rhine.
rèo *a* guilty.
repàrto *nm* department; (*mil*) detachment, party.
repellènte *a* repellent, repulsive.
repentàglio *nm* danger, risk.
repènte, repentíno *a* sudden.
reperíbile *a* to be found.
repèrto *nm* report, evidence, exhibit.
repertòrio *nm* repertory, inventory.
rèplica *nf* reply, retort; repetition.
replicàre *vt* to reply, retort; repeat.
repressióne *nf* repression.
reprímere *vt* to repress, check.
rèprobo *a nm* reprobate.
repúbblica *nf* republic.
repubblicàno *a nm* republican.
reputàre *vt* to consider, deem.
reputàto *a* esteemed, well thought of.
reputazióne *nf* reputation.
rèquie *nf* rest, peace.
requiṣíre *vt* to requisition.
requiṣitòria *nf* charge, indictment.
requiṣizióne *nf* requisition.
résa *nf* surrender; rendering, return, yield.
residènte *a* residing; *nmf* resident.
residènza *nf* residence, residency.
resíduo *a* residual; *nm* residue.
rèsina *nf* resin.
resistènte *a* resistant, strong; (*color*) fast; **r. a** proof against.
resistènza *nf* resistance, endurance.
resístere *vi* to resist, hold out, be proof against.
resocónto *nm* report; account.
respíngere *vt* to drive back, reject.
respiràre *vti* to breathe.
respirazióne *nf* respiration, breathing.
respíro *nm* breath; respite.
responsàbile *a* responsible.
responsabilità *nf* responsibility.
respònso *nm* response, answer.
rèssa *nf* crowd, throng.
restàre *v* **rimanére.**
restauràre *vt* to restore.
restàuro *nm* restoration, repair.
restío *a* restive, reluctant, unmanageable.
restituíre *vt* to return, restore.
restituzióne *nf* restitution, reinstatement.
rèsto *nm* remainder, rest; (*money*) change; **rèsti** *pl* remains *pl*; **del r.** besides.
restríngere *vt* to narrow, contract, restrict, tighten; **-rsi** *vr* to contract, narrow, shrink.
restrizióne *nf* restriction.
resurrezióne *nf* **risurrezióne.**
retàggio *nm* heritage, inheritance.
réte *nf* net, network, share.
reticènza *nf* reticence.
Rètiche, (Àlpi) *nf pl* (*geogr*) Rhaetian Alps.
reticolàto *nm* barbed wire entanglement; wire-netting.
retòrica *nf* rhetoric.
retòrico *a* rhetorical.
retribuíre *vt* to pay, reward.
retribuzióne *nf* pay; retribution.
rètro *ad* behind; *nm* back; **védi r.** please turn over (P.T.O.).
retrobottéga *nf* back-shop.
retrocèdere *vt* to degrade, reduce in rank; *vi* to retreat.
retrocucína *nm* scullery.
retrògrado *a nm* retrograde, reactionary.
retroscèna *nm* behind the scenes; underhand dealing.
retrotèrra *nf* hinterland.
rètta *nf* charge, terms *pl*; (*geom*) straight line; **dàr r. a qlcu** to follow s.o.'s advice.
rettàngolo *nm* rectangle.
rettífica *nf* amendment; alteration.
rettificàre *vt* to rectify, correct.
rettificazióne *nf* rectification, correction.
rèttile *nm* reptile.
rettitúdine *nf* honesty, uprightness.
rètto *a* straight; honest, right.
rettóre *nm* rector.
reumatiṣmo *nm* rheumatism.
reverèndo *a* reverend; *nm* padre.
reviṣióne *nf* revision; **r. dèi cónti** audit.
rèvoca *nf* revocation, repeal.
revocàbile *a* revokable.
revocàre *vt* to repeal, revoke.
revòlver *nm* revolver.
revolveràta *nf* revolver shot.
ri: *common prefix to Italian verbs meaning again or back; thus*: **richiúdere** to shut again; **ridàre** to give back *etc. For verbs with prefix* **ri-** *not given below, see entries without prefix.*
riabilitàre *vt* to rehabilitate, requalify; **-rsi** *vr* to regain one's good name.

riabilitazióne *nf* rehabilitation.
rialzàre *vt* to lift up again, heighten; *vi* go up.
riàlzo *nm* rise.
riàrso *a* dry, parched.
riassúnto *nm* summary, summing-up.
riavérsi *vr* to recover.
ribadíre *vt* to clinch, fix; rivet.
ribaldería *nf* foul deed, knavish trick.
ribàldo *nm* rascal, scoundrel.
ribàlta *nf* (*theat*) footlights, front of the stage.
ribaltàre *vti* to capsize, overturn.
ribassàre *vt* to lower, reduce.
ribàsso *nm* fall, decline; reduction.
ribàttere *vt* to beat again; repel; (*fig*) confute.
ribellàrsi *vr* to rebel, rise (against).
ribèlle *a nm* rebel.
ribellióne *nf* rebellion.
ríbes *nm* redcurrant; blackcurrant.
ribrézzo *nm* horror, loathing.
ributtànte *a* revolting.
ricadére *vi* to fall down again; (have a) relapse.
ricadúta *nf* relapse.
ricamàre *vt* to embroider.
ricamatríce *nf* embroiderer.
ricambiàre *vt* to change again, reciprocate, repay, return.
ricàmbio *nm* exchange, return; **pèzzo di r.** (*tec*) spare (part).
ricàmo *nm* embroidery.
ricapitolàre *vti* to recapitulate, sum up.
ricattàre *vt* to blackmail.
ricattatóre *nm* blackmailer.
ricàtto *nm* blackmail(ing).
ricavàre *vt* to draw, extract; gain.
ricàvo, ricavàto *nm* proceeds *pl*, return.
Riccàrdo *nm pr* Richard.
ricchézza *nf* riches *pl*, richness, wealth.
ríccio *a* curly; *nm* lock; hedgehog; sea urchin.
ricciúto *a* curly.
rícco *pl* **rícchi** *a* rich.
ricérca *nf* search, pursuit, research, inquiry, demand; **àlla r. di** in search of.
ricercàre *vt* to look for again, seek, pursue, investigate.
ricercatézza *nf* affectation.
ricètta *nf* prescription; recipe.
ricettàcolo *nm* receptacle.
ricettàre *vt* to shelter; receive (*stolen goods*).
ricettazióne *nf* receiving stolen goods.
ricévere *vt* to receive, welcome.
riceviménto *nm* receiving, reception.
ricevitóre *nm* receiver.
recevúta *nf* receipt.
richiamàre *vt* to (re)call; reprimand.
richiàmo *nm* recall, call; admonition.
richièdere *vt* to ask again for; require; send for; apply for.
richièsta *nf* demand, request.
richièsto *a* in demand, required, sought after.
rícino, òlio di *nm* castor oil.
ricognizióne *nf* (*mil*) reconnaissance.
ricolmàre *vt* to fill, overload (with).
ricólmo *a* brimful.
ricompènsa *nf* recompense, reward.
ricompensàre *vt* to recompense, reward.
ricompórre *vt* to reassemble; (re) compose; **-rsi** *vr* to recover oneself.
riconciliàre *vt* to reconcile.
riconférma *nf* confirmation.
riconoscènte *a* grateful, thankful.
riconoscènza *nf* gratitude.
riconóscere *vt* to recognize, acknowledge.
riconosciménto *nm* recognition, acknowledgment; identification.
ricopríre *vt* to cover, hide.
ricordànza *nf* (*poet*) recollection, remembrance.
ricordàre *vti* to remember, recall; remind; mention; **-rsi** *vr* to remember, recall.
ricòrdo *nm* memory, record, souvenir; *pl* memories *pl*.
ricorrènza *nf* recurrence; anniversary; occasion.
ricórrere *vi* to apply, resort; recur; occur.
ricórso *nm* petition, claim; recurrence.
ricostituènte *a nm* tonic.
ricostruzióne *nf* rebuilding, reconstruction.
ricòtta *nf* buttermilk curd.
ricoveràre *vt* to shelter, admit (into hospital); **-rsi** *vr* to find shelter.
ricóvero *nm* refuge, shelter.
ricreàre *vt* to recreate, refresh; **-rsi** *vr* to find recreation.
ricreazióne *nf* pastime, recreation.
ricrédersi *vr* to change one's mind.
ricuperàre *vt* to recover; salvage; make up for.
ricúpero *nm* recovery; rescue.
ricusàre *vt* to refuse, reject.
rídda *nf* confusion, turmoil.
ridènte *a* smiling, pleasant, bright.
rídere *vi* to laugh; **-rsi (di)** *vr* to laugh (at).
ridícolo *a* ridiculous; *nm* ridicule.
ridíre, trovàre da *vi* to find fault.
ridondànte *a* redundant.
ridòsso, a *ad* close by, very near.
ridótta *nf* (*mil*) redoubt.
ridúrre *vt* to reduce.
riduzióne *nf* reduction; adaptation, (*mus*) arrangement.
rielezióne *nf* re-election.
rièmpiere, riempíre *vt* to fill, stuff; **-rsi** *vr* to fill (oneself).
rientràre *vi* to re-enter, return; be part of; **r. in sè** to come to oneself.
riepilogàre *vti* to recapitulate.

riepílogo *pl* **-ghi** *nm* recapitulation.
rifaciménto *nm* remaking, reconstruction.
rifàre *vt* to do again, (re)make; **-rsi** *vr* to make up one's losses.
rifàtto *a* done again, rebuilt, remade.
riferíre *vt* to relate, report, attribute; **-rsi** *vr* to refer, relate.
rifiatàre *vi* to breathe (*also fig*); utter a word.
rifiníre *vt* to finish, give the last touch to; satisfy.
rifioríre *vi* to bloom again, (*fig*) flourish again.
rifiutàre *vti* **-rsi** *vr* to refuse, deny.
rifiúto *nm* refusal; **rifiúti** *pl* refuse, scum.
riflessióne *nf* reflection, deliberation.
riflessívo *a* thoughtful; (*gram*) reflexive.
riflèttere *vti* to reflect.
riflettóre *nm* searchlight, floodlight, reflector.
rifluíre *vi* to flow back, ebb.
riflússo *nm* ebb(-tide), reflux.
rifocillàre *vt* to supply (with food and drink); **-rsi** *vr* to take refreshment.
rifóndere *vt* to refund; melt again.
rifórma *nf* reform(ation).
riformàre *vt* to amend, reform; (*mil*) to declare unfit for service.
riforniménto *nm* supplying, supply; (*av, aut*) refuelling; **stazióne di r.** (*aut*) filling station, gas station.
riforníre *vt* to provide, supply; **-rsi** *vr* to take in a fresh supply.
rifràngere *vt* to refract.
rifrazióne *nf* refraction.
rifréddo *nm* cold dish.
rifugiàrsi *vr* to hide oneself, take refuge.
rifugiàto *nm* refugee.
rifúgio *nm* refuge, shelter.
rifúlgere *vi* to shine brightly.
ríga *nf* line; ruler; row, stripe; (hair) parting.
rigàglie *nf pl* giblets *pl*.
rigàgnolo *nm* brook; gutter.
rigàre *vt* to rule (lines).
rigattière *nm* second-hand dealer.
rigeneràre *vt* **-rsi** *vr* to regenerate.
rigenerazióne *nf* regeneration.
rigettàre *vti* to throw again, throw back, reject; vomit; bud again.
rigidézza, rigidità *nf* rigidity; strictness.
rígido *a* rigid; severe, strict; very cold.
rigiràre *vt* to turn again; surround; trick; **-rsi** *vr* to turn around.
rigíro *nm* turning around; trick.
rígo *pl* **ríghi** *nm* line.
rigóglio *nm* bloom, luxuriance.
rigogliόso *a* luxuriant, flourishing.
rigónfio *a* puffed up, swollen; *nm* swelling.
rigóre *nm* rigor, severity, strictness; **a r. di tèrmini** in the strict sense.
rigorosità *nf* rigorousness, strictness.
rigoróso *a* rigorous, severe, strict.
rigovernàre *vti* to clean, wash up.
riguardànte *a* regarding, concerning.
riguardàre *vt* to look at again; regard; concern; **-rsi** *vr* to take care of oneself.
riguàrdo *nm* care, consideration, regard, respect; **r. a** concerning.
rigurgitànte *a* overflowing, swarming.
rigurgitàre *vi* to flow back, overflow; regurgitate; swarm with.
rilasciàre *vt* to leave again; release, grant, issue; relax.
rilassaménto *nm* slackening, relaxation.
rilassàre *vt* **-rsi** *vr* to loosen, relax, slacken.
rilegàre *vt* to bind (again).
rilegatóre *nm* **-tríce** *nf* bookbinder.
rilegatúra *nf* binding, bookbinding.
rilevànte *a* considerable, important.
rilevàre *vt* to take away again; raise; notice, point out; survey; take; call for.
rilièvo *nm* relief; importance; remark.
rilúcere *vi* to glitter, shine.
riluttànte *a* reluctant.
ríma *nf* rhyme; **rispóndere per le ríme** to give as good as one gets.
rimandàre *vt* to send again; send back; defer; reject; refer.
rimaneggiàre *vt* to rearrange, alter, (*pol*) shuffle.
rimanènte *a* remaining; *nm* remainder.
rimanènza *nf* remainder, remnant.
rimanére *vi* to remain; be located; be surprised; rest with.
rimasúglio *nm* remainder; **rimasúgli** *pl* remains *pl*.
rimbàlzo *nm* rebound; **di r.** on the rebound.
rimbambíre *vi* to grow childish.
rimbeccàre *vt* to retort.
rimboccàre *vt* (*trousers*) to turn up; (*sheets*) turn down; (*sleeves*) roll up.
rimbombàre *vi* to roar, thunder.
rimbómbo *nm* roar.
rimborsàbile *a* repayable.
rimborsàre *vt* to reimburse, repay.
rimbórso *nm* reimbursement, repayment.
rimbròtto *nm* rebuke, reproach.
rimediàre *vti* to remedy; **r. a** find a remedy for.
rimédio *nm* cure, remedy.
rimembrànza *nf* remembrance.
rimeritàre *vt* to recompense, reward.
rimescolàre *vt* to mix up, (*cards*) shuffle; **-rsi** *vr* to be upset.
riméssa *nf* garage, shed; remittance.
riméssο *a* fit again; remitted; meek; **r. a nuòvo** done up; **dénte r.** false tooth.
rimestàre *vt* to stir up.

riméttere *vt* to put again, put back, return; remit; lose; defer, refer; vomit; **-rsi** *vr* to recover; resume; improve; rely on.
rimodernàre *vt* to modernize, remodel.
rimontàre *vti* to remount; go up; date back, go back.
rimorchiàre *vt* to tow.
rimorchiatóre *nm* (*naut*) tug(boat).
rimòrchio *nm* tow; trailer.
rimòrso *nm* remorse.
rimostrànza *nf* complaint, protest.
rimostràre *vt* to show again; *vi* to remonstrate.
rimozióne *nf* removal.
rimpàsto *nm* rearrangement, (*pol*) shuffle.
rimpatriàre *vti* to repatriate.
rimpàtrio *nm* repatriation.
rimpètto *v* **dirimpètto.**
rimpiàngere *vt* to lament, regret.
rimpiànto *nm* regret.
rimpicciolíre *vti* to lessen.
rimproveràre *vt* to reproach, blame; grudge; **-rsi** *vr* to blame oneself, repent.
rimpròvero *nm* rebuke, reproach.
rimuneràre *vt* to remunerate, reward.
rimunerazióne *nf* remuneration, reward.
rimuòvere *vt* to remove; deter, dissuade.
Rinàldo *nm pr* Reginald, Ronald.
Rinascènza *nf v* **Rinasciménto.**
rinàscere *vi* to be born again, revive.
rinasciménto *nm* rebirth; **R.** Renaissance.
rinàscita *nf* rebirth, revival.
rincalzàre *vt* (*a plant*) to earth up; (*bedclothes*) tuck in.
rincantucciàrsi *vr* to creep into a corner, hide oneself.
rincaràre *vt* (*prices*) to raise; *vi* to grow dearer.
rincàro *nm* rise in prices.
rincasàre *vi* to return home.
rinchiúdere *vt* to shut up.
rincórrere *vt* to chase, pursue.
rincórsa *nf* run-up.
rincréscere *v impers* to be sorry, regret, mind.
rincresciménto *nm* regret.
rincrudíre *vt* to aggravate, embitter; *vi* to get worse.
rinculàre *vi* to draw back, recoil.
rinfacciàre *vt* to cast in s.o.'s teeth, taunt.
rinforzàre *vt* to make stronger, reinforce; *vi* to strengthen.
rinfòrzo *nm* reinforcement.
rinfrancàre *vt* to reanimate; **-rsi** *vr* to take heart again; improve.
rinfrescànte *a* refreshing.
rinfrescàre *vt* to cool; refresh, restore; *vi* to get cooler; **-rsi** *vr* to take refreshment.
rinfrésco *pl* **-éschi** *nm* refreshments *pl.*
rinfusa, àlla *ad* higgledy-piggledy, in confusion.
ringalluzzíre *vt* to elate, make cocky.
ringentilíre *vt* to refine.
ringhiàre *vi* to growl, snarl.
ringhièra *nf* banisters *pl*, railing.
ringhióso *a* snarling.
ringiovaníre *vt* to make young(er), rejuvenate; *vi* to grow young again.
ringraziaménti *nm pl* thanks *pl.*
ringraziàre *vt* to thank.
rinnegaménto *nm* disowning, denial.
rinnegàre *vt* to disown, deny.
rinnegàto *a nm* renegade.
rinnovàbile *a* renewable.
rinnovaménto *nm* renewal; revival.
rinnovàre *vt* to renew; revive.
rinnòvo *nm* renewal.
rinocerónte *nm* rhinoceros.
rinomànza *nf* fame, renown.
rinomàto *a* famous, renowned.
rinsavíre *vi* to return to reason.
rintanàrsi *vr* to hide, shut oneself up.
rintoccàre *vi* (*of clock*) to strike, (*of bell*) toll.
rintócco *pl* **-ócchi** *nm* (*clock*) stroke, (*bell*) tolling, knell.
rintracciàre *vt* to trace, find (out).
rintronàre *vt* to deafen; *vi* resound.
rintuzzàre *vt* to blunt, abate, retort.
rinúncia, rinúnzia *nf* renunciation, renouncement.
rinunciàre, rinunziàre *vti* to give up, renounce.
rinveniménto *nm* discovery; recovery.
rinveníre *vt* to discover, find (out); *vi* to recover one's senses.
rinviàre *vt* to put off, postpone, adjourn; send back.
rinvigoríre *vt* to make strong(er); **-rsi** *vr* to grow strong(er).
rinvío *nm* adjournment, postponement; sending back.
Río délle Amàzzoni (il) *nm* (*geogr*) the river Amazon.
rióne *nm* (*town*) part, quarter, ward.
riordinàre *vt* to put in order, rearrange, reorganize.
riorganizzàre *vt* reorganize.
rípa *nf* bank, escarpment.
riparàbile *a* (that) can be mended, repairable.
riparàre *vt* to shelter, protect; repair, make good; repeat (*an exam*); *vi* to make up for, remedy; take shelter; **-rsi** *vr* to protect oneself.
riparazióne *nf* reparation; repair; esàmi di **r.** *pl* (*exams*) second session.
ripàro *nm* cover, shelter, defense.
ripartíre *vt* to distribute, divide share; *vi* to start again.
ripartizióne *nf* distribution, division.
ripercussióne *nf* repercussion.
ripètere *vt* to repeat.
ripetitóre *nm* **-trice** *nf* repeater; coach, private teacher.

ripetizióne *nf* repetition; coaching, private lesson.
ripiàno *nm* shelf; (*stair*) landing; level place.
ripícco *pl* **-pícchi** *nm* pique.
rípido *a* steep.
ripiegàre *vt* to fold (again); *vi* to bend; give ground, retire; **-rsi** *vr* become bent.
ripiègo *pl* **-ghi** *nm* expedient, remedy.
ripièno *a* full, stuffed (with); *nm* stuffing.
ripórre *vt* to put away, put back, place; conceal.
riportàre *vt* to bring again, bring back, report; receive; (*com*) carry forward; **-rsi** *vr* to go back, refer.
ripórto *nm* (*com*) balance forward.
riposàre *vt* to rest; put down again; *vi* **-rsi** *vr* to rest.
ripóso *nm* rest, quiet, pause.
ripostíglio *nm* lumber-room; hiding-place.
riprèndere *vt* to take again, resume, take back; recover; reprove; *vi* to begin again; revive; **-rsi** *vr* to recover, collect oneself; correct oneself.
riprésa *nf* resumption, revival; recapture, recovery; (*cin*) shot; (*aut*) acceleration; recording; (*boxing*) round.
ripristinàre *vt* to restore.
ripristino *nm* restoration.
riprodúrre *vt* to reproduce; **-rsi** *vr* to reproduce.
riproduttóre, *f* **-tríce** *a* reproducing; *nm* **r. acústico** pick-up.
riproduzióne *nf* reproduction.
ripromèttersi *vr* to intend, propose, expect.
ripròva *nf* new evidence; confirmation.
riprovàre *vt* to try again; criticize; (*in exams*) fail.
ripudiàre *vt* to repudiate, (*leg*) renounce.
ripugnànte *a* disgusting, repugnant.
ripugnànza *nf* aversion, reluctance.
ripugnàre *vi* to be repugnant, disgust.
ripúlsa *nf* refusal, repulse.
risàia *nf* rice-field.
risalíre *vti* to go up (again), go back.
risaltàre *vt* to jump again; *vi* stand out.
risàlto *nm* prominence, relief; **dàre r. a** to show up.
risanaménto *nm* healing, recovery, reformation; (*of marsh land*) reclamation.
risanàre *vt* to cure, heal; reclaim, reform.
risarciménto *nm* compensation, indemnity.
risarcíre *vt* to compensate, indemnify.
risàta *nf* laugh(ter).
riscaldaménto *nm* heating.
riscaldàre *vt* to heat, warm; **-rsi** *vr* to warm up, get warm.
riscaldatóre *nm* **-tríce** *nf* heater, radiator.
riscattàre *vt* to ransom, redeem.
riscàtto *nm* redemption, ransom.
rischiaràre *vt* to illuminate, light up, enlighten; **-rsi** *vr* to brighten, clear up.
rischiàre *vt* to risk; *vi* to run the risk.
rischio *nm* risk.
rischióso *a* risky, dangerous, daring.
risciacquàre *vt* to rinse.
riscontràre *vt* to check, compare; find.
riscóntro *nm* checking, comparison; reply.
riscòssa *nf* insurrection, recovery.
riscuòtere *vt* (*money*) to draw, get, receive; rouse, shake; **-rsi** *vr* to start, be startled.
risentiménto *nm* resentment.
risentíre *vt* to feel again, hear again; experience, feel, suffer; *vi* to feel, show traces; **-rsi** *vr* to take offense; come to oneself, wake up; **-rsi di** *vr* to resent.
risentíto *a* angry, resentful; heard again.
risèrbo *nm* reserve, discretion, self-restraint.
risèrva *nf* reserve, reservation; stock, preserve.
riservàre *vt* to reserve, put off; **-rsi** *vr* to reserve (to) oneself; intend.
riservatézza *nf* reserve, prudence.
riservàto *a* reserved; confidential, private.
riservista *nm* reservist.
risíbile *a* laughable, ridiculous.
risièdere *vi* to reside.
ríso *pl f* **rísa** *nm* laughter.
ríso *nm* rice.
risolúto *a* determined, resolute, resolved.
risoluzióne *nf* resolution; solution.
risòlvere *vt* to resolve, settle, solve; **-rsi** *vr* to decide, make up one's mind, be resolved.
risonànza *nf* resonance, sound.
risonàre *vi* to resound, echo, ring; *vt* to ring again; play again.
risórgere *vi* to rise (again), revive.
risorgiménto *nm* renascence, revival.
risórsa *nf* resource.
risparmiàre *vt* to save, spare.
rispàrmio *nm* saving.
rispecchiàre *vt* to reflect; (*fig*) to mirror.
rispettàbile *a* respectable, considerable.
rispettàre *vt* to respect.
rispètto *nm* respect; regard.
rispettóso *a* respectful.
risplèndere *vi* to shine, glitter.
rispondènte *a* answering, in keeping, in conformity.
rispondènza *nf* correspondence, agreement.

rispóndere *vi* to answer, reply, respond.
rispósta *nf* answer, reply, response.
rissa *nf* brawl, fray.
ristabilíre *vt* to re-establish, restore; **-rsi** *vr* to recover one's health.
ristàmpa *nf* reprint, new impression; **il libro è in r.** the book is being reprinted.
ristampàre *vt* to reprint.
ristorànte *a* restorative; *nm* restaurant, refreshment room.
ristoràre *vt* to refresh, restore; **-rsi** *vr* to refresh oneself.
ristoratóre, *f* **-trice** *a* restorative; *nm* restorer, restaurant.
ristòro *nm* relief, refreshment.
ristrettézza *nf* narrowness, meanness, lack; **r. di mèzzi** lack of means, straitened circumstances.
ristrétto *a* narrow, limited, restricted, condensed.
risúcchio *nm* eddy, swirl.
risultàre *vi* to result, follow; appear, become known.
risultàto *nm* result.
risurrezióne *nf* resurrection.
risuscitàre *vti* to resuscitate, revive.
risvegliàre *vt* to (a)wake, excite, rouse, stir up; **-rsi** *vr* to wake up, be roused.
risvéglio *nm* awakening, revival.
risvólto *nm* lapel, cuff; (*pocket*) flap; (*trousers*) turn-up, cuff.
ritàglio *nm* (*of material*) length, remnant; (*newspaper*) clipping, cutting; **ritàgli di témpo** *pl* spare time.
ritardàre *vt* to delay, put off, retard; *vi* to be late, delay.
ritardatàrio *nm* latecomer.
ritàrdo *nm* delay; **èssere in r.** to be late.
ritégno *nm* reserve, restraint.
ritempràre *vt* to fortify, restore, retemper.
ritenére *vt* to keep back, hold; consider, think; **-rsi** *vr* to consider oneself; restrain oneself.
ritenúta *nf* deduction.
ritiràre *vt* to retract, take back, withdraw; **-rsi** *vr* to retire, retreat, withdraw; subside; shrink.
ritiràta *nf* retreat; lavatory, rest room.
ritíro *nm* retreat, withdrawal.
rítmo *nm* rhythm.
ríto *nm* rite, custom.
ritócco *pl* **-ócchi** *nm* (finishing) touch.
ritornàre *vi* to return, come (go) back, recur; *vt* to return.
ritornèllo *nm* refrain.
ritórno *nm* return, recurrence; **bigliétto di andàta e r.** round-trip ticket; **èssere di r.** to be back.
ritorsióne *nf* retort, retaliation.
ritràrre *vt* to withdraw, draw back; get; represent; deduce; *vr* to withdraw; represent oneself.
ritrattàre *vt* to treat again; retract; portray; **-rsi** *vr* to recant; draw oneself.
ritràtto *nm* portrait.
ritrosía *nf* reluctance, shyness.
ritróso *a* bashful, reluctant; **a r.** backwards.
ritrovàre *vt* to find again, recover; **-rsi** *vr* to find oneself; meet again; see one's way.
ritrovàto *nm* invention; discovery; device, gadget.
ritròvo *nm* meeting-place, haunt.
rítto *a* erect, straight; *nm* (*of material*) right side.
rituàle *a nm* ritual.
riunióne *nf* gathering, meeting.
riuníre *vt* to re-unite, gather, combine, bring together; **-rsi** *vr* to come together again, unite.
riuscíre *vi* to succeed, manage, be able; be good at; be, arrive; go out again.
riuscíta *nf* result; success; **riuscíto** *a* successful.
ríva *nf* bank, shore.
rivàle *a nmf* rival.
rivaleggiàre *vi* to rival, compete.
rivalérsi *vr* to make good one's losses.
rivalità *nf* rivalry.
rivàlsa *nf* revenge.
rivedére *vt* to see again, meet again; revise, check; **r. bòzze** to read proofs.
rivelàre *vt* to reveal, show, display.
rivelazióne *nf* revelation.
rivéndere *vt* to resell, retail.
rivendicàre *vt* to claim, vindicate.
rivéndita *nf* resale; shop.
rivèrbero *nm* reflection; **reverberation.**
riverènte *a* reverent, respectful.
riverènza *nf* reverence, respect; bow, curtsey.
riveríre *vt* to respect, venerate, pay one's respects to.
riversàre *vt* to pour (again), pour out (again); throw; **-rsi** *vr* to flow, pour, rush.
riversíbile *a* reversible.
riversióne *nf* reversion.
rivèrso *a* on one's back.
rivestiménto *nm* covering, coating, lining.
rivestíre *vt* to dress again; clothe, cover, line; (*fig*) hold.
rivièra *nf* coast.
rivíncita *nf* return match; revenge.
rivísta *nf* revision; magazine; parade, review.
rívo *nm* (*poet*) brook, stream.
rivòlgere *vt* to turn; **r. la paròla a** to address; **-rsi** *vr* to apply, turn.
rivolgiménto *nm* upheaval, change.
rivòlta *nf* revolt, insurrection.
rivoltàre *vt* to turn (over) (again), turn inside out; mix, upset; **-rsi** *vr* to turn; rebel, revolt.
rivoltèlla *nf* revolver.
rivoluzionàrio *a nm* revolutionary.

rivoluzióne *nf* revolution.
ròba *nf* stuff, things *pl*; **r. da chiòdi** (*person*) bad lot, (*things*) rubbish.
Robèrto *nm pr* Robert.
robustézza *nf* robustness, strength.
robústo *a* robust, strong, sturdy.
rócca *nf* distaff.
ròcca *nf* fortress, rock, stronghold.
rocchétto *nm* reel; (*eccl*) surplice.
ròccia *nf* cliff, rock.
rocciόso *a* rocky.
ròco *pl* **ròchi** *a* hoarse.
rodàggio *nm* (*aut*) running in.
Ròdano *nm* (*geogr*) Rhone.
ròdere *vt* to gnaw, nibble; corrode; **-rsi** *vr* to worry, be consumed with.
Rodèsia *nf* (*geogr*) Rhodesia.
rodiménto *nm* gnawing; erosion, worry.
rododèndro *nm* rhododendron.
Rodòlfo *nm pr* Rudolph, Rudolf.
Rodrígo *nm pr* Roderick.
rógna *nf* scabies, mange; (*fig*) nuisance.
rognóne *nm* kidney of animals.
rognóso *a* scabby, mangy.
rògo *pl* **ròghi** *nm* stake, pyre, bonfire.
Róma *nf* (*geogr*) Rome; **romàno** *a nm* Roman.
romanésco *a nm* Roman dialect.
Romanía *nf* (*geogr*) Rumania.
romànico *pl* **-ici** *a* (*arch*) Romanesque; (*language*) Romance.
romanticismo *nm* Romanticism.
romàntico *pl* **-ici** *a* romantic.
romànza *nf* ballad, song.
romanzésco *pl* **-chi** *a* romantic, adventurous.
romanzière *nm* novelist.
romànzo *nm* romance, novel; *a* (*language*) Romance.
rombàre *vi* to roar.
rómbo *nm* roar; thunder.
romitàggio *nm* hermitage.
romíto *a* lonely, solitary; *nm* hermit.
rómpere *vti* to break.
rompicàpo *nm* puzzle; worry.
rompicòllo *nm* thoughtless person; **a r.** headlong.
rompighiàccio *nm* ice-breaker.
rompiscàtole *inv nmf* bore, tiresome person.
róncola *nf* pruning knife.
rónda *nf* (*mil*) patrol, rounds.
róndine *nf* swallow.
rondóne *nm* (*bird*) swift.
ronzàre *vi* to buzz, hum.
ronzíno *nm* jade, worn-out horse.
ronzío *nm* buzzing, humming.
ròrido *v* **rugiadóso.**
ròsa *nf* rose; **colór r.** pink.
rosàio *nm* rose-bush.
rosàrio *nm* rosary.
ròseo *a* rosy.
roséto *nm* rose-garden.
rosicchiàre *vt* to gnaw, nibble.
rosmaríno *nm* rosemary.
róso *a* corroded, gnawed.
rosolàccio *nm* field poppy.
rosolàre *vt* to brown.
rosolía *nf* German measles.
rosóne *nm* rose window, rosette.
ròspo *nm* toad.
rossàstro, rossíccio *a* reddish.
rossétto *nm* lipstick, rouge; **r. indelèbile** kiss-proof lipstick.
rósso *a nm* red.
rossóre *nm* flush, blush, redness; shame.
rosticcería *nf* cook shop.
ròstro *nm* dais, rostrum.
rotàia *nf* rail.
rotàre *vi* to rotate, revolve.
rotazióne *nf* rotation.
rotèlla *nf* small wheel, castor; (*anat*) kneecap; **pàttini a rotèlle** roller skates.
rotocàlco *nm* rotogravure process.
rotolàre *vti* to roll (up); **-rsi** *vr* to roll, wallow.
ròtolo *nm* roll; **andàre a ròtoli** to go to rack and ruin.
rotolóne *nm* tumble.
rotondàre *vt* to make round.
rotondeggiànte *a* roundish.
rotondità *nf* roundness, rotundity.
rotóndo *a* round, plump, rotund.
rótta *nf* course; breach; rout; **a r. di còllo** at breakneck speed.
rottàme *nm* wreck, fragment; **rottàmi** *pl* scraps *pl*, rubbish.
rótto *a* broken; addicted to, accustomed; *nm* break; **per il r. dèlla cúffia** by the skin of one's teeth.
rottúra *nf* breakage, break, breaking-off, rupture.
rovènte *a* red-hot, fiery.
róvere *nm* oak.
rovesciàre *vt* to overthrow, overturn; pour; upset; **-rsi** *vr* to be overturned, capsize; fall (down).
rovèscio *a* inside out; upside down; supine; *nm* reverse, opposite; set back; (*tennis*) backhand; **a r.** inside out, upside down, the wrong way.
rovína *nf* ruin.
rovinàre *vt* to ruin; *vi* to fall with a crash; **-rsi** *vr* to ruin oneself.
rovinóso *a* ruinous.
rovistàre *vti* to rummage, search.
róvo *nm* blackberry bush, bramble.
rozzaménte *ad* roughly, clumsily, rudely.
rozzézza *nf* roughness, rudeness.
rózzo *nm* rough, rude.
rúba, a *ad* in great quantities.
rubacuòri *inv nm* ladykiller.
rubàre *vt* to steal (from).
rubicóndo *a* rubicund, ruddy.
Rubicóne *nm* (*geogr*) Rubicon.
rubinétto *nm* tap, faucet.
rubíno *nm* ruby.
rúblo *nm* rouble.
rubríca *nf* newspaper column; address book; rubric.
rúde *a* rough, harsh, hard.
rúdere *nm* remains, ruin *pl*.
rudimentàle *a* rudimentary.

rudiménto *nm* first principle, rudiment.
ruffiàno *nm* pander, procurer.
rúga *nf* wrinkle.
rúggine *nf* rust, blight; ill-feeling.
rugginóso *a* rusty.
ruggíre *vi* to roar.
ruggíto *nm* roar(ing).
rugiàda *nf* dew.
rugiadóso *a* dewy.
rugóso *a* wrinkled.
ruína *etc v* **rovína** *etc.*
rullàre *vi* to roll.
rullío *nm* rolling.
rúllo *nm* (*drum etc*) roll; (*mech*) drum-roller, cylinder.
rumèno *a nm* R(o)umanian.
ruminànte *a nm* ruminant.
ruminàre *vti* to ruminate.
rumóre *nm* noise, rumor.
rumoreggiàre *vi* to make a noise, rumble.
rumoróso *a* noisy, loud.
ruòlo *nm* list, roll, role; **di r.** regular, on the staff.
ruòta *nf* wheel.
rúpe *nf* cliff, rock.
ruràle *a* rural; *nm* countryman.
ruscèllo *nm* brook.
russàre *vi* to snore.
Rússia *nf* (*geogr*) Russia.
rússo *a nm* Russian.
rústico *pl* **-ici** *a* country, rustic; unsociable.
ruttàre *vi* to belch.
rútto *nm* belching.
ruvidézza *nf* roughness, coarseness.
rúvido *a* rough, coarse.
ruzzàre *vi* to romp.
ruzzolàre *vi* to roll, tumble down.
ruzzolóne *nm* fall, tumble; **ruzzolóni, (a)** *ad* headlong.

S

sàbato *nm* Saturday.
sàbbia *nf* sand.
sabotàggio *nm* sabotage.
saccarína *nf* saccharine.
saccheggiàre *vt* to sack, plunder.
sacchéggio *nm* plunder, sack.
sàcco *pl* **sàcchi** *nm* bag, sack; **un s. di** a lot of; **mèttere nel s.** to outwit; **vuotàre il s.** to speak one's mind.
saccóne *nm* straw mattress.
sacerdòte *nm* priest.
sacerdotéssa *nf* priestess.
sacerdòzio *nm* priesthood.
sacramentàle *a* sacramental.
sacramentàre *vi* to swear.
sacraménto *nm* sacrament.
sacrificàre *vti* to sacrifice.
sacrifício, sacrifízio *nm* sacrifice.
sacrilègio *nm* sacrilege.
sacrílego *pl* **-eghi** *a* impious, sacrilegious.
sàcro *a* holy, sacred.
sacrosànto *a* sacrosanct; indisputable; well-merited.
sàdico *pl* **-ici** *a nm* sadist(ic).
sadíşmo *nm* sadism.
saétta *nf* arrow; lightning, thunderbolt.
saettàre *vti* to dart, shoot.
sagàce *a* sagacious, shrewd, wise.
sagàcia, sagacità *nf* sagacity, shrewdness.
saggézza *nf* wisdom.
saggiàre *vt* to assay, test.
sàggio *a* wise, sensible; *nm* wise man; (*liter*) essay; test, example, sample.
sàgoma *nf* shape; outline; pattern; character.
sàgra *nf* annual festival.
sagràto *nm* hallowed ground (in front of church).
sagrestàno *nm* sexton.
sagrestía *nf* sacristy, vestry.
sàio *nm* sackcloth; (*eccl*) monk's habit.
sàla *nf* hall, room; **s. d'aspètto** waiting room.
salamàndra *nf* salamander.
salàme *nm* sausage, salami.
salamòia *nf* brine, pickle.
salàre *vt* to salt.
salariàre *vt* to pay wages to.
salariàto *a* wage-earning; *nm* wage-earner.
salàrio *nm* pay, wages.
salàsso *nm* blood-letting; extortion.
salàto *a* salty, salted.
saldàre *vt* to solder, weld, join; (*com*) to settle.
saldatúra *nf* soldering, welding.
saldézza *nf* firmness, steadiness.
sàldo *a* firm, steady; *nm* (*com*) balance; settlement.
sàle *nm* salt; common-sense; **s. inglése** Epsom salts.
salgèmma *nm* rock-salt.
sàlice *nm* willow.
saliènte *a nm* salient.
salièra *nf* salt-cellar.
salína *nf* salt-mine salt-pan.
salíno *a* saline, salt(y).
salíre *vi* to rise, climb, go up, mount; *vt* to climb, go up.
Salisbúrgo *nf* (*geogr*) Salzburg.
saliscéndi (*inv*) *nm* latch.
salíta *nf* ascent, slope.
salíva *nf* saliva.
sàlma *nf* corpse.
salmàstro *a* brackish.
sàlmo *nm* psalm.
salmóne *nm* salmon.
salnítro *nm* saltpeter.
Salomóne *nm pr* Solomon.
salóne *nm* hall, reception room.
salòtto *nm* drawing room, sitting room.
salpàre *vi* to (set) sail, weigh anchor.
sàlsa *nf* sauce.
salsèdine *nf* salt(iness).
salsíccia *nf* sausage.
sàlso *a* salt, salty.
saltàre *vt* to clear, jump (over), skip, miss out; *vi* to jump, leap, spring.

salterellàre *vi* to hop (about), skip (about).
saltimbànco *pl* **-chi** *nm* acrobat; mountebank.
sàlto *nm* jump, leap; **s. mortàle** somersault.
saltuàrio *a* desultory.
salúbre *a* healthy, wholesome.
salúme *nm* salt meat.
salumería *nf* pork-butcher's (shop); **salumière** *nm* pork-butcher.
salutàre *vt* to greet, salute, say good-bye to, welcome; *a* healthy, salutary.
salúte *nf* health, safety, salvation; **s.!** bless you!; **alla s.!** here's health!; **càsa di s.** nursing-home.
salúto *nm* greeting, salute; **salúti** *pl* regards *pl*.
sàlva *nf* salvo, volley.
salvacondótto *nm* safe-conduct.
salvadanàio *nm* money-box.
salvagènte (*inv*) *nm* lifebelt, life preserver; traffic island.
salvaguardàre *vt* to safeguard.
salvaguàrdia *nf* protection, safeguard.
salvàre *vt* to rescue, save; **-rsi** *vr* to save oneself, escape.
salvatàggio *nm* rescue, salvage.
salvatóre *a* saving; *nm* rescuer, saver, savior.
salvazióne *nf* salvation.
salvézza *nf* salvation, safety, escape.
sàlvia *nf* (*plant*) sage.
salviétta *nf* napkin, serviette.
sàlvo *a* safe, secure; **sàno e s.** safe and sound; **in s.** in a safe place; *prep* except, save.
samaritàno *a nm* Samaritan.
sambúco *pl* **-chi** *nm* elder-tree.
Samuèle *nm pr* Samuel.
san *a* Saint.
sanàre *vt* to heal.
sanatòrio *nm* sanatorium.
sancíre *vt* to sanction; ratify.
sàndalo *nm* sandal; sandalwood.
sàngue *nm* blood; **s. fréddo** composure.
sanguígno *a* (of) blood; blood-red; sanguine.
sanguinàrio *a* bloodthirsty; sanguinary.
sanguinàccio *nm* blood sausage.
sanguinàre *vi* to bleed.
sanguinolènto *a* bleeding; bloodstained.
sanguinóso *a* bloody.
sanguisúga *nf* leech; (*fig*) extortioner.
sanità *nf* health, sanity, soundness.
sanitàrio *a* medical, sanitary; *nm* physician.
sàno *a* healthy, sane; sound, wholesome.
santificàre *vt* to consecrate, hallow, sanctify.
santità *nf* holiness, sanctity.
sànto *a* holy, hallowed; *nm* saint.
santuàrio *nm* sanctuary, shrine.
sanzionàre *vt* to authorize, sanction.
sanzióne *nf* sanction, approval.
sapére *vt* to be able; be acquainted with, get to know; hear; know (how to); learn; smell (of), taste (of); *nm* knowledge, learning.
sapiènte *a nm* learned, wise (man).
sapiènza *nf* learning, wisdom.
saponàta *nf* lather, soapsuds.
sapóne *nm* soap; **saponétta** *nf* cake of soap.
sapóre *nm* taste, flavor.
saporitaménte *ad* tastily; **pagàre s.** to pay a very high price.
saporíto, saporóso *a* delicious, savory.
Sàra *nf pr* Sara(h).
saracinésca *nf* rolling shutter; portcullis.
sarcàsmo *nm* sarcasm.
sarcàstico *pl* **-ici** *a* sarcastic.
sàrchio, sarchièllo *nm* hoe.
sarcòfago *pl* **-gi, -ghi** *nm* sarcophagus.
Sardégna *nf* (*geogr*) Sardinia.
sardína *nf* sardine.
sàrdo *a nm* Sardinian.
sàrta *nf* dressmaker.
sàrtie *nf pl* (*naut*) rigging, shrouds *pl*.
sàrto *nm* tailor.
sartoría *nf* tailor's shop.
sassàta *nf* blow from a stone.
sàsso *nm* stone; **rimanére di s.** to be astonished.
sassòfono *nm* saxophone.
Sàtana *nm pr* Satan.
satèllite *a nm* satellite.
sàtira *nf* satire, lampoon.
satireggiàre *vt* to satirize.
satírico *pl* **-ici** *a* satiric(al); *nm* satirist.
satollàre *vt* to fill up, satiate.
satóllo *a* full, overfed, satiated.
saturàre *vt* to saturate, glut.
Satúrno *nm* Saturn.
sàturo *a* saturated.
Sàul *nm pr* Saul.
Savèrio *nm pr* Xavier.
sàvio *a* wise; *nm* sage.
Savòia *nf* (*geogr*) Savoy.
saziàre *vt* to satiate, satisfy; **-rsi** *vr* to get tired of.
sazietà *nf* satiety.
sàzio *a* sated; satiated.
ṣbadatàggine *nf* carelessness, thoughtlessness.
ṣbadàto *a* careless, heedless.
ṣbadigliàre *vi* to yawn.
ṣbadíglio *nm* yawn.
ṣbagliàre *vt* to mistake; **s. stràda** to take the wrong turning; *vi and* **-rsi** *vr* to be mistaken, make a mistake.
ṣbàglio *nm* error, mistake.
ṣbalestràto *a* unbalanced, wild.
ṣballàre *vt* to unpack; *vi* to tell tall tales.
ṣbalordiménto *nm* astonishment, bewilderment, daze.
ṣbalordíre *vt* to amaze, astound.
ṣbalorditívo *a* amazing.
ṣbalzàre *vt* to throw, toss, emboss.

sbàlzo *nm* bound; sudden change; **a sbàlzi** by fits and starts; **lavóro a s.** embossed work.
sbandàre *vt* to disband; *vi* to skid; (*naut*) list.
sbaragliàre *vt* to rout.
sbaràglio *nm* rout; risk.
sbarazzàre *vt* to rid; **-rsi** *vr* to get rid of.
sbarazzíno *nm* scamp.
sbarbàre *vt* **-rsi** *vr* to shave.
sbarbàto *a* clean-shaven.
sbarcàre *vi* to disembark, land; **s. il lunàrio** to make both ends meet.
sbàrco *pl* **sbàrchi** *nm* landing, unloading.
sbàrra *nf* bar.
sbarraménto *nm* (*mil*) barrage; obstruction.
sbarràre *vt* to bar, obstruct; (*eyes*) open wide; (*check*) cross.
sbassàre *vt* to lower.
sbatacchiàre *vt* to slam, bang.
sbàttere *vti* to knock, bang, shake.
sbiadíre *vti* to fade.
sbièco *pl* **-chi** *a* awry, oblique; **di s.** askance.
sbigottiménto *nm* dismay, astonishment.
sbigottíre *vt* to dismay, bewilder.
sbilanciàre *vt* to unbalance, unsettle; **-rsi** *vr* to speak freely; spend beyond one's means.
sbilàncio *nm* lack of balance, disproportion.
sbilènco *pl* **-chi** *a* crooked, twisted.
sbirciàre *vti* to cast a sidelong glance.
sbloccàre *vt* to unblock, clear; decontrol.
sblòcco *nm* unblocking; (*fig*) unfreezing.
sboccàre *vi* to flow into, open into.
sboccàto *a* foul-mouthed.
sbocciàre *vi* to blossom, open.
sbócco *pl* **sbócchi** *nm* outlet; (*river*) mouth; (*road*) end.
sbòrnia *nf* drunkenness.
sborsàre *vt* pay out, spend.
sbórso *nm* disbursement, outlay, payment.
sbottonàre *vt* to unbutton; **-rsi** *vr* to unbutton one's clothes; unbosom oneself.
sbozzàre *vt* to sketch out; **sbòzzo** *nm* rough draft, sketch.
sbraitàre *vi* to bawl, shout.
sbranàre *vt* to tear to pieces.
sbriciolàre *vt* **-rsi** *vr* to crumble.
sbrigàre *vt* to dispatch, finish; **-rsi** *vr* to hurry up, make haste.
sbrigatívo *a* hasty, summary.
sbrigliàto *a* lively, unbridled, wild.
sbrogliàre *vt* to disentangle, extricate.
sbucàre *vi* to come out, spring out.
sbucciàre *vt* to pare, peel, shell, skin.
sbuffàre *vi* to pant, puff, snort.
scàbbia *nf* scabies, mange.
scabróso *a* difficult, rough, rugged.
scacchièra *nf* chessboard, checkerboard; **scacchière** *nm* Exchequer; **Cancellière dello s.** Chancellor of the Exchequer.
scacciàre *vt* to dispel, drive out.
scàcco *pl* **scàcchi** *nm* square, check; **s. (màtto)** check(mate); **scàcchi** chess; **a s.** checked, checkered.
scadènte *a* inferior, of poor quality.
scadènza *nf* (*com*) maturity; **a brève s.** in a short time.
scadére *vi* (*com*) to be due; expire; lose value; sink.
scafàndro *nm* diving suit.
scaffàle *nm* shelf; bookcase.
scàfo *nm* hull.
scagionàre *vt* to exculpate, justify.
scàglia *nf* flake, chip, scale.
scagliàre *vt* to fling, hurl, throw; **-rsi** *vr* to hurl oneself, rush.
scaglióne *nm* echelon.
scàla *nf* ladder; staircase, stairs *pl*; scale.
scalàre *vt* to climb up, to scale; (*com*) scale down.
scalàta *nf* climbing.
scalatóre *nm* **-trice** *nf* climber.
scalcinàto *a* seedy, shabby.
scaldabàgno *nm* water-heater.
scaldàre *vt* to heat, warm; **-rsi** *vr* to warm oneself; get excited.
scaldavivànde (*inv*) *nm* dish-warmer.
scaldíno *nm* hand-warmer, portable warming-pan.
scalfíre *vt* to graze, scratch.
scalinàta *nf* (flight of) steps.
scalíno *nm* step.
scalmanàrsi *vr* to get agitated.
scàlmo *nm* (*naut*) rowlock, oarlock.
scàlo *nm* landing-place, stop; (*rly*) **s. mèrci** freight station.
scaloppína *nf* veal cutlet.
scalpellíno *nm* stone-cutter, small chisel.
scalpèllo *nm* chisel.
scalpóre *nm* fuss.
scàltro *a* shrewd, crafty.
scàlzo *a* barefoot(ed).
scambiàre *vt* to exchange; mistake.
scambiévole *a* mutual, reciprocal.
scàmbio *nm* exchange; (*rly*) points *pl*, switch.
scamiciàto *a* shirt-sleeved; *nm* revolutionary.
scamosciàto *a* chamois, suède.
scampagnàta *nf* country excursion.
scampàre *vt* to rescue, save; *vi* to escape; **scampàrela bèlla** to have a narrow escape.
scàmpo *nm* escape, safety; shrimp.
scàmpolo *nm* remnant.
scancellàre *v* **cancellàre.**
scandagliàre *vt* to sound.
scandàglio *nm* sounding, sounding-rod.
scandalizzàre *vt* to scandalize, shock.
scàndalo *nm* scandal.
scandalóso *a* scandalous, shocking.
Scandinàvia *nf* (*geogr*) Scandinavia.

scandínavo *a nm* Scandinavian.
scandíre *vt* to scan; pronounce clearly.
scannàre *vt* to butcher, cut someone's throat.
scannellatúra *nf* groove, fluting.
scànno *nm* bench, seat.
scansafatíche *inv nmf* loafer.
scansàre *vt* to avoid, shun; **-rsi** *vr* to step aside.
scansía *nf* bookcase, set of shelves.
scansióne *nf* scansion.
scantonàre *vi* to turn the corner; sneak off.
scanzonàto *a* free and easy, unconventional.
scapestràto *a* wild, dissolute; *nm* waster.
scapigliàre *vt* to ruffle; **scapigliàto** *a* dishevelled, disorderly, unconventional.
scapitàre *vi* to lose, suffer loss.
scàpito *nm* detriment, loss.
scàpola *nf* shoulder-blade.
scàpolo *a* single; *nm* bachelor.
scappàre *vi* to escape, run away.
scappàta *nf* escapade; short call; trip.
scappaménto *nm* (*mech*) exhaust.
scappatóia *nf* loophole, way out.
scarabèo *nm* beetle; scarab.
scarabocchiàre *vt* to scrawl, scribble.
scarabòcchio *nm* scribble, scribbling.
scarafàggio *nm* cockroach, roach.
scaramúccia *nf* skirmish.
scaramucciàre *vt* to skirmish.
scaraventàre *vt* to fling, hurl.
scarceràre *vt* to release (from prison).
scardinàre *vt* to unhinge.
scàrica *nf* volley, shower; (*el*) discharge.
scaricàre *vt* to discharge, unload.
scàrico *pl* **-chi** *a* unloaded, discharged, (*clock*) run down; light; *nm* discharge, unloading, waste; **túbo di s.** exhaust-pipe, waste-pipe.
scarlattína *nf* scarlet fever.
scarlàtto *a nm* scarlet.
scarmigliàre *vt* to ruffle.
scàrno *a* lean, thin.
scàrpa *nf* shoe; **scarpóne** *nm* boot; **s. da sci** ski-boot.
scarseggiàre *vi* to be scarce, lack.
scarsézza, scarsità *nf* scarcity, lack.
scàrso *a* scanty, scarce, short.
scartàre *vt* unwrap, reject, discard.
scàrto *nm* discard(ing), refuse; *nm* swerve; **di s.** of inferior quality.
scassinàre *vt* to force open.
scassinatóre *nm* burglar, housebreaker.
scàsso *nm* housebreaking.
scatenàre *vt* to unchain, let loose; cause; **-rsi** *vr* to break out.
scàtola *nf* box, tin, can, case; **in s.** canned.
scatolàme *nm* tins *pl*, cans *pl*, canned food.
scattàre *vi* to be released, go off, spring (up); get angry; *vt* (*phot*) to shoot.
scàtto *nm* click, jerk; impulse; (*tec*) release.
scaturíre *vi* to gush, spring.
scavalcàre *vt* to climb over; oust; excel.
scavàre *vt* to dig out, excavate.
scavezzacòllo *nm* (*fig*) reckless person.
scàvo *nm* excavation.
scégliere *vt* to choose, pick out, select.
scelleratézza *nf* wickedness, crime.
scelleràto *a nm* wicked (man).
scellíno *nm* shilling.
scélta *nf* choice, selection; **di prima s.** choice, top quality.
scélto *a* choice, picked, select(ed).
scemàre *vti* to diminish, lessen.
scèmo *a* foolish, stupid; *nm* fool.
scémpio *a* silly; single; *nm* slaughter.
scèna *nf* scene, stage; **mèttere in s.** (*theat*) to produce, stage.
scenàta *nf* scene; row.
scenàrio *nm* scenario; scenery.
scéndere *vti* to come (go) down, descend.
sceneggiatúra *nf* staging; (*cin*) scenario.
scènico *pl* **-ici** scenic; stage.
sceríffo *nm* sheriff.
scervellàrsi *vr* to cudgel (rack) one's brains.
scèttico *pl* **-ici** *a* skeptical; *nm* skeptic.
scèttro *nm* scepter.
scévro *a* exempt, free (from).
schèda *nf* card, file-card; voting paper.
schedàre *vt* to file, catalogue.
schedàrio *nm* card-index.
schéggia *nf* splinter.
scheggiàre *vt* **-rsi** *vr* to splinter.
schèletro *nm* skeleton.
schèma *nm* plan, scheme; diagram.
schérma *nf* fencing.
schermírsi *vr* to defend oneself.
schérmo *nm* protection; (*cin, tv*) screen; (*phot*) filter.
schernire *vt* to despise, flout, scoff at.
schérno *nm* derision, taunt.
scherzàre *vi* to jest, joke, make fun.
schérzo *nm* jest, joke, trick.
scherzóso *a* facetious, joking, playful.
schettinàre *vi* to roller-skate.
schettíno *nm* roller skate.
schiaccianóci *nm* nutcrackers *pl*.
schiacciànte *a* crushing, overwhelming.
schiacciàre *vt* to crush, squash.
schiaffeggiàre *vt* to slap, smack.
schiàffo *nm* box on the ear, slap; insult.
schiamazzàre *vi* to make a din.
schiamàzzo *nm* din, uproar.
schiantàre *vt* **-rsi** *vr* to break.
schiànto *nm* crash; pang; **di s.** suddenly.

schiariménto *nm* clearing up; explanation.
schiaríre *vt* to clear up; explain; **-rsi** *vr* to become clear, light, brighten, light up.
schiaríta *nf* clearing; (*fig*) improvement.
schiàtta *nf* race, stock.
schiavitú *nf* slavery.
schiàvo *a* slave; *nm* slave, bondsman.
schièna *nf* back.
schièra *nf* band, group; **mèttersi in s.** to fall in.
schieràre *vt* **-rsi** *vr* to draw up, side with.
schiettézza *nf* purity, frankness.
schiètto *a* pure, unadulterated; frank.
schifézza *nf* disgusting thing, disgust.
schifiltóso *a* fastidious, hard to please.
schífo *nm* disgust.
schifosàggine *nf* disgusting action (thing), loathsomeness.
schifóso *a* disgusting, loathsome.
schiòppo *nm* gun.
schiúdere *vt* **-rsi** *vr* to open.
schiúma *nf* foam, froth; scum.
schivàre *vt* to avoid.
schivo *a* shy; averse.
schizzàre *vt* to splash, squirt; sketch; *vi* spurt, rush.
schízzo *nm* splash; sketch.
sci *nm* ski; **s. nàutico** waterski.
scía *nf* track, wake.
sciàbola *nf* saber.
sciacàllo *nm* jackal.
sciacquàre *vt* to rinse; **sciàcquo** *nm* gargling, mouthwash.
sciagúra *nf* disaster, misfortune.
sciaguratamènte *ad* unfortunately, miserably; wickedly.
sciaguràto *a* unlucky, wretched; *nm* wretch.
scialacquàre *vt* to squander, waste.
scialàre *vi* to be wasteful, dissipate; enjoy oneself.
sciàlbo *a* pale, wan.
sciàlle *nm* shawl.
scialúppa *nf* (*naut*) launch.
sciàme *nm* crowd, swarm.
sciancàto *a* lame.
Sciangai *nf* (*geogr*) Shanghai.
sciàre *vi* to ski.
sciàrpa *nf* scarf, sash.
sciàtto *a* slovenly, untidy, careless.
scíbile *nm* knowledge.
scientemènte *ad* knowingly.
scientificamènte *ad* scientifically.
scientífico *pl* **-ici** *a* scientific.
sciènza *nf* science, knowledge.
scienziàto *nm* scientist.
scímmia *nf* ape, monkey.
scimmiottàre *vt* to ape, mimic.
scimunito *a* foolish, silly.
scíndere *vt* to divide, separate.
scintílla *nf* spark.
scintillàre *vi* to sparkle, glitter.
scintillío *nm* sparkling, twinkling.
sciocchézza *nf* foolishness, nonsense, trifle.
sciòcco *pl* **sciòcchi** *a* foolish, silly; *nm* fool.
sciògliere *vt* to dissolve, melt; release, untie; **-rsi** *vr* to dissolve, melt; free oneself.
scioglilíngua *inv nm* tonguetwister.
sciòlto *a* melted; loose, free; nimble.
scioperànte *nm* striker.
scioperàre *vi* to (go on) strike.
scioperàto *a* lazy; *nm* loafer.
sciòpero *nm* strike.
sciorinàre *vt* (*clothes*) hang out; display.
scipíto *a* insipid, tasteless.
sciròcco *pl* **-chi** *nm* south-east wind.
sciròppo *nm* syrup.
scisma *nm* schism.
scissióne *nf* division, split.
sciupàre *vt* to ruin, spoil, waste.
sciupío *nm* waste.
sciupóne *nm* waster, spendthrift.
scivolàre *vi* to slide, slip, skid; **scivolo** *nm* chute.
scoccàre *vt* to dart, to throw; *vi* to strike.
scocciàre *vt* (*fam*) to bore, bother.
scocciatóre *nm* **-trice** *nf* (*fam*) bore.
scodèlla *nf* bowl, soup plate.
scodellàre *vt* to dish up, serve out; (*fig*) pour out.
scodinzolàre *vi* to wag (the tail).
scoglièra *nf* cliff.
scòglio *nm* rock, reef; stumbling-block.
scoiàttolo *nm* squirrel.
scolàre *vti* to drain, drip.
scolàstico *pl* **-ici** *a* scholastic.
scolàro *nm* pupil, schoolboy.
scollàto *a* (*dress*) low-necked.
scollatúra *nf* neckline.
scòllo *nm* neck-opening.
scólo *nm* drainage; drain-pipe.
scoloríre *vt* to discolor; *vi* to fade.
scolpàre *vt* to exculpate, justify; **-rsi** *vr* to apologize; justify oneself.
scolpíre *vt* sculpture, carve, engrave.
scombinàre *vt* to disarrange.
scombussolàre *vt* to disturb, upset.
scommèssa *nf* bet, wager.
scommèttere *vt* to bet, wager.
scomodàre *vt* **-rsi** *vr* to trouble, bother.
scomodità *nf* inconvenience.
scòmodo *a* uncomfortable, inconvenient; *nm* trouble.
scompaginàre *vt* to upset.
scomparíre *vi* disappear, be lost.
scompàrsa *nf* disappearance, death.
scompartiménto *nm* compartment.
scompigliàre *vt* to upset, confuse.
scompíglio *nm* confusion, fuss.
scompórre *vt* to take to pieces, disarrange; **-rsi** *vr* to be upset, lose one's temper.
scompósto *a* dismantled, disordered; upset.
scomúnica *nf* excommunication.
scomunicàre *vt* to excommunicate.

sconcertàre *vt* to baffle, disconcert, puzzle.
sconcézza *nf* obscenity, disgusting thing.
scóncio *a* indecent, nasty.
sconclusionàto *a* rambling.
sconfessàre *vt* to disavow, disown.
sconfíggere *vt* to defeat.
sconfinàto *a* boundless, unlimited.
sconfítta *nf* defeat.
sconfortàto *a* discouraged, disheartened.
sconfòrto *nm* discouragement, dejection.
scongiuràre *vt* to implore; remove.
scongiúro *nm* exorcism.
sconnèttere *vt* to disconnect.
sconoscènte *a* ungrateful.
sconosciúto *a nm* unknown.
sconquassàre *vt* to smash.
sconquassàto *a* rickety, tumble-down.
sconsideràto *a* thoughtless.
sconsigliàre *vt* to advise against, dissuade.
sconsolàto *a* disconsolate, depressed.
scontàre *vt* (*com*) to deduct, discount; to expiate, pay for; to take for granted.
scontentézza *nf* discontent.
scontènto *a* disappointed, dissatisfied; *nm* discontent.
scónto *nm* discount.
scontràrsi *vr* to clash, crash, collide.
scontríno *nm* check, receipt, ticket.
scóntro *nm* collision.
scontrosàggine, scontrosità *nf* cantankerousness, bad temper, peevishness.
scontróso *a* sulky, peevish, bad-tempered.
sconveniènte *a* unseemly, unprofitable.
sconveniènza *nf* unseemliness, discourtesy.
sconvòlgere *vt* to derange, upset.
sconvolgiménto *nm* upset, confusion.
scópa *nf* broom.
scopàre *vi* to sweep.
scopèrta *nf* discovery.
scopèrto *a* bare, open, unprotected.
scòpo *nm* aim, end, object, purpose.
scoppiàre *vi* to burst (out), explode.
scòppio *nm* burst(ing), explosion; outburst, outbreak.
scoprίre *vt* to discover, find out; reveal; **-rsi** *vr* to uncover oneself.
scoraggiàre *vt* to dishearten; **-rsi** *vr* to get disheartened.
scorbutíco *pl* **-ici** *a* scorbutic; cantankerous; awkward.
scorciàre *vt* to shorten; **scorciatóia** *nf* short-cut.
scórcio *nm* foreshortening; end.
scordàre *vt* **-rsi** *vr* to forget; untune.
scòrgere *vt* to discern, perceive.
scornàto *a* humiliated, ridiculed, disgraced.
scòrno *nm* disgrace, shame.
scorpacciàta *nf* bellyful.
scorpióne *nm* scorpion.
scorrazzàre *vi* to run about.
scórrere *vt* to run through; raid; glance over; *vi* to run, slide, flow.
scorrería *nf* incursion, raid.
scorrettézza *nf* mistake; bad manners; dishonesty.
scorrètto *a* incorrect; improper; dishonest, dissolute.
scorrévole *a* flowing, fluent, gliding.
scorrevolézza *nf* fluency, smoothness.
scórsa *nf* glance.
scórso *a* last, past.
scorsóio *a* running; **nódo s.** slip-knot.
scòrta *nf* escort; supply.
scortàre *vt* to escort.
scortecciàre *vt* to strip, peel.
scortése *a* discourteous, rude, uncivil.
scortesía *nf* rudeness, rude act.
scorticàre *vt* to flay, fleece, skin.
scorticatúra *nf* scratch, graze.
scòrza *nf* bark, peel, rind, skin.
scoscéso *a* steep.
scòssa *nf* shake, shock.
scòsso *a* shaken, upset.
scostàre *vt* **-rsi** *vr* to move (away), shift (aside).
scostumàto *a* dissolute; rude.
scottàre *vt* to burn, scald, scorch.
scottatúra *nf* burn, scald.
scòtto *a* (*cook*) overdone; *nm* score, reckoning.
scovàre *vt* to dislodge, rouse, find out.
Scòzia *nf* (*geogr*) Scotland.
scozzése *a* Scottish; *nm* Scot, Scotsman, (*language*) Scots.
screditàre *vt* to discredit.
scrédito *nm* discredit, disgrace.
scremàre *vt* to skim.
screpolàre *vt* **-rsi** *vr* to chap, crack.
screzio *nm* dispute, quarrel.
scribacchiàre *vi* to scribble.
scricchiolàre *vi* to creak.
scricchiolío *nm* creaking.
scrígno *nm* casket, jewel-case.
scriminatúra *nf* (*hair*) parting.
scrítta *nf* inscription, notice.
scrítto *a* written; *nm* writing; document.
scrittóio *nm* writing desk.
scrittóre *nm* **-tríce** *nf* writer.
scrittúra *nf* (hand)writing; contract.
scritturàre *vt* (*theat*) to engage.
scrivanía *nf* (writing-)desk.
scrívere *vt* to write.
scroccàre *vt* to scrounge.
scròcco *pl* **scròcchi** *nm* scrounging; swindle.
scròfa *nf* sow.
scrollàre *vt* to shake, shrug.
scrosciàre *vi* (*rain*) to pelt; (*fig*) thunder.
scròscio *nm* roar; downpour; **piòvere a s.** to pour.
scrúpolo *nm* scruple.
scrupolóso *a* scrupulous.

scrutàre *vt* to investigate, scan.
scrutinàre *vt* to scrutinize.
scrutínio *nm* list of marks; voting; scrutiny.
scucíre *vt* to unstitch.
scudería *nf* stable.
scudíscio *nm* lash, whip.
scúdo *nm* shield, protection.
scultóre *nm* sculptor.
scultúra *nf* carving, sculpture.
scuòla *nf* school, schoolhouse; **s. diúrna** day-school; **s. seràle** night school.
scuòtere *vt* to shake; stir up; **-rsi** *vr* to rouse oneself, stir.
scúre *nf* ax, hatchet.
scúro *a* dark; grim; *nm* darkness; shutter.
scurríle *a* scurrilous.
scúșa *nf* excuse, pretext.
scușàre *vt* to excuse, forgive, justify; **-rsi** *vr* to apologize, justify oneself; **scúsi** excuse me; I beg your pardon.
șdebitàrsi *vr* to pay one's debts.
șdegnàre *vt* to disdain, scorn; **-rsi** to get angry.
șdégno *nm* disdain; indignation.
șdegnóso *a* disdainful, haughty.
sdentàto *a* toothless.
șdoganàre *vt* to clear (through the customs).
șdolcinàto *a* maudlin, sugary, affected.
șdraiàre *vt* to stretch at full length; **-rsi** *vr* to lie down, stretch oneself out; **sdràio** *nm* deck chair.
șdrucciolàre *vi* to slip, slide.
șdrucíre *vt* to tear, unstitch.
se *cj* if, whether; **se no** or else, otherwise.
sè *refl pron* oneself, himself, herself, itself, themselves *pl*.
sebbène *cj* although, though.
Sebastiàno *nm pr* Sebastian.
seccaménte *ad* drily, bluntly.
seccànte *a* tiresome, irritating; **persóna s.** a nuisance.
seccàre *vt* to dry; bother, irritate; **-rsi** *vr* to dry (up); get tired, get annoyed.
seccatúra *nf* nuisance, bother; desiccation.
sécchia *nf* **-o** *nm* bucket, pail.
sécco *pl* **sécchi** *a* dry; thin; **lavàre a s.** to dry-clean.
secolàre *a* age-old; secular, lay; *nm* layman.
sècolo *nm* century, age.
secondàre *v* **assecondàre.**
secondàrio *a* secondary.
secóndo *a* second; favorable; *nm* second, main dish; **di secónda màno** second-hand; *prep* according to; **s. me** in my opinion.
sèdano *nm* celery.
sedàre *vt* to soothe, calm.
sedatívo *a nm* sedative.
sède *nf* center, seat; residence; office; see.
sedentàrio *a* sedentary.
sedére *vi* to sit; **-rsi** *vr* to sit down, take a seat.
sèdia *nf* chair.
sedicènte *a* self-styled.
sédici *a* sixteen; **sedicènne** sixteen-year-old; **sedicèsimo** sixteenth.
sedíle *nm* seat, bench.
sedizióne *nf* sedition.
sedizióso *a* seditious.
sedúrre *vt* to seduce; entice, charm.
sedúta *nf* sitting; meeting.
seduttóre *nm* **-trice** *nf* seducer.
seduzióne *nf* seduction, enticement; charm.
séga *nf* saw.
ségala, ségale *nf* rye.
segàre *vt* to saw.
segatúra *nf* sawing; sawdust.
sèggio *nm* chair, seat; see.
sèggiola *v* **sèdia.**
segnalàre *vt* to signal; point out; **-rsi** *vr* to distinguish oneself.
segnalazióne *nf* signal(ling).
segnàle *nm* signal.
segnalíbro *nm* bookmark.
segnàre *vt* to mark, note; (*sport*) score; **-rsi** *vr* to cross oneself.
ségno *nm* sign, mark.
ségo *pl* **séghi** *nm* tallow.
segregaménto *nm* **segregazióne** *nf* segregation, isolation.
segregàre *vt* to isolate, segregate.
segretàrio *nm* **-ria** *nf* secretary.
segretería *nf* secretary's office.
segretézza *nf* secrecy.
segréto *a nm* secret.
seguàce *nmf* follower, supporter.
seguènte *a* following; next.
seguíre *vt* to follow; supervise; *vi* to follow; result.
seguitàre *vi* to continue, go on, keep on.
séguito *nm* continuation; followers *pl*, retinue; sequel; series; succession; **di s.** in succession; **in s.** later on; **in s. a** *prep* owing to.
sèi *a* six.
seicènto *a* six hundred; *nm* 17th century.
sèlce *nf* flint(stone).
selciàto *nm* pavement; road surface.
selezionàre *vt* to select, choose.
selezióne *nf* selection; digest.
sèlla *nf* saddle.
sellàre *vt* to saddle.
seltz *nm* soda(-water), seltzer.
sélva *nf* forest, wood.
selvaggína *nf* game.
selvàggio *a* savage; wild; rough; *nm* savage.
selvatichézza *nf* wildness; unsociability; uncouthness.
selvàtico *pl* **-ici** *a* wild, rough.
semàforo *nm* traffic lights.
sembiànte *nm* **sembiànza** *nf* appearance.
sembràre *v* **parére.**
sème *nm* seed; cause; **semènza** seeds *pl*; (*liter*) progeny.
semestràle *a* half-yearly.

semèstre *nm* half-year.
semi- *prefix* half-, semi-.
semicùpio *nm* hip-bath.
sémina, seminagióne *nf* sowing; sowing season.
seminàre *vt* to sow; scatter.
seminàrio *nm* seminary; seminar.
seminàto *a* sown; strewn; *nm* sown field.
seminterràto *nm* basement.
sémola *nf* bran; fine flour; freckles *pl*.
semovènte *a* self-moving, self-propelled.
Sempióne *nm* (*geogr*) Simplon.
sempitèrno *a* everlasting.
sémplice *a* simple, easy; mere, plain; **soldàto s.** *nm* private (soldier).
semplicità *nf* simplicity.
semplificàre *vt* to simplify.
sèmpre *ad* always, ever; still; **per s.** forever; **s. méno** less and less; **s. più** more and more; **s. che** *cj* provided (that).
sènapa, sènape *nf* mustard.
senàto *nm* senate.
senatóre *nm* senator.
senése *a nmf* Sienese.
senìle *a* senile.
senilità *nf* senility.
senióre *a nm* senior.
Sènna *nf* (*geogr*) Seine.
sénno *nm* judgment, sense, wisdom.
séno *nm* bosom, breast; cove, inlet.
sensàle *nm* broker, middleman.
sensàto *a* sensible, judicious.
sensazionàle *a* sensational, thrilling.
sensazióne *nf* sensation, feeling.
senserìa *nf* brokerage.
sensìbile *a* sensitive; considerable.
sensibilità *nf* sensitiveness, feeling, sensitivity.
sensitìvo *a* sensory; sensitive.
sènso *nm* sense; feeling; meaning; sensation; **s. ùnico** one way; **prìvo di sènsi** unconscious; **sensòrio** *a* sensory; *nm* sense organ.
sensuàle *a* sensual.
sensualità *nf* sensuality.
sentènza *nf* decree; judgment; maxim.
sentenziàre *vi* to judge; talk sententiously.
sentièro *nm* footpath, path(way).
sentimentàle *a* sentimental.
sentiménto *nm* sentiment; feeling; *pl* senses *pl*.
sentìna *nf* bilge.
sentinèlla *nf* (*mil*) sentinel, sentry.
sentìre *vi* to feel; hear, listen to; **-rsi** *vr* to feel; *nm* feelings *pl*.
sentìto *a* heart-felt, sincere.
sentóre *nm* vague suspicion, inkling.
sènza *prep* without; **sènz'àltro** *ad* immediately; of course.
separàre *vt* to separate, divide; **-rsi** *vr* to part, separate.
separataménte *ad* separately.
separazióne *nf* separation, parting.
sepólcro *nm* sepulcher, grave.
sepoltùra *nf* burial; grave; **luògo di s.** burial place.
seppelliménto *nm* interment, burial.
seppellìre *vt* to bury.
séppia *nf* cuttlefish.
sequèla *nf* series, sequence.
sequestràre *vt* to sequester, sequestrate, distrain upon.
sequèstro *nm* sequestration, distraint.
séra *nf* evening.
seràle *a* evening.
seràta *nf* evening; evening party; (*theat*) evening performance.
serbàre *vt* to put aside; to keep.
serbatóio *nm* reservoir, tank.
sèrbo *nm* **in s.** in reserve; aside.
serenàta *nf* serenade.
serenità *nf* serenity, calmness.
seréno *a* serene, clear, calm.
sergènte *nm* sergeant.
seriaménte *ad* seriously, gravely.
sèrie *nf* series; set; succession; **in s.** mass-produced; **fuòri s.** special, custom-built.
serietà *nf* seriousness, gravity.
sèrio *a* serious, earnest; grave; reliable; **sul s.** in earnest.
sermóne *nm* sermon; reproof.
sèrpe *nf* **-pènte** *nm* serpent, snake.
serpeggiàre *vi* to meander, wind; spread.
sèrra *nf* greenhouse, hothouse.
serràglio *nm* menagerie; seraglio.
serramànico, coltèllo a claspknife.
serrànda *nf* (*of a shop*) shutter.
serràre *vt* to lock (up); shut, close; clench; **-rsi** *vr* to stand close; close up.
serratùra *nf* lock.
sèrva *nf* maid, (woman)servant.
servìle *a* servile, slavish.
servìre *vti* to serve; **-rsi** *vr* to (make) use (of); help oneself.
servitóre *nm* servant.
servitù *nf* servitude; servants *pl*, staff.
serviziévole *a* obliging.
servìzio *nm* service; favor; kindness; **di s.** on duty; **fuòri s.** off duty; **dònna di s.** *nf* maid; **mezzo s.** part-time service.
sèrvo *nm* (man)servant.
sessànta *a nm* sixty; **sessantènne** *a nmf* sixty-year-old (person); **sessantèsimo** *a* sixtieth; **sessantìna** *nf* about sixty.
sessióne *nf* session.
sèsso *nm* sex.
sessuàle *a* sexual.
sèsto *a* sixth; *nm* order; **méttere in s.** to put in order, tidy.
séta *nf* silk.
setàccio *nm* sieve.
séte *nf* thirst; **avèr s.** to be thirsty.
seterìa *nf* silk shop; silk goods.
sétola *nf* bristle.
setolóso *a* bristly.
sètta *nf* sect.
settànta *a nm* seventy; **settantènne**

a nmf seventy-year-old (person); **settantèsimo** *a* seventieth; **settantína** *nf* about seventy.
sètte *a* seven; **settènne** seven-year-old.
settecènto *a* seven hundred; *nm* 18th century.
settèmbre *nm* September.
settentrionàle *a* north(ern), northerly; *nm* northerner.
settentrióne *nm* north.
sèttico *pl* **-ici** *a* septic.
settimàna *nf* week.
settimanàle *a nm* weekly.
sèttimo *a* seventh.
settóre *nm* sector.
settuagenàrio *a nm* septuagenarian.
severaménte *ad* severely, sternly.
severità *nf* severity, strictness, sternness.
sevèro *a* severe, strict, stern.
sevízie *nf pl* cruelty, ill-treatment.
sezionàre *vt* to cut up, dissect.
sezióne *nf* section; department.
sfaccendàre *vi* to bustle about.
sfaccendàto *nm* idler, loafer.
sfacchinàre *vi* to drudge.
sfacchinàta *nf* heavy piece of work.
sfacciatàggine *nf* impudence, insolence.
sfacciàto *a* impudent, shameless.
sfacèlo *nm* break-up, collapse, ruin.
sfamàre *vt* to appease someone's hunger.
sfàrzo *nm* pomp, splendor.
sfarzóso *a* gorgeous, sumptuous.
sfasàto *a* (*el*) out of phase; (*fig*) inconsistent, inconsequent.
sfasciàre *vt* to unbandage; demolish, dismantle.
sfatàre *vt* to disprove, discredit.
sfavillàre *vi* to sparkle, shine.
sfavorévole *a* unfavorable.
sfèra *nf* sphere, circle, globe.
sfèrico *pl* **-ici** *a* spherical.
sferràre *vt* (*a horse*) to unshoe; (*a blow*) deliver; (*an attack*) launch.
sfèrza *nf* lash, whip.
sferzàre *vt* to whip, lash, scourge.
sfiatàrsi *vr* to talk oneself hoarse.
sfida *nf* challenge, defiance.
sfidàre *vt* to challenge, dare, defy; **sfido!** *interj* of course.
sfidúcia *nf* distrust, mistrust, lack of confidence.
sfiduciàto *a* discouraged, disheartened.
sfiguràre *vt* to disfigure; *vi* to cut a poor figure.
sfilàre *vt* to unstring, unthread; *vi* to file (past).
sfilàta *nf* row, parade.
sfinge *nf* sphinx.
sfiniménto *nm* exhaustion.
sfiníto *a* exhausted, worn out.
sfioràre *vt* to graze, skim over, touch lightly, touch on.
sfioríre *vi* to wither, fade.
sfoderàre *vt* to remove the lining; (*sword etc*) draw, display, show off.
sfogàre *vt* to vent, let out; **-rsi** *vr* to give vent to one's feelings, speak frankly.
sfoggiàre *vti* to show off, flaunt.
sfòggio *nm* show, display.
sfogliàre *vt* to pick off leaves; turn over the pages of, run through (a book).
sfógo *pl* **sfóghi** *nm* vent, outlet; eruption.
sfolgorànte *a* blazing, flaming.
sfolgoràre *vi* to blaze, flash.
sfollàre *vt* to disperse; *vi* to disperse, evacuate.
sfondàre *vt* to break (down), knock the bottom out.
sfóndo *nm* background.
sformàto *a* shapeless; *nm* pie, pudding.
sfornàre *vt* to take out of the oven, bring out.
sfortúna *nf* ill-luck, misfortune.
sfortunàto *a* unlucky.
sforzàre *vt* to force strain; **-rsi** *vr* to strive, try hard.
sfòrzo *nm* effort, strain.
sfracellàre *vt* to shatter, smash.
sfrattàre *vt* to turn out, evict.
sfràtto *nm* notice to quit, eviction.
sfrégio *nm* disfigurement; affront.
sfrenatézza *nf* wildness, licentiousness.
sfrenàto *a* unbridled, unrestrained, wild.
sfrontatézza *nf* effrontery, impudence.
sfrontàto *a* brazen, impudent.
sfruttaménto *nm* exploitation.
sfruttàre *vt* to exploit.
sfuggíre *vi* to escape.
sfumàre *vi* to end in smoke, vanish; *vt* (*of colors*) to shade.
sfumatúra *nf* nuance; shade, shading.
ṣgabèllo *nm* stool.
ṣgabuzzíno *nm* closet.
ṣgambettàre *vi* to kick the legs about; toddle.
ṣgambétto *nm* caper, jump; **fàre uno s. a** to trip (s.o.) up.
ṣganciàre *vt* to unhook.
ṣgangheràto *a* ramshackle, rickety, unhinged.
ṣgarbatézza *nf* rudeness; clumsiness.
ṣgarbàto *a* rude, unmannerly.
ṣgarbería *nf* **ṣgàrbo** *nm* rudeness, offense.
ṣgargiànte *a* gaudy, showy.
ṣgelàre *vti* to melt, thaw.
ṣghémbo *a* crooked, oblique, slanting.
ṣghignazzàre *vi* to guffaw.
ṣgobbàre *vi* to drudge, toil, work hard.
ṣgobbóne *nm* slogger.
ṣgocciolàre *vi* to drip, trickle.
ṣgomb(e)ràre *vt* to clear; (*mil*) to abandon; *vi* to clear out, move out.
ṣgómb(e)ro *a* clear, empty, free; *nm* removal.

sgomentàre *vt* to dismay, frighten.
sgoménto *a* dismayed, frightened; *nm* dismay, fright.
sgominàre *vt* to rout.
sgonfiàre *vt* to deflate.
sgòrbio *nm* scrawl; (*fig*) ugly dwarf.
sgorgàre *vi* to gush, spout (out).
sgozzàre *vt* to cut s.o.'s throat.
sgradévole *a* disagreeable, unpleasant.
sgrammaticàto *a* ungrammatical.
sgranàre *vt* to shell, husk; **s. gli òcchi** to open the eyes wide.
sgranchíre *vt* **-rsi** *vr* to stretch.
sgravàre *vt* to lighten, relieve, unload; **-rsi** *vr* to relieve oneself, bring forth.
sgraziàto *a* ungraceful, clumsy.
sgretolàre *vt* to crumble, grind, smash.
sgridàre *vt* to rebuke, scold.
sgridàta *nf* rebuke, scolding.
sgualàto *a* unbecoming, uncomely, coarse.
sgualcíre *vt* to crumple; **-rsi** *vr* to crease.
sgualdrína *nf* strumpet.
sguàrdo *nm* glance, look.
sguarníre *vt* to untrim; (*mil*) withdraw the garrison.
sguàttera *nf* scullery-maid; **sguàttero** *nm* scullery-boy.
sguazzàre *vi* to wallow (*also fig*).
sgusciàre *vt* to hull, shell; *vi* to slip away, steal away.
sí *ad* yes; **díre di s.** to agree.
si *refl pron* oneself, himself, herself, itself, themselves *pl*; *indef pron* one, people, they; *pron* each other, one another.
sía . . . sía *cj* whether . . . or; both . . . and.
siamése *a nmf* Siamese.
siberiàno *a nm* Siberian.
sibilàre *vi* to hiss, whizz.
síbilo *nm* hiss, whistle, whizzing.
sicàrio *nm* hired assassin.
sicchè *cj* so that.
siccità *nf* drought, dryness.
siccóme *ad cj* as.
Sicília *nf* (*geogr*) Sicily; **siciliàno** *a nm* Sicilian.
sicomòro *nm* sycamore.
sicuraménte *ad* certainly; safely.
sicurézza *nf* certainty, safety, security; **s. di sè** self-possession.
sicúro *a* sure, certain; safe, secure, trusty; *interj* quite so; **al s.** in safety.
sicurtà *nf* security, guarantee; insurance.
siderúrgico *pl* **-ici** *a* iron; **stabiliménto s.** ironworks.
sièpe *nf* hedge.
sièro *nm* serum; whey.
sifílide *nf* syphilis.
sifóne *nm* siphon.
sigarétta *nf* cigarette.
sígaro *nm* cigar.
Sigfrído *nm pr* Siegfried.
sigillàre *vt* to seal.
sigillo *nm* seal.
Sigismóndo *nm pr* Siegmund.
sígla *nf* monogram, initials.
significànte, significatívo *a* significant; expressive.
significàre *vt* to mean, signify.
significàto *nm* meaning, significance.
signóra *nf* lady; madam, Mrs; **signóre** *nm* gentleman; Mr; sir; **vívere da s.** to live like a lord.
signoreggiàre *vti* to rule, dominate.
signoría *nf* lordship; dominion, rule.
signoríle *a* gentlemanly; ladylike; high-class.
signorína *nf* miss, young lady; **signoríno** *nm* (young) master.
silenziatóre *nm* silencer, (*aut*) muffler.
silènzio *nm* silence.
silenzióso *a* silent, quiet.
sílice *nf* silica.
síllaba *nf* syllable.
sillabàre *vt* to spell out.
sílo *nm* silo.
sillogísmo *nm* syllogism.
siluràre *vt* to torpedo; (*fig*) give the sack.
silúro *nm* torpedo.
silvèstre *a* sylvan.
Silvèstro *nm pr* Silvester; **la nòtte di San S.** New Year's Eve.
Sílvia *nf pr* Sylvia, Silvia.
simboleggiàre *vti* to symbolize.
simbòlico *pl* **-ici** *a* symbolical.
símbolo *nm* symbol.
similàre *a* similar.
símile *a* alike, such, like; *nm* fellow-creature, like.
similitúdine *nf* simile; similitude.
similménte *ad* the same, likewise.
simmetría *nf* symmetry.
Simóne *nm pr* Simon.
simpatía *nf* liking, attraction; sympathy.
simpàtico *pl* **-ici** *a* agreeable, congenial, nice, pleasant; sympathetic.
simpatizzànte *a* sympathizing; *nmf* sympathizer.
simpatizzàre *vi* to sympathize; take a liking.
simpòsio *nm* symposium, conference.
simulàcro *nm* image, shadow.
simulàre *vt* to simulate, feign, sham.
simulazióne *nf* simulation, shamming.
simultàneo *a* simultaneous.
sinagòga *nf* synagogue.
sinceraménte *ad* sincerely, honestly.
sinceràrsi *vr* to make sure.
sincerità *nf* sincerity, truthfulness, candor.
sincèro *a* sincere, candid, frank.
sincopàto *a* syncopated.
sincronizzatóre *nm* synchronizer.
sindacàto *nm* syndicate, trade union.
síndaco *pl* **-aci** *nm* mayor, (*Scotland*) provost; (*com*) auditor.
sinfonía *nf* symphony.

sinfònico *pl* **-ici** *a* symphonic, symphony.
singhiozzàre *vi* to sob.
singhiózzo *nm* hiccup; sob.
singolàre *a* singular; peculiar, eccentric; rare; single.
singolarità *nf* singularity, strangeness.
síngolo *a* single, each, individual.
sinístra *nf* left (hand).
sinistràto *a* homeless; injured.
sinístro *a* left; ominous, sinister; *nm* accident, mishap.
síno *v* **fíno.**
sínodo *nm* synod.
sinònimo *a* synonymous; *nm* synonym.
sintàssi *nf* syntax.
síntesi *nf* synthesis.
sintètico *pl* **-ici** *a* synthetic(al); concise.
síntomo *nm* symptom.
sinuosità *nf* sinuosity.
sinuóso *a* sinuous, winding.
sinusíte *nf* sinusitis.
sipàrio *nm* (*theat*) (drop) curtain.
Siracúsa *nf* (*geogr*) Syracuse; **siracusàno** *a nm* Syracusan.
sirèna *nf* mermaid; siren, hooter.
Síria *nf* (*geogr*) Syria.
siriàno *a nm* Syrian.
sirínga *nf* (*med*) syringe.
sistèma *nm* system.
sistemàre *vt* to arrange, settle.
sistemàtico *pl* **-ici** *a* systematic, methodical, businesslike.
sistemazióne *nf* arrangement, settlement; position.
síto *nm* place, site, spot.
situàto *a* placed.
situazióne *nf* situation, set-up, position, site.
slacciàre *vt* to unbind, undo, unlace, untie.
slanciàre *vt* to fling, hurl; **-rsi** *vr* to hurl oneself, rush upon, venture.
slanciàto *a* slim, slender.
slàncio *nm* impetus, enthusiasm, impulse.
slattàre *vt* to wean.
slavàto *a* (*of color*) washed out, pale; dull, insipid.
slàvo *a nm* Slav.
sleàle *a* disloyal; unfair.
slealtà *nf* disloyalty.
slegàre *vt* to untie.
slegàto *a* untied, unbound; incoherent.
slítta *nf* sledge, sleigh.
slittaménto *nm* skidding, skid; (*mech*) slipping.
slittàre *vi* to skid; sleigh; slip.
slogàre *vt* to dislocate.
slogatúra *nf* dislocation.
sloggiàre *vt* to dislodge, drive out; *vi* to clear out, decamp.
smacchiàre *vt* to clean, remove stains.
smàcco *pl* **smàcchi** *nm* humiliation, let down.
smagliànte *a* dazzling, gaudy.
smagliàrsi *vr* (*stockings*) to run; (*knitting, net*) to get undone.
smagliatúra *nf* (*of stocking*) ladder, run.
smaltàre *vt* to enamel, glaze.
smaltíre *vt* to digest, work off.
smàlto *nm* enamel.
smània *nf* longing, mania, frenzy.
smaniàre *vi* to long for, fret.
smarriménto *nm* loss; bewilderment.
smarríre *vt* to lose, mislay; **-rsi** *vr* to lose one's way, stray; get confused.
smascheràre *vt* to unmask.
smembràre *vt* to dismember.
smemoràto *a* absent-minded, forgetful.
smentíre *vt* to deny; **-rsi** *vr* to eat one's words; **smentíta** *nf* denial, refutation.
smeràldo *nm* emerald.
smèrcio *nm* sale.
smerigliàto *a* **càrta smerigliàta** emery paper; **vètro s.** frosted glass.
smeríglio *nm* emery.
sméttere *vt* to give up, stop wearing; *vi* to give up, leave off, stop.
smílzo *a* slender, slim.
sminuzzàre *vt* to cut up, chop finely.
smistaménto *nm* clearing; (*rly*) shunting, switching; (*letters*) sorting.
smistàre *vt* to clear; (*letters*) sort; (*rly*) shunt, switch.
smisuràto *a* enormous, immeasurable.
smobiliàre *vt* to strip of furniture.
smobilitàre *vt* to demobilize.
smodàto, smoderàto *a* excessive, immoderate.
smòking *nm* dinner-jacket, tuxedo.
smontàre *vt* to take down, take to pieces; discourage; *vi* to alight, get out of.
smórfia *nf* grimace, wry face.
smorfióso *a* mincing, affected.
smòrto *a* pale, wan.
smorzàre *vt* to dim, tone down; quench.
smúnto *a* pale, emaciated.
smuòvere *vt* to shift, move; affect.
smussàre *vt* to bevel, blunt, smooth.
snaturàre *vt* to alter the nature of, pervert.
snellézza *nf* slimness; agility, nimbleness.
snèllo *a* slim; nimble, agile.
snervàre *vt* to enervate, exhaust.
snobbàre *vt* to look down on, cut.
snobísmo *nm* snobbery.
snodàre *vt* to loosen, untie; make supple; **-rsi** *vr* to get untied; wind.
snudàre *vt* to bare, unsheathe.
soàve *a* sweet, soft, gentle.
soavità *nf* sweetness, softness, gentleness.
sobbalzàre *vi* to start, jump.

sobbarcàrsi *vr* to take on oneself.
sobbórgo *pl* **-ghi** *nm* suburb.
sobillàre *vt* to incite, instigate, stir up.
sobrietà *nf* sobriety, temperance.
sòbrio *a* sober, temperate.
socchiúdere *vt* to leave ajar.
soccómbere *vi* to give in, succumb, yield.
soccórrere *vt* to help, relieve, succor.
soccórso *nm* aid, help, relief.
socièle *a* social; (*com*) of partnership.
socialísmo *nm* socialism.
socialísta *nm* socialist; **socialístico** *a* socialist.
società *nf* society, community; (*com*) company, partnership; **s. a responsabilità limitàta** limited liability company, corporation.
sociévole *a* companionable, sociable.
sòcio *nm* member, fellow, associate, partner.
sociología *nf* sociology.
sociòlogo *pl* **-gi, -ghi** *nm* sociologist.
sodalízio *nm* association, guild, society.
soddisfacènte *a* satisfactory.
soddisfàre *vt* to satisfy, fulfill; make amends.
soddisfazióne *nf* satisfaction.
sòdio *nm* sodium.
sòdo *a* solid, hard, sound, firm.
sofà *nm* sofa.
sofferènte *a* suffering, poorly,
sofferènza *nf* suffering, endurance.
soffermàrsi *vr* to linger, pause.
soffiàre *vti* to blow.
sòffice *a* soft.
soffiétto *nm* bellows; *pl* (*of carriage*) folding top, puff; (*fig*) blurb.
sóffio *nm* puff, whiff, breath.
soffítta *nf* attic, garret.
soffítto *nm* ceiling.
soffocàre *vti* to choke, suffocate.
soffocazióne *nf* choking, suffocation.
soffríre *vti* to suffer, bear.
Sòfia *nf pr* (*geogr*) Sofia.
Sofía *nf pr* Sophia, Sophie, Sophy.
sofísma *nm* sophism.
sofisticàre *vi* to sophisticate, quibble; *vt* to adulterate.
soggettísta *nmf* (*cin*) scenario writer.
soggettívo *a* subjective.
soggètto *a* subject, liable; *nm* subject, topic; **s. agli incidènti** accident-prone.
soggezióne *nf* awe, timidity; subjection.
sogghignàre *vi* to sneer, grin.
soggiacére *vi* to be subjected, be liable; succumb.
soggiogàre *vt* to subdue, subjugate.
soggiornàre *vi* to sojourn, stay.
soggiórno *nm* sojourn, stay; **permèsso di s.** permission to stay.
soggiúngere *vti* to add, reply.
sòglia *nf* threshold.
sògliola *nf* (*fish*) sole.
sognànte *a* dreaming, dreamy.
sognàre *vt* to dream of; **-rsi** *vr* to imagine, fancy.
sognatóre *nm* **-trice** *nf* dreamer.
sógno *nm* dream, fancy.
sol *nm* (*mus*) sol, G.
solàio *nm* loft.
solaménte *ad* only, solely.
solcàre *vt* to furrow, plow.
sólco *pl* **-chi** *nm* furrow, track, wrinkle, groove.
soldatésca *nf* soldiery.
soldatésco *pl* **-chi** *a* soldierly.
soldàto *nm* soldier.
sòldo *nm* (*old Italian coin*) soldo; **sòldi** *pl* pay, money.
sóle *nm* sun(shine); **al s.** in the sun.
soleggiàto *a* sunny.
solènne *a* solemn.
solennità *nf* solemnity.
solére *vi* to use, be in the habit of.
solèrte *a* active, attentive, zealous.
solèrzia *nf* diligence, industriousness.
solétto *a* alone; **sólo s.** all alone.
solfàto *nm* sulphate.
solidàle *a* joint; loyal to.
solidarietà *nf* solidarity.
solidità *nf* solidity; (*of colors*) fastness.
sòlido *a* solid; (*of colors*) fast; sound, reliable.
solilòquio *nm* soliloquy.
solísta *nmf* soloist.
solitàrio *a* solitary, lonely; *nm* hermit; (*gem and game*) solitaire; (*game*) patience.
sòlito *a nm* usual, di s. usually.
solitúdine solitude.
sollàzzo *nm* amusement, pastime, laughing-stock.
sollecitàre *vt* to urge, solicit; hasten.
sollécito *a* prompt; solicitous; *nm* soliciting (*payment etc*).
sollecitúdine *nf* diligence, speed; attention.
solleóne *nm* dog-days *pl*.
solleticàre *vt* to tickle; stimulate.
sollético *pl* **-ichi** *nm* tickle.
sollevàre *vt* to lift, raise; relieve; **-rsi** *vr* to rise.
sollevàto *a* relieved, cheered up.
sollièvo *nm* relief, comfort.
sólo *a* alone, only, sole; **da s.** by oneself; *ad* but, only.
solstízio *nm* solstice.
soltànto *ad* only, solely.
solúbile *a* soluble.
solubilità *nf* solubility.
soluzióne *nf* solution.
solvènte *a nm* solvent.
solvènza, solvibilità *nf* solvency.
sòma *nf* load, burden.
Somàlia *nf* (*geogr*) Somaliland.
somàro *nm* ass, donkey.
somigliànte *a* like, resembling.
somigliànza *nf* likeness, resemblance.
somigliàre *vi* to be like, look like, resemble.
sómma *nf* addition, sum, amount.

sommaménte *ad* extremely, highly.
sommàre *vt* to add up; *vi* to amount to.
sommàrio *a nm* summary.
sommèrgere *vt* to submerge, flood; **-rsi** *vr* to sink, dive.
sommergíbile *a* submergible; *nm* submarine.
somméssо *a* meek, subdued.
somministràre *vt* to administer.
somministrazióne *nf* administration; provision, supply.
sommità *nf* summit, top.
sómmo *a* highest, very great; *nm* summit.
sommòssa *nf* rising, rebellion.
sommozzatóre *nm* frogman, skin-diver.
sommuòvere *vt* to excite, rouse, stir up.
sonàglio *nm* harness-bell; rattle.
sonàre *v* **suonàre.**
sónda *nf* sounding line; probe, feeler; drill.
sondàggio *nm* sounding.
sondàre *vt* to sound, probe.
sonería *nf* striking mechanism; alarm-bell.
sonétto *nm* sonnet.
sonnàmbulo *nm* sleepwalker, somnambulist.
sonnecchiàre *vi* to doze.
sonnellíno *nm* doze, nap.
sonnífero *nm* soporific, narcotic.
sónno *nm* sleep; **avér s.** to be sleepy.
sonnolènto *a* drowsy, sleepy.
sonnolènza *nf* drowsiness.
sonorità *nf* sonorousness, sonority.
sonòro *a* resonant, sonorous; sound.
sontuosità *nf* sumptuousness.
sontuóso *a* sumptuous.
sopíre *vt* to make drowsy; calm.
sopóre *nm* drowsiness, light sleep.
soporífero *a nm* soporific.
sopperíre a *vi* to provide for.
soppiantàre *vt* to oust, supplant.
sopportàbile *a* bearable, endurable.
sopportàre *vt* to bear, endure, tolerate.
soppressióne *nf* suppression, abolition.
sopprímere *vt* to suppress, abolish, kill.
sópra *prep* above, on, over; **di s.** upstairs.
soprabbondàre *etc v* **sovrabbondàre** *etc.*
sopràbito *nm* overcoat.
sopraccíglio *nm* eyebrow.
sopraddétto *a* above-mentioned.
sopraffàre *vt* to overcome, overwhelm.
sopraffazióne *nf* act of tyranny, abuse of power.
sopraffíno *a* first-class, superfine, exceptional.
sopraggiúngere *vi* to arrive, come up, happen.
sopr(a)intendènte *nm* superintendent.
sopraluògo *pl* **-òghi** *nm* investigation on the spot.
soprammòbile *nm* knick-knack.
soprannaturàle *a nm* supernatural.
soprannóme *nm* nickname.
soprannúmero *nm* excess, surplus.
sopràno *nm* (*mus*) soprano.
soprappassàggio *nm* overpass.
soprappensièro *ad* sunk in thought.
soprappiù *nm* extra.
soprapprèzzo *nm* increase in price, surcharge.
soprascàrpa *nf* overshoe, galosh.
soprascrítta *nf* address; superscription.
soprascrítto *a* above(-written).
soprassàlto *nm* start; **di s.** with a start.
soprassedére *vi* to wait, postpone.
soprattàssa *nf* surtax.
soprattútto *ad* above all, especially.
sopravanzàre *vt* to surpass, exceed; *vi* to be left over.
sopravvenire *vi* to turn up, happen, occur.
sopravvènto *nm* advantage, superiority.
sopravvívere *vi* to outlive, survive.
sopruso *nm* abuse of power; insult, outrage.
soqquàdro *nm* confusion, disorder; **a s.** topsy-turvy.
sorbíre *vt* to sip; **-rsi** *vr* to put up with; swallow.
Sorbóna *nf pr* Sorbonne.
sórcio *nm* mouse.
sordaménte *ad* with a dull sound, with a thud; secretly.
sòrdido *a* dirty, filthy.
sordità *nf* deafness.
sórdo *a* deaf; hollow, dull.
sordomúto *a* deaf-and-dumb; *nm* deaf-mute.
sorèlla *nf* sister.
sorellàstra *nf* half-sister.
sorgènte *nf* spring, source; cause.
sórgere *vi* to (a)rise, rise up.
sormontàre *vt* to overcome, surmount.
sornióne *a* sly.
sorpassàre *vt* to overtake; excel, outdo; **sorpàsso** *nm* (*aut*) overtaking.
sorpassàto *a* out of date.
sorprendènte *a* surprising, astonishing.
sorprèndere *vt* to surprise; catch.
sorprésa *nf* surprise.
sorrèggere *vt* to support.
sorridènte *a* smiling.
sorrídere *vi* to smile (at); appeal.
sorriso *nm* smile.
sórso *nm* draft; drop; sip.
sòrta *nf* kind, sort.
sòrte *nf* destiny, fortune; lot.
sorteggiàre *vt* to draw by lot.
sortéggio *nm* draw.
sortilègio *nm* witchcraft.
sortíre *vi* to be drawn (by lot); to go out.
sortíta *nf* sally, witty remark.

sorveglianza *nf* surveillance, supervision.
sorvegliàre *vt* to oversee, watch (over).
sorvolàre *vt* to fly over, pass over.
sospèndere *vt* to suspend; hang; adjourn, interrupt.
sospensióne *nf* suspension.
sospéso *a* hanging, suspended; in suspense, uncertain.
sospettàre *vti* to suspect.
sospètto *a* suspicious; suspect; *nm* suspicion.
sospettóso *a* suspicious, distrustful.
sospiràre *vt* to long for, sigh for; *vi* to sigh.
sospíro *nm* sigh.
sossópra *ad* topsy-turvy, upside-down.
sòsta *nf* halt, stop; respite.
sostantívo *nm* noun, substantive.
sostànza *nf* substance; **in s.** essentially, in short.
sostanziàle *a* substantial, fundamental.
sostanzióso *a* substantial, nourishing.
sostàre *vi* to pause, stop.
sostégno *nm* support.
sostenére *vt* to support, sustain, carry, maintain, keep up, endure, hold; **-rsi** *vr* to lean on, support oneself.
sostenibile *a* sustainable, tenable; bearable.
sostentaménto *nm* sustenance, support.
sostentàre *vt* to support.
sostenúto *a* stiff, reserved, distant.
sostituíre *vt* to replace, take the place of.
sostitúto *nm* substitute.
sostituzióne *nf* replacement, substitution.
sottacéti *nm pl* pickles *pl*.
sottàna *nf* skirt, petticoat; (*eccl*) cassock.
sottentràre (a) *vi* to take the place (of).
sotterfúgio *nm* subterfuge.
sottèrra *ad* underground.
sotterràneo *a* subterranean, underground; *nm* cave, vault, dungeon.
sotterràre *vt* to bury.
sottigliézza *nf* thinness, fineness; subtlety, quibble.
sottíle *a* thin, slender; subtle.
sottintèndere *vt* to imply, understand.
sottintéso *a* understood, implied; *nm* allusion.
sótto *ad prep* under(neath), below; **al di s.** di below.
sottòcchio *ad* before one's eyes.
sottochiàve *ad* under lock and key.
sottocommissióne *nf* sub-commission.
sottolineàre *vt* to underline; emphasize.
sottomàno, di *ad* underhand(edly).
sottomarino *a nm* submarine.
sottomésso *a* subject; submissive, respectful.
sottométtere *vt* to conquer, subdue, subject; **-rsi** *vr* to give in, submit, yield.
sottomissióne *nf* submission, subjection.
sottopassàggio *nm* subway, underpass.
sottopórre *vt* to subject; submit; **-rsi** *vr* to submit.
sottoscrívere *vt* to sign, underwrite; *vi* subscribe; **-rsi** *vr* to sign.
sottoscrizióne *nf* subscription.
sottosegretàrio *nm* under-secretary.
sottosópra *ad* topsy-turvy, upside-down.
sottostànte *a* below.
sottostàre *vi* to be subjected; lie below; submit.
sottosuòlo *nm* subsoil.
sottotenènte *nm* second lieutenant.
sottovèste *nf* petticoat, slip.
sottovóce *ad* in a low voice, in an undertone.
sottràrre *vt* to subtract; steal; take away, deduct; **-rsi** *vr* to escape from, evade.
sottrazióne *nf* subtraction, taking away.
sottufficiàle *nm* non-commissioned officer.
sovènte *ad* often.
soverchiàre *vt* to overflow; overcome; surpass.
soverchiería *nf* insolence, imposition.
sovèrchio *a* excessive.
sovièttico *pl* **-ici** *a* Soviet.
sóvra *v* **sópra.**
sovrabbondànza *nf* superabundance.
sovrabbondàre *vi* to superabound.
sovraccàrico *pl* **-ichi** *a* overloaded; *nm* overload; **per s.** in addition, moreover.
sovranità *nf* sovereignty.
sovrannaturàle *v* **soprannaturàle.**
sovràno *nm* sovereign.
sovrastàre *vi* to hang over, surpass.
sovrumàno *a* superhuman.
sovvenire *vti* to assist, help; **far s.** to remind; **-rsi** *vr* to remember.
sovvenzióne *nf* subsidy, subvention.
sovversióne *nf* overthrow, subversion.
sovversívo *a* subversive; *nm* subverter.
sovvertíre *vt* to overthrow, subvert.
sózzo *a* filthy, loathsome.
sozzúra *nf* filth.
spaccalégna (*inv*) *nm* wood-cutter.
spaccapiètre (*inv*) *nm* stone-breaker.
spaccàre *vt* to cleave, split, break.
spaccatúra *nf* crack, split.
spacciàre *vt* to sell; pass off; dispatch; **-rsi** *vr* to set up as.
spacciàto *a* done for.
spàccio *nm* sale; shop.
spàcco *pl* **spàcchi** *nm* cleft, split.

spaccóne *nm* boaster, braggart.
spàda *nf* sword; *pl* (*cards*) spades *pl.*
Spàgna *nf* (*geogr*) Spain.
spagnolétta *nf* spool; (*fam*) peanut.
spagn(u)òlo *a* Spanish; *nm* Spaniard.
spàgo *pl* **spàghi** *nm* string, twine.
spaiàre *vt* to uncouple.
spalancàre *vt* to open wide, throw open.
spàlla *nf* shoulder, back.
spalleggiàre *vt* to back, support.
spallièra *nf* (*of chair*) back.
spallína *nf* epaulet, shoulder-strap.
spalmàre *vt* to spread, smear.
spàlto *nm* glacis.
spàndere *vt* to spread, divulge; shed; squander.
spànna *nf* span.
sparàre *vt* to shoot, fire, discharge.
sparàto *a* shot; *nm* shirt-front.
sparatòria *nf* shooting, exchange of shots.
sparecchiàre *vt* to clear (away).
spàrgere *vt* to scatter, shed, spread.
sparíre *vi* to disappear.
sparizióne *nf* disappearance.
sparlàre *vi* to speak ill.
spàro *nm* shot.
sparpagliàre *vt* to scatter, spread.
spàrso *a* shed, loose.
spartiàcque (*inv*) *nm* watershed, divide.
spartíre *vt* to divide, separate.
spartíto *nm* (*mus*) score.
spartitràffico (*inv*) *nm* traffic island.
spartizióne *nf* distribution, division, partition.
sparúto *a* gaunt, lean, thin.
sparvière, sparvièro *nm* hawk.
spaşimànte *nm* lover, wooer.
spaşimàre *vi* to suffer terribly; yearn.
spàşimo *nm* pang, (*med*) spasm.
spassàrsi *vr* to amuse oneself, enjoy oneself; **spassàrsela** to have a very good time.
spassionàto *a* dispassionate, impartial.
spàsso *nm* amusement, pastime; **andàre a s.** to go for a walk.
spassóso *a* amusing.
spatriàre *v* **espatriàre.**
spauràcchio *nm* scarecrow; bugbear.
spauríre *vt* to frighten.
spavaldería *nf* boldness, defiance; boast.
spavàldo *a* bold, defiant; *nm* bold fellow, braggart.
spaventapàsseri (*inv*) *nm* scarecrow.
spaventàre *vt* to frighten, scare.
spaventévole *a* dreadful, frightful.
spaziàle *a* space.
spavènto *nm* fright, fear.
spaventóso *a* dreadful, frightful.
spaziàre *vi* to soar.
spazientírsi *vr* to lose one's patience.
spàzio *nm* space, distance; interval; room; period of time.
şpazióso *a* broad, roomy, spacious.
spazzacamíno *pl* **-íni** *nm* chimney-sweep.
spazzamíne *inv nm* minesweeper.
spazzanéve (*inv*) *nm* snowplow.
spazzàre *vt* to sweep.
spazzatúra *nf* sweeping; sweepings *pl.*
spazzaturàio, spazzino *nm* sweeper; garbageman.
spàzzola *nf* brush.
spazzolàre *vt* to brush.
spazzolíno *nm* small brush; **s. da dènti** toothbrush.
specchiàrsi *vr* to look at oneself in the glass, be reflected.
specchièra *nf* looking-glass, dressing-table.
spècchio *nm* mirror, looking-glass.
speciàle *a* special, particular.
specialísta *nmf* specialist.
specialità *nf* speciality.
specializzàrsi *vr* to specialize.
specializzazióne *nf* specialization.
specialménte *ad* especially.
spècie (*inv*) *nf* kind, species, sort; **far s.** to amaze; **in s.** especially.
specífica *nf* (*com*) detailed list.
specificàre *vt* to specify.
specificazióne *nf* specification.
specífico *pl* **-ici** *a nm* specific.
specióso *a* specious.
speculàre *vti* to speculate (upon).
speculazióne *nf* speculation.
spedíre *vt* send, mail, dispatch, forward.
speditaménte *ad* quickly, promptly; fluently.
speditézza *nf* expedition, quickness; fluency.
spedíto *a* prompt, quick; fluent.
spedizióne *nf* dispatch, expedition, forwarding, consignment.
spedizionière *nm* forwarding agent, shipping agent, carrier, express company.
spègnere *vt* to extinguish, put out, switch off; stifle; kill; **-rsi** *vr* to be extinguished, go out; fade away, pass away.
spelàto *a* hairless; threadbare, worn.
spelónca *nf* cave, den.
spèndere *vti* to spend.
spennàre *vt* to pluck (poultry).
spensieratézza *nf* light-heartedness.
spensieràto *a* light-hearted, care-free.
spènto *a* extinguished; extinct; (*of colors, eyes etc*) dull.
speràbile *a* to be hoped for.
sperànza *nf* hope, expectation.
speranzóso *a* hopeful.
speràre *vt* to hope for, expect.
spèrdersi *vr* to get lost, go astray.
sperdúto *a* secluded, wild; lost (*also fig*); ill at ease.
spergiuràre *vi* to perjure oneself, swear falsely.
spergiúro *a* perjured; *nm* perjurer; perjury.
sperimentàle *a* experimental.

sperimentàre *vt* to experiment with.
speróne *nm* spur.
sperperàre *vt* to dissipate, squander, waste.
spèrpero *nm* dissipation, waste.
spésa *nf* expense, cost; shopping; purchase; **spése generàli** running cost, operating cost.
spèsso *a* dense; thick; *ad* frequently, often.
spessóre *nm* thickness.
spettàcolo *nm* sight, spectacle; performance.
spettànza *nf* concern; *pl* dues *pl*; **èssere di s. di** to be the duty of, concern.
spettàre *vi* to be the duty of; be the turn of.
spettatóre *nm* **-trice** *nf* spectator, bystander, onlooker.
spettinàto *a* dishevelled, unkempt.
spèttro *nm* ghost, specter.
spettràle *a* ghostly, spectral.
spettroscòpio *nm* spectroscope.
spèzie *nf pl* spices *pl*.
spezzàre *vt* to break.
spezzóne *nm* incendiary bomb.
spía *nf* spy; telltale.
spiacènte *a* sorry.
spiacére *v* **dispiacére**.
spiacévole *a* unpleasant.
spiàggia *nf* beach, shore.
spianàre *vt* to level, raze, smooth.
spianàta *nf* open space, clearing; esplanade.
spiantàre *vt* to uproot; ruin.
spiantàto *nm* penniless person.
spiàre *vt* to spy upon, watch for.
spiccàre *vt* to pick; *vi* stand out; **s. un salto** to leap; **s. le paròle** to enunciate clearly.
spícchio *nm* (*of garlic*) clove, (*of fruit*) segment, quarter.
spicciàre *vt* to dispatch; **-rsi** *vr* to hurry up, make haste.
spicciolàta, alla *ad* a few at a time.
spícciolo *a* small; *nm* small coin; *pl* change.
spíder *nm* (*aut*) two-seater sports car.
spièdo *nm* spit.
spiegàbile *a* explicable, justifiable.
spiegàre *vt* to explain; spread out, display; **-rsi** *vr* to make oneself understood; open out.
spiegazióne *nf* explanation.
spietàto *a* pitiless, ruthless.
spíffero *nm* draft (of air).
spíga *nf* stalk of wheat.
spighétta *nf* braid.
spigliatézza *nf* ease, nimbleness.
spigliàto *a* easy, nimble.
spígo *pl* **spíghi** *nm* lavender.
spigolàre *vt* to glean.
spígolo *nm* (*of table etc*) corner.
spílla *nf* pin, brooch.
spillàre *vt* to broach, tap, draw.
spíllo *nm* pin; **spillóne** brooch, (hat-)pin.
spilòrcio *a* miserly, niggardly, stingy; *nm* miser.
spína *nf* thorn; (*fish*) bone; (*elec*) plug; **s. dorsàle** backbone, spine.
spinàci *nm pl* spinach.
spíngere *vt* to push; drive, induce.
spíno *nm* thorn.
spinóso *a* thorny.
spínta *nf* push, shove.
spinterògeno *nm* (*aut*) coil ignition.
spínto *a* pushed, driven; excessive; daring.
spionàggio *nm* espionage, spying.
spiovènte *a* drooping, sloping.
spiòvere *vi* to stop raining.
spíra *nf* coil.
spiràglio *nm* air-hole; gleam of light; breath of air.
spiràle *a nf* spiral.
spiràre *vi* to blow; die, expire; *vt* to exhale.
spiritàto *a* possessed.
spiritísmo *nm* spiritualism.
spírito *nm* spirit, ghost; wit.
spiritóso *a* witty; alcoholic.
spirituàle *a* spiritual.
splendènte *a* bright, brilliant, shining.
splèndere *vt* to shine, glitter.
splèndido *a* gorgeous, magnificent, splendid.
splendóre *nm* splendor, magnificence.
Splúga, (Pàsso déllo) *nm* (*geogr*) Splugen Pass.
spodestàre *vt* to dispossess, oust.
spòglia *nf* booty, spoil; **spòglie** *pl* remains *pl*.
spogliàre *vt* to strip, undress; despoil; **-rsi** *vr* to strip oneself, undress.
spogliarèllo *nm* striptease.
spogliatóio *nm* dressing-room, cloakroom.
spòglio *a* bare, undressed; *nm* examination; **spògli** *pl* cast-off clothes *pl*.
spòla *nf* shuttle; **fàre la s.** to go to and fro, commute.
spolétta *nf* reel of cotton, spool; (*mil*) fuse.
spolpàre *vt* to remove flesh; bleed white.
spolveràre *vt* to dust; eat up.
spolveràta *nf* dust(ing), brush(ing).
spónda *nf* bank, edge.
sponsàli *nm pl* (*poet*) wedding.
spontaneità *nf* spontaneousness, spontaneity.
spontàneo *a* spontaneous.
spopolàre *vt* to depopulate.
sporàdico *pl* **-ici** *a* sporadic.
sporcàre *vt* to dirty, soil.
sporcízia *nf* dirt, filth.
spòrco *pl* **spòrchi** *a* dirty, unclean.
sporgènte *a* jutting out.
spòrgere *vt* to put out; *vi* to jut out; **-rsi** *vr* to lean out.
spòrta *nf* (shopping)basket.
sportèllo *nm* (*of carriage etc*) door, (*of booking office*) window; counter.

sportívo *a* sporting, sports, sportsmanlike; *nm* sportsman.
spòṣa *nf* bride, young wife; **spòso** *nm* bridegroom.
spoṣalízio *nm* wedding.
spoṣàre *vt* to marry, wed; **-rsi** *vr* to get married.
spossànte *a* exhausting, enervating.
spossàre *vt* to exhaust, wear out.
spossatézza *nf* exhaustion, weariness.
spossessàre *vt* to dispossess.
spostaménto *nm* shifting, displacement, change.
spostàre *vt* to shift, displace, change.
spostàto *a* out of its place; ill-adjusted; *nm* misfit.
sprànga *nf* bolt, (cross-)bar.
spràzzo *nm* flash, gleam.
sprecàre *vt* to waste, squander.
sprèco *pl* **sprèchi** *nm* waste.
sprecóne *nm* waster, squanderer.
spregévole *a* despicable, mean.
spregiàre *v* **sprezzàre.**
sprègio *nm* disdain, scorn.
spregiudicatézza *nf* open-mindedness.
spregiudicàto *a* unbiased, unprejudiced.
sprèmere *vt* to squeeze (*also fig*).
spremúta *nf* squash.
sprezzànte *a* scornful, contemptuous.
sprigionàre *vt* to give off, release; **-rsi** *vr* to spring out, burst forth.
sprizzàre *vi* to spout, spurt.
sprofondaménto *nm* sinking, subsidence, collapse.
sprofondàre *vi* to founder, sink; **-rsi** *vr* to sink, collapse; be absorbed.
spronàre *vt* to spur, urge.
spróne *nm* spur.
sproporzionàto *a* disproportionate.
sproporzióne *nf* disproportion.
spropòsito *nm* blunder, gaffe.
sprovvedére *vt* to leave unprovided; **-rsi** *vr* to deprive oneself.
sprovvísta, alla *ad* unawares, unexpectedly.
sprovvísto *a* lacking, unprovided with, unprepared.
spruzzàre *vt* to spray, sprinkle.
sprúzzo *nm* spray, sprinkling.
ṣpudoràto *a* shameless, impudent.
spúgna *nf* sponge.
spugnosità *nf* sponginess.
spugnóso *a* spongy.
spumànte *a* foaming, frothing; *nm* sparkling wine.
spuntàre *vt* to blunt; cut off the end; *vi* to appear, rise.
spuntíno *nm* snack.
sputàre *vti* to spit.
spúto *nm* spit, spittle.
squàdra *nf* square; squad, team.
squadràre *vt* to look up and down; square.
squadríglia *nf* squadron.
squagliàrsi *vr* to melt, thaw; steal away.
squàllido *a* dismal, dreary.
squallóre *nm* dreariness, gloom.
squàlo *nm* shark.
squàma *nf* (*of fish etc*) scale.
squamóso *a* scaly.
squarciagóla, a *ad* at the top of one's voice.
squarciàre *vt* to rend, tear asunder; dispel.
squàrcio *nm* gash, rent, tear; (*of a book etc*) passage.
squartàre *vt* to quarter, cut up.
squassàre *vt* to shake.
squattrinàto *a* penniless.
squilibràto *a* unbalanced.
squilíbrio *nm* want of balance; **s. mentàle** madness.
squílla *nf* (small) bell; ring.
squillànte *a* blaring, shrill.
squillàre *vi* to blare; ring, peal.
squíllo *nm* blare, ring.
squiṣitézza *nf* exquisiteness, deliciousness.
squiṣíto *a* exquisite, delicious.
squittíre *vi* to squeak.
ṣradicàre *vt* to eradicate, uproot.
ṣragionàre *vi* to talk nonsense, reason falsely.
ṣregolatézza *nf* disorder, dissoluteness.
ṣregolàto *a* disorderly, dissolute.
stàbile *a* stable, firm, lasting.
stabiliménto *nm* factory, works, plant, establishment.
stabilíre *vt* to establish, fix; ascertain; decide; set; **-rsi** *vr* to settle.
stabilità *nf* stability, firmness.
stabiliẓẓatóre *nm* (*av naut*) stabilizer.
staccaménto *nm* detachment.
staccàre *vt* to detach, remove, separate; **-rsi** *vr* to be different; become detached, break off; leave.
stacciàre *vt* to sieve, sift.
stàccio *nm* sieve.
stàcco *pl* **stàcchi** *nm* separation.
stadèra *nf* (*tec*) steelyard.
stàdio *nm* stadium, sports-ground; phase.
stàffa *nf* footboard; stirrup; **pèrdere le stàffe** to lose one's temper.
staffière *nm* groom.
staffilàre *vt* to whip, lash.
staffíle *nm* whip, lash.
stagionàle *a* seasonal.
stagionàre *vi* to season.
stagióne *nf* season.
stagnàio, stagníno *nm* tin-smith.
stagnànte *a* stagnant.
stagnàre *vt* to solder, tin; *vi* to stagnate.
stàgno *nm* tin; pond, pool.
stàio *pl m* **stài** *f* **stàia** *nm* bushel.
Stalingràdo *nf* (*geogr*) Stalingrad.
stàlla *nf* stable, cowshed.
stallàggio *nm* stabling.
stallière *nm* groom, stableman.
stallóne *nm* stallion.
stamàne, stamàni, stamattína *ad* this morning.

stambúgio *nm* cubby-hole, little dark room.
stàmpa *nf* press, print; **stàmpe** *pl* printed matter.
stampàre *vt* to print, publish; coin; **-rsi** *vr* to impress.
stampatèllo *nm* block letters.
stampàto *a* printed; *nm* printed matter; form.
stampèlla *nf* crutch.
stampería *nf* printing press, printing works.
stàmpo *nm* die, stamp, kind, sort.
stancàre *vt* to tire; bore.
stanchézza *nf* tiredness, weariness.
stànco *pl* **-chi** *a* tired, weary.
stànga *nf* bar; (*of carriage*) shaft.
stangàre *vt* to bar; thrash.
stanòtte *ad* last night; tonight.
stànte *a* being; **sedúta s.** during the sitting; at once.
stantío *a* stale.
stantúffo *nm* piston.
stànza *nf* room; (*poet*) stanza; **èssere di s.** (*mil*) to be stationed.
stanziàre *vt* to set apart (funds).
stappàre *vt* to uncork.
stàre *vi* to stay, remain; stand; live; be.
stàrna *nf* partridge.
starnutíre *vi* to sneeze.
starnúto *nm* sneeze.
staséra *ad* this evening, tonight.
statàle *a* (of the) state; *nm* civil servant.
Stàti Uníti *nm pl* United States *pl*.
stàtico *pl* **-ici** *a* static.
statísta *nm* statesman.
statística *nf* statistics.
statístico *pl* **-ici** *a* statistical.
stàto *nm* state, condition, situation; **s. maggióre** (*mil*) general staff.
stàtua *nf* statue.
statuària *nf* statuary.
statunitènse *a nmf* United States (citizen).
statúra *nf* height, size, stature.
statúto *nm* statute; constitution.
stazionàrio *a* stationary.
stazióne *nf* station; **s. climàtica** health resort.
stàzza *nf* (*naut*) tonnage.
stazzàre *vt* to gauge, measure; *vi* (*naut*) to have a tonnage of.
stécca *nf* (*billiards*) cue; (*mus*) false note; small stick; (*umbrella*) rib.
steccàto *nm* fence, paling, rails *pl*.
stecchíno *nm* toothpick.
stecchíto *a* dried up; skinny; stiff and stark.
Stéfano *nm pr* Stephen.
stélla *nf* star.
stellàto *a* starry.
stellétta *nf* asterisk; (*mil*) star.
stèlo *nm* stalk, stem.
stèmma *nm* coat of arms.
stemperàre *vt* to melt; mix.
stempiàrsi *vr* to lose one's hair at the temples, to go bald.
stendàrdo *nm* standard.
stèndere *vt* to spread, lay out, hang out, (out)stretch; draw up.
stenografàre *vt* to write in shorthand.
stenografía *nf* shorthand.
stenògrafo *nm* **stenògrafa** *nf* shorthand-writer, stenographer.
stentàre *vi* to find it hard to.
stènto *nm* difficulty; privation, suffering; **a s.** hardly, with difficulty.
stéppa *nf* steppe.
stereofònico *pl* **-ici** *a* stereophonic.
stèrile *a* sterile, barren, unproductive.
sterilità *nf* sterility, barrenness.
sterilizzàre *vt* to sterilize.
sterlína *nf* pound (sterling).
sterminàre *vt* to exterminate.
sterminàto *a* exterminated; boundless.
stermínio *nm* extermination.
sterràre *vt* to dig up, excavate.
sterzàre *vt* (*aut*) to steer; **stèrzo** *nm* (*aut*) steering wheel, steering.
stésso *a pron* same, self; *nm* same.
stesúra *nf* drawing up, drafting.
stilàre *vt* to draw up.
stíle *nm* style.
stílla *nf* drop.
stillàre *vti* to drip, ooze, exude.
stílo *nm* stylus.
stilogràfica, (pénna) *nf* fountain pen.
stíma *nf* estimate, estimation, valuation; esteem.
stimàre *vt* to estimate, value; esteem; consider; **-rsi** *vr* to think oneself.
stimolànte *a* stimulating; *nm* stimulant.
stimolàre *vt* to drive, goad, stimulate, urge.
stímolo *nm* goad, spur, stimulus.
stínco *pl* **-chi** *nm* shin, shinbone.
stipàre *vt* **-rsi** *vr* to crowd, throng.
stipèndio *nm* salary, wages *pl*; **s. ridótto (mèzzo s.)** half-pay.
stípite *nm* (door-)post; (*family*) stock.
stipulàre *vt* to stipulate.
stipulazióne *nf* stipulation.
stiracchiàre *vt* to stretch; bargain over.
stiracchiàto *a* forced, unconvincing.
stiràre *vt* to iron; stretch (out); **-rsi** *vr* to stretch (oneself).
stíro, fèrro da *nm* iron.
stírpe *nm* birth, descent, race.
stitichézza *nf* constipation.
stítico *pl* **-ici** *a* constipated.
stíva *nf* (*naut*) hold.
stivàle *nm* boot; **stivalétto** *nm* ankle-boot.
stivàre *vt* to stow.
stízza *nf* anger.
stizzírsi *vr* to get angry, get cross.
stizzóso *a* irritable, ill-tempered.
stoccafísso *nm* stockfish.
Stoccólma *nf* (*geogr*) Stockholm.
stòffa *nf* material, stuff.

stòico *pl* **-ici** *a* stoical; *nm* stoic.
stòla *nf* stole.
stolidità, stolidézza *nf* stolidity; stupidity.
stòlido *a* stolid; stupid.
stoltézza *nf* foolishness, folly.
stólto *a* foolish; *nm* fool.
stomacàre *vt* to disgust, sicken; **-rsi** *vr* to be disgusted with, be sick of.
stomachévole *a* disgusting, loathsome.
stòmaco *pl* **-chi** *nm* stomach.
stonàre *vi* to be out of tune; be out of place.
stonatúra *nf* false note (*also fig*).
stóppa *nf* tow, oakum.
stóppia *nf* stubble.
stoppíno *nm* wick.
stòrcere *vt* to twist, distort; **-rsi** *vr* to twist, writhe.
stordiménto *nm* dazed state, dizziness.
stordíre *vt* to daze, stun, stupefy.
storditàggine *nf* absent-mindedness, carelessness, foolishness.
stòria *nf* history, story, tale.
stòrico *pl* **-ici** *a* historical; *nm* historian.
storióne *nm* sturgeon.
stormíre *vi* to rustle.
stórmo *nm* flight, flock; **suonàre a s.** to sound the tocsin.
stornàre *vt* to avert, ward off.
stórno, stornèllo *nm* starling.
storpiàre *vt* to cripple, maim, mangle.
storpiatúra *nf* crippling, maiming, mangling.
stórpio *a* crippled; *nm* cripple.
stòrta *nf* sprain.
stòrto *a* twisted, crooked; wrong.
stovíglie *nf pl* crockery.
stra- *prefix* over.
stràbico *pl* **-ici** *a* squint-eyed.
strabiliàre *vi* to be amazed, be astounded.
strabíşmo *nm* squint, squinting.
straboccàre *vi* to overflow.
stracciàre *vt* to tear.
stràccio *a* ragged, torn; *nm* rag.
straccióne *nm* ragamuffin.
stràda *nf* road, street, way; **s. facèndo** on the way.
stradàle *a* road, of the road; *nm* road.
stradóne *nm* large street, main road.
strafalcióne *nm* blunder.
strafàre *vi* to overdo.
stràge *nf* massacre, slaughter, havoc.
stralunàre *vt* to open wide, roll (one's eyes).
stramazzàre *vi* to fall heavily.
strambería *nf* eccentricity, oddity.
stràmbo *a* odd, eccentric.
stràme *nm* litter, straw.
strampalàto *a* odd, eccentric.
stranézza *nf* oddness, strangeness.
strangolàre *vt* to strangle, throttle, choke.
stranièro *a* foreign; *nm* foreigner.
stràno *a* strange, odd, queer, funny.
straordinariaménte *ad* extraordinarily, unusually, enormously.
straordinàrio *a* extraordinary, astonishing, unusual; **edizióne straordinària** *nf* (*newspaper*) special edition; **lavóro s.** *nm* overtime work.
strapazzàre *vt* to ill-treat, ill-use; **-rsi** *vr* to overwork oneself.
strapazzàta *nf* scolding; overwork.
strapàzzo *nm* overwork, over-exertion.
strappàre *vt* to tear, wrench, snatch; **-rsi** *vr* to get torn; tear oneself away.
stràppo *nm* tear, jerk; infringement; **fàre úno s. àlla règola** to make an exception.
straripàre *vi* to overflow.
Strasbúrgo *nf* (*geogr*) Strasbourg.
strascicàre *vt* to drag, shuffle; drawl.
stràscico *pl* **-ichi** *nm* train; sequel.
stratagèmma *nm* stratagem.
strategía *nf* strategy.
stratègico *pl* **-ici** *a* strategic.
stràto *nm* layer, stratum.
stravagànte *a* odd, strange; *nm* eccentric.
stravagànza *nf* eccentricity, oddness.
straviziàre *vi* to be intemperate.
stravízio *nm* excess, intemperance.
stravòlto *a* twisted, convulsed.
straziàre *vt* to rend, torture.
stràzio *nm* torment, torture; heartbreak, trouble.
stréga *nf* witch; **stregóne** *nm* wizard.
stregàre *vt* to bewitch.
stregonería *nf* witchcraft.
strégua *nf* standard, way.
stremàre *vt* to exhaust.
strènna *nf* Christmas box; gift.
strènuo *a* brave; strenuous, vigorous.
strepitàre *vi* to make an uproar, shout.
strèpito *nm* din, uproar.
strepitóso *a* uproarious, clamorous.
streptocòcco *pl* **-còcchi** *nm* streptococcus.
streptomicína *nf* streptomycin.
strétta *nf* clasp, embrace, grasp, hold; **s. di màno** handshake.
strettézza *nf* narrowness; poverty; **in strettézze** hard up.
strétto *a* narrow, tight; strict; *nm* strait.
strettóia *nf* difficult situation.
strettóio *nm* (*mech*) press.
stricnína *nf* strychnine.
stridènte *a* shrill, sharp, strident; jarring, clashing.
strídere *vi* to creak, screech, jar.
strído *nm* cry, screech.
stridóre *nm* screeching, jarring.
strídulo *a* piercing, shrill.
stríglia *nf* curry-comb.
strigliàre *vt* to curry; rebuke.
strillàre *vi* to scream, shout.

strillo *nm* scream, shriek, cry.
strillóne *nm* (news)paper-boy.
striminzíto *a* thin, stunted.
strimpellàre *vt* to strum, thrum.
strinàto *a* singed.
strínga *nf* (shoe)lace.
stringàto *a* laced; tight; (*of style*) concise.
stríngere *vt* to press, tighten, grasp; **-rsi** *vr* to press (against); shrug; squeeze.
stríscia *nf* strip, stripe.
strisciàre *vt* to drag, shuffle; graze; *vi* to crawl, creep.
strìscio *nm* graze; **di s.** grazingly.
stritolàre *vt* to crush.
strizzàre *vt* to squeeze, wring; **s. l'òcchio** to wink.
stròfa *nf* strophe.
strofinàccio *nm* duster, floor-cloth.
strofinàre *vt* to rub.
strombazzàre *vt* to trumpet; boast.
stroncàre *vt* to break (off); criticize harshly.
stroncatúra *nf* devastating criticism.
stropicciàre *vt* to rub, shuffle.
stròzza *nf* throat.
strozzàre *vt* to strangle, throttle, suffocate; (*fig*) fleece.
strozzinàggio *nm* usury.
strozzíno *nm* usurer.
strúggere *vt* to melt; consume; **-rsi** *vr* to be consumed; long (for); melt.
struggiménto *nm* torment; longing.
struménto *nm* implement, tool, instrument.
strútto *nm* lard.
struttúra *nf* structure.
strúzzo *nm* ostrich.
stuccàre *vt* to coat with stucco, plaster; surfeit; **-rsi** *vr* to grow weary.
stuccatúra *nf* plastering.
stucchévole *a* filling; sickening, tedious.
stúcco *pl* **-chi** *nm* plaster, stucco; **rimanére di s.** to be dumbfounded; *a* fed-up, sick.
studènte *nm* **studentéssa** *nf* student.
studentésco *pl* **-chi** *a* student, student-like.
studiàre *vti* to study; **-rsi** *vr* to do one's best, try.
studiataménte *ad* deliberately; with affectation.
stúdio *nm* study; plan; office; studio; **a bèllo s.** on purpose.
studióso *a* studious; *nm* scholar.
stúfa *nf* stove; **s. elèttrica** electric fire, electric heater.
stufàto *nm* stew.
stúfo *a* bored, sick, tired.
stuòia *nf* mat, matting.
stuòlo *nm* band, group, troop.
stupefacènte *a* stupefying; *nm* drug, narcotic.
stupefàre *vt* to astonish, stupefy.
stupefazióne *nf* astonishment, stupefaction.
stupèndo *a* splendid, stupendous.
stupidàggine *nf* foolishness; nonsense.
stupidità *nf* stupidity.
stúpido *a* stupid; *nm* fool.
stupíre *vt* to amaze, astound.
stupóre *nm* amazement, stupor, daze.
stupràre *vt* to rape, violate.
stúpro *nm* rape.
sturàre *vt* to uncork.
stuzzicadènti (*inv*) *nm* toothpick.
stuzzicànte *a* appetizing.
stuzzicàre *vt* to prod, pick; tease; whet.
su *prep* on, upon, over, above; about; towards; *ad* up, upstairs; on.
subàcqueo *a* underwater, subaqueous; **pésca subàcquea** underwater fishing.
subaltèrno *a nm* subordinate.
subbúglio *nm* turmoil, upheaval.
subcosciènte *a nm* subconscious.
súbdolo *a* shifty, underhand.
subentràre *vi* to take the place of.
subíre *vt* to undergo, suffer.
subissàre *vt* to sink, ruin, overwhelm; *vi* to sink, fall into ruin.
subitàneo *a* sudden.
súbito *a* sudden; *ad* at once, immediately.
sublimàre *vt* to sublimate.
sublimàto *nm* sublimate.
sublíme *a* sublime.
subodoràre *vt* to get wind of, suspect.
subordinàre *vt* to subordinate.
subordinazióne *nf* subordination.
subornàre *vt* to suborn, bribe.
subornazióne *nf* subornation.
suburbàno *a* suburban.
subúrbio *nm* suburb(s).
subúrra *nf* slums *pl*.
succèdere *vi* to succeed; follow; happen; **-rsi** *nm* succession.
successióne *nf* succession.
successívo *a* following, subsequent.
succèsso *nm* success.
successóre *nm* successor.
succhiàre *vt* to suck.
succhièllo *nm* gimlet.
succínto *a* scanty, succinct.
súcco *pl* **súcchi** *nm* juice, essence.
succóso *a* juicy.
súccubo *a* (entirely) dominated; *nm* succubus.
succulènto *a* succulent.
succursàle *nf* branch (office).
sud *nm* (*geogr*) south; **s. est** south-east; **s. ovest** south-west.
sudafricàno *a nm* South African.
sudamericàno *a nm* South American.
sudàre *vti* to perspire, sweat.
súddito *nm* subject.
súdicio *a* dirty, filthy.
sudiciúme *nm* dirt, filth.
sudóre *nm* perspiration, sweat.
sufficiènte *a* sufficient, enough; *nm* haughty person.
sufficiènza *nf* enough, sufficient

quantity; (*in exams*) pass mark; self-sufficiency.
suffísso *nm* suffix.
suffragàre *vt* to support.
suffragétta *nf* suffragette.
suffràgio *nm* suffrage; approval; **mèssa in s.** Mass for the repose of a soul.
suggellàre *vt* to seal (up).
suggèllo *nm* seal.
suggeriménto *nm* suggestion.
suggerire *vt* to suggest; (*theat*) prompt.
suggeritóre *nm* (*theat*) prompter.
suggestionàre *vt* to hypnotize; influence.
suggestióne *nf* suggestion; influence.
suggestívo *a* evocative, suggestive.
súghero *nm* cork, cork-tree.
súgo *pl* **-ghi** *nm* gravy, juice; (*fig*) pleasure.
suicída *a* suicidal; *nm* suicide (*person*).
suicidàrsi *vr* to commit suicide.
suicídio *nm* suicide (*act*).
suíno *a nm* swine.
sulfamídico *pl* **-ici** *a* sulphamidic; *nm* sulphonamide.
sulfúreo *a* sulphureous.
sultàno *nm* sultan.
súo *nm* property; *poss a and pron* his, hers, its, one's.
suòcero *nm* father-in-law; **suòcera** *nf* mother-in-law.
suòla *nf* (*of a shoe*) sole.
suòlo *nm* soil, ground.
suonàre *vti* to sound, play, strike, ring.
suòno *nm* sound.
suòra *nf* nun, sister.
superàre *vt* to outrun; excel; get over, get through; surpass, exceed; **s. di número** outnumber.
supèrbia *nf* arrogance, pride.
supèrbo *a* arrogant, proud; superb; lofty.
superficiàle *a* superficial.
superficialità *nf* superficiality.
superfície *pl* **-ci** *nf* surface, area.
supèrfluo *a* superfluous, unnecessary; *nm* surplus.
superióre *a* higher; superior; upper; above; senior; *nm* superior.
superiorità *nf* superiority.
superlatívo *a* superlative.
supermercàto *nm* supermarket.
supersònico *pl* **-ici** *a* supersonic.
supèrstite *a* surviving; *nmf* survivor.
superstizióne *nf* superstition.
superstizióso *a* superstitious.
supíno *a* supine.
suppellèttili *nf pl* equipment; fittings *pl*, furnishings *pl*.
suppergiú *ad* approximately, nearly, roughly.
supplementàre *a* supplementary, additional.
suppleménto *nm* supplement, addition, extra.
supplènte *a nmf* substitute, temporary (teacher).
supplènza *nf* temporary post.
súpplica *nf* entreaty, petition.
supplicàre *vt* to entreat, implore.
supplichévole *a* imploring, entreating.
supplíre *vi* to make up for, replace, substitute for.
supplízio *nm* torture, torment.
suppórre *vt* to suppose.
suppòrto *nm* support; (*of an object*) rest, stand, bracket, mount.
suppoşizióne *nf* supposition.
suppuràre *vi* to suppurate.
supremazía *nf* supremacy.
suprèmo *a* supreme, extraordinary, greatest, highest, last.
surgelaménto *nm* deep freeze.
surgelàto *a nm* deep frozen food.
surrealişmo *nm* surrealism.
surrealísta *a nm* surrealist.
surriscaldàre *vt* to overheat.
surrogàre *vt* to replace, substitute
surrogàto *nm* substitute.
Suşànna *nf pr* Susan.
suscettíbile *a* susceptible, touchy.
suscettibilità *nf* susceptibility, touchiness.
suscitàre *vt* to give rise to, provoke, rouse.
susína *nf* plum; **susíno** *nm* plum-tree.
susseguènte *a* subsequent, successive.
sussidiàre *vt* to subsidize, support, help.
sussídio *nm* subsidy, aid.
sussiègo *pl* **-ghi** *nm* exaggerated dignity, haughtiness.
sussistènza *nf* existence, subsistence.
sussístere *vi* to exist, subsist.
sussultàre *vi* to start, tremble.
sussúlto *nm* start, tremor.
sussurràre *vti* to whisper, murmur.
sussúrro *nm* whisper, murmur.
şvagàre *vt* to amuse; distract someone's attention.
şvagàto *a* absent-minded.
şvàgo *pl* **-ghi** *nm* amusement, recreation.
şvaligiàre *vt* to rob, burgle.
şvalutàre *vt* to depreciate, undervalue.
şvalutazióne *nf* depreciation, devaluation.
şvaníre *vi* to disappear, vanish.
şvaníto *a* vanished, faded; feeble-minded.
şvantàggio *nm* disadvantage.
şvantaggióso *a* unfavorable, detrimental.
şvaporàre *vi* to evaporate, vanish, lose strength.
şvariàto *a* varied, various.
şvedése *a* Swedish; *nmf* Swede.
şvéglia *nf* waking-up; alarm clock; (*mil*) reveille.
şvegliàre *vt* to (a)rouse, wake (up); **-rsi** *vr* to wake (up).

şvegliatézza *nf* alertness, readiness of mind.
şvéglio *a* awake; quick-witted, alert.
şvelàre *vt* to reveal, disclose.
şvèllere *vt* to extirpate, eradicate.
şveltézza *nf* quickness, rapidity.
şveltíre *vt* to make lively, nimble, quick, slender.
şvèlto *a* quick, alert; slender; *ad* fast, quickly.
şvéndere *vt* to undersell; sell below cost.
şvéndita *nf* clearance sale.
şveniménto *nm* fainting fit, swoon.
şveníre *vi* to faint, swoon.
şventàre *vt* to baffle, foil, thwart.
şventatézza *nf* thoughtlessness, rashness.
şventàto *a* thwarted; heedless, scatter-brained; *nm* scatter-brain.
şventolàre *vt* to wave, flutter.
şventràre *vt* to disembowel; destroy.
şventúra *nf* bad luck, misfortune, mishap.
şventuràto *a* unfortunate, unlucky.
şvergognàre *vt* to disgrace.
şvergognàto *a* shameless.
şvernàre *vi* to winter.
şvestíre *vt* to undress.
Şvezia *nf* (*geogr*) Sweden.
şvezzàre *vt* to wean.
şviaménto *nm* deviation; leading astray; going astray.
şviàre *vt* to divert; lead astray; **-rsi** *vr* to diverge; go astray.
şvignàrsela *vr* to slip away.
şviluppàre *vt* to develop, work out; **-rsi** *vr* to develop, grow; break out.
şvilúppo *nm* development, growth, increase.
şvincolàre *vt* to free, redeem, clear.
şvişàre *vt* to disfigure, misrepresent.
şvisceràre *vt* to disembowel; examine thoroughly.
şviscerato *a* ardent, passionate.
şvísta *nf* oversight.
şvitàre *vt* to unscrew.
Şvízzera *nf* (*geogr*) Switzerland.
şvízzero *a nm* Swiss.
şvogliatézza *nf* listlessness, laziness.
şvogliàto *a* lazy, listless; *nm* lazy-bones.
şvolazzàre *vi* to fly about, flit, flutter.
şvòlgere *vt* to unwind, unroll; develop; carry out; **-rsi** *vr* to unfold, unroll; happen, take place.
şvolgiménto *nm* unwinding, unrolling; treatment; development.
şvòlta *nf* turn, turning point; winding, bend.
şvoltàre *vi* to turn, bend.
şvoltolàre *vt* to roll; **-rsi** *vr* to roll about, wallow.
şv(u)otàre *vt* to empty.

T

tabaccàio *nm* **-àia** *nf* tobacconist.
tabaccheria *nf* tobacconist's shop; cigar store.
tabacchièra *nf* snuff-box.
tabàcco *pl* **-chi** *nm* tobacco; **t. da nàso** snuff.
tabèlla *nf* table; list, schedule.
tabellóne *nm* notice board, bulletin board; **t. d'affissióne** billboard.
tabernàcolo *nm* tabernacle, shrine.
tabù *nm* taboo.
tàcca *nf* notch; defect.
taccàgno *a* miserly, stingy.
tacchíno *nm* turkey.
tàccia *nf* bad reputation; accusation, charge.
tacciàre *vt* to accuse (of), charge (with).
tàcco *pl* **-chi** *nm* (*of a shoe*) heel; **t. a spillo** stiletto heel.
taccuíno *nm* memorandum book, notebook, pocket-book.
tacére *vi* to be silent, keep silence; *vt* to be silent about, leave out, conceal.
tachímetro *nm* (*aut*) speedometer.
tàcito *a* tacit; silent.
tacitúrno *a* taciturn, sulky.
tafàno *nm* gadfly.
tafferúglio *nm* brawl, fray.
tàglia *nf* ransom, tribute, price on someone's head; size.
tagliabòschi (*inv*) *nm* woodcutter, woodman.
tagliacàrte (*inv*) *nm* paper-cutter, paperknife.
tagliàndo *nm* coupon.
tagliàre *vt* to cut, cut off, cut out.
tagliatèlle *nf pl* noodles.
tagliàto *a* cut; cut out; fit.
tagliènte *a* cutting; sharp.
tàglio *nm* cut; (*of bills etc*) denomination; dress length, (*of knife etc*) edge.
tagli(u)òla *nf* trap.
tailleur (*Fr*) *nm* costume
tàlamo *nm* nuptial bed.
tàlco *pl* **-chi** *nm* talc, talcum powder.
tàle *a* such, like, similar; *pron* someone; **tal dei tàli** so-and-so.
talènto *nm* talent; intelligence; will.
talismàno *nm* talisman.
tallóne *nm* heel.
talménte *ad* so, so much, to such a degree.
talóra *v* **talvòlta.**
tàlpa *nf* mole.
talúno *a* some, certain; *pron* somebody, someone.
talvòlta *ad* sometimes.
tamaríndo *nm* tamarind.
tamburíno *nm* drummer.
tambúro *nm* drum; cylinder.
tameríce *nf* tamarisk.
tamponàre *vt* to stop, plug.
tampóne *nm* stopper; (*med*) tampon.
tàna *nf* den, hole, lair.

tànfo *nm* bad smell, stench.
Tanganíca *nm* (*geogr*) Tanganyika.
tangènte *a* tangent.
Tàngeri *nf* (*geogr*) Tangier.
tànghero *nm* boor, bumpkin.
tangíbile *a* tangible.
tànto *a* so much, as much; *ad* so, so long, so much; **t. . . . quànto** as . . . as, both . . . and; **tànti** *a and pron pl* as many.
tapíno *a* miserable, wretched; *nm* wretch.
tàppa *nf* halting place; stage; lap.
tappàre *vt* to cork, plug, stop (up); **-rsi** *vr* to shut oneself up; to stop one's ears.
tapparèlla *nf* rolling shutter.
tappéto *nm* carpet, rug.
tappezzàre *vt* to upholster; paper.
tappezzería *nf* wallpaper; hangings; upholstery.
tappezzière *nm* paper-hanger; upholsterer.
tàppo *nm* cork, plug, stopper.
tàra *nf* tare; defect
tarchiàto *a* thickset.
tardàre *vi* to be late, be long, delay; *vt* to defer.
tàrdi *ad* late; **far t.** to be late.
tàrdo *a* slow; dull; tardy, late.
tàrga *nf* nameplate, number-plate.
taríffa *nf* tariff.
tarlàto *a* worm-eaten.
tàrlo *nm* woodworm, clothes moth.
tàrma *nf* moth.
taròcchi *nm pl* tarot.
tàrsia *nf* inlaid work, marquetry.
tartagliàre *vi* to stammer, stutter.
tartaglióne *nm* stammerer.
tàrtaro *nm* tartar; *a nm* Tartar.
tartarúga *nf* tortoise, turtle.
tartassàre *vt* to harass, bully.
tartína *nf* canapé.
tartúfo *nm* truffle.
tàsca *nf* pocket.
tascàbile *a* pocket.
tàssa *nf* tax; (*school etc*) fee.
tassàmetro *nm* (*aut*) taximeter; **t. di parchéggio** parking meter.
tassàre *vt* to tax; assess.
tassatívo *a* definite, compulsory.
tassí *nm* taxi, taxicab.
tassísta *nm* taxidriver, taximan.
tàsso *nm* badger; (*com*) rate; yew-tree.
tastàre *vt* to touch; feel; sound.
tastièra *nf* keyboard.
tàsto *nm* (*of musical instrument, typewriter etc*) key; touch; subject.
tastóni, a *ad* gropingly.
tàttica *nm* tactics *pl*.
tàttico *pl* **-ici** *a* tactical; *nm* tactician.
tàtto *nm* touch; tact.
tatuàggio *nm* tattoo, tattooing.
tatuàre *vt* to tattoo.
taumatúrgo *nm* miracle-worker.
tavèrna *nf* public house.
tàvola *nf* table; board; slab.
tavolétta *nf* tablet, small board; **t. di cioccolàta** bar of chocolate.
tavolíno *nm* small table, writing-desk.
tàvolo *nm* table.
tavolòzza *nf* palette.
tàzza *nf* cup.
te *pron 2nd pers sing oblique case and object* you, yourself.
tè *nm* tea; **pastína da t.** teacake, scone, biscuit.
teatràle *a* theatrical.
teàtro *nm* theater; **t. di varietà** music-hall, vaudeville theater.
tècnica *nf* technique.
tècnico *pl* **-ici** *a* technical; *nm* technician.
tedésco *pl* **-chi** *a nm* German.
tediàre *vt* to bore, tire, weary.
tèdio *nm* boredom, tedium, weariness.
tedióso *a* tedious, irksome, tiresome.
tegàme *nm* pan.
téglia *nf* oven-pan.
tégola *nf* **-olo** *nm* brickbat, tile.
teièra *nf* teapot.
téla *nf* cloth; linen; (*painter's*) canvas; (*theat*) curtain; painting.
telàio *nm* loom; frame.
teleàrma *pl* **-i** *nf* guided missile.
telecàmera *nf* (*tv*) telecamera.
telefèrica *nf* cable way.
telefonàre *vt* to telephone.
telefonàta *nf* telephone call; **t. urbàna** local call; **t. interurbàna** long-distance call.
telefònico *pl* **-ici** *a* telephone.
telèfono *nm* telephone.
telegiornàle *nm* television news.
telegrafàre *vt* to telegraph, cable.
telegràfico *pl* **-ici** *a* telegraph(ic).
telegràmma *nm* telegram, cable.
telepatía *nf* telepathy.
telería *nf* linen and cotton goods *pl*; **negoziànte di telerie** (linen-)draper.
telescòpio *nm* telescope.
telescrivènte *a nf* teletype; teleprinter.
televiṣióne *nf* television; **t. a gettóne** coin television, pay television; **trasmèttere per t.** to televise.
televiṣóre *nm* television set.
tellína *nf* cockle.
télo *nm* (*of material*) length, width.
telóne *nm* (*theat*) drop-curtain.
tèma *nm* theme; composition.
temeràrio *a* rash, arrogant, foolhardy.
temére *vti* to be afraid of, dread, fear.
temerità *nf* rashness, temerity.
tèmpera *nf* (*painting*) tempera; distemper; (*metal*) temper.
temperaménto *nm* temperament; mitigation.
temperànza *nf* temperance, moderation.
temperàre *vt* to mitigate; (*pencil*) sharpen; temper.
temperatúra *nf* temperature.
temperíno *nm* penknife.
tempèsta *nf* storm, tempest.

tempestàre *vi* to storm; *vt* to harass, assail (*also fig*); adorn.
tempestívo *a* opportune, timely.
tempestóso *a* stormy.
tèmpia *nf* (*anat*) temple.
tèmpio *pl* **-pii** *nm* temple.
tèmpo *nm* time; weather; (*gram*) tense; stage; **che t. fa?** what kind of weather is it?
temporàle *nm* storm.
temporalésco *pl* **-chi** *a* stormy.
temporàneo *a* temporary.
temporeggiàre *vi* to temporize.
tèmpra *nf* temper; character; timbre.
tempràre *vt* to temper; strengthen; mold.
tenàce *a* tenacious, persevering; obstinate.
tenàcia *nf* tenacity, stubbornness.
tenàglia *nf pl* tongs *pl*; pincers *pl*; pliers *pl*.
tènda *nf* curtain; tent; awning.
tendàggio *nm* curtain, drape.
tendènza *nf* tendency, trend.
tèndere *vt* to hold out; stretch (out); *vi* to be inclined to; aim.
tendína *nf* curtain.
tènebre *nf pl* darkness.
tenebróso *a* dark; obscure; mysterious.
tenènte *nm* lieutenant.
teneraménte *ad* tenderly, gently.
tenére *vt* to hold, keep; **t. a** to be proud of, care for, like; **t. da** to take after; **t. per** to side with; **-rsi** *vr* to consider oneself; keep to.
tenerézza *nf* tenderness, affection.
tènero *a* tender, loving; *nm* tender part; affection.
tènia *nf* tapeworm.
tènnis *nm* tennis; **t. su pràto** lawn-tennis; **tennísta** tennis-player.
tenóre *nm* tenor; **t. di víta** standard of living; way of living.
tensióne *nf* tension, strain.
tentàcolo *nm* tentacle.
tentàre *vt* to try, attempt; tempt; (*med*) probe.
tentatívo *nm* attempt, endeavor; trial.
tentatóre *f* **-tríce** *a* tempting; *nm* tempter; *nf* temptress.
tentazióne *nf* temptation.
tentennaménto *nm* wavering.
tentennàre *vi* to stagger; waver.
tènue *a* slight, thin, fine; soft.
tenuità *nf* thinness, smallness, slightness; softness.
tenúta *nf* estate; uniform.
teología *nf* theology.
teològico *pl* **-ici** *a* theological.
teòlogo *pl* **-ogi** *nm* theologian.
teorèma *nm* theorem.
teoría *nf* theory.
teòrico *pl* **-ici** *a* theoretical; *nm* theorist.
tèpido *v* **tièpido**.
tepóre *nm* warmth.
terapèutico *pl* **-ici** *a* therapeutic.
terapía *nf* therapy.
Terèsa *nf pr* T(h)eresa.
tèrgere *vt* to wipe off, dry.
tergicristàllo *nm* (*aut*) windshield wiper.
tergiversàre *vi* to beat about the bush, hesitate.
tergiversazióne *nf* hesitation.
tèrgo *nm* back; **a t.** overleaf; **da t.** from behind.
termàle *a* thermal.
tèrme *nf pl* hot baths *pl*; hot springs *pl*; spa.
terminàre *vti* to finish, end.
tèrmine *nm* boundary; date; term; limit; **a rigór di tèrmini** strictly speaking.
termoconvettóre *nm* convector.
termòforo *nm* warming pad.
termòmetro *nm* thermometer.
tèrmos *nm* thermos.
termosifóne *nm* radiator.
tèrno *nm* treble; jackpot.
tèrra *nf* earth, land, ground.
terracòtta *nf* terracotta; baked clay.
terrafèrma *nf* mainland.
terràglia *nf* earthenware, pottery.
terramicína *nf* terramycin.
Terranòva *nf* Newfoundland.
terrapièno *nm* bank, earthwork.
terràzza *nf* **-àzzo** *nm* terrace.
terremòto *nm* earthquake.
terréno *a* earthly, worldly; *nm* ground, soil; land; **pian t.** ground floor.
terrèstre *a* earthly, terrestrial.
terríbile *a* terrible, awful, frightful.
territòrio *nm* territory.
terróre *nm* terror, dread.
tèrso *a* clear, terse.
terziàrio *a nm* tertiary.
tèrzo *a* third; *nm* third party.
tésa *nf* (*of hat*) brim; (*of cap*) visor; (*of nets*) cast.
tèschio *nm* skull.
tèşi *nf* thesis.
téso *a* taut, tight, strained.
teşorería *nf* treasury.
teşorière *nm* treasurer.
teşòro *nm* treasure; treasury.
tèssera *nf* card; ticket; (*mosaic*) tessera.
tesseraménto *nm* rationing.
tesseràre *vt* to ration.
tèssere *vt* to weave.
tèssile *a nm* textile.
tessitóre *nm* **-tríce** *nf* weaver.
tessitúra *nf* weaving.
tessúto *nm* cloth, fabric; tissue; web; **negòzio di tessúti** dry-goods store; **un t. de menzogne** a tissue of lies.
tèsta *nf* head; **t. càlda** hot-head.
testaménto *nm* testament, will.
testàrdo *a* headstrong, stubborn.
testàta *nf* (*of bed, bridge etc*) head; (*newspaper*) heading; butt.
tèste *nmf* witness; **bànco dei tèsti** witness box, witness stand.
testícolo *nm* testicle.
testimòne *nmf* witness; **t. oculàre** eyewitness.

testimoniànza *nf* evidence, testimony, witness.
testimoniàre *vti* to testify, witness.
tèsto *nm* text.
testuàle *a* exact, precise; textual.
testúggine *nf* tortoise, turtle.
tètano *nm* tetanus.
tètro *a* dismal, gloomy.
tétto *nm* roof; house; **sénza t.** homeless.
tettóia *nf* penthouse; (*of market, station etc*) roof.
teutònico *pl* **-ici** *a* Teutonic.
Tévere *nm* (*geogr*) Tiber.
ti *pron 2nd pers sing object and oblique* you, yourself.
tiàra *nf* tiara.
Tíbet *nm* (*geogr*) Tibet.
tibetàno *a nm* Tibetan.
tíbia *nf* (*mus*) pipe; (*anat*) shinbone, tibia.
ticchettío *nm* ticking.
tícchio *nm* caprice, whim.
tiepidézza *nf* (*fig*) lukewarmness.
tièpido *a* lukewarm (*also fig*).
tífo *nm* (*med*) typhus; **fàre il t. per** to be a fan of.
tifòide *nf* (*med*) typhoid.
tifóne *nm* typhoon.
tifóso *a* typhous; *nm* (*fig cinema, football etc*) fan.
tíglio *nm* lime(tree); fiber.
tígna *nf* ringworm.
tignòla *nf* moth.
tigràto *a* striped, tabby (cat).
tígre *nf* tiger, tigress.
timbràre *vt* to stamp, postmark.
tímbro *nm* stamp; **t. postàle** postmark; timbre.
timidézza *nf* shyness, timidity.
tímido *a* bashful, shy, timid.
tímo *nm* thyme.
timóne *nm* (*naut*) helm, rudder.
timonière *nm* helmsman, steersman.
timoràto *a* respectful; scrupulous; devout.
timóre *nm* fear, awe.
timoróso *a* timorous, timid.
Timòteo *nm pr* Timothy.
tímpano *nm* eardrum; (*mus*) kettledrum.
tínca *nf* tench.
tinèllo *nm* breakfast room; small vat.
tíngere *vt* to dye, paint, stain.
tíno *nm* tub, vat.
tinòzza *nf* (bath-)tub, wash-tub.
tínta *nf* color, dye, hue, tint.
tintarélla *nf* (*fam*) sun-tan.
tintinnàre *vi* to tinkle, jingle.
tintóre *nm* dyer.
tintoría *nf* dyer's, dye-works; cleaners' shop.
tintúra *nf* dyeing; tincture.
típico *pl* **-ici** *a* typical.
típo *nm* type; model; specimen; **un bel t.** a queer fellow.
tipografía *nf* typography; printing works.
tipogràfico *pl* **-ici** *a* typographical.
tipògrafo *nm* printer, typographer.
tiranneggiàre *vt* to oppress, tyrannize.
tirànnico *pl* **-ici** *a* tyrannical.
tirànnide, tirannía *nf* tyranny.
tirànno *nm* tyrant.
tiràre *vt* to draw, pull, drag; throw; (*typ*) print; *vi* shoot at; blow; **tíra vènto** it is windy; **quèsta màcchina tíra béne** this car goes like a bird.
tiràta *nf* draw, pull; stretch; tirade.
tiratóre *nm* marksman, shooter.
tiratúra *nf* drawing, pulling; (*typ*) circulation; edition.
tirchiería *nf* stinginess.
tírchio *a* miserly, stingy; *nm* miser.
tíro *nm* draft; fire; throw; trick; **animàle da t.** draft animal.
tirocínio *nm* apprenticeship; training.
tiròide *nf* thyroid.
Tirólo *nm* (*geogr*) Tyrol; **tirolése** *a nm* Tyrolese.
Tirrèno *a nm* (*geogr*) Tyrrhenian.
tísi *nf* (*med*) consumption.
tísico *pl* **-ici** *a nm* consumptive.
titillàre *vt* to titillate, tickle.
titolàre *a* regular; titular; *nm* regular holder; owner; (*of a chair*) professor.
títolo *nm* title; headline; right; qualification; (*com*) security; stock.
titubànte *a* hesitating, undecided.
titubànza *nf* hesitation.
titubàre *vi* to hesitate, waver.
tízio *nm* fellow; **Tízio, Càio e Sempronio** Tom, Dick and Harry.
tízzo, tizzóne *nm* (fire)brand.
toccàre *vt* to touch, handle; strike; move; (*naut*) call at; *vi* to fall on; be the duty of.
tócco *pl* **-chi** *nm* touch; knock; stroke; piece; **al t.** at one o'clock.
tòga *nf* toga; gown.
tògliere *vt* to take (away); take off; free; prevent; **t. di mèzzo** to get rid of; **-rsi** *vr* to get away, get off, get out.
tolétta, toilette (*Fr*) dressing table; toilet.
tolleràbile *a* tolerable.
tollerànte *a* indulgent, tolerant.
tollerànza *nf* tolerance, endurance; **càsa di t.** brothel.
tolleràre *vt* to bear, tolerate.
tómba *nf* grave, tomb.
tómbola *nf* bingo.
Tommàso *nm pr* Thomas.
tòmo *nm* tome, volume.
tònaca *nf* (monk's) habit, (priest's) cassock; tunic.
tonàre *v* **tuonàre**.
tondíno *nm* saucer, small plate.
tóndo *a* round; *nm* round; circle; **chiàro e t.** plainly.
tónfo *nm* splash; thud.
tònico *pl* **-ici** *a nm* tonic.
tonificànte *a* tonic, bracing.
tonnellàggio *nm* tonnage.
tonnellàta *nf* ton.
tónno *nm* tuna.

tòno *nm* tone; **èssere fuòri t.** to be out of tune.
tonsílla *nf* tonsil.
tonsillíte *nf* tonsillitis.
tonsúra *nf* tonsure.
tónto *a nm* stupid, simpleton.
topàia *nf* rats' nest; hovel.
topàzio *nm* topaz.
tòpica *nf* blunder, gaffe.
tòpo *nm* mouse, rat; **t. di bibliotèca** bookworm.
topografía *nf* topography.
tòppa *nf* patch; door-lock.
toràce *nm* thorax.
tórba *nf* peat.
tórbido *a* turbid, muddy; gloomy; *nm* disorder, trouble.
tòrcere *vt* to wring, twist.
tòrchio *nm* press.
tòrcia *nf* torch, candle.
torcicòllo *nm* stiff neck.
tórdo *nm* thrush.
Toríno *nf* (*geogr*) Turin; **torinése** *a nm* Torinese.
tórma *nf* crowd; swarm; herd.
torménta *nf* blizzard, snowstorm.
tormentàre *vt* to torment, torture, worry; **-rsi** *vr* to worry.
torménto *nm* torment, torture.
tormentóso *a* tormenting, vexing.
tornacónto *nm* profit.
tornànte *a* returning; *nm* bend, turning.
tornàre *vi* to return; turn out; be correct; fit.
tornèo *nm* tournament.
tórnio *nm* (*tec*) turning lathe.
torníre *vt* (*tec*) to turn.
tornitóre *nm* turner.
tórno *nm* period; **in quél t.** thereabouts; **tórno tórno** all round.
tòro *nm* bull.
torpedinàre *vt* to torpedo.
torpèdine *nm* torpedo.
torpedinièra *nf* torpedo boat.
torpedóne *nm* (motor) coach.
tòrpido *a* torpid, sluggish, dull.
torpóre *nm* torpor, sluggishness.
tórre *nf* tower.
torrefazióne *nf* coffee roasting; coffee store.
torreggiàre *vi* to loom, tower.
torrènte *nm* torrent, stream, flood.
torrenziàle *a* torrential.
tòrrido *a* torrid; scorching.
torróne *nm* nougat.
torsióne *nf* torsion, twist.
tórso *nm* torso, trunk.
tórsolo *nm* (*fruit*) core, (*vegetable*) stump.
tórta *nf* cake, tart, pie.
tortièra *nf* baking tin.
tòrto *nm* wrong, fault; **avér t.** to be wrong; **a t.** unjustly, wrongly; bent, crooked.
tórtora *nf* turtle-dove.
tortuóso *a* tortuous, crooked.
tortúra *nf* torture.
torturàre *vt* to torture.
torvaménte *ad* grimly, surlily.
tórvo *a* grim, surly.
tosàre *vt* to clip, cut (s.o.'s) hair, shear.
tosatúra *nm* (sheep-)shearing.
Toscàna *nf* Tuscany; **toscàno** *a nm* Tuscan.
tósse *nf* cough.
tòssico *pl* **-ici** *a* poisonous; *nm* poison.
tossíre *vi* to cough.
tostapàne *nm* toaster; **pàne tostato** toast.
tostàre *vt* to roast (*coffee*); toast.
tòsto *a* hard; **fàccia tòsta** impudence; *ad* immediately; **t. che** *cj* as soon as.
totàle *a nm* total.
totalità *nf* totality, whole.
totalitàrio *a* absolute, totalitarian.
totalizzàre *vt* to totalize, score.
totalménte *ad* totally, completely.
tòtano *nm* cuttlefish.
tovàglia *nf* (table)cloth.
tovagliòlo *nm* napkin, serviette.
tòzzo *a* squat, stocky, thickset; *nm* piece; **un t. di pàne** a piece of bread.
tra *prep* among, between; **t. pòco** in a short time.
traballànte *a* unsteady, staggering.
traballàre *vi* to stagger, totter; jolt.
trabíccolo *nm* bed-warmer; rickety vehicle.
traboccàre *vi* to brim over, overflow.
trabocchétto *nm* trap.
tracannàre *vt* to gulp down.
tràccia *nf* trail, trace, track; outline.
tracciàre *vt* to trace, draw, mark out, sketch.
tracòlla *nf* shoulder-belt.
tracòllo *nm* breakdown, collapse; ruin.
tracotànte *a* arrogant, overbearing.
tracotànza *nf* arrogance.
tradiménto *nm* treason, betrayal, treachery; **a t.** treacherously.
tradíre *vt* to betray, deceive, be unfaithful to.
traditóre *nm* **-tríce** *nf* traitor; *a* treacherous.
tradizionàle *a* traditional.
tradizióne *nf* tradition.
tradúrre *vt* to translate; bring into effect; take to; turn.
traduttóre *nm* **-tríce** *nf* translator.
traduzióne *nf* translation.
trafelàto *a* breathless, panting.
trafficànte *nm* dealer, trafficker.
trafficàre *vi* to deal, trade, traffic.
tràffico *pl* **-ichi, -ici** *nm* traffic; trade, trading.
trafíggere *vt* to transfix, pierce.
trafítta *nf* pang, stabbing pain.
traforàre *vt* to bore, perforate, pierce.
trafóro *nm* boring, piercing; tunnelling; tunnel.
trafugàre *vt* to steal, purloin.
tragèdia *nf* tragedy.
traghettàre *vt* to ferry.

traghétto *nm* ferry.
tràgico *pl* **-ici** *a* tragic; *nm* tragedian.
tragítto *nm* passage, way, journey.
traguàrdo *nm* winning post; (*fig*) goal.
trainàre *v* **trascinàre.**
tràino *nm* haulage; truck; load.
tralasciàre *vt* to omit; interrupt.
tràlcio *nm* vine-shoot.
tralíccio *nm* trellis; ticking.
tralignàre *vi* to degenerate.
tram *nm* tram(car), streetcar.
tràma *nf* weft; plot.
tramandàre *vt* to hand down.
tramàre *vt* to weave; plot.
trambústo *nm* bustle.
tramestío *nm* stir, bustle.
tramezzàre *vt* to partition off; interpose.
tramèzzo *nm* partition.
tràmite *nm* way; **per t. di** through.
tramontàna *nf* north wind.
tramontàre *vi* to set, fade, wane.
tramónto *nm* setting, sunset; end.
tramortíre *vt* to stun; *vi* to faint.
trampolíno *nm* springboard; (*fig*) stepping stone.
tràmpolo *nm* stilt.
tramutàre *vt* to alter, change, transform.
tranèllo *nm* snare, trap.
trangugiàre *vt* to bolt, gulp down, swallow.
trànne *prep* but, except, save.
tranquillànte *a* tranquilizing; *nm* tranquilizer.
tranquillizzàre *vt* to tranquillize.
tranquillità *nf* calm, tranquillity.
tranquíllo *a* calm, quiet, tranquil.
transatlàntico *pl* **-ici** *a* transatlantic; *nm* liner.
transazióne *nf* arrangement; composition; transaction.
transígere *vi* to come to terms; yield; (*com*) compound.
transístor *nm* transistor.
transitàbile *a* (*of a road etc*) practicable.
transitàre *vi* to pass (through).
trànsito *nm* transit; **t. interrótto** road closed; **vietàto il t.** no thoroughfare.
transitòrio *a* transitory, transient.
transizióne *nf* transition.
tranvài *v* **tram.**
tranvière *nm* tram conductor; tram driver; streetcar operator.
trapanàre *vt* to drill; (*med*) trepan.
tràpano *nm* drill; (*med*) trepanning saw.
trapassàre *vt* to pierce, run through; *vi* to pass (away).
trapàsso *nm* death; passage; transfer.
trapelàre *vi* to transpire, leak out.
trapèzio *nm* trapeze.
trapiantàre *vt* to transplant; **-rsi** *vr* to emigrate, settle.
trapiànto *nm* transplantation, grafting.
tràppola *nf* snare, trap.
trapúnta *nf* quilt, comforter.
trapúnto *a* quilted.
tràrre *vt* to draw; get; lead; **tràrsi** *vr* to draw; get (out); stand (back).
trasalíre *vi* to start, startle.
traşandàre *vt* to neglect.
traşandàto *a* careless, slatternly.
traşbordàre *vt* to transship, transfer; (*train etc*) change.
trascèndere *vti* to transcend, go beyond; lose one's control.
trascinàre *vt* to drag, trail; fascinate.
trascórrere *vt* to pass, spend; *vi* to elapse, pass.
trascórso *a* past; *nm* fault, slip.
trascrívere *vt* to transcribe.
trascrizióne *nf* transcription.
trascuràbile *a* negligible.
trascurànza *nf* carelessness, negligence, slovenliness.
trascuràre *vt* to neglect, disregard.
trascuràto *a* careless, negligent, indifferent, slovenly.
trasecolàre *vi* to be amazed, startled.
trasferíbile *a* transferable.
trasferiménto *nm* change; removal; transfer.
trasferíre *vt* **-rsi** *vr* to transfer, remove.
trasfèrta *nf* transfer; travelling allowance.
trasfiguràre *vt* to transfigure.
trasfigurazióne *nf* transfiguration.
trasfóndere *vt* to transfuse, instill.
trasformàre *vt* to transform.
trasformatóre *nm* (*elec*) transformer.
trasformazióne *nf* transformation.
trasfuşióne *nf* transfusion.
traşgredíre *vti* to infringe, transgress.
traşgressióne *nf* infringement, transgression.
traşgressóre *nm* infringer, transgressor, offender.
traşlocàre *vti* to move; change one's address.
traşlòco *pl* **-chi** *nm* removal.
traşméttere *vt* to pass on, send, transmit; **t. per ràdio** to broadcast.
traşmissióne *nf* transmission; broadcast.
traşmodàre *vi* to exaggerate; exceed.
traşmodàto *a* excessive, immoderate.
traşmutàre *vt* to transmute, transform.
trasognàre *vi* to (day)dream.
trasognàto *a* dreamy, lost in reverie.
trasparènte *a* transparent.
trasparíre *vi* to appear (through); be evident; **lasciàre t.** to betray, reveal.
traspiràre *vi* to perspire; transpire, leak out.
traspirazióne *nf* perspiration.
trasportàbile *a* transportable.
trasportàre *vt* to carry, convey, transport; transfer.

traspòrto *nm* transport (*also fig*).
trastullàrsi *vr* to amuse oneself, toy with.
trastúllo *nm* plaything, amusement; (*fig*) laughing stock.
traşversàle *a* transverse, cross; *nf* transversal line, side street.
traşvolàta *nf* flight across.
traşvolàre *vt* to fly across.
tràtta *nf* (*com*) draft; trade.
trattaménto *nm* treatment; reception; salary.
trattàre *vti* to deal with; treat; deal in; discuss; **-rsi** *vr impers* to be a question (of).
trattatíva *nf* negotiation.
trattàto *nm* treaty; treatise.
tratteggiàre *vt* to outline, sketch.
trattenére *vt* to keep (back); restrain; deduct; entertain; **-rsi** *vr* to stay; stop; restrain oneself; help (doing).
tratteniménto *nm* entertainment; party.
trattenúta *nf* deduction.
trattíno *nm* hyphen; dash.
tràtto *nm* pull; stroke; line, stretch; trait, feature; way of dealing; **tútt'ad un tràtto** all of a sudden.
trattóre *nm* tractor.
trattoría *nf* eating house, restaurant.
travagliàre *vt* to torment, trouble; -rsi *vr* to worry, toil.
travàglio *nm* labor, toil; trouble.
travaşàre *vt* to decant, pour off.
tràve *nf* beam.
travèrsa *nf* crossbar; side street; (*rly*) sleeper, tie.
traversàle *a* transversal.
traversàre *vt* to cross.
traversàta *nf* crossing, passage.
traversía *nf* misfortune, trouble.
travèrso *a* oblique, transverse; **di t.** askance, the wrong way.
travertíno *nm* travertine.
travestiménto *nm* disguise; travesty.
travestíre *vt* to disguise, travesty.
traviaménto *nm* going astray; corruption.
traviàre *vt* to mislead; pervert; **-rsi** *vr* to go astray.
travicèllo *nm* joist.
travişàre *vt* to distort, misrepresent.
travolgènte *a* overwhelming, overpowering.
travòlgere *vt* to carry away; overcome, overwhelm; sweep away.
travolgiménto *nm* overthrow.
trazióne *nf* traction.
tre *a* three.
trebbiàre *vt* to thrash, thresh.
trebbiatrice *nf* thresher, threshing machine.
trebbiatúra *nf* threshing.
tréccia *nf* plait, pigtail, tress.
trecentísta *nm* painter or writer of the 14th century.
trecènto *a* three hundred; *nm* 14th century.
trédici *a* thirteen; **tredicènne** thirteen-year-old; **tredicèsimo** thirteenth.
trégua *nf* truce, respite.
tremànte *a* trembling, quivering, shuddering.
tremàre *vi* to tremble, quake, shake.
tremèndo *a* awful, dreadful, tremendous; **tremendaménte** *ad* awfully, dreadfully.
trementína *nf* turpentine.
trèmito *nm* shaking, tremble, trembling.
tremolàre *vi* to quiver, flicker.
tremolío *nm* quivering, flickering.
trèmulo *a* tremulous, trembling.
trèno *nm* train; **t. di víta** way of living.
trénta *a* thirty; **trentènne** thirty-year-old; **trentèsimo** thirtieth; **trentína** some thirty.
Trènto *nf* (*geogr*) Trent, Trento.
trepidàre *vi* to be anxious; be in a flutter; tremble.
trepidazióne *nf* anxiety, trepidation.
trèpido *a* anxious; fluttering, trembling.
treppièdi (*inv*) *nm* trivet, tripod.
trésca *nf* intrigue.
tréspolo *nm* trestle; rickety vehicle.
triangolàre *a* triangular.
triàngolo *nm* triangle.
tribolàre *vi* to suffer, toil; **far t.** to vex.
tribolazióne *nf* suffering, tribulation.
tríbolo *nm* suffering, tribulation.
tribórdo *nm* (*naut*) starboard.
tribú *nf* tribe.
tribúna *nf* platform; gallery; stand.
tribunàle *nm* (law) court; tribunal.
tribúno *nm* tribune.
tributàre *vt* to give; offer; pay.
tributàrio *a* fiscal; *nm* tributary.
tribúto *nm* tribute; tax.
trichèco *pl* **-chi** *nm* walrus.
tricolóre *a nm* tricolor; (*usu*) Italian flag.
tricòrno *nm* three-cornered hat.
tridènte *nm* hay-fork; trident.
triennàle *a* triennial.
trifòglio *nm* clover; shamrock; trefoil.
tríglia *nf* mullet.
tríllo *nm* trill.
trimestràle *a* quarterly.
trimèstre *nm* quarter; term.
trína *nf* lace.
trincèa *nf* trench.
trinceraménto *nm* entrenchment.
trinceràre *vt* to entrench; **-rsi** *vr* to take refuge.
trinchétto, àlbero di *nm* (*naut*) foremast.
trinciànte *a nm* carving (knife).
trinciàre *vt* to cut.
trinciàto *a* cut up; *nm* cut tobacco.
Trinità *nf* Trinity.
trionfàle *a* triumphal.
trionfànte *a* exultant, triumphal.

trionfàre *vi* to be triumphant, triumph over.
trióнfo *nm* triumph.
tríplice *a* threefold, treble, triple.
tríplo *a* triple; *nm* triple the amount.
trípode *nm* tripod.
tríppa *nf* tripe; (*vulg*) paunch.
tripudiàre *vi* to exult.
tripúdio *nm* exultation.
tríste *a* sad, sorrowful; depressing.
tristézza *nf* sadness, sorrow; gloominess.
trísto *a* wicked, wretched; *nm* rogue.
tritàre *vt* to mince; pound.
tritàto *a* minced; *nm* mince.
tritatútto *inv nm* mincing machine.
tríto *a* minced; worn out; trite.
tríttico *pl* **-ici** *nm* triptych.
trivèlla *nf* (*tec*) borer.
trivellàre *vt* (*tec*) to bore.
trivіàle *a* low; vulgar.
trivialità *nf* coarseness, vulgarity; vulgar expression.
trívio *nm* crossroad(s).
trofèo *nm* trophy.
trògolo *nm* trough.
tròia *nf* sow.
trómba *nf* trumpet; bugle; (*anat*) tube; (*of staircase*) well.
trombettière *nm* trumpeter.
troncaménto *nm* cutting off; breaking off.
troncàre *vt* to break off; cut off; cut short; interrupt.
trónco *pl* **-chi** *a* broken; truncated; *nm* trunk.
trónfio *a* puffed up; conceited.
tròno *nm* throne.
tròpico *pl* **-ici** *nm* tropic.
tròppo *ad* too (much); *a and pron* too much; **tròppi** *pl* too many.
tròta *nf* trout.
trottàre *vi* to trot; walk fast.
tròtto *nm* trot.
tròttola *nf* (whipping) top.
trovàre *vt* to find (out); meet (with); **andàre a t.** to go and see; **-rsi** *vr* to be, find oneself, meet.
trovàta *nf* invention, expedient.
trovatèllo *nm* foundling.
trovatóre *nm* troubadour.
truccàre *vt* to make up; **-rsi** *vr* to make up one's face.
trúcco *pl* **-cchi** *nm* trick, deceit, make-up.
trúce *a* fierce, grim.
trucidàre *vt* to slay, murder.
trúciolo *nm* chip, shaving.
trucolènto, truculènto *a* truculent.
trúffa *nf* cheat, swindle; **t. alla americàna** confidence trick, confidence game.
truffàre *vt* to cheat, swindle.
truffatóre *nm* **-tríce** *nf* cheat, swindler.
trúppa *nf* troop, band, troupe.
tu *pron* thou, you (*sing*); **dàre del t.** to be on first name terms.
tubàre *vi* to coo.
tubercolàre *a* tubercular.
tubercolòsi *nf* consumption, tuberculosis.
tubercolóso, tubercolòtico *a nm* consumptive.
túbero *nm* tuber.
túbo *nm* pipe, tube.
tubolàre *a* tubular.
tuffàre *vt* to plunge; **-rsi** *vr* to dive, plunge.
túffo *nm* dive, plunge.
túfo *nm* tufa; tuff.
tugúrio *nm* hovel.
tulipàno *nm* tulip.
túmido *a* tumid, swollen; (*style*) pompous.
tumóre *nm* tumor.
tumulàre *vt* to bury, inter.
túmulo *nm* grave; tumulus.
tumúlto *nm* tumult, uproar; riot.
tumultuóso *a* tumultuous; riotous.
túnica *nf* tunic.
Túnisi *nf* (*geogr*) Tunis; **tunisíno** *a nm* Tunisian.
Tunisía *nf* (*geogr*) Tunisia.
túo *poss a* thy, your; *poss pron* thine, yours.
tuonàre *vi* to thunder.
tuòno *nm* thunder.
t(u)órlo *nm* (egg) yolk.
turàcciolo *nm* cork, stopper.
turàre *vt* to stop, plug, fill up.
túrba *nf* crowd, mob, rabble.
turbaménto *nm* perturbation; excitement; commotion.
turbànte *nm* turban.
turbàre *vt* to upset, trouble, disturb; **-rsi** *vr* to get upset.
turbína *nf* turbine; **t. idràulica** waterwheel.
turbinàre *vi* to eddy; whirl.
túrbine *nm* whirl, eddy (*also fig*); hurricane.
turbinío *nm* whirling.
turbolènto *a* turbulent; riotous, stormy.
turchése *nf* turquoise.
Turchía *nf* (*geogr*) Turkey.
turchíno *nm* dark blue.
túrco *pl* **-chi** *a* Turkish; *nm* **Turk.**
túrgido *a* turgid; pompous.
turísmo *nm* tourism.
turísta *nmf* tourist.
turístico *pl* **-ici** *a* tourist.
túrno *nm* turn; **di t.** on duty.
túrpe *a* base, vile; disgraceful.
turpitúdine *nf* baseness, turpitude.
túta *nf* mechanic's overall.
tutèla *nf* guardianship, tutelage; defense.
tutelàre *vt* to guard, defend, protect.
tutóre *nm* **-tríce** *nf* guardian.
tutòrio *a* tutelar; tutorial.
tuttavía *ad and cj* nevertheless, still, yet.
tútto *a* all, whole; *pron* all, everything; **tútti** *pl* all *pl*, everyone; *ad* wholly, all; *nm* whole; **del t.** quite; **t. ad un tràtto** all of a sudden.
tuttóra *ad* still.

U

ubbía *nf* false idea; superstition; nonsense.
ubbidiènte *a* obedient.
ubbidiènza *nf* obedience.
ubbidíre *vti* to obey.
ubertà *nf* fertility.
ubertóso *a* fertile, fruitful.
ubicazióne *nf* position, situation.
ubiquità *nf* ubiquity, omnipresence.
ubriacàre *vt* to intoxicate, make drunk; **-rsi** *vr* to get drunk.
ubriacatúra, ubriachézza *nf* drunkenness, intoxication.
ubriàco *pl* **-chi** *a* drunk.
ubriacóne *nm* drunkard.
uccellàre *vi* to go fowling.
uccellatóre *nm* fowler.
uccèllo *nm* bird; **u. di bòsco** fugitive from the law.
uccídere *vt* to kill.
uccisióne *nf* killing, murder.
Ucràina *nf* (*geogr*) Ukraine.
udiènza *nf* audience; hearing; **dàre u.** to receive.
udíre *vt* to hear, listen to.
udíto *nm* (sense of) hearing.
uditóre *nm* **-tríce** *nf* listener, hearer.
uditório *nm* audience, hearers *pl*.
ufficiàle *a* official; formal; *nm* officer; official.
ufficialménte *ad* officially.
ufficiàre *vi* to officiate.
uffício *nm* office; agency; department; duty; **d'u.** officially.
ufficióso *a* unofficial.
uffízio *nm* (religious) office.
úfo, a *ad* gratis.
úggia *nf* boredom; dislike; **avére in u.** to dislike.
uggióso *a* tiresome; dull; gloomy.
Úgo *nm pr* Hugh.
ugonòtto *nm* Huguenot.
uguagliànza *nf* equality.
uguagliàre *vt* to (be) equal (to); equalize; **-rsi** *vr* to claim equality; compare oneself.
uguàle *a* equal; same; like, similar.
ugualménte *ad* equally.
uh! *interj* ah!
úlcera *nf* ulcer.
ulíva *etc v* **olíva** *etc*.
ulterióre *a* further; ulterior.
ultimaménte *ad* lately; recently.
ultimàre *vt* to complete, finish.
ultimàtum *nm* ultimatum.
última *a* last, latest; utmost; lowest; ultimate.
última *prefix* ultra, extremely; **non plus últra** *nm* height, acme.
ultrasònico *pl* **-ici** *a* ultrasonic.
ultraviolétto *a* ultra-violet.
ululàre *vi* to howl.
ululàto, úlulo *nm* howl, howling.
umanaménte *ad* humanly, humanely.
umanésimo *nm* humanism.
umanísta *nm* humanist.
umanità *nf* humanity; mankind.
umanitàrio *a* humanitarian.
umàno *a* human; humane.
Umbèrto *nm pr* Humbert.
umidità *nf* dampness, moisture.
úmido *a* damp, moist; *nm* dampness; stew.
úmile *a* humble; modest.
umiliànte *a* humiliating.
umiliàre *vt* to humble; humiliate; mortify; **-rsi** *vr* to abase oneself, humble oneself.
umiliazióne *nf* humiliation, mortification.
umilménte *ad* humbly; modestly.
umiltà *nf* humility; humbleness.
umóre *nm* humor; mood; **di buòn u.** in a good humor.
umorísmo *nm* humor.
umorísta *nm* humorist.
umorístico *pl* **-ici** *a* humorous, funny.
un *v* **úno.**
unànime *a* unanimous.
unanimità *nf* unanimity.
uncinétto *nm* crochet hook.
uncíno *nm* hook.
úndici *a* eleven; **undicènne** eleven-year-old; **undicèsimo** eleventh.
úngere *vt* to grease; smear; anoint.
ungherése *a nmf* Hungarian.
Ungheria *nf* (*geogr*) Hungary.
únghia *nf* nail; claw; hoof.
unguènto *nm* ointment.
único *pl* **-ici** *a* only, single, sole; unique.
unificàre *vt* to unify.
unificazióne *nf* unification.
uniformàre *vt* to conform; make uniform; **-rsi (a)** *vr* to comply (with), conform (to).
unifórme *a nf* uniform.
uniformità *nf* uniformity.
unigènito *a* only-begotten.
unióne *nf* union, harmony.
uníre *vt* to unite, join; enclose.
unísono *nm* unison; harmony.
unità *nf* unity; unit.
uníto *a* united; **tínta uníta** plain color.
universàle *a* universal; **giudízio u.** the Last Judgment.
universalità *nf* universality.
università *nf* university.
universitàrio *a* (of a) university; *nm* university student.
univèrso *nm* universe.
úno *indef art* a(n), one; *a* one; *indef pron* one, someone; **l'úno e l'àltro** both.
únto *nm* grease; fat; *a* greasy.
untuóso *a* greasy, oily; unctuous.
unzióne *nf* unction.
uòmo *nm* man.
uòpo *nm* necessity, need; **èssere d'u.** *impers* to be necessary; **fàre all'u.** to meet the case.
uòvo *pl f* **uòva** *nm* egg.

uragàno *nm* hurricane.
Uràli (gli) *nm pl* (the) Urals.
uràngo *pl* **-ghi** *nm* orangutang.
urànio *nm* uranium.
urbanística *nf* town planning.
urbanità *nf* civility; courtesy; urbanity.
urbanizzàre *vt* to urbanize.
urbàno *a* urban; urbane; civil, courteous.
Úrbe (l') *nf* the 'city', Rome.
urgènte *a* urgent, pressing.
urgènza *nf* urgency.
úrgere *vi* to be urgent, be pressing.
urína *v* **orína.**
urlàre *vt* to shout, howl, shriek.
úrlo *pl* **úrli** *or f* (*of humans*) **úrla** *nm* cry; shout; howl, shriek.
úrna *nf* urn; ballot-box; **andàre àlle úrne** to go to the polls.
urtànte *a* irritating, annoying.
urtàre *vti* to knock against; (*fig*) annoy; hit.
urticària *nf* nettle-rash, urticaria.
úrto *nm* collision; push, shove; **èssere in u.** to be at variance, be on bad terms.
usànza *nf* usage; custom.
usàre *vt* to use, make use of; *vi* to be accustomed; be fashionable.
usàto *a* second-hand; usual; in use.
uscière *nm* usher.
úscio *nm* door.
uscíre *vi* to go (come) out; go off; get out; retire.
uscíta *nf* going (coming) out; exit; outlet; witty remark; **vía di u.** escape.
usign(u)òlo *nm* nightingale.
úso *a* used; accustomed; *nm* usage; custom.
ússaro, ússero *nm* hussar.
ustionàre *vt* to burn, scorch.
ustióne *nf* burn.
usuàle *a* usual.
usualménte *ad* usually.
usufruíre *vi* to benefit by; take advantage of.
usufrútto *nm* usufruct.
usúra *nf* usury.
usuràio *nm* usurer.
usurpàre *vt* to usurp.
usurpazióne *nf* usurpation.
utensíle *nm* implement, tool, utensil.
utènte *nm* user; consumer.
útero *nm* uterus, womb.
útile *a* useful; *nm* profit; interest.
utilità *nf* utility, usefulness, benefit.
utilitària *nf* (*aut*) minicar, compact.
utilitàrio *a* utilitarian.
utilitarísmo *nm* utilitarianism.
utilizzàbile *a* utilizable, that can be made use of.
utilizzàre *vt* to make use of, utilize.
utilizzazióne *nf* utilization, use.
utilménte *ad* usefully.
utopía *nf* utopia; chimerical project.
úva *nf* grapes *pl*; **u. spína** gooseberry.
úzzolo *nm* whim, fancy.

V

vacànte *a* vacant.
vacànza *nf* holiday, vacation; vacancy; **v. scolàstica** school holidays, recess.
vàcca *nf* cow.
vaccàro *nm* cowherd.
vaccinàre *vt* to vaccinate.
vaccinazióne *nf* vaccination.
vaccíno *nm* vaccine.
vacillaménto *nm* staggering, wobbling; unsteadiness; (*fig*) hesitation.
vacillànte *a* tottering, unsteady; wavering, irresolute.
vacillàre *vi* to totter; be irresolute.
vàcuo *a* empty; vacuous; vain.
vagabondàggio *nm* vagabondage, vagrancy; wandering.
vagabondàre *vi* to roam, rove, wander.
vagabóndo *a* wandering; *nm* vagabond; wanderer.
vagaménte *ad* vaguely; prettily.
vagànte *a* wandering, roving.
vagàre *vi* to wander, ramble.
vagheggiàre *vt* to cherish; long for; look lovingly at; **-rsi** *vr* to look at oneself complacently.
vagheggíno *nm* dandy, beau.
vaghézza *nf* beauty; longing; delight; vagueness.
vagíre *vi* to wail, whimper.
vagíto *nm* wail(ing), whimper(ing).
vàglia *nf* ability; merit; worth; **v. postàle** *nm* postal order.
vagliàre *vt* to sift; (*fig*) weigh.
vàglio *nm* sieve.
vàgo *pl* **-ghi** *a* vague; pretty.
vagóne *nm* (*rly*) coach, car; **v. letto** sleeping car; **v. mèrci** freight car; **v. ristorante** dining car.
vainíglia *v* **vaníglia.**
vaiòlo *nm* smallpox.
valànga *nf* avalanche.
valdése *a nmf* Waldensian.
valènte *a* skillful, clever; valiant.
valentía *nf* skill, ability, worth.
Valentíno *nm pr* Valentine.
valentuòmo *pl* **-uòmini** *nm* worthy man.
Valènza *nf* (*geogr*) Valencia.
valére *vi* to be worth; be valid; **v. la péna** to be worth while; **vàle a díre** that is to say; **-rsi** *vr* to avail oneself, make use.
Valèria *nf pr* Valerie.
valetudinàrio *a nm* valetudinarian.
valévole *a* valid; efficacious.
valicàre *vt* to cross, pass.
vàlico *pl* **-ichi** *nm* crossing; passage; pass.
validità *nf* validity.
vàlido *a* valid, efficacious.
valigería *nf* leather-goods shop; trunk manufactory.
valígia *pl* **-ie** *nf* suitcase.
valigiàio *nm* trunk-maker; leatherware merchant.

vallàta, vàlle *nf* valley.
vallétto *nm* valet.
valligiàno *nm* dalesman, inhabitant of a valley.
valóre *nm* value, worth; valor.
valorizzàre *vt* to employ to advantage, turn to account.
valorosaménte *ad* bravely.
valoróso *a* brave, valiant.
valsènte *nm* value, price.
valúta *nf* value; money.
valutàre *vt* to value, appraise.
valutazióne *nf* estimation, valuation.
vàlva *nf* valve.
vàlvola *nf* (*el*) fuse; valve.
vàlzer *nm* waltz.
vàmpa *nf* flame; flush.
vampàta *nf* blaze; blast; flush.
vampíro *nm* vampire.
vanaglòria *nf* vainglory, conceit.
vanaglorióso *a* vainglorious, conceited.
vanaménte *ad* in vain, vainly.
vandalísmo *nm* vandalism.
vàndalo *nm* vandal.
vaneggiàre *vi* to be delirious, rave.
vànga *nf* spade.
vangàre *vt* to dig.
vangélo *nm* Gospel.
vaníglia *nf* vanilla.
vanità *nf* vanity.
vanitóso *a* vain, conceited.
vàno *a* vain, useless; *nm* space, room.
vantàggio *nm* advantage; profit; odds.
vantaggiosaménte *ad* advantageously, to good profit.
vantaggióso *a* advantageous, profitable.
vantàre *vt* to boast of; **-rsi** *vr* to be proud, boast.
vantería *nf* boast(ing), brag(ging).
vànto *nm* boast.
vànvera, a *ad* at random, nonsensically.
vapóre *nm* vapor, steam; fume; **bastiménto a v.** steamer; **màcchina a v.** steam-engine.
vaporétto *nm* steamboat.
vaporizzatóre *nm* vaporizer, atomizer.
vaporóso *a* airy, filmy, vaporous.
varàre *vt* to launch.
varcàre *vt* to cross, pass.
vàrco *pl* **-chi** *nm* passage, way; **aspettàre al v.** to lie in wait for.
varechína *nf* chlorine; **àcqua di v.** bleach.
variàbile *a* variable, changeable; unsettled.
variaménte *ad* variously.
variànte *a* varying; *nf* variant.
variàre *vti* to vary, change.
variazióne *nf* variation, change.
varicèlla *nf* chicken-pox.
varicóso *a* varicose.
variegàto *a* variegated.
varietà *nf* variety, (*theat*) vaudeville.
vàrio *a* varied, various.
variopínto *a* many-colored.
vàro *nm* launch(ing).
Varsàvia *nf* (*geogr*) Warsaw.
vàsca *nf* basin; tub; bath; pond.
vascèllo *nm* vessel, ship.
vascolàre *a* vascular.
vaselína *nf* vaseline.
vasellàme *nm* crockery, china.
vàso *nm* vase; pot; vessel; **v. da nòtte** chamber-pot.
vassàllo *a nm* vassal, subject.
vassóio *nm* tray.
vastità *nf* vastness; expanse, extent.
vàsto *a* vast, wide.
vàte *nm* (*poet*) bard, poet; prophet.
Vaticàno *nm* Vatican.
vaticínio *nm* prophecy.
vecchiàia, vecchiézza *nf* old age.
vècchio *a* old.
véccia *nf* tare, vetch.
véce *nf* stead, place; **in mía v.** in my stead; **in v. di** instead of; **fàre le véci di** to act as.
vedére *vt* to see; **fàrsi v.** to appear, show oneself.
vedétta *nf* look-out, sentinel.
védova *nf* widow; **védovo** *nm* widower.
vedovànza *nf* widowhood.
vedovíle *a* widower's, widow's.
vedúta *nf* sight, view.
veemènte *a* vehement.
veemènza *nf* vehemence.
vegetàle *a nm* vegetable.
vegetàre *vi* to vegetate.
vegetariàno *a nm* vegetarian.
vegetazióne *nf* vegetation.
vègeto *a* strong, thriving, vigorous.
veggènte *a* seeing; *nmf* seer, prophet, prophetess.
véglia *nf* waking; watch; wake.
vegliàrdo *nm* old man.
vegliàre *vi* to be awake; watch over; watch by.
veglióne *nm* masked ball.
veícolo *nm* vehicle.
véla *nf* sail; **a gónfie véle** very well.
velàre *vt* to veil; cloud; conceal.
velataménte *ad* covertly, by allusions.
velàto *a* veiled; (*fig*) covert; (*of voice*) husky.
veleggiàre *vti* to sail.
veléno *nm* poison, venom.
velenóso *a* poisonous.
velièro *nm* sailing-boat.
velína, *nf* flimsy; **càrta v.** tissue-paper.
velívolo *nm* airplane.
velleità *nf* foolish ambition, foolish idea.
vèllo *nm* fleece.
vellutàto *a* velvety, velvet-like.
vellúto *nm* velvet.
vélo *nm* veil.
velóce *a* swift, quick, rapid.
veloceménte *ad* swiftly, quickly, fast.
velocità *nf* speed, velocity.
velòdromo *nm* cycle-racing track.

véltro *nm* greyhound.
véna *nf* vein; **èssere in v.** to be in form; be in the mood.
venàle *a* venal; market(able).
venatúra *nf* vein; (*of wood*) grain.
vendémmia *nf* grape-gathering; vintage.
vendemmiàre *vi* to gather grapes.
vendemmiatóre *nm* **-tríce** *nf* vine-harvester.
véndere *vt* to sell.
vendétta *nf* revenge, vengeance.
vendicàre *vt* to avenge, revenge.
vendicatívo *a* revengeful, vindictive.
véndita *nf* sale.
venditóre *nm* **-tríce** *nf* seller, vendor; **v. ambulànte** hawker, peddler.
veneràbile *a* venerable.
veneràre *vt* to worship; venerate.
venerazióne *nf* veneration; worship.
venerdì *nm* Friday; **gli mànca un v.** he has a screw loose.
venèreo *a* venereal.
Vèneto *nm* (*geogr*) Venetia; *a* of Venetia.
Venèzia *nf* (*geogr*) Venice; **veneziàno** *a nm* Venetian.
veniàle *a* venial.
veníre *vi* to come; **v. méno** to faint.
ventàglio *nm* fan.
ventàta *nf* gust of wind.
vénti *a* twenty; **ventènne** twenty-year-old; **ventènnio** *nm* period of twenty years; **ventèsimo** twentieth; **ventína** *nf* a score.
ventilàre *vt* to ventilate.
ventilatóre *nm* ventilator; (*aut*) fan.
ventilazióne *nf* ventilation.
vènto *nm* wind.
ventósa *nf* sucker.
ventóso *a* windy.
vèntre *nm* abdomen, belly.
ventúra *nf* chance, luck.
ventúro *a* next, coming, future.
venúta *nf* arrival, coming.
veràce *a* truthful; true.
veracità *nf* veracity.
veraménte *ad* really, truly, indeed.
verànda *nf* veranda(h), porch.
verbàle *a* verbal; *nm* minutes *pl.*
verbalménte *ad* verbally, orally.
verbèna *nf* vervain, verbena.
vèrbo *nm* verb; word.
verbosità *nf* verbosity, prolixity.
verbóso *a* verbose, prolix.
verdàstro *a* greenish.
vérde *a nm* green; **èssere al v.** to be penniless.
verdeggiànte *a* verdant.
verdeggiàre *vi* to be (grow) green.
verdétto *nm* verdict.
verdúra *nf* vegetables *pl*; verdure.
verecóndia *nf* modesty, bashfulness.
verecóndo *a* modest, bashful.
vérga *nf* rod; **v. pastoràle** (*eccl*) crozier.
verginàle *a* maidenly, virgin.
vérgine *nf* virgin.
verginità *nf* virginity.
vergógna *nf* shame; shyness.
vergognàrsi *vr* to be ashamed; be shy.
vergognóso *a* shameful; shy; ashamed.
verífica *nf* check; verification; (*com*) audit.
verificàre *vt* to check; verify; (*com*) audit; **-rsi** *vr* to come to pass; come true.
verisímile *etc v* **verosímile.**
veríṣmo *nm* realism.
verità *nf* truth.
veritièro *a* truthful.
vèrme *nm* worm.
vermíglio *a* vermilion.
vèrmut *nm* vermouth.
vernàcolo *a nm* vernacular.
verníce *nf* paint, varnish; (*fig*) smattering; patent leather; **úna màno di v.** a coat of paint.
verniciàre *vt* to paint, varnish; polish.
verniciatúra *nf* painting, varnishing; polishing.
véro *a* true *nm* truth; **dàl v.** from life, from nature.
verosimigliànza *nf* likelihood; verisimilitude.
verosímile *a* likely, probable.
verrúca *nf* wart.
versaménto *nm* pouring; spilling; payment.
versànte *nm* side; slope; (*com*) depositor; payer.
versàre *vt* to pour; spill; shed; pay; *vi* to be, live.
versàtile *a* versatile.
versàto *a* poured out; spilled; shed; versed; paid.
verseggiàre *vti* to versify.
versióne *nf* version; translation.
vèrso *nm* line; verse; sound; note; way; **non c'è v.** it is impossible; *prep* towards.
vertènte *a* regarding.
vertènza *nf* dispute.
vèrtere *vi* to be about, concern, regard.
verticàle *a* vertical.
vèrtice *nm* vertex; top; height.
vertígine *pl* **-ini** *nf* dizziness, giddiness.
vertiginóso *a* dizzy.
vescíca *nf* bladder; blister.
vescovàdo *nm* bishopric; bishop's palace.
vescovíle *a* episcopal, of a bishop.
véscovo *nm* bishop.
vèspa *nf* wasp; (*motor-scooter*) 'Vespa'.
vespàio *nm* wasp's nest; (*fig*) hornet's nest.
vespaṣiàno *nm* (public) urinal.
vèspro *nm* evening; evensong; vespers.
vessàre *vt* to vex; oppress.
vessazióne *nf* vexation.
vessíllo *nm* flag, standard.

vestàglia *nf* dressing-gown, bathrobe.
vestàle *nf* vestal.
vèste *nf* dress; guise; (*fig*) capacity; **vèsti** *pl* clothes *pl*.
vestiàrio *nm* clothes *pl*, clothing.
vestíbolo *nm* hall, vestibule.
vestígio *pl f* **-gia** *f* footprint, track, vestige, trace.
vestíre *vt* to dress, clothe; **-rsi** *vr* to dress.
vestíto *nm* dress; suit.
veteràno *a* veteran; *nm* (*mil*) ex-serviceman, veteran.
veterinària *nf* veterinary science.
veterinàrio *a* veterinary; *nm* veterinary surgeon.
vèto *nm* veto.
vetràio *nm* glass-blower; glazier.
vetràta *nf* glass door; (stained-)glass window.
vetrería *nf* glass manufactory; glassware.
vetrína *nf* shop-window; glass case, showcase.
vetriòlo *nm* vitriol.
vétro *nm* glass; window-pane.
vétta *nm* summit, top.
vettovàglie *nf pl* provisions *pl*, victuals *pl*.
vettúra *nf* car; cab; carriage; coach; (*rly*) **v. ristorànte** restaurant car, diner (dining-car).
vetturíno *nm* driver, cabby.
vetústo *a* ancient, old.
vezzeggiàre *vt* to fondle.
vézzo *nm* (bad) habit; charm; necklace.
vezzóso *a* charming; pretty.
vi *pron acc and dat* you, to you; *ad* there.
vía *nf* street; road; way; **v. di mézzo** compromise.
viabilità *nf* condition of a road.
viadótto *nm* viaduct.
viaggiàre *vt* to travel, journey.
viaggiatóre *nm* **-tríce** *nf* traveler; passenger.
viàggio *nm* journey; tour; voyage; viàggi *pl* travels *pl*.
viàle *nm* avenue.
viandànte *nm* passer-by; traveler.
viavài *nm* coming and going.
vibràre *vti* to vibrate; strike; quiver.
vibrazióne *nf* vibration; quivering.
vicàrio *nm* vicar.
více *prefix* vice-, assistant, deputy.
vicènda *nf* event; vicissitude; **a v.** in turn; reciprocally.
vicendévole *a* mutual; reciprocal.
vicendevolménte *ad* mutually, each other, one another.
vichíngo *pl* **-ghi** *nm* Viking.
vicinànza *nf* closeness, nearness; neighborhood, vicinity.
vicinàto *nm* neighborhood; neighbors *pl*.
vicíno *a* near, neighboring; *nm* neighbor; *ad* close by, near; **v. a** *prep* beside, close to, near.
vicissitúdine *nf* vicissitude.
vícolo *nm* alley, lane.
vídeo *inv nm* (*tv*) video.
vidimàre *vt* to authenticate; visa.
vidimazióne *nf* authentication; visa.
viennése *a nmf* Viennese.
vieppiù *ad* more (and more).
vietàre *vt* to forbid, prohibit.
vigènte *a* in force.
vígere *vi* to be in force.
vigilànte *a* vigilant, watchful.
vigilànza *nf* vigilance, watchfulness; look-out.
vigilàre *vt* to watch over, to keep an eye on; *vi* to be on one's guard; keep watch.
vígile *a* watchful, vigilant; *nm* policeman.
vigília *nf* eve; vigil.
vigliaccheria *nf* cowardice, cowardly action.
vigliàcco *pl* **-àcchi** *a* cowardly; *nm* coward.
vígna *nf* **vignéto** *nm* vineyard.
vignétta *nf* vignette; cartoon.
vigóre *nm* vigor; strength; force.
vigoría *nf* vigor; strength.
vigoróso *a* vigorous; strong.
víle *a* cowardly; vile; *nm* coward.
vilipèndere *vt* to despise, scorn.
vílla *nf* villa, country house.
villàggio *nm* village.
villanía *nf* rudeness, abuse.
villàno *a* rude, uncivil; *nm* boor, ill-bred fellow; peasant.
villeggiànte *nmf* holidaymaker, vacationer.
villeggiàre *vi* to spend one's summer holidays.
villeggiatúra *nf* holiday (in the country); **luògo di v.** holiday resort.
villeréccio *a* rustic, rural.
villíno *nm* small villa.
vilménte *ad* cowardly; meanly.
viltà *nf* cowardice; meanness.
vímine *nm* osier, withy; **di vímini** wicker.
vinàio *nm* wine merchant.
Vincènzo *nm pr* Vincent.
víncere *vt* to win; defeat, overcome, vanquish; **-rsi** *vr* to master oneself.
víncita *nf* winning(s).
vincitóre *nm* **-tríce** *nf* winner, conqueror.
vincolàre *vt* to bind; (*com*) tie up.
víncolo *nm* bond, tie.
viníco lo *a* wine.
viníle *nm* (*chem*) vinyl.
víno *nm* wine.
viòla *nf* (*mus*) viola, viol; (*bot*) viola; **v. del pensièro** pansy; *a nm* (*color*) violet.
violacciòcca *nf* wallflower.
violàre *vt* to violate.
violazióne *nf* violation.
violentàre *vt* to rape; violate.
violènto *a* violent.
violènza *nf* violence.
violétta *nf* violet.
violinísta *nmf* violinist.

violíno *nm* violin, fiddle.
violoncèllo *nm* violoncello.
viòttola *nf* **-olo** *nm* lane.
vípera *nf* viper.
viràre *vi* (*naut*) to tack, turn.
viràta *nf* tacking, turn.
Virgílio *nm pr* Virgil.
vírgola *nf* comma; **púnto e vírgola** semi-colon; **virgolétte** *nf pl* quotation marks.
viríle *a* manly, virile.
virilità *nf* manliness, virility; manhood.
virtù *nf* virtue.
virtualménte *ad* virtually.
virtuosísmo *nm* virtuousness; virtuosity.
virtuóso *a* virtuous; virtuoso.
virulènto *a* virulent.
víscere *nm* (*anat*) vital organ; **vísceri** *m pl* viscera *pl*; **víscere** *f pl* bowels (*fig*).
víschio *nm* mistletoe; bird-lime.
vischióso *a* viscous; slimy.
víscido *a* sticky; slippery.
viscónte *nm* viscount.
visíbile *a* visible.
visibílio *nm* a lot; **andàre in v.** to go into raptures.
visibilità *nf* visibility.
visibilménte *ad* visibly; clearly.
visièra *nf* visor; (*of cap*) peak.
visionàrio *a nm* visionary.
visióne *nf* vision; **préndere in v.** to examine.
vísita *nf* visit; **v. mèdica** medical examination.
visitàre *vt* to visit; to call on; (*med*) examine.
visitatóre *nm* **-tríce** *nf* visitor.
visívo *a* visual.
víso *nm* face; **a v. apèrto** frankly, openly.
visóne *nm* mink.
víspo *a* brisk, lively.
vísta *nf* sight; outlook, view; **conóscere di v.** to know by sight; **fàr v. di** to pretend.
vistàre *vt* to visa.
vísto *a* seen; *nm* visa; **méttere il v.** to visa.
vistóso *a* gaudy, showy; large.
visuàle *a* visual; *nf* sight; view.
víta *nf* life; living; waist.
vitàlba *nf* (*bot*) traveler's joy, clematis.
vitàle *a* vital.
vitalità *nf* vitality.
vitalízio *a* lasting for life; *nm* life annuity.
vitamína *nf* vitamin(e).
vitamínico *pl* **-ici** *a* vitaminic.
víte *nf* vine; (*tec*) screw.
vitèllo *nm* calf; **càrne di v.** veal.
vitellóne *nm* bullock; (*fig*) representative of contemporary jeunesse dorée.
víttima *nf* victim.
vítto *nm* food; board; living.
vittòria *nf* victory.
Vittòrio *nm pr* Victor.
vittorióso *a* victorious.
vituperàre *vt* to vituperate.
vitupèrio *nm* insult, shame, disgrace.
viúzza *nf* narrow street, lane.
víva *interj* hurrah, hurray.
vivàce *a* lively, live; bright; quick.
vivacità *nf* vivacity; quickness; brightness.
vivàio *nm* (*of fish or plants*) nursery.
vivaménte *ad* deeply, warmly.
vivànda *nf* food; dish.
vivènte *a* living.
vívere *vti* to live; *nm* life, living; **v. àlla giornàta** to live from hand to mouth.
víveri *nm pl* provisions *pl*, supplies *pl*, victuals *pl*.
vivézza *nf* liveliness; brightness; vividness.
vívido *a* vivid.
vivificàre *vt* to enliven; give life to.
vivisezióne *nf* vivisection.
vívo *a* living; alive; lively; bright; deep; **a víva vóce** orally; **toccàre nel v.** to pierce to the quick.
viziàre *vt* to spoil, vitiate.
viziàto *a* spoilt, vitiated.
vízio *nm* vice; bad habit; defect.
vizióso *a* vicious, depraved.
vízzo *a* withered.
vocabolàrio *nm* vocabulary; dictionary.
vocàbolo *nm* word; term.
vocàle *a* vocal; *nf* vowel.
vocazióne *nf* calling, vocation.
vóce *nf* voice; rumor; **a v.** orally; **ad àlta v.** loudly.
vociferàre *vi* to shout; vociferate; rumor.
vociferazióne *nf* shouting; vociferation.
vóga *nf* fashion, vogue; energy; **in v.** fashionable.
vogàre *vi* to row.
vòglia *nf* desire, wish; will; birthmark.
vói *pron 2nd pers pl nom and oblique* you.
volàno *nm* badminton; shuttlecock; flywheel.
volànte *a* flying; *nm* (*aut*) steering-wheel; *nf* (*police*) flying-squad.
volantíno *nm* leaflet.
volàre *vi* to fly.
volàta *nf* flight; rush.
volàtile *a* winged; volatile.
volenteróso *v.* **volonteróso.**
volentièri *ad* willingly; **màl v.** unwillingly.
volére *vti* to will; want; wish; like; take, require; *nm* wish; will.
volgàre *a* vulgar; *nm* vernacular.
volgarità *nf* vulgarity.
vòlgere *vti* **-rsi** *vr* to turn.
vólgo *pl* **-ghi** *nm* common herd; populace.
volitívo *a* strong-willed.
vólo *nm* flight; **a v.** immediately.
volontà *nf* will.

volontàrio *a* voluntary; *nm* volunteer.
volonteróso *a* willing.
vólpe *nf* fox.
volpíno *a* foxy; crafty; *nm* Pomeranian dog.
vòlta *nf* time; turn; **úna v.** once; **dúe vòlte** twice; (*arch*) vault.
voltàggio *nm* (*el*) voltage.
voltàre *vti* **-rsi** *vr* to turn.
voltàta *nf* turn(ing), bend.
volteggiàre *vi* to fly about, whirl; vault.
vólto *nm* face, countenance; *a* turned.
volúbile *a* fickle, inconstant.
volúme *nm* volume, quantity.
voluminóso *a* voluminous, bulky.
volutaménte *ad* intentionally, deliberately.
voluttà *nf* delight, pleasure; voluptuousness.
voluttuóso *a* voluptuous.
vómere *nm* plowshare.
vomitàre *vt* to vomit.
vòmito *nm* vomiting.
vóngola *nf* clam.
voràce *a* voracious, greedy.
voracità *nf* voracity, greed(iness).
voràgine *nf* gulf, abyss.
vòrtice *nm* vortex; whirl(pool).
vorticóso *a* whirling, swirling.
vòstro *poss a* your; *poss pron* yours.
votànte *a* voting; *nm* voter.
votàre *vi* to vote; *vt* to approve; consecrate; offer; **-rsi** *vr* to devote oneself.
votazióne *nf* voting.
votívo *a* votive.
vóto *nm* vow; votive offering; prayer; (*school*) mark; vote.
vulcànico *pl* **-ici** *a* volcanic.
vulcanizzàre *vt* to vulcanize.
vulcàno *nm* volcano.
vulneràbile *a* vulnerable.
vuotàre *vt* to empty.
vuòto *a* empty; vacant; *nm* empty space; vacuum; void; **andàre a v.** to fail.

Z

zafferàno *nm* saffron.
zàffiro *nm* sapphire.
zàino *nm* knapsack, pack.
zàmpa *nf* paw.
zampillànte *a* gushing.
zampillàre *vi* to spurt; spring.
zampíllo *nm* spurt, jet.
zampíno *nm* little paw; (*fig*) finger.
zampógna *nf* bagpipes *pl*; reedpipe.
zampognàro *nm* piper.
zàna *nf* basket; cradle.
zàngola *nf* churn.
zànna *nf* fang; tusk.
zanzàra *nf* mosquito.
zanzarièra *nf* mosquito net.
zàppa *nf* hoe.
zappàre *vt* to dig; hoe.
zappatóre *nm* hoer; (*mil*) pioneer.
zar *nm* czar, tzar.
zàttera *nf* (*naut*) lighter; raft.
zavòrra *nf* ballast.
zàzzera *nf* shock of hair; mane.
zèbra *nf* zebra.
zécca *nf* mint; **nuòvo di z.** brand-new.
zecchíno *nm* sequin.
zèffiro *nm* zephyr.
Zelànda *nf* (*geogr*) Zealand; **Nuòva Z.** New Zealand.
zelànte *a* zealous.
zèlo *nm* zeal.
zènit *nm* zenith.
zènzero *nm* ginger; **pàn di z.** gingerbread.
zéppo *a* full; **piéno z.** crowded, packed.
zerbíno *nm* doormat; dandy.
zerbinòtto *nm* beau, dandy.
zèro *nm* zero, nought.
zía *nf* aunt.
zibaldóne *nm* miscellany, medley.
zibellíno *nm* sable.
zígomo *nm* cheek-bone.
zigzagàre *vi* to zigzag.
zimbèllo *nm* decoy(-bird); laughing-stock.
zincàto *a* zinc plated.
zínco *pl* **-chi** *nm* zinc.
zíngaro *nm* gypsy.
zío *nm* uncle.
zitèlla *nf* spinster; old maid.
zittíre *vti* to hiss.
zítto *a* silent; **stàre z.** to keep quiet.
zizzània *nf* darnel; **seminàre z.** to sow dissension.
zoccolàio *nm* clog-maker.
zòccolo *nm* clog, wooden shoe; hoof; skirting-board.
zodíaco *pl* **-chi** *nm* zodiac.
zolfanèllo *nm* (sulphur) match.
zólfo *nm* sulphur.
zòlla *nf* clod; lump; **zollétta di zúcchero** lump of sugar.
zóna *nf* zone, area.
zónzo, a *ad* idling; strolling.
zoología *nf* zoology.
zoològico *pl* **-ici** *a* zoological.
zoppicànte *a* limping, lame.
zoppicàre *vi* to limp.
zòppo *a* lame, limping.
zòtico *pl* **-ici** *a* boorish, rough; *nm* boor, uncouth fellow.
zúcca *nf* pumpkin; squash; (*fig*) pate.
zuccheràre *vt* to sugar; sweeten (*also fig*).
zuccherièra *nf* sugar-basin.
zuccherifício *nm* sugar-refinery.
zúcchero *nm* sugar.
zucchíno *nm* zucchini, Italian squash.
zúffa *nf* brawl, scuffle.
zufolàre *vi* to whistle.
zúfolo *nm* whistle.
zulú *nm* Zulu.
zúppa *nf* soup; **z. inglése** trifle.
zuppièra *nf* (soup) tureen.
zúppo *a* drenched, soaked.
Zurígo *nf* (*geogr*) Zurich.

English-Italian

A

a [ə] *indef art* un(o), una.
aback [ə'bæk] *ad* all'indietro; **taken a.** sconcertato.
abandon [ə'bændən] *n* abbandono, trasporto; *vt* abbandonare.
abandonment [ə'bændənmənt] *n* abbandono.
abase [ə'beis] *vt* abbassare, umiliare.
abasement [ə'beismənt] *n* umiliazione.
abash [ə'bæʃ] *vt* confondere.
abate [ə'beit] *vt* diminuire, abbassare; *vi* calmarsi, indebolirsi.
abatement [ə'beitmənt] *n* diminuzione, riduzione.
abbé ['æbei] *n* abate.
abbess ['æbis] *n* badessa.
abbey ['æbi] *n* badia.
abbot ['æbət] *n* abate.
abbreviate [ə'bri:vieit] *vt* abbreviare.
abbreviation [ə.bri:vi'eiʃən] *n* abbreviazione.
abc ['eibi:'si:] *n* abbicci.
abdicate ['æbdikeit] *vti* abdicare.
abdomen ['æbdəmen] *n* addome.
abdominal [æb'dɔminl] *a* addominale.
abduct [æb'dʌkt] *vt* rapire.
abduction [æb'dʌkʃən] *n* ratto.
Abel ['eibəl] *nm pr* Abele.
aberration [.æbə'reiʃən] *n* aberrazione.
abet [ə'bet] *vt* favoreggiare, incitare.
abeyance [ə'beiəns] *n* sospensione.
abhor [əb'hɔ:] *vt* aborrire, detestare.
abhorrence [əb'hɔrəns] *n* odio, ripugnanza.
abhorrent [əb'hɔrənt] *a* ripugnante, contrario a.
abide [ə'baid] *vti* sopportare; **a. by** conformarsi a; tener fede a, attenersi a.
ability [ə'biliti] *n* abilità, talento.
abject ['æbdʒekt] *a* abietto, reietto, vile.
abjuration [.æbdʒuə'reiʃən] *n* abiura.
abjure [əb'dʒuə] *vt* abiurare, ripudiare.
ablative ['æblətiv] *a n* ablativo.
ablaze [ə'bleiz] *a* in fiamme; risplendente.
able ['eibl] *a* abile, capace, in grado di.
ablution [ə'blu:ʃən] *n* abluzione.
abnegation [.æbni'geiʃən] *n* abnegazione, rinunzia.
abnormal [æb'nɔ:məl] *a* anormale.
abnormality [.æbnɔ:'mæliti] *n* anormalità; anomalia.
aboard [ə'bɔ:d] *ad prep* (*naut*) a bordo.
abode [ə'boud] *n* dimora, domicilio.
abolish [ə'bɔliʃ] *vt* abolire.
abolition [.æbə'liʃən] *n* abolizione.
abominable [ə'bɔminəbl] *a* abominevole.
abomination [ə.bɔmi'neiʃən] *n* abominazione, disgusto.
aboriginal [.æbə'ridʒənl] *a n* aborigeno, indigeno.
abortion [ə'bɔ:ʃən] *n* aborto.
abortive [ə'bɔ:tiv] *a* abortivo, prematuro; (*fig*) fallito.
abound [ə'baund] *vi* abbondare.
abounding [ə'baundiŋ] *a* abbondante, ricco.
about [ə'baut] *prep* circa, intorno a, per; *ad* intorno, presso, qua e là; **to be about to** stare per.
above [ə'bʌv] *ad prep* in alto, al di sopra di; più (alto) che, lassù, più in alto, sopra.
Abraham ['eibrəhæm] *nm pr* Abramo.
abrasion [ə'breiʒən] *n* abrasione, scalfittura.
abreast [ə'brest] *ad* di fianco.
abridge [ə'bridʒ] *vt* abbreviare, ridurre.
abridg(e)ment [ə'bridʒmənt] *n* abbreviazione, compendio.
abroad [ə'brɔ:d] *ad* all'estero, fuori.
abrogate ['æbrougeit] *vt* abrogare.
abrogation [.æbrou'geiʃən] *n* abrogazione.
abrupt [ə'brʌpt] *a* brusco, improvviso; ripido.
abscess ['æbsis] *n* ascesso.
abscond [əb'skɔnd] *vi* rendersi latitante, fuggire.
absence ['æbsəns] *n* assenza, mancanza; **a. of mind** distrazione.
absent ['æbsənt] *a* assente; *vr* [əb'sent] **to absent oneself** assentarsi.
absentee [.æbsən'ti:] *n* persona abitualmente assente dal suo domicilio o dal lavoro, scuola, etc.
absently ['æbsəntli] *ad* distrattamente.
absinthe ['æbsinθ] *n* assenzio.
absolute ['æbsəlu:t] *a* assoluto, completo; puro.
absolutely ['æbsəlu:tli] *ad* assolutamente.
absoluteness ['æbsəlu:tnis] *n* assolutezza.
absolution [.æbsə'lu:ʃən] *n* assoluzione.

absolutism ['æbsəlu:tizəm] *n* assolutismo.
absolve [əb'zɔlv] *vt* assolvere.
absorb [əb'sɔ:b] *vt* assorbire.
absorbed [əb'sɔ:bd] *a* assorbito, assorto.
absorbent [əb'sɔ:bənt] *a n* assorbente; **a. cotton** (*US*) cotone idrofilo.
absorbing [əb'sɔ:biŋ] *a* assorbente, interessante.
absorption [əb'sɔ:pʃən] *n* assorbimento.
abstain [əb'stein] *vi* astenersi.
abstemious [æb'sti:miəs] *a* astemio, frugale, moderato.
abstension [æb'stenʃən] *n* astensione.
abstinence ['æbstinəns] *n* astinenza.
abstinent ['æbstinənt] *a* astinente, sobrio.
abstract ['æbstrækt] *a* astratto; *n* astrazione, astratto; *vt* [æb'strækt] astrarre; sottrarre.
abstraction [æb'strækʃən] *n* astrazione; distrazione; sottrazione.
abstruse [æb'stru:s] *a* astruso.
absurd [əb'sə:d] *a* assurdo, ridicolo.
absurdity [əb'sə:diti] *n* assurdità.
absurdly [əb'sə:dli] *ad* assurdamente.
abundance [ə'bʌndəns] *n* abbondanza.
abundant [ə'bʌndənt] *a* abbondante.
abuse [ə'bju:s] *n* abuso, cattivo uso; insulto; *vt* [ə'bju:z] abusare di, far cattivo uso; insultare.
abusive [ə'bju:siv] *a* abusivo; ingiurioso.
abysmal [ə'bizməl] *a* abissale.
abyss [ə'bis] *n* abisso.
Abyssinia [,æbi'siniə] *n* Abissinia.
Abyssinian [æbi'siniən] *a n* abissino.
acacia [ə'keiʃə] *n* acacia.
academic [,ækə'demik] *a n* accademico.
academician [ə,kædə'miʃən] *n* accademico.
academy [ə'kædəmi] *n* accademia.
accede [æk'si:d] *vi* accedere; aderire.
accelerate [æk'seləreit] *vti* accelerare.
acceleration [æk,selə'reiʃən] *n* accelerazione.
accelerator [ək'seləreitə] *n* acceleratore.
accent ['æksənt] *n* accento, tono; **accent, accentuate** *vt* accentuare.
accentuation [æk,sentju'eiʃən] *n* accentuazione.
accept [ək'sept] *vt* accettare, approvare.
acceptable [ək'septəbl] *a* accetto, gradevole.
acceptance [ək'septəns] *n* accettazione, accoglienza.
accepter, acceptor [ək'septə] *n* (*com*) accettante.
access ['ækses] *n* accesso.
accessible [æk'sesəbl] *a* accessibile.
accession [æk'seʃən] *n* accessione; aggiunta.
accessory [æk'sesəri] *a n* accessorio; complice.
accident ['æksidənt] *n* accidente, caso; incidente; **by a.** per caso; **a.-prone** soggetto agli incidenti.
accidental [,æksi'dentl] *a* casuale, fortuito; *n* (*mus*) accidente.
accidentally [,æksi'dentəli] *ad* accidentalmente, per caso.
acclaim [ə'kleim] *vt* acclamare.
acclamation [,æklə'meiʃən] *n* acclamazione.
acclimatization [ə,klaimətai'zeiʃən] *n* acclimatazione.
acclimatize [ə'klaimətaiz] *vt* acclimatare.
accommodate [ə'kɔmədeit] *vt* accomodare, comporre; alloggiare.
accommodating [ə'kɔmədeitiŋ] *a* accomodante; compiacente.
accommodation [ə,kɔmə'deiʃən] *n* accomodamento, adattamento; alloggio; sistemazione.
accompaniment [ə'kʌmpənimənt] *n* accompagnamento.
accompanist [ə'kʌmpənist] *n* accompagnatore, -trice.
accompany [ə'kʌmpəni] *vt* accompagnare.
accomplice [ə'kʌmplis] *n* complice.
accomplish [ə'kʌmpliʃ] *vt* compiere, completare, effettuare.
accomplishment [ə'kʌmpliʃmənt] *n* compimento, realizzazione; dote.
accord [ə'kɔ:d] *n* accordo, consenso; *vti* accordare, concedere.
accordance [ə'kɔ:dəns] *n* accordo, conformità.
according to [ə'kɔ:diŋtu] *prep* secondo.
accordingly [ə'kɔ:diŋli] *ad* in conseguenza, in conformità.
accordion [ə'kɔ:diən] *n* (*mus*) fisarmonica.
accost [ə'kɔst] *vt* rivolgere la parola a, abbordare.
account [ə'kaunt] *n* conto; acconto; importanza; relazione; **on a. of** a causa, (motivo) di; **on no a.** a nessun patto.
account [ə'kaunt] *vt* considerare, stimare; **a. for** spiegare la ragione di.
accountability [ə,kauntə'biliti] *n* responsabilità.
accountable [ə'kauntəbl] *a* responsabile.
accountant [ə'kauntənt] *n* contabile; **certified public a.** ragioniere.
accredit [ə'kredit] *vt* accreditare, fornire di credenziali.
accretion [æ'kri:ʃən] *n* accrescimento.
accrue [ə'kru:] *vi* derivare, provenire; accumularsi.
accumulate [ə'kju:mjuleit] *vt* accumulare, ammassare; *vi* accumularsi.

accumulation [ə,kju:mju'leiʃən] *n* accumulamento, ammasso.
accumulative [ə'kju:mjulətiv] *a* accumulativo.
accumulator [ə'kju:mjuleitə] *n* accumulatore.
accuracy ['ækjurəsi] *n* esattezza, precisione.
accurate ['ækjurit] *a* esatto, preciso.
accursed [ə'kə:sid] *a* maledetto.
accusation [,ækju'zeiʃən] *n* accusa.
accusative [ə'kju:zətiv] *a n* accusativo.
accuse [ə'kju:z] *vt* accusare.
accustom [ə'kʌstəm] *vt* abituare; **a. oneself** *vr* abituarsi.
ace [eis] *n* asso; **within an a.** lì per lì.
acerbity [ə'sə:biti] *n* acerbità, asprezza.
acetate ['æsitit] *n* acetato.
acetone ['æsitoun] *n* acetone.
acetylene [ə'setili:n] *n* acetilene.
ache [eik] *n* dolore, male; *vi* dolere.
achieve [ə'tʃi:v] *vt* compiere, condurre a termine; raggiungere.
achievement [ə'tʃi:vmənt] *n* compimento; raggiungimento; successo.
aching ['eikiŋ] *a* dolorante.
acid ['æsid] *a n* acido.
acidify [ə'sidifai] *vt* acidificare.
acidity [ə'siditi] *n* acidità.
acknowledge [ək'nɔlidʒ] *vt* ammettere; riconoscere; accusare (ricezione di).
acknowledgment [ək'nɔlidʒmənt] *n* ammissione; riconoscimento; l'accusare ricezione
acme ['ækmi] *n* acme, culmine.
acne ['ækni] *n* acne.
acolyte ['ækəlait] *n* accolito.
acorn ['eikɔ:n] *n* ghianda.
acoustic [ə'ku:stik] *a* acustico; **acoustics** *n pl* acustica.
acquaint [ə'kweint] *vt* informare, mettere al corrente.
acquaintance [ə'kweintəns] *n* conoscenza; conoscente.
acquiesce [,ækwi'es] *vi* accettare, acconsentire tacitamente.
acquiescence [,ækwi'esns] *n* acquiescenza.
acquiescent [,ækwi'esnt] *a* acquiescente, rassegnato.
acquire [ə'kwaiə] *vt* acquisire, acquistare.
acquisition [,ækwi'ziʃən] *n* acquisizione; acquisto.
acquit [ə'kwit] *vt* assolvere; **a. oneself** *vr* comportarsi.
acquittal [ə'kwitl] *n* assoluzione.
acre ['eikə] *n* acro.
acrid ['ækrid] *a* acre, aspro.
acrimonious [,ækri'mouniəs] *a* aspro, astioso.
acrimony ['ækriməni] *n* acrimonia.
acrobat ['ækrəbæt] *n* acrobata.
across [ə'krɔs] *ad prep* attraverso, da un lato all'altro, dall'altra parte.
acrostic [ə'krɔstik] *n* acrostico.
act [ækt] *n* atto; azione; *vti* agire, fare, comportarsi; rappresentare, recitare.
acting ['æktiŋ] *a* facente; avente funzione di; *n* rappresentazione; modo di recitare.
action ['ækʃən] *n* azione; combattimento; gesto; processo.
activate ['æktiveit] *vt* attivare; rendere radioattivo.
active ['æktiv] *a* attivo, energico.
actively ['æktivli] *ad* attivamente.
activity [æk'tiviti] *n* attività, energia.
actor ['æktə] *n* attore; **actress** *n* attrice.
actual ['æktjuəl] *a* reale, effettivo.
actuality [,æktju'æliti] *n* realtà.
actually ['æktjuəli] *ad* realmente, effettivamente.
actuate ['æktjueit] *vt* mettere in azione; trascinare.
acumen ['ækjumən] *n* acume.
acute [ə'kju:t] *a* acuto; perspicace.
acuteness [ə'kju:tnis] *n* acutezza; perspicacia.
adage ['ædidʒ] *n* adagio, detto, proverbio.
Adam ['ædəm] *nm pr* Adamo.
adamant ['ædəmənt] *a* adamantino, inflessibile.
adapt [ə'dæpt] *vt* adattare, modificare.
adaptability [ə,dæptə'biliti] *n* adattabilità.
adaptable [ə'dæptəbl] *a* adattabile.
adaptation [,ædæp'teiʃən] *n* adattamento.
adapter [ə'dæptə] *n* (*phot*) adattatore; (*el*) pezzo di raccordo.
add [æd] *vti* aggiungere, soggiungere; addizionare, sommare; **to a. up** fare la somma.
adder ['ædə] *n* vipera.
addict ['ædikt] *n* tossicomane; [ə'dikt] *vt* abituare, dedicare.
addiction [ə'dikʃən] *n* dedizione, inclinazione.
addition [ə'diʃən] *n* addizione, somma; aggiunta; **in a. to** oltre a.
additional [ə'diʃənl] *a* aggiunto; supplementare.
additionally [ə'diʃnəli] *ad* in aggiunta; inoltre.
addled ['ædld] *a* guasto; confuso.
address [ə'dres] *n* indirizzo; discorso; destrezza; *vt* indirizzare; rivolgere la parola o lo scritto a.
addressee [,ædre'si:] *n* destinatario.
adduce [ə'dju:s] *vt* addurre; citare.
Adela ['ædilə] *nf pr* Adele.
adenoids ['ædinɔidz] *n pl* adenoidi.
adept ['ædept] *a n* esperto.
adequate ['ædikwit] *a* adeguato.
adhere [əd'hiə] *vi* aderire, attaccarsi.
adherence [əd'hiərəns] *n* aderenza.
adherent [əd'hiərənt] *a* aderente, attaccato; *n* partigiano, seguace.
adhesion [əd'hi:ʒən] adesione.
adhesive [əd'hi:siv] *a* adesivo, appiccicaticcio; **a. paper** carta gom-

mata; **a. plaster** cerotto adesivo.
adieu [ə'dju:] *interj n* addio.
adipose ['ædipous] *a* adiposo.
adjacent [ə'dʒeisənt] *a* adiacente, attiguo.
adjective ['ædʒiktiv] *n* aggettivo.
adjoin [ə'dʒɔin] *vti* essere adiacente.
adjoining [ə'dʒɔiniŋ] *a* adiacente, contiguo.
adjourn [ə'dʒə:n] *vt* aggiornare; rimandare.
adjournment [ə'dʒə:nmənt] *n* rinvio.
adjudge [ə'dʒʌdʒ] *vt* aggiudicare; assegnare.
adjudicate [ə'dʒu:dikeit] *vt* giudicare; aggiudicare.
adjudication [ə,dʒu:di'keiʃən] *n* aggiudicazione; sentenza.
adjudicator [ə'dʒu:dikeitə] *n* giudice; arbitro.
adjunct ['ædʒʌŋkt] *n* aggiunta; aggiunto.
adjure [ə'dʒuə] *vt* implorare, scongiurare.
adjust [ə'dʒʌst] *vt* aggiustare; adattare; regolare.
adjustable [ə'dʒʌstəbl] *a* aggiustabile; regolabile.
adjustment [ə'dʒʌstmənt] *n* adattamento; regolamento.
adjutant ['ædʒutənt] *n* aiutante.
ad lib [æd'lib] *ad* all'impronto, estemporaneamente; *vti* improvvisare; *n.* improvvisazione.
adman ['ædmæn] *n* agente pubblicitario.
admass ['ædmæs] *n* 'il grosso pubblico'.
administer [əd'ministə] *vt* amministrare; somministrare.
administration [əd,minis'treiʃən] *n* amministrazione; somministrazione.
administrative [əd'ministrətiv] *a* amministrativo.
administrator [əd'ministreitə] *n* amministratore.
admirable ['ædmərəbl] *a* ammirabile, ammirevole.
admiral ['ædmərəl] *n* ammiraglio.
admiralty ['ædmərəlti] *n* ammiragliato; Ministero della Marina.
admiration [,ædmə'reiʃən] *n* ammirazione.
admire [əd'maiə] *vt* ammirare.
admirer [əd'maiərə] *n* ammiratore; corteggiatore.
admiring [əd'maiəriŋ] *a* ammirativo.
admissible [əd'misəbl] *a* ammissibile.
admission [əd'miʃən] *n* ammissione.
admit [əd'mit] *vt* ammettere; riconoscere; lasciar entrare; **a. of** *vi* permettere.
admittance [əd'mitəns] *n* ammissione; ingresso.
admittedly [əd'mitidli] *ad* certo, certo che.
admonish [əd'mɔniʃ] *vt* ammonire.
admonishment [əd'mɔniʃmənt] *n* ammonimento; esortazione.
ado [ə'du:] *n* confusione, trambusto; difficoltà.
adolescence [,ædou'lesns] *n* adolescenza.
adolescent [,ædou'lesnt] *a n* adolescente.
adopt [ə'dɔpt] *vt* adottare; **adopted** *a* adottato; **adopted son** figlio adottivo.
adoption [ə'dɔpʃən] *n* adozione.
adoptive [ə'dɔptiv] *a* adottivo.
adorable [ə'dɔ:rəbl] *a* adorabile.
adoration [,ædɔ:'reiʃən] *n* adorazione; venerazione.
adore [ə'dɔ:] *vt* adorare, venerare.
adorer [ə'dɔ:rə] *n* adoratore.
adorn [ə'dɔ:n] *vt* adornare.
adornment [ə'dɔ:nmənt] *n* ornamento.
Adrian ['eidriən] *nm pr* Adriano.
Adriatic [,eidri'ætik] *a n* Adriatico.
adrift [ə'drift] *ad* alla deriva.
adroit [ə'drɔit] *a* destro, abile.
adroitness [ə'drɔitnis] *n* destrezza, abilità.
adulation [,ædju'leiʃən] *n* adulazione.
adult ['ædʌlt] *a n* adulto.
adulterate [ə'dʌltəreit] *vt* adulterare.
adulteration [ə,dʌltə'reiʃən] *a* adulterazione, sofisticazione.
adulterer [ə'dʌltərə] *n* adultero; **adulteress** *n* adultera.
adultery [ə'dʌltəri] *n* adulterio.
advance [əd'vɑ:ns] *n* avanzamento, marcia in avanti, progresso; (*com*) rialzo; anticipo; *vt* avanzare; aumentare; anticipare; *vi* avanzare; progredire.
advanced [əd'vɑ:nst] *a* avanzato, progredito.
advancement [əd'vɑ:nsmənt] *n* avanzamento, progresso, promozione.
advantage [əd'vɑ:ntidʒ] *n* vantaggio.
advantageous [,ædvən'teidʒəs] *a* vantaggioso.
advent ['ædvənt] *n* avvento.
adventitious [,ædven'tiʃəs] *a* avventizio, casuale.
adventure [əd'ventʃə] *n* avventura, impresa.
adventurer [əd'ventʃərə] *n* avventuriero.
adventurous [əd'ventʃərəs] *a* avventuroso.
adverb ['ædvə:b] *n* avverbio.
adverbial [əd'və:biəl] *a* avverbiale.
adversary ['ædvəsəri] *n* avversario, antagonista.
adverse ['ædvə:s] *a* avverso, contrario, opposto.
adversity [əd'və:siti] *n* avversità.
advertise ['ædvətaiz] *vti* fare della pubblicità per; mettere annunci, rendere noto.
advertisement [əd'və:tismənt] *n* annuncio, avviso; inserzione; reclame.

advertiser ['ædvətaizə] *n* inserzionista; **advertising** *a* pubblicitario; *n* pubblicità.
advice [əd'vais] *n* consigli(o), avviso.
advisable [əd'vaizəbl] *a* consigliabile, raccomandabile.
advise [əd'vaiz] *vt* consigliare; avvisare.
advisedly [əd'vaizidli] *ad* consideratamente, giudiziosamente.
adviser [əd'vaizə] *n* consigliere.
advisory [əd'vaizəri] *a* che consiglia; consultivo.
advocate ['ædvəkit] *n* avvocato; *vt* ['ædvəkeit] difendere, patrocinare; sostenere.
Aegean [i'dʒi:ən] *a n* (*geogr*) Egeo.
aerated ['eiəreitid] *a* gassoso.
aerial ['ɛəriəl] *a* aereo, etereo; *n* (*rad*) antenna.
aerobatics ['ɛərou'bætiks] *n pl* acrobazie aeree.
aerodrome ['ɛərədroum] *n* aerodromo.
aerodynamics ['ɛəroudai'næmiks] *n* aerodinamica; **aerodynamic** *a* aerodinamico.
aeronaut ['ɛərənɔ:t] *n* aeronauta.
aeronautics [,ɛərə'nɔ:tiks] *n* aeronautica.
aerosol ['ɛərəsɔl] *n* aerosol.
aerostat ['ɛərostæt] *n* aerostato.
aerostatics [,ɛero'stætiks] *np* aerostatica.
aesthete ['i:sθi:t] *n* esteta.
aesthetic [i:s'θetik] *a* estetico; **aesthetics** *n* estetica.
afar, afar off [ə'fɑ:, ə'fɑ:r'ɔf] *ad* lontano, in lontananza; **from a.** da lontano.
affability [,æfə'biliti] *n* affabilità.
affable ['æfəbl] *a* affabile.
affair [ə'fɛə] *n* affare; avventura, relazione.
affect [ə'fekt] *vt* affettare; riguardare; influire su; commuovere.
affectation [,æfek'teiʃən] *n* affettazione.
affected [ə'fektid] *a* affettato; affetto; commosso.
affection [ə'fekʃən] *n* affetto, affezione.
affectionate [ə'fekʃnit] *a* affettuoso.
affidavit [,æfi'deivit] *n* deposizione scritta e giurata, affidavit.
affiliate [ə'filieit] *vt* affiliare, associare.
affiliation [ə,fili'eiʃən] *n* affiliazione.
affinity [ə'finiti] *n* affinità; parentela.
affirm [ə'fə:m] *vt* affermare, confermare.
affirmation [,æfə:'meiʃən] *n* affermazione, asserzione.
affirmative [ə'fə:mətiv] *a* affermativo; *n* affermativa.
affix [ə'fiks] *vt* affiggere, apporre, attaccare; ['æfiks] *n* affiso.
afflict [ə'flikt] *vt* affliggere.
affliction [ə'flikʃən] *n* afflizione.
affluence ['æfluəns] *n* affluenza, abbondanza.
affluent ['æfluənt] *a* ricco; *n* affluente.
afford [ə'fɔ:d] *vt* fornire, offrire; permettersi il lusso di.
afforestation [æ'fɔris'teiʃən] *n* imboschimento.
affranchise [ə'fræntʃaiz] *vt* affrancare, liberare.
affront [ə'frʌnt] *n* affronto; insulto; *vt* affrontare; insultare.
afloat [ə'flout] *ad* a galla.
afoot [ə'fut] *ad* (*fig*) in moto, in ballo.
aforesaid [ə'fɔ:sed] *a* predetto.
afraid [ə'freid] *a* impaurito, pauroso; **to be a.** aver paura.
afresh [ə'freʃ] *ad* di nuovo, un'altra volta.
Africa ['æfrikə] *n* Africa.
African ['æfrikən] *a n* africano.
Afrikan(d)er [,æfri'kæn(d)ə] *a n* sud-africano, di origine olandese.
aft [ɑ:ft] *ad* (*naut*) a poppa.
after ['ɑ:ftə] *ad prep cj* dopo, dietro, in seguito a; ad imitazione di; dopo che; **a. all** in fin dei conti.
after-effect ['ɑ:ftəri'fekt] *n* conseguenza.
aftermath ['ɑ:ftəmæθ] *n* secondo taglio del fieno; (*fig*) conseguenze *pl*, risultati *pl*.
afternoon ['ɑ:ftə'nu:n] *n* pomeriggio.
afterthought ['ɑ:ftəθɔ:t] *n* riflessione, ripensamento.
afterwards ['ɑ:ftəwədz] *ad* dopo, più tardi.
again [ə'gen] *ad* ancora, di nuovo; altrettanto; **a. and a.** ripetutamente; **now and a.** di quando in quando.
against [ə'genst] *prep* contro, in opposizione a; di fronte a; **a. the grain** (*fig*) contro voglia.
agate ['ægət] *n* agata.
Agatha ['ægəθə] *nf pr* Agata.
age ['eidʒ] *n* età; periodo; **of a.** maggiorenne; **under a.** minorenne.
age ['eidʒ] *vti* invecchiare.
aged ['eidʒid] *a* vecchio; ['eidʒd] dell'età di.
ageless ['eidʒlis] *a* di età invariata, sempre giovane.
agency ['eidʒənsi] *n* agenzia, rappresentanza.
agenda [ə'dʒendə] *n* ordine del giorno.
agent ['eidʒənt] *n* agente, rappresentante.
agglomeration [ə,glɔmə'reiʃən] *n* agglomerazione.
aggrandizement [ə'grændizmənt] *n* accrescimento (di potenza).
aggravate ['ægrəveit] *vt* aggravare; (*fam*) esasperare.
aggravating ['ægrəveitiŋ] *a* (*fam*) irritante, insopportabile.
aggregate ['ægrigit] *a n* aggregato; **in the a.** nel complesso.
aggregation [,ægri'geiʃən] *n* aggregazione.
aggression [ə'greʃən] *n* aggressione.

aggressive [ə'gresiv] *a* aggressivo.
aggressiveness [ə'gresivnis] *n* aggressività.
aggressor [ə'gresə] *n* aggressore.
aghast [ə'gɑ:st] *a* stupefatto: terrorizzato.
agile ['ædʒail] *a* agile.
agility [ə'dʒiliti] *n* agilita.
agitate ['ædʒiteit] *vt* agitare; commuovere; discutere.
agitation [,ædʒi'teiʃən] *n* agitazione, commozione.
agitator ['ædʒiteitə] *n* agitatore.
Agnes ['ægnis] *nf pr* Agnese.
agnostic [æg'nɔstik] *a n* agnostico.
ago [ə'gou] *ad* fa.
agog [ə'gɔg] *a* ansioso, desideroso; *ad* con ansia.
agonized ['ægənaizd] **agonizing** ['ægənaiziŋ] *a* angoscioso.
agony ['ægəni] *n* agonia; angoscia.
agrarian [ə'grɛəriən] *a* agrario.
agree [ə'gri:] *vi* accordarsi, convenire; acconsentire; confarsi.
agreeable [ə'griəbl] *a* piacevole, simpatico; disposto; conveniente.
agreeableness [ə'griəblnis] *n* piacevolezza, conformità.
agreement [ə'gri:mənt] *n* accordo, contratto, patto.
agricultural [,ægri'kʌltʃərəl] *a* agricolo.
agriculture ['ægrikʌltʃə] *n* agricoltura.
aground [ə'graund] *ad a* (*naut*) in secco; **to run a.** incagliarsi.
ahead [ə'hed] *ad* (in) avanti.
aid [eid] *n* aiuto, assistenza, sussidio; **first a.** pronto soccorso; *vt* aiutare.
aide-de-camp ['eiddə'kɑ̃:ŋ] *n* aiutante di campo.
ail [eil] *vi* sentirsi male; *vt* affliggere.
ailing ['eiliŋ] *a* sofferente.
ailment ['eilmənt] *n* indisposizione, malattia.
aim [eim] *n* mira, scopo, proposito; *vti* puntare; *vi* mirare a; aspirare a.
aimless ['eimlis] *a* senza scopo.
air [ɛə] *n* aria; aspetto; atmosfera; (*mus*) aria; *vt* arieggiare, ventilare; **a.-hostess** assistente di volo, 'hostess'; **a. conditioner** condizionatore dell'aria; **a. station** scalo aereo; **a.-raid** incursione aerea.
aircraft (*inv*) ['ɛəkrɑ:ft] *n* aereo, aerei; **a .carrier** porta erei.
airdrome ['ɛədroum] *n* aerodromo.
air force ['ɛəfɔ:s] *n* aeronautica, aviazione.
airily ['ɛərili] *ad* gaiamente; spensieratamente.
airiness ['ɛərinis] *n* leggerezza; spensieratezza.
airing ['ɛəriŋ] *n* ventilazione; giretto all'aria aperta.
airless ['ɛəlis] *a* privo d'aria.
airline ['ɛəlain] *n* aviolinea.
airmail ['ɛəmeil] *n* posta aerea.
airman ['ɛəmən] *n* aviatore.
airplane ['ɛəplein] *n* aeroplano; **fighter a.** aeroplano da caccia.
airport ['ɛəpɔ:t] *n* aeroporto.
air-pump ['ɛəpʌmp] *n* pompa pneumatica.
airship ['ɛəʃip] *n* dirigibile.
airtight ['ɛətait] *a* a tenuta d'aria.
airway ['ɛəwei] *n* via aerea.
airy ['ɛəri] *a* arioso; leggero; spensierato: aereo; vano.
aisle [ail] *n* navata.
ajar [ə'dʒɑ:] *ad* socchiuso.
akimbo [ə'kimbou] *ad* le mani su i fianchi e i gomiti in fuori.
akin [ə'kin] *a* affine, parente.
alabaster ['æləbɑ:stə] *a n* (di) alabastro.
alacrity [ə'lækriti] *n* alacrità.
Alan ['ælən] *nm pr* Alano.
alarm [ə'lɑ:m] *n* allarme; *vt* allarmare, spaventare.
alarm-clock [ə'lɑ:mklɔk] *n* (orologio a) sveglia.
alas! [ə'læs] *interj* ahimè!
Albania [æl'beiniə] *n* (*geogr*) Albania.
Albanian [æl'beiniən] *a n* albanese.
albatross ['ælbətrɔs] *n* albatro.
albeit [ɔ:l'bi:it] *cj* quantunque.
Albert ['ælbət] *nm pr* Alberto.
albino [æl'bi:nou] *pl* **albinos** albino.
album ['ælbəm] *n* album.
albumen ['ælbjumin] *n* albume.
alchemy ['ælkimi] *n* alchimia.
alcohol ['ælkəhɔl] *n* alcool.
alcoholic [,ælkə'hɔlik] *a* alcoolico; *n* alcoolizzato.
alcoholism ['ælkəhɔlizəm] *n* alcoolismo.
alcove ['ælkouv] *n* alcova, recesso.
alder ['ɔ:ldə] *n* ontano.
alderman ['ɔ:ldəmən] *n* assessore comunale.
ale [eil] *n* birra; **a.-house** birrería.
alert [ə'lə:t] *a* vigilante, attento; *n* allarme; **on the a.** all'erta.
alertness [ə'lə:tnis] *n* vigilanza; vivacità.
Alexander [,ælig'zɑ:ndə] *nm pr* Alessandro.
Alexandria [,ælig'zɑ:ndriə] *n* (*geogr*) Alessandria (d'Egitto).
Alfred ['ælfrid] *nm pr* Alfredo.
algebra ['ældʒibrə] *n* algebra.
Algeria [æl'dʒiəriə] *n* (*geogr*) Algeria.
Algerian [æl'dʒiəriən] *a n* algerino.
alias ['eiliæs] *ad* alias; *n* falso nome.
alibi ['ælibai] *n* alibi.
Alice ['ælis] *nf pr* Alice.
alien ['eiliən] *a* estraneo; *n* straniero.
alienate ['eiliəneit] *vt* alienare.
alienation [,eiliə'neiʃən] *n* alienazione.
alight [ə'lait] *a* acceso; illuminato; infiammato; *vi* scendere; atterrare.
alike [ə'laik] *a* simile; *ad* parimenti.
alimentary [,æli'mentəri] *a* alimentare; alimentario.
alimentation [,ælimen'teiʃən] *n* alimentazione.
alimony ['æliməni] *n* alimonia, alimenti.

alive [ə'laiv] *a* vivo, vivente; vivace.
alkaline ['ælkəlain] *a* alcalino.
all [ɔ:l] *a* tutto; *n pron* tutto; *ad* completamente, del tutto; **not at all!** niente affatto!
allay [ə'lei] *vt* calmare; alleviare; diminuire.
allegation [,æle'geiʃən] *n* allegazione, asserzione.
allege [ə'ledʒ] *vt* allegare, asserire.
allegiance [ə'li:dʒəns] *n* fedeltà, obbedienza (al sovrano *etc*).
allegorical [,æle'gɔrikəl] *a* allegorico.
allegory ['æligəri] *n* allegoria.
allergic [ə'lə:dʒik] *a* allergico.
allergy ['ælədʒi] *n* allergia.
alleviate [ə'li:vieit] *vt* alleviare, mitigare.
alley ['æli] *n* vicolo.
alliance [ə'laiəns] *n* alleanza; unione.
allied ['ælaid] *a* alleato.
alligator ['æligeitə] *n* alligatore.
alliteration [ə,litə'reiʃən] *n* allitterazione.
allocate ['æləkeit] *vt* assegnare; distribuire.
allocation [,ælə'keiʃən] *n* assegnazione.
allot [ə'lɔt] *vt* distribuire; assegnare.
allotment [ə'lɔtmənt] *n* assegnazione, lotto; piccolo pezzo di terreno da coltivare.
allow [ə'lau] *vt* permettere, accordare; **to a. for** tener conto di.
allowable [ə'lauəbl] **allowed** [ə'laud] *a* lecito.
allowance [ə'lauəns] *n* assegno; indennità; riduzione, sconto.
alloy ['ælɔi] *n* lega (metallica); *vt* fondere, mescolare.
All Saints' Day ['ɔ:l'seintsdei] *n* Ognissanti.
All Souls' Day ['ɔ:l'soulzdei] *n* giorno dei morti.
allude [ə'lu:d] *vi* alludere.
allure [ə'ljuə] *vt* allettare, sedurre.
allurement [ə'ljuəmənt] *n* allettamento.
alluring [ə'ljuəriŋ] *a* allettante, seducente.
allusion [ə'lu:ʒən] *n* allusione.
ally ['ælai] *n* alleato; *vt* [ə'lai] alleare, collegare, unire.
almanac ['ɔ:lmənæk] *n* almanacco.
almighty [ɔ:l'maiti] *a* onnipotente; **the A.** Dio.
almond ['ɑ:mənd] *n* mandorla; **a.-tree** mandorlo.
almoner ['ɑ:mənə] *n* elemosiniere.
almost ['ɔ:lmoust] *ad* quasi.
alms [ɑ:mz] (*inv*) *n* elemosina; **a.-house** ospizio di mendicità.
aloft [ə'lɔft] *ad* in alto.
alone [ə'loun] *a* solo; **to let a.** lasciar stare.
along [ə'lɔŋ] *ad prep* avanti, lungo, per; **come a.!** su via!; **a. with** con.
aloof [ə'lu:f] *ad* a distanza; in disparte; *a* freddo, distante, sostenuto.
aloud [ə'laud] *ad* a voce alta, forte.
alphabet ['ælfəbit] *n* alfabeto.
alpine ['ælpain] *a* alpino.
Alps [ælps] *n pl* (*geogr*) Alpi.
already [ɔ:l'redi] *ad* già, di già.
Alsace ['ælzæs] *n* Alsazia.
Alsatian [æl'seiʃjən] *a n* alsaziano; **A. (dog)** cane lupo.
also ['ɔ:lsou] *ad* anche, inoltre, pure.
altar ['ɔ:ltə] *n* altare; **high a.** altare maggiore.
alter ['ɔ:ltə] *vti* cambiare, cambiarsi, alterare.
alterable ['ɔ:ltərəbl] *a* alterabile.
alteration [,ɔ:ltə'reiʃən] *n* modificazione, alterazione.
altercation [,ɔ:ltə'keiʃən] *n* alterco.
alternate [ɔ:l'tə:nit] *a* alternato, alterno; *vti* ['ɔ:ltəneit] alternar(si), avvicendar(si); **alternately** vicendevolmente.
alternation [,ɔ:ltə:'neiʃən] *n* alternazione.
alternative [ɔ:l'tə:nətiv] *a* alternativo; *n* alternativa; **alternatively** *ad* alternativamente.
although [ɔ:l'ðou] *cj* sebbene, quantunque, benché.
altitude ['æltitju:d] *n* altitudine, altezza; (*av*) quota.
altogether [,ɔ:ltə'gəðə] *ad* completamente, nell'insieme.
altruism ['æltruizəm] *n* altruismo.
altruistic [,æltru'istik] *a* altruistico.
alum ['æləm] *n* allume.
aluminum [ə'lu:minəm] *n* alluminio.
alveolar ['ælviolə] *a* alveolato.
always ['ɔ:lwəz] *ad* sempre.
amalgam [ə'mælgəm] *n* amalgama.
amalgamate [ə'mælgəmeit] *vti* amalgamar(si).
amalgamation [ə,mælgə'meiʃən] *n* amalgamazione, fusione.
amass [ə'mæs] *vt* accumulare, ammassare.
amateur ['æmətə] *a n* dilettante.
amaze [ə'meiz] *vt* meravigliare, stupire.
amazement [ə'meizmənt] *n* meraviglia.
amazing [ə'meiziŋ] *a* sorprendente.
Amazon ['æməzən] *n* (*geogr*) Rio delle Amazzoni.
ambassador [æm'bæsədə] *n* ambasciatore.
ambassadress [æm'bæsədris] *n* ambasciatrice.
amber ['æmbə] *n* ambra.
ambiguity [,æmbi'gjuiti] *n* ambiguità.
ambiguous [æm'bigjuəs] *a* ambiguo.
ambition [æm'biʃən] *n* ambizione.
ambitious [æm'biʃəs] *a* ambizioso.
amble ['æmbl] *vi* andare lemme lemme; *n* passo lento.
Ambrose ['æmbrouz] *nm pr* Ambrogio; **Ambrosian** *a* ambrosiano.
ambulance ['æmbjuləns] *n* ambulanza.

ambush ['æmbuʃ] *n* agguato, imboscata.
ameliorate [ə'mi:liəreit] *vti* migliorare.
amelioration [ə,mi:liə'reiʃən] *n* miglioramento.
amen ['ɑ:'men] *interj* amen, così sia.
amenable [ə'mi:nəbl] *a* trattabile.
amend [ə'mend] *vti* emendare, emendarsi.
amendment [ə'mendmənt] *n* emendamento.
amends [ə'mendz] *n pl* compenso, riparazione; to **make a.** fare ammenda.
amenity [ə'mi:niti] *n* amenità; **amenities** *n pl* comodità *pl.*
America [ə'merikə] *n* America.
American [ə'merikən] *a n* americano.
amethyst ['æmiθist] *n* ametista.
amiability [,eimiə'biliti] *n* amabilità.
amiable ['eimiəbl] *a* amabile.
amicable ['æmikəbl] *a* amichevole.
amid(st) [ə'mid(st)] *prep* fra, in mezzo a, tra.
amiss [ə'mis] *a* sbagliato; *ad* inopportunamente, in mala parte.
amity ['æmiti] *n* amicizia.
ammonia [ə'mouniə] *n* ammoniaca.
ammunition [,æmju'niʃən] *n* munizioni *pl.*
amnesia [æm'ni:ziə] *n* amnesia.
amnesty ['æmnesti] *n* amnistia.
amok [ə'mɔk] *v* **amuck.**
among(st) [ə'mʌŋ(st)] *prep* fra, in mezzo a, tra.
amoral [æ'mɔrəl] *a* amorale.
amorous ['æmərəs] *a* amoroso.
amorphous [ə'mɔ:fəs] *a* amorfo.
amount [ə'maunt] *n* ammontare, quantità, somma; *vi* ammontare.
amphibious [æm'fibiəs] *a* anfibio.
amphitheatre ['æmfi,θiətə] *n* anfiteatro.
ample ['æmpl] *a* ampio; abbondante.
amplification [,æmplifi'keiʃən] *n* amplificazione.
amplifier ['æmplifaiə] *n* amplificatore.
amplify ['æmplifai] *vti* ampliare, amplificare.
amputate ['æmpjuteit] *vt* amputare.
amputation [,æmpju'teiʃən] *n* amputazione.
amuck [ə'mʌk] *ad* in un accesso di pazzia sanguinaria.
amulet ['æmjulit] *n* amuleto.
amuse [ə'mju:z] *vt* divertire, svagare.
amusement [ə'mju:zmənt] *n* divertimento, svago.
amusing [ə'mju:ziŋ] *a* divertente; faceto.
an [æn] *indef art* un(o), una.
anachronism [a'nækrənizəm] *n* anacronismo.
anagram ['ænəgræm] *n* anagramma.
analogous [ə'næləgəs] *a* analogo.
analogy [ə'nælədʒi] *n* analogia.
analysis [ə'næləsis] *pl* **analyses** *n* analisi; **analyst** *n* analizzatore.
analytic(al) [,ænə'litik(əl)] *a* analitico.
analyze ['ænəlaiz] *vt* analizzare.
anarchist ['ænəkist] *n* anarchico.
anarchy ['ænəki] *n* anarchia.
anathema [ə'næθimə] *n* anatema.
anatomical [,ænə'tɔmikəl] *a* anatomico.
anatomy [ə'nætəmi] *n* anatomia.
ancestor ['ænsistə] *n* antenato.
ancestral [æn'sestrəl] *a* avito.
ancestry ['ænsistri] *n* lignaggio, stirpe.
anchor ['æŋkə] *n* àncora, (*fig*) salvezza; **at a.** ancorato; *vti* ancorar (si).
anchorage ['æŋkəridʒ] *n* ancoraggio.
anchovy ['æntʃəvi] *n* acciuga.
ancient ['einʃənt] *a* antico, venerabile.
and [ænd, ənd, ən] *cj* e, ed.
andiron ['ændaiən] *n* alare.
Andrew ['ændru:] *nm pr* Andrea.
anecdote ['ænikdout] *n* aneddoto.
anemia [ə'ni:miə] *n* anemia.
anemone [ə'neməni] *n* anemone; **sea a.** attinia.
anesthetic [,ænis'θetik] *a n* anestetico.
anew [ə'nju:] *ad* di nuovo.
angel ['eindʒəl] *n* angelo; **guardian a.** angelo custode.
angelic [æn'dʒelik] *a* angelico.
anger ['æŋgə] *n* ira, rabbia; *vt* adirare, far arrabbiare.
angle ['æŋgl] *n* angolo; punto di vista; *vi* pescare all'amo.
angler ['æŋglə] *n* pescatore.
Anglican ['æŋglikən] *a n* anglicano.
angling ['æŋgliŋ] *n* pesca all'amo.
Anglo-Saxon ['æŋglou'sæksən] *a n* anglo-sassone.
angry ['æŋgri] *a* arrabbiato, irato.
anguish ['æŋgwiʃ] *n* angoscia.
angular ['æŋgjulə] *a* angolare.
aniline ['ænili:n] *n* anilina.
animadversion [,ænimæd'və:ʃən] *n* censura, critica.
animal ['æniməl] *a n* animale.
animate ['ænimit] *a* animato; *vt* animare.
animation [,æni'meiʃən] *n* animazione.
animosity [,æni'mɔsiti] *n* animosità.
aniseed ['ænisi:d] *n* seme di anice.
anisette [,æni'zet] *n* anisetta.
ankle ['æŋkl] *n* caviglia.
Ann(e) [æn] *nf pr* Anna.
annals ['ænlz] *n pl* annali.
annex ['æneks] *n* annesso; edificio supplementare.
annex [ə'neks] *vt* annettere.
annexation [,ænek'seiʃən] *n* annessione.
annihilate [ə'naiəleit] *vt* annichilire.
annihilation [ə,naiə'leiʃən] *n* annientamento.
anniversary [,æni'və:səri] *a n* anniversario.

annotate ['ænouteit] *vt* annotare.
announce [ə'nauns] *vt* annunciare.
announcement [ə'naunsmənt] *n* annuncio, avviso.
announcer [ə'naunsə] *n* annunziatore, -trice; (*rad*) annunciatore, -trice, presentatore, -trice.
annoy [ə'nɔi] *vt* disturbare, irritare.
annoyance [ə'nɔiəns] *n* fastidio, irritazione.
annoying [ə'nɔiiŋ] *a* noioso, fastidioso.
annual ['ænjuəl] *a* annuale, annuo; *n* annuario; pianta annuale.
annuity [ə'njuiti] *n* annualità.
annul [ə'nʌl] *vt* annullare, abolire.
annulment [ə'nʌlmənt] *n* annullamento.
annunciation [ə'nʌnsi'eiʃən] *n* annunciazione.
anodyne ['ænoudain] *a* anodino.
anoint [ə'nɔint] *vt* ungere; consacrare.
anomalous [ə'nɔmələs] *a* anomalo, irregolare.
anomaly [ə'nɔməli] *n* anomalia, irregolarità.
anon [ə'nɔn] *ad* subito; **ever and a.** di quando in quando.
anonymous [ə'nɔniməs] *a* anonimo.
anorak ['ænəræk] *n* giacca a vento.
another [ə'nʌðə] *a pron* (un) altro; (un) secondo; **one a.** l'un l'altro.
Anselm ['ænselm] *nm pr* Anselmo.
answer ['ɑ:nsə] *n* risposta; *vt* rispondere a; **to answer for** rispondere di.
answerable ['ɑ:nsərəbl] *a* responsabile.
answering ['ɑ:nsəriŋ] *a* in risposta; corrispondente.
ant [ænt] *n* formica.
antagonism [æn'tægənizəm] *n* antagonismo, opposizione.
antagonist [æn'tægənist] *n* antagonista.
Antarctic [ænt'ɑ:ktik] *a* antartico; *n* Antartico, Antartide.
antecedent [,ænti'si:dənt] *a n* antecedente.
antechamber ['ænti,tʃeimbə] *n* anticamera.
antedate ['ænti'deit] *vt* anticipare, antidatare.
antediluvian ['æntidi'lu:viən] *a n* antidiluviano.
antelope ['æntiloup] *n* antilope.
antenatal ['ænti'neitl] *a* prenatale.
anteroom ['æntirum] *n* anticamera.
anthem ['ænθəm] *n* antifona; inno.
anthology [æn'θɔlədʒi] *n* antologia.
Anthony ['æntəni] *nm pr* Antonio.
anthracite ['ænθrəsait] *n* antracite.
anthropologist [,ænθrə'pɔlədʒist] *n* antropologo.
anthropology [,ænθrə'pɔlədʒi] *n* antropologia.
anti-aircraft ['ænti'ɛəkrɑ:ft] *a* antiaereo.
antibiotic ['æntibai'ɔtik] *a n* antibiotico.
antics ['æntiks] *n pl* stramberie, eccessi *pl*.
antichrist ['æntikraist] *n* anticristo.
anticipate [æn'tisipeit] *vt* anticipare; aspettarsi; pregustare.
anticipation [æn,tisi'peiʃən] *n* anticipazione, anticipo; previsione.
anticlimax ['ænti'klaimæks] *n* improvviso crollo discesa nel banale.
antidote ['æntidout] *n* antidoto.
antifogging ['æntifɔgiŋ] *a n* antiappannante, antinebbia.
antifreeze ['æntifri:z] *n* (*aut*) anticongelante.
antifriction ['ænti'frikʃən] *n* antiattrito.
anti-glare ['ænti'glɛə] *a* antiabbagliante; **a. headlights** (*aut*) fari anabbaglianti.
antihistamine ['ænti'histəmi:n] *n* antistamina.
antimacassar ['æntimə'kæsə] *n* copridivano, copripoltrona.
antimilitarism ['ænti'militərizəm] *n* antimilitarismo.
antimony ['æntiməni] *n* antimonio.
antipathy [æn'tipəθi] *n* antipatia, avversione.
antipodes [æn'tipədi:z] *n pl* antipodi *pl*.
antipope ['æntipoup] *n* antipapa.
antiquarian [,ænti'kwɛəriən] *a n* antiquario.
antiquated ['æntikweitid] *a* antiquato, fuori uso.
antique [æn'ti:k] *a* antico; *n* oggetto antico.
antiquity [æn'tikwiti] *n* antichità, tempi antichi *pl*.
anti-rust ['æntirʌst] *a n* antiruggine.
antiseptic [,ænti'septik] *a n* antisettico.
antisocial ['ænti'souʃəl] *a* antisociale.
anti-theft ['æntiθeft] *a n* antifurto.
antithesis [æn'tiθisis] *pl* **antitheses** *n* antitesi.
antler ['æntlə] *n* corno di cervo.
Antwerp ['æntwə:p] *n* (*geogr*) Anversa.
anvil ['ænvil] *n* incudine.
anxiety [æŋ'zaiəti] *n* ansia, ansietà.
anxious ['æŋkʃəs] *a* ansioso, preoccupato; desideroso.
any ['eni] *a* alcuno, -ni, del, dei, nessuno, qualche, un po' di; ogni, qualsiasi, qualunque; *pron* alcuno, nessuno.
anybody ['eni,bɔdi], **anyone** ['eniwʌn] *pron* alcuno, qualcuno; nessuno; chiunque.
anyhow ['enihau] *ad* in ogni caso, ad ogni modo; in qualsiasi modo.
anything ['eniθiŋ] *pron* qualche cosa, alcuna cosa; qualunque cosa.
anyway ['eniwei] *ad* in ogni caso, ad ogni modo.
anywhere ['eniwɛə] *ad* dovunque, in qualsiasi luogo.
apart [ə'pɑ:t] *ad* a parte, in disparte.

apartheid [ə'pa:theit] *n* segregazione razziale.
apartment [ə'pa:tmənt] *n* stanza, appartamento; **a. hotel** appartamento d'affitto con servizio.
apathetic [,æpə'θetik] *a* apatico, indifferente.
apathy ['æpəθi] *n* apatia, indifferenza.
ape [eip] *n* scimmia; *vt* imitare, scimmiottare.
Apennines ['æpinainz] *n pl* Appennini.
aperient [ə'piəriənt] *a n* lassativo.
aperitif [ə'peritif] *n* aperitivo.
aperture ['æpətjuə] *n* apertura, foro.
apex ['eipeks] *pl* **apexes, apices** *n* apice, vertice.
aphorism ['æfərizəm] *n* aforisma.
apiary ['eipjəri] *n* apiario.
apiece [ə'pi:s] *ad* per ognuno, a testa.
aplomb ['æplɔm] *n* perpendicolarità; sicurezza di sè.
apocalypse [ə'pɔkəlips] *n* apocalisse.
apocryphal [ə'pɔkrifəl] *a* apocrifo.
apogee ['æpoudʒi:] *n* apogeo.
apologetic [ə,pɔlə'dʒetik] *a* pieno di scuse.
apologize [ə'pɔledʒaiz] *vi* scusarsi.
apology [ə'pɔlədʒi] *n* scusa, giustificazione; apologia.
apoplectic [,æpə'plektik] *a* apoplettico.
apoplexy ['æpəpleksi] *n* apoplessia.
apostle [ə'pɔsl] *n* apostolo.
apostolic [,æpəs'tɔlik] *a* apostolico.
apostrophe [ə'pɔstrəfi] *n* apostrofe; (*gram*) apostrofo.
apostrophize [ə'pɔstrəfaiz] *vt* apostrofare.
appall [ə'pɔ:l] *vt* spaventare, atterrire.
appalling [ə'pɔ:liŋ] *a* spaventoso.
apparatus [,æpə'reitəs] *n* (*anat*) apparato; (*tec*) apparecchio.
apparent [ə'pærənt] *a* chiaro, manifesto; **heir a.** *n* erede legittimo.
apparition [,æpə'riʃən] *n* apparizione, fantasma.
appeal [ə'pi:l] *n* appello; attrattiva; *vi* appellarsi; attrarre.
appealing [ə'pi:liŋ] *ad* supplichevole; attraente.
appear [ə'piə] *vi* apparire; comparire; sembrare.
appearance [ə'piərəns] *n* apparenza; aspetto; apparizione; comparizione.
appease [ə'pi:z] *vt* calmare; pacificare.
appeasement [ə'pi:zmənt] *n* pacificazione; appagamento.
append [ə'pend] *vt* apporre, aggiungere.
appendicitis [ə,pendi'saitis] *n* appendicite.
appendix [ə'pendiks] *pl* **appendixes, appendices** *n* appendice.
appertain [,æpə'tein] *vi* appartenere; riferirsi.
appetite ['æpitait] *n* appetito.
appetizing ['æpitaiziŋ] *a* appetitoso.
applaud [ə'plɔ:d] *vti* applaudire.
applause [ə'plɔ:z] *n* applauso, -si *pl.*
apple ['æpl] *n* mela; **a.-tree** melo.
appliance [ə'plaiəns] *n* apparecchio; applicazione.
applicable ['æplikəbl] *a* applicabile.
applicant ['æplikənt] *n* candidato.
application [,æpli'keiʃən] *n* applicazione; domanda; diligenza.
apply [ə'plai] *vti* applicare; applicarsi; rivolgersi, fare domanda.
appoint [ə'pɔint] *vt* stabilire; nominare.
appointed [ə'pɔintid] *a* fissato; arredato, equipaggiato.
appointment [ə'pɔintmənt] *n* appuntamento; nomina; impiego; decreto.
apportion [ə'pɔ:ʃən] *vt* distribuire.
apportionment [ə'pɔ:ʃənmənt] *n* ripartizione.
apposite ['æpəzit] *a* apposito, appropriato.
apposition [,æpə'ziʃən] *n* apposizione.
appraisal [ə'preizəl] *n* stima, valutazione.
appraise [ə'preiz] *vt* stimare, valutare.
appreciable [ə'pri:ʃəbl] *a* apprezzabile; considerevole.
appreciate [ə'pri:ʃieit] *vt* apprezzare; tenere in giusto conto; *vi* aumentare di valore.
appreciation [ə,pri:ʃi'eiʃən] *n* apprezzamento; stima; rivalutazione.
apprehend [,æpri'hend] *vt* arrestare; comprendere; temere.
apprehension [,æpri'henʃən] *n* comprensione; apprensione; timore; arresto.
apprehensive [,æpri'hensiv] *a* timoroso; perspicace.
apprentice [ə'prentis] *n* apprendista.
apprenticeship [ə'prentiʃip] *n* apprendistato, tirocinio.
approach [ə'proutʃ] *n* avvicinamento; approccio; accesso; *vti* avvicinare, avvicinarsi.
approachable [ə'proutʃəbl] *a* avvicinabile, accessibile.
approbation [,æprə'beiʃən] *n* approvazione, sanzione.
appropriate [ə'proupriit] *a* appropriato, proprio; [ə'proupreit] *vt* appropriarsi; stanziare denaro.
appropriately [ə'proupriitli] *ad* appropriatamente.
appropriation [ə,proupri'eiʃən] *n* appropriazione; stanziamento.
approval [ə'pru:vəl] *n* approvazione, (*com*) prova.
approve [ə'pru:v] *vt* approvare, sanzionare.
approximate [ə'prɔksimit] *a* approssimativo; *vti* approssimar(si).
approximately [ə'prɔksimitli] *ad* approssimativamente.

apricot ['eiprikɔt] *n* albicocca; **a. tree** albicocco.
April ['eiprəl] *n* aprile.
apron ['eiprən] *n* grembiule.
apropos ['æprəpou] *ad* a proposito.
apse [æps] *n* abside.
apt [æpt] *a* adatto, atto; **a. at** bravo in; **a. to** avente tendenza a.
aptitude ['æptitju:d] *n* attitudine.
Apulia [ə'pju:liə] *n* (*geogr*) Puglia; **Apulian** *a n* pugliese.
aqualung ['ækwəlʌŋ] *n* autorespiratore.
aquarium [ə'kwɛəriəm] *n* acquario.
aquatic [ə'kwætik] *a* acquatico.
aqueduct ['ækwidʌkt] *n* acquedotto.
aquiline ['ækwilain] *a* aquilino.
Arab ['ærəb] *a n* arabo.
arabesque [,ærə'besk] *a* arabesco.
Arabia [ə'reibiə] *n* (*geogr*) Arabia.
Arabian [ə'reibiən] *a n* arabo, arabico; **Arabic** *a n* arabico la lingua araba.
arable ['ærəbl] *a* arabile.
arbiter ['ɑ:bitə] *n* arbitro, giudice.
arbitrary ['ɑ:bitrəri] *a* arbitrario.
arbitrate ['ɑ:bitreit] *vti* arbitrare.
arbitration [,ɑ:bi'treiʃən] *n* arbitrato.
arbor ['ɑ:bə] *n* pergolato.
arc [ɑ:k] *n* arco; **a. lamp** lampada ad arco.
arcade [ɑ:'keid] *n* galleria; porticato; portici *pl*.
arch [ɑ:tʃ] *a* birichino, furbetto; *n* arco, volta; *vti* arcuar(si).
archaeologist [,ɑ:ki'ɔlədʒist] *n* archeologo.
archaeology [,ɑ:ki'ɔledʒi] *n* archeologia.
archaic [ɑ:'keiik] *a* arcaico.
archangel ['ɑ:k,eindʒəl] *n* arcangelo.
archbishop ['ɑ:tʃ'biʃəp] *n* arcivescovo.
archbishopric [ɑ:tʃ'biʃəprik] *n* arcivescovado.
archdeacon ['ɑ:tʃ'di:kən] *n* arcidiacono.
archduke ['ɑ:tʃ'dju:k] *n* arciduca.
arched [ɑ:tʃt] *a* ad arco, arcuato.
archer ['ɑ:tʃə] *n* arciere.
archery ['ɑ:tʃəri] *n* tiro con l'arco.
archetype ['ɑ:kitaip] *n* archetipo.
Archibald ['ɑ:tʃibəld] *nm pr* Arcibaldo.
archipelago [,ɑ:ki'peligou] *pl* **archipelagoes** *n* arcipelago.
architect ['ɑ:kitekt] *n* architetto.
architecture ['ɑ:kitektʃə] *n* architettura.
archives ['ɑ:kaivz] *n pl* archivi.
archway ['ɑ:tʃwei] *n* arcata.
Arctic ['ɑ:ktik] *a n* artico.
Ardennes [ɑ:'den] *pl* (*geogr*) Ardenne.
ardent ['ɑ:dənt] *a* ardente.
ardor ['ɑ:də] *n* ardore.
arduous ['ɑ:djuəs] *a* arduo; strenuo.
area ['ɛəriə] *n* area; zona.
arena [ə'ri:nə] *n* arena.
Argentina [,ɑ:dʒən'ti:nə] *n* (*geogr*) Argentina.
Argentine ['ɑ:dʒəntain] *n* (*geogr*) Argentina.
Argentinian [,ɑ:dʒən'tiniən] *a n* argentino.
argue ['ɑ:gju:] *vti* argomentare, discutere.
argument ['ɑ:gjumənt] *n* discussione, ragionamento.
argumentative [,ɑ:gju'mentətiv] *a* polemico.
arid ['ærid] *a* arido.
aridity [æ'riditi] *n* aridità.
aright [ə'rait] *ad* bene, giustamente.
arise [ə'raiz] *vi* alzarsi; sorgere.
aristocracy [,æris'tɔkrəsi] *n* aristocrazia.
aristocrat ['æristəkræt] *n* nobile, aristocratico.
aristocratic [,æristə'krætik] *a* aristocratico.
arithmetic [ə'riθmətik] *n* aritmetica.
arithmetical [,æriθ'metikəl] *a* aritmetico.
ark [ɑ:k] *n* arca.
arm [ɑ:m] *n* braccio; bracciuolo; *pl* **arms** (*mil*) armi *pl*; *vti* armar(si).
armament ['ɑ:məmənt] *n* armamento.
armchair ['ɑ:m'tʃɛə] *n* poltrona.
Armenia [ɑ:'miniə] *n* (*geogr*) Armenia.
Armenian [ɑ:'mi:niən] *a n* armeno.
armful ['ɑ:mful] *n* bracciata.
armistice ['ɑ:mistis] *n* armistizio.
armlet ['ɑ:mlit] *n* bracciale.
armor ['ɑ:mə] *n* armatura, corazza; blindatura; forze corazzate *pl*.
armored ['ɑ:məd] *a* corazzato, blindato; **a. car** autoblindo.
armory ['ɑ:məri] *n* arsenale; armeria.
armpit ['ɑ:mpit] *n* ascella.
army ['ɑ:mi] *n* esercito; armata.
Arnold ['ɑ:nld] *nm pr* Arnaldo, Arnoldo.
aromatic(al) [,ærou'mætik(əl)] *a* aromatico.
around [ə'raund] *ad* all'intorno, in ogni parte; *prep* intorno a.
arouse [ə'rauz] *vt* (ri)svegliare; suscitare.
arraign [ə'rein] *vt* accusare, chiamare in giudizio.
arrange [ə'reindʒ] *vt* accomodare; disporre; ordinare; (*mus*) adattare; *vi* prendere accordi.
arrangement [ə'reindʒmənt] *n* accomodamento; accordo.
array [ə'rei] *n* ordine, schiera; mostra; abbigliamento.
arrears [ə'riəz] *n pl* arretrati.
arrest [ə'rest] *n* arresto, fermata; *vt* arrestare, fermare.
arrival [ə'raivəl] *n* arrivo.
arrive [ə'raiv] *vi* arrivare, giungere.
arrogance ['ærəgəns] *n* arroganza.
arrogant ['ærəgənt] *a* arrogante.

arrogate ['ærougeit] *vt* arrogarsi, pretendere.
arrow ['ærou] *n* freccia.
arsenal ['ɑːsinl] *n* arsenale.
arsenic ['ɑːsnik] *n* arsenico.
arson ['ɑːsn] *n* incendio doloso.
art [ɑːt] *n* arte; **fine arts** *pl* belle arti *pl*; **Arts** *pl* lettere *pl*.
artery ['ɑːtəri] *n* arteria.
artesian [ɑː'tiːziən] *a* artesiano.
artful ['ɑːtful] *a* abile; astuto; ingannevole.
arthritis [ɑː'θraitis] *n* artrite.
Arthur ['ɑːθə] *nm pr* Arturo.
artichoke ['ɑːtitʃouk] *n* carciofo.
article ['ɑːtikl] *n* articolo; **leading a.** articolo di fondo; *vt* mettere come apprendista.
articulate [ɑː'tikjulit] *a* articolato; distinto, chiaro; *n* animale articolato; *vti* [ɑː'tikjuleit] articolare; pronunciare distintamente; esprimersi.
articulation [ɑː,tikju'leiʃən] *n* articolazione; pronuncia distinta.
artifice ['ɑːtifis] *n* artificio, astuzia.
artificial [ɑːti'fiʃəl] *a* artificiale; artificioso.
artificiality [,ɑːtifiʃi'æliti] *n* artificiosità.
artillery [ɑː'tiləri] *n* artiglieria.
artilleryman [ɑː'tilərimən] *a* artigliere.
artisan [,ɑːti'zæn] *n* artigiano.
artist ['ɑːtist] *n* artista; pittore.
artistic [ɑː'tistik] *a* artistico.
artless ['ɑːtlis] *a* ingenuo, semplice.
artlessness ['ɑːtlisnis] *n* ingenuità, semplicità.
as [æz] *ad cj* come, nello stesso modo in cui; siccome, mentre; *rel pron* che; **as . . . as** così . . . come, tanto . . . quanto; **as for** in quanto a; **as long as** finchè, purchè.
asbestos [æz'bestəs] *n* amianto.
ascend [ə'send] *vti* ascendere, salire.
ascendency [a'sendənsi] *n* ascendente, influenza.
ascension [ə'senʃən] *n* ascensione.
ascent [ə'sent] *n* ascesa, salita.
ascertain [,æsə'tein] *vt* accertarsi, scoprire.
ascetic [ə'setik] *a* ascetico; *n* asceta.
ascribe [əs'kraib] *vt* ascrivere; attribuire.
ash [æʃ] *n* cenere.
ash(tree) ['æʃ(triː)] *n* frassino.
ashamed [ə'ʃeimd] *a* vergognoso; **to be a. of** vergognarsi.
ashen ['æʃn] *a* cinereo, di color cinerino.
ashore [ə'ʃɔː] *ad* a riva, a terra.
ashtray ['æʃtrei] *n* portacenere.
Asia ['eiʃə] *n* (*geogr*) Asia.
Asian ['eiʃən], **Asiatic** [,eiʃi'ætik] *a n* asiatico.
aside [ə'said] *n* parole pronunziate a parte; *ad* a parte; in disparte.
ask [ɑːsk] *vti* chiedere; invitare; informarsi.
askance [əs'kæns] *ad* obliquamente.
asleep [ə'sliːp] *a* addormentato; **to fall a.** addormentarsi.
asparagus [əs'pærəgəs] *n* (*coll*) asparago, asparagi.
aspect ['æspekt] *n* apparenza, aspetto; (*of houses etc*) esposizione.
aspen ['æspən] *n* pioppo tremulo.
asperity [æs'periti] *n* asperità; asprezza; rigore.
asperse [əs'pəːs] *vt* aspergere; calunniare, denigrare.
aspersion [əs'pəːʃən] *n* aspersione; calunnia.
asphalt ['æsfælt] *n* asfalto.
asphodel ['æsfədel] *n* asfodelo.
asphyxiate [æs'fiksieit] *vt* asfissiare.
aspirate ['æspəreit] *vt* aspirare.
aspiration [,æspə'reiʃən] *n* aspirazione.
aspire [əs'paiə] *vi* aspirare, bramare.
aspirin ['æspərin] *n* aspirina.
aspiring [əs'paiəriŋ] *a* ambizioso.
ass [æs] *n* asino; **to make an a. of oneself** rendersi ridicolo.
assail [ə'seil] *vt* assalire, attaccare.
assailant [ə'seilənt] *n* assalitore.
assassin [ə'sæsin] *n* assassino.
assassinate [ə'sæsineit] *vt* assassinare.
assassination [ə,sæsi'neiʃən] *n* assassinio.
assault [ə'sɔːlt] *vt* assalire; *n* assalto.
assemble [ə'sembl] *vti* riunir(si); (*mech*) montare.
assembly [ə'sembli] *n* assemblea, riunione; (*mech*) montaggio.
assent [ə'sent] *n* assenso, consenso; *vi* acconsentire, approvare.
assert [ə'səːt] *vt* asserire; rivendicare (un diritto).
assertion [ə'səːʃən] *n* asserzione, rivendicazione.
assess [ə'ses] *vt* valutare, stimare; tassare.
assessable [ə'sesəbl] *a* tassabile, imponibile.
assessment [ə'sesmənt] *n* tassa; valutazione.
assessor [ə'sesə] *n* assessore; agente del fisco.
asset ['æset] *n* bene, vantaggio; *pl* (*com*) attivo.
assiduity [,æsi'djuiti] *n* assiduità, diligenza.
assiduous [ə'sidjuəs] *a* assiduo, diligente.
assign [ə'sain] *vt* assegnare; fissare.
assignee [,æsi'niː] *n* (*com*) mandatario.
assignment [ə'sainmənt] *n* assegnazione; stanziamento; nomina, incarico.
assimilate [ə'simileit] *vt* assimilare.
assimilation [ə,simi'leiʃən] *n* assimilazione.
assist [ə'sist] *vt* assistere, aiutare.
assistance [ə'sistəns] *n* assistenza, aiuto.
assistant [ə'sistənt] *a n* assistente; aiuto, aggiunto.

assizes [ə'saiziz] *n pl* corte d'assise.
associate [ə'souʃiit] *a* associato *n*; socio; *vti* [ə'souʃieit] associar(si).
association [ə,sousi'eiʃən] *n* associazione; **A. football** giuoco del calcio.
assort [ə'sɔːt] *vt* assortire.
assortment [ə'sɔːtmənt] *n* assortimento.
assuage [ə'sweidʒ] *vt* calmare, mitigare.
assume [ə'sjuːm] *vt* assumere; arrogarsi; presumere.
assuming [ə'sjuːmiŋ] *a* presuntuoso.
assumption [ə'sʌmpʃən] *n* assunto; assunzione; supposizione.
assurance [ə'ʃuərəns] *n* assicurazione; certezza; fiducia in sè.
assure [ə'ʃuə] *vt* assicurare; rassicurare.
assuredly [ə'ʃuəridli] *ad* certamente.
asterisk ['æstərisk] *n* asterisco.
astern [əs'təːn] *ad* (*naut*) a poppa.
asthma ['æsmə] *n* asma.
asthmatic [æs'mætik] *a* asmatico.
astigmatism [æs'tigmətizəm] *n* astigmatismo.
astir [ə'stəː] *ad a* in moto.
astonish [əs'tɔniʃ] *vt* sorprendere; stupire.
astonishing [əs'tɔniʃiŋ] *a* sorprendente, straordinario.
astonishingly [əs'tɔniʃiŋli] *ad* sorprendentemente.
astonishment [əs'tɔniʃmənt] *n* sorpresa, stupore.
astound [əs'taund] *vt* stupefare.
astrakhan [,æstrə'kæn] *n* astracan.
astral ['æstrəl] *a* astrale.
astray [əs'trei] *ad* fuori della giusta via; **to go a.** sviarsi.
astride [əs'traid] *ad* a cavalcioni.
astringent [əs'trindʒənt] *a n* astringente.
astrologer [əs'trɔlədʒə] *n* astrologo.
astrology [əs'trɔlədʒi] *n* astrologia.
astronaut ['æstrənɔːt] *n* astronauta.
astronautics [,æstrə'nɔːtiks] *n* astronautica.
astronomer [əs'trɔnəmə] *n* astronomo.
astronomical ['æstrə'nɔmikəl] *a* astronomico.
astronomy [əs'trɔnəmi] *n* astronomia.
astute [əs'tjuːt] *a* astuto, sagace.
astuteness [əs'tjuːtnis] *n* astuzia, scaltrezza.
asunder [ə'sʌndə] *ad* a pezzi; separatamente.
asylum [ə'sailəm] *n* asilo; casa di ricovero; **lunatic a.** manicomio.
at [æt] *prep* a, da, di, in.
atheism ['eiθiizəm] *n* ateismo.
atheist ['eiθiist] *n* ateo.
Athenian [ə'θiːniən] *a n* ateniese.
Athens ['æθinz] *n* (*geogr*) Atene.
athlete ['æθliːt] *n* atleta.
athletic [æθ'letik] *a* atletico.
athletics [æθ'letiks] *n* atletica.
at-home [ət'houm] *n* ricevimento (a casa).
Atlantic [ət'læntik] *a n* atlantico.
atlas ['ætləs] *n* atlante.
atmosphere ['ætməsfiə] *n* atmosfera.
atmospherics [,ætməs'feriks] *n pl* (*rad*) scariche *pl*.
atom ['ætəm] *n* atomo.
atomic [ə'tɔmik] *a* atomico.
atomize ['ætəmaiz] *vt* atomizzare.
atomizer ['ætəmaizə] *n* polverizzatore; spruzzatore.
atone [ə'toun] *vi* espiare.
atonement [ə'tounmənt] *n* espiazione, riparazione.
atrocious [ə'trouʃəs] *a* atroce.
atrocity [ə'trɔsiti] *n* atrocità.
atrophy ['ætrəfi] *n* atrofia.
attach [ə'tætʃ] *vt* attaccare; attribuire; fissare; *vi* attaccarsi, aderire.
attaché [ə'tæʃei] *n* diplomatico, addetto ad un'ambasciata; **a.-case** valigetta.
attached [ə'tætʃt] *a* addetto, assegnato; affezionato.
attachment [ə'tætʃmənt] *n* attaccamento; affetto; (*mech*) accessorio.
attack [ə'tæk] *n* attacco, offensiva; accesso; *vt* attaccare, assalire.
attain [ə'tein] *vt* conseguire, ottenere, raggiungere; *vi* arrivare.
attainable [ə'teinəbl] *a* conseguibile, raggiungibile.
attainment [ə'teinmənt] *n* conseguimento; *pl* cultura.
attempt [ə'tempt] *n* tentativo; attentato; *vt* provare, tentare; attentare.
attend [ə'tend] *vi* attendere a; prestare attenzione; dare assistenza; essere presente; *vt* accompagnare, frequentare.
attendance [ə'tendəns] *n* servizio; assistenza; frequenza; persone presenti.
attendant [ə'tendənt] *n* servitore, custode; (*theat*) maschera. *pl* seguito.
attention [ə'tenʃən] *n* attenzione, premura; **to pay a.** stare attento.
attentive [ə'tentiv] *a* attento; premuroso.
attenuate [ə'tenjueit] *vt* attenuare.
attest [ə'test] *vti* attestare, testimoniare.
attestation [,ætes'teiʃən] *n* attestazione, conferma.
attic ['ætik] *n* soffitta, solaio; attico.
attire [ə'taiə] *n* abbigliamento.
attitude ['ætitjuːd] *n* atteggiamento; posa.
attorney [ə'təːni] *n* procuratore, procura; **A. General** Procuratore Generale; Ministro della Giustizia; **district a.** pubblico ministero.
attract [ə'trækt] *vt* attirare.
attraction [ə'trækʃən] *n* attrazione, attrattiva.
attractive [ə'træktiv] *a* attraente, attrattivo.

attribute ['ætribju:t] *n* attributo, qualità; *vt* [ə'tribju(:)t] attribuire.
attrition [ə'triʃən] *n* attrito.
attune [ə'tju:n] *vt* armonizzare.
aubergine ['oubəʒi:n] *n* melanzana.
auburn ['ɔ:bən] *a* color rame, ramato.
auction ['ɔ:kʃən] *n* asta, vendita all'incanto; *vt* vendere all'asta.
auctioneer [,ɔ:kʃə'niə] *n* banditore.
audacious [ɔ:'deiʃəs] *a* audace.
audacity [ɔ:'dæsiti] *n* audacità.
audibility [,ɔ:di'biliti] *n* udibilità.
audible ['ɔ:dəbl] *a* udibile.
audibly ['ɔ:dəbli] *ad* distintamente.
audience ['ɔ:diəns] *n* pubblico; udienza.
audio-visual [,ɔ:diou'vizjuəl] *a* audiovisivo.
audit ['ɔ:dit] *n* controllo; *vt* rivedere (conti).
audition [ɔ:'diʃən] *n* audizione; *vti* ascoltare, esibirsi in audizione.
auditor ['ɔ:ditə] *n* revisore di conti.
auditorium [,ɔ:di'tɔ:riəm] *n* sala, auditorio.
auger ['ɔ:gə] *n* succhiello.
augment [ɔ:g'ment] *vt* aumentare; *vi* crescere.
augmentation [,ɔ:gmen'teiʃən] *n* aumento.
augur ['ɔ:gə] *n* augure; *vti* predire, presagire.
augury ['ɔ:gjuri] *n* presagio, pronostico.
August ['ɔ:gəst] *n* agosto.
august [ɔ:'gʌst] *a* augusto, maestoso.
Augustin(e) [ɔ:'gʌstin] *nm pr* Agostino.
Augustus [ɔ:'gʌstəs] *nm pr* Augusto.
aunt [ɑ:nt] *n* zia.
aureomycin [,ɔ:riou'maisin] *n* aureomicina.
auspice ['ɔ:spis] *n* auspicio, augurio.
auspicious [ɔ:s'piʃəs] *a* di buon augurio.
austere [ɔs'tiə] *a* austero.
austerity [ɔs'teriti] *n* austerità.
Australia [ɔs'treiliə] *n* (*geogr*) Australia.
Australian [ɔs'treiliən] *a n* australiano.
Austria ['ɔstriə] *n* (*geogr*) Austria.
Austrian ['ɔstriən] *a n* austriaco.
authentic [ɔ:'θentik] *a* autentico.
authenticate [ɔ:'θentikeit] *vt* autenticare.
authentication [ɔ:,θenti'keiʃən] *n* autenticazione.
authenticity [,ɔ:θen'tisiti] *n* autenticità.
author ['ɔ:θə] *n* autore.
authoritative [ɔ:'θɔritətiv] *a* autorevole, autoritario.
authority [ɔ:'θɔriti] *n* autorità.
authorization [,ɔ:θərai'zeiʃən] *n* autorizzazione.
authorize ['ɔ:θəraiz] *vt* autorizzare.
autobiography [,ɔ:toubai'ɔgræfi] *n* autobiografia.
autobus ['ɔ:toubʌs] *n* autobus.
autocamp ['ɔ:toukæmp] *n* accampamento per automobilisti.
autocrat ['ɔ:təkræt] *n* autocrate.
autodrome ['ɔ:toudroum] *n* autodromo.
autograph ['ɔ:təgrɑ:f] *n* autografo; *vt* firmare; (*typ*) autografare.
automatic [,ɔ:tə'mætik] *a* automatico; *n* rivoltella.
automatically [,ɔ:tə'mætikəli] *ad* automaticamente.
automation [,ɔ:tə'meiʃən] *n* automazione.
automobile ['ɔ:təməbi:l] *n* automobile.
autonomy [ɔ:'tɔnəmi] *n* autonomia.
autopsy ['ɔ:təpsi] *n* autopsia.
autumn ['ɔ:təm] *n* autunno.
autumnal [ɔ:'tʌmnəl] *a* autunnale, d'autunno.
auxiliary [ɔ:g'ziljəri] *a* ausiliario, -re; *n* ausiliare; *pl* milizie ausiliarie.
avail [ə'veil] *n* utilità, vantaggio; *vi* giovare (a), essere utile (a); *vt* aiutare, favorire; **to a. oneself of** valersi di.
availability [ə'veilə'biliti] *n* disponibilità.
available [ə'veiləbl] *a* disponibile.
avalanche ['ævəlɑ:nʃ] *n* valanga.
avarice ['ævəris] *n* avarizia.
avaricious [,ævə'riʃəs] *a* avaro.
avenge [ə'vendʒ] *vt* vendicare.
avenger [ə'vendʒə] *n* vendicatore.
avenue ['ævinju:] *n* viale; accesso.
aver [ə'və:] *vt* affermare, asserire.
average ['ævəridʒ] *a* di media categoria, medio; *n* media; (*naut*) avaria; *vt* fare la media.
averse [ə'və:s] *a* avverso, contrario.
aversion [ə'və:ʃən] *n* avversione, antipatia.
avert [ə'və:t] *vt* schivare; distogliere.
aviary ['eivjəri] *n* aviario.
aviation [,eivi'eiʃən] *n* aviazione.
avid ['ævid] *a* avido.
avidity [ə'viditi] *n* avidità.
avoid [ə'vɔid] *vt* evitare, schivare.
avoidance [ə'vɔidəns] *n* l'evitare; fuga, scampo.
avowed [ə'vaud] *a* manifesto, aperto, dichiarato.
await [ə'weit] *vt* aspettare.
awake [ə'weik] *a* sveglio; *vti* svegliar(si).
awaken [ə'weikən] *vti* risvegliare, risvegliarsi.
awakening [ə'weikniŋ] *n* risveglio (*also fig*).
award [ə'wɔ:d] *n* giudizio; ricompensa; *vt* aggiudicare, assegnare.
aware [ə'weə] *a* conscio.
away [ə'wei] *ad* lontano, via.
awe [ɔ:] *n* timore misto a venerazione.
awful ['ɔ:ful] *a* terribile, spaventevole.
awfully ['ɔ:fuli] *ad* terribilmente; straordinariamente, molto.
awhile [ə'wail] *ad* un momento.
awkward ['ɔ:kwəd] *a* goffo; imbarazzante; imbarazzato; scomodo.

awkwardly ['ɔːkwədli] *ad* goffamente; in modo imbarazzato.
awkwardness ['ɔːkwədnis] *n* goffaggine; difficoltà.
awl [ɔːl] *n* lesina.
awning ['ɔːniŋ] *n* tenda.
awry [ə'rai] *n* storto.
ax [æks] *n* ascia.
axiom ['æksiəm] *n* assioma.
axis ['æksis] *pl* **axes** ['æksiːz] *n* asse.
axle ['æksl] *n* (*mech*) asse.
ay(e) [ai] *ad* sì.
azalea [ə'zeiliə] *n* azalea.
azure ['eiʒə] *a* azzurro.

B

babble ['bæbl] *vti* balbettare; parlare scioccamente.
babbling ['bæbliŋ] *n* balbettio; discorso senza senso.
Babel ['beibəl] *n* Babele; **babel** *n* confusione.
baboon [bə'buːn] *n* babuino.
baby ['beibi] *n* neonato, bimbo; **b. carriage** carrozzina.
babyhood ['beibihud] *n* prima infanzia.
babyish ['beibiiʃ] *a* bambinesco, infantile, puerile.
bachelor ['bætʃələ] *n* celibe, scapolo; baccelliere.
bachelorhood ['bætʃələhud] *n* celibato.
bacillus [bə'siləs] *pl* **bacilli** *n* bacillo.
back [bæk] *n* dorso, parte posteriore, schiena; schienale; spalle *pl*; spalliera; *a* posteriore, di dietro, indietro, di ritorno; **be b.** essere di ritorno; **come b.** ritornare.
back [bæk] *vti* spalleggiare; indietreggiare; (*com*) avallare; **b. a horse** puntare su un cavallo.
backbite ['bækbait] *vti* calunniare.
backbone ['bækboun] *n* spina dorsale.
background ['bækgraund] *n* sfondo; ambiente.
backslider ['bæk'slaidə] *n* recidivo.
backward ['bækwəd] *a* riluttante; tardivo.
backwardness ['bækwədnis] *n* lentezza d'intelligenza, ritardo di sviluppo.
backwards ['bækwədz] *ad* (all') indietro, a ritroso.
bacon ['beikən] *n* lardo affumicato, pancetta.
bacterium [bæk'tiəriəm] *pl* **bacteria** *n* batterio.
bacteriology [bæk,tiəri'ɔlədʒi] *n* batteriologia.
bad [bæd] *a* cattivo, colpevole, dannoso, grave, sfavorevole; *n* male; **to go b.** andare a male; **badly** *ad* male, malamente.
badge [bædʒ] *n* distintivo, emblema.
badger ['bædʒə] *n* (*zool*) tasso; *vt* tormentare, molestare.
badness ['bædnis] *n* cattiveria; (*quality*) inferiorità.
baffle ['bæfl] *vt* impedire, frustrare; sconcertare; rendere vano.
baffling ['bæfliŋ] *a* sconcertante.
bag [bæg] *n* borsa, borsetta, sacco, carniere; pesci o selvaggina presi; *vt* insaccare, prendere, rubare.
baggage ['bægidʒ] *n* bagagli(o); **b. car** bagagliaio.
bagpipe(s) ['bægpaip(s)] *n* (*usu pl*) cornamusa.
bagpiper ['bægpaipə] *n* suonatore di cornamusa.
bail [beil] *n* cauzione, garanzia, garante; **to go b. for** essere garante di; *vt* procurare la libertà provvisoria a; aggottare (una barca).
bailiff ['beilif] *n* ufficiale giudiziario; fattore di campagna.
bait [beit] *n* esca; *vt* fornire di esca, adescare; tormentare; alimentare; *vi* prendere cibo.
bake [beik] *vt* cuocere al forno; *vi* indurirsi per effetto del calore.
bake-house ['beikhaus] **bakery** ['beikəri] *n* forno.
baker ['beikə] *n* fornaio; **b.'s (shop)** panetteria.
baking ['beikiŋ] *n* cottura al forno; **b. powder** lievito.
balance ['bæləns] *n* bilancia; equilibrio; armonia; (*com*) bilancio, saldo; **b. sheet** bilancio; **to lose one's b.** perdere l'equilibrio; *vti* pesare, bilanciare, mantener l'equilibrio.
balcony ['bælkəni] *n* balcone.
bald [bɔːld] *a* calvo; (*style*) disadorno.
baldness ['bɔːldnis] *n* calvizie *pl*.
Baldwin ['bɔːldwin] *nm pr* Baldovino.
bale [beil] *n* balla; *vt* imballare.
balk [bɔːk] *n* trave rozzamente digrossata; *vt* evitare, ostacolare.
Balkan ['bɔːlkən] *a* balcanico.
Balkans ['bɔːlkənz] *n* Balcani.
ball [bɔːl] *n* palla, pallone, (*thread*) gomitolo; (*dance*) ballo; **ballpoint (pen)** penna a sfera.
ballad ['bæləd] *n* ballata.
ballast ['bæləst] *n* (*naut*) zavorra.
ballet ['bælei] *n* balletto, danza classica.
balloon [bə'luːn] *n* pallone; pallone aerostatico; (*cartoons*) fumetto.
ballot ['bælət] *n* scheda (di votazione), scrutinio; *vi* votare a scrutinio segreto; **b. box** urna.
balm [bɑːm] *n* balsamo.
balmy ['bɑːmi] *a* balsamico, fragrante.
balsam ['bɔːlsəm] *n* balsamo.
Baltic ['bɔːltik] *a n* Baltico.
Baltimore ['bɔːltimɔː] *n* Baltimora.
balustrade [,bæləs'treid] *n* balustrata.
bamboo [bæm'buː] *n* bambù.

bamboozle [bæm'bu:zl] *vt* (*sl*) ingannare, mistificare.
ban [bæn] *n* bando; scomunica; *vt* proibire, mettere all'indice.
banal [bə'nɑ:l] *a* banale.
banality [bə'næliti] *n* banalità.
banana [bə'nɑ:nə] *n* banana.
band [bænd] *n* banda; legame; striscia; *vt* legare insieme; *vi* unirsi.
bandage ['bændidʒ] *n* benda, fascia.
bandbox ['bændbɔks] *n* cappelliera.
bandit ['bændit] *n* bandito.
bandolier [,bændə'liə] *n* bandoliera.
bandsman ['bændzmən] *n* bandista.
bandy ['bændi] *a* curvo, storto; *vt* ribattere, disputare, scambiare parole.
baneful ['beinful] *a* dannoso, velenoso.
bang [bæŋ] *n* colpo rumoroso, esplosione, fracasso; *vt* colpire rumorosamente, sbatacchiare.
bangle ['bæŋgl] *n* braccialetto.
banish ['bæniʃ] *vt* bandire, esiliare.
banishment ['bæniʃmənt] *n* bando, esilio.
banister ['bænistə] *n* ringhiera, balaustra.
bank [bænk] *n* argine, riva; banca, banco; *vt* depositare in una banca; **b.-note, b. bill** banconota; **to b. on** contare su.
banker ['bæŋkə] *n* banchiere.
bank holiday ['bæŋk'hɔlədi] *n* festa civile.
banking ['bæŋkiŋ] *n* professione bancaria; *a* bancario.
bankrupt ['bæŋkrəpt] *a n* fallito; **to go b.** fallire.
bankruptcy ['bæŋkrəptsi] *n* fallimento, bancarotta.
banner ['bænə] *n* bandiera, stendardo.
banns [bænz] *n pl* pubblicazioni matrimoniali *pl*.
banquet ['bæŋkwit] *n* banchetto; *vi* banchettare.
banter ['bæntə] *n* beffa; *vti* prendere in giro, beffarsi.
baptism ['bæptizəm] *n* battesimo.
baptismal [bæp'tizməl] *a* battesimale.
baptist(e)ry ['bæptist(ə)ri] *n* battistero.
baptize [bæp'taiz] *vt* battezzare.
bar [bɑ:] *n* (s)barra; ostacolo; bar; **the bar** ordine degli avvocati; *vt* (s)barrare; escludere; ostacolare; **b. tender** barista; **to be called to the b. to be admitted to the b.** essere iscritto all'albo degli avvocati.
barbarian [bɑ:'bɛəriən] *n* barbaro.
barbaric [bɑ:'bærik] *a* barbarico, primitivo.
barbarism ['bɑ:bərizem] *n* barbarie, barbarismo.
barbarity [bɑ:'bæriti] *n* barbarie, crudeltà.
barbarous ['bɑ:bərəs] *a* barbaro
barbecue ['bɑ:bikju:] *n* animale arrostito intero; festa campestre.
barbed [bɑ:bd] *a* dentellato, spinato; pungente; **b. wire** filo di ferro spinato.
barber ['bɑ:bə] *n* barbiere, parrucchiere.
barbiturate [bɑ:'bitjurit] *n* barbiturico.
bare [bɛə] *a* nudo, spoglio, scoperto; *vt* denudare, scoprire.
barefaced ['bɛəfeist] *a* sfacciato.
barefoot(ed) ['bɛə'fut(id)] *a* scalzo; *ad* a piedi nudi.
bareheaded ['bɛə'hedid] *a ad* a capo scoperto.
barely ['bɛəli] *ad* appena.
bareness ['bɛənis] *n* nudità.
bargain ['bɑ:gin] *n* affare; occasione; **into the b.** per giunta, in più; *vi* contrattare; **to b. for** aspettarsi.
barge [bɑ:dʒ] *n* chiatta; lancia di parata; *vi* **to b. into** urtare.
baritone ['bæritoun] *a n* baritono.
bark [bɑ:k] *n* latrato; corteccia, scorza; *vi* abbaiare; *vt* scorticare, scorzare.
barley ['bɑ:li] *n* orzo.
barm [bɑ:m] *n* fermento, lievito di birra.
barmaid ['bɑ:meid] *n* barista.
barman ['bɑ:mən] *n* barista.
barn [bɑ:n] *n* granaio; **barnyard** aia, cortile (di fattoria).
barnacle ['bɑ:nəkl] *n* cirripede.
barometer [bə'rɔmitə] *n* barometro.
baron(ess) ['bærən(is)] *n* barone(ssa).
baronet ['bærənit] *n* baronetto.
baroque [bə'rouk] *a n* barocco.
barrack ['bærək] *n usu pl* caserma; *vt* alloggiare in caserma; schernire, fischiare.
barrage ['bærɑ:ʒ] *n* (*mil*) sbarramento.
barrel ['bærəl] *n* barile, botte; (*gun*) canna.
barren ['bærən] *a* sterile.
barrenness ['bærənnis] *n* sterilità.
barricade [,bæri'keid] *n* barricata; *vt* barricare, ostruire.
barrier ['bæriə] *n* barriera; **sound b.** muro del suono.
barrister ['bæristə] *n* avvocato.
barrow ['bærou] *n* carriola, carretto.
barter ['bɑ:tə] *n* baratto; *vt* barattare, scambiare.
Bartholomew [bɑ:'θɔləmju:] *nm pr* Bartolomeo.
basalt ['bæsɔ:lt] *n* basalto.
base [beis] *n* base, fondamento; *a* basso, indegno, vile; *vt* basare, fondare.
baseball ['beisbɔ:l] *n* 'baseball', palla a basi.
baseless ['beislis] *a* infondato, senza base.
basement ['beismənt] *n* seminterrato.
baseness ['beisnis] *n* bassezza, viltà.
bash [bæʃ] *n* colpo forte; *vt* colpire violentemente.

bashful ['bæʃful] *a* timido.
bashfulness ['bæʃfulnis] *n* timidezza.
basic ['beisik] *a* basilare, fondamentale.
basil ['bæzl] *n* basilico.
basin ['beisn] *n* bacino, bacinella; scodella; lavabo; **sugar b.** zuccheriera.
basis ['beisis] *pl* **bases** *n* base, fondamento.
bask [bɑ:sk] *vi* godersi il caldo o il sole.
basket ['bɑ:skit] *n* cesta, cesto, paniere; **b.ball** pallacanestro.
Basle [bɑ:l] *n* (*geogr*) Basilea.
Basque [bæsk] *a n* basco.
bas-relief ['bæsri,li:f] *n* basso rilievo.
bass [bæs] *n* (*fish*) pesce persico; (*mus*) basso.
bassoon [bə'su:n] *n* (*mus*) fagotto.
bastard ['bæstəd] *a n* bastardo.
baste [beist] *vt* imbastire; spruzzare di grasso l'arrosto; bastonare.
bastion ['bæstiən] *n* bastione.
bat [bæt] *n* (*zool*) pipistrello; (*cricket etc*) mazza, (*ping-pong*) racchetta.
batch [bætʃ] *n* (*bread*) infornata; (*goods*) lotto.
bath [bɑ:θ] *n* bagno *anche di mare*), tinozza; **to take a b.** fare il bagno; *vt* bagnare; *vi* bagnarsi, fare un bagno; **bathrobe** accappatoio.
bathe [beið] *n* (*di mare etc*) bagno; *vti* bagnar(si), (*nel mare etc*) fare il bagno.
bather ['beiðə] *n* bagnante.
bathing ['beiðiŋ] *n* bagnare, bagno, bagni *pl*; **b. costume, b. suit** costume da bagno; **b. cap** cuffia da bagno.
bathos ['beiθɔs] *n* discesa dal sublime al ridicolo.
bathysphere ['bæθisfiə] *n* batiscafo.
baton ['bætən] *n* bacchetta; bastone di comando.
battalion [bə'tæljən] *n* battaglione.
batten ['bætn] *n* assicella, traversa in legno; *vt* rinforzare con legno; **to b. down** (*naut*) chiudere un boccaporto.
batter ['bætə] *n* pastella; *vti* battere violentemente; cannoneggiare.
battering-ram ['bætəriŋræm] *n* ariete.
battery ['bætəri] *n* (*mil, el*) batteria, pila.
battle ['bætl] *n* battaglia, combattimento; *vi* combattere, lottare.
battlement ['bætlmənt] *n* merlo, bastione.
bauble ['bɔ:bl] *n* ornamento di poco valore; bastone del buffone.
Bavaria [bə'veəriə] *n* (*geogr*) Baviera.
Bavarian [bə'veəriən] *a n* bavarese.
bawd [bɔ:d] *n* mezzana.
bawdiness ['bɔ:dinis] *n* oscenità.
bawdy ['bɔ:di] *a* osceno.
bawl [bɔ:l] *vi* gridare ad alta voce, schiamazzare.
bay [bei] *n* baia, insenatura del mare; (*bot*) lauro; (*window*) recesso; latrato di grosso cane; *vi* abbaiare, latrare; **to hold at b.** tenere a bada.
bayonet ['beiənit] *n* baionetta.
bazaar [bə'zɑ:] *n* bazar.
be [bi:] *vi and aux* essere, esistere, vivere, stare, dovere, costare; **to b. in** essere in casa; **to b. long** tardare; **to be two years old** avere due anni.
beach [bi:tʃ] *n* lido, spiaggia.
beacon ['bi:kən] *n* faro, segnale.
bead [bi:d] *n* (*necklace etc*) grano; (*liquids*) goccia; (*rifle*) mirino; **beads** *pl* rosario.
beadle ['bi:dl] *n* bidello, sagrestano.
beagle ['bi:gl] *n* piccolo cane da caccia.
beak [bi:k] *n* becco, rostro.
beaker ['bi:kə] *n* coppa, bicchiere.
beam [bi:m] *n* trave; (*light*) raggio; sorriso; *vi* risplendere; sorridere.
beaming ['bi:miŋ] *a* raggiante.
bean [bi:n] *n* fagiolo, fava; **full of beans** (*sl*) energico, vivace.
bear [bɛə] *n* orso.
bear [bɛə] *vt* portare, sopportare; produrre; *vi* dirigersi, inclinare; **to b. oneself** comportarsi.
bearable ['bɛərəbl] *a* sopportabile.
beard [biəd] *n* barba *vt* sfidare.
bearded ['biədid] *a* barbuto.
beardless ['biədlis] *a* imberbe.
bearer ['bɛərə] *n* latore, portatore.
bearing ['bɛəriŋ] *n* portamento, contegno; **bearings** *pl* orientamento; (*mech*) cuscinetto.
beast [bi:st] *n* bestia, animale.
beastly ['bi:stli] *a* bestiale; (*sl*) orribile.
beat [bi:t] *n* battito, palpito; (*of policeman etc*) giro; *vti* battere, vincere; palpitare; **to b. about the bush** menare il can per l'aia.
beatification [bi:,ætifi'keiʃən] *n* beatificazione.
beatify [bi:'ætifai] *vt* beatificare.
beating ['bi:tiŋ] *n* azione del battere, busse *pl*; sconfitta.
beatitude [bi:'ætitju:d] *n* beatitudine.
beatnik ['bi:tnik] *n* beatnik, capellone.
Beatrice ['biətris] **Beatrix** ['biətrix] *nf pr* Beatrice.
beau [bou] *pl* **beaux** *n* damerino; cicisbeo.
beautician [bju:'tiʃən] *n* estetista.
beautiful ['bju:təful] *a* bello.
beautifully ['bju:təfli] *ad* meravigliosamente, perfettamente.
beautify ['bju:tifai] *vt* abbellire.
beauty ['bju:ti] *n* bellezza.
beaver ['bi:və] *n* castoro, castorino.
becalm [bi'kɑ:m] *vt* abbonacciare.
because [bi'kɔz] *cj* perchè; **b. of** a causa di.
beckon ['bekən] *vti* chiamare con un cenno.
become [bi'kʌm] *vi* divenire, acca-

dere; *vi* convenire **a**, star bene a.
becoming [bi'kʌmiŋ] *a* conveniente, che s'addice a.
bed [bed] *n* letto; **bedding** biancheria da letto; (*of animals*) lettiera.
bedclothes ['bedklouðz] *n pl* coperte e biancheria da letto.
bedlam ['bedləm] *n* grande confusione; manicomio.
bedouin ['beduin] *a n* beduino.
bedraggle [bi'drægl] *vt* inzaccherare.
bedridden ['bed,ridn] *a* allettato.
bedroom ['bedrum] *n* camera (da letto).
bedside ['bedsaid] *n* capezzale.
bedstead ['bedsted] *n* fusto del letto.
bee [bi:] *n* ape; **beeline** linea diretta.
beech [bi:tʃ] *n* faggio.
beef [bi:f] *n* manzo; **beefsteak** bistecca; **b.** tea brodo ristretto.
beehive ['bi:haiv] *n* alveare.
beer [biə] *n* birra; **b.-house** birreria.
beeswax ['bi:zwæks] *n* cera vergine.
beet ['bi:t] *n* barbabietola, bietola.
beetle ['bi:tl] *n* scarabeo, scarafaggio.
befall [bi'fɔ:l] *vti* accadere a, capitare a, succedere.
befit [bi'fit] *vt* essere adatto a, andar bene per.
befitting [bi'fitiŋ] *a* adatto, conveniente.
before [bi'fɔ:] *ad* prima, già, avanti; *prep* prima di, davanti a; *cj* prima che.
beforehand [bi'fɔ:hænd] *ad* in anticipo.
befriend [bi'frend] *vt* mostrarsi amico di, aiutare.
beg [beg] *vti* domandare, pregare; elemosinare.
beget [bi'get] *vt* generare.
beggar ['begə] *n* mendicante.
beggarly ['begəli] *a* meschino, gretto.
beggary ['begəri] *n* mendicità.
begin [bi'gin] *vti* cominciare, iniziare, intraprendere, mettersi a.
beginner [bi'ginə] *n* principiante.
beginning [bi'giniŋ] *n* principio.
begonia [bi'gouniə] *n* begonia.
begrudge [bi'grʌdʒ] *vt* invidiare, lesinare.
beguile [bi'gail] *vt* ingannare.
behalf [bi'hɑ:f] *n* **on b. of** da parte di.
behave [bi'heiv] *vi* comportarsi; (*machines*) funzionare.
behavior [bi'heivjə] *n* comportamento, condotta; funzionamento.
behead [bi'hed] *vt* decapitare.
behind [bi'haind] *ad* indietro; *prep* dietro a; **b. time** in ritardo; **b. the times** antiquato.
behindhand [bi'haindhænd] *ad a* in arretrato, in ritardo.
behold [bi'hould] *vt* guardare, vedere, contemplare.
beholder [bi'houldə] *n* osservatore, spettatore.
being ['bi:iŋ] **for the time b.** per ora; *n* essere vivente, ente, esistenza.
belabor [bi'leibə] *vt* bastonare.
belated [bi'leitid] *a* tardivo, in ritardo.
belch [beltʃ] *vti* (e)ruttare; *n* rutto.
beleaguer [bi'li:gə] *vt* assediare.
belfry ['belfri] *n* campanile.
Belgian ['beldʒən] *a n* belga.
Belgium ['beldʒəm] *n* Belgio.
Belgrade [bel'greid] *n* Belgrado.
belief [bi'li:f] *n* credenza, fede, opinione.
believable [bi'li:vəbl] *a* credibile.
believe [bi'li:v] *vti* aver fede, credere, pensare, supporre.
believer [bi'li:və] *n* credente.
belittle [bi'litl] *vt* denigrare.
bell [bel] *n* campana, campanello; **bellboy, bellhop** fattorino d'albergo.
bellicose ['belikous] *a* bellicoso.
belligerent [bi'lidʒərənt] *a n* belligerante.
bellow ['belou] *vi* mugghiare, muggire, ruggire; *n* muggito.
bellows ['belouz] *n pl* mantice, soffietto.
belly ['beli] *n* pancia, ventre.
belong [bi'lɔŋ] *vi* appartenere, spettare.
belongings [bi'lɔŋiŋs] *n pl* effetti *pl.*
beloved [bi'lʌv(i)d] *a n* amato, diletto.
below [bi'lou] *prep* sotto (a); al di sotto di; *ad* (al di) sotto, giù.
belt [belt] *n* cinghia, cintura; zona; regione.
bemoan [bi'moun] *vt* compiangere; *vi* lamentarsi.
bench [bentʃ] *n* banco, panca, seggio; ufficio di giudice.
bend [bend] *n* curva, inclinazione; *vt* curvare, piegare; *vi* chinarsi, piegarsi.
beneath [bi'ni:θ] *ad prep* al di sotto (di), in basso, sotto.
Benedictine [,beni'diktin] *a n* benedettino.
benediction [,beni'dikʃən] *n* benedizione.
benefaction [,beni'fækʃən] *n* beneficenza.
benefactor ['benifæktə] *n* benefattore.
beneficence [bi'nefisəns] *n* beneficenza.
beneficent [bi'nefisənt] *a* benefico.
beneficial [,beni'fiʃəl] *a* benefico, utile, vantaggioso.
beneficiary [,beni'fiʃəri] *n* beneficiario.
benefit ['benifit] *n* vantaggio, profitto, (*leg*) beneficio; *vt* beneficare; *vi* trarre profitto.
benevolence [bi'nevələns] *n* benevolenza.
benevolent [bi'nevələnt] *a* benevolo, caritatevole.
benign [bi'nain] **benignant** [bi'nignənt] *a* benevolo, benigno.

Benjamin ['bendʒəmin] *nm pr* Beniamino.
bent [bent] *n* curva, inclinazione naturale, tendenza; *a* curvo, deciso; **to be b. on** essere deciso a.
benumb [bi'nʌm] *vt* intorpidire.
benzine ['benzi:n] *n* benzina.
bequeath [bi'kwi:ð] *vt* lasciare per testamento.
bequest [bi'kwest] *n* lascito, eredità.
bereave [bi'ri:v] *vt* privare, spogliare.
bereavement [bi'ri:vmənt] *n* perdita di parente, lutto.
beret ['berei] *n* berretto, basco.
bergamot ['bə:gəmɔt] *n* (*bot*) bergamotto.
Berlin [bə:'lin] *n* (*geogr*) Berlino; **Berliner** berlinese.
Bermuda [bə:'mju:də] *n* **1.** (le) Bermude **2.** *pl.*
Bernard ['bə:nəd] *nm pr* Bernardo.
berry ['beri] *n* bacca.
berserk ['bə:sə:k] **to go b.** abbandonarsi a violenza cieca.
berth [bə:θ] *n* cuccetta; (*fig*) impiego; (*naut*) posto d'ancoraggio d'una nave; *vi* (*naut*) ancoreggiare.
Bertha ['bə:θə] *nf pr* Berta.
beryl ['beril] *n* (*min*) berillo.
beseech [bi'si:tʃ] *vt* implorare, supplicare.
beset [bi'set] *vt* assediare, assalire.
beside [bi'said] *prep* accanto a, vicino a; **b. oneself** fuori di sè.
besides [bi'saidz] *ad prep* inoltre, per di più, oltre a.
besiege [bi'si:dʒ] *vt* assediare.
besom ['bizəm] *n* granata, scopa.
best [best] *a* il migliore; *ad* il meglio, nel miglior modo, nel più alto grado; *n* il meglio.
bestial ['bestiəl] *a* bestiale, brutale.
bestiality [,besti'æliti] *n* bestialità, brutalità.
bestir [bi'stə:] *vi* **b. oneself** muoversi, scuotersi.
bestow [bi'stou] *vt* conferire, dare, depositare.
bestowal [bi'stouəl] *n* donazione, concessione.
bestride [bi'straid] *vt* stare a cavallo (a cavalcioni) di.
bet [bet] *n* scommessa; *vti* scommettere.
Bethlehem ['beθlihem] *n* Betlemme.
betoken [bi'touken] *vt* indicare, presagire.
betray [bi'trei] *vt* tradire, palesare.
betrayal [bi'treiəl] *n* tradimento.
betrothal [bi'trouðəl] *n* fidanzamento.
betrothed [bi'trouðd] *a n* fidanzato.
better ['betə] *a* migliore; *ad* meglio; **our betters** *pl* i nostri superiori; *vti* migliorar(e).
betting ['betiŋ] *n* lo scommettere.
between [bi'twi:n] *prep* fra, tra; **betwixt and b.** mezzo e mezzo.
beverage ['bevəridʒ] *n* bevanda.
bevy ['bevi] *n* compagnia; stormo.
bewail [bi'weil] *vti* lamentar(si), deplorare.
beware [bi'weə] *vi* stare in guardia.
bewilder [bi'wildə] *vt* confondere, rendere perplesso.
bewildering [bi'wildəriŋ] *a* sbalorditivo, sconcertante.
bewilderment [bi'wildəmənt] *n* confusione.
bewitch [bi'witʃ] *vt* ammaliare, stregare.
beyond [bi'jɔnd] *prep ad n* al di là (di); **the back of b.** il più remoto angolo della terra.
bias ['baiəs] *n* inclinazione, pregiudizio; **on the b.** per sbieco; *vt* far inclinare; influenzare.
bib [bib] *n* bavaglino.
Bible ['baibl] *n* Bibbia.
biblical ['biblikəl] *a* biblico.
bibliography [,bibli'ɔgrəfi] *n* bibliografia.
bibliophile ['biblioufail] *n* bibliofilo.
bicarbonate [bai'ka:bənit] *n* bicarbonato.
biceps ['baiseps] *n* bicipite.
bicker ['bikə] *vi* litigare, altercare.
bicycle ['baisikl] *n* bicicletta; *vi* andare in bicicletta.
bid [bid] *n* (*at an auction*) offerta, proposta; *vti* comandare; dire.
bidder ['bidə] *n* (*at an auction*) offerente.
biennial [bai'eniəl] *a* biennale.
bier [biə] *n* bara.
big [big] *a* grosso, grande, importante; **bigwig** (*sl*) pezzo grosso.
bigamist ['bigəmist] *n* bigamo.
bigamous ['bigəməs] *a* bigamo.
bigamy ['bigəmi] *n* bigamia.
bigot ['bigət] *n* **bigoted** ['bigətid] *a* bigotto.
bigotry ['bigətri] *n* bigottismo.
bike [baik] *n* (*fam*) bicicletta.
bilateral [bai'lætərəl] *a* bilaterale.
bilberry ['bilbəri] *n* mirtillo.
bile [bail] *n* bile.
bilge [bildʒ] *n* (*naut*) sentina; (*sl*) sciocchezze.
bilingual [bai'liŋgwəl] *a* bilingue.
bilious ['biljəs] *a* biliare; bilioso.
bill [bil] *n* (*bird*) becco; (*notice etc*) cartellone, cartello; (*account*) conto, fattura; biglietto di banca, banconota; (*com*) cambiale; (*leg*) progetto di legge; **billboard** spazio per la pubblicità.
billet ['bilit] *n* (*mil*) accantonamento; *vt* accantonare truppe.
billiards ['biljəds] *n pl* biliardo; **billiard saloon** sala del biliardo.
billion ['biljən] *n* bilione, miliardo.
billow ['bilou] *n* flutto, maroso.
billowy ['biloui] *a* pieno di marosi; ondeggiante.
bimetallism [bai'metəlizəm] *n* bimetallismo.

bin [bin] *n* recipiente per grano, carbone *etc.*
binary ['bainəri] *a* binario.
bind [baind] *vti* (ri)legare; obbligare; **it was bound to happen** doveva accadere.
binding ['baindiŋ] *a* obbligatorio, impegnativo; *n* legatura, rilegatura.
bindweed ['baindwi:d] *n* convolvolo.
binoculars [bi'nɔkjuləz] *n pl* binocolo.
biographer [bai'ɔgrəfə] *n* biografo.
biographical [baiou'græfikəl] *a* biografico.
biography [bai'ɔgrəfi] *n* biografia.
biological [,baiə'lɔdʒikəl] *a* biologico.
biology [bai'ɔlədʒi] *n* biologia.
biped ['baiped] *a n* bipede.
birch [bə:tʃ] *n* (*bot*) betulla; sferza.
bird [bə:d] *n* uccello.
bird-lime ['bə:dlaim] *n* vischio.
bird's-eye view ['bə:dzai'vju:] *n* panorama a volo d'uccello.
birth [bə:θ] *n* nascita; origine.
birthday ['bə:θdei] *n* compleanno.
birthplace ['bə:θpleis] *n* luogo di nascita.
birthright ['bə:θrait] *n* diritto ereditario; primogenitura.
Biscay ['biskei] *n* Biscaglia.
biscuit ['biskit] *n* biscotto, pastina da tè; **soda b.** galletta, 'cracker'.
bisect [bai'sekt] *vt* bisecare.
bishop ['biʃəp] *n* vescovo; (*chess*) alfiere.
bismuth ['bizməθ] *n* bismuto.
bison ['baisn] *n* bisonte.
bit [bit] *n* pezzo, pezzetto; (*bread*) boccone; (*bridle*) morso; (*tec*) morsa; punta.
bitch [bitʃ] *n* cagna; lupa; volpe femmina.
bite [bait] *n* morsicatura, morso; boccone; *vt* mordere; abboccare.
biting ['baitiŋ] *a* pungente; sarcastico.
bitter ['bitə] *a* amaro, aspro.
bitterness ['bitənis] *n* amarezza; rancore; (*of climate*) rigidità.
bitumen ['bitjumin] *n* bitume.
bivouac ['bivuæk] *n* bivacco.
bizarre [bi'zɑ:] *a* bizzarro, eccentrico.
blab [blæb] *vt* rivelare indiscretamente; *vi* chiacchierare.
black [blæk] *a* nero; minaccioso; oscuro; triste.
blackberry ['blæk,beri] *n* mora.
blackbird ['blækbə:d] *n* merlo.
blackboard ['blækbɔ:d] *n* lavagna.
blacken ['blækən] *vt* annerire; diffamare.
blackguard ['blægɑ:d] *n* mascalzone.
blacking ['blækiŋ] *n* lucido nero per scarpe.
blackish ['blækiʃ] *a* nerastro.
blackleg ['blækleg] *n* crumiro.
blackmail ['blækmeil] *n* ricatto; *vt* ricattare; **blackmailer** ricattatore.
blackness ['blæknis] *n* nerezza, oscurità.
blackout ['blækaut] *n* oscuramento; perdita temporanea dei sensi.
blacksmith ['blæksmiθ] *n* fabbroferraio.
bladder ['blædə] *n* vescica.
blade [bleid] *n* filo (d'erba); lama.
blame [bleim] *n* biasimo, censura; colpa; *vt* biasimare, censurare.
blameless ['bleimlis] *a* irreprensibile, innocente.
blameworthy ['bleim,wə:ði] *a* biasimevole.
blanch [blɑ:ntʃ] *vt* scolorire; *vi* impallidire.
Blanche [blɑ:ntʃ] *nf pr* Bianca.
blancmange [blə'mɔnʒ] *n* biancomangiare.
bland [blænd] *a* blando.
blandishment ['blændiʃmənt] *n* blandizia.
blank [blæŋk] *a* bianco; vuoto; *n* lacuna; spazio in bianco; modulo; **b. check** assegno in bianco; **b. verse** verso sciolto.
blanket ['blæŋkit] *n* coperta; copertura.
blankly ['blæŋkli] *ad* senza espressione; recisamente.
blare [blɛə] *n* squillo; *vi* squillare; *vt* annunciare a gran voce.
blaspheme [blæs'fi:m] *vti* bestemmiare.
blasphemous ['blæsfiməs] *a* blasfemo; empio.
blasphemy ['blæsfimi] *n* bestemmia.
blast [blɑ:st] *n* raffica, colpo di vento; esplosione; squillo; *vt* far esplodere; distruggere; maledire; **b. off** blast-off; **b. furnace** altoforno.
blasting ['blɑ:stiŋ] *n* esplosione.
blatant ['bleitənt] *a* rumoroso; sguaiato; evidente.
blaze [bleiz] *n* fiamma, vampata; *vi* divampare, fiammeggiare.
blazer ['bleizə] *n* giacca sportiva; giacca di uniforme scolastica.
bleach [bli:tʃ] *vt* imbiancare.
bleak [bli:k] *a* esposto al vento; squallido; desolato; triste.
blear [bliə] *a* oscuro, confuso; **b.-eyed** dagli occhi cisposi.
bleat [bli:t] *vi* belare; **bleat(ing)** *n* belato.
bleed [bli:d] *vi* sanguinare; *vt* salassare; **bleeding** *n* emorragia.
blemish ['blemiʃ] *n* macchia; difetto (morale o fisico).
blench [blentʃ] *vi* indietreggiare.
blend [blend] *n* miscela, mistura; *vti* mescolar(si).
bless [bles] *vt* benedire, consacrare.
blessed ['blesid] *a* benedetto; beato, santo.
blessing ['blesiŋ] *n* benedizione.
blight [blait] *n* golpe, carbonchio; (*fig*) influenza maligna; *vt* inaridire.
blind [blaind] *a* cieco; *n* tendina, persiana; finzione; *vt* accecare.

blindfold ['blaindfould] *ad* ad occhi bendati; *vt* bendare gli occhi.
blindly ['blaindli] *ad* ciecamente, alla cieca.
blindness ['blaindnis] *n* cecità; mancanza di discernimento.
blink [bliŋk] *n* occhiata, sguardo rapido; guizzo di luce; *vi* battere le palpebre; ammiccare.
blinker ['bliŋkə] *n* (*aut*) lampeggiatore; paraocchi.
bliss [blis] *n* beatitudine; felicità.
blissful ['blisful] *a* beato; delizioso.
blister ['blistə] *n* bolla, vescica; *vt* far venire vesciche a; *vi* coprirsi di vesciche.
blithe [blaið] *a* giocondo.
blitheness ['blaiðnis] *n* giocondità.
blizzard ['blizəd] *n* bufera di neve, tormenta.
bloat [blout] *vti* gonfiar(si).
bloater ['bloutə] *n* aringa affumicata.
blob [blɔb] *n* goccia; macchia.
block [blɔk] *b* blocco; ceppo; gruppo di case; ostacolo; *vt* bloccare, ostacolare.
blockade [blɔ'keid] *n* blocco, assedio.
blockhead ['blɔkhed] *n* stupido.
blond(e) [blɔnd] *a n* biondo.
blood [blʌd] *n* sangue; discendenza, parentela, bellimbusto; **b.-donor** donatore di sangue; **b.-curdling** raccapricciante; **b.-stained** macchiato di sangue.
bloodhound ['blʌdhaund] *n* segugio.
bloodless ['blʌdlis] *a* esangue, pallido.
bloodshed ['blʌdʃed] *n* spargimento di sangue.
bloodshot ['blʌdʃɔt] *a* iniettato di sangue.
bloody ['blʌdi] *a* sanguinoso; sanguinario; insanguinato; (*vulg*) maledetto; *ad* (*vulg*) maledettamente, molto.
bloom [blu:m] *n* fiore, fioritura; incarnato; *vi* fiorire, sbocciare.
blooming ['blu:miŋ] *a* fiorente.
blossom ['blɔsəm] *n* fiore, fioritura; *vi* fiorire.
blot [blɔt] *n* macchia; cancellatura; difetto, colpa; *vt* macchiare; asciugare con carta assorbente; **b. out** cancellare.
blotch [blɔtʃ] *n* macchia, chiazza; sgorbio; pustola; **blotched, blotchy** chiazzato; bitorzoluto.
blotting-paper ['blɔtiŋ,peipə] *n* carta assorbente.
blouse [blauz] *n* blusa, camicetta.
blow [blou] *n* colpo; raffica, soffio; soffiata; *vti* soffiare; suonare (*a wind instrument*); ansare.
blowy ['bloui] *a* ventoso.
blowzy ['blauzi] *a* scapigliato.
blubber ['blʌbə] *n* grasso di balena; *vi* piangere rumorosamente.
bludgeon ['blʌdʒən] *n* randello.
blue [blu:] *a n* azzurro, blu, celeste, turchino; *a* nervoso, depresso, triste; **to have the blues** essere depresso.
bluebell ['blu:bel] *n* giacinto selvatico; campanula.
bluebottle ['blu:,bɔtl] *n* moscone.
blue-stocking ['blu:,stɔkiŋ] *n* donna intellettuale, donna saccente.
bluff [blʌf] *a* brusco, franco; *n* inganno, montatura; *vt* ingannare.
bluish ['blu(:)iʃ] *a* bluastro, azzurrognolo.
blunder ['blʌndə] *n* errore grossolano, sbaglio; *vti* condurre maldestramente (un affare); fare un errore.
blunt [blʌnt] *a* smussato; franco; rude; ottuso; *vt* smussare; ottundere.
bluntly ['blʌntli] *ad* bruscamente; esplicitamente.
bluntness ['blʌntnis] *n* rudezza; franchezza; ottusità.
blur [blə:] *n* macchia; offuscamento; *vt* macchiare; offuscare.
blurb [blə:b] *n* soffietto editoriale.
blurt out ['blə:t'aut] *vt* spifferare, riferire senza discrezione.
blush [blʌʃ] *n* rossore; *vi* arrossire.
bluster ['blʌstə] *n* fanfaronata; millanteria; *vi* tempestare; smargiassare; **blusterer** *n* spaccone.
boar [bɔə] *n* verro; cinghiale.
board [bɔ:d] *n* asse, tavola; comitato, commissione; ministero; (*naut*) bordo; **above b.** a carte scoperte; pensione; *pl* (*theat*) palcoscenico; *vti* coprire di assi; prendere a pensione, tenere a pensione; salire a bordo.
boarder ['bɔ:də] *n* convittore, pensionante.
boarding house ['bɔ:diŋhaus] *n* pensione.
boarding school ['bɔ:diŋsku:l] *n* convitto.
boast [boust] *n* vanteria, vanto; *vti* vantar(si).
boastful ['boustful] *a* millantatore.
boat [bout] *n* barca; battello, vapore; **in the same b.** trovarsi nelle stesse condizioni.
boatman ['boutmən] *n* barcaiuolo.
boatswain ['boutswein, 'bousn] *n* (*naut*) nostromo.
bob [bɔb] *vt* tagliare corti (i capelli); *vi* fare inchini; muoversi in su e in giù; **b. up** tornare a galla.
bobbin ['bɔbin] *n* bobina, rocchetto.
bobsled ['bɔbsled] *n* bob, guidoslitta.
bodice ['bɔdis] *n* corpetto.
bodiless ['bɔdilis] *a* incorporeo.
bodily ['bɔdili] *a* corporeo; *ad* corporalmente; di peso, in massa.
bodkin ['bɔdkin] *n* punteruolo, passanastro.
Bodleian [bɔd'li(:)ən] *a* bodleiano.
body ['bɔdi] n corpo; torso; cadavere; ente; **in a b.** tutti insieme.
bodyguard ['bɔdigɑ:d] *n* guardia del corpo.
Boer ['bouə] *a n* boero.
bog [bɔg] *n* palude, pantano.

boggle ['bɔgl] *vi* trasalire; esitare.
boggy ['bɔgi] *a* paludoso.
bogie ['bougi] *n* carrello.
bogus ['bougəs] *a* falso, finto; simulato.
Bohemia [bou'hi:miə] *n* Boemia.
Bohemian [bou'hi:miən] *a n* boemo; 'bohemien'.
boil [bɔil] *n* (punto di) ebollizione; foruncolo; *vti* (far) bollire; lessare.
boiler ['bɔilə] *n* bollitore; caldaia.
boisterous ['bɔistərəs] *a* chiassoso; turbolento.
bold [bould] *a* audace, temerario; sfacciato; vigoroso; **boldly** *ad* arditamente; sfacciatamente.
boldness ['bouldnis] *n* audacia; sfacciataggine.
bole [boul] *n* tronco d'albero.
bolshevik ['bɔlʃivik] *a n* bolscevico.
bolshevism ['bɔlʃivizəm] *n* bolscevismo.
bolster ['boulstə] *n* cuscino, traversino; *vt* sostenere.
bolt [boult] *n* bullone, catenaccio; spranga; freccia; fulmine; *vt* chiudere a catenaccio; inghiottire in fretta; *vi* darsela a gambe.
bomb [bɔm] *n* bomba; *vti* bombardare.
bombard [bɔm'ba:d] *vt* bombardare.
bombardment [bɔm'ba:dmənt] *n* bombardamento.
bombast ['bɔmbæst] *n* linguaggio ampolloso.
bombastic [bɔm'bæstik] *a* ampolloso.
bomber ['bɔmə] *n* bombardiere.
bombshell ['bɔmʃel] *n* obice, granata; notizia, evento sconvolgente.
bond [bɔnd] *n* legame, vincolo; obbligazione; (*com*) deposito doganale.
bondage ['bɔndidʒ] *n* schiavitù, servitù.
bondsman ['bɔndzmən] *n* (*com*) garante.
bone [boun] *n* osso; *vt* disossare.
boneless ['bounlis] *a* senz'osso.
bonfire ['bɔn.faiə] *n* falò.
Boniface ['bɔnifeis] *nm pr* Bonifazio.
bonnet ['bɔnit] *n* berretto scozzese, cappellino legato con nastri sotto il mento.
bonny ['bɔni] *a* bello, grazioso.
bonus ['bounəs] *n* compenso; gratifica; extradividendo.
bony ['bouni] *a* ossuto.
boo [bu:] *vti* fischiare.
booby ['bu:bi] *n* individuo sciocco.
book [buk] *n* libro; *vt* prendere nota di; prenotare; registrare; *vi* fare un biglietto (ferroviario).
book-binder ['buk.baində] *n* rilegatore di libri.
book-binding ['buk.baindiŋ] *n* rilegatura di libri.
book case ['bukkeis] *n* libreria, scaffale.
booking ['bukiŋ] *n* prenotazione; **b. clerk** bigliettario; **b. office** biglietteria.
book-keeper ['buk.ki:pə] *n* contabile.
book-keeping ['buk.ki:piŋ] *n* contabilità.
booklet ['buklit] *n* libretto, opuscolo.
bookmaker ['buk.meikə] *n* allibratore.
bookmark(er) ['buk'ma:k(ə)] *n* segnalibro.
bookseller ['buk.selə] *n* libraio.
bookshop ['bukʃɔp] *n* libreria.
bookstall ['bukstɔ:l] *n* edicola, chiosco; bancarella.
bookworm ['bukwə:m] *n* tignuola; (*fig*) topo di biblioteca.
boom [bu:m] *n* rimbombo; palo che tien tesa una rete; barriera galleggiante in un porto; improvviso aumento di attività commerciale; *vi* rimbombare; avere un improvviso aumento di attività.
boon [bu:n] *n* dono, favore, vantaggio.
boor [buə] *n* persona zotica, villana.
boorish ['buəriʃ] *a* rozzo, zotico.
boost [bu:st] *vt* lanciare un prodotto con gran pubblicità; (*el*) elevare la tensione di.
boot [bu:t] *n* stivale; (*aut*) portabagagli.
booth [bu:ð] *n* baracca; **telephone b.** cabina telefonica.
booty ['bu:ti] *n* bottino.
booze [bu:z] *n* (*fam*) bevande alcooliche *pl*; *vi* bere all'eccesso.
borax ['bɔ:ræks] *n* borace.
border ['bɔ:də] *n* bordo; confine; *a* di confine; *vti* confinare (con); orlare; rasentare.
borderer ['bɔ:dərə] *n* abitante di confine.
bordering ['bɔ:dəriŋ] *a* di confine, limitrofo.
bore [bɔ:] *n* buco, foro; calibro di fucile; noia, seccatura; seccatore; *vt* (per)forare; seccare, annoiare.
boredom ['bɔ:dəm] *n* noia.
boric ['bɔ:rik] *a* borico.
boring ['bɔ:riŋ] *a* noioso.
born [bɔ:n] *a* nato; nativo.
borough ['bʌrə] *n* città avente amministrazione autonoma; collegio elettorale; mandamento.
borrow ['bɔrou] *vt* prendere a prestito.
bosom ['buzəm] *n* petto, seno; il davanti di una camicia; **b. friend** amico intimo.
boss [bɔs] *n* borchia, ornamento in rilievo; (*sl*) padrone; capo.
bossy ['bɔsi] *a* prepotente; autoritario.
botanic [bə'tænik] *a* botanico.
botanist ['bɔtənist] *n* botanico.
botany ['bɔtəni] *n* botanica.
botch [bɔtʃ] *vt* rappezzare inabilmente.
both [bouθ] *a pron* ambedue, l'uno e

l'altro; **both . . . and** tanto . . . quanto.

bother ['bɔðə] *n* fastidio; *vt* seccare; *vi* preoccuparsi.

bothersome ['bɔðəsəm] *a* seccante, noioso.

bottle ['bɔtl] *n* bottiglia; fascio di fieno; *vt* imbottigliare.

bottom ['bɔtəm] *n* fondo, base; sedere; **at b.** in fondo.

bottomless ['bɔtəmlis] *a* senza fondo.

bough [bau] *n* ramo d'albero.

boulder ['bouldə] *n* masso roccioso.

bounce [bauns] *n* rimbalzo, salto; *vi* (rim)balzare.

bouncer ['baunsə] *n* (*sl*) chi getta fuori da un locale gli intrusi.

bouncing ['baunsiŋ] *a* vigoroso; vivace.

bound [baund] *n* confine; limite; salto, rimbalzo; *a* diretto; connesso con; destinato a; *vt* limitare; *vi* saltare, rimbalzare.

boundary ['baundəri] *n* linea di confine.

boundless ['baundlis] *a* illimitato.

bounteous ['bauntiəs] *a* benefico, generoso.

bountiful ['bauntiful] *a* generoso, liberale.

bounty ['baunti] *n* generosità; premio d'incoraggiamento.

bouquet ['bukei] *n* mazzolino; profumo.

bourgeois ['buəʒwɑ:] *a n* borghese; **bourgeoisie** borghesia.

bout [baut] *n* assalto; accesso; partita.

bovine ['bouvain] *a* bovino.

bow [bou] *n* arco; nodo.

bow [bau] *n* inchino; (*ship*) prua; *vi* inchinarsi; sottomettersi.

bowel ['bauəl] *n* budello; **bowels** *pl* budella *pl*; (*fig*) viscere.

bowl [boul] *n* ciotola; vaso; recipiente; boccia; palla di legno; *vti* rotolare.

bowler ['boulə] *n* bombetta, cappello duro; giocatore di bocce; (*cricket*) giocatore che serve la palla.

bowling ['bouliŋ], **bowls** [boulz] *n* gioco delle bocce.

bowsprit ['bousprit] *n* (*naut*) bompresso.

box [bɔks] *n* scatola; cassetta; (*driver's*) cassetta; (*jury*) banco; (*theat*) palco; schiaffo; **b. car** vagone merci chiuso; *vt* mettere in scatola; *vi* fare del pugilato.

boxer ['bɔksə] *n* pugilatore, pugile.

boxing ['bɔksiŋ] *n* pugilato; **b. match** partita di pugilato.

box number ['bɔks,nʌmbə] *n* casella postale.

box-office ['bɔks'ɔfis] *n* botteghino del teatro, biglietteria.

boy [bɔi] *n* ragazzo.

boycott ['bɔikət] *vt* boicottare.

boyhood ['bɔihud] *n* fanciullezza.

boyish ['bɔiiʃ] *a* fanciullesco.

brace [breis] *n* qualunque cosa che tiene unito; palo; **braces** *pl* bretelle *pl*; *vt* assicurare strettamente.

bracelet ['breislit] *n* braccialetto.

bracing ['breisiŋ] *a* invigorante, salubre.

bracken ['brækən] *n* felce.

bracket ['brækit] *n* mensola; parentesi; *vt* mettere fra parentesi.

brackish ['brækiʃ] *a* salso, salmastro.

brag [bræg] *n* millanteria, vanteria; *vi* vantarsi.

braggart ['brægət] *n* millantatore, spaccone.

braid [breid] *n* (*of hair*) treccia; gallone; *vt* intrecciare; guarnire.

brain [brein] *n* cervello; (*fig, usu pl*) intelligenza; **b. washing** lavaggio del cervello; **b.-drain** emigrazione pesante di studiosi e scienziati.

brain [brein] *vt* accoppare.

brainy ['breini] *a* (*fam*) intelligente.

braise [breiz] *vt* brasare.

brake [breik] *n* macchia di cespugli; (*mech*) freno; *vt* frenare; **b. horsepower** potenza del freno; **foot b.** (*aut*) freno a pedale; **hand b.** freno a mano.

bramble ['bræmbl] *n* pruno, rovo.

bran [bræn] *n* crusca.

branch [brɑ:ntʃ] *n* ramo; diramazione; filiale; *vi* ramificarsi; **to b. off** biforcarsi; **to b. out** estendersi.

brand [brænd] *n* marchio; tizzone; *vt* marchiare; stigmatizzare; imprimere.

brandish ['brændiʃ] *vt* brandire.

brandy ['brændi] *n* acquavite, cognac.

brash [bræʃ] *a* impudente; fragile.

brass [brɑ:s] *n* ottone; (*fig*) sfrontatezza.

brassiere ['bræsiə] *n* reggipetto, reggiseno.

brassy ['brɑ:si] *a* di ottone; impudente.

brat [bræt] *n* marmocchio; monello.

bravado [brə'vɑ:dou] *n* bravata, spavalderia.

brave [breiv] *a* coraggioso; *n* prode; *vt* affrontare, sfidare.

bravely ['breivli] *ad* coraggiosamente.

bravery ['breivəri] *n* coraggio.

brawl [brɔ:l] *n* rissa; *vi* rissare.

brawn [brɔ:n] *n* muscolo, forza muscolare; soprassata.

brawny ['brɔ:ni] *a* forte, muscoloso.

bray [brei] *vi* ragliare.

brazen ['breizn] *a* d'ottone; impudente; **b.-faced** sfrontato.

brazenly ['breiznli] *ad* sfacciatamente.

brazier ['breiziə] *n* braciere.

Brazil [brə'zil] *n* Brasile.

Brazilian [brə'ziljən] *a n* brasiliano.

breach [bri:tʃ] *n* breccia, rottura; *vt* far breccia in, rompere.

bread [bred] *n* pane.

breadth [bredθ] *n* ampiezza, larghezza; (*of material*) altezza.
break [breik] *n* rottura; intervallo; *vti* rompere, spezzare; rompersi, spezzarsi; venir meno a.
breakable ['breikəbl] *a* fragile.
breakage ['breikidʒ] *n* rottura.
breakaway ['breikəwei] *n* separazione; (*rly*) sbandamento.
breakdown ['breikdaun] *n* collasso; crollo; esaurimento nervoso; (*aut*) panna, guasto.
breaker ['breikə] *n* rompitore; violatore; (*of horses*) domatore; maroso.
breakfast ['brekfəst] *n* (prima) colazione.
breaking ['breikiŋ] *n* rottura; interruzione; infrazione.
breakneck ['breiknek] *a* rompicollo.
breakwater ['breik.wɔ:tə] *n* frangiflutti, diga.
breast [brest] *n* mammella; petto; seno; *vt* affrontare, lottare con.
breath [breθ] *n* respiro; fiato; soffio.
breathalyser ['breθəlaizə] *n* analizzatore del tasso alcoolico.
breathe [bri:ð] *vti* respirare; prender fiato; mormorare; infondere; **b. forth** esalare.
breathing ['bri:ðiŋ] *n* respiro, respirazione.
breathless ['breθlis] *a* ansimante, senza fiato.
breathlessly ['breθlisli] *ad* con il fiato sospeso.
breathlessness ['breθlisnis] *n* mancanza di respiro, affanno.
breeches ['britʃiz] *n pl* calzoni *pl*, brache *pl*.
breed [bri:d] *n* discendenza, razza; *vti* generare; partorire; (ri)prodursi; allevare.
breeder ['bri:də] *n* allevatore; **b. reactor** reattore nucleare autofertilizzante.
breeding ['bri:diŋ] *n* allevamento; educazione, buone maniere *pl*.
breeze [bri:z] *n* brezza, vento leggero.
breezy ['bri:zi] *a* battuto dal vento, fresco; gioviale.
brethren ['breðrən] *n pl* confratelli *pl*.
breviary ['bri:vjəri] *n* breviario.
brevity ['breviti] *n* brevità, concisione.
brew [bru:] *vt* fare (*un infuso*); fare (*la birra*); (*fig*) tramare; *vi* essere in fermentazione; prepararsi.
brewer ['bru(:)ə] *n* fabbricante di birra.
brewery ['bruəri] *n* fabbrica di birra.
briar *v* **brier**
bribe [braib] *n* dono (per corrompere o influenzare); *vt* corrompere (per mezzo di doni).
bribery ['braibəri] *n* corruzione.
brick [brik] *n* mattone; *a* di mattoni; **to drop a b.** commettere un'indiscrezione.
bridal ['braidl] *a* nuziale; *n* sposalizio.
bride [braid] *n* sposa; **bridegroom** sposo.
bridesmaid ['braidzmeid] *n* damigella d'onore della sposa.
bridge [bridʒ] *n* ponte, (*naut*) ponte di comando; (*cards*) 'bridge', ponte.
Bridget ['bridʒit] *nf pr* Brigida.
bridle ['braidl] *n* briglia, freno.
brief [bri:f] *a* breve, conciso; *n* (*leg*) riassunto.
briefness ['bri:fnis] *n* brevità.
brier ['braiə] *n* rosa di macchia, rovo; (pipa di) radica.
brig [brig] *n* brigantino.
brigade [bri'geid] *n* brigata.
brigadier [.brigə'diə] *n* comandante di brigata.
brigand ['brigənd] *n* bandito, brigante.
brigandage ['brigəndidʒ] *n* brigantaggio, banditismo.
bright [brait] *a* brillante, luminoso, risplendente; gaio, vivace; sveglio; intelligente.
brighten ['braitn] *vt* rallegrare, rendere più brillante; *vi* illuminarsi, rischiararsi.
brightness ['braitnis] *n* splendore; vivacità.
brilliancy ['briljənsi] *n* splendore.
brilliant ['briljənt] *a* brillante, lucente; *n* brillante.
brim [brim] *n* orlo; bordo, margine; (*of hat*) tesa, ala; *vti* colmar(si); **to b. over** traboccare.
brimless ['brimlis] *a* senza orlo, senz'ala.
brindled ['brindld] *a* chiazzato.
brine [brain] *n* acqua salata.
bring [briŋ] *vt* portare; procurare; addurre; causare; indurre; **to b. up** educare.
brink [briŋk] *n* orlo; limite estremo.
brisk [brisk] *a* vivace, svelto.
briskly ['briskli] *ad* vivacemente; speditamente.
briskness ['brisknis] *n* vivacità, sveltezza.
bristle ['brisl] *n* setola, pelo duro e rado; *vi* andare in collera.
bristly ['brisli] *a* setoloso.
Britain ['britn] *n* Britannia; **Great B.** Gran Bretagna.
Britannic [bri'tænik] *a* britannico.
British ['britiʃ] *a* britannico, inglese.
Briton ['britn] *n* britanno.
brittle ['britl] *a* fragile, friabile.
brittleness ['britlnis] *n* fragilità friabilità.
broach [broutʃ] *n* spiedo; *vt* spillare; cominciare una discussione.
broad [brɔ:d] *a* ampio, largo; indelicato, volgare, (*accent*) marcato.
broadcast ['brɔ:dkɑ:st] *n* trasmissione radiofonica; *vt* trasmettere per radio; *vi* parlare alla radio; **broad-**

caster apparecchio trasmittente; chi parla alla radio; **broadcasting** radiodiffusione.
broaden ['brɔːdn] *vti* allargar(si), estender(si).
broadly ['brɔːdli] *ad* largamente; **b. speaking** generalmente parlando.
broadness ['brɔːdnis] *n* larghezza, ampiezza; grossolanità; accento marcato.
brocade [brə'keid] *n* broccato.
brochure ['brouʃjuə] *n* opuscolo.
broil [brɔil] *n* lite, tumulto; *vt* arrostire alla griglia o allo spiedo.
broken ['broukən] *a* rotto; (*of weather*) incerto; (*of ground*) accidentato; scoraggiato; scorretto.
broker ['broukə] *n* mediatore, sensale.
bromide ['broumaid] *n* bromuro.
bronchial ['brɔnkiəl] *a* bronchiale.
bronchitis [brɔŋ'kaitis] *n* bronchite.
bronze [brɔnz] *n* bronzo; *a* bronzeo, di bronzo; *vti* abbronzar(si).
brooch [broutʃ] *n* spilla.
brood [bruːd] *n* covata; *vti* covare; meditare, preoccuparsi.
brook [bruk] *n* ruscello.
broom [brum] *n* ginestra; scopa.
broomstick ['brumstik] *n* manico di scopa.
broth [brɔθ] *n* brodo.
brothel ['brɔθl] *n* bordello.
brother ['brʌðə] *n* fratello; confratello (*pl* **brethren**); **b. in arms** compagno d'armi; **b. in law** cognato.
brotherhood ['brʌðəhud] *n* fratellanza, fraternità; confratérnita.
brotherly ['brʌðəli] *a* fraterno.
brow [brau] *n* fronte; sopracciglio; (*cliff*) orlo; (*hill*) sommità.
browbeat ['braubiːt] *vt* intimidire.
brown [braun] *a* marrone, scuro, abbronzato; *n* color marrone; *vti* rendere (divenire) marrone, abbronzare; rosolare.
brownie ['brauni] *n* folletto; giovane esploratrice.
browse [brauz] *vti* brucare; scorrere libri.
bruise [bruːz] *n* contusione, ammaccatura, livido; *vt* ammaccare.
brunette [bruː'net] *a n* bruna.
brunt [brʌnt] *n* urto; **to bear the b.** sopportare il peso.
brush [brʌʃ] *n* spazzola; spazzolata; pennello; *vt* spazzolare; sfiorare.
brushwood ['brʌʃwud] *n* macchia.
brusque [brusk] *a* brusco, rude.
Brussels ['brʌslz] *n* (*geogr*) Bruxelles; **B. sprouts** cavolini di Bruxelles.
brutal ['bruːtl] *a* brutale.
brutality [bruː'tæliti] *n* brutalità.
brutalize ['bruːtəlaiz] *vt* abbrutire.
brute [bruːt] *a* brutale; *n* bruto.
brutish ['bruːtiʃ] *a* brutale, bestiale.
bubble ['bʌbl] *n* bolla; progetto vano; rumore di liquido che bolle; *vi* gorgogliare; far bolle; bollire.
buccaneer [ˌbʌkə'niə] *n* pirata.
Bucharest ['bjuːkərest] *n* (*geogr*) Bucarest.
buck [bʌk] *n* daino; coniglio; leprotto; maschio di molti animali; (*sl*) dollaro.
bucket ['bʌkit] *n* secchia, secchio.
buckle ['bʌkl] *n* fibbia; *vt* affibbiare, fermare; piegare.
buckler ['bʌklə] *n* scudo rotondo; (*fig*) protettore.
buckwheat ['bʌkwiːt] *n* grano saraceno.
bucolic [bjuː'kɔlik] *a* bucolico, pastorale.
bud [bʌd] *n* bocciolo; gemma; germoglio; *vi* germogliare.
Buddha ['budə] *n* Budda.
Buddhist ['budist] *a* buddistico; *n* buddista.
budge [bʌdʒ] *vi* fare un piccolo movimento, muoversi.
budgerigar ['bʌdʒərigɑː] *n* pappagallino.
budget ['bʌdʒit] *n* bilancio preventivo; *vi* fare un bilancio preventivo.
buff [bʌf] *a* scamosciato, marrone; *n* pelle di bufalo; color camoscio.
buffalo ['bʌfəlou] *a* bufalo.
buffer ['bʌfə] *n* (*mech*) respingente.
buffet ['bʌfit] *n* schiaffo; *vt* schiaffeggiare.
buffet ['bufei] *n* credenza, 'buffet'.
buffoon [bʌ'fuːn] *n* buffone.
buffoonery [bʌ'fuːnəri] *n* buffoneria.
bug [bʌg] *n* cimice; (*sl*) virus; piccolo insetto; **big bug** (*sl*) persona importante.
bugbear ['bʌgbɛə] *n* spauracchio.
buggy ['bʌgi] *n* carrozzino scoperto, calesse.
bugle ['bjuːgl] *n* buccina.
bugler ['bjuːglə] *n* sonatore di buccina.
build [bild] *n* costruzione; corporatura; *vt* costruire; edificare, fabbricare; *vi* nidificare.
builder ['bildə] *n* costruttore; impresario di costruzioni.
building ['bildiŋ] *a* edile, edilizio; *n* edificio, costruzione.
built [bilt] *a* costruito, formato; **well-b.** ben messo, ben piantato.
bulb [bʌlb] *n* bulbo; lampadina elettrica.
bulbous ['bʌlbəs] *a* bulboso.
Bulgaria [bʌl'gɛəriə] *n* (*geogr*) Bulgaria.
Bulgarian [bʌl'gɛəriən] *a n* bulgaro.
bulge [bʌldʒ] *n* gonfiore, protuberanza; *vi* gonfiarsi.
bulging ['bʌldʒiŋ] *a* sporgente, protuberante.
bulk [bʌlk] *n* massa; la maggior parte; *vi* ammontare, essere voluminoso.
bulkiness ['bʌlkinis] *n* voluminosità.
bulky ['bʌlki] *a* ingombrante, voluminoso.
bull [bul] *n* toro; bolla papale.
bulldog ['buldɔg] *n* bulldog, mastino.

bulldozer ['bul,douzə] *n* 'bulldozer', scavatrice.
bullet ['bulit] *n* pallottola; proiettile.
bulletin ['bulitin] *n* bollettino, notiziario; **news b.** giornale radio; **b. board** tabellone per affissi.
bullfight ['bulfait] *n* corrida.
bullfinch ['bulfintʃ] *n* ciuffolotto.
bullion ['buljən] *n* oro o argento in verghe.
bullock ['bulək] *n* bue giovane.
bull's eye ['bulzai] *n* oblò; lente convessa; centro del bersaglio.
bully ['buli] *n* prepotente, tiranno; manzo lesso in scatola; *vt* tiranneggiare, fare il bravaccio con.
bulrush ['bulrʌʃ] *n* giunco.
bulwark ['bulwək] *n* baluardo; bastione; (*naut*) parapetto.
bum-boat ['bʌmbout] *n* battello di rifornimento viveri.
bump [bʌmp] *n* collisione, colpo, urto; bernoccolo, gonfiore; *vti* urtare, collidere.
bumper ['bʌmpə] *a* pieno, abbondante; *n* (*aut*) paraurti; (*rly*) respingente.
bumpkin ['bʌmpkin] *n* zotico.
bumptious ['bʌmpʃəs] *a* presuntuoso.
bumpy ['bʌmpi] *a* (*of road*) sassoso, ineguale; bernoccoluto.
bun [bʌn] *n* panetto, piccola focaccia; crocchia di capelli.
bunch [bʌntʃ] *n* fascio, mazzo; grappolo; *vi* raggrupparsi.
bundle ['bʌndl] *n* fagotto, fastello; *vt* affastellare; **b. off** mandare via senza cerimonie.
bung [bʌŋ] *n* tappo, grosso turacciolo; *vt* tappare, otturare.
bungalow ['bʌŋgəlou] *n* 'bungalow', casetta di costruzione leggera, a un piano.
bungle ['bʌŋgl] *n* lavoro malfatto, pasticcio; *vti* fare o aggiustare malamente, guastare.
bunion ['bʌnjən] *n* callo, infiammazione ai piedi.
bunk [bʌŋk] *n* cuccetta; sciocchezze.
bunny ['bʌni] *n* coniglietto.
buoy [bɔi] *n* boa, gavitello.
buoyancy ['bɔiənsi] *n* galleggiabilità; (*fig*) elasticità, brio.
buoyant ['bɔiənt] *a* capace di stare a galla; leggero; vivace.
burden ['bə:dn] *n* peso, carico, fardello, onere; ritornello; (*naut*) tonnellaggio; *vt* caricare, gravare.
burdensome ['bə:dnsəm] *a* gravoso, opprimente.
burdock ['bə:dɔk] *n* (*bot*) lappola.
bureau [bjuə'rou] *pl* **bureaus** *n* scrittoio; ufficio.
bureaucracy [bjuə'rɔkrəsi] *n* burocrazia.
bureaucrat ['bjuəroukræt] *n* burocrate.
bureaucratic [,bjuərou'krætik] *a* burocratico.
burglar ['bə:glə] *n* scassinatore; **b. alarm** campanello antifurto.
burglary ['bə:gləri] *n* furto mediante scasso.
burgle ['bə:gl] *vt* scassinare.
Burgundy ['bə:gəndi] *n* (*geogr*) Borgogna; **b.** vino di Borgogna.
burial ['beriəl] *n* sepoltura; **b. ground** cimitero; **b. place** sepoltura, tomba.
burlesque [bə:'lesk] *a* burlesco; *n* 'burlesque'; farsa.
burly ['bə:li] *a* grosso e robusto.
Burma ['bə:mə] *n* Birmania.
Burmese [bə:'mi:z] *a n* birmano.
burn [bə:n] *n* bruciatura, scottatura; (*scozzese*) ruscello; *vti* bruciare, ardere.
burner ['bə:nə] *n* becco di lampada o di fornello a gas.
burning ['bə:niŋ] *a* bruciante, ardente; *n* bruciatura.
burnish ['bə:niʃ] *vt* brunire, lustrare.
burrow ['bʌrou] *n* tana; *vi* rintanarsi; investigare.
bursar ['bə:sə] *n* economo; borsista.
bursary ['bə:səri] *n* borsa di studio.
burst [bə:st] *n* esplosione, scoppio; *vti* (far) esplodere, (far) scoppiare; rompere.
bury ['beri] *vt* seppellire; (*fig*) dimenticare, nascondere alla vista.
bus [bʌs] *pl* **buses** *n* autobus.
busman ['bʌsmən] *pl* **busmen** *n* conducente di autobus.
bush ['buʃ] *n* cespuglio, macchia; (*mech*) boccola.
bushel ['buʃel] *n* staio.
bushy ['buʃi] *a* folto; cespuglioso.
busily ['bizili] *ad* attivamente.
business ['bizinis] *n* affare, affari *pl*; commercio; occupazione; azienda commerciale; **business-like** metodico, pratico; **b. suit** abito maschile da passeggio.
bust [bʌst] *n* busto; petto.
bustard ['bʌstəd] *n* ottarda.
bustle ['bʌsl] *n* andirivieni, tramestio; *vi* agitarsi, affaccendarsi.
busy ['bizi] *a* occupato, affaccendato.
busybody ['bizi,bɔdi] *n* ficcanaso.
but [bʌt] *cj* ma, però, se non che; *ad prep* eccetto, fuorchè, non . . . che; *n* ma.
butane ['bju:tein] *n* (*chem*) butano.
butcher ['butʃə] *n* macellaio; *vt* macellare; massacrare.
butchery ['butʃəri] *n* macello; strage.
butler ['bʌtlə] *n* maggiordomo.
butt [bʌt] *n* barile, botte; calcio di fucile; bersaglio; zimbello; cozzo, cornata; *vt* cozzare.
butter ['bʌtə] *n* burro; *vt* imburrare.
buttercup ['bʌtəkʌp] *n* ranuncolo.
butterfly ['bʌtəflai] *n* farfalla.
buttock ['bʌtək] *n* natica.
button ['bʌtn] *n* bottone; **collar b.** bottoncino per colletto; **b. hook** allacciabottoni; *vt* abbottonare; **to b. oneself up** abbottonarsi.

buttonhole ['bʌtnhoul] *n* occhiello; fiore portato all'occhiello; *vt* far occhielli; (*fig*) attaccar bottone; **buttonholer** attaccabottoni.
buttress ['bʌtris] *n* contrafforte; sostegno.
buxom ['bʌksəm] *a* grassoccio; formoso.
buy [bai] *vt* acquistare, comp(e)rare.
buyer ['baiə] *n* acquirente, compratore.
buzz [bʌz] *vi* ronzare; *n* ronzio.
buzzing ['bʌziŋ] *a* ronzante; *n* ronzio.
by [bai] *prep* da, di, a fianco di, per, vicino a; non più tardi di; **by the way, by the by** a proposito; *ad* vicino, da parte; **to stand by** stare vicino, parteggiare per, essere spettatore; **to put by** metter via.
bye-bye ['baibai] *interj* addio, arrivederci, ciao; *n* (*fam*) nanna.
bygone ['baigɔn] *a* finito, passato.
bye-law ['bailɔ:] *n* regolamento locale.
by-pass ['baipa:s] *n* strada che evita il passaggio per una città.
byre ['baiə] *n* stalla per buoi.
by-road ['bairoud] **byway** ['baiwei] *n* strada secondaria.
bystander ['bai,stændə] *n* spettatore.
by-word ['baiwə:d] *n* detto comune; oggetto di rimprovero.
Byzantine [bi'zænti:n] *a n* bizantino.
Byzantium [bi'zæntiəm] *n* Bisanzio.

C

cab [kæb] *n* vettura pubblica; **taxi-c.** tassì; **c. rank, c. stand** posteggio di tassì.
cabbage ['kæbidʒ] *n* cavolo.
cabin ['kæbin] *n* cabina, capanna; **c. boy** mozzo di nave.
cabinet ['kæbinit] *n* gabinetto, armadietto, stipo; **c.-maker** ebanista; **C.** Consiglio dei Ministri.
cable ['keibl] *n* cavo; cablogramma; *vi* spedire un cablogramma; **c. car** funicolare.
caboose [kə'bu:s] *n* (*naut*) cucina, cambusa, (*rly*) furgone.
cacao [kə'ka:ou] *n* cacao.
cackle ['kækl] *n* schiamazzo; *vi* schiamazzare.
cactus ['kæktəs] *pl* **cactuses, cacti** *n* cactus, pianta grassa.
cad [kæd] *n* furfante.
caddy ['kædi] *n* scatola per custodire il tè; (*golf*) porta-mazze.
cadence ['keidəns] *n* cadenza.
cadet [kə'det] *n* cadetto.
cadge [kædʒ] *vti* scroccare.
Caesar ['si:zə] *nm pr* Cesare.
café ['kæfei] *n* caffè, ristorante.
cafeteria [,kæfi'tiəriə] *n* ristorante 'self-service'.
cage [keidʒ] *n* gabbia.
Cain [kein] *nm pr* Caino.
caique [kai'i:k] *n* caicco, scialuppa.
cairngorm ['kεən'gɔ:m] *n* quarzo giallo.
cajole [kə'dʒoul] *vt* blandire, lusingare.
cajolery [kə'dʒouləri] *n* adulazione, allettamento.
cake [keik] *n* torta, dolce, pasticcino; **c. of soap** saponetta; *vti* incrostar (si).
Calabrian [kə'læbriən] *a n* calabrese.
calamitous [kə'læmitəs] *a* calamitoso, disastroso.
calamity [kə'læmiti] *n* calamità, sventura.
calcium ['kælsiəm] *n* (*chem*) calcio.
calculable ['kælkjuləbl] *a* calcolabile.
calculate ['kælkjuleit] *vti* calcolare; contare (su).
calculation [,kælkju'leiʃən] *n* calcolo; previsione.
calculator ['kælkjuleitə] *n* calcolatore; macchina calcolatrice.
calculus ['kælkjuləs] *pl* **calculi** *n* (*math, med*) calcolo.
Caledonia [,kæli'douniə] *n* Caledonia, Scozia; **Caledonian** caledone, scozzese.
calendar ['kælində] *n* calendario; annuario; lista.
calender ['kælində] *n* (*mech*) cilindratoio; calandra; *vt* calandrare.
calf [ka:f] *pl* **calves** *n* vitello; pelle di vitello; piccolo di elefante e di altri mammiferi.
caliber ['kælibə] *n* calibro.
calipers ['kælipəz] *n pl* compassi.
call [kɔ:l] *n* chiamata, richiamo; grido; breve visita; diritto; **within c.** a portata di voce; **c. boy** (*theat*) buttafuori; **c. up** chiamata alle armi; **telephone c.** telefonata; *vti* chiamare; gridare; chiamarsi; invocare; fare una breve visita.
caller ['kɔ:lə] *n* visitatore.
calling ['kɔ:liŋ] *n* occupazione, professione; vocazione.
callous ['kæləs] *a* calloso; insensibile.
callow ['kælou] *a* implume; inesperto; imberbe.
calm [ka:m] *a* calmo, sereno; *n* calma, tranquillità; *vt* calmare, tranquillare.
calmly ['ka:mli] *ad* tranquillamente, con calma.
calmness ['ka:mnis] *n* calma, tranquillità.
calomel ['kæloumel] *n* calomelano.
calorie ['kæləri] *n* caloria.
calumniate [kə'lʌmnieit] *vt* calunniare.
calumny ['kæləmni] *n* calunnia.
Calvary ['kælvəri] *n* Calvario; **c.** Via Crucis, calvario.
Calvinism ['kælvinizəm] *n* calvinismo.
calypso [kæ'lipso] *n* calipso.
camber ['kæmbə] *n* curvatura, inarcamento; *vt* curvare.

cambric ['keimbrik] *n* cambri, batista.
camel ['kæməl] *n* cammello.
cameo ['kæmiou] *n* cammeo.
camera ['kæmərə] *n* macchina fotografica; **cameraman** fotoreporter; operatore cinematografico, televisivo; in **c.** a porte chiuse.
camomile ['kæməmail] *n* camomilla.
camouflage ['kæmuflɑːʒ] *n* camuffamento, mimetizzazione.
camp [kæmp] *n* campeggio; campo; accampamento; *vi* accamparsi, attendarsi; **camp site** camping.
campaign [kæm'pein] *n* campagna; *vi* fare una campagna.
camphor ['kæmfə] *n* canfora.
campus ['kæmpəs] *n* insieme di terreni, campi di gioco, edifici universitari.
can [kæn] *n* bidone; scatola di latta per cibi conservati.
can [kæn] *vi* (*3rd sing*) essere in grado di; potere; sapere; *vt* mettere in scatola.
Canada ['kænədə] *n* Canadà.
Canadian [kə'neidiən] *a n* canadese.
canal [kə'næl] *n* canale.
canary [kə'nɛəri] *n* canarino.
Canary (Islands) [kə'nɛəri ('ailəndz)] *n* (Isole) Canarie.
cancel ['kænsəl] *vt* annullare; cancellare; sopprimere.
cancellation [,kænse'leiʃən] *n* annullamento, soppressione.
cancer ['kænsə] *n* cancro.
candid ['kændid] *a* franco, sincero.
candidate ['kændidit] *n* candidato.
candidature ['kændiditʃə] *n* candidatura.
candidness ['kændidnis] *n* franchezza.
candied ['kændid] *a* candito.
candle ['kændl] *n* candela.
Candlemas ['kændlməs] *n* Candelora.
candlestick ['kændlstik] *n* candeliere.
candor ['kændə] *n* franchezza, sincerità.
candy ['kændi] *n* candito; dolciumi *pl*; **c. floss, cotton c.** zucchero filato.
cane [kein] *n* bastone da passeggio; canna; bacchetta; **sugar c.** canna da zucchero; *vt* bastonare.
canine ['keinain] *a* canino.
canister ['kænistə] *n* barattolo.
canker ['kæŋkə] *n* cancro; brutto difetto; influenza corruttrice; *vti* corromper(si).
cankerous ['kæŋkərəs] *a* cancrenoso.
canned [kænd] *a* conservato in scatola; **c. meat** carne in scatola.
cannibal ['kænibəl] *n* cannibale.
cannon ['kænən] *n* cannone, cannoni *pl*; (*billiards*) carambola.
cannonade [,kænə'neid] *n* bombardamento, cannoneggiamento.
canny ['kæni] *a* astuto, abile.
canoe [kə'nuː] *n* canoa.
canon ['kænən] *n* canone; canonico.
canonical [kə'nɔnikəl] *a* canonico.
canonization [,kænənai'zeiʃən] *n* canonizzazione.
canonize ['kænənaiz] *vt* canonizzare.
canopy ['kænəpi] *n* baldacchino.
cant [kænt] *n* pendenza, inclinazione; gergo; ipocrisia.
cantankerous [kən'tæŋkərəs] *a* intrattabile, litigioso.
canteen [kæn'tiːn] *n* borraccia da soldato; cantina militare; cassetta per posateria.
canter ['kæntə] *n* piccolo galoppo; *vi* andare a piccolo galoppo.
canticle ['kæntikl] *n* cantico.
cantilever ['kæntiliːvə] *n* mensola che regge balconi *etc*; modiglione; **c. bridge** ponte a mensola.
canton ['kæntɔn] *n* cantone.
canvas ['kænvəs] *n* canovaccio, tela; vele *pl*.
canvass ['kænvəs] *vti* sollecitare voti, ordini *etc*.
canvasser ['kænvəsə] *n* galoppino elettorale.
canyon ['kænjən] *n* 'canyon', burrone.
cap [kæp] *n* berretto, copricapo, cuffietta; *vt* coprire; superare.
capability [,keipə'biliti] *n* capacità, abilità.
capable ['keipəbl] *a* abile, capace.
capacious [kə'peiʃəs] *a* spazioso, capace.
capaciousness [kə'peiʃəsnis] *n* spaziosità, capacità.
capacity [kə'pæsiti] *n* capacità; competenza; ufficio.
cape [keip] *n* capo, promontorio; cappa, mantello.
caper ['keipə] *n* cappero; capriola; (*fig*) stramberia.
Capetown ['keiptaun] *n pr* (*geogr*) Città del Capo.
capillary [kə'piləri] *a* capillare.
capital ['kæpitl] *a* capitale; eccellente; maiuscolo; *n* capitale; lettera maiuscola; (*arch*) capitello.
capitalism ['kæpitəlizəm] *n* capitalismo.
capitalist ['kæpitəlist] *n* capitalista
capitalize [kə'pitəlaiz] *vt* capitalizzare.
Capitol ['kæpitl] (**the**) *n* Campidoglio; **Capitoline** *a* capitolino.
capitulate [kə'pitjuleit] *vi* capitolare arrendersi.
capitulation [kə,pitju'leiʃən] *n* capitolazione, resa.
capon ['keipən] *n* cappone.
caprice [kə'priːs] *n* capriccio.
capricious [kə'priʃəs] *a* capriccioso volubile.
capriciousness [kə'priʃəsnis] *n* capricciosità.
capsize [kæp'saiz] *vti* capovolger(si)
capstan ['kæpstən] *n* (*naut*) argano.

capsule ['kæpsju:l] *n* capsula; schema.
captain ['kæptin] *n* capitano, comandante; capo.
caption ['kæpʃən] *n* intestazione, titolo; (*cin*) didascalia.
captious ['kæpʃəs] *a* capzioso; sofistico.
captiousness ['kæpʃəsnis] *n* capziosità.
captivate ['kæptiveit] *vt* attrarre; cattivarsi.
captivating ['kæptiveitiŋ] *a* seducente, affascinante.
captive ['kæptiv] *a n* prigioniero.
captor ['kæptə] *n* chi fa prigioniero, catturatore.
capture ['kæptʃə] *n* cattura; *vt* catturare.
Capuchin ['kæpjuʃin] *n* frate cappuccino.
car [kɑ:] *n* automobile; carro; (*rly*) vagone, (*rly*) carrozza; **armored c.** (*mil*) autoblinda; **baggage c.** bagagliaio; **cable c.** funicolare; **freight c.** vagone merci; **mail c.** vagone postale; **restaurant c., dining c.** vagone ristorante; **sleeping c.** vagone letto; **carpark** parcheggio.
carafe [kə'rɑ:f] *n* caraffa.
caramel ['kærəmel] *n* caramello; caramella.
carat ['kærət] *n* carato.
caravan ['kærəvæn] *n* carovana, carrozzone; (*aut*) roulotte.
caraway ['kærəwei] *n* (*bot*) comino.
carbine ['kɑ:bain] *n* carabina.
carbohydrate ['kɑ:bou'haidreit] *n* (*chem*) carboidrato.
carbolic [kɑ:'bɔlik] *a* fenico.
carbon ['kɑ:bən] *n* carbonio; **c. paper** carta carbone.
carbonate ['kɑ:bənit] *n* carbonato.
carbonic [kɑ:'bɔnik] *a* carbonico.
carboniferous [,kɑ:bə'nifərəs] *a* carbonifero.
carbonize ['kɑ:bənaiz] *vt* carbonizzare.
carbuncle ['kɑ:bʌŋkl] *n* carbonchio.
carburetor ['kɑ:bjuretə] *n* carburatore.
carcass ['kɑ:kəs] *n* carcassa.
card [kɑ:d] *n* biglietto da visita; cartoncino; carta da giuoco; cartolina; tessera; *vt* cardare.
cardboard ['kɑ:dbɔ:d] *n* cartone.
cardiac ['kɑ:diæk] *a* cardiaco.
cardigan ['kɑ:digən] *n* giacca a maglia.
cardinal ['kɑ:dinl] *a n* cardinale.
care [kεə] *n* cura, attenzione; preoccupazione; **(in) c. of** (*in indirizzi*) presso; *vi* importare; interessarsi; **to care for** voler bene a; curare; piacere.
careen [kə'ri:n] *vti* (*naut*) carenare.
career [kə'riə] *n* carriera; corsa.
careful ['kεəful] *a* accurato; attento, premuroso.
carefully ['kεəfuli] *ad* attentamente; con cura.
carefulness ['kεəfulnis] *n* accuratezza; attenzione.
careless ['kεəlis] *a* negligente, trascurato.
carelessness ['kεəlisnis] *n* negligenza, trascuratezza.
caress [kə'res] *n* carezza; *vt* accarezzare.
caretaker ['kεə,teikə] *n* custode, guardiano, portiere.
cargo ['kɑ:gou] *pl* **cargoes** *n* (*d'una nave*) carico.
Caribbean [,kæri'bi:ən] *a* caraibico.
caricature [,kærikə'tjuə] *n* caricatura; *vt* caricaturare.
caricaturist [,kærikə'tjuərist] *n* caricaturista.
Carmelite ['kɑ:milait] *a n* carmelitano.
carnage ['kɑ:nidʒ] *n* carneficina, strage.
carnal ['kɑ:nl] *a* carnale, sensuale.
carnation [kɑ:'neiʃən] *n* garofano.
carnival ['kɑ:nivəl] *n* carnevale.
carnivorous [kɑ:'nivərəs] *a* carnivoro.
carob ['kærəb] *n* (*bot*) carruba; **c.-tree** carrubo.
carol ['kærəl] *n* carola, inno natalizio.
Caroline ['kærəlain] *nf pr* Carolina.
carotid [kə'rɔtid] *n* (*anat*) carotide.
carouse [kə'rauz] *vi* far baldoria, gozzovigliare.
carousel [kə'rauzəl] *n* carosello.
carp [kɑ:p] *n* carpa; **c. at** *vi* trovare sempre da ridire su.
carpenter ['kɑ:pintə] *n* carpentiere, falegname.
carpentry ['kɑ:pintri] *n* carpenteria.
carpet ['kɑ:pit] *n* tappeto.
carping ['kɑ:piŋ] *a* cavilloso.
carriage ['kæridʒ] *n* carrozza, vettura; (*com*) trasporto, prezzo di trasporto; portamento; **baby c.** carrozzina per bambini.
carrier ['kæriə] *n* portatore; corriere, spedizioniere; portapacchi di bicicletta.
carrion ['kæriən] *n* carogna.
carrot ['kærət] *n* carota.
carry ['kæri] *vti* portare; trasportare; riportare; raggiungere; **to carry oneself** comportarsi.
cart [kɑ:t] *n* carro, calesse; *vt* trasportare con carro.
cartage ['kɑ:tidʒ] *n* trasporto con carri; prezzo di trasporto.
carter ['kɑ:tə] *n* carrettiere.
Carthusian [kɑ:'θju:ziən] *a n* certosino.
cartilage ['kɑ:tilidʒ] *n* cartilagine.
carton ['kɑ:tən] *n* cartone; scatola.
cartoon [kɑ:'tu:n] *n* cartone; vignetta; cartone animato; **cartoonist** vignettista; disegnatore di cartoni animati.
cartridge ['kɑ:tridʒ] *n* cartuccia.

carve [ka:v] *vt* intagliare, scolpire; trinciare.
carving ['ka:viŋ] *n* scultura, intaglio; il trinciare; **c. knife** trinciante.
cascade [kæs'keid] *n* cascata; *vi* scrosciare; sparpagliarsi.
case [keis] *n* caso, avvenimento; causa; cassa; astuccio, fodero; valigia.
casement ['keismənt] *n* finestra a due battenti.
cash [kæʃ] *n* cassa; contanti *pl*; *vt* incassare, prelevare.
cashier [kæ'ʃiə] *n* cassiere; *vt* (*mil*) destituire.
cashmere ['kæʃmiə] *n* cachemire, cashmere.
cask [ka:sk] *n* barile.
casket ['ka:skit] *n* cofanetto, scrigno.
casserole ['kæsəroul] *n* casseruola.
cassock ['kæsək] *n* tunica del clero anglicano.
cast [ka:st] *n* getto, lancio; stampo; insieme degli attori in una rappresentazione; *vti* gettare, lanciare; dedurre; distribuire parti agli attori.
castanets [,kæstə'nets] *n pl* nacchere *pl*.
castaway ['ka:stəwei] *n* naufrago; reietto.
caste [ka:st] *n* casta.
castigate ['kæstigeit] *vt* castigare, punire.
Castile [kæs'ti:l] *n* Castiglia; **Castilian** *a n* castigliano.
casting ['ka:stiŋ] *n* getto; colata; distribuzione di parti ad attori.
cast iron ['ka:st'aiən] *n* ghisa.
castle ['ka:sl] *n* castello; (*chess*) torre.
castor ['ka:stə] *n* rotella da mobili; saliera; ampolla; **c. sugar** zucchero raffinato.
castor oil ['ka:stər'ɔil] *n* olio di ricino.
castrate [kæs'treit] *vt* castrare.
castration [kæs'treiʃən] *n* castrazione.
casual ['kæʒjuəl] *a* casuale, fortuito; (*clothes*) semplice, sportivo.
casually ['kæʒjuəli] *ad* per caso; con noncuranza.
casualty ['kæʒjuəlti] *n* disgrazia; vittima; **c. list** lista delle vittime.
casuist ['kæzjuist] *n* casista.
casuistry ['kæzjuistri] *n* casistica.
cat [kat] *n* gatto.
cataclysm ['kætəklizəm] *n* cataclisma.
catacomb ['kætəkoum] *n* catacomba.
Catalan ['kætələn] *a n* catalano.
catalepsy ['kætəlepsi] *n* catalessi.
catalogue ['kætəlɔg] *n* catalogo; *vt* catalogare.
Catalonia [,kætə'louniə] *n* Catalogna.
catapult ['kætəpʌlt] *n* catapulta; fionda; *vti* catapultare.
cataract ['kætərækt] *n* cateratta; (*falls*) cascata.
catarrh [kə'ta:] *n* catarro.
catastrophe [kə'tæstrəfi] *n* catastrofe.
catch [kætʃ] *n* presa, cattura; preda; guadagno fatto; pesca; trappola; paletto di porta; *vti* acchiappare, afferrare; sorprendere; capire.
catching ['kætʃiŋ] *a* contagioso; orecchiabile.
catchword ['kætʃwə:d] *n* richiamo, slogan.
catechism ['kætikizəm] *n* catechismo.
catechize ['kætikaiz] *vt* catechizzare.
categorical [,kæti'gɔrikəl] *a* categorico.
category ['kætigəri] *n* categoria.
cater ['keitə] *vi* provvedere cibo; procurare divertimento.
caterer ['keitərə] *n* provveditore di cibo *etc*.
caterpillar ['kætəpilə] *n* bruco (*mech*) cingola.
catgut ['kætgʌt] *n* minugia.
cathedral [kə'θi:drəl] *n* cattedrale, duomo.
Catherine ['kæθərin] *nf pr* Caterina.
cathode ['kæθoud] *n* catodo.
catholic ['kæθəlik] *a n* cattolico.
Catholicism [kə'θɔlisizəm] *n* cattolicismo.
cattle ['kætl] *n pl* bestiame.
catty ['kæti] *a* (*fig*) sarcastico, acido.
Caucasus ['kɔ:kəsəs] *n* Caucaso; **Caucasian** *a n* caucasico.
cauldron ['kɔ:ldrən] *n* caldaia.
cauliflower ['kɔliflauə] *n* cavolfiore.
cause [kɔ:z] *n* causa, motivo, ragione; *vt* causare, produrre.
causeway ['kɔ:zwei] *n* strada rialzata.
caustic ['kɔ:stik] *a n* caustico.
causticity [kɔ:s'tisiti] *n* causticità.
cauterize ['kɔ:təraiz] *vt* cauterizzare.
caution ['kɔ:ʃən] *n* prudenza, cautela; avvertimento; cauzione; *vt* mettere in guardia.
cautious ['kɔ:ʃəs] *a* cauto, prudente.
cautiously ['kɔ:ʃəsli] *ad* cautamente, con prudenza.
cautiousness ['kɔ:ʃəsnis] *n* cautela.
cavalcade [,kævəl'keid] *n* cavalcata.
cavalier [,kævə'liə] *a* brusco, scortese; *n* cavaliere.
cavalry ['kævəlri] *n* cavalleria.
cave [keiv] *n* cava, caverna; **to cave in** cedere schiacciare.
cavern ['kævən] *n* caverna, grotta.
cavernous ['kævənəs] *a* cavernoso.
caviar(e) ['kævia:] *n* caviale.
cavil ['kævil] *n* cavillo; *vi* cavillare.
cavity ['kæviti] *n* cavità.
caw [kɔ:] *n* gracchiamento; *vi* gracchiare.
Cayenne [kei'en] *n* Caienna; **c. (pepper)** pepe di Caienna.
cease [si:s] *vti* cessare, fermarsi, finire.
ceaseless ['si:slis] *a* continuo, incessante.
ceaselessly ['si:slisli] *ad* incessantemente, di continuo.

Cecil [sesl] *nm pr* Cecilio.
Cecilia [sə'si:liə] **Cecily** ['sesili] *nf pr* Cecilia.
cedar ['si:də] *n* cedro.
ceiling ['si:liŋ] *n* soffitto.
celebrate ['selibreit] *vti* celebrare.
celebrated ['selibreitid] *a* celebre, famoso.
celebration [,seli'breiʃən] *n* celebrazione.
celebrity [si'lebriti] *n* celebrità.
celerity [si'leriti] *n* celerità, rapidità.
celery ['seləri] *n* sedano.
celestial [si'lestiəl] *a* celeste; celestiale.
celibacy ['selibəsi] *n* celibato.
celibate ['selibit] *a n* celibe.
cell [sel] *n* cella; (*anat*) cellula; (*el*) pila; **fuel c.** pila a combustibile.
cellar ['selə] *n* cantina.
cellarer ['selərə] *n* cantiniere.
cellist ['tʃelist] *n* violoncellista.
cello ['tʃelou] *n* violoncello.
cellophane ['seləfein] *n* cellofane.
cellular ['seljulə] *a* cellulare.
celluloid ['seljulɔid] *a n* (di) celluloide.
cellulose ['seljulous] *a* celluloso; *n* cellulosa.
Celtic ['keltik] *a* celtico.
cement [si'ment] *n* cemento; *vt* cementare.
cemetery ['semitri] *n* cimitero.
censer ['sensə] *n* incensiere, turibolo.
censor ['sensə] *n* censore; *vt* censurare; **censorship** censura, censorato.
censorious [sen'sɔ:riəs] *a* ipercritico.
censurable ['senʃərəbl] *a* censurabile.
censure ['senʃə] *n* censura, giudizio avverso; *vt* censurare, criticare.
census ['sensəs] *n* censimento, censo.
cent [sent] *n* centesimo di dollaro; (*fam*) soldo.
centaur ['sentɔ:] *n* centauro.
centenarian [,senti'nɛəriən] *a n* (*persona*) centenario.
centenary [sen'ti:nəri] *a n* centenario.
centennial [sen'teniəl] *a* centennale.
center ['sentə] *n* centro; *vti* concentrar(si); (*sport*) centrare.
centigrade ['sentigreid] *a* centigrado.
centimeter ['senti'mi:tə] *n* centimetro (*0.393 inches*).
centipede ['sentipi:d] *n* millepiedi.
central ['sentrəl] *a* centrale.
centralization [,sentrəlai'zeiʃən] *n* accentramento.
centralize ['sentrəlaiz] *vt* accentrare.
centrifugal [sen'trifjugəl] *a* centrifugo.
centuple ['sentjupl] *a n* centuplo.
century ['sentʃuri] *n* secolo.
ceramics [si'ræmiks] *n* ceramica.
cereal ['siəriəl] *a n* cereale.
cerebral ['seribrəl] *a* cerebrale.
ceremonial [,seri'mouniəl] *a* da cerimonia; *n* cerimoniale, etichetta.
ceremonious [,seri'mouniəs] *a* cerimonioso.
ceremony ['seriməni] *n* cerimonia; **to stand on c.** fare complimenti.
certain ['sə:tn] *a* certo, sicuro; **for c.** sicuramente; **to make c.** assicurarsi.
certainly ['sə:tnli] *ad* certamente, sicuramente.
certainty ['sə:tnti] *n* certezza, sicurezza.
certifiable ['sə:tifaiəbl] *a* attestabile; che dovrebbe essere attestato pazzo.
certificate [sə'tifikit] *n* certificato.
certification [,sə:tifi'keiʃən] *n* certificazione.
certify ['sə:tifai] *vt* attestare, certificare; (*leg*) autenticare, legalizzare.
certitude ['sə:titju:d] *n* certezza.
cervical ['sə:vikəl] *a* (*anat*) cervicale.
cessation [se'seiʃən] *n* cessazione.
cession ['seʃən] *n* cessione.
cesspit ['sespit] **cesspool** ['sespu:l] *n* pozzo nero.
cetacean [si'teiʃjən] *n* cetaceo.
Ceylonese [si'lɔni:z] *a n* cingalese.
chafe [tʃeif] *n* irritazione; *vti* irritar(si) (la pelle); frizionare; (*fig*) irritare, irritarsi.
chaff [tʃa:f] *n* pula; paglia; (*fam*) burla.
chaffer ['tʃæfə] *vi* comprare lesinando sul prezzo.
chaffinch ['tʃæfintʃ] *n* fringuello.
chagrin ['ʃægrin] *n* cruccio, dispetto.
chain [tʃein] *n* catena; *vt* incatenare.
chair [tʃeə] *n* sedia; seggio; cattedra; **chairlift** seggiovia; **to take the c.** assumere la presidenza.
chairman ['tʃɛəmən] *n* presidente, presidentessa.
chairmanship ['tʃɛəmənʃip] *n* presidenza.
chalice ['tʃælis] *n* calice.
chalk [tʃɔ:k] *n* gesso; (*min*) calcare; **by a long c.** di gran lunga.
chalky ['tʃɔ:ki] *a* gessoso; calcareo; pallido, terreo.
challenge ['tʃælindʒ] *n* sfida; *vt* sfidare; obbiettare; provocare.
chamber ['tʃeimbə] *n* aula, sala; (*tec*) camera; **Chamber** Camera; **c. music** musica da camera.
chamberlain ['tʃeimbəlin] *n* ciambellano.
chambermaid ['tʃeimbəmeid] *n* cameriera d'albergo.
chameleon [kə'mi:liən] *n* camaleonte.
chamois ['ʃæmwa:] *n* camoscio.
champagne [ʃæm'pein] *n* sciampagna.
champion ['tʃæmpiən] *n* campione; *vt* sostenere (una causa); **championship** campionato.
chance [tʃa:ns] *a* fortuito, casuale; *n* caso, sorte, fortuna; occasione; **by c.** per caso; *vti* accadere; (*fam*) arrischiare.
chancel ['tʃa:nsəl] *n* presbiterio, coro.
chancellor ['tʃa:nsələ] *n* cancelliere.

chancery ['tʃɑ:nsəri] *n* cancelleria.
chancy ['tʃɑ:nsi] *a* incerto, rischioso.
chandelier [.ʃændi'liə] *n* lampadario.
chandler ['tʃɑ:ndlə] *n* droghiere, fornitore.
change [tʃeindʒ] *n* cambio, mutamento; danaro spicciolo; resto; *vti* cambiar(si).
changeable ['tʃeindʒəbl] *a* mutabile, incostante.
changeableness ['tʃeindʒəblnis] *n* inconstanza.
changeless ['tʃeindʒlis] *a* costante, immutabile.
changeling ['tʃeindʒliŋ] *n* (*poet*) bimbo sostituito.
changing ['tʃeindʒiŋ] *a* cangiante, mutevole; *n* cambio.
channel ['tʃænl] *n* canale, stretto; **the (English) C.** la Manica; (*fig*) via; *vt* incanalare, (*arch*) scanalare.
chant [tʃɑ:nt] *n* canto, recitativo monotono.
chaos ['keiɔs] *n* caos.
chaotic [kei'ɔtik] *a* caotico.
chap [tʃæp] *n* screpolatura; (*fam*) ragazzo, individuo; *vti* screpolar(si).
chapel ['tʃæpəl] *n* cappella.
chaperon ['ʃæpəroun] *n* 'chaperon', accompagnatrice di signorine; *vt* scortare.
chaplain ['tʃæplin] *n* cappellano.
chaplaincy ['tʃæplinsi] *n* carica di cappellano.
chaplet ['tʃæplit] *n* corona, ghirlanda.
chapter ['tʃæptə] *n* capitolo.
char [tʃɑ:] *vti* carbonizzar(si).
char(woman) ['tʃɑ:(wumən)] *n* domestica a ore.
character ['kæriktə] *n* carattere, caratteristica; scrittura; attestato di servizio; individuo eccentrico; personaggio.
characteristic [.kæriktə'ristik] *a* caratteristico; *n* caratteristica.
characterize ['kæriktəraiz] *vt* caratterizzare; definire.
charade [ʃə'rɑ:d] *n* sciarada.
charcoal ['tʃɑ:koul] *n* carbone di legna; (*drawing*) carboncino.
charge [tʃɑ:dʒ] *n* prezzo, spesa; carica; incarico, cura; accusa; attacco; *vti* far pagare; incaricare; accusare; caricare di; attaccare.
chargeable ['tʃɑ:dʒəbl] *a* a carico di, addebitabile.
charger ['tʃɑ:dʒə] *n* destriero; (*of gun*) caricatore; accumulatore elettrico.
chariot ['tʃæriət] *n* cocchio.
charitable ['tʃæritəbl] *a* caritatevole.
charitableness ['tʃæritəblnis] *n* filantropia.
charity ['tʃæriti] *n* carità, beneficenza.
charlatan ['ʃɑ:lətən] *n* ciarlatano.
Charles [tʃɑ:lz] *nm pr* Carlo.
Charlotte ['ʃɑ:lət] *nf pr* Carlotta.
charm [tʃɑ:m] *n* attrattiva, fascino; incantesimo; amuleto, ciondolo; *vt* affascinare, incantare.
charmer ['tʃɑ:mə] *n* incantatore, incantatrice.
charming ['tʃɑ:miŋ] *a* incantevole.
chart [tʃɑ:t] *n* carta nautica, quadro statistico; *vt* fare la carta di.
charter ['tʃɑ:tə] *n* carta, documento; *vt* concedere statuto; noleggiare.
chary ['tʃεəri] *a* cauto, prudente, parco di.
chase [tʃeis] *n* caccia, inseguimento; *vt* cacciare, inseguire; cesellare.
chasing ['tʃeisiŋ] *n* cesellatura.
chasm ['kæzəm] *n* abisso, baratro.
chassis ['ʃæsi:] *n inv* chassis, telaio, intelaiatura.
chaste [tʃeist] *a* casto, puro.
chastise [tʃæs'taiz] *vt* castigare.
chastisement ['tʃæstizmənt] *n* castigo, punizione.
chastity ['tʃæstiti] *n* castità, purezza.
chat [tʃæt] *n* chiacchierata; *vi* chiacchierare.
chattels ['tʃætls] *n pl* beni mobili pl.
chatter ['tʃætə] *vi* chiacchierare; (*teeth*) battere.
chatterbox ['tʃætəbɔks] *n* chiacchierone, chiacchierona.
chatty ['tʃæti] *a* ciarliero, chiacchierone.
chauffeur ['ʃoufə] *n* autista.
cheap [tʃi:p] *a* a buon mercato; **cheaply** *ad* a buon mercato.
cheapen ['tʃi:pən] *vt* diminuire il prezzo; screditare, sottovalutare.
cheapness ['tʃi:pnis] *n* basso prezzo, buon mercato.
cheat [tʃi:t] *n* inganno; ingannatore, imbroglione; *vti* ingannare, truffare.
cheating ['tʃi:tiŋ] *n* inganno, truffa.
check [tʃek] *n* scacco; arresto; freno; controllo; quadretto su stoffa o carta; scontrino; conto; assegno bancario; **check room** deposito bagagli; *vt* controllare; far arrestare, fermare; (*chess*) dare scacco.
checkers ['tʃekəz] *n* giuoco della dama.
checkmate ['tʃek'meit] *n* scacco matto; *vt* dare scacco matto a.
checkpoint ['tʃekpɔint] *n* posto di controllo.
cheek [tʃi:k] *n* guancia, gota; sfrontatezza.
cheer [tʃiə] *n* disposizione d'animo, buon umore; applauso; vivande *pl*; *vti* applaudire; incoraggiare rallegrare.
cheerful ['tʃiəful] *a* allegro, di buon umore.
cheerfully ['tʃiəfuli] *ad* allegramente.
cheerfulness ['tʃiəfulnis] *n* allegria, buon umore.
cheering ['tʃiəriŋ] *a* incoraggiante; *n* acclamazioni.
cheerio ['tʃiəri'ou] *interj* (*fam*) ciao, arrivederci!
cheerless ['tʃiəlis] *a* triste.
cheery ['tʃiəri] *a* allegro.

cheese [tʃi:z] *n* formaggio.
chemical ['kemikəl] *a* chimico.
chemicals ['kemikəlz] *n pl* prodotti chimici.
chemist ['kemist] *n* chimico; farmacista.
chemistry ['kemistri] *n* chimica.
chenille [ʃə'ni:l] *n* ciniglia.
cherish ['tʃeriʃ] *vt* nutrire; curare con affetto, tener caro.
cherry ['tʃeri] *n* ciliegia; **c.-tree** ciliegio.
cherub ['tʃerəb] *n* cherubino.
chess [tʃes] *n* (gioco degli) scacchi.
chessboard ['tʃesbɔ:d] *n* scacchiera.
chessman ['tʃesmæn] *n* scacco.
chest [tʃest] *n* petto, torace; cassa, cassetta; **c. of drawers** cassettone.
chestnut ['tʃesnʌt] *n* castagna; **c.-tree** castagno; **horse c.** ippocastano.
chew [tʃu:] *vt* masticare; **to c. the cud** ruminare; **to c. over** meditare.
chick [tʃik] *n* pulcino.
chicken ['tʃikin] *n* pollastro, pollo.
chicken-pox ['tʃikinpɔks] *n* varicella.
chicory ['tʃikəri] *n* cicoria.
chide [tʃaid] *vt* sgridare, biasimare.
chief [tʃi:f] *a* principale, il più importante; *n* capo.
chiefly ['tʃi:fli] *ad* sopratutto, principalmente.
chieftain ['tʃi:ftən] *n* (*di tribù, clan*) capo.
chilblain ['tʃilblein] *n* gelone.
child [tʃaild] *pl* **children** ['tʃildrən] *n* bambino, figlio; **c.-bearing** gravidanza.
childbirth ['tʃaildbə:θ] *n* parto.
childhood ['tʃaildhud] *n* infanzia.
childish ['tʃaildiʃ] *a* infantile, puerile.
childless ['tʃaildlis] *a* senza figli.
childlike ['tʃaildlaik] *a* infantile, da bambino.
Chile ['tʃili] *n* Cile.
Chilean ['tʃiliən] *a n* cileno.
chili ['tʃili] *n* pepe di Caienna.
chill [tʃil] *a* freddo; *n* colpo di freddo; sensazione di freddo; *vt* raffreddare.
chilly ['tʃili] *a* freddoloso, piuttosto freddo.
chime [tʃaim] *n* scampanio armonioso; *vti* battere, scampanare.
chimney ['tʃimni] *n* camino, fumaiuolo; **c.-corner** angolo del focolare.
chimneysweep ['tʃimniswi:p] *n* spazzacamino.
chimpanzee [ˌtʃimpən'zi:] *n* (*zool*) scimpanzè.
chin [tʃin] *n* mento.
China ['tʃainə] *n* Cina.
china ['tʃainə] *n* porcellana.
Chinese ['tʃai'ni:z] *a n* cinese.
chink [tʃiŋk] *n* crepa, fessura.
chintz [tʃints] *n* cotone stampato.
chip [tʃip] *n* frammento, scheggia, truciolo; patata fritta; *vt* scheggiare, tagliare a piccoli pezzi.
chipboard ['tʃipbɔ:d] *n* legno ricostituito.
chipmunk ['tʃipmʌŋk] *n* (*zool*) tamia orientale.
chiropodist [ki'rɔpədist] *n* pedicure, callista.
chirp [tʃə:p] *n* cinguettio; *vi* cinguettare.
chisel ['tʃizl] *n* cesello, scalpello; *vi* cesellare.
chivalrous ['ʃivəlrəs] *a* cavalleresco.
chivalry ['ʃivəlri] *n* (*fig*) cavalleria.
chive [tʃaiv] *n* aglio di serpe.
chloride ['klɔ:raid] *n* cloruro.
chlorine ['klɔ:ri:n] *n* cloro.
chloroform ['klɔrəfɔ:m] *n* cloroformio; *vt* cloroformizzare.
chlorophyl(l) ['klɔrəfil] *n* (*bot*) clorofilla.
chocolate ['tʃɔkəlit] *n* cioccolata; cioccolato, cioccolatino.
choice [tʃɔis] *a* prelibato, scelto, squisito; *n* scelta.
choir ['kwaiə] *n* coro; **choirmaster** maestro di cappella.
choke [tʃouk] *n* soffocazione; strozzameeto; (*mech*) regolatore; *vti* soffocare, soffocarsi; ingombrare.
cholera ['kɔlərə] *n* colera.
choleric ['kɔlərik] *a* collerico, irascibile.
choose [tʃu:z] *vti* scegliere.
choos(e)y ['tʃu:zi] *a* (*fam*) schizzinoso, pignolo.
chop [tʃɔp] *n* colpo d'ascia; costoletta di maiale o di montone; *vt* tagliare, tagliuzzare.
chopper ['tʃɔpə] *n* corta ascia, mannaia.
choppy ['tʃɔpi] *a* increspato, mosso.
choral ['kɔ:rəl] *a n* corale.
chord [kɔ:d] *n* (*mus*) corda, (*mus*) accordo.
choreographer [ˌkɔri'ɔgræfə] *n* coreografo.
choreography [ˌkɔri'ɔgrəfi] *n* coreografia.
chorister ['kɔristə] *n* corista.
chorus ['kɔ:rəs] *n* coro; ritornello.
Christ [kraist] *nm pr* Cristo.
christen ['krisn] *vt* battezzare.
Christendom ['krisndəm] *n* cristianità.
christening ['krisniŋ] *n* battesimo.
Christian ['kristjən] *a n* cristiano; **C. name** nome proprio; nome di battesimo.
Christianity ['kristi'æniti] *n* cristianesimo.
christianize ['kristjənaiz] *vt* convertire al cristianesimo.
Christina [kris'ti:nə] **Christine** ['kristi:n] *nf pr* Cristina.
Christmas ['krisməs] *n* Natale; **C. gift** [gift] strenna natalizia.
Christopher ['kristəfə] *nm pr* Cristoforo.
chromatic [krə'mætik] *a* cromatico.
chrome [kroum] *n* cromo; *vt* cromare.

chromium ['kroumiəm] *n* (*chem*) cromo.
chromosome ['kroumәsoum] *n* cromosoma.
chronic ['krɔnik] *a* cronico; (*sl*) terribile.
chronicle ['krɔnikl] *n* cronaca.
chronicler ['krɔniklə] *n* cronista.
chronological [,krɔnə'lɔdʒikəl] *a* cronologico.
chronology [krə'nɔlədʒi] *n* cronologia.
chronometer [krə'nɔmitə] *n* cronometro.
chrysalis ['krisəlis] *n* crisalide.
chrysanthemum [kri'sænθəməm] *n* crisantemo.
chubby ['tʃʌbi] *a* paffuto, pienotto.
chuck [tʃʌk] *vt* dare un buffetto a; (*fam*) gettare; (*fam*) sperperare; **c. out** (*fam*) mettere alla porta; **chucker-out** chi getta fuori da un locale gli intrusi.
chuckle ['tʃʌkl] *n* riso soffocato; *vi* ridere sotto i baffi.
chum [tʃʌm] *n* (*fam*) amico intimo, compagno; *vi* (*fam*) essere amici.
chunk [tʃʌŋk] *n* grosso pezzo, tozzo.
church [tʃə:tʃ] *n* chiesa.
churchman ['tʃə:tʃmən] *n* ecclesiastico.
churchyard ['tʃə:tʃ'ja:d] *n* camposanto.
churl [tʃə:l] *n* zotico, uomo sgarbato o tirchio.
churlish ['tʃə:liʃ] *a* rozzo, sgarbato, tirchio.
churlishness ['tʃə:liʃnis] *n* sgarbatezza, tirchieria.
churn [tʃə:n] *n* zangola; *vti* battere il latte dentro la zangola per farne burro; agitar(si).
chute [ʃu:t] *n* canale di scolo.
ciborium [si'bɔ:riəm] *n* ciborio.
cicada [si'ka:də] *n* cicala.
cicatrize ['sikətraiz] *vti* cicatrizzar(si).
cider ['saidə] *n* sidro.
cigar [si'ga:] *n* sigaro; **c. store** tabaccheria.
cigarette [,sigə'ret] *n* sigaretta; **c. case** portasigarette.
cinder ['sində] *n* brace, cenere.
Cinderella [,sində'relə] *n* Cenerentola.
cine-camera [sini'kæmərə] *n* macchina da presa, cinepresa.
cinema ['sinimə] *n* cinema(tografo).
cinematographic [,sini,mætə'græfik] *a* cinematografico.
cinematography [,sinimə'tɔgrəfi] *n* cinematografia.
cinnamon ['sinəmən] *n* cannella, cinnamomo.
cipher ['saifə] *n* zero; nulla, nullità; cifrario, cifra.
circle ['sə:kl] *n* cerchio, circolo; orbita; (*theat*) galleria; *vti* circondare, girare intorno a.
circuit ['sə:kit] *n* circuito; giro; circoscrizione.
circuitous [sə'kju:itəs] *a* tortuoso, indiretto.
circular ['sə:kjulə] *a n* circolare.
circularize ['sə:kjuləraiz] *vt* inviare circolari a.
circulate ['sə:kjuleit] *vti* (far) circolare.
circulation [,sə:kju'leiʃən] *n* circolazione.
circulatory ['sə:kju:lətəri] *n* circolatorio.
circumcise ['sə:kəmsaiz] *vt* circoncidere.
circumcision [,sə:kəm'siʒən] *n* circoncisione.
circumference [sə'kʌmfərəns] *n* circonferenza.
circumflex ['sə:kəmfleks] *a* circonflesso.
circumlocution [,sə:kəmlə'kju:ʃən] *n* circonlocuzione, perifrasi.
circumscribe ['sə:kəmskraib] *vt* circoscrivere.
circumspect ['sə:kəmspekt] *a* circospetto, cauto.
circumspection [,sə:kəm'spekʃən] *n* circospezione.
circumstance ['sə:kəmstəns] *n* circostanza, condizione.
circumstantial [,sə'kəm'stænʃəl] *a* circostanziato; indiziario.
circumvent [,sə:kəm'vent] *vt* ingannare, circuire.
circumvention [,sə:kəm'ventʃən] *n* circonvenzione, raggiro.
circus ['sə:kəs] *n* circo.
Cistercian [sis'tə:ʃjən] *a n* cistercense.
cistern ['sistən] *n* cisterna, serbatoio.
citadel ['sitədl] *n* cittadella, fortezza.
cite [sait] *vt* citare.
citizen ['sitizn] *n* cittadino; **citizenship** *n* cittadinanza.
citrate ['sitrit] *n* (*chem*) citrato.
citric ['sitrik] *a* citrico.
citron ['sitrən] *n* cedro.
city ['siti] *n* città, centro d'una grande città.
civet ['sivit] *n* zibetto.
civic ['sivik] *a* civico.
civil ['sivl] *a* civile, educato, gentile.
civilian [si'viljən] *n* civile, borghese.
civility [si'viliti] *n* cortesia, educazione.
civilization [,sivilai'zeiʃən] *n* civilizzazione, civiltà.
civilize ['sivilaiz] *vt* incivilire, civilizzare.
claim [kleim] *n* diritto, pretesa; reclamo, rivendicazione; concessione mineraria; *vt* pretendere; reclamare, rivendicare; asserire.
claimant ['kleimənt] *n* pretendente.
clairvoyance [klɛə'vɔiəns] *n* chiaroveggenza.
clairvoyant [klɛə'vɔiənt] *a n* chiaroveggente.

clam [klæm] *n* mollusco bivalve; (*mech*) grappa, morsa.
clamant ['kleimənt] *a* insistente, rumoroso.
clamber ['klæmbə] *vi* arrampicarsi.
clamminess ['klæminis] *n* viscosità.
clammy ['klæmi] *a* freddo umido; viscoso.
clamor ['klæmə] *vi* chiedere clamorosamente, fare molto rumore.
clamorous ['klæmərəs] *a* clamoroso.
clamp [klæmp] *n* pinza, morsa; *vt* tener fermo, assicurare.
clan [klæn] *n* tribù, 'clan'.
clandestine [klæn'destin] *a* clandestino.
clang [klæŋ] **clangor** ['klæŋgə] *n* fragore.
clang [klæŋ] *vti* far risuonare con fragore.
clank [klæŋk] *n* suono metallico, clangore; *vi* produrre un rumore secco, metallico.
clap [klæp] *n* battimano; colpo; *vti* battere le mani, applaudire.
clapper ['klæpə] *n* applauditore; battente, battaglio.
Clara ['klɛərə] **Clare** [klɛə] *n f pr* Clara, Chiara.
claret ['klærət] *n* bordò.
clarification [,klærifi'keiʃən] *n* chiarificazione.
clarify ['klærifai] *vt* chiarire; raffinare.
clarinet [,klæri'net] *n* (*mus*) clarinetto.
clarity ['klæriti] *n* chiarezza.
clash [klæʃ] *n* collisione, scontro; conflitto; rumore, strepito; *vti* urtar(si), fare strepito.
clashing ['klæʃiŋ] *a* opposto, contrastante.
clasp [klɑ:sp] *n* fermaglio, gancio; stretta di mano, abbraccio; *vt* agganciare; stringere, abbracciare.
class [klɑ:s] *n* classe; *vt* classificare.
classic ['klæsik] *a n* classico.
classical ['klæsikəl] *a* classico.
classicism ['klæsisizəm] *n* classicismo.
classification [,klæsifi'keiʃən] *n* classifica, classificazione.
classify ['klæsifai] *vt* classificare.
clatter ['klætə] *n* acciottolio, fracasso; *vti* far fracasso.
Claud(e) [klɔ:d] *nm pr* Claudio.
clause [klɔ:z] *n* clausola.
claustrophobia [,klɔ:strə'foubiə] *n* claustrofobia.
claw [klɔ:] *n* artiglio; *vti* artigliare.
clay [klei] *n* argilla, creta.
clean [kli:n] *a* pulito, netto; innocente, puro; completo; *vt* pulire.
cleaning ['kli:niŋ] *n* pulitura, pulizia; **dry-c.** lavaggio a secco; **spring c.** pulizia di Pasqua.
cleanliness ['klenlinis] *n* pulizia.
cleanly ['klenli] *a* pulito; ['kli:nli] *ad* in modo pulito.
cleanness ['kli:nnis] *n* pulizia, chiarezza, purezza.
cleanse [klenz] *vt* purificare; pulire.
cleansing ['klenziŋ] *a* purificante; *n* purificazione; detersione; **c. cream** crema detergente.
clear [kliə] *a* chiaro, evidente; libero da ostacoli; *vti* chiarire, chiarificare, schiarir(si); sdoganare.
clearance ['kliərəns] *n* liquidazione; sdoganamento.
clearing ['kliəriŋ] *n* tratto di terreno disboscato per la coltivazione; **c. house** (*com*) stanza di compensazione.
clearly ['kliəli] *ad* chiaramente, distintamente.
clearness ['kliənis] *n* chiarezza.
cleavage ['kli:vidʒ] *n* sfaldamento.
cleaver ['kli:və] *n* mannaia del macellaio.
clef [klef] *n* (*mus*) chiave.
cleft [kleft] *n* spaccatura, fessura.
clemency ['klemənsi] *n* clemenza.
clement ['klemənt] *a* clemente, mite.
clench [klentʃ] *vt* stringere; (*tec*) ribadire; (*fig*) definire.
clergy ['klə:dʒi] *n* clero.
clergyman ['klə:dʒimən] *n* pastore evangelico, ecclesiastico.
cleric ['klerik] *n* ecclesiastico.
clerical ['klerikəl] *a* clericale; di impiegato; **c. work** lavoro d'ufficio.
clerk [klə:k] *n* impiegato d'ufficio; commesso.
clever ['klevə] *a* intelligente, abile, ingegnoso.
cleverness ['klevənis] *n* intelligenza, abilità, ingegnosità.
click [klik] *n* suono metallico; scatto.
client ['klaiənt] *n* cliente.
clientele [,kli:ɑ̃:n'teil] *n* clientela.
cliff [klif] *n* rupe a picco, scarpata.
climate ['klaimit] *n* clima.
climatic [klai'mætik] *a* climatico.
climax ['klaimæks] *n* culmine, punto culminante.
climb [klaim] *vti* arrampicarsi, scalare; *n* salita; scalata.
climber ['klaimə] *n* scalatore, (*bot*) pianta rampicante; (*fig*) arrivista.
clinch [klintʃ] *v* **clench.**
cling [kliŋ] *vi* avviticchiarsi, aggrapparsi.
clinic ['klinik] *n* clinica.
clinical ['klinikəl] *a* clinico.
clink [kliŋk] *n* tintinnio; (*sl*) prigione; *vti* (far) tintinnare.
clip [klip] *n* fermaglio, gancio; taglio, tosatura; ritaglio; *vt* tagliare, tosare.
clipper ['klipə] *n* goletta; forbici per tosare.
clipping ['klipiŋ] *n* taglio, tosatura; ritaglio di un giornale.
clique [kli:k] *n* cricca.
cloak [klouk] *n* mantello; (*fig*) pretesto; *vt* (*fig*) mascherare.
clock [klɔk] *n* orologio (da muro), pendola; *vti* cronometrare.

clockwork ['klɔkwə:k] *n* meccanismo d'orologio.
clod [klɔd] *n* zolla di terra.
clog [klɔg] *n* zoccolo; intoppo; *vt* ingombrare, ostruire.
cloister ['klɔistə] *n* chiostro, convento.
close [klous] *a* chiuso, rinchiuso; afoso; fitto, stretto; vicino; *ad* (da) vicino; *prep* vicino a; *n* recinto.
close [klouz] *n* conclusione, fine; *vt* chiudere, concludere, finire; **closed-circuit television** *n* televisione a circuito chiuso.
closely ['klousli] *ad* strettamente; attentamente.
closeness ['klousnis] *n* prossimità, vicinanza; pesantezza dell'aria.
closet ['klɔzit] *n* gabinetto, salotto privato, studio; armadio a muro.
closing ['klouziŋ] *a* di chiusura, ultimo; *n* chiusura.
closure ['klouʒə] *n* chiusura, fine.
clot [klɔt] *n* coagulo, grumo; *vi* coagularsi, raggrumarsi.
cloth [klɔθ] *n* stoffa, tela, tessuto; tovaglia.
clothe [klouð] *vt* (ri)vestire.
clothes [klouðz] *n pl* indumenti, vestiti *pl*; **clothespeg, clothespin** molletta ferma-bucato.
clothier ['klouðiə] *n* commerciante in vestiti e stoffe.
clothing ['klouðiŋ] *n* vestiario, indumenti.
cloud [klaud] *n* nube, nuvola; *vi* rannuvolarsi; *vt* annuvolare, oscurare.
cloudless ['klaudlis] *a* senza nubi, sereno.
cloudy ['klaudi] *a* nuvoloso, oscuro.
clove [klouv] *n* chiodo di garofano.
clover ['klouvə] *n* trifoglio.
clown [klaun] *n* buffone, pagliaccio.
clownish ['klauniʃ] *a* pagliaccesco; rustico.
cloy [klɔi] *vt* saziare, nauseare.
club [klʌb] *n* bastone, randello; circolo; (*cards*) fiori; *vt* bastonare; **to c. together** pagare il proprio tributo.
cluck [klʌk] *vi* chiocciare.
clue [klu:] *n* bandolo, indizio.
clump [klʌmp] *n* gruppo d'alberi o di cespugli; *vi* camminare pesantemente.
clumsiness ['klʌmzinis] *n* goffaggine, mancanza di tatto.
clumsy ['klʌmzi] *a* goffo, senza tatto.
cluster ['klʌstə] *n* grappolo, gruppo, sciame; *vi* crescere in grappoli; raccogliersi in gruppo.
clutch [klʌtʃ] *n* presa fortissima, stretta; (*mech*) innesto; *vti* afferrare, agguantare; **clutches** *pl* artigli, grinfie *pl*.
clutter ['klʌtə] *n* confusione, massa confusa; *vti* far confusione, ingombrare.
coach [koutʃ] *n* carrozza, (*rly*) carrozza, vagone, vettura; pullman; insegnante privato, ripetitore; allenatore di atleti; *vt* allenare; dare ripetizioni a; **baby c.** carrozzina per bambini.
coagulate [kou'ægjuleit] *vti* coagulare, coagularsi.
coagulation [kou,ægju'leiʃən] *n* coagulazione.
coal [koul] *n* carbone; **c. field** bacino carbonifero.
coalesce [,kouə'les] *vi* fondersi, unirsi.
coalition [,kouə'liʃən] *n* coalizione.
coal-mine ['koulmain] *n* miniera di carbone.
coarse [kɔ:s] *a* ruvido, rozzo, grossolano, volgare.
coarseness ['kɔ:snis] *n* ruvidezza, grossolanità.
coast [koust] *n* costa; *vt* costeggiare.
coastal ['koustl] *a* costiero.
coastguard ['koustgɑ:d] *n* guardiacoste.
coat [kout] *n* giacca; mantello; paltò; mano (di vernice); *vt* rivestire; verniciare; **c.-of-arms** stemma.
coating ['koutiŋ] *n* rivestimento, strato.
coax [kouks] *vt* persuadere con le moine, blandire.
cob [kɔb] *n* cavallo da tiro; cigno maschio; pannocchia di frumentone.
cobalt ['koubɔ:lt] *n* cobalto.
cobble ['kɔbl] *n* ciottolo; *vt* selciare con ciottoli; rattoppare.
cobbler ['kɔblə] *n* ciabattino.
cobra ['koubrə] *n* (*zool*) cobra.
cobweb ['kɔbweb] *n* ragnatela.
cocaine [kə'kein] *n* cocaina.
cochineal ['kɔtʃini:l] *n* cocciniglia.
cock [kɔk] *n* gallo, maschio di uccelli; rubinetto, spina; mucchio di fieno; cane di fucile; *vti* drizzar(si); ammucchiare fieno; **c.-eyed** strabico.
cockade [kɔ'keid] *n* coccarda.
cockchafer ['kɔk,tʃeifə] *n* maggiolino.
cockerel ['kɔkərəl] *n* galletto.
cockle ['kɔkl] *n* (*zool*) cardio; (*bot*) loglio; **c.-shell** conchiglia.
cockney ['kɔkni] *a n* londinese (spesso con senso spregiativo).
cockpit ['kɔkpit] *n* arena da combattimento; (*av*) carlinga.
cockroach ['kɔkroutʃ] *n* scarafaggio.
cockscomb ['kɔkskoum] *n* cresta di gallo; (*bot*) amaranto.
cocksure ['kɔk'ʃuə] *a* presuntuoso.
cocktail ['kɔkteil] *n* 'cocktail'; **c. cabinet** mobile bar.
cocky ['kɔki] *a* impertinente, presuntuoso.
cocoa ['koukou] *n* cacao.
coconut ['koukənʌt] *n* noce di cocco.
cocoon [kə'ku:n] *n* bozzolo.
cod [kɔd] *n* (*inv*) merluzzo.

coddle ['kɔdl] *vt* vezzeggiare, coccolare.
code [koud] *n* codice, cifrario.
codeine ['koudi:n] *n* codeina.
codex ['koudeks] *pl* **codices** *n* codice.
codicil ['kɔdisil] *n* codicillo.
codification [,kɔdifi'keiʃən] *n* codificazione.
codify ['kɔdifai] *vt* codificare.
coeducation ['kou,edju:'keiʃən] *n* istruzione in scuola mista.
coefficient [,koui'fiʃənt] *n* coefficiente.
coerce [kou'ə:s] *vt* costringere.
coercion [kou'ə:ʃən] *n* coercizione.
coercive [kou'ə:siv] *a* coercitivo.
coexistence ['kouig'zistəns] *n* coesistenza.
coffee ['kɔfi] *n* caffè; **c. mill** macinino da caffè; **c. pot** caffettiera; **ground c.** caffè tostato; **white c.** caffellatte.
coffer ['kɔfə] *n* cofano, scrigno.
coffin ['kɔfin] *n* cassa da morto, bara.
cog [kɔg] *n* dente d'una ruota; *vt* dentare una ruota.
cogency ['koudʒənsi] *n* forza di persuasione.
cogent ['koudʒənt] *a* convincente, persuasivo.
cogitate ['kɔdʒiteit] *vti* cogitare, ponderare.
cogitation [,kɔdʒi'teiʃən] *n* cogitazione.
cognate ['kɔgneit] *a n* congiunto, parente.
cognizance ['kɔgnizəns] *n* conoscenza, percezione.
cohabit [kou'hæbit] *vi* coabitare.
cohabitation [,kouhæbi'teiʃən] *n* coabitazione.
co-heir ['kou'ɛə] (*m*) **co-heiress** ['kou'ɛəris] (*f*) *n* coerede.
cohere [kou'hiə] *vi* aderire; essere coerente.
coherence [kou'hiərəns] *n* coerenza.
coherent [kou'hiərənt] *a* coerente.
cohesion [kou'hi:ʒən] *n* coesione.
cohesive [kou'hi:siv] *a* coesivo.
coiffure [kwɑ:'fjuə] *n* pettinatura, acconciatura.
coil [kɔil] *n* rotolo, gomitolo; (*snake*) spira; (*el*) bobina; *vt* arrotolare, avvolgere in spire.
coin [kɔin] *n* moneta; *vt* coniare.
coinage ['kɔinidʒ] *n* conio; sistema monetario.
coincide [kouin'said] *vi* coincidere.
coincidence [,kou'insidəns] *n* coincidenza; combinazione.
coincidental [kou,insi'dentl] *a* coincidente, di coincidenza.
coke [kouk] *n* carbone coke.
colander ['kʌləndə] *n* colapasta, colatoio.
cold [kould] *a* freddo; *n* freddo; raffreddore; **to be c.** aver freddo; **to catch a c.** infreddarsi.
coldly ['kouldli] *ad* freddamente.
coldness ['kouldnis] *n* freddezza.
colic ['kɔlik] *n* colica.
collaborate [kə'læbəreit] *vi* collaborare.
collaboration [kə,læbə'reiʃən] *n* collaborazione.
collaborator [kə'læbəreitə] *n* collaboratore.
collapse [kə'læps] *n* crollo, caduta; (*med*) collasso; *vi* crollare; avere un collasso.
collar ['kɔlə] *n* colletto; (*dogs*) collare; **c. stud, c. button** bottone del colletto; *vt* afferrare, prendere per il collo.
collate [kɔ'leit] *vt* collazionare.
collateral [kɔ'lætərəl] *a n* collaterale.
collation [kɔ'leiʃən] *n* collazione.
colleague ['kɔli:g] *n* collega.
collect ['kɔlekt] *n* colletta; [kə'lekt] *vt* raccogliere, mettere insieme, radunare, fare una collezione; *vi* radunarsi; **to c. oneself** riprendersi.
collected [kɔ'lektid] *a* raccolto, riunito; padrone di sè.
collection [kə'lekʃən] *n* riunione, raccolta, colletta, collezione.
collective [kə'lektiv] *a* collettivo.
collectivity [kəlek'tiviti] *n* collettività.
collector [kə'lektə] *n* collezionista; esattore.
college ['kɔlidʒ] *n* collegio; università.
collide [kə'laid] *vi* scontrarsi.
collier ['kɔliə] *n* minatore; nave carboniera.
collision [kə'liʒən] *n* collisione, scontro.
colloquial [kə'loukwiəl] *a* usato nella conversazione familiare, d'uso corrente; **colloquialism** espressione familiare.
colloquy ['kɔləkwi] *n* colloquio.
collusion [kə'lu:ʒən] *n* collusione.
Colombia [kə'lʌmbiə] *n* (*geogr*) Colombia.
colon ['koulən] *n* due punti; **semi-c.** punto e virgola.
colonel ['kə:nl] *n* colonnello.
colonial [kə'louniəl] *a* coloniale.
colonist ['kɔlənist] *n* abitante di colonia.
colonization [,kɔlənai'zeiʃən] *n* colonizzazione.
colonize ['kɔlənaiz] *vti* colonizzare.
colonnade [,kɔlə'neid] *n* colonnato.
colony ['kɔləni] *n* colonia.
color ['kʌlə] *n* colore, colorito, tinta; apparenza; pretesto; **colors** *pl* bandiera; *vti* colorare, colorire, colorirsi, dipingere; arrossire.
colored ['kʌləd] *a* colorato, colorito, di colore; **c. person** persona di colore.
colorful ['kʌləful] *a* pieno di colore, pittoresco.
coloring ['kʌləriŋ] *n* colorante; colorito; arrossimento.
colorless ['kʌləlis] *a* incolore, pallido; insipido.

colossal [kə'lɔsl] *a* colossale.
Colosseum [,kɔlə'siəm] *n* Colosseo.
colt [koult] *n* puledro.
column ['kɔləm] *n* colonna.
columnist ['kɔləmnist] *n* giornalista, cronista.
coma ['koumə] *n* coma, torpore.
comb [koum] *n* pettine; (*crest*) cresta; favo; *vt* pettinare, strigliare; (*fig*) rastrellare, perlustrare.
combat ['kɔmbət] *n* combattimento, lotta; *vti* combattere, lottare.
combatant ['kɔmbətənt] *a n* combattente.
combination [,kɔmbi'neiʃən] *n* combinazione.
combine ['kɔmbain] *n* associazione, sindacato; [kəm'bain] *vti* combinar(si).
combined [kɔm'baind] *a* combinato, congiunto; **c. ticket** biglietto misto.
combing ['koumiŋ] *n* pettinata; (*fig*) rastrellamento, perlustramento.
combustible [kəm'bʌstəbl] *a n* combustibile.
combustion [kəm'bʌstʃən] *n* combustione.
come [kʌm] *vi* venire, arrivare, giungere; accadere; **to c. back** ritornare; **to c. in** entrare; **to c. around** passare da; riprendere i sensi.
comedian [kə'mi:diən] *n* commediante, (attore) comico.
comedown ['kʌmdaun] *n* (*fig*) crollo.
comedy ['kɔmidi] *n* commedia.
comeliness ['kʌmlinis] *n* avvenenza.
comely ['kʌmli] *a* avvenente.
comet ['kɔmit] *n* cometa.
comfort ['kʌmfət] *n* conforto, consolazione, comodità, agio; *vt* confortare, consolare.
comfortable ['kʌmfətəbl] *a* comodo, confortevole; adeguato.
comfortably ['kʌmfətəbli] *ad* comodamente, con agio.
comforter ['kʌmfətə] *n* consolatore; lunga sciarpa di lana; trapunta.
comic(al) ['kɔmik(l)] *a* comico, buffo; *n pl* giornale a fumetti.
coming ['kʌmiŋ] *a* venturo, prossimo; *n* venuta, arrivo.
comma ['kɔmə] *n* virgola.
command [kə'mɑ:nd] *n* comando, ordine; dominio; *vti* comandare, ordinare; controllare, dominare.
commandant [,kɔmən'dænt] *n* comandante.
commandeer [,kɔmən'diə] *vt* requisire.
commander [kɔ'mɑ:ndə] *n* comandante.
commanding [kɔ'mɑ:ndiŋ] *a* che comanda; maestoso, dominante.
commandment [kɔ'mɑ:ndmənt] *n* comandamento.
commemorate [kə'memәreit] *vt* commemorare.
commemoration [kə,memə'reiʃən] *n* commemorazione.
commence [kə'mens] *vti* cominciare.
commencement [kə'mensmənt] *n* principio; cerimonia per il conferimento di lauree.
commend [kə'mend] *vt* lodare; raccomandare.
commendable [kə'mendəbl] *a* lodevole.
commendation [,kɔmen'deiʃən] *n* elogio, raccomandazione.
commensurable [kə'menʃərəbl] *a* commensurabile.
commensurate [kə'menʃərit] *a* adeguato, commisurato.
comment ['kɔment] *n* commento; *vi* commentare.
commentary ['kɔməntəri] *n* commentario, commento.
commentator ['kɔmenteitə] *n* commentatore, radiocronista.
commerce ['kɔmə:s] *n* commercio.
commercial [kə'mə:ʃəl] *a* commerciale; (*tv etc*) pubblicità.
commercialize [kə'mə:ʃəlaiz] *vt* rendere commerciabile.
commiserate [kə'mizəreit] *vt* compiangere.
commiseration [kə,mizə'reiʃən] *n* commiserazione, pietà.
commissariat [,kɔmi'sɛəriət] *n* (*mil*) commissariato.
commission [kə'miʃən] *n* commissione, incarico, mandato; brevetto da ufficiale; *vt* incaricare, dare una carica a, armare, equipaggiare (una nave).
commissionaire [kə,miʃə'nɛə] *n* portiere gallonato.
commissioned [kə'miʃənd] *a* delegato; **non-c. officer** sottufficiale.
commissioner [kə'miʃənə] *n* commissario.
commit [kə'mit] *vt* affidare. consegnare, mandare in prigione, commettere **to c. oneself** impegnarsi.
commitment [kə'mitmənt] *n* impegno.
committal [kə'mitl] *n* consegna, perpretazione; il mandare in prigione.
committee [kə'miti] *n* comitato, commissione.
commode [kə'moud] *n* cassettone.
commodious [kə'moudiəs] *a* spazioso.
commodity [kə'mɔditi] *n* merce, prodotto, genere di prima necessità.
commodore ['kɔmədɔ:] *n* (*naut*) commodoro.
common ['kɔmən] *a* comune, usuale, ordinario; *n* terreno demaniale; **c. market** mercato comune; **c.-sense** buonsenso, senso comune; **c. stock** (*com*) azioni ordinarie; **in c.** in comune.
commoner ['kɔmənə] *n* borghese o popolano.
commonly ['kɔmənli] *ad* comunemente.
commonplace ['kɔmənpleis] *a* banale, trito; *n* banalità, luogo comune.
commons ['kɔmənz] *n pl* popolo;

House of C. Camera dei Comuni; (*food*) cibo, razioni *pl*; **short c.** scarse razioni *pl*.
commonwealth ['kɔmənwelθ] *n* comunità indipendente.
commotion [kə'mouʃən] *n* agitazione, trambusto.
communal ['kɔmjunl] *a* della comunità, comunale.
communicant [kə'mju:nikənt] *n* (*eccl*) comunicando; informatore.
communicate [kə'mju:nikeit] *vti* comunicar(si).
communication [kə,mju:ni'keiʃən] comunicazione.
communicative [kə'mju:nikətiv] *a* comunicativo.
communion [kə'mju:njən] *n* comunione, comunanza.
communiqué [kə'mju:nikei] *n* comunicato ufficiale.
communism ['kɔmjunizəm] *n* comunismo.
communist ['kɔmjunist] *n* comunista.
community [kə'mju:niti] *n* comunità.
commutation [,kɔmju:'teiʃən] *n* commutazione; **c. passenger** (*rly*) abbonato; **c. ticket** (*rly*) biglietto di abbonamento.
commute [kə'mju:t] *vt* commutare; *vi* fare la spola.
commuter [kə'mju:tə] *n* (*rly*) abbonato.
compact ['kɔmpækt] *n* patto, contratto; portacipria.
compact [kəm'pækt] *a* compatto, conciso.
compactness [kəm'pæktnis] *n* compattezza, concisione.
companion [kəm'pænjən] *n* compagno, socio; dama di compagnia.
companionable [kəm'pænjənəbl] *a* socievole.
companionship [kəm'pænjənʃip] *n* amicizia, compagnia.
company ['kʌmpəni] *n* compagnia, associazione, società; (*naut*) ciurma; **joint stock c.** società per azioni; **limited liability c.** società a responsabilità limitata.
comparable ['kɔmpərəbl] *a* paragonabile.
comparative [kəm'pærətiv] *a n* comparativo; comparato; relativo; **comparatively** relativamente, comparativamente.
compare [kəm'pεə] *vti* paragonare, confrontare.
comparison [kəm'pærisn] *n* paragone, confronto.
compartment [kəm'pɑ:tmənt] *n* scompartimento.
compass ['kʌmpəs] *n* circonferenza, spazio, portata; bussola; *vt* circondare; realizzare.
compasses ['kʌmpəsiz] *n pl* compasso.
compassion [kəm'pæʃən] *n* compassione, pietà.
compassionate [kəm'pæʃənit] *a* pieno di compassione; *vt* compassionare.
compatibility [kəm,pætə'biliti] *n* compatibilità.
compatible [kəm'pætəbl] *a* compatibile.
compatriot [kəm'pætriət] *n* compatriota.
compel [kəm'pel] *vt* costringere, forzare.
compelling [kəm peliŋ] *a* irresistibile.
compendious [kəm'pendiəs] *a* compendioso.
compendium [kəm'pendiəm] *pl* **compendiums, compendia** *n* compendio.
compensate ['kɔmpenseit] *vti* compensare, ricompensare.
compensation [,kɔmpen'seiʃən] *n* compenso, indennità.
compère ['kɔmpεə] *n* (*theat*) presentatore, gareggiare, concorrere.
compete [kəm'pi:t] *vi* competere; *vti* presentare.
competence ['kɔmpitəns] *n* competenza, capacità.
competent ['kɔmpitənt] *a* competente, capace.
competition [,kɔmpi'tiʃən] *n* competizione, concorso, gara; (*com*) concorrenza.
competitive [kəm'petitiv] *a* di competizione, di concorso; (*com*) di concorrenza; **c. prices** prezzi di concorrenza.
competitor [kəm'petitə] *n* competitore, concorrente.
compilation [,kɔmpi'leiʃən] *n* compilazione.
compile [kəm'pail] *vt* compilare.
complacency [kəm'pleisnsi] *n* compiacenza, compiacimento.
complacent [kəm'pleisnt] *a* compiaciuto, compiacente.
complain [kəm'plein] *vi* lamentarsi.
complaint [kəm'pleint] *n* lagnanza, reclamo; malattia.
complaisance [kəm'pleizəns] *n* compiacenza, cortesia.
complement ['kɔmplimənt] *n* complemento.
complementary [,kɔmpli'mentəri] *a* complementare.
complete [kəm'pli:t] *a* completo, intero, perfetto; *vt* completare, finire; riempire.
completely [kəm'pli:tli] *ad* completamente.
completion [kəm'pli:ʃən] *n* completamento; compimento.
complex ['kɔmpleks] *a* complesso, complicato; *n* complesso.
complexion [kəm'plekʃən] *n* carnagione, colorito.
complexity [kəm'pleksiti] *n* complessità.

compliance [kəm'plaiəns] *n* condiscendenza; in c. with d'accordo con.
compliant [kəm'plaiənt] *a* accondiscendente.
complicate ['kɔmplikeit] *vt* complicare.
complicated ['kɔmplikeitid] *a* complicato.
complication [,kɔmpli'keiʃən] *n* complicazione.
complicity [kəm'plisiti] *n* complicità.
compliment ['kɔmplimənt] *n* complimento; *vt* [,kɔmpli'ment] congratularsi con.
complimentary [,kɔmpli'mentəri] *a* di complimento, di omaggio, di favore; **c. tickets** biglietti di omaggio.
comply [kəm'plai] *vi* accondiscendere, conformarsi.
component [kəm'pounənt] *a n* componente.
compose [kəm'pouz] *vt* comporre; calmare.
composed [kəm'pouzd] *a* composto, calmo.
composer [kəm'pouzə] *n* compositore.
composite ['kɔmpəzit] *a* composto, composito.
composition [,kɔmpə'ziʃən] *n* composizione; concordato; tema.
compositor [kəm'pɔzitə] *n* (*typ*) compositore.
compost ['kɔmpɔst] *n* composto, concime; *vt* concimare.
composure [kəm'pouʒə] *n* calma, compostezza.
compound ['kɔmpaund] *a* composto; *n* miscela, composto; *vt* [kɔm'paund] comporre, mescolare; *vi* accordarsi.
comprehend [,kɔmpri'hend] *vt* comprendere, includere.
comprehensible [,kɔmpri'hensəbl] *a* comprensibile.
comprehension [,kɔmpri'henʃən] *n* comprensione.
comprehensive [,kɔmpri'hensiv] *a* comprensivo.
compress ['kɔmpres] *n* compressa.
compress [kəm'pres] *vt* comprimere; condensare.
compression [kəm'preʃən] *n* compressione; (*fig*) concentrazione.
comprise [kəm'praiz] *vt* comprendere, includere.
compromise ['kɔmprəmaiz] *n* compromesso; *vti* compromettere, accomodare, sistemare.
comptometer [kɔmp'tɔmitə] *n* macchina calcolatrice.
compulsion [kəm'pʌlʃən] *n* costrizione, obbligo.
compulsive [kəm'pʌlsiv] *a* coercitivo.
compulsory [kəm'pʌlsəri] *a* obbligatorio, forzato.
compunction [kəm'pʌŋkʃən] *n* compunzione.
computation [,kɔmpju:'teiʃən] *n* computo, calcolo.
compute [kəm'pju:t] *vt* computare.
computer [kəm'pju:tə] *n* calcolatore, (macchina) calcolatrice.
comrade ['kɔmrid] *n* camerata, compagno.
con [kɔn] *vt* imparare a memoria.
concave ['kɔn'keiv] *a* concavo, a volta.
conceal [kən'si:l] *vt* celare, nascondere.
concealment [kən'si:lmənt] *n* occultamento, nascondiglio.
concede [kən'si:d] *vt* ammettere; concedere.
conceit [kən'si:t] *n* vanità, presunzione; ricercatezza; concettismo.
conceited [kən'si:tid] *a* presuntuoso, vanesio, affettato.
conceivable [kən'si:vəbl] *a* concepibile.
conceive [kən'si:v] *vt* concepire.
concentrate ['kɔnsentreit] *vti* concentrar(si).
concentration [,kɔnsen'treiʃən] *n* concentramento, concentrazione.
concentric [kɔn'sentrik] *a* concentrico.
concept ['kɔnsept] *n* concetto.
conception [kən'sepʃən] *n* concezione.
concern [kən'sə:n] *n* ansietà, faccenda, ditta, impresa; *vt* avere a che fare con, concernere, riguardare.
concerned [kən'sə:nd] *a* interessato; preoccupato.
concerning [kən'sə:niŋ] *prep* riguardo a, circa.
concert ['kɔnsət] *n* concerto; accordo.
concert [kən'sə:t] *vt* concertare.
concertina [,kɔnsə'ti:nə] *n* piccola fisarmonica.
concerto [kən'tʃə:tou] *n* (*mus*) concerto; **piano c.** concerto per pianoforte.
concession [kən'seʃən] *n* concessione; **concessionary** *a* concessionario.
concession(n)aire [kən seʃə'nɛə] *n* concessionario.
conciliate [kən'silieit] *vt* conciliare, guadagnarsi.
conciliation [kən,sili'eiʃən] *n* conciliazione.
conciliatory [kən'siliətəri] *a* conciliante.
concise [kən'sais] *a* breve, conciso.
conciseness [kən'saisnis] *n* concisione, brevità.
concision [kən'siʒən] *n* concisione.
conclave ['kɔnkleiv] *n* conclave.
conclude [kən'klu:d] *vti* concludere, finire.
concluding [kən'klu:diŋ] *a* finale, ultimo.
conclusion [kən'klu:ʒən] *n* conclusione, fine.

conclusive [kən'klu:ziv] *a* conclusivo.
concoct [kən'kɔkt] *vt* mescolare ingredienti; architettare, tramare.
concoction [kən'kɔkʃən] *n* miscuglio, macchinazione.
concomitance [kən'kɔmitəns] *n* concomitanza.
concomitant [kən'kɔmitənt] *a* concomitante; *n* fatto concomitante.
concord ['kɔŋkɔ:d] *n* concordia; (*mus*) accordo.
concordance [kən'kɔ:dəns] *n* accordo; concordanza; indice alfabetico.
concordant [kən'kɔ:dənt] *a* concorde, armonioso.
concourse ['kɔŋkɔ:s] *n* affluenza, concorso.
concrete ['kɔnkri:t] *a* concreto; *n* calcestruzzo; **reinforced c.** cemento armato.
concubine ['kɔŋkjubain] *n* concubina.
concur [kən'kə:] *vi* concorrere, accordarsi.
concurrence [kən'kʌrəns] *n* concorso, consenso.
concurrent [kən'kʌrənt] *a* concorrente; concorde.
concussion [kən'kʌʃən] *n* scossa, urto; **c. (of the brain)** commozione cerebrale.
condemn [kən'dem] *vt* condannare, biasimare; confiscare.
condemnation [,kɔndem'neiʃən] *n* condanna, biasimo.
condensation [,kɔnden'seiʃən] *n* condensazione.
condense [kən'dens] *vti* condensar (si); (*fig*) compendiare.
condescend [,kɔndi'send] *vi* (ac) condiscendere, degnarsi.
condescending [,kɔndi'sendiŋ] *a* condiscendente.
condescension [,kɔndi'senʃən] *n* condiscendenza.
condiment ['kɔndimənt] *n* condimento.
condition [kən'diʃən] *n* condizione, stato, patto; *vt* condizionare, porre condizioni; rimandare (uno studente).
conditional [kən'diʃənl] *a n* condizionale.
condole [kən'doul] *vi* fare le condoglianze.
condolence [kən'douləns] *n* condoglianza.
condone [kən'doun] *vt* condonare, perdonare.
conducive [kən'dju:siv] *a* contribuente, tendente.
conduct ['kɔndəkt] *n* condotta, direzione *vt* [kən'dʌkt] condurre, dirigere.
conductor [kən'dʌktə] *n* conduttore, guida, (*tram etc*) bigliettario, (*rly*) capotreno; controllore; direttore d'orchestra.
conductress [kən'dʌktris] *n* bigliettaria.
conduit ['kɔndit] *n* condotto.
cone [koun] *n* cono (*bot*) pigna.
confection [kən'fekʃən] *n* confezione, composizione; *vt* preparare, confezionare.
confectioner [kən'fekʃənə] *n* pasticciere.
confectionery [kən'fekʃnəri] *n* dolci *pl*, pasticceria.
confederacy [kən'fedərəsi] *n* confederazione; lega; cospirazione.
confederate [kən'fedərit] *a n* confederato, alleato.
confederation [kən,fedə'reiʃən] *n* confederazione.
confer [kən'fə:] *vti* conferire.
conference ['kɔnfərəns] *n* conferenza, abboccamento, congresso.
conferment [kən'fə:mənt] *n* conferimento.
confess [kən'fes] *vti* confessar(si).
confession [kən'feʃən] *n* confessione.
confessional [kən'feʃənl] *a n* confessionale.
confessor [kən'fesə] *n* confessore.
confetti [kən'feti] *n pl* coriandoli.
confidant(e) [,kɔnfi'dænt] *n* confidente.
confide [kən'faid] *vti* confidare.
confidence ['kɔnfidəns] *n* fiducia, confidenza; **self-c.** sicurezza di sè; **c. trick, c. game** truffa all'americana.
confident ['kɔnfidənt] *a* fiducioso, presuntuoso.
confidently ['kɔnfidəntli] *ad* con sicurezza, con fiducia.
confidential [,kɔnfi'denʃəl] *a* confidenziale, privato.
confidentially [,kɔnfi'denʃəli] *ad* confidenzialmente.
configuration [kən,figju'reiʃən] *n* configurazione.
confine [kən'fain] *vti* confinare; limitar(si).
confines ['kɔnfainz] *n pl* confini *pl*.
confinement [kən'fainmənt] *n* confino, reclusione; parto.
confirm [kən'fə:m] *vt* confermare, ratificare; cresimare.
confirmation [,kɔnfə'meiʃən] *n* conferma, ratifica; cresima.
confirmed [kən'fə:md] *a* inveterato, convinto; cresimato.
confiscate ['kɔnfiskeit] *vt* confiscare.
confiscation [,kɔnfis'keiʃən] *n* confisca.
conflagration [,kɔnflə'greiʃən] *n* conflagrazione.
conflict ['kɔnflikt] *n* conflitto, lotta, urto; *vi* [kən'flikt] lottare, urtarsi.
conflicting [kən'fliktiŋ] *a* opposto, in conflitto.
confluence ['kɔnfluəns] *n* confluenza.
confluent ['kɔnfluənt] *a n* confluente.
conform [kən'fɔ:m] *vti* conformar(si).
conformation [kɔn,fɔ:'meiʃən] *n* conformazione, adattamento.

conformist [kən'fɔːmist] *n* conformista.
conformity [kən'fɔːmiti] *n* conformità.
confound [kən'faund] *vt* confondere; mandare al diavolo; **c. it!** accidenti!
confounded [kən'faundid] *a* confuso, sconcertato; (*fam*) maledetto.
confraternity [,kɔnfrə'təːniti] *n* confraternita.
confront [kən'frʌnt] *vt* affrontare, mettere a confronto.
confrontation [,kɔnfrʌn'teiʃən] *n* confronto.
confuse [kən'fjuːz] *vt* confondere, sconcertare.
confused [kən'fjuːzd] *a* confuso, disorientato.
confusion [kən'fjuːʒən] *n* confusione, disordine; imbarazzo.
confute [kən'fjuːt] *vt* confutare.
congeal [kən'dʒiːl] *vti* congelar(si).
congealment [kən'dʒiːlmənt] *n* congelamento.
congenial [kən'dʒiːniəl] *a* affine; simpatico; adatto.
congenital [kən'dʒenitl] *a* congenito.
congest [kən'dʒest] *vt* congestionare; ingorgare.
congested [kən'dʒestid] *a* congestionato; sovrappopolato.
congestion [kən'dʒestʃən] *n* congestione; ingorgamento.
conglomerate [kən'glɔməreit] *vti* conglomerar(si).
conglomeration [kən,glɔmə'reiʃən] *n* conglomerazione, conglomerato.
congratulate [kən'grætjuleit] *vt* congratularsi con, rallegrarsi con.
congratulation [kən,grætju'leiʃən] *n* congratulazione, rallegramento.
congregate ['kɔŋgrigeit] *vti* congregare, unirsi.
congregation [,kɔŋgri'geiʃən] *n* congregazione, riunione.
congress ['kɔŋgres] *n* congresso.
congruous ['kɔŋgruəs] *a* congruo.
conic(al) ['kɔnik(əl)] *a* conico.
conjectural [kən'dʒektʃərəl] *a* congetturale.
conjecture [kən'dʒektʃə] *n* congettura; *vti* congetturare.
conjoin [kən'dʒɔin] *vti* congiunger(si).
conjoint ['kɔndʒɔint] *a* congiunto, unito.
conjugal ['kɔndʒugəl] *a* coniugale.
conjugate ['kɔndʒugeit] *vti* coniugar (si).
conjugation [,kɔndʒu'geiʃən] *n* coniugazione.
conjunction [kən'dʒʌŋkʃən] *n* congiunzione, unione.
conjunctive [kən'dʒʌŋktiv] *a n* congiuntivo.
conjuncture [kən'dʒʌŋktʃə] *n* congiuntura.
conjure ['kʌndʒə] *vti* evocare; far giochi di prestigio; **c. up** evocare; [kən'dʒuə] scongiurare.
conjurer ['kʌndʒərə] *n* prestigiatore.
connect [kə'nekt] *vti* connetter(si), far coincidenza; associare; **connected** connesso, imparentato.
connectedly [kə'nektidli] *ad* coerentemente, logicamente.
connecting [kə'nektiŋ] *a* che connette; di comunicazione, di collegamento.
connection, [kə'nekʃən] *n* collegamento, connessione; legame, rapporto; parentela; (*rly*) coincidenza; **in this c.** a questo proposito.
connective [kə'nektiv] *a* connettivo.
connivance [kə'naivəns] *n* connivenza.
connive [kə'naiv] *vi* essere connivente.
connoisseur [,kɔni'səː] *n* conoscitore, intenditore.
connotation [,kɔnou'teiʃən] *n* significato implicito.
conquer ['kɔŋkə] *vti* conquistare, vincere; **conquering** vincente, vittorioso.
conqueror ['kɔŋkərə] *n* conquistatore.
conquest ['kɔŋkwest] *n* conquista.
Conrad ['kɔnræd] *nm pr* Corrado.
conscience ['kɔnʃəns] *n* coscienza.
conscientious [,kɔnʃi'enʃəs] *a* coscienzioso.
conscientiousness [,kɔnʃi'enʃəsnis] *n* coscienziosità.
conscious ['kɔnʃəs] *a* consapevole, conscio, cosciente.
consciousness ['kɔnʃəsnis] *n* consapevolezza, coscienza, conoscenza.
conscript ['kɔnskript] *a n* coscritto.
conscription [kən'skripʃən] *n* coscrizione, leva.
consecrate ['kɔnsikreit] *vt* consacrare.
consecration [,kɔnsi'kreiʃən] *n* consacrazione.
consecutive [kən'sekjutiv] *a* consecutivo.
consensus [kən'sensəs] *n* consenso unanime.
consent [kən'sent] *n* consenso, accordo; *vi* acconsentire.
consequence ['kɔnsikwəns] *n* conseguenza, effetto; importanza.
consequent ['kɔnsikwənt] *a* conseguente.
consequently ['kɔnsikwəntli] *ad cj* di conseguenza, conseguentemente.
conservative [kən'səːvətiv] *a n* conservatore.
conservatory [kən'səːvətri] *n* serra, conservatorio.
conserve [kən'səːv] *n* conserva; *vt* conservare.
consider [kən'sidə] *vti* considerare, riflettere.
considerable [kən'sidərəbl] *a* considerevole.
considerate [kən'sidərit] *a* riguardoso; premuroso.
consideration [kən,sidə'reiʃən] *n*

considerazione; importanza; ricompensa.
considering [kən'sidəriŋ] *prep* tenuto conto di, visto che.
consign [kən'sain] *vt* consegnare, mandare.
consignee [,kɔnsai'ni:] *n* (*com*) destinatario.
consignment [kən'sainmənt] *n* consegna; (*com*) partita di merci.
consignor [kən'sainə] *n* (*com*) mittente.
consist [kən'sist] *vi* consistere.
consistence [kən'sistəns] **consistency** [kən'sistənsi] *n* consistenza, densità.
consistent [kən'sistənt] *a* coerente; costante.
consolation [,kɔnsə'leiʃən] *n* consolazione.
console [kən'soul] *vt* consolare.
consoling [kən'souliŋ] *a* consolante.
consolidate [kən'sɔlideit] *vti* consolidar(si).
consolidation [kən,sɔli'deiʃən] *n* consolidamento.
consonance ['kɔnsənəns] *n* consonanza, armonia, accordo.
consonant ['kɔnsənənt] *a* consono, armonioso; *n* (*gram*) consonante.
consort ['kɔnsɔ:t] *n* consorte, compagno; [kən'sɔ:t] *vi* accompagnar(si).
conspicuous [kən'spikjuəs] *a* cospicuo, eminente.
conspiracy [kən'spirəsi] *n* cospirazione, congiura.
conspirator [kən'spirətə] *n* cospiratore.
conspire [kən'spaiə] *vti* cospirare, tramare.
constable ['kʌnstəbl] *n* conestabile, guardia, poliziotto.
Constance ['kɔnstəns] *nf pr* Costanza.
constancy ['kɔnstənsi] *n* costanza, perseveranza.
constant ['kɔnstənt] *a* costante, fedele.
Constantinople [,kɔnstænti'noupl] *n* Costantinopoli.
constantly ['konstəntli] *ad* costantemente, continuamente.
constellation [,kɔnstə'leiʃən] *n* costellazione.
consternation [,kɔnstə:'neiʃən] *n* costernazione.
constipate ['kɔnstipeit] *vt* costipare.
constipated ['kɔnstipeitid] *a* stitico.
constipation [,kɔnsti'peiʃən] *n* stitichezza.
constituency [kən'stitjuənsi] *n* circoscrizione elettorale.
constituent [kən'stitjuənt] *a* costituente; *n* elettore.
constitute ['kɔnstitju:t] *vt* costituire.
constitution [,kɔnsti'tju:ʃən] *n* costituzione, legge.
constitutional [,kɔnsti'tju:ʃənl] *a* costituzionale; *n* passeggiata igienica.
constrain [kən'strein] *vt* costringere; reprimere.
constraint [kən'streint] *n* costrizione, repressione; imbarazzo.
constrict [kən'strikt] *vt* comprimere, contrarre.
constriction [kən'strikʃən] *n* costrizione, contrazione.
construct [kən'strʌkt] *vt* costruire.
construction [kən'strʌkʃən] *n* costruzione.
constructive [kən'strʌktiv] *a* costruttivo.
construe [kən'stru:] *vt* (*gram*) analizzare; tradurre; interpretare.
consul ['kɔnsəl] *n* console.
consular ['kɔnsjulə] *a* consolare.
consulate ['kɔnsjulit] *n* consolato.
consult [kən'sʌlt] *vti* consultar(si).
consultant [kən'sʌltənt] *n* consulente.
consultation [,kɔnsəl'teiʃən] *n* consultazione, consulto.
consulting [kən'sʌltiŋ] *a* di consultazione.
consume [kən'sju:m] *vti* consumar(si).
consumer [kən'sju:mə] *n* consumatore, utente.
consummate [kən'sʌmit] *a* consumato, perfetto.
consummate ['kɔnsʌmeit] *vt* compiere, consumare.
consummation [,kɔnsʌ'meiʃən] *n* consumazione.
consumption [kən'sʌmpʃən] *n* consumo; (*med*) consunzione, tisi.
consumptive [kən'sʌmptiv] *a n* tisico.
contact ['kɔntækt] *n* contatto; *vti* [kən'tækt] metter(si) in contatto con; essere in contatto.
contagion [kən'teidʒən] *n* contagio.
contagious [kən'teidʒəs] *a* contagioso.
contain [kən'tein] *vt* contenere, includere; reprimere.
container [kən'teinə] *n* recipiente.
contaminate [kən'tæmineit] *vt* contaminare, infettare.
contamination [kən,tæmi'neiʃən] *n* contaminazione.
contemplate ['kɔntempleit] *vt* contemplare, meditare; progettare.
contemplation [,kɔntem'pleiʃən] *n* contemplazione; progetto.
contemplative [kən'templətiv] *a* contemplativo, meditativo.
contemporary [kən'tempərəri] *a n* contemporaneo; coetaneo.
contempt [kən'tempt] *n* disprezzo.
contemptible [kən'temptəbl] *a* spregevole.
contemptuous [kən'temptjuəs] *a* sprezzante.
contend [kən'tend] *vi* contendere, lottare; contestare; sostenere.
content [kən'tent] *a* contento, soddisfatto; *n* contentezza, soddisfazione; *vt* accontentare, soddisfare.

contented [kən'tentid] *a* contento.
contention [kən'tenʃən] *n* contesa, discordia, opinione.
contentious [kən'tenʃəs] *a* litigioso; controverso; (*leg*) contenzioso.
contentment [kən'tentmənt] *n* il contentarsi; contentezza.
contents ['kɔntents] *n pl* contenuto.
contest ['kɔntest] *n* competizione; contesa; *vt* [kən'test] contestare, disputare.
contestant [kən'testənt] *n* competitore, concorrente.
context ['kɔntekst] *n* contesto.
contiguous [kən'tigjuəs] *a* contiguo.
continence ['kɔntinəns] *n* continenza.
continent ['kɔntinənt] *a* casto, continente, moderato; *n* continente.
continental [,kɔnti'nentl] *a n* continentale.
contingency [kən'tindʒənsi] *n* contingenza.
contingent [kən'tindʒənt] *a n* contingente.
continual [kən'tinjuəl] *a* continuo.
continuation [kən,tinju'eiʃən] *n* continuazione, seguito.
continue [kən'tinju:] *vti* continuare, persistere, proseguire.
continuity [,kɔnti'nju:iti] *n* continuità.
continuous [kən'tinjuəs] *a* continuo, ininterrotto.
continuously [kən'tinjuəsli] *ad* continuamente, ininterrottamente.
contort [kən'tɔ:t] *vt* contorcere.
contortion [kən'tɔ:ʃən] *n* contorsione.
contour ['kɔntuə] *n* contorno, profilo.
contraband ['kɔntrəbænd] *a n* (di) contrabbando.
contract ['kɔntrækt] *n* contratto, appalto; *vt* [kən'trækt] contrarre; contrattare, appaltare.
contraction [kən'trækʃən] *n* contrazione.
contractor [kən'træktə] *n* contraente; appaltatore; imprenditore.
contradict [,kɔntrə'dikt] *vt* contraddire.
contradiction [,kɔntrə'dikʃən] *n* contraddizione.
contradictory [,kɔntrə'diktəri] *a* contraddittorio.
contralto [kən'træltou] *n* (*mus*) contralto.
contrariety [,kɔntrə'raiəti] *n* contrarietà, opposizione.
contrary ['kɔntrəri] *a* contrario; ostinato; *n* contrario; *ad* contrariamente; **on the c.** al contrario.
contrast ['kɔntræst] *n* contrasto; *vt* [kən'træst] mettere in contrasto, confrontare; *vi* contrastare.
contravene [,kɔntrə'vi:n] *vt* contravvenire.
contravention [,kɔntrə'venʃən] *n* contravvenzione.
contribute [kən'tribju:t] *vti* contribuire.
contribution [,kɔntri'bju:ʃən] *n* contributo; collaborazione.
contributor [kən'tribjutə] *n* contributore; collaboratore.
contrite ['kɔntrait] *a* contrito.
contrition [kən'triʃən] *n* contrizione.
contrivance [kən'traivəns] *n* invenzione, congegno.
contrive [kən'traiv] *vt* inventare; escogitare, fare in modo di.
control [kən'troul] *n* controllo, freno, autorità; *vt* controllare, frenare, dirigere.
controversial [,kɔntrə'və:ʃəl] *a* controverso.
controversy ['kɔntrəvə:si] *n* controversia.
contumacious [,kɔntju:'meiʃəs] *a* contumace.
contuse [kən'tju:z] *vt* ammaccare, contundere.
contusion [kən'tju:ʒən] *n* contusione.
conundrum [kə'nʌndrəm] *n* indovinello.
convalesce [,kɔnvə'les] *vi* rimettersi in salute.
convalescence [,kɔnvə'lesns] *n* convalescenza.
convalescent [,kɔnvə'lesnt] *a n* convalescente.
convector [kən'vektə] *n* convettore, termo convettore.
convene [kən'vi:n] *vti* convocare; convenire.
convenience [kən'vi:niəns] *n* comodità, convenienza, vantaggio; **public c.** gabinetto pubblico.
convenient [kən'vi:niənt] *a* comodo, conveniente, adatto.
convent ['kɔnvənt] *n* convento.
conventicle [kən'ventikl] *n* conventicola.
convention [kən'venʃən] *n* convenzione.
conventional [kən'venʃənl] *a* convenzionale.
conventual [kən'ventjuəl] *a* conventuale.
converge [kən'və:dʒ] *vi* convergere.
convergent [kən'və:dʒənt] *a* convergente.
conversant [kən'və:sənt] *a* versato (in), bene informato.
conversation [,kɔnvə'seiʃən] *n* conversazione.
converse ['kɔnvə:s] *a n* converso, contrario; *vi* [kən'və:s] conversare.
conversely ['kɔnvə:sli] *ad* viceversa.
conversion [kən'və:ʃən] *n* conversione.
convert ['kɔnvə:t] *n* convertito; *vt* [kən'və:t] convertire.
convertible [kən'və:təbl] *a* convertibile; **c. car** automobile decappottabile.
convex ['kɔn'veks] *a* convesso.
convey [kən'vei] *vt* portare, trasportare; trasmettere; esprimere.

conveyance [kən'veiəns] *n* mezzo di trasporto.
conveyor [kən'veiə] *n* portatore; **c.-belt** (*ind*) trasportatore a cinghia.
convict ['kɔnvikt] *n* ergastolano; *vt* [kən'vikt] dichiarare colpevole.
conviction [kən'vikʃən] *n* condanna; convinzione.
convince [kən'vins] *vt* convincere.
convincing [kən'vinsiŋ] *a* convincente.
convivial [kən'viviəl] *a* conviviale.
convocation [kɔnvə'keiʃən] *n* convocazione, assemblea.
convoke [kən'vouk] *vt* convocare.
convoy ['kɔnvɔi] *n* convoglio, scorta; *vt* convogliare, scortare.
convulse [kən'vʌls] *vt* sconvolgere, agitare, mettere in convulsioni.
convulsion [kən'vʌlʃən] *n* convulsione.
convulsive [kən'vʌlsiv] *a* convulsivo.
coo [ku:] *vi* tubare.
cook [kuk] *n* cuoco, cuoca; *vti* cucinare, cuocere; **cookbook** libro di cucina.
cooker ['kukə] *n* fornello, cucina; pentola.
cookery ['kukəri] *n* arte culinaria; **c. book** libro di cucina.
cookie ['kuki] *n* biscotto.
cooking ['kukiŋ] *n* cottura; arte culinaria; cucina.
cool [ku:l] *a* fresco; calmo; impudente; *n* fresco, frescura; *vti* rinfrescar(si).
cooler ['ku:lə] *n* refrigerante; (*sl*) gattabuia; **air c.** condizionatore dell'aria.
cooling ['ku:liŋ] *a* rinfrescante.
coolly ['ku:lli] *ad* freddamente, con calma.
coolness ['ku:lnis] *n* fresco; sangue freddo; sfacciataggine.
coop [ku:p] *n* stia; *vt* mettere nella stia, rinchiudere.
co-operate [kou'ɔpəreit] *vi* cooperare.
co-operation [kou,ɔpə'reiʃən] *n* cooperazione.
co-operative [kou'ɔpərətiv] *a* cooperativo.
co-operator [kou'ɔpəreitə] *n* cooperatore.
co-ordinate [kou'ɔ:dineit] *vt* coordinare; *n* coordinata.
co-ordination [kou,ɔ:di'neiʃən] *n* coordinazione.
co-owner ['kou'ounə] *n* comproprietario.
copartner ['kou'pɑ:tnə] *n* (*com*) consocio; **copartnership** società in nome collettivo.
cope [koup] *n* cappa di ecclesiastico; **c. with** *vi* far fronte a, lottare contro.
Copenhagen [,koupn'heigən] *n* Copenaghen.
co-pilot ['kou'pailət] *n* (*av*) secondo pilota.
copious ['koupiəs] *a* abbondante, copioso.
copiousness ['koupiəsnis] *n* abbondanza.
copper ['kɔpə] *a* di rame, color di rame; *n* rame, moneta di rame, caldaia; (*sl*) poliziotto; **coppers** *pl* moneta spicciola; **copperplate engraving** incisione su rame.
coppice ['kɔpis] *n* bosco ceduo.
copulate ['kɔpjuleit] *vi* accoppiarsi.
copulation [,kɔpju'leiʃən] *n* copulazione, accoppiamento.
copy ['kɔpi] *n* copia; trascrizione; (*journalism*) materiale; **c. book** quaderno; **c. reader** revisore di stampa; **fair c.** bella copia; **rough c.** brutta copia; *vt* copiare; imitare; trascrivere.
copyright ['kɔpirait] *n* diritti d'autore *pl*, proprietà letteraria.
coquet(te) [kou'ket] *vi* civettare.
coquette [kou'ket] *n* (donna) civetta.
coral ['kɔrəl] *a n* (di) corallo.
cord [kɔ:d] *n* corda, funicella; **spinal c.** spina dorsale; *vt* legare con una corda.
cordial ['kɔ:diəl] *a n* cordiale.
cordiality [,kɔ:di'æliti] *n* cordialità.
cordially ['kɔ:diəli] *ad* cordialmente.
cordon ['kɔ:dn] *n* cordane; *vt* cordonare.
corduroy ['kɔ:dərɔi] *n* velluto a coste.
core [kɔ:] *n* torsolo; (*fig*) centro, cuore.
cork [kɔ:k] *n* sughero; tappo, turacciolo; *vt* tappare, turare.
corkscrew ['kɔ:k'skru:] *n* cavatappi.
corn [kɔ:n] *n* mais, granturco; callo durone; **c.-cob** pannocchia; **cornflakes** fiocchi di granturco; **cornflour**, **cornmeal** farina di gran turco, polenta.
cornelian [kɔ:'ni:liən] *n* (*min*) corniola.
corner ['kɔ:nə] *n* angolo; spigolo; (*com*) accaparramento; *vt* (*fig*) mettere alle strette; svoltare; accaparrare; **cornerstone** pietra angolare.
cornet ['kɔ:nit] *n* (*mus*) cornetta; cartoccio conico.
cornflower ['kɔ:nflauə] *n* fiordaliso.
cornice ['kɔ:nis] *n* cornicione.
Cornwall ['kɔ:nwəl] *n* Cornovaglia; **Cornish** *a n* della Cornovaglia.
coronary ['kɔrənəri] *a* (*anat*) coronario; **c. thrombosis** trombosi delle coronarie.
coronation [,kɔrə'neiʃən] *n* incoronazione.
coroner ['kɔrənə] *n* magistrato inquirente nei casi di sospetta morte violenta.
coronet ['kɔrənit] *n* corona nobiliare, diadema.
corporal ['kɔ:pərəl] *a n* corporale; *a* corporeo; *n* caporale.

corporate ['kɔ:pərit] *a* corporativo.
corporation [,kɔ:pə'reiʃən] *n* corporazione, (*com*) società a responsabilità limitata, azienda municipale; (*fam*) pancia.
corporative ['kɔ:pərətiv] *a* corporativo.
corporeal [kɔ:'pɔ:riəl] *a* corporeo.
corps [kɔ:] *pl* **corps** *n* (*mil*) corpo.
corpse [kɔ:ps] *n* cadavere.
corpulence ['kɔ:pjuləns] *n* corpulenza.
corpulent ['kɔ:pjulənt] *a* corpulento.
corpuscle ['kɔ:pʌsl] *n* corpuscolo.
correct [kə'rekt] *a* corretto, esatto, giusto; *vt* correggere.
correction [kə'rekʃən] *n* correzione; punizione.
correctly [kə'rektli] *ad* correttamente.
correctness [kə'rektnis] *n* correttezza.
correlate ['kɔrileit] *vti* essere, mettere in correlazione.
correlation [,kɔri'leiʃən] *n* correlazione.
correspond [,kɔris'pɔnd] *vi* corrispondere.
correspondence [,kɔris'pɔndəns] *n* corrispondenza.
correspondent [,kɔris'pɔndənt] *a n* corrispondente.
corresponding [,kɔris'pɔndiŋ] *a* corrispondente.
corridor ['kɔridɔ:] *n* corridoio.
corroborate [kə'rɔbəreit] *vt* corroborare.
corroboration [kə,rɔbə'reiʃən] *n* conferma, corroborazione.
corrode [kə'roud] *vti* corroder(si).
corrosive [kə'rousiv] *a n* corrosivo.
corrugate ['kɔrugeit] *vti* corrugar(si); **corrugated iron** lamiera ondulata; **corrugated paper** carta increspata.
corrupt [kə'rʌpt] *a* corrotto, depravato; *vti* corromper(si).
corruption [kə'rʌpʃən] *n* corruzione.
corsair ['kɔ:sɛə] *n* corsaro.
corset ['kɔ:sit] *n* corsetto, busto; **c.-maker** bustaia.
Corsican ['kɔ:sikən] *a n* corso, corsa.
cosmetic [kɔz'metik] *a n* cosmetico.
cosmic ['kɔzmik] *a* cosmico.
cosmodrome ['kɔzmədroum] *n* cosmodromo.
cosmogony [kɔz'mɔgəni] *n* cosmogonia.
cosmography [kɔz'mɔgrəfi] *n* cosmografia.
cosmonaut ['kɔzmənɔ:t] *n* cosmonauta.
cosmopolitan [,kɔzmə'pɔlitən] *a n* cosmopolita.
cosmos ['kɔzmɔs] *n* cosmo.
Cossack ['kɔsæk] *n* cosacco.
cost [kɔst] *n* costo, prezzo; **costs** *pl* spese processuali *pl*; *vt* costare; (*com*) fissare il prezzo; **running c.** spese generali.
costermonger ['kɔstə,mʌŋgə] *n* venditore ambulante di frutta etc.
costive ['kɔstiv] *a* stitico.
costiveness ['kɔstivnis] *n* stitichezza.
costliness ['kɔstlinis] *n* costosità.
costly ['kɔstli] *a* costoso.
costume ['kɔstju:m] *n* costume; completo.
cot [kɔt] *n* lettino per bambini.
coterie ['koutəri] *n* circolo.
cottage ['kɔtidʒ] *n* casetta di campagna, 'cottage'.
Cottian Alps ['kɔtiən,ælps] *n pl* Alpi Cozie.
cotton ['kɔtn] *n* cotone, tela di cotone; *a* di cotone; **absorbent c.** cotone idrofilo.
couch [kautʃ] *n* divano.
cough [kɔf] *n* tosse; *vti* tossire.
council ['kaunsl] *n* consiglio, concilio.
councilor ['kaunsilə] *n* consigliere.
counsel ['kaunsəl] *n* consigli(o), parere; consulente legale.
counselor ['kaunslə] *n* consigliere, avvocato.
count [kaunt] *n* conto, conteggio; conte; **c. of indictment** capo d'accusa; **countdown** conteggio all'indietro; *vti* contare, numerare, includere.
countenance ['kauntinəns] *n* viso, espressione; *vt* approvare, incoraggiare.
counter ['kauntə] *n* gettone; (*in a shop etc*) banco, cassa; *ad* contro, in opposizione.
counteract [,kauntə'rækt] *vt* agire in opposizione a, neutralizzare.
counter-attack ['kauntərə,tæk] *n* (*mil*) contrattacco.
counterbalance ['kauntə,bæləns] *n* contrappeso.
counterfeit ['kauntəfit] *a* contraffatto, falsificato; *n* contraffazione, falsificazione; *vt* contraffare, falsificare, fingere.
counterfoil ['kauntəfɔil] *n* (*com*) matrice.
countermand [,kauntə'mɑ:nd] *vt* disdire, revocare.
counterpane ['kauntəpein] *n* copriletto.
counterpart ['kauntəpɑ:t] *n* controparte, doppio, duplicato.
counterpoint ['kauntəpɔint] *n* (*mus*) contrappunto.
counterpoise ['kauntəpɔiz] *n* contrappeso; *vt* controbilanciare.
countersign ['kauntəsain] *n* contrassegno; controfirma; parola d'ordine; *vt* controfirmare.
counterweight ['kauntəweit] *n* contrappeso.
countess ['kauntis] *n* contessa.
counting-house ['kauntiŋhaus] *n* ufficio contabile, amministrazione.
countless ['kauntlis] *a* innumerevole.
country ['kʌntri] *n* paese, nazione, patria; campagna; **countryman** compatriota; contadino.

county ['kaunti] *n* contea
coup [ku:] *n* colpo.
couple ['kʌpl] *n* coppia, paio; *vti* accoppiar(si); (*rly*) agganciare.
coupling ['kʌpliŋ] *n* accoppiamento, (*tec*) agganciamento.
coupon ['ku:pɔn] *n* cedola, tagliando, buono.
courage ['kʌridʒ] *n* coraggio.
courageous [kə'reidʒəs] *a* coraggioso.
courageously [kə'reidʒəsli] *ad* coraggiosamente.
courier ['kuriə] *n* corriere, messaggero.
course [kɔ:s] *n* corso, direzione; pista; (*meal*) portata.
court [kɔ:t] *n* corte; tribunale; (*tennis*) campo; *vt* corteggiare.
courteous ['kə:tiəs] *a* cortese.
courteousness ['kə:tiəsnis] *n* cortesia.
courtesan [,kɔ:ti'zæn] *n* cortigiana, prostituta.
courtesy ['kə:tisi] *n* cortesia, gentilezza.
courtier ['kɔ:tiə] *n* cortigiano.
courtly ['kɔ:tli] *a* cortigianesco, cerimonioso.
courtship ['kɔ:tʃip] *n* corte, corteggiamento.
courtyard ['kɔ:tjɑ:d] *n* corte, cortile.
cousin ['kʌzn] *n* cugino, cugina.
cove [kouv] *n* insenatura, piccola baia.
covenant ['kʌvinənt] *n* convenzione, patto; *vti* stipulare, convenire.
cover ['kʌvə] *n* coperta; copertura; coperchio; copertina; riparo; *vt* coprire, nascondere, ricoprire, proteggere; far la cronaca di.
coverage ['kʌvəridʒ] *n* copertura; (*journalism*) servizio d'informazione.
covering ['kʌvəriŋ] *n* coperta; (*com*) garanzia.
coverlet ['kʌvəlit] *n* copriletto.
covet ['kʌvit] *vt* bramare.
covetous ['kʌvitəs] *a* cupido, avido.
covey ['kʌvi] *n* covata (di uccelli).
cow [kau] *n* vacca, mucca, (*di mammiferi*) femmina; *vt* intimidire.
coward ['kauəd] *n* codardo.
cowardice ['kauədis] *n* codardia.
cowardly ['kauədli] *a* codardo; *ad* vilmente.
cower ['kauə] *vi* acquattarsi, farsi piccolo, tremare.
cowl [kaul] *n* cappuccio.
coxcomb ['kɔkskoum] *n* damerino, zerbinotto.
coxswain ['kɔkswein, 'kɔksn] *n* timoniere.
coy [kɔi] *a* ritroso, timido.
coyness ['kɔinis] *n* timidezza, ritrosia.
coziness ['kouzinis] *n* agio, tepore confortevole, intimità.
cozy ['kouzi] *a* comodo, intimo; **tea c.** *n* copriteiera.
crab [kræb] *n* granchio; (*mech*) argano; **c. apple** mela selvatica.
crabbed ['kræbid] *a* ruvido, sgarbato; (*writing*) illegibile.
crack [kræk] *n* fessura, crepa, spacco; incrinatura; schianto, schiocco; *a* di prim'ordine, ottimo; *vti* spaccar(si); **to c. a joke** dire una spiritosaggine.
cracked ['krækt] *a* fesso, incrinato; scervellato.
cracker ['krækə] *n* petardo; galletta.
crackle ['krækl] *vi* crepitare, scricchiolare.
crackling ['krækliŋ] *n* crepitio, scoppiettio.
cracknel ['kræknl] *n* biscotto croccante.
Cracow ['krækou] *n* Cracovia.
cradle ['kreidl] *n* culla; (*for broken limbs*) gabbia, alzacoperte; *vt* cullare.
craft [krɑ:ft] *n* abilità; arte; furberia, inganno; piccola imbarcazione.
craftily ['krɑ:ftili] *ad* abilmente, astutamente.
craftiness ['krɑ:ftinis] *n* furbizia.
craftsman ['krɑ:ftsmən] *n* artigiano; **craftsmanship** arte dell'artigiano.
crafty ['krɑ:fti] *a* furbo, abile.
crag [kræg] *n* picco, roccia scoscesa.
craggy ['krægi] *a* roccioso, dirupato.
cram [kræm] *vti* rimpinzar(si); (*fam*) imbottire di nozioni in vista di un esame.
cramp [kræmp] *n* crampo; *vt* impacciare; cagionare crampi a; impedire nei movimenti.
cranberry ['krænbəri] *n* mirtillo nero.
crane [krein] *n* gru; *vti* allungare il collo, sporgersi.
cranium ['kreiniəm] *pl* **crania** *n* cranio.
crank [kræŋk] *n* manovella; (*fig*) individuo eccentrico.
cranny ['kræni] *n* fessura.
crape [kreip] *n* crespo, gramaglie *pl*.
crash [kræʃ] *n* schianto, crollo; cozzo; scontro; *vi* crollare con fracasso, precipitare; urtare (contro).
crass [kræs] *a* crasso, grossolano.
crate [kreit] *n* cassa da imballaggio.
crater ['kreitə] *n* cratere.
cravat [krə'væt] *n* fazzoletto da collo, cravatta.
crave [kreiv] *vti* bramare, implorare.
craven ['kreivn] *a n* codardo.
craving ['kreiviŋ] *a* ardente, insaziabile; *n* brama, voglia.
crawl [krɔ:l] *vi* strisciare, andare carponi.
crayfish ['kreifiʃ] *n* gambero d'acqua dolce.
crayon ['kreiən] *n* pastello.
craze [kreiz] *n* mania, pazzia; passione; moda.
craziness ['kreizinis] *n* follia; instabilità d'un edificio.
crazy ['kreizi] *a* folle, pazzo; instabile.
creak [kri:k] *n* cigolio; *vi* cigolare, scricchiolare.

cream [kri:m] *n* panna, crema; (*fig*) fior fiore; **c. jug** lattiera.
creamer ['kri:mə] *n* lattiera.
creamery ['kri:məri] *n* caseificio, latteria.
crease [kri:s] *n* grinza, piega; *vt* piegare; sgualcir(si).
create [kri:'eit] *vt* creare.
creation [kri:'eiʃən] *n* creazione, creato.
creative [kri:'eitiv] *a* creativa.
creator [kri'eitə] *n* creatore.
creature ['kri:tʃə] *n* creatura.
credentials [kri'denʃəls] *n pl* credenziali *pl*.
credibility [,kredi'biliti] *n* credibilità.
credible ['kredəbl] *a* credibile.
credit ['kredit] *n* credito, fiducia; reputazione, onore, merito; *vt* credere, prestar fede a; attribuire, accreditare a.
creditable ['kreditəbl] *a* degno di fede, di stima, che torna all'onore di.
creditor ['kreditə] *n* creditore.
credulity [kri'dju:liti] *n* credulità.
creduious ['kredjuləs] *a* credulo.
creed [kri:d] *n* credo, somma degli articoli di fede.
creek [kri:k] *n* cala, piccola baia, insenatura.
creep [kri:p] *vi* (*of plants*) arrampicarsi; insinuarsi; strisciare; *n* strisciamento; *pl* brividi *pl*, pelle d'oca.
creeper ['kri:pə] *n* pianta rampicante; (*fig*) persona strisciante.
creepy ['kri:pi] *a* strisciante, che dà i brividi.
cremate [kri'meit] *vt* cremare.
cremation [kri'meiʃən] *n* cremazione.
crematorium [,kremə'tɔ:riəm] *pl* **crematoria** forno crematorio.
creole ['kri:oul] *a n* creolo.
creosote ['kriəsout] *n* (*chem*) creosoto.
crêpe [kreip] *n* crespo, tessuto di seta.
crescent ['kresnt] *a* crescente, a mezzaluna; *n* fila di case disposte a semicerchio.
cress [kres] *n* crescione.
crest [krest] *n* cresta, ciuffetto, criniera.
crestfallen ['krest,fɔ:lən] *a* abbattuto, mortificato.
crevasse [kri'væs] *n* crepaccio.
crevice ['krevis] *n* crepa, fessura.
crew [kru:] *n* ciurma, equipaggio.
crib [krib] *n* lettino per bimbo; mangiatoia, presepio; (*fam*) plagio; (*sl*) traduttore, bigino; *vt* copiare, plagiare.
cricket ['krikit] *n* grillo; (*sport*) 'cricket'.
crime [kraim] *n* delitto, misfatto.
criminal ['kriminl] *a* criminale, penale; *n* criminale, delinquente.
criminology [,krimi'nɔlədʒi] *n* criminologia.
crimson ['krimzn] *a n* cremisi.
cringe [krindʒ] *vi* essere servile, comportarsi servilmente.
crinkle ['kriŋkl] *n* grinza, crespa; *vti* increspar(si), spiegazzare.
crinoline ['krinəlin] *n* crinolina.
cripple ['kripl] *n* sciancato, zoppo, invalido; *vt* azzoppare; (*fig*) diminuire la capacità di.
crisis ['kraisis] *n* crisi.
crisp [krisp] *a* croccante; (*hair*) crespo; (*air*) frizzante; (*style*) incisivo.
crispness ['krispnis] *n* friabilità; crespositià; freddo intenso; chiarezza.
criterion [krai'tiəriən] *pl* **criteria** *n* criterio.
critic ['kritik] *n* critico.
critical ['kritikəl] *a* critico.
criticism ['kritisizəm] *n* critica, giudizio critico.
criticize ['kritisaiz] *vt* criticare, fare la critica a.
croak [krouk] *vi* gracchiare, gracidare; (*fig*) predire malanni.
croaky ['krouki] *a* rauco.
crochet ['krouʃei] *n* lavoro ad uncinetto.
crockery ['krɔkəri] *n* terraglie *pl*, vasellame.
crocodile ['krɔkədail] *n* coccodrillo.
crocus ['kroukəs] *n* croco.
croft [krɔft] *n* piccolo podere, campicello.
crone [kroun] *n* vecchia rugosa.
crony ['krouni] *n* (*fam*) vecchio amico.
crook [kruk] *n* ricurvatura; gancio; bastone da pastore; (*sl*) malvivente; *vti* curvar(si).
crooked ['krukid] *a* curvo, storto; disonesto.
crookedness ['krukidnis] *n* tortuosità, disonestà.
croon [kru:n] *vi* canticchiare sotto voce.
crop [krɔp] *n* raccolto; gozzo d'uccello; frusta; capelli corti; *vt* mozzare, tosare; mietere, raccogliere; brucare.
croquet ['kroukei] *n* (*sport*) 'croquet', pallamaglio.
crosier ['krouʒə] *n* pastorale.
cross [krɔs] *a* obliquo, trasversale; di cattivo umore; *n* croce; incrocio; *vt* attraversare; incrociare; segnare con una croce; *vi* incrociarsi.
cross-examine ['krɔsig'zæmin] *vt* interrogare a contraddittorio.
crossing ['krɔsiŋ] *n* traversata; incrocio; **level c., grade c.** passaggio a livello.
crossroads ['krɔsroudz] *n pl* crocevia.
crossword ['krɔswə:d] *n* cruciverba.
crotchet ['krɔtʃit] *n* capriccio; **crotchety** capriccioso.
crouch [krautʃ] *vi* accucciarsi, rannicchiarsi.
croup [kru:p] *n* groppa; (*med*) crup, difterite.

crow [krou] *n* cornacchia, corvo; (*cock's*) canto; *vi* cantare; **c. over** vantarsi sopra.
crowd [kraud] *n* folla, massa; *vti* affollar(si); **crowded** affollato, popoloso.
crown [kraun] *n* corona; (*head*) sommità; (*hat*) fondo; coronamento; *vt* (in)coronare; **to c. it all** per colmo (di fortuna, di disgrazia).
crucial ['kru:ʃəl] *a* cruciale, critico.
crucible ['kru:sibl] *n* crogiuolo.
crucifix ['kru:sifiks] *n* crocifisso.
crucifixion [,kru:si'fikʃən] *n* crocifissione.
crucify ['kru:sifai] *vt* crocifiggere.
crude [kru:d] *a* crudo, grezzo, immaturo, primitivo.
cruel ['kruəl] *a* crudele.
cruelly ['kruəli] *ad* crudelmente.
cruelty ['kruəlti] *n* crudeltà.
cruet ['kru:it] *n* ampolla, ampollina; **c.-stand** ampolliera.
cruise [kru:z] *n* crociera; *vi* fare una crociera; incrociare.
cruiser ['kru:zə] *n* incrociatore; automobile della polizia.
crumb [krʌm] *n* briciola, mollica.
crumble ['krʌmbl] *vti* sbriciolar(si), sgretolar(si).
crumple ['krʌmpl] *vti* raggrinzar(si), sgualcir(si).
crunch [krʌntʃ] *vti* sgranocchiare rumorosamente, scricchiolare.
crusade [kru:'seid] *n* crociata.
crusader [kru:'seidə] *n* crociato.
crush [krʌʃ] *n* compressione, schiacciamento; calca; (*sl*) infatuazione, cotta; *vt* schiacciare, frantumare; sgualcire; annientare.
crushing ['krʌʃiŋ] *a* schiacciante; **c. mill** frantoio; **c. plant** impianto di frantumazione.
crust [krʌst] *n* crosta, incrostazione; *vti* incrostar(si).
crustiness ['krʌstinis] *n* irascibilità.
crusty ['krʌsti] *a* crostoso; irritabile.
crutch [krʌtʃ] *n* gruccia, stampella; forcella; inforcatura.
crux [krʌks] *n* punto, nodo.
cry [krai] *n* grido, richiamo, urlo, pianto; *vti* gridare, piangere.
crying ['kraiiŋ] *a* evidente, patente; *n.* pianto.
crypt [kript] *n* cripta.
cryptic ['kriptik] *a* misterioso, nascosto.
crystal ['kristl] *a* di cristallo; *n* cristallo.
crystalline ['kristəlain] *a n* cristallino.
crystallize ['kristəlaiz] *vti* cristallizzar(si).
cub [kʌb] *n* cucciolo di animali selvatici; **c. scout** lupetto.
Cuba ['kju:bə] *n* Cuba: **Cuban** *a n* cubano, cubana.
cube [kju:b] *n* cubo.
cubic ['kju:bik] *a* cubico.
cubicle ['kju:bikl] *n* stanzetta, piccolo locale, cubicolo.
cuckold ['kʌkəld] *n* becco, cornuto.
cuckoo ['kuku:] *n* cuculo, cucù; (*sl*) mezzo scemo.
cucumber ['kju:kəmbə] *n* cetriolo.
cud [kʌd] *n* bolo alimentare di ruminante.
cuddle ['kʌdl] *vt* abbracciare stretto.
cudgel ['kʌdʒəl] *n* clava, randello; *vt* picchiare con la clava, randellare; **to c. one's brains** scervellarsi.
cue [kju:] *n* (*theat*) battuta d'entrata; suggerimento; stecca da biliardo.
cuff [kʌf] *n* polsino; risvolto dei pantaloni; pugno, scapaccione; *vt* percuotere, picchiare.
cuisine [kwi:'zi:n] *n* cucina, modo di cucinare.
cul-de-sac ['kuldə'sæk] *n* vicolo cieco.
culinary ['kʌlinəri] *a* culinario.
culminate ['kʌlmineit] *vi* culminare.
culmination [,kʌlmi'neiʃən] *n* culminazione, culmine.
culpable ['kʌlpəbl] *a* colpevole.
culprit ['kʌlprit] *n* colpevole; imputato.
cult [kʌlt] *n* culto, venerazione.
cultivate ['kʌltiveit] *vt* coltivare.
cultivated ['kʌltiveitid] *a* coltivato; colto, educato.
cultivation [,kʌlti'veiʃən] *n* coltivazione; cultura.
cultivator ['kʌltiveitə] *n* coltivatore, cultore.
cultural ['kʌltʃərəl] *a* culturale.
culture ['kʌltʃə] *n* coltura, allevamento; (*of the mind*) cultura.
cultured ['kʌltʃəd] *a* colto.
cumber ['kʌmbə] *vt* impacciare, ingombrare.
cumbersome ['kʌmbəsəm] *a* ingombrante, poco maneggevole.
cumulative ['kju:mjulətiv] *a* cumulativo.
cunning ['kʌniŋ] *a* astuto, furbo; *n* astuzia, furberia, accortezza.
cup [kʌp] *n* tazza, calice, coppa.
cupboard ['kʌbəd] *n* armadio.
cupidity [kju:'piditi] *n* cupidigia.
cur [kə:] *n* cane bastardo.
curable ['kjuərəbl] *a* guaribile.
curate ['kjuərit] *n* curato.
curative ['kjuərətiv] *a* curativo.
curator [kjuə'reitə] *n* sovrintendente.
curb [kə:b] *n* costrizione, freno; bordo di marciapiede; *vt* frenare, soggiogare.
curds [kə:dz] *n pl* latte cagliato.
curdle ['kə:dl] *vti* cagliare, coagular(si); (*fig*) agghiacciar(si).
cure [kjuə] *n* cura, guarigione, rimedio; *vt* guarire; (*fish*) affumicare.
curfew ['kə:fju:] *n* coprifuoco.
curio ['kjuəriou] *pl* **curios** *n* oggetti rari.
curiosity [,kjuəri,ɔsiti] *n* curiosità.
curious ['kjuəriəs] curioso, raro, singolare.

curiously ['kjuəriəsli] *ad* curiosamente, stranamente; **c. enough** strano a dirsi.
curl [kə:l] *n* ricciolo; curva; *vt* arricciare, arricciarsi, sollevarsi in onde, in spire.
curler ['kə:lə] *n* bigodino, ferro per arricciare i capelli; giocatore di 'curling'.
curly ['kə:li] *a* ricciuto.
currant ['kʌrənt] *n* uva sultanina; ribes.
currency ['kʌrənsi] *n* circolazione monetaria, moneta circolante; corso.
current ['kʌrənt] *a n* corrente.
curry ['kʌri] *n* salsa fatta di spezie e di aromi; *vt* stufare con aromi; (*leather*) conciare; (*horse*) strigliare; **to c. favor with** adulare, ingraziarsi.
currycomb ['kʌri,koum] *n* striglia.
curse [kə:s] *n* imprecazione, maledizione; sventura, calamità; *vti* bestemmiare, maledire; (*passive*) essere afflitto.
cursed [kə:st] *a* maledetto.
cursive ['kə:siv] *a n* corsivo.
cursory ['kə:səri] *a* frettoloso, rapido.
curt [kə:t] *a* asciutto, brusco.
curtail [kə:'teil] *vt* abbreviare, accorciare.
curtain ['kə:tn] *n* cortina, tenda, sipario.
curtsey ['kə:tsi] *n* inchino, riverenza.
curve [kə:v] *n* curva; *vti* curvar(si).
cushion ['kuʃən] *n* cuscino; (*mech*) cuscinetto.
custard ['kʌstəd] *n* crema.
custody ['kʌstədi] *n* custodia, imprigionamento.
custom ['kʌstəm] *n* uso, costume, abitudine, clientela; *pl* dazio, dogana; **customhouse** dogana.
customary ['kʌstəməri] *a* abituale, consueto.
customer ['kʌstəmə] *n* avventore, cliente; (*sl*) tipo, individuo.
cut [kʌt] *n* taglio, ferita; affronto; riduzione; (*meat, material etc*) pezzo; *vt* tagliare, trinciare; togliere il saluto a; (*prices*) ridurre; (*cards*) alzare; **short c.** scorciatoia; **cutoff** scorciatoia; ritaglio di giornale.
cuticle ['kju:tikl] *n* cuticola.
cutler ['kʌtlə] *n* coltellinaio.
cutlery ['kʌtləri] *n* posateria.
cutlet ['kʌtlit] *n* cotoletta.
cutter ['kʌtə] *n* tagliatore; (*mech*) fresa.
cut-throat ['kʌtθrout] *a* accanito; *n* assassino.
cutting ['kʌtiŋ] *a* tagliente; (*fig*) pungente, mordace; *n* taglio; ritaglio, riduzione.
cuttle ['kʌtl] *n* **cuttlefish** seppia; **c.-bone** osso di seppia.
cyanide ['saiənaid] *n* (*chem*) cianuro.
cycle ['saikl] *n* ciclo, bicicletta; *vi* andare in bicicletta.
cyclist ['saiklist] *n* ciclista.
cyclone ['saikloun] *n* ciclone.
cylinder ['silində] *n* cilindro.
cylindrical [si'lindrikəl] *a* cilindrico.
cynic ['sinik] *n* cinico.
cynical ['sinikəl] *a* cinico.
cynicism ['sinisizəm] *n* cinismo.
cypress ['saipris] *n* cipresso.
Cyprus ['saiprəs] *n* Cipro; **Cyprian, Cypriot** *n* cipriota.
cyst [sist] *n* ciste.
czar [zɑ:] *n* zar.
Czechoslovakia ['tʃekouslou'vækiə] *n* Cecoslovacchia; **Czech** *a n* ceco; **Czechoslovak** *a n* cecoslovacco.

D

dab [dæb] *n* pezzettino, spalmatina, tocco, schizzo; *vt* toccare leggermente.
dabble ['dæbl] *vi* sguazzare; **to d. in** fare una cosa da dilettante.
dachshund ['dækshund] *n* cane bassotto.
dad [dæd] **daddy** ['dædi] *n* (*fam*) babbo, papà.
daffodil ['dæfədil] *n* narciso.
daft [dɑ:ft] *a* pazzerello, sciocco.
dagger ['dægə] *n* daga, pugnale.
dahlia ['deiliə] *n* (*bot*) dalia.
daily ['deili] *a* giornaliero, quotidiano; *n* (*giornale*) quotidiano.
daintiness ['deintinis] *n* delicatezza, raffinatezza, ricercatezza.
dainty ['deinti] *a* squisito, delicato, grazioso; schizzinoso; *n* leccornia.
dairy ['deəri] *n* latteria, cascina, caseificio; **dairymaid** lattaia; **dairyman** lattaio.
dais ['deiis] *n* pedana.
daisy ['deizi] *n* margherita, pratolina.
dale [deil] *n* vallata.
dally ['dæli] *vi* perdere tempo, gingillarsi, trastullarsi.
Dalmatia [dæl'meiʃə] *n* Dalmazia.
Dalmatian [dæl'meiʃjən] *a n* dalmata.
dam [dæm] *n* argine, diga; (*of animals*) madre; *vt* arginare.
damage ['dæmidʒ] *n* danno, danni *pl*; perdita; *vt* danneggiare.
damaged ['dæmidʒd] *a* guastato, avariato.
damaging ['dæmidʒiŋ] *a* dannoso, nocivo.
damask ['dæməsk] *n* damasco.
dame [deim] *n* dama, nobildonna.
damn [dæm] *vt* dannare, maledire.
damnation [dæm'neiʃən] *n* dannazione.
damned [dæmd] *a* dannato, maledetto; *ad* (*sl*) maledettamente; molto.
damning ['dæmiŋ] *a* che condanna, schiacciante; che maledice; *n* condanna; maledizione.
damp [dæmp] *a* umido; *n* umidità; *vt* inumidire; (*fig*) scoraggiare.
dampness ['dæmpnis] *n* umidità.

damsel ['dæmzəl] *n* (*poet*) donzella.
damson ['dæmzən] *n* susina damascena.
dance [dɑːns] *n* ballo, danza; *vi* ballare, danzare.
dancer ['dɑːnsə] *n* ballerino, ballerina.
dancing ['dɑːnsiŋ] *a* danzante; *n* il ballo, la danza.
dandelion ['dændilaiən] *n* (*bot*) tarassico, (*fam*) soffione.
dandle ['dændl] *vt* dondolare, far ballare sulle ginocchia, vezzeggiare.
dandruff ['dændrif] *n* forfora.
dandy ['dændi] *n* bellimbusto, damerino.
Dane [dein] *n* danese.
danger ['deindʒə] *n* pericolo.
dangerous ['deindʒrəs] *a* pericoloso.
dangle ['dængl] *vti* (far) dondolare.
dangling ['dæŋgliŋ] *a* ciondolante, penzoloni.
Daniel ['dænjəl] *nm pr* Daniele.
Danish ['deiniʃ] *a n* danese.
dank [dæŋk] *a* umido e freddo.
Danube ['dænjuːb] *n* Danubio.
dapper ['dæpə] *a* arzillo, vivace.
dappled ['dæpld] *a* chiazzato, pomellato.
dare [dɛə] *vi* osare; *vt* sfidare; **I dare say** forse, probabilmente; **dare-devil** scavezzacollo.
daring ['dɛəriŋ] *a* audace, intrepido; *n* audacia.
dark [dɑːk] *a* buio, (o)scuro, tenebroso; *n* oscurità, tenebre *pl*.
darken ['dɑːkən] *vti* oscurar(si).
darkness ['dɑːknis] *n* oscurità, tenebre *pl*, buio.
darling ['dɑːliŋ] *a* caro, diletto; *n* prediletto.
darn [dɑːn] *n* rammendo; *vt* rammendare.
darning ['dɑːniŋ] *n* rammendo; **d. needle** ago da rammendo; **d. wool** lana da rammendo.
dart [dɑːt] *n* dardo; balzo, movimento rapido; *vt* dardeggiare, lanciare; *vi* balzare, slanciar(si).
dash [dæʃ] *n* slancio, impeto, attacco, colpo; goccio; lineetta; **dashboard** (*aut*) cruscotto; *vti* precipitarsi, urtare violentemente, frantumare, frantumarsi, distruggere; **to d. off** fare qualcosa velocemente, scappar via.
dashing ['dæʃiŋ] *a* impetuoso; sgargiante.
dastard ['dæstəd] *n* codardo, vile; **dastardly** *a* vile, codardo.
dastardliness ['dæstədlinis] *n* viltà.
data ['deitə] *n pl* dati, elementi.
date [deit] *n* dattero; data, scadenza; appuntamento; **out of d.** antiquato; **up to d.** aggiornato; *vti* datare; avere (fissare) un appuntamento.
dative ['deitiv] *a n* dativo.
daub [dɔːb] *n* imbrattamento, pittura malfatta, intonaco; *vt* imbrattare, impiastrare.
daughter ['dɔːtə] *n* figlia; **d.-in-law** nuora.
daunt [dɔːnt] *vt* scoraggiare, spaventare.
dauntless ['dɔːntlis] *a* intrepido.
David ['deivid] *nm pr* Davide.
dawdle ['dɔːdl] *vi* bighellonare.
dawn [dɔːn] *n* alba, aurora; inizio; *vi* albeggiare, cominciare ad apparire.
day [dei] *n* giorno, giornata, dì; **d. boy** allievo esterno; **d. school** scuola diurna.
daybreak ['deibreik] *n* alba.
daydream ['deidriːm] *n* sogno ad occhi aperti.
day-laborer ['dei͵leibərə] *n* lavoratore a giornata.
daylight ['deilait] *n* (luce del) giorno.
daytime ['deitaim] *n* il giorno, la giornata.
daze [deiz] *n* intontimento, stupore.
dazzle ['dæzl] *vt* abbagliare.
deacon ['diːkən] *n* diacono.
dead [ded] *a* morto; completo, assoluto; *n* morto, morti, (*fig*) profondità; **at d. of night** nel cuor della notte; *ad* completamente, assolutamente.
deaden ['dedn] *vt* ammortire, smorzare; *vi* affievolirsi.
deadlock ['dedlɔk] *n* punto morto.
deadly ['dedli] *a* mortale; *ad* mortalmente.
deadness ['dednis] *n* ammortimento, stato di torpore.
deaf [def] *a* sordo.
deafen ['defn] *vt* assordare, stordire; **deafening** assordante.
deaf-mute ['def'mjuːt] *n* sordomuto.
deafness ['defnis] *n* sordità.
deal [diːl] *n* affare, accordo; (*at cards*) mano; legno d'abete o di pino; quantità; **a good d. (of)** molto; *vi* commerciare, trattare; comportarsi; *vt* distribuire; assestare (un colpo).
dealer ['diːlə] *n* commerciante, negoziante.
dealing ['diːliŋ] *n* commercio; distribuzione; condotta; *pl* rapporti *pl*.
dean [diːn] *n* arciprete, decano; preside di facoltà.
dear [diə] *a* caro, costoso; **dear me!** *interj* Dio mio!
dearly ['diəli] *ad* teneramente; a caro prezzo.
dearness ['diənis] *n* caro prezzo.
dearth [dəːθ] *n* carestia, scarsità.
death [deθ] *n* morte; **deathbed** letto di morte; **d.-rate** mortalità.
debar [di'bɑː] *vt* escludere.
debase [di'beis] *vt* abbassare, svilire.
debatable [di'beitəbl] *a* discutibile, contestabile.
debate [di'beit] *n* dibattito, discussione; *vti* dibattere, discutere.
debauch [di'bɔːtʃ] *n* crapula, orgia; *vt* pervertire.

debauchery [di'bɔ:tʃəri] *n* pervertimento, scostumatezza.
debenture [di'bentʃə] *n* (*com*) obbligazione.
debilitate [di'biliteit] *vt* debilitare.
debility [di'biliti] *n* debolezza, languore.
debit ['debit] *n* (*com*) debito; *vt* addebitare.
debris ['debri] *n* macerie, detriti.
debt [det] *n* debito.
debtor ['detə] *n* debitore.
debunk [di:'bʌŋk] *vt* ridurre alle giuste proporzioni.
debut ['deibu:] *n* debutto.
débutante ['debju:tɑ:nt] *n* debuttante.
decade ['dekeid] *n* decade, decennio.
decadence ['dekədəns] *n* decadenza.
decadent ['dekədənt] *a n* decadente.
decalogue ['dekəlɔg] *n* decalogo.
decant [di'kænt] *vt* versare, travasare.
decanter [di'kæntə] *n* caraffa.
decapitate [di'kæpiteit] *vt* decapitare.
decasyllable ['dekəsiləbl] *a n* (*poet*) decasillabo.
decay [di'kei] *n* decomposizione, decadenza, rovina; *vi* decadere, decomporsi, deperire, (*teeth*) cariarsi.
decease [di'si:s] *vi* decedere, morire.
deceased [di'si:st] *a n* deceduto, defunto, fu.
deceit [di'si:t] *n* inganno, frode, falsità.
deceitful [di'si:tful] *a* ingannevole, falso.
deceitfulness [di'si:tfulnis] *n* doppiezza, falsità.
deceive [di'si:v] *vt* ingannare, deludere.
decelerate [di:'seləreit] *vti* rallentare.
December [di'sembə] *n* dicembre.
decency ['di:snsi] *n* decenza, decoro.
decent ['di:snt] *a* decente, decoroso, onesto, per bene.
decentralize [di'sentrəlaiz] *vt* decentrare.
deception [di'sepʃən] *n* inganno; illusione.
deceptive [di'septiv] *a* ingannevole.
deceptiveness [di'septivnis] *n* carattere ingannevole, fallacia.
decibel ['desibel] *n* (*phys*) decibel.
decide [di'said] *vti* decidere.
decided [di'saidid] *a* deciso, risoluto, inconfutabile.
decidedly [di'saididli] *ad* decisamente, indubbiamente.
decimal ['desiməl] *a n* decimale.
decimate ['desimeit] *vt* decimare.
decimation [,desi'meiʃən] *n* decimazione.
decipher [di'saifə] *vt* decifrare.
deciphering [di'saifəriŋ] *n* decifrazione.
decision [di'siʒən] *n* decisione, giudizio; risolutezza.
decisive [di'saisiv] *a* decisivo; deciso.
decisiveness [di'saisivnis] *n* risolutezza.
deck [dek] *n* (*naut*) ponte, coperta; mazzo di carte da gioco; *vt* ornare, coprire, rivestire; **d. chair** sedia a sdraio.
declaim [di'kleim] *vti* declamare.
declamation [,deklə'meiʃən] *n* declamazione.
declamatory [di'klæmətəri] *a* declamatorio.
declaration [,deklə'reiʃən] *n* dichiarazione.
declare [di'klɛə] *vt* dichiarare, proclamare; *vi* dichiararsi.
declension [di'klenʃən] *n* (*gram*) declinazione.
decline [di'klain] *n* declino, decadimento; declivio; (*price*) ribasso; *vti* declinare, rifiutare; inclinarsi; diminuire.
declivity [di'kliviti] *n* declivio.
decode [di:'koud] *vt* decifrare, tradurre.
décolleté [dei'kɔltei] *a n* scollato; scollatura.
decompose [,di:kəm'pouz] *vti* decomporre, decomporsi; scomporre, scomporsi.
decomposition [,di:kɔmpə'ziʃən] *n* decomposizione.
decontrol ['di:kən'troul] *vt* togliere i controlli a.
decorate ['dekəreit] *vt* decorare, ornare, (*a room*) verniciare.
decoration [,dekə'reiʃən] *n* decorazione, ornamento.
decorator ['dekə'reitə] *n* (pittore) decoratore; **interior d.** arredatore.
decorous ['dekərəs] *a* decoroso.
decorum [di'kɔ:rəm] *n* decoro.
decoy [di'kɔi] *n* esca, richiamo; *vt* allettare, adescare.
decrease ['di:kri:s] *n* diminuzione; *vti* [di:'kri:s] diminuire.
decree [di'kri:] *n* decreto: *vt* decretare.
decrepit [di'krepit] *a* decrepito.
decry [di'krai] *vt* denigrare, screditare.
dedicate ['dedikeit] *vt* dedicare.
dedicated ['dedikeitid] *a* dedicato; votato, consacrato; scrupoloso.
dedication [,dedi'keiʃən] *n* dedica; dedicazione.
deduce [di'dju:s] *vt* dedurre, desumere.
deduct [di'dʌkt] *vt* dedurre, sottrarre.
deduction [di'dʌkʃən] *n* deduzione.
deed [di:d] *n* azione, atto, fatto, impresa; titolo, contratto.
deem [di:m] *vti* giudicare, stimare, pensare.
deep [di:p] *a* profondo; alto; sprofondato; cupo; *ad* profondamente; *n* abisso, alto mare.
deep-freeze [di:p'fri:z] *n* surgelamento.
deepen ['di:pən] *vti* approfondir(si).
deeply ['di:pli] *ad* profondamente.

deepness ['di:pnis] *n* profondità.
deer [diə] *n* (*inv*) cervo, daino.
deface [di'feis] *vt* sfigurare; cancellare.
defacement [di'feismənt] *n* sfregio, cancellazione.
defamation [,defə'meiʃən] *n* diffamazione, calunnia.
defamatory [di'fæmətəri] *a* diffamatorio, calunnioso.
defame [di'feim] *vt* diffamare, calunniare.
default [di'fɔ:lt] *n* mancanza; insolvenza contumacia; *vti* render(si) contumace, mancare di pagare.
defaulter [di'fɔ:ltə] *n* debitore moroso; imputato contumace.
defeat [di'fi:t] *n* disfatta, sconfitta; *vt* sconfiggere.
defeatist [di'fi:tist] *n* disfattista.
defect [di'fekt] *n* difetto, imperfezione.
defection [di'fekʃən] *n* defezione.
defective [di'fektiv] *a* difettoso, imperfetto; **mentally d.** infermo di mente.
defend [di'fend] *vt* difendere.
defendant [di'fendənt] *n* convenuto, imputato.
defender [di'fendə] *n* difensore.
defense [di'fens] *n* difesa.
defenseless [di'fenslis] *a* indifeso.
defensive [di'fensiv] *a* difensivo; *n* difensiva.
defer [di'fə:] *vt* differire, rimandare; essere deferente.
deference ['defərəns] *n* deferenza.
deferent ['defərənt] *a* deferente.
deferentially [,defə'renʃəli] *ad* con deferenza.
deferment [di'fə:mənt] *n* differimento, rimando; dilazione.
defiance [di'faiəns] *n* sfida; spavalderia.
defiant [di'faiənt] *a* ardito, provocante; spavaldo.
deficiency [di'fiʃənsi] *n* deficienza; (*com*) disavanzo.
deficient [di'fiʃənt] *a* deficiente, difettoso, insufficiente.
deficit ['defisit] *n* disavanzo, deficit.
defile ['di:fail] *n* gola di montagna, stretto passaggio; *vt* [di'fail] insozzare; violare; *vi* procedere in fila, sfilare.
defilement [di'failmənt] *n* contaminazione, violazione.
define [di'fain] *vt* definire, determinare, delimitare.
definite ['definit] *a* definito, preciso.
definition [,defi'niʃən] *n* definizione.
definitive [di'finitiv] *a* definitivo; decisivo.
deflate [di'fleit] *vt* (*tire*) sgonfiare; (*fin*) deflazionare.
deflect [di'flekt] *vt* (far) deflettere.
deflection [di'flekʃən] *n* deviazione.
deforest [di'fɔrist] *vt* disboscare.
deform [di'fɔ:m] *vt* deformare.
deformed [di'fɔ:md] *a* deforme.
deformity [di'fɔ:miti] *n* deformità.
defraud [di'frɔ:d] *vt* defraudare.
defray [di'frei] *vt* pagare, sostenere le spese.
defrost [di'frɔst] *vt* (*also com*) sgelare; disgelare; (*refrigerator*) sbrinare; **defroster** (*aut*) riscaldatore.
deft [deft] *a* lesto; agile; abile.
defunct [di'fʌŋkt] *a n* defunto, deceduto.
defy [di'fai] *vt* sfidare.
degenerate [di'dʒenərit] *a n* degenerato; *vi* [di'dʒenəreit] degenerare.
degradation [,degrə'deiʃən] *n* degradazione.
degrade [di'greid] *vt* degradare.
degrading [di'greidiŋ] *a* degradante.
degree [di'gri:] *n* grado, laurea.
deign [dein] *vti* degnar(si).
deity ['di:iti] *n* deità, divinità.
deject [di'dʒekt] *vt* deprimere, scoraggiare.
dejected [di'dʒektid] *a* abbattuto, scoraggiato.
dejection [di'dʒekʃən] *n* scoraggiamento.
delay [di'lei] *n* ritardo, indugio; *vt* ritardare; *vi* indugiare.
delegate ['deligit] *n* delegato; ['deligeit] *vt* delegare.
delegation [,deli'geiʃən] *n* delegazione.
delete [di'li:t] *vt* cancellare.
deleterious [,deli'tiəriəs] *a* deleterio.
deletion [di'li:ʃən] *n* cancellatura.
deliberate [di'libərit] *a* cauto, deliberato, misurato; *vti* [di'libəreit] deliberare.
deliberately [di'libəritli] *ad* deliberatamente, apposta.
deliberation [di,libə'reiʃən] *n* deliberazione; decisione.
delicacy ['delikəsi] *n* delicatezza; leccornia.
delicate ['delikit] *a* delicato.
delicately ['delikitli] *ad* delicatamente.
delicious [di'liʃəs] *a* delizioso, squisito.
deliciousness [di'liʃəsnis] *n* squisitezza.
delight [di'lait] *n* diletto, gioia; *vti* dilettar(si), divertir(si).
delightful [di'laitful] *a* delizioso, dilettevole, incantevole, molto piacevole.
delightfully [di'laitfuli] *ad* deliziosamente.
delineate [di'linieit] *vt* delineare.
delineation [di,lini'eiʃən] *n* delineazione.
delinquency [di'liŋkwənsi] *n* delinquenza.
delinquent [di'liŋkwənt] *n* delinquente.
delirious [di'liriəs] *a* delirante.
delirium [di'liriəm] *n* delirio.
deliver [di'livə] *vt* liberare, salvare;

(*med*) partorire; consegnare; (*speech*) pronunciare; (*blow*) vibrare.
deliverance [di'livərəns] *n* liberazione; parto; consegna; pronunziamento.
deliverer [di'livərə] *n* liberatore, salvatore.
delivery [di'livəri] *n* consegna, distribuzione di posta; parto; il pronunciare un discorso; **cash on d.** (**C.O.D.**) contro assegno; **deliveryman** fattorino, ragazzo; **general d.** fermo posta.
dell [del] *n* valletta, conca.
delphinium [del'finiəm] *n* (*bot*) fiorcappuccio.
delta ['deltə] *n* delta; **d.-wing** (*av*) ala a delta.
delude [di'lju:d] *vt* illudere, ingannare.
deluge ['delju:dʒ] *n* diluvio.
delusion [di'lu:ʒən] *n* illusione; allucinazione.
delusive [di'lju:siv] *a* ingannevole, illusorio.
delve [delv] *vt* zappare; (*fig*) penetrare, sondare.
demagogue ['deməgɔg] *n* demagogo.
demand [di:'ma:nd] *n* domanda, richiesta; *vt* richiedere; domandare, esigere.
demeanor [di'mi:nə] *n* comportamento.
demented [di'mentid] *a* demente, pazzo.
demise [di'maiz] *n* decesso; cessione.
demobilization ['di:,moubilai'zeiʃən] *n* smobilitazione.
demobilize [di:'moubilaiz] *vt* smobilitare.
democracy [di'mɔkrəsi] *n* democrazia.
democrat ['deməkræt] *n* democratico.
democratic [,demə'krætik] *a* democratico.
demolish [di'mɔliʃ] *vt* demolire.
demolition [,demə'liʃən] *n* demolizione.
demon ['di:mən] *n* demonio, spirito maligno.
demoniac [di'mouniæk] *a* demoniaco; *n* indemoniato.
demonstrate ['demənstreit] *vti* dimostrare.
demonstration [,demənsʼtreiʃən] *n* dimostrazione.
demonstrative [di'mɔnstrətiv] *a* dimostrativo; espansivo.
demoralization [di,mɔrəlai'zeiʃən] *n* demoralizzazione.
demoralize [di'mɔrəlaiz] *vt* demoralizzare.
demur [di'mə:] *n* esitazione, irresolutezza; *vi* esitare; obiettare.
demure [di'mjuə] *a* affettatamente modesto.
demureness [di'mjuənis] *n* modestia, affettato candore.
den [den] *n* covo, tana; (*fam*) studiolo.
denationalize [di:'næʃnəlaiz] *vt* snazionalizzare.
denial [di'naiəl] *n* diniego, rifiuto.
denigrate ['denigreit] *vt* denigrare.
denigration [,deni'greiʃən] *n* denigrazione.
denim ['denim] *n* tessuto di cotone; *pl* tuta.
Denis ['denis] *nm pr* Dionigi.
denizen ['denizn] *n* abitante; straniero naturalizzato.
Denmark ['denma:k] *n* Danimarca.
denominate [di'nɔmineit] *vt* denominare.
denomination [di,nɔmi'neiʃən] *n* denominazione; (*com*) taglio, valore.
denote [di'nout] *vt* denotare, indicare.
denounce [di'nauns] *vt* denunciare.
dense [dens] *a* denso, spesso; ottuso.
density ['densiti] *n* densità; stupidità.
dent [dent] *n* incavo, intaccatura; (*mech*) dente; *vt* intaccare; *vi* dentellarsi.
dental ['dentl] *a n* dentale.
dentifrice ['dentifris] *n* dentifricio.
dentist ['dentist] *n* dentista.
denture ['dentʃə] *n* dentiera.
denude [di'nju:d] *vt* denudare.
denunciation [di,nʌnsi'eiʃən] *n* denuncia, accusa.
deny [di'nai] *vt* negare; rifiutare.
deodorant [di:'oudərənt] *n* deodorante.
depart [di'pa:t] *vi* partire; (*fig*) derogare da; **departed** *a* passato; **the departed** il defunto, i defunti.
department [di'pa:tmənt] *n* dipartimento, reparto; **d. store** emporio.
departure [di'pa:tʃə] *n* partenza; allontanamento; **new d.** nuovo orientamento.
depend [di'pend] *vi* dipendere, contare su.
dependability [di'pendəbiliti] *n* fidatezza; (*of machine etc*) sicurezza di funzionamento.
dependable [di'pendəbl] *a* fidato, sicuro, attendibile.
dependant, dependent [di'pendənt] *n* dipendente.
dependence [di'pendəns] *n* dipendenza; fiducia.
depict [di'pikt] *vt* dipingere, descrivere.
depilate ['depileit] *vt* depilare.
depilatory [di'pilətəri] *a n* depilatorio.
deplete [di'pli:t] *vt* esaurire, vuotare.
deplorable [di'plɔ:rəbl] *a* deplorevole.
deplore [di'plɔ:] *vt* deplorare.
deploy [di'plɔi] *vti* (*mil*) spiegar(si).
depopulate [di'pɔpjuleit] *vt* spopolare.
depopulation [di:,pɔpju'leiʃən] *n* spopolamento.

deport [di'pɔ:t] *vt* deportare, esiliare.
deportation [,di:pɔ:'teiʃən] *n* deportazione.
deportment [di'pɔ:tmənt] *n* portamento, contegno.
depose [di'pouz] *vt* deporre, togliere di carica.
deposit [di'pɔzit] *n* deposito; versamento; *vt* depositare; versare.
depositary [di'pɔzitəri] *n* depositario.
deposition [,depə'ziʃən] *n* deposizione.
depositor [di'pɔzitə] *n* depositante.
depository [di'pɔzitəri] *n* deposito.
depot ['depou] *n* deposito, magazzino.
depravation [,deprə'veiʃən] *n* corruzione, depravazione.
deprave [di'preiv] *vt* corrompere, depravare.
depravity [di'præviti] *n* depravazione.
deprecate ['deprikeit] *vt* deprecare.
deprecation [,depri'keiʃən] *n* deprecazione.
depreciate [di'pri:ʃieit] *vt* deprezzare, screditare; *vi* diminuire di valore.
depreciation [di,pri:ʃi'eiʃən] *n* deprezzamento.
depredation [,depri'deiʃən] *n* depredazione.
depress [di'pres] *vt* deprimere.
depressing [di'presiŋ] *a* deprimente.
depression [di'preʃən] *n* depressione.
deprivation [,depri'veiʃən] *n* privazione.
deprive [di'praiv] *vt* privare.
depth [depθ] *n* profondità, fondo; **d.-charge** bomba di profondità; **d.-finder** scandaglio.
deputation [,depju:'teiʃən] *n* deputazione.
depute [di'pju:t] *vt* deputare.
deputize ['depjutaiz] *vi* sostituire, fare le veci di.
deputy ['depjuti] *n* delegato, deputato, rappresentante.
derail [di'reil] *vt* far deragliare; *vi* deragliare.
derailment [di'reilmənt] *n* deragliamento.
derange [di'reindʒ] *vt* disordinare, scombussolare.
derangement [di'reindʒmənt] *n* sconvolgimento, confusione.
derelict ['derilikt] *a* abbandonato, derelitto; *n* relitto.
dereliction [,deri'likʃən] *n* abbandono; negligenza.
deride [di'raid] *vt* deridere.
derision [di'riʒən] *n* derisione, sarcasmo.
derisive [di'raisiv] *a* derisorio.
derivation [,deri'veiʃən] *n* derivazione.
derivative [di'rivətiv] *a n* derivato.
derive [di'raiv] *vti* derivare.
derogate ['derəgeit] *vi* derogare.
derogation [,derə'geiʃən] *n* deroga.
derogatory [di'rɔgətəri] *a* derogatorio.
derrick ['derik] *n* argano, gru.
descend [di'send] *vti* scendere, discendere; trasmettersi.
descendant [di'sendənt] *a n* discendente.
descent [di'sent] *n* discesa, pendio; discendenza, lignaggio.
describe [dis'kraib] *vt* descrivere.
description [dis'kripʃən] *n* descrizione; genere, specie.
descriptive [dis'kriptiv] *a* descrittivo.
descry [dis'krai] *vt* discernere, scorgere.
desecrate ['desikreit] *vt* profanare.
desecration [,desi'kreiʃən] *n* profanazione.
desert [di'zə:t] *vti* disertare.
desert ['dezət] *n* deserto.
desert [di'zə:t] *n* (*usu pl*) merito.
deserted [di'zə:tid] *a* deserto, abbandonato.
deserter [di'zə:tə] *n* disertore.
desertion [di'zə:ʃən] *n* diserzione.
deserve [di'zə:v] *vt* meritare.
deserving [di'zə:viŋ] *a* degno, meritevole.
desiccate ['desikeit] *vt* essiccare.
design [di'zain] *n* disegno, proposito; *vt* disegnare, proporsi.
designate ['dezigneit] *vt* designare.
designation [,dezig'neiʃən] *n* designazione.
designer [di'zainə] *n* disegnatore, modellista.
designing [di'zainiŋ] *a* astuto, intrigante.
desirable [di'zaiərəbl] *a* desiderabile.
desire [di'zaiə] *n* desiderio, passione, voglia, preghiera; *vt* desiderare, pregare.
desirous [di'zaiərəs] *a* desideroso.
desist [di'zist] *vi* desistere.
desk [desk] *n* tavolo, scrittoio, scrivania; cattedra, banco di scuola.
desolate ['desəlit] *a* desolato; ['desəleit] *vt* desolare, devastare.
desolation [,desə'leiʃən] *n* desolazione, distruzione.
despair [dis'pɛə] *n* disperazione; *vi* disperar(si).
despairing [dis'pɛəriŋ] *a* disperato, che fa disperare.
despatch [dis'pætʃ] *v* **dispatch.**
desperate ['despərit] *a* disperato; furioso.
desperately ['despəritli] *ad* disperatamente; gravemente.
desperation [,despə'reiʃən] *n* disperazione, accanimento.
despicability [,despikə'biliti] *n* spregevolezza.
despicable ['despikəbl] *a* spregevole.
despise [dis'paiz] *vt* disprezzare.
despite [dis'pait] *n* dispetto; *prep* a dispetto di, nonostante, malgrado.
despoil [dis'pɔil] *vt* derubare, spogliare.

despondency [dis'pɔndənsi] *n* abbattimento, scoraggiamento.
despondent [dis'pɔndənt] *a* abbattuto, scoraggiato.
despot ['despɔt] *n* despota.
despotic [des'pɔtik] *a* dispotico.
despotism ['despətizəm] *n* dispotismo.
dessert [di'zə:t] *n* 'dessert', dolci e frutta (alla fine del pasto) *pl.*
destination [,desti'neiʃən] *n* destinazione.
destine ['destin] *vt* destinare.
destiny ['destini] *n* destino, fato.
destitute ['destitju:t] *a* bisognoso, privo di mezzi.
destitution [,desti'tju:ʃən] *n* destituzione, miseria.
destroy [dis'trɔi] *vt* distruggere.
destroyer [dis'trɔiə] *n* distruttore; (*naut*) cacciatorpediniere.
destruction [dis'trʌkʃən] *n* distruzione, rovina.
destructive [dis'trʌktiv] *a* distruttivo.
destructiveness [dis'trʌktivnis] *n* potenza distruttiva, mania distruttiva.
desultory ['desəltəri] *a* saltuario, sconnesso.
detach [di'tætʃ] *vt* (di)staccare, separare.
detached [di'tætʃt] *a* distaccato, isolato, obiettivo.
detachment [di'tætʃmənt] *n* distacco; (*mil*) distaccamento.
detail ['di:teil] *n* dettaglio, particolare; *vt* dettagliare; (*mil*) distaccare.
detain [di'tein] *vt* detenere, trattenere.
detect [di'tekt] *vt* scoprire.
detection [di'tekʃən] *n* scoperta, rivelazione.
detective [di'tektiv] *n* 'detective', agente investigativo.
detention [di'tenʃən] *n* detenzione.
deter [di'tə:] *vt* distogliere, scoraggiare.
detergent [di'tə:dʒənt] *a n* detergente; detersivo.
deteriorate [di'tiəriəreit] *vti* deteriorar(si).
deterioration [di,tiəriə'reiʃən] *n* deterioramento.
determinate [di'tə:minit] *a* determinato, definito, deciso.
determination [di,tə:mi'neiʃən] *n* determinazione, risolutezza.
determine [di'tə:min] *vt* determinare, decidere; *vi* decidersi.
determined [di'tə:mind] *a* deciso, risoluto.
deterrent [di'terənt] *n* azione avente un effetto preventivo, freno.
detest [di'test] *vt* detestare.
detestable [di'testəbl] *a* detestabile.
detestation [,di:test'teiʃən] *n* avversione, odio.
dethrone [di'θroun] *vt* detronizzare.
detonate ['detouneit] *vti* (far) detonare.
detonation [,detou'neiʃən] *n* detonazione.
detonator ['detouneitə] *n* detonatore.
detour ['deituə] *n* deviazione d'itinerario, giro; deviazione stradale.
detract [di'trækt] *vti* detrarre, sottrarre.
detraction [di'trækʃən] *n* detrazione; diffamazione.
detractor [di'træktə] *n* detrattore; diffamatore.
detriment ['detrimənt] *n* detrimento, danno.
detrimental [,detri'mentl] *a* dannoso.
deuce [dju:s] *n* diavolo, diamine; (*cards*) due; (*tennis*) quaranta pari.
devaluate [di:'væljueit] *vt* svalutare.
devaluation [,di:vælju'eiʃən] *n* svalutazione.
devalue [di:'vælju:] *v* **devaluate.**
devastate ['devəsteit] *vt* devastare.
devastating ['devəsteitiŋ] *a* rovinoso, devastante.
devastation [,devəs'teiʃən] *n* devastazione.
develop [di'veləp] *vt* sviluppare; *vi* svilupparsi.
development [di'veləpmənt] *n* sviluppo.
deviate ['di:vieit] *vti* (far) deviare.
deviation [,di:vi'eiʃən] *n* deviazione.
device [di'vais] *n* mezzo, espediente, progetto, stratagemma; aggeggio; dispositivo.
devil ['devl] *n* diavolo.
devilish ['deviiʃ] *a* diabolico.
devilry ['devlri] *n* diavoleria.
devious ['di:viəs] *a* indiretto, tortuoso, falso.
devise [di'vaiz] *vt* escogitare, progettare; lasciare per testamento.
devoid [di'vɔid] *a* privo.
devolution [,di:və'lu:ʃən] *n* devoluzione.
devolve [di'vɔlv] *vt* devolvere; *vi* ricadere.
devote [di'vout] *vt* consacrare, dedicare.
devoted [di'voutid] *a* devoto, votato.
devotee [,devou'ti:] *n* devoto.
devotion [di'vouʃən] *n* devozione, dedizione.
devour [di'vauə] *vt* divorare.
devout [di'vaut] *a* devoto, pio.
devoutness [di'vautnis] *n* religiosità.
dew [dju:] *n* rugiada.
dewy ['dju:i] *a* rugiadoso.
dexterity [deks'teriti] *n* destrezza.
dexterous ['dekstərəs] *a* destro, abile.
diabetes [,daiə'bi:ti:z] *n* diabete.
diabetic [,daiə'betik] *a* diabetico.
diabolic(al) [,daiə'bɔlik(əl)] *a* diabolico.
diadem ['daiədem] *n* diadema.
diagnose ['daiəgnouz] *vt* diagnosticare.

diagnosis [ˌdaiəg'nousis] *n* diagnosi.
diagonal [dai'ægənl] *a n* diagonale.
diagram ['daiəgræm] *n* diagramma.
dial ['daiəl] *n* meridiana, (*clock etc*) quadrante; (*tel*) disco combinatore.
dialect ['daiəlekt] *n* dialetto.
dialectal [ˌdaiə'lektəl] *a* dialettale.
dialogue ['daiəlɔg] *n* dialogo.
diameter [dai'æmitə] *n* diametro.
diametrically [ˌdaiə'metrikəli] *ad* diametralmente.
diamond ['daiəmənd] *n* diamante, brillante; (*geom*) rombo; **diamonds** *pl* (*cards*) quadri.
diaper ['daiəpə] *n* tela operata; pannolino.
diaphanous [dai'æfənəs] *a* diafano.
diaphragm ['daiəfræm] *n* diaframma.
diarrhea [ˌdaiə'riə] *n* diarrea.
diatribe ['daiətraib] *n* diatriba.
diary ['daiəri] *n* diario; agenda.
dictaphone ['diktəfoun] *n* dittafono.
dictate ['dikteit] *vti* dettare.
dictation [dik'teiʃən] *n* dettatura; comando.
dictator [dik'teitə] *n* chi detta; dittatore.
dictatorial [ˌdiktə'tɔːriəl] *a* dittatorio, dittatoriale.
dictatorship [dik'teitəʃip] *n* dittatura.
diction ['dikʃən] *n* dizione.
dictionary ['dikʃənri] *n* dizionario, vocabolario.
didactic [di'dæktik] *a* didattico.
die [dai] *pl* **dice** *n* dado; *pl* **dies** *n* (*tec*) conio, stampo; *vi* morire; **to d. out** scomparire.
diesel ['diːzəl] *n pr* diesel; **d. oil** nafta.
diet ['daiət] *n* dieta, regime; *vt* mettere a dieta, a regime; *vi* seguire una dieta.
differ ['difə] *vi* differire; dissentire.
difference ['difrəns] *n* differenza; contesa.
different ['difrənt] *a* differente, diverso.
differential [ˌdifə'renʃəl] *a* differenziale.
differentiate [ˌdifə'renʃieit] *vti* differenziar(si).
difficult ['difikəlt] *a* difficile.
difficulty ['difikəlti] *n* difficoltà; ostacolo.
diffidence ['difidəns] *n* diffidenza, sfiducia in sè, timidezza.
diffident ['difidənt] *a* diffidente, timido.
diffuse [di'fjuːs] *a* diffuso; *vti* diffonder(si).
diffusion [di'fjuːʒən] *n* diffusione.
dig [dig] *vti* scavare, vangare.
digest ['daidʒest] *n* riassunto, digesto; *vti* [dai'dʒest] digerire, assimilare.
digestible [di'dʒestəbl] *a* digeribile.
digestion [di'dʒestʃən] *n* digestione.
digestive [di'dʒestiv] *a* digestivo.
digger ['digə] *n* scavatore.
digit ['didʒit] *n* dito, cifra.
dignified ['dignifaid] *a* composto, dignitoso.
dignify ['dignifai] *vt* investire di dignità.
dignitary ['dignitəri] *n* dignitario.
dignity ['digniti] *n* dignità.
digress [dai'gres] *vi* fare delle digressioni.
digression [dai'greʃən] *n* digressione.
dike [daik] *n* diga.
dilapidate [di'læpideit] *vt* dilapidare; **dilapidated** in rovina.
dilate [dai'leit] *vti* dilatar(si).
dilatory ['dilətəri] *a* dilatorio.
dilemma [di'lemə] *n* dilemma.
diligence ['diliʒəns] *n* diligenza.
diligent ['dilidʒənt] *a* diligente.
dilute [dai'ljuːt] *vt* diluire *a* diluito.
dilution [dai'ljuːʃən] *n* diluzione.
dim [dim] *a* indistinto, oscuro; appannato; debole; (*intelligence*) ottuso; *vti* offuscar(si), oscurar(si).
dime [daim] *n* moneta d'argento equivalente ad un decimo di dollaro.
dimension [di'menʃən] *n* dimensione.
dimensional [di'menʃənl] *a* di dimensioni; (*phys*) dimensionale.
diminish [di'miniʃ] *vti* diminuire.
diminution [ˌdimi'njuːʃən] *n* diminuzione.
diminutive [di'minjutiv] *a n* diminutivo.
dimness ['dimnis] *n* oscurità, offuscamento; imprecisione.
dimple ['dimpl] *n* fossetta.
din [din] *n* frastuono, rumore; assordante.
dine [dain] *vi* pranzare.
diner ['dainə] *a* commensale; (*rly*) vagone ristorante.
dinette [di'net] *n* saletta da pranzo.
dinginess ['dindʒinis] *n* squallore; sudiciume.
dingy ['dindʒi] *a* scuro, sporco.
dining ['dainiŋ] *n* il pranzare; **d. car** vagone ristorante; **d. room** sala da pranzo.
dinner ['dinə] *n* desinare, pranzo, cena
dint [dint] *n* tacca, ammaccatura; **by d. of** *prep* a forza di.
diocese ['daiəsis] *n* diocesi.
dioxide [dai'ɔksaid] *n* (*chem*) biossido.
dip [dip] *n* immersione; inclinazione; candela di sego; *vti* immerger(si); inclinar(si); abbassarsi.
diphtheria [dif'θiəriə] *n* difterite.
diphthong ['difθɔŋ] *n* dittongo.
diplomacy [di'ploumәsi] *n* diplomazia.
diplomat ['dipləmæt] *n* diplomatico.
diplomatic [ˌdiplə'mætik] *a* diplomatico.
dipper ['dipə] *n* chi (s')immerge; mestolo; **Big Dipper or Great Bear** l'Orsa Maggiore.

dire ['daiə] *a* spaventoso, terribile.
direct [di'rekt] *a* diretto; esplicito; *ad* immediatamente; *vt* avviare, dirigere, indirizzare.
direction [di'rekʃən] *n* direzione, indicazione.
directive [di'rektiv] *a* direttivo; *n* direttiva, istruzione.
directly [di'rektli] *ad cj* immediatamente, appena che.
directness [di'rektnis] *n* franchezza.
director [di'rektə] *n* direttore.
directory [di'rektəri] *n* (*tel*) elenco, guida, consiglio d'amministrazione.
dirge [də:dʒ] *n* canto funebre, nenia.
dirt [də:t] **dirtiness** ['də:tinis] *n* sporcizia, sudiciume.
dirty ['də:ti] *a* sporco, sudicio; *vt* insudiciare, sporcare.
disability [,disə'biliti] *n* incapacità, invalidità.
disable [dis'eibl] *vt* inabilitare, rendere incapace.
disabled [dis'eibld] *a* incapace, invalido.
disabuse [,disə'bju:z] *vt* disingannare.
disadvantage [,disəd'vɑ:ntidʒ] *n* svantaggio.
disadvantageous [,disædvɑ:n'teidʒəs] *a* svantaggioso.
disagree [,disə'gri:] *vi* dissentire, non andar d'accordo; nucere.
disagreeable [,disə'griəbl] *a* sgradevole, antipatico.
disagreement [,disə'gri:mənt] *n* disaccordo, dissenso.
disallow ['disə'lau] *vt* non permettere, non ammettere.
disappear [,disə'piə] *vi* scomparire, svanire.
disappearance [,disə'piərəns] *n* scomparsa.
disappoint [,disə'pɔint] *vt* deludere.
disappointed [,disə'pɔintid] *a* deluso, scontento.
disappointing [,disə'pɔintiŋ] *a* deludente, spiacevole.
disappointment [,disə'pɔintmənt] *n* delusione, disappunto.
disapproval [,disə'pru:vəl] *n* disapprovazione.
disapprove [,disə'pru:v] *vt* disapprovare.
disapproving [,disə'pru:viŋ] *a* di disapprovazione.
disapprovingly [,disə'pru:viŋli] *ad* con disapprovazione.
disarm [dis'ɑ:m] *vti* disarmare.
disarmament [dis'ɑ:məmənt] *n* disarmo.
disarrange ['disə'reindʒ] *vt* scompigliare, scomporre, disorganizzare.
disarray ['disə'rei] *n* disordine, scompiglio.
disarray ['disə'rei] *vt* scompigliare.
disaster [di'zɑ:stə] *n* disastro.
disastrous [di'zɑ:strəs] *a* disastroso.
disavow ['disə'vau] *vt* disconoscere, sconfessare, ripudiare.
disavowal ['disə'vauəl] *n* rinnegazione, disconoscimento.
disband [dis'bænd] *vti* sbandar(si).
disbelief ['disbi'li:f] *n* incredulità.
disbelieve ['disbi'li:v] *vt* non credere a; **disbeliever** *n* miscredente.
disburden [dis'bə:dn] *vt* alleggerire d'un peso.
disburse [dis'bə:s] *vt* sborsare.
disbursement [dis'bə:smənt] *n* sborso.
disc [disk] *n* disco; **d.-brake** (*aut*) freno a disco; **identity d.** (*mil*) piastrina d'identità; **slipped d.** (*med*) ernia del disco.
discard [dis'kɑ:d] *vt* scartare.
discern [di'sə:n] *vt* discernere.
discerning [di'sə:niŋ] *a* acuto, penetrante.
discernment [di'sə:nmənt] *n* discernimento, acutezza di giudizio.
discharge [dis'tʃɑ:dʒ] *n* scarico, scarica; emissione; suppurazione; liberazione; pagamento; adempimento; *vi* scaricarsi; suppurare; *vt* scaricare, emettere; liberare; licenziare.
disciple [di'saipl] *n* discepolo.
disciplinarian [,disipli'neəriən] *n* chi mantiene una rigida disciplina.
disciplinary ['disiplinəri] *a* disciplinare.
discipline ['disiplin] *n* disciplina; *vt* disciplinare, castigare.
disclaim [dis'kleim] *vt* negare, ripudiare, non riconoscere.
disclose [dis'klouz] *vt* dischiudere, rivelare.
disclosure [dis'klouʒə] *n* rivelazione.
discolor [dis'kʌlə] *vt* scolorire, macchiare; *vi* scolorirsi, macchiarsi.
discoloration [dis,kʌlə'reiʃən] *n* scoloramento, macchia.
discomfiture [dis'kʌmfitʃə] *n* sconfitta, scoraggiamento.
discomfort [dis'kʌmfət] *n* disagio, incomodo.
disconcert [,diskən'sə:t] *vt* sconcertare.
disconcerting [,diskən'sə:tiŋ] *a* sconcertante.
disconnect ['diskə'nekt] *vt* sconnettere, staccare.
disconsolate [dis'kɔnsəlit] *a* sconsolato, triste.
discontent(ment) ['diskən'tent(mənt)] *n* scontento.
discontented ['diskən'tentid] *a* malcontento.
discontinuance [,diskən'tinjuəns] *n* cessazione, interruzione.
discontinue ['diskən'tinju:] *vt* cessare, interrompere.
discord ['diskɔ:d] *n* discordia; (*mus*) dissonanza.
discordance [dis'kɔ:dəns] *n* discordanza.
discordant [dis'kɔ:dənt] *a* di-

scorde, dissenziente; discordante; dissonante.
discotheque ['diskɔtek] *n* discoteca.
discount ['diskaunt] *n* sconto, tara; *vt* [dis'kaunt] scontare, fare la tara a.
discourage [dis'kʌridʒ] *vt* scoraggiare, dissuadere.
discouragement [dis'kʌridʒmənt] *n* scoraggiamento.
discouraging [dis'kʌridʒiŋ] *a* scoraggiante.
discourse ['diskɔ:s] *n* discorso; *vi* [dis'kɔ:s] discorrere.
discourteous [dis'kə:tiəs] *a* scortese.
discover [dis'kʌvə] *vt* scoprire.
discoverer [dis'kʌvərə] *n* scopritore.
discovery [dis'kʌvəri] *n* scoperta.
discredit [dis'kredit] *n* discredito; *vt* screditare.
discreditable [dis'kreditəbl] *a* vergognoso.
discreet [dis'kri:t] *a* discreto, prudente, riservato.
discrepancy [dis'krepənsi] *n* discrepanza.
discretion [dis'kreʃən] *n* discrezione, prudenza.
discriminate [dis'krimineit] *vti* discriminare.
discrimination [dis,krimi'neiʃən] *n* discriminazione.
discursive [dis'kə:siv] *a* discorsivo, digressivo, saltuario.
discus ['diskəs] *n* (*sport*) disco.
discuss [dis'kʌs] *vt* discutere.
discussion [dis'kʌʃən] *n* discussione.
disdain [dis'dein] *n* sdegno; *vt* sdegnare.
disdainful [dis'deinful] *a* sdegnoso.
disdainfully [dis'deinfuli] *ad* sdegnosamente.
disease [di'zi:z] *n* malattia.
diseased [di'zi:zd] *a* malato.
disembark ['disim'bɑ:k] *vti* sbarcare.
disembarkation [,disembə'keiʃən] *n* sbarco.
disenchant ['disin'tʃɑ:nt] *vt* disincantare, disilludere.
disengage ['disin'geidʒ] *vt* svincolare, liberare.
disentangle ['disin'tæŋgl] *vt* districare, sbrogliare.
disfavor ['dis'feivə] *n* disistima, sfavore.
disfigure [dis'figə] *vt* deturpare, sfregiare.
disfigurement [dis'figəmənt] *n* deturpazione, sfregio.
disgorge [dis'gɔ:dʒ] *vt* buttar fuori.
disgrace [dis'greis] *n* disonore, vergogna, disgrazia; *vt* disonorare, far cadere in disgrazia.
disgraceful [dis'greisful] *a* vergognoso, disonorevole.
disgruntled [dis'grʌntld] *a* malcontento, di cattivo umore, irritato.
disguise [dis'gaiz] *n* travestimento, maschera; *vt* travestire, mascherare.
disgust [dis'gʌst] *n* disgusto; *vt* disgustare.
disgusted [dis'gʌstid] *a* disgustato, indignato.
disgusting [dis'gʌstiŋ] *a* disgustoso.
dish [diʃ] *n* piatto; portata; recipiente; **dishwasher** lavapiatti; *vt* mettere nel piatto, servire.
dishearten [dis'hɑ:tn] *vt* scoraggiare.
dishevel [di'ʃevəl] *vt* scapigliare.
disheveled [di'ʃevəld] *a* scarmigliato, arruffato; disordinato.
dishonest [dis'ɔnist] *a* disonesto.
dishonesty [dis'ɔnisti] *n* disonestà.
dishonor [dis'ɔnə] *n* disonore; (*com*) mancato pagamento; *vt* disonorare; (*com*) rifiutarsi di pagare.
dishonorable [dis'ɔnərəbl] *a* disonorevole.
disillusion [disi'lu:ʒən] *n* disillusione; *vt* disilludere.
disinclination [,disinkli'neiʃən] *n* antipatia, avversione.
disincline ['disin'klain] *vt* rendere avverso a.
disinfect [,disin'fekt] *vt* disinfettare.
disinfectant [,disin'fektənt] *n* disinfettante.
disinherit ['disin'herit] *vt* diseredare.
disintegrate [dis'intigreit] *vti* disintegrar(si).
disinterested [dis'intristid] *a* disinteressato, imparziale.
disjointed [dis'dʒɔintid] *a* disarticolato; incoerente; sconnesso.
disk [disk] *v* **disc**.
dislike [dis'laik] *n* antipatia; *vt* sentire antipatia per; **I d.** it non mi piace.
dislocate ['disləkeit] *vt* slogare.
dislocation [,dislə'keiʃən] *n* dislocazione, slogatura.
dislodge [dis'lɔdʒ] *vti* sloggiare.
disloyal ['dis'lɔiəl] *a* sleale, infedele.
disloyalty ['dis'lɔiəlti] *n* slealtà, infedeltà.
dismal ['dizməl] *a* tetro, triste, squallido.
dismantle [dis'mæntl] *vt* smantellare.
dismay [dis'mei] *n* costernazione, sbigottimento; *vt* costernare, sbigottire.
dismember [dis'membə] *vt* smembrare.
dismiss [dis'mis] *vt* licenziare, bandire, allontanare.
dismissal [dis'misəl] *n* licenziamento, rigetto.
dismount ['dis'maunt] *vi* smontare.
disobedience [,disə'bi:djəns] *n* disobbidienza.
disobedient [,disə'bi:djənt] *a* disubbidiente.
disobey ['disə'bei] *vti* disubbidire (a).
disoblige ['disə'blaidʒ] *vt* rifiutare un favore a.
disorder [dis'ɔ:də] *n* disordine; indisposizione; *vt* disordinare; far ammalare.
disorderly [dis'ɔ:dəli] *a* disordinato, sregolato.

disorganization [dis,ɔ:gənai'zeiʃən] *n* disorganizzazione.
disorganize [dis'ɔ:gənaiz] *vt* disorganizzare.
disown [dis'oun] *vt* rinnegare, disconoscere.
disparage [dis'pæridʒ] *vt* deprezzare, screditare.
disparagement [dis'pæridʒmənt] *n* denigrazione.
disparaging [dis'pæridʒiŋ] *a* sprezzante, spregiativo.
disparagingly [dis'pæridʒiŋli] *ad* con disprezzo, in modo spregiativo.
disparity [dis'pæriti] *n* disparità, differenza.
dispassionate [dis'pæʃnit] *a* spassionato, imparziale.
dispatch [dis'pætʃ] *n* dispaccio; spedizione; prontezza; *vt* spedire, sbrigare.
dispel [dis'pel] *vt* dissipare, scacciare.
dispensary [dis'pensəri] *n* dispensario.
dispensation [dispen'seiʃən] *n* dispensa, dispensazione.
dispense [dis'pens] *vt* dispensare; distribuire.
disperse [dis'pə:s] *vt* disperdere; *vi* disperdersi.
dispersion [dis'pə:ʃən] *n* dispersione.
displace [dis'pleis] *vt* spostare, sostituire; (*naut*) dislocare, stazzare; **displaced person** profugo.
displacement [dis'pleismənt] *n* spostamento, sostituzione; (*naut*) dislocamento.
display [dis'plei] *n* mostra, esibizione, ostentazione; *vt* mettere in mostra, esporre, ostentare.
displease [dis'pli:z] *vt* dispiacere, offendere.
displeasure [dis'pleʒə] *n* dispiacere, scontento.
disposal [dis'pouzəl] *n* disposizione; eliminazione; **at your d.** a sua disposizione.
disposable [dis'pouzəbl] *a* disponibile.
dispose [dis'pouz] *vt* disporre; **to d. of** disfarsi di, vendere.
disposition [,dispə'ziʃən] *n* disposizione, carattere, temperamento.
dispossess ['dispə'zes] *vt* privare, spossessare.
disproportion ['disprə'pɔ:ʃən] *n* sproporzione.
disproportionate [,disprə'pɔ:ʃnit] *a* sproporzionato.
disprove ['dis'pru:v] *vt* confutare.
disputable [dis'pju:təbl] *a* discutibile, disputabile; contestabile.
dispute [dis'pju:t] *n* disputa, controversia, vertenza; *vti* disputare.
disqualification [dis,kwɔlifi'keiʃən] *n* squalifica.
disqualify [dis'kwɔlifai] *vt* squalificare.
disquieting [dis'kwaiətiŋ] *a* inquietante.
disregard [,disri'gɑ:d] *n* noncuranza; *vt* ignorare, trascurare, non curarsi di.
disregardful [,disri'gɑ:dful] *a* noncurante.
disrepair ['disri'pεə] *n* cattivo stato, rovina.
disreputable [dis'repjutəbl] *a* disonorevole, losco, malfamato.
disrepute ['disri'pju:t] *n* scredito; disistima; cattiva fama.
disrespect ['disris'pekt] *n* mancanza di rispetto, irriverenza.
disrupt [dis'rʌpt] *vt* rompere, disorganizzare.
disruption [dis'rʌpʃən] *n* rottura, scissione.
dissatisfaction ['dis,sætis'fækʃən] *n* malcontento.
dissatisfied ['dis'sætisfaid] *a* insoddisfatto, scontento.
dissatisfy ['dis'sætisfai] *vt* non soddisfare.
dissect [di'sekt] *vt* sezionare; (*fig*) criticare.
dissection [di'sekʃən] *n* dissezione.
dissemble [di'sembl] *vti* simulare, nascondere.
disseminate [di'semineit] *vt* disseminare, diffondere.
dissemination [di,semi'neiʃən] *n* disseminazione; (*fig*) divulgazione.
dissension [di'senʃən] *n* discordia, dissenso.
dissent [di'sent] *n* dissenso, dissentimento; *vt* dissentire.
dissenter [di'sentə] *n* dissidente.
disservice ['dis'sə:vis] *n* disservizio.
dissident ['disidənt] *a n* dissidente.
dissimilar ['di'similə] *a* dissimile.
dissimilarity [,disimi'læriti] *n* dissomiglianza.
dissipate ['disipeit] *vti* dissipar(si).
dissipated ['disipeitid] *a* dissoluto, dissipato.
dissipation [,disi'peiʃən] *n* dissipazione, dispersione.
dissociate [di'souʃieit] *vti* dissociar (si).
dissociation [di,sousi'eiʃən] *n* dissociazione, sdoppiamento.
dissoluble [di'sɔljubl] *a* dissolubile.
dissolute ['disəlu:t] *a* dissoluto.
dissolution [,disə'lu:ʃən] *n* dissoluzione, scioglimento.
dissolve [di'zɔlv] *vti* disciogler(si), dissolver(si), disfar(si); *n* (*cin*) dissolvenza
dissolvent [di'zɔlvənt] *a n* dissolvente.
dissonance ['disənəns] *n* dissonanza.
dissonant ['disənənt] *a* dissonante; discordante.
dissuade [di'sweid] *vt* dissuadere.
dissuasion [di'sweiʒən] *n* dissuasione.
distaff ['distɑ:f] *n* conocchia.
distance ['distəns] *n* distanza.
distant ['distənt] *a* distante, remoto; (*fig*) freddo, riservato.

distaste ['dis'teist] *n* ripugnanza.
distasteful [dis'teistful] *a* ripugnante, sgradevole.
distemper [dis'tempə] *n* indisposizione; (*vet*) cimurro.
distemper [dis'tempə] *vt* dipingere a tempera, intonacare.
distend [dis'tend] *vti* gonfiar(si), dilatar(si).
distill [dis'til] *vt* distillare; *vi* stillare.
distillation [,disti'leiʃən] *n* distillazione.
distillery [dis'tiləri] *n* distilleria.
distinct [dis'tiŋkt] *a* ben definito, distinto, diverso.
distinction [dis'tiŋkʃən] *n* distinzione.
distinctive [dis'tiŋktiv] *a* distintivo, caratteristico.
distinguish [dis'tiŋgwiʃ] *vti* distinguere, differenziare.
distinguished [dis'tiŋgwiʃd] *a* distinto, insigne.
distinguishing [dis'tiŋgwiʃiŋ] *a* distintivo, caratteristico.
distort [dis'tɔ:t] *vt* distorcere, deformare; svisare.
distortion [dis'tɔ:ʃən] *n* distorsione, deformazione.
distract [dis'trækt] *vt* distrarre; far impazzire.
distracted [dis'træktid] *a* sconvolto, pazzo.
distraction [dis'trækʃən] *n* distrazione, svago; follia; disperazione.
distrain [dis'trein] *vi* sequestrare, fare un sequestro.
distraught [dis'trɔ:t] *a* sconvolto, disperato.
distress [dis'tres] *n* dolore; miseria, difficoltà; *vt* affliggere.
distressed [dis'trest] *n* angustiato, afflitto, in angustie.
distressing [dis:'tresiŋ] *a* penoso, doloroso.
distribute [dis'tribju(:)t] *vt* distribuire.
distribution [distri'bju:ʃən] *n* distribuzione.
distributor [dis'tribjutə] *n* distributore, distributrice; (*merchandise*) grossista.
district ['distrikt] *n* distretto; quartiere.
distrust [dis'trʌst] *n* diffidenza, sfiducia; *vt* diffidare di.
distrustful [dis'trʌstful] *a* diffidente, sospettoso.
disturb [dis'tə:b] *vt* disturbare.
disturbance [dis'tə:bəns] *n* agitazione, tumulto.
disunion ['dis'ju:njən] *n* disunione.
disuse ['dis'ju:s] *n* disuso.
ditch [ditʃ] *n* fossa, fossato.
ditto ['ditou] *n* lo stesso; *ad* come sopra.
ditty ['diti] *n* canzone popolare, ritornello.
divan [di'væn] *n* divano.
dive [daiv] *n* tuffo; **d. bombing** bombardamento in picchiata; *vi* immergersi, tuffarsi; (*av*) scendere in picchiata.
diver ['daivə] *n* tuffatore; palombaro; **skin d.** nuotatore subacqueo, sommozzatore.
diverge [dai'və:dʒ] *vi* divergere.
divergence [dai'və:dʒəns] **divergency** [dai'və:dʒənsi] *n* divergenza.
divergent [dai'və:dʒənt] *a* divergente.
diverse ['daivə(:)z] *a* diverso.
diversify [dai'və:sifai] *vt* diversificare, variare.
diversion [dai'və:ʃən] *n* diversione; **road d., traffic d.** deviazione stradale.
diversity [dai'və:siti] *n* diversità.
divert [dai'və:t] *vt* deviare, divertire.
divest [dai'vest] *vt* spogliare, svestire.
divide [di'vaid] *vti* divider(si).
dividend ['dividend] *n* (*com*) dividendo.
dividers [di'vaidəz] *n pl* compasso a punte fisse.
divine [di'vain] *a* divino; *n* teologo; *vti* divinare, predire.
diviner [di'vainə] *n* indovino; **water d.** rabdomante.
diving ['daiviŋ] *n* il tuffarsi, immersione; **d. board** trampolino; **d. suit** scafandro.
divinity [di'viniti] *n* divinità; teologia.
divisible [di'vizəbl] *a* divisibile.
division [di'viʒən] *n* divisione.
divorce [di'vɔ:s] *n* divorzio; *vt* divorziare da.
divorcee [di'vɔ:sei] *n* divorziato, divorziata.
divulge [dai'vʌldʒ] *vt* divulgare.
dizziness ['dizinis] *n* capogiro, vertigine.
dizzy ['dizi] *a* vertiginoso; preso da vertigine; **to feel d.** sentirsi girar la testa.
do [du:] *vt* fare, compiere, eseguire; cucinare; (*sl*) ingannare; *vi* comportarsi; stare di salute; andar bene; bastare.
docile ['dousail] *a* docile.
docility [dou'siliti] *n* docilità.
dock [dɔk] *n* bacino portuario; **dockyard** arsenale; *vt* mozzare; (*fam*) ridurre; *vi* entrare in porto.
docker ['dɔkə] *n* scaricatore di porto.
doctor ['dɔktə] *n* dottore, medico.
doctrine ['dɔktrin] *n* dottrina.
document ['dɔkjumənt] *n* documento.
documentary [,dɔkju'mentəri] *a n* documentario.
dodge [dɔdʒ] *vti* scansare, schivare, eludere.
doe [dou] *n* (*deer*) daina, (*hare*) lepre femmina, (*rabbit*) coniglia; **doeskin** pelle di daino.
dog [dɔg] *n* cane; **d. days** *pl* la canicola; **top d.** (*fam*) persona autorevole; **dogfish** pescecane; **d.**

rose rosa canina; *vt* seguire, pedinare.
dogged ['dɔgid] *a* ostinato, tenace.
doggedly ['dɔgidli] *ad* ostinatamente, indefessamente.
dogma ['dɔgmə] *n* dogma.
dogmatic [dɔg'mætik] *a* dogmatico.
dogmatize ['dɔgmətaiz] *vi* dogmatizzare.
doings ['du(:)iŋz] *n pl* fatti, azioni, occupazioni.
dole [doul] *n* distribuzione caritatevole; **the d.** sussidio dato ai disoccupati; *vt* distribuire in piccole quantità, dare in elemosina.
doleful ['doulful] *a* malinconico, triste.
doll [dɔl] *n* bambola.
dollar ['dɔlə] *n* dollaro.
Dolomites ['dɔləmaits] *n pl* le Dolomiti.
dolphin ['dɔlfin] *n* delfino.
dolt [doult] *n* individuo ottuso.
domain [də'mein] *n* dominio, proprietà terriera.
dome [doum] *n* cupola.
domestic [də'mestik] *a n* domestico, domestica; **d. mail** posta per l'interno.
domicile ['dɔmisail] *n* domicilio.
dominant ['dɔminənt] *a* dominante.
dominate ['dɔmineit] *vti* dominare.
domination [,dɔmi'neiʃən] *n* dominazione, dominio.
domineer [,dɔmi'niə] *vi* spadroneggiare, tiranneggiare.
domineering [,dɔmi'niəriŋ] *a* dispotico, imperioso, prepotente.
Dominic ['dɔminik] *nm pr* Domenico.
Dominican [də'minikən] *a n* domenicano.
dominion [də'minjən] *n* dominio.
domino ['dɔminou] *pl* **dominoes** *n* domino.
don [dɔn] *n* insegnante universitario; *vt* indossare, mettersi.
donate [dou'neit] *vt* donare.
donation [dou'neiʃən] *n* donazione.
donkey ['dɔŋki] *n* asino, somaro; **d.-engine** locomotiva di manovra.
donor ['dounə] *n* donatore; **blood d.** donatore di sangue.
doom [du:m] *n* condanna; destino, sorte; *vt* condannare.
doomsday ['du:mzdei] *n* giorno del giudizio.
door [dɔ:] *n* porta, uscio; **doorway** vano della porta.
dope [doup] *n* lubrificante; stimolante; narcotico.
dormant ['dɔ:mənt] *a* assopito; inattivo; caduto in disuso; **d. partner** (*com*) socio occulto.
dormitory ['dɔ:mitri] *n* dormitorio.
dormouse ['dɔ:maus] *n* ghiro.
dorsal ['dɔ:səl] *a* dorsale.
dose [dous] *n* dose; *vt* dosare, somministrare a dosi; (*drinks*) adulterare.
dot [dɔt] *n* punto, puntino.
dotage ['doutidʒ] *n* rimbambimento.
dotard ['doutəd] *n* vecchio rimbambito.
dote [dout] *vi* essere rimbambito, essere infatuato.
double ['dʌbl] *a* doppio; finto; *n* doppio; *ad* due volte; *vt* raddoppiare; passar intorno a; *vi* voltare improvvisamente.
doubt [daut] *n* dubbio, incertezza; sospetto; *vti* dubitare; sospettare.
doubtful ['dautful] *a* incerto, dubbio, dubbioso.
doubtless ['dautlis] *ad* indubbiamente, senza dubbio.
dough [dou] *n* pasta.
dove [dʌv] *n* colomba.
dowager ['dauədʒə] *n* vedova (che ha un titolo o un patrimonio ereditato dal marito).
dowdy ['daudi] *a* sciatto, trasandato.
down [daun] *n* duna, collinetta; lanugine, peluria; piumino; *a* depresso; *prep* in basso, giù per; *ad* giù, in basso, in giù; **d. with . . .** *interj* a abbasso; *vt* (*fam*) abbattere, gettare terra.
downcast ['daunka:st] *a* abbattuto.
downfall ['daunfɔ:l] *n* caduta, rovescio di fortuna.
downhearted ['daun'ha:tid] *a* scoraggiato, abbattuto.
downhill ['daun'hil] *a* discendente; *n* discesa; *ad* in discesa.
downpour ['daunpɔ:] *n* acquazzone.
downright ['daunrait] *a* netto, chiaro; onesto *ad* categoricamente.
downstairs ['daun'stεəz] *a* del (al) piano di sotto; *ad* giù.
downward ['daunwəd] *a* verso il basso, discendente; **downwards** *ad* in giù, in basso.
dowry ['dauəri] *n* dote.
doze [douz] *n* sonnellino; *vt* sonnecchiare.
dozen ['dʌzn] *n* dozzina.
drab [dræb] *a* grigio, scialbo.
draft [dra:ft] *n* (*outline*) abbozzo; brutta copia; assegno, tratta; (*mil*) distaccamento; bevanda, pozione; corrente d'aria, (*naut*) pescaggio; trazione; *vt* redigere; abbozzare; arruolare.
draftsman ['dra:ftsmən] *n* disegnatore.
drafty ['dra:fti] *a* pieno di correnti d'aria.
drag [dræg] *n* (*naut*) draga; (*agr*) erpice; carrozza a quattro cavalli; (*fig*) ostacolo, peso; *vt* trascinare, dragare.
dragon ['drægən] *n* drago(ne); **dragonfly** libellula.
dragoon [drə'gu:n] *n* (*mil*) dragone.
drain [drein] *n* canale di scolo, fogna, tubo di scarico, tubo per drenaggio; *vt* prosciugare per drenaggio; scolare, bere fino in fondo.
drainage ['dreinidʒ] *n* fognatura,

drenaggio, prosciugamento.
drake [dreik] *n* anitra maschio.
drama ['drɑ:mə] *n* dramma.
dramatic [drə'mætik] *a* drammatico.
dramatist ['dræmətist] *n* drammaturgo.
dramatize ['dræmətaiz] *vt* drammatizzare; adattare per il teatro.
drape [dreip] *vt* coprire, drappeggiare.
draper ['dreipə] *n* merciaio, negoziante in tessuti.
drapery ['dreipəri] *n* tessuti, drappeggi, commercio in tessuti.
drastic ['dræstik] *a* drastico, energico.
draught [drɑ:ft] *v* **draft.**
draughts [drɑ:fts] *n pl* (*game*) gioco della dama.
draw [drɔ:] *n* trazione; attrazione; sorteggio; (*sport*) pareggio; *vti* tirare, (ri)tirarsi, attirare, trascinare; disegnare; tirare a sorte; (*com*) emettere; riscuotere, (*sport*) pareggiare.
drawback ['drɔ:bæk] *n* inconveniente, svantaggio.
drawbridge ['drɔ:bridʒ] *n* ponte levatoio.
drawer ['drɔ:ə] *n* disegnatore; redattore; (*com*) traente; cassetto; **drawers** *pl* mutande *pl.*
drawing ['drɔ:iŋ] *n* disegno; sorteggio; tiraggio; **d. room** salotto.
drawl [drɔ:l] *n* pronuncia strascicata; *vi* strascicare le parole.
dray [drei] *n* carro pesante.
dread [dred] *n* terrore; *vt* temere.
dreadful ['dredful] *a* terribile.
dreadnought ['drednɔ:t] *n* (*naut*) supercorazzata.
dream [dri:m] *n* sogno: *vti* sognare.
dreamer ['dri:mə] *n* sognatore.
dreamy ['dri:mi] *a* sognante, vago.
dreary ['driəri] *a* triste, cupo.
dredge [dredʒ] *n* draga; *vt* dragare; (*with flour, sugar etc*) spolverizzare (di).
dregs [dregz] *n pl* feccia, fondo, sedimento.
drench [drentʃ] *vt* bagnare, inzuppare; **drenching rain** pioggia dirotta.
dress [dres] *n* abito, vestito, veste, modo di vestirsi; *vti* vestire, vestirsi; (*mil*) allineare; medicare; (*dish*) guarnire.
dresser ['dresə] *n* assistente chirurgo; (*theat*) vestiarista; credenza, dispensa; toletta.
dressing ['dresiŋ] *n* abbigliamento; medicazione; condimento.
dressing-gown ['dresiŋgaun] *n* vestaglia.
dressmaker ['dres,meikə] *n* sarta.
dribble ['dribl] *n* gocciolamento; bava; (*football*) palleggio; *vi* gocciolare; sbavare; (*football*) palleggiare, dribblare.
drift [drift] *n* spinta, direzione, velocità; deriva; *vti* lasciarsi trasportare, andare alla deriva, ammucchiare.
drifter ['driftə] *n* (*naut*) motopeschereccio con tramaglio.
drill [dril] *n* (*mech*) perforatrice, trapano; (*mil*) esercitazioni *pl*; *vt* trapanare; esercitare; *vi* fare esercitazioni.
driller ['drilə] *n* macchina perforatrice.
drilling ['driliŋ] *n* trapanazione; (*mil*) esercitazione; **d. machine** trapano.
drink [driŋk] *n* bevanda, bibita; intemperanza nel bere; *vti* bere.
drinkable ['driŋkəbl] *a* bevibile, potabile.
drinking ['driŋkiŋ] *a* da bere, potabile; *n* il bere, alcoolismo.
drip [drip] *n* gocciolamento, stillicidio; *vi* gocciolare.
dripping ['dripiŋ] *n* grasso sciolto di carne.
drive [draiv] *n* passeggiata in carrozza o in auto; viale; spinta, propulsione; (*aut*) guida; *vt* condurre, guidare; costringere; trasportare; *vi* andare in carrozza, in auto.
drivel ['drivl] *n* bava, saliva; insulsaggine; *vi* sbavare; parlare da sciocco.
driver ['draivə] *n* autista, conducente, conduttore, guidatore, vetturino.
driving ['draiviŋ] *a* propulsore; dinamico; sferzante; **d. rain** pioggia sferzante; *n* (*aut*) guida; (*mech*) comando; **d. school** scuola guida; **d. wheel** (*aut*) volante.
drizzle ['drizl] *n* pioggerella; *vi* piovigginare.
droll [droul] *a* buffo, divertente.
drollery ['drouləri] *n* buffoneria.
dromedary ['drɔmədəri] *n* dromedario.
drone [droun] *n* (*bee*) fuco; ronzio; fannullone; *vi* ronzare, parlare con tono monotono.
droop [dru:p] *n* portamento curvo; accasciamento; *vi* pendere, curvarsi, abbassare, languire.
drop [drɔp] *n* goccia, goccio; caduta; (*prices*) ribasso; (*temperature*) abbassamento; *vt* lasciar cadere; *vi* cadere, diminuire.
dropper ['drɔpə] *n* contagocce.
dropsy ['drɔpsi] *n* (*med*) idropisia.
dross [drɔs] *n* scoria; (*fig*) rifiuto.
drought [draut] *n* siccità.
drove [drouv] *n* branco, gregge, mandria.
drover ['drouvə] *n* mandriano.
drown [draun] *vti* affogare, annegare; **drowning** annegamento, sommersione.
drowse [drauz] *vi* assopirsi, sonnecchiare.
drowsiness ['drauzinis] *n* sonnolenza.
drowsy ['drauzi] *a* sonnolento.
drudge [drʌdʒ] *n* schiavo; sgobbone.

drudge [drʌdʒ] *vi* sfacchinare.
drudgery ['drʌdʒəri] *n* lavoro faticoso, ingrato.
drug [drʌg] *n* droga, prodotto farmaceutico; stupefacente; **drugstore** farmacia.
druggist ['drʌgist] *n* farmacista.
drum [drʌm] *n* tamburo; (*anat*) timpano; (*mech*) rullo; *vi* suonare il tamburo, tamburellare; *vt* inculcare.
drummer ['drʌmə] *n* tamburino, batterista; viaggiatore di commercio; propagandista.
drunk [drʌŋk] *a* ubriaco.
drunkard ['drʌŋkəd] *n* ubriacone.
drunken ['drʌŋkən] *a* ubriaco.
drunkenness ['drʌŋkənnis] *n* ubriachezza.
dry [drei] *a* asciutto, arido, secco; privo d'interesse; *vt* asciugare, seccare, esaurire; *vi* evaporare completamente, seccarsi; **to d. clean** lavare a secco; **d.-goods store** negozio di tessuti.
dryly ['draili] *ad* seccamente.
dryness ['dramis] *n* aridità, secchezza.
dual ['dju:əl] *a* doppio, duplice; **d. highway** strada a doppia carreggiata.
dub [dʌb] *vt* (*cin*) doppiare; **dubbing** *n* doppiaggio.
dubious ['dju:biəs] *a* dubbio, equivoco, incerto.
Dublin ['dʌblin] *n* Dublino.
duchess ['dʌtʃis] *n* duchessa.
duchy ['dʌtʃi] *n* ducato.
duck [dʌk] *n* anitra, anatra; *vti* immerger(si), tuffar(si); *vi* abbassare il capo improvvisamente.
duckling ['dʌkliŋ] *n* anatroccolo.
duct [dʌkt] *n* canale, tubo, condotto; (*anat*) vaso.
due [dju:] *a* dovuto, debito, adeguato; *n* dovuto, quota, tassa; **to be d.** dover arrivare.
duel ['dju:əl] *n* duello.
duet [dju:'et] *n* duetto.
duke [dju:k] *n* duca.
dukedom ['dju:kdəm] *n* ducato.
dull [dʌl] *a* tardo, lento; (*color*) smorto; (*sound*) sordo; triste, monotono; *vt* intorpidire, smorzare, istupidire.
dullard ['dʌləd] *n* individuo ottuso.
dullness ['dʌlnis] *n* lentezza, mancanza di vivacità, monotonia, ottusità.
duly ['dju:li] *ad* debitamente, a tempo debito.
dumb [dʌm] *a* muto; **dumbwaiter** montavivande.
dumbfound [dʌm'faund] *vt* stupefare, confondere.
dumbness ['dʌmnis] *n* mutismo.
dummy ['dʌmi] *n* fantoccio, manichino, uomo di paglia; **baby's d.** succhiotto, tettarella.
dump [dʌmp] *n* deposito di rifiuti; (*mil*) deposito di munizioni; *vt* scaricare.
dumpling ['dʌmpliŋ] *n* grossa polpetta di pasta bollita; (*sl*) individuo, animale piccolo e rotondetto.
dumpy ['dʌmpi] *a* tarchiato, tozzo.
dun [dʌn] *a* grigio scuro; *n* creditore importuno; *vt* domandare insistentemente il pagamento.
dunce [dʌns] *n* ignorante, stupido.
dune [dju:n] *n* duna.
dung [duŋ] *n* letame, sterco.
dungarees [,dʌŋgə'ri:z] *n pl* tuta.
dungeon ['dʌndʒən] *n* prigione sotterranea, segreta.
dupe [dju:p] *n* credulone, gonzo; *vt* gabbare, ingannare.
duplicate ['dju:plikit] *a n* duplicato; *vt* ['djuplikeit] duplicare.
duplicator ['dju:plikeitə] *n* copialettere.
duplicity [dju:'plisiti] *n* doppiezza.
durability [,djuərə'biliti] *n* durabilità.
durable ['djuərəbl] *a* durevole.
duration [djuə'reiʃən] *n* durata.
duress [djuə'res] *n* costrizione, violenza, imprigionamento.
during ['djuəriŋ] *prep* durante.
dusk [dʌsk] *n* crepuscolo.
dusky ['dʌski] *a* oscuro, fosco.
dust [dʌst] *n* polvere; **dustbin** pattumiera; *vt* spolverare; impolverare, cospargere di.
duster ['dʌstə] *n* strofinaccio.
dusting ['dʌstiŋ] *n* spolverare, spolveratura; (*fig*) bastonatura.
dusty ['dʌsti] *a* polveroso.
Dutch [dʌtʃ] *a n* olandese; **D. courage** finto coraggio, coraggio dato da stimolanti.
dutiful ['dju:tiful] *a* ubbidiente, rispettoso.
duty ['dju:ti] *n* dovere; rispetto; servizio; imposta, tassa.
dwarf [dwɔ:f] *a n* nano; *vt* rimpicciolire.
dwell [dwel] *vi* dimorare, abitare; soffermarsi.
dwelling ['dweliŋ] *n* abitazione, dimora.
dwindle ['dwindl] *vi* consumarsi, rimpicciolirsi.
dye [dai] *n* tintura, tinta; *vt* tingere; *vi* tingersi, prendere il colore di.
dyer ['daiə] *n* tintore.
dying ['daiiŋ] *a* morente, moribondo.
dynamic [dai'næmik] *a* dinamico; **dynamics** *n pl* dinamica.
dynamite ['dainəmait] *n* dinamite.
dynamo ['dainəmou] *pl* **dynamos** *n* dinamo.
dynasty ['dinəsti] *n* dinastia.
dysentery ['disntri] *n* dissenteria.
dyspepsia [dis'pepsiə] *n* dispepsia.

E

each [i:tʃ] *a pron* ciascuno, ogni, ognuno; **e. other** l'un l'altro.
eager ['i:gə] *a* ardente, avido.
eagerly ['i:gəli] *ad* ardentemente, avidamente.
eagerness ['i:gənis] *n* premura, ansia, brama.
eagle ['i:gl] *n* aquila.
ear [iə] *n* orecchio, orecchia; spiga.
earl [ə:l] *n* conte dell'aristocrazia inglese.
earldom ['ə:ldəm] *n* contea.
earliness ['ə:linis] *n* ora mattutina; precocità.
early ['ə:li] *a* primo; mattutino, prossimo, prematuro; *ad* di buon'ora, presto.
earn [ə:n] *vt* guadagnare, meritare.
earnest ['ə:nist] *a* serio, fervido; *n* anticipo, caparra, pegno; **in e.** seriamente, sul serio.
earnestness ['ə:nistnis] *n* serietà.
earnings ['ə:niŋz] *n pl* guadagni *pl.*
ear-ring ['iə:riŋ] *n* orecchino.
earth [ə:θ] *n* terra, suolo; tana; **e. wire** (*el*) filo di terra.
earthen ['ə:θən] *a* di terra, di terracotta.
earthenware ['ə:θənwɛə] *n* terraglia.
earthly ['ə:θli] *a* terreno, terrestre.
earthquake ['ə:θkweik] *n* terremoto.
earthworm ['ə:θwə:m] *n* lombrico.
earthy ['ə:θi] *a* di terra, terroso; grossolano.
earwig ['iəwig] *n* forfecchia.
ease [i:z] *n* agio, comodo, riposo; *vt* calmare, dar sollievo a, allentare, alleggerire.
easel ['i:zl] *n* cavalletto.
easily ['i:zili] *ad* facilmente, comodamente.
easiness ['i:zinis] *n* disinvoltura, facilità.
east [i:st] *n* est, oriente; *a* orientale.
Easter ['i:stə] *n* Pasqua.
easterly ['i:stəli] *a* (*vento, direzione*) d'est, dell'est.
eastern ['i:stən] *a* orientale, dell'est.
eastward ['i:stwəd] *a* ad est, verso est.
easy ['i:zi] *a* agevole, comodo, disinvolto, facile.
eat [i:t] *vti* mangiare.
eatable ['i:təbl] *a* mangiabile; *a n* commestibile.
eating ['i:tiŋ] *a* che consuma, (*fig*) che rode; *n* il mangiare.
eaves [i:vz] *n pl* gronda.
eavesdrop ['i:vzdrɔp] *vi* origliare.
ebb [eb] *n* riflusso; **e.-tide** bassa marea; *vi* rifluire, abbassarsi.
ebony ['ebəni] *a* d'ebano; *n* ebano.
eccentric [ik'sentrik] *a n* eccentrico.
eccentricity [.eksen'trisiti] *n* eccentricità.
ecclesiastic [i.kli:zi'æstik] *a n* ecclesiastico.
echelon ['eʃəlɔn] *n* (*mil*) scaglione.
echo ['ekou] *n* eco; *vt* ripetere; *vi* echeggiare.
eclectic [ek'lektik] *a n* eclettico.
eclipse [i'klips] *n* eclissi; *vt* eclissare.
economic [.i:ke'nɔmik] *a* economico; **economical** economico, economo; **economics** *n pl* economia, scienze economiche.
economist [i:'kɔnəmist] *n* economista.
economize [i:'kɔnəmaiz] *vti* economizzare.
economy [i:'kɔnəmi] *n* economia.
ecstasy ['ekstəsi] *n* estasi.
ecstatic [eks'tætik] *a* estatico.
eczema ['eksimə] *n* eczema.
eddy ['edi] *n* vortice; *vi* girar vorticosamente, turbinare.
Eden ['i:dn] *n* Eden, Paradiso Terrestre.
Edgar ['edgə] *nm pr* Edgardo.
edge [edʒ] *n* bordo, margine, orlo, filo tagliente; *vt* bordare, orlare; *vi* avanzare obliquamente; **to be on e.** avere i nervi tesi.
edgeways ['edʒweiz] **edgewise** [edʒwaiz] *ad* di taglio; a mala pena.
edgy ['edʒi] *a* affilato, tagliente; (*fig*) nervoso.
edible ['edibl] *a* commestibile, mangereccio.
edict ['i:dikt] *n* editto.
edification [.edifi'keiʃən] *n* edificazione.
edifice ['edifis] *n* edificio.
edify ['edifai] *vt* (*fig*) edificare.
edifying ['edifaiiŋ] *a* edificante.
Edinburgh ['edinbərə] *n* Edimburgo.
edit ['edit] *vt* curare l'edizione di; (*cin*) curare il montaggio.
edition [i'diʃən] *n* edizione.
editor ['editə] *n* editore, direttore, redattore d'un giornale *etc.*
editorial [.edi'tɔ:riəl] *a* editoriale; redazionale; *n* articolo di fondo.
educate ['edju:keit] *vt* istruire, educare.
education [.edju:'keiʃən] *n* istruzione.
educational [.edju:'keiʃənl] *a* educativo.
Edward ['edwəd] *nm pr* Edoardo.
eel [i:l] *n* anguilla.
eerie ['iəri] *a* misterioso, che ispira paura, soprannaturale.
efface [i'feis] *vt* cancellare.
effect [i'fekt] *n* effetto, conseguenza; significato; **effects** *pl* beni, effetti, oggetti personali *pl*; *vt* effettuare, compiere.
effective [i'fektiv] *a* efficace, effettivo.
effectively [i'fektivli] *ad* efficacemente, effettivamente.
effectual [i'fektjuəl] *a* efficace, valido.
effectuate [i'fektjueit] *vt* effettuare.
effeminacy [i'feminəsi] *n* effeminatezza.
effeminate [i'feminit] *a* effeminato.

effervesce [ˌefəˈves] *vi* essere effervescente, spumare.
effervescence [ˌefəˈvesns] *n* effervescenza.
effervescent [ˌefəˈvesnt] *a* effervescente; vivace, spumeggiante.
effete [eˈfi:t] *a* indebolito, esausto.
efficacious [ˌefiˈkeiʃəs] *a* efficace.
efficacy [ˈefikəsi] *n* efficacia.
efficiency [iˈfiʃənsi] *n* efficienza.
efficient [iˈfiʃənt] *a* efficiente.
efficiently [iˈfiʃəntli] *ad* con competenza, efficacemente.
effigy [ˈefidʒi] *n* effigie.
effort [ˈefət] *n* sforzo.
effortless [ˈefətlis] *a* senza sforzo, agevole, piano; passivo.
effrontery [eˈfrʌntəri] *n* sfrontatezza.
effusion [iˈfju:ʒən] *n* effusione.
effusive [iˈfju:siv] *a* espansivo, esuberante.
egg [eg] *n* uovo; *vt* incitare, istigare; **eggcup** porta-uovo.
egoism [ˈegouizəm] *n* egoismo.
egoist [ˈegouist] *n* egoista.
egotism [ˈegoutizəm] *n* egotismo.
egotist [ˈegoutist] *n* egotista.
Egypt [ˈi:dʒipt] *n* Egitto.
Egyptian [iˈdʒipʃən] *a n* egiziano.
eight [eit] *a n* otto; **eighth** *a n* ottavo.
eighteen [ˈeiˈti:n] *a n* diciotto; **eighteenth** *a n* diciottesimo.
eighty [ˈeiti] *a n* ottanta; **eightieth** *a n* ottantesimo.
Eire [ˈɛərə] *n* Irlanda.
either [ˈaiðə] *a pron* l'uno o l'altro, ognuno dei due; *ad* neanche, nemmeno; **e. . . . or** *cj* o . . . o.
ejaculate [iˈdʒækjuleit] *vt* emettere; *vi* esclamare.
ejaculation [iˌdʒækjuˈleiʃən] *n* esclamazione.
eject [i:ˈdʒekt] *vt* emettere, espellere.
elaborate [iˈlæbərit] *a* elaborato; *vt* [iˈlæbəreit] elaborare.
elaboration [iˌlæbəˈreiʃən] *n* elaborazione.
elapse [iˈlæps] *vi* passare, trascorrere.
elastic [iˈlæstik] *a n* elastico.
elasticity [ˌelæsˈtisiti] *n* elasticità.
elate [iˈleit] *vt* esaltare, inebriare.
elation [iˈleiʃən] *n* esaltazione, esultanza.
elbow [ˈelbou] *n* gomito; *vt* prendere a gomitate; *vi* farsi largo a gomitate; **e. room** spazio, agio.
elder [ˈeldə] *a* più vecchio, maggiore; *n* maggiore; dignitario della chiesa; (*bot*) sambuco.
elderly [ˈeldəli] *a* anziano.
Eleanor [ˈelinə] *nf pr* Eleonora.
elect [iˈlekt] *a* eletto, scelto; *vti* eleggere, scegliere.
election [iˈlekʃən] *n* elezione.
elector [iˈlektə] *n* elettore.
electoral [iˈlektərəl] *a* elettorale.
electorate [iˈlektərit] *n* elettorato, elettori *pl*.
electric [iˈlektrik] *a* elettrico; **e. heater** stufa elettrica.
electrical [iˈlektrikəl] *a* elettrico.
electrician [ilekˈtriʃən] *n* elettricista.
electricity [ilekˈtrisiti] *n* elettricità.
electrification [iˌlektrifiˈkeiʃən] *n* elettrificazione.
electrify [iˈlektrifai] *vt* elettrificare; elettrizzare.
electrocardiogram [iˈlektrouˈkɑ:diogram] *n* elettrocardiogramma.
electrocute [iˈlektrəkju:t] *vt* fulminare; giustiziare sulla sedia elettrica.
electrocution [iˌlektrəˈkju:ʃən] *n* elettroesecuzione.
electronic [ilekˈtrɔnik] *a* elettronico.
electronics [ilekˈtrɔniks] *n* elettronica.
elegance [ˈeligəns] *n* eleganza.
elegant [ˈeligənt] *a* elegante.
elegy [ˈelidʒi] *n* elegia.
element [ˈelimənt] *n* elemento.
elemental [ˌeliˈmentl] *a* degli elementi; fondamentale.
elementary [ˌeliˈmentəri] *a* elementare, rudimentale.
elephant [ˈelifənt] *n* elefante.
elevate [ˈeliveit] *vt* elevare, innalzare.
elevation [ˌeliˈveiʃən] *n* elevazione.
elevator [ˌeliˈveitə] n ascensore, montacarichi.
eleven [iˈlevn] *a n* undici; **eleventh** *a n* undicesimo.
elf [elf] *n* elfo, folletto.
Elia(h) Elias [ˈi:liə, iˈlaiəs] *nm pr* Elia.
elicit [iˈlicit] *vt* tirar fuori, attirare.
elide [iˈlaid] *vt* elidere.
eligibility [ˌelidʒəˈbiliti] *n* eleggibilità.
eligible [ˈelidʒəbl] *a* eleggibile, desiderabile.
eliminate [iˈlimineit] *vt* eliminare.
elimination [iˌlimiˈneiʃən] *n* eliminazione.
elision [iˈliʒən] *n* elisione.
Elizabeth [iˈlizəbəθ] *nf pr* Elisabetta.
Elizabethan [iˌlizəˈbi:θən] *a* elisabettiano.
elk [elk] *n* alce.
ellipse [iˈlips] *n* ellisse.
ellipsis [iˈlipsis] *pl* **ellipses** *n* ellissi.
elliptic(al) [iˈliptik(əl)] *a* ellittico.
elm [elm] *n* olmo.
elocution [ˌeləˈkju:ʃən] *n* elocuzione.
elongate [ˈi:lɔŋgeit] *vti* allungar(si); prolungare.
elope [iˈloup] *vi* fuggire (con un amante).
elopement [iˈloupmənt] *n* fuga di amanti.
eloquence [ˈeləkwəns] *n* eloquenza.
eloquent [ˈeləkwənt] *a* eloquente.
eloquently [ˈeləkwəntli] *ad* con eloquenza, con calore.
else [els] *ad* altrimenti; *a* altro.
elsewhere [ˈelsˈwɛə] *ad* altrove.
elucidate [iˈlu:sideit] *vt* delucidare, chiarire.

elucidation [iˌluːsiˈdeiʃən] *n* delucidazione, (s)chiarimento.
elude [iˈluːd] *vt* eludere, sfuggire a.
elusive [iˈluːsiv] *a* evasivo, sfuggevole.
emaciate [iˈmeiʃieit] *vt* emaciare, far dimagrire.
emaciation [iˌmeisiˈeiʃən] *n* macilenza.
emanate [ˈeməneit] *vti* emanare.
emanation [ˌeməˈneiʃən] *n* emanazione.
emancipate [iˈmænsipeit] *vt* emancipare.
emancipation [iˌmænsiˈpeiʃən] *n* emancipazione.
Emanuel [iˈmænjuəl] *nm pr* Emanuele.
embalm [imˈbɑːm] *vt* imbalsamare.
embankment [imˈbæŋkmənt] *n* argine, diga.
embargo [emˈbɑːgou] *n* embargo.
embark [imˈbɑːk] *vti* imbarcar(si); (*fig*) intraprendere.
embarkation [ˌembɑːˈkeiʃən] *n* imbarco.
embarrass [imˈbærəs] *vt* imbarazzare.
embarrassing [imˈbærəsiŋ] *a* imbarazzante.
embarrassment [imˈbærəsmənt] *n* imbarazzo.
embassy [ˈembəsi] *n* ambiasciata.
embellish [imˈbeliʃ] *vt* abbellire.
embellishment [imˈbeliʃmənt] *n* abbellimento.
ember [ˈembə] *n* (*usu pl*) brace, ceneri ardenti *pl*; **e. days** i tre giorni di digiuno delle quattro Tempora.
embezzle [imˈbezl] *vt* appropriarsi fraudolentemente.
embezzlement [imˈbezlmənt] *n* appropriazione indebita.
embitter [imˈbitə] *vt* amareggiare, inasprire.
emblem [ˈembləm] *n* emblema, simbolo.
embody [imˈbɔdi] *vt* incarnare, personificare; includere.
embolden [imˈbouldən] *vt* incoraggiare, imbaldanzire.
embolism [ˈembəlizəm] *n* (*med*) embolia.
emboss [imˈbɔs] *vt* ornare con rilievi.
embrace [imˈbreis] *n* abbraccio; *vt* abbracciare; comprendere.
embrasure [imˈbreiʒə] *n* (*mil*) feritoia; (*arch*) strombatura di porta (o finestra).
embroider [imˈbrɔidə] *vt* ricamare.
embroidery [imˈbrɔidəri] *n* ricamo.
embroil [imˈbrɔil] *vt* imbrogliare.
embryo [ˈembriou] *pl* **embryos** *n* embrione.
emerald [ˈemərəld] *n* smeraldo.
emerge [iˈməːdʒ] *vi* emergere; sbucare.
emergence [iˈməːdʒəns] *n* emersione, apparizione improvvisa.
emergency [iˈməːdʒənsi] *n* emergenza.
emergent [iˈməːdʒənt] *a* emergente, sorgente.
emery [ˈeməri] *n* smeriglio; **e. paper** carta smerigiata.
emetic [iˈmetik] *a n* emetico.
emigrant [ˈemigrənt] *a n* emigrante.
emigrate [ˈemigreit] *vi* emigrare.
emigration [ˌemiˈgreiʃən] *n* emigrazione.
Emily [ˈemili] *nf pr* Emilia.
eminence [ˈeminəns] *n* eminenza; altura.
eminent [ˈeminənt] *a* eminente.
emissary [ˈemisəri] *a n* emissario.
emission [iˈmiʃən] *n* emissione.
emit [iˈmit] *vt* emettere.
Emmanuel [iˈmænjuəl] *nm pr* Emanuele.
emollient [iˈmɔliənt] *a n* emolliente.
emolument [iˈmɔljumənt] *n* emolumento.
emotion [iˈmouʃən] *n* commozione, emozione.
emotional [iˈmouʃənəl] *a* emotivo, impressionabile, commovente.
emperor [ˈempərə] *n* imperatore.
emphasis [ˈemfəsis] *n* enfasi.
emphasize [ˈemfəsaiz] *vt* dare enfasi a, mettere in rilievo, sottolineare.
emphatic [imˈfætik] *a* enfatico.
empire [ˈempaiə] *n* impero.
empirical [emˈpirikəl] *a* empirico.
employ [imˈplɔi] *n* impiego; *vt* impiegare.
employee [ˌemplɔiˈiː] *n* impiegato.
employer [imˈplɔiə] *n* datore di lavoro, padrone.
employment [imˈplɔimənt] *n* impiego, occupazione.
emporium [emˈpɔːriəm] *n* emporio.
empower [imˈpauə] *vt* autorizzare.
empress [ˈempris] *n* imperatrice.
emptiness [ˈemptinis] *n* vuoto, vacuità.
empty [ˈempti] *a* vuoto, vacante; *n pl* i vuoti; **to return the empties** restituire i vuoti; *vti* vuotar(si).
emulate [ˈemjuleit] *vt* emulare.
emulation [ˌemjuˈleiʃən] *n* emulazione.
emulsion [iˈmʌlʃən] *n* emulsione.
enable [iˈneibl] *vt* mettere in grado (di), permettere.
enact [iˈnækt] *vt* mettere in atto; recitare.
enactment [iˈnæktmənt] *n* decreto, legge.
enamel [iˈnæməl] *n* smalto; *vt* smaltare.
enamor [iˈnæmə] *vt* innamorare.
encamp [inˈkæmp] *vti* accampar(si).
encampment [inˈkæmpmənt] *n* accampamento.
enchant [inˈtʃɑːnt] *vt* incantare.
enchanter [inˈtʃɑːntə] *n* incantatore, mago.
enchanting [inˈtʃɑːntiŋ] *a* incantevole, affascinante.

enchantment [in'tʃɑ:ntmənt] *n* incantesimo, incanto.
enchantress [in'tʃɑ:ntris] *n* incantatrice, maga.
encircle [in'sə:kl] *vt* accerchiare.
enclose [in'klouz] *vt* accludere; rinchiudere, circondare.
enclosure [in'klouʒə] *n* recinto; (*com*) allegato.
encompass [in'kʌmpəs] *vt* circondare, abbracciare.
encore [ɔŋ'kɔ:] *interj n* bis; *vt* chiedere il bis (di).
encounter [in'kauntə] *n* incontro; scontro; *vt* incontrare, affrontare.
encourage [in'kʌridʒ] *vt* incoraggiare.
encouragement [in'kʌridʒmənt] *n* incoraggiamento.
encroach [in'kroutʃ] *vi* intromettersi illegalmente, usurpare i diritti altrui.
encroachment [in'kroutʃmənt] *n* usurpazione, abuso.
encumber [in'kʌmbə] *vt* ingombrare, gravare.
encumbrance [in'kʌmbrəns] *n* impedimento, ingombro; ipoteca.
encyclical [en'siklikəl] *a* (*eccl*) enciclico; *n* (*eccl*) enciclica.
encyclopedia [en,saiklou'pi:diə] *n* enciclopedia.
end [end] *n* fine; scopo; morte; estremità; *vti* finire.
endanger [in'deindʒə] *vt* mettere in pericolo.
endear [en'diə] *vt* rendere caro.
endearing [en'diəriŋ] *a* tenero, affettuoso.
endearment [en'diə:mənt] *n* tenerezza, carezza; **term of e.** vezzeggiativo.
endeavor [in'devə] *n* sforzo, tentativo; *vi* sforzarsi, tentare.
endemic [en'demik] *a* endemico.
ending ['endiŋ] *n* conclusione, termine; (*gram*) desinenza.
endive ['endiv] *n* indivia.
endless ['endlis] *a* interminabile.
endorse [in'dɔ:s] *vt* firmare, girare, confermare, sanzionare.
endorsement [in'dɔ:smənt] *n* (*com*) girata; approvazione.
endow [in'dau] *vt* dotare.
endowment [in'daumənt] *n* dotazione; dote, pregio.
endurance [in'djuərəns] *n* resistenza, pazienza, sopportazione.
endure [in'djuə] *vt* sopportare, tollerare; *vi* durare, continuare.
enduring [in'djuəriŋ] *a* tollerante, paziente; durevole.
enema ['enimə] *n* clistere.
enemy ['enimi] *a n* nemico.
energetic [,enə'dʒetik] *a* energico.
energy ['enədʒi] *n* energia.
enervate ['enə:veit] *vt* snervare.
enfeeble [in'fi:bl] *vt* indebolire.
enfold [in'fould] *vt* avvolgere, abbracciare.
enforce [in'fɔ:s] *vt* imporre, far osservare.
enforcement [in'fɔ:smənt] *n* imposizione; applicazione.
enfranchise [in'fræntʃaiz] *vt* affrancare, liberare; dare il diritto di voto.
enfranchisement [in'fræntʃizmənt] *n* affrancamento, liberazione.
engage [in'geidʒ] *vt* impegnare, prenotare; assumere in servizio; *vi* entrare in, occuparsi di, impegnarsi.
engaged [in'geidʒd] *a* impegnato; fidanzato; occupato.
engagement [in'geidʒmənt] *n* impegno; fidanzamento.
engaging [in'geidʒiŋ] *a* attraente.
engender [in'dʒendə] *vt* generare, produrre.
engine ['endʒin] *n* macchina, motore.
engineer [,endʒi'niə] *n* ingegnere; macchinista; (*mil*) soldato del Genio.
engineer [,endʒi'niə] *vt* (*fam*) macchinare, architettare.
engineering [,endʒi'niəriŋ] *n* ingegneria.
England ['iŋglənd] *n* Inghilterra.
English ['iŋgliʃ] *a n* inglese; **Englishman** Inglese.
engrave [in'greiv] *vt* incidere; (*fig*) imprimere.
engraving [in'greiviŋ] *n* incisione.
engross [in'grous] *vt* assorbire (attenzione); **to become engrossed** astrarsi.
engulf [in'gʌlf] *vt* inghiottire, sommergere.
enhance [in'hɑ:ns] *vt* aumentare, intensificare.
enigma [i'nigmə] *n* enigma.
enigmatic [,enig'mætik] *a* enigmatico.
enjoin [in'dʒɔin] *vt* ingiungere, ordinare.
enjoy [in'dʒɔi] *vt* divertirsi, godere.
enjoyable [in'dʒɔiəbl] *a* piacevole, divertente.
enjoyment [in'dʒɔimənt] *n* godimento, piacere.
enlarge [in'lɑ:dʒ] *vt* espandere, estendere, ingrandire; *vi* allargarsi; dilungarsi.
enlargement [in'lɑ:dʒmənt] *n* allargamento, ingrandimento.
enlighten [in'laitn] *vt* (*fig*) illuminare.
enlightenment [in'laitnmənt] *n* spiegazione, schiarimento.
enlist [in'list] *vti* arruolar(si).
enlistment [in'listmənt] *n* arruolamento.
enliven [in'laivn] *vt* ravvivare.
enmity ['enmiti] *n* inimicizia, ostilità.
ennoble [i'noubl] *vt* nobilitare.
ennui [ɑ̃:'nwi] *n* noia.
enormity [i'nɔ:miti] *n* enormità.
enormous [i'nɔ:məs] *a* enorme.
enough [i'nʌf] *a* sufficiente; *ad* abbastanza, sufficientemente; *n* il necessario, sufficienza.
enquire [in'kwaiə] *v* **inquire.**

enrage [in'reidʒ] *vt* far arrabbiare, imbestialire.
enrapture [in'ræptʃə] *vt* estasiare, incantare.
enrich [in'ritʃ] *vt* arricchire.
enroll [in'roul] *vt* iscrivere, registrare; arruolare.
enrollment [in'roulmənt] *n* iscrizione, registrazione; arruolamento.
enshrine [in'ʃrain] *vt* custodire come cosa sacra, rinchiudere.
ensign ['ensain] *n* bandiera, insegna.
enslave [in'sleiv] *vt* asservire, fare schiavo.
enslavement [in'sleivmənt] *n* asservimento, schiavitù.
ensnare [in'snεə] *vt* irretire, prendere al laccio.
ensue [in'sju:] *vi* risultare, seguire.
ensure [in'ʃuə] *vt* assicurare.
entail [in'teil] *n* assegnazione, eredità inalienabile; *vt* comportare, implicare; intestare a.
entangle [in'tæŋgl] *vt* aggrovigliare, impegolare.
entanglement [in'tæŋglmənt] *n* groviglio, imbroglio.
enter ['entə] *vt* entrare; iscrivere; **to e. into** (*fig*) entrare in, iniziare.
enterprise ['entəpraiz] *n* impresa.
enterprising ['entəpraiziŋ] *a* intraprendente.
entertain [,entə'tein] *vt* divertire, intrattenere, ricevere; nutrire (sospetti).
entertaining [,entə'teiniŋ] *a* divertente, piacevole.
entertainment [,entə'teinmənt] *n* divertimento, trattenimento.
enthralling [in'θrɔ:liŋ] *a* ammaliante, incantevole.
enthusiasm [in'θju:ziæzəm] *n* entusiasmo.
enthusiast [in'θju:ziæst] *n* entusiasta.
enthusiastic [in,θju:zi'æstik] *a* entusiastico.
entice [in'tais] *vi* adescare, allettare.
enticement [in'taismənt] *n* seduzione, allettamento, lusinga.
enticing [in'taisiŋ] *a* seducente, attraente.
entire [in'taiə] *a* completo, intero.
entirely [in'taiəli] *ad* interamente, completamente.
entirety [in'tairəti] *n* interezza; integrità.
entitle [in'taitl] *vt* intitolare, aver diritto a.
entity ['entiti] *n* entità.
entomb [in'tu:m] *vt* inumare.
entombment [in'tu:mmənt] *n* inumazione.
entrails ['entreilz] *n pl* intestini, viscere *pl.*
entrance ['entrəns] *n* entrata, ingresso; **e. fee** tassa d'iscrizione.
entrance [in'trɑ:ns] *vt* incantare, estasiare.
entrap [in'træp] *vt* intrappolare, raggirare.
entreat [in'tri:t] *vt* implorare, supplicare.
entreaty [in'tri:ti] *n* preghiera, supplica.
entrench [in'trentʃ] *vt* trincerare.
entrenchment [in'trentʃmənt] *n* trinceramento.
entrust [in'trʌst] *vt* affidare, commettere.
entry ['entri] *n* entrata, ingresso, iscrizione, annotazione.
entwine [in'twain] *vt* intrecciare.
enumerate [i'nju:məreit] *vt* enumerare.
enunciate [i'nʌnsieit] *vt* enunciare.
enunciation [i,nʌnsi'eiʃən] *n* enunciazione.
envelop [in'veləp] *vt* avvolgere; (*mil*) accerchiare.
envelope ['enviloup] *n* busta, involucro.
enviable ['enviəbl] *a* invidiabile.
envious ['enviəs] *a* invidioso.
environment [in'vaiərənmənt] *n* ambiente.
environs [in'vaiərənz] *n pl* dintorni *pl.*
envisage [in'vizidʒ] *vt* immaginare, vedere, figurarsi.
envoy ['envɔi] *n* inviato, ministro plenipotenziario.
envy ['envi] *n* invidia; *vt* invidiare.
epaulet(te) ['epoulet] *n* (*mil*) spallina.
ephemeral [i'femərəl] *a* effimero, fuggevole.
epic ['epik] *a* epico; *n* epica.
epicure ['epikjuə] *n* epicureo.
epicurean [,epikjuə'ri:ən] *a n* epicureo.
epidemic [,epi'demik] *a* epidemico; *n* epidemia.
epigram ['epigræm] *n* epigramma.
epigraph ['epigrɑ:f] *n* epigrafe.
epilepsy ['epilepsi] *n* epilessia.
epileptic [,epi'leptik] *a n* epilettico.
epilogue ['epilɔg] *n* epilogo.
Epiphany [i'pifəni] *n* Epifania.
episcopacy [i'piskəpəsi] *n* episcopato.
episcopal [i'piskəpəl] *a* episcopale.
episode ['episoud] *n* episodio.
epistle [i'pisl] *n* epistola.
epitaph ['epitɑ:f] *n* epitaffio.
epithet ['epiθet] *n* epiteto.
epitome [i'pitəmi] *n* epitome, compendio.
epitomize [i'pitəmaiz] *vt* compendiare, riassumere.
epoch ['i:pɔk] *n* epoca.
equable ['ekwəbl] *a* equo.
equal ['i:kwəl] *a n* uguale; *vt* uguagliare.
equality [i:'kwɔliti] *n* uguaglianza.
equalize ['i:kwəlaiz] *vt* uguagliare, pareggiare.
equally ['i:kwəli] *ad* ugualmente.
equanimity [,i:kwə'nimiti] *n* equanimità.

equate [i'kweit] *vt* uguagliare; paragonare.
equation [i'kweiʃən] *n* equazione.
equator [i'kweitə] *n* equatore.
equatorial [,ekwə'tɔ:riəl] *a* equatoriale.
equerry [i'kweri] *n* scudiero.
equestrian [i'kwestriən] *a* equestre.
equilibrium [,i:kwi'libriəm] *n* equilibrio.
equinox ['i:kwinɔks] *n* equinozio.
equip [i'kwip] *vt* equipaggiare, attrezzare.
equipage ['ekwipidʒ] *n* attrezzatura; equipaggio.
equipment [i'kwipmənt] *n* equipaggiamento, attrezzatura.
equitable ['ekwitəbl] *a* equo, giusto.
equity ['ekwiti] *n* equità.
equivalent [i'kwivələnt] *a n* equivalente.
equivocal [i'kwivəkəl] *a* ambiguo, equivoco, sospetto.
era ['iərə] *n* era.
eradicate [i'rædikeit] *vt* sradicare.
erase [i'reiz] *vt* cancellare, raschiare.
eraser [i'reizə] *n* raschietto; gomma per cancellare.
erasure [i'reiʒə] *n* cancellatura.
erect [i'rekt] *a* eretto, ritto; *vt* erigere, innalzare.
erection [i'rekʃən] *n* elevazione, erezione.
ermine ['ə:min] *n* ermellino.
Ernest ['ə:nist] *nm pr* Ernesto.
erode [i'roud] *vt* erodere, consumare.
erosion [i'rouʒən] *n* erosione.
erotic [i'rɔtik] *a* erotico.
err [ə:] *vi* errare, sbagliare.
errand ['erənd] *n* commissione, incarico.
errant ['erənt] *a* errante.
erratic [i'rætik] *a* irregolare; eccentrico; erratico.
erroneous [i'rouniəs] *a* erroneo, scorretto.
error ['erə] *n* errore, sbaglio; colpa.
erudite ['erju:dait] *a* erudito.
erudition [,erju:'diʃən] *n* erudizione.
erupt [i'rʌpt] *vi* (*volcano*) eruttare, entrare in eruzione.
eruption [i'rʌpʃən] *n* eruzione, scoppio.
erysipelas [,eri'sipiləs] *n* erisipela.
escalator ['eskəleitə] *n* scala meccanica; scala mobile.
escapade [,eskə'peid] *n* (*fig*) scappata.
escape [is'keip] *n* fuga, scampo, scappamento; *vti* fuggire; evitare; sfuggire.
escapism [is'keipizəm] *n* evasione (dalla realtà).
eschew [is'tʃu:] *vt* astenersi da, evitare.
escort ['eskɔ:t] *n* scorta; [is'kɔ:t] *vt* scortare.
Eskimo ['eskimou] *pl* **Eskimoes** *a n* esquimese.
especial [is'peʃəl] *a* speciale.
especially [is'peʃəli] *ad* specialmente, sopratutto.
espionage [,espiə'nɑ:ʒ] *n* spionaggio.
esplanade [,esplə'neid] *n* spianata; lungomare.
esquire [is'kwaiə] *n* signore (usato negli indirizzi dopo il cognome); **John Smith Esq.** Egregio Signor John Smith.
essay ['esei] *n* saggio; tema; prova; *vt* tentare, provare.
essence ['esns] *n* essenza.
essential [i'senʃəl] *a n* essenziale.
essentially [i'senʃəli] *ad* essenzialmente, fondamentalmente.
establish [is'tæbliʃ] *vt* stabilire, fondare, istituire; constatare; **established** stabilito, affermato.
establishment [is'tæbliʃmənt] *a* stabilimento, istituzione; ordine costituito; accertamento.
estate [is'teit] *n* tenuta, proprietà; stato.
esteem [is'ti:m] *n* considerazione, stima; *vt* considerare, stimare.
Esther ['estə] *nf pr* Ester.
estimable ['estiməbl] *a* stimabile, degno di stima.
estimate ['estimit] *n* stima, valutazione, preventivo; ['estimeit] *vt* stimare, valutare.
estimation [,esti'meiʃən] *n* stima, valutazione.
estrange [is'treindʒ] *vt* alienare, estraniare, inimicarsi.
estrangement [is'treindʒmənt] *n* alienazione, allontanamento.
estuary ['estjuəri] *n* estuario.
etch [etʃ] *vt* incidere all'acquaforte.
etching ['etʃiŋ] *n* acquaforte, incisione.
eternal [i:'tə:nl] *a* eterno.
eternity [i:'tə:niti] *n* eternità.
ether ['i:θə] *n* etere.
ethereal [i:'θiəriəl] *a* etereo.
ethics ['eθiks] *n* etica.
Ethiopia [,i:θi'oupiə] *n* Etiopia.
Ethiopian [,i:θi'oupiən] *a* etiopico; *n* etiope.
etiquette [,eti'ket] *n* etichetta.
Etna ['etnə] *n* Etna.
Etruscan [i'trʌskən] *a n* etrusco.
etymology [,eti'mɔlədʒi] *n* etimologia.
Eucharist ['ju:kərist] *n* Eucarestia.
Eugene [ju:'ʒein] *nm pr* Eugenio.
eulogy ['ju:lədʒi] *n* elogio.
eunuch ['ju:nək] *n* eunuco.
euphemism ['ju:fimizəm] *n* eufemismo.
euphony ['ju:fəni] *n* eufonia.
Europe ['juərəp] *n* Europa.
European [,juərə'pi:ən] *a n* europeo.
euthanasia [,ju:θə'neiziə] *n* eutanasia.
evacuate [i'vækjueit] *vt* evacuare, sfollare.
evacuation [i,vækju'eiʃən] *n* evacuazione, sfollamento.
evacuee [i vækju:'i:] *n* sfollato.

evade [i'veid] *vt* evitare, schivare.
evaluate [i'væljueit] *vt* valutare.
evanescence [.i:və'nesns] *n* evanescenza.
evanescent [.i:və'nesnt] *a* evanescente.
evangelic(al) [.i:væn'dʒelikəl] *a* evangelico; **evangelist** *n* evangelista.
evaporate [i'væpəreit] *vti* (far) evaporare.
evaporation [i væpə'reiʃən] *n* evaporazione.
evasion [i'veiʒən] *n* evasione, sotterfugio.
evasive [i'veisiv] *a* evasivo.
Eve [i:v] *nf pr* Eva.
eve [i:v] *n* vigilia.
even ['i:vən] *a* pari; uguale; piatto; uniforme; *ad* anche, perfino; *vt* uguagliare, uniformare.
evening ['i:vəniŋ] *n* sera.
evenly ['i:vənli] *ad* uniformemente; in parti uguali; pianamente; con calma.
evenness ['i:vənnis] *n* uguaglianza, uniformità.
event [i'vent] *n* avvenimento, evento.
eventful [i'ventful] *a* pieno di avvenimenti, memorabile.
eventual [i'ventjuəl] *a* finale, eventuale; **eventually** *ad* finalmente.
ever ['evə] *ad* mai, sempre.
evergreen ['evəgri:n] *a n* sempreverde.
everlasting [.evə'lɑ:stiŋ] *a* eterno; *n* eternità.
evermore [.evə'mɔ:] *ad* sempre; **for e.** per sempre.
every ['evri] *a* ogni, ciascuno, tutti; **e. now and then** di quando in quando; **e. other day** un giorno sì, e un giorno no.
everybody ['evribɔdi] **everyone** ['evriwʌn] *pron* ognuno, tutti *pl.*
everyday ['evridei] *a* di ogni giorno, quotidiano.
everything ['evriθiŋ] *pron* ogni cosa, tutto.
everywhere ['evriwɛə] *ad* in ogni luogo, ovunque.
evict [i:'vikt] *vt* espellere, sfrattare.
eviction [i:'vikʃən] *n* espulsione, sfratto.
evidence ['evidəns] *n* evidenza, prova, testimonianza; **to give e.** deporre.
evident ['evidənt] *a* evidente, chiaro.
evil ['i:vl] *a* cattivo, maligno, funesto; *ad* male; *n* male.
evince [i'vins] *vt* manifestare, dimostrare.
evocative [i:'vɔkətiv] *a* evocatore.
evoke [i'vouk] *vt* evocare.
evolution [.i:və'lu:ʃən] *n* evoluzione, sviluppo.
evolve [i'vɔlv] *vti* evolver(si).
ewe [ju:] *n* pecora (femmina).
ewer ['ju:ə] *n* brocca.
exact [ig'zækt] *a* esatto, preciso; *vt* esigere.
exacting [ig'zæktiŋ] *a* esigente, impegnativo.
exactitude [ig'zæktitju:d] **exactness** [ig'zæktnis] *n* esattezza, precisione.
exactly [ig'zæktli] *ad* esattamente; proprio; precisamente.
exaggerate [ig'zædʒəreit] *vt* esagerare.
exaggeration [ig.zædʒə'reiʃən] *n* esagerazione.
exalt [ig'zɔ:lt] *vt* esaltare.
exaltation [.egzɔ:l'teiʃən] *n* esaltazione.
examination [ig.zæmi'neiʃən] *n* esame; visita (medica).
examine [ig'zæmin] *vt* esaminare; visitare.
examiner [ig'zæminə] *n* esaminatore.
example [ig'zɑ:mpl] *n* esempio.
exasperate [ig'zɑ:spəreit] *vt* esasperare.
exasperation [ig.zɑ:spə'reiʃən] *n* esasperazione.
excavate ['ekskəveit] *vt* scavare.
excavation [.ekskə'veiʃən] *n* scavo.
exceed [ik'si:d] *vti* eccedere, superare.
exceedingly [ik'si:diŋli] *ad* estremamente.
excel [ik'sel] *vi* eccellere, essere superiore a.
excellence ['eksələns] *n* eccellenza, superiorità.
excellency ['eksələnsi] *n* (*titolo*) eccellenza.
excellent ['eksələnt] *a* eccellente, ottimo.
except [ik'sept] *prep* eccetto, eccettuato, ad eccezione di, tranne; *vt* eccettuare; *vi* obiettare; **excepting** eccetto, tranne.
exception [ik'sepʃən] *n* eccezione, obiezione.
exceptional [ik'sepʃənl] *a* eccezionale.
exceptionally [ik'sepʃənəli] *ad* eccezionalmente, in via eccezionale.
excerpt ['eksə:pt] *n* estratto, citazione.
excess [ik'ses] *n* eccesso; **e. fare** supplemento.
excessive [ik'sesiv] *a* eccessivo, smoderato.
exchange [iks'tʃeindʒ] *n* cambio, scambio; borsa; (*tel*) centrale telefonica; *vt* (s)cambiare.
exchequer [iks'tʃekə] *n* Scacchiere, Tesoro, Fisco.
excise [ek'saiz] *n* imposta indiretta, dazio sul consumo.
exciseman [ek'saizmæn] *pl* **-men** *n* daziere.
excitable [ik'saitəbl] *a* eccitabile, impressionabile.
excite [ik'sait] *vt* eccitare, provocare, entusiasmare.
excitement [ik'saitmənt] *n* agitazione, eccitazione; trambusto.
exciting [ik'saitiŋ] *a* eccitante, emozionante.
exclaim [iks'kleim] *vi* esclamare.

exclamation [,ekskləˈmeiʃən] *n* esclamazione.
exclude [iksˈklu:d] *vt* escludere.
exclusion [iksˈklu:ʒən] *n* esclusione.
exclusive [iksˈklu:siv] *a* esclusivo, scelto.
excommunicate [,ekskəˈmju:nikeit] *vt* scomunicare.
excommunication [ˈekskə,mju:niˈkeiʃən] *n* scomunica.
excrement [ˈekskrimənt] *n* escremento.
excrete [eksˈkri:t] *vt* espellere, secernere.
excruciating [iksˈkru:ʃieitiŋ] *a* atroce, lancinante.
excursion [iksˈkə:ʃən] *n* escursione, gita.
excusable [iksˈkju:zəbl] *a* scusabile, perdonabile.
excuse [iksˈkju:z] *n* scusa, pretesto; *vt* scusare, perdonare, dispensare da.
execrable [ˈeksikrəbl] *a* esecrabile.
execrate [ˈeksikreit] *vt* esecrare.
execute [ˈeksikju:t] *vt* eseguire, mettere in esecuzione; giustiziare.
execution [,eksiˈkju:ʃən] *n* esecuzione; sequestro.
executioner [,eksiˈkju:ʃənə] *n* boia, carnefice.
executive [igˈzekjutiv] *a* esecutivo; *n* direzione, dirigente.
executor [igˈzekjutə] *n* esecutore.
exemplar [igˈzemplə] *n* esemplare, modello.
exemplary [igˈzempləri] *a* esemplare.
exemplify [igˈzemplifai] *vt* illustrare con esempi; fare copia autentica di.
exempt [igˈzempt] *a* esente; *vt* esentare.
exemption [igˈzempʃən] *n* esenzione.
exercise [ˈeksəsaiz] *n* esercizio, esercitazione; *vti* esercitar(si).
exert [igˈzə:t] *vt* esercitare, fare uso di; **to e. oneself** sforzarsi.
exertion [igˈzə:ʃən] *n* sforzo; impiego, uso.
exhalation [,ekshəˈleiʃən] *n* esalazione.
exhale [eksˈheil] *vt* esalare.
exhaust [igˈzɔ:st] *n* (*mech*) scarico, scappamento; *vt* esaurire, vuotare; (*gas etc*), aspirare; *vi* (*gas etc*) scaricarsi.
exhauster [igˈzɔ:stə] *n* aspiratore; ventilatore di scarico.
exhaustion [igˈzɔ:stʃən] *n* esaurimento.
exhaustive [igˈzɔ:stiv] *a* esauriente.
exhibit [igˈzibit] *n* oggetto mandato ad un'esposizione; (*leg*) reperto; *vt* esibire, esporre.
exhibition [,eksiˈbiʃən] *n* esibizione, esposizione, mostra; borsa di studio.
exhibitioner [,eksiˈbiʃenə] *n* chi usufruisce di una borsa di studio.
exhibitor [igˈzibitə] *n* espositore.
exhilarate [igˈziləreit] *vt* esilarare.
exhilaration [ig,ziləˈreiʃən] *n* eccitazione, entusiasmo, allegria.
exhort [igˈzɔ:t] *vt* esortare.
exhortation [,egzɔ:ˈteiʃən] *n* esortazione.
exigency [ekˈsidʒənsi] *n* esigenza.
exigent [ˈeksidʒənt] *a* esigente.
exile [ˈeksail] *n* esilio; esule; *vt* bandire, esiliare.
exist [igˈzist] *vi* esistere.
existence [igˈzistəns] *n* esistenza.
existentialism [egzisˈtenʃəlizəm] *n* esistenzialismo.
existentialist [,egzisˈtenʃəlist] *a n* esistenzialista.
existing [igˈzistiŋ] *a* esistente, attuale.
exit [ˈeksit] *n* uscita.
exodus [ˈeksədəs] *n* esodo.
exonerate [igˈzɔnəreit] *vt* esonerare.
exoneration [ig,zɔnəˈreiʃən] *n* esonero.
exorbitant [igˈzɔ:bitənt] *a* esorbitante.
exorcism [ˈeksɔ:sizəm] *n* esorcismo.
exorcize [ˈeksɔ:saiz] *vt* esorcizzare.
exotic [egˈzɔtik] *a* esotico; *n* pianta esotica.
expand [iksˈpænd] *vti* espander(si), sviluppar(si).
expanse [iksˈpæns] *n* spazio, distesa.
expansion [iksˈpænʃən] *n* espansione, estensione.
expansive [iksˈpænsiv] *a* espansivo.
expatiate [eksˈpeiʃieit] *vi* diffondersi, spaziare.
expatriate [eksˈpætrieit] *vt* espatriare.
expect [iksˈpekt] *vt* aspettar(si); prevedere; supporre; sperare.
expectancy [iksˈpektənsi] *n* aspettativa, attesa; aspettazione.
expectant [iksˈpektənt] *a* in attesa; **e. mother** donna incinta.
expectation [,ekspekˈteiʃən] *n* aspettativa, speranza.
expectorate [eksˈpektəreit] *vt* espettorare.
expediency [iksˈpi:diənsi] *n* convenienza, opportunità.
expedient [iksˈpi:diənt] *a* conveniente; *n* espediente, mezzo ingegnoso.
expedite [ˈekspidait] *vt* accelerare, sbrigare.
expedition [,ekspiˈdiʃən] *n* impresa, spedizione; prontezza.
expel [iksˈpel] *vt* espellere, cacciare.
expend [iksˈpend] *vt* consumare, spendere.
expenditure [iksˈpenditʃə] *n* spesa.
expense [iksˈpens] *n* spesa.
expensive [iksˈpensiv] *a* costoso, dispendioso.
experience [iksˈpiəriəns] *n* esperienza; *vt* provare, sperimentare.
experiment [iksˈperimənt] *n* esperimento, prova; *vi* sperimentare.
experimental [eks,periˈmentl] *a* sperimentale.
expert [ˈekspə:t] *a* abile, esperto; *n* esperto, perito, specialista.

expertise ['ekspə:ti:z] *n* abilità, pratica (di).
expertly ['ekspə:tli] *ad* espertamente, abilmente.
expiate ['ekspieit] *vt* espiare.
expiation [,ekspi'eiʃən] *n* espiazione.
expiration [,ekspaiə'reiʃən] *n* scadenza, termine.
expire [iks'paiə] *vti* scadere, spirare.
expiry [iks'paiəri] *n* termine, scadenza.
explain [iks'plein] *vti* spiegare.
explanation [,eksplə'neiʃən] *n* spiegazione, chiarimento.
explanatory [iks'plænətəri] *a* esplicativo, chiarificatore.
explicit [iks'plisit] *a* esplicito, chiaro.
explode [iks'ploud] *vti* (far) esplodere; (*fig*) rivelare la falsità di.
exploit ['eksplɔit] *n* gesta, impresa; [iks'plɔit] *vt* sfruttare, utilizzare.
exploitation [,eksplɔi'teiʃən] *n* sfruttamento, utilizzazione.
exploration [,eksplɔ:'reiʃən] *n* esplorazione.
explore [iks'plɔ:] *vt* esplorare.
explorer [iks'plɔ:rə] *n* esploratore, esploratrice.
explosion [iks'plouʒən] *n* esplosione, scoppio.
explosive [iks'plousiv] *a n* esplosivo.
exponent [eks'pounənt] *n* esponente, interprete.
export ['ekspɔ:t] *n* esportazione, genere esportabile; *vt* [eks'pɔ:t] esportare.
expose [iks'pouz] *vt* esporre, smascherare.
exposition [,ekspə'ziʃən] *n* esposizione.
expostulate [iks'pɔstjuleit] *vi* fare rimostranze, protestare.
expostulation [iks'pɔstju'leiʃən] *n* rimostranza, protesta.
exposure [iks'pouʒə] *n* esposizione, (*phot*) esposizione, posa; smascheramento, scandalo.
expound [iks'paund] *vt* commentare, spiegare.
express [iks'pres] *a* esplicito, espresso; *n* (*letter*) espresso; (*train*) direttissimo; *vt* esprimere; spremere; spedire per espresso; **e. company** servizio corriere.
expression [iks'preʃən] *n* espressione.
expressive [iks'presiv] *a* espressivo.
expropriate [eks'prouprieit] *vt* espropriare.
expulsion [iks'pʌlʃən] *n* espulsione.
expurgate ['ekspə:geit] *vt* (es)purgare.
expurgation [,ekspə:'geiʃən] *n* espurgazione.
exquisite ['ekskwizit] *a* squisito; (*pain*) acuto.
exquisiteness ['ekskwizitnis] *n* squisitezza.
ex-service ['eks'sə:vis] *a* che ha prestato servizio militare; **ex-serviceman** *n* ex-combattente.
extant [eks'tænt] *a* esistente ancora.
extemporary [iks'tempərəri] *a* estemporaneo, improvvisato.
extempore [eks'tempəri] *a* improvvisato, estemporaneo; *ad* estemporaneamente.
extemporize [iks'tempəraiz] *vt* improvvisare.
extend [iks'tend] *vti* estender(si); prolungare; prorogare; porgere.
extension [iks'tenʃən] *n* estensione, prolungamento; proroga; **e. wire** (*el*) filo flessibile.
extensive [iks'tensiv] *a* esteso, largo.
extensively [iks'tensivli] *ad* ampiamente, estensivamente.
extent [iks'tent] *n* estensione; grado; punto; portata.
extenuate [eks'tenjueit] *vt* attenuare, scusare.
extenuating [eks'tenjueitiŋ] *a* attenuante.
extenuation [eks,tenju'eiʃən] *n* attenuazione.
exterior [eks'tiəriə] *a n* esterno, esteriore.
exterminate [eks'tə:mineit] *vt* sterminare.
extermination [eks,tə:mi'neiʃən] *n* sterminio.
external [eks'tə:nl] *a n* esterno.
extinct [iks'tiŋkt] *a* estinto, spento.
extinction [iks'tiŋkʃən] *n* estinzione.
extinguish [iks'tiŋgwiʃ] *vt* estinguere, spegnere.
extinguisher [iks'tiŋgwiʃə] *n* spegnitoio, estintore.
extirpate ['ekstə:peit] *vt* estirpare.
extirpation [,ekstə:'peiʃən] *n* estirpazione.
extol [iks'tɔl] *vt* esaltare, estollere.
extort [iks'tɔ:t] *vt* estorcere.
extortion [iks'tɔ:ʃən] *n* estorsione.
extortionate [iks'tɔ:ʃnit] *a* (*price*) eccessivo, esorbitante.
extra ['ekstrə] *a* extra, straordinario; superiore; *ad* extra, in più; straordinariamente *n* extra; supplemento; (*theat*) comparsa; **e.-postage** soprattassa.
extract ['ekstrækt] *n* estratto; *vt* [iks'trækt] estrarre.
extraction [iks'trækʃən] *n* estrazione, origine.
extradite ['ekstrədait] *vt* (*leg*) estradare.
extradition [,ekstrə'diʃən] *n* estradizione.
extraneous [eks'treiniəs] *a* estraneo.
extraordinary [iks'trɔ:dnri] *a* straordinario.
extrasensory ['ekstrə'sensəri] *a* al di là dei sensi.
extraterritorial ['ekstrə,teri'tɔ:riəl] *a* estraterritoriale.
extravagance [iks'trævigəns] *n* prodigalità; stravaganza.
extravagant [iks'trævigənt] *a* prodigo; stravagante.
extreme [iks'tri:m] *a n* estremo.

extremely [iks'tri:mli] *ad* estremamente.
extremism [iks'tri:mizəm] *n* (*pol*) estremismo.
extremity [iks'tremiti] *n* estremità; estremo; eccesso; estremo pericolo; bisogno; dolore.
extricate ['ekstrikeit] *vt* districare.
extrinsic [eks'trinsik] *a* estrinseco.
extrovert ['ekstrouvə:t] *n* estroverso.
exuberance [ig'zju:bərəns] *n* esuberanza.
exuberant [ig'zju:bərənt] *a* esuberante.
exult [ig'zʌlt] *vi* esultare.
exultation [,egzʌl'teiʃən] *n* esultanza.
eye [ai] *n* occhio; sguardo; vista.
eyeball ['aibɔ:l] *n* bulbo oculare.
eyebrow ['aibrau] *n* sopracciglio.
eyelash ['ailæʃ] *n* ciglio.
eyelid ['ailid] *n* palpebra.
eyesight ['aisait] *n* vista, potere visivo.
eyewitness ['æ,witnis] *n* testimonio oculare; *vt* guardare, osservare.

F

fable ['feibl] *n* favola.
fabric ['fæbrik] *n* tessuto; struttura.
fabricate ['fæbrikeit] *vt* inventare, (*fig*) fabbricare.
fabrication [,fæbri'keiʃən] *n* contraffazione, invenzione.
fabulous ['fæbjuləs] *a* favoloso.
façade [fə'sɑ:d] *n* facciata.
face [feis] *n* faccia, viso; facciata; faccetta; (*of a watch*) quadrante; *vt* affrontare, fronteggiare; guardare verso.
facet ['fæsit] *n* sfaccettatura, faccetta.
facetious [fə'si:ʃəs] *a* faceto, gioviale.
facial ['feiʃəl] *a* facciale.
facile ['fæsail] *a* facile; scorrevole; superficiale; affrettato.
facilitate [fə'siliteit] *vt* facilitare, agevolare.
facility [fə'siliti] *n* facilità; destrezza; *pl* agevolazioni; attrezzature.
facing ['feisiŋ] *a* che sta di fronte; *n* (*buildings*) rivestimento; (*dress*) risvolto.
facsimile [fæk'simili] *n* facsimile.
fact [fækt] *n* fatto, realtà.
faction ['fækʃən] *n* fazione.
factious ['fækʃəs] *a* fazioso.
factor ['fæktə] *n* fattore.
factory ['fæktəri] *n* fabbrica, manifattura.
factual ['fæktjuəl] *a* effettivo, reale.
faculty ['fækəlti] *n* facoltà.
fad [fæd] *n* mania.
fade [feid] *n* (*cin*) dissolvenza; *vi* appassire; sbiadire; dileguarsi; svanire.
faded ['feidid] *a* appassito; sbiadito.
fag [fæg] *n* lavoro faticoso; (*sl*) sigaretta.
fag(g)ot ['fægət] *n* fascina.
fail [feil] *n* fallo; *vt* abbandonare; mancare a; bocciare; *vi* fallire; mancare, essere insufficiente; (*com*) fallire.
failing ['feiliŋ] *a* debole, scarso; *n* debolezza, difetto, mancanza; *prep* in mancanza di.
faille [feil] *n* faglia, tessuto di seta.
failure ['feiljə] *n* fallimento, fiasco, insuccesso; mancanza.
faint [feint] *a* debole, lieve, (*of colors*) pallido; *n* svenimento; *vi* svenire.
faintness ['feintnis] *n* debolezza, languore.
fair [fɛə] *a* bello; biondo; chiaro; sereno; giusto; leale; onesto; *ad* bene, onestamente; *n* fiera, mercato.
fairly ['fɛəli] *ad* lealmente; abbastanza.
fairness ['fɛənis] *n* bellezza; bianchezza, biondezza; onestà, equità.
fairy ['fɛəri] *a* fatato; *n* fata; **fairy tale** fiaba.
fairyland ['fɛərilænd] *n* paese delle fate.
faith [feiθ] *n* fede, fiducia.
faithful ['feiθful] *a* fedele, leale.
faithfully ['feiθfəli] *ad* fedelmente; **Yours f.** distinti saluti.
faithless ['feiθlis] *a* miscredente; sleale, falso.
fake [feik] *n* contraffazione, falso; *vti* falsificare; fingere.
falcon ['fɔ:lkən] *n* falcone.
fall [fɔ:l] *n* caduta; abbassamento; ribasso; rovina; cascata; autunno; *vi* cadere; diminuire; toccare in sorte.
fallacious [fə'leiʃəs] *a* fallace.
fallacy ['fæləsi] *n* errore; sofisma; fallacia.
fallibility [,fæli'biliti] *n* fallibilità.
fallible ['fæləbl] *a* fallibile.
falling ['fɔ:liŋ] *a* cadente; *n* caduta; scadenza.
fall-out ['fɔ:laut] *n* pioggia radioattiva.
fallow ['fælou] *a* incolto; *n* maggese.
false ['fɔ:ls] *a* falso, finto, ingannevole.
falsehood ['fɔ:lshud] *n* menzogna.
falsify ['fɔ:lsifai] *vt* falsificare.
falsity ['fɔ:lsiti] *n* falsità.
falter ['fɔ:ltə] *vi* balbettare; esitare; vacillare.
fame [feim] *n* fama.
famed [feimd] *a* rinomato, famoso, celebre.
familiar [fə'miljə] *a n* familiare.
familiarity [fə,mili'æriti] *n* familiarità.
familiarize [fə'miljəraiz] *vt* familiarizzare.
family ['fæmili] *n* famiglia; **f. name** cognome.
famine ['fæmin] *n* carestia.
famish ['fæmiʃ] *vti* affamare; morire di fame.
famous ['feiməs] *a* famoso, celebre.

fan [fæn] *n* ventaglio, ventilatore; (*sl*) tifoso d'uno sport; *vt* sventolare, ventilare; (*fig*) stimolare, alimentare.
fanatic [fə'nætik] *a n* fanatico.
fanaticism [fə'nætisizəm] *n* fanatismo.
fanciful ['fænsiful] *a* capriccioso, fantasioso; immaginario.
fancy ['fænsi] *n* fantasia, capriccio, desiderio; *vt* creare con la fantasia, immaginare, desiderare.
fanfare ['fænfεə] *n* fanfara.
fang [fæŋ] *n* zanna.
fantastic [fæn'tæstik] *a* fantastico.
fantasy ['fæntəsi] *n* fantasia, immaginazione.
far [fɑ:] *a* lontano, remoto; *ad* a grande distanza; di gran lunga, molto; **so f.** finora, fin qui; **faraway** lontano; **f.-fetched** esagerato, ricercato, stiracchiato; **f. off** molto lontano; **f.-reaching** di lunga portata.
farce [fɑ:s] *n* farsa.
farcical ['fɑ:sikəl] *a* farsesco.
fare [fεə] *n* cibo, nutrimento; (*train etc*) prezzo di una corsa, passeggero; *vi* stare, trovarsi, vivere, mangiare.
farewell ['fεə'wel] *n* addio.
farm [fɑ:m] *n* fattoria, podere; **farmyard** aia; *vt* coltivare, prendere, dare in appalto; *vi* fare l'agricoltore.
farmer ['fɑ:mə] *n* agricoltore, fittavolo.
farming ['fɑ:miŋ] *n* il lavoro dei campi; agricoltura; coltivazione.
farrier ['færiə] *n* maniscalco.
farther ['fɑ:ðə] *a* più lontano, ulteriore *ad* anche, inoltre, più a lungo; più lontano.
farthest ['fɑ:ðist] *a* il più lontano, estremo; *ad* più lontano.
farthing ['fɑ:ðiŋ] *n* quarto di 'penny'; (*fig*) cosa di nessun valore.
fascinate ['fæsineit] *vt* affascinare.
fascination [,fæsi'neiʃən] *n* fascino.
fascism ['fæʃizəm] *n* (*pol*) fascismo.
fascist ['fæʃist] *a n* fascista.
fashion ['fæʃən] *n* moda, modello; modo, stile; *vt* fare, foggiare, creare secondo un modello.
fashionable ['fæʃnəbl] *a* alla moda, di moda; elegante.
fast [fɑ:st] *a* fermo, fisso, saldo; rapido, veloce; (*fig*) dissoluto; *n* astinenza, digiuno; *ad* rapidamente; fermamente, saldamente; *vi* digiunare.
fasten ['fɑ:sn] *vt* assicurare, attaccare, fissare; *vi* attaccarsi.
fastener ['fɑ:snə] *n* chiusura, fermaglio; **zip f.** chiusura lampo.
fastening ['fɑ:sniŋ] *n* chiusura, fermatura.
fastidious [fæs'tidiəs] *a* di gusti difficili, schizzinoso.
fastidiousness [fæs'tidiəsnis] *n* l'essere di gusti difficili.
fasting ['fɑ:stiŋ] *a* di digiuno; *n* digiuno.
fat [fæt] *a* grasso; corpulento; ricco, fertile; *n* grasso.
fatal ['feitl] *a* fatale, funesto.
fatalism ['feitəlizəm] *n* fatalismo.
fatality [fə'tæliti] *n* fatalità, sventura, morte accidentale.
fate [feit] *n* fato, destino.
fated ['feitid] *a* destinato.
fateful ['feitful] *a* fatale, decisivo.
father ['fɑ:ðə] *n* padre; *vt* procreare; **f.-in-law** suocero.
fatherhood ['fɑ:ðəhud] *n* paternità.
fatherless ['fɑ:ðəlis] *a* orfano di padre.
fatherly ['fɑ:ðəli] *a* paterno.
fathom ['fæðəm] *n* misura di profondità (*metri* 1,83 *circa*); *vt* scandagliare; (*fig*) capire.
fathomless ['fæðəmlis] *a* incommensurabile, impenetrabile.
fatigue [fə'ti:g] *n* fatica; *vt* affaticare, stancare.
fatiguing [fə'ti:giŋ] *a* faticoso, sfibrante.
fatness ['fætnis] *n* grassezza.
fatten ['fætn] *vti* ingrassare.
fatty ['fæti] *a* adiposo, grasso.
fatuity [fə'tju:iti] *n* fatuità.
fatuous ['fætjuəs] *a* fatuo.
faucet ['fɔ:sit] *n* rubinetto.
fault [fɔ:lt] *n* difetto, colpa, fallo; **to a f.** all'eccesso.
faultless ['fɔ:ltlis] *a* irreprensibile, perfetto.
faulty ['fɔ:lti] *a* difettoso, imperfetto.
faun [fɔ:n] *n* fauno.
favor ['feivə] *n* favore, parzialità; *vt* favorire.
favorable ['feivərəbl] *a* favorevole, propizio.
favorite ['feivərit] *a n* favorito.
fawn [fɔ:n] *a n* cerbiatto; color fulvo; *vi* accarezzare, adulare.
fear [fiə] *n* paura, timore; *vti* temere, aver paura.
fearful ['fiəful] *a* spaventoso, timoroso.
fearless ['fiəlis] *a* ardimentoso, impavido.
fearsome ['fiəsəm] *a* spaventoso.
feasible ['fi:zəbl] *a* fattibile, possibile.
feast [fi:st] *n* festa, festino, *vt* festeggiare; *vi* banchettare, far festa.
feat [fi:t] *n* atto eroico, prodezza.
feather ['feðə] *n* penna, piuma.
feature ['fi:tʃə] *n* fattezza, lineamento; configurazione; caratteristica.
February ['februəri] *n* febbraio.
feckless ['feklis] *a* inefficiente.
fecund ['fi:kənd] *a* fecondo.
fecundity [fi'kʌnditi] *n* fecondità.
federal ['fedərəl] *a* federale.
federate ['fedərit] *a* (con)federato.
federation [,fedə'reiʃən] *n* (con) federazione.
fee [fi:] *n* onorario, emolumento; (*enrollment, examination etc*) tassa; *vt* pagare un onorario a.
feeble ['fi:bl] *a* debole.

feebleness ['fi:blnis] *n* debolezza.
feed [fi:d] *n* alimento, (*fam*) mangiata; (*mech*) alimentazione, rifornimento; *vti* nutrir(si).
feeder ['fi:də] *n* alimentatore; (*bib*) bavaglino; (*stream*) affluente; (*rly*) linea secondaria; (*feeding bottle*) biberon, poppatoio.
feeding ['fi:diŋ] *n* alimentazione, nutrimento.
feel [fi:l] *n* sensazione (tattile); *vti* sentir(si), avere la sensazione di, percepire.
feeler ['fi:lə] *n* antenna; tentacolo; (*fig*) sondaggio, approccio; (*mech*) sonda.
feeling ['fi:liŋ] *a* sensibile; *n* sentimento, sensazione, sensibilità.
feign [fein] *vti* fingere, simulare.
feint [feint] *n* finta; (*mil*) finto attacco; *vi* fare una finta.
felicitate [fi'lisiteit] *vt* felicitarsi con, congratularsi con.
felicitation [fi,lisi'teiʃən] *n* felicitazione, congratulazione.
felicitous [fi'lisitəs] *a* felice, appropriato.
felicity [fi'lisiti] *n* felicità.
feline ['fi:lain] *a n* felino.
fell [fel] *n* collina brulla; pelle, vello; *a* feroce *vt* abbattere.
fellow ['felou] *n* individuo; camerata, compagno, socio; **fellowship** compagnia; amicizia; associazione; borsa di studio.
felon ['felən] *n* criminale.
felony ['feləni] *n* crimine.
felt [felt] *n* feltro.
female ['fi:meil] *a* femminile, di sesso femminile; *n* femmina.
feminine ['feminin] *a* femminile.
fen [fen] *n* terreno acquitrinoso.
fence [fens] *n* recinto, stecconato; ricettatore; *vt* chiudere con un recinto; ricettare; *vi* tirar di scherma; (*fig*) schermirsi.
fencing ['fensiŋ] *n* scherma; recinto.
fend [fend] *vt* **f. off** parare; **f. for oneself** provvedere a se stesso.
fender ['fendə] *n* paraurti; parafuoco; (*aut*) parafango.
fennel ['fenl] *n* finocchio.
Ferdinand ['fə:dinənd] *nm pr* Ferdinando.
ferment ['fə:ment] *n* fermento; [fə:'ment] *vti* (far) fermentare; (*fig*) fomentare.
fermentation [,fə:men'teiʃən] *n* fermentazione.
fern [fə:n] *n* felce.
ferocious [fə'rouʃəs] *a* feroce.
ferocity [fə'rɔsiti] *n* ferocia.
ferret ['ferit] *n* furetto; **f. out** *vt* scoprire.
ferrule ['feru:l] *n* ghiera.
ferry ['feri] *n* traghetto, ferryboàt; *vt* traghettare.
fertile ['fə:tail] *a* fertile.
fertility [fə:'tiliti] *n* fertilità.
fertilize ['fə:tilaiz] *vt* fertilizzare.
fervent ['fə:vənt] *a* fervente.
fervid ['fə:vid] *a* fervido.
fervor ['fə:və] *n* fervore.
fester ['festə] *vi* suppurare.
festival ['festivəl] *n* festa, celebrazione; (*mus etc*) festival.
festive ['festiv] *a* festivo, gioioso.
festivity [fes'tiviti] *n* festività, festa.
festoon [fes'tu:n] *n* festone; *vt* adornare con festoni.
fetch [fetʃ] *vt* andare a prendere; valere, fruttare.
fête [feit] *n* festa; *vt* festeggiare.
fetid ['fetid] *a* fetido.
fetish ['fi:tiʃ] *n* feticcio.
fetter ['fetə] *n* catena; **fetters** *pl* ceppi *pl*; *vt* mettere in ceppi; intralciare.
fettle ['fetl] *n* condizione, stato.
feud [fju:d] *n* contesa, inimicizia.
feudal ['fju:dəl] *a* feudale.
feudalism ['fju:dəlizəm] *n* feudalismo.
fever ['fi:və] *n* febbre.
feverish ['fi:vəriʃ] *a* febbricitante, febbrile.
few [fju:] *a pron pl* pochi; **a f.** alcuni, un certo numero; **the f.** la minoranza.
fiancé [fi'ɑ̃:nsei] *n* fidanzato; **fiancée** fidanzata.
fiasco [fi'æskou] *n* insuccesso, fiasco.
fib [fib] *n* (*fam*) piccola bugia.
fiber ['faibə] *n* fibra.
fiberglass ['faibəglɑ:s] *n* lana di vetro.
fibrous ['faibrəs] *a* fibroso.
fickle ['fikl] *a* incostante, volubile.
fickleness ['fiklnis] *n* incostanza, volubilità.
fiction ['fikʃən] *n* prosa narrativa; finzione, invenzione.
fictitious [fik'tiʃəs] *a* fittizio.
fiddle ['fidl] *n* (*fam*) violino; *vti* (*fam*) suonare il violino; gingillarsi
fidelity [fi'deliti] *n* fedeltà.
fidget ['fidʒit] *n* irrequietezza; *vi* essere irrequieto, agitarsi.
fidgety ['fidʒiti] *a* irrequieto.
field [fi:ld] *n* campo.
fiend [fi:nd] *n* demonio, spirito maligno.
fiendish ['fi:ndiʃ] *a* demoniaco, diabolico.
fiendishly ['fi:ndiʃli] *ad* diabolicamente.
fierce [fiəs] *a* feroce, violento; ardente.
fiercely ['fiəsli] *ad* ferocemente; ardentemente; furiosamente.
fierceness ['fiəsnis] *n* ferocia; ardore, furia.
fiery ['faiəri] *n* infiammato, focoso.
fife [faif] *n* piffero.
fifteen ['fif'ti:n] *a n* quindici; **fifteenth** *a n* quindicesimo, decimo quinto.
fifth [fifθ] *a n* quinto.
fifty ['fifti] *a n* cinquanta; **fiftieth** *a n* cinquantesimo.

fig (tree) ['fig(tri:)] *n* (pianta di) fico.
fight [fait] *n* battaglia, combattimento; *vti* combattere, lottare.
fighter ['faitə] *n* combattente; (*av*) caccia.
figment ['figmənt] *n* finzione, invenzione.
figurative ['figjurətiv] *a* figurativo; figurato; ornato.
figure ['figə] *n* cifra; figura; *vti* figurarsi, raffigurare; **f. out** calcolare; **figurehead** uomo di paglia.
filament ['filəmənt] *n* filamento.
filch [filtʃ] *n* refurtiva; *vt* rubacchiare.
file [fail] *n* lima; fila; filza, schedario; *vti* archiviare, ordinare; (far) marciare in fila; limare.
filial ['filiəl] *a* filiale.
filibuster ['filibʌstə] *n* ostruzionista; *vi* ostruzionare.
filigree ['filigri:] *n* filigrana.
fill [fil] *n* sazietà; *vt* riempire; (*position*) occupare; (*tooth*) otturare; *vi* riempirsi.
fillet ['filit] *n* nastro; filetto.
filling ['filiŋ] *n* riempitura; ripieno; (*tooth*) otturazione; **f. station** (*aut*) stazione di rifornimento.
fillip ['filip] *n* lo schioccare delle dita; (*fig*) stimolo; *vti* schioccare le dita; (*fig*) stimolare.
filly ['fili] *n* puledra.
film [film] *n* film, pellicola; patina; (*fig*) velo; *vt* filmare.
filmy ['filmi] *a* velato, vaporoso.
filter ['filtə] *n* filtro; *vti* filtrare; **f.-tip cigarette** sigaretta con filtro.
filth [filθ] **filthiness** ['filθinis] *n* sudiciume; oscenità.
filthy ['filθi] *a* sudicio; osceno.
fin [fin] *n* pinna.
final ['fainl] *a* finale, ultimo, decisivo; *n* (*sport*) gara finale; *pl* esami finali *pl*; **finalist** *n* (*sport*) finalista.
finale [fi'nɑ:li] *n* (*mus*) finale.
finally ['fainəli] *ad* finalmente, alla fine; definitivamente.
finance [fai'næns] *n* finanza; *vt* finanziare.
financial [fai'nænʃəl] *a* finanziario.
financier [fai'nænsiə] *n* finanziere.
finch [fintʃ] *n* fringuello.
find [faind] *n* scoperta, ritrovamento; *vt* trovare; **f. out** scoprire.
fine [fain] *a* bello; delicato; fine, raffinato; *ad* bene; *n* multa; *vt* multare.
fineness ['fainnis] *n* bellezza; finezza.
finery ['fainəri] *n* abiti delle feste *pl*, fronzoli *pl*.
finesse [fi'nes] *n* finezza, sottigliezza.
finger ['fingə] *n* dito; *vt* tastare, toccare delicatamente; **fingerprint** impronta digitale.
finical ['finikəl], **finicky** ['finiki] *a* pignolo, affettato, schizzinoso.
finish ['finiʃ] *n* rifinitura, ultimo tocco; fine; *vti* finire, perfezionare.
finite ['fainait] *a* definito, limitato; (*gram*) finito.
Finland ['finlənd] *n* Finlandia.
Finn [fin] *n* finlandese.
Finnish ['finiʃ] *a* finlandese.
fiord [fjɔ:d] *n* fiordo.
fir (tree) ['fə:(tri:)] *n* abete.
fire ['faiə] *n* fuoco, incendio; (*gun*) tiro; *vt* incendiare; sparare.
firearms ['faiərɑ:mz] *n pl* armi da fuoco *pl*.
fire brigade ['faiəbri,geid] *n* corpo dei pompieri.
fire department ['faiədi:'pɑ:tmənt] *n* corpo dei pompieri.
fire-escape ['faiəris,keip] *n* uscita di sicurezza.
fire-extinguisher ['faiəriks,tiŋgwiʃə] *n* estintore, pompa antincendio.
firefly ['faiəflai] *n* lucciola.
fireman ['faiəmən] *pl* **firemen** *n* pompiere.
fireplace ['faiəpleis] *n* caminetto, camino.
fireproof ['faiəpru:f] *a* incombustibile.
fireside ['faiəsaid] *n* focolare.
firewood ['faiəwud] *n* legna da ardere.
firework ['faiəwə:k] *n* fuoco d'artifizio.
firing ['faiəriŋ] *n* combustione; scarica, sparo; **f. party, f. squad** (*mil*) plotone d'esecuzione.
firm [fə:m] *a* duro; saldo, stabile; deciso; *n* ditta.
firmament ['fə:məmənt] *n* firmamento.
firmly ['fə:mli] *ad* fermamente; saldamente.
firmness ['fə:mnis] *n* fermezza; stabilità.
first [fə:st] *n* primo; *ad* prima, in primo luogo.
firth [fə:θ] *n* (*scozzese*) estuario.
fish [fiʃ] *pl* **fishes, fish** *n* pesce; *vti* pescare.
fisher(man) ['fiʃə(mən)] *pl* **fishermen** *n* pescatore.
fishery ['fiʃəri] *n* pesca; riserva di pesca; vivaio.
fishing ['fiʃiŋ] *a* di pesca, per la pesca; *n* pesca; **f. hook** amo; **f. line** lenza; **f. rod** canna da pesca.
fishmonger ['fiʃ,mʌŋgə] *n* pescivendolo.
fish-pond ['fiʃpɔnd] *n* vasca per pesci.
fishy ['fiʃi] *a* di pesce; (*fig*) dubbio, equivoco.
fission ['fiʃən] *n* fissione.
fissure ['fiʃə] *n* crepa, fessura.
fist [fist] *n* pugno.
fit [fit] *a* adatto, appropriato, conveniente, idoneo; in buona salute; *n* misura; accesso, convulsione; *vti* adattare; prepararsi a; convenire, star bene.
fitful ['fitful] *a* spasmodico, irregolare.

fitfully ['fitfuli] *ad* a sbalzi; irregolarmente.
fitness ['fitnis] *n* opportunità; buona salute.
fitting ['fitiŋ] *a* adatto, conveniente; *n* (*of a dress etc*) prova; (*usu pl*) accessori, arredi, infissi *pl*.
fittingly ['fitiŋli] *ad* convenientemente.
five [faiv] *a n* cinque.
fix [fiks] *n* (*fam*) dilemma, difficoltà; *vt* fissare, aggiustare; stabilire; **to f. up** accomodare.
fixation [fik'seiʃən] *n* fissazione.
fixative ['fiksətiv] *a* fissativo; *n* fissativo, fissatore.
fixed [fikst] *a* fisso, fissato.
fixing ['fiksiŋ] *n* (*phot*) fissaggio.
fixture ['fikstʃə] *n* infisso; (*sport*) data fissata; impianto di gas, luce *etc*.
fizz [fiz] *n* (*sl*) spumante, bevanda effervescente; *vi* frizzare.
fizzle ['fizl] *vi* frizzare, sibilare; **to f. out** far fiasco.
flabbergast ['flæbəgɑ:st] *vt* (*fam*) sbalordire.
flabbiness ['flæbinis] *n* flaccidezza.
flabby ['flæbi] *a* cascante, floscio.
flaccid ['flæksid] *a* flaccido.
flag [flæg] *n* bandiera; (*bot*) iride; (*stone*) pietra da lastrico; *vi* perdere le forze.
flagellate ['flædʒileit] *vt* flagellare.
flagellation [flædʒe'leiʃən] *n* flagellazione.
flagon ['flægən] *n* bottiglione.
flagrancy ['fleigrənsi] *n* flagranza.
flagrant ['fleigrənt] *a* flagrante.
flair [flɛə] *n* fiuto, intuizione.
flake [fleik] *n* fiocco; lamina, scaglia; *vti* sfaldar(si).
flaky ['fleiki] *a* scaglioso; fioccoso; (*pastry*) sfogliato.
flamboyant [flæm'bɔiənt] *a* sgargiante.
flame [fleim] *n* fiamma; *vi* fiammeggiare.
flaming ['fleimiŋ] *a* infuocato, ardente.
Flanders ['flɑ:ndəz] *n* (*geogr*) Fiandre.
flank [flæŋk] *n* fianco; *vt* fiancheggiare.
flannel ['flænl] *a n* (di) flanella.
flap [flæp] *n* falda, lembo, tesa, colpo d'ala; *vt* agitare, sbattere.
flare [flɛə] *n* chiarore intenso, fiammata improvvisa; (*av*) razzo; *vi* brillare di luce viva, avvampare.
flash [flæʃ] *n* baleno, lampo, vampata; **flashback** (*cin*) scena retrospettiva; **flashbulb** lampada per fotolampo; **flashlight** lampadina elettrica; (*naut*) luce intermittente; **flashpoint** temperatura di infiammabilità; *vti* lanciare, balenare, sfavillare.
flashy ['flæʃi] *a* (*fam*) sgargiante, vistoso, appariscente.
flask [flɑ:sk] *n* fiasco.
flat [flæt] *a* piano, piatto; monotono, uniforme; reciso; *n* appartamento; piano di casa; **service flats** appartamenti di affitto con servizio.
flatly ['flætli] *ad* freddamente, recisamente.
flatness ['flætnis] *n* monotonia, uniformità.
flatten ['flætn] *vt* appiattire.
flatter ['flætə] *vt* adulare, lusingare.
flattering ['flætəriŋ] *a* adulatorio.
flattery ['flætəri] *n* adulazione.
flatulence ['flætjuləns] *n* flatulenza.
flaunt [flɔ:nt] *vt* ostentare.
flautist ['flɔ:tist] *n* flautista.
flavor ['fleivə] *n* aroma, gusto, sapore; *vt* dare gusto a, aromatizzare.
flaw [flɔ:] *n* difetto, pecca.
flax [flæks] *n* lino.
flaxen ['flæksən] *a* di lino; biondo.
flay [flei] *vt* scorticare, pelare.
flea [fli:] *n* pulce.
fleck [flek] *n* lentiggine; macchietta; particella.
fledge [fledʒ] *vi* mettere le ali.
fledged [fledʒd] *a* (*of bird*) pennuto; piumato.
fledgling ['fledʒliŋ] *n* uccellino appena uscito dal nido.
flee [fli:] *vi* fuggire.
fleece [fli:s] *n* vello; *vt* (*sl*) pelare, derubare.
fleecy ['fli:si] *a* lanoso, velloso.
fleet [fli:t] *n* flotta.
fleeting ['fli:tiŋ] *a* fugace, transitorio.
Fleming ['flemiŋ] *n* fiammingo.
Flemish ['flemiʃ] *a n* fiammingo.
flesh [fleʃ] *n* carne.
fleshy ['fleʃi] *a* polposo, grasso.
flex [fleks] *n* (*el*) filo flessibile.
flexibility [,fleksə'biliti] *n* flessibilità.
flexible ['fleksəbl] *a* flessibile.
flick [flik] *n* colpetto, schiocco; buffetto; (*sl*) cinema; *vt* colpire; dare un buffetto; **f. knife** coltello a molla.
flicker ['flikə] *n* barlume; tremolio; battito; *vi* tremolare, vacillare; brillare debolmente.
flight [flait] *n* volo; stormo; (*av*) squadriglia; rampa di scale; fuga.
flightily ['flaitili] *ad* capricciosamente, leggermente.
flighty ['flaiti] *a* frivolo, incostante.
flimsiness ['flimzinis] *n* tenuità, inconsistenza; frivolezza.
flimsy ['flimzi] *a* tenue, leggero; frivolo.
flinch [flintʃ] *vi* indietreggiare, ritirarsi.
fling [fliŋ] *n* getto, lancio; godimento completo, baldoria; *vt* gettare, lanciare.
flint [flint] *n* pietra focaia, selce; (*of cigarette lighter*) pietrina.
flinty ['flinti] *a* petroso; crudele, duro.
flip [flip] *vt* sbattere leggermente; **egg-flip** uova sbattute, zabaione.

flippancy ['flipənsi] *n* leggerezza, mancanza di serietà.
flippant ['flipənt] *a* leggero, irrispettoso.
flipper ['flipə] *n* pinna, ala natatoria.
flirt [flə:t] *n* ragazza civettuola; damerino; amoreggiamento, 'flirt'; *vt* agitare; *vi* civettare, 'flirtare'.
flirtation [flə:'teiʃən] *n* amoreggiamento, 'flirt'.
flit [flit] *vi* volare, svolazzare; sloggiare.
float [flout] *n* galleggiante; carro per processione; *vti* galleggiare, far galleggiare.
floater ['floutə] *n* galleggiante.
floating ['floutiŋ] *a* galleggiante, fluttuante; **f. capital** (*com*) capitale circolante.
flock [flɔk] *n* branco, gregge; bioccolo, fiocco di lana; *vi* riunirsi a stormi.
floe [flou] *n* banchisa.
flog [flɔg] *vt* frustare.
flogging ['flɔgiŋ] *n* bastonatura, fustigazione.
flood [flʌd] *n* diluvio, inondazione, allagamento; *vt* inondare, sommergere.
floodlight ['flʌdlait] *n* riflettore; *vt* illuminare con riflettori.
floor [flɔ:] *n* pavimento; piano (di casa); *vt* pavimentare, ridurre al silenzio; atterrare.
flop [flɔp] *n* tonfo; fiasco, insuccesso; *vi* camminare (sedersi) goffamente; (*sl*) far fiasco; **flophouse** dormitorio pubblico.
floral ['flɔ:rəl] *a* floreale.
Florence ['flɔ:rəns] *n* (*geogr*) Firenze; **Florentine** *a n* fiorentino, fiorentina.
florid ['flɔrid] *a* florido, prosperoso.
florin ['flɔrin] *n* fiorino (*in Inghilterra, moneta da due scellini*).
florist ['flɔrist] *n* fiorista, fioraio, floricultore.
flotilla [flou'tilə] *n* flottiglia.
flotsam ['flɔtsəm] *n* relitti *pl*; merci ritrovate galleggianti sul mare *pl*.
flounce [flauns] *n* falpalà; *vt* ornare di volani; *vi* dimenarsi, muoversi in modo agitato.
flounder ['flaundə] *n* (*fish*) passerino; *vi* agitarsi, dibatersi; condurre una cosa male, fare errori.
flour ['flauə] *n* (fior di) farina.
flourish ['flʌriʃ] *n* fioritura; (*of trumpets*) squillo; (*writing*) svolazzo; *vi* fiorire; (*fig*) prosperare; *vt* (*stick etc*) brandire.
flout [flaut] *vt* insultare, schernire.
flow [flou] *n* flusso, corso, corrente; abbondanza; **f. of words** facilità; *vi* fluire, scorrere.
flower ['flauə] *n* fiore; **flowerbed** aiuola; fiorire, produrre fiori.
flowery ['flauəri] *a* fiorito.
flowing ['flouiŋ] *a* fluente, corrente, sciolto, fluido; *n* flusso, corso.
flu [flu:] *n* (*fam*) influenza.
fluctuate ['flʌktjueit] *vi* fluttuare.
fluctuation [,flʌktju'eiʃən] *n* oscillazione, fluttuazione.
flue [flu:] *n* conduttura d'un camino, tubo.
fluency ['flu:ənsi] *n* fluidità, scioltezza, facilità (di parola).
fluent ['flu:ənt] *a* fluente, scorrevole, dalla parola facile.
fluff [flʌf] *n* lanugine, peluria.
fluid ['flu:id] *a n* fluido.
fluke ['flu:k] *n* (*naut*) marra; (*zool*) distoma epatico; (*fam*) vantaggio inaspettato, colpo di fortuna.
flunkey ['flʌŋki] *n* valletto.
fluorescent [fluə'resnt] *a* fluorescente.
flurry ['flʌri] *n* agitazione; improvviso colpo di vento, o scroscio di pioggia.
flush [flʌʃ] *n* rossore, afflusso di sangue al volto; *vt* sciacquare (con acqua abbondante); *vi* arrossire.
fluster ['flʌstə] *n* agitazione, eccitazione; *vti* agitare, agitarsi.
flute [flu:t] *n* flauto.
flutter ['flʌtə] *n* svolazzamento; agitazione; (*sl*) speculazione; *vt* agitare; *vi* agitarsi, svolazzare.
flux [flʌks] *n* flusso.
fly [flai] *n* mosca; *vti* (far) volare.
flying ['flaiiŋ] *a* volante, sventolante; breve.
foal [foul] *n* puledro.
foam [foum] *n* schiuma, spuma; *vi* schiumare, spumeggiare.
fob (**off**) [fɔb] *vt* imbrogliare, appioppare *qc* a *qlcu*.
focus ['foukəs] *n* fuoco; **in f.** a fuoco; **out of f.** fuori fuoco, sfocato.
fodder ['fɔdə] *n* foraggio.
foe [fou] *n* avversario, nemico.
fog [fɔg] *n* nebbia.
foggy ['fɔgi] *a* nebbioso.
foible ['fɔibl] *n* lato debole.
foil [fɔil] *n* foglia sottile di metallo; cosa che serve a porre in risalto; *vt* frustrare; far perdere le tracce.
foist [fɔist] *vt* introdurre di nascosto, far accettare con un trucco.
fold [fould] *n* piega, spira; ovile; (*fig*) Chiesa; *vt* piegare; (*arms*) incrociare; *vi* ripiegarsi.
folder ['fouldə] *n* (manifestino) pieghevole; cartella, cartellatta; piegatore.
folding ['fouldiŋ] *a* pieghevole; *n* piega; **f. bed** branda.
foliage ['fouliidʒ] *n* fogliame.
folk [fouk] *n* gente, popolo; (*fam*) la propria famiglia.
folklore ['fouklɔ:] *n* folclore.
follow ['fɔlou] *vt* seguire; inseguire; *vi* conseguire, derivare.
follower ['fɔlouə] *n* seguace, discepolo, *pl* ammiratori *pl*; **following** *a* seguente; *n* seguito.
folly ['fɔli] *n* follia.
foment [fou'ment] *vt* fomentare.

fond [fɔnd] *a* affezionato, appassionato; **to be f. of** voler bene a, amare.
fondle ['fɔndl] *vt* accarezzare.
fondly ['fɔndli] *ad* appassionatamente, amorevolmente.
fondness ['fɔndnis] *n* affettuosità indulgente, tenerezza, passione.
font [fɔnt] *n* fonte battesimale.
food [fu:d] *n* cibo, alimento, nutrimento.
fool [fu:l] *n* idiota, sciocco; (*court*) buffone; *vt* imbrogliare, ingannare; *vi* fare lo sciocco.
foolery ['fu:ləri] *n* buffonata, sciocchezza.
foolhardy ['fu:l,ha:di] *a* temerario.
foolish ['fu:liʃ] *a* sciocco, stolto.
foolishness ['fu:liʃnis] *n* sciocchezza, stoltezza.
foot [fut] *pl* **feet** *n* piede; fanteria; misura lineare corrispondente a 30,5 cm. circa.
football ['futbɔ:l] *n* calcio, pallone per il calcio; **association f.** gioco del calcio; **Rugby f.** pallovale, rugby; **footballer** giocatore di calcio.
foot-bridge ['futbridʒ] *n* ponte per soli pedoni, cavalcavia.
foothold ['futhould] *n* punto d'appoggio; (*fig*) piede.
footlights ['futlaits] *n pl* (*theat*) luci della ribalta.
footman ['futmən] *n* servo in livrea.
footnote ['futnout] *n* poscritto, postilla.
footpath ['futpa:θ] *n* sentiero.
footprint ['futprint] *n* orma, impronta.
footstep ['futstep] *n* passo, suono di passi.
footstool ['futstu:l] *n* sgabello.
for [fɔ:] *prep* per, a, di, a causa di; *cj* perchè.
forage ['fɔridʒ] *n* foraggio.
foray ['fɔrei] *n* incursione, scorreria.
forbear [fɔ:'bɛə] *vi* trattenersi da.
forbearance [fɔ:'bɛərəns] *n* pazienza, sopportazione.
forbearing [fɔ:'bɛəriŋ] *a* paziente.
forbid [fə'bid] *vt* proibire, vietare.
forbidding [fə'bidiŋ] *a* severo; ripugnante.
force [fɔ:s] *n* forza, violenza; (*of law*) vigore; **forces** *pl* truppe *pl*; *vt* costringere, forzare.
forceful ['fɔ:sful] *a* energico.
forceps ['fɔ:seps] *n pl* pinze chirurgiche *pl*, forcipe.
forcible ['fɔ:səbl] *a* impetuoso, violento.
ford [fɔ:d] *n* guado; *vt* passare a guado.
fordable ['fɔ:dəbl] *a* guadabile.
fore [fɔ:] *a* anteriore; *n* davanti, parte anteriore.
fore-arm ['fɔ:ra:m] *n* avambraccio.
forebear ['fɔ:bɛə] *n* antenato.
foreboding [fɔ:'boudiŋ] *n* presagio, presentimento.
forecast ['fɔ:ka:st] *n* previsione; *vt* pronosticare.
forecastle ['fouksl] *n* (*naut*) castello di prua.
forefather ['fɔ:,fa:ðə] *n* antenato.
forefinger ['fɔ:,fiŋgə] *n* indice.
forefront ['fɔ:frʌnt] *n* prima linea; posizione d'importanza.
foregoing ['fɔ:gouiŋ] *a* precedente; **foregone** *a* previsto.
foreground ['fɔ:graund] *n* primo piano.
forehead ['fɔrid] *n* fronte.
foreign ['fɔrin] *a* estero, straniero, forestiero, estraneo.
foreigner ['fɔrinə] *n* straniero, (*fam*) forestiero.
foreman ['fɔ:mən] *pl* **foremen** *n* capo-officina; capomastro; capo dei giurati.
foremost ['fɔ:moust] *a* primo; *ad* in testa, in avanti.
forenoon ['fɔ:nu:n] *n* mattino.
forensic [fə'rensik] *a* forense.
forerunner ['fɔ:,rʌnə] *n* precursore.
foresee [fɔ:'si:] *vt* prevedere.
foreshadow [fɔ:'ʃædou] *vt* adombrare; presagire.
foresight ['fɔ:sait] *n* preveggenza; prudenza.
forest ['fɔrist] *a* forestale; *n* foresta; **forestry** silvicultura.
forestall [fɔ:'stɔ:l] *vt* prevenire, anticipare; (*com*) fare incetta.
forester ['fɔristə] *n* guardia forestale.
foretaste ['fɔ:teist] *n* pregustazione.
foretell [fɔ:'tel] *vt* predire, pronosticare.
forethought ['fɔ:θɔ:t] *n* previdenza.
forever [fə'revə] *ad* per sempre, eternamente.
forewarn [fɔ:'wɔ:n] *vt* (pre)avvertire.
foreword ['fɔ:wə:d] *n* prefazione.
forfeit ['fɔ:fit] *n* multa, pegno; perdita; *vt* perdere il diritto a, dover pagare, essere privato di.
forfeiture ['fɔ:fitʃə] *n* multa, perdita.
for(e)gather [fɔ:'gæðə] *vi* adunarsi; incontrarsi, fraternizzare.
forge [fɔ:dʒ] *n* fornace, fucina; *vt* forgiare, contraffare, falsificare; **to f. ahead** avanzare.
forger ['fɔ:dʒə] *n* falsificatore.
forgery ['fɔ:dʒəri] *n* contraffazione, documento falso.
forget [fə'get] *vti* dimenticare.
forgetful [fə'getful] *a* dimentico, distratto, immemore.
forgetfulness [fə'getfulnis] *n* smemorataggine, oblio.
forgivable [fə'givəbl] *a* perdonabile.
forgive [fə'giv] *vt* perdonare.
forgiveness [fə'givnis] *n* perdono, remissione.
forgiving [fə'giviŋ] *a* clemente, indulgente.
forgo [fɔ:'gou] *vt* rinunziare a, privarsi di.
fork [fɔ:k] *n* forchetta; *vi* biforcarsi.
forlorn [fə'lɔ:n] *a* abbandonato,

infelice; **f.** **hope** vana speranza, impresa disperata.
form [fɔ:m] *n* forma; modulo; banco di scuola, classe; covo di lepre; *vti* formar(si).
formal ['fɔ:məl] *a* formale, cerimonioso.
formality [fɔ:'mæliti] *n* formalità.
formally ['fɔ:məli] *ad* formalmente.
formation [fɔ:'meiʃən] *n* formazione.
former ['fɔ:mə] *a* precedente, primo, antico; *pron* (di due persone) il primo.
formerly ['fɔ:məli] *ad* già, un tempo.
formidable ['fɔ:midəbl] *a* formidabile.
formula ['fɔ:mjulə] *pl* **formulae, formulas** *n* formula.
formulate ['fɔ:mjuleit] *vt* formulare.
forsake [fə'seik] *vt* abbandonare.
fort [fɔ:t] *n* forte, fortezza.
forte ['fɔ:ti] *n* attitudine speciale, forte; (*mus*) forte.
forth [fɔ:θ] *ad* (in) avanti, fuori.
forthcoming [fɔ:θ'kʌmiŋ] *a* prossimo, presso a venire, vicino alla pubblicazione.
forthright ['fɔ:θrait] *a* franco; esplicito; *ad* immediatamente, esplicitamente.
forthwith ['fɔ:θ'wiθ] *ad* immediatamente, senz'altro.
fortification [,fɔ:tifi'keiʃən] *n* fortificazione.
fortify ['fɔ:tifai] *vt* fortificare.
fortitude ['fɔ:titju:d] *n* forza d'animo.
fortnight ['fɔ:tnait] *n* due settimane *pl*, quindici giorni, quindicina.
fortnightly ['fɔ:t,naitli] *a* quindicinale; *ad* ogni quindici giorni.
fortress ['fɔ:tris] *n* fortezza, roccaforte.
fortuitous [fɔ:'tju:itəs] *a* fortuito, casuale.
fortunate ['fɔ:tʃnit] *a* fortunato, favorevole.
fortune ['fɔ:tʃən] *n* fortuna, destino; **f.-telling** predizione dell'avvenire.
forty ['fɔ:ti] *a n* quaranta; **fortieth** *a n* quarantesimo.
forward ['fɔ:wəd] *a* avanzato; precoce; spinto; *ad* (in) avanti, in poi; *vt* far proseguire, spedire, promuovere.
forwarding ['fɔ:wədiŋ] *n* spedizione; **f. agent** (*com*) spedizioniere.
forwards ['fɔ:wədz] *ad v* **forward.**
fossil ['fɔsl] *n* fossile.
fossilize ['fɔsilaiz] *vti* fossilizzar(si).
foster ['fɔstə] *vt* allevare, nutrire; incoraggiare.
foul [faul] *a* sporco, sudicio, osceno; (*sport*) sleale; **f. play** intrigo, azione disonesta; *n* (*sport*) fallo.
foully ['faulli] *ad* sudiciamente; ignobilmente.
foulness ['faulnis] *n* sporcizia, oscenità.
found [faund] *vt* fondare; fondere; *vi* fondarsi.
foundation [faun'deiʃən] *n* fondazione; fondamenta *pl*; istituzione.
founder ['faundə] *n* fondatore; fonditore.
founder ['faundə] *vt* affondare, (*a horse*) azzoppare; *vi* affondare, sprofondarsi.
foundling ['faundliŋ] *n* trovatello.
foundry ['faundri] *n* fonderia.
fountain ['fauntin] *n* fontana, fonte; **f. pen** penna stilografica.
four [fɔ:] *a n* quattro; **fourth** *a n* quarto.
fourfold ['fɔ:fould] *a* quadruplo.
fourteen ['fɔ:'ti:n] *a n* quattordici; **fourteenth** *a n* quattordicesimo.
fowl [faul] *n* pollo, uccello.
fox [fɔks] *n* volpe.
foxhound ['fɔkshaund] *n* bracco.
foxy ['fɔksi] *a* (*fig*) astuto, scaltro.
fraction ['frækʃən] *n* frazione.
fractious ['frækʃəs] *a* litigioso, permaloso.
fracture ['fræktʃə] *n* frattura; *vti* fratturar(si).
fragile ['frædʒail] *a* fragile.
fragment ['frægmənt] *n* frammento.
fragrance ['freigrəns] *n* fragranza.
fragrant ['freigrənt] *a* fragrante.
frail [freil] *a* fragile, debole.
frailty ['freilti] *n* fragilità.
frame [freim] *n* cornice; struttura, intelaiatura; (*bicycle*) telaio; (*spectacles*) montatura; *vt* incorniciare; dar forma a; inventare.
framework ['freimwə:k] *n* struttura, ossatura.
franc [fræŋk] *n* franco (moneta).
France [frɑ:ns] *n* Francia.
Frances ['frɑ:nsis] *nf pr* Francesca.
franchise ['fræntʃaiz] *n* franchigia, diritti di voto *pl*.
Francis ['frɑ:nsis] *nm pr* Francesco.
Franciscan [fræn'siskən] *a n* francescano.
Frank [fræŋk] *nm pr* Franco.
frank [fræŋk] *a* aperto, franco, schietto.
frankness ['fræŋknis] *n* franchezza, schiettezza.
frantic ['fræntik] *a* fuori di sè, frenetico.
frantically ['fræntikəli] *ad* freneticamente; terribilmente.
fraternal [frə'tə:nəl] *a* fraterno.
fraternity [frə'tə:niti] *n* fraternità, confraternità.
fraternize ['frætənaiz] *vi* fraternizzare.
fratricide ['frætrisaid] *n* fratricida, fratricidio.
fraud [frɔ:d] *n* frode, truffa; impostore.
fraudulent ['frɔ:djulənt] *a* fraudolento.
fraught [frɔ:t] *a* carico (di).
fray [frei] *n* zuffa, rissa; *vti* logorar (si).

freak [fri:k] *n* capriccio, anomalia.
freakish ['fri:kiʃ] *a* capriccioso.
freckle ['frekl] *n* lentiggine; *vti* macchiar(si) di lentiggini.
Frederic(k) ['fredrik] *nm pr* Federico.
free [fri:] *a* libero; gratis, gratuito; (*com*) franco; *vt* liberare.
freedom ['fri:dəm] *n* libertà; disinvoltura; familiarità.
freely ['fri:li] *ad* liberamente; gratuitamente.
freeman ['fri:mən] *pl* **freemen** *n* cittadino onorario.
freemason ['fri:,meisn] *n* frammassone.
freemasonry ['fri:,meisnri] *n* frammassoneria.
freethinker ['fri:'θiŋkə] *n* libero pensatore.
freeze [fri:z] *n* (*of prices etc*) congelamento, blocco; *vti* congelar(si), gelare, irrigidir(si).
freezer ['fri:zə] *n* congelante; frigorifero; cella frigorifera.
freezing ['fri:ziŋ] *a* gelido, glaciale; *n* congelamento; **below f. point** sotto zero.
freight [freit] *n* nolo, carico; *vt* (*ship*) caricare, noleggiare; **f. car** vagone merci.
French [frentʃ] *a n* francese; **Frenchman** *n* francese; **F. fries** patate fritte.
frenzied ['frenzid] *a* frenetico.
frenzy ['frenzi] *n* frenesia.
frequency ['fri:kwənsi] *n* frequenza.
frequent ['fri:kwənt] *a* frequente; *vt* [fri'kwent] frequentare.
frequently ['fri:kwəntli] *ad* frequentemente.
fresco ['freskou] *pl* **frescos, frescoes** *n* affresco.
fresh [freʃ] *a* fresco; nuovo; (*of water*) dolce; inesperto.
freshen ['freʃn] *vti* rinfrescar(si), rinvigorir(si).
freshly ['freʃli] *ad* in modo fresco; di fresco, recentemente.
freshness ['freʃnis] *n* freschezza.
fret [fret] *n* inquietudine, irritazione; (*arch*) fregio, greca; *vt* agitare, irritare; fregare, rodere; *vi* impazientirsi, irritarsi.
fretful ['fretful] *a* irritabile.
fretwork ['fretwə:k] *n* lavoro d'intaglio, lavoro a greca.
friar ['fraiə] *n* frate.
friction ['frikʃən] *n* attrito, frizione.
Friday ['fraidi] *n* venerdì.
friend [frend] *n* amico; **F.** quacchero.
friendless ['frendlis] *a* senza amici.
friendliness ['frendlinis] *n* cordialità.
friendly ['frendli] *a* amichevole, amico; *ad* amichevolmente.
friendship ['frendʃip] *n* amicizia.
frieze [fri:z] *n* fregio.
frigate ['frigit] *n* fregata.
fright [frait] *n* spavento, paura.
frighten ['fraitn] *vt* spaventare.
frightful ['fraitful] *a* spaventoso.
frigid ['fridʒid] *a* glaciale, frigido, freddo.
frigidity [fri'dʒiditi] *n* freddezza, frigidità.
frill [fril] *n* frangia, gala increspata.
fringe [frindʒ] *n* frangia, frangetta; bordo, limite; *vt* ornare di frangia.
frisk [frisk] *vi* far salti, salterellare.
frisky ['friski] *a* saltellante, vivace.
fritter ['fritə] *n* frittella; frammento; *vt* suddividere in frammenti; (*time*) sciupare.
frivolity [fri'vɔliti] *n* frivolezza, vanità.
frivolous ['frivələs] *a* frivolo.
frizzle ['frizl] *vti* arricciar(si); sfriggere.
fro [frou] *ad* indietro; **to and f.** avanti e indietro.
frock [frɔk] *n* veste, vestito intero; (*monk's*) tonaca.
frog [frɔg] *n* rana; alamaro.
frolic ['frɔlik] *n* scherzo, spasso; *vi* far salti, scherzare.
frolicsome ['frɔliksəm] *a* allegro, gaio.
from [frɔm] *prep* da, per.
front [frʌnt] *a* di fronte, davanti; *n* parte anteriore, facciata; (*mil*) fronte; *vti* essere di fronte a; affrontare.
frontage ['frʌntidʒ] *n* facciata, prospetto.
frontal ['frʌntl] *a n* frontale.
frontier ['frʌntiə] *a n* (di) frontiera.
frontispiece ['frʌntispi:s] *n* frontespizio.
frost [frɔ:st] *n* gelo; (*sl*) fiasco; **hoar-f.** brina.
frostbite ['frɔstbait] *n* congelamento.
frosty ['frɔsti] *a* gelato, gelido.
froth [frɔθ] *n* schiuma, spuma; chiacchierata vuota.
frothy ['frɔθi] *a* schiumoso, spumoso; vuoto.
frown [fraun] *n* aggrottamento delle ciglia, cipiglio; *vi* aggrottare le ciglia.
frowsy ['frauzi] *a* sciatto, sporco; di cattivo odore.
fructify ['frʌktifai] *vi* fruttificare.
frugal ['fru:gəl] *a* frugale.
fruit [fru:t] *n* frutto, frutta *pl*.
fruit dealer ['fru:t di:lə] *n* commerciante in frutta, fruttivendolo.
fruitful ['fru:tful] *a* fruttifero, produttivo, fecondo.
fruitfulness ['fru:tfulnis] *n* fertilità, fecondità.
fruition [fru:'iʃən] *n* fruizione; (*fig*) godimento.
fruitless ['fru:tlis] *a* infruttuoso, sterile.
fruity ['fru:ti] *a* che sa di frutta; (*fig*) piccante.
frump [frʌmp] *n* donna vestita di abiti fuori moda.
frustrate [frʌs'treit] *vt* frustrare.

frustration [frʌs'treiʃən] *n* frustrazione, delusione.
fry [frai] *n* fritto, frittura; (*zool*) avannotto; (*fig*) persone di poca importanza; **small f.** *vti* friggere.
frying pan ['fraiiŋ,pæn] *n* padella.
fuddle ['fʌdl] *vt* confondere, intontire, ubriacare.
fuel [fjuəl] *n* combustibile, carburante; (*fig*) esca, alimento.
fueling ['fjuəliŋ] *n* approvvigionamento, rifornimento combustibili.
fugitive ['fju:dʒitiv] *a n* fuggitivo.
fugue [fju:g] *n* (*mus*) fuga.
fulfill [ful'fil] *vt* soddisfare, compiere.
fulfillment [ful'filmənt] *n* adempimento, realizzazione, compimento.
full [ful] *a* pieno; *ad* completamente, perfettamente, in pieno; *n* pieno, colmo; *vt* follare, gualcare.
fuller ['fulə] *n* follatore.
fullness ['fulnis] *n* pienezza, abbondanza.
fully ['fuli] *ad* completamente, interamente.
fulminate ['fʌlmineit] *vti* fulminare.
fulsome ['fulsəm] *a* disgustoso, nauseante.
fumble ['fʌmbl] *vti* frugare, maneggiare senza abilità, annaspare.
fume [fju:m] *n* fumo, vapore; accesso di rabbia; *vt* sottoporre a vapori chimici; *vi* emettere vapori; essere in collera.
fumigate ['fju:migeit] *vt* fumigare.
fumigation [,fju:mi'geiʃən] *n* fumigazione.
fun [fʌn] *n* allegria, divertimento, svago.
function ['fʌnkʃən] *n* funzione; cerimonia; *vi* funzionare.
functional ['fʌnkʃənl] *a* funzionale.
fund [fʌnd] *n* fondo, capitale.
fundamental [,fʌndə'mentl] *a* fondamentale.
funeral ['fju:nərəl] *a* funebre, funerario; *n* funerale.
funereal [fju:'niəriəl] *a* funereo, lugubre, funebre.
fungus ['fʌŋgəs] *n* fungo.
funicular [fju'nikjulə] *a n* funicolare.
funk [fʌŋk] *n* (*sl*) panico, timore.
funnel ['fʌnl] *n* imbuto; ciminiera di nave.
funny ['fʌni] *n* buffo, comico, strano.
fur [fə:] *n* pelliccia, pelo; incrostazione.
furbish ['fə:biʃ] *vt* forbire, lustrare.
furious ['fjuəriəs] *a* furioso, furibondo.
furl [fə:l] *vt* ammainare, chiudere.
furlough ['fə:lou] *n* (*mil etc*) licenza, permesso.
furnace ['fə:nis] *n* fornace; caldaia di termosifone.
furnish ['fə:niʃ] *vt* fornire, rifornire; ammobiliare.
furnishings ['fə:niʃiŋs] *n pl* arredamento.
furniture ['fə:nitʃə] *n* mobilia, mobili *pl*.
furrier ['fʌriə] *n* pellicciaio.
furrow ['fʌrou] *n* solco; ruga; traccia; *vt* solcare.
furry ['fə:ri] *a* peloso; di pelliccia; coperto di pelliccia; patinoso.
further ['fə:ðə] *a* altro, ulteriore; *ad* oltre, più avanti; *vt* favorire, promuovere.
furthermore ['fə:ðə'mɔ:] *ad* per di più, inoltre.
furtive ['fə:tiv] *a* furtivo.
fury ['fjuəri] *n* furore, furia.
furze [fə:z] *n* ginestra spinosa.
fuse [fju:z] *n* spoletta, (*el*) valvola; *vti* fonder(si), far esplodere.
fuselage ['fju:zilɑ:ʒ] *n* (*av*) fusoliera.
fusillade [,fju:zi'leid] *n* scarica di fucili.
fusion ['fju:ʒən] *n* fusione.
fuss ['fʌs] *n* trambusto, scalpore; *vi* agitarsi; far confusione.
fussily ['fʌsili] *ad* con esagerata attenzione; con inutile indaffaramento.
fussy ['fʌsi] *a* brontolone; di difficile contentatura.
fustian ['fʌstiən] *n* fustagno.
fusty ['fʌsti] *a* ammuffito, che sa di muffa.
futile ['fjutail] *a* futile.
future ['fju:tʃə] *a n* futuro, avvenire.
futurity ['fju:tuəriti] *n* avvenire.
fuzz [fʌz] *n* lanugine; increspatura di capelli.
fuzzy ['fʌzi] *a* lanuginoso; dai capelli crespi; confuso; (*phot*) sfocato.

G

gabardine ['gæbədi:n] *n* gabardina.
gabble ['gæbl] *n* barbugliamento; *vt* pronunciare in modo inarticolato o confuso; *vi* parlare indistintamente.
gable ['geibl] *n* (*arch*) timpano, frontone; **g. roof** tetto a due spioventi.
Gabriel ['geibriəl] *nm pr* Gabriele.
gad [gæd] *vi* bighellonare; **g. about** *a n* vagabondo.
gadfly ['gædflai] *n* tafano.
gadget ['gædʒit] *n* (*fam*) congegno, aggeggio.
Gaelic ['geilik] *a* gaelico.
gag [gæg] *n* bavaglio; (*sl*) battuta improvvisata; *vt* imbavagliare; *vi* (*sl*) improvvisare battute.
gage [geidʒ] *n* pegno.
gaiety ['geiəti] *n* gaiezza.
gaily ['geili] *ad* gaiamente.
gain [gein] *n* guadagno; *vt* guadagnare; *vi* (*clock*) andare avanti.
gainings ['geiniŋz] *n pl* utili, profitti.
gainsay [gein'sei] *vt* contraddire.
gait [geit] *n* andatura.
gaiter ['geitə] *n* [illegible]hetta.
galaxy ['gæləks[illegible] *n* galassia; (*fig*) assemblea brilla[illegible].
gale [geil] *n* bufera di vento.
gall [gɔ:l] *n* bile, fiele; malignità; *vt*

irritare; scorticare; **gallstone** calcolo biliare.
gallant ['gælənt] *a* intrepido, valoroso; galante; *n* galante, cavaliere.
gallantry ['gæləntri] *n* valore; galanteria.
galleon ['gæliən] *n* (*naut*) galeone.
gallery ['gæləri] *n* galleria; (*theat*) loggione.
galley ['gæli] *n* galea; (*naut*) cambusa.
gallivant [,gæli'vænt] *vi* andare a zonzo.
gallon ['gælən] *n* gallone (*misura inglese di capacita = litri 4,543*).
gallop ['gæləp] *n* galoppo; *vti* (far) galoppare.
gallows ['gælouz] *n pl* forca, patibolo.
galore [gə'lɔ:] *n* abbondanza; *ad* a bizzeffe.
galosh [gə'lɔʃ] *n* galoscia; soprascarpa.
galvanic [gæl'vænik] *a* (*el*) galvanico; (*fig*) galvanizzante.
galvanize ['gælvənaiz] *vt* galvanizzare.
gambit ['gæmbit] *n* (*chess*) gambetto; (*fig*) iniziativa, attacco.
gamble ['gæmbl] *n* gioco d'azzardo; *vti* giocare d'azzardo, speculare rischiosamente.
gambler ['gæmblə] *n* giocatore d'azzardo, speculatore.
gambling ['gæmbliŋ] *n* giochi d'azzardo *pl*, **g. house** bisca.
gambol ['gæmbəl] *n* piroetta, capriola; *vi* piroettare.
game [geim] *n* gioco, partita; caccia, selvaggina.
gamekeeper ['geim,ki:pə] *n* guardacaccia.
gammon ['gæmən] *n* parte più bassa d'un prosciutto, prosciutto affumicato; (*fig*) inganno.
gamut ['gæmət] *n* gamma, serie completa.
gander ['gændə] *n* papero.
gang [gæŋ] *n* banda; squadra; combriccola.
ganglion ['gæŋgliən] *n* ganglio.
gangrene ['gæŋgri:n] *n* cancrena.
gangster ['gæŋstə] *n* 'gangster' bandito.
gangway ['gæŋwei] *n* corridoio, passaggio; passerella.
gannet ['gænit] *n* gabbiano.
gantry ['gæntri] *n* gru a cavalletto.
gap [gæp] *n* breccia, fenditura; passo di montagna; (*fig*) divergenza; lacuna.
gape [geip] *n* spaccatura; apertura della bocca; sbadiglio; *vi* sbadigliare; spalancare la bocca.
garage ['gærɑ:ʒ] *n* autorimessa, 'garage'.
garb [gɑ:b] *n* abbigliamento
garbage ['gɑ:bidʒ] *n* rifiuti *pl*; **g. can** pattumiera.
garble ['gɑ:bl] *vt* falsificare (una storia).
garden ['gɑ:dn] *n* giardino; *vi* lavorare di giardinaggio.
gardener ['gɑ:dnə] *n* giardiniere.
gardening ['gɑ:dniŋ] *n* giardinaggio.
gargle ['gɑ:gl] *n* gargarismo; *vi* fare gargarismi.
gargoyle ['gɑ:gɔil] *n* gargolla; figura grottesca.
garish ['gɛəriʃ] *a* abbagliante, sgargiante.
garland ['gɑ:lənd] *n* ghirlanda.
garlic ['gɑ:lik] *n* aglio.
garment ['gɑ:mənt] *n* articolo di vestiario, indumento.
garnish ['gɑ:niʃ] *n* (*cook*) guarnizione, contorno; *vt* guarnire, ornare.
garret ['gærət] *n* abbaino, soffitta.
garrison ['gærisn] *n* guarnigione; *vt* fornire di guarnigione.
garrulity [gæ'ru:liti] *n* loquacità.
garrulous ['gæruləs] *a* garrulo, loquace.
garter ['gɑ:tə] *n* giarrettiera.
gas [gæs] *pl* **gases** *n* gas; **g. cooker** cucina a gas, fornello a gas; **g. meter** contatore del gas; **g. stove** cucina a gas.
gash [gæʃ] *n* squarcio; *vt* fare uno squarcio.
gasoline ['gæsəli:n] benzina.
gasp [gɑ:sp] *n* respiro affannoso, rantolo; sussulto; *vti* boccheggiare, ansare; soffocare un'esclamazione.
gassy ['gæsi] *a* gassoso.
gastric ['gæstrik] *a* gastrico.
gastritis [gæs'traitis] *n* gastrite.
gastronomical [,gæstrə'nɔmikəl] *n* gastronomico.
gastronomy [gæs'trɔnəmi] *n* gastronomia.
gate [geit] *n* cancello, (*of town*) porta.
gateway ['geitwei] *n* portone, entrata.
gather ['gæðə] *vt* (rac)cogliere, radunare; fare le pieghe; *vi* radunarsi; (*med*) venire a suppurazione.
gathering ['gæðəriŋ] *n* adunata, assemblea; (*med*) ascesso.
gaudy ['gɔ:di] *a* sfarzoso e di cattivo gusto.
gauge [geidʒ] *n* apparecchio misuratore, misura base, stima; *vt* misurare con esattezza; (*fig*) formarsi un concetto di.
gauger ['geidʒə] *n* collaudatore.
gaunt [gɔ:nt] *a* macilento, sparuto.
gauntlet ['gɔ:ntlit] *n* grosso guanto che copre il polso, guanto di armatura.
gauntness ['gɔ:ntnis] *n* macilenza.
gauze [gɔ:z] *n* garza, velo.
gawky ['gɔ:ki] *a* goffo, sguaiato, balordo.
gay [gei] *a* allegro, gaio; vistoso; brillante; (*fig*) dissoluto.
gaze [geiz] *n* sguardo fisso; *vi* guardare fisso.
gazelle [gə'zel] *n* gazzella.
gazette [gə'zet] *n* gazzetta.

gazetteer [,gæzi'tiə] *n* dizionario geografico.
gear [giə] *n* equipaggiamento, congegno, ingranaggio, meccanismo, (*aut*) marcia; **in g.** in marcia.
gelatin(e) ['dʒelətiːn] *n* gelatina.
geld [geld] *vt* castrare.
gelding ['geldiŋ] *n* cavallo castrato.
gelignite ['dʒelignait] *n* (*chem*) nitroglicerina.
gem [dʒem] *n* gemma, gioiello.
gender ['dʒendə] *n* genere; sesso.
genealogical [,dʒiːniə'lɔdʒikəl] *a* genealogico.
genealogy [,dʒiːni'ælədʒi] *n* genealogia.
general ['dʒenərəl] *a n* generale.
generality [,dʒenə'ræliti] *n* generalità, maggioranza.
generalization [,dʒenərəlai'zeiʃən] *n* generalizzazione.
generalize ['dʒenərəlaiz] *vti* generalizzare.
generally ['dʒenərəli] *ad* generalmente, di solito.
generate ['dʒenəreit] *vt* generare.
generation [,dʒenə'reiʃən] *n* generazione.
generative ['dʒenərətiv] *a* generativo, produttivo.
generator ['dʒenəreitə] *n* generatore, (*aut*) dinamo, generatore.
generosity [,dʒenə'rɔsiti] *n* generosità.
generous ['dʒenərəs] *a* generoso.
generously ['dʒenərəsli] *ad* generosamente.
genetic [dʒi'netik] *a* genetico.
Geneva [dʒi'niːvə] *n* Ginevra.
Genevieve [,dʒenə'viːv] *nf pr* Genoveffa.
genial ['dʒiːniəl] *a* amabile, piacevole; (*climate*) mite.
geniality [,dʒiːni'æliti] *n* amabilità, giovialità.
genital ['dʒenitl] *a* genitale.
genitals ['dʒenitlz] *n pl* organi genitali.
genitive ['dʒenitiv] *a n* genitivo.
genius ['dʒiːniəs] *n* genio, talento.
Genoa ['dʒenouə] *n* Genova; **Genoese** *a n* genovese.
genocide ['dʒenousaid] *n* genocidio.
genteel [dʒen'tiːl] *a* (*ironic*) compito, manieroso.
gentle ['dʒentl] *a* dolce, mite; nobile.
gentlefolk ['dʒentlfouk] *n* gente che appartiene alle classi elevate.
gentleman ['dʒentlmən] *n* gentiluomo, signore.
gentlemanly ['dʒentlmənli] *a* da gentiluomo, signorile.
gentleness ['dʒentlnis] *n* dolcezza, tenerezza, grazia.
gentlewoman ['dʒentl,wumən] *n* gentildonna, signora.
gently ['dʒentli] *ad* con delicatezza, dolcemente.
gentry ['dʒentri] *n* piccola nobiltà.
genuine ['dʒenjuin] *a* genuino.
genuineness ['dʒenjuinis] *n* genuinità.
geodesy [dʒiː'ɔdisi] *n* geodesia.
Geoffrey ['dʒefri] *nm pr* Goffredo.
geographic(al) [dʒiə'græfik(əl)] *a* geografico.
geography [dʒi'ɔgrəfi] *n* geografia.
geology [dʒi'ɔlədʒi] *n* geologia.
geometric [dʒiə'metrik] *a* geometrico.
geometry [dʒi'ɔmitri] *n* geometria.
George [dʒɔːdʒ] *nm pr* Giorgio.
Georgian ['dʒɔːdʒiən] *a n* georgiano, georgiana.
geranium [dʒi'reiniəm] *n* geranio.
geriatric [,dʒeri'ætrik] *a* geriatrico.
geriatrics [,dʒeri'ætriks] *n* geriatria.
germ [dʒəːm] *n* germe.
German ['dʒəːmən] *a n* tedesco.
Germany ['dʒəːməni] *n* Germania.
germinate ['dʒəːmineit] *vi* germinare.
germination [,dʒəːmi'neiʃən] *n* germinazione.
Gertrude ['gəːtruːd] *nf pr* Gertrude.
gestation [dʒes'teiʃən] *n* gestazione.
gesticulate [dʒes'tikjuleit] *vi* gesticolare.
gesticulation [dʒes,tikju'leiʃən] *n* il gesticolare.
gesture ['dʒestʃə] *n* gesto; *vi* gestire. gesticolare.
get [get] *vt* ottenere, ricevere, guadagnare, prendere, portare, persuadere; *vi* arrivare, raggiungere, divenire.
gewgaw ['gjuːgɔː] *n* ninnolo.
geyser ['giːzə] *n* sorgente calda; apparecchio scaldabagno.
ghastly ['gɑːstli] *a* spaventoso, spettrale.
gherkin ['gəːkin] *n* cetriolino.
ghetto ['getou] *pl* **ghettos** *n* ghetto.
ghost [goust] *n* spirito, fantasma; **The Holy G.** lo Spirito Santo.
ghostly ['goustli] *a* spettrale.
ghoul [guːl] *n* spirito maligno che divora i cadaveri; (*fig*) persona orribile e crudele.
ghoulish ['guːliʃ] *a* demoniaco, macabro.
giant ['dʒaiənt] *a n* gigante; **giantess** *n* gigantessa.
gibber ['dʒibə] *vi* parlare rapidamente e senza senso.
gibberish ['gibəriʃ] *n* parole senza senso.
gibbet ['dʒibit] *n* forca, patibolo.
gibe [dʒaib] *n* beffa, scherno; *vti* beffar(si), schernire.
giblets ['dʒiblits] *n pl* rigaglie *pl*.
Gibraltar [dʒi'brɔːltə] *n* Gibilterra.
giddiness ['gidinis] *n* vertigine; incostanza.
giddy ['gidi] *a* in preda a vertigini; incostante.
gift [gift] *n* dono, regalo, donazione.
gig [gig] *n* calessino; (*naut*) lancia.
gigantic [dʒai'gæntik] *a* gigantesco.

giggle ['gigl] *n* risatina sciocca; *vi* ridere scioccamente.
gigue [ʒi:g] *n* (*mus*) giga.
gild [gild] *vt* (in)dorare.
gilding ['gildiŋ] *n* doratura.
Giles [dʒailz] *nm pr* Egidio.
gill [gil] *n* misura di capacità liquida (*litri* ,0142).
gilt [gilt] *a* dorato; *n* doratura.
gimcrack ['dʒimkræk] *a* appariscente e di nessun valore; *n* cianfrusaglia.
gimlet ['gimlit] *n* succhiello.
gin [dʒin] *n* gin; trappola.
ginger ['dʒindʒə] *n* zenzero; **gingerbread** pan di zenzero.
gingerly ['dʒindʒəli] *a* guardingo; *ad* con precauzione.
gingham ['giŋəm] *n* percalle a righe o quadretti, rigatino.
gipsy, gypsy ['dʒipsi] *n* zingaro, zingara; *a* zingaresco.
giraffe [dʒi'rɑ:f] *n* giraffa.
gird [gə:d] *vt* cingere, circondare; *vi* beffare.
girder ['gə:də] *n* (*mech*) trave maestra, putrella.
girdle ['gə:dl] *n* cintura; cerchia; busto; *vt* recingere; chiudere con una cintura.
girl [gə:l] *n* ragazza, fanciulla.
girlhood ['gə:lhud] *n* adolescenza (di ragazza).
girlish ['gə:liʃ] *a* di (da) ragazza.
girth [gə:θ] *n* circonferenza; sottopancia; *vt* cingere.
gist [dʒist] *n* punto essenziale, sostanza.
give [giv] *vti* dare, cedere; **g. and take** *n* compromesso, concessione reciproca.
gizzard ['gizəd] *n* (*of birds*) ventriglio.
glacial ['gleisiəl] *a* glaciale.
glacier ['glæsiə] *n* ghiacciaio.
glad [glæd] *a* contento, lieto.
glade [gleid] *n* radura.
gladiator ['glædieitə] *n* gladiatore.
gladiolus [.glædi'ouləs] *pl* **gladioli** *n* gladiolo.
gladly ['glædli] *ad* con piacere, volentieri.
gladness ['glædnis] *n* contentezza.
glamor ['glæmə] *n* fascino, magia.
glamorous ['glæmərəs] *a* affascinante.
glance [glɑ:ns] *n* occhiata, sguardo; *vi* dare un'occhiata, gettare uno sguardo.
glancing ['glɑ:nsiŋ] *a* fugace, rapido.
gland [glænd] *n* glandola.
glanders ['glændəz] *n pl* cimurro.
glandular ['glændjulə] *a* glandolare.
glare [glεə] *n* bagliore, luce abbagliante; sguardo furibondo; *vi* risplendere di luce abbagliante; guardare con rabbia.
glaring ['glεəriŋ] *a* abbagliante; manifesto.
glass [glɑ:s] *n* vetro, vetri *pl*; bicchiere; cristallo; telescopio; **glasses** *pl* occhiali *pl*.
glassy ['glɑ:si] *a* vitreo.
Glaswegian [glæs'wi:dʒjən] *a n* abitante di Glasgow.
glaze [gleiz] *n* smalto, vernice; *vt* fornire di vetri; smaltare, verniciare.
glazier ['gleiziə] *n* vetraio.
gleam [gli:m] *n* barlume, debole raggio di luce; *vi* luccicare, balugínare.
glean [gli:n] *vti* spigolare, raccogliere.
gleaning ['gli:niŋ] *n* spigolatura.
glebe [gli:b] *n* gleba.
glee [gli:] *n* giubilo; (*mus*) canone.
glen [glen] *n* valletta.
glib [glib] *a* liscio, scorrevole, pronto.
glide [glaid] *vi* scivolare, trascorrere.
glider ['glaidə] *n* (*av*) aliante; (*naut*) idroplano.
gliding ['glaidiŋ] *a* scorrevole, (*av*) che plana; *n* (*av*) volo a vela.
glimmer ['glimə] *n* luce debole e incerta; *vi* mandare una luce fioca.
glimpse [glimps] *n* rapida visione; *vt* intravvedere.
glint [glint] *n* luccichio; *vi* luccicare.
glisten ['glisn] *n* scintillio, luccichio; *vi* scintillare, luccicare.
glitter ['glitə] *n* scintillio; *vi* scintillare.
glittering ['glitəriŋ] *a* scintillante, brillante; *n* scintillio.
gloaming ['gloumiŋ] *n* crepuscolo.
gloat [glout] *vi* guardare con gioia perversa, gongolare.
globe [gloub] *n* globo.
gloom [glu:m] *n* tenebre *pl*, tristezza.
gloomy ['glu:mi] *a* fosco, tetro, triste.
glorification [.glɔ:rifi'keiʃən] *n* glorificazione.
glorify ['glɔ:rifai] *vt* glorificare.
glorious ['glɔ:riəs] *a* glorioso, magnifico.
gloriously ['glɔ:riəsli] *ad* gloriosamente, splendidamente.
glory ['glɔ:ri] *n* gloria, splendore; *vi* esultare, gloriarsi.
gloss [glɔs] *n* chiosa, glossa; lucentezza; (*fig*) vernice; *vt* lucidare; chiosare.
glossary ['glɔsəri] *n* glossario.
glossy ['glɔsi] *a* lucido, lucente.
glove [glʌv] *n* guanto.
glow [glou] *n* incandescenza, calore; ardore; *vi* rosseggiare; essere incandescente; ardere.
glow-worm ['glouwə:m] *n* lucciola.
glower ['glauə] *vi* guardare con cipiglio.
glucose ['glu:kous] *n* (*chem*) glucosio.
glue [glu:] *n* colla; *vt* incollare.
glum [glʌm] *a* accigliato, taciturno.
glut [glʌt] *n* sovrabbondanza, sazietà.
glutinous ['glu:tinəs] *a* gluttinoso.
glutton ['glʌtn] *n* ghiottone.
gluttonous ['glʌtənəs] *a* ghiotto, goloso.

gluttony ['glʌtni] *n* golosità, ingordigia.
glycerine ['glisəri:n] *n* glicerina.
gnarled [nɑ:ld] *a* nodoso, nocchieruto, pieno di nodi.
gnash [næʃ] *vt* digrignare (i denti).
gnat [næt] *n* moscerino.
gnaw [nɔ:] *vt* rodere, rosicchiare.
gnome [noum] *n* gnomo.
go [gou] *vi* andare, farsi; **g.-ahead** *a* (*fam*) intraprendente; *n* segnale di passare all'azione; **g.-between** intermediario; **g.-getter** (*fam*) arrivista.
goad [goud] *n* pungolo, stimolo; *vt* mandar avanti col pungolo, stimolare.
goal [goul] *n* meta, traguardo; (*football*) porta, rete; "gol."
goat [gout] *n* capra; **g.-herd** capraio.
gobble ['gɔbl] *vt* ingoiare a grossi bocconi.
goblet ['gɔblit] *n* calice, coppa.
goblin ['gɔblin] *n* folletto, spirito maligno.
god [gɔd] *n* dio, divinità; idolo.
godchild ['gɔdtʃaild] *n* figlioccio.
goddess ['gɔdis] *n* dea.
godfather ['gɔd,fɑ:ðə] *n* padrino.
godhead ['gɔdhed] *n* divinità.
godless ['gɔdlis] *a* ateo, empio.
godlessness ['gɔdlisnis] *n* ateismo; empietà.
godliness ['gɔdlinis] *n* devozione, religiosità.
godly ['gɔdli] *a* devoto, religioso.
godmother ['gɔd,mʌðə] *n* madrina.
godsend ['gɔdsend] *n* dono del cielo, fortuna inaspettata.
godson ['gɔdsʌn] *n* figlioccio.
goggle ['gɔgl] *vi* stralunare (gli occhi).
goggles ['gɔglz] *n pl* occhiali di protezione; (*sl*) occhialoni.
going ['gouiŋ] *n* partenza; l'andare; andamento; *a* ben avviato.
goiter ['gɔitə] *n* gozzo.
gold [gould] *a* aureo, d'oro; *n* oro, danaro.
golden ['gouldən] *a* aureo, d'oro, dorato.
goldfinch ['gouldfintʃ] *n* cardellino.
goldfish ['gouldfiʃ] *n* pesce rosso.
goldsmith ['gouldsmiθ] *n* orefice.
golosh [gə'lɔʃ] *v* **galosh.**
gondolier [,gɔndə'liə] *n* gondoliere.
gong [gɔŋ] *n* gong.
good [gud] *a* buono; *n* bene; **g. day** buon giorno; **g. night** buona sera, buona notte.
good-bye ['gud'bai] *interj* addio, arrivederci.
good-for-nothing ['gudfə,nʌθiŋ] *a* inutile; *n* buono a nulla.
goodly ['gudli] *a* bello, buono; considerevole.
good-natured ['gud'neitʃəd] *a* di buon carattere.
goodness ['gudnis] *n* bontà, generosità.
goods ['gudz] *n pl* beni *pl*, effetti *pl*, merci *pl*.
goodwill ['gud'wil] *n* buona volontà, benevolenza, favore.
goose [gu:s] *pl* **geese** *n* oca; **g. flesh** pelle d'oca.
gooseberry ['guzbəri] *n* uva spina.
gorge ['gɔ:dʒ] *n* strozza; *vt* ingozzare; *vi* rimpinzarsi; gola di montagna.
gorgeous ['gɔ:dʒəs] *a* magnifico, sontuoso, sgargiante.
gorilla [gə'rilə] *n* gorilla.
gorse [gɔ:s] *n* ginestra spinosa.
gory ['gɔ:ri] *a* insanguinato.
gosling ['gɔzliŋ] *n* paperetto.
gospel ['gɔspəl] *n* vangelo.
gossamer ['gɔsəmə] *n* sottile filo di ragnatela, velo finissimo.
gossip ['gɔsip] *n* chiacchiera, pettegolezzo; individuo pettegolo; *vi* pettegolare.
Gothic ['gɔθik] *a* gotico.
gouache [gu'ɑ:ʃ] *n* guazzo.
gourd [guəd] *n* zucca.
gourmet ['guəmei] *n* buongustaio, conoscitore.
gout [gaut] *n* gotta.
gouty ['gauti] *a* gottoso.
govern ['gʌvən] *vti* governare.
governable ['gʌvənəbl] *a* docile.
governess ['gʌvənis] *n* istitutrice.
governing ['gʌvəniŋ] *a* governante, dirigente.
government ['gʌvənmənt] *n* governo.
governor ['gʌvənə] *n* governatore; (*sl*) padrone, capo, padre.
gown [gaun] *n* veste, vestito, toga; **dressing g.** veste da camera, vestaglia.
grab [græb] *vt* afferrare, impadronirsi con la violenza di.
grabble ['græbl] *vi* andare a tastoni.
grace [greis] *n* grazia, favore; *vt* adornare, favorire.
Grace [greis] *nf pr* Grazia.
graceful ['greisful] *a* aggraziato, grazioso.
gracefulness ['greisfulnis] *n* grazia.
gracious ['greiʃəs] *a* condiscendente, grazioso.
gradation [gre'deiʃən] *n* gradazione.
grade [greid] *n* grado; pendenza; classe; classificazione; *vt* classificare, graduare; **g. crossing** passaggio a livello.
gradient ['greidiənt] *n* pendenza, gradiente.
gradual ['grædjuəl] *a n* graduale.
gradually ['grædjuəli] *ad* gradualmente, gradatamente; a poco a poco.
graduate ['grædjuit] *n* laureato; diplomato; ['gradjueit] *vt* graduare; *vi* laurearsi.
graduation [,grædju'eiʃən] *n* laurea, licenza, diploma; graduazione.
graft [grɑ:ft] *n* innesto; *vt* innestare.
grain [grein] *n* grano; grana; venatura.

gram [græm] *n* grammo.
grammar ['græmə] *n* grammatica.
grammarian [grə'mɛəriən] *n* grammatico.
grammatical [grə'mætikəl] *a* grammaticale.
gramophone ['græməfoun] *n* grammofono.
granary ['grænəri] *n* granaio.
grand [grænd] *a* grande, grandioso, imponente, maestoso, principale.
grandchild ['græntʃaild] *pl* **grandchildren** *n* nipote, nipotino, nipotina.
granddaughter ['græn,dɔ:tə] *n* nipote, nipotina.
grandeur ['grændʒə] *n* magnificenza, splendore.
grandfather ['grænd,fɑ:ðə] *n* nonno.
grandiose ['grændious] *a* grandioso, pomposo.
grandmother ['græn,mʌðə] *n* nonna.
grandparent ['græn,pɛərənt] *n* nonno, nonna.
grandson ['grænsʌn] *n* nipote, nipotino.
grandstand ['grænstænd] *n* tribuna d'onore.
grange [greindʒ] *n* fattoria, casa signorile di campagna.
granite ['grænit] *n* granito.
grant [grɑ:nt] *n* concessione, borsa di studio, donazione; *vt* ammettere, concedere.
grape [greip] *n* (acino d') uva; (*mil*) carica di mitraglia; **grapefruit** pompelmo.
graph [grɑ:f] *n* grafico.
graphic ['græfik] *a* grafico.
graphite ['græfait] *n* grafite.
grapnel ['græpnəl] *n* ancoretta, uncino.
grapple ['græpl] *n* ancoretta, rampone; lotta corpo a corpo; *vt* assicurare con l'ancoretta; *vi* venire alle prese; lottare.
grasp [grɑ:sp] *n* presa, stretta; comprensione; *vt* afferrare.
grasping ['grɑ:spiŋ] *a* avaro, avido.
grass [grɑ:s] *n* erba.
grasshopper ['grɑ:s,hɔpə] *n* grillo, saltamartino; (*av mil*) apparecchio di collegamento.
grassy ['grɑ:si] *a* erboso.
grate [greit] *n* grata, griglia, inferriata; *vt* munire di grata; grattugiare; *vi* stridere; irritare.
grateful ['greitful] *a* grato, riconoscente.
grater ['greitə] *n* grattugia.
gratification [,grætifi'keiʃən] *n* gratificazione, soddisfazione.
gratify ['grætifai] *vt* gratificare.
grating ['greitiŋ] *a* irritante; stridente; *n* grata, inferriata.
gratitude ['grætitju:d] *n* gratitudine, riconoscenza.
gratuitous [grə'tju:itəs] *a* gratuito, ingiustificato.
gratuity [grə'tju:iti] *n* gratifica, mancia.
grave [greiv] *a* austero, grave, serio; *n* tomba.
gravel ['grævəl] *n* ghiaia; *vt* ricoprire di ghiaia; (*fig*) imbarazzare.
graveyard ['greivjɑ:d] *n* camposanto, cimitero.
gravitate ['græviteit] *vi* gravitare.
gravitation [,grævi'teiʃən] *n* gravitazione.
gravity ['græviti] *n* gravità.
gravy ['greivi] *n* sugo di carne, salsa.
gray [grei] *a n* grigio.
grayness ['greinis] *n* grigiore.
graze [greiz] *n* abrasione; *vt* escoriare, scalfire, sfiorare; *vt* pascere, pascolare.
grazing ['greiziŋ] *n* pascolo, pastura.
grease [gri:s] *n* grasso, unto; materia lubrificante; *vt* lubrificare, ungere.
greasy ['gri:zi] *a* grasso, unto, untuoso.
great [greit] *a* grande, nobile.
Great Britain ['greit'britn] *n* Gran Bretagna.
greatly ['greitli] *ad* grandemente, molto.
greatness ['greitnis] *n* grandezza.
Greece [gri:s] *n* Grecia.
greed [gri:d] *n* bramosia, cupidigia.
greedily ['gri:dili] *ad* avidamente, golosamente.
greediness ['gri:dinis] *n* avidità, golosità.
greedy ['gri:di] *a* ghiotto, goloso, avido.
Greek [gri:k] *a n* greco.
green [gri:n] *a* verde; *n* verde, verzura; **greens** *pl* erbaggi *pl*, verdura.
greenery ['gri:nəri] *n* verdura.
greenfinch ['gri:nfintʃ] *n* verdone.
greengage ['gri:ngeidʒ] *n* susina claudia.
greengrocer ['gri:n,grousə] *n* erbivendolo, ortolano.
greenhouse ['gri:nhaus] *n* serra.
Greenland ['gri:nlənd] *n* Groenlandia.
Greenlander ['gri:nləndə] *n* groenlandese.
greenness ['gri:nnis] *n* color verde; (*fig*) immaturità, inesperienza.
greet [gri:t] *vt* salutare (all'arrivo).
greeting ['gri:tiŋ] *n* saluto.
Gregory ['gregəri] *nm pr* Gregorio.
grenade [gre'neid] *n* (*mil*) granata.
grenadier [,grenə'diə] *n* granatiere.
grey [grei] *v* **gray**.
greyhound ['greihaund] *n* levriero.
grid [grid] *n* grata, griglia; (*map*) quadrettatura.
grief [gri:f] *n* afflizione, dolore.
grievance ['gri:vəns] *n* lagnanza; torto.
grieve [gri:v] *vti* addolorar(si), affligger(si).
grievous ['gri:vəs] *a* doloroso, penoso, grave, serio.

grill [gril] *n* (vivanda alla) griglia; *vt* arrostire alla griglia; sottoporre ad un severo interrogatorio; *vi* esser tormentato (dal caldo).
grim [grim] *a* fosco, torvo, severo.
grimace [gri'meis] *n* smorfia.
grime [graim] *n* sudiciume.
grimy ['graimi] *a* sudicio.
grin [grin] *n* sogghigno, largo sorriso; *vi* sogghignare.
grind [graind] *n* lavoro faticoso e ingrato; *vt* arrotare, macinare; (*fig*) opprimere; *vi* sgobbare.
grinder ['graində] *n* arrotino; macina, dente molare.
grindstone ['graindstoun] *n* macina, mola.
grip [grip] *n* presa, stretta; controllo; impugnatura; capacità di fermare l'attenzione; *vi* afferrare, tenere fermo.
gripe [graip] *vt* afferrare; causare dolori al ventre.
grisly ['grizli] *a* orribile, spaventoso.
grist [grist] *n* grano da macinare, malto preparato per la fabbricazione della birra.
gristle ['grisl] *n* cartilagine.
grit [grit] *n* sabbia, grana; (*fam*) forza di carattere.
grizzled ['grizld] *a* brizzolato.
groan [groun] *n* gemito, lamento; *vi* gemere, lamentarsi.
grocer ['grousə] *n* droghiere.
grocery ['grousəri] *n* (generi di) drogheria, (negozio, generi di) drogheria.
grog [grɔg] *n* (*fam*) bevanda alcoolica calda, 'grog'.
groggy ['grɔgi] *a* brillo; barcollante; vacillante; malfermo.
groin [grɔin] *n* inguine.
groom [grum] *n* stalliere; palafreniere; *vt* strigliare.
groove [gru:v] *n* scanalatura, solco; *vt* scanalare, solcare.
grope [group] *vi* andare tentoni, brancolare.
groping(ly) ['groupiŋ(li)] *ad* (a) tentoni.
gross [grous] *a* grossolano, volgare, (*com*) lordo, complessivo; *n* grossa.
grossness ['grousnis] *n* grossolanità, volgarità.
grotesque [grou'tesk] *a n* grottesco; **grotesqueness** *n* bizzarria, grottesco.
grotto ['grɔtou] *pl* **grottos, grottoes** *n* grotta.
ground [graund] *n* terra, terreno, suolo; base; motivo; sfondo; *vt* basare, fondare; istruire bene; *vi* incagliarsi; **grounds** *pl* deposito, fondi *pl*; (*of mansion*) parco, giardini *pl*; **g. floor** pianterreno; **g. wire** (*rad*) filo di terra.
grounding ['graundiŋ] *n* base, conoscenza.
groundless ['graundlis] *a* infondato.
group [gru:p] *n* gruppo; *vti* raggruppar(si).
grouse [graus] *n* gallo di montagna; *vi* (*fam*) brontolare.
grove [grouv] *n* boschetto.
grovel ['grɔvl] *vi* strisciare a terra, umiliarsi.
grow [grou] *vi* crescere, aumentare, svilupparsi, divenire; *vt* coltivare.
grower ['grouə] *n* coltivatore.
growl [graul] *n* borbottio rabbioso; *vi* brontolare, borbottare irosamente.
grown-up ['grounʌp] *a n* adulto.
growth [grouθ] *n* crescita, sviluppo, progresso; (*med*) escrescenza morbosa, tumore.
grub [grʌb] *n* larva, bruco; (*sl*) cibo; *vt* zappare, sgobbare.
grubby ['grʌbi] *a* sporco, verminoso.
grudge [grʌdʒ] *n* astio, rancore; *vt* lesinare;, invidiare.
grudgingly ['grʌdʒiŋli] *ad* a malincuore, malvolentieri.
gruel ['gruəl] *n* pappa d'avena; **to give s.o. his g.** darne un fracco a *qlcu*.
grueling ['gruəliŋ] *a* estenuante.
gruesome ['gru:səm] *a* orribile, orripilante.
gruff [grʌf] *a* burbero, sgarbato.
gruffness ['grʌfnis] *n* burbanza.
grumble ['grʌmbl] *vi* borbottare, brontolare.
grumpy ['grʌmpi] *a* (*fam*) irritabile, bisbetico.
grunt [grʌnt] *n* grugnito, brontolio; *vti* grugnire, brontolare.
guarantee [,gærən'ti:] *n* garanzia, garante; *vt* garantire, essere garante per.
guarantor [,gærən'tɔ:] *n* garante; (*com*) avallante.
guard [gɑ:d] *n* guardia; (*rly*) capotreno; *vt* custodire, proteggere, sorvegliare.
guarded ['gɑ:did] *a* prudente, guardingo, cauto.
guardedly ['gɑ:didli] *ad* in modo guardingo, con circospezione.
guardian ['gɑ:diən] *n* guardiano, tutore; **guardianship** protezione, tutela.
guerrilla [gə'rilə] *pl* **guerrillas** *n* guerriglia; guerrigliere.
guess [ges] *n* congettura, supposizione; *vti* congetturare, indovinare, supporre.
guest [gest] *n* ospite.
guffaw [gʌ'fɔ:] *n* risata fragorosa.
guidance ['gaidəns] *n* guida, direzione.
guide [gaid] *n* guida, cicerone; *vt* guidare, dirigere.
guild [gild] *n* corporazione.
guile [gail] *n* artificio, astuzia, inganno.
guileless ['gaillis] *a* semplice, ingenuo.
guillotine [,gilə'ti:n] *n* ghigliottina; *vt* ghigliottinare.
guilt [gilt] *n* colpa, colpevolezza.

guiltless ['giltlis] *a* innocente.
guilty ['gilti] *a* colpevole.
Guinea ['gini] *n* Guinea.
guinea ['gini] *n* ghinea (*moneta inglese antica, che valeva ventun scellini*).
guinea-pig ['ginipig] *n* porcellino d'india, cavia.
guise [gaiz] *n* apparenza, foggia, guisa.
guitar [gi'tɑ:] *n* chitarra.
gulf [gʌlf] *n* golfo; abisso; vortice.
gull [gʌl] *n* gabbiano; *vt* gabbare, ingannare.
gullet ['gʌlit] *n* gola, esofago.
gully ['gʌli] *n* burrone.
gulp [gʌlp] *n* atto dell'inghiottire, quantità inghiottita in una volta; *vt* inghiottire voracemente, trangugiare.
gum [gʌm] *n* gomma; gengiva; *vt* ingommare.
gun [gʌn] *n* cannone, fucile, arma da sparo; **gunfire** sparatoria, cannoneggiamento; **gunman** (*sl*) rapinatore.
gunboat ['gʌnbout] *n* (*naut*) cannoniera.
gunner ['gʌnə] *n* artigliere.
gunpowder ['gʌn,paudə] *n* polvere da sparo.
gunshot ['gʌnʃɔt] *n* colpo di arma da fuoco.
gunsmith ['gʌnsmiθ] *n* armaiolo.
gurgle ['gə:gl] *n* gorgoglio; *vi* gorgogliare.
gush [gʌʃ] *n* fiotto, zampillo; effusione sentimentale; *vti* sgorgare in gran copia, zampillare; fare esagerate effusioni.
gushing ['gʌʃiŋ] *a* zampillante; espansivo.
gust ['gʌst] *n* (*of wind, rain*) raffica, (*of wind*) colpo; (*of rage*) scoppio.
gusto ['gʌstou] *n* entusiasmo, piacere.
gusty ['gʌsti] *a* burrascoso.
gut [gʌt] *n* budello, intestino; *vt* sbudellare, sventrare.
gutter ['gʌtə] *n* grondaia, cunetta.
guttural ['gʌtərəl] *a* gutturale.
Guy [gai] *nm pr* Guido.
guy [gai] *n* (*mech*) cavo; figura grottesca, spauracchio; individuo.
guzzle ['gʌzl] *vti* mangiare o bere a crepapelle.
gymnasium [dʒim'neiziəm] *n* palestra.
gymnast ['dʒimnæst] *n* ginnasta.
gymnastics [dʒim'næstiks] *n pl* ginnastica.
gypsy ['dʒipsi] *v* **gipsy**.
gyrate [,dʒaiə'reit] *vi* girare, turbinare.

H

haberdasher ['hæbədæʃə] *n* merciaio.
haberdashery ['hæbədæʃəri] *n* merceria.
habit ['hæbit] *n* abitudine; abito.
habitable ['hæbitəbl] *a* abitabile.
habitation [,hæbi'teiʃən] *n* abitazione.
habitual [hə'bitjuəl] *a* abituale.
hack ['hæk] *n* intaccatura, taglio; cavallo da nolo; individuo sfruttato in un lavoro gravoso; *vt* colpire con arma da taglio; tagliuzzare; *vi* tossire a colpi secchi.
hackney ['hækni] *n* **h. cab** vettura da nolo; **hackneyed** *a* banale.
haddock ['hædək] *n* specie di merluzzo.
haft [hɑ:ft] *n* elsa, manico.
hag [hæg] *n* megera, strega.
haggard ['hægəd] *a* magro, sparuto; **haggardness** sparutezza, pallore, magrezza.
haggle ['hægl] *vi* disputare, lesinare sul prezzo, contrattare.
Hague (the) [ðə'heig] *n* l'Aja.
hail [heil] *n* grandine; saluto; *vi* grandinare; *vt* chiamare a gran voce.
hair [hɛə] *n* capello, capelli *pl*; pelo; **h.'s breadth** spessore di un capello, distanza minima; **haircut** taglio di capelli; **hairline** corda di crine; **hairpin** forcina.
hairdresser ['hɛə,dresə] *n* parrucchiere, parrucchiera.
hairless ['hɛəlis] *a* calvo, senza peli.
hairy ['hɛəri] *a* peloso, irsuto.
halcyon ['hælsiən] *a* calmo; *n* alcione.
hale [heil] *a* robusto, sano, vigoroso.
half [hɑ:f] *pl* **halves** *a* mezzo; *n* metà, mezzo; *ad* a metà, (a) mezzo; **half-brother** fratellastro; **half-hour** mezz'ora; **half-pay** mezzo stipendio; **half-way** a mezza strada; **half-witted** corto d'intelletto; **half-yearly** semestrale, due volte all'anno.
halfpenny ['heipni] *pl* **halfpennies, halfpence** *n* mezzo penny.
halibut ['hælibət] *n* (*fish*) passera.
hall [hɔ:l] *n* aula, salone, sala di ricevimento; vestibolo.
hallo(a)! [hə'lou] *interj* salve!; (*tel*) pronto!
hallow ['hælou] *vt* consacrare; **hallowed** *a* santo, benedetto.
hallucination [hə,lu:si'neiʃən] *a* allucinazione.
halo ['heilou] *pl* **halos, haloes** *n* alone, aureola.
halt [hɔ:lt] *n* sosta, fermata; *vi* fare una sosta, fermarsi; esitare; zoppicare.
halter ['hɔ:ltə] *n* capestro; cavezza.
halve [hɑ:v] *vt* dimezzare.
ham [hæm] *n* prosciutto; coscia.
Hamburg ['hæmbə:g] *n* Amburgo.
hamburger ['hæmbə:gə] *n* polpetta di carne e cipolla tritata; panino imbottito di tale polpetta.
hamlet ['hæmlit] *n* piccolo villaggio.
hammer ['hæmə] *n* martello; (*gun*)

cane; *vt* martellare; (*fam*) ficcare in testa; battere.
hammering ['hæməriŋ] *a* martellamento, battuta.
hammock ['hæmək] *n* amaca.
hamper ['hæmpə] *n* cesta; (*naut*) accessori ingombranti; *vt* impedire, ostacolare.
hamster ['hæmstə] *n* criceto.
hand [hænd] *n* mano; (*of clocks etc*) lancetta; calligrafia; (*cards*) mano; (*worker*) operaio; *vt* consegnare, porgere.
handbag ['hændbæg] *n* borsetta.
handbill ['hændbil] *n* volantino.
handbook ['hændbuk] *n* manuale.
handcuff ['hændkʌf] *n usu pl* manette *pl*; *vt* mettere le manette a.
handful ['hændful] *n* manata, pugno; (*fam*) persona, cosa difficile da trattarsi.
handicap ['hændikæp] *n* ostacolo; (*sport*) 'handicap', corsa pareggiata.
handicraft ['hændikrɑ:ft] *n* arte, lavoro dell'artigiano.
handiwork ['hændiwə:k] *n* lavoro (a mano).
handkerchief ['hæŋkətʃif] *n* fazzoletto.
handle ['hændl] *n* manico; maniglia; (*fig*) occasione; *vt* maneggiare, manipolare.
handlebar ['hændlbɑ:] *n* manubrio di bicicletta.
handshake ['hændʃeik] *n* stretta di mano.
handsome ['hænsəm] *a* bello, ben proporzionato; generoso.
handwriting ['hænd,raitiŋ] *n* calligrafia, scrittura.
handy ['hændi] *a* abile, destro; a portata di mano.
hang [hæŋ] *vt* appendere, attaccare, impiccare; *vi* dipendere, pendere.
hangar ['hæŋə] *a* aviorimessa, 'hangar'.
hangman ['hæŋmən] *pl* **-men** *n* boia, carnefice.
hank [hæŋk] *n* matassa; (*naut*) anello della randa.
hanker ['hæŋkə] *vi* bramare.
haphazard ['hæp'hæzəd] *n* puro caso; *ad* a caso.
hapless ['hæplis] *a* sfortunato.
happen ['hæpən] *vi* accadere, avvenire, capitare, succedere.
happening ['hæpəniŋ] *n* avvenimento.
happily ['hæpili] *ad* felicemente, fortunatamente.
happiness ['hæpinis] *n* felicità.
happy ['hæpi] *a* felice, propizio.
harangue [hə'ræŋ] *n* arringa; *vt* arringare.
harass ['hærəs] *vt* seccare, tormentare.
harbinger ['hɑ:bindʒə] *n* messaggero; precursore.
harbor ['hɑ:bə] *n* porto, rifugio; *vt* accogliere, albergare; (*fig*) nutrire.
hard [hɑ:d] *a* duro, difficile; *ad* con insistenza, con difficoltà, molto.
harden ['hɑ:dn] *vt* indurire, rendere insensibile; *vi* indurirsi, diventare insensibile.
hardihood ['hɑ:dihud] *n* ardimento, arditezza.
hardiness ['hɑ:dinis] *n* robustezza, resistenza fisica.
hardly ['hɑ:dli] *ad* appena, a mala pena, scarsamente.
hardness ['hɑ:dnis] *n* durezza.
hardship ['hɑ:dʃip] *n* avversità, disagio, privazione.
hardware ['hɑ:dwɛə] *n* ferramenta *pl*.
hardy ['hɑ:di] *a* ardito; resistente.
hare [hɛə] *n* lepre.
harem ['hɛərem] *n* harem.
haricot ['hærikou] *n* fagiolo.
hark! [hɑ:k] *interj* ascolta(te)!
harlequin ['hɑ:likwin] *n* arlecchino.
harlot ['hɑ:lət] *n* prostituta.
harm [hɑ:m] *n* danno, male; *vt* danneggiare, far male a.
harmful ['hɑ:mful] *a* dannoso, nocivo.
harmless ['hɑ:mlis] *a* innocuo.
harmlessly ['hɑ:mlisli] *ad* in modo innocuo.
harmonica [hɑ:'mɔnikə] *n* armonica; armonica a bocca.
harmonics [hɑ:'mɔniks] *n pl* armonia.
harmonious [hɑ:'mouniəs] *a* armonioso.
harmonium [hɑ:'mouniəm] *n* armonium.
harmonize ['hɑ:mənaiz] *vti* armonizzare.
harmony ['hɑ:məni] *n* armonia.
harness ['hɑ:nis] *n* bardatura, finimenti *pl*; *vt* bardare; (*fig*) utilizzare.
harp [hɑ:p] *n* arpa; *vi* insistere fino ad annoiare.
harpoon [hɑ:'pu:n] *n* fiocina; *vt* fiocinare.
harpsichord ['hɑ:psikɔ:d] *n* clavicembalo.
harpy ['hɑ:pi] *n* arpia; (*fig*) megera.
harrow ['hærou] *n* erpice; *vt* erpicare; (*fig*) straziare.
harsh [hɑ:ʃ] *a* aspro, crudele, severo.
harshness ['hɑ:ʃnis] *n* asprezza, severità.
hart [hɑ:t] *n* cervo, daino.
harum-scarum ['hɛərəm'skɛərəm] *a* avventato, irresponsabile.
harvest ['hɑ:vist] *n* messe, raccolto; *vt* mietere, raccogliere.
harvester ['hɑ:vistə] *n* mietitore.
hash [hæʃ] *n* specie di ragù; (*fig*) pasticcio; *vt* sminuzzare; (*fig*) fare un pasticcio di.
hasp [hɑ:sp] *n* fermaglio.
hassock ['hæsək] *n* grosso cuscino usato come inginocchiatoio.
haste [heist] *n* fretta, furia.
hasten ['heisn] *vti* affrettar(si).

hastily ['heistili] *ad* frettolosamente, di furia.
hastiness ['heistinis] *n* fretta, precipitazione; irritabilità.
hasty ['heisti] *a* frettoloso, avventato; irritabile.
hat [hæt] *n* cappello; **hatbox** cappelliera.
hatch [hætʃ] *n* mezza porta; (*naut*) boccaporto; covata; *vt* covare; macchinare; *vi* (*of eggs*) schiudersi; (*of birds*) nascere.
hatchet ['hætʃit] *n* accetta.
hate [heit] *n* odio; *vt* odiare.
hateful ['heitful] *a* odioso.
hatpin ['hætpin] *n* spillone (da cappello).
hatred ['heitrid] *n* odio; astio.
hatter ['hætə] *n* cappellaio.
haughtiness ['hɔ:tinis] *n* arroganza, superbia.
haughty ['hɔ:ti] *a* arrogante, superbo.
haul [hɔ:l] *n* retata; tirata; (*fig*) guadagno; refurtiva; *vt* tirare, trascinare, rimorchiare.
haulage ['hɔ:lidʒ] *n* trasporto.
haulier ['hɔ:liə] *n* imprenditore di trasporti, impresa autotrasporti.
haunch [hɔ:ntʃ] *n* anca, coscia.
haunt [hɔ:nt] *n* ritrovo; *vt* frequentare; ossessionare, perseguitare; **haunted** *a* frequentato, perseguitato, infestato da fantasmi.
Havana [hə'vænə] *n* Avana.
have [hæv] *vt aux* avere, ricevere, fare; **h.** to dovere.
haven ['heivn] *n* porto, rifugio.
haversack ['hævəsæk] *n* zaino, sacco da montagna.
havoc ['hævək] *n* devastazione, distruzione.
hawk [hɔ:k] *n* falco; *vt* portare in giro (merci) per la vendita; *vi* cacciare col falco.
hawker ['hɔ:kə] *n* venditore ambulante.
hawser ['hɔ:zə] *n* (*naut*) gomena, piccolo cavo.
hawthorn ['hɔ:θɔ:n] *n* biancospino.
hay [hei] *n* fieno.
haycock ['heikɔk] **haystack** ['heistæk] *n* mucchio di fieno.
hazard ['hæzəd] *n* azzardo, rischio; *vt* arrischiare, azzardare.
hazardous ['hæzədəs] *a* rischioso.
haze [heiz] *n* nebbia, nebbiolina; (*fig*) confusione di mente.
hazel [heizl] *n* nocciolo, nocciola.
hazy ['heizi] *a* nebbioso, indistinto, vago.
he [hi:] *pron* egli, lui; (*prefix with names of animals*) maschio.
head [hed] *n* capo, testa; (*arrow*) punta; (*bed*) capezzale; (*page*) testata; *vt* capeggiare; intestare; *vi* colpire con la testa; dirigersi; **headmaster** n direttore di scuola, preside.
headache ['hedeik] *n* male di capo, emicrania.
heading ['hediŋ] *n* intestazione, titolo, (*av*) rotta.
headland ['hedlənd] *n* capo, promontorio.
headlight ['hedlait] *n* (*aut*) faro (anteriore).
headlong ['hedlɔŋ] *a* impetuoso, precipitoso; *ad* (a) capofitto.
headmost ['hedmoust] *a* il più avanzato.
headquarters ['hed'kwɔ:təz] *n pl* Quartier Generale.
headstrong ['hedstrɔŋ] *a* ostinato, testardo.
headway ['hedwei] *n* progresso, cammino.
heady ['hedi] *a* violento; testardo; inebriante.
heal ['hi:l] *vt* guarire, sanare.
healing ['hi:liŋ] *a* salutare; *n* guarigione.
health ['helθ] *n* salute.
healthy ['helθi] *a* sano, salutare, salubre.
heap [hi:p] *n* cumulo, mucchio; *vt* accumulare, ammucchiare.
hear [hiə] *vt* ascoltare; *vti* sentire, udire; apprendere.
hearing ['hiəriŋ] *n* udito; udienza; ascolto; **within h.** a portata di voce.
hearsay ['hiəsei] *n* diceria, voce.
hearse [hə:s] *n* carro funebre.
heart [hɑ:t] *n* cuore; **heartbeat** pulsazione; **heartbreak** crepacuore.
heartache ['hɑ:teik] *n* crepacuore.
heartbroken ['hɑ:t,broukən] *a* straziato.
heartburn ['hɑ:tbə:n] *n* bruciore di stomaco.
hearten ['hɑ:tn] *vt* incoraggiare, rincorare.
heartening ['hɑ:tniŋ] *a* incoraggiante.
hearth [hɑ:θ] *n* focolare.
heartily ['hɑ:tili] *ad* cordialmente; vigorosamente.
heartless ['hɑ:tlis] *a* senza cuore, insensibile.
hearty ['hɑ:ti] *a* cordiale; vigoroso.
heat [hi:t] *n* calore, caldo; *vt* riscaldare, infiammare.
heater ['hi:tə] *n* riscaldatore; **electric h.** stufetta elettrica.
heath [hi:θ] *n* brughiera, erica.
heathen ['hi:ðən] *a n* pagano.
heather ['heðə] *n* erica.
heating ['hi:tiŋ] *n* riscaldamento; **h. element** resistenza.
heave [hi:v] *n* spinta; conato di vomito; *vt* alzare con fatica; (far) sollevare; *vi* spingere; ansimare; sollevarsi.
heaven ['hevn] *n* cielo.
heavenly ['hevnli] *a* celeste, celestiale, divino.
heavily ['hevili] *ad* pesantemente; molto.
heaviness ['hevinis] *n* pesantezza; oppressione.
heavy ['hevi] *a* pesante, opprimente;

h. sea mare grosso; **h.-hearted** col cuore triste; **heavyweight** (*boxing*) peso massimo.
Hebrew ['hi:bru:] *a n* ebraico, ebreo.
Hebrides ['hebridiz] *n* (isole) Ebridi.
heckle ['hekl] *n* carda; *vt* cardare; tempestare di domande.
hectic ['hektik] *a* (*med*) etico, tisico; agitato; febbrile.
Hector ['hektə] *nm pr* Ettore.
hedge [hedʒ] *n* siepe.
hedgehog ['hedʒhɔg] *n* porcospino, riccio (*also fig*).
heed [hi:d] *n* attenzione; *vt* fare attenzione a, badare a.
heedful ['hi:dful] *a* attento, cauto.
heedless ['hi:dlis] *a* disattento, incurante.
heel [hi:l] *a* calcagno, tacco, tallone; *vt* mettere i tacchi a.
hefty ['hefti] *a* forte, vigoroso; piuttosto pesante.
hegemony [hi:'geməni] *n* egemonia.
heifer ['hefə] *n* giovenca.
height [hait] *n* altezza, altura; culmine.
heighten ['haitn] *vt* innalzare, intensificare.
heinous ['heinəs] *a* atroce, odioso.
heir [ɛə] *n* erede; **heiress** ereditiera.
heirloom ['ɛəlu:m] *n* cimelio di famiglia.
Helen ['helin] *nf pr* Elena.
helicopter ['helikɔptə] *n* elicottero.
hell [hel] *n* inferno.
hello [he'lou] *interj* salve!; (*tel*) pronto!
helm [helm] *n* (*naut*) timone.
helm(et) ['helm(it)] *n* elmetto, casco.
helmsman ['helmzmən] *pl* **-men** *n* timoniere.
help [help] *n* aiuto, assistenza, rimedio; *vt* aiutare, soccorrere; evitare; servire (cibo a tavola).
helper ['helpə] *n* aiuto, aiutante, soccorritore, soccorritrice.
helpful ['helpful] *a* servizievole, utile.
helping ['helpiŋ] *n* (*food*) porzione.
helpless ['helplis] *a* impotente.
helplessness ['helplisnis] *n* impotenza; mancanza di iniziativa.
helpmate ['helpmeit] *n* collaboratore, compagno.
helter-skelter ['heltə'skeltə] *ad* alla rinfusa.
hem [hem] *n* orlo, bordura; *vt* orlare; **to h. in** circondare.
hemisphere ['hemisfiə] *n* emisfero.
hemlock ['hemlɔk] *n* cicuta.
hemorrhage ['hemərid3] *n* emorragia.
hemp [hemp] *n* canapa.
hemstitch ['hemstitʃ] *n* orlo a giorno.
hen [hen] *n* gallina; femmina di vari uccelli.
hence [hens] *ad* di qui a, perciò, quindi.
henceforth ['hens'fɔ:θ] *ad* d'ora in avanti.
henchman ['hentʃmən] *pl* **henchmen** *n* (*pol*) seguace, accolito.
Henry ['henri] *nm pr* Enrico.
her [hə:] *pron a* la, lei; di lei, suo (sua, sue, suoi); **to h.** le, a lei; **herself** *pron* ella medesima, lei stessa.
herald ['herəld] *n* araldo; *vt* annunciare, proclamare.
heraldry ['herəldri] *n* araldica.
herb [hə:b] *n* erba aromatica.
herbalist ['hə:bəlist] *n* erborista.
herd [hə:d] *n* branco, gregge, mandria; *vt* custodire bestiame; *vi* formare gregge.
herdsman ['hə:dzmən] *pl* **-men** *n* mandriano.
here [hiə] *ad* qui, costì.
hereabout(s) ['hiərə,baut(s)] *ad* all'intorno, qui vicino.
hereafter [hiər'ɑ:ftə] *n* vita futura; *ad* d'ora in poi.
hereditary [hi'reditəri] *a* ereditario.
heredity [hi'rediti] *n* eredità.
heresy ['herəsi] *n* eresia.
heretic ['herətik] *a n* eretico.
herewith ['hiə'wið] *ad* con questo, qui accluso.
heritage ['heritid3] *n* eredità (*also fig*).
hermetically [hə:'metikəli] *ad* ermeticamente.
hermit ['hə:mit] *n* eremita.
hermitage ['hə:mitid3] *n* eremitaggio.
hernia ['hə:niə] *n* ernia.
hero ['hiərou] *n* eroe; protagonista.
heroic [hi'rouik] *a* eroico.
heroine ['herouin] *n* eroina; protagonista.
heroism ['herouizəm] *n* eroismo.
heron ['herən] *n* airone.
herring ['heriŋ] *n* aringa; **smoked h.** aringa affumicata.
hers [hə:z] *pron* il suo, la sua, i suoi, le sue; di lei.
hesitant ['hezitənt] *a* esitante, titubante.
hesitate ['heziteit] *vi* esitare.
hesitation [,hezi'teiʃən] *n* esitazione.
heterogeneous ['hetərou'dʒi:niəs] *a* eterogeneo.
hew [hju:] *vt* abbattere; spaccare.
heyday ['heidei] *n* apogeo, apice.
hiatus [hai'eitəs] *n* iato; lacuna.
hibernate ['haibəneit] *vi* svernare, essere in ibernazione.
hiccup, hiccough ['hikʌp] *vi* (avere il) singhiozzo; *n* singhiozzo.
hide [haid] *n* cuoio, pelle; *vti* nasconder(si), celar(si).
hideous ['hidiəs] *a* mostruoso, ripugnante.
hideousness ['hidiəsnis] *n* mostruosità.
hideout ['haidaut] *n* nascondiglio.
hiding ['haidiŋ] *n* nascondiglio; (*fam*) fustigazione.
hierarchy ['haiərɑ:ki] *n* gerarchia.
higgledy-piggledy ['higldi'pigldi] *ad* alla rinfusa.

high [hai] *a* alto; importante; (*time*) avanzato; (*color*) acceso; **h. altar** altare maggiore; **h. school** scuola media; **h. water** alta marea.
highbrow ['haibrau] *an* intellettuale.
highland ['hailənd] *a* montanaro; *n usu pl* regione montuosa.
highlander ['hailəndə] *n* montanaro.
highly ['haili] *ad* molto, estremamente.
highness ['hainis] *n* (*title*) altezza.
highway ['haiwei] *n* strada maestra; autostrada; **highwayman** bandito.
hike [haik] *vi n* (fare una) escursione a piedi.
hiker ['haikə] *n* escursionista (a piedi).
hilarious [hi'lɛəriəs] *a* ilare, allegro.
hill [hil] *n* colle, collina.
hilliness ['hilinis] *n* natura collinosa.
hillock ['hilək] *n* collinetta, poggio.
hillside ['hilsaid] *n* pendio.
hilltop ['hiltɔp] *n* sommità della collina.
hilly ['hili] *a* collinoso.
hilt [hilt] *n* elsa, impugnatura.
him [him] *pron* lui, lo; **to h.** gli, a lui; **himself** egli stesso, proprio lui, si, se stesso, quello.
Himalaya [,himə'leiə] *n* Imalaia.
Himalayan [,himə'leiən] *a n* imalaiano, imalaiana.
hind [haind] *n* cerva, daina; *a* posteriore.
hinder ['haində] *a* posteriore; *vt* ['hində] impedire, ostacolare.
hindrance ['hindrəns] *n* impedimento, ostacolo.
hinge [hindʒ] *n* cardine; *vt* munire di cardini; *vi* dipendere.
hint [hint] *n* allusione, accenno; *vti* alludere, accennare.
hinterland ['hintəlænd] *n* retroterra.
hip [hip] *n* anca, fianco.
hippopotamus [,hipə'pɔtəməs] *n* ippopotamo.
hire ['haiə] *n* nolo, affito; *vt* affittare, noléggiare; **for h.** da nolo; **to h. out** dare a nolo.
hireling ['haiəliŋ] *n* mercenario.
hirsute ['hə:sju:t] *a* irsuto, ispido.
his [hiz] *a pron* (il) suo, di lui.
hiss [his] *n* fischio, sibilo; *vti* fischiare, sibilare.
historian [his'tɔ:riən] *n* storico.
historic [his'tɔrik] *a* importante; (*gram*) storico.
historical [his'tɔrikəl] *a* storico.
history ['histəri] *n* storia.
histrionic [,histri'ɔnik] *a* istrionico.
hit [hit] *n* colpo; successo; tentativo fortunato; *vt* colpire.
hitch [hitʃ] *n* nodo, impedimento, ostacolo.
hitch-hike ['hitʃhaik] *vi* fare l'autostop.
hitch-hiker ['hitʃ,haikə] *n* chi fa l'autostop.
hitch-hiking ['hitʃ,haikiŋ] *n* autostop.
hither ['hiðə] *ad* qui, qua; **h. and thither** qua e là.
hitherto ['hiðə'tu:] *ad* finora.
hive [haiv] *n* alveare.
hoar [hɔ:] *a* canuto, grigio; **h.-frost** *n* brina.
hoard [hɔ:d] *n* ammasso, tesoro; *vti* ammassare, fare incetta di.
hoarder ['hɔ:də] *n* risparmiatore.
hoarding ['hɔ:diŋ] *n* accumulazione, incetta, risparmio.
hoarse [hɔ:s] *a* rauco.
hoarsely ['hɔ:sli] *ad* raucamente.
hoarseness ['hɔ:snis] *n* raucedine.
hoary ['hɔ:ri] *a* canuto, venerabile.
hoax [houks] *n* inganno, tiro scherzoso; *vt* ingannare.
hobble ['hɔbl] *n* zoppicamento, pastoia; *vi* zoppicare; *vt* impastoiare.
hobbledehoy ['hɔbldi'hɔi] *n* adolescente goffo.
hobby ['hɔbi] *n* svago preferito, 'hobby'.
hock [hɔk] *n* garretto (di cavallo).
hockey ['hɔki] *n* pallamaglio, 'hockey'; **ice h.** hockey sul ghiaccio.
hoe [hou] *n* zappa; *vti* zappare.
hog [hɔg] *n* maiale, porco.
hogmanay [,hɔgmə'nei] *n* (*in Scozia*) ultimo giorno dell'anno.
hogshead ['hɔgzhed] *n* grossa botte della capacità di galloni 52½ (= *litri* 238,5).
hoist [hɔist] *n* montacarichi; *vt* innalzare, sollevare.
hold [hould] *n* presa, stretta; luogo fortificato; (*naut*) stiva; *vt* contenere; tenere; trattenere; *vi* tenere (duro).
holder ['houldə] *n* detentore, possessore.
holding ['houldiŋ] *n* possesso, tenuta.
hole [houl] *n* buca, buco, cavità; tana; (*sl*) situazione difficile.
holiday ['hɔlidei] *n* giorno festivo, vacanza; **holidaymaker** villeggiante.
holiness ['houlinis] *n* santità.
Holland ['hɔlənd] *n* Olanda.
hollow ['hɔlou] *a* cavo, vuoto; (*fig*) falso; *n* cavità, buca; *vt* incavare, scavare.
holly ['hɔli] *n* agrifoglio.
holm [houm] *n* leccio.
holster ['houlstə] *n* fondina di pistola.
holy ['houli] *n* sacro, santo.
homage ['hɔmidʒ] *n* omaggio.
home [houm] *n* casa, focolare domestico, patria; *a* domestico, familiare, nazionale; **homecoming** ritorno al focolare.
homeland ['houmlænd] *n* patria.
homeless ['houmlis] *a* senza tetto, senza patria.
homely ['houmli] *a* casalingo; insignificante; semplice.
home-made ['houm'meid] *a* fatto in casa.
homesick ['houmsik] *a* nostalgico.

homesickness ['houmsiknis] *n* nostalgia.
homeward ['houmwəd] *a ad* verso casa, verso il proprio paese.
homework ['houmwə:k] *n* compito per casa.
homicide ['hɔmisaid] *n* omicida; omicidio.
homogeneous [,hɔmə'dʒi:niəs] *a* omogeneo.
homosexual ['houmou'seksjuəl] *a* omosessuale.
hone [houn] *n* cote; *vt* affilare.
honest ['ɔnist] *a* onesto, leale.
honestly ['ɔnistli] *ad* onestamente, sinceramente.
honesty ['ɔnisti] *n* onestà, lealtà.
honey ['hʌni] *n* miele.
honeycomb ['hʌnikoum] *n* favo.
honeymoon ['hʌnimu:n] *n* luna di miele; viaggio di nozze.
honeysuckle ['hʌni,sʌkl] *n* caprifoglio.
honor ['ɔnə] *n* onore, onoranza; (*title*) eccellenza; *vt* onorare.
honorable ['ɔnərəbl] *a* onorevole.
honorary ['ɔnərəri] *a* onorario.
hood [hud] *n* cappuccio; cofano di automobile; mantice di carrozza; *vt* incappucciare.
hoodwink ['hudwiŋk] *vt* bendare gli occhi a; (*fig*) ingannare.
hoof [hu:f] *pl* **hoofs, hooves** *n* zoccolo.
hook [huk] *n* uncino, gancio, amo; *vt* agganciare, prendere all'amo.
hooked [hukt] *a* adunco.
hooligan ['hu:ligən] *n* giovinastro.
hoop [hu:p] *n* cerchio.
hoot [hu:t] *n* grido della civetta; schiamazzo; (*train*) fischio; *vi* gridare; suonare il clacson; *vt* deridere.
hooter ['hu:tə] *n* sirena; clacson.
hop [hɔp] *n* balzo, salto su un piede; luppolo; *vi* saltare su un piede.
hope [houp] *n* speranza; *vti* sperare.
hopeful ['houpful] *a* speranzoso, ottimista.
hopeless ['houplis] *a* disperato, senza rimedio, senza speranza.
hopelessly ['houplisli] *ad* irrimediabilmente, senza speranza.
Horace ['hɔrəs] *nm pr* Orazio.
horde [hɔ:d] *n* orda.
horizon [hə'raizn] *n* orizzonte.
horizontal [,hɔri'zɔntl] *a* orizzontale.
hormone ['hɔ:moun] *n* ormone.
horn ['hɔ:n] *n* corno; (*insect*) antenna; (*aut*) clacson.
hornet ['hɔ:nit] *n* calabrone.
horoscope ['hɔrəskoup] *n* oroscopo.
horrible ['hɔrəbl] *a* orribile.
horrid ['hɔrid] *a* orrido, odioso.
horrify ['hɔrifai] *vt* far inorridire.
horror ['hɔrə] *n* orrore.
horse [hɔ:s] *n* cavallo, *pl* cavalleria; **horseshoe** ferro di cavallo.
horseback ['hɔ:sbæk] *n* groppa; **on h.** *ad* a cavallo, in sella.
horseman ['hɔ:smən] *n* cavaliere; **horsewoman** amazzone.
horsemanship ['hɔ:smənʃip] *n* equitazione.
horticultural [,hɔ:ti'kʌltʃərəl] *a* riguardante l'orticultura.
horticulture ['hɔ:tikʌltʃə] *n* orticultura.
hose [houz] *n* tubo flessibile; idrante; calze *pl.*
hosiery ['houʒəri] *n* maglieria.
hospice ['hɔspis] *n* ospizio.
hospitable ['hɔspitəbl] *a* ospitale.
hospital ['hɔspitl] *n* (o)spedale.
hospitality [,hɔspi'tæliti] *n* ospitalità.
host [houst] *n* ospite (che ospita); albergatore, oste; moltitudine, schiera; ostia.
hostage ['hɔstidʒ] *n* ostaggio.
hostel ['hɔstəl] *n* pensionato; ostello.
hostess ['houstis] *n* padrona di casa, ospite; (*av*) "hostess."
hostile ['hɔstail] *a* ostile.
hostility [hɔs'tiliti] *n* ostilità.
hot [hɔt] *a* caldo, ardente, veemente, (*food*) piccante; **hothead** testa calda, persona impulsiva; **h. line** linea diritta; **hotplate** fornello, piastra riscaldante; **h.-water bottle** borsa dell'acqua calda.
hotel [hou'tel] *n* albergo; **hotelier** albergatore.
hound [haund] *n* cane da caccia; *vt* inseguire, perseguitare.
hour ['auə] *n* ora.
hourly ['auəli] *a ad* ogni ora.
house [haus] *n* casa; *vt* alloggiare; (*harvest*) portare dentro il raccolto; **full h.** (*theat*) tutto esaurito.
housebreaker ['haus,breikə] *n* scassinatore.
housecoat ['hauskout] *n* vestaglia.
household ['haushould] *n* famiglia, compresi i domestici; *a* di (da) famiglia, casalingo, domestico.
householder ['haus,houldə] *n* capofamiglia.
housekeeper ['haus,ki:pə] *n* governante, di casa.
housekeeping ['haus,ki:piŋ] *n* governo della casa.
housetop ['haustɔp] *n* tetto della casa.
housewife ['hauswaif] *n* massaia, casalinga; astuccio da lavoro tascabile.
housework ['hauswə:k] *n* lavoro domestico.
housing ['hauziŋ] *n* l'accogliere, l'alloggiare; alloggio, abitazione.
hovel ['hɔvəl] *n* casupola, tugurio.
hover ['hɔvə] *vi* librarsi, gravitare; ronzare intorno; sorvolare.
how [hau] *ad* come, quanto.
however [hau'evə] *ad cj* comunque, però, tuttavia.
howitzer ['hauitsə] *n* obice.
howl [haul] *n* ululato, urlo; *vi* ululare, urlare.

hub [hʌb] *n* (*mech*) mozzo di ruota; (*fig*) punto centrale.
hubbub ['hʌbʌb] *n* suono confuso, tumulto.
huddle ['hʌdl] *n* folla disordinata; *vti* ammucchiare confusamente, affollarsi, accalcarsi, stringersi insieme.
hue [hju:] *n* colore, tinta; clamore.
huff [hʌf] *n* risentimento, stizza.
hug [hʌg] *n* (*fam*) abbraccio, stretta; *vt* (*fam*) abbracciare stretto; (*fig*) restare attaccato a.
huge [hju:dʒ] *a* enorme.
hugeness ['hju:dʒnis] *n* grandezza smisurata.
Hugh [hju:] *nm pr* Ugo.
Huguenot ['hju:gənɔt] *n* ugonotto.
hulk [hʌlk] *n* (*naut*) carcassa.
hull [hʌl] *n* baccello; (*naut*) scafo.
hullabaloo ['hʌləbə'lu:] *n* fracasso, baccano, confusione.
hullo [hʌ'lou] *interj* ciao, salve!; (*tel*) pronto!
hum [hʌm] *n* ronzio; *vi* ronzare; canticchiare a labbra chiuse; (*fam*) essere in grande attività.
human ['hju:mən] *a* umano.
humane [hju:'mein] *a* umano, umanitario.
humanism ['hju:mənizəm] *n* umanesimo.
humanist ['hju:mənist] *n* umanista.
humanitarian [hju:,mæni'teəriən] *a* filantropico, umanitario; *n* filantropo.
humanity [hju:'mæniti] *n* umanità.
humanly ['hju:mənli] *ad* umanamente.
humble ['hʌmbl] *a* umile; *vt* umiliare; **to eat h. pie** scusarsi umilmente.
humbly ['hʌmbli] *ad* umilmente, con sottomissione.
humbug ['hʌmbʌg] *n* (*fam*) frottola, inganno, ipocrisia; impostore, ipocrita; *interj* sciocchezze!
humdrum ['hʌmdrʌm] *a* noioso, monotono.
humid ['hju:mid] *a* umido.
humidity [hju:'miditi] *n* umidità.
humiliate [hju:'milieit] *vi* umiliare.
humiliation [hju:,mili'eiʃən] *n* umiliazione.
humility [hju:'militi] *n* umiltà.
humor ['hju:mə] *n* senso dell'umorismo, vena; *vt* assecondare.
humorist ['hju:mərist] *n* umorista.
humorous ['hju:mərəs] *a* umoristico, spiritoso.
hump [hʌmp] *n* gobba, protuberanza; (*fig*) malumore; **humpbacked** gobbo.
hunch [hʌntʃ] *n* gobba, protuberanza; (*fig*) impressione, sospetto; **hunchbacked** gobbo.
hundred ['hʌndrəd] *a n* cento.
hundredfold ['hʌndrədfould] *a n* centuplo.
hundredth ['hʌndrədθ] *a n* centesimo.
hundredweight ['hʌndrədweit] *n* (**cwt**) misura di peso di 112 libbre (=*chili* 50,8).
Hungarian [hʌŋ'geəriən] *a n* ungherese.
Hungary ['hʌŋgəri] *n* Ungheria.
hunger ['hʌŋgə] *n* fame; *vi* bramare; *vt* affamare.
hungry ['hʌngri] *a* affamato, desideroso; **be h.** aver fame.
hunk [hʌŋk] *n* grosso pezzo.
hunt [hʌnt] *n* caccia, gruppo di cacciatori; *vti* cacciare.
hunter ['hʌntə] *n* cacciatore.
hunting ['hʌntiŋ] *n* caccia.
huntsman ['hʌntsmən] *pl* **-men** *n* cacciatore.
hurdle ['hə:dl] *n* graticcio, ostacolo; **h. race** corsa ad ostacoli.
hurdy-gurdy ['hə:di,gə:di] *n* organetto a manovella.
hurl [hə:l] *vt* scagliare.
hurly-burly ['hə:li,bə:li] *n* mischia, tumulto.
hurrah [hu'rɑ:] *interj* urrah!
hurricane ['hʌrikən] *n* ciclone, uragano.
hurriedly ['hʌridli] *ad* in gran fretta, precipitosamente.
hurry ['hʌri] *n* fretta, premura; *vti* affrettarsi.
hurt [hə:t] *n* ferita, danno; *vti* far male a, danneggiare, dolere.
hurtful ['hə:tful] *a* dannoso, nocivo.
hurtle ['hə:tl] *vti* scagliar(si). precipitarsi.
husband ['hʌzbənd] *n* marito; *vt* amministrare con parsimonia, risparmiare.
husbandman ['hʌzbəndmən] *pl* **-men** *n* agricoltore.
husbandry ['hʌzbəndri] *n* agricoltura; amministrazione domestica.
hush [hʌʃ] *n* silenzio, quiete; *vti* (far) tacere.
husk [hʌsk] *n* buccia.
husky ['hʌski] *a* pieno di bucce; (*voice*) rauco, velato.
hussar [hu'zɑ:] *n* ussaro.
hussy ['hʌsi] *n* civetta, donna leggera.
hustle ['hʌsl] *n* spinta, trambusto; *vt* spingere.
hut [hʌt] *n* capanna; (*mil*) baracca.
hutch [hʌtʃ] *n* conigliera; gabbia; casotto.
hyacinth ['haiəsinθ] *n* giacinto.
hybrid ['haibrid] *a n* ibrido.
hydrant ['haidrənt] *n* idrante.
hydrate ['haidreit] *n* idrato.
hydroelectric ['haidroui'lektrik] *a* idroelettrico.
hydroplane ['haidrouplein] *n* idroplano, idrovolante.
hydrogen ['haidridʒən] *n* idrogeno.
hydropsy ['haidrɔpsi] *n* idropisia.
hyena [hai'i:nə] *n* iena.
hygiene ['haidʒi:n] *n* igiene.

hygienic [hai'dʒi:nik] *a* igienico.
hymn [him] *n* inno.
hyperbole [hai'pə:bəli] *n* iperbole.
hypersensitive ['haipə:'sensitiv] *a* ipersensibile, ipersensitivo.
hyphen ['haifən] *n* lineetta, tratto d'unione.
hypnotism ['hipnətizəm] *n* ipnotismo.
hypochondriac [,haipou'kɔndriæk] *a n* ipocondriaco.
hypocrisy [hi'pɔkrəsi] *n* ipocrisia.
hypocrite ['hipəkrit] *n* ipocrita.
hypocritical [,hipə'kritikəl] *a* ipocrita.
hypodermic [,haipə'də:mik] *a* ipodermico.
hypothesis [hai'pɔθisis] *pl* **hypotheses** *n* ipotesi.
hypothetical [,haipou'θetikəl] *a* ipotetico.
hysteria [his'tiəriə] *n* isterismo.
hysterical [his'terikəl] *a* isterico.
hysterics [his'teriks] *n* attacco isterico.

I

I [ai] *pron* io.
Ia(i)n [iən] *nm pr* (*scozzese*) Giovanni.
ice [ais] *n* ghiaccio, gelato; *vt* ghiacciare; (*cook*) glassare.
iceberg ['aisbə:g] *n* massa di ghiacci galleggianti, 'iceberg'.
ice-cream ['ais'kri:m] *n* gelato.
Iceland ['aislənd] *n* Islanda.
Icelander ['aisləndə] *n* islandese.
Icelandic [ais'lændik] *a n* islandese.
icicle ['aisikil] *n* ghiacciolo.
icing ['aisiŋ] *a* (*sugar*) al velo; *n* (*cook*) glassa.
icy ['aisi] *a* gelato, gelido, ghiacciato.
idea [ai'diə] *n* idea.
ideal [ai'diəl] *a n* ideale.
idealism [ai'diəlizəm] *n* idealismo.
idealist [ai'diəlist] *n* idealista.
identikit [ai'dentikit] *n* identi-kit.
identic(al) [ai'dentik(əl)] *a* identico.
identification [ai,dentifi'keiʃən] *n* identificazione, riconoscimento; **i. tag** (*mil*) piastrina di riconoscimento.
ideology [,aidi'ɔlədʒi] *n* ideologia.
idiocy ['idiəsi] *n* idiozia.
idiom ['idiəm] *n* idiotismo, espressione idiomatica; idioma.
idiomatic [,idiə'mætik] *a* idiomatico.
idiot ['idiət] *n* idiota.
idiotic [,idi'ɔtik] *a* idiota, stupido.
idle ['aidl] *a* indolente, ozioso, inutile, vano; *vi* oziare; *vt* sprecare (tempo) in ozio.
idleness ['aidlnis] *n* indolenza, ozio.
idly ['aidli] *ad* pigramente, inutilmente.
idol ['aidl] *n* idolo.
idolater [ai'dɔlətə] *n* idolatra.
idolatry [ai'dɔlətri] *n* idolatria.
idolize ['aidəlaiz] *vt* idolatrare.
idyll ['idil] *n* idillio.
if [if] *cj* se; **if anything** se mai; **if so** in tal caso.
ignition [ig'niʃən] *n* ignizione, accensione; **i. key** (*aut*) chiavetta dell'accensione.
ignoble [ig'noubl] *a* ignobile.
ignominious [,ignə'miniəs] *a* ignominioso.
ignominy ['ignəmini] *n* ignominia.
ignoramus [,ignə'reiməs] *n* ignorante.
ignorance ['ignərəns] *n* ignoranza.
ignorant ['ignərənt] *a* ignorante.
ignore [ig'nɔ:] *vt* far finta di non sentire, di non vedere, ignorare, trascurare.
ill [il] *a* (am)malato; dannoso, malefico; *ad* male; *n* male, danno.
illegal [i'li:gəl] *a* illegale.
illegality [,ili:'gæliti] *n* illegalità.
illegible [i'ledʒəbl] *a* illeggibile.
illegitimacy [,ili'dʒitiməsi] *n* illegittimità.
illegitimate [,ili'dʒitimit] *a* illegittimo.
illiberal [i'libərəl] *a* illiberale, tirchio.
illicit [i'lisit] *a* illecito.
illiterate [i'litərit] *a n* analfabeta.
illness ['ilnis] *n* malattia.
illogical [i'lɔdʒikəl] *a* illogico.
illuminate [i'lju:mineit] *vt* illuminare; miniare.
illumination [i,lju:mi'neiʃən] *n* illuminazione; miniatura.
illusion [i'lu:ʒən] *n* illusione.
illusive [i'lu:siv] *a* illusorio.
illustrate ['iləstreit] *vt* illustrare.
illustration [,iləs'treiʃən] *n* illustrazione.
illustrious [i'lʌstriəs] *a* illustre.
image ['imidʒ] *n* immagine.
imagery ['imidʒəri] *n pl* immagini; linguaggio figurato.
imaginable [i'mædʒinəbl] *a* immaginabile.
imaginary [i'mædʒinəri] *a* immaginario.
imagination [i,mædʒi'neiʃən] *n* immaginazione.
imaginative [i'mædʒinətiv] *a* immaginativo, fantasioso.
imagine [i'mædʒin] *vti* immaginare, figurarsi, farsi un'idea.
imbecile ['imbisi:l] *a n* imbecille.
imbibe [im'baib] *vt* assimilare, assorbire, bere.
imbue [im'bju:] *vt* imbevere, impregnare.
imitate ['imiteit] *vt* imitare.
imitation [,imi'teiʃən] *n* imitazione.
immaculate [i'mækjulit] *a* immacolato.
immaterial [,imə'tiəriəl] *a* immateriale, di nessuna importanza.
immature [,imə'tjuə] *a* immaturo.
immeasurable [i'meʒərəbl] *a* incommensurabile.

immediacy [i'mi:diəsi] *n* immediatezza.
immediate [i'mi:diet] *a* immediato.
immediately [i'mi:diətli] *ad* immediatamente.
immemorial [,imi'mɔ:riəl] *a* immemorabile.
immense [i'mens] *a* immenso.
immensity [i'mensiti] *n* immensità.
immerse [i'mə:s] *vt* immergere.
immersion [i'mə:ʃən] *n* immersione.
immigrant ['imigrənt] *a n* immigrante.
immigrate ['imigreit] *vi* immigrare.
immigration [,imi'greiʃən] *n* immigrazione.
imminent ['iminənt] *a* imminente.
immobility [,imou'biliti] *n* immobilità.
immobilize [i'moubilaiz] *vt* immobilizzare.
immoderate [i'mɔdərit] *a* smodato.
immodest [i'mɔdist] *a* immodesto, impudico.
immolate ['imouleit] *vt* immolare.
immoral [i'mɔrəl] *a* immorale.
immorality [,imə'ræliti] *a* immoralità.
immortal [i'mɔ:tl] *a n* immortale.
immortality [,imɔ:'tæliti] *n* immortalità.
immortalize [i'mɔ:təlaiz] *vt* immortalare.
immovable [i'mu:vəbl] *a* immobile, inamovibile.
immune [i'mju:n] *a* immune.
immunity [i'mju:niti] *n* immunità.
immunization [,imju:nai'zeiʃən] *n* immunizzazione.
immutability [i,mju:tə'biliti] *n* immutabilità.
immutable [i'mju:təbl] *a* immutabile.
imp [imp] *n* diavoletto.
impact ['impækt] *n* collisione, urto.
impair [im'pεə] *vt* danneggiare, menomare.
impalpable [im'pælpəbl] *a* impalpabile.
impart [im'pɑ:t] *vt* impartire, comunicare.
impartial [im'pɑ:ʃəl] *a* imparziale.
impartiality ['im,pɑ:ʃi'æliti] *n* imparzialità.
impassible [im'pɑ:səbl] *a* impassibile.
impassioned [im'pæʃənd] *a* appassionato, eloquente.
impassive [im'pæsiv] *a* impassibile.
impatience [im'peiʃəns] *n* impazienza.
impatient [im'peiʃənt] *a* impaziente.
impeach [im'pi:tʃ] *vt* accusare, imputare.
impeccable [im'pekəbl] *a* impeccabile.
impecunious [,impi'kju:niəs] *a* senza denaro, povero.
impede [im'pi:d] *vt* impedire, ostacolare.
impediment [im'pedimənt] *n* impedimento, ostacolo.
impel [im'pel] *vt* costringere, spingere.
impend [im'pend] *vi* sovrastare, incombere.
impenetrable [im'penitrəbl] *a* impenetrabile.
impenitent [im'penitənt] *a* impenitente.
imperative [im'perətiv] *a n* imperativo.
imperceptible [,impə'septəbl] *a* impercettibile.
imperfect [im'pə:fikt] *a n* imperfetto.
imperfection [,impə'fekʃən] *n* imperfezione.
imperial [im'piəriəl] *a* imperiale; *n* (*beard*) pizzo; imperiale.
imperialism [im'piəriəlizəm] *n* imperialismo.
imperil [im'peril] *vt* mettere in pericolo.
imperious [im'piəriəs] *a* imperioso.
imperishable [im'periʃəbl] *a* imperituro.
impermeable [im'pə:miəbl] *a* impermeabile.
impersonal [im'pə:snl] *a* impersonale.
impersonate [im'pə:səneit] *vt* interpretare, impersonare.
impertinence [im'pə:tinəns] *n* impertinenza.
impertinent [im'pə:tinənt] *a* impertinente.
imperturbable [,impə:'tə:bəbl] *a* imperturbabile.
impervious ['im'pə:viəs] *a* impervio, inaccessibile (*also fig*).
impetuosity [im,petju'ɔsiti] *n* impetuosità.
impetuous [im'petjuəs] *a* impetuoso.
impetus ['impitəs] *n* impeto.
impiety [im'paiəti] *n* empietà.
impinge [im'pindʒ] *vi* venire in urto (con); interferire (in).
impious ['impiəs] *a* empio.
implacable [im'plækəbl] *a* implacabile.
implant [im'plɑ:nt] *vt* impiantare, instillare.
implement ['implimənt] *n* arnese, utensile; *vt* ['impliment] effettuare, completare.
implicate ['implikeit] *vt* implicare.
implication [,impli'keiʃən] *n* implicazione; **by i.** implicitamente, per induzione.
implicit [im'plisit] *a* implicito.
implicitly [im'plisitli] *ad* implicitamente.
implied [im'plaid] *a* implicito, sottinteso.
imploration [,implɔ:'reiʃən] *n* implorazione.
implore [im'plɔ:] *vt* implorare.
imply [im'plai] *vt* implicare, significare; insinuare.
impolite [,impə'lait] *a* scortese, sgarbato.
import ['impɔ:t] *n* (articolo di) importazione; importanza; significa-

to; *vt* [im'pɔ:t] significare; (*com*) importare.
importance [im'pɔ:təns] *n* importanza.
important [im'pɔ:tənt] *a* importante.
importation [,impɔ:'teiʃən] *n* importazione.
importer [im'pɔ:tə] *n* importatore.
importunate [im'pɔ:tjunit] *a* importuno, insistente.
importune [,impɔ:'tju:n] *vt* importunare.
impose [im'pouz] *vt* imporre.
imposing [im'pouziŋ] *a* maestoso, imponente.
imposition [,impə'ziʃən] *n* imposizione, imposta; inganno.
impossibility [im,pɔsə'biliti] *n* impossibilità.
impossible [im'pɔsəbl] *a* impossibile.
impostor [im'pɔstə] *n* impostore.
imposture [im'pɔstʃə] *n* impostura, inganno.
impotence ['impətəns] *n* impotenza.
impotent ['impətənt] *a* impotente.
impound [im'paund] *vt* sequestrare, confiscare.
impoverish [im'pɔvəriʃ] *vt* impoverire.
impracticable [im'præktikəbl] *a* impraticabile.
impregnable [im'pregnəbl] *a* impregnabile.
impregnate [im'pregneit] *vt* impregnare.
impress [im'pres] *vt* imprimere, impressionare.
impression [im'preʃən] *n* impressione, impronta; stampa.
impressionability [im,preʃnə'biliti] *n* impressionabilità, sensibilità.
impressionable [im'preʃnəbl] *a* impressionabile.
impressive [im'presiv] *a* impressionante, solenne.
imprint [im'print] *vt* imprimere, stampare; *n* ['imprint] impressione; impronta; stampa.
imprison [im'prizn] *vt* imprigionare.
imprisonment [im'priznmənt] *n* prigionia, carcere.
improbable [im'prɔbəbl] *a* improbabile.
impromptu [im'prɔmptju:] *a* improvvisato, estemporaneo; *ad* all'impronto, estemporaneamente.
improper [im'prɔpə] *a* improprio, sconveniente, scorretto.
impropriety [,imprə'praiəti] *n* improprietà, sconvenienza.
improve [im'pru:v] *vti* migliorare.
improvement [im'pru:vmənt] *n* miglioramento, progresso, progressi *pl*.
improvidence [im'prɔvidəns] *n* imprevidenza.
improvident [im'prɔvidənt] *a* imprevidente.
improvise ['imprəvaiz] *vt* improvvisare.
imprudence [im'pru:dəns] *n* imprudenza.
imprudent [im'pru:dənt] *a* imprudente.
impudence ['impjudəns] *n* impudenza, sfacciataggine.
impudent ['impjudənt] *a* impudente, sfacciato.
impulse ['impʌls] *n* impulso.
impulsive [im'pʌlsiv] *a* impulsivo.
impulsiveness [im'pʌlsivnis] *n* impulsività.
impunity [im'pju:niti] *n* impunità.
impure [im'pjuə] *a* impuro.
impurity [im'pjuəriti] *n* impurità.
imputation [,impu:'teiʃən] *n* imputazione.
impute [im'pju:t] *vt* imputare, attribuire.
in [in] *prep ad* a, in, entro, dentro, durante, secondo.
inability [,inə'biliti] *n* inabilità.
inaccessible [,inæk'sesəbl] *a* inaccessibile.
inaccuracy [in'ækjurəsi] *n* inaccuratezza, imprecisione.
inaccurate [in'ækjurit] *a* inaccurato, impreciso.
inaction [in'ækʃən] *n* inattività.
inactive [in'æktiv] *a* inattivo.
inadequate [in'ædikwit] *a* inadeguato, insufficiente.
inadmissible [,inəd'misəbl] *a* inammissibile.
inadvertent [,inəd'və:tənt] *a* involontario.
inane [i'nein] *a* inane, sciocco, vacuo.
inanimate [in'ænimit] *a* inanimato.
inanity [i'næniti] *n* inanità, vacuità.
inapplicable [in'æplikəbl] *a* inapplicabile.
inappropriate [,inə'proupriit] *a* non appropriato, improprio.
inapt ['in'æpt] *a* inadatto, inetto.
inarticulate [,inɑ:'tikjulit] *a* inarticolato, indistinto.
inasmuch as [inəz'mʌtʃæz] *ad* visto che, poichè, in quanto che.
inattention [,inə'tenʃən] *n* disattenzione, distrazione.
inattentive [,inə'tentiv] *a* disattento, distratto.
inaudible [in'ɔ:dəbl] *a* impercettibile, inafferabile.
inaugurate [i'nɔ:gjureit] *vt* inaugurare.
inborn ['in'bɔ:n] *a* innato.
inbreeding ['in'bri:diŋ] *n* incrocio tra animali affini.
incalculable [in'kælkjuləbl] *a* incalcolabile.
incandescence [,inkæn'desns] *n* incandescenza.
incandescent [,inkæn'desnt] *a* incandescente.
incantation [,inkæn'teiʃən] *n* incantesimo, parole magiche.
incapability [in,keipə'biliti] *n* incapacità, inettitudine.

incapable [in'keipəbl] *a* incapace, inetto.
incapacitate [,inkə'pæsiteit] *vt* rendere inabile, incapace.
incapacity [,inkə'pæsiti] *n* inabilità, incapacità.
incarcerate [in'kɑ:səreit] *vt* incarcerare.
incarceration [in,kɑ:sə'reiʃən] *n* incarcerazione.
incarnate [in'kɑ:nit] *a* incarnato; *vt* ['inkɑ:neit] incarnare.
incautious [in'kɔ:ʃəs] *a* incauto.
incendiary [in'sendjəri] *a n* incendiario.
incense ['insens] *n* incenso; *vt* [in'sens] incensare; *vi* fare arrabbiare.
incentive [in'sentiv] *n* incentivo, motivo.
incessant [in'sesnt] *a* continuo, incessante.
incest ['insest] *n* incesto.
incestuous [in'sestjuəs] *a* incestuoso.
inch [intʃ] *n* pollice (*misura lineare = cm* 2,54); *vt* spostarsi gradatamente.
incidence ['insidəns] *n* incidenza.
incident ['insidənt] *n* avvenimento, episodio, incidente; *a* incidente, inerente.
incidental [,insi'dentl] *a* casuale, fortuito.
incision [in'siʒən] *n* incisione.
incisive [in'saisiv] *a* incisivo, penetrante.
incite [in'sait] *vt* incitare, stimolare.
incitement [in'saitmənt] *n* incitamento, stimolo.
incivility [,insi'viliti] *n* scortesia.
inclemency [in'klemənsi] *n* inclemenza.
inclement ['inklemənt] *a* inclemente.
inclination [,inkli'neiʃən] *n* inclinazione, propensità; pendio.
incline [in'klain] *n* pendio, piano inclinato; *vti* inclinare, essere incline.
include [in'klu:d] *vt* includere, comprendere.
inclusion [in'klu:ʒən] *n* inclusione.
inclusive [in'klu:siv] *a* compreso, inclusivo.
incoherence [,inkou'hiərəns] *n* incoerenza.
incoherent [,inkou'hiərənt] *a* incoerente.
income ['inkəm] *n* reddito, entrata.
incoming ['in,kʌmiŋ] *a* entrante, che succede ad altri; *n* l'entrare, il flusso; *pl* entrate.
incommunicability [,inkə'mju:nikəbiliti] *n* incomunicabilità.
incomparable [in'kɔmpərəbl] *a* incomparabile.
incompatible [,inkəm'pætəbl] *a* incompatibile.
incompetence [in'kɔmpitəns] *n* incompetenza.
incompetent [in'kɔmpitənt] *a* incompetente.
incomplete [,inkəm'pli:t] *a* incompleto, incompiuto.
incomprehensible [in,kɔmpri'hensəbl] *a* incomprensibile.
inconceivable [,inkən'si:vəbl] *a* inconcepibile.
inconclusive [,inkən'klu:siv] *a* inconcludente.
incongruous [in'kɔŋgruəs] *a* incongruo.
inconsequent [in'kɔnsikwənt] *a* illogico, inconseguente.
inconsequential [in'kɔnsikwəntʃəl] *a* inconseguente, irrilevante.
inconsiderable [,inkən'sidərəbl] *a* trascurabile.
inconsiderate [,inkən'sidərit] *a* sconsiderato; senza riguardi.
inconsistent [,inkən'sistənt] *a* inconsistente, incompatibile.
inconsolable [,inkən'souləbl] *a* inconsolabile.
inconspicuous [,inkən'spikjuəs] *a* incospicuo, insignificante.
inconstancy [in'kɔnstənsi] *n* incostanza.
inconstant [in'kɔnstənt] *a* incostante.
incontinent [in'kɔntinənt] *a* incontinente.
inconvenience [,inkən'vi:niəns] *n* disturbo, inconveniente, disagio; *vt* incomodare, disturbare.
inconvenient [,inkən'vi:niənt] *a* incomodo, scomodo.
inconvertible [,inkən'və:təbl] *a* inconvertibile.
incorporate [in'kɔ:pəreit] *vt* incorporare; *a* [in'kɔ:pərit] unito in corporazione.
incorporeal [,inkɔ:'pɔ:riəl] *a* immateriale, incorporeo.
incorrect [,inkə'rekt] *a* inesatto, scorretto, sbagliato.
incorrectness [,inkə'rektnis] *n* inesattezza, scorrettezza.
incorrigible [in'kɔridʒəbl] *a* incorreggibile.
incorruptible [,inkə'rʌptəbl] *a* incorruttibile.
increase ['inkri:s] *n* aumento, incremento; *vti* [in'kri:s] aumentare, (far) crescere.
incredible [in'kredəbl] *a* incredibile.
incredulity [,inkri'dju:liti] *n* incredulità.
incredulous [in'kredjuləs] *a* incredulo.
increment ['inkrimənt] *n* incremento, guadagno.
incriminate [in'krimineit] *vt* incriminare, incolpare.
incubate ['inkjubeit] *vti* covare; essere in incubazione.
incubation [,inkju'beiʃən] *n* incubazione.
incubator ['inkjubeitə] *n* incubatrice.
inculcate ['inkʌlkeit] *vt* inculcare.
inculpate ['inkʌlpeit] *vt* incolpare.
incumbent [in'kʌmbənt] *a* incombente, obbligatorio; *n* titolare d'un beneficio ecclesiastico.

incur [in'kə:] *vt* incorrere in.
incurable [in'kjuərəbl] *a* incurabile.
incursion [in'kə:ʃən] *n* incursione.
indebted [in'detid] *a* indebitato, grato.
indecency [in'di:snsi] *n* indecenza.
indecent [in'di:snt] *a* indecente.
indecipherable ['indi'saifərəbl] *a* indecifrabile.
indecision [,indi'siʒən] *n* indecisione.
indecisive [,indi'saisiv] *a* indeciso, non decisivo.
indecorous [in'dekərəs] *a* indecoroso, sconveniente.
indeed [in'di:d] *ad* davvero, infatti, in realtà.
indefatigable [,indi'fætigəbl] *a* instancabile.
indefensible [,indi'fensəbl] *a* indefensibile.
indefinite [in'definit] *a* indefinito.
indelible [in'delibl] *a* indelebile.
indelicacy [in'delikəsi] *n* indelicatezza.
indelicate [in'delikit] *a* indelicato.
indemnify [in'demnifai] *vt* indennizzare, risarcire.
indemnity [in'demniti] *n* indennità, risarcimento.
indent ['indent] *n* dentellatura, tacca; contratto, documento; requisizione; *vti* [in'dent] dentellare, intaccare; stendere un documento in due copie; requisire.
indentation [,inden'teiʃən] *n* dentellatura.
indenture [in'dentʃə] *n* dentellatura; contratto.
independence [,indi'pendəns] *n* indipendenza.
independent [,indi'pendənt] *a* indipendente.
independently [,indi'pendəntli] *ad* indipendentemente, separatamente.
indescribable [indis'kraibəbl] *a* indescrivibile.
indestructible [,indis'trʌktəbl] *a* indistruttibile.
indeterminate [,indi'tə:minit] *a* indeterminato.
index ['indeks] *n* indice.
India ['indiə] *n* India.
Indian ['indiən] *a n* indiano.
indicate ['indikeit] *vt* indicare.
indication [,indi'keiʃən] *n* indicazione, segno, sintomo.
indicative [in'dikətiv] *a* indicativo, che indica.
indicator ['indikeitə] *n* indicatore; **mileage i.** contachilometri.
indict [in'dait] *vt* accusare.
indictment [in'daitmənt] *n* accusa, imputazione.
indifference [in'difrəns] *n* indifferenza.
indifferent [in'difrənt] *a* indifferente, mediocre.
indigence ['indidʒəns] *n* indigenza.
indigenous [in'didʒinəs] *a* indigeno.
indigent ['indidʒənt] *a* indigente.
indigestible [,indi'dʒestəbl] *a* indigeribile, indigesto.
indigestion [,indi'dʒestʃən] *n* imbarazzo di stomaco; dispepsia.
indignant [in'dignənt] *a* indignato, sdegnato.
indignantly [in'dignəntli] *ad* con indignazione, con sdegno.
indignation [,indig'neiʃən] *n* indignazione, sdegno.
indignity [in'digniti] *n* offesa, trattamento indegno.
indigo ['indigou] *n* indaco.
indirect [,indi'rekt] *a* indiretto.
indiscernible [,indi'sə:nəbl] *a* indiscernibile.
indiscreet [,indis'kri:t] *a* indiscreto; sconsiderato.
indiscretion [,indis'kreʃən] *n* indiscrezione; imprudenza.
indiscriminate [,indis'kriminit] *a* indiscriminato.
indispensable [,indis'pensəbl] *a* indispensabile.
indispose [,indis'pouz] *vt* indisporre.
indisposed [,indis'pouzd] *a* indisposto; maldisposto.
indisposition [,indispə'ziʃən] *n* indisposizione.
indisputable ['indis'pju:təbl] *a* indiscutibile, sicuro.
indisputed ['indis'pju:tid] *a* indiscusso.
indissoluble [,indi'sɔljubl] *a* indissolubile.
indistinct [,indis'tiŋkt] *a* indistinto, confuso.
indistinctness [,indis'tiŋktnis] *n* mancanza di chiarezza.
indistinguishable [,indis'tiŋgwiʃəbl] *a* indistinguibile.
indite [in'dait] *vt* comporre, redigere.
individual [,indi'vidjuəl] *a* singolo, individuale; *n* individuo.
individuality [,indi,vidju'æliti] *n* individualità.
indivisible [,indi'vizəbl] *a* indivisibile.
Indo-China ['indou'tʃainə] *n* Indocina.
Indo-Chinese ['indou'tʃai'ni:z] *a n* indocinese.
indolence ['indələns] *n* indolenza.
indolent ['indələnt] *a* indolente.
indomitable [in'dɔmitəbl] *a* indomabile; indomito.
indoor ['indɔ:] *a* che ha luogo in casa, da eseguirsi in casa; **indoors** *ad* dentro, in casa.
indrawn ['in'drɔ:n] *a* chiuso in se stesso, introverso.
indubitable [in'dju:bitəbl] *a* indubitabile.
induce [in'dju:s] *vt* indurre.
inducement [in'dju:smənt] *n* allettamento, incentivo.
induction [in'dʌkʃən] *n* induzione; investitura.
inductive [in'dʌktiv] *a* induttivo.
indulge [in'dʌldʒ] *vti* indulgere,

lasciar libero corso a; abbandonarsi.
indulgence [in'dʌldʒəns] *n* indulgenza, compiacenza; licenza.
indulgent [in'dʌldʒənt] *a* indulgente.
industrial [in'dʌstriəl] *a* industriale.
industrialist [in'dʌstriəlist] *n* industriale.
industrialization [in'dʌstriəlai'zeiʃən] *n* industrializzazione.
industrious [in'dʌstriəs] *a* attivo, operoso.
industry ['indəstri] *n* industria, attività.
inebriate [i'ni:briit] *vt* inebriare, ubriacare.
ineffable [in'efəbl] *a* ineffabile.
ineffective [,ini'fektiv] *a* inefficace.
ineffectual [,ini'fektjuəl] *a* inefficace, vano.
inefficacy [in'efikəsi] *n* inefficacia.
inefficiency [,ini'fiʃənsi] *n* inefficienza; inefficacia; incapacità.
inefficient [,ini'fiʃənt] *a* inefficiente, poco capace.
inelegant [in'eligənt] *a* inelegante.
ineligible [in'elidʒəbl] *a* ineleggibile.
inept [i'nept] *a* inetto.
ineptitude [i'neptitju:d] *n* inettitudine.
inequality [,ini:'kwɔliti] *n* ineguaglianza.
inert [i'nə:t] *a* inerte.
inertia [i'nə:ʃjə] *n* inerzia.
inertness [i'nə:tnis] *n* inerzia, apatia.
inestimable [in'estiməbl] *a* inestimabile.
inevitability [in,evitə'biliti] *n* inevitabilità.
inevitable [in'evitəbl] *a* inevitabile.
inexact [,inig'zækt] *a* inesatto.
inexcusable [,iniks'kju:zəbl] *a* imperdonabile.
inexhaustible [,inig'zɔ:stəbl] *a* inesauribile.
inexorable [in'eksərəbl] *a* inesorabile.
inexpensive [,iniks'pensiv] *a* poco costoso, a buon mercato.
inexperience [,iniks'piəriəns] *n* inesperienza.
inexperienced [,iniks'piəriənst] *a* inesperto.
inexplicable [in'eksplikəbl] *a* inesplicabile, inspiegabile.
inexpressible [,iniks'presəbl] *a* inesprimibile.
inexpressive [,iniks'presiv] *a* inespressivo.
infallibility [in,fælə'biliti] *n* infallibilità.
infallible [in'fæləbl] *a* infallibile.
infamous ['infəməs] *a* infame.
infamy ['infəmi] *n* infamia.
infancy ['infənsi] *n* infanzia.
infant ['infənt] *a* infantile, nascente; *n* neonato, bambino, infante.
infantry ['infəntri] *n* fanteria.
infatuate [in'fætjueit] *vt* infatuare.
infatuated [in'fætjueitid] *a* infatuato; fanatico di.
infatuation [in,fætju'eiʃən] *n* infatuazione.
infect [in'fekt] *vt* infettare.
infection [in'fekʃən] *n* infezione.
infectious [in'fekʃəs] *a* infettivo, contagioso.
infer [in'fə:] *vt* inferire, dedurre.
inference ['infərəns] *n* conclusione, deduzione.
inferior [in'fiəriə] *a n* inferiore.
inferiority [in,fiəri'ɔriti] *n* inferiorità.
infernal [in'fə:nl] *a* infernale.
infertile [in'fə:tail] *a* improduttivo, non fertile.
infest [in'fest] *vt* infestare.
infidel ['infidəl] *a n* infedele, miscredente.
infidelity [,infi'deliti] *n* infedeltà.
infiltrate ['infiltreit] *vti* infiltrar(si).
infinite ['infinit] *a n* infinito.
infinitive [in'finitiv] *a n* (*gram*) infinito.
infinity [in'finiti] *n* infinità.
infirm [in'fə:m] *a* infermo, debole; irresoluto.
infirmary [in'fə:məri] *n* infermeria, ospedale.
infirmity [in'fə:miti] *n* infermità; irresolutezza.
inflame [in'fleim] *vt* infiammare.
inflammable [in'flæməbl] *a* infiammabile.
inflammation [,inflə'meiʃən] *n* infiammazione.
inflammatory [in'flæmətəri] *a* infiammatorio.
inflate [in'fleit] *vti* gonfiare, gonfiarsi.
inflation [in'fleiʃən] *n* gonfiamento; inflazione.
inflect [in'flekt] *vt* inflettere.
inflection [in'flekʃən] *n* inflessione.
inflexible [in'fleksəbl] *a* inflessibile rigido.
inflict [in'flikt] *vt* infliggere.
infliction [in'flikʃən] *n* inflizione.
influence ['influəns] *n* ascendente, influenza, influsso; *vt* influenzare.
influential [,influ'enʃəl] *a* influente, autorevole.
influenza [,influ'enzə] *n* (*med*) influenza.
influx ['inflʌks] *n* afflusso, flusso.
inform [in'fɔ:m] *vt* informare.
informal [in'fɔ:ml] *a* non ufficiale, senza formalità; irregolare.
informality [,infɔ:'mæliti] *n* assenza di formalità; (*leg*) irregolarità.
informant [in'fɔ:mənt] *n* informatore.
information [,infə'meiʃən] *n* informazione, informazioni *pl*; accusa.
informer [in'fɔ:mə] *n* delatore.
infrequent [in'fri:kwənt] *a* infrequente, raro.
infringe [in'frindʒ] *vt* trasgredire.
infringement [in'frindʒmənt] *n* infrazione, trasgressione.
infuriate [in'fjuərieit] *vt* infuriare, rendere furioso.

infuse [in'fju:z] *vt* infondere, instillare, mettere in infusione; stare in infusione.
infusion [in'fju:ʒən] *n* infusione, infuso.
ingenious [in'dʒi:niəs] *a* ingegnoso.
ingenuity [,indʒi'nju:iti] *n* abilità inventiva, ingegnosità.
ingenuous [in'dʒenjuəs] *a* ingenuo; **ingenuousness** *n* ingenuità.
ingle-nook ['iŋglnuk] *n* angolo del focolare.
inglorious [in'glɔ:riəs] *a* inglorioso.
ingot ['iŋgət] *n* lingotto.
ingrained ['in'greind] *a* radicato; inveterato.
ingratiate [in'greiʃieit] *vt* ingraziarsi.
ingratitude [in'grætitju:d] *n* ingratitudine.
ingredient [in'gri:diənt] *n* ingrediente.
inhabit [in'hæbit] *vt* abitare, occupare.
inhabitable [in'hæbitəbl] *a* abitabile.
inhabitant [in'hæbitənt] *n* abitante.
inhale [in'heil] *vt* aspirare.
inhaler [in'heilə] *n* inalatore.
inhere [in'hiə] *vi* essere inerente.
inherent [in'hiərənt] *a* inerente, intrinseco.
inherit [in'herit] *vti* ereditare.
inheritance [in'heritəns] *n* eredità.
inhibit [in'hibit] *vt* inibire, impedire.
inhibition [,inhi'biʃən] *n* inibizione.
inhospitable [in'hɔspitəbl] *a* inospitale.
inhuman [in'hju:mən] *a* barbaro, inumano.
inhumanity [,inhu:'mæniti] *n* inumanità.
inimical [i'nimikəl] *a* nemico, ostile.
inimitable [i'nimitəbl] *a* inimitabile.
iniquity [i'nikwiti] *n* iniquità.
initial [i'niʃəl] *a n* iniziale; *vt* firmare con le sole iniziali.
initiate [i'niʃiit] *n* iniziato; *vt* [i'niʃieit] iniziare.
initiation [i,niʃi'eiʃən] *n* iniziazione.
initiative [i'niʃiətiv] *n* iniziativa.
inject [in'dʒekt] *vt* iniettare.
injection [in'dʒekʃən] *n* iniezione.
injudicious [,indʒu:'diʃəs] *a* sconsiderato, avventato.
injunction [in'dʒʌŋkʃən] *n* ingiunzione.
injure ['indʒə] *vt* danneggiare, ferire, nuocere a.
injurious [in'dʒuəriəs] *a* nocivo, ingiurioso.
injury ['indʒəri] *n* ferita, torto, danno.
injustice [in'dʒʌstis] *n* ingiustizia.
ink [iŋk] *n* inchiostro; **inkstand** calamaio; **inkwell** calamaio, infisso.
inkling ['iŋkliŋ] *n* indizio, sospetto.
inky ['iŋki] *a* d'inchiostro, nero come l'inchiostro, macchiato d'inchiostro.
inland ['inlənd] *a n* (di un paese) interno, nell'interno, verso l'interno; **i. revenue** fisco.
inlay ['inlei] *n* intarsio; *vt* intarsiare.
inlet ['inlet] *n* insenatura, piccola baia.
inmate ['inmeit] *n* inquilino; persona alloggiata in un istituto.
inmost ['inmoust] *a* il più interno, profondo.
inn [in] *n* albergo, locanda; **innkeeper** locandiere, oste.
innate ['i'neit] *a* innato, istintivo.
inner ['inə] *a* interiore, interno.
innocence ['inəsns] *n* innocenza.
innocent ['inəsnt] *a n* innocente.
innocuous [i'nɔkjuəs] *a* innocuo.
innovate ['inouveit] *vt* innovare.
innovation [,inou'veiʃən] *n* innovazione.
innuendo [,inju:'endou] *n* allusione, insinuazione.
innumerable [i'nju:mərəbl] *a* innumerevole.
inoculate [i'nɔkjuleit] *vt* inoculare; vaccinare; innestare; inculcare.
inoculation [i,nɔkju'leiʃən] *n* inoculazione.
inoffensive [,inə'fensiv] *a* inoffensivo.
inopportune [in'ɔpətju:n] *a* inopportuno, intempestivo.
inordinate [i'nɔ:dinit] *a* eccessivo, smoderato.
in-patient ['in,peiʃənt] *n* ammalato degente in ospedale.
input ['input] *n* (*mech, el*) entrata, alimentazione; **i. energy** energia immessa.
inquest ['inkwest] *n* inchiesta.
inquire [in'kwaiə] *vt* domandare; *vi* indagare, informarsi, fare ricerche *pl*.
inquiringly [in'kwaiəriŋli] *ad* interrogativamente, con aria interrogativa.
inquiry [in'kwaiəri] *n* investigazione, inchiesta.
inquisition [,inkwi'ziʃən] *n* inquisizione.
inquisitive [iŋ'kwizitiv] *a* curioso, indagatore.
inquisitively [in'kwizitivli] *ad* con curiosità; indiscretamente.
inquisitor [in'kwizitə] *n* inquisitore.
inroad ['inroud] *n* incursione; scorreria, sottrazione.
insane [in'sein] *a* folle, pazzo.
insanity [in'sæniti] *n* follia, pazzia.
insatiable [in'seiʃjəbl] *a* insaziabile.
inscribe [in'skraib] *vt* iscrivere; incidere.
inscription [in'skripʃən] *n* iscrizione.
inscrutable [in'skru:təbl] *a* inscrutabile.
insect ['insekt] *n* insetto.
insecticide [in'sektisaid] *n* insetticida.
insecure [,insi'kjuə] *a* malsicuro.
insecurity [,insi'kjuəriti] *n* mancanza di sicurezza.
insemination [in,semi'neiʃən] *n*

(*med*) fecondazione; **artificial i.** fecondazione artificiale.
insensibility [in,sensə'biliti] *n* incoscienza, insensibilità.
insensible [in'sensəbl] *a* inconscio; insensibile; privo di sensi.
insensitive [in'sensitiv] *a* insensibile.
inseparable [in'sepərəbl] *a* inseparabile.
insert [in'sə:t] *vt* inserire.
insertion [in'sə:ʃən] *n* inserzione, aggiunta.
inside ['in'said] *a* interno, interiore; *n* interno; *ad* dentro; *prep* dentro; **i. out** rivoltato, a rovescio.
insider ['in'saidə] *n* chi è addentro, iniziato.
insidious [in'sidiəs] *a* insidioso.
insight ['insait] *n* penetrazione, intuito.
insignificant [.insig'nifikənt] *a* insignificante.
insincere [.insin'siə] *a* insincero, falso.
insincerity [.insin'seriti] *n* insincerità, falsità.
insinuate [in'sinjueit] *vt* insinuare; introdurre.
insinuation [in.sinju'eiʃən] *n* insinuazione.
insipid [in'sipid] *a* insipido, insulso.
insipidity [.insi'piditi] *n* insipidezza; insulsaggine.
insist [in'sist] *vi* insistere.
insistence [in'sistəns] *n* insistenza.
insistent [in'sistənt] *a* insistente.
insolence ['insələns] *n* insolenza.
insolent ['insələnt] *a* insolente.
insoluble [in'sɔljubl] *a* insolubile.
insolvency [in'sɔlvənsi] *n* insolvenza.
insolvent [in'sɔlvənt] *a* insolvente.
insomnia [in'sɔmniə] *n* insonnia.
inspect [in'spekt] *vt* ispezionare, controllare.
inspection [in'spekʃən] *n* ispezione, controllo.
inspector [in'spektə] *n* ispettore, controllore.
inspiration [.inspə'reiʃən] *n* ispirazione.
inspire [in'spaiə] *vt* ispirare.
instability [.instə'biliti] *n* instabilità.
install [in'stɔ:l] *vt* installare, insediare.
installation [.instə'leiʃən] *n* insediamento; (*el etc*) impianto, installazione.
installment [in'stɔ:lmənt] *n* rata; puntata; **i. plan** (sistema di) vendita a rate.
instance ['instəns] *n* esempio, istanza; **for i.** ad esempio.
instant ['instənt] *a* immediato; (*month*) corrente; *n* istante, momento.
instantaneous [.instən'teiniəs] *a* istantaneo.
instantly ['instəntli] *ad* immediatamente.
instead [in'sted] *ad* invece (di).
instep ['instep] *n* collo del piede.
instigate ['instigeit] *vt* istigare.
instigation [.insti'geiʃən] *n* istigazione.
instigator ['instigeitə] *n* istigatore, istigatrice.
instill [in'stil] *vt* instillare.
instinct ['instiŋkt] *n* istinto.
instinctive [in'stiŋktiv] *a* istintivo.
institute ['institju:t] *n* istituto, istituzione; *vt* istituire.
institution [.insti'tju:ʃən] *n* istituzione, ente; (*eccl*) nomina.
instruct [in'strʌkt] *vt* istruire, informare.
instruction [in'strʌkʃən] *n* istruzione, insegnamento; *pl* istruzione, disposizione.
instructive [in'strʌktiv] *a* istruttivo.
instructor [in'strʌktə] *n* istruttore, maestro, lettore universitario; **instructress** maestra, insegnante.
instrument ['instrumənt] *n* strumento; arnese.
instrumental [.instru'mentl] *a* strumentale.
insubordinate [.insə'bɔ:dnit] *a* insubordinato, indisciplinato.
insufficiency [.insə'fiʃənsi] *n* insufficienza.
insufficient [.insə'fiʃənt] *a* insufficiente.
insular ['insjulə] *a* insulare.
insulate ['insjuleit] *vt* isolare.
insulation [.insju'leiʃən] *n* isolamento.
insult ['insʌlt] *n* insulto; *vt* [in'sʌlt] insultare.
insuperable [in'sju:pərəbl] *a* insuperabile, insormontabile.
insurance [in'ʃuərəns] *n* (*com*) assicurazione.
insure [in'ʃuə] *vt* assicurare.
insurer [in'ʃuərə] *n* (*com*) assicuratore.
insurgency [in'sə:dʒənsi] *n* sollevarsi; insurrezione.
insurgent [in'sə:dʒənt] *a n* insorto.
insurmountable [.insə:'mauntəbl] *a* insormontabile.
insurrection [.insə'rekʃən] *n* insurrezione.
intact [in'tækt] *a* intatto, intero.
intake ['inteik] *n* immissione; presa (*pump*) aspirazione.
intangible [in'tændʒəbl] *a* intangibile.
integer ['intidʒə] *n* numero intero.
integral ['intigrəl] *a n* integrale.
integrate ['intigreit] *a* integrale, intero; *vt* integrare, completare.
integration [.inti'greiʃən] *n* integrazione.
integrity [in'tegriti] *n* integrità.
intellect ['intilekt] *n* intelletto.
intellectual [.inti'lektjuəl] *a n* intellettuale.
intelligence [in'telidʒəns] *n* intelligenza; informazioni *pl*, notizie *pl*.
intelligent [in'telidʒənt] *a* intelligente.

intelligentsia [in,teli'dʒentsiə] *n* intellettuali, classe colta.
intelligibility [in,telidʒə'biliti] *n* intelligibilità.
intelligible [in'telidʒəbl] *a* intelligibile; comprensibile; chiaro.
intemperance [in'tempərəns] *n* intemperanza.
intemperate [in'tempərit] *a* smoderato, violento; dedito al bere; (*climate*) rigido.
intend [in'tend] *vti* intendere, proporsi.
intended [in'tendid] *a* intenzionale, deliberato.
intense [in'tens] *a* intenso; (*fig*) profondo, ipersensibile.
intensification [in,tensifi'keiʃən] *n* intensificazione.
intensify [in'tensifai] *vti* intensificar (si).
intensity [in'tensiti] *n* intensità.
intensive [in'tensiv] *a* intensivo, intenso.
intent [in'tent] *a* intento; *n* scopo.
intention [in'tenʃən] *n* intenzione, proposito.
intentional [in'tenʃənl] *a* intenzionale, premeditato.
inter [in'tə:] *vt* interrare, seppellire.
interact [,intər'ækt] *vt* esercitare azione reciproca.
interaction [,intər'ækʃən] *n* azione reciproca.
intercede [,intə:'si:d] *vi* intercedere.
intercept [,intə:'sept] *vt* intercettare.
interception [,intə:'sepʃən] *n* intercettamento; interruzione.
interchange ['intə:'tʃeindʒ] *n* scambio; *vti* scambiar(si).
interchangeable [,intə:'tʃeindʒəbl] *a* scambievole.
intercourse ['intə:kɔ:s] *n* relazione, rapporto; **sexual i.** rapporti sessuali *pl*.
interdependent [,intədi'pendənt] *a* interdipendente.
interdict ['intə:dikt] *n* interdetto (papale); *vt* [,intə:'dikt] interdire, vietare.
interdiction [,intə:'dikʃən] *n* divieto, interdizione, interdetto.
interest ['intrist] *n* interesse, interessi *pl*, interessamento; *vt* interessare.
interesting ['intristiŋ] *a* interessante.
interfere [,intə'fiə] *vi* intervenire, intromettersi, ostacolare, interferire.
interference [,intə'fiərəns] *n* interferenza, ingerenza, intralcio.
interim ['intərim] *n* interim, lasso di tempo; *ad* nel frattempo; *a* provvisorio, temporaneo.
interior [in'tiəriə] *a* interiore, interno; *n* interno.
interject [,intə:'dʒekt] *vti* interporre.
interjection [,intə:'dʒekʃən] *n* interiezione; (*fig*) intromissione.
interlace [,intə:'leis] *vt* intrecciare.
interleave ['intəli:v] *vt* interfogliare.
interlock [,intə:'lɔk] *n* (*cin*) sincronizzazione; *vti* allacciar(si); (*cin*) sincronizzare.
interlocutor [,intə:'lɔkjutə] *n* interlocutore.
interloper ['intə:loupə] *n* intruso.
interlude ['intə:lu:d] *n* interludio, intervallo.
intermediate [,intə:'mi:diət] *a* intermedio.
interment [in'tə:mənt] *n* inumazione, seppellimento.
interminable [in'tə:minəbl] *a* interminabile.
intermingle [,intə:'miŋgl] *vti* inframmischiar(si).
intermission [,intə:'miʃən] *n* intervallo, interruzione, pausa.
intermittent [,intə:'mitənt] *a* intermittente.
intern [in'tə:n] *vt* internare.
internal [in'tə:nl] *a* interno; **i. revenue** fisco.
international [,intə:'næʃənl] *a n* internazionale.
internment [in'tə:nmənt] *n* internamento.
interpellation [in,tə:pe'leiʃən] *n* interpellanza.
interplay ['intə:'plei] *n* gioco (di colori etc.); azione reciproca.
interpolate [in'tə:pouleit] *vt* interpolare.
interpose [,intə:'pouz] *vti* interpor (si).
interpret [in'tə:prit] *vti* interpretare; fare da interprete.
interpreter [in'tə:pritə] *n* interprete.
interrogate [in'terəgeit] *vt* interrogare.
interrogation [in,terə'geiʃən] *n* interrogazione.
interrogative [,intə'rɔgətiv] *a n* interrogativo.
interrogatory [,intə'rɔgətəri] *a n* interrogatorio.
interrupt [,intə'rʌpt] *vt* interrompere.
interruption [,intə'rʌpʃən] *n* interruzione.
intersect [,intə:'sekt] *vti* intersecar (si).
intersection [,intə:'sekʃən] *n* intersecazione.
intersperse [,intə:'spə:s] *vt* spargere qua e là, disseminare, inframmezzare.
intertwine [,intə:'twain] *vti* intrecciar(si).
interval ['intəvəl] *n* intervallo.
intervene [,intə:'vi:n] *vi* intervenire, intromettersi; **intervening** interveniente; **in the intervening time** nel frattempo.
intervention [,intə:'venʃən] *n* intervento.
interview ['intəvju:] *n* intervista, abboccamento; *vt* intervistare.
intestate [in'testit] *a* intestato, senza disposizioni testamentarie.

intestinal [in'testinl] *a* intestinale.
intestine [in'testin] *a* intestino, interno; *n* intestino; *n pl* intestino.
intimacy ['intimәsi] *n* intimità.
intimate ['intimit] *a* intimo; *vt* ['intimeit] intimare, comunicare, suggerire.
intimation [,inti'meiʃәn] *n* intimazione, avviso.
intimidate [in'timideit] *vt* intimidire.
intimidation [in,timi'deiʃәn] *n* intimidazione.
into ['intu] *prep* in.
intolerable [in'tɔlәrәbl] *a* intollerabile.
intolerance [in'tɔlәrәns] *n* intolleranza.
intolerant [in'tɔlәrәnt] *a* intollerante.
intonation [,intou'neiʃәn] *n* intonazione.
intone [in'toun] *vt* intonare.
intoxicate [in'tɔksikeit] *vt* ubriacare, inebriare.
intoxication [in,tɔksi'keiʃәn] *n* ubriachezza, ebbrezza.
intransigent [in'trænsidʒәnt] *a* intransigente.
intrepid [in'trepid] *a* intrepido.
intrepidity [,intri'piditi] *n* intrepidità.
intricacy ['intrikәsi] *n* groviglio, viluppo.
intricate ['intrikit] *a* intricato, involuto.
intrigue [in'tri:g] *n* intrigo, macchinazione; *vi* intrigare, macchinare; *vt* (*sl*) stuzzicare la curiosità di.
intriguing [in'tri:giŋ] *a* intrigante; interessante.
intrinsic [in'trinsik] *a* intrinseco.
introduce [,intrә'dju:s] *vt* introdurre, presentare.
introduction [,intrә'dʌkʃәn] *n* introduzione, presentazione.
introductory [,intrә'dʌktәri] *a* introduttivo, preliminare.
introspection [,introu'spekʃәn] *n* introspezione.
introspective [,introu'spektiv] *a* introspettivo.
introvert ['introuvә:t] *a n* introvertito, introverso.
intrude [in'tru:d] *vti* intromettersi.
intruder [in'tru:dә] *n* intruso.
intrusion [in'tru:ʒәn] *n* intrusione.
intuition [,intju:'iʃәn] *n* intuito, intuizione.
intuitive [in'tju:itiv] *a* intuitivo.
inundate ['inʌndeit] *vt* inondare.
inure [i'njuә] *vt* indurire, abituare.
invade [in'veid] *vt* invadere.
invader [in'veidә] *n* invasore.
invalid ['invәli:d] *a n* invalido, infermo; *vt* (*mil*) riformare; [in'vælid] *a* non valido, nullo.
invalidate [in'vælideit] *vt* infirmare.
invalidity [,invә'liditi] *n* invalidità.
invaluable [in'væljuәbl] *a* inestimabile.
invariable [in'vєәriәbl] *a* invariabile.
invasion [in'veiʒәn] *n* invasione.
invective [in'vektiv] *n* invettiva.
inveigh [in'vei] *vi* inveire.
inveigle [in'vi:gl] *vt* adescare, sedurre.
invent [in'vent] *vt* inventare.
invention [in'venʃәn] *n* invenzione.
inventive [in'ventiv] *a* inventivo.
inventor [in'ventә] *n* inventore.
inventory ['invәntri] *n* inventario; *vt* inventariare.
inversion [in'vә:ʃәn] *n* inversione.
invert [in'vә:t] *vt* invertire.
invest [in'vest] *vt* investire.
investigate [in'vestigeit] *vti* investigare.
investigation [in,vesti'geiʃәn] *n* investigazione, indagine.
investigator [in'vestigeitә] *n* investigatore, investigatrice.
investiture [in'vestitʃә] *n* investitura.
investment [in'vestmәnt] *n* (*com*) investimento.
inveterate [in'vetәrit] *a* inveterato, ostinato.
invidious [in'vidiәs] *a* sgradevole, odioso.
invigorate [in'vigәreit] *vt* invigorire, rinforzare.
invincible [in'vinsәbl] *a* invincibile.
inviolate [in'vaiәlit] *a* inviolato.
invisible [in'vizәbl] *a* invisibile.
invitation [,invi'teiʃәn] *n* invito.
invite [in'vait] *vt* invitare.
inviting [in'vaitiŋ] *a* invitante, attraente.
invocation [,invou'keiʃәn] *n* invocazione.
invoice ['invɔis] *n* (*com*) fattura; *vt* (*com*) fatturare.
invoke [in'vouk] *vt* invocare.
involuntary [in'vɔlәntәri] *a* involontario.
involve [in'vɔlv] *vt* implicare, coinvolgere, comportare.
inward ['inwәd] *a* interno, intimo; verso l'interno.
inwardly ['inwәdli] *ad* internamente, (*fig*) intimamente.
iodine ['aiәdi:n] *n* iodio.
Ionian [ai'ouniәn] *a n* ionio.
irascible [i'ræsibl] *a* irascibile; irritabile.
irate [ai'reit] *a* irato.
Ireland ['aiә:lәnd] *n* Irlanda.
iris ['aiәris] *n* iride, (*bot*) iris, giaggiolo.
Irish ['aiәriʃ] *a n* irlandese
irksome ['ә:ksәm] *a* fastidioso, tedioso.
iron ['aiәn] *a* ferreo, di ferro, in ferro; *n* ferro; ferro da stiro; *vt* stirare; ferrare; **i. age** età del ferro; **i. industry** industria siderurgica; **i. foundry** fonderia; **i. ore** minerale di ferro.
ironclad ['aiәnklæd] *a* corazzato; *n* corazzata.
ironical [ai'rɔnikәl] *a* ironico.

ironmonger ['aiən,mʌŋgə] *n* negoziante in ferramenta.
ironmongery ['aiən,mʌŋgəri] *n* ferramenta.
ironwork ['aiənwəːk] *n* lavoro in ferro, costruzione in ferro.
irony ['aiərəni] *n* ironia.
irradiate [i'reidieit] *vti* irradiare.
irrational [i'ræʃənl] *a* irrazionale.
irreconcilable [i'rekənsailəbl] *a* irreconciliabile.
irrefutable [i'refjutəbl] *a* irrefutabile.
irregular [i'regjulə] *a* irregolare, anormale.
irrelevant [i'relivənt] *a* non appropriato, non pertinente.
irremovable [,iri'muːvəbl] *a* irremovibile.
irreparable [i'repərəbl] *a* irreparabile.
irreplaceable [,iri'pleisəbl] *a* insostituibile.
irrepressible [,iri'presəbl] *a* irreprimibile, irrefrenabile.
irreproachable [,iri'proutʃəbl] *a* irreprensibile.
irresistible [,iri'zistəbl] *a* irresistibile.
irresolute [i'rezəluːt] *a* irresoluto.
irresolution ['i,rezə'luːʃən] *n* irresolutezza.
irrespective [,iris'pektiv] *a* senza riguardo a.
irresponsible [,iris'pɔnsəbl] *a* irresponsabile.
irreverent [i'revərənt] *a* irriverente.
irrevocable [i'revəkəbl] *a* irrevocabile.
irrigate ['irigeit] *vt* irrigare.
irrigation [,iri'geiʃən] *n* irrigazione.
irritable ['iritəbl] *n* irritabile.
irritably ['iritəbli] *ad* irritabilmente.
irritant ['iritənt] *a n* irritante.
irritate ['iriteit] *vt* irritare.
irritation [,iri'teiʃən] *n* irritazione.
irruption [i'rʌpʃən] *n* irruzione.
Isabel ['izəbel] *nf pr* Isabella.
Islam ['izlɑːm] *n pr* Islam.
Islamic [iz'læmik] *a* islamico, maomettano.
island ['ailənd] *n* isola; (*road*) salvagente.
islander ['ailəndə] *n* isolano.
isolate ['aisəleit] *vt* isolare.
isolation [,aisə'leiʃən] *n* isolamento.
Israel ['izreiəl] *n* Israele.
Israeli [iz'reili] *a n* israeliano.
Israelite ['izriəlait] *n* israelita.
issue ['isjuː] *n* uscita, sbocco; (*notes etc*) emissione; (*publication*) tiratura, edizione; (*offspring*) discendenza; *vt* pubblicare; rilasciare; *vi* uscire.
isthmus ['isməs] *n* istmo.
it [it] *pron* esso, essa, lo, la; **its** *a* (il) suo, (la) sua; **itself** *pron* si, se stesso, se stessa.
Italian [i'tæliən] *a n* italiano.
italics [i'tæliks] *n pl* corsivo.
Italy ['itəli] *n* Italia.
itchy ['itʃi] *a* che prude.
itch [itʃ] *n* prurito, scabbia; *vi* prudere.
item ['aitəm] *n* articolo, numero; (*com*) voce.
iterate ['itəreit] *vt* ripetere.
itinerant [i'tinərənt] *a* ambulante, girovago.
itinerary [ai'tinərəri] *n* itinerario.
ivory ['aivəri] *a* di (in) avorio; *n* avorio.
ivy ['aivi] *n* edera.

J

jab [dʒæb] *vt* colpire con oggetto appuntito.
jabber ['dʒæbə] *vti* pronunciare rapidamente e indistintamente, mormorare, borbottare.
jack [dʒæk] *n* (*naut*) bandiera; (*mech*) cricco; (*spit*) girarrosto; (*cards*) fante; (*bowls*) boccino; **j. of all trades** factotum.
jackal ['dʒækɔːl] *n* sciacallo.
jackass ['dʒækæs] *n* somaro.
jackdaw ['dʒækdɔː] *n* cornacchia, taccola.
jacket ['dʒækit] *n* giacca, giacchetta; buccia; rivestimento; copertina di libro.
jackknife ['dʒæknaif] *n* coltello a serramanico.
jackpot ['dʒækpɔt] *n* (*poker*) posta; **to hit the j.** fare una grossa vincita.
Jacob ['dʒeikəb] *nm pr* Giacobbe.
Jacobite ['dʒækəbait] *n* giacobita.
jade [dʒeid] *n* giada; vecchia cavalla; donnaccia.
jag [dʒæg] *n* punta di roccia, sporgenza appuntita.
jagged ['dʒægid] *a* dentellato, frastagliato.
jail [dʒeil] *n* carcere, prigione; *vt* incarcerare.
jailer ['dʒeilə] *n* carceriere.
jam [dʒæm] *n* conserva di frutta, marmellata; blocco; compressione; ingorgo di traffico; *vt* comprimere, bloccare, bloccarsi.
Jamaica [dʒə'meikə] *n* Giamaica.
Jamaican [dʒə'meikən] *a n* giamaicano.
James [dʒeimz] *nm pr* Giacomo.
Jane [dʒein] *nf pr* Giovanna, Gianna.
jangle ['dʒæŋgl] *n* suono aspro e discordante; *vti* (far) fare rumori discordanti; vociare sgarbatamente, berciare.
janitor ['dʒænitə] *n* bidello; portiere.
January ['dʒænjuəri] *n* gennaio.
Japan [dʒə'pæn] *n* Giappone.
Japanese [,dʒæpə'niːz] *a n* giapponese.
jar [dʒɑː] *n* giara, vaso, barattolo; suono aspro; *vi* vibrare; discordare; produrre un'impressione sgradevole; *vt* scuotere.

jargon ['dʒɑ:gən] *n* gergo, linguaggio professionale.
jasmine ['dʒæsmin] *n* gelsomino.
jasper ['dʒæspə] *n* diaspro.
jaundice ['dʒɔ:ndis] *n* itterizia.
jaunt [dʒɔ:nt] *n* gita, scampagnata.
jaunty ['dʒɔ:nti] *a* arzillo, vivace.
javelin ['dʒævlin] *n* giavellotto.
jaw [dʒɔ:] *n* mascella; **jaws** *pl* fauci *pl*, mandibola.
jay [dʒei] *n* ghiandaia.
jealous ['dʒeləs] *a* geloso.
jealousy ['dʒeləsi] *n* gelosia.
Jean [dʒi:n] *nf pr* Giovanna.
jeans [dʒi:nz] *n pl* calzoni di tela; tuta.
jeer [dʒiə] *n* derisione, scherno; *vti* beffarsi, deridere, schernire.
Jeffrey ['dʒefri] *nm pr* Goffredo.
jelly ['dʒeli] *n* gelatina.
jellyfish ['dʒelifiʃ] *n* medusa.
jeopardize ['dʒepədaiz] *vt* mettere in pericolo.
jeopardy ['dʒepədi] *n* repentaglio, pericolo.
Jericho ['dʒerikou] *n* Gerico.
jerk [dʒə:k] *n* scatto, strattone; *vti* dare uno strattone; sobbalzare.
jerkin ['dʒə:kin] *n* giacca a vento; giustacuore.
Jerome [dʒə'roum] *nm pr* Gerolamo.
jersey ['dʒə:zi] *n* camicetta a maglia; maglione; maglia sportiva.
Jerusalem [dʒə'ru:sələm] *n* Gerusalemme.
jest [dʒest] *n* scherzo, beffa, zimbello; *vi* scherzare.
jester ['dʒestə] *n* burlone, buffone.
Jesuit ['dʒezjuit] *n* gesuita; ipocrita.
Jesus ['dʒi:zəs] *nm pr* Gesù.
jet [dʒet] *n* zampillo, getto; (*chem*) becco; gialetto.
jetsam ['dʒetsəm] *n* (*naut*) relitti *pl* di mare.
jettison ['dʒetisn] *vt* gettare in mare (un carico); (*fig*) disfarsi di.
jetty ['dʒeti] *n* gettata, molo.
Jew [dʒu:] *n* ebreo, giudeo, israelita.
jewel ['dʒu:əl] *n* gioiello.
jeweler ['dʒu:ələ] *n* gioielliere.
jewelry ['dʒu:əlri] *n* gioielli *pl*, gioielleria.
Jewess ['dʒu(:)is] *n* ebrea, israelita.
Jewish ['dʒu(:)iʃ] *a* ebreo, giudaico, israelitico.
jib [dʒib] *vi* recalcitrare; *vt* (*naut*) orientare.
jig [dʒig] *n* giga.
jigsaw ['dʒigsɔ:] *n* sega da traforo; **j. puzzle** gioco di pazienza.
jilt [dʒilt] *n* donna capricciosa; *vt* abbandonare il fidanzato o la fidanzata.
jingle ['dʒiŋgl] *n* tintinnio; *vti* far tintinnare.
Joan [dʒoun] *nf pr* Giovanna.
job [dʒɔb] *n* lavoro, occupazione, posto, faccenda.
jockey ['dʒɔki] *n* fantino.
jocose [dʒə'kous] *a* giocoso.
jocular ['dʒɔkjulə] *a* allegro, scherzoso.
jocund ['dʒɔkənd] *a* giocondo.
jog [dʒɔg] *n* gomitata, spinta; andatura lenta; *vti* urtare col gomito, spingere; procedere adagio.
joggle ['dʒɔgl] *n* leggera scossa.
John [dʒɔn] *nm pr* Giovanni.
join [dʒɔin] *n* giuntura, congiunzione; *vti* associarsi a, congiungere, unirsi a; raggiungere.
joiner ['dʒɔinə] *n* falegname.
joint [dʒɔint] *a* articolazione, giuntura; parte di bestia macellata.
jointly ['dʒɔintli] *ad* unitamente, assieme, collettivamente.
joke [dʒouk] *n* facezia, scherzo, tiro, barzalletta, burla; *vi* scherzare.
jolly ['dʒɔli] *a* allegro, festoso, giovanile.
jolt [dʒoult] *n* scossa, sobbalzo; *vti* (far) sobbalzare.
Jonathan ['dʒɔnəθən] *nm pr* Gionata.
Jordan ['dʒɔ:dn] *n* Giordano, Giordania.
Jordanian [dʒɔ:'deiniən] *a n* giordanico, giordano.
Joseph ['dʒouzif] *nm pr* Giuseppe; **Josephine** *nf pr* Giuseppina.
Joshua ['dʒɔʃwə] *nm pr* Giosuè.
jostle ['dʒɔsl] *vt* spingere, urtare col gomito; *vi* lottare.
jot [dʒɔt] *n* iota, particella minima.
journal ['dʒə:nl] *n* giornale, periodico; diario.
journalism ['dʒə:nəlizəm] *n* giornalismo.
journalist ['dʒə:nəlist] *n* giornalista.
journalistic [ˌdʒə:nə'listik] *a* giornalistico.
journey ['dʒə:ni] *n* viaggio; *vi* viaggiare, fare un viaggio.
journeyman ['dʒə:nimən] *n* meccanico o operaio qualificato che lavora a giornata.
joust [dʒaust] *n* torneo.
jovial ['dʒouviəl] *a* allegro, gioviale.
joviality [ˌdʒouvi'æliti] *n* giovialità.
joy [dʒɔi] *n* gioia.
Joy [dʒɔi] *nf pr* Gioia.
joyful ['dʒɔiful] *a* gioioso.
joyfully ['dʒɔifuli] *ad* gioiosamente, allegramente.
joyfulness ['dʒɔifulnis] *n* allegrezza, gioia.
joyless ['dʒɔilis] *a* senza gioia, triste.
joyous ['dʒɔiəs] *a* gioioso, gaio.
jubilant ['dʒu:bilənt] *a* esultante, giubilante.
jubilation [ˌdʒu:bi'leiʃən] *n* esultanza, giubilo.
jubilee ['dʒu:bili:] *n* giubileo.
Judaic [dʒu(:)'deiik] *a* giudaico, ebraico.
Judaism ['dʒu:deiizəm] *n* giudaismo.
Judas ['dʒu:dəs] *nm pr* Giuda.
judge [dʒʌdʒ] *n* giudice; *vti* giudicare.
judgment ['dʒʌdʒmənt] *n* giudizio, sentenza, punizione divina.

judicial [dʒu(:)'diʃəl] *a* giudiziario, imparziale.
judicious [dʒu(:)'diʃəs] *a* giudizioso.
Judith ['dʒu:diθ] *nf pr* Giuditta.
jug [dʒʌg] *n* brocca, caraffa, boccale.
juggle ['dʒʌgl] *n* gioco di prestigio; *vi* far giochi di destrezza o di prestigio, raggirare.
juggler ['dʒʌglə] *n* prestigiatore; impostore.
Jugoslav ['ju:gou'slɑ:v] *a n* iugoslavo.
Jugoslavia ['ju:gou'slɑ:viə] *n* Iugoslavia.
jugular ['dʒʌgjulə] *a n* (vena) giugulare.
juice [dʒu:s] *n* succo; (*sl*) benzina.
juicy ['dʒu:si] *a* succoso; (*sl*) interessante.
jukebox ['dʒu:kbɔks] *n* grammofono a gettone, 'jukbox'.
Juliet ['dʒu:liət] *nf pr* Giulietta.
Julius ['dʒu:liəs] *nm pr* Giulio.
July [dʒu(:)'lai] *n* luglio.
jumble ['dʒʌmbl] *n* confusione, mescolanza; *vt* mescolare, gettare insieme alla rinfusa.
jump [dʒʌmp] *n* salto; *vti* saltare, fare un salto.
jumper ['dʒʌmpə] *n* saltatore; maglione, golf.
jumpy ['dʒʌmpi] *n* nervoso, irrequieto, teso.
junction ['dʒʌŋkʃən] *n* congiunzione, unione; nodo ferroviario.
juncture ['dʒʌŋktʃə] *n* congiuntura, giuntura, stato di cose.
June [dʒu:n] *n* giugno.
jungle ['dʒʌŋgl] *n* giungla.
junior ['dʒu:niə] *a n* chi è più giovane, chi ha grado o posizione inferiore.
juniper ['dʒu:nipə] *n* ginepro.
junk [dʒʌŋk] *n* articoli marinareschi *pl*, articoli *pl* di scarto.
junket ['dʒʌŋkit] *n* giuncata.
jurisdiction [,dʒuəris'dikʃən] *n* giurisdizione.
jurisprudence ['dʒuəris,pru:dəns] *n* giurisprudenza.
jurist ['dʒuərist] *n* giurista.
juror ['dʒuərə] *n* giurato.
jury ['dʒuəri] *n* giuria.
just [dʒʌst] *a* giusto, retto; *ad* appena; esattamente, proprio; **j. now** or ora.
justice ['dʒʌstis] *n* giustizia, giudice.
justifiable ['dʒʌstifaiəbl] *a* giustificabile.
justification [,dʒʌstifi'keiʃən] *n* giustificazione.
justify ['dʒʌstifai] *vt* giustificare.
justly ['dʒʌstli] *ad* giustamente, a buon diritto.
justness ['dʒʌstnis] *n* giustizia.
jut [dʒʌt] *n* sporgenza; *vi* sporgere.
juvenile ['dʒu:venail] *a* giovane, giovanile; *n* giovane, minorenne.
juxtaposition [,dʒʌkstəpə'ziʃən] *n* giustapposizione.

K

kale, kail [keil] *n* cavolo riccio.
kangaroo [,kæŋgə'ru:] *n* canguro.
kapok ['keipɔk] *n* capoc.
Katharine, Katherine ['kæθərin] **Kathleen** ['kæθli:n] *nf pr* Caterina.
kedge [kedʒ] *n* (*naut*) ancorotto.
keel [ki:l] *n* (*naut*) chiglia; chiatta; *vt* (*naut*) carenare.
keen [ki:n] *a* acuminato, acuto; amante, appassionato, forte, intenso; **be keen on** essere amante di.
keenness ['ki:nnis] *n* acutezza, perspicacia; passione; entusiasmo.
keep [ki:p] *n* mantenimento; (*of castle*) torrione; *vt* tenere, mantenere, conservare, trattenere; festeggiare; *vi* continuare, conservarsi, mantenersi.
keeper ['ki:pə] *n* custode, guardiano.
keeping ['ki:piŋ] *n* custodia, armonia.
keepsake ['ki:pseik] *n* ricordo, pegno d'affetto.
keg [keg] *n* bariletto.
ken [ken] *n* comprensione, conoscenza.
kennel ['kenl] *n* canile.
Kenya ['kenjə] *n* Kenia.
kerchief ['kə:tʃif] *n* fazzoletto da capo, fisciù.
kernel ['kə:nl] *n* mandorla, gheriglio; (*fig*) nocciolo.
kerosene ['kerəsi:n] *n* petrolio raffinato.
kestrel ['kestrəl] *n* gheppio.
kettle ['ketl] *n* bollitore, bricco.
key [ki:] *n* chiave; (*mus*) chiave, tasto.
kick [kik] *n* calcio; (*mil*) rinculo; *vti* dare (tirare) calci (a).
kid [kid] *n* capretto; (*fam*) ragazzino; *vti* (*sl*) prendere in giro, scherzare.
kidnap ['kidnæp] *vt* rapire una persona.
kidney ['kidni] *n* rene, rognone; carattere, tipo.
kill [kil] *vt* ammazzare, uccidere.
killer ['kilə] *n* uccisore, assassino; **lady k.** dongiovanni.
killing ['kiliŋ] *a* mortale, distruttivo; (*fam*) affascinante; *n* uccisione, carneficina.
kiln [kiln] *n* fornace.
kilogram ['kiləgræm] *n* chilo (grammo).
kilometer ['kilə,mi:tə] *n* chilometro.
kilt [kilt] *n* 'kilt', gonnellino degli scozzesi.
kin [kin] *n* parentela, congiunti, parenti *pl*.
kind [kaind] *a* buono, gentile; *n* genere, sorta, specie, tipo.
kindergarten ['kində,gɑ:tn] *n* giardino d'infanzia.
kindle ['kindl] *vt* accendere, destare, infiammare, suscitare.

kindly ['kaindli] *a* benevolo, gentile; *ad* benevolmente, gentilmente.
kindness ['kaindnis] *n* benevolenza, bontà, gentilezza.
kindred ['kindrid] *a* affine; *n* affinità, parentela, parenti *pl*.
king [kiŋ] *n* re.
kingdom ['kiŋdəm] *n* regno, reame.
kingfisher ['kiŋ,fiʃə] *n* martin pescatore.
kingly ['kiŋli] *a* da re, regale.
kink [kiŋk] *n* nodo; (*fig*) capriccio, ghiribizzo.
kinsfolk ['kinzfouk] *n* congiunti, parenti *pl*.
kinsman ['kinzmən] *n* congiunto, parente.
kiosk ['ki:ɔsk] *n* chiosco, edicola.
kipper ['kipə] *n* aringa salata e affumicata.
kiss [kis] *n* bacio; *vt* baciare.
kit [kit] *n* utensili, attrezzi *pl*; borsa utensili; **kitbag** sacco militare.
kitchen ['kitʃin] *n* cucina.
kitchenette [,kitʃin'et] *n* cucinino.
kite [kait] *n* nibbio; aquilone.
kitten ['kitn] *n* gattino, micino.
knack [næk] *n* abilità, facoltà.
knapsack ['næpsæk] *n* zaino.
knave [neiv] *n* briccone, furfante; (*cards*) fante.
knavery ['neivəri] *n* bricconeria.
knavish ['neiviʃ] *a* da briccone, disonesto.
knead [ni:d] *vt* impastare; massaggiare.
knee [ni:] *n* ginocchio.
kneel [ni:l] *vi* inginocchiarsi.
knell [nel] *n* rintocco funebre.
knickerbockers ['nikəbɔkəz] *n pl* calzoni *pl* alla zuava.
knickers ['nikəz] *n pl* mutande da donna *pl*; *v also* **knickerbockers**.
knick-knack ['niknæk] *n* ninnolo.
knife [naif] *n* coltello; *vt* accoltellare.
knight [nait] *n* cavaliere; (*chess*) cavallo.
knighthood ['naithud] *n* titolo di cavaliere.
knightly ['naitli] *a* cavalleresco.
knit [nit] *vti* lavorare a maglia; saldar(si); corrugare (la fronte); congiunger(si).
knitting ['nitiŋ] *n* lavoro a maglia; **k. needle, k. pin** ferro da calza.
knob [nɔb] *n* bernoccolo; pomo.
knock [nɔk] *n* colpo, urto; il bussare (alla porta); *vti* bussare; colpire, urtare, picchiare; **to k. down** abbattere; assegnare all'asta; **to k. out** mettere fuori combattimento.
knocker ['nɔkə] *n* battente.
knoll [noul] *n* collinetta, poggio.
knot [nɔt] *n* nodo, groviglio; *vti* annodar(si).
knotty ['nɔti] *a* nodoso; ingarbugliato.
know [nou] *vti* conoscere, sapere.
knowing ['nouiŋ] *a* abile, accorto.
knowingly ['nouiŋli] *ad* scientemente, a bello studio.
knowledge ['nɔlidʒ] *n* conoscenza, cognizioni *pl*, sapere.
knowledgeable ['nɔlidʒəbl] *a* intelligente, ben informato.
knuckle ['nʌkl] *n* nocca (delle dita), articolazione, giuntura; **k.-duster** pugno di ferro.

L

label ['leibl] *n* cartellino, etichetta; *vt* mettere le etichette a, classificare.
labor ['leibə] *n* fatica, lavoro faticoso; doglie del parto *pl*; *vi* affaticarsi, lavorare faticosamente; **hard l.** *n* lavori forzati *pl*; **L. Party** partito laburista.
laboratory [lə'bɔrətəri] *n* laboratorio.
laborer ['leibərə] *n* bracciante.
laborious [lə'bɔ:riəs] *a* faticoso; laborioso.
laboriousness [lə'bɔ:riəsnis] *n* laboriosità; fatica.
laburnum [lə'bə:nəm] *n* avorno, laburno.
labyrinth ['læbərinθ] *n* labirinto.
lace [leis] *n* merletto, pizzo; laccio da scarpe; *vt* allacciare; guarnire con merletti.
lacerate ['læsəreit] *vt* lacerare.
laceration [,læsə'reiʃən] *n* lacerazione.
lachrymose ['lækrimous] *a* lacrimoso.
lack [læk] *n* mancanza; *vt* mancare di; *vi* mancare.
lackadaisical [,lækə'deizikəl] *a* affettato, languido.
lackey ['læki] *n* lacchè.
laconic [lə'kɔnik] *a* laconico.
lacquer ['lækə] *n* lacca.
lad [læd] *n* giovanetto, ragazzo.
ladder ['lædə] *n* scala a piuoli.
lade [leid] *vt* caricare una nave.
lading ['leidiŋ] *n* carico.
ladle ['leidl] *n* mestolo.
lady ['leidi] *n* signora, gentildonna; **L. Day** Festa dell'Annunciazione.
ladybird ['leidibə:d] *n* coccinella.
ladylike ['leidilaik] *a* da signora, distinto, signorile.
ladyship ['leidiʃip] *n* Eccellenza (*titolo delle signore dell'aristocrazia*).
lag [læg] *vi* indugiare; farsi tirare; **to l. behind** restare indietro.
lagoon [lə'gu:n] *n* laguna.
lair [lɛə] *n* covo, tana.
laird [lɛəd] *n* (*scozzese*) proprietario terriero.
laity ['leiiti] *n* laicato.
lake [leik] *n* lago.
lamb [læm] *n* agnello.
lame [leim] *a* zoppo; *vt* azzoppare.
lameness ['leimnis] *n* zoppaggine.
lament [lə'ment] *n* lamento, pianto,

elegia funebre; *vt* lamentar(si), rimpiangere.
lamentable ['læməntəbl] *a* lamentevole, deplorevole.
lamentation [,læmen'teiʃən] *n* lamentazione, lamento.
lamented [lə'mentid] *a* deplorato; compianto.
lamp [læmp] *n* lampada, lampione, lucerna, fanale; (*fig*) lume.
lampoon [læm'pu:n] *n* satira, pasquinata.
lamprey ['læmpri] *n* lampreda.
lance [lɑ:ns] *n* lancia; rampone; *vt* tagliare col bisturi.
lancer ['lɑ:nsə] *n* lanciere.
lancet ['lɑ:nsit] *n* bisturi.
land [lænd] *n* terra, suolo, terreno; paese; *vt* sbarcare, atterrare; porsi (in una situazione).
landed ['lændid] *a* terriero.
landing ['lændiŋ] *n* approdo, sbarco; atterraggio; pianerottolo.
landlord ['lænlɔ:d] **landlady** ['lænd,leidi] *n* padrone, padrona di terre o case affittate, locandiere, locandiera.
landmark ['lænmɑ:k] *n* punto di riferimento, pietra miliare, pietra di confine.
landowner ['lænd,ounə] *n* proprietario di terre.
landscape ['lænskeip] *n* paesaggio.
lane [lein] *n* vicolo, viottolo.
language ['læŋgwidʒ] *n* lingua, linguaggio.
languid ['læŋgwid] *a* languido.
languish ['læŋgwiʃ] *vi* languire.
languor ['læŋgə] *n* languore.
lank [læŋk] **lanky** ['læŋki] *a* alto e magro.
lanolin(e) ['lænəlin] *n* lanolina.
lantern ['læntən] *n* lanterna.
lap [læp] *n* grembo; lembo, falda; (*races*) giro di pista; *vt* lambire; avvolgere, ripiegare; bere rumorosamente; (*of dogs*) lappare; **to l. up** leccare il piatto, mangiar tutto; **lapping waves** maretta.
lapdog ['læpdɔg] *n* cagnolino.
lapel [lə'pel] *n* risvolto.
Lapland ['læplænd] *n* Lapponia.
Lapp [læp] **Laplander** ['læplændə] *a n* lappone.
lapse [læps] *n* decorso, lasso (di tempo), intervallo; errore; perdita di validità; *vi* passare, trascorrere, decadere; (*fig*) cadere.
larboard ['lɑ:bəd] *n* (*naut*) babordo.
larceny ['lɑ:sni] *n* furto, ladrocinio.
larch [lɑ:tʃ] *n* larice.
lard [lɑ:d] *n* lardo.
larder ['lɑ:də] *n* dispensa.
large [lɑ:dʒ] *a* grande, ampio, spazioso; considerevole; numeroso.
largely ['lɑ:dʒli] *ad* largamente, in gran misura.
largeness ['lɑ:dʒnis] *n* grandezza, estensione.
lark [lɑ:k] *n* allodola; (*fam*) burla, scherzo.
larynx ['læriŋks] *n* laringe.
lascivious [lə'siviəs] *a* lascivo.
lasciviousness [lə'siviəsnis] *n* lascivia.
lash [læʃ] *n* ciglio; frusta(ta), sferza(ta); sarcasmo; *vt* frustare, sferzare, incitare; assicurare con una corda; **to l. its tail** agitare la coda; **to l. out** prorompere (in); (*horse*) sferrare calci.
lashing ['læʃiŋ] *n* frustata; *pl* (*fam*) abbondanza.
lass [læs] *n* fanciulla, ragazza.
last [lɑ:st] *n* ultimo, scorso, estremo; *ad* per ultimo; l'ultima volta; finalmente; *n* ultimo; fine; (*shoe*) forma; *vi* durare.
lasting ['lɑ:stiŋ] *a* duraturo, durevole.
lastly ['lɑ:stli] *a* in conclusione, per ultimo.
latch [lætʃ] *n* saliscendi, serratura a scatto; *vt* chiudere con saliscendi.
late [leit] *a* tardivo; in ritardo; recente; ultimo; fu, defunto; *ad* tardi; **latecomer** ritardatario.
lately ['leitli] *ad* recentemente, ultimamente.
latent ['leitənt] *a* latente.
lateral ['lætərəl] *a* laterale.
latest ['leitist] *a* recentissimo, ultimo.
lathe [leið] *n* tornio.
lather ['lɑ:ðə] *n* schiuma, saponata; sudore schiumoso; *vt* insaponare, coprir(si) di schiuma.
latin ['lætin] *a n* latino.
latitude ['lætitju:d] *n* latitudine; (*fig*) larghezza, libertà.
latrine [lə'tri:n] *n* latrina.
latter ['lætə] *a pron* (*di due*) quest'ultimo, il secondo.
latterly ['lætəli] *ad* di recente.
lattice ['lætis] *n* grata, traliccio.
laudable ['lɔ:dəbl] *a* lodevole.
laugh(ter) ['lɑ:f(tə)] *n* risata, riso.
laugh [lɑ:f] *vi* ridere.
laughable ['lɑ:fəbl] *a* buffo, comico.
launch [lɔ:ntʃ] *n* (*naut*) lancia, varo; *vt* varare; *vti* lanciar(si) in.
launder ['lɔ:ndə] *vti* lavare e stirare, fare il bucato.
launderette [lɔ:nd'ret] *n*. lavanderia automatica (dove il cliente fa il bucato da sè).
laundress ['lɔ:ndris] *n* lavandaia.
laundry ['lɔ:ndri] *n* lavanderia, bucato; **laundryman** lavandaio.
Laura ['lɔ:rə] *nf pr* Laura.
laurel ['lɔrəl] *n* alloro, lauro.
Laurence ['lɔrəns] *nm pr* Lorenzo.
lavatory ['lævətəri] *n* gabinetto, latrina.
lavender ['lævində] *n* lavanda.
lavish ['læviʃ] *a* generoso, prodigo; *vt* prodigare, profondere.
law [lɔ:] *n* diritto, legge.
lawful ['lɔ:ful] *a* legale, legittimo.
lawfully ['lɔ:fuli] *ad* legittimamente, legalmente.

lawfulness ['lɔ:fulnis] *n* legalità, legittimità.
lawgiver ['lɔ:,givə] *n* legislatore.
lawless ['lɔ:lis] *a* illegale, illegittimo.
lawn [lɔ:n] *n* prato; batista; **lawnmower** falciatrice per prati; **l. tennis** tennis su prato.
Lawrence ['lɔrəns] *nm pr* Lorenzo.
lawsuit ['lɔ:su:t] *n* causa, procedimento legale.
lawyer ['lɔ:jə] *n* avvocato.
lax [læks] *a* negligente, rilassato.
laxative ['læksətiv] *n* lassativo.
lay [lei] *a* laico, secolare; *n* (*of ground*) configurazione; *vti* collocare, (de)porre, stendere, adagiare; coricarsi; scommettere; **to l. down** deporre; (*law*) dettare; (*project*) tracciare; (*life*) fare sacrifizio di; **to l. out** spendere; spiegare; **to l. up** ammassare; **laid up** allettato; **to l. waste** devastare.
layer ['leiə] *n* strato; (*agr*) propaggine.
layette [lei'et] *n* corredino da neonato.
layman ['leimən] *n* laico, secolare.
laze [leiz] *vi* passare (il tempo) in ozio, oziare.
laziness ['leizinis] *n* indolenza, pigrizia.
lazy ['leizi] *a* indolente, pigro.
lead [li:d] *n* direzione, guida; (*dog*) guinzaglio; *vt* condurre, dirigere, guidare; *vi* fare da guida.
lead [led] *n* piombo, scandaglio; *vt* impiombare, saldare col piombo.
leaden ['ledn] *a* di piombo, plumbeo.
leader ['li:də] *n* capo, duce; articolo di fondo d'un giornale.
leadership ['li:dəʃip] *n* direzione, comando.
leading ['li:diŋ] *a* dominante, eminente, principale; **l. article** articolo di fondo.
leaf [li:f] *pl* **leaves** *n* foglia; foglio, pagina; (*door*) battente; (*table*) asse.
leafless ['li:flis] *a* senza foglie, sfrondato.
leaflet ['li:flit] *n* manifestino, volantino.
leafy ['li:fi] *a* coperto di foglie, fronzuto.
league [li:g] *n* lega, società; *vt* unir(si) in lega.
leak [li:k] *n* falla; *vi* far acqua, perdere; **to l. out** trapelare.
leakage ['li:kidʒ] *n* perdita, indiscrezione.
leaky ['li:ki] *a* che perde, che cola.
lean [li:n] *a* magro, scarno; *vti* appoggiare, appoggiarsi, inclinarsi.
leaning ['li:niŋ] *a* pendente, inclinato; *n* inclinazione; **the Leaning Tower of Pisa** la Torre pendente di Pisa.
leanness ['li:nnis] *n* magrezza.
leap [li:p] *n* balzo, salto; *vi* balzare, saltare; **l. year** anno bisestile.
earn [lə:n] *vt* imparare.
learned ['lə:nid] *a* dotto, erudito.
learning ['lə:niŋ] *n* erudizione, sapere.
lease [li:s] *n* contratto d'affitto; *vt* affittare; **leasehold** *a* in affitto; *n* durata di un contratto d'affitto; **leaseholder** *n* affittuario.
leash [li:ʃ] *n* guinzaglio.
least [li:st] *a* il più piccolo, il minimo; *n* il meno; *ad* meno, minimamente; **at l.** almeno.
leather ['leðə] *n* cuoio, pelle; *a* di cuoio, di pelle.
leave [li:v] *n* licenza, permesso; congedo, commiato; *vt* abbandonare, lasciare; *vi* partire.
leaven ['levn] *n* lievito; *vt* far lievitare.
leaving ['li:viŋ] *n* partenza; *pl* avanzi, rifiuti.
Lebanese [,lebə'ni:z] *a n* libanese.
Lebanon ['lebənən] *n* Libano.
lecherous ['letʃərəs] *a* lascivo, vizioso.
lechery ['letʃəri] *n* lascivia; libertinaggio.
lecture ['lektʃə] *n* conferenza; lezione universitaria; ramanzina; *vti* tenere una conferenza, o lezione; ammonire.
lecturer ['lektʃərə] *n* conferenziere; libero docente.
lectureship ['lektʃəʃip] *n* carica di libero docente.
ledge [ledʒ] *n* ripiano, sporgenza.
ledger ['ledʒə] *n* (*com*) libro mastro.
lee [li:] *n* (*naut*) sottovento.
leech [li:tʃ] *n* sanguisuga.
leek [li:k] *n* porro.
leer [liə] *n* occhiata bieca, occhiata maliziosa; *vi* guardar di traverso.
leeward ['li:wəd] *a* di sottovento; *ad* in direzione di sottovento.
left [left] *a* sinistro, manco, mancino; *n* sinistra; *ad* a sinistra; **l.-handed** mancino.
leftovers ['left,ouvəz] *n pl* rimasugli, resti *pl.*
leg [leg] *n* gamba; (*fowl*) coscia; (*birds etc*) zampa; (*table etc*) piede.
legacy ['legəsi] *n* legato, lascito.
legal ['li:gəl] *a* legale.
legality [li(:)'gæliti] *n* legalità.
legalization [,ligəlai'zeiʃən] *n* legalizzazione.
legalize ['li:gəlaiz] *vt* legalizzare.
legate ['legit] *n* legato.
legatee [,legə'ti:] *n* legatario.
legation [li'geiʃən] *n* legazione.
legend ['ledʒənd] *n* leggenda.
legendary ['ledʒəndəri] *a* leggendario.
legging ['legiŋ] *n* gambale; *pl* ghette *pl.*
Leghorn ['leg'hɔ:n] *n* Livorno.
legible ['ledʒəbl] *a* leggibile.
legion ['li:dʒən] *n* legione.
legionary ['li:dʒənəri] *a* legionario.
legislation [,ledʒis'leiʃən] *n* legislazione.
legislative ['ledʒislətiv] *a* legislativo.

legislator ['ledʒisleitə] *n* legislatore.
legislature ['ledʒisleitʃə] *n* legislatura, corpo legislativo.
legitimacy [li'dʒitiməsi] *n* legittimità.
legitimate [li'dʒitimit] *a* legittimo.
leisure ['leʒə] *n* agio, ozio, comodo, ritagli di tempo.
leisurely ['leʒəli] *a* fatto con comodo, a proprio agio; *ad* senza fretta.
lemon ['lemən] *n* limone.
lemonade ['lemə'neid] *n* limonata.
lend [lend] *vt* prestare; *vi* fare un prestito.
lending ['lendiŋ] *n* prestito.
length [leŋθ] *n* lunghezza; taglio di stoffa.
lengthen ['leŋθən] *vti* allungar(si).
lengthy ['leŋθi] *a* lungo, prolisso.
lenient ['li:niənt] *a* indulgente.
lens [lenz] *n* lente.
Lent [lent] *n* quaresima.
Lenten ['lentən] *a* quaresimale, da quaresima.
lentil ['lentl] *n* lenticchia.
Leo ['li(:)ou] *nm pr* Leone.
Leonard ['lenəd] *nm pr* Leonardo.
leopard ['lepəd] *n* leopardo.
Leopold ['liəpould] *nm pr* Leopoldo.
leper ['lepə] *n* lebbroso.
leprosy ['leprəsi] *n* lebbra.
lesbian ['lezbiən] *a* lesbico; *n* lesbica.
lesion ['li:ʒən] *n* lesione.
less [les] *a* meno, minore; *n* meno; *ad prep* meno.
lessee [le'si:] *n* locatario.
lessen ['lesn] *vti* diminuire, rimpicciolir(si).
lessening ['lesniŋ] *n* diminuzione, attenuazione.
lesser ['lesə] *a* minore.
lesson ['lesn] *n* lezione.
lest [lest] *cj* per paura che.
let [let] *vt* lasciare, permettere; dare in affitto; **l. down** abbassare; allungare; sciogliere; deludere; **l. off** lasciar andare; perdonare, (*a shot etc*) far partire.
lethal ['li:θəl] *a* letale, mortale.
lethargic [le'θɑ:dʒik] *a* letargico.
lethargy ['leθədʒi] *n* letargo.
letter ['letə] *n* lettera.
lettuce ['letis] *n* lattuga.
leukemia [lju'ki:miə] *n* leucemia.
Levantine ['levəntain] *a* levantino.
level ['levl] *a* livellato, orizzontale, pari; *n* spianata, livello; **l. crossing** passaggio a livello; *vt* livellare, spianare, pareggiare; (*fig*) dirigere.
lever ['li:və] *n* (*mech*) leva.
leverage ['li:vəridʒ] *n* (*mech*) azione d'una leva, sistema di leve.
levity ['leviti] *n* frivolezza, leggerezza.
levy ['levi] *n* leva; imposta, tributo; *vt* arruolare; (*tax etc*) imporre.
lewd [lju:d] *a* impudico, lascivo.
lewdness ['lju:dnis] *n* lascivia.
Lewis ['lu(:)is] *nm pr* Luigi.
lexicographer [,leksi'kɔgrəfə] *n* lessicografo.
lexicon ['leksikən] *n* lessico.
liability [,laiə'biliti] *n* obbligo; disposizione a; responsabilità; *pl* (*com*) passività.
liable ['laiəbl] *a* soggetto, responsabile.
liar ['laiə] *n* bugiardo.
libation [lai'beiʃən] *n* libagione.
libel ['laibəl] *n* libello, calunnia, diffamazione; *vt* diffamare a mezzo di libello.
libelous ['laibləs] *a* diffamatorio.
liberal ['libərəl] *a n* liberale.
liberality [,libə'ræliti] *n* liberalità.
liberate ['libəreit] *vt* liberare.
liberation [,libə'reiʃən] *n* liberazione.
Liberia [lai'biəriə] *n* Liberia.
libertine ['libə(:)ti:n] *a n* libertino.
liberty ['libəti] *n* libertà; licenza.
librarian [lai'brɛəriən] *n* bibliotecario.
library ['laibrəri] *n* biblioteca.
libretto [li'bretou] *pl* **librettos** *n* libretto (d'opera).
Libya ['libiə] *n* Libia.
Libyan ['libiən] *a* libico.
license ['laisəns] *n* licenza, patente, permesso.
license ['laisəns] *vt* autorizzare, dar permesso a.
licentious [lai'senʃəs] *a* licenzioso.
lichen ['laiken] *n* lichene.
lick [lik] *n* leccata; *vt* leccare, lambire.
lid [lid] *n* coperchio.
lie [lai] *n* bugia, menzogna; (*of ground*) configurazione; *vi* mentire; giacere, stare, trovarsi; **l. down** sdraiarsi.
lieutenant [lu:'tenənt] *n* luogotenente, tenente.
life [laif] *n* vita; **l. insurance** assicurazione sulla vita; **l. preserver** salvagente; bastone sfollagente.
lifebelt ['laifbelt] *n* cintura di salvataggio, salvagente.
lifeboat ['laifbout] *n* scialuppa di salvataggio.
life-giving ['laif,giviŋ] *a* vivificante.
lifeguard ['laifgɑ:d] *n* bagnino.
lifeless ['laiflis] *a* inanimato, senza vita.
lifelike ['laiflaik] *a* realistico, vivido.
life-long ['laiflɔŋ] *a* che dura tutta la vita.
lifetime ['laiftaim] *n* durata della vita.
lift [lift] *n* ascensore, montacarichi; passaggio; *vt* alzare, elevare, sollevare; *vi* (*of weather*) schiarire.
ligament ['ligəmənt] *n* legamento.
ligature ['ligətʃuə] *n* legatura.
light [lait] *a* chiaro, biondo, luminoso; leggero; *n* luce, lampada, lume; finestra; *vt* accendere; *vi* illuminar (si).
lighten ['laitn] *vti* alleggerir(si), accender(si), rischiararsi.

lighter ['laitə] *n* accendisigaro, accendino; (*naut*) chiatta.
light-hearted ['lait'hɑ:tid] *a* allegro, ottimista.
lighthouse ['laithaus] *n* faro.
lighting ['laitiŋ] *n* illuminazione.
lightless ['laitlis] *a* privo di luce.
lightly ['laitli] *ad* leggermente; agilmente; un poco.
light-minded ['lait'maindid] *a* frivolo, sconsiderato.
lightning ['laitniŋ] *n* lampi *pl*; (**flash of**) **l.** lampo.
lightsome ['laitsəm] *a* allegro, gaio.
lightweight ['laitweit] *n* peso leggero.
Ligurian [li'gjuəriən] *a n* ligure.
like [laik] *a* simile, uguale, somigliante; *prep* come, a somiglianza di; *n* altrettanto, la stessa cosa, *pl* simpatia; *vti* amare, piacere, volere; **I l. that** ciò mi piace; **as you l.** come vuoi.
likelihood ['laiklihud] *n* verosimiglianza, probabilità.
likely ['laikli] *a* probabile, verosimile; *ad* probabilmente.
liken ['laikən] *vt* paragonare.
likeness ['laiknis] *n* somiglianza, aspetto, ritratto.
likewise ['laikwaiz] *ad* parimenti, inoltre, altrettanto.
liking ['laikiŋ] *n* gusto, inclinazione, simpatia.
lilac ['lailək] *a* (di) color lilla; *n* lilla.
lilt [lilt] *n* cadenza, ritmo.
lily ['lili] *n* giglio.
limb [lim] *n* arto, membro; ramo; (*sl*) ragazzo sventato.
limber ['limbə] *vt* **l. up** (*sport*) scaldarsi i muscoli, mettersi in forma.
lime [laim] *n* calce; vischio; tiglio; cedro.
limelight ['laimlait] *n* (*theat*) luce della ribalta.
limit ['limit] *n* limite; (*sl*) il colmo; *vt* limitare.
limitation [,limi'teiʃən] *n* limitazione.
limited ['limitid] *a* limitato; **l. liability company** (*com*) società a responsabilità limitata.
limp [limp] *a* debole, floscio, inerte; *n* andatura zoppicante; *vi* zoppicare.
limpet ['limpit] *n* patella.
limpid ['limpid] *a* limpido.
linden ['lindən] *n* tiglio.
line [lain] *n* linea; equatore; limite; lenza; ruga; (*com*) ramo; *pl* (*of an actor*) parte.
line [lain] *vt* rigare, segnare; foderare; riempire; **to l. up** allinear(si), fare la coda.
lineage ['liniidʒ] *n* lignaggio.
lineal ['liniəl] *a* diretto, in linea diretta.
lineament ['liniəmənt] *n* lineamento, tratto.
linear ['liniə] *a* lineare.
linen ['linin] *n* biancheria, tela di lino; *a* di lino.
liner ['lainə] *n* (*naut*) transatlantico.
linger ['liŋgə] *vi* indugiare, andare lentamente, attardarsi.
linguist ['liŋgwist] *n* linguista, poliglotta.
linguistics [liŋ'gwistiks] *n* linguistica.
lining ['lainiŋ] *n* fodera.
link [liŋk] *n* anello (di catena), legame, vincolo; *vt* congiungere, vincolare; *vi* collegarsi; **cufflinks** gemelli per polsini.
links [liŋks] *n pl* (*costruzione sing.*) campo da golf.
linnet ['linit] *n* fanello.
linoleum [li'nouliəm] *n* linoleum.
linseed ['linsi:d] *n* seme di lino.
lint [lint] *n* filaccia, garza.
lintel ['lintl] *n* architrave, mensola di caminetto.
lion ['laiən] *n* leone; (*fig*) celebrità.
lioness ['laiənis] *n* leonessa.
lip [lip] *n* labbro; (*sl*) discorso impudente; **l. service** fedeltà a parole, ipocrisia.
lipstick ['lipstik] *n* rossetto, matita per labbra.
liquefy ['likwifai] *vti* liquefar(si).
liqueur [li'kjuə] *n* liquore.
liquid ['likwid] *a n* liquido.
liquidate ['likwideit] *vti* liquidare.
liquidation [,likwi'deiʃən] *n* liquidazione.
liquor ['likə] *n* bevanda alcoolica.
liquorice ['likəris] *n* liquiriza.
Lisbon ['lizbən] *n* Lisbona.
lisp [lisp] *n* pronuncia blesa; *vi* parlare bleso.
lissom(e) ['lisəm] *a* flessibile, pieghevole.
list [list] *n* elenco, lista, ruolo; (*prices etc*) bollettino; (*naut*) sbandamento; *vt* elencare.
listen ['lisn] *vi* ascoltare.
listener ['lisnə] *n* ascoltatore.
listless ['listlis] *a* indifferente, svogliato.
listlessness ['listlisnis] *n* svogliatezza.
litany ['litəni] *n* litania.
liter ['li:tə] *n* litro.
literacy ['litərəsi] *n* grado di istruzione.
literal ['litərəl] *a* letterale.
literary ['litərəri] *a* letterario.
literate ['litərit] *a* non analfabeta; letterato.
literature ['litəritʃə] *n* letteratura.
lithe [laið] *a* flessibile, flessuoso.
lithograph ['liθəgrɑ:f] *n* litografia.
lithography [li'θɔgrəfi] *n* litografia.
Lithuania [,liθju(:)'einiə] *n* Lituania.
Lithuanian [,liθju(:)'einiən] *a n* lituano.
litigant ['litigənt] *n* litigante, parte in causa.
litigate ['litigeit] *vti* essere in causa, contestare.
litigation [,liti'geiʃən] *n* lite, causa.

litter ['litə] *n* lettiera, lettiga; (*of animals*) figliata; scarti e rifiuti *pl*; confusione; *vt* spargere disordinatamente; apprestare la lettiera per; *vi* (*of animals*) figliare.
little ['litl] *a* piccolo, breve, poco, un po' di; *ad* poco; *n* poco.
live [laiv] *a* vivente, vivo; [liv] *vi* vivere, abitare.
livelihood ['laivlihud] *n* mezzi di sussistenza *pl*, mantenimento.
liveliness ['laivlinis] *n* vivacità, animazione.
lively ['laivli] *a* vivo, vivace.
liven ['laivn] *vt* ravvivare.
liver ['livə] *n* fegato.
livery ['livəri] *n* livrea; **l.-stable** stallaggio.
livid ['livid] *a* livido; (*fam*) furioso.
living ['liviŋ] *a* vivente; *n* (*mezzi per vivere*) vita; beneficio ecclesiastico.
lizard ['lizəd] *n* lucertola.
llama ['lɑːmə] *n* (*zool*) lama.
load [loud] *n* carico, peso; *vt* caricare, colmare.
loaf [louf] *pl* **loaves** *n* pane in cassetta; pagnotta; (*sl*) testa; *vi* oziare.
loafer ['loufə] *n* fannullone.
loam [loum] *n* argilla sabbiosa.
loan [loun] *n* prestito.
loath [louθ] *a* restio, riluttante.
loathe [louð] *vt* detestare, sentire ripugnanza per.
loathing ['louðiŋ] *n* ripugnanza.
loathsome ['louðsəm] *a* nauseante, ripugnante.
lobby ['lɔbi] *n* corridoio (in un pubblico edificio).
lobster ['lɔbstə] *n* aragosta.
local ['loukəl] *a* locale, del luogo.
locality [lou'kæliti] *n* località.
localize ['loukəlaiz] *vt* localizzare.
locally ['loukəli] *ad* localmente.
locate [lou'keit] *vt* individuare, situare.
location [lou'keiʃən] *n* posizione, (*com*) locazione.
lock [lɔk] *n* serratura; (*canal*) chiusa; (*hair*) ciocca, ciuffo; *vt* chiudere a chiave, serrare.
locker ['lɔkə] *n* armadietto.
locket ['lɔkit] *n* medaglione.
locksmith ['lɔksmiθ] *n* fabbro.
locomotion [ˌloukə'mouʃən] *n* locomozione.
locomotive ['loukəˌmoutiv] *a* locomotivo, locomotore; *n* locomotiva.
locust ['loukəst] *n* locusta.
lode [loud] *n* filone metallifero.
lodge [lɔdʒ] *n* casetta (*spesso al cancello d'un parco*); (*freemasons*) loggia; *vti* alloggiare; collocare; (*appeal*) presentare, sporgere.
lodger ['lɔdʒə] *n* inquilino.
lodging ['lɔdʒiŋ] *n* alloggio, *usu pl* stanze prese in affitto.
loft [lɔft] *n* abbaino, solaio.
loftiness ['lɔftinis] *n* altezza, elevatezza, nobiltà; superbia.
lofty ['lɔfti] *a* alto; altero; elevato, nobile.
log [lɔg] *n* ceppo, tronco; (*naut*) diario di bordo.
logarithm ['lɔgəriθəm] *n* logaritmo.
loggerhead ['lɔgəhed] **at loggerheads with** *ad* in urto con.
logic ['lɔdʒik] *n* logica.
logical ['lɔdʒikəl] *a* logico.
logician [lou'dʒiʃən] *n* logico.
loin [lɔin] *n* lombo, lombata; *pl* (*poet*) fianchi, lombi *pl*.
loiter ['lɔitə] *vi* bighellonare, indugiare.
loiterer ['lɔitərə] *n* bighellone, perdigiorno.
loll [lɔl] *vi* adagiarsi; pigramente; (*tongue*) penzolare.
lollipop ['lɔlipɔp] *n* lecca-lecca.
Lombard ['lɔmbəd] *a n* lombardo.
Lombardy ['lɔmbədi] *n* Lombardia.
London ['lʌndən] *n* Londra; **Londoner** *n* Londinese.
lone [loun] *a* solitario, solo, isolato.
loneliness ['lounlinis] *n* solitudine.
lonely ['lounli] *a* solo, solitario; desolato.
lonesome ['lounsəm] *a* solitario, malinconico.
long [lɔŋ] *a* lungo; *ad* a lungo, lungamente, per molto tempo; *n* molto tempo; *vi* bramare, desiderare ardentemente; **l.-sighted** presbite; preveggente; **l.-suffering** paziente, tollerante; **l.-standing** di lunga data.
longing ['lɔŋiŋ] *n* brama, desiderio ardente.
longitude ['lɔŋitjuːd] *n* longitudine.
longwinded ['lɔŋ'windid] *a* prolisso, noioso.
look [luk] *n* sguardo, occhiata, espressione; aspetto; bellezza; *vi* guardare, sembrare; **to l. for** cercare; **to l. like** somigliare a.
looking-glass ['lukiŋglɑːs] *n* specchio.
lookout ['luk'aut] *n* guardia; vigilanza; vista; (*fig*) prospettiva.
loom [luːm] *n* telaio; *vi* apparire all'orizzonte.
loop [luːp] *n* cappio, laccio, nodo scorsoio; gancio; punto a maglia; *vti* far cappio, annodare.
loophole ['luːphoul] *n* feritoia; (*fig*) scappatoia.
loose [luːs] *a* sciolto, libero, slegato, rilassato; scorretto; sfrenato; *vt* sciogliere, slegare, liberare.
loosen ['luːsn] *vti* allentar(si).
looseness ['luːsnis] *n* scioltezza; (*fig*) rilassatezza; libertinaggio; (*style etc*) imprecisione.
loot [luːt] *n* bottino; *vt* saccheggiare.
lop [lɔp] *vt* potare, tagliare.
lopsided ['lɔp'saidid] *a* asimmetrico, sbilenco.
loquacious [lou'kweiʃəs] *a* loquace.
loquacity [lou'kwæsiti] *n* loquacità.

lord [lɔ:d] *n* signore.
lordly ['lɔ:dli] *a* signorile; altero; sontuoso.
lordship ['lɔ:dʃip] *n* signoria.
lore [lɔ:] *n* tradizioni *pl*.
lorry ['lɔri] *n* autocarro, camion.
lose [lu:z] *vti* perdere, perdersi; sciupare.
loser ['lu:zə] *n* chi perde, perdente; **to be a good l.** saper perdere.
loss [lɔs] *n* perdita.
lot [lɔt] *n* destino, sorte; lotto, quantità, quota.
lotion ['louʃən] *n* lozione.
lottery ['lɔtəri] *n* lotteria.
lotus ['loutəs] *n* loto.
loud [laud] *a* rumoroso, sonoro, alto, forte; (*colors*) vistoso; *ad* ad alta voce, forte.
loudness ['laudnis] *n* frastuono, rumorosità, vistosità.
Louis ['lu(:)i] *nm pr* Luigi.
Louisa [lu(:)'i:zə] **Louise** [lu(:)'i:z] *nf pr* Luisa, Luigia.
lounge [laundʒ] *n* (*theat*) ridotto; (*hotel*) salone, vestibolo; salotto; **l. suit** abito maschile da passeggio; *vi* andare a zonzo, bighellonare, poltrire.
lour ['lauə] *vi* corrugare le sopracciglia; (*weather*) minacciare, oscurarsi.
louse [laus] *pl* **lice** *n* pidocchio.
lousy ['lauzi] *a* pidocchioso; (*fig*) sporco, vile, schifoso.
lout [laut] *n* zoticone.
lovable ['lʌvəbl] *a* amabile.
love [lʌv] *n* amore; saluti affettuosi *pl*; *vti* amare.
loveliness ['lʌvlinis] *n* leggiadria.
lovely ['lʌvli] *a* bello, attraente.
lover ['lʌvə] *n* amante; innamorato, innamorata.
loving ['lʌviŋ] *a* affettuoso, tenero; d'amore.
lovingly ['lʌviŋli] *ad* amorosamente, affettuosamente, teneramente.
low [lou] *a* basso, abbattuto, depresso; *ad* in basso, a voce bassa; *vi* muggire.
lower ['louə] *vti* abbassar(si).
lowering ['louəriŋ] *n* abbassamento, ribasso.
lowland ['loulənd] *n* bassopiano, pianura.
Lowlands ['louləndz] *n pl* Scozia meridionale.
lowly ['louli] *a* basso, umile; *ad* umilmente.
loyal ['lɔiəl] *a* leale, fedele.
loyalty ['lɔiəlti] *n* lealtà, fedeltà.
lozenge ['lɔzindʒ] *n* pasticca, losanga.
lubricant ['lu:brikənt] *n* lubrificante.
lubricate ['lu:brikeit] *vt* lubrificare.
lubrication [,lu:bri'keiʃən] *n* lubrificazione.
lucid ['lu:sid] *a* chiaro, lucido.
lucidity [lu:'siditi] *n* lucidità.
Lucie, Lucy ['lu:si] *nf pr* Lucia.
luck [lʌk] *n* fortuna, sorte.
luckless ['lʌklis] *a* sfortunato.
lucky ['lʌki] *a* fortunato, propizio.
lucrative ['lu:krətiv] *a* lucrativo.
lucre ['lu:kə] *n* lucro.
ludicrous ['lu:dikrəs] *a* ridicolo, comico.
luff [lʌf] *n* (*naut*) orzata; *vi* (*naut*) orzare.
lug [lʌg] *vti* trascinare, tirare.
luggage ['lʌgidʒ] *n* bagagli(o); **l. office (room)** deposito bagagli; **l. rack** portabagagli.
lugubrious [lu:'gu:briəs] *a* lugubre.
Luke [lu:k] *nm pr* Luca.
lukewarm ['lu:kwɔ:m] *a* tiepido; indifferente.
lull [lʌl] *n* calma, tregua; *vti* acquietar(si); cullare.
lullaby ['lʌləbai] *n* ninna-nanna.
lumbago [lʌm'beigou] *n* lombaggine.
lumber ['lʌmbə] *n* legname da costruzione; mobili *pl*; di scarto; cianfrusaglie.
luminary ['lu:minəri] *n* luminare.
luminous ['lu:minəs] *a* luminoso.
lump [lʌmp] *n* massa, pezzo, pezzetto, blocco; gonfiore; *vt* ammassare, riunire in blocco.
lumpy ['lʌmpi] *a* grumoso, bernoccoluto.
lunacy ['lu:nəsi] *n* demenza, pazzia.
lunar ['lu:nə] *a* lunare.
lunatic ['lu:nətik] *a n* demente, pazzo.
lunch [lʌntʃ] *n* (seconda) colazione; spuntino; *vi* fare (la seconda) colazione; fare uno spuntino.
luncheon ['lʌntʃən] *n* seconda colazione, pasto del mezzogiorno; spuntino.
lung [lʌŋ] *n* polmone.
lupin(e) ['lu:pin] *n* (*bot*) lupino.
lurch [lə:tʃ] *n* traballamento; *vi* traballare; **to leave in the l.** lasciare nelle peste.
lure [ljuə] *n* adescamento; *vt* adescare.
lurid ['ljuərid] *a* livido, spettrale, terribile.
lurk [lə:k] *vi* appiattarsi, stare in agguato.
luscious ['lʌʃəs] *a* dolce, succolento, delizioso.
lush [lʌʃ] *a* lussureggiante; succoso.
lust [lʌst] *n* lussuria, concupiscenza, brama; *vi* desiderare ardentemente, bramare.
luster ['lʌstə] *n* lucentezza, lustro; lampadario a gocce.
lustful ['lʌstful] *a* lussurioso, bramoso.
lustrous ['lʌstrəs] *a* lustro, rilucente.
lusty ['lʌsti] *a* sano e robusto, vigoroso.
lute [lu:t] *n* (*mus*) liuto.
Lutheran ['lu:θərən] *a n* luterano.
Luxemburg ['lʌksəmbə:g] *n* Lussemburgo.
luxuriance [lʌg'zjuəriəns] *n* esuberanza, rigoglio.

luxuriant [lʌg'zjuəriənt] *a* lussureggiante, rigoglioso.
luxurious [lʌg'zjuəriəs] *a* lussuoso.
luxury ['lʌkʃəri] *n* lusso.
lyceum [lai'siəm] *n* liceo.
lye [lai] *n* lisciva.
lying ['laiiŋ] *a* bugiardo, menzognero; *n* menzogna.
lying-in ['laiiŋ'in] *n* parto.
lymph [limf] *n* linfa, vaccino.
lynch [lintʃ] *vt* linciare.
lynx [liŋks] *n* lince.
Lyons ['laiənz] *n* Lione.
lyre ['laiə] *n* (*mus*) lira.
lyric ['lirik] *n* lirica, poesia lirica.
lyrical ['lirikəl] *a* lirico.

M

macabre [mə'kɑ:br] *a* macabro.
macadam [mə'kædəm] *n* macadam.
macadamize [mə'kædəmaiz] *vt* macadamizzare.
macaroon [,mækə'ru:n] *n* amaretto, spumiglia.
macaroni [,mækə'rouni] *n* maccheroni *pl*, pasta.
mace [meis] *n* mazza; (*chem*) macis.
macerate ['mæsəreit] *vt* macerare.
machination [,mæki'neiʃən] *n* macchinazione, trama.
machine [mə'ʃi:n] *n* macchina.
machinery [mə'ʃinəri] *n* macchinario, meccanismo; (*fig*) macchina.
mackerel ['mækrəl] *n* sgombro.
mackintosh ['mækintɔʃ] *n* impermeabile.
mad [mæd] *a* matto, furioso; (*of dog*) idrofobo.
madam ['mædəm] *n* (*vocative*) signora.
madden ['mædn] *vt* far impazzire.
maddening ['mædniŋ] *a* che fa impazzire; esasperante.
Madeira [mə'diərə] *n* Madera.
madly ['mædli] *ad* pazzamente, alla follia.
madness ['mædnis] *n* pazzia, follia.
madrigal ['mædrigəl] *n* madrigale.
maecenas [mi'si:næs] *n* mecenate.
magazine [,mægə'zi:n] *n* magazzino; periodico, rivista; caricatore di arma.
Magdalen(e) ['mægdəlin] *nf pr* Maddalena.
maggot ['mægət] *n* baco; (*fig*) capriccio, ubbia.
magic ['mædʒik] *n* magia; **magic(al)** *a* magico.
magician [mə'dʒiʃən] *n* mago.
magistrate ['mædʒistrit] *n* magistrato.
magnanimous [mæg'næniməs] *a* magnanimo.
magnate ['mægnit] *n* magnate.
magnesia [mæg'ni:ʃə] *n* magnesia.
magnesium [mæg'ni:ziəm] *n* magnesio.
magnet ['mægnit] *n* magnete, calamita.
magnetic [mæg'netik] *a* magnetico.
magnetism ['mægnitizəm] *n* magnetismo.
magnetize ['mægnitaiz] *vt* magnetizzare.
magnificence [mæg'nifisns] *n* magnificenza.
magnificent [mæg'nifisnt] *a* magnifico, sontuoso.
magnify ['mægnifai] *vt* ampliare, ingrandire; **magnifying glass** *n* lente d'ingrandimento.
magnitude ['mægnitju:d] *n* grandezza, vastità.
magnolia [mæg'nouliə] *n* magnolia.
magpie ['mægpai] *n* gazza.
mahogany [mə'hɔgəni] *n* mogano.
maid [meid] *n* domestica; fanciulla; zitella; **old m.** vecchia zitella.
maiden ['meidn] *a* verginale, nubile; *n* fanciulla, vergine.
maidenhood ['meidnhud] *n* verginità.
maidenly ['meidnli] *a* di fanciulla, delicato, modesto.
mail [meil] *n* posta, corrispondenza; maglia di ferro; **m. car** vagone postale; **mailman** portalettere; *vt* mandare per posta.
maim [meim] *vt* mutilare, storpiare.
main [mein] *a* principale; *n* conduttura principale; l'essenziale.
mainland ['meinlənd] *n* continente.
mainly ['meinli] *ad* per lo più, principalmente.
maintain [men'tein] *vt* mantenere, sostenere.
maintenance ['meintinəns] *n* mantenimento, manutenzione.
maize [meiz] *n* granturco, mais.
majestic [mə'dʒestik] *a* maestoso.
majesty ['mædʒisti] *n* maestà.
major ['meidʒə] *a* maggiore; *n* (*mil*) maggiore.
Majorca [mə'dʒɔ:kə] *n* Maiorca.
majority [mə'dʒɔriti] *n* maggioranza; maggiore età.
make [meik] *n* fabbricazione, fattura, marca; *vt* fare, creare, fabbricare; rendere; **m. for** *vi* dirigersi; **m.-believe** finta, finzione.
maker ['meikə] *n* creatore, fabbricante.
makeshift ['meikʃift] *a* improvvisato; *n* espediente, ripiego.
make-up ['meikʌp] *n* confezione, composizione; comportamento; trucco, cosmetici.
making ['meikiŋ] *n* creazione, fattura, confezione.
maladjusted ['mælə'dʒʌstid] *a* disadatto, incapace di inserirsi (in una società *etc*).
maladjustment ['mælə'dʒʌstmənt] *n* incapacità di adattamento, inadattabilità.
malady ['mælədi] *n* malattia.
malaise [mæ'leiz] *n* malessere.
malaria [mə'lɛəriə] *n* malaria.
Malay [mə'lei] *a n* malese.

male [meil] *a* maschile; *n* maschio.
malevolence [mə'levələns] *n* malevolenza.
malevolent [mə'levələnt] *a* malevolo.
malice ['mælis] *n* malizia, malignità.
malicious [mə'liʃəs] *a* maligno, malevolo.
malign [mə'lain] *a* maligno; *vti* calunniare, malignare.
malignant [mə'lignənt] *a* maligno, malevolo.
malinger [mə'liŋgə] *vi* fingersi malato.
malleable ['mæliəbl] *a* malleabile.
mallet ['mælit] *n* mazzuolo, martello di legno.
mallow ['mælou] *n* malva.
malnutrition ['mælnju(:)'triʃən] *n* malnutrizione; denutrizione.
malt [mɔ:lt] *n* malto.
Malta ['mɔ:ltə] *n* Malta; **Maltese** *a n* maltese.
maltreat [mæl'tri:t] *vt* maltrattare.
mamma [mə'mɑ:] *n* (*fam*) mamma.
mammal ['mæməl] *n* mammifero.
man [mæn] *pl* **men** *n* uomo, persona, essere umano; (*checkers*) pedina; (*chess*) pezzo; *vt* presidiare; far funzionare; farsi coraggio.
manacle ['mænəkl] *n usu pl* manetta; restrizione, impedimento; *vt* ammanettare.
manage ['mænidʒ] *vt* amministrare, dirigere, gestire; riuscire.
manageable ['mænidʒəbl] *a* trattabile, maneggevole.
management ['mænidʒmənt] *n* amministrazione, gestione, direzione.
manager ['mænidʒə] *n* amministratore, direttore.
managing ['mænidʒiŋ] *a* dirigente; **m. director** consigliere delegato.
Manchuria [mænt'tʃuəriə] *n* Manciuria.
mandarin ['mændərin] *n* mandarino; (*bot*) mandarino.
mandate ['mændeit] *n* mandato.
mandolin ['mændəlin] *n* mandolino.
mane [mein] *n* criniera.
maneuver [mə'nu:və] *n* manovra; *vti* manovrare.
manful ['mænful] *a* maschio, virile.
mange [meindʒ] *n* rogna, scabbia.
manger ['meindʒə] *n* greppia, mangiatoia.
mangle ['mæŋgl] *n* mangano; *vt* manganare, maciullare, straziare.
mangy ['meindʒi] *a* rognoso.
manhole ['mænhoul] *n* botola.
manhood ['mænhud] *n* età virile, virilità.
mania ['meiniə] *n* mania.
maniac ['meiniæk] *a n* pazzo furioso; maniaco.
manicure ['mænikjuə] *n* manicure.
manifest ['mænifest] *a* manifesto, evidente; *n* (*com*) manifesto, nota di carico; *vti* manifestar(si), rivelare.
manifestation [,mænifes'teiʃən] *n* manifestazione
manifesto [,mæni'festou] *n* manifesto, *pl* **manifesto(e)s** *n* manifesto, proclama.
manifold ['mænifould] *a* molteplice, multiforme.
manikin ['mænikin] *n* nano, omino; manichino.
manipulate [mə'nipjuleit] *vt* manipolare, maneggiare.
manipulation [mə,nipju'leiʃən] *n* manipolazione.
mankind [mæn'kaind] *n* genere umano, umanità.
manliness ['mænlinis] *n* virilità, mascolinità.
manly ['mænli] *a* maschio, virile.
mannequin ['mænikin] *n* indossatore, indossatrice.
manner ['mænə] *n* maniera, modo; **manners** *pl* buone maniere *pl*, educazione.
mannerism ['mænərizəm] *n* manierismo; affettazione; (*fam*) gesto consueto, ticchio.
mannerly ['mænəli] *a* cortese, educato.
mannish ['mæniʃ] *a* mascolino.
manor ['mænə] *n* grande proprietà terriera; maniero.
manse [mæns] *n* (*Scozia*) residenza d'un parroco presbiteriano.
mansion ['mænʃən] *n* palazzo, villa.
manslaughter ['mæn,slɔ:tə] *n* omicidio colposo.
mantelpiece ['mæntlpi:s] *n* mensola del camino, caminetto.
mantle ['mæntl] *n* mantello, manto.
Mantua ['mæntjuə] *n* Mantova; **Mantuan** *a n* mantovano.
manual ['mænjuəl] *a n* manuale.
manufactory ['mænju'fæktəri] *n* fabbrica.
manufacture [,mænju'fæktʃə] *n* fabbricazione, manifattura; manufatto; *vt* fabbricare, confezionare.
manufacturer [,mænju'fæktʃərə] *n* fabbricante; industriale.
manure [mə'njuə] *n* concime; *vt* concimare.
manuscript ['mænjuskript] *a n* manoscritto.
many ['meni] *a pl* molti, -te *pl*; *n* molti; **a good m.** un buon numero di; **a great m.** moltissimi; **the m.** la folla.
map [mæp] *n* carta geografica, mappa; *vt* rappresentare su una carta; **to m. out** progettare in ogni particolare.
maple ['meipl] *n* acero; **m. sugar** zucchero d'acero.
mar [mɑ:] *vt* guastare, sciupare.
marble ['mɑ:bl] *n* marmo, pallina (di vetro).
March [mɑ:tʃ] *n* marzo.
march [mɑ:tʃ] *n* frontiera, confine; (*mil*) marcia; (*mus*) marcia; *vi* confinare, (far) marciare.
marchioness ['mɑ:ʃənis] *n* marchesa.
mare [mɛə] *n* cavalla, giumenta;

shank's m. il cavallo di S. Francesco.
Margaret ['mɑ:gərit] **Marguerite** [,mɑ:gə'ri:t] *nf pr* Margherita.
margarine [,mɑ:dʒə'ri:n] *n* margarina.
margin ['mɑ:dʒin] *n* bordo, margine.
marginal ['mɑ:dʒinəl] *a* marginale; di confine.
marigold ['mærigould] *n* calendula.
marinade ['mærineid] *n* (*cook*) salsa marinata; *vt* marinare.
marine [mə'ri:n] *a* marino, marittimo; *n* marina.
mariner ['mærinə] *n* marinaio.
marionette [,mæriə'net] *n* marionetta.
marital ['mæritl] *a* coniugale.
maritime ['mæritaim] *a* marittimo.
marjoram ['mɑ:dʒərəm] *n* maggiorana.
mark [mɑ:k] *n* segno, marca, marchio; bersaglio; (*school*) voto, (*German coin*) marco; *vt* marcare, segnare; prestare attenzione a.
Mark [mɑ:k] *nm pr* Marco.
market ['mɑ:kit] *n* mercato; *vt* esporre o vendere in mercato; **m. gardener** ortolano, orticoltore.
marketable ['mɑ:kitəbl] *a* vendibile.
marketing ['mɑ:kitiŋ] *n* compravendita.
marking-ink ['mɑ:kiŋ'iŋk] *n* inchiostro indelebile.
marksman ['mɑ:ksmən] *n* tiratore scelto.
marl [mɑ:l] *n* marna.
marmalade ['mɑ:məleid] *n* marmellata (di agrumi).
marmot ['mɑ:mət] *n* marmotta.
maroon [mə'ru:n] *a* marrone rossastro; *n* individuo abbandonato su qualche isola o spiaggia deserta; *vt* abbandonare su un'isola o spiaggia deserta.
marquess, -quis ['mɑ:kwis] *n* marchese.
marriage ['mæridʒ] *n* matrimonio, nozze.
marriageable ['mæridʒəbl] *a* ammogliabile, maritabile.
marrow ['mærou] *n* midollo; zucchino.
marry ['mæri] *vti* maritar(si), sposar(si).
Marseilles [mɑ:'seilz] *n* Marsiglia.
marsh [mɑ:ʃ] *n* acquitrino, palude.
marshal ['mɑ:ʃəl] *n* maresciallo; *vt* ordinare, disporre per ordine.
marshy ['mɑ:ʃi] *a* paludoso.
marten ['mɑ:tin] *n* martora.
Martha ['mɑ:θə] *nf pr* Marta.
martial ['mɑ:ʃəl] *a* marziale.
Martin ['mɑ:tin] *nm pr* Martino.
martin ['mɑ:tin] *n* rondicchio.
martinet [,mɑ:ti'net] *n* zelante della disciplina, castigamatti.
martyr ['mɑ:tə] *n* martire.
martyrdom ['mɑ:tədəm] *n* martirio.
marvel ['mɑ:vəl] *n* meraviglia; *vi* meravigliarsi.
marvelous ['mɑ:viləs] *a* meraviglioso.
Marxist ['mɑ:ksist] *a n* marxista.
Mary ['meəri] *nf pr* Maria.
mascot ['mæskət] *n* portafortuna, mascotte.
masculine ['mɑ:skjulin] *a* maschile; mascolino; (*fig*) maschio.
mash [mæʃ] *vt* mescolare, schiacciare; **mashed potatoes** purè di patate; **potato masher** schiacciapatate.
mask [mɑ:sk] *n* maschera; *vt* mascherare.
masochism ['mæzəkizəm] *n* masochismo.
mason ['meisn] *n* muratore; massone.
masonic [mə'sɔnik] *a* massonico.
masonry ['meisnri] *n* lavoro in muratura; massoneria.
masque [mɑ:sk] *n* rappresentazione allegorica.
masquerade [,mæskə'reid] *n* mascherata; *vi* mascherarsi, travestirsi.
mass [mæs] *n* messa; massa; *vti* ammassar(si); **m. meeting** adunata popolare, comizio.
massacre ['mæsəkə] *n* massacro; *vt* massacrare.
massage ['mæsɑ:ʒ] *n* massaggio.
massive ['mæsiv] *a* compatto, massiccio.
massy ['mæsi] *a* massiccio, imponente.
mast [mɑ:st] *n* (*naut*) albero.
master ['mɑ:stə] *n* signore, signorino; professore, maestro; **M. of Arts** laureato in lettere; **m. of ceremonies** (*theat*) presentatore; *vt* dominare, impadronirsi (di).
masterful ['mɑ:stəful] *a* imperioso.
masterly ['mɑ:stəli] *a* abile.
masterpiece ['mɑ:stəpi:s] *n* capolavoro.
mastery ['mɑ:stəri] *n* maestria, padronanza, supremazia.
masticate ['mæstikeit] *vt* masticare.
mastiff ['mæstif] *n* mastino.
mat [mæt] *a* opaco; *n* stuoia, sottopiatto, sottovaso *etc*; *vt* coprire con stuoie; **matted hair** capelli arruffati.
match [mætʃ] *n* fiammifero; uguale; gara, partita; matrimonio, partito; avversario; *vti* accoppiare, maritare; armonizzare; opporre; uguagliare.
matchless ['mætʃlis] *a* incomparabile, senza pari.
mate [meit] *n* compagno; (*naut*) secondo; scacco matto; *vti* accoppiar(si); dare scacco matto.
material [mə'tiəriəl] *a* materiale, essenziale; *n* materiale, materia.
materialism [mə'tiəriəlizəm] *n* materialismo.
materialistic [mə,tiəriə'listik] *a* materialistico.
materialize [mə'tiəriəlaiz] *vti* materializzare, materializzarsi, avverarsi.

materially [mə'tiəriəli] *ad* materialmente, fisicamente.
maternal [mə'tə:nl] *a* materno.
maternity [mə'tə:niti] *n* maternità; **m. hospital** casa di maternità.
mathematical [ˌmæθi'mætikəl] *a* matematico.
mathematician [ˌmæθimə'tiʃən] *n* matematico.
mathematics [ˌmæθi'mætiks] *n* matematica.
matin ['mætin] *n* mattutino.
matinée ['mætinei] *n* (*theat*) 'matinée', mattinata.
matriculate [mə'trikjuleit] *vti* immatricolar(si).
matriculation [məˌtrikju'leiʃən] *n* immatricolazione.
matrimonial [ˌmætri'mouniəl] *a* matrimoniale, coniugale.
matrimony ['mætriməni] *n* matrimonio.
matron ['meitrən] *n* matrona, capoinfermiera; vigilatrice.
matter ['mætə] *n* affare, faccenda; materia, questione; *vi* importare; (*med*) emettere pus; **m.-of-fact** *a* positivo, pratico; **what is the m.?** che c'è?
Matterhorn ['mætəhɔ:n] *n* Monte Cervino.
Matthew ['mæθju:] *nm pr* Matteo.
mattress ['mætris] *n* materasso.
mature [mə'tjuə] *a* maturo; (*com*) scaduto; *vti* (far) maturare; (*com*) scadere.
maturation [ˌmætju'reiʃən] *n* maturazione.
maturity [mə'tjuəriti] *n* maturità; (*com*) scadenza.
maudlin ['mɔ:dlin] *a* brillo e piagnucoloso.
maul [mɔ:l] *n* maglio; *vt* malmenare, percuotere.
Maurice ['mɔris] *nm pr* Maurizio.
mauve [mouv] *a n* (color) ciclamino.
mawkish ['mɔ:kiʃ] *a* sdolcinato, sentimentale.
mawkishness ['mɔ:kiʃnis] *n* sentimentalità sdolcinata.
maxim ['mæksim] *n* massima.
maximum ['mæksiməm] *a* massimo.
May [mei] *n* maggio; **M. Day** il 1 maggio.
may [mei] *v difettivo* potere, avere il permesso di.
mayflower ['mei'flauə] *n* biancospino.
mayonnaise [ˌmeiə'neiz] *n* (*cook*) maionese.
mayor [mɛə] *n* sindaco.
maze [meiz] *n* labirinto.
me [mi:] *pron* mi, me.
meadow ['medou] *n* prato.
meager ['mi:gə] *a* povero, scarso, scarno.
meal [mi:l] *n* pasto; farina.
mean [mi:n] *a* basso, vile, gretto, mediocre; (*average*) medio; *n* mezzo; media; *vti* significare, proporsi, destinare.
meander [mi'ændə] *n* meandro, tortuosità; *vi* vagare; (*fig*) divagare.
meaning ['mi:niŋ] *a* espressivo, significativo; *n* significato, intenzione.
meaningful ['mi:niŋful] *a* pieno di significato, significativo, espressivo.
meanness ['mi:nnis] *n* bassezza, tirchieria.
meantime, -while [mi:n'taim, -wail] *n* frattempo; *ad* nel frattempo, intanto.
measles ['mi:zlz] *n* (*med*) morbillo.
measurable ['meʒərəbl] *a* misurabile.
measure ['meʒə] *n* misura; *vti* misurare.
measured ['meʒəd] *a* misurato, cadenzato, ritmico.
measurement ['meʒəmənt] *n* misura.
meat [mi:t] *n* carne; cibo.
meaty ['mi:ti] *a* carnoso, polposo; sostanzioso.
mechanic [mi'kænik] *n* meccanico.
mechanical [mi'kænikəl] *a* meccanico.
mechanics [mi'kæniks] *n pl* meccanica.
mechanism ['mekənizəm] *n* meccanismo.
medal ['medl] *n* medaglia.
medallion [mi'dæliən] *n* medaglione.
meddle ['medl] *vi* immischiarsi, intromettersi.
meddler ['medlə] *n* persona inframettente.
meddlesome ['medlsəm] *a* inframettente.
mediate ['mi:dieit] *vi* far da mediatore, interporsi.
mediation [ˌmi:di'eiʃən] *n* mediazione, intervento.
medical ['medikəl] *a* medico; *n* (*fam*) studente di medicina.
medicate ['medikeit] *vt* medicare.
medicinal [me'disinl] *a* medicinale.
medicine ['medsin] *n* medicina.
medieval [ˌmedi'i:vəl] *a* medi(o)evale.
mediocre [ˌmi:di'oukə] *a* mediocre.
mediocrity [ˌmi:di'ɔkriti] *n* mediocrità.
meditate ['mediteit] *vti* macchinare; meditare.
meditation [ˌmedi'teiʃən] *n* meditazione.
mediterranean [ˌmeditə'reiniən] *a* mediterraneo; *a n* Mediterraneo.
medium ['mi:djəm] *a* medio; *n* mezzo, strumento; medium
medlar ['medlə] *n* (*bot*) nespola, -o.
medley ['medli] *n* miscellanea, miscuglio.
meek [mi:k] *a* mite, remissivo.
meekness ['mi:knis] *n* mansuetudine, sottomissione.
meet [mi:t] *n* riunione di cacciatori; *vti* incontrar(si), far la conoscenza di.

meeting ['mi:tiŋ] *n* incontro, riunione, duello; **m. place** luogo di ritrovo.
megalomania ['megəlou'meiniə] *n* megalomania.
megaphone ['megəfoun] *n* megafono.
melancholy ['melənkəli] *a* malinconico; *n* malinconia.
mellifluous [me'lifluəs] *a* mellifluo.
mellow ['melou] *a* maturo, succoso, tenero; *vti* ammorbidir(si), maturar(si).
mellowness ['melounis] *n* maturità, succosità; (*fig*) comprensione, maturità.
melodious [mi'loudiəs] *a* melodioso.
melodrama ['melə,drɑ:mə] *n* dramma a lieto fine.
melodramatic [,melədrə'mætik] *a* melodrammatico.
melody ['melədi] *n* melodia.
melon ['melən] *n* melone, popone; **water m.** anguria, cocomero.
melt [melt] *n* fusione; *vt* fondere, sciogliere; *vi* fondersi, sciogliersi, dissolversi; (*fig*) intenerirsi.
member ['membə] *n* membro.
membership ['membəʃip] *n* insieme dei membri di una associazione, funzione di membro.
membrane ['membrein] *n* membrana.
memento [mə'mentou] *n* memento; oggetto ricordo.
memoir ['memwɑ:] *n* (*pl book*) ricordi *pl*.
memorable ['memərəbl] *a* memorabile.
memorandum [,memə'rændəm] *pl* **memoranda** *n* memorandum, appunto; **m. book** taccuino, agenda.
memorial [mi'mɔ:riəl] *a* commemorativo; *n* memoriale, monumento (alla memoria).
memorize ['meməraiz] *vt* imparare a memoria.
memory ['meməri] *n* memoria, ricordo.
menace ['menəs] *n* minaccia; *vt* minacciare.
menacing ['menisiŋ] *a* minaccioso, torvo.
mend [mend] *n* rammendo; riparazione; *vt* accomodare, rammendare, riparare, correggere; *vi* correggersi; rimettersi (in salute).
mendacious [men'deiʃəs] *a* mendace.
mendicant ['mendikənt] *a n* mendicante.
menial ['mi:niəl] *a* servile, umile; *n* servo.
menstruation [,menstru'eiʃən] *n* mestruazione.
mental ['mentl] *a* mentale.
mentality [men'tæliti] *n* mentalità.
mention ['menʃən] *n* accenno, menzione; *vt* accennare a, menzionare; **don't m. it!** *interj* di niente!
mercantile ['mə:kəntail] *a* mercantile.
mercenary ['mə:sinəri] *a n* mercenario.
merchandise ['mə:tʃəndaiz] *n* mercanzie *pl*, merce.
merchant ['mə:tʃənt] *n* mercante, commerciante.
merciful ['mə:siful] *a* misericordioso, pietoso.
merciless ['mə:silis] *a* spietato.
mercurial [mə:'kjuəriəl] *a* mutevole, eccitabile.
mercury ['mə:kjuri] *n* mercurio.
mercy ['mə:si] *n* misericordia, pietà, carità.
mere [miə] *a* mero, puro, schietto, semplice.
merely ['miəli] *ad* puramente, semplicemente.
merge [mə:dʒ] *vti* immergersi, assorbire, amalgamarsi.
meridian [mə'ridiən] *a n* meridiano.
meringue [mə'ræŋ] *n* meringa.
merit ['merit] *n* merito; *vt* meritare.
meritorious [,meri'tɔ:riəs] *a* meritorio.
mermaid ['mə:meid] *n* sirena.
merriment ['merimənt] *a* allegria.
merry ['meri] *a* allegro, brioso.
mesh [meʃ] *n* maglia, rete; *vt* prendere nella rete; (*mech*) ingranare.
mesmerize ['mezməraiz] *vt* ipnotizzare.
mess [mes] *n* confusione, pasticcio; mensa, pasto preso da una comunità; *vt* fare confusione in, un pasticcio di; *vi* mangiare alla mensa.
message ['mesidʒ] *n* ambasciata, messaggio.
messenger ['mesindʒə] *n* messaggero.
Messiah [me'saiə] *n* Messia.
metal ['metl] *n* metallo; **m. fatigue** fatica del metallo.
metallic [mi'tælik] *a* metallico, di metallo.
metallurgy [me'tælədʒi] *n* metallurgia.
metamorphosis [,metə'mɔ:fəsis] *n* metamorfosi.
metaphor ['metəfə] *n* metafora.
metaphoric(al) [,metə'fɔrik(əl)] *a* metaforico.
metaphysical [,metə'fizikəl] *a* metafisico.
metaphysics [,metə'fiziks] *n pl* metafisica.
meteor ['mi:tiə] *n* meteora.
meteorological [,mi:tiərə'lɔdʒikəl] *a* metereologico; **m. office** ufficio metereologico.
meter ['mi:tə] *n* contatore, misuratore; metro; metro poetico; ritmo.
method ['meθəd] *n* metodo.
methodical [mi'θɔdikəl] *a* metodico; **methodically** metodicamente.
Methodist ['meθədist] *n* metodista.
methyl ['meθil] *n* (*chem*) metile.
meticulous [me'tikjuləs] *a* meticoloso.

metric ['metrik] *a* metrico.

metrical ['metrikəl] *a* (*linear measure*) metrico.

metropolis [mi'trɔpəlis] *n* metropoli.

metropolitan [ˌmetrə'pɔlitən] *a n* metropolitano.

mettle ['metl] *n* ardore, coraggio, foga.

mew [mju:] *n* miagoliò; gabbia (per falchi); **mews** *pl* scuderie, stalle *pl* (disposte intorno ad un cortile).

mew [mju:] *vi* miagolare.

Mexican ['meksikən] *a n* messicano.

Mexico ['meksikou] *n* Messico.

Michael ['maikl] *nm pr* Michele.

Michaelmas ['miklməs] *n* festa di S. Michele.

microbe ['maikroub] *n* microbo.

microgroove ['maikrouˌgru:v] *n* microsolco.

microphone ['maikrəfoun] *n* microfono.

microscope ['maikrəskoup] *n* microscopio.

microscopic(al) [ˌmaikrə'skɔpik(əl)] *a* microscopico.

mid [mid] *a* medio, mezzo.

midday ['middei] *n* mezzogiorno.

middle ['midl] *a* intermedio, medio, di mezzo; *n* mezzo, centro; **M. Ages** Medioevo; **m.-aged** di mezza età; **m. class** borghesia.

middleman ['midlmæn] *pl* **-men** *n* (*com*) intermediario.

middling ['midliŋ] *a* medio, mediocre; *ad* discretamente.

midge [midʒ] *n* moscerino.

midget ['midʒit] *n* omiciattolo, cosa piccolissima.

midland ['midlənd] *a* centrale; **the Midlands** *pl* contee dell'Inghilterra centrale.

midnight ['midnait] *a n* (di) mezzanotte.

midshipman ['midʃipmən] *pl* **-men** *n* (*naut*) cadetto.

midst [midst] *n* mezzo, centro.

midsummer ['midˌsʌmə] *n* periodo del solstizio d'estate.

midway ['mid'wei] *ad* a metà strada.

midwife ['midwaif] *n* levatrice.

midwifery ['midwifəri] *n* ostetricia.

might [mait] *past tense of* **may**; *n* forza, potenza.

mighty ['maiti] *a* possente, potente; *ad* (*fam*) molto.

mignonette [ˌminjə'net] *n* reseda.

migraine ['mi:grein] *n* emicrania.

migrate [mai'greit] *vi* emigrare, trasmigrare.

migration [mai'greiʃən] *n* migrazione, emigrazione.

migratory ['maigrətəri] *a* migratore, migratorio.

Milan [mi'læn] *n* Milano; **Milanese** *a n* milanese.

mild [maild] *a* dolce, mite, blando.

mildew ['mildju:] *n* muffa.

mildness ['maildnis] *n* dolcezza, mitezza.

mile [mail] *n* miglio (= *metri 1609*).

mileage ['mailidʒ] *n* distanza in miglia; **m. recorder** contachilometri.

milestone ['mailstoun] *n* pietra miliare.

militant ['militənt] *a* militante; *n* attivista.

military ['militəri] *a* militare; **the m.** i militari.

militate ['militeit] *vi* **m. against** opporsi a.

militia [mi'liʃə] *n* milizia.

milk [milk] *n* latte; *vti* mungere.

milkmaid ['milkmeid] *n* mungitrice.

milkman ['milkmən] *n* lattaio.

milky ['milki] *a* latteo, di latte; **the M. Way** la Via Lattea.

mill [mil] *n* mulino, fabbrica; *vt* macinare.

millennium [mi'leniəm] *n* millennio.

millepede ['milipi:d] *n* millepiedi.

miller ['milə] *n* mugnaio.

millet ['milit] *n* miglio.

milliard ['milia:d] *n* miliardo, bilione.

milliner ['milinə] *n* modista.

million ['miljən] *a n* milione; **millionaire** milionario.

millpond ['milpɔnd] *n* gora di mulino.

millstone ['milstoun] *n* macina di mulino.

mimic ['mimik] *a* imitativo; *n* mimo; imitatore; contraffazione.

mimicry ['mimikri] *n* mimesi; mimica; mimetismo.

mince [mins] *n* carne tritata; *vt* tritare; abbreviare; (*fig*) mitigare; parlare con affettazione.

mincing ['minsiŋ] *a* affettato.

mind [maind] *n* mente, intelligenza; animo, opinione; memoria; *vt* badare a, occuparsi di, fare attenzione a, importare; spiacere.

mindful ['maindful] *a* attento, memore.

mine [main] *n* mina, miniera; *pron* (il) mio *etc*; *vti* scavare, estrarre; minare.

miner ['mainə] *n* minatore.

mineral ['minərəl] *a n* minerale.

mingle ['miŋgl] *vti* mescolar(si), mischiar(si).

miniature ['minətʃə] *a n* (in) miniatura.

minim ['minim] *n* (*mus*) minima.

minimize ['minimaiz] *vt* minimizzare.

minimum ['miniməm] *a n* minimo.

mining ['mainiŋ] *a* minerario; *n* lavoro nelle miniere.

minion ['minjən] *n* favorito; **m. of the law** (*fam*) poliziotto.

miniskirt ['miniskə:t] *n* minigonna.

minister ['ministə] *n* ministro; *vi* dare aiuto.

ministration [ˌminis'treiʃən] *n* aiuto, assistenza.

ministry ['ministri] *n* ministero.

mink [miŋk] *n* visone.

minnow ['minou] *n* pesciolino d'acqua dolce.
minor ['mainə] *a* minore; *n* minorenne.
minority [mai'nɔriti] *n* minoranza; minorità.
minster ['minstə] *n* chiesa d'un monastero, cattedrale.
minstrel ['minstrəl] *n* menestrello.
mint [mint] *n* zecca; (*fig*) grossa somma; menta; *vt* coniare.
minuet [,minju'et] *n* minuetto.
minus ['mainəs] *prep* meno, privo di; *a n* meno.
minute [mai'nju:t] *a* minuto, piccolissimo; ['minit] *n* minuto; nota, minuta; **minutes** *pl* verbale.
minuteness [mai'nju:tnis] *n* minutezza, piccolezza.
minx [miŋks] *n* ragazza sfacciata.
miracle ['mirəkl] *n* miracolo.
miraculous [mi'rækjuləs] *a* miracoloso.
mirage [mi'rɑ:ʒ] *n* miraggio.
mire ['maiə] *n* fango, pantano.
mirror ['mirə] *n* specchio; *vt* rispecchiare.
mirth [mə:θ] *n* allegria.
miry ['maiəri] *a* fangoso.
misadventure ['misəd'ventʃə] *n* disgrazia.
misanthrope ['mizənθroup] *n* misantropo.
misanthropy [mi'sænθrəpi] *n* misantropia.
misapply ['misə'plai] *vt* applicare erroneamente.
misapprehend ['mis,æpri'hend] *vt* fraintendere.
misbehave ['misbi'heiv] *vi* comportarsi male.
misbehavior ['misbi'heivjə] *n* cattivo contegno.
miscalculate ['mis'kælkjuleit] *vti* calcolare male.
miscarriage [mis'kæridʒ] *n* aborto; disguido postale; insuccesso; errore.
miscarry [mis'kæri] *vi* abortire; andare smarrito; fallire.
miscellaneous [,misi'leiniəs] *a* miscellaneo.
miscellany [mi'seləni] *n* miscellanea.
mischance [mis'tʃɑ:ns] *n* disgrazia, sventura.
mischief ['mistʃif] *n* male, danno, malizia, birichinata.
mischievous ['mistʃivəs] *a* cattivo, dannoso; malizioso, furbo.
misconception ['miskən'sepʃən] *n* concetto erroneo, malinteso.
misconduct [mis'kɔndəkt] *n* cattiva condotta; cattiva amministrazione; adulterio.
misconstrue ['miskən'stru:] *vt* fraintendere.
misdeed ['mis'di:d] *n* misfatto.
misdemeanor [,misdi'mi:nə] *n* cattiva condotta, infrazione alla legge.
misdirection ['misdi'rekʃən] *n* indirizzo sbagliato, informazione sbagliata.
miser ['maizə] *n* avaro.
miserable ['mizərəbl] *a* triste, infelice; miserabile.
miserly ['maizəli] *a* avaro, sordido.
misery ['mizəri] *n* infelicità; indigenza, *pl* avversità.
misfire ['mis'faiə] *vi* far cilecca (*also fig*).
misfit ['misfit] *n* indumento mal riuscito; (*fam*) individuo spostato.
misfortune [mis'fɔ:tʃən] *n* disgrazia, sfortuna.
misgiving [mis'giviŋ] *n* apprensione; presentimento.
mishap ['mishæp] *n* disgrazia, incidente.
misinform ['misin'fɔ:m] *vt* informar male.
misinterpret ['misin'tə:prit] *vt* interpretar male.
misjudge ['mis'dʒʌdʒ] *vt* giudicare male.
mislay [mis'lei] *vt* smarrire, metter fuori posto.
mislead [mis'li:d] *vt* sviare, ingannare.
misleading [mis'li:diŋ] *a* ingannevole, che fa sbagliare.
mismanage ['mis'mænidʒ] *vt* amministrar male, dirigere male.
mismanagement ['mis'mænidʒmənt] *n* cattiva amministrazione.
misplace ['mis'pleis] *vt* collocare male.
misprint ['mis'print] *n* errore di stampa; [mis'print] *vt* stampare con errori.
misrepresent ['mis,repri'zent] *vt* travisare.
misrule ['mis'ru:l] *n* malgoverno.
miss [mis] *n* signorina (*premesso al nome di donna non sposata*); colpo mancato, insuccesso; *vti* non afferrare, non colpire, perdere, sbagliare; sentire la mancanza di; (*fig*) far cilecca, mancare; **to m. out** tralasciare, saltare.
missal ['misəl] *n* messale.
missile ['misail] *n* proiettile, missile; **guided m.** missile teleguidato.
missing ['misiŋ] *a* mancante, assente, disperso.
mission ['miʃən] *n* missione.
missionary ['miʃnəri] *a n* missionario.
misspell ['mis'spel] *vt* sbagliar l'ortografia di, scrivere erratamente.
mist [mist] *n* foschia, caligine; **Scotch m.** pioggia leggera.
mistake [mis'teik] *n* errore, sbaglio; *vti* scambiare, fraintendere, sbagliarsi.
mistaken [mis'teikən] *a* erroneo, sbagliato.
Mister ['mistə] *n* **Mr** Signor(e).
mistletoe ['misltou] *n* vischio.
mistress ['mistris] *n* padrona; maestra; amante; **Mrs** ['misiz] Signora.

mistrust ['mis'trʌst] *n* diffidenza, sfiducia; *vt* diffidare di.
mistrustful ['mis'trʌstful] *a* diffidente.
misty ['misti] *a* nebbioso.
misunderstand ['misʌndə'stænd] *vt* capir male, fraintendere.
misunderstanding ['misʌndə'stændiŋ] *n* malinteso; dissapore.
misuse ['mis'ju:s] *n* abuso, uso sbagliato; maltrattamento; *vt* ['mis'ju:z] maltrattare; usar male; abusare di.
mite [mait] *n* piccola moneta, piccolo contributo; (*child*) piccino.
miter ['maitə] *n* mitra.
mitigate ['mitigeit] *vt* mitigare, attenuare.
mitten ['mitn] *n* mezzo guanto, manopola.
mix [miks] *vti* mescolare, mescolarsi, armonizzare, associarsi; **to m. up** confondere.
mixture ['mikstʃə] *n* miscela, miscuglio, mistura.
mix-up ['miks'ʌp] *n* confusione, baruffa.
moan [moun] *n* gemito, lamento; *vi* gemere, lamentarsi.
moat [mout] *n* fosso, fossato.
mob [mɔb] *n* folla tumultuante, plebaglia; *vt* àssalire, accalcarsi.
mobile ['moubail] *a* mobile.
mobility [mou'biliti] *n* mobilità.
mobilization [,moubilai'zeiʃən] *n* mobilitazione.
mobilize ['moubilaiz] *vt* mobilitare.
mock [mɔk] *a* falso, finto, imitato; *vti* ingannare; deridere, burlarsi di.
mockery ['mɔkəri] *n* derisione, scherno, beffa.
mode [moud] *n* modo, maniera, moda.
model ['mɔdl] *a* modello; *n* modello, modella; *vt* modellare.
moderate ['mɔdərit] *a* moderato, modico; *vti* ['mɔdəreit] moderare, moderarsi, (*weather*) calmarsi.
moderation [,mɔdə:'reiʃən] *n* moderazione.
modern ['mɔdən] *a n* moderno.
modernity [mɔ'də:niti] *n* modernità.
modernization [,mɔdə:nai'zeiʃən] *n* rimodernamento.
modernize ['mɔdə:naiz] *vt* rimodernare.
modest ['mɔdist] *a* modesto.
modesty ['mɔdisti] *n* modestia.
modification [,mɔdifi'keiʃən] *n* modificazione.
modify ['mɔdifai] *vt* modificare.
modulation [,mɔdju'leiʃən] *n* modulazione.
Mohammed [mou'hæmid] *nm pr* Maometto.
Mohammedan [mou'hæmidən] *a n* maomettano.
moist [mɔist] *a* umido.
moisten ['mɔisn] *vti* inumidir(si).
moistness ['mɔistnis] **moisture** ['mɔistʃə] *n* umidità.
molar ['moulə] *a n* molare.
mold [mould] *n* muffia; terriccio; modello, forma, stampo; *vt* formare, modellare, plasmare.
moldy ['mouldi] *a* ammuffito.
mole [moul] *n* molo, talpa.
molest [mou'lest] *vt* molestare.
mollify ['mɔlifai] *vt* addolcire, ammollire.
mollusc ['mɔləsk] *n* mollusco.
molt [moult] *n* muda; *vi* mudare.
moment ['moumənt] *n* momento; importanza.
momentary ['moumәntəri] *a* momentaneo, transitorio.
momentous [mou'mentəs] *a* grave, importante.
Monaco ['mɔnəkou] *n* Monaco (Principato di).
monarch ['mɔnək] *n* monarca.
monarchy ['mɔnəki] *n* monarchia.
monastery ['mɔnəstəri] *n* monastero.
monastic [mə'næstik] *a* monastico.
Monday ['mʌndi] *n* lunedì.
monetary ['mʌnitəri] *a* monetario.
money ['mʌni] *n* denaro, moneta, soldi *pl*.
Mongol ['mɔŋgɔl] *a n* mongolo.
Mongolian [mɔŋ'gouliən] *a* mongolo; *n* lingua mongolica.
mongoloid ['mɔŋ gɔlɔid] *a n* mongoloide.
mongoose ['mɔŋgu:s] *n* mangosta.
mongrel ['mʌŋgrəl] *n* meticcio; cane bastardo; *a* ibrido, misto.
monitor ['mɔnitə] *n* consigliere; (*el*) monitore; dispositivo di controllo.
monk [mʌŋk] *n* monaco.
monkey ['mʌŋki] *n* scimmia.
monocle ['mɔnəkl] *n* monocolo.
monogram ['mɔnəgræm] *n* monogramma.
monograph ['mɔnəgrɑ:f] *n* monografia.
monologue ['mɔnəlɔg] *n* monologo.
monopolize [mə'nɔpəlaiz] *vt* monopolizzare; **monopoly** *n* monopolio.
monosyllable ['mɔnə,siləbl] *n* monosillabo.
monotonous [mə'nɔtənəs] *a* monotono.
monotony [mə'nɔtəni] *n* monotonia.
monsoon [,mɔn'su:n] *n* monsone.
monster ['mɔnstə] *a* enorme, mostruoso; *n* mostro.
monstrance ['mɔnstrəns] *n* ostensorio.
monstrosity [mɔns'trɔsiti] *n* mostruosità.
monstrous ['mɔnstrəs] *a* mostruoso.
Mont Blanc [mɔ̃:m'blɑ̃:ŋ] *n* Monte Bianco.
Mont Cenis [,mɔ̃:nsə'ni:] *n* Moncenisio.
month [mʌnθ] *n* mese.
monthly ['mʌnθli] *a* mensile; *ad* mensilmente; *n* rivista mensile.

monument ['mɔnjumənt] *n* monumento.
monumental [,mɔnju'mentl] *a* monumentale.
mood [mu:d] *n* stato d'animo, umore; (*verb*) modo.
moody ['mu:di] *a* di malumore; lunatico.
moon [mu:n] *n* luna.
moonlight ['mu:nlait] *n* chiaro di luna.
moor [muə] *n* brughiera; *vt* (*naut*) ormeggiare.
Moor [muə] *n* moro, marocchino.
mooring ['muəriŋ] *n* (*naut*) ormeggio.
Moorish ['muəriʃ] *a* moro, moresco.
mop [mɔp] *n* scopa di stracci, strofinaccio; *vt* pulire, asciugare (un pavimento).
mope [moup] *vi* essere abbattuto, depresso.
moral ['mɔrəl] *a n* morale; **morals** *pl* condotta, costumi *pl*.
morale [mɔ'rɑ:l] *n* il morale, lo stato d'animo.
moralist ['mɔrəlist] *n* moralista.
morality [mə'ræliti] *n* morale, moralità.
moralize ['mɔrəlaiz] *vi* moralizzare.
morass [mə'ræs] *n* palude.
morbid ['mɔ:bid] *a* morboso.
morbidity [mɔ:'biditi] *n* morbosità.
mordant ['mɔ:dənt] *a* pungente, acuto.
more [mɔ:] *a* più; *ad* più, di più.
moreover [mɔ:'rouvə] *ad* inoltre, per di più.
morganatic [,mɔ:gə'nætik] *a* morganatico.
morgue [mɔ:g] *n* 'morgue', obitorio.
moribund ['mɔribʌnd] *a n* morente, moribondo.
Mormon ['mɔ:mən] *a n* mormone.
morning ['mɔ:niŋ] *n* mattina -no, mattinata.
Moroccan [mə'rɔkən] *a n* marocchino.
Morocco [mə'rɔkou] *n* (*geogr*) Marocco.
morocco [mə'rɔkou] *n* (*leather*) marocchino.
moron ['mɔ:rɔn] *n* deficiente, idiota.
morose [mə'rous] *a* tetro, imbronciato, non socievole.
moroseness [mə'rousnis] *n* tetraggine.
morphia ['mɔ:fiə] **morphine** ['mɔ:fi:n] *n* (*chem*) morfina.
Morris ['mɔris] *nm pr* Maurizio.
morsel ['mɔ:səl] *n* boccone, pezzetto.
mortal ['mɔ:tl] *a n* mortale.
mortality [mɔ:'tæliti] *n* mortalità.
mortar ['mɔ:tə] *n* mortaio, calcina.
mortgage ['mɔ:gidʒ] *n* ipoteca; *vt* ipotecare.
mortify ['mɔ:tifai] *vti* mortificar(si); incancrenire.
mortmain ['mɔ:tmein] *n* (*leg*) manomorta.
mortuary ['mɔ:tjuəri] *a* mortuario; *n* camera mortuaria.
mosaic [mə'zeiik] *a n* (di) mosaico.
Moscow ['mɔskou] *n* Mosca.
Moses ['mouziz] *nm pr* (*Bibl*) Mosè.
Moslem ['mɔzlem] **Muslim** ['mʌzlim] *a n* musulmano.
mosque [mɔsk] *n* moschea.
mosquito [məs'ki:tou] *n* zanzara.
moss [mɔs] *n* muschio; terreno paludoso.
most [moust] *a* il più, la maggior parte; *ad* il più, di più, molto; **mostly** principalmente, per lo più.
mote [mout] *n* bruscolo, pagliuzza.
motel [mou'tel] *n* 'motel' autostello.
moth [mɔθ] *n* falena; tarma, tignola.
mother ['mʌðə] *n* madre; **m.-in-law** suocera; **m.-of-pearl** madreperla; **m. tongue** madre lingua.
motherhood ['mʌðəhud] *n* maternità.
motherly ['mʌðəli] *a* materno.
motif [mou'ti:f] *n* motivo idea dominante.
motion ['mouʃən] *n* moto, movimento; mozione; *vi* fare cenno a.
motionless ['mouʃənlis] *a* senza moto, immobile.
motivation [,mouti'veiʃən] *n* motivazione; motivo, movente.
motive ['moutiv] *a* motore; *n* motivo, movente; causa.
motley ['mɔtli] *a* multicolore, eterogeneo.
motor ['moutə] *a* motore; *n* motore, macchina; **m. car** automobile; **motorway** autostrada.
motorcade ['moutəkeid] *n* sfilata di automobili.
motoring ['moutəriŋ] *a* automobilismo.
motorist ['moutərist] *n* automobilista.
mottle ['mɔtl] *vt* chiazzare, macchiare.
motto ['mɔtou] *pl* **mottoes** *n* motto.
mound [maund] *n* montagnola; tumulo, mucchio.
mount [maunt] *n* colle, monte; cavallo, montatura; *vt* ascendere, salire, montare, far salire su; incorniciare.
mountain ['mauntin] *n* montagna, monte.
mountaineer [,maunti'niə] *n* montanaro, alpinista.
mountainous ['mauntinəs] *a* montuoso.
mountebank ['mauntibæŋk] *n* ciarlatano, saltimbanco.
mourn [mɔ:n] *vti* piangere, lamentarsi, portare il lutto.
mourner ['mɔ:nə] *n* persona in lutto; chi accompagna un funerale; prefica.
mournful ['mɔ:nful] *a* lugubre, triste.

mourning ['mɔ:niŋ] *n* lutto.
mouse [maus] *pl* **mice** *n* topo, sorcio.
moustache [məs'tɑ:ʃ] *n* baffo, baffi *pl*.
mousy ['mausi] *a* grigio topo; scialbo, insignificante, (*person*) timido, silenzioso.
mouth [mauθ] *n* bocca; foce; apertura.
mouthful ['mauθful] *n* boccone.
mouthpiece ['mauθpi:s] *n* (*mus instrument*) imboccatura; bocchino; (*fig*) portavoce.
movable ['mu:vəbl] *a* mobile, (*leg*) mobiliare; **movables** *n pl* beni mobili.
move [mu:v] *n* movimento; mossa; *vti* muovere, muoversi, traslocare; commuovere; spingere; procedere.
movement ['mu:vmənt] *n* movimento, moto.
movies ['mu:viz] *n pl* (*fam*) cinematografo.
moving ['mu:viŋ] *a* commovente; mobile.
mow [mou] *vt* falciare, mietere.
mower ['mouə] *n* falciatore; (*mech*) falciatrice.
Mr *v* **Mister.**
Mrs *v* **mistress.**
much [mʌtʃ] *ad* molto, pressappoco; *a pron* molto.
muck [mʌk] *n* concime, letame; sudiciume.
mud [mʌd] *n* fango; **m.-bath** (*med*) fangature *pl*; **mudguard** (*aut*) parafango; **m.-pie** formina di terra, di sabbia.
muddle ['mʌdl] *n* confusione, disordine; *vt* confondere, guastare; **muddler** *n* confusionario, pasticcione.
muddy ['mʌdi] *a* fangoso.
muff [mʌf] *n* manicotto.
muffin ['mʌfin] *n* piccola focaccia.
muffle ['mʌfl] *vt* imbacuccare, avvolgere, bendare, coprire, soffocare.
muffler ['mʌflə] *n* sciarpa pesante; (*aut*) silenziatore.
mufti ['mʌfti] *n* abito borghese.
mug [mʌg] *n* bicchiere, boccale; (*sl*) faccia.
muggy ['mʌgi] *a* afoso, umido.
mulberry ['mʌlbəri] *n* gelso moro, mora.
mule [mju:l] *n* mulo; pianella.
mull [mʌl] *vt* **mulled wine** vino caldo.
mullet ['mʌlit] *n* triglia; muggine.
mullion ['mʌliən] *n* (*arch*) colonnina divisoria d'una finestra bifora.
multiform ['mʌltifɔ:m] *a* multiforme.
multiple ['mʌltipl] *a n* multiplo.
multiplication [,mʌltipli'keiʃən] *n* moltiplicazione.
multiplicity [,mʌlti'plisiti] *n* molteplicità.
multiply ['mʌltiplai] *vti* moltiplicar(si).
multiracial ['mʌlti,reiʃəl] *a* dalle molte razze, plurirazziale.
multitude ['mʌltitju:d] *n* moltitudine.
mumble ['mʌmbl] *n* borbottìo; *vi* borbottare.
mummy ['mʌmi] *n* mummia; (*fam*) mamma.
mumps [mʌmps] *n* parotite, (*fam*) orecchioni.
munch [mʌntʃ] *vt* masticare, sgranocchiare.
mundane ['mʌndein] *a* mondano, del mondo.
Munich ['mju:nik] *n* Monaco (di Baviera).
municipal [mju:'nisipəl] *a* municipale.
municipality [mju:,nisi'pæliti] *n* municipalità.
munificent [mju:'nifisnt] *a* munifico.
munitions [mju:'niʃəns] *n pl* munizioni *pl*.
mural ['mjuərəl] *a* murale; *n* affresco.
murder ['mə:də] *n* assassinio; *vt* assassinare.
murderer ['mə:dərə] *n* assassino.
murderous ['mə:dərəs] *a* assassino, micidiale.
murky ['mə:ki] *a* fosco, tenebroso.
murmur ['mə:mə] *n* mormorio; *vi* mormorare.
muscle ['mʌsl] *n* muscolo.
Muscovite ['mʌskəvait] *a n* moscovita.
muscular ['mʌskjulə] *a* muscolare; muscoloso.
muse [mju:z] *n* musa; *vi* meditare, essere assorto in un pensiero.
museum [mju:'ziəm] *n* museo.
mushroom ['mʌʃrum] *n* fungo.
music ['mju:zik] *n* musica; **m.-hall** teatro di varietà.
musical ['mju:zikəl] *a* musicale.
musician [mju:'ziʃən] *n* musicista.
musk [mʌsk] *n* muschio.
musket ['mʌskit] *n* moschetto.
musketeer [,mʌski'tiə] *n* moschettiere.
musketry ['mʌskitri] *n* moschetteria, fucileria.
Muslim ['muslim] *a n* musulmano.
muslin ['mʌzlin] *n* mussola.
mussel ['mʌsl] *n* arsella, cozza, muscolo.
Mussulman ['mʌslmən] *a n* musulmano.
must [mʌst] *n* mosto, muffa.
must [mʌst] *v* dovere.
mustard ['mʌstəd] *n* senape; difettivo mostarda.
muster ['mʌstə] *a* adunata, parata; *vti* raccoglier(si), radunar(si).
mustiness ['mʌstinis] *n* muffa.
musty ['mʌsti] *a* ammuffito.
mute [mju:t] *a n* muto.
mutilate ['mju:tileit] *vt* mutilare.
mutilation [,mju:ti'leiʃən] *n* mutilazione.

mutineer [,mju:ti'niə] *n* ammutinato.
mutinous ['mju:tinəs] *a* ammutinato, rivoltoso; ribelle.
mutiny ['mju:tini] *n* ammutinamento; *vi* ammutinarsi.
mutter ['mʌtə] *n* borbottio; *vi* borbottare.
mutton ['mʌtn] *n* carne di montone o di pecora.
mutual ['mju:tjuəl] *a* mutuo, reciproco.
muzzle ['mʌzl] *n* muso; museruola; (*gun etc*) bocca; *vt* mettere la museruola a; (*fig*) costringere al silenzio.
muzzy ['mʌzi] *a* confuso, inebetito; instupidito (dall'alcool).
my [mai] *a* (il) mio, (la) mia *etc*; **myself** *pron* io stesso, mi, me stesso.
myriad ['miriəd] *a n* miriade.
myrrh [mə:] *n* mirra.
myrtle ['mə:tl] *n* mirto.
mysterious [mis'tiəriəs] *a* misterioso.
mystery ['mistəri] *n* mistero.
mystic(al) ['mistik(əl)] *a n* mistico.
mystify ['mistifai] *vt* mistificare; ingannare; disorientare.
myth [miθ] *n* mito.
mythological [,miθə'lɔdʒikəl] *a* mitologico.
mythology [mi'θɔlədʒi] *n* mitologia.

N

nag [næg] *n* (*fam*) cavallo, -lino; *vti* (*fam*) brontolare; tormentare.
nail [neil] *n* unghia; artiglio; chiodo; *vt* inchiodare; **on the n.** puntualmente, senz'indugio.
naïve [nai'i:v] *a* ingenuo, semplice.
naked ['neikid] *a* nudo, disadorno; evidente; indifeso.
nakedness ['neikidnis] *n* nudità.
name [neim] *n* nome; reputazione; *vt* chiamare, designare, nominare.
nameless ['neimlis] *a* senza nome, anonimo, innominato; indicibile.
namely ['neimli] *ad* cioè.
namesake ['neimseik] *n* omonimo.
nanny ['næni] *n* bambinaia, balia.
nap [næp] *n* pisolino, sonnellino; (*of material*) pelo; *vi* fare un pisolino, sonnecchiare.
nape [neip] *n* nuca.
naphtha ['næfθə] *n* nafta.
napkin ['næpkin] *n* tovagliolo, pannolino.
Naples ['neiplz] *n* Napoli.
Napoleon [nə'pouliən] *nm pr* Napoleone.
narcissus [nɑ:'sisəs] *n* narciso.
narcotic [nɑ:'kɔtik] *a n* narcotico.
narrate [næ'reit] *vt* narrare.
narration [næ'reiʃən] *n* narrazione.
narrative ['nærətiv] *a* narrativo; *n* narrazione, racconto.
narrator [næ'reitə] *n* narratore.
narrow ['nærou] *a* stretto, ristretto; minuzioso; *n* (*usu pl*) stretto, gola; *vt* restringere.
narrowly ['nærouli] *ad* a stento; minuziosamente.
narrowness ['nærounis] *n* strettezza, ristrettezza.
nasal ['neizəl] *a n* nasale.
nastiness ['nɑ:stinis] *n* cattiveria; sporcizia; indecenza.
nasturtium [nəs'tə:ʃəm] *n* nasturzio.
nasty ['nɑ:sti] *a* disgustoso; cattivo; indecente.
nation ['neiʃən] *n* nazione.
national ['næʃənl] *a* nazionale.
nationalism ['næʃnəlizəm] *n* nazionalismo.
nationality [,næʃə'næliti] *n* nazionalità.
nationalization [,næʃnəlai'zeiʃən] *n* nazionalizzazione.
nationalize ['næʃnəlaiz] *vt* nazionalizzare.
native ['neitiv] *a n* indigeno, nativo.
nativity [nə'tiviti] *n* natività, nascita.
natty ['næti] *a* ben aggiustato, in ghingheri.
natural ['nætʃrəl] *a* naturale.
naturalist ['nætʃrəlist] *n* naturalista.
naturalization [,nætʃrəlai'zeiʃən] *n* naturalizzazione.
naturalize ['nætʃrəlaiz] *vt* naturalizzare.
naturally ['nætʃrəli] *ad* naturalmente, per natura.
nature ['neitʃə] *n* natura.
naught [nɔ:t] *n* nulla, zero.
naughtiness ['nɔ:tinis] *n* cattiveria, disubbidienza, impertinenza.
naughty ['nɔ:ti] *a* cattivo, disubbidiente.
nausea ['nɔ:siə] *n* nausea.
nauseate ['nɔ:sieit] *vt* nauseare.
nauseous ['nɔ:siəs] *a* disgustoso, nauseante.
nautical ['nɔ:tikəl] *a* nautico.
naval ['neivəl] *a* navale.
nave [neiv] *n* navata.
navel ['neivəl] *n* ombelico.
navigability [,nævigə'biliti] *n* navigabilità.
navigable ['nævigəbl] *a* navigabile.
navigate ['nævigeit] *vti* navigare.
navigation [,nævi'geiʃən] *n* navigazione.
navigator ['nævigeitə] *n* navigatore.
navy ['neivi] *n* flotta; marina; **n. yard** arsenale marittimo.
Nazarene [,næzə'ri:n] *a n* nazzareno.
Nazareth ['næzəriθ] *n* Nazaret.
Nazi ['nɑ:tsi] *a n* nazista.
Neapolitan [niə'pɔlitən] *a n* napoletano.
near [niə] *a* vicino, intimo; *ad* presso, vicino; *prep* vicino a; *vti* approssimar(si), avvicinar(si).
nearby ['niəbai] *a ad prep* vicino.
nearly ['niəli] *ad* quasi; da vicino, strettamente.

nearness ['niənis] *n* prossimità, vicinanza, intimità.
neat [ni:t] *a* lindo, accurato; (*of drinks*) liscio; chiaro e conciso.
neatly ['ni:tli] *ad* accuratamente; abilmente; elegantemente.
neatness ['ni:tnis] *n* pulizia, ordine, accuratezza, proprietà.
necessarily ['nesisərili] *ad* necessariamente.
necessary ['nesisəri] *a n* necessario.
necessitate [ni'sesiteit] *vt* richiedere, necessitare.
necessity [ni'sesiti] *n* necessità.
neck [nek] *n* collo.
neckerchief ['nekətʃif] *n* fazzoletto da collo.
necklace ['neklis] *n* collana.
necktie ['nektai] *n* cravatta.
necrology [ne'krɔlədʒi] *n* necrologia; necrologio.
necromancer ['nekroumænsə] *n* negromante.
necromancy ['nekroumænsi] *n* negromanzia.
nectar ['nektə] *n* nettare.
need [ni:d] *n* bisogno; *vti* aver bisogno di; essere necessario, occorrere.
needful ['ni:dful] *a* necessario.
neediness ['ni:dinis] *n* indigenza, miseria.
needle ['ni:dl] *n* ago; **knitting n.** ferro da calza.
needless ['ni:dlis] *a* inutile.
needy ['ni:di] *a* bisognoso, indigente.
nefarious [ni'fɛəriəs] *a* abominevole.
negation [ni'geiʃən] *n* negazione.
negative ['negətiv] *a* negativo; *n* negativa.
neglect [ni'glekt] *n* negligenza, trascuratezza; *vi* negligere, trascurare.
neglectful [ni'glektful] *a* negligente, trascurato.
negligence ['neglidʒəns] *n* negligenza, trascuratezza.
negligent ['neglidʒənt] *a* negligente, trascurato.
negligible ['neglidʒəbl] *a* trascurabile.
negotiate [ni'gouʃieit] *vti* negoziare, trattare.
negotiation [ni,gouʃi'eiʃən] *n* trattativa, negoziati *pl*.
Negro ['ni:grou] *n* negro; **Negro woman** negra.
neigh [nei] *vi* nitrire.
neighbor ['neibə] *n* prossimo, vicino.
neighborhood ['neibəhud] *n* vicinato, dintorni, vicinanze *pl*.
neighboring ['neibəriŋ] *a* limitrofo, vicino.
neighborly ['neibərli] *a* amichevole, da buon vicino.
neither ['naiðə] *a pron* nè l'uno nè l'altro; *cj* nè, neppure; **neither . . . nor** nè . . . nè.
neon ['ni:ɔn] *n* (*chem*) neon; **n. lights** luci al neon.
nephew ['nevju] *n* nipote (di zio).
nerve [nə:v] *n* nervo; *pl* nervi *pl*; sangue freddo; (*fam*) sfrontatezza.
nervous ['nə:vəs] *a* eccitabile, nervoso; pauroso, timido.
nervousness ['nə:vəsnis] *n* nervosismo; timidezza.
nervy ['nə:vi] *a* (*fam*) eccitabile, nervoso.
nest [nest] *n* nido; covo; *vi* nidificare.
nestle ['nesl] *vi* annidarsi; accoccolarsi.
nestling ['nesliŋ] *n* uccellino di nido.
net [net] *a* netto; *n* rete; *vt* prendere con la rete, pescare; (*fig*) irretire; *vi* far le reti.
Netherlands ['neðələndz] *n pl* Paesi Bassi.
netting ['netiŋ] *n* rete; reticolato.
nettle ['netl] *n* ortica.
network ['netwə:k] *n* rete, reticolato.
neuralgia [njuə'rældʒə] *n* nevralgia.
neurasthenia [,njuərəs'θiniə] *n* neurastenia, nevrastenia.
neurasthenic [,njuərəs'θenik] *a* nevrastenico.
neurosis [njuə'rousis] *n* neurosi, nevrosi.
neurotic [njuə'rɔtik] *a* nervoso; *n* neurotico, neuropatico.
neuter ['nju:tə] *a* neutrale, neutro; *n* neutro; individuo che si tiene neutrale.
neutral ['nju:trəl] *n* neutrale; *a* neutro.
neutrality [nju'træliti] *n* neutralità.
neutralize ['nju:trəlaiz] *vt* neutralizzare.
never ['nevə] *ad* non . . . mai, mai.
nevertheless [,nevəðə'les] *ad cj* nondimeno, ciò nonostante, tuttavia.
new [nju:] *a* nuovo, fresco, novello; **n.-born child** neonato.
New Guinea [nju'gini] *n* Nuova Guinea.
New Hebrides [nju'hebrədi:z] *n pl* Nuove Ebridi.
newly ['nju:li] *ad* di fresco, di recente.
news [nju:z] *n* (*sing*) notizie *pl*; **a piece of n.** una notizia; **newsagent** giornalaio; **newsreel** cinegiornale; **newsstand** edicola.
newspaper ['nju:s,peipə] *n* giornale.
newt [nju:t] *n* (*zool*) tritone.
New York ['nju:'jɔ:k] *n* Nuova York.
New Zealand [nju:'zi:lənd] *n* Nuova Zelanda.
New Zealander [nju:'zi:ləndə] *n* neozelandese.
next [nekst] *a* prossimo, seguente, più vicino; *ad* poi, subito, dopo; *prep* accanto a, vicino a.
nib [nib] *n* pennino.
nibble ['nibl] *vti* rosicchiare; abboccare.
Nice [ni:s] *n* Nizza.
nice [nais] *a* buono; amabile, simpatico; grazioso, bello; esatto, scrupoloso; difficile (di gusti); sottile.
nicety ['naisiti] *n* delicatezza; sotti-

gliezza; **to a n.** con estrema esattezza.
niche [nitʃ] *n* nicchia.
Nicholas ['nikələs] *nm pr* Nicola, Niccolò.
nick [nik] *n* tacca; **in the n. of time** appena in tempo.
nickel ['nikl] *n* nichel.
nickname ['nikneim] *n* nomignolo, soprannome.
niece [ni:s] *n* nipote (di zio).
Nigeria [nai'dʒiəriə] *n* (*geogr*) Nigeria.
Nigerian [nai'dʒiəriən] *a n* (abitante) della Nigeria.
niggard ['nigəd] *n* avaro.
niggardliness ['nigədlinis] *n* avarizia.
niggardly ['nigədli] *a* avaro.
niggling ['nigliŋ] *a* insignificante.
night [nait] *n* notte, sera.
nightfall ['naitfɔ:l] *n* tramonto, crepuscolo; **at n.** sull'imbrunire.
nightingale ['naitiŋgeil] *n* usignuolo.
nightly ['naitli] *a* notturno; di ogni notte; *ad* di notte; ogni notte.
nightmare ['naitmɛə] *n* incubo.
nihilist ['naiilist] *n* nichilista.
Nile [nail] *n* Nilo.
nimble ['nimbl] *a* agile; svelto, sveglio.
nimbleness ['nimblnis] *n* agilità, sveltezza.
nine [nain] *a n* nove; **ninth** *a* nono.
nineteen ['nain'ti:n] *a n* diciannove; **nineteenth** *a* diciannovesimo.
ninetieth ['naintiiθ] *a* novantesimo.
ninth [nainθ] *a n* nono.
ninety ['nainti] *a n* novanta.
nip [nip] *n* morso, pizzicotto, detto sarcastico, aria gelida, (*of liquor*) goccia.
nip [nip] *vt* pizzicare; mordere; stroncare.
nipper ['nipə] *n* pinza, pinzetta; (*sl*) monello, ragazzo.
nipple ['nipl] *n* capezzolo.
nippy ['nipi] *a* pungente; (*sl*) svelto.
niter ['naitə] *n* nitrato di potassio.
nitrate ['naitreit] *n* nitrato.
no [nou] *a* nessuno; *ad* no, non, niente.
nobility [nou'biliti] *n* nobiltà.
noble [noubl] *a n* nobile.
nobleman ['noublmən] *pl* **-men** *n* nobile, nobiluomo.
nobleness ['noublnis] *n* nobiltà.
nobody ['noubədi] *pron* nessuno.
nocturnal [nɔk'tə:nl] *a* notturno.
nocturne ['nɔktə:n] *n* (*mus*) notturno.
nod [nɔd] *n* cenno affermativo del capo; *vti* annuire; chinare il capo; sonnecchiare.
noise [nɔiz] *n* rumore, chiasso, clamore.
noiseless ['nɔizlis] *a* senza rumore, silenzioso.
noisily ['nɔizili] *ad* rumorosamente.
noisiness ['nɔizinis] *n* rumorosità.
noisy ['nɔizi] *a* rumoroso; turbolento.
nomad ['noumәd] *n* nomade.
nomadic [nou'mædik] *a* nomade.
nominal ['nɔminl] *a* nominale.
nominate ['nɔmineit] *vt* designare, proporre, nominare.
nomination [,nɔmi'neiʃən] *n* designazione, nomina.
nominative ['nɔminətiv] *a n* nominativo.
nonchalant ['nɔnʃələnt] *a* noncurante, indifferente.
nonconformist ['nɔnkən'fɔ:mist] *a n* anticonformista.
nonconformity ['nɔnkən'fɔ:miti] *n* anticonformismo.
nondescript ['nɔndiskript] *a* non classificabile, qualunque.
none [nʌn] *pron* nessuno; *ad* niente, affatto, per nulla; **n. the less** nondimeno.
nonentity [nɔ'nentiti] *n* persona insignificante, nullità.
non-existent ['nɔnig'zistənt] *a* inesistente.
nonsense ['nɔnsəns] *n* assurdità, schiocchezza.
nonsensical [nɔn'sensikəl] *a* assurdo, privo di senso.
non-stop ['nɔn'stɔp] *a* ininterrotto; *ad* ininterrottamente.
noodle ['nu:dl] *n* semplicione; (*cook*) taglierini.
nook [nuk] *n* angolo, cantuccio, recesso.
noon [nu:n] *n* mezzogiorno; **noonday** *a n* mezzogiorno.
noose [nu:s] *n* nodo scorsoio; (*fig*) trappola.
nor [nɔ:] *cj* nè, neppure, nemmeno.
Nordic ['nɔ:dik] *a* nordico.
normal ['nɔ:məl] *a* normale; perpendicolare; *n* perpendicolare; norma.
Norman ['nɔ:mən] *a n* normanno.
Normandy ['nɔ:məndi] *n* Normandia.
Norse [nɔ:s] *a n* norvegese, lingua norvegese.
Norseman ['nɔ:smən] *pl* **-men** *n* norvegese.
north [nɔ:θ] *a* nordico, settentrionale; *ad* a (verso) nord; *n* nord, settentrione; **n.-east** nord-est; **n.-west** nord-ovest.
northerly ['nɔ:ðəli] *a* del nord.
northern ['nɔ:ðən] *a* del nord nordico.
northward(s) ['nɔ:θwəd(s)] *ad* verso nord.
Norway ['nɔ:wei] *n* Norvegia.
Norwegian [nɔ:'wi:dʒən] *a n* norvegese.
nose [nouz] *n* naso.
nosegay ['nouzgei] *n* mazzolino di fiori.
nostalgia [nɔs'tældʒiə] *n* nostalgia.
nostalgic [nɔs'tældʒik] *n* nostalgico.
nostril ['nɔstril] *n* narice.
not [nɔt] *ad* non.

notable ['noutəbl] *a* notevole; *n* notabile.
notably ['noutəbli] *ad* notevolmente; considerevolmente; sensibilmente.
notary ['noutəri] *n* notaio.
notation [nou'teiʃən] *n* notazione.
notch [nɔtʃ] *n* incisione, tacca; *vt* dentellare.
note [nout] *n* (*mus*) nota; segno; appunto, biglietto; *vt* notare, prender nota di; **notepaper** carta da lettere.
notebook ['noutbuk] *n* taccuino, bloc-notes.
noted ['noutid] *a* noto, rinomato.
noteworthy ['nout,wə:ði] *a* degno di nota.
nothing ['nʌθiŋ] *pron* niente, nulla; *ad* per nulla; *n* zero, niente.
nothingness ['nʌθiŋnis] *n* il nulla, inesistenza.
notice ['noutis] *n* avviso; notifica; preavviso; disdetta; recensione; **noticeboard** tabellone per affissi.
noticeable ['noutisəbl] *a* notevole, visibile.
noticeably ['noutisəbli] *ad* notevolmente; percettibilmente.
notification [,noutifi'keiʃən] *n* notificazione, notifica.
notify ['noutifai] *vt* notificare.
notion ['nouʃən] *n* nozione, idea, opinione.
notoriety [,noutə:'raiəti] *n* notorietà.
notorious [nou'tɔ:riəs] *a* notorio.
notwithstanding ['nɔtwiθ'stændiŋ] *ad prep* nonostante, malgrado, tuttavia.
nougat ['nu:gɑ:] *n* torrone.
nought [nɔ:t] *n* niente, zero.
noun [naun] *n* nome, sostantivo.
nourish ['nʌriʃ] *vt* nutrire.
nourishment ['nʌriʃmənt] *n* nutrimento, nutrizione.
novel ['nɔvəl] *a* nuovo, insolito; *n* romanzo.
novelist ['nɔvəlist] *n* romanziere.
novelty ['nɔvəlti] *n* novità.
November [nou'vembə] *n* novembre.
novice ['nɔvis] *n* novizio.
noviciate, novitiate [nou'viʃiit] *n* noviziato.
now [nau] *ad cj* ora, allora, ora che; *n* questo momento.
nowadays ['nauədeiz] *ad* al giorno d'oggi.
nowhere ['nouwɛə] *ad* in nessun luogo, da nessuna parte.
noxious ['nɔkʃəs] *a* dannoso, nocivo.
nozzle ['nɔzl] *n* becco, beccuccio; (*pump*) beccaglio.
nuance [nju'ɑ̃:ns] *n* sfumatura.
nuclear ['nju:kliə] *a* nucleare.
nucleus ['nju:kliəs] *n* nucleo.
nude [nju:d] *a n* nudo.
nudge [nʌdʒ] *n* gomitata; *vt* toccare col gomito.
nudist ['nju:dist] *n* nudista.
nudity ['nju:diti] *n* nudità.
nugget ['nʌgit] *n* pepita d'oro.
nuisance ['nju:sns] *n* fastidio, seccatura.
null [nʌl] *a* nullo.
nullify ['nʌlifai] *vt* annullare.
nullity ['nʌliti] *n* nullità.
numb [nʌm] *a* intorpidito.
number ['nʌmbə] *n* numero.
numbness ['nʌmnis] *n* intorpidimento, torpore.
numeral ['nju:mərəl] *a n* numerale.
numerous ['nju:mərəs] *a* numeroso.
nun [nʌn] *n* monaca, suora.
nunnery ['nʌnəri] *n* convento (di monache).
nuptial ['nʌpʃəl] *a* nuziale; *n pl* nozze *pl*.
Nuremberg ['njuərəmbə:g] *n* Norimberga.
nurse [nə:s] *n* infermiera; bambinaia, balia, nutrice; *vt* assistere, curare, nutrire; (*fig*) covare (*hatred etc*); coltivare, accarezzare.
nursery ['nə:sri] *n* stanza dei bambini; (*of plants*) vivaio.
nursing ['nə:siŋ] *a* che allatta, nutre; *n* allattamento, nutrire; professione di infermiera.
nurture ['nə:tʃə] *n* allevamento, cura, educazione; *vt* nutrire, allevare, educare.
nut [nʌt] *n* noce, nocciola; (*mech*) dado; **a hard n.** (*sl*) un osso duro.
nutcracker ['nʌt,krækə] *n* (*usu pl*) schiaccianoci.
nutmeg ['nʌtmeg] *n* noce moscata.
nutrition [nju'triʃən] *n* nutrizione.
nutritious [nju'triʃəs] *a* nutriente.
nutshell ['nʌtʃel] *n* guscio di noce; **in a n.** in poche parole.
nuzzle ['nʌzl] *vti* frugare (col muso); accoccolarsi (vicino a).
nylon ['nailən] *n* nailon.
nymph [nimf] *n* ninfa.

O

oaf [ouf] *pl* **oafs,** *n* persona goffa, semplicione.
oak [ouk] *n* quercia.
oakum ['oukəm] *n* stoppa.
oar [ɔ:] *n* remo; **oarlock** scalmo; *vt* remare.
oarsman ['ɔ:zmən] *n* rematore.
oasis [ou'eisis] *pl* **oases** *n* oasi.
oat [out] *n* (*usu pl*) avena.
oath [ouθ] *n* bestemmia, giuramento.
oatmeal ['outmi:l] *n* farina d'avena.
obduracy ['ɔbdjurəsi] *n* ostinazione.
obdurate ['ɔbdjurit] *a* ostinato.
obedience [ə'bi:diəns] *n* ubbidienza.
obedient [ə'bi:diənt] *a* ubbidiente.
obeisance [ou'beisəns] *n* inchino; omaggio.
obelisk ['ɔbilisk] *n* obelisco.
obey [ə'bei] *vti* ubbidire a; ubbidire.
obituary [ə'bitjuəri] *n* necrologia.
object ['ɔbdʒikt] *n* oggetto; fine, scopo; persona o cosa di aspetto

ridicolo; *vti* [əb'dʒekt] obiettare, opporre, opporsi.
objection [əb'dʒekʃən] *n* obiezione.
objectionable [əb'dʒekʃnəbl] *a* offensivo.
objective [əb'dʒektiv] *a n* obiettivo, oggettivo.
oblation [ou'bleiʃən] *n* oblazione.
obligation [,ɔbli'geiʃən] *n* obbligo, debito, dovere, impegno.
obligatory [ɔ'bligətəri] *a* obbligatorio.
oblige [ə'blaidʒ] *vt* obbligare; fare un favore a.
obliging [ə'blaidʒiŋ] *a* gentile, compiacente.
oblique [ə'bli:k] *a* obliquo.
obliterate [ə'blitəreit] *vt* cancellare.
obliteration [ə,blitə'reiʃən] *n* obliterazione, cancellatura.
oblivion [ə'bliviən] *n* oblio.
oblivious [ə'bliviəs] *a* dimentico, immemore.
oblong ['ɔblɔŋ] *a* oblungo.
obnoxious [əb'nɔkʃəs] *a* detestabile; nocivo.
oboe ['oubou] *n* (*mus*) oboe.
obscene [ɔb'si:n] *a* osceno.
obscenity [ɔb'seniti] *n* oscenità.
obscure [əb'skjuə] *a* oscuro; *vt* oscurare.
obscurity [əb'skjuəriti] *n* oscurità.
obsequies ['ɔbsikwiz] *n pl* esequie, funerali *pl*.
obsequious [əb'si:kwiəs] *a* ossequioso, servile.
observance [əb'zə:vəns] *n* osservanza; (*religious*) pratica.
observant [əb'zə:vənt] *a n* osservante; *a* attento, rispettoso.
observation [,ɔbzə'veiʃən] *n* osservazione.
observatory [əb'zə:vətri] *n* osservatorio.
observe [əb'zə:v] *vti* osservare, praticare; rilevare.
observer [əb'zə:və] *n* osservatore.
obsess [əb'ses] *vt* ossessionare.
obsession [əb'seʃən] *n* ossessione.
obsolete ['ɔbsəli:t] *a* caduto in disuso, antiquato.
obstacle ['ɔbstəkl] *n* ostacolo, impedimento.
obstetrics [ɔb'stetriks] *n* ostetricia.
obstinacy ['ɔbstinəsi] *n* ostinazione.
obstinate ['ɔbstinit] *a* ostinato.
obstinately ['ɔbstinitli] *ad* ostinatamente.
obstreperous [əb'strepərəs] *a* indisciplinato, rumoroso.
obstruct [əb'strʌkt] *vt* ostruire; ritardare, impedire.
obstruction [əb'strʌkʃən] *n* ostacolo, ostruzione.
obstructive [ɔb'strʌktiv] *a* ostruente, ostruttivo.
obtain [əb'tein] *vt* ottenere.
obtrude [əb'tru:d] *vti* imporre, imporsi, intromettersi.
obtuse [əb'tju:s] *a* ottuso.
obviate ['ɔbvieit] *vt* ovviare a.
obvious ['ɔbviəs] *a* ovvio, evidente.
occasion [ə'keiʒən] *n* occasione; motivo.
occasional [ə'keiʒənl] *a* occasionale, accidentale, di quando in quando.
occasionally [ə'keiʒənli] *ad* di quando in quando, occasionalmente.
occult [ɔ'kʌlt] *a* occulto.
occupancy ['ɔkjupənsi] *n* occupazione, presa di possesso.
occupant ['ɔkjupənt] *n* occupante, locatario.
occupation [,ɔkju'peiʃən] *n* occupazione; impiego, professione.
occupy ['ɔkjupai] *vt* occupare, prendere possesso di; impiegare.
occur [ə'kə:] *vi* accadere; venire in mente a; ricorrere.
occurrence [ə'kʌrəns] *n* avvenimento, evento.
ocean ['ouʃən] *n* oceano.
ocher ['oukə] *n* ocra.
o'clock [ə'klɔk] **it is two o.** sono le due.
octave ['ɔktiv] *n* ottava.
October [ɔk'toubə] *n* ottobre.
octopus ['ɔktəpəs] *n* piovra, polipo.
octosyllable ['ɔktou,siləbl] *a* ottosillabico; *n* ottonario.
ocular ['ɔkjulə] *a* oculare.
oculist ['ɔkjulist] *n* oculista.
odd [ɔd] *a* dispari, scompagnato; occasionale; bizzarro, strano.
oddity ['ɔditi] *n* stranezza, singolarità; persona eccentrica.
oddment ['ɔdmənt] *n* (*usu pl*) scampoli, rimanenze.
oddness ['ɔdnis] *n* disparità; bizzarria; stranezza.
odds [ɔdz] *n pl* differenza; disaccordo; probabilità; vantaggio; **o. and ends** *pl* avanzi, resti, cianfrusaglie *pl*.
ode [oud] *n* ode.
odious ['oudiəs] *a* odioso.
odium ['oudiəm] *n* odio, odiosità.
odor ['oudə] *n* odore; reputazione.
odorous ['oudərəs] *a* fragrante, odoroso.
odyssey ['ɔdisi] *n* odissea.
of [ɔv] *prep* di; a, in; da; **of course** per certo.
off [ɔf] *ad* via, lontano, a distanza; *prep* (via) da, distante da; *a* esterno; laterale; remoto; libero; **o.-peak** di consumo ridotto.
offal ['ɔfəl] *n* regaglie; rifiuti *pl*.
offend [ə'fend] *vti* offendere; trasgredire.
offender [ə'fendə] *n* offensore, delinquente, reo.
offense [ə'fens] *n* offesa; colpa, reato, trasgressione.
offensive [ə'fensiv] *n* offensiva; *a* offensivo; aggressivo.
offer ['ɔfə] *n* offerta, proposta; *vti* offrir(si), presentar(si).
offering ['ɔfəriŋ] *n* offerta; sacrificio.
offertory ['ɔfətəri] *n* offertorio; (*collection*) colletta.

offhand ['ɔf'hænd] *a* casuale; improvvisato; alla buona; *ad* lì per lì.
office ['ɔfis] *n* ufficio, carica, ministero; gabinetto medico.
officer ['ɔfisə] *n* ufficiale.
official [ə'fiʃəl] *a* ufficiale; *n* funzionario, impiegato, ufficiale.
officiate [ə'fiʃieit] *vi* esercitare le funzioni di; (*eccl*) officiare.
officious [ə'fiʃəs] *a* intromettente; ufficioso.
offing ['ɔfiŋ] *n* largo, mare aperto, distanza dalla costa; **in the o.** al largo; (*fig*) in vista.
offset ['ɔfsət] *n* compenso, equivalente; germoglio; rampollo; *vt* controbilanciare.
offshoot ['ɔfʃu:t] *n* germoglio; derivato.
offside ['ɔf'said] *n* (*football etc*) fuori gioco.
offspring ['ofspriŋ] *n* prole, rampollo; prodotto.
often ['ɔfn] *ad* spesso.
ogle ['ougl] *vt* adocchiare, guardare sottecchi.
ogre ['ougə] *n* orco.
oil [ɔil] *n* olio; petrolio; *vt* lubrificare, ungere; **oilcloth** tela cerata; **o. pan** (*aut*) coppa; **oilskin** tela impermeabile; **fuel o.** nafta.
oily ['ɔili] *a* oleoso, untuoso.
ointment ['ɔintmənt] *n* unguento, pomata.
old [ould] *a* vecchio; antico; usato; **o.-fashioned** antiquato.
olden ['ouldən] *a* antico.
oleander [,ouli'ændə] *n* oleandro.
oligarchy ['ɔliga:ki] *n* oligarchia.
olive ['ɔliv] *a* d'oliva; d'olivo; olivastro; *n* olivo, oliva.
omelet(te) ['ɔmlit] *n* frittata.
omen ['oumen] *n* augurio, presagio.
ominous ['ɔminəs] *a* sinistro, infausto.
omission [ou'miʃən] *n* omissione.
omit [ou'mit] *vt* omettere.
omnibus ['ɔmnibəs] *pl* **-buses** *n* (*usu* **bus**) autobus, omnibus.
omnipotence [ɔm'nipətəns] *n* onnipotenza.
omnipotent [ɔm'nipətənt] *a* onnipotente.
on [ɔn] *prep* su, sopra; a; di; in; per; *ad* addosso; indosso; avanti; in poi; **off and o.** di quando in quando, intermittentemente.
once [wʌns] *ad* una volta, un tempo; *cj* una volta che.
on-coming ['ɔn,kʌmiŋ] *a* prossimo, che si avvicina.
one [wʌn] *a* uno; unico, uno solo; *pron* uno; si; questo, quello, codesto; **o. another** l'un l'altro; si; **o.-sided** unilaterale; **o.-way ticket** biglietto d'andata; **o.-way traffic** circolazione a senso unico.
oneness ['wʌnnis] *n* identità, unione, accordo.
onerous ['ɔnərəs] *a* oneroso.
onion ['ʌnjən] *n* cipolla.
onlooker ['ɔn,lukə] *n* spettatore.
only ['ounli] *a* solo, unico; *ad* solo, solamente, soltanto, unicamente: *cj* eccetto che.
onset ['ɔnset] *n* inizio.
onslaught ['ɔnslɔ:t] *n* aggressione, assalto.
onto ['ɔntu] *prep* su, sopra.
onus ['ounəs] *n* peso, onere, responsabilità.
onward ['ɔnwəd] *a* avanzato; progressivo; *ad* (in) avanti.
onyx ['ɔniks] *n* onice.
ooze [u:z] *n* melma, fango; *vi* colare, fluire lentamente; **to o. out** trapelare.
oozy ['u:zi] *a* melmoso.
opal ['oupəl] *n* opale.
opaque [ou'peik] *a* opaco.
open ['oupən] *a* aperto; franco; libero; **in the o.** *ad* all'aperto; **o. air** l'aria aperta, l'aperto; *vti* aprir(si).
opener ['oupnə] *n* **tin, can o.** apriscatole; **bottle o.** apribottiglie.
open-eyed ['oupn'aid] *a ad* ad occhi aperti.
open-handed ['oupn'hændid] *a* generoso.
open-hearted ['oupən,ha:tid] *a* cordiale, espansivo.
opening ['oupəniŋ] *a* che si apre, inaugurale, iniziale; *n* apertura, inaugurazione, inizio.
openly ['oupənli] *ad* apertamente; pubblicamente.
openness ['oupənnis] *n* (*fig*) franchezza.
opera ['ɔpərə] *pl* **operas** *n* opera.
operate ['ɔpəreit] *vti* operare; **operating room** (*or* **theatre**) *n* sala operatoria.
operation [,ɔpə'reiʃən] *n* operazione; azione.
operative ['ɔpərətiv] *a* efficace; operativo, operante; operatorio; attivo, *n* lavorante, operaio.
operator ['ɔpəreitə] *n* operatore.
Ophelia [ɔ'fi:liə] *nf pr* Ofelia.
ophthalmic [ɔf'θælmik] *a* oftalmico.
opiate ['oupiit] *a* oppiato; *n* narcotico.
opine [ou'pain] *vi* opinare, essere del parere.
opinion [ə'pinjən] *n* opinione, parere.
opinionated [ə'pinjəneitid] *a* ostinato, dogmatico.
opium ['oupiəm] *n* oppio.
opponent [ə'pounənt] *n* antagonista, rivale; *a* contrario, opposto.
opportune ['ɔpətju:n] *a* opportuno.
opportunity [,ɔpə'tju:niti] *n* occasione, opportunità.
oppose [ɔ'pouz] *vt* opporre, contrapporre, opporsi a.
opposite ['ɔpəzit] *a* contrario, opposto; *prep* dirimpetto a, di faccia a; *n* opposto.
opposition [,ɔpə'ziʃən] *n* opposizione.
oppress [ə'pres] *vt* opprimere.

oppression [ə'preʃən] *n* oppressione.
oppressive [ə'presiv] *a* oppressivo.
opprobrious [ə'proubriəs] *a* obbrobrioso.
opt [ɔpt] *vi* optare.
optic ['ɔptik] *a* ottico.
optical ['ɔptikəl] *a* ottico.
optician [ɔp'tiʃən] *n* ottico.
optics ['ɔptiks] *n* ottica.
optimism ['ɔptimizəm] *n* ottimismo.
optimist ['ɔptimist] *n* ottimista.
optimistic [,ɔpti'mistik] *a* ottimistico.
option ['ɔpʃən] *n* opzione, scelta.
optional ['ɔpʃənl] *a* facoltativo.
opulence ['ɔpjuləns] *n* opulenza.
opulent ['ɔpjulənt] *a* opulento.
or [ɔ:] *cj* o, oppure.
oracle ['ɔrəkl] *n* oracolo.
oral ['ɔ:rəl] *a* orale.
orange ['ɔrindʒ] *a* di color arancio, arancione; *n* arancia; (*tree, color*) arancio.
oration [ɔ:'reiʃən] *n* orazione; discorso.
orator ['ɔrətə] *n* oratore.
oratory ['ɔrətəri] *n* oratorio.
orb [ɔ:b] *n* cerchio; globo; orbita.
orbit ['ɔ:bit] *n* orbita.
Orcadian [ɔ:'keidiən] *a* delle isole Orcadi; *n* abitante delle isole Orcadi.
orchard ['ɔ:tʃəd] *n* frutteto.
orchestra ['ɔ:kistrə] *n* orchestra; **o. seat** (*theat*) poltrona.
orchid ['ɔ:kid] *n* orchidea.
ordain [ɔ:'dein] *vt* ordinare; decretare.
ordeal [ɔ:'di:l] *n* cimento, dura prova.
order ['ɔ:də] *n* ordine; (*com*) ordinazione; **in o. that** affinchè; *vt* ordinare.
orderliness ['ɔ:dəlinis] *n* ordine, disciplina.
orderly ['ɔ:dəli] *a* ordinato, disciplinato; *n* (*mil*) ordinanza.
ordinal ['ɔ:dinl] *a n* ordinale.
ordinance ['ɔ:dinəns] *n* decreto, ordinanza.
ordinary ['ɔ:dnri] *a* ordinario, comune, solito.
ordination [,ɔ:di'neiʃən] *n* (*eccl*) ordinazione.
ordnance ['ɔ:dnəns] *n* (*mil*) artiglieria; sussistenza.
ore [ɔ:] *n* minerale.
organ ['ɔ:gən] *n* organo.
organic [ɔ:'gænik] *a* organico.
organism ['ɔ:gənizəm] *n* organismo.
organist ['ɔ:gənist] *n* organista.
organization [,ɔ:gənai'zeiʃən] *n* organizzazione.
organize ['ɔ:gənaiz] *vt* organizzare.
organizer ['ɔ:gənaizə] *n* organizzatore.
orgasm ['ɔ:gæzəm] *n* orgasmo, eccitazione.
orgy ['ɔ:dʒi] *n* orgia.
oriel ['ɔ:riəl] *n* (*arch*) finestra sporgente.
orient ['ɔ:riənt] *a n* (*poet*) orientale, oriente; *vti* orientare, orientarsi.
oriental [,ɔ:ri'entl] *a* orientale.
origin ['ɔridʒin] *n* origine.
original [ə'ridʒənl] *a n* originale; *a* originario.
originality [ə,ridʒi'næliti] *n* originalità.
originate [ə'ridʒineit] *vt* originare, dare origine a; *vi* avere origine.
Orkney Islands ['ɔ:kni'ailəndz] *n* Isole Orcadi.
ornament ['ɔ:nəmənt] *n* ornamento; *vt* adornare, ornare.
ornamental [,ɔ:nə'mentl] *a* ornamentale.
ornate [ɔ:'neit] *a* adorno, ornato, riccamente decorato.
ornithology [,ɔ:ni'θɔlədʒi] *n* ornitologia.
ornithologist [,ɔ:ni'θɔlədʒist] *n* ornitologo.
orphan ['ɔ:fən] *a n* orfano; *vt* rendere orfano.
orphanage ['ɔ:fənidʒ] *n* brefotrofio, orfanotrofio.
Orpheus ['ɔ:fju:s] *nm pr* Orfeo.
orthodox ['ɔ:θədɔks] *a* ortodosso.
orthodoxy ['ɔ:θədɔksi] *n* ortodossia.
orthography [ɔ:'θɔgrəfi] *n* ortografia.
orthopedic [,ɔ:θou'pi:dik] *a* ortopedico.
Oscar ['ɔskə] *nm pr* Oscar.
oscillate ['ɔsileit] *vi* oscillare; *vt* (far) oscillare.
oscillation [,ɔsi'leiʃən] *n* oscillazione.
osier ['ouʒə] *n* vimine.
osprey ['ɔspri] *n* ossifraga.
Ostend [ɔs'tend] *n* Ostenda.
ostensible [ɔs'tensəbl] *a* apparente; finto.
ostensibly [ɔs'tensibli] *ad* apparentemente, con il pretesto di.
ostentation [,ɔsten'teiʃən] *n* ostentazione; sfarzo.
ostentatious [,ɔsten'teiʃəs] *a* ostentato; sfarzoso.
ostracism ['ɔstrəsizəm] *n* ostracismo.
ostracize ['ɔstrəsaiz] *vt* dare l'ostracismo a, bandire.
ostrich ['ɔstriʃ] *n* struzzo.
Othello [ou'θelou] *nm pr* Otello.
other ['ʌðə] *a pron* altro; **every o. day** ogni due giorni.
otherwise ['ʌðəwaiz] *ad* altrimenti.
otter ['ɔtə] *n* lontra.
ought [ɔ:t] *v aux impers* (*al condizionale*) dovere.
ounce [auns] (*abbr* **oz**) oncia.
our ['auə] *a* (il) nostro *etc*; **ours** *pron* (il) nostro *etc*; **ourselves** *pron* ci, noi stessi.
oust [aust] *vt* espellere; soppiantare.
out [aut] *ad* fuori; **o. of** *prep* fuori da, fuori di; a motivo di, per; **o. of date** fuori moda; arcaico; **o. of door(s)** all'aperto, fuori di casa.

outbid [aut'bid] *vt* offrire un prezzo più alto.
outbreak ['aut'breik] *n* eruzione; scoppio; sommossa.
outburst ['aut'bə:st] *n* esplosione; (*fig*) scoppio, accesso.
outcast ['autkɑ:st] *a n* abbandonato, reietto.
outcome ['autkʌm] *n* esito, risultato.
outcry ['autkrai] *n* clamore, grido; scalpore.
outdo [aut'du:] *vt* superare.
outdoor ['autdɔ:] *a* all'aperto.
outer ['autə] *a* esteriore; esterno.
outermost ['autəmoust] *a* estremo; il più remoto.
outfit ['autfit] *n* corredo, equipaggiamento.
outfitter ['autfitə] *n* fornitore (di articoli di abbigliamento).
outgoing [aut'gouiŋ] *a* uscente; in partenza; *n* uscita; *pl* spese.
outgrow [aut'grou] *vt* sorpassare in crescita, diventare troppo grande per.
outhouse ['authaus] *n* edificio annesso.
outing ['autiŋ] *n* passeggiata; gita, scampagnata.
outlandish [aut'lændiʃ] *a* strano; remoto.
outlaw ['aut'lɔ:] *n* bandito, fuori legge; *vt* bandire.
outlay ['aut'lei] *n* spesa.
outlet ['autlet] *n* sbocco, uscita.
outline ['autlain] *n* contorno, schizzo; *vt* schizzare, tracciare i contorni di.
outlive [aut'liv] *vt* sopravvivere a.
outlook ['autluk] *n* vista, prospettiva, modo di vedere.
outlying ['aut,laiiŋ] *a* fuori mano, periferico.
outnumber [aut'nʌmbə] *vt* superare in numero.
outpatient ['aut,peiʃənt] *n* malato esterno.
outplay [aut'plei] *vt* superare in un gioco, battere.
outpost ['autpoust] *n* (*mil*) avamposto.
outpouring [aut'pɔ:riŋ] *n* sfogo, effusione.
output ['autput] *n* produzione.
outrage ['autreidʒ] *n* oltraggio; *vt* oltraggiare; violare.
outrageous [aut'reidʒəs] *a* oltraggioso; atroce; eccessivo.
outright ['autrait] *ad* immediatamente, completamente, in blocco; *a* completo.
outrun [aut'rʌn] *vt* oltrepassare, superare.
outset ['autset] *n* inizio, principio.
outside ['aut'said] *a* esteriore, esterno, superficiale; *prep* fuori di; all'infuori di; *ad* all'esterno, esternamente, fuori, all'aperto; *n* l'esterno, apparenza esteriore; massimo.
outsider ['aut'saidə] *n* estraneo; (*horse*) cavallo non classificato.
outskirts ['autskə:ts] *n pl* periferia.
outspoken [aut'spoukən] *a* esplicito, franco.
outstanding [aut'stændiŋ] *a* prominente; di rilievo, eminente; (*com*) arretrato, in sospeso.
outstretched [aut'stretʃt] *a* disteso, spiegato, aperto.
outstrip [aut'strip] *vt* distanziare, vincere.
outward ['autwəd] *a* esterno; esteriore, **o. bound** (*naut*) diretto a un porto straniero; **outwards** esternamente.
outwear [aut'wɛə] *vt* durare più a lungo di, logorare con continuo uso.
outweigh [aut'wei] *vt* superare di peso; superare in importanza.
outwit [aut'wit] *vt* superare in furberia.
oval ['ouvəl] *a n* ovale.
ovary ['ouvəri] *n* (*anat*) ovaia; ovario.
ovation [ou'veiʃən] *n* ovazione.
oven ['ʌvn] *n* forno.
over ['ouvə] *prep* su, sopra, al di sopra di; attraverso a; *ad* al di sopra; dall'altra parte; in aggiunta; di nuovo, completamente, dal principio alla fine; *a* eccessivo.
overall ['ouvərɔ:l] *a* completo, globale; *n* (*usu pl*) grembiule; tuta.
overbalance [,ouvə'bæləns] *n* eccedenza; *vti* superare di peso; (far) perdere l'equilibrio.
overbearing [,ouvə'bɛəriŋ] *a* imperioso, prepotente.
overboard ['ouvəbɔ:d] *ad* fuori bordo, in mare.
overburden [,ouvə'bə:dn] *vt* sovraccaricare.
overcast ['ouvəkɑ:st] *a* coperto di nubi; *vt* offuscare; cucire a sopraggitto.
overcharge ['ouvə'tʃɑ:dʒ] *n* sovrapprezzo; *vti* sovraccaricare; chiedere troppo di prezzo.
overcloud [,ouvə'klaud] *vti* coprire di nubi, (r)annuvolarsi.
overcoat ['ouvəkout] *n* soprabito, cappotto.
overcome [,ouvə'kʌm] *vt* vincere, sopraffare.
overconfidence ['ouvə'kɔnfidəns] *n* presunzione; eccessiva sicurezza di sè.
overcrowd [,ouvə'kraud] *vt* affollare all'eccesso.
overdo [,ouvə'du:] *vti* esagerare; cuocere troppo; strafare; affaticare.
overdose ['ouvədous] *n* dose eccessiva.
overdraft ['ouvədrɑ:ft] *n* (*com*) credito allo scoperto.
overdraw ['ouvə'drɔ:] *vt* (*com*) trarre allo scoperto; (*fig*) esagerare.
overdress ['ouvə'dres] *vi* vestire in modo troppo vistoso.

overdrive ['ouvə'draiv] *n* eccessivo sforzo; eccessivo sfruttamento; (*tec*) moltiplicatore di velocità; *vt* affaticare, sfruttare troppo.
overdue ['ouvə'dju:] *a* (*com*) in sofferenza, scaduto; in ritardo.
overeat ['ouvər'i:t] *vi* mangiare troppo.
overestimate ['ouvər'estimeit] *vt* sopravvalutare.
overexcited ['ouvərik'saitid] *a* sovraeccitato.
overflow ['ouvəflou] *n* traboccamento; [,ouvə'flou] *vt* inondare; *vi* straripare, traboccare.
overgrown ['ouvə'groun] *a* cresciuto troppo; coperto di.
overhang ['ouvəhæŋ] *vti* incombere su, sovrastare (a).
overhaul ['ouvəhɔ:l] *n* revisione, verifica, esame accurato; riparazione.
overhead ['ouvəhed] *a* superiore; *ad* di sopra, in alto; *n pl* spese generali *pl*.
overhear [,ouvə'hiə] *vt* udire per caso.
overlap [,ouvə'læp] *vti* sovrapporre, sovrapporsi.
overleaf ['ouvə'li:f] *ad* sul verso, sul retro (della pagina).
overload ['ouvəloud] *n* sovraccarico; *vt* sovraccaricare.
overlook [,ouvə'luk] *vt* guardare dall'alto, sorvegliare; passar sopra, trascurare, non accorgersi di.
overnight ['ouvə'nait] *a ad* durante la notte.
overpass ['ouvəpɑ:s] *n* soprappassaggio; *vt* [,ouvə'pɑ:s] sorpassare; trasgredire; ignorare.
overpay ['ouvə'pei] *vt* pagare più del dovuto.
overpower [,ouvə'pauə] *vt* sopraffare, vincere.
overpowering [,ouvə'pauəriŋ] *a* schiacciante, irresistibile.
overrate ['ouvə'reit] *vt* sopravvalutare.
overreach [,ouvə'ri:tʃ] *vti* oltrepassare, spingersi al di là di; **to o. oneself** fare il passo più lungo della gamba.
override ['ouvə'raid] *vti* far scorrerie; (*fig*) infrangere, annullare, non tener conto di.
overrun [,ouvə'rʌn] *vt* invadere; oltrepassare.
oversea(s) ['ouvə'si:(z)] *a* d'oltre mare; *ad* oltremare.
overseer ['ouvəsiə] *n* capo operaio, sopraintendente.
overshadow [,ovə'ʃædou] *vt* ombreggiare; (*fig*) oscurare, eclissare.
overshoe ['ouvəʃu:] *n* soprascarpa.
oversight ['ouvəsait] *n* svista; sorveglianza.
oversleep ['ouvə'sli:p] *vi* dormire oltre l'ora giusta.
overspill ['ouvəspil] *n* l'eccesso, l'in più.
overstate ['ouvə'steit] *vt* esagerare.
overstatement ['ouvə'steitmənt] *n* esagerazione.
overstrain ['ouvə'strein] *vti* sforzar (si) eccessivamente.
overt ['ouvə:t] *a* aperto, pubblico, visibile.
overtake [,ouvə'teik] *vt* raggiungere; sorpassare.
overtax ['ouvə'tæks] *vt* abusare di; gravare di imposte.
overthrow ['ouvəθrou] *n* rovesciamento, disfatta; *vt* [,ouvə'θrou] rovesciare, abbattere.
overtime ['ouvətaim] *n* lavoro straordinario.
overtire ['ouvə'taiə] *vt* stancare troppo, strapazzare.
overtop ['ouvə'tɔp] *vt* sovrastare, superare di altezza.
overture ['ouvətjuə] *n* offerta, proposta; (*mus*) preludio, sinfonia.
overturn ['ouvətə:n] *vti* capovolgere, rovesciar(si).
overweight ['ouvəweit] *a* che supera il peso; *n* eccedenza di peso.
overwhelm [,ouvə'welm] *vt* sopraffare, opprimere, schiacciare.
overwork ['ouvə'wə:k] *vti* (far) lavorare troppo.
overwrought ['ouvə'rɔ:t] *a* esausto; sovreccitato; troppo ornato.
owe [ou] *vt* dovere, essere in debito di.
owing ['ouiŋ] *a* dovuto, che resta da pagare; **o. to** *prep* a causa di.
owl [aul] *n* civetta; gufo.
own [oun] *a* proprio; *vti* possedere; confessare, riconoscere.
owner ['ounə] *n* possessore, proprietario.
ownership ['ounəʃip] *n* proprietà, possesso.
ox [ɔks] *pl* **oxen** *n* bue.
oxide ['ɔksaid] *n* ossido.
oxygen ['ɔksidʒən] *n* ossigeno.
oyster ['ɔistə] *n* ostrica.

P

pace [peis] *n* andatura, passo; *vt* misurare a passi; *vi* andare al passo.
Pacific [pə'sifik] *n* Pacifico.
pacific [pə'sifik] *a* pacifico.
pacifism ['pæsifizəm] *n* pacifismo.
pacifist ['pæsifist] *n* pacifista.
pacify ['pæsifai] *vt* pacificare.
pack [pæk] *n* pacco, involto; peso; (*mil*) zaino; (*hounds*) muta; (*cards*) mazzo; (*ice*) banchisa; (*thieves*) banda; *vt* imballare, impaccare, stipare; (*med*) fare impacchi a; **to p. up** fare le valigie.
package ['pækidʒ] *n* balla, collo, pacco; **p. holiday** (*or* **tour**) villeggiatura o gita turistica spesata in anticipo.

packet ['pækit] *n* pacchetto; **p.-boat** (*naut*) vapore postale.
packing ['pækiŋ] *n* imballaggio; fare le valigie; (*of food*) confezione.
pact [pækt] *n* patto.
pad [pæd] *n* blocco di carta; cuscinetto; imbottitura; zampa di animale; (*med*) tampone; *vt* imbottire; tamponare.
padding ['pædiŋ] *n* imbottitura.
paddle ['pædl] *n* (*naut*) pagaia; *vt* remare con la pagaia; sguazzare nell'acqua.
paddock ['pædək] *n* recinto per i cavalli da corsa; chiuso.
padlock ['pædlɔk] *n* lucchetto.
Padua ['pædjuə] *n* Padova; **Paduan** *a n* padovano.
pagan ['peigən] *a n* pagano.
page [peidʒ] *n* pagina; paggio; **pageboy** fattorino d'albergo.
pageant ['pædʒənt] *n* corteo o spettacolo storico.
pageantry ['pædʒəntri] *n* sfarzo, spettacolo sfarzoso.
pail [peil] *n* secchia, secchio.
pain [pein] *n* dolore, male, sofferenza, pena; *vt* affliggere, far soffrire.
painful ['peinful] *a* doloroso, penoso.
painfully ['peinfuli] *ad* dolorosamente, penosamente.
painless ['peinlis] *a* indolore.
painstaking ['peinz,teikiŋ] *a* coscienzioso.
paint [peint] *n* pittura; vernice; colore; belletto; *vt* dipinger(si).
painter ['peintə] *n* pittore; decoratore; imbianchino.
painting ['peintiŋ] *n* pittura; quadro.
pair [pɛə] *n* paio, coppia; *vt* accoppiare, appaiare; *vi* accoppiarsi.
pajamas [pə'dʒɑ:məz] *n pl* pigiama.
Pakistan [,pɑ:kis'tɑ:n] *n* Pakistan.
Pakistani [,pɑ:kis'tɑ:ni] *a n* pachistano.
palace ['pælis] *n* palazzo.
paladin ['pælədin] *n* paladino.
palatable ['pælətəbl] *a* gradevole.
palate ['pælit] *n* palato; gusto.
palaver [pə'lɑ:və] *n* discussione, chiacchiere.
pale [peil] *a* pallido, scialbo, chiaro; *n* palo; palizzata; *vi* impallidire.
paleness ['peilnis] *n* pallore.
Palestine ['pælistain] *n* Palestina.
Palestinian [,pæles'tiniən] *a n* palestinese.
palette ['pælit] *n* tavolozza.
palisade [,pæli'seid] *n* palizzata.
pall [pɔ:l] *n* coltre funebre; *vi* diventare insipido, non essere più interessante.
pallet ['pælit] *n* giaciglio, paglericcio.
palliate ['pælieit] *vt* mitigare.
palliative ['pæliətiv] *a n* palliativo.
pallid ['pælid] *a* pallido.
pallor ['pælə] *n* pallore.
palm [pɑ:m] *n* (*tree*) palma; (*hand*) palmo.
palpable ['pælpəbl] *a* palpabile; evidente.
palpitate ['pælpiteit] *vi* palpitare.
palpitation [,pælpi'teiʃən] *n* palpitazione.
palsy ['pɔ:lzi] *n* paralisi.
palter ['pɔ:ltə] *vi* tergiversare.
paltry ['pɔ:ltri] *a* di poco valore, meschino.
pamper ['pæmpə] *vt* trattare con soverchia indulgenza, viziare.
pamphlet ['pæmflit] *n* opuscolo.
pan [pæn] *n* padella, tegame.
pancake ['pænkeik] *n* frittella.
pandemonium ['pændi'mouniəm] *n* pandemonio.
pander ['pændə] *n* mezzano, ruffiano; *vi* fare il mezzano; (*fig*) accarezzare i gusti.
pane [pein] *n* vetro di finestra.
panegyric [,pæni'dʒirik] *n* panegirico.
panel ['pænl] *n* pannello; commissione; **p. doctor** dottore della mutua.
pang [pæŋ] *n* dolore acuto, spasimo.
panic ['pænik] *n* panico.
panorama [,pænə'rɑ:mə] *n* panorama.
pansy ['pænzi] *n* viola del pensiero.
pant [pænt] *n* palpitazione, palpito; *vi* ansimare; desiderare ardentemente.
pantaloons [,pæntə'lu:ns] *n pl* pantaloni *pl*.
pantheism ['pænθi:izəm] *n* panteismo.
panther ['pænθə] *n* pantera.
pantomime ['pæntəmaim] *n* pantomima.
pantry ['pæntri] *n* dispensa.
pap [pæp] *n* pappa.
papa [pə'pɑ:] *n* papà, babbo.
papacy ['peipəsi] *n* papato.
papal ['peipəl] *a* papale.
paper ['peipə] *n* carta; documento; giornale; dissertazione, saggio; *vt* tappezzare; **wrapping p.** carta da imballaggio; **waste p.** carta straccia.
paper-hanger ['peipə,hæŋə] *n* tappezziere.
paper-mill ['peipəmil] *n* cartiera.
papist ['peipist] *n* papista.
papyrus [pə'paiərəs] *n* papiro.
par [pɑ:] *n* pari, parità.
parable ['pærəbl] *n* parabola.
parachute ['pærəʃu:t] *n* paracadute.
parachutist ['pærəʃu:tist] *n* paracadutista.
parade [pə'reid] *n* mostra; parata, sfilata, rivista; *vt* far mostra di; *vi* sfilare in parata.
paradise ['pærədais] *n* paradiso.
paradox ['pærədɔks] *n* paradosso.
paradoxical [pærə'dɔksikəl] *a* paradossale.
paraffin ['pærəfin] *n* paraffina, petrolio.
paragon ['pærəgən] *n* paragone, modello.

paragraph ['pærəgrɑːf] *n* paragrafo, capoverso.
Paraguay ['pærəgwai] *n* Paraguai.
Paraguayan [ˌpærə'gwaiən] *a n* paraguaiano.
parallel ['pærəlel] *a* parallelo; *n* parallela; parallelo; confronto.
paralysis [pə'rælisis] *n* paralisi.
paralytic [ˌpærə'litik] *a n* paralitico.
paralyze ['pærəlaiz] *vt* paralizzare.
paramount ['pærəmaunt] *a* sovrano, supremo.
parapet ['pærəpit] *n* parapetto.
paraphernalia [ˌpærəfə'neiliə] *n* (*fam*) armamentario, roba.
paraphrase ['pærəfreiz] *n* parafrasi.
parapsychology ['pærəsai'kɔlədʒi] *n* metapsichica.
parasite ['pærəsait] *n* parassita.
parasol ['pærəsol] *n* ombrellino, parasole.
paratrooper ['pærətruːpə] *n* paracadutista.
paratyphoid ['pærə'taifɔid] *n* paratifo.
parboil ['pɑːbɔil] *vt* bollire parzialmente.
parcel ['pɑːsl] *n* pacco; pezzo di terra; *vt* **to p. up** impaccare.
parch [pɑːtʃ] *vt* disseccare, inaridire; *vi* diventare riarso.
parchment ['pɑːtʃmənt] *n* pergamena.
pardon ['pɑːdn] *n* perdono, amnistia; *vt* perdonare.
pardonable ['pɑːdnəbl] *a* perdonabile, scusabile.
pare [pɛə] *vt* (*fruit*) sbucciare; (*nails*) tagliare.
parent ['pɛərənt] *n* genitore *m*, genitrice *f* genitori *pl*.
parentage ['pɛərəntidʒ] *n* origini, natali *pl*.
parental [pə'rentl] *a* paterno, materno, di genitori.
parenthesis [pə'renθisis] *n* parentesi.
Paris ['pæris] *n* Parigi.
parish ['pæriʃ] *n* parrocchia.
parishioner [pə'riʃənə] *n* parrocchiano.
Parisian [pə'riziən] *a n* parigino.
park [pɑːk] *n* parco; (*aut*) posteggio.
parking ['pɑːkiŋ] *n* (*aut*) parcheggio, posteggio; aiuola spartitraffico; **p. meter** contatore per parcheggio; **p. place, p. lot** area per parcheggio, posteggio.
parlance ['pɑːləns] *n* parlata, gergo.
parley ['pɑːli] *n* discussione, parlamento; *vi* discutere, parlamentare.
parliament ['pɑːləmənt] *n* parlamento.
parliamentary [ˌpɑːlə'mentəri] *a* parlamentare.
parlor ['pɑːlə] *n* salotto.
Parmesan [ˌpɑːmi'zæn] *a* parmigiano.
parochial [pə'roukiəl] *a* parrocchiale.
parody ['pærədi] *n* parodia; *vt* parodiare.
paroxysm ['pærəksizəm] *n* parossismo.
parricide ['pærisaid] *n* parricida, parricidio.
parrot ['pærət] *n* pappagallo.
parry ['pæri] *n* parata; *vt* evitare; parare.
parse [pɑːz] *vt* fare l'analisi (grammaticale o logica) di.
parsimonious [ˌpɑːsi'mouniəs] *a* parsimonioso, economo.
parsimony ['pɑːsiməni] *n* parsimonia, economia.
parsley ['pɑːsli] *n* prezzemolo.
parsnip ['pɑːsnip] *n* pastinaca.
parson ['pɑːsn] *n* parroco (anglicano); (*fam*) pastore.
part [pɑːt] *n* parte; *vti* divider(si), separar(si).
partake [pɑː'teik] *vi* partecipare.
partial ['pɑːʃəl] *a* parziale, propenso verso.
partiality [ˌpɑːʃi'æliti] *n* parzialità; favoritismo; predilezione.
participant [pɑː'tisipənt] *a* partecipe; *n* partecipante.
participate [pɑː'tisipeit] *vi* partecipare; prendere parte a.
participation [pɑːˌtisi'peiʃən] *n* partecipazione.
participle ['pɑːtisipl] *n* (*gram*) participio.
particle ['pɑːtikl] *n* particella; (*eccl*) particola.
particular [pə'tikjulə] *a* particolare, speciale; minuzioso; *n* particolare, dettaglio; informazione; **in p.** in particolare.
particularly [pə'tikjuləli] *ad* particolarmente, dettagliatamente.
parting ['pɑːtiŋ] *n* separazione; congedo; (*hair*) scriminatura, divisa.
partisan [ˌpɑːti'zæn] *a n* partigiano.
partition [pɑː'tiʃən] *n* divisione; spartizione; tramezzo.
partly ['pɑːtli] *ad* in parte.
partner ['pɑːtnə] *n* compagno, ballerina, -no, marito, moglie; (*com*) socio; **partnership** (*com*) società, associazione.
partridge ['pɑːtridʒ] *n* pernice.
party ['pɑːti] *n* partito; brigata; trattenimento, festa, festicciola; (*leg*) parte in causa.
pass [pɑːs] *n* passo, valico; situazione; passaggio; (*mil*) permesso, lasciapassare; *vti* passare; accadere; *vt* attraversare; superare; approvare (una legge); **to p. away** morire; **to p. by** passare davanti a; passare sotto silenzio.
passable ['pɑːsəbl] *a* discreto, passabile; attraversabile.
passage ['pæsidʒ] *n* passaggio; traversata; varco; corridoio; brano.
passenger ['pæsindʒə] *n* passeggiero, viaggiatore.

passer-by ['pɑ:sə'bai] *n* passante.
passing ['pɑ:siŋ] *a* passante; passeggiero, casuale; *n* passaggio; trapasso, morte.
passion ['pæʃən] *n* passione.
passionate ['pæʃənit] *a* appassionato; passionale; irascibile.
passive ['pæsiv] *a n* passivo.
passport ['pɑ:spɔ:t] *n* passaporto.
password ['pɑ:swə:d] *n* parola d'ordine.
past [pɑ:st] *a* passato, scorso; finito; *prep* al di là di; *ad* oltre; *n* passato.
paste [peist] *n* pasta; colla; *vt* incollare.
pasteboard ['peistbɔ:d] *n* cartone grosso.
pastel ['pæstəl] *n* pastello.
pastime ['pɑ:staim] *n* passatempo.
pastor ['pɑ:stə] *n* (*eccl*) pastore.
pastoral ['pɑ:stərəl] *a n* pastorale.
pastry ['peistri] *n* pasticceria; **p. board** asse per la pasta.
pasture ['pɑ:stʃə] *n* pascolo, pastura; *vti* far pascolare.
pat [pæt] *n* colpetto, tocco leggero; panetto di burro; *a* pronto, adatto; *ad* a proposito; *vt* accarezzare, dare un piccolo colpo su, dare un buffetto a.
patch [pætʃ] *n* toppa; piccolo pezzo di terreno; macchia; *vt* rattoppare, mettere insieme alla meglio; **patchwork** rappezzatura, mescolanza, mosaico.
patent ['peitənt] *a* evidente, ovvio; brevettato, patentato; *n* brevetto; **p. leather** *n* cuoio verniciato; *vt* brevettare.
patentee [,peitən'ti:] *n* detentore di brevetto.
paternal [pə'tə:nl] *a* paterno.
paternity [pə'tə:niti] *n* paternità.
path [pɑ:θ] *n* sentiero, viottolo.
pathetic [pə'θetik] *a* commovente, patetico.
pathfinder ['pɑ:θ,faində] *n* esploratore, pioniere.
pathologic(al) [,pæθə'lɔdʒik(əl)] *a* patologico.
pathology [pə'θɔlədʒi] *n* patologia.
pathos ['peiθɔs] *n* pathos, commozione.
pathway ['pɑ:θwei] *n* sentiero.
patience ['peiʃəns] *n* pazienza.
patient ['peiʃənt] *a n* paziente.
patriarch ['peitriɑ:k] *n* patriarca.
patriarchal [,peitri'ɑ:kəl] *a* patriarcale.
Patricia [pə'triʃə] *nf pr* Patrizia.
patrician [pə'triʃən] *a n* patrizio.
Patrick ['pætrik] *nm pr* Patrizio.
patrimony ['pætriməni] *n* patrimonio.
patriot ['peitriət] *n* patriota.
patriotic [,pætri'ɔtik] *a* patriottico.
patriotism ['pætriətizəm] *n* patriottismo.
patrol [pə'troul] *n* (*mil*) pattuglia; *vt* perlustrare; *vi* pattugliare.
patrolman [pə'troulmæn] *pl* **-men** *n* poliziotto.
patron ['peitrən] *n* patrono, mecenate.
patronage ['pætrənidʒ] *n* patronato, patrocinio; (*shop*) concorso di avventori.
patronize ['pætrənaiz] *vt* patrocinare; trattare con aria condiscendente; essere cliente abituale di.
patter ['pætə] *n* picchiettio, scalpitio; (*rain*) ticchettio; parlata, cicaleccio; *vi* picchiettare; camminare con passetti rapidi; parlare meccanicamente.
pattern ['pætən] *n* campione, modello.
Paul [pɔ:l] *nm pr* Paolo.
Pauline ['pɔ:li:n] *nf pr* Paola, Paolina.
paunch ['pɔ:ntʃ] *n* pancia, pancione.
pauper ['pɔ:pə] *n* povero, mendicante.
pauperism ['pɔ:pərizəm] *n* indigenza.
pauperize ['pɔ:pəraiz] *vt* impoverire.
pause [pɔ:z] *n* pausa; *vi* fare una pausa, fermarsi.
pave [peiv] *vt* pavimentare; (*fig*) preparare il terreno.
pavement ['peivmənt] *n* marciapiede, selciato.
pavilion [pə'viljən] *n* padiglione.
paw [pɔ:] *n* zampa.
pawn [pɔ:n] *n* pegno; (*chess*) pedina; *vt* impegnare.
pawnbroker ['pɔ:n,broukə] *n* chi presta denaro su pegno.
pawnshop ['pɔ:nʃɔp] *n* monti di pegni.
pay [pei] *n* paga, salario, retribuzione; *vt* pagare, rimunerare; *vi* dar frutti, rendere.
payable ['peiəbl] *a* pagabile.
payment ['peimənt] *n* pagamento, saldo.
pea [pi:] *n* pisello.
peace [pi:s] *n* pace, ordine pubblico; **peacemaker** paciere.
peaceable ['pi:səbl] **peaceful** ['pi:sful] *a* pacifico, tranquillo.
peach [pi:tʃ] *n* pesca.
peacock ['pi:kɔk] *n* pavone.
peak [pi:k] *n* cima, picco; punta; visiera.
peal [pi:l] *n* scampanio; salva d'artiglieria; scroscio; rombo; *vi* risuonare, scampanare, tuonare.
peanut ['pi:nʌt] *n* arachide, nocciolina americana; **p. butter** pasta di arachidi.
pear [pεə] *n* pera; **p. tree** pero.
pearl [pə:l] *n* perla.
peasant ['pezənt] *n* contadino; *a* contadinesco, rustico.
peasantry ['pezəntri] *n* contadini *pl.*
peat [pi:t] *n* torba.
pebble ['pebl] *n* ciottolo, sassolino.
peck [pek] *vti* beccare.

peculiar [pi'kju:liə] *a* peculiare, particolare; strano.
peculiarity [pi,kju:li'æriti] *n* caratteristica.
peculiarly [pi'kju:liəli] *ad* particolarmente; stranamente.
pecuniary [pi'kju:niəri] *a* pecuniario.
pedagogue ['pedəgɔg] *n* pedagogo.
pedal ['pedl] *n* pedale.
pedant ['pedənt] *n* pedante.
pedantic [pe'dæntik] *a* pedantesco, pedante.
pedantry ['pedəntri] *n* pedanteria.
peddle ['pedl] *vt* vendere al minuto; *vi* fare il venditore ambulante.
peddler ['pedlə] *n* venditore ambulante.
pedestal ['pedistl] *n* piedistallo.
pedestrian [pi'destriən] *a* pedestre; *n* pedone.
pedigree ['pedigri:] *n* albero genealogico; (*animals*) pedigree.
peel [pi:l] *n* buccia; *vt* sbucciare.
peep [pi:p] *n* occhiata, sguardo furtivo o timido; *vi* far capolino, guardare furtivamente, lasciarsi intravedere, spuntare.
peer [piə] *n* pari; *vi* spuntare; scrutare.
peerage ['piəridʒ] *n* la nobiltà; almanacco nobiliare.
peevish ['pi:viʃ] *a* stizzoso, irritabile.
peewit ['pi:wit] *n* pavoncella.
peg [peg] *n* cavicchio, piuolo; molletta; (*fam*) bevanda alcoolica.
Pekinese [,pi:ki'ni:z] *a n* pechinese.
Peking [pi:'kiŋ] *n* Pechino.
pelf [pelf] *n* denaro, lucro.
pelican ['pelikən] *n* pellicano.
pellet ['pelit] *n* pallina; pallottola; pillola.
pell-mell ['pel'mel] *n* confusione, mischia; *ad* confusamente, alla rinfusa.
pelt [pelt] *n* pelle grezza; scroscio di pioggia; velocità; colpo di proiettile; *vt* colpire; *vi* (*of rain*) battere con violenza, correre.
pelvis ['pelvis] *n* (*anat*) pelvi, bacino.
pen [pen] *n* penna; piccolo recinto per animali; *vt* scrivere; chiudere (animali) in un recinto; **penpoint** pennino; **ballpoint p.** penna a sfera; **fountain p.** penna stilografica.
penal ['pi:nl] *a* penale.
penalize ['pi:nəlaiz] *vt* penalizzare.
penalty ['penlti] *n* penalità, punizione; **p. kick** (*football*) calcio di rigore; **p. stroke** (*golf*) colpo di ammenda.
penance ['penəns] *n* penitenza.
pencil ['pensl] *n* matita.
pendant ['pendənt] *n* ciondolo, pendente.
pending ['pendiŋ] *a* pendente; in sospeso; *prep* durante, fino a.
pendulum ['pendjuləm] *n* pendolo.
penetrate ['penitreit] *vti* penetrare.
penetration [,peni'treiʃən] *n* penetrazione, acutezza.
penguin ['peŋgwin] *n* pinguino.
penicillin [,peni'silin] *n* penicillina.
peninsula [pi'ninsjulə] *n* penisola.
peninsular [pi'ninsjulə] *a* peninsulare.
penitence ['penitəns] *n* penitenza.
penitent ['penitənt] *a n* penitente.
penitentiary [,peni'tenʃəri] *a* penitenziale; *n* riformatorio, penitenzario.
penknife ['pennaif] *n* temperino.
penniless ['penilis] *a* senza un soldo.
penny ['peni] *n* 'penny', soldo; **penny-farthing** bicicletta antiquata; **penny-worth** un soldo di.
pension ['penʃən] *n* pensione; *vt* pensionare.
pensioner ['penʃənə] *n* pensionato, pensionata.
pensive ['pensiv] *a* malinconico, pensoso.
pensiveness ['pensivnis] *n* malinconia.
Pentecost ['pentikɔst] *n* Pentecoste.
penthouse *n* tettoia; appartamento sul tetto di un edificio.
penurious [pi'njuəriəs] *a* bisognoso; avaro.
penury ['penjuri] *n* penuria.
peony ['piəni] *n* peonia.
people ['pi:pl] *n* popolo, nazione; (*costruzione pl*) gente, parenti *pl*; *vt* popolare.
pep [pep] *n* (*sl*) iniziativa, vigore.
pepper ['pepə] *n* pepe.
peppercorn ['pepəkɔ:n] *n* grano di pepe.
peppermint ['pepəmint] *n* menta peperita, caramella di menta.
peppery ['pepəri] *a* pepato; pungente; collerico.
perambulator ['præmbjuleitə] **pram** [præm] *n* carrozzina per bambini.
perceive [pə'si:v] *vt* percepire, accorgersi di, scorgere.
percentage [pə'sentidʒ] *n* percentuale.
perceptible [pə'septəbl] *a* percettibile.
perceptibly [pə'septəbli] *ad* in modo percettibile.
perception [pə'sepʃən] *n* percezione; intuizione.
perceptiveness [pə'septivnis] *n* percettività.
perch [pə:tʃ] *n* (*bird's*) posatoio, gruccia; (*measure 25,293 sq meters*) pertica; pesce persico; *vi* appollaiarsi, posarsi.
perchance [pə'tʃa:ns] *ad* (*arc*) forse, per caso.
percolate ['pə:kəleit] *vti* filtrare.
percolator ['pə:kəleitə] *n* filtro; macchina per il caffè.
percussion [pə:'kʌʃən] *n* percussione.
perdition [pə:'diʃən] *n* perdizione.

peremptory [pə'remptəri] *a* perentorio.
perennial [pə'reniəl] *a n* (*of plant*) perenne.
perfect ['pə:fikt] *a n* perfetto; *vt* perfezionare.
perfection [pə'fekʃən] *n* perfezione.
perfectionist [pə'fekʃənist] *n* perfezionista.
perfidious [pə'fidiəs] *a* perfido.
perfidy ['pə:fidi] *n* perfidia.
perforate ['pə:fəreit] *vti* forare; penetrare; (*mech*) perforare.
perform [pə'fɔ:m] *vt* adempiere, compiere; eseguire; rappresentare.
performance [pə'fɔ:məns] *a* adempimento; rappresentazione, recita.
performer [pə'fɔ:mə] *n* esecutore, attore.
perfume ['pə:fju:m] *n* profumo; *vt* profumare.
perfunctory [pə'fʌŋktəri] *a* meccanico, superficiale.
perhaps [pə'hæps] *ad* forse.
peril ['peril] *n* pericolo.
perilous ['periləs] *a* pericoloso.
perilously ['periləsli] *ad* pericolosamente.
period ['piəriəd] *n* epoca, periodo.
periodic [,piəri'ɔdik] *a* periodico.
periodical [,piəri'ɔdikəl] *a n* periodico.
periphery [pə'rifəri] *n* periferia.
periscope ['periskoup] *n* periscopio.
perish ['periʃ] *vti* (far) perire.
perishable ['periʃəbl] *a* deperibile, perituro, deteriorabile.
periwinkle ['peri,wiŋkl] *n* pervinca.
perjure ['pə:dʒə] *vr*; **p. oneself** spergiurare.
perjury ['pə:dʒəri] *n* spergiuro.
perk [pə:k] *vti* **to p. up** drizzare; (*fig*) rallegrare.
perky ['pə:ki] *a* birichino; impertinente.
perm [pə:m] *v* **permanent wave.**
permanence ['pə:mənəns] *n* permanenza.
permanent ['pə:mənənt] *a* permanente; **p. wave** (ondulazione) permanente.
permeate ['pə:mieit] *vt* permeare.
permissible [pə'misəbl] *a* lecito.
permission [pə'miʃən] *n* permesso.
permissive [pə'misiv] *a* che permette, tollerante; permissivo.
permit ['pə:mit] *n* permesso, autorizzazione; *vti* [pə'mit] permettere.
pernicious [pə:'niʃəs] *a* pernicioso, nocivo.
peroration [,perə'reiʃən] *n* perorazione.
peroxide [pə'rɔksaid] *n* (*chem*) perossido.
perpendicular [,pə:pən'dikjulə] *a n* perpendicolare.
perpetrate ['pə:pitreit] *vt* perpetrare.
perpetual [pə'petjuəl] *a* perpetuo.
perpetuate [pə'petjueit] *vt* perpetuare.
perplex [pə'pleks] *vt* imbarazzare, rendere perplesso.
perplexity [pə'pleksiti] *n* perplessità.
perquisite ['pə:kwizit] *n* mancia; guadagno occasionale.
perquisition [,pə:kwi'ziʃən] *n* perquisizione.
persecute ['pə:sikju:t] *vt* perseguitare; importunare.
persecution [,pə:si'kju:ʃən] *n* persecuzione.
persecutor ['pə:sikju:tə] *n* persecutore.
perseverance [,pə:si'viərəns] *n* perseveranza.
persevere [,pə:si'viə] *vi* perseverare
Persia ['pə:ʃə] *n* Persia.
Persian ['pə:ʃən] *a n* persiano.
persist [pə'sist] *vi* persistere, durare.
persistence [pə'sistəns] *n* persistenza, perseveranza.
persistent [pə'sistənt] *a* persistente, tenace.
persistently [pə'sistəntli] *ad* persistentemente, tenacemente.
person ['pə:sn] *n* persona.
personage ['pə:snidʒ] *n* personaggio, personalità.
personal ['pə:snl] *a* personale; **p. business** questione personale.
personality [,pə:sə'næliti] *n* personalità.
personally ['pə:snəli] *ad* personalmente.
personification [pə:,sɔnifi'keiʃən] *n* personificazione.
personify [pə:'sɔnifai] *vt* personificare.
personnel [,pə:sə nel] *n* personale.
perspective [pə spektiv] *n* prospettiva.
perspicacious [,pə:spi'keiʃəs] *a* perspicace.
perspicacity [,pə:spi'kæsiti] *n* perspicacia.
perspiration [,pə:spə'reiʃən] *n* traspirazione, sudore.
perspire [pəs'paiə] *vi* sudare, traspirare.
persuade [pə'sweid] *vt* persuadere.
persuasion [pə'sweiʒən] *n* persuasione, fede.
persuasive [pə'sweisiv] *a* persuasivo; *n* motivo.
pert [pə:t] *a* impertinente; sveglio.
pertain [pə:'tein] *vi* concernere.
pertinacious [,pə:ti'neiʃəs] *a* pertinace.
pertinent ['pə:tinənt] *a* pertinente, proprio.
pertness ['pə:tnis] *n* impertinenza; vivacità.
perturb [pə'tə:b] *vt* perturbare, turbare.
perturbation [,pə:tə:'beiʃən] *n* turbamento.
Peru [pə'ru:] *n* Perù.
perusal [pə'ru:zəl] *n* lettura attenta.
peruse [pə'ru:z] *vt* leggere attentamente; esaminare.

Peruvian [pə'ru:viən] *a n* peruviano.
pervade [pə:'veid] *vt* pervadere, permeare.
pervasive [pə:'veisiv] *a* penetrante; invadente.
perverse [pə'və:s] *a* perverso.
perversion [pə'və:ʃən] *n* perversione, pervertimento.
perversity [pə'və:siti] *n* perversità.
pervert [pə'və:t] *vt* pervertire.
pessimism ['pesimizəm] *n* pessimismo.
pessimist ['pesimist] *n* pessimista.
pessimistic [.pesi'mistik] *a* pessimistico.
pest [pest] *n* peste, individuo noiosissimo.
pester ['pestə] *vt* importunare, infastidire; infestare.
pestilence ['pestiləns] *n* pestilenza.
pestilent ['pestilənt] *a* pestilenziale.
pestle ['pesl] *n* pestello.
pet [pet] *a* favorito; vezzeggiato; *n* animale favorito, beniamino; cattivo umore, collera; *vt* vezzeggiare.
petal ['petl] *n* petalo.
Peter ['pi:tə] *nm pr* Pietro.
petition [pi'tiʃən] *n* petizione, supplica; *vt* presentare una petizione a.
petitioner [pi'tiʃənə] *n* supplicante, postulante.
petrify ['petrifai] *vt* pietrificare.
petrol ['petrəl] *n* benzina.
petroleum [pi'trouliəm] *n* petrolio.
petticoat ['petikout] *n* sottoveste, sottana.
petty ['peti] *a* piccolo, insignificante, meschino; **p. officer** sottufficiale di marina.
petulant ['petjulənt] *a* petulante.
petunia [pi'tju:niə] *n* (*bot*) petunia.
pew [pju:] *n* banco in chiesa.
pewter ['pju:tə] *n* peltro.
phantom ['fæntəm] *n* fantasma.
Pharaoh ['fɛərou] *n* faraone.
Pharisee ['færisi:] *n* fariseo.
pharmacy ['fɑ:məsi] *n* farmacia, scienza farmaceutica.
phase [feiz] *n* fase.
pheasant ['feznt] *n* fagiano.
phenomenon [fi'nɔminən] *n* fenomeno.
phenomenal [fi'nɔminl] *a* fenomenale; (*phil*) fenomenico.
phial ['faiəl] *n* fiala.
Philadelphia [.filə'delfiə] *n* Filadelfia.
philanderer [fi'lændərə] *n* donnaiolo.
philanthropic [.filən'θrɔpik] *a* filantropico.
philanthropist [fi'lænθrəpist] *n* filantropo.
philanthropy [fi'lænθrəpi] *n* filantropia.
philatelist [fi'lætəlist] *n* filatelico.
philately [fi'lætəli] *n* filatelia.
Philip ['filip] *nm pr* Filippo.
philologist [fi'lɔlədʒist] *n* filologo.
philology [fi'lɔlədʒi] *n* filologia.
philosopher [fi'lɔsəfə] *n* filosofo.
philosophic(al) [.filə'sɔfik(l)] *a* filosofico.
philosophy [fi'lɔsəfi] *n* filosofia.
philter ['filtə] *n* filtro.
phlegm [flem] *n* flemma.
phlegmatic [fleg'mætik] *a* flemmatico.
phobia ['foubiə] *n* fobia.
phoenix ['fi:niks] *n* fenice.
phonetic [fə'netik] *a* fonetico.
phonetics [fou'netiks] *n pl* fonetica.
phonograph ['founəgrɑ:f] *n* fonografo.
phosphate ['fɔsfeit] *n* fosfato.
phosphorous ['fɔsfərəs] *n* fosforo.
photocopy ['foutoukɔpi] *n* fotocopia.
photoflash ['foutouflæʃ] *n* fotografia al lampo di magnesio.
photograph ['foutəgrɑ:f] *n* fotografia; *vt* fotografare.
photographer [fə'tɔgrəfə] *n* fotografo.
photographic [.foutə'græfik] *a* fotografico.
photography [fə'tɔgrəfi] *n* (*arte fotografica*) fotografia.
photostat ['foutoustæt] *n* apparecchio fotostatico; copia fotostatica.
phrase [freiz] *n* frase.
phraseology [.freizi'ɔlədʒi] *n* fraseologia.
physical ['fizikəl] *a* fisico.
physician [fi'ziʃən] *n* medico.
physicist ['fizisist] *n* fisico.
physics ['fiziks] *n pl* fisica.
physiognomy [.fizi'ɔnəmi] *n* fisionomia.
physiotherapy [.fiziə'θerəpi] *n* fisioterapia.
physique [fi'zi:k] *n* fisico, costituzione fisica,
pianist ['piənist] *n* pianista.
piano [pi'ænou] *n* pianoforte.
pick [pik] *n* piccone; scelta; *vt* cogliere; **p. up** raccogliere; (*rad*) captare; scegliere.
picket ['pikit] *n* (*mil*) picchetto.
pickle ['pikl] *n* salamoia; situazione spiacevole.
pickpocket ['pik.pɔkit] *n* borsaiolo.
pick-up ['pikʌp] *n* (*el*) riproduttore acustico, fonorivelatore, 'pick-up'; (*tv*) dispositivo di presa.
picnic ['piknik] *n* 'pic-nic', scampagnata.
pictorial [pik'tɔ:riəl] *a* pittorico, illustrato.
picture ['piktʃə] *n* dipinto, quadro. ritratto; **pictures** *pl* (*fam*) cinematografo.
picture ['piktʃə] *vt* dipingere, descrivere, figurarsi.
picturesque [.piktʃə'resk] *a* pittoresco.
pie [pai] *n* pasticcio di carne, torta di frutta; (*ornit*) gazza.
piece [pi:s] *n* pezzo; (*material*) pezza;

(*mus*) composizione; **piecework** lavoro a cottimo.
piecemeal ['pi:smi:l] *ad* pezzo a pezzo, a pezzi e a bocconi.
Piedmont ['pi:dmənt] *n* Piemonte; **piedmontese** *a n* piemontese.
pier [piə] *n* banchina, molo; pilastro.
pierce [piəs] *vti* penetrare, forare.
piercing ['piəsiŋ] *a* penetrante; *n* perforamento.
piety ['paiəti] *n* religiosità, pietà.
pig [pig] *n* maiale, porco.
pigeon ['pidʒin] *n* piccione, colombo.
pigeonhole ['pidʒinhoul] *n* nicchia di colombaia; casella; **set of pigeonholes** casellario; *vt* incasellare, archiviare.
pigtail ['pigteil] *n* treccina stretta di capelli, codino.
pike [paik] *n* picca; (*fish*) luccio.
pilchard ['piltʃəd] *n* sardella.
pile [pail] *n* ammasso, mucchio; pira; (*el*) pila; palafitta; (*nap*) pelo; **piles** *pl* (*med*) emorroidi.
pile [pail] *vt* accumulare, ammucchiare, esagerare.
pilfer ['pilfə] *vt* rubacchiare.
pilgrim ['pilgrim] *n* pellegrino.
pilgrimage ['pilgrimidʒ] *n* pellegrinaggio.
pill [pil] *n* pillola.
pillage ['pilidʒ] *n* saccheggio; *vt* saccheggiare.
pillar ['pilə] *n* colonna, pilastro.
pillory ['piləri] *n* berlina, gogna; *vt* mettere alla berlina.
pillow ['pilou] *n* guanciale, cuscino; (*mech*) cuscinetto.
pilot ['pailət] *n* pilota; *vt* pilotare.
pimple ['pimpl] *n* foruncolo.
pin [pin] *n* spillo; **pins and needles** (*fig*) formicolio.
pincers ['pinsəz] *n pl* pinze; tanaglie *pl*.
pinch [pintʃ] *n* pizzico; (*snuff*) presa; *vti* pizzicare; stringere; privare del necessario; far soffrire.
pincushion ['pin,kuʃin] *n* portaspilli.
pine [pain] *n* pino; *vi* languire, struggersi.
pink [piŋk] *a* rosa; *n* color rosa; garofano; (*fig*) fiore, modello, perfezione.
pinnacle ['pinəkl] *n* pinnacolo; (*fig*) apogeo.
pinpoint ['pinpɔint] *vt* localizzare, determinare con esattezza.
pint [paint] *n* pinta (*circa mezzo litro*).
pioneer [,paiə'niə] *n* pioniere.
pious ['paiəs] *a* pio, devoto.
pip [pip] *n* seme di frutto; (*cards etc*) macchia; (*officer's*) stelletta; (*sl*) malumore.
pipe [paip] *n* tubo; canna; cornamusa, zampogna; pipa; vena di minerale; *vi* suonare (la cornamusa *etc*).
piper ['paipə] *n* sonatore di cornamusa, pifferaio.
piquant ['pi:kənt] *a* piccante.
pique [pi:k] *n* picca, risentimento; *vt* ferire l'orgoglio di, offendere.
piracy ['paiərəsi] *n* pirateria.
pirate ['paiərit] *n* pirata.
pistol ['pistl] *n* pistola.
piston ['pistən] *n* pistone, stantuffo.
pit [pit] *n* abisso; buca, cava, cavità; miniera.
pitch [pitʃ] *n* pec (*degree*) grado; intensità; massimo punto; (*mus*) tono; *vt* lanciare, piantare, fissare al suolo; *vi* (*naut*) beccheggiare.
pitcher ['pitʃə] *n* brocca.
piteous ['pitiəs] *a* commovente, pietoso.
pitfall ['pitfɔ:l] *n* trappola; (*fig*) inganno.
pith [piθ] *n* midollo, parte essenziale.
pitiable ['pitiəbl] *a* compassionevole.
pitiful ['pitiful] *a* pietoso, miserando.
pitiless ['pitilis] *a* crudele, spietato.
pittance ['pitəns] *n* elemosina, piccola parte o quantità, piccola somma.
pity ['piti] *n* pietà, compassione; **what a p.!** *interj* che peccato!; *vt* compiangere.
Pius ['paiəs] *nm pr* Pio.
pivot ['pivət] *n* pernio.
placard ['plækɑ:d] *n* affisso, manifesto.
placate [plə'keit] *vt* placare.
place [pleis] *n* luogo, località, posto; *vt* collocare, mettere, posare.
placid ['plæsid] *a* placido.
plagiarize ['pleidʒjəraiz] *vt* plagiare.
plague [pleig] *n* peste, pestilenza; *vt* tormentare, vessare.
plain [plein] *a* piano, liscio; chiaro, evidente, sincero; insignificante; *n* pianura, piano; **p. clothes** abiti borghesi.
plainly ['pleinli] *ad* chiaramente; semplicemente.
plaintiff ['pleintif] *a* querelante.
plaintive ['pleintiv] *a* lamentoso.
plait [plæt] *n* piega; treccia; *vt* pieghettare; intrecciare.
plan [plæn] *n* piano, progetto, disegno; (*building etc*) pianta; *vt* progettare, pianificare.
plane [plein] *a* piano; *n* piano, (*tool*); pialla; (*tree*) platano; aereo.
planet ['plænit] *n* pianeta.
plank [plæŋk] *n* asse, tavola.
plant [plɑ:nt] *n* pianta, impianto; *vt* piantare.
plantation [plæn'teiʃən] *n* piantagione.
planter ['plɑ:ntə] *n* piantatore, colono.
plaque [plɑ:k] *n* placca.
plaster ['plɑ:stə] *n* cerotto; impiastro; gesso, intonaco, stucco; *vt* applicare un cerotto a; intonacare.
plasterer ['plɑ:stərə] *n* imbianchino; gessaio.
plastic ['plæstik] *a* plastico; **plastics** *n sing* plastica.
plasticine ['plæstisi:n] *n* plastilina.
plate [pleit] *n* piatto; lamina; placca,

targa; argenteria; (*book*) tavola fuori testo; dentiera; *vt* placcare, rivestire.
plateau ['plætou] *pl* **plateaux, plateaus** *n* altipiano.
platform ['plætfɔ:m] *n* piattaforma; pianoro; (*rly*) marciapiede.
platinum ['plætinəm] *n* platino.
platitude ['plætitju:d] *n* banalità.
platonic [plə'tɔnik] *a* platonico.
platoon [plə'tu:n] *n* (*mil*) plotone.
platter ['plætə] *n* piatto grande.
plausibility [,plɔ:zə'biliti] *n* plausibilità.
plausible ['plɔ:zəbl] *a* plausibile.
play [plei] *n* gioco, divertimento; commedia, dramma; *vti* giocare, rappresentare; suonare; **playground** *n* cortile (di scuola) per la ricreazione; **playmate** compagno di giuochi; **plaything** giocattolo.
player ['pleiə] *n* giocatore; suonatore; attore.
playful ['pleiful] *a* giocoso, scherzoso.
plea [pli:] *n* difesa, scusa.
plead [pli:d] *vti* addurre come pretesto; dichiararsi; perorare, supplicare.
pleading ['pli:diŋ] *a* supplichevole; *n* discussione d'una causa.
pleasant ['pleznt] *a* piacevole, simpatico.
please [pli:z] *vti* piacere (a).
pleasing ['pli:ziŋ] *a* piacente, attraente, ameno, piacevole.
pleasure ['pleʒə] *n* piacere.
plebeian [pli'bi:ən] *a n* plebeo.
plebiscite ['plebisit] *n* plebiscito.
pledge [pledʒ] *n* pegno, garanzia; promessa; brindisi; *vt* impegnare; brindare a.
plenipotentiary [,plenipə'tenʃəri] *a n* plenipotenziario.
plentiful ['plentiful] *a* abbondante, copioso.
plenty ['plenti] *n* abbondanza.
pleurisy ['pluərisi] *n* pleurite.
pliable ['plaiəbl] **pliant** ['plaiənt] *a* pieghevole, flessibile; docile, influenzabile.
pliers ['plaiəz] *n pl* pinze *pl*.
plight [plait] *n* condizione, situazione.
plimsolls ['plimsəls] *n pl* scarpe di tela.
plod [plɔd] *vi* camminare con passi lenti e pesanti; sgobbare.
plodder ['plɔdə] *n* sgobbone.
plot [plɔt] *n* complotto, cospirazione; (*novel etc*) intreccio, trama; piccolo pezzo di terreno; *vt* fare la pianta di; *vti* complottare.
plotter ['plɔtə] *n* cospiratore.
plover ['plʌvə] *n* piviere, pavoncella.
plow [plau] *n* aratro; *vti* arare, solcare; **to put one's hand to the p.** intraprendere un lavoro.
pluck [plʌk] *n* (*fig*) coraggio; frattaglie; *vt* strappare, pelare, tirare.
plucky ['plʌki] *a* coraggioso.
plug [plʌg] *n* tappo; tampone; (*el*) spina, tabacco compresso.
plum [plʌm] *n* prugna; susina.
plumage ['plu:midʒ] *n* penne *pl*.
plumb [plʌm] *vt* misurare la profondità di, scandagliare; *ad* a piombo; (*fig*) esattamente; assolutamente.
plumber ['plʌmə] *n* idraulico.
plumbing ['plʌmiŋ] *n* impiombatura; impianto idraulico.
plume [plu:m] *n* piuma; (*mil*) pennacchio.
plump [plʌmp] *a* grassoccio, paffuto.
plumpness ['plʌmpnis] *n* rotondità di forme.
plunder ['plʌndə] *n* saccheggio, bottino; *vt* depredare, saccheggiare.
plunge [plʌndʒ] *n* immersione, tuffo; *vti* immerger(si), tuffar(si).
plural ['pluərəl] *a n* plurale.
plus [plʌs] *a* in più; *n* più, quantità addizionale, quantità positiva.
plush [plʌʃ] *n* felpa; *a* felpato; comodo, elegante.
ply [plai] *vt* maneggiare; occuparsi di; importunare; *vi* andare avanti e indietro regolarmente.
plywood ['plaiwud] *n* legno compensato.
pneumatic [nju:'mætik] *a n* pneumatico.
pneumonia [nju:'mouniə] *n* polmonite.
poach [poutʃ] *vt* cuocere (uova) in camicia; *vi* andare a caccia di frodo.
poacher ['poutʃə] *n* cacciatore di frodo; bracconiere.
pocket ['pɔkit] *n* tasca; *vt* intascare, appropriarsi di; **p.-book** taccuino, libro formato tascabile.
pod [pɔd] *n* baccello.
poem ['pouim] *n* poesia, poema.
poet ['pouit] *n* poeta.
poetic [pou'etik] *a* poetico.
poetics [pou'etiks] *n* poetica.
poetry ['pouitri] *n* poesia.
poignancy ['pɔinənsi] *n* (*of grief*) acutezza; commozione; mordacità.
poignant ['pɔinənt] *a* acuto, vivo, cocente; mordace.
point [pɔint] *n* punto, punta, promontorio; *vt* (*sharpen*) fare la punta a; (*emphasize*) dar rilievo a; **to p. at** additare; **to p. out** indicare, far osservare.
point-blank ['pɔint'blæŋk] *a* diretto; orizzontale; *ad* orizzontalmente; chiaro e tondo; a bruciapelo.
pointed ['pɔintid] *a* appuntito, aguzzo; (*fig*) evidente; mordace.
pointer ['pɔintə] *n* indicatore; lancetta; cane da ferma.
pointless ['pɔintlis] *a* senza punta; (*fig*) inutile.
poise [pɔiz] *n* equilibrio; portamento; *vt* equilibrare.
poison ['pɔizn] *n* veleno; *vt* avvelenare.
poisonous ['pɔiznəs] *a* velenoso.

poke [pouk] *n* spinta; *vt* spingere; (*fire*) attizzare; frugare; **to buy a pig in a p.** comperare la gatta nel sacco.
poker ['poukə] *n* attizzatoio.
Poland ['poulənd] *n* (*geogr*) Polonia.
polar ['poulə] *a* polare; (*el*) magnetico; (*fig*) opposto.
Pole [poul] *n* polacco.
pole [poul] *n* palo; pertica (misura di lunghezza uguale a m. 5 circa); polo.
polemic [pɔ'lemik] *n* polemica.
police [pə'li:s] *n* polizia.
policeman [pə'li:smən] *n* poliziotto, agente di polizia, vigile urbano.
policy ['pɔlisi] *n* politica; linea di condotta; polizza.
poliomyelitis [,poulioumaiə'laitis] *n* poliomielite.
Polish ['pouliʃ] *a n* polacco.
polish ['pɔliʃ] *n* lucidatura; lucido, vernice; raffinatezza; *vt* lucidare, lustrare; raffinare.
polite [pə'lait] *a* cortese, educato, gentile.
politeness [pə'laitnis] *n* cortesia, educazione.
political [pə'litikəl] *a* uomo politico, politicante.
politician [,pɔli'tiʃən] *n* uomo politico, politicante.
politics ['pɔlitiks] *n pl* politica, scienza politica.
poll [poul] *n* votazione; scrutinio; lista elettorale; voti; **polling** *a* votante; *n* votazione elettorale.
pollen ['pɔlin] *n* polline.
pollute [pə'lu:t] *vt* contaminare; corrompere.
pollution [pə'lu:ʃən] *n* contaminazione.
polygamy [pɔ'ligəmi] *n* poligamia.
polyvinyl ['pɔli'vinl] *a* polivinilico; *n* polivinile.
poliphony [pə'lifəni] *n* (*mus*) polifonia.
polythene ['pɔliθi:n] *n* politene.
pomade [pə'mɑ:d] *n* pomata.
pomegranate ['pɔm,grænit] *n* melagrana.
pomp [pɔmp] *n* pompa, fasto.
Pompeian [pɔm'pi:ən] *a* pompeiano.
Pompeii ['pɔmpiai] *n* Pompei.
pompous ['pɔmpəs] *a* pomposo.
pompousness ['pɔmpəsnis] *n* sussiego.
pond [pɔnd] *n* laghetto, stagno; vivaio.
ponder ['pɔndə] *vti* meditare, ponderare.
ponderous ['pɔndərəs] *a* ponderoso, pesante.
pontiff ['pɔntif] *n* pontefice, papa.
pontoon [pɔn'tu:n] *n* pontone.
pony ['pouni] *n* cavallino, "pony".
poodle ['pu:dl] *n* cane barbone, barboncino.
pool [pu:l] *n* stagno, pozzanghera; (*com*) fondo comune; (*com*) 'pool'; sindacato; **football p.** totocalcio; **p. room** sala del biliardo.
poop [pu:p] *n* (*naut*) poppa.
poor [puə] *a* povero, scarso.
poorly ['puəli] *a* indisposto; *ad* poveramente, dimessamente.
pop [pɔp] *n* scoppio, sparo; *vti* (far) esplodere; entrare, uscire (di colpo); (*cork*) saltare.
Pope [poup] *n* papa; (*Russian priest*) pope.
popery ['poupəri] *n* papismo.
poplar ['pɔplə] *n* pioppo.
poppy ['pɔpi] *n* papavero.
populace ['pɔpjuləs] *n* plebaglia, popolaccio.
popular ['pɔpjulə] *a* popolare.
popularity [,pɔpju'læriti] *n* popolarità.
populate ['pɔpjuleit] *vt* popolare.
population [,pɔpju'leiʃən] *n* popolazione.
populous ['pɔpjuləs] *a* popoloso.
porcelain ['pɔ:slin] *n* porcellana.
porch [pɔ:tʃ] *n* portico, porticato.
porcupine ['pɔ:kjupain] *n* porcospino.
pore [pɔ:] *n* poro; *vi* studiare assiduamente.
pork [pɔ:k] *n* carne di maiale.
pornographic [,pɔ:nə'græfik] *a* pornografico.
porous ['pɔ:rəs] *a* poroso.
porphyry ['pɔ:firi] *n* porfido.
porpoise ['pɔ:pəs] *n* focena.
porridge ['pɔridʒ] *n* pappa di farina d'avena.
port [pɔ:t] *n* porto; (*naut*) fianco sinistro della nave; vino d'Oporto.
portable ['pɔ:təbl] *a* portatile.
portal ['pɔ:tl] *n* portale; **p. vein** vena porta.
portend [pɔ:'tend] *vt* presagire.
portent ['pɔ:tent] *n* portento; presagio.
porter ['pɔ:tə] *n* facchino; portiere, portinaio.
porterage ['pɔ:təridʒ] *n* facchinaggio.
portfolio [pɔ:t'fouliou] *n* cartella; portafoglio ministeriale.
portion ['pɔ:ʃən] *n* porzione, parte; destino.
portly ['pɔ:tli] *a* corpulento; di portamento dignitoso.
portmanteau [pɔ:t'mæntou] *n* baule armadio.
portrait ['pɔ:trit] *n* ritratto.
portray [pɔ:'trei] *vt* ritrarre; rappresentare.
Portugal ['pɔ:tjugəl] *n* Portogallo.
Portuguese [,pɔ:tju'gi:z] *a n* portoghese.
pose [pouz] *n* posa, affettazione.
position [pə'ziʃən] *n* posizione; condizione; impiego, posto.
positive ['pɔzətiv] *a* preciso, certo, reale, positivo; *n* cosa positiva, (il) positivo; (*phot*) positiva.
posse ['pɔsi] *n* manipolo di persone incaricate di far rispettare l'ordine pubblico.

possess [pə'zes] *vt* possedere.
possession [pə'zeʃən] *n* possesso, possedimento.
possessive [pə'zesiv] *a* possessivo.
possibility [ˌpɔsə'biliti] *n* possibilità.
possible ['pɔsəbl] *a* possibile.
possibly ['pɔsəbli] *ad* possibilmente, forse; (*in the negative*) assolutamente.
post [poust] *n* posta; impiego, posto; palo, pilastro; *vt* affiggere; impostare; imbucare;; pubblicare; (*com*) registrare, collocare; **p. office** ufficio postale.
postage ['poustidʒ] *n* affrancatura.
postal ['poustəl] *a* postale; **p. order** vaglia postale.
poster ['poustə] *n* affisso, manifesto pubblicitario, cartellone.
poste-restante ['poust'restɑ̃:nt] *n* fermo posta.
posterior [pɔs'tiəriə] *a* posteriore; *n* deretano, sedere.
posterity [pɔs'teriti] *n* posterità.
posthumous ['pɔstjuməs] *a* postumo.
postman ['poustmən] *n* portalettere, postino.
postpone [poust'poun] *vt* posporre, rimandare.
postponement [poust'pounmənt] *n* rinvio.
postscript ['pousskript] *n* poscritto.
postulate ['pɔstjuleit] *vti* richiedere; supporre.
posture ['pɔstʃə] *n* posizione, atteggiamento.
posy ['pouzi] *n* mazzo di fiori.
pot [pɔt] *n* vaso; pentola.
potash ['pɔtæʃ] *n* potasso.
potassium [pə'tæsiəm] *n* potassio.
potato [pə'teitou] *pl* **potatoes** *n* patata; **p. chips** patatine fritte; **mashed p.** *pl* purè di patate.
potent ['poutənt] *a* potente, forte.
potentate ['poutənteit] *n* potentato.
potential [pə'tenʃəl] *a* potenziale.
pother ['pɔðə] *n* confusione, pandemonio.
potion ['pouʃən] *n* pozione.
potted ['pɔtid] *a* conservato, in conserva.
pottery ['pɔtəri] *n* terraglie, stoviglie *pl*.
pouch [pautʃ] *n* bisaccia, borsa; carniera.
poulterer ['poultərə] *n* pollivendolo.
poultice ['poultis] *n* cataplasma.
poultry ['poultri] *n* pollame, gallinacei domestici *pl*.
pounce [pauns] *n* balzo; *vti* avventarsi, piombare (su).
pound [paund] (*abbr* **lb**) *n* libbra (*uguale a grammi* 453); (*abbr* **£**) lira sterlina; recinto per bestiame; *vt* pestare, frantumare.
pour [pɔə] *vt* versare; *vi* diluviare.
pout [paut] *vi* fare il broncio.
poverty ['pɔvəti] *n* miseria, povertà.
powder ['paudə] *n* polvere; cipria; *vt* incipriare; polverizzare; spolverizzare; **p.-puff** piumino per la cipria;
powdery *a* friabile; polveroso.
power ['pauə] *n* potere, potenza, forza, energia; **p. station** centrale elettrica.
powerful ['pauəful] *a* potente, possente.
powerless ['pauəlis] *a* impotente.
practical ['præktikəl] *a* pratico, fattibile.
practically ['præktikəli] *ad* praticamente; quasi, virtualmente.
practice ['præktis] *n* pratica, abitudine; esercizio; clientela; lavoro professionale.
practice ['præktis] *vti* esercitar(si), praticare.
practitioner [præk'tiʃnə] *n* professionista (medico); **general p.** medico generico.
prairie ['prεəri] *n* prateria.
praise [preiz] *n* elogio, lode; *vt* lodare.
praiseworthy ['preizˌwə:ði] *a* lodevole, degno di lode.
prance [prɑ:ns] *vi* (*of horses*) impennarsi; camminare con spavalderia.
prank [præŋk] *n* scherzo, tiro.
prattle ['prætl] *n* cicaleccio infantile; *vi* cianciare, cinguettare.
prawn [prɔ:n] *n* gambero.
pray [prei] *vti* pregare.
prayer ['preiə] *n* preghiera; **p.-book** libro di preghiere.
preach [pri:tʃ] *vti* predicare.
preacher ['pri:tʃə] *n* predicatore.
precarious [pri'kεəriəs] *a* precario.
precaution [pri'kɔ:ʃən] *n* precauzione.
precede [pri:'si:d] *vti* precedere.
precedence [pri:'si:dəns] *n* precedenza.
precedent ['presidənt] *n* precedente.
preceding [pri:'si:diŋ] *a* precedente.
precept ['pri:sept] *n* precetto.
precinct ['pri:siŋkt] *n* recinto; **precincts** *pl* confini, limiti *pl*.
preciosity [ˌpreʃi'ɔsiti] *n* preziosità, ricercatezza.
precious ['preʃəs] *a* prezioso, ricercato.
precipice ['presipis] *n* precipizio.
precipitate [pri'sipiteit] *a* precipitoso, avventato; *vti* precipitare.
precipitous [pri'sipitəs] *a* erto, scosceso.
precise [pri'sais] *a* preciso.
precisely [pri'saisli] *ad* precisamente, esattamente, in punto.
precision [pri'siʒən] *n* precisione.
preclude [pri'klu:d] *vt* precludere, escludere.
precocious [pri'kouʃəs] *a* precoce.
preconceived ['pri:kən'si:vd] *a* preconcetto.
precursor [pri:'kə:sə] *n* precursore.
predecessor ['pri:disesə] *n* predecessore.
predicament [pri'dikəmənt] *n* situazione difficile o pericolosa.

predict ['pri'dikt] *vt* predire.
predilection [,pri:di'lekʃən] *n* predilezione.
predispose ['pri:dis'pouz] *vt* predisporre.
predominance [pri'dɔminəns] *n* predominio.
predominant [pri'dɔminənt] *a* predominante.
predominate [pri'dɔmineit] *vi* predominare.
pre-eminent [pri:'eminənt] *a* preminente.
prefab ['pri:'fæb] *n* (*fam*) casa prefabbricata.
prefabricate ['pri:'fæbrikeit] *vt* prefabbricare.
preface ['prefis] *n* prefazione; (*eccl*) prefazio.
prefect ['pri:fekt] *n* prefetto.
prefer [pri'fə:] *vt* preferire; **preferred shares** (*com*) azioni privilegiate (*or* preferenziali).
preferable ['prefərəbl] *a* preferibile.
preference ['prefərəns] *n* preferenza.
prefix ['pri:fiks] *n* prefisso.
pregnancy ['pregnənsi] *n* gravidanza.
pregnant ['pregnənt] *a* gravida, incinta; pregno, significativo.
prejudice ['predʒudis] *n* pregiudizio; *vt* compromettere, pregiudicare.
prejudicial [,predʒu'diʃəl] *a* pregiudizievole, dannoso.
prelate ['prelit] *n* prelato.
preliminary [pri'liminəri] *a n* preliminare.
prelude ['prelju:d] *n* preludio.
premature [,premə'tjuə] *a* prematuro.
premier ['premiə] *a* primo; *n* primo ministro.
premiere ['premjɛ:r] *n* (*theat*) prima.
premise ['premis] *n* premessa.
premise [pri'maiz] *vt* premettere.
premises ['premisiz] *n pl* edificio, locali *pl*.
premium ['pri:miəm] *n* (*com*) premio, aggio.
premonition [,pri:mə:'niʃən] *n* premonizione, presentimento.
preparation [,prepə'reiʃən] *n* preparazione, preparativo.
preparatory [pri'pærətəri] *a* preparatorio.
prepare [pri'pɛə] *vti* preparar(si).
prepay ['pri:'pei] *vt* pagare in anticipo.
preponderant [pri'pɔndərənt] *a* preponderante.
preponderate [pri'pɔndəreit] (**over**) *vi* predominare, prevalere.
preposition [,prepə'ziʃən] *n* preposizione.
prepossess [,pri:pə'zes] *vt* influenzare.
prepossessing [,pri:pə'zesiŋ] *a* simpatico, attraente.
prepossession [,pri:pə'zeʃən] *n* prevenzione; predisposizione.
preposterous [pri'pɔstərəs] *a* assurdo.
prerogative [pri'rɔgətiv] *n* prerogativa.
presage ['presidʒ] *n* presagio.
presbyterian [,prezbi'tiəriən] *a n* presbiteriano.
prescribe [pris'kraib] *vti* prescrivere.
prescription [pris'kripʃən] *n* ricetta medica.
presence ['prezns] *n* presenza.
present ['preznt] *a* presente; attuale; *n* presente, regalo, dono; *vt* presentare; regalare a.
presentation [,prezen'teiʃən] *n* presentazione; dono, omaggio.
presentiment [pri'zentimənt] *n* presentimento.
presently ['prezntli] *ad* tra poco, presto, poco dopo, di li a poco.
preservation [,prezə:'veiʃən] *n* conservazione, preservazione.
preservative [pri'zə:vətiv] *a n* preservativo.
preserve [pri'zə:v] *n* conserva, marmellata; (*game etc*) riserva; *vt* preservare, conservare, mettere in conserva.
preside [pri'zaid] *vi* presiedere.
presidency ['prezidənsi] *n* presidenza.
president ['prezidənt] *n* presidente.
presidential [,prezi'denʃəl] *a* presidenziale.
press [pres] *n* torchio; pressione; folla; (*mech*) pressa; stampa; armadio; *vti* premere, comprimere, stringere; urgere, affollarsi.
pressing ['presiŋ] *a* pressante, insistente, urgente.
pressure ['preʃə] *n* pressione.
prestige [pres'ti:ʒ] *n* prestigio.
presume [pri'zju:m] *vti* presumere, supporre.
presumption [pri'zʌmpʃən] *n* presunzione; supposizione.
presumptive [pri'zʌmptiv] *a* presuntivo, presunto.
presumptuous [pri'zʌmptjuəs] *a* presuntuoso.
presuppose [,pri:sə'pouz] *vt* presupporre.
pretend [pri'tend] *vt* fingere, pretendere; *vi* aspirare, vantare diritti su.
pretense [pri'tens] *n* pretesa; pretesto, finzione.
pretension [pri'tenʃən] *n* pretensione, pretesa, diritto.
pretentious [pri'tenʃəs] *a* pretenzioso.
pretext ['pri:tekst] *n* pretesto.
prettiness ['pritinis] *n* grazia, leggiadria.
pretty ['priti] *a* grazioso, carino; *ad* discretamente, piuttosto, un po'.
prevail [pri'veil] *vi* prevalere; **to p. (up)on** persuadere.
prevalent ['prevələnt] *a* prevalente.

prevaricate [pri'værikeit] *vi* tergiversare; mentire.
prevarication [pri,væri'keiʃən] *n* tergiversazione; menzogna.
prevent [pri'vent] *vt* impedire.
prevention [pri'venʃən] *n* impedimento; misura preventiva.
preventive [pri'ventiv] *a* preventivo; *n* misura preventiva.
preview ['pri:vju:] *n* visione privata, anteprima; 'prossimamente'.
previous ['pri:viəs] *a* anteriore, precedente.
previously ['pri:viəsli] *ad* precedentemente.
prevision [pri:'viʒən] *n* previsione.
prey [prei] *n* preda; **p. upon** *vi* predare; consumare.
price [prais] *n* prezzo.
priceless ['praislis] *a* inestimabile; (*sl*) impagabile.
prick [prik] *n* puntura; (*fig*) pungolo, rimorso; *vt* pungere, punzecchiare; drizzare (gli orecchi).
prickle ['prikl] *n* pungiglione; puntura.
prickly ['prikli] *a* spinoso; **p. pear** fico d'India.
pride [praid] *n* orgoglio, superbia; **p. oneself on** gloriarsi di, vantarsi.
priest [pri:st] *n* prete, sacerdote.
priesthood ['pri:sthud] *n* sacerdozio.
prig [prig] *n* pedante, saccente.
priggish ['prigiʃ] *a* affettato, pedante.
prim [prim] *a* affettato, cerimonioso.
primacy ['praiməsi] *n* primato, supremazia.
primarily ['praimərili] *ad* in primo luogo, essenzialmente.
primary ['praiməri] *a* primario, originario, fondamentale, principale.
primate ['praimeit] *n* arcivescovo, primate.
prime [praim] *a* primo; di prima qualità; *n* fiore, rigoglio.
primeval [prai'mi:vəl] *a* primitivo, primordiale.
primitive ['primitiv] *a* primitivo.
primordial [prai'mɔ:diəl] *a* primordiale.
primrose ['primrouz] *n* primula.
prince [prins] *n* principe.
princely ['prinsli] *a* principesco.
princess [prin'ses] *n* principessa.
principal ['prinsəpəl] *a* principale; *n* principale, capo, direttore, superiore, rettore; (*com*) capitale.
principality [,prinsi'pæliti] *n* principato.
principle ['prinsəpl] *n* principio.
print [print] *n* impronta, orma, stampa; tessuto di cotone stampato; *vt* imprimere; pubblicare, stampare.
printer ['printə] *n* tipografo, stampatore.
printing ['printiŋ] *n* stampa, tiratura.
prior ['praiə] *a* antecedente, precedente; *n* priore; *ad* anteriormente, prima di.
priority [prai'ɔriti] *n* priorità.
prism ['prizəm] *n* prisma.
prison ['prizn] *n* prigione, penitenziario, carcere.
prisoner ['priznə] *n* prigioniero, detenuto.
pristine ['pristain] *a* pristino.
privacy ['praivəsi] *n* intimità, segreto, ritiro, vita privata.
private ['praivit] *n* soldato semplice; *a* privato; **p. business** questione personale.
privateer [,privə'tiə] *n* nave corsara.
privation [prai'veiʃən] *n* privazione.
privet ['privit] *n* ligustro.
privilege ['privilidʒ] *n* privilegio.
privy ['privi] *a* privato; **p. to** a conoscenza di.
prize [praiz] *n* premio; *vt* apprezzare, valutare.
probability [,prɔbə'biliti] *n* probabilità.
probable ['prɔbəbl] *a* probabile.
probate ['proubit] *n* verifica di testamento.
probation [prə'beiʃən] *n* prova; noviziato; libertà condizionata.
probationer [prə'beiʃnə] *n* apprendista; novizio; chi si trova in libertà condizionata.
probe [proub] *n* (*med*) sonda; *vt* sondare; scandagliare.
probity ['proubiti] *n* probità.
problem ['prɔbləm] *n* problema.
problematic [,prɔbli'mætik] *a* problematico.
procedure [prə'si:dʒə] *n* procedimento; procedura.
proceed [prə'si:d] *vi* procedere, avanzare; derivare.
proceeding [prə'si:diŋ] *n* atto, azione, condotta, procedimento.
proceeds ['prousi:dz] *n pl* provento, ricavo.
process ['prouses] *n* corso, processo; *vt* sottoporre a procedimento.
procession [prə'seʃən] *n* processione, corteo.
proclaim [prə'kleim] *vt* proclamare.
proclamation [,prɔklə'meiʃən] *n* proclama(zione).
proclivity [prə'kliviti] *n* inclinazione, tendenza.
procrastinate [prou'kræstineit] *vti* procrastinare.
procrastination [prou,kræsti'neiʃən] *n* indugio, procrastinazione.
procreate ['proukrieit] *vt* procreare.
procreation [,proukri'eiʃən] *n* procreazione.
procure [prə'kjuə] *vt* procurar(si).
prod [prɔd] *n* pungolo, stimolo; *vt* stimolare.
prodigal ['prɔdigəl] *a n* prodigo.
prodigious [prə'didʒəs] *a* prodigioso.
prodigy ['prɔdidʒi] *n* prodigio.
produce ['prɔdju:s] *n* prodotti *pl*; *vti* [prə'dju:s] produrre; presentare.
producer [prə'dju:sə] *n* produttore; (*theat*) regista, impresario.

product ['prɔdəkt] *n* prodotto.
production [prə'dʌkʃən] *n* produzione.
productive [prə'dʌktiv] *a* produttivo.
productivity [,prɔdʌk'tiviti] *n* produttività.
profanation [,prɔfə'neiʃən] *n* profanazione.
profane [prə'fein] *a* profano; *vt* profanare.
profess [prə'fes] *vti* professare; esercitare; insegnare.
profession [prə'feʃən] *n* professione.
professional [prə'feʃənl] *a* di professione, professionale; *n* professionista.
professor [prə'fesə] *n* professore; **professorship** professorato.
proffer ['prɔfə] *vt* offrire.
proficiency [prə'fiʃənsi] *n* abilità, perizia.
proficient [prə'fiʃənt] *a n* esperto, competente.
profile ['proufail] *n* profilo.
profit ['prɔfit] *n* guadagno, profitto, utile, vantaggio; *vt* giovare; *vi* (ap)profittare, trarre vantaggio.
profitable ['prɔfitəbl] *a* vantaggioso.
profiteer [,prɔfi'tiə] *n* profittatore; (*fig*) pescecane.
profligacy ['prɔfligəsi] *n* dissolutezza, licenziosità.
profligate ['prɔfligit] *a n* dissoluto.
profound [prə'faund] *a* profondo.
profuse [prə'fju:s] *a* abbondante; prodigo.
profusion [prə'fju:ʒən] *n* profusione.
progeny ['prɔdʒini] *n* progenie.
prognosticate [prəg'nɔstikeit] *vt* pronosticare.
program ['prougræm] *n* programma.
progress ['prougres] *n* avanzata; corso; progresso; *vi* [prə'gres] progredire, fare progressi.
progressive [prə'gresiv] *a* progressivo.
prohibit [prə'hibit] *vt* proibire, vietare.
prohibition [,proui'biʃən] *n* proibizione, divieto.
prohibitive [prə'hibitiv] *a* proibitivo.
project ['prɔdʒekt] *n* progetto; *vt* [prə'djekt] proiettare; *vi* sporgere.
projectile ['prɔdʒiktail] *n* proiettile.
projection [prə'dʒekʃən] *n* proiezione; sporgenza.
proletariat [,proule'tɛəriət] *n* proletariato.
prolific [prə'lifik] *a* prolifico.
prolix ['prouliks] *a* prolisso.
prologue ['proulɔg] *n* prologo.
prolong [prə'lɔŋ] *vt* prolungare.
promenade [,prɔmi'nɑ:d] *n* passeggiata; lungomare.
prominence ['prɔminəns] *n* prominenza, risalto.
prominent ['prɔminənt] *a* prominente, cospicuo.
promiscuity [,prɔmis'kju:iti] *n* promiscuità.
promiscuous [prə'miskjuəs] *a* promiscuo.
promise ['prɔmis] *n* promessa; *vti* promettere.
promising ['prɔmisiŋ] *a* promettente.
promissory ['prɔmisəri] *a* che contiene una promessa, promettente.
promontory ['prɔməntri] *n* promontorio.
promote [prə'mout] *vt* incoraggiare, promuovere.
promotion [prə'mouʃən] *n* promozione.
prompt [prɔmpt] *a* pronto, sollecito; *vt* incitare; suggerire.
prompter ['prɔmptə] *n* (*theat*) suggeritore.
promptitude ['prɔmptitju:d] *n* prontezza, sollecitudine.
promptness ['prɔmptnis] *n* prontezza.
promulgate ['prɔməlgeit] *vt* promulgare.
promulgation [,prɔməl'geiʃən] *n* promulgazione.
prone [proun] *a* incline, propenso; prono, prostrato.
proneness ['prounnis] *n* inclinazione, propensione.
prong [prɔŋ] *n* rebbio; punta.
pronoun ['prounaun] *n* pronome.
pronounce [prə'nauns] *vt* pronunciare, -ziare; dichiarare.
pronounced [prə'naunst] *a* pronunziato.
pronunciation [prə,nʌnsi'eiʃən] *n* pronuncia, -zia.
proof [pru:f] *n* prova; (*print*) bozza di stampa.
prop [prɔp] *n* appoggio, puntello; (*theat*) attrezzo scenico; *vt* puntellare, sostenere.
propaganda [,prɔpə'gændə] *n* propaganda.
propagate ['prɔpəgeit] *vti* propagar(si).
propagation [,prɔpə'geiʃən] *n* propagazione.
propel [prə'pel] *vt* spingere avanti.
propeller [prə'pelə] *n* (*mech*) elica; propulsore.
propensity [prə'pensiti] *n* propensione, tendenza.
proper ['prɔpə] *a* proprio, appropriato, vero e proprio.
properly ['prɔpəli] *ad* per bene, come si deve. correttamente.
property ['prɔpəti] *n* proprietà, beni; qualità.
prophecy ['prɔfisi] *n* profezia.
prophesy ['prɔfisai] *vti* profetizzare.
prophet ['prɔfit] *n* profeta.
prophetic [prə'fetik] *a* profetico.
propinquity [prə'piŋkwiti] *n* vicinanza.
propitiate [prə'piʃieit] *vt* propiziare.

propitious [prə'piʃəs] *a* propizio.
proportion [prə'pɔ:ʃən] *n* proporzione.
proportional [prə'pɔ:ʃənl] *a* proporzionale.
proportionate [prə'pɔ:ʃnit] *a* proporzionato.
proposal [prə'pouzəl] *n* proposta; proposta di matrimonio.
propose [prə'pouz] *vt* proporre; **p. a toast to** fare un brindisi a; *vi* proporre; fare una proposta di matrimonio.
proposition [,prɔpə'ziʃən] *n* asserzione; proposta; proposizione.
propound [prə'paund] *vt* proporre.
proprietor [prə'praiətə] *n* proprietario.
propriety [prə'praiəti] *n* correttezza, proprietà; opportunità.
prorogation [,prourə'geiʃən] *n* proroga, rinvio.
prosaic [prou'zeiik] *a* prosaico.
proscribe [prous'kraib] *vt* proscrivere.
proscription [prous'kripʃən] *n* proscrizione.
prose [prouz] *n* prosa; **p. writer** prosatore.
prosecute ['prɔsikju:t] *vti* perseguire, proseguire; procedere contro, querelare.
prosecution [,prɔsi'kju:ʃən] *n* prosecuzione; (*leg*) processo.
prosecutor ['prɔsikju:tə] *n* prosecutore; querelante; **public p.** pubblico ministero.
proselyte ['prɔsilait] *n* proselito.
proselytize ['prɔsilitaiz] *vi* fare proseliti.
prosody ['prɔsədi] *n* prosodia.
prospect ['prɔspekt] *n* vista; prospettiva, speranza; *vt* [prəs'pekt] esplorare.
prospective [prəs'pektiv] *a* eventuale, probabile.
prospectus [prəs'pektəs] *n* programma, prospetto.
prosper ['prɔspə] *vi* prosperare.
prosperity [prɔs'periti] *n* prosperità.
prosperous ['prɔspərəs] *a* prospero.
prostitute ['prɔstitju:t] *n* prostituta.
prostitution [,prɔsti'tju:ʃən] *n* prostituzione.
prostrate ['prɔstreit] *a* prosternato; (*fig*) prostrato; *vt* [prɔs'treit] prosternare; (*fig*) prostrare.
prostration [prɔs'treiʃən] *n* prostrazione.
protagonist [prə'tægənist] *n* protagonista.
protect [prə'tekt] *vt* proteggere.
protection [prə'tekʃən] *n* protezione; salvacondotto.
protective [prə'tektiv] *a* protettivo.
protector [prə'tektə] *n* protettore.
protégé ['prouteʒei] *n* protetto.
protein ['prouti:n] *n* proteina.
protest ['proutest] *n* protesta; (*com*) rotesto; *vti* [prə'test] protestare.
protestant ['prɔtistənt] *a n* protestante.
Protestantism ['prɔtistəntizəm] *n* protestantesimo.
protocol ['proutəkɔl] *n* protocollo.
protoplasm ['proutə,plæzəm] *n* protoplasma.
prototype ['proutətaip] *n* prototipo.
protract [prə'trækt] *vt* protrarre.
protraction [prə'trækʃən] *n* protrazione; disegno su scala.
protrude [prə'tru:d] *vt* sporgere, spingere avanti; *vi* proiettarsi, sporgere.
protuberance [prə'tju:bərəns] *n* protuberanza.
proud [praud] *a* fiero, orgoglioso; superbo.
prove [pru:v] *vt* dimostrare, provare; *vi* mostrarsi, riuscire.
Provençal [,prɔvɑ̃:n'sɑ:l] *a n* provenzale; lingua provenzale.
Provence [prɔ'vɑ̃:s] *n* Provenza.
provender ['prɔvində] *n* foraggio.
proverb ['prɔvəb] *n* proverbio.
proverbial [prə'və:biəl] *a* proverbiale.
provide [prə'vaid] *vti* provvedere, fornire; **to p. against** premunirsi contro.
provided [prə'vaidid] *cj* purchè, a patto che.
providence ['prɔvidəns] *n* provvidenza; previdenza.
provident ['prɔvidənt] *a* provvido; previdente.
providential [,prɔvi'denʃəl] *a* provvidenziale.
province ['prɔvins] *n* provincia; (*fig*) competenza, sfera d'azione.
provincial [prə'vinʃəl] *a n* provinciale.
provision [prə'viʒən] *n* preparativo, provvedimento; clausola; *pl* provviste, viveri; *vt* approvvigionare.
provisional [prə'viʒənl] *a* provvisorio.
provocation [,prɔvə'keiʃən] *n* provocazione.
provocative [prə'vɔkətiv] *a* provocante.
provoke [prə'vouk] *vt* provocare.
provoking [prə'voukiŋ] *a* provocante.
prow [prau] *n* (*naut*) prora, prua.
prowess ['prauis] *n* prodezza.
prowl [praul] *vi* vagare in cerca di preda.
proximity [prɔk'simiti] *n* prossimità.
proxy ['prɔksi] *n* procura; procuratore.
prude [pru:d] *n* donna eccessivamente pudica.
prudence ['pru:dəns] *n* prudenza.
prudent ['pru:dənt] *a* prudente, circospetto, giudizioso.
prudery ['pru:dəri] *n* eccessiva pudicizia.
prudish ['pru:diʃ] *a* pudibondo; schifiltoso.

prune ['pru:n] *n* prugna secca; *vt* potare, sfrondare.
prurient ['pruəriənt] *a* lascivo.
Prussia ['prʌʃə] *n* Prussia.
pry [prai] *vi* curiosare, ficcare il naso.
psalm [sɑ:m] *n* salmo.
pseudonym ['sju:dənim] *n* pseudonimo.
psychedelic [,saikə'delik] *a* psichedelico.
psychiatrist [sai'kaiətrist] *n* psichiatra.
psychiatry [sai'kaiətri] *n* psichiatria.
psychic ['saikik] *a* psichico.
psychologic(al) [,saikə'lɔdʒik(l)] *a* psicologico.
psychology [sai'kɔlədʒi] *n* psicologia.
psychosis [sai'kousis] *n* psicosi.
puberty ['pju:bəti] *n* pubertà.
public ['pʌblik] *a n* pubblico; **p. convenience, p. comfort station** gabinetto pubblico; **p. house** spaccio di birra e bevande alcooliche.
publican ['pʌblikən] *n* oste; proprietario di bar.
publication [,pʌbli'keiʃən] *n* pubblicazione.
publicity [pʌb'lisiti] *n* pubblicità.
publish ['pʌbliʃ] *vt* pubblicare; promulgare.
publisher ['pʌbliʃə] *n* editore; (*of newspaper*) proprietario.
pucker ['pʌkə] *n* crespa, grinza; *vt* corrugare, increspare; *vi* raggrinzirsi.
pudding ['pudiŋ] *n* budino, dolce.
puddle ['pʌdl] *n* pozzanghera.
puerility [pjuə'riliti] *n* puerilità.
Puerto Rican ['pwə:tou'ri:kən] *a n* portoricano.
Puerto Rico ['pwə:tou'ri:kou] *n* Portorico.
puff [pʌf] *n* sbuffo; soffio; piumino da cipria, pubblicità con elogi esagerati; *vt* gonfiare soffiando; fare una pubblicità esagerata a; *vi* ansimare; sbuffare; soffiare; **p. pastry** pasta sfoglia.
pug [pʌg] *n* (*clay*) argilla; (*dog*) cagnolino; **p. nose** naso camuso.
pugilist ['pju:dʒilist] *n* pugile.
pugnacious [pʌg'neiʃəs] *a* pugnace, battagliero.
pugnacity [pʌg'næsiti] *n* spirito battagliero.
pull [pul] *n* strattone, tirata; (*sl*) influenza; vantaggio; *vt* strappare, tirare.
pullet ['pulit] *n* pollastrella.
pulley ['puli] *n* (*mech*) puleggia.
pullover ['pul,ouvə] *n* 'pullover', golf.
pulmonary ['pʌlmənəri] *a* polmonare.
pulp [pʌlp] *n* polpa; (*paper making*) pasta.
pulpit ['pulpit] *n* pulpito.
pulsate [pʌl'seit] *vti* battere, pulsare.
pulsation [pʌl'seiʃən] *n* pulsazione.
pulse [pʌls] *n* polso, battito.
pulverize ['pʌlvəraiz] *vti* polverizzar(si).
pumice ['pʌmis] *n* pomice.
pump [pʌmp] *n* pompa; *vti* pompare; (*fam*) cercare di estrarre informazioni.
pumpkin ['pʌmpkin] *n* zucca.
pun [pʌn] *n* gioco di parole.
punch [pʌntʃ] *n* pugno; (*fam*) vigore; punzone; ponce; *vt* perforare; dare pugni a.
punctual ['pʌŋktjuəl] *a* puntuale.
punctuality [,puŋktju'æliti] *n* puntualità.
punctuate ['puŋktjueit] *vt* punteggiare.
punctuation [,puŋktju'eiʃən] *n* punteggiatura.
puncture ['pʌŋktʃə] *n* puntura; (*tire*) foratura.
pungent ['pʌndʒənt] *a* pungente, acuto, mordace.
punish ['pʌniʃ] *vt* punire.
punishable ['pʌniʃəbl] *a* punibile.
punishment ['pʌniʃmənt] *n* punizione.
punt [pʌnt] *n* chiatta, pontone; barchino; *vti* navigare su chiatta.
punter ['pʌntə] *n* puntatore (alle corse *etc*).
puny ['pju:ni] *a* piccolo e debole.
pup [pʌp] **puppy** ['pʌpi] *n* cucciolo.
pupil ['pju:pil] *n* alunno, -na; scolaro, -ra, (*eye*) pupilla.
puppet ['pʌpit] *n* burattino, marionetta.
purchase ['pə:tʃəs] *n* acquisto; *vt* acquistare, comperare.
purchaser ['pə:tʃəsə] *n* acquirente, compratore.
pure [pjuə] *a* puro.
pureness ['pjuənis] *n* purezza.
purgative ['pə:gətiv] *a* purgativo; *n* purgante.
purgatory ['pə:gətəri] *n* purgatorio.
purge [pə:dʒ] *n* purga(nte); epurazione; *vti* purgar(si), purificar(si).
purification [,pjuərifi'keiʃən] *n* purificazione.
purify ['pjuərifai] *vt* purificare.
puritan ['pjuəritən] *a n* puritano.
puritanism ['pjuəritənizəm] *n* puritanismo.
purity ['pjuəriti] *n* purezza, purità.
purl [pə:l] *vi* mormorare, gorgogliare; **p. knitting** lavoro a punto rovescio.
purloin [pə:'lɔin] *vt* rubare, sottrarre.
purple ['pə:pl] *a* purpureo, violaceo; *n* porpora.
purport ['pə:pət] *n* significato; tenore; *vt* [pə:'pɔ:t] significare.
purpose ['pə:pəs] *n* fine, proposito, scopo; *vti* proporsi, avere intenzione di.
purr [pə:] *vi* far le fusa.
purse [pə:s] *n* borsa, portamonete.
purser ['pə:sə] *n* (*naut*) commissario di bordo.

pursuance [pə'sju:əns] *n* continuazione; esecuzione.
pursue [pə'sju:] *vti* inseguire; continuare; perseguire.
pursuer [pə'sju:ə] *n* inseguitore; (*Scots law*) attore.
pursuit [pə'sju:t] *n* inseguimento; occupazione.
purvey [pə:'vei] *vti* provvedere, fornire.
purveyor [pə:'veiə] *n* fornitore.
pus [pʌs] *n* (*med*) pus.
push [puʃ] *n* spinta; (*el*) pulsante; pressione; energia; momento critico; **p.-button switch** interruttore a pulsante; **p. cart** carretto a mano; passeggino; *vt* spingere, far pressioni su.
pushing ['puʃiŋ] *a* energico; intraprendente; invadente.
pusillanimous [.pju:si'læniməs] *a* pusillanime.
puss [pus] *n* micio; **pussy** micino.
put [put] *vt* mettere, porre; **p. off** differire; (*fig*) scoraggiare; distrarre; **p. on** indossare; **p. out** mettere fuori; spegnere; **p. up** contribuire; costruire; (*cards*) puntare; alloggiare; **p. up with** sopportare.
putrefaction [.pju:tri'fækʃən] *n* putrefazione.
putrefy ['pju:trifai] *vti* putrefar(si).
putrid ['pju:trid] *a* putrido.
puttee ['pʌti:] *n* mollettiera.
putty ['pʌti] *n* stucco; mastice.
puzzle ['pʌzl] *n* enigma, indovinello, rebus; perplessità; *vt* rendere perplesso.
puzzling ['pʌzliŋ] *a* sconcertante, imbarazzante.
pygmy ['pigmi] *a n* pigmeo.
pyjamas [pə'dʒɑ:məz] *n pl* pigiama.
pylon ['pailɔn] *n* pilone.
pyramid ['pirəmid] *n* piramide.
pyre ['paiə] *n* pira, rogo.
pyrotechnic ['pairou'teknik] *a* pirotecnico.

Q

quack [kwæk] *n* ciarlatano; verso dell'anatra; *vi* (*duck*) schiamazzare.
quackery ['kwækəri] *n* ciarlataneria; empirismo.
quadrangle ['kwɔ.dræŋgl] *n* quadrangolo; corte quadrangolare interna.
quadrant ['kwɔdrənt] *n* quadrante.
quadrille [kwə'dril] *n* quadriglia.
quadruped ['kwɔdruped] *a n* quadrupede.
quadruple ['kwɔdrupl] *a* quadruplice, quadruplo; *n* quadruplo.
quaff [kwɑ:f] *vt* tracannare.
quagmire ['kwægmaiə] *n* pantano, palude.
quail [kweil] *n* quaglia; *vi* scoraggiarsi.
quaint [kweint] *a* curioso, strano; caratteristico.
quaintness ['kweintnis] *n* bizzarria, singolarità.
quake [kweik] *n* scossa, tremito; *vi* tremare.
Quaker ['kweikə] *a n* quacquero.
qualification [.kwɔlifi'keiʃən] *n* requisito, titolo, qualifica; condizione.
qualify ['kwɔlifai] *vt* qualificare, abilitare; autorizzare; modificare; restringere; *vi* rendersi idoneo.
quality ['kwɔliti] *n* qualità.
qualm [kwɔ:m] *n* nausea; (*fig*) scrupolo.
quandary ['kwɔndəri] *n* imbarazzo, incertezza, situazione difficile.
quantity ['kwɔntiti] *n* quantità.
quarantine ['kwɔrənti:n] *n* quarantena.
quarrel ['kwɔrəl] *n* litigio, lite; *vi* litigare.
quarrelsome ['kwɔrəlsəm] *a* litigioso.
quarry ['kwɔri] *n* cava; preda.
quarryman ['kwɔrimən] *n* cavatore.
quart [kwɔ:t] *n* quarto di gallone.
quarter ['kwɔ:tə] *n* quarto; quartiere; direzione; località; trimestre; *vt* dividere in quarti; (*mil*) acquartierare.
quarter-deck ['kwɔ:tədek] *n* (*naut*) cassero.
quarterly ['kwɔ:təli] *a* trimestrale; *ad* trimestralmente; *n* pubblicazione trimestrale.
quartermaster ['kwɔ:tə.mɑ:stə] *n* (*mil*) furiere.
quartet [kwɔ:'tet] *n* (*mus*) quartetto.
quartz [kwɔ:ts] *n* quarzo.
quash [kwɔʃ] *vt* schiacciare, annullare.
quatrain ['kwɔtrein] *n* quartina.
quaver ['kweivə] *n* trillo, tremolio, vibrazione; (*mus*) croma; *vi* tremolare, vibrare.
quay [ki:] *n* banchina, molo.
queasy ['kwi:zi] *a* delicato di stomaco; nauseato; scrupoloso.
queen [kwi:n] *n* regina.
queenly ['kwi:nli] *a* da (di) regina, regale.
queer [kwiə] *a* strano, bizzarro, eccentrico; dubbio, sospetto; debole, che ha le vertigini.
quell [kwel] *vt* reprimere, soffocare.
quench [kwentʃ] *vt* spegnere, estinguere, calmare.
querulous ['kwerjuləs] *a* querulo, lamentevole.
query ['kwiəri] *n* domanda, punto interrogativo; *vt* mettere in dubbio, interrogare.
quest [kwest] *n* ricerca, inchiesta.
question ['kwestʃən] *n* domanda; questione; *vt* interrogare, mettere in dubbio.
questionable ['kwestʃənəbl] *a* discutibile, dubbio.

questionnaire [ˌkwestiəˈnɛə] *n* questionario.
queue [kju:] *n* coda; *vi* **to q. up** fare la coda.
quibble [ˈkwibl] *n* gioco di parole, cavillo; *vi* far giochi di parole, cavillare.
quick [kwik] *a* rapido, svelto, pronto, vivace, vivo; *ad* presto, rapidamente; *n* vivo, parte vitale.
quicken [ˈkwikən] *vt* affrettare, stimolare; *vi* animarsi, affrettarsi..
quickness [ˈkwiknis] *n* rapidità, prontezza, acutezza.
quicksand [ˈkwiksænd] *n* sabbia mobile.
quicksilver [ˈkwikˌsilvə] *n* mercurio, argento vivo.
quiet [ˈkwaiət] *a* quieto, tranquillo, dolce, sobrio; *n* quiete, tranquillità.
quiet(en) [ˈkwaiət(n)] *vti* acquietar(si), calmar(si).
quietness [ˈkwaiətnis] *n* quiete, riposo, silenzio.
quill [kwil] *n* penna, penna d'oca.
quilt [kwilt] *n* trapunta; *vt* trapuntare.
quince [kwins] *n* cotogna.
quinine [kwiˈni:n] *n* chinino.
quinsy [ˈkwinzi] *n* (*med*) tonsillite.
quintal [ˈkwintl] *n* quintale.
quintet [kwinˈtet] *n* (*mus*) quintetto.
quip [kwip] *n* battuta spiritosa, motto pungente.
quire [ˈkwaiə] *n* quaderno, insieme di 24 fogli di carta da scrivere.
quirk [kwə:k] *n* arguzia; svolazzo.
quit [kwit] *a* sdebitato, libero; *vt* abbandonare, lasciare; *vi* andarsene.
quite [kwait] *ad* completamente, del tutto, proprio.
quits [kwits] *a* pari.
quiver [ˈkwivə] *n* brivido, fremito; faretra; *vi* fremere, tremare.
quiz [kwiz] *n* beffa, scherzo, indovinello, 'quiz'; *vt* burlare, porre quesiti, esaminare.
quizzical [ˈkwizikəl] *a* canzonatorio.
quoit [kɔit] *n* grosso anello piatto di metallo o di gomma.
quorum [ˈkwɔ:rəm] *n* 'quorum'.
quota [ˈkwoutə] *n* quota.
quotation [kwou teiʃən] *n* citazione; (*com*) quotazione; **q. marks** virgolette.
quote [kwout] *vt* citare; (*com*) quotare.
quotidian [kwɔˈtidiən] *a* quotidiano.
quotient [ˈkwouʃənt] *n* quoziente.

R

rabbi [ˈræbai] *n* rabbino.
rabbit [ˈræbit] *n* coniglio; (*fam*) giocatore scadente; **r.-warren** conigliera.
rabble [ˈræbl] *n* folla tumultuante, plebaglia.
rabid [ˈræbid] *a* rabbioso, fanatico; **r. dog** cane idrofobo.
rabies [ˈreibi:z] *n* idrofobia.
race [reis] *n* corsa; razza, stirpe; **racecourse, racetrack** ippodromo; *vt* far andar a gran velocità, far correre; *vi* correre, gareggiare in velocità.
racehorse [ˈreishɔ:s] *n* cavallo da corsa.
Rachel [ˈreitʃəl] *nf pr* Rachele.
racial [ˈreiʃəl] *a* razziale.
rack [ræk] *n* (*luggage, rly*) rete; (*fodder*) rastrelliera; (*plates etc*) scolapiatti; tortura della ruota; rovina; *vt* torturare; **to r. one's brains** scervellarsi.
racket [ˈrækit] *n* racchetta; chiasso.
racy [ˈreisi] *a* piccante; vigoroso; vivace.
radar [ˈreida:] *n* radar.
radiance [ˈreidiəns] *n* splendore.
radiant [ˈreidiənt] *a* raggiante.
radiate [ˈreidieit] *vi* irradiare; brillare.
radiation [ˌreidiˈeiʃən] *n* radiazione, irradiazione.
radiator [ˈreidieitə] *n* radiatore, termosifone.
radical [ˈrædikəl] *a n* radicale.
radio [ˈreidiou] *pl* **radios** *n* radio; **r. set** apparecchio radio(fonico).
radioactive [ˈreidiouˈæktiv] *a* radioattivo.
radiogram [ˈreidiougræm] *n* radiogramma; radiogrammofono.
radiography [ˌreidiˈɔgrəfi] *n* radiografia.
radish [ˈrædiʃ] *n* ravanello.
radius [ˈreidiəs] *n* raggio.
raffle [ˈræfl] *n* lotteria; *vt* estrarre a sorte.
raft [ˈra:ft] *n* chiatta, zattera.
rafter [ˈra:ftə] *n* trave, puntone.
rag [ræg] *n* cencio, straccio, brandello; (*sl*) baldoria.
ragamuffin [ˈrægəˌmʌfin] *n* piccolo straccione.
rage [reidʒ] *n* collera, rabbia; (*fam*) persona o cosa di gran moda; *vi* essere furibondo, infuriarsi.
ragged [ˈrægid] *a* cencioso, stracciato; imperfetto; senza uniformità.
raid [reid] *n* incursione, scorreria; *vt* razziare, fare un'incursione.
rail [reil] *n* inferriata, ringhiera; (*rly*) rotaia; sbarra; *vt* chiudere con, cingere di, cancellata o sbarre; **to r.** at ingiuriare.
railing [ˈreiliŋ] *n* ringhiera, parapetto di ferro, inferriata, cancellata.
raillery [ˈreiləri] *n* leggera satira.
railway [ˈreilwei] **railroad** [reilroud] *n* ferrovia, strada ferrata.
rain [rein] *n* pioggia; *vi* piovere; **r. water** acqua piovana.
rainbow [ˈreinbou] *n* arcobaleno.
raincoat [ˈreinkout] *n* impermeabile.
rainfall [ˈreinfɔ:l] *n* piovosità, caduta di pioggia.

rainy ['reini] *a* piovoso.
raise [reiz] *n* (di stipendio) aumento; *vt* alzare, levare, sollevare; allevare, coltivare; elevare, innalzare, aumentare; dare occasione a; raccogliere.
raisin ['reizn] *n* uva passa.
rake [reik] *n* rastrello; (*fig*) libertino; *vt* rastrellare; passare in rassegna; abbracciare con lo sguardo; (*mil*) colpire d'infilata.
rakish ['reikiʃ] *a* dissoluto.
rally ['ræli] *n* adunata; ricupero di forze; *vt* raccogliere; rianimare; *vi* rianimarsi, schierarsi.
ram [ræm] *n* ariete, montone; (*mil*) ariete; (*naut*) sperone; *vt* conficcare; (*naut*) speronare; sbattere contro.
ramble ['ræmbl] *n* passeggiata senza meta precisa; *vi* vagare; divagare.
rambler ['ræmblə] *n* chi passeggia senza meta; divagatore.
rambling ['ræmbliŋ] *a* errante, vagante; incoerente, sconnesso; (*plants*) rampicante.
ramification [ˌræmifi'keiʃən] *n* ramificazione.
ramify ['ræmifai] *vi* ramificar(si).
ramp [ræmp] *n* salita, rampa.
rampant ['ræmpənt] *a* aggressivo; violento; esuberante; rampante.
rampart ['ræmpɑːt] *n* bastione.
ramrod ['ræmrɔd] *n* bacchetta di fucile.
ramshackle ['ræmˌʃækl] *a* sgangherato.
ranch [rɑːntʃ] *n* 'ranch', grande fattoria con bestiame.
rancid ['rænsid] *a* rancido.
rancidity [ræn'siditi] *n* rancidezza.
rancor ['ræŋkə] *n* rancore.
Randolph ['rændɔlf] *nm pr* Rodolfo.
random ['rændəm] *a* fatto a caso; **at r.** *ad* a casaccio.
range [reindʒ] *n* serie; fila; (*mountains*) catena; distesa; campo, sfera; gamma; campo da tiro, raggio, gittata; cucina economica; *vt* collocare, disporre; *vi* (e)stendersi, distribuirsi; errare, vagare.
rank [ræŋk] *a* lussureggiante; rancido, puzzolente; indecente; *vt* classificare, assegnare un grado a; *vi* essere nel grado di; *n* rango, grado, fila.
rankle ['ræŋkl] *vi* inasprirsi, bruciare.
rankness ['ræŋknis] *n* esuberanza, rigoglio; rancidezza; indecenza.
ransack ['rænsæk] *vt* frugare, saccheggiare.
ransom ['rænsəm] *n* riscatto; *vt* riscattare.
rant [rænt] *vti* declamare, usare un linguaggio ampolloso.
rap [ræp] *n* colpo, colpetto, picchio; *vt* battere, colpire, picchiare.
rapacious [rə'peiʃəs] *a* rapace.
rape [reip] *n* ratto; stupro; *vt* rapire; stuprare; violentare.
Raphael ['ræfeiəl] *nm pr* Raffaele.
rapid ['ræpid] *a* rapido, veloce; erto; *n* rapida.
rapidity [ræ'piditi] *n* rapidità, velocità.
rapier ['reipiə] *n* stocco, spadino.
rapine ['ræpain] *n* rapina.
rapture ['ræptʃə] *n* estasi, rapimento.
rapturous ['ræptʃərəs] *a* estatico.
rare [rɛə] *a* raro; poco cotto.
rareness ['rɛənis] **rarity** ['rɛəriti] *n* rarità; rarefazione.
rascal ['rɑːskəl] *n* briccone, furfante.
rascality [rɑːs'kæliti] *n* furfanteria.
rash [ræʃ] *a* avventato, imprudente, sconsiderato; *n* eruzione cutanea.
rasher ['ræʃə] *n* fetta sottile di pancetta o prosciutto.
rashness ['ræʃnis] *n* avventatezza, imprudenza, sconsideratezza.
rasp [rɑːsp] *n* raspa, raschietto; *vt* raspare, raschiare; *vi* stridere.
raspberry ['rɑːzbəri] *n* lampone.
rat [ræt] *n* topo, ratto; (*pol*) disertore, girella; (*blackleg*) crumiro; *vi* andare alla caccia dei topi; (*pol*) defezionare.
rate [reit] *n* tasso; aliquota, prezzo, tariffa; (con)tributo; passo, velocità; *vt* calcolare, valutare; tassare, considerare; classificare; *vi* classificarsi.
rather ['rɑːðə] *ad* piuttosto, alquanto, un po'.
ratification [ˌrætifi'keiʃən] *n* ratifica.
ratify ['rætifai] *vt* ratificare.
rating ['reitiŋ] *n* valutazione, stima; classifica, posizione; classificazione.
ratio ['reiʃiou] *pl* **ratios** *n* rapporto, proporzione, ragione.
ration ['ræʃən] *n* razione; *vt* razionare.
rational ['ræʃənl] *a* razionale, ragionevole.
rattle ['rætl] *n* sonaglio; tintinnio; strepito, rumore; rantolo; chiacchierio vuoto; chiacchierone; *vi* produrre un rumore secco; ciarlare; *vt* (*sl*) innervosire.
raucous ['rɔːkəs] *a* rauco, aspro.
ravage ['rævidʒ] *n* danno, devastazione; *vt* devastare, saccheggiare.
rave [reiv] *n* delirio; infatuazione; *vi* delirare; (*fam*) andare in estasi; infuriare.
ravel ['rævəl] *vti* ingarbugliar(si), sfilacciarsi.
raven ['reivn] *a* corvino; *n* corvo.
ravenous ['rævinəs] *a* affamato, vorace.
ravine [rə'viːn] *n* burrone.
raving ['reiviŋ] *a* delirante; *n* delirio.
ravish ['ræviʃ] *vt* rapire, violentare; (*fig*) estasiare.
ravishing ['ræviʃiŋ] *a* incantevole.
raw [rɔː] *a* crudo; greggio; (*wound*) scoperto, vivo; (*fig*) inesperto; (*weather*) freddo e umido.
rawness ['rɔːnis] *n* crudezza; inesperienza; (*weather*) rigore.

ray [rei] *n* raggio.
rayon ['reiɔn] *n* raion, seta artificiale.
Raymond ['reimənd] *nm pr* Raimondo.
raze, rase [reiz] *vt* radere al suolo, distruggere completamente.
razor ['reizə] *n* rasoio.
re- ['ri:] *prefisso usato davanti a verbi e sostantivi* ri- (*qualora non si trovasse il vocabolo sotto la forma composta si cerchi la forma senza prefisso*).
reach [ri:tʃ] *n* portata; possibilità; estensione; tiro; **out of r.** *a* irraggiungibile; *vt* arrivare a, (rag)giungere, tendere; *vi* estendersi.
react [ri:'ækt] *vi* reagire.
reaction [ri:'ækʃən] *n* reazione.
reactive [ri:'æktiv] *a* reattivo, reagente.
reactor [ri:'æktə] *n* reattore.
read [ri:d] *vt* leggere; (*of instruments*) segnare.
readable ['ri:dəbl] *a* interessante, piacevole.
reader ['ri:də] *n* lettore, lettrice; libro di lettura.
readily ['redili] *ad* prontamente; volentieri; facilmente.
readiness ['redinis] *n* prontezza, facilità.
reading ['ri:diŋ] *n* lettura interpretazione; **r. desk** leggio; **r. room** sala di lettura.
ready ['redi] *a* pronto, preparato; facile, disinvolto; **r.-made** confezionato; **r. money** denaro in contanti.
real ['ri:əl] *a n* reale; *a* autentico; vero; (*leg*) immobile.
realism ['riəlizəm] *n* realismo.
realist ['riəlist] *n* realista.
realistic [riə'listik] *a* realistico.
reality [ri:'æliti] n realtà.
realization [,riəlai'zeiʃən] *n* percezione; realizzazione; compimento.
realize ['riəlaiz] *vt* accorgersi, capire, rendersi conto; realizzare; convertire in denaro.
really ['riəli] *ad* davvero, realmente.
realm [relm] *n* reame, regno.
ream [ri:m] *n* risma.
reap [ri:p] *vti* mietere, raccogliere.
reaper ['ri:pə] *n* mietitore, mietitrice, (*mech*) mietitrice.
rear [riə] *n* (*mil*) retroguardia; coda, parte posteriore, retro; *vt* allevare, coltivare, educare; costruire, ergere; *vi* (*horse*) impennarsi; **r. admiral** (*naut*) contrammiraglio; **in the r., at the r.** indietro.
reason ['ri:zn] *n* ragione, ragionevolezza; *vi* ragionare, persuadere.
reasonable ['ri:znəbl] *a* ragionevole.
reasonableness ['ri:znəblnis] *n* ragionevolezza.
reasoning ['ri:zniŋ] *n* ragionamento, argomentazione.
reassure [,ri:ə'ʃuə] *vt* rassicurare.
rebate ['ri:beit] *n* (*com*) riduzione, sconto, rimborso.
rebel ['rebl] *a n* ribelle; *vi* [ri'bel] ribellarsi.
rebellion [ri'beljən] *n* ribellione, rivolta.
rebellious [ri'beljəs] *a* ribelle.
rebound [ri'baund] *n* reazione, rimbalzo; *vi* rimbalzare.
rebuff [ri'bʌf] *n* rifiuto; rabbuffo; *vt* respingere.
rebuke [ri'bju:k] *n* rimprovero; *vt* rimproverare.
recall [ri'kɔ:l] *n* richiamo; revoca; *vt* richiamare, ricordare; revocare.
recant [ri'kænt] *vti* abiurare, ritrattar(si).
recantation [,ri:kæn'teiʃən] *n* abiura, ritrattazione.
recapitulate [,ri:kə'pitjuleit] *vt* riassumere, ricapitolare.
recapitulation [,ri:kəpitju'leiʃən] *n* ricapitolazione.
recede [ri:'si:d] *vt* recedere; diminuire.
receding [ri:'si:diŋ] *a* rientrante, sfuggente; **r. chin** mento sfuggente; **r. hair** calvizie incipiente.
receipt [ri'si:t] *n* ricevimento, ricevuta, quietanza.
receive [ri'si:v] *vti* ricevere.
receiver [ri'si:və] *n* ricevitore; (*rad*) apparecchio radioricevente.
recent ['ri:snt] *a* recente.
receptacle [ri'septəkl] *n* ricettacolo.
reception [ri'sepʃən] *n* ricevimento, accoglienza.
recess [ri'ses] *n* luogo appartato, nicchia, recesso; tregua; vacanza scolastica.
recipe ['resipi] *n* ricetta.
recipient [ri'sipiənt] *n* ricevente, chi riceve.
reciprocal [ri'siprəkl] *a* reciproco.
reciprocate [ri'siprəkeit] *vt* contraccambiare, ricambiare.
reciprocity [,resi'prɔsiti] *n* reciprocità.
recital [ri'saitl] *n* esposto, racconto, "recital", esibizione di un solista, di un attore.
recitation [,resi'teiʃən] *n* recitazione.
recite [ri'sait] *vt* recitare: (*leg*) esporre.
reckless ['reklis] *a* avventato, temerario.
reckon ['rekən] *vti* calcolare, contare, considerare, supporre, contare su.
reckoning ['rekəniŋ] *n* computo, calcolo, resa dei conti.
reclaim [ri'kleim] *vt* (*land*) bonificare, rivendicare.
reclamation [,reklə'meiʃən] *n* bonifica, rivendicazione.
recline [ri'klain] *vi* essere o mettersi in posizione inclinata.
recluse [ri'klu:s] *n* anacoreta.
recognition [,rekəg'niʃən] *n* riconoscimento.
recognize ['rekəgnaiz] *vt* riconoscere.
recoil [ri'kɔil] *n* indietreggiamento, rinculo; *vi* indietreggiare, rinculare.

recollect [,rekə'lekt] *vt* ricordare, ricordarsi.
recollection [,rekə'lekʃən] *n* reminiscenza, ricordo.
recommend [,rekə'mend] *vt* raccomandare.
recommendation [,rekəmen'deiʃən] *n* raccomandazione.
recompense ['rekəmpens] *n* ricompensa; *vt* ricompensare.
reconcile ['rekənsail] *vt* (ri)conciliare.
reconcilement [,rekən'sailmənt] **reconciliation** [,rekənsili'eiʃən] *n* (ri) conciliazione.
recondite [ri'kɔndait] *a* recondito.
reconstruct ['ri:kəns'trʌkt] *vt* ricostruire.
reconstruction ['ri:kəns'trʌkʃən] *n* ricostruzione.
record ['rekɔ:d] *n* registrazione; documento; verbale, atto; archivio, (*sport*) record, primato; (*gramophone*) disco; **r.-player** giradischi, grammofono; *vt* [ri'kɔ:d] mettere a verbale; registrare, riportare, notare; (*disc*) incidere.
recorder [ri'kɔ:də] *n* apparecchio registratore; (*leg*) cancelliere; (*mus*) flauto dolce; **tape r.** magnetofono, registratore a nastro.
recount ['ri:'kaunt] *vt* raccontare.
recourse [ri'kɔ:s] *n* ricorso.
recover [ri'kʌvə] *vt* ricuperare, riprendere; *vi* riaversi, ricuperare la salute.
recovery [ri:'kʌvəri] *n* guarigione; ricupero.
re-create ['ri:kri'eit] *vt* ricreare.
recreate ['rekrieit] *vt* ricreare, divertire.
recreation [,rekri'eiʃən] *n* ricreazione, divertimento.
recruit [ri'kru:t] *n* recluta; (*fig*) novizio; *vt* reclutare; rinvigorire; *vi* ricuperare la salute.
rectangle ['rek,tæŋgl] *n* rettangolo.
rectification [,rektifi'keiʃən] *n* rettificazione.
rectify ['rektifai] *vt* rettificare, correggere.
rectitude ['rektitju:d] *n* rettitudine.
rector ['rektə] *n* parroco; rettore.
rectory ['rektəri] *n* canonica.
recumbent [ri'kʌmbənt] *a* appoggiato, semi-sdraiato.
recuperate [ri'kju:pəreit] *vti* ricuperare, ristabilirsi.
recur [ri'kə:] *vi* ricorrere, ritornare.
recurrence [ri'kʌrəns] *n* ricorrenza, ritorno.
recurrent [ri'kʌrənt] *a* ricorrente, periodico.
red [red] *a n* rosso; **r.-hot** rovente; (*fig*) ardente.
redden ['redn] *vti* arrossare, arrossire.
reddish ['rediʃ] *a* rossastro, rossiccio.
redeem [ri'di:m] *vt* redimere, riabilitare, riscattare, salvare.
redeemer [ri'di:mə] *n* redentore.
redemption [ri'dempʃən] *n* redenzione, salvezza.
redness ['rednis] *n* rossore.
redolent ['redoulənt] *a* fragrante, profumato.
redouble [ri'dʌbl] *vti* raddoppiar(si), intensificar(si).
redoubt [ri'daut] *n* (*mil*) ridotta.
redoubtable [ri'dautəbl] *a* formidabile.
redound [ri'daund] *vi* ridondare.
redress [ri'dres] *n* atto di giustizia riparatrice, riparazione; *vt* riparare, raddrizzare.
reduce [ri'dju:s] *vt* ridurre.
reduction [ri'dʌkʃən] *n* riduzione.
redundant [ri'dʌndənt] *a* ridondante, sovrabbondante.
re-echo [ri:'ekou] *vt* ripetere; *vi* riecheggiare.
reed [ri:d] *n* canna; (*poet*) zampogna.
reef [ri:f] *n* scoglio, scogliera, banco; (*naut*) terzaruolo.
reek [ri:k] *n* fumo, esalazione, fetore; *vi* fumare, puzzare.
reel [ri:l] *n* arcolaio, aspo, bobina, spoletta, rocchetto; rotolo, rullo; vacillamento; danza scozzese; *vt* avvolgere su un rocchetto; *vi* girare; vacillare.
re-election ['ri:i'lekʃən] *n* rielezione.
refectory [ri'fektəri] *n* refettorio.
refer [ri'fə:] *vt* ascrivere, attribuire, riferire; rimandare a; *vi* alludere, riferire, rivolgersi a.
referee [,refə'ri:] *n* arbitro; *vti* fare da arbitro, arbitrare.
reference ['refrəns] *n* riferimento, allusione; referenza; competenza; **r. book** libro di consultazione.
refill ['ri:'fil] *n* ricambio; *vti* riempire, riempirsi; ricaricare.
refine [ri'fain] *vt* ingentilire, (r)affinare; *vi* ingentilirsi, raffinarsi; sottilizzare.
refinement [ri'fainmənt] *n* raffinamento; (*fig*) raffinatezza, finezza.
reflect [ri'flekt] *vt* riflettere; *vi* riflettere, meditare; gettare biasimo.
reflection [ri'flekʃən] *n* riflessione; riflesso.
reflective [ri'flektiv] *a* riflessivo.
reflector [ri'flektə] *n* riflettore.
reflex ['ri:fleks] *a n* riflesso.
reflexive [ri'fleksiv] *a* (*gram*) riflessivo.
reform [ri'fɔ:m] *n* riforma; *vti* riformar(si).
reformation [,refə'meiʃən] *n* riforma.
reformer [ri'fɔ:mə] *n* riformatore.
refract [ri'frækt] *vt* rifrangere.
refraction [ri'frækʃən] *n* rifrazione.
refractor [ri'fræktə] *n* rifrattore.
refractory [ri'fræktəri] *a* refrattario, ribelle.
refrain [ri'frein] *n* ritornello; *vi* frenarsi, trattenersi.
refresh [ri'freʃ] *vt* ravvivare, riani-

mare, rinfrescare, rinvigorire; *vi* ristorarsi.
refreshing [ri'freʃiŋ] *a* rinfrescante, ristoratore.
refresher [ri'freʃə] *n* chi, cosa che rinfresca; **r. course** corso di aggiornamento.
refreshment [ri'freʃmənt] *n* rinfresco, ristoro.
refrigerator [ri'fridʒəreitə] *n* frigorifero.
refuel [ri'fjuəl] *vti (av, aut)* rifornire, rifornirsi di carburante.
refuge ['refju:dʒ] *n* rifugio.
refugee [refju:'dʒi:] *n* profugo, rifugiato.
refund ['ri:fʌnd] *n* rimborso; [ri'fʌnd] *vt* rifondere, rimborsare.
refusal [ri'fju:zəl] *n* rifiuto; diritto di opzione.
refuse ['refju:s] *n* rifiuti, scarti *pl.*
refuse [ri'fju:z] *vti* rifiutare, negare.
refute [ri'fju:t] *vt* confutare, ribattere.
regain [ri'gein] *vt* riguadagnare, riacquistare, ricuperare; raggiungere di nuovo.
regal ['ri:gəl] *a* regale.
regale [ri'geil] *vt* intrattenere.
regality [ri'gæliti] *n* regalità.
regard [ri'gɑ:d] *n* considerazione, stima; *vt* riguardare, considerare, concernere; **regards** *pl* ossequi, saluti; **with r. to. regarding** riguardo a, per quanto riguarda.
regardless [ri'gɑ:dlis] *a* incurante, senza riguardo; **r. of** a dispetto di, nonostante.
regatta [ri'gætə] *n* regata.
regency ['ri:dʒənsi] *n* reggenza.
regenerate [ri'dʒenəreit] *vti* rigenerare, rigenerarsi.
regent ['ri:dʒənt] *n* reggente.
regicide ['redʒisaid] *n* regicida, regicidio.
regime [rei'ʒi:m] *n* regime.
regiment ['redʒimənt] *n* reggimento.
regimental [,redʒi'mentl] *a* reggimentale.
Reginald ['redʒinld] *nm pr* Reginaldo.
region ['ri:dʒən] *n* regione.
regional ['ri:dʒənl] *a* regionale.
register ['redʒistə] *n* registro; registratore; *(mech)* valvola di regolazione; *(mus, type)* registro; *vt* registrare; *(post)* raccomandare; *(luggage)* assicurare; *vi* (far) iscrivere il proprio nome su un registro; **r. of voters** lista elettorale.
registrar [,redʒis'trɑ:] *n* archivista, ufficiale dello stato civile.
registration [,redʒis'treiʃən] *n* registrazione; iscrizione; *(post)* raccomandazione; *(luggage)* assicurazione.
registry ['redʒistri] *n* ufficio del registro, ufficio di stato civile; ufficio di collocamento.
regression [ri'greʃən] *n* regresso.
regret [ri'gret] *n* rammarico, rimpianto; *vt* rimpiangere, deplorare, rammaricarsi di.
regretful [ri'gretful] *a* dolente.
regrettable [ri'gretəbl] *a* deplorevole, increscioso.
regrettingly [ri'gretiŋli] *ad* con rammarico, con dispiacere.
regular ['regjulə] *a n* regolare.
regularity [,regju'læriti] *n* regolarità.
regulate ['regjuleit] *vt* regolare.
regulation [,regju'leiʃən] *a* regolamentare; *n* regolamento, regola.
regulator ['regjuleitə] *n* regolatore.
rehabilitation ['ri:ə bili'teiʃən] *n* riabilitazione.
rehearsal [ri'hə:səl] *n* prova.
rehearse [ri'hə:s] *vt* provare.
reign [rein] *n* regno; *vi* regnare.
reimburse [,ri:im'bə:s] *vt* rimborsare, rifondere.
rein [rein] *n* redine.
reindeer ['reindiə] *n* renna.
reinforce [,ri:in'fɔ:s] *vt* rinforzare, rafforzare.
reinforcement [,ri:in'fɔ:smənt] *n* rinforzo.
reinstate ['ri:in'steit] *vt* ricollocare, rimettere, reintegrare.
reiterate [ri:'itəreit] *vt* reiterare.
reiteration [ri:'itəreiʃən] *n* reiterazione.
reject [ri'dʒekt] *vt* rigettare, respingere; *(mil)* riformare.
rejection [ri'dʒekʃən] *n* rigetto, rifiuto.
rejoice [ri'dʒɔis] *vi* gioire, rallegrarsi; *vt* rallegrare.
rejoicing [ri'dʒɔisiŋ] *n* gioia, letizia; **rejoicings** *pl* festeggiamenti *pl.*
rejoin [ri'dʒɔin] *vt* raggiungere, riunire; *vi* ribattere, rispondere.
rejoinder [ri'dʒɔində] *n* risposta.
rejuvenate [ri'dʒu:vineit] *vti* ringiovanire.
relapse [ri'læps] *n* ricaduta; *vi* ricadere.
relate [ri'leit] *vt* narrare; *vi* aver rapporto, riferirsi.
relation [ri'leiʃən] *n* relazione, rapporto; parente.
relationship [ri'leiʃənʃip] *n* relazione, rapporto; parentela.
relative ['relətiv] *a* relativo; *n* parente.
relativity [,relə'tiviti] *n* relatività.
relax [ri'læks] *vt* allentare, rilassare, diminuire; *vi* allentarsi, rilassarsi.
relaxation [,ri:læk'seiʃən] *n* rilassamento, distensione, ricreazione, riposo, diminuzione.
relay ['ri:lei] *n (horses)* cavalli di ricambio, *(dogs)* muta di ricambio; **r. race** corsa a staffetta; *vt* sostituire; *(rad)* ritrasmettere.
release [ri'li:s] *n* liberazione; *(mech)* scarico; *vt* liberare, sciogliere.
relegate ['religeit] *vt* relegare.
relent [ri'lent] *vi* piegarsi, intenerirsi.
relentless [ri'lentlis] *a* inflessibile, rigido.

relevance ['relivəns] **relevancy** ['relivənsi] *n* attinenza, pertinenza.
relevant ['relivənt] *a* attinente, pertinente.
reliability [ri,laiə'biliti] *n* attendibilità; fidatezza.
reliable [ri'laiəbl] *a* fidato; attendibile.
reliance [ri'laiəns] *n* fiducia.
reliant [ri'laiənt] *a* fiducioso; che fa assegnamento.
relic ['relik] *n* reliquia; **relics** *pl* reliquie, avanzi, resti *pl.*
relief [ri'li:f] *n* sollievo; aiuto, soccorso; cambio; diversivo; rilievo.
relieve [ri'li:v] *vt* alleviare, mitigare, soccorrere, sollevare, liberare, dare il cambio a.
religion [ri'lidʒən] *n* religione.
religious [ri'lidʒəs] *a* religioso; *a* devoto, pio.
relinquish [ri'liŋkwiʃ] *vt* abbandonare, rinunziare a.
relish ['reliʃ] *n* gusto, sapore, piacere, condimento; *vt* (far) gustare, trovar piacere.
reluctance [ri'lʌktəns] *n* riluttanza.
reluctant [ri'lʌktənt] *a* riluttante.
rely [ri'lai] *vi* fare assegnamento (su), contare (su), fidarsi (di).
remain [ri'mein] *vi* restare, rimanere; avanzare.
remainder [ri'meində] *n* resto, rimanenza.
remaining [ri'meiniŋ] *a* restante, rimanente.
remains [ri'meins] *n pl* avanzi, resti, reliquie *pl*, resti mortali *pl*, spoglie *pl.*
remand [ri'mɑ:nd] *vt* rimandare in carcere.
remark [ri'mɑ:k] *n* commento, osservazione; *vti* notare, osservare.
remarkable [ri'mɑ:kəbl] *a* eccezzionale, notevole.
remedy ['remidi] *n* rimedio, medicina; *vt* porre rimedio a.
remember [ri'membə] *vt* ricordare, ricordar(si di), rammentar(si di).
remembrance [ri'membrəns] *n* ricordo, memoria, rimembranza; **remembrances** *pl* saluti, ossequi *pl.*
remind [ri'maind] *vt* ricordare a, richiamare alla memoria di, rammentare a.
reminder [ri'maində] *n* ricordo, promemoria.
reminiscence [,remi'nisns] *n* reminiscenza.
reminiscent [,remi'nisnt] *a* che richiama alla memoria.
remiss [ri'mis] *a* negligente, trascurato.
remission [ri'miʃən] *n* remissione, condono.
remit [ri'mit] *vt* rimettere, perdonare.
remittance [ri'mitəns] *n* (*com*) rimessa.
remnant ['remnənt] *n* resto, scampolo.
remonstrance [ri'mɔnstrəns] *n* rimostranza.
remonstrate ['remənstreit] *vi* protestare, fare rimostranza.
remorse [ri'mɔ:s] *n* rimorso.
remorseful [ri'mɔ:sful] *a* pieno di rimorsi.
remorseless [ri'mɔ:slis] *a* spietato.
remote [ri'mout] *a* lontano, remoto.
removal [ri'mu:vəl] *n* rimozione, trasferimento, trasloco.
remove [ri'mu:v] *vti* rimuovere; levare; trasferirsi, traslocare.
remunerate [ri'mju:nəreit] *vt* rimunerare.
remuneration [ri,mju:nə'reiʃən] *n* rimunerazione.
remunerative [ri'mu:nərətiv] *a* rimunerativo.
renaissance, renascence [rə'neisəns] *n* rinascimento.
rend [rend] *vt* lacerare, strappare.
render ['rendə] *vt* rendere, tradurre; (*fats*) sciogliere; (*oil*) raffinare.
rendering ['rendəriŋ] *n* resa, traduzione, interpretazione.
rendezvous ['rɔndeivu:] *n* (*mil*) luogo di raduno; appuntamento; *vi* riunirsi.
renegade ['renigeid] *n* rinnegato, traditore.
renew [ri'nju:] *vt* rinnovare.
renewal [ri'nju:əl] *n* rinnovamento.
rennet ['renit] *n* caglio; mela ranetta.
renounce [ri'nauns] *vt* rinunciare a, ripudiare.
renouncement [ri'naunsmənt] *n* rinunzia.
renovate ['renouveit] *vt* rinnovare.
renovation [,renou'veiʃən] *n* rinnovamento.
renown [ri'naun] *n* fama, rinomanza.
renowned [ri'naund] *a* celebre, famoso.
rent [rent] *n* affitto, nolo; strappo; *vt* dare o prendere in affitto; *vi* venire affittato; **rental** canone d'affitto; **rental library** biblioteca circolante.
renunciation [ri,nʌnsi'eiʃən] *n* rinuncia.
repair [ri'peə] *n* riparazione, restauro; *vt* riparare, restaurare, rimediare a; *vi* recarsi, rifugiarsi; **in good r.** in buono stato.
reparation [,repə'reiʃən] *n* riparazione, risarcimento.
repartee [,repɑ:'ti:] *n* risposta pronta.
repast [ri'pɑ:st] *n* pasto.
repatriate [ri:'pætrieit] *n* rimpatriato; *vti* rimpatriare.
repay [ri:'pei] *vt* ripagare; restituire; ricompensare.
repayment [ri:'peimənt] *n* rimborso; ricompensa.
repeal [ri'pi:l] *vt* abrogare, revocare.
repeat [ri'pi:t] *vt* ripetere.

repel [ri'pel] *vt* respingere; ripugnare a.
repent [ri'pent] *vti* pentirsi (di).
repentance [ri'pentəns] *n* pentimento.
repentant [ri'pentənt] *a* pentito.
repertoire ['repətwa:] *n* repertorio.
repertory ['repətəri] *n* repertorio.
repetition [,repi'tiʃən] *n* ripetizione.
replace [ri'pleis] *vt* ricollocare, rimettere; sostituire.
replacement [ri'pleismənt] *n* ricollocamento; sostituzione.
replenish [ri'pleniʃ] *vt* riempire.
replete [ri'pli:t] *a* pieno, sazio.
repletion [ri'pli:ʃən] *n* pienezza, sazietà.
replica ['replikə] *n* replica, copia.
reply [ri'plai] *n* risposta; *vi* rispondere.
report [ri'pɔ:t] *n* rapporto, relazione, resoconto; detonazione; *vt* fare un rapporto di, riferire, fare la cronaca di; *vi* fare il cronista.
reporter [ri'pɔ:tə] *n* corrispondente, cronista.
repose [ri'pouz] *n* riposo; *vi* riposarsi, basarsi.
repository [ri'pɔzitəri] *n* deposito, magazzino; (*fig*) confidente.
reprehensible [,repri'hensəbl] *a* biasimevole.
represent [,repri'zent] *vt* rappresentare.
representation [,reprizen'teiʃən] *n* rappresentazione.
representative [,repri'zentətiv] *a* rappresentativo; *n* rappresentante.
repress [ri'pres] *vt* reprimere, frenare.
repression [ri'preʃən] *n* repressione.
reprieve [ri'pri:v] *n* dilazione; *vt* accordare una dilazione a.
reprimand ['reprima:nd] *n* rimprovero; *vt* rimproverare.
reprint ['ri:'print] *n* ristampa; *vt* ristampare.
reprisal [ri'praizəl] *n* rappresaglia.
reproach [ri'proutʃ] *n* rimprovero, vergogna; *vt* rimproverare.
reproachful [ri'proutʃful] *a* di rimprovero.
reprobate ['reproubeit] *a n* reprobo; *vt* riprovare.
reproduce [,ri:prə'dju:s] *vti* riprodur(si).
reproduction [,ri:prə'dʌkʃən] *n* riproduzione.
reproductive [,ri:prə'dʌktiv] *a* riproduttivo.
reproof [ri'pru:f] *n* biasimo, rimprovero.
reprove [ri'pru:v] *vt* biasimare, rimproverare.
reptile ['reptail] *n* rettile.
republic [ri'pʌblik] *n* repubblica.
republican [ri'pʌblikən] *a n* repubblicano.
repudiate [ri'pju:dieit] *vt* ripudiare, rinnegare.
repugnance [ri'pʌgnəns] *n* ripugnanza.
repugnant [ri'pʌgnənt] *a* ripugnante.
repulse [ri'pʌls] *n* ripulsa, rifiuto; *vt* respingere.
repulsion [ri'pʌlʃən] *n* repulsione.
repulsive [ri'pʌlsiv] *a* repellente, ripulsivo.
reputable ['repjutəbl] *a* rispettabile.
reputation [,repju:'teiʃən] *n* reputazione; rispettabilità.
repute [ri'pju:t] *n* reputazione, fama; *vt* giudicare, reputare.
request [ri'kwest] *n* domanda, richiesta; *vt* domandare, pregare, richiedere.
require [ri'kwaiə] *vt* richiedere, esigere; aver bisogno di.
requirement [ri'kwaiəmənt] *n* richiesta, esigenza; bisogno; requisito.
requisite ['rekwizit] *a* necessario, richiesto; *n* requisito.
requisition [,rekwi'ziʃən] *n* requisizione; *vt* requisire.
requital [ri'kwaitl] *n* contraccambio; ricompensa.
requite [ri'kwait] *vt* ricompensare; contraccambiare.
rescue ['reskju:] *n* liberazione, salvezza, soccorso; *vt* liberare, salvare.
research [ri:'sə:tʃ] *n* indagine, ricerca; **r. worker** ricercatore, investigatore.
resemblance [ri'zembləns] *n* (ras) somiglianza.
resemble [ri'zembl] *vt* (as)somigliare a, rassomigliare.
resent [ri'zent] *vt* risentirsi di, risentire.
resentment [ri'zentmənt] *n* risentimento, rancore.
reservation [,rezə'veiʃən] *n* riserva; prenotazione.
reserve [ri'zə:v] *n* reticenza, riserbo, riserva; *vt* riservare, prenotare.
reservoir ['rezəvwa:] *n* serbatoio.
reside [ri'zaid] *vi* risiedere.
residence ['rezidəns] *n* residenza.
resident ['rezidənt] *a n* residente.
residential [,rezi'denʃəl] *a* adatto per case di abitazione, residenziale.
residue ['rezidju:] *n* residuo, resto.
resign [ri'zain] *vt* rinunziare a; *vi* dimettersi, rassegnare le dimissioni.
resignation [,rezig'neiʃən] *n* dimissioni *pl*; rassegnazione.
resilience [ri'ziliəns] *n* elasticità, capacità di ricupero.
resilient [ri'ziliənt] *a* elastico, rimbalzante; che ha la capacità di ricupero.
resin ['rezin] *n* resina.
resist [ri'zist] *vt* resistere a; *vi* resistere.
resistance [ri'zistəns] *n* resistenza.
resistant [ri'zistənt] *a* resistente.
resolute ['rezəlu:t] *a* risoluto.
resolution [,rezə'lu:ʃən] *n* risolutezza, decisione; soluzione, risoluzione.
resolve [ri'zɔlv] *n* decisione; *vt*

risolvere, sciogliere; *vi* decidere, risolversi.
resonance ['reznəns] *n* risonanza.
resonant ['reznənt] *a* risonante.
resort [ri'zɔ:t] *n* ricorso, risorsa; luogo di soggiorno; *vi* ricorrere a; affluire.
resound [ri'zaund] *vi* risuonare, echeggiare.
resource [ri'sɔ:s] *n* risorsa, mezzo, espediente, ingegnosità.
resourceful [ri'sɔ:sful] *a* pieno di risorse.
respect [ris'pekt] *n* rispetto, stima; riguardo, aspetto; *vt* rispettare, tenere in considerazione; **respects** *pl* ossequi *pl*.
respectability [ri,spektə'biliti] *n* rispettabilità.
respectable [ris'pektəbl] *a* rispettabile, per bene, considerevole.
respectably [ri'spektəbli] *ad* rispettabilmente; decentemente.
respectful [ris'pektful] *a* rispettoso.
respecting [ris'pektiŋ] *prep* riguardo a.
respective [ris'pektiv] *a* rispettivo, relativo.
respiration [,respə'reiʃən] *n* respirazione.
respirator ['respəreitə] *n* (*med*) respiratore; (*mil*) maschera anti-gas.
respite ['respait] *n* tregua, respiro.
resplendent [ris'plendənt] *a* (ri) splendente.
respond [ris'pɔnd] *vi* rispondere.
respondent [ris'pɔndənt] *n* (*leg*) convenuto, imputato.
response [ris'pɔns] *n* risposta, responso; reazione; (*eccl*) responsorio.
responsibility [ris,pɔnsə'biliti] *n* responsabilità.
responsible [ris'pɔnsəbl] *a* responsabile.
responsive [ris'pɔnsiv] *a* sensibile a.
responsiveness [ris'pɔnsivnis] *n* rispondenza, sensibilità.
rest [rest] *n* riposo; resto, rimanente; *pron pl* gli altri, le altre *pl*; *vt* posare, appoggiare; *vi* riposarsi, stare quieto.
restaurant ['restərɔ̃:ŋ] *n* ristorante; **r. car** vettura ristorante.
restful ['restful] *a* riposante, tranquillo.
restitution [,resti'tju:ʃən] *n* restituzione, risarcimento.
restive ['restiv] *a* restio, recalcitrante.
restless ['restlis] *a* irrequieto, agitato.
restlessness ['restlisnis] *n* irrequietezza, agitazione.
restoration [,restə'reiʃən] *n* restauro, restaurazione, restituzione, ricupero, ripristino.
restore [ris'tɔ:] *vt* rimettere, restaurare, restituire, ricuperare, ripristinare.
restrain [ris'trein] *vt* reprimere, trattenere.
restraint [ris'treint] *n* controllo, freno, ritegno; detenzione.
restrict [ris'trikt] *vt* restringere, limitare.
restriction [ris'trikʃən] *n* restrizione.
restrictive [ris'triktiv] *a* restrittivo.
result [ri'zʌlt] *n* risultato, esito; *vi* risultare, risolversi.
resultant [ri'zʌltənt] *a n* risultante.
resume [ri'zju:m] *vti* riprendere.
resumption [ri'zʌmpʃən] *n* ripresa.
resurrection [,rezə'rekʃən] *n* risurrezione.
resuscitate [ri'sʌsiteit] *vti* risuscitare.
retail ['ri:teil] *n* vendita al minuto; *ad* al minuto; *vt* vendere al minuto; raccontare dettagliatamente.
retailer ['ri:teilə] *n* venditore al minuto.
retain [ri'tein] *vt* mantenere; conservare.
retaliate [ri'tælieit] *vt* ricambiare; *vi* rendere la pariglia.
retaliation [ri,tæli'eiʃən] *n* rappresaglia.
retard [ri'tɑ:d] *vt* ritardare.
retch [ri:tʃ] *vi* avere conati di vomito.
retention [ri'tenʃən] *n* ritenzione, conservazione; memoria.
retentive [ri'tentiv] *a* ritentivo, tenace.
reticence ['retisəns] *n* reticenza.
reticent ['retisənt] *a* reticente, riservato.
retinue ['retinju:] *n* seguito.
retire [ri'taiə] *vti* ritirar(si).
retirement [ri'taiəmənt] *n* ritiro, collocamento a riposo.
retort [ri'tɔ:t] *n* ritorsione, risposta incisiva; (*chem*) storta; *vti* ritorcere, ribattere.
retrace [ri'treis] *vt* rintracciare, ripercorrere, tornare indietro.
retract [ri'trækt] *vt* ritrattare; *vi* disdirsi.
retreat [ri'tri:t] *n* (*mil*) ritirata; ritiro; *vi* ritirarsi.
retrench [ri'trentʃ] *vt* diminuire, ridurre; *vi* economizzare.
retribution [,retri'bju:ʃən] *n* retribuzione, ricompensa.
retrieve [ri'tri:v] *vt* ricuperare, riacquistare il possesso di, riparare; (*game*) riportare.
retriever [ri'tri:və] *n* cane da presa.
retrograde ['retrougreid] *a* retrogrado; inverso.
retrospect ['retrouspekt] *n* sguardo retrospettivo.
retrospective [,retrə'spektiv] *a* retrospettivo.
return [ri'tə:n] *n* ritorno; restituzione; prospetto statistico; *usu pl* provento, guadagno; *vt* contraccambiare; restituire; rimandare; *vi* (ri)tornare; replicare, rispondere.

reunion ['ri:'ju:njən] *n* riunione.
reveal [ri'vi:l] *vt* rivelare.
revel ['revl] *n* baldoria, gozzoviglia; *vi* fare baldoria, gozzovigliare, dilettarsi.
revelation [,revi'leiʃən] *n* rivelazione.
revenge [ri'vendʒ] *n* vendetta, rivincita; *vti* vendicar(si).
revengeful [ri'vendʒful] *a* vendicativo.
revenue ['revinju:] *n* entrata; reddito; fisco; **r. stamp** marca da bollo; **r. tax** imposta sull'entrata.
reverberate [ri'və:bəreit] *vti* riverberar(si), riecheggiare, rimbombare.
reverberation [ri,və:bə'reiʃən] *n* riverbero; riverberazione.
revere [ri'viə] *vt* riverire, venerare.
reverence ['revərəns] *n* riverenza, venerazione.
reverend ['revərənd] *a n* reverendo.
reverent ['revərənt] *a* riverente.
reverie ['revəri] *n* sogno ad occhi aperti, fantasticheria.
reversal [ri'və:səl] *n* rovesciamento, inversione.
reverse [ri'və:s] *a* contrario, inverso, rovescio, opposto; *n* il rovescio, l'opposto, il contrario; *vt* rovesciare, capovolgere, invertire; *vi* girare in senso inverso.
reversible [ri'və:səbl] *a* reversibile, revocabile; (*mech*) a inversione di marcia.
reversion [ri'və:ʃən] *n* reversione, ritorno.
revert [ri'və:t] *vi* ritornare.
review [ri'vju:] *n* rivista, recensione; revisione; sguardo retrospettivo; *vt* passare in rivista; recensire; rivedere; *vi* scrivere recensioni.
reviewer [ri'vju:ə] *n* recensore, critico d'una rivista.
revile [ri'vail] *vt* ingiuriare, insultare; *vi* inveire.
revise [ri'vaiz] *vt* rivedere, correggere.
revision [ri'viʒən] *n* revisione, correzione.
revival [ri'vaivəl] *n* rinascita, risveglio, riesumazione.
revive [ri'vaiv] *vt* far rivivere, risvegliare, riesumare; *vi* riprendere i sensi, ritornare in uso, in vita.
revoke [ri'vouk] *vt* revocare, ritirare.
revolt [ri'voult] *n* rivolta, insurrezione; senso di disgusto; *vt* rivoltare; *vi* ribellarsi, rivoltarsi; provar disgusto.
revolting [ri'voultiŋ] *a* disgusting.
revolution [,revə'lu:ʃən] *n* rivoluzione; giro.
revolutionary [,revə'lu:ʃnəri] *a n* rivoluzionario.
revolve [ri'vɔlv] *vt* rivolgere; meditare; *vi* girare.
revolver [ri'vɔlvə] *n* rivoltella, "revolver".
revue [ri'vju:] *n* (*theat*) rivista.
revulsion [ri'vʌlʃən] *n* revulsione, ripugnanza.
reward [ri'wɔ:d] *n* compenso, ricompensa; *vt* (ri)compensare.
Reynold ['renld] *nm pr* Rinaldo
rhapsody ['ræpsədi] *n* rapsodia.
rhetoric ['retərik] *n* retorica.
rhetorical [ri'tɔrikəl] *a* retorico.
rheumatic [ru:'mætik] *a* reumatico; **rheumatics** *n pl* reumatismi *pl*.
rheumatism ['ru:mætizəm] *n* reumatismo.
Rhine [rain] *n* Reno.
rhinoceros [rai'nɔsərəs] *n* rinoceronte.
Rhodes [roudz] *n* Rodi.
Rhodesia [rou'di:ziə] *n* Rodesia.
Rhodesian [rou'di:ziən] *a n* di Rodesia, della Rodesia.
rhododendron [,roudə'dendrən] *n* rododendro.
Rhone [roun] *n* Rodano.
rhubarb ['ru:bɑ:b] *n* rabarbaro.
rhyme, rime [raim] *n* rima; *vt* mettere in rima; *vi* rimare.
rhythm ['riðəm] *n* ritmo.
rhythmic(al) ['riðmik(əl)] *a* ritmico.
rib [rib] *n* costola; (*umbrella etc*) stecca.
ribald ['ribəld] *a* osceno, sboccato.
ribaldry ['ribəldri] *n* linguaggio osceno.
ribbon ['ribən] *n* nastro; **to tear to ribbons** stracciare, far a brandelli.
rice [rais] *n* riso.
rich [ritʃ] *a* ricco.
Richard ['ritʃəd] *nm pr* Riccardo.
riches ['ritʃiz] *n pl* ricchezza, -ze.
richly ['ritʃli] *ad* riccamente; ampiamente.
richness ['ritʃnis] *n* ricchezza, sontuo sità.
rick [rik] *n* (*of straw etc*) cumulo, mucchio.
rickets ['rikits] *n* rachitismo.
rickety ['rikiti] *a* rachitico; sgangherato, traballante.
rid [rid] *vt* liberare, sbarazzare.
riddance ['ridəns] *n* liberazione.
riddle ['ridl] *n* enigma, indovinello; crivello; vaglio; *vt* crivellare; vagliare; *vi* proporre indovinelli.
ride [raid] *n* cavalcata, galoppata, corsa; *vt* cavalcare, percorrere a cavallo; *vi* cavalcare, andare a cavallo; in bicicletta *etc*; (*naut*) essere all'ancora; (*fig*) opprimere.
rider ['raidə] *n* cavaliere, cavallerizzo; aggiunta, codicillo.
ridge [ridʒ] *n* (*of mountains*) cresta, spartiacque; (*agr*) porca.
ridicule ['ridikju:l] *n* ridicolo; *vt* mettere in ridicolo.
ridiculous [ri'dikjuləs] *a* ridicolo.
ridiculously [ri'dikjuləsli] *ad* ridicolamente; in modo assurdo.
riding ['raidiŋ] *n* cavalcata; equitazione; **r. school** scuola di equitazione, maneggio.
rife [raif] *a* comune; prevalente; rigoglioso.
riff-raff ['rifræf] *n* plebaglia.

rifle ['raifl] *n* fucile, carabina; **rifleman** fuciliere; *vt* derubare, vuotare.
rift [rift] *n* crepa, spaccatura.
rig [rig] *n* (*naut*) attrezzatura; (*fam*) abbigliamento; *vt* (*naut*) attrezzare.
right [rait] *a* giusto, retto, esatto; destro; corretto; *n* il giusto, il bene; il diritto; destra; *vt* correggere; (*rad*) drizzare; vendicare; *vi* raddrizzarsi; **to be r.** aver ragione; *ad* bene, direttamente; a destra; **r. away** immediatamente.
righteous ['raitʃəs] *a* retto, virtuoso.
rightful ['raitful] *a* legittimo, giusto.
rightly ['raitli] *ad* giustamente; esattamente.
rigid ['ridʒid] *a* rigido, inflessibile.
rigidity [ri'dʒiditi] *n* rigidezza, inflessibilità.
rigmarole ['rigməroul] *n* filastrocca.
rigor ['rigə] *n* rigore; intransigenza.
rigorous ['rigərəs] *a* rigido, rigoroso.
rill [ril] *n* ruscelletto.
rim [rim] *n* orlo, bordo, margine; (*wheel*) cerchione; (*spectacles*) montatura.
rind [raind] *n* buccia, corteccia; (*cheese, bread*) crosta.
ring [riŋ] *n* anello; cerchio; scampanellata; colpo di telefono; crocchio; (*boxing*) 'ring', quadrato; (*sport*) pista, recinto; *vt* accerchiare; suonare (il campanello); *vi* suonare, tintinnare; **to r. up** chiamare per telefono.
ringleader ['riŋˌli:də] *n* capo d'una sommossa.
ringlet ['riŋlit] *n* ricciolo.
rink [riŋk] *n* recinto per pattinaggio.
rinse [rins] *vt* risciacquare; *n* risciucquata.
riot ['raiət] *n* schiamazzo, tumulto, rivolta; *vi* tumultuare.
riotous ['raiətəs] *a* sedizioso, tumultuante; dissoluto.
rip [rip] *n* squarcio, strappo; persona dissoluta; *vt* squarciare, strappare; (*fam*) andare a tutta velocità.
ripe [raip] *a* maturo.
ripen ['raipən] *vti* maturare.
ripeness ['raipnis] *n* maturità.
ripple ['ripl] *n* increspatura, piccola onda; *vi* incresparsi.
rise [raiz] *n* (*sun*) levata; sorgere, ascesa, salita, aumento; *vi* alzarsi, levarsi, salire, sorgere, aumentare, insorgere.
risk [risk] *n* rischio; *vt* rischiare, mettere in pericolo.
risky ['riski] *a* arrischiato, rischioso.
rite [rait] *n* rito.
ritual ['ritjuəl] *a n* rituale.
rival ['raivəl] *a n* rivale; *vt* rivaleggiare.
rivalry ['raivəlri] *n* rivalità.
river ['rivə] *n* fiume.
rivet ['rivit] *n* chiodo, rivetto; *vt* inchiodare, ribadire, fissare.
rivulet ['rivjulit] *n* fiumicello.
roach [routʃ] *n* (*fish*) carpa; scarafaggio.
road [roud] *n* strada, via; (*naut*) rada; **r. detour** deviazione stradale; **r. haulier(s)** impresa autotrasporti.
roadhouse ['roudhaus] *n* albergo, locanda, trattoria sulla strada.
roadside ['roudsaid] *n* bordo della strada.
roam [roum] *vt* percorrere; *vi* girovagare, vagare.
roan [roun] *a n* roano.
roar [rɔ:] *n* mugghio, muggito; rombo; (*laughter, applause*) scroscio; *vti* mugghiare, ruggire; urlare.
roast [roust] *a n* arrosto; *vti* arrostir(si), (*coffee*) tostar(si).
rob [rɔb] *vt* (de)rubare, spogliare, svaligiare.
robber ['rɔbə] *n* ladro, rapinatore; ladrone.
robbery ['rɔbəri] *n* furto, rapina.
robe [roub] *n* lungo manto da cerimonie, toga; *vti* vestirsi.
Robert ['rɔbət] *nm pr* Roberto.
robin (redbreast) ['rɔbin('redbrest)] *n* pettirosso.
robot ['roubɔt] *n* 'robot', automa.
robust [rə'bʌst] *a* robusto, vigoroso.
rock [rɔk] *n* roccia, scoglio; rocca; *vti* cullar(si), dondolar(si).
rocket ['rɔkit] *n* razzo, missile; *vi* elevarsi come un razzo, (*of prices*) salire vertiginosamente.
rocking ['rɔkiŋ] *a* a dondolo, barcollante; **r. chair** sedia a dondolo.
rocky ['rɔki] *a* roccioso.
rod [rɔd] *n* bacchetta; verga; canna (da pesca), (*measure*) pertica.
rodent ['roudənt] *a n* roditore.
Roderick ['rɔdərik] *nm pr* Rodrigo.
roe [rou] *n* capriolo; (*fish*) uova di pesce.
Roger ['rɔdʒə] *nm pr* Ruggero.
rogue [roug] *n* briccone, furfante; birichino, bricconcello.
roguery ['rougəri] *n* furfanteria.
roguish ['rougiʃ] *a* furbo, malizioso.
roguishness ['rougiʃnis] *n* bricconeria; furberia, malizia.
roister ['rɔistə] *vi* far baccano.
Roland ['roulənd] *nm pr* Orlando.
role [roul] *n* ruolo.
roll [roul] *n* rotolo; rullo, elenco; (*naut*) rullio, (*thunder etc*) rombo; panino; *vt* avvolgere, rotolare; *vi* rotolare, ruzzolare, rullare; (*time*) scorrere.
roller ['roulə] *n* rullo, cilindro; (*sea*) maroso; **r. skates** pattini a rotelle.
rolling stock ['rouliŋstɔk] *n* (*rly*) materiale rotabile.
Roman ['roumən] *a n* romano.
romance [rə'mæns] *n* romanzo cavalleresco; (*mus*) romanza; romanticheria, idillio; *vi* romanzare; **R.** *a* romanzo.

Romanesque [ˌroumə'nesk] *a* romanico; *n* (*arch*) stile romanico.
romantic [rə'mæntik] *a* romantico; romanzesco.
romanticism [rə'mæntisizəm] *n* romanticismo.
Rome [roum] *n* Roma.
romp [rɔmp] *n* giuoco rumoroso; ragazza indiavolata; *vi* giocare rumorosamente.
Ronald ['rɔnld] *nm pr* Rinaldo.
roof [ru:f] *n* tetto; *vt* ricoprire con tetto, fare il tetto a.
rook [ruk] *n* cornacchia; (*chess*) torre.
room [rum] *n* camera, stanza; posto, spazio; possibilità.
roomy ['rumi] *a* spazioso, vasto.
roost [ru:st] *n* posatoio di uccelli; pollaio; *vi* appollaiarsi; (*fam*) andare a dormire.
rooster ['ru:stə] *n* gallo domestico.
root [ru:t] *n* radice; *vt* fissare saldamente; **to r. up** sradicare; *vi* radicarsi.
rope [roup] *n* corda, fune; (*pearls*) filo.
Rosalind ['rɔzəlind] *nf pr* Rosalinda.
rosary ['rouzəri] *n* rosario.
rose [rouz] *n* rosa.
rosemary ['rouzməri] *n* rosmarino.
rosy ['rouzi] *a* roseo.
rot [rɔt] *n* marciume, putrefazione; malattia delle pecore; (*sl*) sciocchezze; *vt* far marcire; *vi* imputridire, marcire.
rotate [rou'teit] *vti* (far) rotare; coltivare a rotazione.
rotation [rou'teiʃən] *n* rotazione, successione.
rote [rout] *n* memoria meccanica.
rotten ['rɔtn] *a* marcio, putrido; (*sl*) disgustoso; (*fig*) corrotto.
rotund [rou'tʌnd] *a* rotondo.
rotundity [rou'tʌnditi] *n* rotondità.
rouble ['ru:bl] *n* rublo.
rouge [ru:ʒ] *n* rossetto; *vt* imbellettare; *vi* mettersi il rossetto.
rough [rʌf] *a* (*ground*) accidentato; grossolano, rozzo, rude, ruvido; approssimativo; violento, (*sea*) agitato, (*weather*) tempestoso.
roughen ['rʌfən] *vti* irruvidir(si), diventare (rendere) rozzo.
roughly ['rʌfli] *ad* approssimativamente; ruvidamente, violentemente.
roughness ['rʌfnis] *n* rozzezza, ruvidezza; grossolanità, violenza.
Roumania [ru:'meiniə] *v* **Rumania.**
round [raund] *a* circolare, rotondo, tondo; *n* cerchio, sfera; (*tour*) giro; (*rung*) piolo; (*applause*) scoppio, ronda; *ad* all'intorno, in giro; *prep* intorno a; *vt* arrotondare; completare; girare; *vi* completarsi; **r.-up** raduno, accolta.
roundabout ['raundəbaut] *a* indiretto, tortuoso; *n* giostra.
roundly ['raundli] *ad* vigorosamente; chiaro e tondo.
rouse [rauz] *vt* destare, (ri)svegliare; incitare, provocare; *vi* svegliarsi.
rout [raut] *n* folla tumultuante, sommossa; (*mil*) rotta, sconfitta; *vt* (*mil*) mettere in rotta, sbaragliare; **to r. out** cacciar fuori, snidare.
route [ru:t] *n* via, rotta; (*mil*) (ordini di) marcia; **r. march** marcia d'allenamento.
routine [ru:'ti:n] *n* 'routine', pratica, abitudine meccanica.
rove [rouv] *vi* errare, vagabondare.
rover ['rouvə] *n* giramondo; (*scouts*) 'rover'; pirata.
row [rou] *n* (*fam*) baccano, lite rumorosa.
row [rau] *n* fila, filare; gita in barca a remi; *vt* far andare a forza di remi; *vi* remare, vogare.
rowdy ['raudi] *a* rumoroso, litigioso.
rowel ['rauəl] *n* stella di sperone.
royal ['rɔiəl] *a* reale, regale, regio; eccellente.
royalist ['rɔiəlist] *n* realista, monarchico.
royalty ['rɔiəlti] *n* regalità, sovranità; membro di famiglia reale; diritto d'autore.
rub [rʌb] *n* fregata, frizione; (*fig*) difficoltà, ostacolo; *vt* fregare, strofinare, lucidare; *vi* fregarsi, logorarsi.
rubber ['rʌbə] *n* gomma, caucciù; strofinaccio; (*cards*) partita tripla; *pl* soprascarpe di gomma.
rubbish ['rʌbiʃ] *n* rifiuti, scarti *pl*; cosa di nessun valore, sciocchezza.
rubble ['rʌbl] *n* pietrisco, frantumi di pietra.
Rubicon ['ru:bikən] *n pr* Rubicone.
rubric ['ru:brik] *n* rubrica.
ruby ['ru:bi] *n* rubino.
rudder ['rʌdə] *n* (*naut*) timone.
ruddy ['rʌdi] *a* rubicondo, vermiglio; rubizzo.
rude [ru:d] *a* rude, offensivo, sgarbato; vigoroso.
rudeness ['ru:dnis] *n* sgarbatezza, grossolanità.
rudiment ['ru:dimənt] *n* rudimento.
rudimental [ˌru:di'mentl] *a* rudimentale.
Rudolf, Rudolph ['ru:dɔlf] *n pr* Rodolfo.
rue [ru:] *n* (*bot*) ruta; *vt* pentirsi di.
rueful ['ru:ful] *a* lamentevole, triste.
ruff [rʌf] *n* gorgiera; (*of bird*) collare.
ruffian ['rʌfiən] *n* malfattore, ribaldo.
ruffle ['rʌfl] *n* guarnizione pieghettata; increspatura; *vt* arruffare, increspare; (*fig*) irritare.
rug [rʌg] *n* coperta (da viaggio); tappetino.
rugby ['rʌgbi] *n* (*sport*) 'rugby', pallaovale.
rugged ['rʌgid] *a* ruvido, scabro, irregolare; aspro, austero, inflessibile; vigoroso.
ruggedness ['rʌgidnis] *n* ruvidezza,

scabrosità, irregolarità; asprezza inflessibilità.
ruin ['ruin] *n* rovina, macerie, ruderi *pl*; *vt* rovinare.
ruinous ['ruinəs] *a* rovinoso; in rovina.
rule [ru:l] *n* regola, norma; regolo, riga; governo; *vt* dominare, governare, regolare; rigare; *vi* aver dominio.
ruler ['ru:lə] *n* sovrano, governatore; regolo, riga.
ruling ['ru:liŋ] *a* dominante, prevalente; *n* regolamento; governo; rigatura.
rum [rʌm] *n* rum.
Rumania [ru:'meiniə] *n* Romania.
Rumanian [ru:'meiniən] *a n* romeno.
rumble ['rʌmbl] *n* (*thunder etc*) rombo; brontolio; rumoreggiamento; *vi* brontolare; rumoreggiare.
ruminate ['ru:mineit] *vti* ruminare; meditare, rumiginare.
rumination [,ru:mi'neiʃən] *n* ruminazione.
rummage ['rʌmidʒ] *vti* frugare, rovistare.
rumor ['ru:mə] *n* diceria.
rump [rʌmp] *n* groppa, posteriore.
rumple ['rʌmpl] *vt* sgualcire; (*hair*) arruffare.
run [rʌn] *n* corsa, gita, giro; tragitto, corso; periodo, successione, serie; recinto di animali; *vt* far correre; condurre, gestire; *vi* correre; decorrere; scorrere; fuggire; diffondersi.
runaway ['rʌnəwei] *n* fuggiasco.
rung [rʌŋ] *n* piolo.
runner ['rʌnə] *n* corridore; messo; (*mil*) staffetta; passatoia; (*millstone*) macina; **r. bean** fagiolo rampicante; **r.-up** (*sport*) secondo arrivato.
runway ['rʌnwei] *n* pista di decollo, pista di lancio.
rupture ['rʌptʃə] *n* rottura; (*med*) ernia.
rural ['ruərəl] *a* rurale, campestre.
ruse [ru:z] *n* astuzia, stratagemma.
rush [rʌʃ] *n* giunco; afflusso, assalto, impeto; *vt* prendere d'assalto; *vi* affluire, precipitarsi.
rusk [rʌsk] *n* pane biscottato.
russet ['rʌsit] *a* color ruggine.
Russia ['rʌʃə] *n* Russia.
Russian ['rʌʃən] *a n* russo.
rust [rʌst] *n* ruggine; *vt* corrodere; *vi* arrugginire.
rustic ['rʌstik] *a* rustico, grezzo.
rusticate ['rʌstikeit] *vt* sospendere (studenti universitari); *vi* vivere in campagna.
rustle ['rʌsl] *n* fruscio, stormire; *vti* (far) frusciare, (far) stormire.
rusty ['rʌsti] *a* arrugginito, rugginoso.
rut [rʌt] *n* (*groove*) solco; (*fig*) abitudine inveterata; (*of animals*) fregola; *vt* solcare; *vi* essere in fregola, in calore.
ruthless ['ru:θlis] *a* spietato.
rye [rai] *n* segale.

S

Sabbath ['sæbəθ] *n* (*Jewish*) sabato, (*Christian*) domenica.
saber ['seibə] *n* sciabola.
sable ['seibl] *a* di zibellino; *n* zibellino.
sabotage ['sæbətɑ:ʒ] *n* sabotaggio; *vt* sabotare.
saccharine ['sækərin] *n* saccarina.
sack [sæk] *n* sacco; saccheggio; (*sl*) licenziamento; *vt* insaccare; saccheggiare; (*sl*) licenziare.
sacking ['sækiŋ] *n* tela da sacchi.
sacrament ['sækrəmənt] *n* sacramento.
sacred ['seikrid] *a* sacro, consacrato.
sacrifice ['sækrifais] *n* sacrificio; *vt* sacrificare.
sacrilege ['sækrilidʒ] *n* sacrilegio.
sacristan ['sækristən] *n* sagrestano.
sacristy ['sækristi] *n* sagrestia.
sad [sæd] *a* triste, doloroso, funesto.
sadden ['sædn] *vt* rattristare.
saddle ['sædl] *n* sella; *vt* sellare; (*fig*) addossare, gravare.
sadistic [sə'distik] *a* sadico.
sadness ['sædnis] *n* tristezza.
safe [seif] *a* sano, salvo, sicuro, intatto, al sicuro, cauto; *n* cassaforte; (*arms*) sicura.
safe conduct ['seif'kɔndəkt] *n* salvacondotto.
safeguard ['seifgɑ:d] *n* salvaguardia, difesa.
safety ['seifti] *n* sicurezza, salvezza; **s. belt** cintura di sicurezza; **s. pin** spilla di sicurezza; **s. island** salvagente (stradale).
saffron ['sæfrən] *n* zafferano.
sag [sæg] *vi* curvarsi, piegarsi, (*of prices*) cedere.
saga ['sɑ:gə] *n* saga; romanzo fiume.
sagacious [sə'geiʃəs] *a* sagace.
sagacity [sə'gæsiti] *n* sagacia, perspicacia.
sage [seidʒ] *a n* saggio; *n* salvia.
sageness ['seidʒnis] *n* saggezza.
sail [seil] *n* vela, gita o viaggio su imbarcazione a vela; *vti* navigare, veleggiare, salpare, sorvolare.
sailer ['seilə] *n* veliero.
sailor ['seilə] *n* marinaio.
saint [seint] *a n* santo (*abbr* St).
saintly ['seintli] *a* santo.
sake [seik] *n* amore, causa, motivo.
salacious [sə'leiʃəs] *a* salace.
salad ['sæləd] *n* insalata.
salamander ['sælə,mændə] *n* salamandra.
salary ['sæləri] *n* stipendio.
sale [seil] *n* vendita; svendita.
saleable ['seiləbl] *a* smerciabile, vendibile.
salesman ['seilzmən] *n* venditore, viaggiatore commesso, piazzista.
salient ['seiliənt] *a n* saliente.
saliva [sə'laivə] *n* saliva; **salivary** *a* salivare.

sallow ['sælou] *a* olivastro; *n* salice.
sally ['sæli] *n* sortita; battuta spiritosa; *vi* balzar fuori, fare una sortita.
salmon ['sæmən] *n* salmone.
salon ['sælɔ̃:ŋ] *n* salone; galleria d'arte.
saloon [sə'lu:n] *n* sala da ricevimenti; bar; **s. keeper** oste, proprietario di bar.
salt [sɔ:lt] *a* amaro, salato, salso; *n* sale; *vt* salare; **s.-cellar** saliera; **s. water** acqua salsa, acqua di mari.
saltiness ['sɔ:ltnis] *n* gusto di sale.
saltpeter ['sɔ:lt,pi:tə] *n* salnitro.
salty ['sɔ:lti] *a* salato, salmastro; piccante.
salutary ['sæljutəri] *a* salutare.
salutation [,sælju:'teiʃən] *n* saluto.
salute [sə'lu:t] *n* saluto; (*mil*) salva; *vt* salutare.
salvage ['sælvidʒ] *n* salvataggio, ricupero; *vt* salvare.
salvation [sæl'veiʃən] *n* salvezza.
salver ['sælvə] *n* vassoio.
salvo ['sælvou] *pl* **salvoes** *n* (*mil*) salva.
same [seim] *a pron* medesimo, stesso.
sameness ['seimnis] *n* identità, uniformità.
sample ['sɑ:mpl] *n* campione, modello, esemplare; **samples** *pl* campionario; *vt* assaggiare.
sanatorium [,sænə'tɔ:riəm] *n* sanatorio.
sanctify ['sæŋktifai] *vt* santificare.
sanctimonious [,sæŋkti'mouniəs] *a* santarello, bigotto, ipocrita.
sanction ['sæŋkʃən] *n* sanzione; *vt* autorizzare, ratificare, sanzionare.
sanctity ['sæŋktiti] *n* santità.
sanctuary ['sæŋktjuəri] *n* santuario, asilo.
sand [sænd] *n* sabbia, rena; **sandbank** banco di sabbia; **sandhill** duna; **sandpaper** cartavetrata.
sandal ['sændl] *n* sandalo.
sandwich ['sænwidʒ] *n* 'sandwich', panino ripieno; **open s.** tartina.
sandy ['sændi] *a* sabbioso; (*color*) giallo-rossastro.
sane [sein] *a* sano di mente, equilibrato.
sanguinary ['sæŋgwinəri] *a* sanguinario.
sanguine ['sæŋgwin] *a* sanguigno, rubicondo; ottimista.
sanitary ['sænitəri] *a* igienico, sanitario.
sanitation [,sæni'teiʃən] *n* igiene.
sanity ['sæniti] *n* sanità di mente.
Santa Claus [,sæntə'klɔ:z] *nm pr* Babbo Natale.
sap [sæp] *n* linfa, succo; (*mil*) scavo d'approccio, trincea; *vt* minare (*also fig*).
sapling ['sæpliŋ] *n* alberello.
sapper ['sæpə] *n* zappatore; (*mil*) geniere, genio.
sapphire ['sæfaiə] *n* zaffiro.
sappy ['sæpi] *a* ricco di linfa, succoso.
Saracen ['særəsn] *a n* saraceno.
Sarah ['sɛərə] *nf pr* Sara.
sarcasm ['sɑ:kæzəm] *n* sarcasmo.
sarcastic [sɑ:'kæstik] *a* sarcastico.
sardine [sɑ:'di:n] *n* sardina.
Sardinia [sɑ:'diniə] *n* Sardegna.
Sardinian [sɑ:'diniən] *a n* sardo.
sardonic [sɑ:'dɔnik] *a* sardonico.
sash [sæʃ] *n* cintura, sciarpa; telaio scorrevole di finestra.
Satan ['seitən] *nm pr* Satana.
satchel ['sætʃəl] *n* cartella di scolaro.
sate [seit] *vt* satollare, saziare.
satellite ['sætəlait] *a n* satellite.
satiate ['seiʃieit] *vt* saziare.
satiation [,seiti'eiʃən] **satiety** [sə'taiəti] *n* sazietà.
satin ['sætin] *n* raso.
satire ['sætaiə] *n* satira.
satiric(al) [sə'tirik(əl)] *a* satirico.
satirist ['sætərist] *n* scrittore satirico.
satirize ['sætəraiz] *vt* satireggiare.
satisfaction [,sætis'fækʃən] *n* soddisfazione.
satisfactorily [,sætis'fæktərili] *ad* soddisfacentemente.
satisfactory [,sætis'fæktəri] *a* soddisfacente.
satisfy ['sætisfai] *vt* soddisfare; convincere, persuadere.
saturate ['sætʃəreit] *vt* saturare.
saturation [,sætʃə'reiʃən] *n* saturazione.
Saturday ['sætədi] *n* sabato.
saturnine ['sætə:nain] *a* cupo, taciturno, tetro.
sauce [sɔ:s] *n* intingolo, salsa; (*fig*) impertinenza.
saucepan ['sɔ:spən] *n* casseruola.
saucer ['sɔ:sə] *n* piattino, sottocoppa.
sauciness ['sɔ:sinis] *n* impertinenza.
saucy ['sɔ:si] *a* impertinente.
saunter ['sɔ:ntə] *vi* andare a zonzo.
sausage ['sɔsidʒ] *n* salsiccia, salame.
sauté ['soutei] *a* (*cook*) saltato in padella, fritto.
savage ['sævidʒ] *a n* selvaggio; *a* barbaro, brutale.
savageness ['sævidʒnis] **savagery** ['sævidʒəri] *n* brutalità, ferocia.
save [seiv] *prep* ad eccezione di, salvo; *vt* salvare, conservare, economizzare, risparmiare; *vi* fare economie.
saving ['seiviŋ] *a* economico; *n* risparmio, economia.
savior ['seivjə] *n* salvatore, redentore.
savor ['seivə] *n* gusto, sapore; *vi* sapere di, aver il gusto; *vt* assaporare, gustare; insaporire.
savory ['seivəri] *a* saporito, piccante; *n* salatino.
Savoy [sə'voi] *n* Savoia.
Savoyard [sə'vɔiɑ:d] *a n* savoiardo.
saw [sɔ:] *n* sega; massima, proverbio; *vt* segare.
sawdust ['sɔ:dʌst] *n* segatura.
sawmill ['sɔ:mil] *n* segheria.

sawyer ['sɔ:jə] *n* segatore.
Saxon ['sæksn] *a n* sassone.
Saxony ['sæksni] *n* Sassonia.
saxophone ['sæksəfoun] *n* sassofono.
say [sei] *vti* dire, affermare, asserire.
saying ['seiiŋ] *n* massima, proverbio.
scab [skæb] *n* crosta, scabbia; crumiro.
scabbard ['skæbəd] *n* fodero, guaina.
scabby ['skæbi] *a* pieno di croste, scabbioso.
scaffold ['skæfəld] *n* patibolo.
scaffolding ['skæfəldiŋ] *n* impalcatura, intelaiatura.
scald [skɔ:ld] *n* scottatura; *vt* scottare, ustionare.
scalding ['skɔ:ldiŋ] *a* bollente, scottante; *n* scottatura.
scale [skeil] *n* gradazione, scala; scaglia, squama; bilancia; *vti* scalare, graduare; *vi* squamarsi.
scalp [skælp] *n* cuoio capelluto; *vt* scotennare.
scalpel ['skælpəl] *n* (*med*) scalpello.
scaly ['skeili] *a* squamoso, coperto di incrostazioni.
scamp [skæmp] *n* birichino, mascalzoncello.
scamper ['skæmpə] *vi* correre; **s. away** svignarsela.
scan [skæn] *vt* scandire; scrutare attentamente; *vi* (*verse*) essere corretto.
scandal ['skændl] *n* scandalo.
scandalize ['skændəlaiz] *vt* scandalizzare.
scandalous ['skændələs] *a* scandaloso.
Scandinavia [,skændi'neiviə] *n* Scandinavia.
Scandinavian [,skændi'neiviən] *a n* scandinavo.
scansion ['skænʃən] *n* scansione.
scant [skænt] *a* esiguo, insufficiente, scarso.
scantiness ['skæntinis] *n* esiguità, scarsezza.
scanty ['skænti] *a* limitato, ristretto, scarso.
scapegoat ['skeipgout] *n* capro espiatorio.
scapegrace ['skeipgreis] *n* scapestrato.
scapular(y) ['skæpjulər(i)] *n* scapolare.
scar [skɑ:] *n* cicatrice, segno.
scarce [skɛəs] *a* scarso, raro.
scarcely ['skɛəsli] *ad* appena, a mala pena, a stento.
scarcity ['skɛəsiti] *n* scarsezza, penuria.
scare [skɛə] *n* panico, spavento; *vt* spaventare.
scarecrow ['skɛəkrou] *n* spauracchio, spaventapasseri.
scarf [skɑ:f] *n* sciarpa.
scarlet ['skɑ:lit] *a n* rosso scarlatto.
scathing ['skeiðiŋ] *a* sarcastico, mordace.
scatter ['skætə] *vti* sparger(si).
scavenger ['skævindʒə] *n* spazzino.
scene [si:n] *n* scena; scenata; spettacolo; **behind the scenes** dietro la scena; **to make a s.** fare una scenata; **the s. of the battle** il teatro del combattimento.
scenery ['si:nəri] *n* scenario, veduta, panorama, paesaggio.
scenic ['si:nik] *a* scenico, teatrale.
scent [sent] *n* odore, profumo; fiuto; *vt* fiutare; profumare.
scepter ['septə] *n* scettro.
schedule ['skedju:l] *n* inventario, lista; orario, programma.
scheme [ski:m] *n* piano, progetto; *vt* progettare; *vi* fare progetti, intrigare.
schism ['sizəm] *n* scisma.
schismatic [siz'mætik] *a n* scismatico.
schizophrenic [,skitsou'frenik] *a n* schizofrenico.
scholar ['skɔlə] *n* erudito, studioso, studente detentore d'una borsa di studio.
scholarly ['skɔləli] *a* dotto, erudito.
scholarship ['skɔləʃip] *n* dottrina, erudizione; borsa di studio.
scholastic [skə'læstik] *a n* scolastico.
school [sku:l] *n* scuola; *vt* disciplinare, domare; **schoolhouse** scuola.
schooling ['sku:liŋ] *n* insegnamento, istruzione.
schoolmaster ['sku:l mɑ:stə] *n* insegnante, maestro, professore.
schoolroom ['sku:lrum] *n* aula scolastica.
schooner ['sku:nə] *n* (*naut*) goletta.
sciatica [sai'ætikə] *n* sciatica.
science ['saiəns] *n* scienza; **s. fiction** fantascienza.
scientific [,saiən'tifik] *a* scientifico.
scientist ['saiəntist] *n* scienziato.
scimitar ['simitə] *n* scimitarra.
scintillate ['sintileit] *vt* scintillare, brillare.
scion ['saiən] *n* (*plants*) pollone; (*fig*) erede, rampollo.
scissors ['sizəz] *n pl* forbici *pl*.
scoff [skɔf] *vti* **s. at** beffare, deridere.
scold [skould] *n* donna bisbetica; *vti* rimproverare, sgridare.
scone [skɔn] *n* pastina da tè.
scoop [sku:p] *n* paletta, ramaiuolo; (*fig, press*) notizia, servizio in esclusiva; *vt* vuotare; (*press*) accaparrarsi una notizia; **to s. up** raccogliere con la pala.
scooter ['sku:tə] *n* monopattino; 'scooter', motoretta.
scope [skoup] *n* portata, campo d'azione, prospettiva.
scorch [skɔ:tʃ] *n* scottatura; *vt* scottare.
score [skɔ:] *n* ventina; punto; punteggio; numero di punti; conto; scotto; tacca; (*mus*) spartito; *vt* intaccare, marcare, segnare; segnare punti, mettere in conto; (*mus*) orche-

strare; *vi* assicurarsi un vantaggio, aver fortuna.
scorn [skɔ:n] *n* disprezzo, sdegno; *vt* disprezzare.
scornful ['skɔ:nful] *a* sdegnoso.
scornfully ['skɔ:nfuli] *ad* sprezzantemente, sdegnosamente.
scorpion ['skɔ:piən] *n* scorpione.
Scot [skɔt] *n* scozzese.
Scotch [skɔtʃ] **Scottish** ['skɔtiʃ] *a* scozzese.
Scotland ['skɔtlənd] *n* Scozia.
Scots [skɔts] *a* scozzese.
Scotsman [skɔtsmən] *n* scozzese.
scoundrel ['skaundrəl] *n* farabutto, mascalzone.
scour ['skauə] *vt* pulire fregando; perlustrare.
scourge [skə:dʒ] *n* frusta, sferza; *vt* fustigare, sferzare.
scout [skaut] *n* esploratore, vedetta; *vt* respingere con sdegno; *vi* esplorare.
scowl [skaul] *n* sguardo torvo; *vi* guardare torvo.
scrabble ['skræbl] *vi* frugare affannosamente.
scraggy ['skrægi] *a* ossuto, scarno.
scramble ['skræmbl] *n* parapiglia, lotta, confusione; *vi* affrettarsi, arrampicarsi con mani e piedi; *vt* arraffare, (*eggs*) strapazzare.
scrap [skræp] *n* frammento, pezzetto; rottame; *vt* scartare; **scrapbook** album di ritagli.
scrape [skreip] *n* raschiatura, graffio; (*fam*) impiccio, situazione difficile; *vt* raschiare, scrostare, sfregare; **to s. through** cavarsela.
scraper ['skreipə] *n* raschietto; (*mat*) pulisciscarpe.
scrapings ['skreipiŋz] *n pl* risparmi.
scrappy ['skræpi] *a* frammentario.
scratch [skrætʃ] *a* male assortito, eterogeneo; *n* graffio; linea di partenza; *vti* graffiare, grattare, raspare; **to start from s.** partire da zero; **to come up to s.** (*fig*) farsi onore; **s. pad** blocco per note, nòtes.
scratchy ['skrætʃi] *a* scarabocchiato; scricchiolante.
scrawl [skrɔ:l] *n* scarabocchio; *vti* scarabocchiare.
scream [skri:m] *n* strillo, urlo; *vi* strillare, urlare.
screech [skri:tʃ] *n* strillo acuto; *vi* strillare.
screed [skri:d] *n* lunga filastrocca.
screen [skri:n] *n* parafuoco, paravento; difesa, riparo; (*cin, TV*) schermo; *vt* proteggere, riparare; proiettare.
screw [skru:] *n* vite; (*sl*) strozzino; (*naut*) elica; *vt* torcere; *vti* avvitare; (*fig*) opprimere.
screwdriver ['skru:ˌdraivə] *n* cacciavite.
scribble ['skribl] *n* scarabocchio; *vti* scarabocchiare; **scribbling block** blocco per note, nòtes.
scribbler ['skriblə] *n* imbrattacarte.
scribe [skraib] *n* copista, scriba.
scrimmage ['skrimidʒ] *n* schermaglia.
script [skript] *n* scrittura; (*typ*) corsivo; (*theat etc*) copione, sceneggiatura.
scripture ['skriptʃə] *n* sacra scrittura.
scroll [skroul] *n* pergamena; rotolo di carta; svolazzo; (*arch*) voluta.
scrub [skrʌb] *n* sottobosco, macchia; *vti* strofinare energicamente.
scruff [skrʌf] *n* (*of the neck*) collottola.
scruple ['skru:pl] *n* scrupolo; *vi* esitare, farsi scrupolo di.
scrupulosity [ˌskru:pju'lɔsiti] *n* scrupolosità.
scrupulous ['skru:pjuləs] *a* scrupoloso.
scrutinize ['skru:tinaiz] *vt* scrutinare.
scrutiny ['skru:tini] *n* esame minuzioso, scrutinio.
scud [skʌd] *n* fuga, rapida corsa; *vi* correre velocemente.
scuffle ['skʌfl] *n* baruffa, parapiglia; *vi* azzuffarsi.
scull [skʌl] *n* remo; *vti* vogare con remi corti.
scullery ['skʌləri] *n* retrocucina.
sculptor ['skʌlptə] *n* scultore.
sculptural ['skʌlptʃərəl] *a* di scultura, scultorio.
sculpture ['skʌlptʃə] *n* scultura; *vt* scolpire.
scum [skʌm] *n* schiuma, (*also fig*) feccia, scoria.
scurf [skə:f] *n* forfora.
scurrility [skʌ'riliti] *n* scurrilità.
scurrilous ['skʌriləs] *a* scurrile.
scurry ['skʌri] *n* corsa frettolosa; *vi* correre, affrettarsi.
scurvy ['skə:vi] *a* basso, vile; *n* scorbuto.
scuttle ['skʌtl] *n* recipiente per il carbone; fuga precipitosa; (*naut*) portello; *vt* (*naut*) affondare; *vi* svignarsela.
scythe [saið] *n* falce.
sea [si:] *n* mare; **s. level** livello del mare; **s. power** potenza navale; **s. shell** conchiglia; **s. voyage** viaggio per mare.
seafarer ['si:ˌfɛərə] *n* navigatore.
seal [si:l] *n* sigillo, suggello, timbro; (*zool*) foca; *vt* bollare, sigillare, suggellare.
sealing wax ['si:liŋwæks] *n* ceralacca.
seam [si:m] *n* costura, cucitura; cicatrice; (*geol*) giacimento.
seaman ['si:mən] *n* marinaio.
seamstress ['semstris] *n* cucitrice.
seaplane ['si:plein] *n* idrovolante.
seaport ['si:pɔ:t] *n* porto di mare.
sear [siə] *vt* bruciare, cauterizzare, disseccare; (*fig*) indurire.
search [sə:tʃ] *n* ricerca, indagine, inchiesta; perquisizione; *vt* per-

quisire; *vi* cercare, fare ricerche, perlustrare.
searching ['sə:tʃiŋ] *a* indagatore, penetrante, minuzioso.
searchlight ['sə:tʃlait] *n* riflettore.
seaside ['si:'said] *n* spiaggia, mare; **s. resort** stazione balneare.
season ['si:zn] *n* stagione; epoca; tempo; *vt* condire; stagionare; acclimatare; *vi* divenire stagionato.
seasonable ['si:znəbl] *a* di stagione; tempestivo.
seasoning ['si:zniŋ] *n* condimento; stagionatura.
seat [si:t] *n* posto (a sedere), panca, sedia, sedile, seggio; sede; residenza; sedere, deretano; *vt* far sedere, offrire posti a sedere a; **four-seater** (*aut*) automobile a quattro posti.
seaweed ['si:wi:d] *n* alga.
Sebastian [si'bæstiən] *nm pr* Sebastiano.
secede [si'si:d] *vi* separarsi.
secession [si'seʃən] *n* secessione, separazione.
secluded [si'klu:did] *a* ritirato, appartato.
seclusion [si'klu:ʒən] *n* ritiro, solitudine, reclusione.
second ['sekənd] *a n* secondo; *vt* appoggiare, assecondare; **s.-hand** di seconda mano.
secondary ['sekəndəri] *a* secondario, subordinato.
secrecy ['si:krisi] *n* segretezza.
secret ['si:krit] *a n* segreto.
secretary ['sekrətri] *n* segretario, -a.
secrete [si'kri:t] *vt* secernere; nascondere.
secretion [si'kri:ʃən] *n* secrezione.
secretive ['si:kritiv] *a* riservato, poco comunicativo.
sect [sekt] *n* setta.
sectarian [sek'tɛəriən] *a n* settario.
section ['sekʃən] *n* sezione, paragrafo; parte.
sector ['sektə] *n* settore.
secular ['sekjulə] *a n* secolare.
secularization ['sekjulərai'zeiʃən] *n* secolarizzazione.
secularize ['sekjuləraiz] *vt* secolarizzare.
secure [si'kjuə] *a* sicuro, al sicuro, fiducioso, tranquillo; *vt* assicurare, garantire; procurarsi.
security [si'kjuəriti] *n* sicurezza, garanzia.
sedan [si'dæn] *n* portantina.
sedate [si'deit] *a* calmo, pacato.
sedateness [si'deitnis] *n* calma, pacatezza.
sedative ['sedətiv] *a n* sedativo, calmante.
sedentary ['sedntəri] *a n* sedentario.
sedge [sedʒ] *n* carice.
sediment ['sedimənt] *n* sedimento.
sedition [si'diʃən] *n* sedizione.
seditious [si'diʃəs] *a* sedizioso.
seduce [si'dju:s] *vt* sedurre.
seduction [si'dʌkʃən] *n* seduzione.
sedulous ['sedjuləs] *a* assiduo, diligente.
see [si:] *n* diocesi, sede; *vti* vedere; capire; visitare.
seed [si:d] *n* seme, semenza; *vi* produrre semi.
seedling ['si:dliŋ] *n* pianticella, alberello.
seedy ['si:di] *a* pieno di semi: (*fig*) male in arnese, indisposto.
seek [si:k] *vti* cercare, perseguire.
seem [si:m] *vi* sembrare, parere.
seeming ['si:miŋ] *a* apparente.
seemly ['si:mli] *a* di bell'aspetto, decoroso.
seep [si:p] *vi* filtrare, penetrare.
seer ['si:ə] *n* veggente, profeta.
seesaw ['si:sɔ:] *n* altalena.
seethe [si:ð] *vi* bollire; essere in fermento.
segment ['segmənt] *n* segmento.
segregate ['segrigeit] *vti* segregar(si).
segregation [,segri'geiʃən] *n* segregazione.
Seine [sein] *n* Senna.
seize [si:z] *vt* afferrare, impadronirsi di, confiscare, sequestrare.
seizure ['si:ʒə] *n* presa, confisca; (*med*) attacco.
seldom ['seldəm] *ad* di rado, raramente.
select [si'lekt] *a* scelto; *vt* scegliere, selezionare.
selection [si'lekʃən] *n* assortimento, scelta, selezione.
self [self] *n* l'io, l'individuo, se stesso.
self-command ['selfkə'mɑ:nd] *n* padronanza di sè.
self-conceit ['selfkən'si:t] *n* presunzione.
self-confidence ['self'kɔnfidəns] *n* sicurezza di sè.
self-conscious ['self'kɔnʃəs] *a* impacciato; (*phil*) autocosciente.
self-contained ['selfkən'teind] *a* riservato; autonomo, indipendente.
self-control ['selfkən'troul] *n* padronanza di sè.
self-defense ['selfdi'fens] *n* autodifesa.
self-denial ['selfdi'naiəl] *n* abnegazione.
self-government ['self'gʌvnmənt] *n* autonomia.
selfish ['selfiʃ] *a* egoista, egoistico.
selfishness ['selfiʃnis] *n* egoismo.
selfless ['selflis] *a* altruistico, disinteressato.
self-made ['self'meid] *a* che deve tutto a se stesso, che si è fatto da sè.
self-reliance ['selfri'laiəns] *n* fiducia in sè.
self-supporting ['selfsə'pɔ:tiŋ] *a* indipendente.
self-service ['self'sə:vis] *a n* 'self service', (di) locale in cui ci si serve da sè.
self-taught ['self'tɔ:t] *a* autodidatta.
sell [sel] *vt* vendere; *vi* trovare smercio, vendersi.

semaphore ['seməfɔ:] *n* semaforo.
semblance ['sembləns] *n* aspetto, apparenza; parvenza; somiglianza.
semicircle ['semi,sə:kl] *n* semicerchio.
seminar ['seminɑ:] *n* (*university*) seminario.
seminary ['seminəri] *n* seminario.
semolina [semə'li:nə] *n* semolino.
senate ['senit] *n* senato.
senator ['senətə] *n* senatore.
send [send] *vt* mandare, inviare, spedire; **to s. for** mandare a chiamare; **sender** mittente, speditore.
senile ['si:nail] *a* senile.
senility [si'niliti] *n* senilità.
senior ['si:niə] *a n* maggiore, più anziano, seniore, decano.
seniority [,si:ni'ɔriti] *n* anzianità.
sensation [sen'seiʃən] *n* sensazione, scalpore.
sensational [sen'seiʃənl] *a* sensazionale.
sense [sens] *n* senso; conoscenza; buon senso; significato.
senseless ['senslis] *a* inanime; assurdo, senza significato.
sensibility [,sensi'biliti] *n* sensibilità.
sensible ['sensəbl] *a* sensato, ragionevole, cosciente.
sensitive ['sensitiv] *a* sensibile, sensitivo, suscettibile.
sensitiveness ['sensitivnis] **sensitivity** [,sensi'tiviti] *n* sensibilità, suscettibilità.
sensorial [sen'sɔ:riəl] *a* sensorio.
sensual ['sensjuəl] *a* sensuale, voluttuoso.
sensuality [,sensju'æliti] *n* sensualità, voluttà.
sensuous ['sensjuəs] *a* dei sensi, sensitivo.
sentence ['sentəns] *n* sentenza, condanna; frase, periodo; massima; *vt* condannare.
sentiment ['sentimənt] *n* sentimento, idea; sentimentalità.
sentimental [,senti'mentl] *a* sentimentale.
sentinel ['sentinl] **sentry** ['sentri] *n* (*mil*) sentinella.
sentry-box ['sentribɔks] *n* garitta.
separate ['sepəreit] *vti* divider(si), separar(si); ['sepərit] *a* separato, distinto.
separately ['sepəritli] *ad* separatamente, singolarmente.
separation [,sepə'reiʃən] *n* separazione.
sepia ['si:piə] *n* seppia; color seppia.
September [səp'tembə] *n* settembre.
septic ['septik] *a* settico.
sepulcher ['sepəlkə] *n* sepolcro; **whited s.** sepolcro imbiancato, ipocrita.
sepulchral [si'pʌlkrəl] *a* sepolcrale.
sequel ['si:kwəl] *n* seguito.
sequence ['si:kwəns] *n* serie, successione.
sequestered [si'kwestəd] *a* remoto, solitario.
sequestrate [si'kwestreit] *vt* sequestrare.
sequestration [,si:kwes'treiʃən] *n* sequestro.
serenade [,seri'neid] *n* serenata.
serene [si'ri:n] *a* calmo, sereno.
serenity [si'reniti] *n* serenità.
serf [sə:f] *n* servo della gleba.
serge [sə:dʒ] *n* 'serge', saia.
sergeant ['sɑ:dʒənt] *n* sergente.
serial ['siəriəl] *a* periodico, a puntate; *n* romanzo a puntate, pubblicazione periodica.
series ['siəri:z] *n* serie.
serious ['siəriəs] *a* serio, grave.
seriously ['siəriəsli] *ad* seriamente, sul serio; gravemente.
seriousness ['siəriəsnis] *n* serietà, gravità.
sermon ['sə:mən] *n* predica, sermone, (*fam*) predicozzo.
serpent ['sə:pənt] *n* serpente.
serrated [se'reitid] *a* dentellato, seghettato.
servant ['sə:vənt] *n* domestico, -ca, servitore, servo, -va; funzionario.
serve [sə:v] *vti* servire.
service ['sə:vis] *n* servizio; ufficio (divino), funzione (religiosa), **s. flats** appartamenti d'affitto con servizio; **s. lift** montavivande.
serviceable ['sə:visəbl] *a* utile, pratico.
serviette [,sə:vi'et] *n* tovagliolo.
servile ['sə:vail] *a* servile, abbietto.
servility [sə:'viliti] *n* servilità.
servitude ['sə:vitju:d] *n* servitù, schiavitù.
session ['seʃən] *n* sessione.
set [set] *a* fisso, stabilito, ostinato; *n* collezione, serie, servizio; cricca, crocchio; partita, gioco; (*rad*) apparecchio; (*teeth*) dentiera; *vt* disporre, mettere; fissare; montare; regolare; (*type*) comporre; *vi* applicarsi; disporsi, mettersi; solidificarsi; tramontare; **set up** sistemazione, situazione, stato di cose.
settee [se'ti:] *n* divano.
setter ['setə] *n* cane da ferma.
setting ['setiŋ] *n* montaggio; messa in scena; solidificazione; (*gem*) montatura; (*typ*) composizione; **hair s.** messa in piega.
settle ['setl] *vt* accomodare, fissare, stabilire, sistemare; calmare; pagare, saldare; *vi* fissarsi, sistemarsi, stabilirsi.
settlement ['setlmənt] *n* contratto, accordo, sistemazione; saldo; colonia, colonizzazione.
settler ['setlə] *n* colonizzatore, colono.
seven ['sevn] *a n* sette; **seventh** *a* settimo.
seventeen ['sevn'ti:n] *a n* diciassette; **seventeenth** *a* diciassettesimo.
seventy ['sevnti] *a n* settanta; **seventieth** *a* settantesimo.

sever ['sevə] *vti* staccar(si), separar (si).
several ['sevrəl] *a* diverso, separato; *a pron pl* parecchi(e) *pl.*
severance ['sevərəns] *n* distacco, separazione.
severe [si'viə] *a* severo, austero; rigido; violento.
severity [si'veriti] *n* severità; rigore.
Seville ['sevil] *n* Siviglia.
sew [sou] *vti* cucire.
sewage ['sju:idʒ] *n* acque di scolo *pl.*
sewer ['sjuə] *n* conduttura, fogna.
sex [seks] *n* sesso.
sexton ['sekstən] *n* sagrestano; becchino.
sexual ['seksjuəl] *a* sessuale.
shabbiness ['ʃæbinis] *n* l'essere male in arnese; grettezza.
shabby ['ʃæbi] *a* male in arnese; gretto.
shackle ['ʃækl] *n* anello di metallo; *vt* mettere in ceppi; (*fig*) ostacolare; **shackles** *pl* **ceppi**, manette, ferri *pl.*
shade [ʃeid] *n* ombra; paralume; riparo dalla luce; sfumatura; tinta; *vt* adombrare; ombreggiare; proteggere, riparare; sfumare.
shading ['ʃeidiŋ] *n* ombreggiatura, sfumatura.
shadow ['ʃædou] *n* ombra; fantasma; *vt* seguire come un'ombra.
shadowy ['ʃædoui] *a* ombroso;, indistinto.
shady ['ʃeidi] *a* fresco, ombreggiato; (*fig*) equivoco, losco.
shaft [ʃɑ:ft] *n* lancia; fusto; freccia, strale; (*light*) raggio; manico; (*mine*) pozzo.
shag [ʃæg] *n* tabacco forte; cormorano crestato.
shaggy ['ʃægi] *a* irsuto, ispido, peloso.
shagreen [ʃæ'gri:n] *n* zigrino.
shake [ʃeik] *n* scossa, urto, tremore; (*mus*) trillo; *vt* scuotere, scrollare; turbare; *vi* tremare, vacillare, agitarsi; (*mus*) trillare; **milk s.** frappè.
shaky ['ʃeiki] *a* tremolante, vacillante; malsicuro; debole; precario.
shale [ʃeil] *n* argilla schistosa; **s. oil** olio minerale, olio di schisto.
shallow ['ʃælou] *a* basso, poco profondo; (*fig*) superficiale; *n* bassofondo, secca.
shallowness ['ʃælounis] *n* poca profondità, superficialità.
sham [ʃæm] *a* finto, simulato; *n* finta, inganno, impostura; *vti* fingere, simulare.
shamble ['ʃæmbl] *vi* avere, camminare con, una andatura goffa o strascicante.
shambles ['ʃæmblz] *n* carneficina, macello, disordine, confusione.
shame [ʃeim] *n* vergogna, obbrobrio, onta; *vt* svergognare, indurre, costringere (per vergogna) a.
shamefaced ['ʃeimfeist] *a* vergognoso; confuso.
shameful ['ʃeimful] *a* vergognoso, disonorevole.
shameless ['ʃeimlis] *a* svergognato, sfacciato, impudente.
shampoo [ʃæm'pu:] *n* lavatura dei capelli, 'shampoo'; *vt* lavare i capelli, fare lo 'shampoo'.
shamrock ['ʃæmrɔk] *n* trifoglio (emblema nazionale dell'Irlanda).
Shanghai [ʃæŋ'hai] *n* Sciangai.
shank [ʃæŋk] *n* gamba, stinco.
shape [ʃeip] *n* forma, figura, stampo; *vt* foggiare, formare, modellare; *vi* assumere forma, presentarsi.
shapeless ['ʃeiplis] *a* informe.
shapely ['ʃeipli] *a* ben fatto, ben proporzionato.
share [ʃɛə] *n* parte, porzione, quota; (*com*) azione; **common s.** azione ordinaria; *vt* (con)dividere, spartire, distribuire; *vi* partecipare.
shareholder ['ʃɛə,houldə] *n* azionista.
shark [ʃɑ:k] *n* pescecane, squalo; furfante, speculatore; *vti* truffare, vivere di truffe.
sharp [ʃɑ:p] *a* acuto, affilato, aguzzo, penetrante; improvviso; piccante; scaltro; vivace; *n* (*mus*) diesis; *ad* in punto, puntualmente.
sharpen ['ʃɑ:pən] *vt* affilare, aguzzare, eccitare.
sharpness ['ʃɑ:pnis] *n* acutezza, acume; astuzia; prontezza, vivacità.
shatter ['ʃætə] *vti* frantumar(si), fracassar(si).
shave [ʃeiv] *n* rasatura; sfioramento; *vt* radere, tagliare; *vti* rader(si), far(si) la barba; **to have a close s.** salvarsi per miracolo, scamparla bella.
shaving ['ʃeiviŋ] *n* il rader(si); truciolo.
shawl [ʃɔ:l] *n* scialle.
she [ʃi:] *pron* ella, lei, colei; *n* femmina.
sheaf [ʃi:f] *n* covone, fascio.
shear [ʃiə] *vti* tosare, pelare; spogliare.
shears [ʃiəz] *n pl* cesoie *pl.*
sheath [ʃi:θ] *n* astuccio, fodero, guaina.
sheathe [ʃi:ð] *vt* rimettere nel fodero, inguainare.
shed [ʃed] *n* capannone, rimessa; *vt* spargere, spogliarsi di, versare.
sheen [ʃi:n] *n* lustro, splendore.
sheep [ʃi:p] *pl* **sheep** *n* pecora.
sheepish ['ʃi:piʃ] *a* vergognoso, timido, impacciato.
sheer [ʃiə] *a* puro, semplice; a piombo, perpendicolare; *ad* a piombo, verticalmente.
sheet [ʃi:t] *n* lenzuolo; foglio; giornale; lamina; (*of ice*) lastra, (*of water*) specchio.
shelf [ʃelf] *n* scaffale; palchetto, ripiano; scoglio.
shell [ʃel] *n* conchiglia; guscio; involucro; proiettile; *vt* sgusciare;

sbucciare; bombardare; **shellfish** crostaceo.
shelter [ˈʃeltə] *n* riparo, rifugio, difesa; *vt* mettere al coperto, riparare; *vi* rifugiarsi; **air-raid s.** rifugio antiaereo.
shelve [ʃelv] *vt* mettere sugli scaffali; (*fig*) differire, mettere in disparte.
shepherd [ˈʃepəd] *n* pastore; **shepherdess** pastorella.
sheriff [ˈʃerif] *n* sceriffo.
sherry [ˈʃeri] *n* 'sherry', vino di Xeres.
shield [ʃi:ld] *n* scudo; difesa, protezione; *vt* difendere, proteggere.
shift [ʃift] *n* cambiamento; espediente; turno; abito da donna; *vt* cambiare, spostare, trasferire; *vi* cambiar di posto, cambiarsi, spostarsi.
shifty [ˈʃifti] *a* volubile, furbo, ambiguo; **s. glance** sguardo sfuggente.
shilling [ˈʃiliŋ] *n* scellino.
shimmer [ˈʃimə] *n* luccichio, scintillio.
shin [ʃin] *n* stinco, coscia; (*beef*) garretto; **s.-bone** tibia.
shindy [ˈʃindi] *n* (*fam*) chiasso, baccano.
shine [ʃain] *n* lucentezza, splendore; *vi* brillare, splendere.
shingle [ˈʃingl] *n* ghiaia; tegola di legno; **shingles** *pl* (*med*) fuoco di S. Antonio; *vt* tagliare (capelli) alla garçonne.
shiny [ˈʃaini] *a* rilucente; lucido.
ship [ʃip] *n* nave, bastimento; *vt* imbarcare, spedire; *vi* imbarcarsi.
shipbroker [ˈʃip,broukə] *n* sensale marittimo.
shipbuilding [ˈʃip,bildiŋ] *n* costruzione navale.
ship-chandler [ˈʃipˈtʃɑ:ndlə] *n* fornitore navale.
shipmate [ˈʃipmeit] *n* compagno di bordo.
shipment [ˈʃipmənt] *n* imbarco, spedizione.
shipping [ˈʃipiŋ] *n* imbarco, marina mercantile, forze navali *pl*.
shipwreck [ˈʃiprek] *n* naufragio.
shipwright [ˈʃiprait] *n* (*naut*) maestro d'ascia.
shipyard [ˈʃipjɑ:d] *n* cantiere navale, arsenale.
shire [ˈʃaiə] *n* contea.
shirk [ʃə:k] *vt* schivare, sfuggire.
shirt [ʃə:t] *n* camicia da uomo; **s. front** sparato di camicia.
shiver [ˈʃivə] *n* brivido; frantume, scheggia; *vi* rabbrividire, tremare; *vti* rompere (andare) in frantumi.
shoal [ʃoul] *n* secca, bassofondo; banco di pesci; folla, ressa.
shock [ʃɔk] *n* colpo, urto, forte emozione, scossa; massa di capelli incolti; *vt* offendere, scandalizzare, urtare.
shocker [ˈʃɔkə] *n* cosa che colpisce, romanzo scandalistico.
shocking [ˈʃɔkiŋ] *a* scandaloso.
shoddy [ˈʃɔdi] *a* scadente e appariscente; *n* cascame; (*fig*) roba scadente e appariscente.
shoe [ʃu:] *n* scarpa; ferro da cavallo; *vt* calzare; ferrare.
shoemaker [ˈʃu:,meikə] *n* calzolaio.
shoot [ʃu:t] *n* germoglio; partita di caccia; *vt* colpire, fucilare; *vi* andare a caccia, sparare; germogliare; lanciarsi.
shooting [ˈʃu:tiŋ] *n* sparatoria; caccia; **s. pain** dolore lancinante; **s. star** stella cadente.
shop [ʃɔp] *n* bottega, negozio, spaccio; *vi* fare delle compere; **s. assistant** commesso; **to talk s.** parlare di affari; **s. window** vetrina.
shopkeeper [ˈʃɔp,ki:pə] *n* negoziante.
shore [ʃɔ:] *n* spiaggia, riva, sponda; puntello; *vt* puntellare.
short [ʃɔ:t] *a* breve, corto, (*height*) basso; brusco, conciso, ristretto; *ad* di botto; **s.-cut** scorciatoia; **s.-sighted** miope.
shortage [ˈʃɔ:tidʒ] *a* scarsezza.
shorten [ˈʃɔ:tn] *vti* accorciar(si); diminuir(si).
shorthand [ˈʃɔ:thænd] *n* stenografia; **s. typist** stenodattilografo; **s. writer** stenografo.
shortly [ˈʃɔ:tli] *ad* in breve, tra poco.
shortness [ˈʃɔ:tnis] *n* brevità, cortezza; insufficenza.
shot [ʃɔt] *n* colpo; sparo; scarica; palla, proiettile; tiratore; tiro; portata.
shotgun [ˈʃɔtgʌn] *n* fucile da caccia.
shoulder [ˈʃouldə] *n* spalla; (*of road*) bordo della strada; *vt* addossarsi, prendere sulle spalle.
shout [ʃaut] *n* grido; *vti* gridare.
shove [ʃʌv] *n* spinta; *vti* spingere.
shovel [ˈʃʌvl] *n* pala, palata; *vt* ammucchiare, spalare; rimpinzarsi la bocca di.
show [ʃou] *n* mostra, esibizione; esposizione; ostentazione, pompa; spettacolo; *vt* far vedere, mostrare.
shower [ˈʃauə] *n* acquazzone, rovescio; doccia; *vt* far piovere; *vi* diluviare.
showery [ˈʃauəri] *a* temporalesco.
showman [ˈʃoumən] *n* imbonitore; direttore, capocomico.
showy [ˈʃoui] *a* appariscente, vistoso.
shrapnel [ˈʃræpnl] *n* shrapnel.
shred [ʃred] *n* brandello, pezzetto, ritaglio; *vt* sminuzzare, tagliuzzare.
shrew [ʃru:] *n* bisbetica.
shrewd [ʃru:d] *a* accorto, perspicace, scaltro.
shrewdness [ˈʃru:dnis] *n* accortezza, perspicacia.
shriek [ʃri:k] *n* grido acuto, strillo; *vti* strillare, gridare.
shrike [ʃraik] *n* averla.

shrill [ʃril] *a* stridulo; *vti* stridere.
shrimp [ʃrimp] *n* gamberetto; (*fig*) omiciattolo.
shrine [ʃrain] *n* reliquario, santuario.
shrink [ʃriŋk] *vt* far restringere; *vi* restringersi, ritirarsi; indietreggiare.
shrivel ['ʃrivl] *vti* raggrinzar(si).
shroud [ʃraud] *n* sudario; velo; *vt* avvolgere, coprire, nascondere.
Shrove Tuesday ['ʃrouv'tju:zdi] *n* martedì grasso.
shrub [ʃrʌb] *n* arbusto, cespuglio; bibita di succo di frutta.
shrug [ʃrʌg] *n* alzata di spalle; *vi* stringersi nelle spalle.
shudder ['ʃʌdə] *n* brivido; *vi* rabbrividire.
shuffle ['ʃʌfl] *n* andatura strascicata; il mescolare le carte; *vt* (*cards*) mescolare; muovere con fatica, strascicare; *vi* muoversi con fatica, strascicarsi; ricorrere a sotterfugi.
shun [ʃʌn] *vt* evitare, scansare.
shunt [ʃʌnt] *n* (*rly*) binario di smistamento; (*el*) derivazione; *vt* (*rly*) smistare; (*el*) derivare.
shut [ʃʌt] *vti* chiuder(si).
shutter ['ʃʌtə] *n* imposta, persiana; (*phot*) otturatore.
shuttle ['ʃʌtl] *n* navetta, spoletta.
shy [ʃai] *a* timido; diffidente, (*horse*) ombroso; *vt* lanciare; *vi* pigliar ombra.
shyness ['ʃainis] *n* timidezza.
Siamese [,saiə'mi:z] *a n* siamese.
Siberia [sai'biəriə] *n* Siberia.
Siberian [sai'biəriən] *a n* siberiano.
sibilant ['sibilənt] *a n* sibilante.
sibyl ['sibil] *n* sibilla.
Sicilian [si'siliən] *a n* siciliano.
Sicily ['sisili] *n* Sicilia.
sick [sik] *a* (am)malato, sofferente; nauseato; stanco.
sicken ['sikn] *vt* disgustare; *vi* ammalarsi, disgustarsi.
sickle ['sikl] *n* falcetto, falce.
sickly ['sikli] *a* di salute cagionevole, malaticcio; nauseante.
sickness ['siknis] *n* malattia; nausea.
sickroom ['sikrum] *n* camera per ammalati.
side [said] *n* fianco, lato; riva; parte, partito; *vi* parteggiare.
sideboard ['saidbɔ:d] *n* credenza.
side-effect ['saidi'fekt] *n* effetto secondario.
sidelong ['saidlɔŋ] *a* obliquo; *ad* obliquamente.
sidewalk ['saidwɔ:k] *n* marciapiede.
sideways ['saidweiz] *ad* lateralmente, a sghembo.
sidle ['saidl] *vi* camminare di sghembo; diportarsi untuosamente.
siding ['saidiŋ] *n* (*rly*) binario morto.
siege [si:dʒ] *n* assedio.
sieve [siv] *n* crivello, staccio; *vt* stacciare.
sift [sift] *vt* setacciare.
sigh [sai] *n* sospiro; *vi* sospirare.
sight [sait] *n* vista, occhi *pl*; (*gun*) mirino; spettacolo, visione; (*fam*) gran quantità; *vt* avvistare; prendere la mira di; **s.-seeing** visita turistica.
sightless ['saitlis] *a* cieco.
sightly ['saitli] *a* avvenente, bello.
Sigismond, Sigismund ['sigismənd] *nm pr* Sigismondo.
sign [sain] *n* segno, cenno; insegna; *vti* firmare, segnare.
signal ['signl] *a* cospicuo, notevole; *n* segnale, segnalazione, segno; *vti* segnalare.
signatory ['signətəri] *n* firmatario.
signature ['signitʃə] *n* firma; (*typ*) segnatura; (*mus*) indicazione.
signet ['signit] *n* sigillo.
significance [sig'nifikəns] *n* significato; espressione; importanza.
significant [sig'nifikənt] *a* significativo, importante.
signify ['signifai] *vt* significare, far sapere, voler dire; *vi* importare.
silence ['sailəns] *n* silenzio.
silencer ['sailənsə] *n* (*aut*) silenziatore.
silent ['sailənt] *a* silenzioso, muto.
silhouette [,silu(:)'et] *n* profilo; *vti* profilar(si).
silk [silk] *a* di seta; *n* seta.
silken ['silkən] *a* serico, di seta; (*fig*) insinuante.
silkiness ['silkinis] *n* morbidezza, lucentezza.
silkworm ['silkwə:m] *n* baco da seta.
silky ['silki] *a* di seta, serico; morbido.
sill [sil] *n* davanzale; soglia.
silliness ['silinis] *n* stupidità, sciocchezza.
silly ['sili] *a* sciocco, stupido.
silt [silt] *n* sedimento di fango o sabbia; *vti* ostruir(si) per fango o sabbia.
silver ['silvə] *a* d'argento; *n* argento.
silversmith ['silvəsmiθ] *n* argentiere.
silvery ['silvəri] *a* argenteo, -tato, -tino.
similar ['similə] *a n* simile; *a* somigliante, analogo.
similarity [,simi'læriti] *n* somiglianza.
simile ['simili] *n* paragone, similitudine.
simmer ['simə] *vti* (far) bollire lentamente; (*fig*) essere sul punto di scoppiare per, ribollire di.
Simon ['saimən] *nm pr* Simone.
simony ['saiməni] *n* simonia.
simper ['simpə] *n* sorriso melenso; *vi* sorridere in modo melenso.
simple ['simpl] *a* semplice; *n* erba medicinale.
simpleton ['simpltən] *n* semplicione.
simplicity [sim'plisiti] *n* semplicità.
simplification [,simplifi'keiʃən] *n* semplificazione.
simplify ['simplifai] *vt* semplificare.
simulate ['simjuleit] *vt* simulare.
simulation [,simju'leiʃən] *n* simulazione.

simultaneous [ˌsiməl'teiniəs] *a* simultaneo.
simultaneously [ˌsiməl'teiniəsli] *ad* simultaneamente.
sin [sin] *n* peccato; *vi* peccare.
since [sins] *ad cj prep* d'allora in poi; da quando; poichè; da.
sincere [sin'siə] *a* sincero.
sincerity [sin'seriti] *n* sincerità.
sinecure ['sinikjuə] *n* sinecura.
sinew ['sinju:] *n* nervo, tendine; nerbo.
sinewy ['sinju:i] *a* nerboruto, gagliardo.
sinful ['sinful] *a* peccaminoso, colpevole.
sing [siŋ] *vti* cantare.
singe [sindʒ] *vt* bruciare, bruciacchiare.
singer ['siŋə] *n* cantante, cantore.
singing ['siŋiŋ] *a* cantante, canterino; *n* canto.
single ['siŋgl] *a* solo, unico; semplice; singolo, celibe, nubile; *vt* distinguere; scegliere; **s. ticket** (*rly*) biglietto d'andata.
singular ['siŋgjulə] *a n* singolare; *a* caratteristico, particolare.
singularity [ˌsiŋgju'læriti] *n* singolarità; stranezza.
singularly ['siŋgjuləli] *ad* singolarmente, particolarmente.
sinister ['sinistə] *a* sinistro, funesto.
sink [siŋk] *n* acquaio; sentina; *vt* affondare, immergere; nascondere; investire denaro a fondo perduto; *vi* affondare; declinare; sparire, tramontare.
sinless ['sinlis] *a* innocente, puro.
sinner ['sinə] *n* peccatore, -trice.
sinuous ['sinjuəs] *a* sinuoso.
sip [sip] *n* sorso; *vti* centellinare.
siphon ['saifən] *n* sifone.
sir [sə:] *n* (*vocative*) signore, 'Sir', titolo premesso a nome proprio di cavaliere, baronetto.
sire ['saiə] *n* sire.
siren ['saiərin] *n* sirena.
sirloin ['sə:lɔin] *n* lombo di manzo.
sister ['sistə] *n* sorella; suora; **s.-in-law** cognata.
sisterhood ['sistəhud] *n* comunità religiosa.
sisterly ['sistəli] *a* da (di) sorella.
sit [sit] *vi* sedere, stare seduto; **to s. down** mettersi a sedere.
site [sait] *n* sito, luogo, posizione.
sitting ['sitiŋ] *a* seduto; in seduta; *n* seduta; posa; riunione; **s. room** salotto, stanza di soggiorno.
situated ['sitjueitid] *a* posto, situato.
situation [ˌsitju'eiʃən] *n* posizione; situazione; condizioni *pl*; impiego, posto.
six [siks] *a n* sei; **sixth** *a* sesto.
sixpence ['sikspəns] *n* mezzo scellino.
sixteen ['siks'ti:n] *a n* sedici; **sixteenth** *a* sedicesimo.
sixty ['siksti] *a n* sessanta; **sixtieth** *a* sessantesimo.
sizable ['saizəbl] *a* piuttosto grande.
size [saiz] *n* grandezza, dimensione; formato; misura; **s. up** *vt* valutare, giudicare.
skate [skeit] *n* pattino; (*fish*) razza; *vi* pattinare; schettinare.
skating ['skeitiŋ] *n* pattinaggio.
skein [skein] *n* matassa.
skeleton ['skelitn] *n* scheletro; ossatura.
skeptic ['skeptik] *n* scettico.
skeptical ['skeptikəl] *a* scettico.
skepticism ['skeptisizəm] *n* scetticismo.
sketch [sketʃ] *n* abbozzo, bozzetto, schizzo; *vti* abbozzare, schizzare, fare degli schizzi.
skew [skju:] *a* obliquo, sbieco.
skewer ['skjuə] *n* spiedo; *vt* infilare sullo spiedo.
ski [ski:] *n* sci; *vi* sciare.
skid [skid] *n* slittamento; (*av*) pattino di coda; **side s.** (*aut*) sbandamento; *vi* sbandare, slittare; scivolare.
skier ['ski:ə] *n* sciatore.
skiff [skif] *n* (*naut*) schifo.
skill [skil] *n* abilità, destrezza, perizia.
skilled [skild] *a* esperto, specializzato.
skillful ['skilful] *a* abile, destro, esperto.
skim [skim] *vt* schiumare, scremare; sfiorare, dare un'occhiata a; **skimmed milk** latte scremato.
skimmer ['skimə] *n* schiumatoio.
skimp [skimp] *vt* lesinare, tenere a stecchetto.
skimpy ['skimpi] *a* scarso, misero.
skin [skin] *n* pelle; *vt* pelare; sbucciare, scorticare; **s. diver** nuotatore subacqueo, sommozzatore; **s. diving** nuoto subacqueo.
skinny ['skini] *a* magro, macilento.
skip [skip] *n* balzo; *vt* omettere, passare sopra; *vi* balzare, saltare.
skipper ['skipə] *n* capitano di nave mercantile o peschereccia.
skirmish ['skə:miʃ] *n* scaramuccia; *vi* scaramucciare.
skirt [skə:t] *n* sottana, gonna; falda, lembo; *vt* costeggiare, rasentare, confinare con.
skit [skit] *n* parodia, frizzo.
skittish ['skitiʃ] *a* capriccioso, volubile, vivace.
skittle ['skitl] *n* birillo.
skulk [skʌlk] *vi* celarsi, nascondersi, sottrarsi al proprio dovere.
skull [skʌl] *n* cranio, teschio.
skunk [skʌŋk] *n* moffetta; (*fig*) individuo ignobile.
sky [skai] *n* cielo, volta del cielo.
skylark ['skailɑ:k] *n* allodola.
skylight ['skailait] *n* lucernario.
skyline ['skailain] *n* orizzonte.
skyscraper ['skaiˌskreipə] *n* grattacielo.
slab [slæb] *n* grossa fetta; lastra.

slack [slæk] *a* allentato, fiacco, indolente; fermo, stagnante.
slacken ['slækən] *vti* allentar(si), moderar(si).
slackness ['slæknis] *n* fiacchezza, rilassatezza; (*com*) fermo.
slag [slæg] *n* scoria, -ie.
slake [sleik] *vt* estinguere; soddisfare.
slam [slæm] *n* sbatacchiamento; *vti* sbatacchiar(si), scaraventare.
slander ['slɑ:ndə] *n* calunnia; *vt* calunniare, diffamare.
slanderer [slɑ:ndərə] *n* calunniatore, diffamatore.
slanderous ['slɑ:ndərəs] *a* calunnioso, diffamatorio.
slang [slæŋ] *n* gergo.
slant [slɑ:nt] *n* inclinazione, pendìo; posizione obliqua; (*fig*) prospettiva; *vt* disporre obliquamente; *vi* inclinarsi.
slap [slæp] *n* colpo, schiaffo; *vt* colpire, schiaffeggiare; gettare, scaraventare.
slapdash ['slæpdæʃ] *a* impetuoso; affrettato, superficiale.
slapstick ['slæpstik] *n* farsa grossolana.
slash [slæʃ] *n* squarcio, taglio; *vt* squarciare, tagliare; criticare ferocemente.
slate [sleit] *n* ardesia; tegola d'ardesia; lavagna.
slattern ['slætə:n] *n* donna sciatta.
slaughter ['slɔ:tə] *n* carneficina, macello; *vt* macellare, massacrare.
Slav [slɑ:v] *a n* slavo.
slave [sleiv] *n* schiavo; *vi* sgobbare.
slaver ['sleivə] *n* negriero; nave negriera.
slaver ['slævə] *n* bava, saliva; *vi* sbavare.
slavery ['sleivəri] *n* schiavitù.
Slavic ['slævik] *a n* slavo, lingua slava.
slavish ['sleiviʃ] *a* abietto, servile.
slavishness ['sleiviʃnis] *n* servilismo.
Slavonic [slə'vɔnik] *a n* slavo, lingua slava.
slay [slei] *vt* ammazzare, trucidare.
sled [sled] *n* slitta.
sledge [sledʒ] *n* slitta; **s.-hammer** mazza da fabbro.
sleek [sli:k] *a* liscio; *vt* lisciare.
sleep [sli:p] *n* sonno; *vi* dormire.
sleeper ['sli:pə] *n* dormiente; (*rly*) traversa, -sina; cuccetta; (*av*) poltrona letto; (*rly*) vagone letto.
sleepiness ['slipinis] *n* sonnolenza.
sleepless ['sli:plis] *a* insonne.
sleeplessness ['sli:plisnis] *n* insonnia.
sleepwalker ['sli:p,wɔ:kə] *n* sonnambulo.
sleepy ['sli:pi] *a* assonnato, sonnolento.
sleet [sli:t] *n* nevischio; *vi* cadere nevischio.
sleeve [sli:v] *n* manica.
sleigh [slei] *n* slitta.
slender ['slendə] *a* slanciato, snello, sottile; esiguo, piccolo, scarso.
slenderness ['slendənis] *n* snellezza; scarsità.
slice [slais] *n* fetta; parte, porzione; *vt* affettare, dividere.
slide [slaid] *n* scivolata; scivolo; (*phot*) diapositiva, lastra; vetrino per microscopio; *vt* far scorrere; *vi* scivolare, sdrucciolare; **sliding** scorrevole, mobile; **sliding scale** scala mobile.
slight [slait] *a* magro, esile, esiguo; insufficiente, scarso; superficiale; *n* affronto, mancanza di riguardo; *vt* mancare di rispetto a, non far caso di.
slim [slim] *a* esile, slanciato, sottile; *vi* dimagrire.
slime [slaim] *n* melma, sostanza viscida in genere.
slimness ['slimnis] *n* snellezza, esilità.
slimy ['slaimi] *a* melmoso, viscido.
sling [sliŋ] *n* fionda; striscia di tela per sostenere un braccio ammalato; **s. shot** fionda; *vt* scagliare con la fionda; sospendere.
slink [sliŋk] *vi* svignarsela, sgattaiolare.
slip [slip] *n* scivolone, sdrucciolone; errore, svista, passo falso; guinzaglio; federa; sottabito; *vt* far scivolare in; *vi* scivolare, sdrucciolare; andare furtivamente; sbagliare, scappare; **s. on** *vt* (*garment*) infilare.
slipper ['slipə] *n* pantofola, ciabatta.
slippery ['slipəri] *a* sdrucciolevole; viscido; (*fig*) incostante, poco scrupoloso.
slipshod ['slipʃɔd] *a* trasandato, trascurato.
slit [slit] *n* fessura, lunga incisione; *vt* fendere, tagliare a strisce.
sloe [slou] *n* prugnola.
slogan ['slougən] *n* grido di guerra; (*com*) motto pubblicitario, motto, "slogan".
sloop [slu:p] *n* (*naut*) scialuppa, corvetta.
slop [slɔp] *n* (*usu pl*) risciacquatura di piatti; liquidi sporchi.
slope [sloup] *n* pendenza, pendio; *vt* inclinare; *vi* essere in pendenza.
sloppy ['slɔpi] *a* bagnato; (*fig*) sciatto; sdolcinato.
slot [slɔt] *n* buco o foro oblungo; **s.-machine** distributore automatico.
sloth [slouθ] *n* pigrizia, ignavia.
slothful ['slouθful] *a* indolente, pigro.
slouch [slautʃ] *n* andatura dinoccolata; *vi* camminare in modo dinoccolato; **s. hat** cappello a cencio.
slough [slau] *n* palude, pantano; [slʌf] *vti* (*of snakes*) cambiare la pelle; (*fig*) liberarsi di.
sloven ['slʌvn] *n* persona trasandata.
slovenliness ['slʌvnlinis] *n* sudiceria, sciatteria.

slovenly ['slʌvnli] *a* disordinato, trasandato.
slow [slou] *a* lento; tardo; in ritardo; *ad* adagio; *vti* rallentare.
slowness ['slounis] *n* lentezza, indolenza.
slug [slʌg] *n* lumaca.
sluggard ['slʌgəd] *n* poltrone.
sluggish ['slʌgiʃ] *a* indolente, neghittoso, lento.
sluggishness ['slʌgiʃnis] *n* indolenza.
sluice [slu:s] *n* cateratta, chiusa; *vt* bagnare abbondantemente; *vi* scorrere violentemente.
slum [slʌm] *n* quartiere popolare e sudicio.
slumber ['slʌmbə] *n* sonno; *vi* dormire.
slump [slʌmp] *n* tracollo, brusco ribasso di prezzi, improvviso arresto nelle richieste di vendita; *vi* cadere, precipitare.
slur [slə:] *n* calunnia, insulto, macchia, pronuncia indistinta; (*mus*) legatura; *vt* pronunciare indistintamente; (*mus*) legare.
slush [slʌʃ] *n* fanghiglia, neve sciolta.
slut [slʌt] *n* donna trasandata, sudiciona.
sly [slai] *a* astuto, furbo, scaltro.
slyness ['slainis] *n* astuzia, furberia, scaltrezza.
smack [smæk] *n* schiaffo; schiocco; gusto, sapore di; peschereccio; *vt* schiaffeggiare; schioccare; *vi* aver sapore di, sapere di.
small [smɔ:l] *a* piccolo; limitato; scarso; umile; meschino.
smallness ['smɔ:lnis] *n* piccolezza.
smallpox ['smɔ:lpɔks] *n* vaiolo.
smart [smɑ:t] *a* acuto, intelligente, sveglio; elegante; *n* bruciore, dolore acuto; *vi* dolere, bruciare; soffrire.
smartness ['smɑ:tnis] *n* vivacità, spirito; eleganza.
smash [smæʃ] *n* scontro, urto; rovina; fallimento; *vt* fracassare, frantumare; *vi* fracassarsi; fallire.
smattering ['smætəriŋ] *n* infarinatura.
smear [smiə] *n* macchia; *vt* imbrattare, macchiare.
smell [smel] *n* fiuto; odorato, olfatto; odore; *vt* fiutare, sentire l'odore di; (*fig*) sospettare; *vi* odorare, aver l'odore di.
smelt [smelt] *vt* fondere.
smelting ['smeltiŋ] *n* fusione.
smile [smail] *n* sorriso; *vi* sorridere.
smirk [smə:k] *n* sorriso affettato; *vi* sorridere affettatamente.
smith [smiθ] *n* fabbro.
smithy ['smiði] *n* fucina.
smock [smɔk] *n* grembiule da bambino; blusa da operaio.
smog [smɔg] *n* 'smog', caligine.
smoke [smouk] *n* fumo; *vt* fumare, affumicare; *vi* emettere fumo; **smoked herring** aringa affumicata.
smoker ['smoukə] *n* fumatore; (*rly*) carrozza per fumatori.
smoky ['smouki] *a* fumoso.
smolder ['smouldə] *vi* bruciare senza fiamma, covare sotto la cenere.
smooth [smu:ð] *a* levigato, liscio; calmo; blando, mellifluo; *vt* levigare, lisciare, piallare, spianare; *vi* calmarsi, rasserenarsi.
smoothness ['smu:ðnis] *n* levigatezza; scorrevolezza; calma.
smother ['smʌðə] *n* nuvola di polvere *etc*; *vt* asfissiare, soffocare; coprire; opprimere; spegnere.
smudge [smʌdʒ] *n* chiazza; sgorbio; *vt* chiazzare, macchiare.
smug [smʌg] *a* ipocrita, soddisfatto di sè.
smuggle ['smʌgl] *vt* far entrare di contrabbando; *vi* esercitare il contrabbando.
smuggler ['smʌglə] *n* contrabbandiere.
smut [smʌt] *n* macchia di fuliggine.
smutty ['smʌti] *a* fuligginoso, sporco; (*fig*) osceno.
snack [snæk] *n* spuntino.
snag [snæg] *n* nodo; sporgenza; (*fig*) intoppo, difficoltà.
snail [sneil] *n* chiocciola; lumaca.
snake [sneik] *n* serpe, serpente.
snap [snæp] *n* schiocco; rumore secco; (*phot*) istantanea; (*fig*) brio, vivacità; *vt* rompere con rumore secco; schioccare; fare l'istantanea a; *vi* fare un rumore secco, rompersi.
snappish ['snæpiʃ] *a* bisbetico, secco, stizzoso.
snapshot ['snæpʃɔt] *n* (*phot*) istantanea.
snare [snɛə] *n* insidia; laccio; trappola; *vt* prendere al laccio, in trappola.
snarl [snɑ:l] *n* groviglio; ringhio; *vt* aggrovigliare; *vi* aggrovigliarsi, ringhiare.
snatch [snætʃ] *vt* afferrare, ghermire, strappare.
sneak [sni:k] *n* (*fam*) persona vile; (*school sl*) spia; *vi* strisciare.
sneaking ['sni:kiŋ] *a* basso, servile; nascosto.
sneer [sniə] *n* (sog)ghigno, sarcasmo; *vi* sogghignare, deridere.
sneeze [sni:z] *n* starnuto; *vi* starnutire; **s. at** disprezzare.
sniff [snif] *n* l'annusare, il fiutare; *vti* annusare, fiutare; aspirare.
snigger ['snigə] *n* risolino cinico; *vi* ridere sotto i baffi, ridacchiare.
snip [snip] *n* forbiciata, ritaglio; *vti* tagliuzzare, tagliare.
snipe [snaip] *n* beccaccino.
sniper ['snaipə] *n* chi caccia beccaccini; (*mil*) franco tiratore.
snippet ['snipit] *n* pezzettino, ritaglio.
snivel ['snivəl] *vi* piagnucolare; simulare contrizione, dolore.

snob [snɔb] *n* 'snob'.
snobbery ['snɔbəri] *n* snobismo.
snobbish ['snɔbiʃ] *a* snobistico, snob.
snooze [snu:z] *n* pisolino, sonnellino; *vi* fare un pisolino.
snore [snɔ:] *n* il russare; *vi* russare.
snorkel ['snɔ:kəl] *n* 'snorkel', presa d'aria per nuotatori e sommergibili.
snort [snɔ:t] *n* sbuffo; *vi* sbuffare.
snout [snaut] *n* muso, grugno.
snow [snou] *n* neve; *vi* nevicare.
snowdrift ['snoudrift] *n* ammasso di neve, raffica di neve.
snowdrop ['snoudrɔp] *n* bucaneve.
snowflake ['snoufleik] *n* fiocco di neve.
snow-plow ['snouplau] *n* spazzaneve.
snowshoe ['snouʃu:] *n* racchetta per la neve.
snowstorm ['snoustɔ:m] *n* tormenta.
snowy ['snoui] *n* nevoso, niveo, candido.
snub [snʌb] *a* (*nose*) camuso; *n* rimprovero, affronto; *vt* rimproverare, umiliare.
snuff [snʌf] *n* tabacco da fiuto; *vti* fiutare, annusare.
snuffers ['snʌfəz] *n pl* smoccolatoio.
snuffle ['snʌfl] *vi* respirare rumorosamente; parlare nel naso; parlare in tono piagnucoloso.
snug [snʌg] *a* comodo, riparato dalle intemperie.
snuggle ['snʌgl] *vi* rannicchiarsi.
so [sou] *ad* così, a questo modo, tanto, perciò, quindi; **s. as to** tanto . . . da; **s. that** *cj* così che, di modo che.
soak [souk] *vt* bagnare, immergere, inzuppare.
soap [soup] *n* sapone.
soapy ['soupi] *a* saponoso.
soar [sɔ:] *vi* librarsi sulle ali, volare in alto.
sob [sɔb] *n* singhiozzo; *vi* singhiozzare.
sober ['soubə] *a* sobrio, moderato nel bere; equilibrato; sensato; serio.
soberness ['soubənis] **sobriety** [sou'braiəti] *n* moderazione, temperanza.
sociable ['souʃəbl] *a* socievole.
social ['souʃəl] *a* sociale.
socialism ['souʃəlizəm] *n* socialismo.
socialist ['souʃəlist] *a n* socialista.
socialite ['souʃəlait] *n* membro dell'alta società.
society [sə'saiəti] *n* società, associazione, compagnia.
sociology [,sousi'ɔlədʒi] *n* sociologia.
sock [sɔk] *n* calzino, soletta; **s. suspender** giarrettiera.
socket ['sɔkit] *n* orbita, cavità; (*teeth*) alveolo.
sod [sɔd] *n* zolla erbosa.
soda ['soudə] *n* soda; **s.-water** (acqua di) seltz; **s. biscuit** galletta, 'cracker'.
sodden ['sɔdn] *a* impregnato d'acqua, fradicio; (*fig*) istupidito dal bere.
sodium ['soudiəm] *n* sodio.
sofa ['soufə] *n* sofa.
Sofia ['soufiə] *n* Sofia.
soft [sɔft] *a* morbido, molle, soffice; cedevole; delicato; mite, conciliante.
soften ['sɔfn] *vti* ammollir(si), mitigar(si), intenerir(si).
softly ['sɔftli] *ad* dolcemente; sommessamente, adagio.
softness ['sɔftnis] *n* morbidezza; delicatezza; mitezza.
soggy ['sɔgi] *a* bagnato; (*bread*) mal cotto.
soil [sɔil] *n* suolo, terra, terreno; macchia; sporcizia; *vt* insozzare, sporcare; *vi* sporcarsi.
sojourn ['sɔdʒə:n] *n* soggiorno; *vi* soggiornare.
solace ['sɔləs] *n* sollievo, consolazione; *vt* consolare, sollevare.
solar ['soulə] *a* solare.
solder ['sɔldə] *n* saldatura; *vt* saldare.
soldier ['souldʒə] *n* soldato, militare.
soldierly ['souldʒəli] *a* marziale, militare.
soldiery ['souldʒəri] *n* soldati *pl*, soldatesca.
sole [soul] *a* solo, unico; *n* pianta del piede; suola; (*fish*) sogliola; *vt* risolare.
solecism ['sɔlisizəm] *n* solecismo.
solemn ['sɔləm] *a* solenne.
solemnity [sə'lemniti] *n* solennità; rito solenne.
solemnize ['sɔləmnaiz] *vt* solennizzare.
solicit [sə'lisit] *vt* chiedere con insistenza.
solicitor [sə'lisitə] *n* avvocato, procuratore legale.
solicitous [sə'lisitəs] *a* premuroso, sollecito; desideroso.
solicitude [sə'lisitju:d] *n* sollecitudine, premura.
solid ['sɔlid] *a* solido; compatto; massiccio; intero; pieno; posato, serio; (*com*) solvibile; *n* corpo solido.
solidarity [,sɔli'dæriti] *n* solidarietà.
solidify [sə'lidifai] *vti* solidificar(si).
solidity [sə'liditi] *n* solidità; (*com*) solvenza.
soliloquy [sə'liləkwi] *n* soliloquio.
solitary ['sɔlitəri] *a* solo, solitario.
solitude ['sɔlitju:d] *n* solitudine.
solo ['soulou] *pl* **solos** *n* (*mus*) assolo; (*av*) volo solitario.
solstice ['sɔlstis] *n* solstizio.
soluble ['sɔljubl] *a* solubile.
solution [sə'lju:ʃən] *n* soluzione, risoluzione.
solve [sɔlv] *vt* risolvere, sciogliere, spiegare.
solvent ['sɔlvənt] *a n* solvente; *a* (*com*) solvibile.
Somali [sou'ma:li] *n* somalo.
Somaliland [sou'ma:lilænd] *n* Somalia.
somber ['sɔmbə] *a* fosco, tenebroso; triste.

some [sʌm] *a* pron qualche, alcuni, del; ne; un po' di; *ad* all'incirca, circa.
somebody ['sʌmbədi] *pron* qualcuno.
somehow ['sʌmhau] *ad* in qualche modo, in un modo o nell'altro.
someone ['sʌmwʌn] *pron* qualcuno.
somersault ['sʌməsɔ:lt] *n* capriola, salto mortale.
something ['sʌmθiŋ] *pron* qual(che) cosa; *ad* un po'.
sometime ['sʌmtaim] *a* di un tempo, antico; *ad* un tempo, un giorno o l'altro; **s. soon** uno di questi giorni.
sometimes ['sʌmtaimz] *ad* talvolta.
somewhat ['sʌmwɔt] *ad* piuttosto, un po'.
somewhere ['sʌmwɛə] *ad* in qualche parte.
somnambulism [sɔm'næmbjulizəm] *n* sonnambulismo.
somnambulist [sɔm'næmbjulist] *n* sonnambulo.
somniferous [sɔm'nifərəs] *a* soporifero, sonnifero.
somnolent ['sɔmnələnt] *a* sonnolento.
son [sʌn] *n* figlio; **s.-in-law** genero.
song [sɔŋ] *n* canto, canzone; romanza.
songster ['sɔŋstə] *n* uccello canterino.
sonnet ['sɔnit] *n* sonetto.
sonorous ['sɔnərəs] *a* sonoro.
soon [su:n] *ad* fra poco, presto, tosto; **sooner** piuttosto.
soot [sut] *n* fuliggine.
soothe [su:ð] *vt* calmare, placare; blandire.
soothing ['su:ðiŋ] *a* calmante, lenitivo.
soothsayer ['su:θˌseiə] *n* indovino.
sooty ['suti] *a* fuligginoso, nero.
sop [sɔp] *n* pezzo di pane o altro inzuppato; (*fig*) dono propiziatorio.
sophism ['sɔfizəm] *n* sofisma.
sophist ['sɔfist] *n* sofista.
sophisticate [sə'fistikeit] *vti* sofisticare.
sophisticated [sə'fistikeitid] *a* sofisticato, raffinato.
sophistry ['sɔfistri] *n* sofisticheria, cavilli *pl*.
soporific [ˌsɔpə'rifik] *a* soporifero; *n* sonnifero, narcotico.
soprano [sə'prɑ:nou] *pl* **sopranos** *n* soprano.
sorcerer ['sɔ:sərə] *n* mago, stregone.
sorceress ['sɔ:səris] *n* strega, fattucchiera.
sorcery ['sɔ:səri] *n* magia, stregoneria.
sordid ['sɔ:did] *a* sordido, spilorcio; ignobile.
sordidness ['sɔ:didnis] *n* sordidezza, grettezza.
sore [sɔ:] *a* dolorante; infiammato; addolorato, irritato; grave; *n* piaga, ulcera.
sorely ['sɔ:li] *ad* gravemente, fortemente.
soreness ['sɔ:nis] *n* dolore, irritazione.
sorrel ['sɔrəl] *n* acetosa; cavallo sauro; *a* di color sauro.
sorrow ['sɔrou] *n* afflizione, dolore; sventura; *vi* addolorarsi, rattristarsi.
sorrowful ['sɔrəful] *a* addolorato, doloroso.
sorry ['sɔri] *a* dispiacente, dolente; meschino, misero.
sort [sɔ:t] *n* sorta, genere, specie, tipo; *vt* selezionare, classificare, smistare.
sortie ['sɔ:ti:] *n* (*mil*) sortita.
so-so ['sousou] *a* discreto; *ad* così così.
sot [sɔt] *n* ubriacone inveterato.
sough [sau] *vi* gemere; (*wind*) sussurrare.
soul [soul] *n* anima, spirito; (*fig*) incarnazione.
soulful ['soulful] *a* pieno di sentimento.
sound [saund] *n* rumore, suono; sonda; (*geogr*) stretto; *a* giusto, logico; profondo; sano, solido, ben fondato; *ad* profondamente; *vt* suonare, far risonare; sondare, scandagliare; *vi* sembrare; suonare, risonare.
sounding ['saundiŋ] *n* sonorità; (*med*) auscultazione; (*naut*) scandaglio.
soundness ['saundnis] *n* sanità, solidità.
soup [su:p] *n* minestra, brodo, zuppa.
sour ['sauə] *a* acido, agro, aspro, amaro; (*of soil*) sterile; *vt* fare inacidire; (*fig*) esacerbare; *vi* inacidire, inasprirsi.
source [sɔ:s] *n* fonte, origine, sorgente.
sourish ['sauəriʃ] *a* acidulo.
sourness ['sauənis] *n* acidità, asprezza; (*fig*) acrimonia.
souse [saus] *n* salamoia; *vt* marinare.
south [sauθ] *n* mezzogiorno, sud; *a* del sud, meridionale; *ad* a sud.
South Africa [ˌsauð'æfrikə] *n* Sud Africa.
southerly ['sʌðəli] *a* del sud, meridionale; *ad* a sud.
southern ['sʌðən] *a* del sud.
southerner ['sʌðənə] *n* meridionale.
southward ['sauθwəd] *a* verso sud; **southwards** *ad* verso sud.
south-west ['sauθ'west] *a* di sud-ovest; *n* sud-ovest; *ad* verso sud-ovest.
souvenir [ˌsu:və'niə] *n* ricordo.
sovereign ['sɔvrin] *a* sovrano, supremo; *n* sovrano; sterlina d'oro.
sovereignty ['sɔvrənti] *n* sovranità.
sow [sou] *vt* seminare, spargere.
sow [sau] *n* scrofa.
spa [spɑ:] *n* stazione termale.
space [speis] *n* spazio, estensione, luogo; periodo di tempo; *a* spaziale; *vt* disporre ad intervalli.
space-craft ['speiskrɑ:ft] **space-ship** ['speisʃip] *n* astronave.

spacious ['speiʃəs] *a* ampio, spazioso.
spaciousness ['speiʃəsnis] *n* ampiezza, spaziosità.
spade [speid] *n* badile, vanga; (*cards*) picche.
Spain [spein] *n* Spagna.
span [spæn] *n* spanna, palmo; apertura; breve durata, periodo; *vt* abbracciare, misurare, estendersi attraverso.
spangle ['spæŋgl] *n* lustrino.
Spaniard ['spænjəd] *n* spagnolo.
spaniel ['spænjəl] *n* 'spaniel', cane spagnolo; (*fig*) persona servile.
Spanish ['spæniʃ] *a* spagnolo.
spank [spæŋk] *vt* sculacciare.
spanner ['spænə] *n* (*mech*) chiave.
spar [spɑ:] *n* (*naut*) alberatura; pugilato; *vi* allenarsi nel pugilato; avere un battibecco.
spare [spɛə] *a* magro; parco, frugale; disponibile, libero; di ricambio, di riserva; *n* pezzo di ricambio; *vt* fare a meno di; risparmiare, mettere da parte; *vi* essere risparmiatore.
sparing ['spɛəriŋ] *a* economo, parco.
sparingly ['spɛəriŋli] *ad* in moderazione; limitatamente.
spark [spɑ:k] *n* favilla, scintilla, barlume; (*fig*) bellimbusto; *vi* emettere scintille; **spark plug** (*aut*) candela.
sparkle ['spɑ:kl] *n* bagliore, scintillio, vivacità; *vi* brillare, scintillare.
sparkling ['spɑ:kliŋ] *a* scintillante, brillante; (*wine*) spumante.
sparrow ['spærou] *n* passero.
sparse [spɑ:s] *a* rado, sparso, che si trova ad intervalli irregolari.
sparsely ['spɑ:sli] *ad* scarsamente, poco; qui e là.
spasm ['spæzəm] *n* contrazione, spasimo.
spasmodic [spæs'mɔdik] *a* spasmodico.
spastic ['spæstik] *a* spastico.
spat [spæt] *n* ghetta.
spate [speit] *n* piena, straripamento.
spatter ['spætə] *vti* impillaccherare, spruzzare.
spawn [spɔ:n] *n* (*of fish etc*) uova *pl*; micelio; *vt* generare, produrre; *vi* deporre le uova.
speak [spi:k] *vi* parlare; *vt* pronunziare.
speaker ['spi:kə] *n* parlatore, oratore; **S. of the House** Presidente della Camera; **loud-s.** alto parlante.
spear [spiə] *n* arpione, lancia; *vt* trafiggere con arpione; o lancia.
special ['speʃəl] *a* speciale, particolare; *n* treno speciale; edizione straordinaria di giornale.
specialist ['speʃəlist] *n* specialista.
speciality [,speʃi'æliti] *n* specialità.
specialize ['speʃəlaiz] *vti* specializzar(si).
species ['spiʃiz] *pl* **species** *n* specie, genere, sorta.
specific [spi'sifik] *a n* specifico; *a* caratteristico.
specification [,spesifi'keiʃən] *n* specificazione.
specify ['spesifai] *vt* specificare.
specimen ['spesimin] *n* campione, esemplare, saggio.
specious ['spi:ʃəs] *a* specioso.
speck [spek] *n* macchiolina; punto; *vt* chiazzare, macchiare.
speckle ['spekl] *n* macchiolina; *vt* segnare con macchioline, variegare.
spectacle ['spektəkl] *n* spettacolo, vista; **spectacles** *pl* occhiali *pl*.
spectacular [spek'tækjulə] *a* spettacolare, spettacoloso.
spectator [spek'teitə] *n* spettatore.
specter ['spektə] *n* fantasma, spettro.
spectral ['spektrəl] *a* spettrale.
speculate ['spekjuleit] *vi* speculare.
speculation [,spekju'leiʃən] *n* speculazione, congettura, meditazione.
speculator ['spekjuleitə] *n* speculatore.
speech [spi:tʃ] *n* discorso, orazione; favella, linguaggio.
speechless ['spi:tʃlis] *a* muto, senza parole; sbalordito.
speed [spi:d] *n* velocità, rapidità, sveltezza; *vti* affrettar(si); **to s. up** accelerare.
speedometer [spi'dɔmitə] *n* (*aut*) tachimetro.
speedway ['spi:dwei] *n* pista, circuito; autostrada.
speedy ['spi:di] *a* pronto, rapido, veloce.
spell [spel] *n* incantesimo, magia, fascino; breve periodo; *vti* compitare; significare.
spellbound ['spelbaund] *a* affascinato, incantato.
spelling ['speliŋ] *n* ortografia.
spend [spend] *vt* spendere; impiegare, passare, trascorrere; *vi* consumarsi; spendere.
spendthrift ['spendθrift] *a n* prodigo.
sperm [spə:m] *n* sperma.
spew [spju:] *vti* vomitare.
sphere [sfiə] *n* sfera; ambiente.
spherical ['sferikəl] *a* sferico.
sphinx [sfiŋks] *n* sfinge.
spice [spais] *n* spezie *pl*; aroma, sapore.
spick-and-span ['spikən'spæn] *a* lucido come uno specchio, lindo e ordinato.
spicy ['spaisi] *a* aromatico, piccante.
spider ['spaidə] *n* ragno.
spigot ['spigət] *n* zipolo; rubinetto.
spike [spaik] *n* aculeo, chiodo, punta; spiga.
spiky ['spaiki] *a* munito di aculei, irto; (*fig*) di carattere difficile, spinoso.
spill [spil] *n* atto del versare; (*fam*) caduta, rovesciamento, (*pipe light*) legnetto; *vt* rovesciare, versare, spargere; *vi* cadere, rovesciarsi.

spin [spin] *n* giro, giretto; rotazione; *vt* filare, far girare, raccontare (una storia); *vi* girare, roteare.
spinach ['spinidʒ] *n* spinaci *pl*.
spindle ['spindl] *n* fuso; perno; *a* **s.-shanked** dalle gambe lunghe e sottili.
spin-drier ['spin'draiə] *n* asciugatrice automatica.
spine [spain] *n* spina (dorsale).
spineless ['spainlis] *a* senza spina dorsale; molle, senza carattere.
spinet ['spinit] *n* (*mus*) spinetta.
spinning ['spiniŋ] *n* filatura; **s. wheel** filatoio.
spinster ['spinstə] *n* zitella.
spiral ['spaiərəl] *a* spirale.
spire ['spaiə] *n* spira, spirale; guglia.
spirit ['spirit] *n* spirito.
spirited ['spiritəd] *a* brioso, vivace, ardente.
spiritless ['spiritlis] *a* avvilito, senz'energia.
spiritual ['spiritjuəl] *a* spirituale; *n* canto religioso dei negri degli S.U.
spiritualism ['spiritjuəlizəm] *n* spiritismo.
spiritualist ['spiritjuəlist] *n* spiritualista; spiritista.
spirt [spə:t] *n* getto, zampillo improvviso.
spit [spit] *n* spiedo; lingua di terra che avanza nel mare; sputo; badile, vanga; *vt* infilzare nello spiedo; sputare; pronunciare con violenza; *vi* sputare; piovigginare; mandar faville.
spite [spait] *n* dispetto, rancore; *vt* contrariare, vessare; **in s. of** *prep* a dispetto di, malgrado.
spiteful ['spaitful] *a* dispettoso, malevolo.
spitefully ['spaitfuli] *ad* per dispetto; con astio.
spitefulness ['spaitfulnis] *n* dispetto, malevolenza.
spittle ['spitl] *n* saliva, sputo.
spittoon [spi'tu:n] *n* sputacchiera.
splash [splæʃ] *n* spruzzo, tonfo; pillacchera; *vt* impillaccherare; spruzzare; *vi* sollevare spruzzi; cadere nell'acqua con un tonfo; **to make a s.** fare un effetone, fare colpo, far furore.
splay [splei] *a* largo e piatto; voltato verso l'esterno; obliquo; *vti* (*arch*) svasare; essere in posizione obliqua; slogare.
spleen [spli:n] *n* milza; bile, ipocondria.
splendid ['splendid] *a* splendido.
splendor ['splendə] *n* splendore.
splice [splais] *n* unione, intrecciatura; (*naut*) impiombatura; *vt* congiungere, unire; impiombare.
splint [splint] *n* scheggia; (*med*) stecca.
splinter ['splintə] *n* scheggia.
split [split] *a* spaccata; *n* fenditura, spaccatura; scisma; *vti* fender(si), spaccar(si), scheggiar(si).
splutter ['splʌtə] *vti* barbugliare; (*in speech*) sputacchiare; (*of pen*) spruzzare.
spoil [spɔil] *n usu pl* bottino; *vti* deteriorar(si), guastar(si), viziare.
spoke [spouk] *n* raggio.
spokesman ['spouksmən] *n* portavoce.
spoliation [,spouli'eiʃən] *n* spoliazione.
sponge [spʌndʒ] *n* spugna; spugnatura; **s. cake** biscotto spugnoso; **sponger** (*fig*) parassita, scroccone; *vt* cancellare, lavare con la spugna; *vi* vivere a scrocco.
spongy ['spʌndʒi] *a* spugnoso, poroso.
sponsor ['spɔnsə] *n* garante, madrina *f*, padrino *m*.
spontaneity [,spɔntə'ni:iti] *n* spontaneità.
spontaneous [spɔn'teiniəs] *a* spontaneo.
spool [spu:l] *n* bobina, rocchetto.
spoon [spu:n] *n* cucchiaio.
spoonful ['spu:nful] *n* cucchiaiata.
sporadic [spə'rædik] *a* sporadico.
spore [spɔ:] *n* spora.
sport [spɔ:t] *n* gioco, divertimento; sport; (*fig*) persona di spirito; *vi* divertirsi, giocare; *vt* ostentare; **sports requisites** (*or* **sports goods**) articoli sportivi.
sporting ['spɔ:tiŋ] *a* sportivo; **s. goods** articoli sportivi.
sportive ['spɔ:tiv] *a* gioviale, sportivo.
sportsman ['spɔ:tsmən] *n* sportivo; giocatore d'azzardo.
spot [spɔt] *n* luogo, posto, punto; macchia, (*fam*) piccola quantità; *vti* macchiar(si); *vt* (*fam*) individuare, scoprire.
spotless ['spɔtlis] *a* immacolato, senza macchia.
spotlight ['spɔtlait] *n* luce della ribalta, riflettore.
spouse [spauz] *n* coniuge, marito *m*, moglie *f*.
spout [spaut] *n* becco; (*of teapot etc*) beccuccio; (*of liquid*) getto; tubo di scarico; *vi* gettare, spruzzare; *vti* scaricare, scaturire, zampillare; (*fig*) declamare.
sprain [sprein] *n* storta; *vt* storcere.
sprat [spræt] *n* spratto; (*fam*) bimbetto.
sprawl [sprɔ:l] *vi* sdraiarsi, stare sdraiato, in modo scomposto.
spray [sprei] *n* schiuma, spruzzo; rametto, ramoscello; *vt* spruzzare.
spread [spred] *n* distesa, estensione; (*fam*) banchetto; *vt* diffondere, propagare, spargere, spiegare, stendere; *vi* spargersi, spiegarsi, stendersi.
spree [spri:] *n* (*fam*) baldoria.
sprig [sprig] *n* rametto; (*fig*) giovincello.

sprightliness ['spraitlinis] *n* spirito, vivacità.
sprightly ['spraitli] *a* spiritoso, vivace.
spring [spriŋ] *n* balzo, salto; molla; fonte, sorgente; (*season*) primavera; *vt* far scattare; *vi* balzare; derivare, provenire; sorgere.
springtime ['spriŋtaim] *n* tempo di primavera.
springy ['spriŋi] *a* elastico.
sprinkle ['spriŋkl] *n* aspersione, spruzzatina; *vt* aspergere, spruzzare.
sprinkling ['spriŋkliŋ] *n* spruzzamento; spruzzatina; aspersione; (*fig*) pizzico, infarinatura.
sprint [sprint] *n* (*sport*) scatto finale, 'sprint'; *vi* correre alla massima velocità.
sprite [sprait] *n* folletto, spiritello.
sprout [spraut] *n* germoglio; (*vegetable*) cavolino di Bruxelles; *vi* germogliare, spuntare.
spruce [spru:s] *a* azzimato, attillato; *n* abete rosso.
spry [sprai] *a* arzillo, vivace.
spur [spə:] *n* sprone, sperone; (*fig*) incitamento; *vt* incitare, spronare, stimolare.
spurious ['spjuəriəs] *a* falso, spurio.
spuriousness ['spjuəriəsnis] *n* contraffazione, falsità.
spurn [spə:n] *vt* respingere a calci; (*fig*) disprezzare, rifiutare con sdegno.
spurt [spə:t] *n* breve sforzo violento; *vti* fare un breve sforzo violento, scattare; schizzare.
sputter ['spʌtə] *vi* parlare incoerentemente, barbugliare, sputacchiare.
spy [spai] *n* spia; *vti* spiare.
squab [skwɔb] *n* piccioncino; cuscinetto.
squabble ['skwɔbl] *n* bisticcio; *vi* bisticciar(si).
squad [skwɔd] *n* squadra.
squadron ['skwɔdrən] *n* (*mil*) squadra, squadrone; (*naut, av*) squadriglia.
squalid ['skwɔlid] *a* squallido, sordido.
squall [skwɔ:l] *n* raffica, turbine; (*fig*) litigio.
squalor ['skwɔlə] *n* squallore, miseria.
squander ['skwɔndə] *vt* scialacquare.
square [skwɛə] *a* quadro, quadrato; robusto; giusto, onesto; preciso; sostanzioso; *n* quadrato; piazza; (*instrument*) squadra; *ad* angolo retto, direttamente; *vt* quadrare; elevare al quadrato; (*fam*) corrompere; *vi* adattarsi, conformarsi.
squash [skwɔʃ] *n* spremuta; cosa schiacciata; (*fam*) ressa; melopopone; **Italian s.** zucchino; *vti* schiacciar(si), spremere; *vt* (*fam*) stroncare, soffocare.
squat [skwɔt] *a* tarchiato, tozzo; rannicchiato; *vi* accosciarsi, rannicchiarsi.
squawk [skwɔ:k] *n* grido rauco; *vti* emettere un grido rauco; lamentarsi.
squeak [skwi:k] *n* grido acuto, squittio, stridore; *vi* squittire, stridere, cigolare; parlare con voce stridula.
squeaky ['skwi:ki] *a* (*voice*) acuto; che squittisce; cigolante, stridente.
squeal [skwi:l] *n* strillo, squittio; *vi* strillare.
squeamish ['skwi:miʃ] *a* delicato di stomaco; schizzinoso.
squeamishness ['skwi:miʃnis] *n* delicatezza di stomaco; schizzinosità.
squeeze [skwi:z] *n* compressione, spremitura, stretta; ressa; *vti* spremere, spremersi, stringere, stringersi; estorcere.
squelch [skweltʃ] *vti* fare il rumore del piede tirato su dal fango molle; diguazzare; (*fig*) soffocare, sopprimere.
squib [skwib] *n* petardo, razzo; pasquinata, satira.
squid [skwid] *n* seppia.
squint [skwint] *n* strabismo; sguardo furtivo; *vi* guardare obliquamente; essere strabico; aver tendenza verso.
squire ['skwaiə] *n* gentiluomo di campagna; (*hist*) scudiero.
squirm [skwə:m] *vi* contorcersi; provare imbarazzo, o umiliazione.
squirrel ['skwirəl] *n* scoiattolo.
squirt [skwə:t] *n* schizzetto; siringa; *vti* schizzare.
stab [stæb] *n* pugnalata; *vt* pugnalare.
stability [stə'biliti] *n* stabilità.
stabilize ['steibilaiz] *vt* stabilizzare.
stable ['steibl] *a* fermo, stabile; *n* scuderia, stalla.
stack [stæk] *n* ammasso, mucchio, catasta; pagliaio, gruppo di camini sul tetto; (*fam*) grande quantità; *vt* ammucchiare, accatastare.
stadium ['steidiəm] *pl* **stadia** *n* stadio, campo sportivo.
staff [stɑ:f] *n* appoggio, sostegno; bastone; personale; corpo insegnante, (*mil*) stato maggiore; *vt* fornire di personale.
stag [stæg] *n* cervo, cerbiatto; **s. beetle** cervo volante.
stage [steidʒ] *n* palcoscenico, teatro; tappa; fase; periodo; scena; *vt* (*theat*) mettere in scena.
stagger ['stægə] *n* barcollamento, passo incerto; *vt* far barcollare; (*fig*) sbalordire; *vi* barcollare, vacillare.
stagnant ['stægnənt] *a* stagnante.
stagnate ['stægneit] *vi* stagnare, subire una stasi ristagnare.
stagnation [stæg'neiʃən] *n* ristagno; stasi.
staid [steid] *a* posato, serio.
stain [stein] *n* macchia; onta; colore, tinta; *vt* macchiare; dipingere.
stainless ['steinlis] *a* senza macchia; **s. steel** acciaio inossidabile.
stair [stɛə] *n* gradino, scalino; *pl* scala.

staircase ['stɛəkeis] *n* scala, tromba delle scale.
stake [steik] *n* palo; rogo; posta, premio; *vt* sostenere, delimitare con pali; rischiare; scommettere.
stale [steil] *a* raffermo, stantio; spossato, trito; *vti* rendere, diventare stantio.
stalemate ['steil'meit] *n* (*chess*) stallo; (*fig*) punto morto; *vt* fare stallo a; (*fig*) portare a un punto morto.
stalk [stɔ:k] *n* gambo, stelo; andatura maestosa; inseguimento di selvaggina; *vi* camminare maestosamente; inseguire selvaggina.
stall [stɔ:l] *n* stalla; stallo; bancherella; chiosco, edicola; scanno; *vr* fermarsi; *vi* non andare innanzi, posporre.
stallion ['stæljən] *n* stallone.
stalwart ['stɔlwət] *a* robusto, vigoroso.
stammer ['stæmə] *n* balbettamento, balbuzie; *vi* balbettare, tartagliare.
stamp [stæmp] *n* francobollo; bollo, marchio, timbro; impronta; *vt* affrancare; bollare, timbrare; imprimere; *vi* pestare i piedi.
stampede [stæm'pi:d] *n* fuga precipitosa e tumultante.
stanch [sta:ntʃ] *v* **staunch.**
stanchion ['sta:nʃən] *n* puntello; sbarra.
stand [stænd] *n* arresto, pausa; posizione; posteggio; posto; banco, edicola; palco, tribuna; leggio, piedistallo; (*exhibition*) "stand"; *vt* appoggiare, mettere in piedi; affrontare, resistere a, sopportare; *vi* stare ritto, stare in piedi; fermarsi.
standard ['stændəd] *n* bandiera, stendardo; modello, livello; *a* classico, normale.
standardize ['stændədaiz] *vt* standardizzare.
standing ['stændiŋ] *n* posizione, riputazione.
standpoint ['stændpɔint] *n* punto di vista.
standstill ['stændstil] *n* punto morto, ristagno.
stanza ['stænzə] *n* (*poet*) stanza, strofa.
staple ['steipl] *a* principale; *n* (*com*) prodotto principale.
star [sta:] *n* stella, astro; asterisco; (*theat etc*) divo, -va; *vt* segnare con l'asterisco; ornare di stelle; *vi* essere attore di cartello.
starboard ['sta:bəd] *n* (*naut*) tribordo.
starch [sta:tʃ] *n* amido; (*fig*) formalismo; *vt* inamidare.
stare [stɛə] *n* sguardo fisso; *vi* fissare, guardare fisso.
starfish ['sta:fiʃ] *n* stella di mare.
stark [sta:k] *a* rigido; completo; *ad* del tutto, completamente.
starling ['sta:liŋ] *n* stornello.
starlit ['sta:lit] *a* stellato.
starry ['sta:ri] *a* stellato; scintillante.
start [sta:t] *n* partenza, avvio, inizio; sobbalzo, sussulto; vantaggio; *vt* mettere in moto, iniziare; *vi* partire; sobbalzare, trasalire.
starter ['sta:tə] *n* iniziatore, fondatore, (*aut*) avviamento.
startle ['sta:tl] *vt* far trasalire.
startling ['sta:tliŋ] *a* impressionante, sensazionale.
starvation [sta:'veiʃən] *n* fame, inedia.
starve [sta:v] *vti* (far) morire di fame; *vi* agognare.
state [steit] *n* stato, nazione; condizioni *pl*; grado, qualità, dignità; pompa; *vt* affermare, asserire, formulare, specificare, stabilire.
stateliness ['steitlinis] *n* imponenza, maestosità.
stately ['steitli] *a* imponente, maestoso, solenne.
statement ['steitmənt] *n* affermazione, dichiarazione; deposizione testimoniale; rendiconto.
statesman ['steitsmən] *pl* **-men** *n* statista, uomo di stato; **statesmanship** arte di governo.
static ['stætik] *a* statico.
station ['steiʃən] *n* stazione; grado; posto, posizione sociale; *vt* assegnare un posto a, collocare.
stationary ['steiʃnəri] *a* stazionario, fisso.
stationer ['steiʃnə] *n* cartolaio.
stationery ['steiʃnəri] *n* cartoleria.
statistic [stə'tistik] *a* statistico; *n pl* statistica.
statuary ['stætjuəri] *a* statuario; *n* scultura, statuaria.
statue ['stætju:] *n* statua.
statuesque [,stætju'esk] *a* statuario.
stature ['stætʃə] *n* statura.
status ['steitəs] *n* stato, condizione sociale, situazione; **s. symbol** simbolo di posizione sociale.
statute ['stætju:t] *n* statuto, legge.
statutory ['stætjutəri] *a* statutario, fissato dalla legge.
staunch [stɔ:ntʃ] *a* fedele, leale; solido; *vt* (*med*) tamponare.
stave [steiv] *n* doga; strofa, stanza; (*mus*) rigo; *vt* praticare un foro in; **to s. off** allontanare, stornare.
stay [stei] *n* permanenza, soggiorno; sostegno; (*leg*) sospensione; *vt* trattenere, arrestare, ritardare; *vi* rimanere, stare, soggiornare; *n pl* busto, corsetto.
stead [sted] *n* luogo, vece.
steadfast ['stedfəst] *a* costante, risoluto.
steadiness ['stedinis] *n* costanza, fermezza.
steady ['stedi] *a* costante, fermo, posato, stabile.
steak [steik] *n* fetta di carne o pesce.
steal [sti:l] *vt* rubare, sottrarre; *vi* rubare; muoversi furtivamente.

stealth [stelθ] *n* movimento, o atto, furtivo.
stealthily ['stelθili] *ad* furtivamente, di nascosto.
stealthy ['stelθi] *a* clandestino, furtivo.
steam [sti:m] *n* vapore; *vt* esporre a vapore; cuocere a vapore; *vi* emettere vapore, fumare; **s. roller** rullo compressore.
steamboat ['sti:mbout] *n* battello a vapore.
steamer ['sti:mə] *n* piroscafo, vapore.
steamship ['sti:mʃip] *n* piroscafo, vapore.
steed [sti:d] *n* destriero, corsiero.
steel [sti:l] *n* acciaio; *vt* ricoprire, rivestire di acciaio; (*fig*) fortificare; indurire; **steelwork** lavoro in acciaio, *pl* acciaierie.
steely ['sti:li] *a* di acciaio; (*fig*) duro, inflessibile, di ferro.
steep [sti:p] *a* erto, ripido, scosceso; (*fam*) esorbitante; *n* erta, precipizio.
steeple ['sti:pl] *n* campanile.
steeplechase ['sti:pltʃeis] *n* corsa ad ostacoli.
steepness ['sti:pnis] *n* ripidezza.
steer [stiə] *vti* dirigere, guidare, governare, dirigersi.
steer [stiə] *n* (*zool*) giovenco.
steerage ['stiəridʒ] *n* governo del timone; parte della nave riservata ai passeggeri di 3ª classe.
steersman ['stiəzmən] *pl* **-men** *n* timoniere.
stem [stem] *n* gambo; stelo; ramo, rampollo, stirpe; (*gram*) tema, radicale; *vt* arginare, arrestare, contenere.
stench [stentʃ] *n* fetore, tanfo.
stencil ['stensl] *n* stampino, decorazione fatta con stampino; **s. copy** copia a ciclostile.
stenographer [ste'nɔgrəfə] *n* stenografo *m*, stenografa *f*.
stenography [ste'nɔgrəfi] *n* stenografia.
step [step] *n* passo; gradino, scalino; piolo, provvedimento; *pl* scalinata; scala a mano; *vt* misurare a passi; *vi* andare, venire, camminare.
stepbrother ['step,brʌðə] *n* fratellastro; **stepdaughter** *n* figliastra; **stepfather** *n* patrigno; **stepmother** *n* matrigna; **stepsister** *n* sorellastra; **stepson** *n* figliastro.
Stephen ['sti:vn] *nm pr* Stefano.
stepping-stone ['stepiŋstoun] *n* pietra per guadare; (*fig*) trampolino.
stereophonic [,steriə'fɔnik] *a* stereofonico.
stereoscope ['stiəriəskoup] *n* stereoscopio.
stereoscopic [,steriə'skɔpik] *a* stereoscopico.
stereotype ['stiəriətaip] *n* stereotipo.
sterile ['sterail] *a* sterile.
sterility [ste'riliti] *n* sterilità.
sterling ['stə:liŋ] *a* genuino, puro, di buona lega; **pound s.** (lira) sterlina.
stern [stə:n] *a* austero, rigido, severo; *n* (*naut*) poppa; deretano.
sternness ['stə:nnis] *n* austerità, severità.
stertorous ['stə:tərəs] *a* affannoso.
stew [stju:] *n* ragù, stufato; vivaio di pesci; *vti* cuocere a fuoco lento.
steward ['stjuəd] *n* amministratore; dispensiere; cameriere di bordo; **stewardess** cameriera di bordo.
stick [stik] *n* bacchetta; bastone; ramo, stecco; *vt* ficcare, conficcare; appiccicare, incollare; *vi* aderire, rimanere attaccato; **s.-in-the-mud** persona priva di iniziativa.
sticker ['stikə] *n* attacchino; scocciatore; etichetta gommata.
stickler ['stiklə] *n* sostenitore accanito; pignolo.
sticky ['stiki] *a* appiccicoso, viscido; (*fig*) poco accomodante.
stiff [stif] *a* duro, inflessibile, rigido; intorpidito; (*price*) caro; difficile; impacciato.
stiffen ['stifn] *vt* indurire, irrigidire; inamidare; indolenzire; *vi* irrigidirsi, rassodarsi.
stiffness ['stifnis] *n* rigidezza; intorpidimento, indolenzimento; difficoltà.
stifle ['staifl] *vti* soffocare; *vt* estinguere.
stifling ['staifliŋ] *s* soffocante.
stigma ['stigmə] *n* marchio, segno (d'infamia).
stigmatize ['stigmətaiz] *vt* stigmatizzare.
stiletto [sti'letou] *pl* **-os, -oes** *n* stiletto; **s. heels** tacchi a spillo.
still [stil] *a* calmo; fermo, immobile; tranquillo, silenzioso; *ad* ancora, tuttora, tuttavia; *n* silenzio, quiete; alambicco; *vt* calmare, far tacere.
stillness ['stilnis] *n* calma, quiete, tranquillità.
stilt [stilt] *n* trampolo.
stilted ['stiltid] *a* ricercato, affettato, privo di naturalezza.
stimulant ['stimjulənt] *a n* stimolante.
stimulate ['stimjuleit] *vt* stimolare.
stimulating ['stimjuleitiŋ] *a* stimolante, eccitante.
stimulation [,stimju'leiʃən] *n* stimolo.
stimulus ['stimjuləs] *n* stimolo; pungolo.
sting [stiŋ] *n* pungiglione; puntura; (*insect*) pungolo; (*fig*) frecciata, sarcasmo; *vt* pungere; (*fig*) irritare, far arrabbiare.
stinginess ['stindʒinis] *n* spilorceria, tirchieria.
stingy ['stindʒi] *a* spilorcio, tirchio.
stink [stiŋk] *n* fetore, puzzo; *vi* puzzare.
stint [stint] *n* limite, restrizione; compito; *vt* lesinare, limitare, tenere a stecchetto.

stipend ['staipend] *n (eccl)* stipendio.
stipulate ['stipjuleit] *vti* pattuire, stipolare.
stipulation [,stipju'leiʃən] *n* patto, stipolazione.
stir [stə:] *n* il rimescolare, l'attizzare; trambusto, movimento; *vt* agitare, muovere, rimescolare; *vi* muoversi; **to s. up** stimolare, eccitare.
stirrup ['stirəp] *n* staffa.
stitch [stitʃ] *n* punto (di cucitura); maglia; *vt* cucire.
stoat [stout] *n* ermellino.
stock [stɔk] *n* riserva, scorta; bestiame; famiglia, stirpe; ceppo, tronco; *(rifle)* calcio; *(com)* azioni *pl*; **s. market** mercato finanziario; **common s.** azioni ordinarie; **stocks and shares** valori di borsa, titoli; *vt* tenere in magazzino; provvedere, rifornire.
stockbroker ['stɔk,broukə] *a* agente di cambio.
stockfish ['stɔkfiʃ] *n* stoccafisso.
Stockholm ['stɔkhoum] *n* Stoccolma.
stocking ['stɔkiŋ] *n* calza (lunga).
stockist ['stɔkist] *n (com)* grossista; fornitore.
stocky ['stɔki] *a* tarchiato.
stodgy ['stɔdʒi] *a* indigesto, pesante.
stoic ['stouik] *a n* stoico; **stoically** stoicamente.
stoke [stouk] *vt* attizzare (il fuoco), alimentare (la caldaia); *vi* fare il fuochista.
stoker ['stoukə] *n* fuochista.
stole [stoul] *n* stola.
stolid ['stɔlid] *a* stolido, imperturbabile.
stolidity [stɔ'liditi] *n* stolidezza, stolidità.
stomach ['stʌmək] *n* stomaco; *(fig)* coraggio; *vt* ingoiare, subire, tollerare.
stone [stoun] *n* pietra, sasso; *(fruit)* nocciolo; misura di peso (= 14 *libbre, kg* 6,45); *(med)* calcolo; *vt* lapidare; togliere il nocciolo a.
stony ['stouni] *a* pietroso; *(fig)* duro, freddo.
stool [stu:l] *n* sgabello; escremento, feci *pl*.
stoop [stu:p] *n* curvatura, inclinazione del corpo in avanti; *vi* curvarsi, chinarsi; umiliarsi; essere curvo.
stop [stɔp] *n* arresto, fermata; punto d'interpunzione; *vt* arrestare, sospendere; ostruire; (ot)turare; *vi* fermarsi, cessare.
stoppage ['stɔpidʒ] *n* arresto, cessazione: ostruzione; *(med)* occlusione.
stopper ['stɔpə] *n* tampone, tappo, turacciolo.
storage ['stɔ:ridʒ] *n* immagazzinamento, deposito, *(com)* magazzinaggio.
store [stɔ:] *n* grande magazzino, emporio, negozio; provvista, *pl* provvigioni, abbondanza; *vt* approvvigionare, immagazzinare; **storehouse** magazzino deposito; **s. clerk** commesso.
stork [stɔ:k] *n* cicogna.
storm [stɔ:m] *n* burrasca, tempesta, temporale; scoppio; *vi* essere violento, infuriare; *vt* prendere d'assalto.
stormily ['stə:mili] *ad* violentemente.
stormy ['stɔ:mi] *a* tempestoso; *(fig)* violento.
story ['stɔ:ri] *n* storia, novella, racconto, favola, frottola; **storyteller** narratore; *(fam)* bugiardo; *n* piano (d'una casa).
stout [staut] *a* forte, robusto, ben piantato, corpulento; *n* birra scura.
stout-hearted ['staut'hɑ:tid] *a* coraggioso, intrepido.
stoutness ['stautnis] *n* corpulenza.
stove [stouv] *n* fornello, stufa, cucina.
stow [stou] *vt* collocare accuratamente, stivare; *(sl)* smettere.
stowage ['stouidʒ] *n (naut)* stivaggio.
stowaway ['stouəwei] *n* passeggero clandestino.
straddle ['strædl] *vti* stare a cavalcioni di, cavalcare, divaricare, stare a gambe divaricate.
straggle ['strægl] *vi* disperdersi, sbandarsi, sparpagliarsi.
straggler ['stræglə] *n* ritardatario; soldato sbandato.
straggling ['stræglin] *a* sparso, isolato; **s. beard** barba rada.
straight [streit] *a* diritto; retto; *drinks)* liscio; *ad* direttamente.
straighten ['streitn] *vti* raddrizzar (si).
straightforward [streit'fɔ:wəd] *a* franco, leale, retto; semplice, facile.
straightforwardness [streit'fɔ:wədnis] *n* franchezza, rettitudine; semplicità, chiarezza.
straightness ['streitnis] *n* dirittura.
strain [strein] *n* tensione, sforzo, strappo muscolare; tono; razza, *pl* melodia; *vt* sforzare, mettere a dura prova; filtrare; *vi* sforzarsi; filtrare; procedere faticosamente.
strainer ['streinə] *n* colino.
strait [streit] *n (geogr)* stretto; difficoltà, imbarazzo; **s.-jacket** camicia di forza; **in straitened circumstances** in difficoltà, in strettezze.
strand [strænd] *n* filo di corda, fune; riva, spiaggia; *vt* far arenare; *vi* arenarsi.
strange [streindʒ] *a* strano, bizzarro; estraneo; insolito, nuovo; forestiero, sconosciuto.
strangeness ['streindʒnis] *n* stranezza, singolarità, novità.
stranger ['streindʒə] *n* estraneo, sconosciuto, forestiero.
strangle ['stræŋgl] *vt* strangolare, soffocare; *(fig)* reprimere.
strap [stræp] *n* cinghia, correggia; *vt* legare con una cinghia.
strapping ['stræpiŋ] *a* robusto, ben piantato.

stratagem ['strætidʒəm] *n* stratagemma.
strategic [strə'ti:dʒik] *a* strategico.
strategist ['strætidʒist] *n* stratega.
strategy ['strætidʒi] *n* strategia.
stratum ['strɑ:təm] *pl* **strata** *n* strato; strato sociale.
straw [strɔ:] *n* paglia; festuca; pagliuzza; (*fig*) cosa da nulla; **the last s.** il colmo, la goccia che fa traboccare il vaso.
strawberry ['strɔ:bəri] *n* fragola.
stray [strei] *a* smarrito; casuale, sporadico; *vi* smarrirsi, sviarsi, errare.
streak ['stri:k] *n* striscia, stria; (*fig*) vena; *vt* striare; *vi* muoversi velocemente.
streaky ['stri:ki] *a* striato, a strisce.
stream [stri:m] *n* corrente, corso d'acqua, fiotto, fiume; *vt* versare a fiotti; *vi* fluire, scorrere.
streamer ['stri:mə] *n* banderuola; nastro; (*newspaper*) testata.
streamline ['stri:mlain] *n* (*aut, av*) linea aerodinamica; *vt* dare linea aerodinamica; (*fig*) ordinare, semplificare.
street [stri:t] *n* via, strada; **streetcar** tram.
strength [streŋθ] *n* forza, forze *pl*, robustezza, vigore.
strengthen ['streŋθən] *vt* fortificare, rafforzare.
strengthless ['streŋθlis] *a* debole, senza forza.
strenuous ['strenjuəs] *a* strenuo; vigoroso; arduo.
strenuousness ['strenjuəsnis] *n* accanimento.
stress [stres] *n* sforzo, tensione; accento, enfasi; importanza; *vt* mettere l'accento su, mettere in rilievo, sottolineare.
stretch [stretʃ] *n* distesa, tratto; stiramento; *vt* (e)stendere; sgranchire; esagerare; *vi* (e)stendersi, stirarsi.
stretcher ['stretʃə] *n* barella.
strew [stru:] *vt* cospargere, disseminare.
strict [strikt] *a* stretto, esatto; (*fig*) severo.
strictness ['striktnis] *n* esattezza, severità.
stricture ['striktʃə] *n* censura, critica.
stride [straid] *n* passo lungo; *vt* scavalcare; *vi* camminare a gran passi.
strident ['straidənt] *a* stridente, stridulo.
strife [straif] *n* conflitto.
strike [straik] *n* sciopero; scoperta di giacimento minerario; *vt* battere, colpire; accendere; impressionare; *vi* colpire; scioperare; (*clock*) suonare.
striker ['straikə] *n* scioperante; battitore.
striking ['straikiŋ] *a* sorprendente, impressionante, rimarchevole.
string [striŋ] *n* corda, spago, stringa; serie; fila, filza; *vt* (*pearls etc*) infilare; **to s. up** (*violin etc*) accordare.
stringent ['strindʒənt] *a* rigoroso, severo.
stringy ['striŋi] *a* filamentoso; fibroso.
strip [strip] *n* striscia; *vt* denudare, privare, spogliare; *vi* spogliarsi, svestirsi.
stripe [straip] *n* striscia; (*mil*) gallone.
strive [straiv] *vi* sforzarsi, lottare.
stroke [strouk] *n* colpo; battuta; (*med*) colpo; sferzata; tratto; carezza; *vt* accarezzare, lisciare.
stroll [stroul] *n* giretto, passeggiata; *vi* andare a zonzo, bighellonare.
strong [strɔŋ] *a* forte, robusto, saldo.
stronghold ['strɔŋhould] *n* roccaforte, cittadella.
strop [strɔp] *n* coramella; *vt* affilare un rasoio.
strophe ['stroufi] *n* strofa.
structure ['strʌktʃə] *n* struttura, costruzione.
struggle ['strʌgl] *n* combattimento, lotta; *vi* lottare, divincolarsi.
strum [strʌm] *n* strimpellamento; *vti* strimpellare.
strut [strʌt] *vi* pavoneggiarsi, camminare impettito.
stub [stʌb] *n* troncone; mozzicone; (*cheque book etc*) matrice; *vt* sradicare; sbattere; spegnere.
stubble ['stʌbl] *n* stoppia, stoppie *pl*; barba ispida.
stubborn ['stʌbən] *a* ostinato, testardo.
stubbornness ['stʌbənnis] *n* ostinazione, testardaggine.
stucco ['stʌkou] *n* stucco.
stud [stʌd] *n* borchia; bottoncino da colletto; allevamento di cavalli da corsa.
student ['stjudənt] *n* studente, studentessa.
studio ['stjudiou] *n* (*artist's*) studio; (*cin*) teatro di posa.
studious ['stjudiəs] *a* studioso.
study ['stʌdi] *n* studio; applicazione; premura; *vt* studiare, esaminare attentamente; *vi* studiare, darsi la pena.
stuff [stʌf] *n* materia; roba; sostanza; stoffa, tessuto; cosa di nessun valore; *vt* imbottire, infarcire, rimpinzare; impagliare; *vi* rimpinzarsi.
stuffing ['stʌfiŋ] *n* imbottitura; (*cook*) ripieno.
stuffy ['stʌfi] *a* chiuso, senz'aria; (*of weather*) afoso, (*fam*) di idee antiquate; noioso.
stultify ['stʌltifai] *vt* infirmare, neutralizzare.
stumble ['stʌmbl] *n* passo falso; (*fig*) errore; *vi* incespicare, inciampare, fare errori.
stump [stʌmp] *n* ceppo, tronco;

moncherino; mozzicone; *vt* confondere, mettere nell'imbarazzo; *vi* camminare goffamente.
stumpy ['stʌmpi] *a* tarchiato, tozzo.
stun [stʌn] *vt* assordare, stordire; far perdere i sensi a.
stunning ['stʌniŋ] *a* stordente, assordante; (*sl*) meraviglioso.
stunt [stʌnt] *n* (*sl*) bravata; trovata pubblicitaria, notizia sensazionale; (*av*) acrobazia; *vt* arrestare lo sviluppo di.
stupefy ['stjupifai] *vt* istupidire.
stupendous [stju'pendəs] *a* stupendo.
stupid ['stjupid] *a* stupido.
stupidity [stju'piditi] *n* stupidità.
stupor ['stjupə] *n* stupore; (*med*) torpore.
sturdiness ['stə:dinis] *n* gagliardia, vigore.
sturdy ['stə:di] *a* robusto, vigoroso, gagliardo.
sturgeon ['stə:dʒən] *n* storione.
stutter ['stʌtə] *n* balbuzie; *vi* essere balbuziente.
sty [stai] *n* porcile.
sty(e) [stai] *n* orzaiolo.
style [stail] *n* stile; distinzione; titolo; stilo; (*com*) ragion sociale.
stylish ['stailiʃ] *a* elegante, distinto, alla moda.
stylus ['stailəs] *n* stilo, puntina per grammofono.
suave [swɑ:v] *a* mellifluo; garbato.
subaltern ['sʌbltən] *a n* subalterno.
subdue [səb'dju:] *vt* domare, soggiogare, vincere.
sub-editor ['sʌb'editə] *n* redattore aggiunto, revisore di stampa.
subject ['sʌbdʒikt] *a* soggetto; suscettibile; *n* argomento; soggetto; materia di studio; suddito; *vt* [səb'dʒekt] assoggettare, sottoporre.
subjection [səb'dʒekʃən] *n* soggezione, sottomissione.
subjective [səb'dʒektiv] *a n* soggettivo.
subjugate ['sʌbdʒugeit] *vt* soggiogare.
subjunctive [səb'dʒʌŋktiv] *n* (*gram*) congiuntivo.
sub-let ['sʌb'let] *vt* subaffittare.
sublime [sə'blaim] *a* sublime.
submarine ['sʌbmərin] *a* sottomarino; *n* sommergibile.
submerge [səb'mə:dʒ] *vti* sommerger (si), immerger(si).
submersion [səb'mə:ʃən] *n* sommersione.
submission [səb'miʃən] *n* sottomissione.
submissive [səb'misiv] *a* remissivo, sottomesso.
submit [səb'mit] *vt* sottomettere, sottoporre; *vi* cedere, rassegnarsi.
subordinate [sə'bɔ:dnit] *a* subordinato; *n* subalterno; *vt* subordinare.
suborn [sʌ'bɔ:n] *vt* subornare.
subscribe [səb'skraib] *vt* sottoscrivere a; *vi* aderire, sottoscriversi.
subscriber [səb'skraibə] *n* sottoscritto; (*com*) contraente; abbonato.
subscription [səb'skripʃən] *n* abbonamento; quota d'iscrizione.
subsequent ['sʌbsikwənt] *a* successivo, susseguente.
subservient [səb'səviənt] *a* ossequiente, servile; subordinato.
subside [səb'said] *vi* abbassarsi, (*waters*) decrescere; cedere, (*ground*) sprofondare; calmarsi, diminuire.
subsidence [səb'saidəns] *n* abbassamento, cedimento.
subsidiary [səb'sidjəri] *a* sussidiario, accessorio, supplementare.
subsidize ['sʌbsidaiz] *vt* sussidiare, sovvenzionare.
subsidy ['sʌbsidi] *n* sussidio, sovvenzione.
subsist [səb'sist] *vi* sussistere.
subsistence [səb'sistəns] *n* sussistenza, sostentamento.
substance ['sʌbstəns] *n* sostanza.
substantial [səb'stænʃəl] *a* sostanzioso; sostanziale.
substantiate [səb'stænʃieit] *vt* provare, dar fondamento a.
substitute ['sʌbstitju:t] *n* sostituto, surrogato; *vt* sostituire.
substitution [,sʌbsti'tju:ʃən] *n* sostituzione.
subterfuge ['sʌbtəfju:dʒ] *n* sotterfugio.
subterranean ['sʌbtə'reiniən] *a* sotterraneo.
subtle ['sʌtl] *a* sottile, delicato, tenue, indefinibile; astuto, ingegnoso.
subtlety ['sʌtlti] *n* sottigliezza; astuzia.
subtract [səb'trækt] *vt* sottrarre.
subtraction [səb'trækʃən] *n* sottrazione.
suburb ['sʌbə:b] *n* sobborgo.
suburban [sə'bə:bən] *a* suburbano, della periferia.
subversive [sʌb'və:siv] *a* sovversivo, sovvertitore.
subvert [sʌb'və:t] *vt* sovvertire.
subway ['sʌbwei] *n* sottopassaggio; metropolitana.
succeed [sək'si:d] *vt* succedere a; *vi* riuscire, aver successo, salire a.
success [sək'ses] *n* successo, fortuna.
successful [sək'sesful] *a* fortunato.
successfully [sək'sesfuli] *ad* con successo, felicemente.
succession [sək'seʃən] *n* successione; serie.
successive [sək'sesiv] *a* successivo, consecutivo.
successor [sək'sesə] *n* successore.
succinct [sək'siŋkt] *a* conciso, succinto.
succor ['sʌkə] *n* soccorso; *vt* aiutare, soccorrere.
succulent ['sʌkjulənt] *a* succulento; squisito.

succumb [sə'kʌm] *vi* soccombere.
such [sʌtʃ] *a pron* tale; questo; simile.
suck [sʌk] *vt* succhiare; poppare; assorbire.
sucker ['sʌkə] *n* (*of insect*) succhiatoio; (*of leech*) ventosa; (*fig*) credulone; parassita.
suckle ['sʌkl] *vt* allattare.
suckling ['sʌkliŋ] *n* lattante, poppante.
suction ['sʌkʃən] *n* succhiamento; aspirazione.
sudden ['sʌdn] *a* improvviso, imprevisto.
suddenly ['sʌdnli] *ad* (tutt')ad un tratto, improvvisamente.
suddenness ['sʌdnnis] *n* subitaneità.
suds [sʌdz] *n* saponata.
sue [sju:] *vt* citare in giudizio.
suède [sweid] *n* pelle scamosciata.
suet ['sjuit] *n* grasso, sugna.
suffer ['sʌfə] *vt* soffrire, subire, tollerare; *vi* soffrire, patire.
sufferance ['sʌfərəns] *n* sopportazione, tolleranza.
suffering ['sʌfəriŋ] *a* sofferente; *n* sofferenza.
suffice [sə'fais] *vt* essere sufficiente per; *vi* bastare.
sufficient [sə'fiʃənt] *a* bastevole, sufficiente; *n* quantità sufficiente.
suffix ['sʌfiks] *n* (*gram*) suffisso.
suffocate ['sʌfəkeit] *vt* soffocare, asfissiare.
suffocation [,sʌfə'keiʃən] *n* soffocazione, asfissia.
suffrage ['sʌfridʒ] *n* suffragio, diritto di voto.
suffragette [,sʌfrə'dʒet] *n* suffragetta.
suffuse [sə'fju:z] *vt* diffondersi su, coprire.
sugar ['ʃugə] *n* zucchero; (*fig*) parole dolci *pl*; **icing s.** zucchero a velo; **powdered s.** zucchero in polvere.
suggest [sə'dʒest] *vt* suggerire, proporre.
suggestion [sə'dʒestʃən] *n* suggerimento, proposta.
suggestive [sə'dʒestiv] *a* che richiama alla mente; allusivo; suggestivo.
suicidal [sui'saidl] *a* suicida; (*fig*) disastroso.
suicide ['sjuisaid] *n* suicida; suicidio.
suit [sju:t] *n* abito completo; petizione, supplica; causa; (*cards*) colore, seme; *vt* soddisfare, convenire a, giovare a; donare a; *vi* addirsi, andar bene, convenire.
suitable ['sju:təbl] *a* adatto, conveniente.
suitably ['sju:təbli] *ad* appropriatamente; opportunamente.
suite [swi:t] *n* sèguito; serie.
suitor ['sju:tə] *n* aspirante, corteggiatore; (*leg*) attore in una causa.
sulk [sʌlk] *vi* tenere il broncio.
sulky ['sʌlki] *a* imbronciato, scontroso.
sullen ['sʌlən] *a* cupo, imbronciato.
sullenness ['sʌlənnis] *n* umor nero, intrattabilità.
sully ['sʌli] *vt* macchiare, disonorare.
sulphur ['sʌlfə] *n* zolfo.
sulphuric [sʌl'fjuərik] *a* solforico.
sultan ['sʌltən] *n* sultano.
sultana [səl'tɑ:nə] *n* sultana, uva sultanina.
sultry ['sʌltri] *a* afoso, soffocante.
sum [sʌm] *n* addizione, somma; *vt* addizionare, sommare; **s. up** riassumere.
summary ['sʌməri] *n* riassunto; *a n* sommario.
summer ['sʌmə] *n* estate.
summery ['sʌməri] *a* estivo.
summit ['sʌmit] *n* sommità, vetta, apice.
summon ['sʌmən] *vt* chiamare, mandare a chiamare, convocare; (*leg*) citare.
summons ['sʌmənz] *n* (*leg*) citazione; convocazione; (*mil*) chiamata.
sump [sʌmp] *n* pozzo nero; (*aut*) coppa.
sumptuous ['sʌmptjuəs] *a* sontuoso.
sun [sʌn] *n* sole.
sunbeam ['sʌnbi:m] *n* raggio di sole.
sunburnt ['sʌnbə:nt] *a* abbronzato.
Sunday ['sʌndi] *n* domenica.
sunder ['sʌndə] *vt* scindere, separare.
sundry ['sʌndri] *a* parecchi, diversi; **sundries** *n pl* bagatelle *pl*; spese varie *pl*.
sunlight ['sʌnlait] *n* luce del sole; **s. treatment** elioterapia.
sunny ['sʌni] *a* pieno di sole, solatio, assolato; (*fig*) allegro.
sunrise ['sʌnraiz] *n* alba, levata del sole.
sunset ['sʌnset] *n* tramonto.
sunshine ['sʌnʃain] *n* (luce del) sole; (*fig*) gioia, felicità.
sup [sʌp] *vi* cenare.
superb [sju'pə:b] *a* superbo, magnifico, splendido.
supercilious [,sju:pə'siliəs] *a* arrogante, sdegnoso.
superficial [,sju:pə'fiʃəl] *a* superficiale.
superfluous [sju'pə:fluəs] *a* superfluo.
superhuman [,sju:pə'hjumən] *a* sovrumano.
superintend [,sju:prin'tend] *vti* sovrintendere (a).
superintendent [,sju:prin'tendənt] *n* sovrintendente.
superior [sju'pieriə] *a n* superiore.
superiority [sju,piəri'ɔriti] *n* superiorità.
superlative [sju'pə:lətiv] *a* superlativo, eccellente; *n* superlativo.
supermarket ['sju:pə,mɑ:kit] *n* 'supermarket', supermercato.
supernatural [,sju:pə'nætʃrəl] *a* sovrannaturale.
supersede [,sju:pə'si:d] *vt* rimpiazzare, sostituire, sostituirsi(a).

supersonic ['sju:pə'sɔnik] *a* ultrasonoro; (*av*) supersonico.
superstition [,sju:pə'stiʃən] *n* superstizione.
superstitious [,sju:pə'stiʃəs] *a* superstizioso.
superstructure ['sju:pə,strʌktʃə] *n* sovrastruttura.
supervene [,sju:pə'vi:n] *vi* sopravvenire.
supervise ['sju:pəvaiz] *vt* sorvegliare, sovrintendere a.
supervision [,sju:pə'viʒən] *n* sorveglianza, sovrintendenza.
supine ['sju:pain] *a* supino; inerte.
supper ['sʌpə] *n* cena.
supplant [sə'plɑ:nt] *vt* soppiantare.
supple ['sʌpl] *a* flessibile, pieghevole, agile; (*fig*) docile.
supplement ['sʌplimənt] *n* supplemento; ['sʌpliment] *vt* aggiungere a, completare, integrare.
suppleness ['sʌplnis] *n* flessibilità, pieghevolezza.
suppliant ['sʌpliənt] *a* supplichevole; *n* supplicante, supplice.
supplicate ['sʌplikeit] *vt* supplicare.
supplication [,sʌpli'keiʃən] *n* supplica(zione).
supplier [sə'plaiə] *n* fornitore, fornitrice.
supply [sə'plai] *n* approvvigionamento, fornitura, rifornimento, scorta; *vt* approvvigionare, (ri)fornire, provvedere; supplire.
support [sə'pɔ:t] *n* sostegno, appoggio, aiuto, mantenimento; *vt* sostenere, mantenere; assecondare.
supportable [sə'pɔ:təbl] *a* sopportabile.
supporter [sə'pɔ:tə] *n* fautore, sostenitore; (*sport*) tifoso.
suppose [sə'pouz] *vt* supporre, ritenere.
supposedly [sə'pouzidli] *ad* presumibilmente, per ipotesi.
supposition [,sʌpə'ziʃən] *n* supposizione, ipotesi.
suppress [sə'pres] *vt* sopprimere; (*fig*) soffocare, nascondere.
suppression [sə'preʃən] *n* soppressione.
suppurate ['sʌpjuəreit] *vi* (*med*) suppurare.
supremacy [sju'preməsi] *n* supremazia.
supreme [sju'pri:m] *a* supremo.
surcharge ['sə:tʃɑ:dʒ] *n* soprattassa, soprapprezzo.
sure [ʃuə] *a* certo, sicuro; *ad* (*fam*) sicuro.
surely ['ʃuəli] *ad* sicuramente, senza dubbio, certo, certamente.
sureness ['ʃuənis] *n* certezza, sicurezza.
surety ['ʃuəti] *n* garanzia; garante, mallevadore.
surf [sə:f] *n* frangente, risacca; **s.-boat** barca piatta per navigare tra i frangenti; **s.-riding** sport dell'acquaplano.
surface ['sə:fis] *n* superficie.
surfeit ['sə:fit] *n* sovrabbondanza, sazietà.
surge [sə:dʒ] *n* onda, onde *pl*; *vi* ondeggiare.
surgeon ['sə:dʒən] *n* chirurgo.
surgery ['sə:dʒəri] *n* chirurgia; gabinetto medico; ambulatorio.
surgical ['sə:dʒikəl] *a* chirurgico.
surliness ['sə:linis] *n* scontrosità, villania.
surly ['sə:li] *a* scontroso, villano.
surmise ['sə:maiz] *n* congettura; *vt* congetturare, sospettare.
surmount [sə'maunt] *vt* sormontare, sorpassare.
surname ['sə:neim] *n* cognome.
surpass [sə'pɑ:s] *vt* sorpassare, superare.
surplice ['sə:pləs] *n* (*eccl*) cotta.
surplus ['sə:pləs] *n* eccedenza, sovrappiù.
surprise [sə'praiz] *n* sorpresa; *vt* sorprendere.
surprisingly [sə'praiziŋli] *ad* sorprendentemente, tra la sorpresa generale.
surrealism [sə'riəlizəm] *n* surrealismo.
surrender [sə'rendə] *n* resa; cessione, consegna; (*com*) riscatto; *vt* cedere; rinunziare a, abbandonare; *vi* arrendersi, sottomettersi.
surreptitious [,sʌrəp'tiʃəs] *a* clandestino.
surround [sə'raund] *vt* attorniare, circondare.
surroundings [sə'raundiŋz] *n pl* dintorni *pl*, ambiente.
survey ['sə:vei] *n* esame; rilevamento topografico; sguardo generale; indagine; [sə'vei] *vt* esaminare, dare uno sguardo generale a, rilevare.
surveyor [sə'veiə] *n* ispettore; agrimensore, geometra.
survival [sə'vaivəl] *n* sopravvivenza.
survive [sə'vaiv] *vt* sopravvivere (a).
survivor [sə'vaivə] *n* superstite.
Susan ['suzn] *nf pr* Susanna.
susceptibility [sə,septi'biliti] *n* suscettibilità.
susceptible [sə'septəbl] *a* suscettibile, sensibile.
suspect ['sʌspekt] *a* sospetto; *n* persona sospetta; *vt* sospettare, diffidare di.
suspend [səs'pend] *vt* sospendere, differire.
suspender [səs'pendə] *n* giarrettiera; *pl* bretelle.
suspense [səs'pens] *n* ansietà, indecisione, sospensione d'animo, incertezza; **in s.** nell'incertezza, in sospeso.
suspension [səs'penʃən] *n* sospensione.
suspicion [səs'piʃən] *n* sospetto.

suspicious [səs'piʃəs] *a* sospettoso, diffidente.
sustain [səs'tein] *vt* sostenere; prolungare; subire; mantenere.
sustenance ['sʌstinəns] *n* nutrimento, vitto, sostentamento.
swab [swɔb] *n* strofinaccio; (*naut*) radazza; (*med*) tampone.
swaddling clothes ['swɔdliŋklouðz] *n* fasce *pl*.
swagger ['swægə] *n* fanfaronata, spavalderia; *vi* camminare con sussiego, vantarsi.
swaggerer ['swægərə] *n* fanfarone.
swain [swein] *n* (*poet*) contadino, rustico innamorato.
swallow ['swɔlou] *n* rondine; *vt* inghiottire, ingoiare.
swamp ['swɔmp] *n* palude.
swampy ['swɔmpi] *a* paludoso.
swan [swɔn] *n* cigno.
swap [swɔp] *n* scambio, baratto; *vt* barattare.
sward [swɔ:d] *n* distesa erbosa.
swarm [swɔ:m] *n* sciame, frotta, gran numero; *vi* sciamare, brulicare.
swarthy ['swɔ:ði] *a* bruno, di carnagione scura.
swastika ['swɔstikə] *n* svastica, croce uncinata.
swathe [sweið] *n* benda, fascia; *vt* fasciare, bendare.
sway [swei] *n* oscillazione; influenza, dominio; *vt* far oscillare; influenzare; *vi* oscillare.
swear [swεə] *vti* (far) giurare; *vi* bestemmiare, imprecare.
sweat [swet] *n* sudore; *vti* sudare; (*fig*) sfruttare.
sweater ['swetə] *n* chi suda; maglione di lana.
Swede [swi:d] *n* svedese; **swede** rapa svedese.
Sweden ['swi:dn] *n* Svezia.
Swedish ['swi:diʃ] *a* svedese.
sweep [swi:p] *n* scopata, spazzata; spazzacamino; distesa; movimento circolare; (*mil*) rastrellamento; *vt* scopare, spazzare; (*mil*) rastrellare; *vi* muoversi rapidamente.
sweeper ['swi:pə] *n* chi scopa; spazzino.
sweeping ['swi:piŋ] *a* vasto, sconfinato; impetuoso; assoluto.
sweepings ['swi:piŋz] *n pl* spazzatura.
sweet [swi:t] *a* dolce, profumato, tenero, amabile; *n* dolce, dolciume.
sweetbread ['swi:tbred] *n* animella.
sweeten ['swi:tn] *vt* addolcire, inzuccherare.
sweetheart ['swi:thɑ:t] *n* innamorato, -a.
sweetmeat ['swi:tmi:t] *n* (*usu pl*) dolciumi, frutta candita.
sweetness ['swi:tnis] *n* dolcezza, tenerezza, profumo.
swell [swel] *n* il sollevarsi delle acque; (*sl*) elegantone; *a* (*fam*) elegante; *vti* gonfiar(si), ingrossar(si).
swelling ['sweliŋ] *n* gonfiamento, gonfiore.
swelter ['sweltə] *vi* essere oppresso dal caldo, sudare; *n* afa, caldo opprimente.
sweltering ['sweltəriŋ] *a* soffocante; molle di sudore.
swerve [swə:v] *vi* deviare, fare uno scarto.
swift [swift] *a* agile, rapido, svelto, veloce; *n* rondone.
swiftness ['swiftnis]*n* agilità, rapidità, velocità.
swill [swil] *n* risciacquatura; *n* risciacquata; *vt* risciacquare; *vi* bere all'eccesso.
swim [swim] *n* nuotata; (*fig*) corrente degli affari, della vita sociale; *vi* nuotare.
swimmer ['swimə] *n* nuotatore.
swimming ['swimiŋ] *n* nuoto; **s. pool** piscina.
swindle ['swindl] *n* truffa; *vti* truffare, imbrogliare.
swindler ['swindlə] *n* imbroglione, truffatore.
swine [swain] *n pl* maiali *pl*, suini *pl*; (*fig*) porco.
swing [swiŋ] *n* dondolio; oscillazione; altalena; ritmo; *vt* dondolare; *vi* dondolare; oscillare; pendere; (*of boat*) muoversi sull'ancora.
swipe [swaip] *n* colpo violento, manata; *vt* colpire violentemente; (*sl*) rubacchiare.
swirl [swə:l] *n* vortice, turbine.
swish [swiʃ] *n* fruscio; sibilo; sferzata.
Swiss [swis] *a n* svizzero.
switch [switʃ] *n* (*mech*) interruttore; commutatore; (*rly*) scambio; bastoncino, verga; treccia finta.
Switzerland ['switsələnd] *n* Svizzera.
swivel ['swivl] *n* (*mech*) perno.
swoon [swu:n] *n* deliquio, svenimento; *vi* svenire, venir meno.
swoop [swu:p] *n* calata improvvisa, attacco; *vt* **to s. down** piombare su.
swop *v* **swap.**
sword [sɔ:d] *n* spada; **s.-cane** stocco; **s. fish** pesce spada; **s. hilt** elsa della spada; **s. thrust** stoccato.
swordsman ['sɔ:dzmən] *pl* **-men** *n* spadaccino.
sycamore ['sikəmɔ:] *n* sicomoro.
syllable ['siləbl] *n* sillaba.
syllabus ['siləbəs] *n* programma scolastico, prospetto.
syllogism ['silədʒizəm] *n* sillogismo.
sylvan ['silvən] *a* silvano, silvestre.
Sylvia ['silviə] *nf pr* Silvia.
symbol ['simbəl] *n* simbolo.
symbolic [sim'bɔlik] *a* simbolico.
symbolize ['simbəlaiz] *vt* simboleggiare.
symmetrical [si'metrikəl] *a* simmetrico.
symmetry ['simitri] *n* simmetria.
sympathetic [,simpə'θetik] *a* sensibile, comprensivo.

sympathetically [,simpə'θetikli] *ad* con comprensione.
sympathize ['simpəθaiz] *vi* condividere i sentimenti altrui, aver comprensione, compassione.
sympathy ['simpəθi] *n* comprensione, partecipazione ai sentimenti altrui, compassione.
symphony ['simfəni] *n* sinfonia.
symposium [sim'pouziəm] *n* simposio.
symptom ['simptəm] *n* sintomo.
symptomatic [,simptə'mætik] *a* sintomatico.
synagogue ['sinagɔg] *n* sinagoga.
synchronize ['siŋkrənaiz] *vti* sincronizzare.
syndicate ['sindikit] *n* sindacato.
synod ['sinəd] *n* sinodo.
synonym ['sinənim] *n* sinonimo.
synonymous [si'nɔniməs] *a* sinonimo.
syntax ['sintæks] *n* (*gram*) sintassi.
synthesis ['sinθisis] *n* sintesi.
synthetic [sin'θetik] *a* sintetico.
syphilis ['sifilis] *n* (*med*) sifilide.
Syracuse ['saiərəkju:z] *n* Siracusa.
Syria ['siriə] *n* Siria.
Syriac ['siriæk] *a n* siriaco, lingua siriaca.
Syrian ['siriən] *a n* siriano.
syringe [si'rindʒ] *n* (*med*) siringa; *vt* (*med*) siringare.
syrup ['sirəp] *n* sciroppo, melassa.
system ['sistim] *n* sistema; organizzazione; metodo.
systematic [,sisti'mætik] *a* sistematico, metodico.

T

tab [tæb] *n* linguetta, (*mil*) mostrina; cartellino; (*av*) aletta compensatrice.
tabernacle ['tæbənækl] *n* tabernacolo.
table ['teibl] *n* tavola, -lo; prospetto, tabella; **t. of contents** *n* indice; **t. d'hôte** pasto a prezzo fisso.
table-cloth ['teiblklɔθ] *n* tovaglia.
tablet ['tæblit] *n* tavoletta; lapide; pastiglia.
taboo [tə'bu:] *a* tabù, proibito; *n* tabù, interdizione.
tabulate ['tæbjuleit] *vt* ordinare in tavole sinottiche; catalogare.
tabulator ['tæbjuleitə] *n* (*mech*) tabulatore, incolonnatore.
tacit ['tæsit] *a* implicito, sottinteso, tacito.
taciturn ['tæsitə:n] *a* taciturno.
tack [tæk] *n* bulletta, chiodo; (*fig*) linea di condotta, tattica; *vt* inchiodare; imbastire; *vi* (*naut*) virare.
tackle ['tækl] *n* (*naut*) sartiame; attrezzi; *vt* affrontare, mettere mano a.
tacky ['tæki] *a* appiccicaticcio.
tact [tækt] *n* tatto.
tactful ['tæktful] *a* pieno di tatto.
tactical ['tæktikəl] *a* tattico.
tactics ['tæktiks] *n pl* tattica; espedienti *pl*.
tactless ['tæktlis] *a* senza tatto.
tadpole ['tædpoul] *n* girino.
taffy ['tæfi] *n* caramella.
tag [tæg] *n* punta metallica; puntale; cartellino di spedizione etichetta; frase o luogo comune; ritornello.
tail [teil] *n* coda, estremità; *vt* mettere la coda a; (*sl*) pedinare; *vi* essere in coda a.
tailor ['teilə] *n* sarto.
taint [teint] *n* infezione; marchio; *vti* corromper(si), infettar(si).
take [teik] *vti* prendere, afferrare; acquistare; accettare; condurre, portare; catturare; rubare; considerare, ritenere; attaccare; **t. in** ricevere; capire; ingannare; **t. off** togliere; (*av*) decollare; fare la caricatura a; **t. on** assumere, intraprendere; **t. over** succedere in.
take-off ['teikɔf] *n* (*av*) decollo; (*sport*) linea di partenza; caricatura.
taking ['teikiŋ] *a* attraente, piacevole; contagioso; *n* presa; *pl* (*com*) incasso.
talcum ['tælkʌm] *n* talco.
tale [teil] *n* racconto, novella.
talent ['tælənt] *n* talento, attitudine.
talk [tɔ:k] *n* abboccamento, colloquio, conversazione, discorso, chiacchiere *pl*; *vti* parlare, conversare; chiacchierare, discorrere (su, di).
talkative ['tɔ:kətiv] *a* loquace.
talkies ['tɔ:kiz] *n pl* (*sl*) film sonoro.
tall [tɔ:l] *a* alto; grande; incredibile.
tallow ['tælou] *n* sego.
tally ['tæli] *n* tacca; conto; piastrina di contrassegno; *vi* concordare concorrispondere a; *vt* calcolare; spuntare.
talon ['tælən] *n* artiglio.
tamarind ['tæmərind] *n* tamarindo.
tamarisk ['tæmərisk] *n* tamerice, tamarisco.
tame [teim] *a* domestico, addomesticato; docile, mansueto; insipido; *vt* domare, addomesticare.
tameness ['teimnis] *n* docilità.
tamper ['tæmpə] *vi* immischiarsi; (*fig*) corrompere, falsificare.
tan [tæn] *n* concia; abbronzatura; tanè; *vt* conciare (*skins*), abbronzare.
tandem ['tændəm] *n* tandem.
tang [tæŋ] *n* sapore; asprigno piccante; odore penetrante; accento speciale.
tangent ['tændʒənt] *n* tangente.
tangerine [,tændʒə'ri:n] *n* mandarino.
tangible ['tændʒəbl] *a* tangibile.
Tangier [tæn'dʒiə] *n* Tangeri.
tangle ['tæŋgl] *n* complicazione, garbuglio; *vti* complicar(si), ingarbugliar(si).
tank [tæŋk] *n* cisterna, serbatoio, vasca; (*mil*) carro armato.

tankard ['tæŋkəd] *n* grosso boccale.
tanker ['tænkə] *n* nave cisterna.
tanner ['tænə] *n* conciatore, conciapelli.
tannery ['tænəri] *n* conceria.
tannin ['tænin] *n* tannino.
tantalize ['tæntəlaiz] *vt* tormentare, lusingare.
tantamount ['tæntəmaunt] *a* equivalente.
tantrum ['tæntrəm] *n* furie, nervi *pl*.
tap [tæp] *n* spina; rubinetto; qualità di birra; colpetto, picchio; *vt* spillare; battere, picchiare leggermente; intercettare.
tape [teip] *n* nastro, passamano, fettuccia; **t.-recorder** registratore a nastro.
taper ['teipə] *vt* affusolar(si); *n* candela, stoppino.
tapering ['teipəriŋ] *a* affusolato, a punta.
tapestry ['tæpistri] *n* arazzi *pl*; tappezzeria.
tapeworm ['teipwə:m] *n* tenia.
tar [tɑ:] *n* catrame; *vt* incatramare.
tardiness ['tɑ:dinis] *n* lentezza; riluttanza.
tardy ['tɑ:di] *a* lento, tardo; riluttante.
tare [tɛə] *n* tara; veccia.
target ['tɑ:git] *n* bersaglio; (*fig*) obiettivo, mira.
tariff ['tærif] *n* tariffa.
tarmac ['tɑ:mæk] *n* macadam al catrame; (*av*) pista di decollo, di atterraggio.
tarnish ['tɑ:niʃ] *vti* appannar(si), offuscar(si), ossidar(si); (*fig*) macchiar(si).
tarpaulin [tɑ:'pɔ:lin] *n* copertone impermeabile, tessuto incerato.
tarry ['tɑ:ri] *a* incatramato, bituminoso; ['tæri] *vi* indugiare, ritardare.
tart [tɑ:t] *a* agro, aspro; *n* torta di frutta; (*sl*) sgualdrina.
tartan ['tɑ:tən] *n* tessuto di ana scozzese; (*naut*) tartana.
tartar ['tɑ:tə] *n* tartaro.
tartaric [tɑ:'tærik] *a* tartarico.
tartness ['tɑ:tnis] *n* asprezza; (*fig*) mordacità.
task [tɑ:sk] *n* compito, mansione, lavoro, incarico; *vt* mettere a prova, affaticare.
tassel ['tæsəl] *n* fiocco, nappa.
taste [teist] *n* gusto, sapore, assaggio; *vt* assaggiare; *vi* avere gusto di, sapere di.
tasteful ['teistful] *a* di buon gusto.
tasteless ['teistlis] *a* senza gusto, insipido.
tasty ['teisti] *a* saporito.
tatter ['tætə] *n* brandello, straccio; *vt* ridurre a brandelli, stracciare.
tattle ['tætl] *n* chiacchierio, ciarla; *vi* chiacchierare, ciarlare.
tattler ['tætlə] *n* chiacchierone, pettegolo.
tattoo [tə'tu:] *n* tatuaggio; (*mil*) ritirata; (il) tamburellare; *vt* tatuare.
taunt [tɔ:nt] *n* sarcasmo, scherno, rimprovero; *vt* rinfacciare; ingiuriare, schernire.
taut [tɔ:t] *a* teso, rigido.
tavern ['tævən] *n* osteria, trattoria.
tawdry ['tɔ:dri] *a* vistoso e di cattivo gusto.
tawny ['tɔ:ni] *a* abbronzato, fulvo, tanè.
tax [tæks] *n* imposta, tassa, gravame, onere; *vt* tassare, mettere a dura prova; accusare, tacciare.
taxable ['tæksəbl] *a* tassabile.
taxation [tæk'seiʃən] *n* tassazione, tasse *pl*.
taxi ['tæksi] *n* auto pubblica, tassì; **taximeter** tassametro; **t.-stand** posteggio di tassì.
tea [ti:] *n* tè; **teacup** tàzza da tè; **teapot** teiera; **teaspoon** cucchiaino da tè.
teach [ti:tʃ] *vt* insegnare, istruire, ammaestrare; **t.-in** 'teach-in'.
teacher ['ti:tʃə] *n* insegnante.
teaching ['ti:tʃiŋ] *n* insegnamento, dottrina.
teak [ti:k] *n* tek (albero, legno).
team [ti:m] *n* (*horses*) tiro; squadra.
tear [tɛə] *vti* lacerar(si), strappar(si); *vi* correre precipitosamente.
tear [tiə] *n* lacrima, lagrima.
tearful ['tiəful] *a* lacrimoso, piangente.
tearless ['tiəlis] *a* senza lacrime.
tease [ti:z] *n* importuno, seccatore; *vt* stuzzicare, tormentare; (*textiles*) cardare.
teasel, teazle ['ti:zl] *n* cardo; (*mech*) scardasso.
teat [ti:t] *n* capezzolo.
technical ['teknikəl] *a* tecnico.
technicality [,tekni'kæliti] *n* tecnicismo, particolare tecnico.
technician [tek'niʃən] *n* tecnico.
technique [tek'ni:k] *n* tecnica.
technology [tek'nɔlədʒi] *n* tecnologia.
tedious ['ti:diəs] *a* tedioso, noioso.
tedium ['ti:diəm] *n* tedio, noia.
teem [ti:m] *vi* abbondare, brulicare di.
teenager ['ti:n,eidʒə] *n* chi ha meno di vent'anni, adolescente.
teens [ti:nz] *n pl* età da 13 a 19 anni.
teething ['ti:ðiŋ] *n* dentizione.
teetotal(er) [ti:'toutl(ə)] *a n* astemio.
telecast ['telikɑ:st] *vt* teletrasmettere; *n* trasmissione televisiva.
telegram ['teligræm] *n* telegramma.
telegraph ['teligrɑ:f] *n* telegrafo; *vti* telegrafare.
telegraphic [teli'græfik] *a* telegrafico.
telepathy [ti'lepəθi] *n* telepatia.
telephone ['telifoun] *n* telefono; *vti* telefonare.
telephonic [,teli'fɔnik] *a* telefonico.
telephonist [ti'lefənist] *n* telefonista.

telescope ['teliskoup] *n* telescopio; cannocchiale.
televiewer ['telivjuə] *n* telespettatore, telespettatrice.
televise ['telivaiz] *vt* teletrasmettere
television ['teli,viʒən] *n* televisione.
tell [tel] *vt* dire; informare; raccontare; ingiungere, ordinare.
teller ['telə] *n* chi riferisce; (*com*) cassiere.
telltale ['telteil] *a*˚ *n* pettegolo; *a* indiscreto.
temerity [ti'meriti] *n* temerità.
temper ['tempə] *n* carattere, indole; umore; collera; (*metal*) tempera; *vt* mitigare, modificare, temperare, temprare; *vi* (*metal*) temprarsi.
temperament ['tempərəmənt] *n* temperamento, carattere.
temperance ['tempərəns] *n* temperanza, moderazione, astinenza dall'alcool.
temperate ['tempərit] *a* (*climate*) temperato, moderato, sobrio.
temperature ['tempritʃə] *n* temperatura, febbre.
tempest ['tempist] *n* tempesta.
tempestuous [tem'pestjuəs] *a* tempestoso, violento.
templar ['templə] *n* templare.
temple ['templ] *n* tempia; tempio.
temporal ['tempərəl] *a* temporale.
temporary ['tempərəri] *a* temporaneo, transitorio.
temporize ['tempəraiz] *vi* temporeggiare.
tempt [tempt] *vt* tentare, indurre.
temptation [temp'teiʃən] *n* tentazione.
tempter ['temptə] *n* tentatore; **the t.** il Diavolo.
tempting ['temptiŋ] *a* allettante, seducente.
ten [ten] *a n* dieci; **tenth** *a n* decimo.
tenable ['tenəbl] *a* difendibile, che si può tenere, sostenibile.
tenacious [ti'neiʃəs] *a* tenace, adesivo.
tenacity [ti'næsiti] *n* tenacia.
tenancy ['tenənsi] *n* affitto, locazione.
tenant ['tenənt] *n* affittuario, locatario, inquilino.
tend [tend] *vi* tendere, essere diretto; *vt* curare, sorvegliare.
tendency ['tendənsi] *n* tendenza .
tender ['tendə] *a* tenero, delicato, sensibile; *n* (*com*) offerta; (*rly*) tender; (*naut*) lancia; *vt* offrire, porgere; *vi* (*com*) concorrere ad un appalto.
tenderness ['tendənis] *n* tenerezza.
tendon ['tendən] *n* tendine.
tenement ['tenimənt] *n* abitazione, appartamento; **t. house** casa popolare; casamento.
tennis ['tenis] *n* tennis.
tenor ['tenə] *n* tenore.
tense [tens] *a* teso; *n* (*gram*) tempo.
tension ['tenʃən] *n* tensione.
tent [tent] *n* tenda.
tentacle ['tentəkl] *n* tentacolo.
tentative ['tentətiv] *a* sperimentale, di prova.
tenuous ['tenjuəs] *a* tenue, sottile.
tenure ['tenjuə] *n* possesso, diritto di possesso, durata di possesso.
tepid ['tepid] *a* tiepido.
term [tə:m] *n* termine, periodo di tempo; trimestre; (*leg*) sessione; *vt* chiamare, denominare; **terms** *pl* condizioni, patti; rapporti *pl*.
termagant ['tə:məgənt] *n* bisbetica, virago.
terminate ['tə:mineit] *vti* finire, terminare.
termination [,tə:mi'neiʃən] *n* conclusione, fine; (*gram*) desinenza.
terminology [,tə:mi'nɔlədʒi] *n* terminologia.
terminus ['tə:minəs] *n* capolinea.
termite ['tə:mait] *n* termite.
terrace ['terəs] *n* terrazzo, terrapieno; terrazza; fila di case.
terrestrial [ti'restriəl] *a* terrestre.
terrible ['terəbl] *a* terribile.
terrier ['teriə] *n* cane terrier.
terrific [tə'rifik] *a* terrificante; (*fam*) magnifico.
terrify ['terifai] *vt* atterrire, terrificare.
territorial [,teri'tɔ:riəl] *a* territoriale; *n* soldato della milizia territoriale.
territory ['teritəri] *n* territorio.
terror ['terə] *n* terrore.
terrorist ['terərist] *n* terrorista.
terse [tə:s] *a* conciso, incisivo.
terseness ['tə:snis] *n* concisione.
test [test] *n* prova, esperimento, saggio; (*chem*) reagente; *vt* collaudare, provare; (*chem*) analizzare.
testament ['testəmənt] *n* testamento.
testify ['testifai] *vt* testimoniare.
testimonial [,testi'mouniəl] *a* testimoniale; *n* benservito, certificato di servizio, attestato.
testimony ['testiməni] *n* testimonianza.
testy ['testi] *a* irritabile, risentito.
tetanus ['tetənəs] *n* tetano.
tether ['teðə] *n* pastoia; *vt* impastoiare; **at the end of one's t.** all'estremo delle proprie risorse, al limite della pazienza.
Teutonic [tju'tɔnik] *a* teutonico.
text [tekst] *n* testo, argomento.
textile ['tekstail] *a* tessile; *n* tessuto, fibra tessile.
textual ['tekstjuəl] *a* testuale.
texture ['tekstʃə] *n* tessitura; tessuto; trama.
Thames [temz] *n* Tamigi.
than [ðæn] *cj prep* di, che, di quello che (non), di quanto.
thank [θæŋk] *vt* ringraziare.
thankful ['θæŋkful] *a* grato, riconoscente.
thankfulness ['θæŋkfulnis] *n* gratitudine, riconoscenza.
thankless ['θæŋklis] *a* ingrato.

thanklessness ['θæŋklisnis] *n* ingratitudine.
thanks [θæŋks] *n pl* grazie, ringraziamenti *pl*.
thanksgiving ['θæŋks giviŋ] *n* ringraziamento solenne; **T. (Day)** (*US*) giorno del ringraziamento.
that [ðæt] *pl* **those** [ðouz] *a pron* quello *etc*, ciò; che, il quale, la quale *etc*; *cj* che; *ad* (*fam*) così, a tal segno, tanto.
thatch [θætʃ] *n* tetto di paglia; *vt* coprire di paglia.
thaw [θɔ:] *n* (di)sgelo; *vti* disgelar(si), scioglier(si); (*fig*) commuover(si).
the [ðə, ði] *def art* il, lo, la, i, gli, le; *ad* (*before comparatives*) quanto . . . tanto.
theater ['θiətə] *n* teatro.
theatrical [θi'ætrikəl] *a* scenico, teatrale; (*fig*) affettato, manierato.
theft [θeft] *n* furto.
their [ðɛə] *poss a* il loro *etc*; **theirs** *poss pron* il loro *etc*.
them [ðem] *pron* li, le, loro; **themselves** *pron pl* se stessi, si *etc*.
theme [θi:m] *n* tema, argomento.
then [ðen] *ad* allora, poi, in sèguito; dunque, perciò, quindi; *a* di allora.
thence [ðens] *ad* di là; quindi, pertanto.
thenceforth ['ðens'fɔ:θ] *ad* d'allora in poi
Theodore ['θiədɔ:] *nm pr* Teodoro.
theologian [θiə'loudʒjən] *n* teologo.
theological [θiə'lɔdʒikəl] *a* teologico.
theology [θi'ɔlədʒi] *n* teologia.
theorem ['θiərəm] *n* teorema.
theoretical [θiə'retikəl] *a* teorico.
theory ['θiəri] *n* teoria.
therapeutic [,θerə'pju:tik] *a* terapeutico.
therapist ['θerəpist] *n* terapeuta.
therapy ['θerəpi] *n* terapia.
there [ðɛə] *ad* là, vi, lì, ci.
thereby ['ðɛə'bai] *ad* così, perciò.
thereabout(s) ['ðɛərəbaut(s)] *ad* all'incirca, a un dipresso, nei dintorni *pl*.
therefore ['ðɛəfɔ:] *ad* perciò.
Theresa [ti'ri:zə] *nf pr* Teresa.
thereupon ['ðɛərə'pɔn] *ad* al che.
thermometer [θə'mɔmitə] *n* termometro.
thermos ['θə:mɔs] *n* termos.
thesis ['θi:sis] *pl* **theses** *n* tesi.
they [ðei] *pron pl* essi, esse, loro.
thick [θik] *a* denso, fitto, folto, grosso, spesso.
thicken ['θikən] *vti* condensar(si), infittire, infoltire.
thicket ['θikit] *n* boschetto, macchia.
thickness ['θiknis] *n* densità, foltezza; spessore, strato.
thief [θi:f] *n* ladro.
thieve [θi:v] *vi* fare il ladro.
thievish ['θi:viʃ] *a* ladresco.
thigh [θai] *n* coscia.
thimble ['θimbl] *n* ditale.
thin [θin] *a* magro, delicato, fine, leggero, rado, sparso sottile; *vti* assottigliar(si), diradar(si).
thing [θiŋ] *n* cosa, coso.
think [θiŋk] *vti* pensare, credere, ritenere.
thinker ['θiŋkə] *n* pensatore.
thinness ['θinnis] *n* magrezza, sottigliezza, tenuità.
third [θə:d] *a* terzo.
thirst [θə:st] *n* sete; (*fig*) avidità, brama.
thirsty ['θə:sti] *a* assetato, avido; **be t.** aver sete.
thirteen ['θə:'ti:n] *a n* tredici; **thirteenth** *a n* tredicesimo.
thirty ['θə:ti] *a n* trenta; **thirtieth** *a n* trentesimo.
this [ðis] *pl* **these** [ði:z] *dem a pron* questo *etc*.
thistle ['θisl] *n* cardo.
thither ['ðiðə] *ad* là, in quella direzione; **hither and t.** qua e là.
Thomas ['tɔməs] *nm pr* Tommaso.
thong [θɔŋ] *n* cinghia, correggia.
thorn [θɔ:n] *n* spina.
thorny ['θɔ:ni] *a* spinoso.
thorough ['θʌrə] *a* completo, intero; perfetto, esauriente.
thoroughbred ['θʌrəbred] *a* purosangue, che ha stile; *n* purosangue.
thoroughfare ['θʌrəfɛə] *n* arteria di gran traffico, strada principale.
thoroughness ['θʌrənis] *n* perfezione
thou [ðau] *pron* tu.
though [ðou] *cj* benchè, quantunque, sebbene.
thought [θɔ:t] *n* pensiero.
thoughtful ['θɔ:tful] *a* pensieroso, pensoso; attento; previdente.
thoughtfully ['θɔ:tfuli] *ad* pensosamente, pensierosamente; premurosamente.
thoughtfulness ['θɔ:tfulnis] *n* meditazione; attenzione; previdenza; premura.
thoughtless ['θɔ:tlis] *a* irriflessivo, sconsiderato.
thoughtlessly ['θɔ:tlisli] *ad* sventatamente; negligentemente, trascuratamente.
thoughtlessness ['θɔ:tlisnis] *n* sconsideratezza, mancanza di riguardo.
thousand ['θauzənd] *a n* mille; **thousandth** *a n* millesimo.
thrall [θrɔ:l] *n* schiavo, schiavitù.
thrash [θræʃ] *vt* bastonare, battere.
thrashing ['θræʃiŋ] *n* bastonatura, legnate.
thread [θred] *n* filo; *vt* infilare, (far) passare attraverso.
threadbare ['θredbɛə] *a* consumato, logoro; (*fig*) vieto, trito.
threat [θret] *n* minaccia.
threaten ['θretn] *vt* minacciare.
three [θri:] *a n* tre.
threefold ['θri:fould] *a* triplice, triplo.
threshold ['θreʃhould] *n* soglia.
thrice [θrais] *ad* tre volte.
thrift [θrift] *n* economia, frugalità.
thrifty ['θrifti] *a* economico, frugale.

thrill [θril] *n* fremito, palpito; *vt* elettrizzare, far rabbrividire; *vi* fremere, vibrare.
thriller ['θrilə] *n* dramma, film poliziesco, libro, film giallo.
thrive [θraiv] *vi* crescere, prosperare, svilupparsi vigorosamente.
throat [θrout] *n* gola.
throb [θrɔb] *n* pulsazione, vibrazione; *vi* battere, pulsare, vibrare.
throes [θrouz] *n pl* sofferenza acuta.
throne [θroun] *n* trono.
throng [θrɔŋ] *n* calca, folla, ressa; *vt* affollare, ingombrare; *vi* affollarsi, affluire.
throttle ['θrɔtl] *n* (*mech*) valvola; (*aut*) acceleratore; *vt* strangolare.
through [θru:] *a* diretto; *prep* attraverso, per; per mezzo di; *ad* da parte a parte.
throughout [θru'aut] *prep* da un capo all'altro di; per tutta la durata di; *ad* completamente, dappertutto.
throw [θrou] *n* getto, lancio, tiro; *vt* buttare, gettare, lanciare.
thrush [θrʌʃ] *n* tordo.
thrust [θrʌst] *n* pressione, spinta; *vti* cacciar(si), conficcar(si), introdur(si) a viva forza.
thud [θʌd] *n* rumore sordo, tonfo.
thug [θʌg] *n* teppista, furfante.
thumb [θʌm] *n* pollice; *vt* sfogliare; lasciar ditate su; **thumbtack** puntina da disegno; **to t. a lift** chiedere un passaggio facendo l'autostop.
thump [θʌmp] *n* rumore sordo, colpo; *vt* battere, percuotere.
thunder ['θʌndə] *n* tuono, -ni *pl*; *vt* pronunciare con voce tonante; *vi* tuonare.
thunderbolt ['θʌndəboult] *n* fulmine.
thunderstruck ['θʌndəstrʌk] *a* fulminato; sbalordito.
Thursday ['θə:zdi] *n* giovedì.
thus [ðʌs] *ad* così, in tal modo.
thwart [θwɔ:t] *n* (*naut*) banco di rematore; *vt* contrariare, frustrare.
thy [ðai] *a poss* tuo, tua, tuoi, tue.
thyme [taim] *n* timo.
tiara [ti'ɑ:rə] *n* tiara; diadema.
tick [tik] *n* battito; ticchettio; (*fam*) attimo; (*insect*) zecca; (*fam*) credito; *vi* battere, fare tic-tac.
ticket ['tikit] *n* biglietto, cartellino; **t. agent** (*rly*) bigliettario; **t. office** (*rly*) biglietteria.
tickle ['tikl] *n* solletico; *vt* solleticare; stuzzicare; divertire; *vt* far solletico.
ticklish ['tikliʃ] *a* che sente molto il solletico; (*fig*) delicato, scabroso.
tidal ['taidl] *a* della marea; **t. wave** onda di marea; (*fig*) impulso travolgente.
tide [taid] *n* marea; (*fig*) corrente.
tidings ['taidiŋz] *n pl* notizie, nuove.
tidy ['taidi] *a* ordinato, preciso, lindo; (*fam*) considerevole; **to t. up** *vt* rassettare, mettere in ordine.
tie [tai] *n* cravatta; legame, vincolo; (*sport*) pareggio; (*rly*) traversina; *vt* legare, unire; *vi* (*sport*) pareggiare; **cup-t.** eliminatoria di torneo; **t.-up** ingorgo stradale.
tier [tiə] *n* fila; ordine graduato (di posti).
tiff [tif] *n* (*fam*) bisticcio.
tiger ['taigə] **tigress** (*f*) *n* tigre.
tight [tait] *a* aderente, attillato, stretto; teso; (*sl*) brillo; *n pl* calzamaglia.
tighten ['taitn] *vti* serrar(si), stringer(si), tirare.
tightness ['taitnis] *n* strettezza; tensione; oppressione di petto.
tile [tail] *n* mattonella, piastrella; tegola; *vt* coprire di tegole *etc*.
till [til] *n* cassa; *prep* fino a, sino a; *cj* finchè (non); *vt* coltivare (la terra).
tillage ['tilidʒ] *n* coltivazione.
tilt [tilt] *n* inclinazione, giostra, torneo; copertone; *vti* (far) inclinare; giostrare.
timber ['timbə] *n* alberi *pl* di alto fusto, legname da costruzione.
time [taim] *n* tempo; epoca; ora; volta; *vt* cronometrare, scegliere il momento giusto per.
timeless ['taimlis] *a* eterno, infinito; senza tempo; fuori del tempo.
timely ['taimli] *a* opportuno, tempestivo.
timid ['timid] *a* timido.
timidity [ti'miditi] *n* timidezza.
timorous ['timərəs] *a* timoroso.
Timothy ['timəθi] *nm pr* Timoteo.
tin [tin] *n* stagno; latta; scatola, barattolo di latta.
tincture ['tiŋktʃə] *n* tintura; tinta; leggero aroma; (*fig*) infarinatura.
tinder ['tində] *n* (per fuoco) esca.
tinfoil ['tinfɔil] *n* lamina di stagno, stagnola.
tinge [tindʒ] *n* lieve coloritura, sfumatura; *vt* colorire leggermente, sfumare.
tingle ['tiŋgl] *vi* sentire un formicolio; fremere.
tinker ['tiŋkə] *n* stagnino; **to t. with** affaccendarsi.
tinkle ['tiŋkl] *n* tintinnio.
tinkle ['tiŋkl] *vti* (far) tintinnare.
tinsel ['tinsəl] *n* 'lamè'; orpello.
tint [tint] *n* tinta; sfumatura; *vt* colorire; sfumare.
tiny ['taini] *a* minuscolo.
tip [tip] *n* punta; cima; puntale; mancia; informazione segreta, suggerimento; *vt* mettere la punta; (far) inclinare; dare la mancia; avvisare; *vi* ribaltare.
tipple ['tipl] *n* (*fam*) forte bevanda alcoolica; *vi* bere parecchio.
tippler ['tiplə] *n* bevitore abituale.
tipsy ['tipsi] *a* alticcio, brillo.
tiptoe ['tiptou] *n* punta dei piedi; **on t.** *ad* in punta di piedi.
tirade [tai'reid] *n* tirata, filippica.

tire ['taiə] *n* cerchione di ruota, pneumatico; *vti* stancar(si).
tired ['taiəd] *a* stanco.
tiredness ['taiədnis] *n* stanchezza.
tiresome ['taiəsəm] *a* faticoso, noioso.
tissue ['tisju:] *n* tessuto; **t. paper** carta velina.
titbit ['titbit] **tidbit** ['tidbit] *n* boccone delicato, leccornia.
tithe [taið] *n* decima, tassa.
Titian ['tiʃiən] *nm pr* Tiziano.
title ['taitl] *n* titolo; appellativo; **t. page** frontespizio.
titter ['titə] *vi* ridacchiare.
titular ['titjulə] *a n* titolare; **t. saint** santo patrono.
to [tu:] *prep* a; per; rispetto a; verso, in; fino a; contro.
toad [toud] *n* rospo.
toady ['toudi] *vt* adulare; *n* parassita.
toast [toust] *n* pane abbrustolito; brindisi; *vt* abbrustolire; fare un brindisi a; *vi* brindare.
toaster ['toustə] *n* graticola; tostino; tostapane.
tobacco [tə'bækou] *n* tabacco.
tobacconist [tə'bækənist] *n* tabaccaio; **t.'s shop** tabaccheria.
toboggan [tə'bɔgən] *n* toboga; *vi* andare in toboga; (*of prices*) calare.
today [tə'dei] *n ad* oggi.
toddle ['tɔdl] *vi* fare i primi passi.
toddler ['tɔdlə] *n* infante ai primi passi.
toe [tou] *n* dito del piede.
toffee ['tɔfi] *n* caramella.
together [tə'geðə] *ad* insieme, assieme.
toil [tɔil] *n* fatica, lavoro faticoso; *vi* faticare.
toilet ['tɔilit] *n* toeletta; gabinetto
toilsome ['tɔilsəm] *a* faticoso, laborioso.
token ['toukən] *n* segno, pegno.
Toledo [tɔ'leidou] *n* Toledo.
tolerable ['tɔlərəbl] *a* tollerabile, sopportabile; discreto.
tolerance ['tɔlərəns] *n* tolleranza, sopportazione, indulgenza.
tolerant ['tɔlərənt] *a* tollerante, indulgente.
tolerate ['tɔləreit] *vt* tollerare, sopportare.
toleration [,tɔlə'reiʃən] *n* tolleranza.
toll [toul] *n* gabella, pedaggio, tassa; rintocco di campana; *vti* suonare a rintocco.
tomato [tə'mɑ:tou] *n* pomodoro.
tomb [tu:m] *n* tomba.
tombstone ['tu:mstoun] *n* pietra sepolcrale.
tom-cat ['tɔm'kæt] *n* gatto (maschio).
tomorrow [tə'mɔrou] *n ad* domani.
ton [tʌn] *n* tonnellata.
tone [toun] *n* tono; *vt* dare il tono a; *vi* armonizzare, intonarsi.
tongs [tɔŋz] *n pl* molle, mollette *pl*.
tongue [tʌŋ] *n* lingua; linguaggio; (*of bell*) battaglio; (*strip*) linguetta.
tonic ['tɔnik] *a n* tonico, ricostituente.
tonight [tə'nait] *n ad* stanotte; stasera.
tonnage ['tʌnidʒ] *n* tonnellaggio.
tonsil ['tɔnsl] *n* tonsilla.
tonsure ['tɔnʃə] *n* tonsura.
too [tu:] *ad* troppo; anche; inoltre, per di più; pure.
tool [tu:l] *n* arnese, attrezzo, strumento, utensile.
tooth [tu:θ] *n* dente.
toothache ['tu:θeik] *n* mal di dente.
toothless ['tu:θlis] *a* senza denti, sdentato.
top [tɔp] *n* cima, culmine; coperchio; (*toy*) trottola; *vt* coprire, coronare, raggiungere la sommità di; sorpassare.
topaz ['toupæz] *n* topazio.
topic ['tɔpik] *n* argomento, soggetto.
topical ['tɔpikəl] *a* d'attualità.
topmost ['tɔpmoust] *a* (il) più alto.
topographic(al) [,tɔpə'græfik(l)] *a* topografico.
topography [tə'pɔgrəfi] *n* topografia.
topsyturvy ['tɔpsi'tə:vi] *ad* sossopra, a soqquadro.
torch [tɔ:tʃ] *n* torcia, fiaccola; lampadina tascabile.
torment ['tɔ:ment] *n* tormento; [tɔ:'ment] *vt* tormentare.
tornado [tɔ:'neidou] *n* tornado, ciclone.
torpedo [tɔ:'pi:dou] *n* torpedine, siluro.
torpid ['tɔ:pid] *a* torpido, apatico, inerte.
torpor ['tɔ:pə] *n* torpore, apatia.
torrent ['tɔrənt] *n* torrente.
torrid ['tɔrid] *a* torrido.
tortoise ['tɔ:təs] *n* tartaruga, testuggine.
tortuous ['tɔ:tjuəs] *a* tortuoso.
torture ['tɔ:tʃə] *n* tortura; *vt* torturare.
Tory ['tɔ:ri] *a n* (*pol*) conservatore.
toss [tɔs] *n* lancio; moto brusco; beccheggio; *vt* buttare in aria; sballottare, scuotere; *vi* dimenarsi; giocare a testa o croce.
tot [tɔt] *n* piccino; bicchierino.
total ['toutl] *a n* totale.
totter ['tɔtə] *vi* barcollare, vacillare.
touch [tʌtʃ] *n* tatto, tocco, colpetto; contatto; leggero attacco; accenno; un po' di; *vt* toccare; commuovere; riguardare; *vi* toccarsi; **to t. at** (*naut*) far scalo; **to t. up** ritoccare.
touching ['tʌtʃiŋ] *a* commovente.
touchstone ['tʌtʃstoun] *n* pietra di paragone.
touchy ['tʌtʃi] *a* suscettibile, permaloso.
tough [tʌf] *a* duro, difficile, resistente, tenace; (*of meat*) tiglioso.
toughen ['tʌfn] *vti* indurir(si).

toughness ['tʌfnis] *n* durezza, tenacia; difficoltà.
tour [tuə] *n* giro, gita, viaggio; *vi* fare un viaggio, una gita, un giro, visitare.
tourism ['tuərizəm] *n* turismo.
tourist ['tuərist] *n* turista.
tournament ['tuənəmənt] *n* torneo.
tousle ['tauzl] *vt* scarmigliare.
tout [taut] *vi* sollecitare ordini; (*com*) fare la piazza.
tow [tou] *n* stoppa; rimorchio; *vt* rimorchiare.
toward(s) [tə'wɔ:d(z)] *prep* verso; a favore di.
towel ['tauəl] *n* asciugamano.
tower ['tauə] *n* torre; *vi* torreggiare.
town [taun] *n* città; **town hall** municipio.
toy [tɔi] *n* balocco, giocattolo; *vi* giocherellare, trastullarsi.
trace [treis] *n* traccia, orma, impronta; residuo; *vt* tracciare; rintracciare; seguire le tracce.
track [træk] *n* traccia, cammino, pista; sentiero; binario; rotta; scia; *vt* seguire la traccia di; snidare.
tract [trækt] *n* tratto, distesa; trattato, opuscolo.
tractable ['træktəbl] *a* trattabile, docile.
traction ['trækʃən] *n* trazione.
tractor ['træktə] *n* (*mech*) trattore, trattrice.
trade [treid] *n* commercio, traffico; mestiere, occupazione; *vti* commerciare, trattare; scambiare; **T. Union** sindacato; **t. winds** (venti) alisei *pl*.
trader ['treidə] *n* commerciante; nave mercantile.
tradesman ['treidzmən] *n* commerciante, negoziante.
tradition [trə'diʃən] *n* tradizione.
traditional [trə'diʃənl] *a* tradizionale.
traduce [trə'dju:s] *vt* calunniare, diffamare.
traffic ['træfik] *n* traffico; circolazione; *vti* trafficare, commerciare; **t. lights** semaforo.
tragedian [trə'dʒi:diən] *n* tragediografo; attore tragico.
tragedy ['trædʒidi] *n* tragedia.
tragic(al) ['trædʒik(əl)] *a* tragico.
trail [treil] *n* traccia, scia, strascico, pista; *vt* seguire la traccia di, strascicare; *vi* strisciare, trascinarsi.
trailer ['treilə] *n* rimorchio; roulotte; (*cin*) 'prossimamente'.
train [trein] *n* treno; sèguito; strascico; serie; *vt* allenare, ammaestrare, allevare; *vi* allenarsi.
trainer ['treinə] *n* allenatore.
training ['treiniŋ] *n* allenamento, ammaestramento, esercitazione.
trait [treit] *n* tratto, caratteristica.
traitor ['treitə] *n* traditore.
tram(car) ['træm(kɑ:)] *n* tram.
trammel ['træməl] *n* tramaglio; *pl* impedimenti, ostacoli *pl*; *vt* impedire, impastoiare.
tramp [træmp] *n* viaggio a piedi; calpestio; vagabondo; *vt* attraversare a piedi; *vi* camminare con passo pesante.
trample ['træmpl] *n* calpestio; *vti* calpestare.
trance [trɑ:ns] *n* trance, catalessi ipnotica.
tranquil ['træŋkwil] *a* tranquillo.
tranquillity [træŋ'kwiliti] *n* tranquillità.
transact [træn'zækt] *vt* eseguire, trattare, negoziare.
transaction [træn'zækʃən] *n* affare, operazione; (*leg*) transazione; *pl* atti, verbali di società.
transatlantic ['trænzət'læntik] *a* transatlantico.
transcend [træn'send] *vti* trascendere.
transcendent [træn'sendənt] *a* trascendente; **transcendental** *a* trascendentale.
transcribe [træns'kraib] *vt* trascrivere.
transcript ['trænskript] *n* copia; riproduzione.
transfer ['trænsfə:] *n* trasferimento; cessione; (*com*) storno; decalcomania.
transfer [træns'fə:] *vt* trasferire; (*com*) stornare; decalcare.
transferable [træns'fə:rəbl] *a* trasferibile.
transfiguration ['trænsfigju'reiʃən] *n* trasfigurazione.
transfigure [træns'figə] *vt* trasfigurare.
transfix [træns'fiks] *vt* trafiggere, trapassare; pietrificare.
transform [træns'fɔ:m] *vt* trasformare.
transformation [,trænsfə'meiʃən] *n* trasformazione, metamorfosi.
transformer [træns'fɔ:mə] *n* trasformatore.
transfuse [træns'fju:z] *vt* travasare; (*fig*) trasfondere.
transfusion [træns'fju:ʒən] *n* trasfusione.
transgress [træns'gres] *vt* contravvenire a, trasgredire.
transgression [træns'greʃən] *n* trasgressione.
transgressor [træns'gresə] *n* trasgressore.
transient ['trænziənt] *a* transitorio fugace.
transistor [træn'sistə] *n* transistor.
transit ['trænsit] *n* transito.
transition [træn'siʒən] *n* transizione, passaggio.
transitive ['trænsitiv] *a* transitivo.
transitory ['trænsitəri] *a* transitorio.
translatable [træns'leitəbl] *a* traducibile.
translate [træns'leit] *vt* tradurre.
translation [træns'leiʃən] *n* traduzione.

translator [træns'leitə] *n* traduttore.
translucent [træns'lu:snt] *a* traslucido, trasparente, diafano.
transmigration [,trænzmai'greiʃən] *n* trasmigrazione.
transmission [trænz'miʃən] *n* trasmissione.
transmit [trænz'mit] *vt* trasmettere.
transmitter [trænz'mitə] *n* trasmettitore.
transparency [træns'pεərənsi] *n* trasparenza; (*phot*) diapositiva.
transparent [træns'pεərənt] *a* trasparente.
transpire [træns'paiə] *vi* trasparire, trapelare.
transplant [træns'pla:nt] *vt* trapiantare.
transport ['trænspɔ:t] *n* trasporto, mezzo di trasporto; violenta emozione; estasi; [træns'pɔ:t] *vt* trasportare, rapire.
transportation [,trænspɔ:'teiʃən] *n* trasporto, deportazione.
transpose [træns'pouz] *vi* trasporre, spostare.
trans-ship [træns'ʃip] *vt* (*naut*) trasbordare.
transubstantiation ['trænsəb,stænʃi'eiʃən] *n* transubstanziazione.
trap [træp] *n* trappola; botola; calesse; *vt* prendere in trappola.
trap-door ['træp'dɔ:] *n* botola.
trapeze [trə'pi:z] *n* trapezio.
trapper ['træpə] *n* cacciatore di pelli.
trappings ['træpiŋz] *n pl* bardatura, finimenti *pl*.
trash [træʃ] *n* robaccia; sciocchezze.
traumatic [trɔ:'mætik] *a* traumatico.
travel ['trævl] *n* viaggi *pl*; *vi* viaggiare.
traveler ['trævlə] *n* viaggiatore.
traverse ['trævə:s] *a* trasversale; *n* traversa; *vt* attraversare; contestare.
travesty ['trævisti] *n* parodia; *vt* parodiare.
trawl [trɔ:l] *n* rete a strascico; *vti* pescare con strascico.
trawler ['trɔ:lə] *n* motopeschereccio a strascico.
tray [trei] *n* vassoio; (*of a trunk*) scompartimento.
treacherous ['tretʃərəs] *a* traditore, sleale.
treachery ['tretʃəri] *n* tradimento, slealtà.
treacle ['tri:kl] *n* melassa.
tread [tred] *n* passo; parte di suola che tocca la terra; (*of tire*) battistrada; (*of stair step*) pedata; *vt* calpestare; *vi* mettere il piede, camminare.
treadle ['tredl] *n* pedale.
treason ['tri:zn] *n* tradimento.
treasonable ['tri:znəbl] *a* proditorio.
treasure ['treʒə] *n* tesoro; *vt* custodire, tener caro.
treasurer ['treʒərə] *n* tesoriere.
treasury ['treʒəri] *n* tesoreria, tesoro.
treat [tri:t] *n* festa, trattenimento; piacere; *vt* trattare; offrire un trattenimento a; (*med*) curare; *vi* negoziare, trattare.
treatise ['tri:tiz] *n* trattato, dissertazione.
treatment ['tri:tmənt] *n* trattamento, cura.
treaty ['tri:ti] *n* trattato, patto.
treble ['trebl] *a n* triplo; (*mus*) soprano; *vti* triplicar(si).
tree [tri:] *n* albero.
trefoil ['trefɔil] *n* trifoglio.
trellis ['trelis] *n* traliccio; graticcio.
tremble ['trembl] *n* trèmito, tremore; *vi* tremare.
tremendous [tri'mendəs] *a* tremendo, terribile; (*fam*) straordinario.
tremor ['tremə] *n* tremore.
tremulous ['tremjuləs] *a* tremulo.
trench [trentʃ] *n* trincea, fosso.
trenchant ['trentʃənt] *a* tagliente, incisivo.
trend [trend] *n* orientamento, direzione, tendenza; *vi* tendere a, dirigersi.
Trent [trent] *n* Trento.
trepidation [,trepi'deiʃən] *n* trepidazione.
trespass ['trespəs] *n* trasgressione, infrazione; violazione di proprietà; *vi* commettere un'infrazione, trasgredire, abusare di.
trespasser ['trespəsə] *n* trasgressore, contravventore.
tress [tres] *n* treccia.
trestle ['tresl] *n* cavalletto, trespolo.
trial ['traiəl] *n* esperimento, prova; processo; *pl* tribolazione.
triangle ['traiæŋgl] *n* triangolo.
triangular [trai'æŋgjulə] *a* triangolare.
tribe [traib] *n* tribù.
tribulation [,tribju'leiʃən] *n* tribolazione.
tribunal [trai'bju:nl] *n* tribunale.
tribune ['tribju:n] *n* tribuno; tribuna.
tributary ['tribjutəri] *n* affluente; *a n* tributario.
tribute ['tribju:t] *n* tributo.
trice [trais] *n* istante; **in a t.** in un batter d'occhio.
trick [trik] *n* tiro; trucco; abitudine; espediente; *vt* ingannare; *vi* giocar tiri.
trickery ['trikəri] *n* inganno, stratagemma.
trickle ['trikl] *n* gocciolio; ruscelletto; *vi* gocciolare.
trickster ['trikstə] *n* raggiratore.
tricky ['triki] *a* furbo, ingannevole; difficile.
tricolor ['trikələ] *a n* tricolore.
tricycle ['traisikl] *n* triciclo.
trident ['traidənt] *n* tridente.
triennial [trai'eniəl] *a* triennale.
trifle ['traifl] *n* bagattella, bazzecola; (*cook*) zuppa inglese; *vti* gingillarsi, scherzare.
trifler ['traiflə] *n* persona frivola.

trifling ['traifliŋ] *a* insignificante; frivolo.
trigger ['trigə] *n* grilletto; **to t. off** *vt* dare inizio a.
trigonometry [,trigə'nɔmitri] *n* trigonometria.
trill [tril] *n* trillo; *vti* trillare.
trim [trim] *a* accurato, azzimato; *n* ordine, assetto, stato; *vt* aggiustare, rassettare; guarnire; tagliare.
trimming ['trimiŋ] *n* guarnizione.
Trinity ['triniti] *n* trinità.
trinket ['triŋkit] *n* gingillo, ninnolo.
trio ['triou] *pl* **trios** *n* (*mus*) trio, terzetto.
trip [trip] *n* gita, viaggio; incespicamento, passo falso, sgambetto; *vt* far inciampare, far sbagliare; *vi* inciampare, far un passo falso; **to t. along** saltellare.
tripe [traip] *n* trippa; (*sl*) sciocchezze *pl*.
triple ['tripl] *a* triplice; *vti* triplicar(si).
triplet ['triplit] *n* terzina; bimbo nato di parto trigemino.
triplicate ['triplikit] *a* triplicato; triplice; ['triplikeit] *vt* triplicare.
tripod ['traipɔd] *n* treppiedi; tripode.
Tripoli ['tripəli] *n* Tripoli.
trite [trait] *n* trito, banale, comune.
triteness ['traitnis] *n* banalità.
triton ['traitn] *n* tritone.
triumph ['traiəmf] *n* trionfo; *vi* trionfare.
triumphant [trai'ʌmfənt] *a* trionfante.
trivet ['trivit] *n* treppiedi.
trivial ['triviəl] *a* insignificante, banale, senza importanza.
triviality [,trivi'æliti] *n* banalità, cosa di nessuna importanza.
troll [troul] *vi* pescare con esca girante.
trolley ['trɔli] *n* carrello; (*el*) rotella di presa; **t. bus** filobus; **t. car** vettura tranviaria.
trombone [trɔm'boun] *n* (*mus*) trombone.
troop [tru:p] *n* (*mil*) truppa; frotta; compagnia teatrale; *vti* radunar(si), sfilare.
trooper ['tru:pə] *n* (*mil*) soldato di cavalleria; cavallo di truppa; (*naut*) nave per il trasporto di truppe.
trophy ['troufi] *n* trofeo.
tropic ['trɔpik] *n* tropico.
tropical ['trɔpikəl] *a* tropicale.
trot [trɔt] *n* trotto, trottata; *vi* trottare.
trotter ['trɔtə] *n* trottatore, zampa, zampino.
troubadour ['trubəduə] *n* trovatore.
trouble ['trʌbl] *n* disturbo, guaio, seccatura, imbroglio, disordine; *vt* disturbare, turbare, importunare, affliggere; *vi* preoccuparsi prendersi la briga di.
troubled ['trʌbld] *a* agitato, inquieto.
troublesome ['trʌblsəm] *a* fastidioso, molesto, noioso.
trough [trɔf] *n* trogolo.
trousers ['trauzəz] *n pl* calzoni pantaloni *pl*.
trout [traut] *n* trota.
trowel ['trauəl] *n* cazzuola; trapiantatoio.
truant ['truənt] *a n* pigro, svogliato, vagabondo; **play t.** marinare la scuola.
truce [tru:s] *n* tregua, armistizio.
truck [trʌk] *n* baratto; roba, robaccio; carro, carretto, autocarro; **t. farmer** ortolano, orticoltore; **t. line** impresa autotrasporti; **t. trailer** rimorchio di autocarro.
truckle ['trʌkl] *vi* mostrarsi servile.
truculent ['trʌkjulənt] *a* truculento.
trudge [trʌdʒ] *vt* percorrere faticosamente; *vi* camminare faticosamente.
true [tru:] *a* vero, fedele, leale.
truffle ['trʌfl] *n* tartufo.
truism ['truizəm] *n* truismo, verità lapalissiana.
truly ['tru:li] *ad* veramente, sinceramente; **yours t.** vostro devotissimo.
trump [trʌmp] *n* (*cards*) briscola, atout; (*fam*) persona eccellente; *vti* giocare una briscola, degli atouts.
trumpery ['trʌmpəri] *a* senza valore; *n* chincaglieria, orpello.
trumpet ['trʌmpit] *n* tromba; *vi* strombazzare, suonare la tromba; (*elephant*) barrire.
trumpeter ['trʌmpitə] *n* trombettiere.
truncate ['trʌŋkeit] *vt* troncare, mozzare.
truncheon ['trʌntʃən] *n* bastone, randello.
trundle ['trʌndl] *vti* (far) correre, ruzzolare.
trunk [trʌŋk] *n* tronco; baule; proboscide; *pl* calzoni corti, calzoncini.
truss [trʌs] *n* fascio, fastello, (*building*) travatura; (*med*) cinto erniario; *vt* (*of chicken etc, before cooking*) legare le ali; immobilizzare.
trust [trʌst] *n* fede, fiducia; custodia; (*com*) credito; *vt* aver fiducia in, fidarsi di; *vi* sperare vivamente.
trustee [trʌs'ti:] *n* fiduciario, amministratore.
trusteeship [trʌs'ti:ʃip] *n* amministrazione fiduciaria.
trustful ['trʌstful] *a* fiducioso.
trustworthy ['trʌst,wəði] *a* fidato, attendibile.
trusty ['trʌsti] *a* fedele, fidato.
truth [tru:θ] *n* verità.
truthful ['tru:θful] *a* veritiero, verace.
truthfully ['tru:θfuli] *ad* sinceramente; fedelmente, esattamente.
truthfulness ['tru:θfulnis] *n* veracità, sincerità
try [trai] *vt* provare, tentare, mettere alla prova, saggiare; (*leg*) processare; *vi* provare, sforzarsi.

trying ['traiiŋ] *a* difficile, penoso.
tsar [tsɑ:] *n* zar.
tub [tʌb] *n* tino, tinozza, vasca da bagno; (*naut*) barcaccia.
tubby ['tʌbi] *a* tondo e grasso.
tube [tju:b] *n* tubo; (*London*) ferrovia sotterranea; (*US rad*) valvola; **test t.** provetta.
tubercle ['tju:bəkl] *n* tubercolo.
tubercular [tju(:)'bə:kjulə] *a* tubercolare; tubercoloso.
tuberculosis [tju(:),bə:kju'lousis] *n* tubercolosi.
tuberculous [tju'bə:kjuləs] *a* tubercoloso, tubercolotico.
tubular ['tju:bjulə] *a* tubolare.
tuck [tʌk] *n* piega, basta; (*sl*) cibo; *vt* fare pieghe in; **t. in** ripiegare; (*fam*) mangiare avidamente; **t. up** rimboccare.
Tuesday ['tju:zdi] *n* martedì.
tuft [tʌft] *n* ciuffo, fiocco, cespuglio.
tug [tʌg] *n* strappo, sforzo; strazio; (*naut*) rimorchiatore; *vti* tirare con forza, rimorchiare.
tuition [tju'iʃən] *n* insegnamento, istruzione.
tulip ['tju:lip] *n* tulipano.
tumble ['tʌmbl] *n* capitombolo; *vt* buttar giù, rovesciare; *vi* cadere, capitombolare, fare acrobazie.
tumbler ['tʌmblə] *n* acrobata; bicchiere.
tumour ['tju:mə] *n* tumore.
tumult ['tju:mʌlt] *n* tumulto.
tumultuous [tju'mʌltjuəs] *a* tumultuoso.
tun [tʌn] *n* botte, tino.
tuna ['tu:nə] *n* tonno.
tune [tju:n] *n* aria, melodia; accordo; *vt* accordare; **to t. in** (*rad*) sintonizzare.
tuneful ['tju:nful] *a* armonioso, melodioso.
tunic ['tju:nik] *n* tunica.
tunnel ['tʌnl] *n* galleria, traforo, tunnel.
tunny ['tʌni] *n* tonno.
turban ['tə:bən] *n* turbante.
turbid ['tə:bid] *a* torbido.
turbine ['tə:bin] *n* turbina.
turbot ['tə:bət] *n* rombo.
turbulence ['tə:bjuləns] *n* turbolenza, agitazione.
turbulent ['tə:bjulənt] *a* turbolento.
tureen [tə'ri:n] *n* zuppiera.
turf [tə:f] *n* zolla erbosa, tappeto, erboso.
turgid ['tə:dʒid] *a* turgido; (*fig*) ampolloso.
Turin [tju:'rin] *n* Torino; **Turinese** *a n* torinese.
Turk [tə:k] *n* turco.
Turkey ['tə:ki] *n* Turchia.
turkey ['tə:ki] *n* tacchino.
Turkish ['tə:kiʃ] *a n* turco.
turmoil ['tə:mɔil] *n* baccano, tumulto.
turn [tə:n] *n* giro, curva, voltata, piega; turno; passeggiata; inclinazione; *vt* cambiare; girare; trasformare; voltare; tornire; tradurre; *vi* girare; divenire, farsi; rivolgersi, voltarsi; trasformarsi. **turntable** (*rly*) piattaforma girevole, (*of record player*) piatto, giradischi.
turncoat ['tə:nkout] *n* girella.
turncock ['tə:nkɔk] *n* fontaniere.
turner ['tə:nə] *n* tornitore.
turning ['tə:niŋ] *a* girevole; *n* svolta, voltata; **t. point** *n* svolta decisiva.
turnip ['tə:nip] *n* rapa.
turnover ['tə:n,ouvə] *n* rovesciamento; (*com*) giro di affari; torta.
turpentine ['tə:pəntain] *n* trementina, acqua ragia.
turquoise ['tə:kwɑ:z] *n* turchese.
turret ['tʌrit] *n* torre, torretta.
turtle ['tə:tl] *n* tartaruga; **t.-dove** *n* tortora.
Tuscan ['tʌskən] *a n* toscano.
Tuscany ['tʌskəni] *n* Toscana.
tusk [tʌsk] *n* zanna.
tussle ['tʌsl] *n* rissa, zuffa; *vi* azzuffarsi.
tutor ['tju:tə] *n* istitutore, precettore; tutore; *vt* istruire, essere il precettore di.
tutorial [tju'tɔ:riəl] *a* tutorio; *n* lezione a un piccolo gruppo di studenti.
twang [twæŋ] *n* suono acuto, suono nasale; *vt* pronunciare con tono nasale; *vi* fare un suono acuto o nasale.
tweed [twi:d] *n* tessuto di lana cardata, "tweed".
tweezers ['twi:zəz] *n pl* pinze, pinzette *pl*.
twelfth [twelfθ] *a n* dodicesimo.
twelve [twelv] *a n* dodici.
twenty ['twenti] *a n* venti; **twentieth** *a n* ventesimo.
twice [twais] *ad* due volte.
twig [twig] *n* rametto, ramoscello.
twilight ['twailait] *n* crepuscolo.
twin [twin] *a n* gemello.
twine [twain] *n* cordicella, spago; *vti* attorcigliar(si), intrecciar(si), torcer(si).
twinge [twindʒ] *n* dolore lancinante, fitta; (*fig*) rimorso.
twinkle ['twiŋkl] *n* luccichio, scintillio; *vi* luccicare, scintillare; ammiccare, strizzare l'occhio.
twinkling ['twiŋkliŋ] *n* scintillio, balenio; **in the t. of an eye** in un baleno, in un batter d'occhio.
twirl [twə:l] *n* ghirigoro, piroetta.
twist [twist] *n* filo ritorto; rotolo di tabacco; filoncino (di pane); torsione; tendenza; capriccio; (*dance*) "twist"; *vti* contorcer(si), intrecciar(si), torcer(si).
twister ['twistə] *n* torcitore; (*sl*) truffatore; compito difficile, situazione ingarbugliata; **tongue-t.** scioglilingua.
twit [twit] *vt* rinfacciare.

twitch [twitʃ] *n* contrazione spasmodica; *vt* dare uno strattone a; *vi* contorcersi spasmodicamente.
twitter ['twitə] *n* cinguettio, pigolio; (*fam*) agitazione; *vi* cinguettare, pigolare.
two [tu:] *a n* due.
twofold ['tu:fould] *a* doppio, duplice.
tycoon [tai'ku:n] *n* (*sl*) capitalista, magnate.
type [taip] *n* tipo, modello, genere; carattere tipografico.
typewrite ['taiprait] *vt* dattilografare.
typewriter ['taip,raitə] *n* macchina per scrivere.
typhoid ['taifɔid] *a* tifoide; *n* febbre tifoidea.
typhoon [tai'fu:n] *n* tifone.
typhus ['taifəs] *n* (*med*) tifo.
typical ['tipikəl] *a* tipico.
typify ['tipifai] *vt* rappresentare, simboleggiare, esemplificare.
typist ['taipist] n dattilografo, -fa.
typographer [tai'pɔgrəfə] *n* tipografo.
typography [tai'pɔgrəfi] *n* tipografia.
tyrannical [ti'rænikəl] *a* tirannico, dispotico.
tyrannize ['tirənaiz] *vti* tiranneggiare.
tyranny ['tirəni] *n* tirannia.
tyrant ['taiərənt] *n* tiranno.
tyro ['tairou] *n* novizio.
Tyrol ['tiroul] *n* Tirolo.
Tyrolean [ti'rouliən] **Tyrolese** [,tiri'li:z] *a n* tirolese.

U

ubiquitous [ju'bikwitəs] *a* onnipresente.
ubiquity [ju'bikwiti] *n* ubiquità.
udder ['ʌdə] *n* mammella.
Uganda [ju'gændə] *n* Uganda.
ugliness ['ʌglinis] *n* bruttezza.
ugly ['ʌgli] *a* brutto.
Ukraine [ju'krein] *n* Ucraina.
ulcer ['ʌlsə] *n* ulcera.
ulcerate ['ʌlsəreit] *vti* ulcerare.
ulceration [,ʌlsə'reiʃən] *n* ulcerazione.
Ulster ['ʌlstə] *n* Ulster.
ulterior [ʌl'tiəriə] *a* ulteriore.
ultimate ['ʌltimit] *a* finale, fondamentale.
ultimatum [,ʌlti'meitəm] *n* ultimatum.
ultraviolet ['ʌltrə'vaiəlit] *a* ultravioletto.
umbrage ['ʌmbridʒ] *n* (*fig*) ombra, sospetto; offesa.
umbrella [ʌm'brelə] *n* ombrello.
Umbria ['ʌmbriə] *n* Umbria; **Umbrian** *a n* umbro.
umpire ['ʌmpaiə] *n* arbitro; *vti* arbitrare.
un- [ʌn] *prefisso* (avente significato negativo se unito ad aggettivi, avverbi e sostantivi, indicante il contrario o l'annullamento dell'azione, se unito a verbi; qualora non si trovasse il vocabolo sotto la forma composta, si cerchi la forma senza prefisso).
unable ['ʌn'eibl] *a* inabile, incapace.
unabridged ['ʌnə'bridʒd] *a* non abbreviato, intero; **u. edition** edizione integrale.
unaccountable ['ʌnə'kauntəbl] *a* inesplicabile; irresponsabile.
unaccustomed ['ʌnə'kʌstəmd] *a* insolito; non abituato.
unacquainted ['ʌnə'kweintid] *a* **to be u. with** non conoscere.
unadulterated [,ʌnə'dʌltəreitid] *a* non adulterato, genuino.
unaffected ['ʌnə'fektid] *a* semplice, senz'affettazione, non influenzato.
unanimity [,junə'nimiti] *n* unanimità.
unanimous [ju'næniməs] *a* unanime.
unanswerable [ʌn'ɑ:nsərəbl] *a* irrefutabile.
unassuming ['ʌnə'sju:miŋ] *a* modesto, senza pretese.
unattended ['ʌnə'tendid] *a* solo, incustodito.
unaware ['ʌnə'wɛə] *a* inconsapevole, inconscio; **unawares** *ad* all'improvviso, di sorpresa.
unbearable [ʌn'bɛərəbl] *a* insopportabile.
unbecoming ['ʌnbi'kʌmiŋ] *a* sconveniente; che non sta bene, che non si addice.
unbelief ['ʌnbi'li:f] *n* incredulità, scetticismo.
unbeliever [,ʌnbi'li:və] *n* persona incredula, miscredente.
unbend ['ʌn'bend] *vt* raddrizzare; *vi* raddrizzarsi, rilassarsi; (*fig*) farsi affabile.
unbending ['ʌn'bendiŋ] *a* inflessibile.
unbidden ['ʌn'bidn] *a* spontaneo, non invitato.
unblemished [ʌn'blemiʃt] *a* senza macchia, perfetto.
unborn ['ʌn'bɔ:n] *a* non ancora nato, futuro.
unbridled [ʌn'braidld] *a* sfrenato.
unburden [ʌn'bə:dn] *vt* alleggerire; **u. oneself** confidarsi con qlcu.
unbutton ['ʌn'bʌtn] *vti* sbottonare, sbottonarsi.
uncanny [ʌn'kæni] *a* misterioso, strano; inquietante.
uncertain [ʌn'sə:tn] *a* incerto, poco sicuro.
uncertainty [ʌn'sə:tnti] *n* incertezza.
unchangeable [ʌn'tʃeindʒəbl] *a* immutabile, invariabile.
uncle ['ʌŋkl] *n* zio.
unclean ['ʌn'kli:n] *a* impuro, sporco.
uncomfortable [ʌn'kʌmfətəbl] *a* scomodo, spiacevole.
uncommon [ʌn'kɔmən] *a* raro.
uncompromising [ʌn'kɔmprəmaiz-

iŋ] *a* intransigente, inflessibile, assoluto.
unconcerned ['ʌnkən'sə:nd] *a* indifferente.
unconditional ['ʌnkən'diʃənl] *a* incondizionato, assoluto.
unconquered ['ʌn'kɔŋkəd] *a* invitto.
unconscious [ʌn'kɔnʃəs] *a* inconscio, inconsapevole, privo di sensi.
uncouth [ʌn'kuθ] *a* goffo, rozzo.
uncouthness [ʌn'kuθnis] *n* goffaggine, rozzezza.
uncover [ʌn'kʌvə] *vt* scoprire, svelare; *vi* scoprirsi.
unction ['ʌnkʃən] *n* unzione, parole melliflue *pl*.
unctuous ['ʌŋktjuəs] *a* untuoso, mellifluo.
undaunted [ʌn'dɔ:ntid] *a* imperterrito, intrepido.
undecided ['ʌndi'saidid] *a* indeciso, indefinito.
under ['ʌndə] *prep* sotto, al di sotto di; in corso di; *ad* sotto.
underclothes ['ʌndəklouðz] *n pl*, **underclothing** ['ʌndəklouðiŋ] *n* biancheria personale, intima.
undercurrent ['ʌndə,kʌrənt] *n* corrente sottomarina, corrente nascosta.
underdeveloped ['ʌndədi'veləpt] *a* sottosviluppato.
underdone ['ʌndə'dʌn] *a* poco cotto, al sangue.
underfed ['ʌndə'fed] *a* denutrito.
undergo [,ʌndə'gou] *vt* subire, sottoporsi a, sopportare.
undergraduate [,ʌndə'grædjuit] *n* studente universitario.
underground ['ʌndəgraund] *a* sotterraneo; *n* sottosuolo; movimento clandestino; metropolitana, ferrovia sotterranea; *ad* sotto terra.
undergrowth ['ʌndəgrouθ] *n* sottobosco.
underhand ['ʌndəhænd] *a* clandestino, subdolo.
underlie [,ʌndə'lai] *vt* costituire la base di.
underline ['ʌndəlain] *vt* sottolineare.
undermine [,ʌndə'main] *vt* minare.
underneath [,ʌndə'ni:θ] *ad prep* sotto, al di sotto (di).
underrate [,ʌndə'reit] *vt* sottovalutare.
undersell ['ʌndə'sel] *vt* vendere sotto prezzo.
undersigned ['ʌndəsaind] *a* sottoscritto.
understand [,ʌndə'stænd] *vti* capire, comprendere; dedurre; sottintendere; apprendere.
understandable [,ʌndə'stændəbl] *a* comprensibile.
understanding [,ʌndə'stændiŋ] *a* comprensivo; intelligente.
understatement ['ʌndə'steitmənt] *n* attenuazione dei fatti.
undertake [,ʌndə'teik] *vti* intraprendere, impegnarsi a.
undertaker ['ʌndə,teikə] *n* imprenditore di pompe funebri.
undertaking [,ʌndə'teikiŋ] *n* impresa.
undervalue ['ʌndə'vælju:] *vt* sottovalutare.
underwrite ['ʌndərait] *vt* sottoscrivere; (*com*) assicurare.
underwriter ['ʌndə,raitə] *n* firmatario; (*com*) assicuratore.
undisturbed ['ʌndis'tə:bd] *a* indisturbato, imperturbato.
undo ['ʌn'du:] *vt* disfare, sciogliere, annullare, rovinare.
undoing ['ʌn'duiŋ] *n* rovina.
undone ['ʌn'dʌn] *a* slacciato, disfatto, rovinato, incompiuto, intentato.
undress ['ʌn'dres] *vti* svestire, svestirsi, spogliar(si).
undue ['ʌn'dju:] *a* indebito, eccessivo.
undulate ['ʌndjuleit] *vi* ondeggiare, fluttuare.
undulation [,ʌndju'leiʃən] *n* ondulazione.
unearth ['ʌn'ə:θ] *vt* dissotterrare.
unearthly [ʌn'ə:θli] *a* soprannaturale, spettrale; (*fam*) impossibile.
uneasiness [ʌn'i:zinis] *n* disagio, inquietudine, ansia.
uneasy [ʌn'i:zi] *a* ansioso, inquieto.
unequal ['ʌn'i:kwəl] *a* ineguale, impari, non all'altezza di.
unequaled ['ʌn'i:kwəld] *a* senza pari.
unerring ['ʌn'ə:riŋ] *a* infallibile.
uneven ['ʌn'i:vən] *a* ineguale; dispari; irregolare, accidentato.
unevenness ['ʌn'i:vənnis] *n* disuguaglianza; natura accidentata, irregolarità.
unexpected ['ʌniks'pektid] *a* inatteso, imprevisto.
unfair ['ʌn'fεə] *a* ingiusto.
unfairness ['ʌn'fεənis] *n* ingiustizia.
unfaithful ['ʌn'feiθful] *a* infedele, sleale; inesatto.
unfavorable ['ʌn'feivərəbl] *a* sfavorevole.
unfeeling [ʌn'fi:liŋ] *a* insensibile, spietato.
unfinished ['ʌn'finiʃt] *a* incompiuto, non rifinito.
unfit ['ʌn'fit] *a* inadatto, inabile; indegno.
unfold ['ʌn'fould] *vt* aprire, spiegare; svelare; svolgere.
unforgettable ['ʌnfə'getəbl] *a* indimenticabile.
unfortunate [ʌn'fɔ:tʃnit] *a* sfortunato, infelice; **unfortunately** sfortunatamente.
unfrock ['ʌn'frɔk] *vt* spretare.
ungainly [ʌn'geinli] *a* goffo.
ungrateful [ʌn'greitful] *a* ingrato.
unguent ['ʌŋgwənt] *n* unguento.
unhappiness [ʌn'hæpinis] *n* infelicità.
unhappy [ʌn'hæpi] *a* infelice, poco felice; inopportuno.

unhealthy [ʌn'helθi] *a* malsano; malaticcio.
unheard of [ʌn'hə:dɔv] *a* inaudito.
unhurt ['ʌn'hə:t] *a* illeso, incolume.
unicorn ['junikɔ:n] *n* unicorno.
uniform ['junifɔ:m] *a* uniforme; *n* divisa, uniforme.
uniformity [,juni'fɔ:miti] *n* uniformità.
unilateral ['juni'lætərəl] *a* unilaterale.
unimpaired ['ʌnim'pɛəd] *a* non danneggiato, intatto.
unintelligence ['ʌnin'telidʒəns] *n* mancanza di intelligenza.
unintelligent ['ʌnin'telidʒənt] *a* ottuso, stupido.
union ['junjən] *n* unione, accordo, alleanza; **u. suit** combinazione.
unique [ju:'ni:k] *a* unico, solo.
unison ['ju:nizn] *a n* unisono.
unit ['ju:nit] *n* unità, unità di misura.
unitarian [,ju:ni'tɛəriən] *a n* unitario.
unite [ju:'nait] *vti* congiunger(si), unir(si).
United States [ju,naitid'steits] *n pl* Stati Uniti (d'America).
unity ['ju:niti] *n* unità, uniformità, armonia.
universal ['ju:ni'və:səl] *a n* universale.
universality [,ju:nivə:'sæliti] *n* universalità.
universe ['ju:nivə:s] *n* universo.
university [,juni'və:siti] *n* università.
unjust ['ʌn'dʒʌst] *a* ingiusto.
unkempt ['ʌn'kempt] *a* spettinato, incolto.
unkind [ʌn'kaind] *a* scortese, cattivo.
unkindness [ʌn'kaindnis] *n* scortesia, cattiveria.
unknown ['ʌn'noun] *a* sconosciuto, ignoto; *n* ignoto.
unless [ən'les] *cj* a meno che non, se non.
unlike ['ʌn'laik] *a* dissimile; *prep* diversamente da.
unlikely [ʌn'laikli] *a* inverosimile, improbabile.
unload ['ʌn'loud] *vt* scaricare, (*fin*) liberarsi di.
unlock ['ʌn'lɔk] *vt* aprire, disserrare.
unlooked-for [ʌn'luktfɔ:] *a* inaspettato, inatteso.
unlucky [ʌn'lʌki] *a* sfortunato; sinistro.
unmake ['ʌn'meik] *vt* disfare.
unman ['ʌn'mæn] *vt* scoraggiare, snervare.
unmannerly [ʌn'mænəli] *a* sgarbato.
unmistakable ['ʌnmis'teikəbl] *a* chiaro, indubbio.
unmoved ['ʌn'mu:vd] *a* immobile, impassibile.
unnatural [ʌn'nætʃrəl] *a* contro natura, artificioso.
unnecessary [ʌn'nesisəri] *a* inutile, superfluo.
unnerve ['ʌn'nə:v] *vt* snervare.
unobtrusive ['ʌnəb'tru:siv] *a* discreto, modesto, riservato.
unpleasant [ʌn'pleznt] *a* sgradevole, spiacevole.
unpopular ['ʌn'pɔpjulə] *a* impopolare.
unpretending ['ʌnpri'tendiŋ] **unpretentious** ['ʌnpri'tenʃəs] *a* modesto, senza pretese.
unpublished ['ʌn'pʌbliʃt] *a* inedito.
unquestionable [ʌn'kwestʃənəbl] *a* indiscutibile, indubitabile.
unreadable ['ʌn'ri:dəbl] *a* (*of writing, of a book*) illeggibile.
unreasonable [ʌn'ri:znəbl] *a* irragionevole.
unreasonableness [ʌn'ri:znəblnis] *n* irragionevolezza, assurdità.
unrequited ['ʌnri'kwaitid] *a* non corrisposto, non compensato.
unrest ['ʌn'rest] *n* fermento, agitazione.
unruly [ʌn'ru:li] *a* sregolato, indisciplinato.
unsavory ['ʌn'seivəri] *a* (*fig*) ripugnante, disgustoso.
unscripted ['ʌn'skriptid] *a* improvvisato, estemporaneo.
unseemly [ʌn'si:mli] *a* indecoroso, sconveniente.
unseen ['ʌn'si:n] *a* non visto; **u. (sight) translation** traduzione a prima vista.
unselfish ['ʌn'selfiʃ] *a* disinteressato, altruista.
unsettle ['ʌn'setl] *vt* sconvolgere, turbare.
unsightly [ʌn'saitli] *a* brutto, deforme.
unspeakable [ʌn'spi:kəbl] *a* indicibile, inqualificabile.
unsteady ['ʌn'stedi] *a* vacillante, instabile, variabile.
unsure [ʌn'ʃuə] *a* malsicuro, incerto.
untidy [ʌn'taidi] *a* disordinato, sciatto.
until [ən'til] *prep* fino a, prima di; *cj* finchè (non).
untimely [ʌn'taimli] *a* prematuro, intempestivo.
untiring [ʌn'taiəriŋ] *a* instancabile.
untold ['ʌn'tould] *a* indicibile; innumerevole.
unusual [ʌn'juʒuəl] *a* insolito.
unwary [ʌn'wɛəri] *a* imprudente, incauto.
unwelcome [ʌn'welkəm] *a* malaccolto, sgradito.
unwell ['ʌn'wel] *a* indisposto, sofferente.
unwilling ['ʌn'wiliŋ] *a* riluttante.
unworthy ['ʌn'wə:ði] *a* indegno.
up [ʌp] *prep* su per; *ad* in alto; in piedi; su, in su; **up to** fino a; *a* che va verso l'alto.
upbraid [ʌp'breid] *vt* rimproverare.
upbraiding [ʌp'breidiŋ] *n* rimproveri *pl*.

upbringing ['ʌp,briŋiŋ] *n* educazione.
upheaval [ʌp'hi:vəl] *n* sollevamento, subbuglio, scompiglio.
uphill ['up'hil] *a* erto, faticoso; *ad* in salita, in su.
uphold [ʌp'hould] *vt* sostenere, mantenere.
upholsterer [ʌp'houlstərə] *n* tappezziere.
upholstery [ʌp'houlstəri] *n* tappezzeria, imbottitura.
upkeep ['ʌpki:p] *n* mantenimento, manutenzione.
upland ['ʌplənd] *a* alto, montagnoso; *n* altipiano.
uplift ['ʌplift] *n* incoraggiamento; *vt* [ʌp'lift] alzare, sollevare.
upon [ə'pɔn] *prep* sopra, su; al momento di.
upper ['ʌpə] *a* più in alto, più elevato, superiore.
uppermost ['ʌpəmoust] *a ad* il più alto, il più importante, sopra a tutti.
upright ['ʌp'rait] *a* diritto, eretto, in piedi; (*fig*) onesto, retto; *ad* in posizione verticale.
uprightness ['ʌp'raitnis] *n* perpendicolarità; rettitudine.
uproar ['ʌp,rɔ:] *n* tumulto, baraonda.
uproarious [ʌp'rɔ:riəs] *a* rumoroso, fragoroso; tumultuoso.
uproariously [ʌp'rɔ:riəsli] *ad* rumorosamente; tumultuosamente.
uproot [ʌp'ru:t] *vt* estirpare, sradicare, svellere.
upset [ʌp'set] *n* capovolgimento, rovesciamento; *vt* capovolgere, rovesciare, sconvolgere.
upshot ['ʌpʃɔt] *n* esito, risultato finale.
upside-down ['ʌpsaid'daun] *ad* in disordine, sottosopra; capovolto.
upstairs ['ʌp'stɛəz] *a* del piano superiore; *ad* su, al piano di sopra.
upstart ['ʌpstɑ:t] *n* villano rifatto, nuovo ricco.
up-to-date ['ʌptu'deit] *a* aggiornato; alla moda.
upward ['ʌpwəd] *a* che si muove verso l'alto; **upwards** *ad* in alto, verso l'alto.
urban ['ə:bən] *a* urbano, di città.
urbane [ə:'bein] *a* urbano, cortese.
urbanity [ə:'bæniti] *n* urbanità, cortesia.
urchin ['ə:tʃin] *n* monello; **sea u.** riccio di mare.
urge [ə:dʒ] *n* stimolo, impulso; sprone; *vt* incalzare, spingere.
urgency ['ə:dʒənsi] *n* urgenza.
urgent ['ə:dʒənt] *a* urgente.
urine ['jɥərin] *n* orina.
urn [ə:n] *n* urna; bricco.
Uruguay ['urugwai] *n* Uruguay.
us [ʌs] *pron* noi, ci.
usage ['ju:zidʒ] *n* uso, trattamento, usanza.
use [ju:s] *n* uso, impiego; utilità; abitudine, usanza; [ju:z] *vt* usare, servirsi di, utilizzare, adoperare.
useful ['ju:sful] *a* utile, vantaggioso.
usefulness ['ju:sfulnis] *n* utilità.
useless ['ju:slis] *a* inutile, vano, inefficace.
uselessness ['ju:slisnis] *n* inutilità.
user ['ju:zə] *n* chi usa, utente; (*leg*) usufruttuario.
usher ['ʌʃə] *n* usciere; **to u. in** *vt* introdurre, annunciare.
usual ['ju:ʒuəl] *a* usuale, solito; **as u.** *ad* come al solito.
usurer ['ju:ʒərə] *n* usuraio.
usurp [ju:'zə:p] *vt* usurpare.
usurpation [,ju:zə:'peiʃən] *n* usurpazione.
usurper [ju:'zə:pə] *n* usurpatore.
usury ['ju:ʒuri] *n* usura.
utensil [ju'tensl] *n* utensile, arnese, strumento.
uterus ['ju:tərəs] *n* utero.
utilitarian [,ju:tili'tɛəriən] *a* utilitario; *n* (*phil*) utilitarista.
utility [ju:'tiliti] *n* utilità, vantaggio.
utilization [,ju:tilai'zeiʃən] *n* utilizzazione.
utilize ['ju:tilaiz] *vt* utilizzare.
utmost ['ʌtmoust] *a n* massimo, estremo.
utter ['ʌtə] *a* assoluto, completo; *vt* emettere, pronunciare.
utterance ['ʌtərəns] *n* pronuncia modo di parlare; espressione, sfogo.

V

vacancy ['veikənsi] *n* posto vacante, vuoto; (*fig*) vacuità.
vacant ['veikənt] *a* vacante, vuoto, libero; vacuo.
vacate [və'keit] *vt* lasciar libero.
vacation [və'keiʃən] *n* vacanza, **-ze** *pl*; **vacationist** villeggiante.
vaccinate ['væksineit] *vt* vaccinare.
vaccination [,væksi'neiʃən] *n* vaccinazione.
vaccine ['væksi:n] *n* vaccino.
vacillate ['væsileit] *vi* vacillare.
vacillation [,væsi'leiʃən] *n* vacillamento, irresolutezza.
vacuity [væ'kjuiti] *n* vacuità.
vacuous ['vækjuəs] *a* vacuo, vuoto, privo di espressione.
vacuum ['vækjuəm] *n* vuoto, vuoto pneumatico.
vagabond ['vægəbənd] *a n* vagabondo.
vagary ['veigəri] *n* capriccio, ghiribizzo.
vagrant ['veigrənt] *a* ambulante, vagabondo; *n* vagabondo, accattone.
vague [veig] *a* vago, impreciso.
vain [vein] *a* vano, vanitoso.
vainglorious [vein'glɔ:riəs] *a* vanaglorioso.
vainglory [vein'glɔ:ri] *n* vanagloria.
vale [veil] *n* (*poet*) valle, vallata.

Valentine ['væləntain] *nm pr* Valentino.
valentine ['væləntain] *n* innamorato, fidanzato; biglietto amoroso (che si invia il giorno di S. Valentino).
valet ['vælit] *n* cameriere personale.
valiant ['væliənt] *a* valoroso, prode.
valid ['vælid] *a* valido.
validity [və'liditi] *n* validità.
valley ['væli] *n* valle.
valor ['vælə] *n* valore, coraggio.
valuable ['væljuəbl] *a* costoso, prezioso; *n* oggetto di valore.
valuation [,vælju'eiʃən] *n* valutazione, stima.
value ['vælju:] *n* valore, pregio; *vt* valutare, stimare.
valueless ['væljulis] *a* di nessun valore.
valve [vælv] *n* (*mech, anat*) valvola.
vamp [væmp] *n* (*shoe*) tomaia, rimonta; (*mus*) accompagnamento improvvisato; (*sl*) donna fatale; *vt* fare la rimonta; (*mus*) improvvisare; (*sl*) adescare.
vampire ['væmpaiə] *n* vampiro.
van [væn] *n* camioncino, furgoncino; avanguardia.
vanadium [və'neidiəm] *n* vanadio.
vandal ['vændəl] *a n* vandalo.
vandalism ['vændəlizəm] *n* vandalismo.
vane [vein] *n* banderuola.
vanguard ['vængɑ:d] *n* avanguardia.
vanilla [və'nilə] *n* vaniglia.
vanish ['væniʃ] *vi* svanire, sparire, dileguarsi.
vanity ['væniti] *n* vanità.
vanquish ['væŋkwiʃ] *vt* sopraffare, vincere.
vantage ['vɑ:ntidʒ] *n* (*tennis*) vantaggio; **v. ground** posizione elevata.
vapor ['veipə] *n* vapore.
vaporize ['veipəraiz] *vti* vaporizzar(si).
vaporous ['veipərəs] *a* vaporoso.
variable ['vɛəriəbl] *a* variabile; *n* (*math*) quantità variabile.
variance ['vɛəriəns] *n* disaccordo; **at v.** *ad* in disaccordo con.
variation [,vɛəri'eiʃən] *n* variazione.
varicose ['værikous] *a* varicoso.
varied ['vɛərid] *a* vario, variato.
variegate ['vɛərigeit] *vt* screziare, variegare.
variety [və'raiəti] *n* varietà; **v. theatre** teatro di varietà.
various ['vɛəriəs] *a* diverso, vario, parecchi.
varnish ['vɑ:niʃ] *n* vernice; *vt* verniciare.
vary ['vɛəri] *vt* variare, modificare; *vi* variare, essere diverso.
vase [vɑ:z] *n* vaso.
vaseline ['væsilin] *n* vaselina.
vassal ['væsəl] *n* vassallo.
vast [vɑ:st] *a* vasto, immenso.
vastness ['vɑ:stnis] *n* vastità, immensità.
vat [væt] *n* tino, tinozza.
Vatican ['vætikən] *n* Vaticano.
vaudeville ['voudəvil] *n* 'vaudeville', operetta, spettacolo di varietà; **v. theater** teatro di varietà.
vault [vɔ:lt] *n* (*arch*) volta; cantina; sotterraneo; tomba; volteggio, salto; *vt* costruire a volta; *vti* saltare.
vaulting ['vɔltiŋ] *n* salto, volteggio; **pole v.** salto con l'asta.
vaunt [vɔ:nt] *n* vanteria, vanto; *vti* vantarsi di.
veal [vi:l] *n* vitello.
veer [viə] *vi* (*wind*) cambiar direzione; (*fig*) cambiar opinione.
vegetable ['vedʒitəbl] *a* vegetale; *n pl* verdura; ortaggio, legume; **v. marrow** zucchino.
vegetarian [,vedʒi'tɛəriən] *a n* vegetariano.
vegetate ['vedʒiteit] *vi* vegetare.
vegetation [,vedʒi'teiʃən] *n* vegetazione.
vehemence ['vi:iməns] *n* veemenza.
vehement ['vi:imənt] *a* veemente.
vehicle ['vi:ikl] *n* veicolo.
veil [veil] *n* velo; *vt* velare.
vein [vein] *n* vena; (*fig*) umore.
vellum ['veləm] *n* pergamena.
velocity [vi'lɔsiti] *n* velocità.
velvet ['velvit] *a n* (di) velluto.
venal ['vi:nl] *a* venale.
vendor ['vendɔ:] *n* venditore.
veneer [vi'niə] *n* impiallacciatura; (*fig*) vernice.
venerable ['venərəbl] *a* venerabile.
venerate ['venəreit] *vt* venerare.
veneration [,venə'reiʃən] *n* venerazione.
venereal [vi'niəriəl] *a* venereo.
Venetian [vi'ni:ʃən] *a n* veneziano.
Venezuela [,vene'zweilə] *n* Venezuela.
vengeance ['vendʒəns] *n* vendetta.
venial ['viniəl] *a* veniale.
Venice ['venis] *n* Venezia.
venison ['venzn] *n* carne di cervo, di daino.
venom ['venəm] *n* veleno.
venomous ['venəməs] *a* velenoso; (*fig*) malevolo.
vent [vent] *n* buco, foro; sbocco; conduttura di camino; (*fig*) sfogo; *vt* dare sfogo a.
ventilate ['ventileit] *vt* ventilare.
ventilation [,venti'leiʃən] *n* ventilazione.
ventilator ['ventileitə] *n* ventilatore.
ventriloquism [ven'triləkwizəm] *n* ventriloquio.
ventriloquist [ven'triləkwist] *n* ventriloquo.
venture ['ventʃə] *n* impresa, avventura; rischio; speculazione; *vti* arrischiarsi, avventurarsi, osare.
venturesome ['ventʃəsəm] *a* avventuroso, ardito.
Venus ['vi:nəs] *n pr* Venere.
veracious [və'reiʃəs] *a* verace, veridico.
veracity [və'ræsiti] *n* veracità.

verb [vɘ:b] *n* (*gram*) verbo.
verbal ['vɘ:bɘl] *a* verbale.
verbatim [vɘ:'beitim] *a* testuale; *ad* testualmente.
verbose [vɘ:'bous] *a* verboso.
verbosity [vɘ'bɔsiti] *n* verbosità.
verdant ['vɘ:dɘnt] *a* verdeggiante.
verdict ['vɘ:dikt] *n* verdetto.
verdure ['vɘ:dʒɘ] *n* vegetazione, verde, verzura.
verge [vɘ:dʒ] *n* bordo, limite, orlo; punto estremo; *vi* confinare; declinare, tendere verso.
verger ['vɘ:dʒɘ] *n* sagrestano.
Vergil ['vɘ:dʒil] *n* Virgilio.
verification [,verifi'keiʃɘn] *n* verifica.
verify ['verifai] *vt* verificare, controllare.
verity ['veriti] *n* verità.
vermilion [vɘ:'miljɘn] *n* cinabro, vermiglione; (*color*) vermiglio.
vermin ['vɘ:min] *n pl* animali nocivi, insetti parassiti *pl*.
verminous ['vɘ:minɘs] *a* infestato da animali nocivi, da insetti parassiti.
vermouth ['vɘ:mɘθ] *n* vermut, vermouth.
vernacular [vɘ:'nækjulɘ] *a n* vernacolo.
vernal ['vɘ:nl] *a* primaverile.
Verona [vi'rounɘ] *n* Verona; **Veronese** *a n* veronese.
versatile ['vɘ:sɘtail] *a* versatile.
versatility [,vɘ:sɘ'tiliti] *n* versatilità.
verse [vɘ:s] *n* verso, -si *pl*, poesia.
versed [vɘ:st] *a* versato, abile.
version ['vɘ:ʃɘn] *n* versione.
vertex ['vɘ:teks] *pl* **vertices** *n* vertice.
vertical ['vɘ:tikɘl] *a* verticale.
vertigo ['vɘ:tigou] *n* vertigine, -ni *pl*.
vervain ['vɘ:'vein] *n* verbena.
verve [vɘ:v] *n* 'verve', brio; energia, vigore.
very ['veri] *a* stesso, proprio; *ad* molto, assai.
vespers ['vespɘz] *n pl* vespri *pl*.
vessel ['vesl] *n* recipiente; nave, vascello; (*anat*) vaso.
vest [vest] *n* maglia; panciotto.
vestibule ['vestibju:l] *n* vestibolo.
vestige ['vestidʒ] *n* vestigio, orma, traccia.
vestment ['vestmɘnt] *n* (*eccl*) paramento sacerdotale.
vestry ['vestri] *n* sagrestia; consiglio d'amministrazione d'una parrocchia.
veteran ['vetɘrɘn] *a n* veterano.
veterinary ['vetɘrinɘri] *a n* veterinario.
veto ['vi:tou] *pl* **vetoes** *n* veto; diritto di veto.
vex [veks] *vt* irritare.
vexation [vek'seiʃɘn] *n* irritazione.
vexatious [vek'seiʃɘs] *a* irritante, fastidioso.
via [vaiɘ] *prep* per la via di, via.
viaduct ['vaiɘdʌkt] *n* viadotto.
vial ['vaiɘl] *n* fiala.
viand ['vaiɘnd] *n* (*usu pl*) cibo, provvista.
vibrant ['vaibrɘnt] *a* vibrante.
vibrate [vai'breit] *vi* vibrare.
vibration [vai'breiʃɘn] *n* vibrazione.
vicar ['vikɘ] *n* parroco, vicario.
vicarage ['vikɘridʒ] *n* canonica, dignità di parroco.
vicarious [vi'kɛɘriɘs] *a* sopportato per un altro, vicario.
vice [vais] *n* vizio; sostituto, vice; **v.-president** vice presidente.
viceroy ['vaisrɔi] *n* vicerè.
vicinity [vi'siniti] *n* vicinanza.
vicious ['viʃɘs] *a* vizioso, cattivo; (*style etc*) scorretto.
vicissitude [vi'sisitju:d] *n* vicissitudine, vicenda.
victim ['viktim] *n* vittima.
victimize ['viktimaiz] *vt* far vittima di.
victor ['viktɘ] *n* vincitore.
Victor ['viktɘ] *nm pr* Vittorio.
Victoria [vik'tɔ:riɘ] *nf pr* Vittoria.
victorious [vik'tɔ:riɘs] *a* vittorioso.
victory ['viktɘri] *n* vittoria.
victual ['vitl] *vt* vettovagliare.
victuals ['vitlz] *n pl* vettovaglie *pl*.
video ['vaidiou] *a* (*tv*) video; *n* televisione.
vie [vai] *vi* gareggiare, rivaleggiare.
Vienna [vi'enɘ] *n* Vienna; **Viennese** *a n* viennese.
view [vju:] *n* vista, veduta, paesaggio; visione; opinione; *vt* guardare attentamente, considerare.
vigil ['vidʒil] *n* veglia; vigilia.
vigilance ['vidʒilɘns] *n* vigilanza.
vigilant ['vidʒilɘnt] *a* vigilante.
vigor ['vigɘ] *n* vigore.
vigorous ['vigɘrɘs] *a* vigoroso.
Viking ['vaikiŋ] *n* vichingo.
vile [vail] *a* vile, abietto.
vileness ['vailnis] *n* viltà, abiezione.
villa ['vilɘ] *n* villa.
village ['vilidʒ] *n* villaggio, paese.
villager ['vilidʒɘ] *n* villico, abitante di villaggio.
villain ['vilɘn] *n* mascalzone, furfante.
villainous ['vilɘnɘs] *a* scellerato, infame.
villainy ['vilɘni] *n* scelleratezza, infamia.
Vincent ['vinsɘnt] *nm pr* Vincenzo.
vindicate ['vindikeit] *vt* rivendicare.
vindication [,vindi'keiʃɘn] *n* rivendicazione.
vindictive [vin'diktiv] *a* vendicativo.
vine [vain] *n* vite.
vinegar ['vinigɘ] *n* aceto.
vineyard ['vinjɘd] *n* vigna, vigneto.
vintage ['vintidʒ] *n* vendemmia, raccolto.
vinyl ['vainil] *n* vinile.
viola [vi'oulɘ] *n* viola.
violate ['vaiɘleit] *vt* violare; trasgredire, infrangere.
violation [,vaiɘ'leiʃɘn] *n* violazione, infrazione.

violence ['vaiələns] *n* violenza.
violent ['vaiələnt] *a* violento.
violet ['vaiəlit] *a* violetto, di color viola; *n* violetta, viola mammola; color viola.
violin [,vaiə'lin] *n* (*mus*) violino.
violinist ['vaiəlinist] *n* violinista.
viper ['vaipə] *n* vipera.
virago [vi'rɑːgou] *n* virago, donna violenta.
Virgil ['vəːdʒil] *nm pr* Virgilio.
virgin ['vəːdʒin] *a n* vergine.
virginity [vəː'dʒiniti] *n* verginità.
virile ['virail] *a* virile.
virility [vi'riliti] *n* virilità.
virtual ['vəːtjuəl] *a* virtuale, di fatto.
virtue ['vəːtjuː] *n* virtù.
virtuous ['vəːtjuəs] *a* virtuoso.
virulence ['viruləns] *n* virulenza.
virulent ['virulənt] *a* virulento.
virus ['vaiərəs] *n* virus.
visa ['viːzə] *n* visto consolare; *vt* vistare.
visage ['vizidʒ] *n* viso.
viscount(ess) ['vaikaunt(is)] *n* visconte(ssa).
viscous ['viskəs] *a* viscoso.
vise [vais] *n* morsa.
visibility [,vizi'biliti] *n* visibilità.
visible ['vizəbl] *a* visibile.
vision ['viʒən] *n* visione; (*sight*) vista.
visionary ['viʒnəri] *a n* visionario; *a* immaginario, chimerico.
visit ['vizit] *n* visita; *vt* visitare, far visita a.
visitation [,vizi'teiʃən] *n* visita ufficiale; (*eccl*) visitazione.
visitor ['vizitə] *n* visitatore, ospite.
visor ['vaizə] *n* visiera.
vista ['vistə] *n* vista, scorcio panoramico, lunga serie; **v. dome car** (*rly*) carrozza panoramica.
visual ['vizjuəl] *a* visuale, visivo.
visualize ['vizjuəlaiz] *vti* immaginare; rendere visibile.
vital ['vaitl] *a* vitale, (*fig*) essenziale, importante; **v. statistics** statistiche anagrafiche; (*fam*) misure femminili.
vitality [vai'tæliti] *n* vitalità.
vitamin ['vitəmin] *n* vitamina.
vitiate ['viʃieit] *vt* viziare; corrompere; invalidare.
vitreous ['vitriəs] *a* vitreo.
vitriol ['vitriəl] *n* vetriolo.
vituperate [vi'tjupəreit] *vt* vituperare.
vituperation [vi,tjupə'reiʃən] *n* vituperazione.
vivacious [vi'veiʃəs] *a* vivace.
vivacity [vi'væsiti] *n* vivacità.
vivid ['vivid] *a* vivace, vivo, vivido.
vividness ['vividnis] *n* vivezza, vivacità.
vivify ['vivifai] *vt* vivificare.
vivisection [,vivi'sekʃən] *n* vivisezione.
vixen ['viksn] *n* volpe femmina.
vizier [vi'ziə] *n* visir.
vocabulary [və'kæbjuləri] *n* vocabolario.
vocal ['voukəl] *a* vocale.
vocalist ['voukəlist] *n* cantante.
vocation [vou'keiʃən] *n* vocazione.
vocative ['vɔkətiv] *n* vocativo.
vociferate [vou'sifəreit] *vi* vociferare, vociare.
vociferous [və'sifərəs] *a* vociferante, clamoroso.
vogue [voug] *n* voga, moda.
voice [vɔis] *n* voce; grido; (*of animals*) verso; *vt* esprimere, intonare.
void [vɔid] *a n* vuoto; *a* privo, nullo.
volatile ['vɔlətail] *a* volatile.
volatility [,vɔlə'tiliti] *n* volatilità.
volatilize [vɔ'lætilaiz] *vti* volatilizzar(si).
volcanic [vɔl'kænik] *a* vulcanico.
volcano [vɔl'keinou] *n* vulcano.
volition [vou'liʃən] *n* volizione.
volley ['vɔli] *n* raffica, scarica, salva.
volt [voult] *n* (*el*) volt.
voltage ['voultidʒ] *n* (*el*) voltaggio.
voluble ['vɔljubl] *a* fluente, loquace.
volume ['vɔljuːm] *n* volume.
voluminous [və'ljuːminəs] *a* voluminoso.
voluntary ['vɔləntəri] *a* volontario.
volunteer [,vɔlən'tiə] *n* soldato volontario; *vti* offrir(si) volontariamente.
voluptuary [və'lʌptjuəri] *n* individuo sensuale.
voluptuous [və'lʌptjuəs] *a* voluttuoso.
voluptuousness [və'lʌptjuəsnis] *n* voluttà.
vomit ['vɔmit] *vti* vomitare.
voracious [və'reiʃəs] *a* vorace.
voracity [vɔ'ræsiti] *n* voracità.
vortex ['vɔːteks] *n* vortice.
votary ['voutəri] *n* devoto, seguace fedele.
vote [vout] *n* voto, votazione; *vti* votare.
voter ['voutə] *n* votante, elettore.
votive ['voutiv] *a* votivo.
vouch [vautʃ] *vt* attestare, confermare; **to v. for** rispondere di, garantire per.
voucher ['vautʃə] *n* documento giustificativo, pezza d'appoggio; buono, tagliando; (*com*) ricevuta.
vouchsafe [vautʃ'seif] *vt* accordare, concedere.
vow [vau] *n* promesso, voto; *vt* far voto di, giurare.
vowel ['vauəl] *n* vocale.
voyage [vɔidʒ] *n* viaggio (per mare); *vi* navigare, fare una traversata.
vulgar ['vʌlgə] *a* volgare.
vulgarity [vʌl'gæriti] *n* volgarità.
vulnerable ['vʌlnərəbl] *a* vulnerabile.
vulture ['vʌltʃə] *n* avvoltoio.

W

wad [wɔd] *n* batuffolo; stoppaccio; (*sl*) denaro.

wadding ['wɔdiŋ] *n* imbottitura, ovatta.
waddle ['wɔdl] *vi* camminare dondolandosi (come le anitre).
wade [weid] *vti* attraversare a guado; procedere faticosamente.
wafer ['weifə] *n* wafer, cialda, ostia.
waft [wɑ:ft] *n* soffio, alito, zaffata; *vt* diffondere, spandere.
wag [wæg] *n* burlone; *vti* scodinzolare.
wage(s) ['weidʒ(iz)] *n* (*usu pl*) paga, salario; **to w. war** muover guerra.
wager ['weidʒə] *n* scommessa; *vt* scommettere.
waggle ['wægl] *n* dimenamento, dondolamento; *vt* dimenare, dondolare.
wagon ['wægən] *n* carro.
wagtail ['wægteil] *n* cutrettola.
waif [weif] *n* trovatello; **waifs and strays** relitti, oggetti smarriti *pl*.
wail [weil] *n* lamento, gemito; *vi* lamentarsi; (*of baby*) vagire.
wainscot ['weinskət] *n* rivestimento in legno; zoccolo (di parete).
waist [weist] *n* vita, cintola.
waistcoat ['weiskout] *n* panciotto, gilè.
wait [weit] *n* attesa; *vi* aspettare, attendere; servire a tavola; **to w. upon** servire.
waiter ['weitə] **waitress** ['weitris] *n* (*d'albergo etc*) cameriere, -ra.
waive [weiv] *vt* rinunziare a, desistere da.
wake [weik] *n* scia; veglia; *vti* risvegliar(si), svegliar(si); vegliare.
wakeful ['weikful] *a* sveglio, insonne, vigile.
wakefulness ['weikfulnis] *n* insonnia, vigilanza.
waken ['weikən] *vti* svegliar(si).
Wales [weilz] *n* Galles.
walk [wɔ:k] *n* passeggiata; percorso; passo; viale; **w. of life** professione, mestiere; ceto; **sidewalk** marciapiede; *vt* far camminare, percorrere; *vi* camminare, passeggiare, andare a piedi.
walker ['wɔ:kə] *n* camminatore, pedone.
walking ['wɔ:kiŋ] *a* che cammina, ambulante; *n* il camminare; **w. stick** bastone da passeggio.
wall [wɔ:l] *n* muro; mura *pl*; parete; *vt* cingere di mura.
wallet ['wɔlit] *n* portafoglio; borsa.
wallow ['wɔlou] *vi* avvoltolarsi, sguazzare.
wallpaper ['wɔ:l,peipə] *n* tappezzeria, carta da parato.
walnut ['wɔ:lnət] *n* noce.
walrus ['wɔ:lrəs] *n* tricheco.
Walter ['wɔ:ltə] *nm pr* Walter, Gualtiero.
waltz [wɔ:ls] *n* valzer; *vi* ballare il valzer.
wan [wɔn] *a* pallido, smorto.
wand [wɔnd] *n* bacchetta.
wander ['wɔndə] *vi* vagabondare, errare, vagare; divagare; vaneggiare.
wanderer ['wɔndərə] *n* vagabondo.
wane [wein] *n* declino, decrescenza; *vi* declinare, decrescere; (*moon*) calare.
want [wɔnt] *n* bisogno, deficienza, mancanza, miseria; *vt* desiderare, volere; aver bisogno di, mancare di; *vi* occorrere, mancare.
wanton ['wɔntən] *a* licenzioso, lascivo; capriccioso; senza scopo.
wantonness ['wɔntənnis] *n* licenziosità; leggerezza.
war [wɔ:] *n* guerra; *vi* guerreggiare, far guerra.
warble ['wɔ:bl] *vti* gorgheggiare, trillare, cantare.
ward [wɔ:d] *n* custodia, guardia; tutela; pupillo; (*of town*) quartiere; (*hospital*) corsia; **to w. off** schivare, evitare, parare, respingere.
warden ['wɔ:dn] *n* custode, guardiano; (*of school, prison etc*) direttore.
warder ['wɔ:də] *n* carceriere.
wardrobe ['wɔ:droub] *n* armadio, guardaroba.
warehouse ['wεəhaus] *n* magazzino.
wares [wεəz] *n pl* merce, mercanzia, articoli *pl*.
warfare ['wɔ:fεə] *n* guerra, stato di guerra.
wariness ['wεərinis] *n* cautela, prudenza.
warlike ['wɔ:laik] *a* bellicoso, marziale.
warm [wɔ:m] *a* caldo; caloroso, cordiale; *vti* riscaldar(si), scaldar(si); eccitar(si).
warmth [wɔ:mθ] *n* calore.
warn [wɔ:n] *vt* avvertire, ammonire, mettere in guardia, avvisare.
warning ['wɔ:niŋ] *n* ammonimento, avvertimento, preavviso; (*leg*) diffida.
warp [wɔ:p] *n* ordito; (*of wood*) curvatura; (*fig*) pervertimento; *vt* curvare, pervertire; *vi* curvarsi, deformarsi.
warrant ['wɔrənt] *n* autorizzazione, mandato, ordine; garanzia; *vt* autorizzare, garantire.
warranty ['wɔrənti] *n* garanzia.
warren ['wɔrin] *n* conigliera.
warrior ['wɔriə] *n* guerriero.
wart [wɔ:t] *n* verruca.
wary ['wεəri] *a* cauto, guardingo.
wash [wɔʃ] *n* lavata, lavatura, (*linen*) bucato; (*art*) acquerello; (*waves*) sciabordio; (*slops*) risciacquatura di piatti; (*walls etc*) mano di colore; *vti* lavar(si); *vt* imbiancare; metallizzare; bagnare; **to w. away** trascinar via, lavar via; **to w. up** lavare i piatti, rigovernare; **w.-out** (*fig*) un fallimento completo; **washday** giorno di bucato.
washer ['wɔʃə] *n* lavatore, -trice; **dishwasher** lavastoviglie.
washing ['wɔʃiŋ] *n* bucato, lavata;

w. day giorno di bucato; **w. machine** lavatrice; **w. powder** detersivo.
wasp [wɔsp] *n* vespa.
wastage ['weistidʒ] *n* consumo, sciupio.
waste [weist] *a* deserto, desolato; *n* rifiuti *pl*; spreco, perdita; consumo; *vt* sprecare, dissipare; *vi* consumarsi, deperire.
wasteful ['weistful] *a* prodigo, spendereccio, dissipatore, rovinoso.
wastefulness ['weistfulnis] *n* prodigalità, sciupio.
wasting ['weistiŋ] *a* che consuma, che indebolisce; *n* sciupio, spreco; devastazione, deperimento.
watch [wɔtʃ] *n* orologio; veglia; guardia, sentinella; osservazione; *vt* osservare, sorvegliare, spiare; *vi* vegliare, vigilare; **watchdog** cane da guardia; **w.-post** posto di guardia; **watchword** parola d'ordine.
watchful ['wɔtʃful] *a* guardingo, vigilante.
watchfulness ['wɔtʃfulnis] *n* vigilanza, cautela.
watchman ['wɔtʃmən] *pl* **-men** *n* guardia (notturna), guardiano.
water ['wɔ:tə] *n* acqua; *vt* innaffiare; (*horse*) abbeverare; (*drink*) diluire; *vi* (*eyes*) piangere; **w. bottle** bottiglia per acqua, borraccia; **hot-w. bottle** bottiglia dell'acqua calda.
water-closet ['wɔ:tə,klɔzit] *n* gabinetto.
water-color ['wɔ:tə,kʌlə] *n* acquarello.
watercourse ['wɔ:təkɔ:s] *n* corso d'acqua, canale.
waterfall ['wɔ:təfɔ:l] *n* cascata.
watering-can ['wɔ:təriŋkæn] *n* annaffiatoio.
waterpipe ['wɔ:təpaip] *n* conduttura d'acqua.
watering-place ['wɔ:təriŋ,pleis] *n* abbeveratoio, luogo di rifornimento d'acqua; stazione balneare, termale.
water-lily ['wɔ:tə,lili] *n* ninfea.
waterproof ['wɔ:təpru:f] *a n* impermeabile.
waterskiing ['wɔ:təskiiŋ] *n* sci nautico.
watertight ['wɔ:tətait] *a* impermeabile, stagno.
waterway ['wɔ:təwei] *n* canale navigabile.
water-wheel ['wɔ:təwi:l] *n* (*mech*) turbina idraulica.
waterworks ['wɔ:təwə:ks] *n* impianto idrico.
watery ['wɔ:təri] *a* acquoso.
wattle ['wɔtl] *n* canniccio, graticcio; (*birds*) bargiglio; (*fish*) barbetta.
wave [weiv] *n* onda, flutto; (*hand*) cenno; (*wand*) colpo; *vt* agitare; ondulare; *vi* ondeggiare, fluttuare; far segno di.
waver ['weivə] *vi* vacillare.
wavy ['weivi] *a* ondulato; ondoso; ondeggiante.
wax [wæks] *n* cera; ceralacca; cerume; *vt* incerare; dare la cera a.
waxen ['wæksən] *a* di cera, cereo.
way [wei] *n* via, strada; mezzo, modo; abitudine; passaggio; direzione; stato; **by the w.** strada facendo; (*fig*) a proposito.
wayfarer ['wei,fɛərə] *n* viandante.
wayside ['weisaid] *n* margine della strada.
wayward ['weiwəd] *a* ostinato; capriccioso.
waywardness ['weiwədnis] *n* ostinazione; capricciosità.
we [wi:] *pron pl* noi.
weak [wi:k] *a* debole.
weaken ['wi:kən] *vti* indebolir(si).
weakling ['wi:kliŋ] *n* creatura debole; debole, inetto.
weakly ['wi:kli] *a* di debole costituzione; *ad* debolmente.
weakness ['wi:knis] *n* debolezza.
wealth [welθ] *n* ricchezza, -ze *pl*.
wealthy ['welθi] *a* ricco.
wean [wi:n] *vt* svezzare; (*fig*) togliere il vezzo di.
weapon ['wepən] *n* arma.
wear [wɛə] *n* uso, consumo; durata; abbigliamento; *vt* portare, indossare, avere; *vti* consumar(si); durare; **to w. on** passare lentamente.
weariness ['wiərinis] *n* stanchezza, tedio, disgusto.
wearisome ['wiərisəm] *a* stancante, faticoso, tedioso.
weary ['wiəri] *a* stanco; *vti* stancar(si).
weasel ['wi:zl] *n* donnola.
weather ['weðə] *n* (*atmosferico*) tempo; *vt* esporre alle intemperie, resistere a, sopportare; **w. bureau** ufficio metereologico.
weathercock ['weðəkɔk] *n* banderuola.
weave [wi:v] *vt* tessere; (*fig*) imbastire, ordire.
weaver ['wi:və] *n* tessitore.
weaving ['wi:viŋ] *n* tessitura.
web [web] *n* tela, tessuto; (*bird's foot*) membrana; (*spider's*) ragnatela; (*fig*) trama.
wed [wed] *vti* sposar(si).
wedding ['wediŋ] *n* nozze *pl*, sposalizio, matrimonio.
wedge [wedʒ] *n* cuneo, bietta; *vt* incuneare, incastrare; *vi* incunearsi.
wedlock ['wedlɔk] *n* matrimonio, stato coniugale.
Wednesday ['wenzdi] *n* mercoledì.
wee [wi:] *a* (*fam*) piccolo, minuscolo.
weed [wi:d] *n* erbaccia, mala erba; *vt* sarchiare; **to w. out** estirpare; (*fig*) eliminare.
weeds [wi:dz] *n pl* gramaglie *pl*.
weedy ['wi:di] *a* pieno di erbacce; (*fig*) magro, sparuto.
week [wi:k] *n* settimana.
weekday ['wi:kdei] *n* giorno feriale, giorno lavorativo.

weekend ['wi:k'end] *n* 'weekend', (vacanza di) fine settimana.
weekly ['wi:kli] *a n* settimanale; *ad* ogni settimana.
weep [wi:p] *vti* piangere; trasudare.
weeping ['wi:piŋ] *a* piangente; trasudante; *n* pianto, lacrime.
weft [weft] *n* (*di tessuto*) trama.
weigh [wei] *vti* pesare; (*naut*) levare l'ancora.
weight [weit] *n* peso; importanza; **lightweight** (*sport*) peso leggero; (*US sl*) persona di nessuna importanza.
weighty ['weiti] *a* pesante, gravoso; importante.
weir [wiə] *n* diga, sbarramento.
weird [wiəd] *a* misterioso, soprannaturale; (*fam*) bizzarro.
welcome ['welkəm] *a* gradito, ben accetto; *n* benvenuto, buona accoglienza; *vt* accogliere cordialmente, dare il benvenuto a; gradire; **w.!** benvenuto!
weld [weld] *vt* saldare.
welding ['weldiŋ] *n* saldatura.
welfare ['welfɛə] *n* benessere, prosperità.
well [wel] *n* pozzo, fonte; tromba delle scale; *vi* scaturire.
well [wel] *a* bene, buono, in buona salute; *ad* bene; **w.-off, w.-to-do** *a* agiato, benestante.
Welsh [welʃ] *a* gallese; *n* (lingua) gallese; **Welshman** *n* gallese.
welt [welt] *n* (*shoe*) tramezza.
welter ['weltə] *n* tumulto, confusione; *vi* avvoltolarsi; essere sballottato; essere immerso; **welterweight** (*sport*) peso medio-leggero.
wen [wen] *n* natta, gozzo.
wench [wentʃ] *n* (*arc*) ragazza; ragazzotta, popolana, donna di servizio.
west [west] *n* occidente, ovest, ponente.
westerly ['westəli] *a* occidentale; *ad* da (verso) ovest.
western ['westən] *a* occidentale.
westward ['westwəd] *a* volto ad ovest; **westwards** *ad* verso ovest.
wet [wet] *a* bagnato; umido, piovoso; (*of paint*) fresco; *n* umidità, pioggia, tempo piovoso; *vt* bagnare, inumidire; **w. blanket** guastafeste; **w. nurse** balia.
wether ['weðə] *n* castrato.
wetness ['wetnis] *n* umidità.
whack [wæk] *n* bastonata, colpo; (*sl*) parte.
whale [weil] *n* balena.
whaler ['weilə] *n* baleniere, (*naut*) baleniera.
wharf [wɔ:f] *n* banchina, molo.
wharfage ['wɔ:fidʒ] *n* diritti di banchina *pl*.
what [wɔt] *a rel interrog* che, quale; *pron interrog rel indef* che cosa, ciò che, quello che.
whatever [wɔt'evə] *a* qualunque, qualsiasi; *pron rel indef* qualunque cosa, tutto ciò che.
whatsoever [ˌwɔtsou'evə] *a pron* (*arc*) qualunque cosa.
wheat [wi:t] *n* grano, frumento.
wheedle ['wi:dl] *vt* ottenere con le moine, persuadere con le moine.
wheel [wi:l] *n* ruota; (*naut*) ruota del timone; (*aut*) volante; *vti* spingere o tirare (veicolo); (far) girare, turbinare.
wheelbarrow ['wi:lˌbærou] *n* carriola.
wheeze [wi:z] *n* respiro affannoso; *vi* ansimare.
whelk [welk] *n* buccina.
when [wen] *ad cj* quando.
whence [wens] *cj ad* da dove, donde, da che cosa; *n* origine.
whenever [wen'evə] *ad* tutte le volte che, in qualunque momento.
where [wɛə] *ad* dove.
whereabouts ['wɛərəbauts] *ad* dove, in che parte.
whereas [wɛər:'æz] *cj* mentre, (*leg*) siccome.
whereby [wɛə'bai] *ad* per la qual cosa.
wherefore ['wɛəfɔ:] *ad* percio; (*interrog*) perchè; *n* causa, motivo.
wherein [wɛər'in] *ad* nel quale; (*interrog*) in che cosa.
whereupon [ˌwɛərə'pɔn] *ad* al che, in conseguenza di che.
wherever [wɛər'evə] *ad* dovunque, in qualunque luogo.
whet [wet] *vt* affilare; stimolare.
whether ['weðə] *cj* se, sia che.
whetstone ['wetstoun] *n* cote.
which [witʃ] *pron rel* (*riferito ad animali o cose*) che, il quale *etc*; *a pron interrog* (*riferito a persone, animali e cose*) quale.
whichever [witʃ'evə] *a pron indef* qualunque.
whiff [wif] *n* boccata (d'aria *etc*).
whig [wig] *a n* liberale, membro del partito liberale.
while [wail] *n* momento, tempo; *cj* mentre; finchè; sebbene.
whilst [wailst] *cj* mentre.
whim [wim] *n* capriccio.
whimper ['wimpə] *n* piagnucolio; *vi* piagnucolare.
whimsical ['wimzikəl] *a* capriccioso, stravagante.
whimsy ['wimzi] *n* capriccio.
whine [wain] *n* (*of dogs*) uggiolio, piagnucolio; *vi* uggiolare, piagnucolare.
whip [wip] *n* frusta, scudiscio; *vt* frustare, sferzare; battere; cucire a sopraggitto; (*of cream*) montare, frullare; **w. hand** vantaggio; **to w. out** cacciar fuori; **to w. around** girarsi bruscamente.
whirl [wə:l] *n* turbine, vortice; *vt* roteare; *vi* girare, roteare, turbinare, susseguirsi vorticosamente.
whirligig ['wə:ligig] *n* giostra; carosello; girandola.

whirlpool ['wə:lpu:l] *n* vortice d'acqua, gorgo.
whirlwind ['wə:lwind] *n* turbine di vento.
whisk [wisk] *n* frullino; movimento rapido; scopetta; *vt* frullare; spazzolare, (*eggs etc*) sbattere; *vti* muover(si) rapidamente, spazzar via.
whisker ['wiskə] *n* basetta; (*cat*) baffo.
whiskey, whisky ['wiski] *n* whisky.
whisper ['wispə] *n* bisbiglio, mormorio; *vti* bisbigliare, mormorare.
whist [wist] *n* 'whist', gioco di carte.
whistle ['wisl] *n* fischio, fischietto; *vti* fischiare.
whit [wit] *n* quantità minima; **W. Sunday** domenica di Pentecoste.
white [wait] *a n* bianco; **w.-collar worker** impiegato.
whiten ['waitn] *vti* imbiancare.
whiteness ['waitnis] *n* bianchezza.
whitewash ['waitwɔʃ] *n* calce per imbiancare, intonaco; (*sport*) vittoria schiacciante; *vt* imbiancare; (*fig*) riabilitare.
whiting ['waitiŋ] *n* merlano.
whittle ['witl] *vt* tagliuzzare; **to w. down** assottigliare.
whiz(z) [wiz] *n* sibilo; *vi* sibilare, passare sibilando.
who [hu:] *pron interrog* chi; *rel* chi, che, il quale *etc*.
whoever [hu'evə] *pron indef* chiunque.
whole [houl] *a* intero, tutto; *n* il tutto, l'intero, il totale; **on the w.** nel complesso, tutto considerato.
whole-hearted ['houl'ha:tid] *a* caloroso, cordiale.
whole-heartedly ['houl'ha:tidli] *ad* calorosamente, cordialmente.
wholesale ['houlseil] *n* vendita all'ingrosso; *a ad* all'ingrosso.
wholesome ['houlsəm] *a* sano, salubre.
wholly ['houlli] *ad* completamente, del tutto.
whom [hu:m] *pron rel interrog* che, chi, il quale, la quale, i quali, le quali.
whooping cough ['hupiŋkɔf] *n* pertosse.
whore [hɔ:] *n* prostituta.
whortleberry ['wə:tl,beri] *n* mirtillo.
whose [hu:z] *pron rel interrog* di cui, il cui, del quale *etc*, di chi? a chi?
whosoever [,husou'evə] *pron indef* chiunque.
why [wai] *ad interrog* perchè; *interj* ma, ma certo, ma via; *n* il perchè, motivo, causa.
wick [wik] *n* lucignolo, stoppino.
wicked ['wikid] *a* maligno, malvagio, perfido, perverso.
wickedness ['wikidnis] *n* malignità, malvagità, perfidia, perversità.
wicker ['wikə] *n* vimine; **wickerwork** lavoro in vimini.
wicket ['wikit] *n* cancellino, porticina; (*cricket*) porta.
wide [waid] *a* largo, vasto; (*of material*) alto; *ad* bene, completamente; **w.-open** spalancato; **w.-awake** completamente sveglio; **widely** *ad* largamente, molto.
widen ['waidn] *vti* allargar(si), ampliar(si).
widespread ['waidspred] *a* esteso, diffuso.
widow ['widou] *n* vedova.
widower ['widouə] *n* vedovo.
width [widθ] *n* larghezza; (*of material*) altezza.
wield [wi:ld] *vt* tenere, maneggiare, reggere.
wieldy ['wi:ldi] *a* maneggevole.
wife [waif] *n* moglie.
wig [wig] *n* parrucca.
wigwam ['wigwæm] *n* 'wigwam', tenda di pellirosse.
wild [waild] *a* selvaggio, selvatico; tempestoso, violento.
wilderness ['wildənis] *n* deserto, landa solitaria, luogo selvaggio.
wildfire ['waild,faiə] *n* fuoco greco; lampo di caldo.
wildness ['waildnis] *n* selvatichezza, ferocia.
wile [wail] *n* astuzia, inganno; *vt* ingannare, adescare.
Wilhelmina [,wilhel'mi:nə] *nf pr* Guglielmina.
wiliness ['wailinis] *n* astuzia.
will [wil] *n* volontà; (*leg*) testamento; *vti* volere; disporre, lasciare per testamento; costringere.
willful ['wilful] *a* caparbio, ostinato; (*leg*) premeditato.
wilfullness ['wilfulnis] *n* ostinazione, caparbietà.
William ['wiljəm] *nm pr* Guglielmo.
willing ['wiliŋ] *a* disposto (a), volonteroso; volontario.
willingly ['wiliŋli] *ad* volontieri.
willingness ['wiliŋnis] *n* buona volontà.
willow ['wilou] *n* salice.
willy-nilly ['wili'nili] *ad* volente o nolente.
Wilma ['wilmə] *nf pr* Vilma.
wilt [wilt] *vt* far appassire; *vi* appassire, languire.
wily ['waili] *a* astuto, malizioso.
wimple ['wimpl] *n* soggolo.
win [win] *n* successo, vittoria; *vt* vincere, conquistare, ottenere; persuadere; *vi* vincere.
wince [wins] *vi* ritrarsi improvvisamente, trasalire.
winch [wintʃ] *n* (*mech*) argano, manovella.
wind [waind] *vt* avvolgere; (*watch etc*) caricare; *vi* serpeggiare.
wind [wind] *n* vento; fiato; soffio; sentore.
windfall ['windfɔ:l] *n* frutto fatto cadere dal vento; (*fig*) fortuna inaspettata.

windlass ['windləs] *n* (*mech*) argano.
windmill ['winmil] *n* mulino a vento.
window ['windou] *n* finestra; vetrina.
windpipe ['windpaip] *n* trachea.
windshield ['windʃi:ld] *n* (*aut*) parabrezza; **w. wiper** tergicristallo.
windward ['windwəd] *n* parte da cui spira il vento; *a* situato dalla parte da cui spira il vento; *ad* contro vento.
windy ['windi] *a* ventoso, esposto al vento; (*fig*) verboso, vuoto.
wine [wain] *n* vino; **wineglass** bicchiere da vino; **wineshop** osteria, spaccio di vini.
wing [wiŋ] *n* ala; volo; *pl* (*theat*) quinte.
winged [wiŋd] *a* alato.
wink [wiŋk] *n* batter d'occhio, ammicco, cenno; *vi* ammiccare, strizzar l'occhio, batter le palpebre; brillare con intermittenza.
winkle ['wiŋkl] *n* chiocciola di mare.
winner ['winə] *n* vincitore.
winning ['winiŋ] *a* vincente, vincitore; avvincente, attraente; *n pl* vincita.
winnow ['winou] *vt* vagliare, spulare, ventilare.
winsome ['winsəm] *a* (*poet*) pieno di grazia, amabile.
winter ['wintə] *n* inverno; *a* d'inverno, invernale; *vi* passare l'inverno, svernare.
wintry ['wintri] *a* invernale, freddo.
wipe [waip] *n* strofinata, asciugatura, spolverata; *vt* asciugare, pulire, strofinare.
wire ['waiə] *n* filo metallico; telegrafo, telegramma; *vti* assicurare con filo metallico; (*el*) installare fili elettrici; telegrafare.
wireless ['waiəlis] *a* senza fili; *n* radio; **w. valve** valvola.
wiry ['waiəri] *a* magro e nerboruto.
wisdom ['wizdəm] *n* saggezza, sapienza, prudenza, giudizio.
wise [waiz] *a* saggio, savio, prudente, avveduto; **none the wiser** senza saperne più di prima.
wish [wiʃ] *n* desiderio; augurio; cosa desiderata; *vti* desiderare, volere; augurare.
wishful ['wiʃful] *a* desideroso, bramoso; **w. thinking** un pio desiderio.
wisp [wisp] *n* ciuffo, ciuffetto, striscia; **will-o'-the-w.** fuoco fatuo.
wistaria [wis'tɛəriə] *n* glicine.
wistful ['wistful] *a* nostalgico, pensoso, preoccupato.
wit [wit] *n* spirito, arguzia; intelligenza; *pl* ingegno, cervello.
witch [witʃ] *n* strega, ammaliatrice.
witchcraft ['witʃkrɑ:ft] *n* magia, stregoneria.
witchery ['witʃəri] *n* incantesimo, fascino.
with [wið] *prep* con, insieme a; da; presso; di, per; **to be w. it** essere aggiornato.
withdraw [wið'drɔ:] *vti* ritirar(si).
wither ['wiðə] *vt* far avvizzire; *vi* avvizzire, inaridirsi.
withhold [wið'hould] *vt* trattenere; rifiutare, negare.
within [wi'ðin] *prep* entro, dentro; in meno di, fra; *ad* dentro, all'interno.
without [wi'ðaut] *prep* senza (di), fuori di; *ad* fuori; *n* esterno.
withstand [wið'stænd] *vt* resistere a, opporsi a, sostenere.
witness ['witnis] *n* testimone, teste, testimonianza; *vti* testimoniare, essere presente a, firmare come teste; **w. box, w. stand** banco dei testi.
witticism ['witisizəm] *n* frizzo, motto di spirito.
witty ['witi] *a* spiritoso.
wizard ['wizəd] *n* mago, stregone.
wizardry ['wizədri] *n* magia, stregoneria.
wizened ['wiznd] *a* raggrinzito.
wobble ['wɔbl] *vi* barcollare, dondolare.
woe [wou] *n* (*poet*) dolore, sventura.
woeful ['wouful] *a* doloroso, triste.
wolf [wulf] *n* lupo; *vt* divorare.
wolfish ['wulfiʃ] *a* da lupo, crudele, vorace.
woman ['wumən] *pl* **women** ['wimin] *n* donna, -ne.
womanhood ['wumənhud] *n* condizione di donna, maturità della donna.
womanish ['wuməniʃ] *a* effeminato.
womanly ['wumənli] *a* femminile, di donna.
womb [wu:m] *n* grembo, utero.
wonder ['wʌndə] *n* meraviglia, miracolo, prodigio; *vi* meravigliarsi, domandarsi.
wonderful ['wʌndəful] *a* meraviglioso, prodigioso.
wonderland ['wʌndəlænd] *n* paese delle meraviglie.
woo [wu:] *vt* corteggiare, fare la corte a.
wood [wud] *n* bosco; legno; botte.
woodcut ['wudkʌt] *n* incisione su legno, xilografia.
wooded ['wudid] *a* boschivo, coperto di boschi.
wooden ['wudn] *a* di legno, legnoso; senz'espressione.
woodland ['wudlənd] *n* luogo boscoso.
woodman ['wudmən] *pl* **-men** *n* guarda boschi, guardia forestale, taglialegna.
woodpecker ['wud,pekə] *n* picchio.
woodwork ['wudwə:k] *n* lavoro in legno.
woodworm ['wudwə:m] *n* tarlo.
woody ['wudi] *a* boscoso; legnoso.
woof [wu:f] *n* tessitura, trama.
wool [wul] *n* lana.

woolen ['wulin] *a* di lana; *n* articolo di lana.
woolly ['wuli] *a* lanoso; *n* indumento di lana.
word [wə:d] *n* parola; *vt* esprimere con parole, mettere in parole.
wordy ['wə:di] *a* verboso; consistente di parole.
work [wə:k] *n* lavoro; *pl* opere, lavori *pl*; meccanismo; macchinario; fabbrica, officina, stabilimento; *vt* lavorare; azionare; *vi* lavorare; funzionare; **to w. out** esaurire; calcolare; **t. w. up** eccitare.
workable ['wə:kəbl] *a* eseguibile, praticabile, realizzabile.
worker ['wə:kə] *n* lavoratore, operaio.
workhouse ['wə:khaus] *n* ospizio di mendicità.
workman ['wə:kmən] *pl* **-men** *n* operaio, artigiano.
workmanship ['wə:kmənʃip] *n* abilità, tecnica, fattura.
workshop ['wə:kʃɔp] *n* laboratorio, officina.
world [wə:ld] *n* mondo; **worldwide** mondiale.
worldliness ['wə:ldlinis] *n* mondanità.
worldly ['wə:ldli] *a* terreno, mondano.
worm [wə:m] *n* verme, baco, lombrico; *vti* muoversi insidiosamente; **w.-eaten** tarlato.
wormwood ['wə:mwud] *n* assenzio; (*fig*) mortificazione.
worn-out ['wɔ:n'aut] *a* logoro; (*fig*) esausto, sfinito.
worry ['wʌri] *n* inquietudine, fastidio, preoccupazione; *vt* infastidire, importunare; *vi* preoccuparsi, tormentarsi.
worse [wə:s] *a* peggiore; *n* (il) peggio; *ad* peggio.
worsen ['wə:sn] *vti* peggiorare, aggravare, aggravarsi.
worship ['wə:ʃip] *n* adorazione, culto; *vt* adorare, venerare; *vi* prestare culto.
worshipper ['wə:ʃipə] *n* adoratore; *pl* i fedeli *pl*.
worst [wə:st] *a* (il) peggiore; *ad* (il) peggio; *vt* sopraffare.
worsted ['wə:stid] *n* pettinato di lana; *a* di lana pettinata.
worth [wə:θ] *a* degno di, meritevole di; del valore di; *n* valore, merito; **to be w.** valere; **to be worthwhile** valere la pena.
worthiness ['wə:ðinis] *n* merito, rispettabilità.
worthless ['wə:θlis] *a* senza valore, indegno.
worthlessness ['wə:θlisnis] *n* mancanza di valore, indegnità.
worthy ['wə:ði] *a* meritevole, degno; *n* persona illustre, personaggio.
would-be ['wudbi:] *a* sedicente; aspirante.
wound [wu:nd] *n* ferita; *vt* ferire.
wraith [reiθ] *n* fantasma, spettro.
wrangle ['ræŋgl] *n* alterco, rissa; *vi* altercare, azzuffarsi.
wrangler ['ræŋglə] *n* attaccabrighe; guardiano di cavalli.
wrangling ['ræŋgliŋ] *n* disputazione, litigio.
wrap [ræp] *n* scialle; *vt* avvolgere; **w. up** *vi* avvolgersi, imbacuccarsi.
wrapper ['ræpə] *n* accappatoio; fascia, copertina di libro; carta da imballo.
wrath [rɔ:θ] *n* collera, ira.
wrathful ['rɔ:θful] *a* furioso, irato.
wreak [ri:k] *vt* sfogare, soddisfare il desiderio di.
wreath [ri:θ] *n* ghirlanda, corona (funeraria).
wreathe [ri:ð] *vti* inghirlandare, intrecciare, attorcigliarsi.
wreck [rek] *n* naufragio, rovina, relitti *pl*; persona che ha ricevuto gravi colpi; *vt* far naufragare, rovinare, distruggere; *vi* naufragare, andare in pezzi.
wreckage ['rekidʒ] *n* naufragio, relitti, rottami *pl*.
wren [ren] *n* scricciolo.
wrench [rentʃ] *n* violento strappo, slogatura, storta; (*fig*) dolore, strazio; (*mech*) chiave inglese; *vt* strappare violentemente, (con)torcere, slogare; (*fig*) svisare.
wrest [rest] *vt* strappare.
wrestle ['resl] *vi* lottare, fare la lotta.
wrestling ['resliŋ] *n* lotta, (*sport*) lotta libera.
wrestler ['reslə] *n* lottatore.
wretch [retʃ] *n* miserabile, sciagurato.
wretched ['retʃid] *a* miserabile, misero, spregevole.
wretchedness ['retʃidnis] *n* infelicità, miseria, squallore.
wriggle ['rigl] *vi* contorcersi, dimenarsi.
wring [riŋ] *vti* torcere, torcersi, stringere, strizzare, spremere; estorcere.
wringer ['riŋə] *n* asciugatrice meccanica.
wrinkle ['riŋkl] *n* ruga, grinza; *vti* corrugare, increspare.
wrist [rist] *n* polso.
wristband ['ristbænd] *n* polsino.
writ [rit] *n* citazione, mandato, ordine.
write [rait] *vti* scrivere.
writer ['raitə] *n* scrivente, scrittore.
writhe [raið] *vi* contorcersi.
writing ['raitiŋ] *n* scrittura, calligrafia, lo scrivere; *pl* scritti *pl*; **w. paper** carta da lettera, carta da scrivere.
wrong [rɔŋ] *a* sbagliato, erroneo, inesatto, scorretto; ingiusto; *n* torto, danno, male; *vt* far torto a, giudicare erroneamente; **be w.** aver torto; *ad* male, erroneamente;

w.-doer peccatore, trasgressore, offensore.
wrongful ['rɔŋful] *a* ingiusto.
wrought [rɔ:t] *a* (*di ferro*) battuto, lavorato; **w.-up** nervoso, agitato.
wry [rai] *a* contorto, storto; ironico.

X

Xanthippe [zæn'θipi] *n pr* Santippe; moglie bisbetica.
Xmas ['krisməs] *see* **Christmas.**
X-ray ['eks'rei] *a* di raggi X; **X-ray photograph** radiografia; *vt* sottoporre a raggi X.
X-rays ['eks'reiz] *n pl* raggi X *pl*.
xylography [zai'lɔgrəfi] *n* xilografia.
xylophone ['zailəfoun] *n* (*mus*) xilofono.

Y

yacht [jɔt] *n* panfilo, yacht.
yankee ['jæŋki] *a n* (*fam*) americano.
yap [jæp] *vi* guaire, uggiolare, abbaiare.
yard [jɑ:d] *n* iarda (*misura di lunghezza=cm 91 circa*); cortile, recinto.
yarn [jɑ:n] *n* filato; (*tale*) racconto, storia; *vi* (*fam*) raccontare storie.
yawn [jɔ:n] *n* sbadiglio; *vi* sbadigliare.
ye [ji:] *pron* (*poet*) voi; *def art* (*arc*) il *etc*.
year [jə:] *n* anno, annata; età.
yearling ['jə:liŋ] *n* animale di un anno.
yearly ['jə:li] *a* annuale, annuo; *ad* annualmente.
yearn [jə:n] *vi* **y. for** agognare, struggersi di.
yearning ['jə:niŋ] *n* desiderio ardente, struggimento.
yeast [ji:st] *n* lievito.
yell [jel] *n* urlo; *vi* urlare.
yellow ['jelou] *a n* giallo.
yellowish ['jelouiʃ] *a* giallastro, giallognolo.
yellowness ['jelounis] *n* color giallastro.
yelp [jelp] *n* guaito; *vi* guaire.
yeoman ['joumən] *n* piccolo proprietario terriero.
yeomanry ['joumənri] *n* classe dei piccoli proprietari terrieri; corpo di cavalleria volontaria.
yes [jes] *ad* sì.
yesterday ['jestədi] *n ad* ieri.
yet [jet] *ad* ancora, finora, tuttora; eppure, cionondimeno; *cj* tuttavia.
yew (tree) ['ju:(tri:)] *n* tasso.
yield [ji:ld] *n* raccolto, produzione; *vt* produrre, rendere; *vi* arrendersi, cedere.
yoghurt ['jɔgə(:)t] *n* yogurt.
yoke [jouk] *n* giogo; coppia, paio; *vt* aggiogare, soggiogare.
yolk [jouk] *n* rosso d'uovo, tuorlo.
yonder ['jɔndə] *a* quello là; *ad* laggiù, lassù.
yore [jɔ:] *n* (*poet*) tempo passato; **of y.** *ad* anticamente.
you [ju:] *pron* tu, voi, ti, te, vi, ve, Lei, Loro.
young [jʌŋ] *a* giovane; *n* piccolo, piccoli, (*of animals*) prole.
youngster ['jʌŋstə] *n* ragazzo, giovane.
your [jɔ:] *a* (il) tuo *etc*, (il) vostro *etc*; **yours** *pron* (il) tuo *etc*, (il) vostro *etc*; **yourself** *pron* tu stesso, te stesso, ti; **yourselves** *pl pron* voi stessi, vi *etc pl*.
youth [ju:θ] *n* giovane, gioventù, giovinezza.
youthful ['ju:θful] *a* giovanile.
youthfulness ['ju:θfulnis] *n* aspetto, spirito giovanile.
Yugoslavia ['jugou'slɑ:viə] *n* Jugoslavia.
Yule [ju:l] *n* Natale, feste natalizie; **y. log** ceppo di Natale.

Z

Zagreb ['zɑ:greb] *n* Zagabria.
zany ['zeini] *n* buffone, zanni.
zeal [zi:l] *n* zelo.
zealot ['zelət] *n* fanatico, zelatore.
zealous ['zeləs] *a* zelante.
zebra ['zi:brə] *n* zebra.
zenith ['zeniθ] *n* zenit; (*fig*) culmine, apice.
zephyr ['zefə] *n* zeffiro, brezza.
zero ['ziərou] *n* zero.
zest [zest] *n* sapore piccante; (*fig*) gusto, interesse.
zigzag ['zigzæg] *n* zig-zag; *a ad* a zig-zag; *vi* andare a zig-zag, zigzagare.
zinc [ziŋk] *n* zinco.
zip [zip] *n* chiusura lampo.
zither ['ziðə] *pl* **zithern** *n* (*mus*) cetra tirolese.
zodiac ['zoudiæk] *n* zodiaco.
zodiacal [zou'daiəkəl] *a* zodiacale.
zone [zoun] *n* zona.
zoo [zu:] *n* giardino zoologico, zoo.
zoologist [zou'ɔlədʒist] *n* zoologo.
zoology [zou'ɔlədʒi] *n* zoologia.
Zulu ['zu:lu:] *a n* Zulù.
Zurich ['zjuərik] *n* Zurigo.

Italian Grammar—Grammatica Italiana

GENDER OF NOUNS

In Italian there are two genders: masculine and feminine.

Masculine: nouns ending in **o** (exceptions: **la màno** etc.) nouns ending in **i** (exceptions: nouns of Greek origin, like **la crísi, la diòcesi, la tèsi** etc.)

Feminine: nouns ending in **a** (exceptions: some words ending in **ta** and **ma** of Greek origin, like **il telegràmma, il dràmma, il poèma** etc.)

Nouns ending in **e** are sometimes masculine, sometimes feminine.

The following are masculine: nouns referring to male human beings and animals, names of fruit trees (whose corresponding fruit is feminine) names of months, days, mountains, lakes.

The following are feminine: nouns referring to female human beings and animals; names of fruits (whose corresponding tree is masculine); names of islands, abstract nouns indicating quality.

PLURAL OF NOUNS AND ADJECTIVES

The plural of masculine nouns and adjectives is **i**: **artísta, artísti; càne, càni; pòrto, pòrti.**

The plural of feminine nouns and adjectives is **e** if the word in the singular ends in **a**: **pàtria, pàtrie.** It is **i** if the singular ends in **e**: **nàve, nàvi**. Exceptions: **àla** (wing), **àli**. The word **màno** (hand) is feminine and its plural is **màni**.

Note:—

1. Nouns and adjectives ending in the singular in **ca** and **ga** end in the plural in **che** and **ghe** if they are feminine; in **chi** and **ghi** if they are masculine: **amíca** (lady friend), **amíche**; **dúca** (duke), **dúchi**; **stréga** (witch), **stréghe**; **collèga** (colleague), **collèghi**. Exception: **bèlga** (Belgian), **bèlgi** (m.)
2. Nouns and adjectives ending in the singular in **cia** and **gia** end in the plural in **e** keeping the **i** if it is stressed, omitting it if it is not: **bugía** (lie), **bugíe**; **fàccia** (face) **fàcce**. Sometimes—to avoid ambiguity—the unaccented **i** is kept, as in the noun **audàcia** (daring), **audàcie**, to distinguish it from the adjective **audàce** (bold).

3. Nouns and adjectives ending in the singular in **io** end in the plural in **ii** if the **i** of **io** is stressed; if it is unstressed the plural is simply **i**: **zío** (uncle), **zíi**; **fàggio** (beech tree), **fàggi**. Again, to avoid ambiguity the **i**, even if unstressed, is sometimes retained: **òdio** (hatred), **òdii**, to distinguish it from **òde** (ode), **òdi**.
4. Nouns and adjectives consisting of two syllables and ending in the singular in **co** and **go** end in the plural in **chi** and **ghi**: **biànco** (white) **biànchi**; **làgo** (lake) **làghi**. Exceptions: **pòrco** (pig), **pòrci**; **grèco** (Greek), **grèci**.
5. Nouns and adjectives of more than two syllables, ending in the singular in **co** and **go** end in the plural in **chi** and **ghi** if **co** and **go** are preceded by a consonant: **almanàcco** (almanac) **almanàcchi**; **albèrgo** (hotel), **albèrghi**. They end in **ci** and **gi** if **co** and **go** are preceded by a vowel: **amíco** (friend), **amíci** etc. This category, however, presents a considerable number of exceptions. To help the student we have indicated in the Dictionary all the exceptions concerning (2) and (3) and the plural of all the words—regular or exceptions —concerning (4) and (5).
6. Some nouns change their gender in the plural: singular **uòvo** (egg), **uòva**; **díti** (finger), **díta** etc. There are nouns which have two plurals with different meanings: **úrlo** (shout), **úrli** (cries of animals), **úrla** (shouts of human beings). Such irregularities and peculiarities have been indicated in the Dictionary.
7. Some nouns are used only in the singular (**pròle, sàngue, mièle, fàme**); some only in the plural (**esèquie, fòrbici, occhiàli, nòzze,** etc.)
8. Some nouns have the same form both for the singular and for the plural. They are: words accented on the last syllable; *e.g.* la **città**, le **città** (city, cities); monosyllables, *e.g.* il **re**, i **re** (king, kings); surnames; words ending in a consonant, *e.g.* il **gas**, i **gas** (gas, gasses); compounds made of a verb and of a plural noun, *e.g.* il **portalèttere**, i **portalèttere** (postman, postmen); nouns ending in **ie**, *e.g.* **progènie** (progeny). Exceptions to this are **superfície** (surface) and **móglie** (wife) which in the plural become **superfíci** and **mógli**.
9. Compounds, other than those mentioned in (8), form their plural as follows: some change into plural only the second part of the word, *e.g.* **cartapècora** (parchment) **cartapècore**. Some have both parts in plural form *e.g.* **mezzanòtte** (midnight) **mezzenòtti**.

Compounds of **càpo** either change both parts *e.g.* **capocuòco** (chef), **capicuòchi**, or use the plural only in the first part, *e.g.* **caposquàdra** (foreman, group-leader), **capisquàdra**, or only in the second, *e.g.* **capolavóro** (masterpiece), **capolavóri**. These plurals are duly indicated in their place in the Dictionary.

10. Some words have an entirely irregular plural: **uòmo** (man), **uòmini**; **dío** (god), **dèi**; **búe** (ox), **buoi**; **mílle** (one thousand), **míla**.

FEMININE OF NOUNS AND ADJECTIVES

When the masculine noun or adjective ends in **o** the feminine ends in **a**: **il maéstro, la maéstra.**

When the masculine noun or adjective ends in **e** the feminine ends in **e**: **il nipóte, la nipóte.**

When the masculine noun or adjective ends in **a** the feminine ends in **a**: **un artísta, un' artísta.**

When the masculine noun or adjective ends in **ière** the feminine ends in **ièra**: **il consiglière,** la **consiglièra.**

When the masculine noun or adjective ends in **tóre** the feminine ends in **tríce**: **il pittóre, la pittríce**. Exception: **il fattóre** (the land agent), **la fattóra,** or **la fattoréssa.**

There are some exceptions like: **studènte**, **studentéssa** (student); **avvocàto**, **avvocatéssa** (lawyer, lady lawyer) etc. These are indicated in the Dictionary. Names of animals ending in **e** and **u** are common: *e.g.* **il lèpre, la lèpre** (the hare); **il gru, la gru** (the crane). Some have no feminine: *e.g.* **il tòpo** (the mouse), **il coníglio** (the rabbit). Some have no masculine: *e.g.* **la vòlpe** (the fox), **l'àquila** (the eagle). In these cases the word **fémmina** (female) or the word **màschio** (male) is added as explicatory: *e.g.* **il tòpo fémmina** (or **la fémmina del tòpo**), **la vòlpe màschio,** etc.

Italian Verbs—Verbi Italiani

PROGRESSIVE FORM

In Italian there are three progressive tenses: the present, the past and the future, formed respectively by the Present Indicative, the Imperfect and the Future of **stàre** and less frequently **andàre**; *e.g.* he is sleeping, **sta dormèndo**; he was sleeping, **stava dormèndo**; he will be sleeping, **starà dormèndo**. These tenses can be rendered in Italian by the simple tense; *e.g.* he is sleeping, **dorme**.

ORTHOGRAPHIC CHANGES OF SOME VERBS IN–ÀRE

1. Verbs ending in **càre** and **gàre**, as **pagàre, cercàre,** when the **c** or **g** is followed by **e** or **i**, take in **h** in order to preserve the hard sound of the consonant; *e.g.* **paghiàmo, cercherò.**
2. Verbs in **ciàre** and **giàre**, as **cominciàre, mangiàre,** drop the **i** before **e** or **i**; *e.g.* **màngi, mangerò.**
3. Verbs in **iàre** having a sounded **i**, as **spiàre**, **inviàre,** retain the **i** except before **iàmo** and **iàte**; *e.g.* **invíi, spierémo, inviàmo, spiàte**.
4. Verbs in **iàre** where the **i** is not sounded, as **pigliàre, invecchiàre, annoiàre**, drop the **i** when followed by another **i**; *e.g.* **pígli, píglio, invècchi.**

NOTE ON THE VERBS IN–ÍRE

Verbs in **–íre** take the terminations **ísco, ísci, ísce, íscono** in the 1st, 2nd, and 3rd singular, and in the 3rd plural of the Indicative. Similarly in the Present Subjunctive and in the Imperative.

Regular Verbs

Conjugation 1	Conjugation 2	Conjugation 3
	INFINITIVE	
Parlàre, to speak	**Temére**, to fear	**Sentíre**, to hear
	PRESENT INDICATIVE	
I speak	*I fear*	*I hear*
io pàrl-o	tém-o	sènt-o
tu pàrl-i	tém-i	sènt-i
egli pàrl-a	tém-e	sènt-e
noi parl-iàmo	tem-iàmo	sent-iàmo
voi parl-àte	tem-éte	sent-íte
essi pàrl-ano	tém-ono	sènt-ono

IMPERFECT

I used to speak	*I used to fear*	*I used to hear*
io parl-àvo	tem-évo	sent-ívo
tu parl-àvi	tem-évi	sent-ívi
egli parl-àva	tem-éva	sent-íva
noi parl-avàmo	tem-evàmo	sent-ivàmo
voi parl-avàte	tem-evàte	sent-ivàte
essi parl-àvano	tem-évano	sent-ívano

GERUND

parl-àndo, *speaking*	tem-èndo, *fearing*	sent-èndo, *hearing*

PAST PARTICIPLE

parl-àto, *spoken*	tem-úto, *feared*	sent-íto, *heard*

Subjunctive

PRESENT

that I speak	*that I fear*	*that I hear*
ch'io-pàrl-i	ch'io tém-a	ch'io sènt-a
che tu pàrl-i	che tu tém-a	che tu sènt-a
ch'egli pàrl-i	ch'egli tém-a	ch'egli sènt-a
che noi parl-iàmo	che noi tem-iàmo	che noi sent-iàmo
che voi parl-iàte	che voi tem-iàte	che voi sent-iàte
ch'essi pàrl-ino	che essi tém-ano	ch'essi sènt-ano

IMPERFECT

if I spoke	*if I feared*	*if I heard*
se io parl-àssi	tem-éssi	sent-íssi
se tu parl-àssi	tem-éssi	sent-íssi
se egli parl-àsse	tem-ésse	sent-ísse
se noi parl-àssimo	tem-éssimo	sent-íssimo
se voi parl-àste	tem-éste	sente-íste
se essi parl-àssero	tem-éssero	sent-íssero

Compound Tenses

Perfect	io ho	parlàto	*I have*	*spoken,*
Pluperfect	io avévo		*I had*	
2nd Pluperf.	io èbbi		*I had*	or
2nd Future	io avrò	or	*I shall have*	
2nd Condit.	io avrèi		*I should have*	*feared,*
		temúto,		
Subj. Perfect.	ch'io àbbia		*that I have*	
Subj. Pluperf.	se io avéssi	or	*if I had*	or
Past Infin.	avér(e)		*to have*	
Past Gerund	avèndo	sentíto	*having*	*heard*

PAST DEFINITE

I spoke	*I feared*	*I heard*
io parl-ài	tem-éi or -ètti	sent-íi
tu parl-àsti	tem-ésti	sent-ísti
egli parl-ò	tem-è or -ètte	sent-í
noi parl-àmmo	tem-émmo	sent-ímmo
voi parl-àste	tem-éste	sent-íste
essi parl-àrono	tem-érono or -èttero	sent-írono

FUTURE

I shall speak	*I shall fear*	*I shall hear*
io parl-erò	tem-erò	sent-irò
tu parl-eròi	tem-erài	sent-irài
egli parl-erà	tem-erà	sent-irà
noi parl-erémo	tem-erémo	sent-irémo
voi parl-eréte	tem-eréte	sent-iréte
essi parl-erànno	tem-erànno	sent-irànno

CONDITIONAL

I should speak	*I should fear*	*I should hear*
io parl-erèi	tem-erèi	sent-irèi
tu parl-erésti	tem-erésti	sent-irésti
egli arl-erèbbe	tem-erèbbe	sent-irèbbe
noi rl-erèmmo	tem-erèmmo	sent-irèmmo
voi pa eréste	tem-eréste	sent-iréste
essi parl-erèbbero	tem-erèbbero	sent-irèbbero

IMPERATIVE

speak	*fear*	*hear*
pàrl-a	tém-i	sènt-i
pàrl-i	tém-a	sènt-a
parl-iàmo	tem-iàmo	sent-iàmo
parl-àte	tem-éte	sent-íte
pàrl-ino	tém-ano	sént-ano

PRESENT INFINITIVE

parl-àre, *to speak*	tem-ére, *to fear*	sent-íre, *to hear*

PRESENT PARTICIPLE

parl-ànte, *speaking*	tem-ènte, *fearing*	sent-ènte, *hearing*

Auxiliary Verbs

NOTE: **Veníre** and **andàre** may be used as auxiliaries instead of **èssere** with a past participle or with a gerund.

Èssere, to be | **Avére,** to have

PRESENT INDICATIVE

I am	*I have*
io sóno	io ho
tu sèi	tu hai
egli / essa } è	egli / essa } ha
noi siàmo	noi abbiàmo
voi siète	voi avéte
essi / esse } sóno	essi / esse } hànno

IMPERFECT

I was	*I had*
io èro	io avévo
tu èri	tu avévi
egli èra	egli avéva
noi eravàmo	noi avevàmo
voi eravàte	voi avevàte
essi èrano	essi avévano

PAST DEFINITE

I was	*I had*
io fúi	io èbbi
tu fósti	tu avésti
egli fu	egli èbbe
noi fúmmo	noi avémmo
voi fóste	voi avéste
essi fúrono	essi èbbero

FUTURE

I shall be	*I shall have*
io sarò	io avrò
tu saràí	tu avràí
egli sarà	egli avrà
noi sarémo	noi avrémo
voi saréte	voi avréte
essi saranno	essi avrànno

CONDITIONAL

I should be	*I should have*
io sarèi	io avrèi
tu sarésti	tu avrésti
egli sarèbbe	egli avrèbbe
noi sarèmmo	noi avrémmo
voi saréste	voi avréste
essi sarèbbero	essi avrèbbero

IMPERATIVE

be	*have*
síi	àbbi
sía	àbbia
siàmo	abbiàmo
siàte	abbiàte
síano	àbbiano

INFINITIVE

èssere, *to be* — avére, *to have*

GERUND

essèndo, *being* — avèndo, *having*

PAST PARTICIPLE

stàto, stàta stàti, stàte	been	avúto, avúta avúti, avúte	had

Compound Tenses

PERFECT

I have been	*I have had*
io sóno stàto	io ho avúto
tu sèi stàto	tu hai avúto
egli è stàto essa è stàta }	egli essa } ha avúto
noi siàmo stàti	noi abbiàmo avúto
voi sième stàti	voi avéte avúto
essi sóno stàti esse sóno stàte }	essi esse } hànno avúto

PLUPERFECT

I had been	*I had had*
io èro stàto	io avevo avúto
tu èri stàto	tu avévi avúto
egli èra stàto essa èra stàta }	egli essa } avéva avúto
noi eravàmo stàti	noi avevàmo avúto
voi eravàte stàti	voi avevàte avúto
essi èrano stàti esse èrano stàte }	essi esse } avévano avúto

SECOND PLUPERFECT

I had been	*I had had*
io fúi stàto	io èbbi avúto
tu fósti stàto	tu avésti avúto
egli fu stàto essa fu stàta }	egli essa } èbbe avúto
noi fúmmo stàti	noi avémmo avúto
voi fóste stàti	voi avéste avúto
essi fúrono stàti esse fúrono stàte }	essi esse } èbbero avúto

FUTURE PERFECT

I shall have been	*I shall have had*
io sarò stàto	io avrò avúto
tu sarài stàto	tu avrài avúto
egli sarà stàto essa sarà stàta }	egli essa } avrà avúto
noi sarémo stàti	noi avrémo avúto
voi saréte stàti	voi avréte avúto
essi sarànno stàti esse sarànno stàte }	essi esse } avrànno avúto

PERFECT CONDITIONAL

I should have been	*I should have had*
io sarèi stàto	io avrèi avúto
tu sarésti stàto	tu avrésti avúto
egli sarèbbe stàto essa sarèbbe stàta }	egli essa } avrèbbe avúto

noi sarèmmo stàti	noi avrémmo avúto
voi saréste stàti	voi avréste avúto
essi sarèbbero stàti }	essi } avrèbbero avúto
esse sarèbbero stàte }	esse }

PERFECT INFINITIVE

to have been	*to have had*
èssere stàto	avére avúto
èssere stàta	avére avúta

PERFECT GERUND

having been	*having had*
essèndo stàto	avèndo avúto
essèndo stàta	avèndo avúta

PRESENT SUBJUNCTIVE

that I be	*that I have*
ch'io sía	ch'io àbbia
che tu sía	che tu àbbia
che egli sía	che egli àbbia
che noi siàmo	che noi abbiàmo
che voi siàte	che voi abbiàte
che essi síano	che essi àbbiano

IMPERFECT

if I were	*if I had*
se io fóssi	se io avéssi
se tu fóssi	se tu avéssi
se egli fósse	se egli avésse
se noi fóssimo	se noi avéssimo
se voi fóste	se voi avéste
se essi fóssero	se essi avéssero

PERFECT

that I have been	*that I have had*
ch'io sía stàto	ch'io àbbia avúto
che tu sía stàto	che tu àbbia avúto
che egli sía stàto }	che egli } àbbia avúto
che essa sía stàta }	che essa }
che noi siàmo stàti	che noi abbiàmo avúto
che voi siàte stàti	che voi abbiàte avúto
che essi síano stàti }	che essi } àbbiano avúto
che esse síano stàte }	che esse }

PLUPERFECT

if I had been	*if I had had*
se io fóssi stàto	se io avéssi avúto
se tu fóssi stàto	se tu avéssi avúto
se egli fósse stàto }	se egli avésse avúto }
se essa fósse stàta }	se essa avésse avúto }
se noi fóssimo stàti	se noi avéssimo avúto
se voi fóste stàti	se voi avéste avúto
se essi fóssero stàti }	se essi avéssero avúto }
se esse fóssero stàte }	se esse avéssero avúto }

The following regular verbs in -íre do not insert **isc:**

apríre	to open	**àpro**	**dormíre**	to sleep	**dòrmo**
copríre	to cover	**còpro**	**fuggíre**	to escape	**fúggo**
cucíre	to sew	**cúcio**	**partíre**	to depart	**pàrto**
pentírsi	to repent	**mi pènto**	**servíre**	to serve	**sèrvo**
seguíre	to follow	**séguo**	**vestíre**	to dress	**vèsto**
sentíre	to hear, feel	**sènto**			

Bollíre (to boil) when used intransitively prefers not to insert **isc.**

Nutríre (to nourish) uses either form.

Irregular Verbs

Accèndere *to light*
past accesi, accendesti, accese, accendemmo, accendeste, accésero
past part. acceso

Acclúdere *to enclose*
past acclusi, accludesti, accluse, accludemmo, accludeste, acclúsero
past part. accluso

Addúrre *to adduce*
past addussi, adducesti, addusse, adducemmo, adduceste, addússero
fut. addurrò
cond. addurrei
past part. addotto

Adémpiere, Adempíre *to accomplish*
pres. ind. adempio, adempi, adempie, adempiamo, adempite, adémpiono
pres. sub. adempia
imper. adempi, adempia, adempite, adémpiano
past adempii, adempisti, adempí, adempimmo, adempiste, adempirono
past part. adempito *or* adempiuto

Affliggere *to afflict*
past afflissi, affliggesti, afflisse, affliggemmo, affliggeste, afflíssero
past part. afflitto

Allúdere *to allude*
past allusi, alludesti, alluse, alludemmo, alludeste, allúsero
past part. alluso

Andàre *to go*
pres. ind. vado, vai, va, andiamo, andate, vanno
pres. sub. vada, vada, vada, andiamo, andiate, vàdano
imp. vai *or* va', vada, andiamo, andate, vàdano
fut. andrò
cond. andrei

Annèttere *to annex*
past annessi, annettesti, annesse, annettemmo, annetteste, annèssero
past part. annesso

Apparíre *to appear*
pres. ind. apparisco *or* appaio, apparisci *or* appari, apparisce *or* appare, appariamo, apparite, appariscono *or* appàiono
past apparvi *or* apparii, apparisti, apparve *or* apparí *or* apparse, apparimmo, appariste, appàrvero *or* apparírono *or* appàrsero
pres. sub. apparisca *or* appaia, apparisca *or* appaia, apparisca *or* appaia, appariamo, appariate, apparíscano *or* appàiano
imper. apparisci *or* appari, apparisca *or* appaia, apparite, apparíscano *or* appàiano
past. part. apparso

Appèndere *to hang*
past appesi, appendesti, appese, appendemmo, appendeste, appésero
past. part. appeso

Apríre *to open*
pres. ind. apro, apri, apre, apriamo, aprite, àprono
past aprii, *or* apersi, apristi, aprí *or* aperse, aprimmo, apriste, aprírono *or* apèrsero
past. part. aperto

Àrdere *to burn*
past arsi, ardesti, arse, ardemmo, ardeste, àrsero
past. part. arso

Aspèrgere *to sprinkle*
past aspersi, aspergesti, asperse, aspergemmo, aspergeste, aspèrsero
past. part. asperso

Assalíre *to assail*
pres. ind. assalgo *or* assalisco, assali *or* assalisci, assale *or* assalisce, assaliamo, assalite, assàlgono *or* assalíscono

past	assalii *or* assalsi, assalisti, assalí *or* assalse, assalimmo, assaliste, assalírono *or* assàlsero
pres. sub.	assalga *or* assalisca, assalga *or* assalisca, assalga *or* assalisca, assaliamo, assaliate, assàlgano *or* assalíscano
Assídersi	*to take one's seat*
past	mi assisi, ti assidesti, si assise, ci assidemmo, vi assideste, si assísero
past part.	assiso
Assístere	*to assist*
past	assistei *or* assistetti, assistesti, assistè *or* assistette, assistemmo, assisteste, assistérono or assistèttero
past part.	assistito
Assòlvere	*to absolve*
past	assolsi *or* assolvei *or* assolvetti, assolvesti, assolse *or* assolvette, assolvemmo, assolveste, assòlsero *or* assolvèttero
past part.	assolto *or* assoluto
Assorbíre	*to absorb*
pres.	assorbo *or* assorbisco, assorbi *or* assorbisci, assorbe *or* assorbisce, assorbiamo, assorbite, assòrbono *or* assorbíscono
past part.	assorbito *or* assorto
Assúmere	*to assume*
past	assunsi, assumesti, assunse, assumemmo, assumeste, assúnsero
past part.	assunto
Assúrgere	*to rise*
past	assursi, assurgesti, assurse, assurgemmo, assurgeste, assursero
past part.	assurto
Bére	*to drink*
pres. ind.	bevo, bevi, beve, beviamo, bevete, bévono
imp. ind.	bevevo, bevevi, beveva, bevevamo, bevevate, bevévano
past	bevvi *or* bevei, bevesti, bevve *or* bevè *or* bevette, bevemmo, beveste, bèvvero *or* bevérono *or* bevèttero
fut.	berrò
cond.	berrei
pres. sub.	beva
imp. sub.	bevessi
imper.	bevi, beva, bevete, bévano
past part.	bevuto

Cadére *to fall*
past caddi, cadesti, cadde, cademmo, cadeste, càddero
fut. cadrò
cond. cadrei
Cèdere *to give*
past cedei *or* cedetti, cedesti, cedè *or* cedette, cedemmo, cedeste, cedérono *or* cedèttero
Chiédere *to ask*
past chiesi, chiedesti, chiese, chiedemmo, chiedeste, chiésero
past part. chiesto
Chiúdere *to close*
past chiusi, chiudesti, chiuse, chiudemmo, chiudeste, chiúsero
past part. chiuso
Cíngere *to gird*
past cinsi, cingesti, cinse, cingemmo, cingeste, cínsero
past part. cinto
Cògliere *to gather*
pres. ind. colgo, cogli, coglie, cogliamo, cogliete, còlgono
past colsi, cogliesti, colse, cogliemmo, coglieste, còlsero
pres. sub. colga, colga, colga, cogliamo, cogliate, còlgano
past part. colto
Còmpiere, Compíre *to complete*
pres. ind. cómpio, compi, cómpie, compiamo, compite, cómpiono
past compii, compisti, compí, compimmo, compiste, compírono
pres. sub. compia
imper. compi, cómpia, compite, cómpiano
past part. compìto *or* compiúto
Comprímere *to compress*
past compressi, comprimesti, compresse, comprimemmo, comprimeste, comprèssero
past part. compresso
Conóscere *to know*
past conobbi, conoscesti, conobbe, conoscemmo, conosceste, conòbbero
Contúndere *to bruise*
past contusi, contundesti, contuse, contundemmo, contundeste, contúsero
past part. contuso

Convèrgere *to converge*

past conversi *or* convergei, convergesti, converse *or* convergè, convergemmo, convergeste, convèrsero *or* convergèrono

past part. converso

Copríre *to cover*

pres. ind. copro, copri, copre, copriamo, coprite, còprono

past coprii *or* copersi, copristi, coprí *or* coperse, coprimmo, copriste, coprírono *or* copèrsero

past part. coperto

Córrere *to run*

past corsi, corresti, corse, corremmo, correste, córsero

past part. corso

Créscere *to grow*

past crebbi, crescesti, crebbe, crescemmo, cresceste, crébbero

Cuòcere *to cook*

pres. ind. cuocio, cuoci, cuoce, cociamo, cocete, cuòciono

past cossi, cocesti, cosse, cocemmo, coceste, còssero

past part. cotto

Dàre *to give*

pres. ind. do, dài, dà, diamo, date, dànno

imp. ind. davo

past diedi, desti, diede, demmo, deste, dièdero

fut. darò

pres. sub. dia

imp. sub. dessi

cond. darei

imper. da, dia, date, díano

pres. part. dando

past part. dato

Decídere *to decide*

past decisi, decidesti, decise, decidemmo, decideste, decísero

past part. deciso

Devòlvere *to devolve*

past devolvei *or* devolvetti, devolvesti, devolvè *or* devolvette, devolvemmo, devolveste, devolvérono *or* devolvèttero

past part. devoluto

Difèndere *to defend*
past difesi, difendesti, difese, difendemmo, difendeste, difésero
past part. difeso

Díre *to say*
pres. ind. dico, dici, dice, diciamo, dite, dícono
imp. ind. dicevo
past dissi, dicesti, disse, dicemmo, diceste, díssero
fut. dirò
pres. sub. dica
imp. subj. dicesse
cond. direi
imper. di', dica, dite, dìcano
pres. part. dicendo
past part. detto

Dirígere *to direct*
past diressi, dirigesti, diresse, dirigemmo, dirigeste, dirèssero
past part. diretto

Discútere *to discuss*
past discussi *or* discutei, discutesti, discusse *or* discutè, discutemmo, discuteste, discússero *or* discutérono
past part. discusso

Distínguere *to distinguish*
past distinsi, distinguesti, distinse, distinguemmo, distingueste, distínsero
past part. distinto

Divídere *to divide*
past divisi, dividesti, divise, dividemmo, divideste, divísero
past part. diviso

Dolérsi *to regret*
pres. ind. mi dolgo, ti duoli, si duole, ci doliamo *or* dogliamo, vi dolete, si dólgono
past mi dolsi, ti dolesti, si dolse, ci dolemmo, vi doleste, si dólsero
fut. mi dorrò
pres. sub. mi dolga, ti dolga, si dolga, ci doliamo, vi doliate, si dólgano
imp. sub. mi dolessi
cond. mi dorrei
imper. duoliti, si dolga, doletevi, si dólgano
pres. part. dolente
past part. dolutosi

Dovére *to have to*

pres. ind. devo *or* debbo, devi, deve, dobbiamo, dovete, dévono *or* dèbbono

past dovei *or* dovetti, dovesti, dovè *or* dovette, dovemmo, doveste, dovérono *or* dovèttero

fut. dovrò

pres. sub. deva *or* debba, deva *or* debba, deva *or* debba, dobbiamo, dobbiate, dévano *or* dèbbono

imper. devi, deve, dovete, dévono

past part. dovuto

Emèrgere *to emerge*

past emersi, emergesti, emerse, emergemmo, emergeste, emèrsero

past part. emerso

Émpiere *to fill: conjugate like* **empíre**

Empíre *to fill*

pres. ind. empio, empi, empie, empiamo, empite, émpiono

pres. sub. empia, empia, empia, empiamo, empiate, émpiano

imper. empi, empia, empite, émpiano

pres. part. empiente

Èrgere *to raise*

past ersi, ergesti, erse, ergemmo, ergeste, èrsero

past part. erto

Esauríre *to exhaust*

past part. esaurito *or* esàusto

Esígere *to exact*

past esigei *or* esigetti, esigesti, esigè *or* esigette, esigemmo, esigeste, esigérono *or* esigèttero

past part. esatto

Esímere *to exempt*

past esimei *or* esimetti, esimesti, esimè *or* esimette, esimemmo, esimeste, esimérono *or* esimèttero

past part. Not used. Use esente or esentato

Espèllere *to expel*

past espulsi, espellesti, espulse, espellemmo, espelleste, espúlsero

past part. espulso

Esplòdere *to explode*

past esplosi, esplodesti, esplose, esplodemmo, esplodeste, esplòsero

past part. esploso

Evàdere *to escape*
past evasi, evadesti, evase, evademmo, evadeste, evàsero
past part. evaso

Fàre *to do, make*
pres. ind. faccio *or* fo, fai, fa, facciamo, fate, fanno
imp. ind. facevo
past feci, facesti, fece, facemmo, faceste, fécero
fut. farò
cond. farei
pres. sub. faccia
imp. sub. facessi
imper. fai *or* fa', faccia, fate, fàcciano
pres. part. facente
past part. fatto

Fèndere *to split*
past fendei *or* fendetti, fendesti, fendè *or* fendette, fendemmo, fendeste, fendérono *or* fendèttero
past part. fesso *or* fenduto

Fíggere *to fix*
past fissi, figgesti, fisse, figgemmo, figgeste, físsero
past part. fitto

Flèttere *to bend*
past flettei *or* flessi, flettesti, flettè *or* flesse, flettemmo, fletteste, flettérono *or* flèssero
past part. flesso

Fóndere *to melt*
past fusi, fondesti, fuse, fondemmo, fondeste, fúsero
past part. fuso

Fràngere *to break*
past fransi, frangesti, franse, frangemmo, frangeste, frànsero
past part. franto

Fríggere *to fry*
past frissi, friggesti, frisse, friggemmo, friggeste, fríssero
past part. fritto

Giacére *to lie*
pres. ind. giaccio, giaci, giace, giacciamo *or* giaciamo, giacete, giàcciono
past giacqui, giacesti, giacque, giacemmo, giaceste, giàcquero
pres. sub. giaccia
past part. giaciuto

Indúlgere *to indulge*
past indulsi, indulgesti, indulse, indulgemmo, indulgeste, indúlsero
past part. indulto
Inferíre *to infer*
past inferii *or* infersi, inferisti, inferí *or* inferse, inferimmo, inferiste, inferírono *or* infèrsero
past part. inferito *or* inferto
Inseríre *to insert*
past part. inserito *or* (*rare*) inserto
Intrúdere *to intrude*
past intrusi, intrudesti, intruse, intrudemmo, intrudeste, intrúsero
past part. intruso
Lèdere *to offend*
past lesi, ledesti, lese, ledemmo, ledeste, lèsero
past part. leso
Lèggere *to read*
past lessi, leggesti, lesse, leggemmo, leggeste, lèssero
past part. letto
Méscere *to pour*
pres. ind. mesco, mesci, mesce, mesciamo, mescete, méscono
pres. sub. mesca, mesca, mesca, mesciamo, mesciate, méscano
past part. mesciuto *or* misto
Méttere *to place*
past misi, mettesti, mise, mettemmo, metteste, mísero
past part. messo
Mòrdere *to bite*
past morsi, mordesti, morse, mordemmo, mordeste, mòrsero
past part. morso
Moríre *to die*
pres. ind. muoio, muori, muore, moriàmo, morite, muòiono
fut. morirò *or* morrò, morirai *or* morrai, morirà *or* morrà, moriremo *or* morremo, morirete *or* morrete, morirànno *or* morrànno
cond. morirei *or* morrei, moriresti *or* morresti, morirebbe *or* morrebbe, moriremmo *or* morremmo, morireste *or* morreste, morirèbbero *or* morrèbbero

pres. sub. muoia, muoia, muoia, moriamo, moriate, muòiano
imper. muori, muoia, morite, muòiano
past part. morto

Múngere *to milk*
past munsi, mungesti, munse, mungemmo, mungeste, múnsero
past part. munto

Muòvere *to move*
past mossi, movesti, mosse, movemmo, moveste, mòssero
past part. mosso

Nàscere *to be born*
past nacqui, nascesti, nacque, nascemmo, nasceste, nàcquero
past part. nato

Nascóndere *to hide*
past nascosi, nascondesti, nascose, nascondemmo, nascondeste, nascósero
past part. nascosto

Nuòcere *to harm*
pres. ind. nuoccio *or* noccio, nuoci, nuoce, nociamo, nocete, nuòcciono *or* nòcciono
past nocqui, nocesti, nocque, nocemmo, noceste, nòcquero
pres. subj. noccia, noccia, noccia, nociamo, nociate, nòcciano
imper. nuoci, noccia, nocete, nocciano
past part. nociuto

Offríre *to offer*
past offrii *or* offersi, offristi, offrí *or* offerse, offrimmo, offriste, offrírono *or* offèrsero
past part. offerto

Parére *to seem*
pres. ind. paio, pari, pare, paiamo, parete, pàiono
past parvi, paresti, parve, paremmo, pareste, pàrvero
fut. parrò
pres. sub. paia, paia, paia, pariamo, pariate *or* paiate, pàiano
cond. parrei
imper. *lacking*
pres. part. parvente
past part. parso

Pèrdere *to lose*

past persi *or* perdetti, perdesti, perse *or* perdette, perdemmo, perdeste, pèrsero *or* perdèttero

past part. perso *or* perduto

Persuadére *to persuade*

past persuasi, persuadesti, persuase, persuademmo, persuadeste, persuàsero

past part. persuaso

Piacére *to please*

pres. ind. piaccio, piaci, piace, piacciamo, piacete, piàcciono

past piacqui, piacesti, piacque, piacemmo, piaceste, piàcquero

pres. sub. piaccia

past part. piaciuto

Piàngere *to weep*

past piansi, piangesti, pianse, piangemmo, piangeste, piànsero

past part. pianto

Piòvere *to rain*

past piovvi, piovesti, piovve, piovemmo, pioveste, piòvvero

Pòrgere *to offer*

past porsi, porgesti, porse, porgemmo, porgeste, pòrsero

past part. porto

Pórre *to place*

pres. ind. pongo, poni, pone, poniamo, ponete, póngono

imp. ind. ponevo

past posi, ponesti, pose, ponemmo, poneste, pósero

fut. porrò

cond. porrei

pres. sub. ponga, ponga, ponga, poniamo, poniate, póngano

imp. sub. ponessi

imper. poni, ponga, ponete, póngano

pres. part. ponente

past part. posto

Potére *to be able*

pres. ind. posso, puoi, può, possiamo, potete, pòssono

fut. potrò

cond. potrei

pres. sub. possa

past part. potuto

Predilígere *to prefer*
past predilessi, prediligesti, predilesse, prediligemmo, prediligeste, predilessero
past part. prediletto

Prèndere *to take*
past presi, prendesti, prese, prendemmo, prendeste, présero
past part. preso

Prescíndere *to leave out of consideration*
past prescindei *or* prescissi, prescindesti, prescindè *or* prescisse, prescindemmo, prescindeste, prescindérono *or* prescíssero
past part. prescisso

Prevedére *to foresee*
see **vedere**

Proferíre *to utter*
past proferii, proferisti, proferí, proferimmo, proferiste, proferírono
past part. proferito

Profferíre *to proffer*
past proffersi, profferisti, profferse, profferimmo, profferiste, proffèrsero
past part. profferto

Protèggere *to protest*
past protessi, proteggesti, protesse, proteggemmo, proteggeste, protèssero
past part. protetto

Púngere *to prick*
past punsi, pungesti, punse, pungemmo, pungeste, púnsero
past part. punto

Ràdere *to shave*
past rasi, radesti, rase, rademmo, radeste, ràsero
past part. raso

Redígere *to draw up*
past redassi, redigesti, redasse, redigemmo, redigeste, redàssero
past part. redatto

Redímere *to redeem*
past redensi, redimesti, redense, redimemmo, redimeste, redénsero
past part. redento

Règgere *to support*
past ressi, reggesti, resse, reggemmo, reggeste, rèssero
past part. retto

Rèndere *to give back*
past resi, rendesti, rese, rendemmo, rendeste, résero
past part. reso

Restríngere *to restrict*
past part. ristretto

Rídere *to laugh*
past risi, ridesti, rise, ridemmo, rideste, rísero
past part. riso

Riflèttere *to reflect*
past riflettei *or* riflessi, riflettesti, riflettè *or* riflesse, riflettemmo, rifletteste, riflettérono *or* riflèssero
past part. riflettuto *or* riflesso

Rifúlgere *to shine*
past rifulsi, rifulgesti, rifulse, rifulgemmo, rifulgeste, rifúlsero
past part. rifulso

Rilúcere *to shine*
past rilucei, rilucesti, rilucè, rilucemmo, riluceste, rilucérono
past part. *lacking*

Rimanére *to remain*
pres. ind. rimango, rimani, rimane, rimaniamo, rimanete, rimàngono
past rimasi, rimanesti, rimase, rimanemmo, rimaneste, rimàsero
fut. rimarrò
cond. rimarrei
pres. sub. rimanga, rimanga, rimanga, rimaniamo, rimaniate, rimàngano
imper. rimani, rimanga, rimanete, rimàngano
past part. rimasto

Rispóndere *to reply*
past risposi, rispondesti, rispose, rispondemmo, rispondeste, rispósero
past part. risposto

Ródere *to gnaw*
past rosi, rodesti, rose, rodemmo, rodeste, rósero
past part. roso

Rómpere *to break*
past ruppi, rompesti, ruppe, rompemmo, rompeste, rúppero
past part. rotto

Salíre *to climb*
pres. ind. salgo, sali, sale, saliamo, salite, sàlgono
pres. sub. salga, salga, salga, saliamo, saliate, sàlgano
imper. sali, salga, salite, sàlgano

Sapére *to know*
pres. ind. so, sai, sa, sappiamo, sapete, sanno
past seppi, sapesti, seppe, sapemmo, sapeste, sèppero
fut. saprò
cond. saprei
pres. sub. sappia
imper. sappi, sappia, sappiate, sàppiano
pres. part. sapiente

Scégliere *to choose*
pres. ind. scelgo, scegli, sceglie, scegliamo, scegliete, scélgono
past scelsi, scegliesti, scelse, scegliemmo, sceglieste scélsero
pres. sub. scelga, scelga, scelga, scegliamo, scegliate, scélgano
imper. scegli, scelga, scegliete, scélgano
past part. scelto

Scéndere *to descend*
past scesi, scendesti, scese, scendemmo, scendeste, scésero
past part. sceso

Scèrnere *to choose*
past scernei *or* scernetti, scernesti, scernè *or* scernette, scernemmo, scernérono *or* scernèttero
past part. *lacking*

Scíndere *to cut*
past scissi, scindesti, scisse, scindemmo, scindeste, scíssero
past part. scisso

Sciògliere *to melt*
past sciolsi, sciogliesti, sciolse, sciogliemmo, sciogli-este, sciòlsero
past part. sciolto

Scolpíre *to carve*
past scolpii, scolpisti, scolpì, scolpimmo, scolpiste,

scolpírono; *poet.* sculsi, scolpisti, sculse, scolpimmo, scolpiste, scúlsero

past part. scolpito; *poet.* sculto

Scòrgere *to perceive*

past scorsi, scorgesti, scorse, scorgemmo, scorgeste, scòrsero

past part. scorto

Scrívere *to write*

past scrissi, scrivesti, scrisse, scrivemmo, scriveste, scríssero

past part. scritto

Scuòtere *to shake*

past scossi, scotesti, scosse, scotemmo, scoteste, scòssero

past part. scosso

Sedére *to sit*

pres. ind. siedo *or* seggo, siedi, siede, sediamo, sedete, sièdono *or* sèggono

past sedei *or* sedetti, sedesti, sedè *or* sedette, sedemmo, sedeste, sedérono *or* sedèttero

pres. sub. sieda *or* segga, sieda *or* segga, sieda *or* segga, sediamo, sediate, sièdano *or* sèggano

imper. siedi, sieda *or* segga, sedete, sièdano *or* sèggano

Seppellíre *to bury*

past part. seppellito *or* sepolto

Soddisfàre *to satisfy*

pres. ind. soddisfo *or* soddisfaccio, soddisfi *or* soddisfai, soddìsfa, soddisfiamo *or* soddisfacciamo, soddisfate, soddísfano *or* soddisfànno

pres. sub. soddisfi *or* soddisfaccia, soddisfi *or* soddisfaccia, soddisfi *or* soddisfaccia, soddisfacciamo, soddisfacciate, soddísfino *or* soddisfàcciano

imper. soddisfa, soddisfi *or* soddisfaccia, soddisfate, soddísfino *or* soddisfàcciano

past part. soddisfatto

Solére *to be used to*

pres. ind. soglio, suoli, suole, sogliamo, solete, sògliono; *or* sono sòlito, sei sòlito è sòlito, siamo sòliti, siete sòliti, sono sòliti

fut. *lacking*

cond. *lacking*

pres. sub. soglia

imp. sub. solessi

past solei, solesti, solè, solemmo, soleste, solérono (*rare*); *now most commonly*: fui sòlito, fosti sòlito, fu sòlito, fummo sòliti, foste sòliti, fúrono sòliti
imper. *lacking*
pres. part. *lacking*
past. part. sòlito

Sórgere *to rise*
past sorsi, sorgesti, sorse, sorgemmo, sorgeste, sórsero
past part. sorto

Spàndere *to spread*
past spandei *or* spansi, spandesti, spandè *or* spanse, spandemmo, spandeste, spandérono *or* spànsero
past part. *Not used. Use* Sparso (pp. of spargere)

Spàrgere *to scatter*
past sparsi, spargesti, sparse, spargemmo, spargeste, spàrsero
past part. sparso

Sparíre *to disappear*
past sparii *or* sparvi, sparisti, sparí *or* sparve, sparimmo, spariste, sparírono *or* spàrvero

Spégnere *or* **Spéngere** *to extinguish*
pres. ind. spengo, spegni *or* spengi, spegne *or* spenge, spegniamo *or* spengiamo, spegnete *or* spengete, spéngono
past spensi, spegnesti *or* spengesti, spense, spegnemmo *or* spengemmo, spegneste *or* spengeste, spénsero
pres. sub. spenga, spenga, spenga, spegniamo *or* spengiamo, spegniate *or* spengiate, spéngano
imper. spegni *or* spengi, spenga, spegnete *or* spengete, spéngano
past part. spento

Stàre *to stay*
pres. ind. sto, stai, sta, stiamo, state, stanno
past stetti, stesti, stette, stemmo, steste, stéttero
fut. starò
cond. starei
pres. sub. stia
imp. sub. stessi
imper. stai *or* sta', stia, state, stíano
past part. stato

Stríngere *to press*
past strinsi, stringesti, strinse, stringemmo, stringeste, strínsero
past part. stretto

Strúggere *to melt*
past strussi, struggesti, strusse, struggemmo, struggeste, strússero
past part. strutto

Svèllere *to eradicate*
pres. ind. svelgo *or* svello, svelli, svelle, svelliamo, svellete, svèlgono *or* svèllono
past svelsi, svellesti, svelse, svellemmo, svelleste, svèlsero
past part. svelto

Tacére *to be silent*
pres. ind. taccio, taci, tace, taciamo, tacete, tàcciono
past. tacqui, tacesti, tacque, tacemmo, taceste, tàcquero
pres. sub. taccia
imper. taci, taccia, tacete, tacciano

Tèndere *to stretch out*
past tesi, tendesti, tese, tendemmo, tendeste, tésero
past part. teso

Tenére *to hold*
pres. ind. tengo, tieni, tiene, teniamo, tenete, tèngono
past tenni, tenesti, tenne, tenemmo, teneste, tènnero
fut. terrò
cond. terrei
pres. sub. tenga, tenga, tenga, teniamo, teniate, tèngano
imper. tieni, tenga, tenete, tèngano

Tèrgere *to dry*
past tersi, tergesti, terse, tergemmo, tergeste, tèrsero
past part. terso

Tíngere *to dye*
past tinsi, tingesti, tinse, tingemmo, tingeste, tínsero
past part tinto

Tògliere *to take away*
pres. ind. tolgo, togli, toglie, togliamo, togliete, tòlgono
past tolsi, togliesti, tolse, togliemmo, toglieste, tòlsero
pres. sub. tolga, tolga, tolga, togliamo, togliate, tòlgano
imper. togli, tolga, togliete, tòlgano
cond. toglierei *or* torrei, toglieresti *or* torresti, toglierebbe *or* torrebbe, toglieremmo *or* torremmo,

	toglieresti *or* torreste, toglierèbbero *or* rèbbero
fut.	toglierò *or* torrò, toglierai *or* torrai, toglierà *or* torrà, toglieremo *or* torremo, toglierete *or* torrete, toglieranno *or* torranno
past part.	tolto

Tòrcere *to twist*

past	torsi, torcesti, torse, torcemmo, torceste, tòrsero
past part.	torto

Tràrre *to draw*

pres. ind.	traggo, trai, trae, traiamo, traete, tràggono
imp. ind.	traevo
fut.	trarrò
past	trassi, traesti, trasse, traemmo, traeste, tràssero
cond.	trarrei
pres. sub.	tragga, tragga, tragga, traiamo, traiate, tràggano
imp. sub.	traessi
imper.	trai, tragga, traete, tràggano
pres. part.	traente
past part.	tratto

Uccídere *to kill*

past	uccisi, uccidesti, uccise, uccidemmo, uccideste, uccísero
past part	ucciso

Udíre *to hear*

pres. ind.	odo, odi, ode, udiamo, udite, òdono
fut.	udirò *or* udrò, udirai *or* udrai, udirà *or* udrà, udiremo *or* udremo, udirete *or* udrete, udiranno *or* udranno
pres. sub.	oda, oda, oda, udiamo, udiate, òdano
imper.	odi, oda, udite, òdano
pres. part.	udente *or* udiente

Uscíre *to go out*

pres. ind.	esco, esci, esce, usciamo, uscite, éscono
pres. sub.	esca, esca, esca, usciamo, usciate, éscano
imper.	esci, esca, uscite, éscano

Valére *to be worth*

pres. ind.	valgo, vali, vale, valiamo, valete, vàlgono
past	valsi, valesti, valse, valemmo, valeste, vàlsero
fut.	varrò
cond.	varrei
pres. sub.	valga, valga, valga, valiamo, valiate, vàlgano
imper.	vali, valga, valete, vàlgano
past part.	valso

Vedére *to see*

past vidi, vedesti, vide, vedemmo, vedeste, vídero
fut. vedrò
cond. vedrei
pres. part. vedente *or* veggente
past part. visto *or* veduto

Veníre *to come*

pres. ind. vengo, vieni, viene, veniamo, venite, vèngono
past venni, venisti, venne, venimmo, veniste, vènnero
fut. verrò
cond. verrei
pres. sub. venga, venga, venga, veniamo, veniate, vèngano
imper. vieni, venga, venite, vèngano
pres. part. veniente
past part. venuto

Víncere *to win*

past vinsi, vincesti, vinse, vincemmo, vinceste, vínsero
past part. vinto

Vívere *to live*

past vissi, vivesti, visse, vivemmo, viveste, víssero
fut. vivrò
cond. vivrei
past part. vissuto

Volére *to want*

pres. ind. voglio, vuoi, vuole, vogliamo, volete, vògliono
past volli, volesti, volle, volemmo, voleste, vòllero
fut. vorrò
cond. vorrei
pres. sub. voglia
past part. voluto

Vòlgere *to turn*

past volsi, volgesti, volse, volgemmo, volgeste, vòlsero
past part. volto

Grammatica Inglese—English Grammar

IL PLURALE DEI SOSTANTIVI

1. Normalmente il plurale si forma aggiungendo **-s**: **chair** (sedia), **chairs**; **table** (tavolo), **tables**.
2. **-ch, -s, -sh, -x, -z.** I sostantivi terminanti in questo modo aggiungono **-es**, che costituisce una sillaba extra: **arch** (arco), **arches**; **kiss** (bacio), **kisses**; **dish** (piatto), **dishes**; **box** (scatola), **boxes**; **buzz** (ronzio), **buzzes**.
3. **-y.** Se la **-y** è preceduta da vocale, il plurale si forma normalmente: **boy** (ragazzo), **boys**. Se la **-y** è precuduto da consonante, il plurale si forma in **-ies**: **lady** (signora), **ladies**.
4. **-fe, -f.** I sostantivi in **-fe**, e molti in **-f**, formano il plurale in **-ves**: **wife** (moglie), **wives**; **leaf** (foglia), **leaves**.
5. **-o.** Alcuni sostantivi formano il plurale in **-oes**: **hero** (eroe), **heroes**; altri in **-os**: **piano** (pianoforte), **pianos**.
6. Molti sostantivi di origine latina o greca fanno il plurale come in latino o in greco, specialmente nel caso di termini scientifici: **radius** (raggio), **radii**; **thesis** (tesi), **theses**; **medium** (mezzo), **media**.
7. Alcuni nomi di animali non cambiano nel plurale: **sheep** (pecora); **deer** (cervo).
8. Alcuni sostantivi hanno il plurale irregolare: **man** (uomo), **men**; **woman** (donna), **women**; **child** (bambino), **children**; **foot** (piede), **feet**; **tooth** (dente), **teeth**; **goose** (oca), **geese**; **mouse** (sorcio), **mice**; **louse** (pidocchio), **lice**; **ox** (bue), **oxen**.

Nel dizionario il plurale è indicato dei sostantivi che entrano nelle categorie trattate nelle note 4-8.

Verbi Inglesi—English Verbs

Verbi Ausiliari

To be, *essere*	**To have,** *avere*
INDICATIVO PRESENTE	
Sono, ecc	*Ho, ecc*
I am	I have
You are (thou art)	You have (thou hast)
He, She, It } is	He, She, It } has
We are	We have
You are	You have
They are	They have
INDICATIVO PASSATO	
Ero, fui, ecc	*Avevo, ebbi, ecc*
I was	I had
You were (thou wert)	You had (thou hadst)
He, She, It } was	He, She, It } had
We were	We had
You were	You had
They were	They had
FUTURO	
sarò, ecc	*Avrò, ecc*
I shall be	I shall have
You will (thou wilt) be	You will (thou wilt) have
He, She, It } will be	He, She, It } will have
We shall be	We shall have
You will be	You will have
They will be	They will have
CONDIZIONALE	
Sarei, ecc	*Avrei, ecc*
I should be	I should have
You would (thou wouldst) be	You would (thou wouldst) have
He, She, It } would be	He, She, It } would have
We should be	We should have
You would be	You would have
They would be	They would have

IMPERATIVO

[*Ch'io sia*], *sii*	[*Ch'io abbia*], *abbi*
Let me be	Let me have
Be	Have
Let him	Let him
her } be	her } have
it	it
Let us be	Let us have
Be	Have
Let them be	Let them have

INFINITO

To be, *essere*	To have, *avere*

GERUNDIO E PARTICIPIO PRESENTE

Being, *essendo*	Having, *avendo*, *avente*

PARTICIPIO PASSATO

Been, *stato*	Had, *avuto*

Tempi Composti

PERFETTO

Sono stato, ecc	*Ho avuto, ecc*
I have been	I have had
You have been	You have had
He	He
She } has been	She } has had
It	It
We have been	We have had
You have been	You have had
They have been	They have had

PIUCCHEPERFETTO

Ero, fui stato, ecc	*Avevo, ebbi avuto, ecc*
I had been	I had had
You had been	You had had
He	He
She } had been	She } had had
It	It
We had been	We had had
You had been	You had had
They had been	They had had

FUTURO PERFETTO

Sarò stato, ecc	*Avrò avuto, ecc*
I shall have been	I shall have had
You will have been	You will have had
He	He
She } will have been	She } will have had
It	It
We shall have been	We shall haye had
You will have been	You will have had
They will have been	They will have had

CONDIZIONALE PERFETTO

Sarei stato, ecc	*Avrei avuto, ecc*
I should have been	I should have had
You would have been	You would have had
He / She / It } would have been	He / She / It } would have had
We should have been	We should have had
You would have been	You would have had
They would have been	They would have had

INFINITO PASSATO

Essere stato	*Avere avuto*
To have been	To have had

GERUNDIO PASSATO

Essendo stato	*Avendo avuto*
Having been	Having had

CONGIUNTIVO PRESENTE

Ch'io sia, ecc	*Ch'io abbia, ecc*
That I be	That I have
That you be	That you have
That he / she / it } be	That he / she / it } have
That we be	That we have
That you be	That you have
That they be	That they have

N.B.—Il congiuntivo presente non si usa ormai più in inglese, se non in qualche frase idiomatica

CONGIUNTIVO PASSATO

Se io fossi, ecc	*Se io avessi, ecc*
If I were	If I had
If you were	If you had
If he / she / it } were	If he / she / it } had
If we were	If we had
If you were	If you had
If they were	If they had

Verbi Irregolari Inglesi
English Irregular Verbs

Infinito		*Passato*	*Part. passato*
abide	dimorare	abode	abode
arise	alzarsi	arose	arisen
awake	svegliare, svegliarsi	awoke	awaked*
bear	portare	bore	borne
beat	battere	beat	beaten

Infinito		*Passato*	*Part. passato*
begin	cominciare	began	begun
bend	piegare	bent	bent
bereave	orbare	bereft	bereft*
beseech	implorare	besought	besought
bid	ordinare	bade (bid)	bidden (bid)
bind	legare	bound	bound
bite	mordere	bit	bitten
bleed	sanguinare	bled	bled
blow	soffiare	blew	blown
break	rompere	broke	broken
breed	generare, allevare	bred	bred
bring	portare	brought	brought
build	costruire	built	built
burn	bruciare	burned	burned*
burst	scoppiare	burst	burst
buy	comperare	bought	bought
cast	gettare	cast	cast
catch	afferrare	caught	caught
chide	sgridare	chid	chidden, chid*
choose	scegliere	chose	chosen
cleave	fendere	cleft, clove	cleft, cloven*
cling	aggrapparsi	clung	clung
come	venire	came	come
cost	costare	cost	cost
creep	strisciare	crept	crept
crow	cantare (del gallo)	crew	crowed
cut	tagliare	cut	cut
dare	osare	(durst)	dared*
deal	trattare	dealt	dealt
dig	scavare	dug	dug
do	fare	did	done
draw	disegnare, trarre	drew	drawn
dream	sognare	dreamt	dreamt*
drink	bere	drank	drunk
drive	guidare	drove	driven
dwell	abitare	dwelled	dwelled*
eat	mangiare	ate	eaten
fall	cadere	fell	fallen
feed	nutrire	fed	fed
feel	sentire	felt	felt
fight	combattere	fought	fought
find	trovare	found	found
flee	fuggire	fled	fled
fling	lanciare	flung	flung
fly	volare	flew	flown
forsake	abbandonare	forsook	forsaken
freeze	gelare	froze	frozen
get	acquisire	got	got, gotten
gild	dorare	gilt	gilt*
gird	cingere	girt	girt*
give	dare	gave	given
go	andare	went	gone

grind	macinare	ground	ground
grow	crescere	grew	grown
hang	appendere	hung	hung (=impiccare)*
hear	udire	heard	heard
hew	spaccare	hewed	hewn
hide	nascondere	hid	hidden, hid
hit	colpire	hit	hit
hold	tenere	held	held
hurt	dolere	hurt	hurt
keep	conservare	kept	kept
kneel	inginocchiarsi	knelt	knelt*
know	conoscere, sapere	knew	known
lay	deporre	laid	laid
lead	guidare	led	led
leave	lasciare	left	left
lend	prestare	lent	lent
let	lasciare, affittare	let	let
lie	giacere	lay	lain (=mentire*)
light	accendere, illuminare	lit	lit*
lose	perdere	lost	lost
make	fare	made	made
mean	significare	meant	meant
meet	incontrare	met	met
mow	mietere	mowed	mown
pay	pagare	paid	paid
put	mettere	put	put
read	leggere	read	read
rend	strappare	rent	rent
rid	liberare	rid	rid
ride	cavalcare	rode	ridden
ring	suonare	rang, rung	rung
rise	alzarsi, sorgere	rose	risen
rive	spaccare	rived	riven
run	correre	ran	run
say	dire	said	said
see	vedere	saw	seen
seek	cercare	sought	sought
sell	vendere	sold	sold
send	mandare	sent	sent
set	mettere	set	set
shake	scuotere	shook	shaken
shear	tosare	sheared	shorn
shed	versare	shed	shed
shine	brillare	shone	shone
shoe	calzare, ferrare	shod	shod
shoot	sparare	shot	shot
show	mostrare	showed	shown
shrink	ritirarsi	shrank	shrunk
shut	chiudere	shut	shut
sing	cantare	sang	sung
sink	affondare	sank	sunk

Infinito		*Passato*	*Part. passato*
sit	sedere	sat	sat
slay	uccidere	slew	slain
sleep	dormire	slept	slept
slide	slittare	slid	slid
sling	lanciare, appendere	slung	slung
slink	sgattaiolare	slunk	slunk
slit	fendere	slit	slit
smell	fiutare	smelled	smelled*
smite	colpire	smote	smitten
sow	seminare	sowed	sown*
speak	parlare	spoke	spoken
spend	spendere	spent	spent
spill	versare	spilled	spilled*
spin	filare	span, spun	spun
spit	sputare	spat, spit	spit
split	spaccare, dividere	split	split
spread	spandere	spread	spread
spring	balzare, scaturire	sprang	sprung
stand	stare in piedi	stood	stood
steal	rubare	stole	stolen
stick	attaccare	stuck	stuck
sting	pungere	stung	stung
stink	puzzare	stank, stunk	stunk
stride	camminare a grandi passi	strode	stridden
strike	colpire	struck	struck
string	infilare	strung	strung
strive	sforzarsi	strove	striven
swear	giurare, imprecare	swore	sworn
sweep	scopare	swept	swept
swell	gonfiarsi	swelled	swollen
swim	nuotare	swam	swum
swing	dondolare	swung	swung
take	prendere	took	taken
teach	insegnare	taught	taught
tear	stracciare	tore	torn
tell	dire, raccontare	told	told
think	pensare	thought	thought
thrive	prosperare	throve	thriven*
throw	gettare	threw	thrown
thrust	spingere	thrust	thrust
tread	camminare, calpestare	trod	trod, trodden
wear	indossare	wore	worn
weave	tessere	wove	woven
weep	piangere	wept	wept
win	vincere	won	won
wind	attorcigliare	wound	wound
work	lavorare	(wrought)	(wrought)*
wring	torcere	wrung	wrung
write	scrivere	wrote	written

NOTE: I verbi contrassegnati da asterisco si coniugano anche regolarmente.

Numerals - Numerali

NUMERI CARDINALI		CARDINAL NUMBERS
uno	1	one
due	2	two
tre	3	three
quattro	4	four
cinque	5	five
sei	6	six
sette	7	seven
otto	8	eight
nove	9	nine
dieci	10	ten
undici	11	eleven
dodici	12	twelve
tredici	13	thirteen
quattordici	14	fourteen
quindici	15	fifteen
sedici	16	sixteen
diciassette	17	seventeen
diciotto	18	eighteen
diciannove	19	nineteen
venti	20	twenty
ventuno	21	twenty-one
ventidue	22	twenty-two
ventitre etc.	23	twenty-three etc.
trenta	30	thirty
trentuno	31	thirty-one
trentadue	32	thirty-two
quaranta	40	forty
cinquanta	50	fifty
sessanta	60	sixty
settanta	70	seventy
ottanta	80	eighty
novanta	90	ninety
cento	100	one hundred
centouno	101	one hundred and one
centodue	102	one hundred and two
duecento	200	two hundred
trecento	300	three hundred
quattrocento	400	four hundred
cinquecento	500	five hundred
mille	1,000	one thousand
mille e cento	1,100	one thousand one hundred
mille e duecento	1,200	one thousand two hundred
duemila	2,000	two thousand
tremila	3,000	three thousand

diecimila	10,000	ten thousand
centomila	100,000	one hundred thousand
un milione	1,000,000	one million
due milioni	2,000,000	two million

NUMERI ORDINALI		ORDINAL NUMBERS
primo	1st	the first
secondo	2nd	the second
terzo	3rd	the third
quarto	4th	the fourth
quinto	5th	the fifth
sesto	6th	the sixth
settimo	7th	the seventh
ottavo	8th	the eighth
nono	9th	the ninth
decimo	10th	the tenth
undicesimo	11th	the eleventh
dodicesimo	12th	the twelfth
tredicesimo	13th	the thirteenth
quattordicesimo	14th	the fourteenth
quindicesimo	15th	the fifteenth
sedicesimo	16th	the sixteenth
diciasettesimo	17th	the seventeenth
diciottesimo	18th	the eighteenth
dicianovesimo	19th	the nineteenth
ventesimo	20th	the twentieth
ventesimoprimo	21st	the twenty-first
ventesimosecondo etc.	22nd	the twenty-second etc.
trentesimo	30th	the thirtieth
quarantesimo	40th	the fortieth
cinquantesimo	50th	the fiftieth
sessantesimo	60th	the sixtieth
settantesimo	70th	the seventieth
ottantesimo	80th	the eightieth
novantesimo	90th	the ninetieth
centesimo	100th	the hundredth
centesimoprimo	101st	the hundred and first
centocinquantesimo	150th	the hundred and fiftieth
centonovantesimo	190th	the hundred and ninetieth
ducentesimo	200th	the two hundredth
millesimo	1,000th	the thousandth
duemillesimo	2,000th	the two thousandth
diecimillesimo	10,000th	the ten thousandth
centomillesimo	100,000th	the hundred thousandth
milionesimo	1,000,000th	the millionth

Italian Measures and Weights
Misure e Pesi Italiani

LUNGHEZZA—LENGTH

1 Millimetro	=·001 Metro	=·0394 inch
1 Centimetro	=·01 Metro	=·394 inch
1 Metro	=39·4 inches	=*1 yard
1 Chilometro	=1000 Metri	=*1094 yards or ⅝ mile
8 Chilometri	=5 miles	

SUPERFICIE—AREA

1 Ettaro	=11960·11 square yards
1 Quadrachilometro	=247·11 acres

CAPACITÀ—CAPACITY

1 Centilitro	=·01 Litro	=·0176 pint	
1 Litro	=*1¾ pints	=·2201 gallon	
1 Ettolitro	=100 Litri	=*22 gallons	=2¾ bushels
1 Chilolitro	=1000 Litri	=*220 gallons	=27½ bushels

PESI—WEIGHTS

1 Milligrammo	=·001 Grammo	=·0154 grain
1 Centigrammo	=·01 Grammo	=·1543 grain
1 Grammo		=15·43 grains
1 Ettogrammo	=1000 Grammi	=*3½ oz
1 Tonnellata	=1000 Chilogrammi	=*1 ton

IL TERMOMETRO—THE THERMOMETER

Punto di Congelamento	=Centigrade 0°
Freezing Point	=Fahrenheit 32°
Punto d'Ebollizione	=Centigrade 100°
Boiling Point	=Fahrenheit 212°

**roughly*

Misure e Pesi Americani
American Weights and Measures

LENGTH—LUNGHEZZA

Inch (in)	=25 Millimetri
Foot (ft) (12 in)	=304 Millimetri
Yard (yd) (3 ft)	=913 Millimetri (quasi 1 Metro)
Fathom (fthm) (2 yards)	=1 Metro 828 Millimetri
Mile (8 furlongs, 1760 yards)	=1609 Metri
Nautical mile, knot	=1853 Metri
5 miles	=8 Chilometri

AREA—SUPERFICIE

Square inch	=6,45 Centimetri quadrati (cm^2)
Square foot	=929 cm^2
Square yard	=0,8360 Metri quadrati (m^2)
Acre	=4047 m^2

CAPACITY—CAPACITÀ

Pint	=0,567 Litro
Quart (2 pints)	=1,136 Litri
Gallon (4 quarts)	=4,53 Litri
Peck (2 gallons)	=9,086 Litri
Bushel (8 gallons)	=36,348 Litri
Quarter (8 bushels)	=290,8 Litri

WEIGHTS (AVOIRDUPOIS)—PESI

Ounce (oz)	=28,35 Grammi
Pound (lb) (16 oz)	=453,59 Grammi
Stone (st) (14 lb)	=6,35 Chili
Quarter (qr) (28 lb)	=12,7 Chili
Hundredweight (cwt) (112 lb)	=50,8 Chili
Ton (T) (20 cwts)	=1016 Chili

THE THERMOMETER—IL TERMOMETRO

Freezing Point	=Fahrenheit 32°
Punto di Congelamento	=Centigrade 0°
Boiling Point	=Fahrenheit 212°
Punto d'Ebollizione	=Centigrade 100°

Italian Abbreviations—Abbreviazioni Italiane

AA Accademia Aeronautica (*Air Force Academy*); Assistenza Automobilistica (*organization for assisting motorists*)
aC avanti Cristo (*before Christ*)
ACDG Associazione Cristiana dei Giovani (*Young Men's Christian Association*)
ACI Automobile Club d'Italia (*Italian Automobile Association*); Azione Cattolica Italiana (*Italian Catholic Action*)
ACIS Alto Commissariato per l'Igiene e la Sanità (*Public Health Board*)
AGIP Azienda Generale Italiana Petroli (*National Italian Oil Company*)
ago agusto (*August*)
AI Aeronautica Italiana (*Italian Air Force*)
ALITALIA Aerolinee Italiane Internazionali (*Italian International Airlines*)
all allegato (*enclosure*)
alt altezza (*height*); altitudine (*altitude*)
ANAS Azienda Nazionale Autonoma della Strada (*National Road Board*)
ANSA Agenzia Nazionale Stampa Associata (*Associated Press*)
apr aprile (*April*)
AR Altezza Reale (*Royal Highness*); andata e ritorno (*round trip*)
ASC Associazione Scoutistica Cattolica (*Catholic Scout Movement*)
ATM Azienda Tranviaria Municipale (*Municipal Tram Company*)
AVIS Associazione Volontari Italiani del Sangue (*Association of Italian Blood Donors*)
avv avverbio (*adverb*); avvocato (*lawyer*)
BI Banca d'Italia (*Bank of Italy*)
brev brevetto (*patent*)
c capitolo (*chapter*); circa (*about*); codice ((*leg*) code); corpo (*type-size*)
cabl cablogramma (*cable*)
cad cadauno (*each*)
CAI Club Alpino Italiano (*Italian Alpine Club*)
Cap Capitano (*Captain*); capitolo (*chapter*)
Cav Cavaliere (*Knight*)
cc conto corrente (*current account*)
CC Corpo Carabinieri (*Carabiniere Corps*); Corte di Cassazione (*Supreme Court of Appeal*)
CCI Camera di Commercio Internazionale (*International Chamber of Commerce*)
ccp conto corrente postale (*current postal account*)
Cd'A Corte d'Assise (*Court of Assizes*)
CdL Camera del Lavoro (*Trade Union*)
CdS Circolo della Stampa (*Press Club*); Codice della Strada (*Highway Code*); Consiglio di Sicurezza (*Security Council*)
CECA Comunità Europea per il Carbone e l'Acciaio (*European Coal and Steel Community*)
CERN Consiglio Europeo per le Ricerche Nucleari (*European Council for Nuclear Research*)

CGIL Confederazione Generale Italiana del Lavoro (*Federation of Italian Trade Unions*)
CIT Compagnia Italiana Turismo (*Italian Travel Agency*)
CLN Comitato di Liberazione Nazionale (*Resistance Movement Committee (World War II)*)
cm corrente mese (*present month*)
CONFINDUSTRIA Confederazione Generale dell'Industria Italiana (*General Confederation of Italian Industry*)
CONI Comitato Olimpico Nazionale Italiano (*Italian Olympic Games Committee*)
CP Casella Postale (*Post Office Box*)
CRI Croce Rossa Internazionale (*International Red Cross*)
Croce Rossa Italiana (*Italian Red Cross*)
c. to conto (*account*)
CV cavallo vapore (*horse power*)
dC dopo Cristo (*Anno Domini, in the year of the Lord*)
DC Democrazia Cristiana (*Christian Democrat Party*)
devmo devotissimo ((*in letters*) *yours truly*)
dic dicembre (*December*)
dott Dottore (*Doctor*)
dr Dottore (*Doctor*)
dr.ssa Dottoressa (*Doctor*)
ecc eccetera (*et cetera*)
Ecc Eccellenza (*Excellency*)
Egr.Sig. Egregio Signore ((*in addresses*) *Mr.;* (*in letters*) Dear Sir)
ENAL Ente Nazionale Assistenza Lavoratori (*National Association for Assistance to Workers*)
ENIC Ente Nazionale Industrie Cinematografiche (*National Association of the Cinema Industry*)
ENIT Ente Nazionale Industrie Turistiche (*National Tourist Office*)
feb febbraio (*February*)
ferr ferrovia (*railway*)
FFSS Ferrovie dello Stato (*State Railways*)
FIAT Fabbrica Italiana Automobili Torino (*Italian Automobile Works Torino*)
FIGC Federazione Italiana Giuoco Calcio (*Italian Football Association*)
FIT Federazione Italiana Tennis (*Italian Lawn Tennis Association*)
Flli Fratelli ((*com*) *Brothers*)
FPI Federazione Pugilistica Italiana (*Italian Boxing Association*)
Fr b franco belga (*Belgian franc*)
Fr f franco francese (*French franc*)
Fr s franco svizzero (*Swiss franc*)
GB Gran Bretagna (*Great Britain*)
GdF Guardia di Finanza (*Revenue Guard*)
GEI Giovani Esploratori Italiani (*Italian Boy Scouts*)
gen genitivo (*genitive*); gennaio (*January*)
GU Gazzetta Ufficiale (*Official Gazette*)
h ora (*hour*)
HF alta frequenza (*high frequency*)
IGE Imposta Generale sull'Entrata (*Income Tax*)
INA Istituto Nazionale Assicurazioni (*National Insurance*)
INAM Istituto Nazionale per l'Assicurazione contro le malattie (*National Health Insurance*)

INCOM	Industria Cortometraggi (*Short-Film Industry*)
INPI	Istituto Nazionale per la Prevenzione degli Infortuni (*National Institute for the Prevention of Accidents*)
INPS	Istituto Nazionale Previdenza Sociale (*National Institute of Social Security*)
IPS	Istituto Poligrafico dello Stato (*Stationery Office*)
Italcable	Compagnia Italiana dei Cavi Telegrafici e Telefonic Sottomarini (*Italian Cable Company*)
kg	chilogrammo (*kilogram*)
lett.	letterario (*literary*); letteratura (*literature*)
LF	bassa frequenza (*low frequency*)
Lit	Lire italiane (*Italian lire*)
LLPP	Lavori Pubblici (*Public Works*)
lm	livello del mare (*sea level*)
Lsr	lira sterlina (*£ pound (sterling)*)
lug	luglio (*July*)
M	Monte (*Mount*)
mag	maggio (*May*)
mar	marzo (*March*)
MAS	motoscafo antisommergibile (*motor torpedo-boat*)
MCD	massimo comun divisore (*highest common factor*)
mcm	minimo comune multiplo (*lowest common multiple*)
ME	Medio Evo (*Middle Ages*)
MEC	Mercato Europeo Comune ((*European*) *Common Market*)
MM	Marina Militare (*Royal Navy*)
M/N	motonave (*motorship*)
Mo	Maestro ((*mus*) *maestro*)
MPPTT	Ministero delle Poste e delle Telecomunicazioni (*Post Office*)
Msa	Marchesa (*Marchioness*)
Mse	Marchese (*Marquis*)
MSI	Movimento Sociale Italiano (*neo-Fascist Party*)
n	nato (*born*); neutro (*neuter*)
ND	Nobil Donna (*lady of a noble family*)
NdA	Nota dell'Autore (*author's note*)
NdE	Nota dell'Editore (*publisher's note*)
NdT	Nota del Traduttore (*translator's note*)
NH	Nobil Uomo (*member of a noble family*)
NN	(L. *Nescio nomen*) di paternità ignota (*name of father unknown*)
nov	novembre (*November*)
NU	Nazioni Unite (*United Nations*)
OdG	ordine del giorno (*agenda*)
OECE	Organizzazione Economica per la Cooperazione Europea (*Organization for European Economic Co-operation*)
OIL	Organizzazione Internazionale del Lavoro (*International Labour Organization*)
OMR	Ordine al Merito della Repubblica (*Order of Merit of the Republic*)
ONMI	Opera Nazionale per il Mezzogiorno d'Italia (*National Board for the South of Italy*); Opera Nazionale per la Protezione della Maternità e dell'Infanzia (*National Board for Maternity and Child Welfare*)
ONU	Organizzazione delle Nazioni Unite (*United Nations Organization*)

OSSSA	Ordine Supremo della Santissima Annunziata (*Supreme Order of the Holy Annunciation*)
ott	ottobre (*October*)
OVRA	Opera Volontaria per la Repressione dell'Antifascismo (*Fascist Secret Police*)
P	Padre (*eccl*) *Father*)
pag	pagina (*page*)
pcc	per copia conforme (*certified copy*)
PCI	Partito Comunista Italiano (*Italian Communist Party*)
PdA	Partito d'Azione (*Action Party*)
PDC	Partito Democratico Cristiano (*Christian Democrat Party*)
PDI	Partito Democratico Italiano (*Italian Democratic Party*)
pes	per esempio (*for example*)
pf	per favore (*please*)
PG	Procuratore Generale (*Attorney General*)
PI	Pubblica Istruzione (*Public Education*)
PLI	Partito Liberale Italiano (*Italian Liberal Party*)
PM	Polizia Militare (*Military Police*); Pubblico Ministero (*Public Prosecutor*)
PNF	Partito Nazionale Fascista (*National Fascist Party*)
pp	pacco postale (*parcel post*)
pr	per ringraziamento (*with thanks*)
PRI	Partito Repubblicano Italiano (*Italian Republican Party*)
Proc Gen	Procuratore Generale (*Attorney General*)
profsta	professionista (*professional man*)
PSDI	Partito Socialista Democratico Italiano (*Italian Socialist Democratic Party*)
PSI	Partito Socialista Italiano (*Italian Socialist Party*)
PT	Poste e Telegrafi (*Post and Telegraph Service*)
PTP	Posto Telefonico Pubblico (*public telephone*)
pza	piazza (*square*)
q	quadrato (*square*)
qb	quanto basta (*a sufficient quantity*)
QG	Quartier Generale (*Headquarters*)
R	raccomandata (*registered letter*)
racc	raccomandata (*registered letter*)
rag	ragioniere (*certified accountant*)
RAI	Radio Audizioni Italiane (*Italian Broadcasting Corporation*)
RAU	Repubblica Araba Unita (*United Arab Republic*)
RI	Repubblica Italiana (*Italian Republic*)
RU	Regno Unito (*United Kingdom*)
S	Santo (*Saint*); Sud (*South*)
SA	Sua Altezza (*His, Her Highness*)
SAR	Sua Altezza Reale (*His, Her Royal Highness*)
sbf	salvo buon fine ((*com*) *under usual reserve*)
SCV	Stato della Città del Vaticano (*Vatican City*)
SEDI	Società Editrice Documentari Italiani (*Italian Newsreel Company*)
SEO	salvo errori ed omissioni (*com*) (*errors and omissions excepted*)
serg	sergente (*sergeant*)
sett	settembre (*September*)
sfr	sotto fascia raccomandata (*registered printed matter*)
sfs	sotto fascia semplice (*unregistered printed matter*)
Sig	Signore (*Mr, Mister*)
Siga	Signora (*Mrs, Mistress*)
Sigg	Signori (*Messrs, Messieurs*)

Signa	Signorina (*Miss*)
SISAL	Società Italiana Sistemi a Lotto (*Italian Society of State Lottery Systems*)
SMG	Stato Maggiore Generale (*General Staff*)
SMOM	Sovrano Militare Ordine di Malta (*Sovereign Military Order of Malta*)
SNDA	Società Nazionale Dante Alighieri (*National Dante Alighieri Society*)
SO	Sud-Ovest (*South-West*)
Soc	Società (*Society*)
Sottte	Sottotenente (*Sub-Lieutenant*)
SpA	Società per Azioni (*joint-stock company or limited liability company*)
SPA	Società Protettrice degli Animali (*Society for the Prevention of Cruelty to Animals*)
Spett	Spettabile (honorable)
SPM	sue proprie mani (*personal* (*for addressee*))
SRC	Santa Romana Chiesa (*Holy Roman Church*)
Srl	Società a responsabilità limitata (*Limited Company*)
SSPP	Santi Padri (*Holy Fathers*)
STIPEL	Società Telefonica Interregionale Piemonte e Lombardia (*Telephone Company* (*Piedmont and Lombardy*))
SU	Stati Uniti (*United States*)
SUA	Stati Uniti d'America (*United States of America*)
SVP	(*German* Südtiroler Volkspartei) Partito Popolare Sudtirolese (*People's Party of South Tyrol*)
tbc, TBC	tubercolosi (*tuberculosis*)
TCI	Touring Club Italiano (*Italian Touring Club*)
tel	telefono (*telephone*)
Ten	Tenente (*Lieutenant*)
TOTIP	Totalizzatore Ippico (*horse-race pools*)
TOTOCALCIO	Totalizzatore Calcistico (*Football Pools*)
tr	tratta (*draft*)
UCDG	Unione Cristiana delle Giovani (*Young Women's Christian Association*)
UCI	Unione Ciclistica Internazionale (*International Cycling Union*)
UDE	Unione Doganale Europea (*European Customs Union*)
UDI	Unione Donne Italiane (*Association of Italian Women*)
urg	urgente (*urgent*)
URSS	Unione Repubbliche Socialiste Sovietiche (*Union of Soviet Socialist Republics*)
US	Ufficio Stampa (*Press Agency*); Uscita di Sicurezza (*Emergency Exit*)
V	Via (*Street*)
Vat	Vaticano (*Vatican*)
VE	Vostra Eccellenza (*Your Excellency*)
VEm	Vostra Eminenza (*Your Eminence*)
Vle	Viale (*avenue*)
VM	Vostra Maestà (*Your Majesty*)
vr	vedi retro (*please turn over*)
vs	vostro (*your, yours*)
W	viva! (*long live*); watt (*watt*)
WL	(F. *wagon-lit*) carrozza-letto (*sleeping car*)
YCI	Yacht Club Italia (*Italian Yacht Club*)

Abbreviazioni Americani—American Abbreviations

A	adults (*adulti*)
AA	Automobile Association (*Automobile Club*); Alcoholics Anonymous (*Alcoolizzati Anonimi*)
AAA	American Automobile Association (*Automobile Club d'America*)
a/c	account (current) *conto* (*corrente*)
AEC	Atomic Energy Commission (*Commissione per l'Energia Atomica*)
AFL-CIO	American Federation of Labor and Congress of Industrial Organizations (*Confederazione Generale Americana del Lavoro*)
A1	first class (*Prima Categoria*)
AID	Artificial Insemination by Donor (*Fecondazione Artificiale da parte di Donatore*)
AMA	American Medical Association (*Ordine Americano dei Medici*)
anon	anonymous (*anonimo*)
AP	Associated Press (*Stampa Associata*)
approx	approximate(ly) (*approssimato, approssimativamente*)
ARC	American Red Cross (*Croce Rossa Americana*)
arr	arrives (*arrivo*)
assn, assoc	association (*associazione*)
asst	assistant (*assistente*)
av	average (*medio*)
Ave	Avenue (*viale*)
b	born (*nato*)
BA	Bachelor of Arts (*Diplomato in Lettere*); British Academy (*Accadèmia Britannica*); British Association (For the Advancement of Sciences) (*Associazione Britannica* (*per il Progresso della Scienza*))
Bart	Baronet (*Baronetto*)
BBC	British Broadcasting Corporation (*Ente Radiofonico Britannico*)
BC	before Christ (*avanti Cristo*); British Columbia (*Colombia Britannica*)
BD	Bachelor of Divinity (*Diplomato in Teologia*)
Bd	Board (*Commissione, Consiglio, Ministero*)
BDS	Bachelor of Dental Surgery (*Diplomato in Odontoiatria*); bomb disposal squad (*gruppo addetto al disinnestamento delle bombe*)
be, B/E	bill of exchange (*cambiale*)
BEA	British European Airways (*Compagnia Britannica delle Linee Europee*)
bibl.	biblical (*biblico*); bibliographical (*bibliografica*)
B Litt	Bachelor of Letters (*Diplomato in Lettere*)
BM	British Museum (*Museo Britannico*); Bachelor of Medicine (*Diplomato in Medicina*)
B. Mus	Bachelor of Music (*Diplomato in Musica*)
BOAC	British Overseas Airways Corporation (*Compagnia Britannica delle Linee Transoceaniche*)
B of A	Bank of America (*Banca d'America*)
B of E	Bank of England (*Banca d'Inghilterra*); Board of Education (*Ministero della Pubblica Istruzione*)
B of T	Board of Trade (*Ministero del Commercio e dell'Industria*)

Brit Britain ((*Gran*) *Bretagna*); British (*Britannico*)
Bros Brothers (*com*) (*Fratelli*)
B/S Bill of Sale (*nota di vendita, fattura*)
BSA Boy Scouts of America (*Giovani Exploratori Americani*)
BSc Bachelor of Science (*Diplomato in Scienze*)
Bt Baronet (*Baronetto*)
BTU British Thermal Unit (*unità* (*inglese*) *de misura de calore*)
BUP British United Press (*Stampa Unita Britannica*)

C Cape (*Capo*); centigrade (*centigrado*); Central (*Centrale*); Conservative (*Conservatore*)
c cent (*centesimo*); century (*secolo*); about (*L. circa*) (*circa*); chapter (*capitolo*)
Cantab Cambridge (*cantabrigense*)
cap capital letter (*lettera maiuscola*); chapter (*capitolo*)
Capt Captain (*Capitano*)
CBS Columbia Broadcasting System (*Rete Radiofonica Colombia*)
CD Civil Defense (*Difesa Civile*)
cf compare (*confronta*)
CIA Central Intelligence Agency (*Agenzia Centrale Informazioni* (*Servizio Segreto*))
CID Criminal Investigation Department (*Polizia Giudiziaria*)
cif cost, insurance, freight (*costo compreso il nolo e l'assicurazione*)
CND Campaign for Nuclear Disarmament (*Campagna per il Disarmo Nucleare*)
CO Commanding Officer (*Ufficiale Comandante*); conscientious objector (*obiettore di coscienza*)
Co Company (*Compagnia*)
c/o care of (*presso*)
COD cash on delivery (*pagamento alla consegna*)
C of E Church of England (*Chiesa d'Inghilterra*)
C of S Chief of Staff (*capo di stato maggiore*)
Col Colonel (*Colonnello*)
cont continued (*continuazione*)
Co-op Co-operative (*Cooperativa*)
CPA certified public accountant (*ragioniere*)
Cpl Corporal (*caporale*)
CUP Cambridge University Press (*Edizioni dell'Università di Cambridge*)
CWS Co-operative Wholesale Society (*Società Cooperativa all' Ingrosso*)
cwt hundredweight(s)

d died (*morta*); date (*data*); daughter (*figlia*); penny
DC District of Columbia (*Distretto di Colombia*); (*mus*) (*da capo*); Direct Current (*corrente continua*)
DD Doctor of Divinity (*Dottore in Teologia*)
Dem Democrat, Democratic (*Democratico, Democratico*)
dep departs (*partenza*); deputy (*vice*)
dept department (*reparto*); deponent (*deponente*)
DG *Deo gratias, Dei gratia*, thanks to God, by the grace of God (*grazie a Dio, per grazia di Dio*)
diam diameter (*diametro*)
dim diminuendo (*diminuendo*); diminutive (*diminutivo*)
D. Litt. Doctor of Letters (*Dottore in Lettere*)
DM Doctor of Medicine (*Dottore in Medicina*)
do ditto (the same) (*suddetto*)

doz dozen (*dozzina*)
Dr. Doctor (*dottore, dottoressa*)
DSC Distinguished Service Cross (*Croce per Meriti Speciali*)
DSM Distinguished Service Medal (*Medaglia per Meriti Speciali*)
DSO Distinguished Service Order (*Ordine dei Meriti Speciali*)
DST Daylight Saving Time (*ora estiva*)

E East (*Est*); Eastern (*Orientale*)
EEC European Economic Community (Common Market) (*Comunità Economica Europea* (*Mercato Comune*)
EFTA European Free Trade Association (*Associazione Europea di Libero Scambio*)
eg for example (L. *exempli gratia*) (*per esempio*)
EP Extended Play (gramophone record)
ESP extra sensory perception (*percezione metapsichica*)
esp especially (*specialmente*)
Esq Esquire (*Signore*)
est established (*fondato*)
et al. and others (*L. et alia*) (*e altri*)
etc and the rest (L. *et cetera*) (*eccetera*)

FA Football Association (*Associazione Calcistica*)
FAO Food and Agriculture Organization (*Organizzazione Alimenti e Agricoltura*)
FBI Federal Bureau of Investigation (*Polizia Federale Statunitense*)
FC Football Club (*Club Calcistico*)
fig figurative (*figurato*)
fin financial (*finanziario*)
FO Foreign Office (*Ministero degli Affari Esteri*)
fob free on board (*franco a bordo*)
FRAM Fellow of the Royal Academy of Music (*Membro della Reale Accadèmia di Musica*)
FRCS Fellow of the Royal College of Surgeons (*Membro del Reale Collegio dei Chirurghi*)
FRS Fellow of the Royal Society (*Membro della "Royal Society"*)
ft foot (*piede*); feet (*piedi*); fort (*forte*); fortification (*fortificazione*)
FTC Federal Trade Commission (*Commissione Federale di Commercio*)

gal gallon(s) (*gallone, galloni*)
GATT General Agreement on Tariffs and Trade (*Accordo Generale Tariffe e Commercio*)
GB Great Britain (*Gran Bretagna*)
gen gender (*genere*); general (*generale*); genitive (*genitivo*)
GHQ General Headquarters (*Quartier Generale*)
GI Government Issue (American private soldier) (*soldato semplice*)
Gib (*fam*) Gibraltar (*Gibilterra*)
gm gram (*grammo*)
GMT Greenwich Mean Time (*Ora di Greenwich*)
GOP (Grand Old Party) Republican Party (*Partito Repubblicano*)
Govt Government (*Governo*)
GP General Practitioner (*medico generico*)
GPO General Post Office (*Posta Centrale*)

h & c hot and cold (water) (*acqua calda e fredda*)
HCF highest common factor *massimo commun divisore*)
HE high-explosive (*alto esplosivo*); His Eminence (*Sua Eminenza*); His Excellency (*Sua Eccellenza*)
HEW (Department of) Health, Education and Welfare (*Ministero di Sanità, Educazione e Salute Pubblica*)
HH His (Her) Highness (*Sua Altezza*); His Holiness (*Sua Santità*)
HF high frequency (*alta frequenza*)
HM His (Her) Majesty (*Sua Maestà*)
Hon Honorary (*Onorario*); Honorable (*Onorevole*)
HP Houses of Parliament (*Palazzo del Parlamento*); House Physician (*medico interno* (*di ospedale*))
hp horse-power (*potenza in cavalli vapore*)
HQ headquarters (*Quartier Generale*)
hr hour (*ora*)
HRH His (Her) Royal Highness (*Sua Altezza Reale*)

I, Is Island(s) (*Isola* (*Isole*))
ib, ibid in the same place (L. *ibidem*) (*nello stesso luogo*)
i/c in charge (*incaricato, addetto*)
ICBM Inter-Continental Ballistic Missile (*Missile Balistico Intercontinentale*)
ICC Interstate Commerce Commission (*Commissione di Commercio Interstatale*)
Ice Iceland(*Islanda*)
id the same (L. *idem*) (*lo stesso*)
ie that is, namely (L. *id est*) (*cioè*)
ILO International Labour Organization (*Organizzazione Internazionale del Lavoro*)
IMF International Monetary Fund (*Fondo Monetario Internazionale*)
in inch (*pollice*); inches (*pollici*)
Inc incorporated (*incorporato*)
incl included, including, inclusive (*incluso, compreso*)
incog incognito (*incognito*)
INS International News Service (*Agenzia Stampa Internazionale*)
Inst Institute (*Istituto*); inst, instant, the present month (*corrente mese*)
IOU I owe you (*com*) (*pagherò*)
IQ Intelligence Quotient (*coefficiente di intelligenza*)
IRA Irish Republican Army (*Esercito della Repubblica Irlandese*)
IS Island(s) (*isola, isole*)

JP Justice of the Peace (*Giudice di Pace*)
jr junior

KBE Knight Commander of the British Empire (*Cavaliere dell'Impero Britannico*)
KC King's Counsel (*Avvocato di Corte suprema*)
KCB Knight Commander of the Bath (*Cavaliere Maestro* (*dell'Ordine*) *del Bagno*))
KG Knight of the Garter (*Cavaliere* (*dell'Ordine*) *della Giarrettiera*)
KKK Ku Klux Klan
KO (*boxing*) knock out; kick off (*calcio d'inizio*)
Kt Knight (*Cavaliere*)

kw	kilowatt (*chilowatt*)
L	Latin (*Latino*); Law (*Legge*); Learner (on motor cars); Liberal (*Liberale*)
l	lake (*lago*); left (*sinistra*); lira
£	pound (*sterlina*)
lab	laboratory (*laboratorio*); Labor (*laburista*)
Lat	Latin (*Latino*)
lb	pound (*libbra*)
LC	Library of Congress (*Biblioteca del Congresso*)
LCM	lowest common multiple (*minimo commune multiplo*)
LF	low frequency (*bassa frequenza*)
Lib	Library (*Biblioteca*); Liberal (*Liberale*)
lit	literal (*letterale*); literally (*letteralmente*); literature (*letteratura*); litre (*litro*)
LLB	Bachelor of Laws (*Diplomato in Legge*)
log	logarithm (*logaritmo*)
LP	Labour Party (*Partito Laburistà*); Long Playing (gramophone record) (*disco lunga durata*)
LSD	lysergic acid diethylamide (*acido lisergico dietilamidico*)
£sd	Pounds Shillings Pence (*L librae, solidi, denarii*) (*sterline, scellini, pence*)
LSE	London School of Economics (*Instituto di Economia di Londra*)
Ltd (Co)	Limited (Company) (*Società a responsabilità limitata*)
Lw	Long wave (*onda lunga*)
m	meter (*metro*); married (*coniugato*); male (*sesso maschile*); masculine (*maschile*); mile (*miglio*); minute (*minuto*); month (*mese*)
MA	Master of Arts (*Dottore in Lettere*)
MB, ChB	Bachelor of Medicine; Bachelor of Surgery (*Dottore in Medicina*)
MBE	Member of the Order of the British Empire (*Membro dell'Ordine dell'Impero Britannico*)
MC	Master of Ceremonies (*Cerimoniere*); Member of Congress (*Membro del Congresso*); Military Cross (*Croce di Guerra*)
MD	Doctor of Medicine (*Dottore in Medicina*); mentally deficient (*deficiente mentale*)
memo	memorandum (*memorandum*)
Messrs	the plural of Mr. (*Signori*); (*com*) *Ditta* (*in indirizzi*))
Mgr	Monsignor (*Monsignore*)
MI	Military Intelligence (*Controspionaggio*)
MO	Medical Officer (*Ufficiale Medico*)
MOH	Medical Officer of Health (*Ufficiale Medico d'Igiene*)
MP	Member of Parliament (*Deputato al Parlamento*); Military Police (*Polizia Militare*); Metropolitan Police (*Polizia Metropolitana*)
mpg	miles per gallon (*miglia per gallone*)
mph	miles per hour (*miglia all'ora*)
Mr	Mister (*Signore*)
MRCP	Member of Royal College of Physicians (*Membro del Reale Collegio dei Medici*)
Mrs	Mistress (*Signora*)
Mt	Mount, mountain (*monte*)
Mw	medium wave (*onda media*)

N	North (*Nord*); Northern (*Settentrionale*)
n	name (*nome*); noun (*sostantivo*); neuter (*neutro*); noon (*mezzogiorno*); born (L. *natus*) (*nato*); nephew (*nipote*)
NAS	National Academy of Sciences (*Academia Nazionale delle Scienze*)
NASA	National Aeronautics and Space Administration (*Ministero Nazionale di Aeronautica e Spazio*)
Nat	National (*nazionale*); nationalist (*nazionalista*)
NBC	National Broadcasting Company (*Ente Radiofonico Nazionale*)
NCO	Non-commissioned officer (*sottufficiale*)
NE	New England (*Nuova Inghilterra*); Northeast(ern) (*Nord-Est, Nord-Orientale*); new edition (*nuova edizione*)
NFL	National Football League (*Associazione Nazionale Calcistica*)
neg	negative (*negativo*)
NSC	National Security Council (*Censiglio di Sicurezza Nazionale*)
NSPCC	National Society for the Prevention of Cruelty to Children (*Società Nazionale per la Protezione dell' Infanzia*)
NW	Northwest (*Nord-Ovest*); Northwestern (*Nord-Occidentale*)
NY	New York
NZ	New Zealand (*Nuova Zelanda*)
OAS	Organization of American States (*Organizzazione Stati Americani*); Organisation Armée Secrète (*Organizzazione Armata segreta*)
OBE	Order of the British Empire (*Ordine dell'Impero Britannico*)
OECD	Organization for Economic Co-operation and Development (*Organizzazione per la Cooperazione e lo Sviluppo Economici*)
OEEC	Organization for European Economic Co-operation (*Organizzazione Economica per la Cooperazione Europea*)
OED	Oxford English Dictionary (*Dizionario Inglese di Oxford*)
OM	Order of Merit (*ordine di merito*)
op	out of print (*esaurito*)
OT	Old Testament (*Antico Testamento*)
OUP	Oxford University Press (*Edizioni dell'Università di Oxford*)
OXFAM	Oxford Committee for Famine Relief
Oxon	Oxford, of Oxford (L. *Oxoniensis*) (*di Oxford, Ossoniano*)
oz	ounce(s) (*oncia, once*)
p	page (*pagina*); participle (*participio*)
pa	per annum, by the year (*all'anno*)
PAA	Pan American Airways (*Linee Aeree Pan Americane*)
P & O	Peninsular and Oriental (Steam Navigation Company) (*Compagnia di Navigazione Peninsulare-Orientale*)
PAYE	Pay as you earn (Income Tax) (*trattenuta imposte su paghe da parte del datore di lavoro*)
PC	police constable (*agente di polizia*); Privy Council (*Consiglio Privato*); Privy Councillor (*Consigliere Privato*); postcard (*cartolina postale*)
pd	paid (*pagato*)
PhD	Doctor of Philosophy (*Dottore in Filosofia*)
PM	Prime Minister (*Primo Ministro*)
PMG	Postmaster-General (*Direttore Generale delle Poste*)

PO	Petty Officer (*naut*) (*sottufficiale*); Pilot Officer (*Ufficiale Pilota*); Post Office (*Ufficio postale*); Postal Order (*Vaglia Postale*)
POB	post office box (*cassetta postale*)
POW	Prisoner of War (*Prigioniero di Guerra*)
p.p.	on behalf of (L. *per procurationem*) (*per procura*); parcel post (*pacco postale*)
Pres	President (*Presidente*); Presbyterian (*Presbiteriano*)
PRO	Public Relations Officer (*Addetto alla Pubblicità*)
PT	Physical Training (*Educazione Fisica*)
pt	part (*parte*); pint(s) (*pinta, pinte*)
PTO	Please Turn Over (*vedi retro*)
PVC	Polyvinyl chloride (*cloruro di polivinile* (*plastica*))
QMG	Quartermaster-General (*mil*) (*capo del dipartimento amministrazione e alloggi*)
qr	Quarter(s)
qt	quart
qv	which see (L. *Quod vide*) (*vedi*)
RA	Royal Academy (*Accademia Reale*)
RADA	Royal Academy of Dramatic Art (*Accademia Reale d'Arte Drammatica*)
RAF	Royal Air Force (*Regia Aeronautica*)
RC	Roman Catholic (*Cattolico Apostolico Romano*); Red Cross (*Croce Rossa*)
Rd	Road (*Via, Corso*)
ref	reference (*riferimento*)
regd	registered (*raccomandato*)
rel	relative (*relativo*); related (*riferentesi*); religion (*religione*)
Rep	Representative (*Rappresentante*); Republic (*Repubblica*) Republican (*Repubblicano*); Repertory (*Repertorio*) Reporter (*cronista, corrispondente*)
Repub	Republic (*Repubblica*)
Rev	Reverend (*Reverendo*); Revelations (*Rivelazioni*); Revised (*riveduto*)
RN	Registered Nurse (*Infermiera Diplomata*)
rpm	revolutions per minute (*giri al minuto*)
Rt. Hon	Right Honorable (*Molto Onorevole*)
S	South (*Sud*); Saint (*Santo*); Socialist (*Socialista*); Society (*Società*)
s	second (*secondo*); shilling (*scellino*); son (*figlio*); singular (*singolare*); substantive (*sostantivo*); solubility (*solubilità*)
SA	South Africa (*Sud-Africa*)
s.a.e.	stamped addressed envelope (*busta indirizzata e affrancata*)
Sch	School (*scuola*)
SE	Southeast (*Sud-Est*); Southeastern (*Sud-Orientale*)
Sec, Secy	Secretary (*segretario*)
SHAPE	Supreme Headquarters Allied Powers, Europe (*Supremo Quartier Generale delle Truppe Alleate in Europa*)
SPCA	Society for the Prevention of Cruelty to Animals) (*Società per la protezione degli animali*)
SS	steamship (*piroscafo*); Social Security (*Previdensa Sociale*)
St	Saint (*Santo*); Strait (*Stretto*); Street (*strada, via*)

SW	Southwest (*Sud-Ovest*); Southwestern (*Sud-Occidentale*)
TB	Tuberculosis (*Tuberculosi*)
TNT	trinitrotoluene (explosive) (*trinitrotoluolo*)
TT	total abstainer (teetotal) (*astemio*); Tourist Trophy; tuberculin tested
TU	Trade Union (*Sindacato*)
TUC	Trade Union Congress (*Congresso dei Sindacati*)
TWA	Trans World Airlines (*Linee Aeree Intercontinentali*)
UAR	United Arab Republic (*Repubblica Araba Unita*)
UDI	Unilateral Declaration of Independence (*Dichiarazione Unilaterale d'Indipendenza*)
UK	United Kingdom (*Regno Unito*)
ult	(L. *ultimo*) last (month) (*ultimo scorso*)
UN(O)	United Nations (Organization) ((*Organizzazione delle*) *Nazioni Unite*)
UNA	United Nations Association (*Associazione delle Nazioni Unite*)
UNICEF	United Nations International Children's Emergency Fund (*fondo di emergenza delle Nazioni Unite per l'Infanzia*)
UP	United Press (*Stampe Associate*)
US	United States (*Stati Uniti*)
USA	United States of America (*Stati Uniti d'America*)
USAF	United States Air Force (*Aeronautica Militare Statunitense*)
USIS	United States Information Service (*Ufficio Informazioni per gli Stati Uniti d'America*)
USLTA	United States Lawn Tennis Association (*Federazione Statunitense Tennis*)
USN	United States Navy (*Marina Militare Statunitense*)
USSR	Union of Soviet Socialist Republics (*Unione delle Repubbliche Socialiste Sovietiche*)
v	(L. *vide*) see (*vedi*); versus (*contro*)
VA	Veterans Administration (*Amministrazione dei Veterani*)
VC	Victoria Cross (*Croce della Regina Vittoria*)
VD	Venereal Disease (*Malattie veneree*)
Vet	Veterinary Surgeon (*veterinario*)
vg	very good (*molto bene, ottimo, lodevole*)
VIP	(*fam*) very important person (*pezzo grosso, persona molto importante*)
viz	(L. *videlicet*) namely (*vale a dire*)
W	West (*Ovest*); Western (*Occidentale*); Welsh (*gallese*)
WD	War Department (*Ministero della Guerra*)
WHO	World Health Organization (*Organizzazione Mondiale della Santtà*)
wk	week (*settimana*)
wp	weather permitting (*tempo permettendo*)
wt	weight (*peso*)
yd	yard(s) (*iarda, iarde*)
YHA	Youth Hostels Association (*Associazione degli Ostelli della Gioventù*)
YMCA	Young Men's Christian Association (*Associazione Cristiana dei Giovani*)

yr year (*anno*); younger (*più giovane*); your (*vostro*)

YWCA Young Women's Christian Association (*Unione Cristiana delle Giovani*)